Market grid for apartments

	Distinctive design	Economy	Common facilities	Privacy	Close-in location	Room size	Interior variety	Strong management
Swingers								
Sophisticates								
Newly married								
Family								
Job centered								
Home centered								
Urban centered								

Marketing strategy planning requires judgment and research because every "market" can be conceived as a grid with many submarkets.

Basic marketing *a managerial approach*

Basic marketing a managerial approach

E. Jerome McCarthy, Ph.D. *Professor of Marketing, Michigan State University*

Fourth Edition, 1971

Richard D. Irwin, Inc. *Homewood, Illinois 60430|Irwin-Dorsey Limited, Georgetown, Ontario*

Fourth Edition

First Printing, March, 1971

Library of Congress Catalog Card No. 75–146730

Printed in the United States of America

Preface

This text is designed for use in an introductory course in marketing, either in schools with one or two marketing courses or in the larger business schools with a full complement of marketing courses.

All business students should be introduced to the basic problems and practices in marketing management. At the same time, it is clearly wishful thinking to assume that a student can be taught all there is to know about marketing in one or two courses. And it is just as clear that, even in larger schools with a range of marketing courses, less than one third of all business students become marketing majors.

This text, then, is an attempt to meet the needs of the majority of beginning marketing students who are taking their first and perhaps only course in marketing. It tries to give the student an understanding and a feel for the marketing manager's job, and the world in which he operates.

Admittedly, this text does not offer a complete and detailed description of all possible problems or solutions in the marketing area. But it does offer a broad and necessary understanding of marketing problems, giving the student a foundation for investigating more comprehensive references. A student must see the whole picture before he can appreciate the details.

As a basic introductory text, *Basic Marketing* differs considerably from other works. It takes an integrated, analytical approach to both macro- and micro-marketing problems. While the text material, of course, is similar to that found in traditional texts, the approach definitely is not. We will be primarily concerned with micro-marketing — that is, we will see marketing through the manager's eyes because he can affect the performance of both his own firm and the macro-marketing system.

Marketing strategy planning, including designing a marketing mix (but not day-to-day implementation), is stressed to give the student the big-picture view of micro-marketing. This planning takes place within a dynamic social and political environment which affects the macro-marketing system, however; therefore, the effect of the environment on the macro-marketing system (and vice versa) is given extensive treatment.

The first chapter begins with a review of the many criticisms of marketing—of both macro- and micro-marketing. These criticisms lead logically to consideration of the nature of the two views of marketing and the evolution of thinking about marketing and marketing systems. The importance of understanding the macro-marketing system is stressed, while emphasizing that changes in our macro system are likely to come from the actions of individual consumer/voters and businessmen. This sets the stage for the transition to a focus on the actions and potential contributions of businessmen and, in particular, marketing managers.

Following the introductory chapter, the vital role of marketing management in the operation of a firm and the macro-marketing system is stressed. The focus upon satisfying varying target markets on a market grid is emphasized especially. Then, the framework within which the marketing manager must operate and the tools with which he works are discussed. These include marketing research and sales forecasting.

The characteristics and buying habits of target customers—both final consumers in the United States and world markets, and intermediate customers, such as businesses, farmers, and governments—are described.

Next, based on the behavior of target markets and the company's own objectives, a marketing mix is developed out of four ingredients called the four P's: Product, Place (that is, channels and institutions), Promotion, and Price. These sections comprise the bulk of the text and are concerned with developing the "right" product and making it available at the "right" place with the "right" promotion and the "right" price, to satisfy target customers and still meet the objectives of the business.

These materials are presented in an integrated, analytical way so that there is a logical, cumulative development of the student's thinking. After a final discussion on integrating the four P's and controlling the marketing process, we return to a consideration of how efficient the marketing process is, and especially to the question "Does marketing cost too much?" Here we return to the many criticisms of marketing and evaluate the effectiveness of both micro- and macro-level marketing, considering whether any changes are needed. This final analysis is important because marketing men must be concerned about their impact on the economy and how they can help our system work more effectively.

Multinational marketing is considered not only in Chapter 7, but throughout the text in recognition of American businesses' growing interest and involvement in the world market. Technical details are not emphasized. The multinational emphasis merely provides perspective and shows the universal applicability of the principles and approaches presented throughout the text.

"Social responsibility" and "consumerism" materials are woven into the text to emphasize that marketing managers must be continually concerned with, and work within, their environment. Isolating such materials in a separate chapter would lead to an unfortunate "compartmentalization" of ideas, when, in fact, a marketing manager must give continual consideration to these issues.

It is hoped that, in this framework, marketing will be looked upon by more students as a useful, fascinating, and very necessary function in our American economy.

This material can be studied in a number of ways. *One,* the reading material can be supplemented by lectures and class discussion of the text material. A separate *Review Guide* has been developed to help the student in this regard. *Two,* understanding of the text material can be enhanced by conventional questions and problems; further, a separate *Workbook* has been developed offering additional opportunities to obtain a deeper understanding of the material. *Three,* thought-provoking questions included at the end of the chapters can be used to encourage the student to investigate the marketing process and organize his own way of thinking about it.

The text is organized so that any of the methods or any combination of them can be used. All are compatible. However, at least experimentation with the third approach is highly recommended.

I reevaluated my approach to teaching beginning marketing when some educators made some interesting observations. Dr. J. S. Bruner, at Harvard, found that a child learned more geography when given a map and asked to predict where the biggest cities *should be,* rather than by straight memorization of where they actually are. Other educators had success using similar methods, such as asking children to "invent" multiplication as a short cut to addition.

Trying to apply these ideas using conventional marketing texts was difficult, however, since most of the "answers" were given early—sometimes in the first chapter or two. Thus it was not possible to have the student read the text and still develop his own ideas as the text moved along.

This text works differently. It assumes that the student comes to the beginning marketing course with some experience—if nothing else, as a consumer—and that he is able to project what "should be" or "probably will be" on the basis of this prior knowledge. Certainly the student's vocabulary, in the sense of conventional marketing terms and definitions, will be lacking. But he can anticipate the nature of these terms and especially the functions which are provided by the various firms.

It is for this reason—that the student should be encouraged to "think ahead"—that this text deliberately avoids introducing certain concepts and definitions before they are needed. Precise definitions of wholesaling and retailing, for example, are delayed until midway in the book, when the entire area of where and how goods should be made available is considered.

When all the details are not presented early, then creative thought can be encouraged by the questions following each chapter. These questions encourage the student to think ahead and develop what "ought to be," and then subsequent chapters present commonly accepted definitions and methods of operation. For example, following the introductory chapters, customers—both intermediate customers and final consumers—are analyzed. The questions here encourage the student to think about the kind of products these customers *might like,* the kinds of shopping behavior they *would exhibit,* where the goods *should be made available,* and how they *should be priced and promoted.*

In the Product area, after the student has had a chance to roughly categorize the products which will be available, the conventional terms are introduced and his past experience is organized for him.

The questions at the end of the Product chapters ask him how these products should be made available. After he has had a try at this, the conventional definitions and institutional material on wholesaling and retailing are introduced in the Place area; and so on.

This approach follows in sequence four basic steps in psychological learning theory:

1. Motivation.
2. Investigation.
3. Organization.
4. Utilization.

The first few chapters attempt to motivate the student by encouraging his interest in the subject and indicating how important marketing and marketing management are to the operation of a whole economy. The questions at the end of the early chapters encourage him to do his own investigation. Then subsequent chapters provide the commonly accepted organization.

In the middle chapters, the approach is to alternate between Steps 2 and 3—from investigation to organization and then to further investigation, building upon the material previously organized. Finally, at the end of the book, a number of cases of various types are included. They can be used to encourage the student to utilize the thinking he has done in the investigation and organization stages. If there is time, a few of these cases (or cases from other sources) should be tried during and at the end of the course to "set" the material and give the student a chance to utilize the fruits of his own thinking. This completes the learning cycle.

As indicated earlier, this third approach need not be used—the first two can be used quite satisfactorily. But I have thoroughly enjoyed teaching the course since experimenting with its use. Most students feel they know quite a bit about marketing when they come into this course. When the entire course is "high spotted" in the first few chapters, it becomes difficult to maintain interest in "old stuff." If, instead, the instructor and text encourage the student to organize and use his experience and common sense to almost "write" the book, he becomes involved. Many even enjoy the course.

Leads for further reading are provided in many comprehensive footnotes, but the literature of marketing and related fields is so voluminous that selection for others is difficult. With the background provided by this text, the student should be able to locate useful material through his library's card catalog, the *Industrial Arts Index, The Business Periodicals Index,* and the *Reader's Guide to Periodical Literature.* For leads to books and articles published through 1949, he should see: David A. Revzan, *A Comprehensive Classified Marketing Bibliography,* Parts I and II (Berkeley: University of California Press, 1951). For more recent references he should see the fine bibliographical series published by the American Marketing Association.

This book is a result of the blending of my experiences in business, at Northwestern University, Michigan State University, and the Universities of Minnesota, Oregon, and Notre Dame. Many people, too numerous to mention, have had an influence on this text. My colleagues at the University of Notre Dame had a profound effect on my thinking during the years we were developing a beginning course emphasizing marketing management. The original edition of this text grew out of this work. To all of them, and especially the many students who suggested case materials and have criticized and made comments about both the original edition and the revised editions, I am most grateful.

Helpful criticisms and comments were made on either the original edition or the revised editions by the following professors: Harry Lipson of the University of Alabama, William Stanton of the University of Colorado, Phillip McVey of the University of Nebraska, Edwin H. Lewis of the University of Minnesota, William T. Kelley of the Wharton School of Finance and Commerce, Fred Kniffin of Pennsylvania State University, Louis Stern of Wayne State University, Henry Gomez of New York University, Walter Gross of the University of Georgia, David Revzan of the University of California, and R. A. Klages of the State University of New York at Albany.

I am especially indebted to Professor Yusaku Furuhashi of the University of Notre Dame for reading several versions of all revised editions and counseling on the multinational marketing emphasis.

Others who have been especially helpful include Professors Ferdinand Mauser at Wayne State University, Gerald Albaum at the University of Oregon, Joseph Siebert and John Maggard at Miami University, Karl Reyer at Louisiana State University, George Schwartz at the University of Massachusetts, Eric S. Stein of Chicago City Junior College, James D. Taylor of State University of South Dakota, G. J. Eberhart of Indiana State College, William G. Panschar of Indiana University, Noel B. Zabriskie at the University of Maryland, and Alan Kelman, Andrew Brogowicz, and Keith Humphries at Michigan State University.

Mr. and Mrs. Durward Humes, Mr. Kenneth Wylie, and Mr. Don M. Smith provided invaluable editorial assistance and many fresh ideas.

Last, but not least, I must thank my wife, Joanne, for considerable patience, advice, and assistance, and finally for proofreading under typically chaotic conditions. Our daughters Kathleen and Mary helped in this final effort too.

To all of these persons as well as the many publishers who graciously granted permission to use their material, I am deeply grateful. Responsibility for any errors or omissions are certainly mine, but the book would not have been possible without the assistance of many others.

East Lansing, Michigan   E. JEROME McCARTHY
February, 1971

Contents

Contents

Contents

Contents

Contents

Appendix

Marketing arithmetic

Cases

Basic marketing *a managerial approach*

...in modern well-developed economies, the grass grows high on the path to the better mousetrap factory – if the mousetrap is not properly marketed.

...in our economy of abundance, businesses *must* cater to their customers.

...there is no mandate from heaven for business firms to operate the way they do. Each firm must continue to earn the right to operate as part of the marketing process.

1

Marketing: a vital topic

Is marketing really necessary? Does it cost too much? Is it truly a useful activity to society?

Some people do feel that marketing is a superfluous activity – that it wastes resources and energies that could be put to better use elsewhere. Often these people look for quick and simple solutions to problems – the cost of living, unemployment, education, and so on. They feel that too much money is spent on activities that produce no lasting good for mankind.

Marketing activity is especially susceptible to this criticism, mostly because the public sees its "end products" every day. There's nothing like a pocketbook issue for getting the average consumer stirred up.

Most consumers have heard about the seemingly high markups taken by wholesalers and retailers. The "proof" is all around them –

the large discounts, for example, offered by automobile and appliance dealers from posted list prices. Certain types of advertising offend some people; they say it wastes money, or it's in poor taste, or it panders to undesirable wants.

Consumer dissatisfaction has prompted the President of the United States to appoint an "Assistant for Consumer Affairs." Many states have similar agencies. Then there are the independent consumer-oriented groups such as "Nader's Raiders." And individual politicians thrive on taking potshots at business.

Because of real or imagined abuses, it is not a safe bet at this point that marketing activities, at least as they work today, would survive a referendum of the American people.

Other people feel that marketing is overrated, that it doesn't have to be so costly or complicated. Their attitude is reflected in Emerson's old adage: "If a man . . . make a better mouse trap . . . the world will beat a path to his door!" A good product, in other words, is all you need to succeed in business. Make that better product and the customers will find you.

The mousetrap theory probably wasn't true in Emerson's time, and it certainly is not true today. In modern well-developed economies, the grass grows high on the path to the Better Mousetrap Factory — if the new mousetrap is *not* properly marketed.

Today, the design and the production of a good product are only two of the many vital steps. A producer (or a wholesaler or a retailer) must continually study his customers' needs and preferences. He may have to advertise his product and arrange for transporting and warehousing. And, of course, he must offer it for sale.

The modern-day firm must design a production and marketing system — a *total system* — which satisfies some consumer needs. This process can be complex and sometimes very expensive. Also it is often subjected to public criticism, and to legislation which ostensibly is designed to make the marketing system work more effectively.

Our study of marketing will begin with a look at the complaints against it. The businessman must be aware of, and realistic about, the climate of opinion in which he must operate and the kinds of criticism he must face.

Next, we will see how marketing systems can be understood at two levels — a "macro" level and a "micro" level, and how various marketing systems have evolved. We will explore the role marketing plays in our economy. Finally, we will define the concept of marketing, explain the thrust of this book, and examine why an understanding of marketing is so important.

Some complaints against marketing

"Distribu-
tion costs
are just
too high . . ."

A frequent complaint heard today is that distribution costs too much in relation to the cost of production. Authoritative estimates indicate that about 50 percent of the consumer's dollar is spent for getting the product into the consumer's hands — for marketing, in other words — as opposed to the remaining 50 percent to produce what he buys. Some people feel that this marketing cost is too high.

Housewives, for example, are especially sensitive to the price of food. Concern for rising prices during the 1960's led to boycotts of some retail food chains. Since distribution activities between the farm and the supermarket shelf are understood to be marketing functions, the housewife often blames the "middlemen" for the high cost of food in the store, especially if the price paid to the farmer falls and then little price change follows at the retail level.

"Poor-quality products, models change too often, products are too numerous, . . ."

Many consumers also have specific objections about product quality. Complaints usually center around the cost of the product in relation to its value. Sometimes there is the implication that businessmen, in their greed, make the cheapest product possible and then put the highest possible price tag on it.

Critics often cite policies of planned product obsolescence to back up their arguments. Examples mentioned include the regular model changes of automobiles, appliances, and household furnishings, and rapid changes in fashions, especially in women's clothing.

There is also criticism about the similarity of merchandise or products offered under different brand names. For example, it is estimated that there are as many as 10,000 brands of wheat flour, 4,500 brands of canned corn, 1,000 brands of canned peaches, 1,000 brands of canned salmon and peas, 500 brands of mustard, and 300 brands of pineapple.[1] Critics feel that obviously there cannot be that many variations in products. This multiplicity of brands further confuses the consumer, who already finds it difficult to determine product quality.

"Packaging and labeling are often confusing . . ."

Confusion about product quality and content has led to complaints about misleading packaging and labeling. Some critics feel that if the products are essentially similar, the labeling should make this clear. Or if they are different, the labels should so indicate. This concern has led to suggestions that the expected life of the product (an appliance, for example) should be included to permit comparison.

A related problem is the confusion about prices for similar or different products. Some observers have promoted the idea of unit pricing to make the housewife's comparisons of prices and quantities easier. Unit pricing would require that the price per ounce or some other basic unit be shown on the package.

"Product performance is a sometimes thing . . ."

Some consumers get very upset with the way that highly touted products actually perform. The product may not work as claimed, or it may be difficult to get repairs and maintenance work done. Service may not be available in the immediate locality, or the product may have to be returned to the factory.

---

[1] S. H. Slichter, *Modern Economic Society* (New York: Henry Holt & Co., Inc., 1951), p. 552.

Mixups over product warranties (or who pays for what repairs) are another source of consumer aggravation, both in terms of inconvenience and cost. What does the car owner who has bought a "lemon" do for the weeks while the dealer is trying to get his car working? What can a customer do who has been beguiled by a fast-talking salesman into buying the wrong product for his particular needs? A low-priced automobile tire, for example, might be quite satisfactory around town but not suitable for high-speed turnpike driving. This tire might look the same as any other in the dealer's showroom, but how can the customer tell how it will perform in use?

Some products may actually be dangerous in normal use. Examples are some toys and household appliances with sharp edges or exposed moving parts. Ralph Nader rose to prominence by questioning the safety of General Motor's Corvair.[2] He is credited with its subsequent withdrawal from the market.

"Too many middlemen adding to the cost . . ."

Another major area of criticism is the complexity of distribution channels for getting the product to consumers. One sore spot is the sheer numer of wholesalers and retailers. Another is the belief that their practices and methods are inefficient. Many wholesalers, for example, operate in older central districts of cities which were designed for horse-drawn carts, trains, and ships rather than modern trucks. This often leads to additional handling, so that costs rise without adding to the value of the product. Sometimes it seems that this middleman setup simply leads to more and more wholesalers in order to get the job done.

Many farmers have been particularly unhappy about the way their products are handled and the costs which are added during distribution. They know what they are paid for a product and what the customer finally has to pay. They frequently feel that they receive far too small a share of the final consumer price. This had led some farmers to try cooperative marketing, to avoid middlemen.

"Too much advertising of the wrong things for the wrong reasons . . ."

Much of the criticism of marketing is leveled at advertising and sales promotion.

The amount of money spent on advertising, which has been rising continually and totaled more than $18 billion in 1969, is one factor that concerns some observers. The main gripe about advertising, however, is that it stimulates people to buy products they don't really need — often to the neglect of their real needs. Examples are frequently given to "prove" this charge.

One husband was sued for divorce because he bought himself an electric train for Christmas while his three children had to depend on a charity organization for Christmas presents. In another case, among 200 homes in an industrial town in England, it was found that

[2] Ralph Nader, *Unsafe at Any Speed*, (New York: Grossman, 1965).

only 3 had bathtubs, 6 had hot water, and 4 had their own toilets, while 125 *had television sets.*[3]

A best seller of a few years ago, *The Hidden Persuaders,* claims to show how advertising and public relations people are "manipulating" consumers.[4] This very readable book probably gives too much credit to the abilities of the advertising and public relations professions, but is significant reading for marketing men because it is a book that many critics of marketing use for ammunition. *The Waste Makers,* by the same author, focuses on the alleged wastefulness being promoted by industry to sell its high output of products.[5]

More recent books have focused on similar themes, with Senator Magnuson emphasizing fraudulent methods.[6]

In many respects, these books are similar to critical works of the early 1930's which appeared under the titles of *Your Money's Worth* and *100,000,000 Guinea Pigs.*[7] They tried to show that most marketing activities were concerned with cheating and defrauding the public.

The earlier books helped to stimulate and crystallize consumer thinking about some of the aggressive and sometimes harmful marketing practices (patent medicines were a particularly sore point) which had developed during the 1920's. Growing public concern led to the development of private consumers' goods testing and rating agencies, such as Consumers' Research and Consumers Union. These organizations attempt to evaluate and rate new products. Although some consumers find such aids helpful, probably only a few million people ever see the magazines published by these organizations.

A well-known historian, Arnold Toynbee, recently joined the attack against advertising and, even more broadly, against our business system.[8] He called for a reform of our way of life and suggested that personal consumption expenditures could be limited to the level of present-day American monks and nuns. Then, he said, "The balance of our productive capacity could be diverted to supplying elementary needs of the poverty-striken three-quarters of the human race."

Many critics of advertising feel that it creates a demand for trivial goods, urges false standards on people, and builds up consumer preferences for products that are not very different from others available. Furthermore, it is charged, advertising tends to create a monopoly for a particular producer by creating a situation where sellers can

[3] *Time,* October 6, 1958, p. 96.

[4] Vance Packard, *The Hidden Persuaders* (New York: Pocket Books, 1958).

[5] Vance Packard, *The Waste Makers* (New York: David McKay Co., Inc., 1960).

[6] Warren G. Magnuson and Jean Carpe, *The Dark Side of the Marketplace: The Plight of the American Consumer* (Englewood Cliffs, N.J.: Prentice-Hall, Inc., 1968); Curt Gentry, *The Vulnerable Americans* (Garden City, N.Y.: Doubleday & Co., Inc., 1966), and James Bishop, *Let the Seller Be-* *ware* (Washington, D.C.: National Press, Inc., 1969).)

[7] S. Chase and F. J. Schlink, *Your Money's Worth* (New York: Macmillan Co., 1931), and A. Kallet and F. J. Schlink, *100,000,000 Guinea Pigs* (New York: Vanguard Press, Inc., 1932).

[8] "Is It Immoral to Stimulate Buying?" *Printers' Ink,* May 11, 1962, p. 43; "The Real Enemy?" *Time,* September 22, 1961, p. 112; "James Webb Young on Toynbee: 'Adrift on Uses of Advertising,'" *Printers' Ink,* October 20, 1961; and "Are Thought-Leaders a Threat?" *Printers' Ink,* April 26, 1963, pp. 54–56.

avoid price competition. Finally, critical observers claim that advertising merely shuffles demand from one brand to another, rather than stimulating innovations and new product development which are basic to the vitality of a free economy.

"Consumer credit is a misused marketing technique..."

The practice of granting liberal credit is also frequently decried, such as "no down payment" and "easy terms," on the basis that it encourages some consumers to overextend themselves. Critics feel this may lead to neglect of truly necessary expenditures and to a burden of indebtedness with all its depressing effects on the family. Some firms are so lax in their credit checks and so anxious to make sales that there have been instances of consumers with monthly payments that totaled more than their income.

Mortgaging a consumer's future income for a home is now accepted practice, but many observers remain critical of letting consumers commit themselves for less durable goods. They feel "easy credit" is mainly a marketing technique to get rid of more goods and are concerned about the easy availability of credit cards.

"Retail service is deteriorating..."

Most people at one time or another have received poor service from some retail store, even though they had to pay a high retail markup. Critics observe that people have little choice but to patronize such high-cost, poor-service outlets, and that is just another proof of the high cost and inefficiency of marketing. They claim that in recent years the personal service in large department stores – and in retail stores generally – has deteriorated considerably.

In recent years, the deteriorating retail service in the inner city has been of special concern. It is said that the poor people in these areas – the ones who can least afford it – are charged higher prices than the people in more affluent areas. Merchants are described as preying on the innocent. It is recognized that there might be some special problems in serving these markets, but it is felt that retailers have a social responsibility to serve all customers equitably.

"Wrong kinds of goods are produced..."

Critics of marketing are concerned with what is produced in the economy. If advertising or other marketing activities encourage consumers to want to buy the "wrong kinds of goods," then the businessmen will produce these goods – and thereby allocate the economy's resources to the "wrong ends." An example might be a television set in a home where there is too little food or clothing, or no toilet.

"Marketing makes men materialistic..."

Some critics, like Toynbee, simply get upset at what they consider America's materialistic orientation. To them, advertising is the arch-villain that creates or encourages this supposed materialistic outlook. If a man moonlights or if a housewife takes a job, then it's just a case of an artificially stimulated desire for more goods. Critics from abroad are even concerned with the spread of the American brand of materialism to other areas of the world. Young people everywhere, they say, are caught up in the demand for more and more goods. Supposedly, this trend is upsetting some traditional social-economic systems – and the "establishment" naturally looks for someone to blame.[9]

"Controlled markets restrict income and employment..."

Another villain in the marketing critic's lineup is the "greedy" businessman who creates his own market (or monopoly) through product design and promotion that allow him to raise prices and to restrict output and employment. Or if he can't corner the market, he may resort to price fixing or market sharing with "competitors" to achieve higher profits.

It is argued that monopolistic practices, since they tend to raise prices for certain goods, restrict the amount of goods consumers can buy. This, in turn, has a dampening effect on employment, national output, and income.

"The big incomes go to the manipulators..."

This line of thinking holds that if marketing activities permit a firm to raise prices and increase profits, the additional profits go to the smart promoter rather than the legitimate producer. In other words, a disproportionate share of the sales dollar goes to the marketing people – who, it is assumed, are paid fabulous salaries for their ability to manipulate the public.

Marketing systems exist at two levels

A brief review of these complaints against marketing suggests that there are basically two levels of criticism against marketing. One level is concerned with the overall role of marketing and the performance of the entire economic system. The second level of criticism is directed to the activities of individual firms. If we are to understand these two types of criticism, we must learn to evaluate marketing systems at two levels – the *macro* level and the *micro* level.

Macro- versus micro- marketing

A *macro*-level marketing evaluation looks at the economy's entire marketing system to see how it operates and how efficient and fair it is. *Micro*-marketing, or the other hand, examines individual firms within the economic system, to see how they operate or how they should function.

The kinds of problems handled at each level and the methods of analysis are quite different, so it is important that a clear distinction be made. We will begin by discussing the macro-marketing concept and then go onto an analysis of micro-marketing. The latter will be emphasized in the bulk of the text. Along the way, the impact of individual businesses on the whole economy will be explored because individual firms must operate within the macro environment.

At the end of the course, we will return to the macro concept and

---

[9] See John K. Galbraith, *The Affluent Society* (Boston: Houghton Mifflin Co., 1958). For further discussion of criticisms, see R. M. Farmer, "Would You Want Your Daughter to Marry a Marketing Man?" *Journal of Marketing,* January, 1967, pp. 1–3.

to the many criticisms of marketing. We will then take a look at how effectively the marketing process operates and what opportunities there are for improvement.

Now, let's take a look at the macro – or "big-picture" – view of marketing.

Macro-marketing takes a big-picture view

All economic systems – whether state-run or free enterprise – must have marketing systems. This means that some kind of mechanism, along with appropriate institutions, must be developed to decide: *what* and *how much* is to be produced and distributed by *whom, when,* and to *whom. How* the decisions are made may vary from system to system, but the macro-level objectives are basically similar: to create goods and services and make them available when and where they are needed.

Basic economic functions done by marketing

A marketing system must perform some basic economic functions. In economic parlance, three of the four basic utilities isolated by economists are part of the marketing job. *Time, place,* and *possession* utility are definitely created by marketing, and it could be argued that the creation of *form* utility, usually considered a production activity, should be directed by marketing. Having goods available *when* and *where* they are wanted, and then completing the sales transaction to provide *possession* utility, are the very essence of marketing. Providing these utilities adds to the consumer welfare and is a very significant part of any economic system.

Marketing, the great regulator

In a modern economy such as the United States, the marketing system is a vital regulating force. It allocates resources to meet consumer needs and wants. It affects the distribution and size of income. It affects every company's survival. A firm's basic source of income is sales. If a firm can't sell enough of its products and/or services to make a profit, it probably will go out of business.

This process can be seen at work in the soft-coal, hat, leather, textile, and many agricultural and mining industries. These industries receive a relatively small share of national income, in part because consumers have not been willing to pay more for the relatively undifferentiated products and services offered by them. Consumers have wants and needs that are as varied as their patterns of living and as numerous as their special interests. They want products that have a clear identity and a specific utility. Quite naturally, they shift their spending to industries and firms that try to satisfy these needs.

Basically, the role assigned to business firms in our economic system is to satisfy consumers, in the aggregate. Businesses are permitted to make a profit, if they can. But it is not guaranteed. Further, by allowing firms to compete freely with each other, it is hoped that the whole marketing and economic system will satisfy consumers effectively. Some laws have been passed (by consumers' representatives) to guide the operation of the system, and more or different ones could be passed if it were desired to modify the marketing system. Within these constraints, however, the many business firms are expected to compete freely, doing a great variety of things, and in the aggregate make the macro-marketing system work.

Macro-marketing system is many faceted

In a modern economy, there is a great deal of marketing activity which few consumers see or are aware of. For example, more goods and services are sold to farmers, manufacturers, wholesalers, and retailers — to business firms in an economy — than are sold to final consumers.

How can more goods and services be sold than are consumed by final consumers? The answer is that in a complex, interdependent society, much buying and selling takes place during the production and distribution process. In fact, the same product may be bought and sold *several* times before it is finally sold to retail customers.

Several "customers" may handle same product

Many farmers or manufacturers do not themselves produce the finished products bought by the consumer. Rather, many producers in our economy specialize in that aspect of production in which they are most efficient and then sell their goods for further processing or sale. Eventually someone assembles the specialized products of many producers and either physically combines them (manufacturers), or presents them in an attractive assortment (wholesalers or retailers) for the customer. And each time these goods change hands, a sale is recorded.

An example may clarify this process. The small manufacturer of electric fans obviously does not produce iron ore, steel, copper, paint, raw materials, or the other basic ingredients of electric fans. He buys the components from firms specializing in motors, metal castings, stampings, and so on. Moreover, when the manufacturer has finished fabricating and assembling the fan, it is doubtful that he would sell it direct to the final consumer. Instead, wholesalers might buy the fans and sell them to commercial customers, such as plants or offices, or to retailers for resale to their customers.

Volume of intermediate activity is large

As you can see, a lot of marketing activity takes place before a product reaches the final consumer. The complexity and magnitude of this flow of goods and services in the United States has been diagrammed in Figure 1–1. The sizes of the various streams represent roughly the value of the goods and services flowing to subsequent customers. Notice the small amount of activity between the retail level and the final consumers compared to the activity between other levels in the distribution chain. Retailing is important, certainly, but a great deal of marketing goes on before this stage is reached — wholesalers sell to other wholesalers and manufacturers for example, as well as manufacturers to other manufacturers.

The main point shown by Figure 1–1 is that a large volume of goods and services flow between the various levels in an economy. And all of these levels are vital to the efficient operation of an interdependent economy.

The critical importance of satisfying all levels of customers in a marketing system such as this should be obvious. A single firm certainly must sell its output at a profit, or it will go out of business.

Figure 1-1 The flow of goods and services in the United States (the width of each channel indicates the sales volume in that flow)

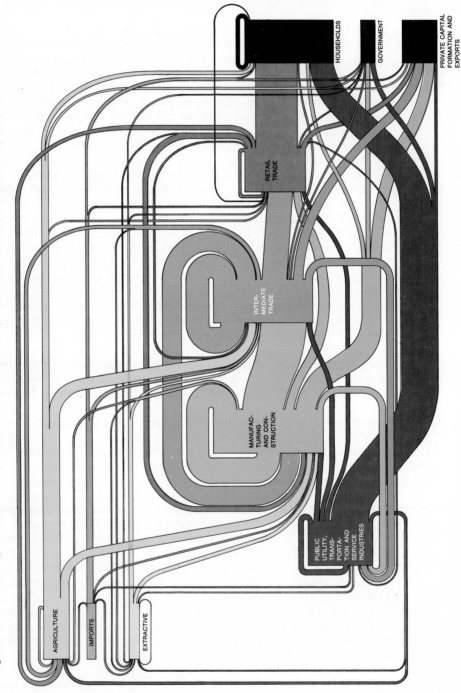

Source: Reavis Cox, *Distribution in a High Level Economy.* © 1965. Reprinted by permission of Prentice-Hall, Inc. Englewood Cliffs, N.J.

But more than this, the repercussions of poor business planning and low sales at one level may be felt throughout the entire system. If you don't sell bicycles at the retail level, for example, this eventually means less business at the wholesale, manufacturing, and raw materials levels too.

Who makes decisions in an economy?

Someone has to make the decisions that make an economic system work. In a traditional society, royal edict or long-accepted customs may decide what is done, by whom, and for whom. These approaches are still used in some less developed parts of the world, while more developed countries, including both "socialist" and "free enterprise" countries, have tended to develop "modern" economies.

In a socialist economy, central planners attempt to make all of the major and many of the minor decisions. As long as the economy is simple and the variety of goods is small, this may work fairly well. However, as economies become more complex, central planning becomes more difficult and may even break down.

In a free enterprise economy, the market directs the economy. There are no central planners who decide how the economy should work. (The American economy today is essentially but not totally market-directed. The federal government controls interest rates and the supply of money, for example, to direct the economy.) Working within a self-regulating mechanism called the "free market," individual business firms compete with each other for the customers' favor.

In a free economy, no consumer is forced to buy any goods or services, except those which society insists are essential. Schools, police, national defense, public health, and food inspection are considered essential services. These are provided by the community, and citizens are taxed to pay for them.

Beyond this, each firm makes its own decisions about what it will produce and sell. If they do their job well—if they satisfy enough customers—they will make a profit and stay in business.

This is the way the needs of a free economy are satisfied without the bureaucratic controls that go along with central planning. Whenever a new need arises, an opportunity is created for some profit-minded businessman. Thus all market needs which can be served profitably will produce businessmen to meet the need.

Micro-marketing is done by businessmen

This version of how a modern market-directed economic system works is accurate, but greatly oversimplified. Some constraints are set by the government—that is, by the consumers' representatives. And the decisions are *not* made automatically—*businessmen must make them.*

This business decision making is not always easy in a dynamic economy where customers have freedom of choice. The customer is under no obligation to buy the products of any business. Business firms must therefore anticipate consumer needs, and be ready to satisfy them when the customer wants to be satisfied, or risk losing the business to other firms. Planning ahead, figuring out what the customer will really need or want, is vital to the business's very survival—and to the working of the system.

The importance of correctly anticipating market needs is sometimes underestimated by students who seem to feel that all business firms are more or less the same and that business decision makers are basically just *reacting* to the needs of the market. The role of individual businesses in creating a dynamic economy and contributing to its growth often is overlooked.

In fact, individual businessmen can and do make a difference in our economy. A great deal depends on how well they do their jobs and how efficiently they manage their businesses.

One of the major thrusts of this text is to demonstrate that: (1) individual businessmen are often positive forces in the economy, *not just reactors* to situations; and that (2) businessmen can take the offensive and be aggressive contributors to change and improvement in our society.

Studies of how businessmen contribute to economic development in other countries have demonstrated that needed marketing activities are not always provided. Money spent to improve the productive capacity in some countries, without a corresponding provision for marketing facilities, has led to increased production but no real improvement in the economy. In some cases, food has actually rotted in the field because there was either no market for it or no distribution system to bring it to the market economically.

This potential for improving the macro or overall marketing process in a free economy is why we will emphasize the micro view of marketing for the bulk of this text. We will examine in depth how business firms can better meet customers' needs and, in the aggregate, make the macro-marketing system work better. We will not spend much time on how present firms work, but rather focus on *why* they do what they do and how they might do it better. Ultimately, you should be able to understand the *why* of present marketing efforts, *how* they might be improved—and *how* you can contribute to the marketing process in the future.

Marketing systems in action

Although our focus will be on how individual firms can and should operate, we must also be concerned with the operation of the total system—not just one level and the buyers and sellers directly above and below that level.

A manufacturer of grocery products, for example, has a wider responsibility than just "dumping" his goods on the wholesaler. He must know whether his products will move through the wholesaler to retail outlets and finally to the consumer. If his products do not move smoothly through to the consumer, inventories will start backing up and the manufacturer soon will be in trouble.

Although individual firms are concerned primarily with their own affairs, and understandably so, in a very real sense we can think of competing "total systems" composed of cooperating producers and middlemen. Sears, Roebuck and associated producers, for instance, compete with General Electric and associated middlemen in the sale of radios. Therefore, in this text, we will be concerned both with a "total system" which is the whole firm itself, and also "total systems" —channel systems—which tie together producers and middlemen.

Marketing functions needed at macro and micro levels

At both the macro and the micro levels of marketing, we find the same basic marketing functions—buying, selling, transporting, storing, grading, financing, risk-taking, and market information. It will be helpful to explain these basic functions and how they serve as a foundation for our approach to marketing.

Buying and selling

Buying and selling involve what is called the exchange process. The *buying* function is directed to the search for, and evaluation of, products and services. For middlemen, this means a search for the products that will appeal to their customers. The *selling* function involves promoting the product and would include the use of personal salesmen and advertising. This is the best-known, and some people feel the only, function of marketing.

Transporting and storing

The functions of *transporting* and *storing* involve the handling and movement of goods. These are the major activities of many marketing institutions, especially warehouses, transportation agencies, wholesalers, and some retailers.

Grading, financing, and risk-taking

Grading, financing, risk-taking, and *market information* assist other functions. *Grading* is dividing the product into the most attractive and useful quantities, thus aiding the storing and selling functions. *Financing* facilitates the exchange of money for goods and provides the credit necessary for storing. *Risk-taking* is inherent in any business activity—because the future is uncertain and is the reason why good management is so highly valued and consequently so well compensated. One of management's jobs is to measure and control the risk.

Market Information

The *market information* function, including collecting, analyzing, and disseminating data, provides the feedback activity that is needed in any system. Without current information, the manager will probably rely on old information—and last year's facts may prove to be the basis of this year's mistakes.

Functions can't be eliminated

No matter how simple or how complex the marketing process is, all the functions of marketing must be performed. If a manager were trying to improve the efficiency of a system, he would attempt to provide these functions with maximum efficiency. In some cases, this might require combining various middlemen into a larger system. In such a system a farmer, for example, would permit a wholesaler to pick up his products at the farm, haul them into town, grade them according to recognized standards, carry the financial burden until

13

they are sold, and throughout this period, take the risk that they can be sold. If this job is complicated, one wholesaler may not be willing to handle all these activities, and two or more wholesalers may become involved.

The important fact is that even if the farmer were to do all of this himself, *none* of the functions could be skipped. He would still have to grade the products on his own farm, store them until needed, and transport them into town. He would have to finance his own activities and bear any risk of price fluctuations or quality deterioration. In either situation, he would feel obligated to watch the newspaper or listen to the radio for market information on prices, supplies, and weather conditions.

From a macro point of view, we can see that these basic marketing functions must be performed by someone. Not every firm needs to do all of them. They can be shifted and shared within the macro system, but someone must do them. An extremely important question at the micro level, then, is who does what and for how much.

We will discuss these matters in more detail later. Now, it is important to note that an efficient macro-marketing system does not just happen. It is the result of considerable decision making and negotiation among business firms.

Development of consumer-oriented economies and customer-oriented companies

In a modern economy, marketing plays an extremely vital role. But it has not always been so important or complex. If we define marketing as a process of getting goods from producers to consumers (a simplified definition), it is obvious that relatively little marketing was done in ancient Egypt, for example, or in feudal Europe. Even today, a marketing structure far less complex than that in the United States operates in many parts of Asia, Africa, and Latin America.

To understand why marketing is so important to modern societies, it will be fruitful to look at the development of economic systems, with primary emphasis on Western civilization.

From subsistence living to money economies

The life of early man, scratching as he did for an existence, could truly be described as *subsistence living*. Yet there are still many parts of the world that have not advanced much beyond this level of living. Such peoples still raise and consume almost everything they produce, living without money and sharing both the output and the work of their communities. In India, for example, approximately 85 percent of the population lives in villages that still operate on a partially communal basis. There is little need there for selling.[10]

[10] Ralph Westfall and Harper W. Boyd, Jr., "Marketing in India," *Journal of Marketing*, October, 1960, pp. 11–15.

In some economies, specialization in production took place at an early stage. About 2100 B.C., the Code of Hammurabi was set down to help regulate the highly developed society that had grown up on the fertile river valleys of the Tigris and the Euphrates. Trade flourished, and these communities rose above the subsistence level because of (1) specialization in production and distribution and (2) an assurance that this specialization would work. That is, artisans were willing to leave the self-sufficient farm economy when they were fairly sure of being fed out of the food production of others. Trade also continued to grow whenever there was political stability—especially during the long period when the Romans ruled the Mediterranean area and controlled its commerce.[11]

Trade between nations dried up when Rome's power was broken. Western Europe moved into feudalism. Basically, feudalism was a return to an almost self-sufficient economy in which each family or manor grew and made what it needed. Eventually, however, the feudal manors began to come out of their isolation. At first, small weekly markets were developed. These markets—from perhaps 5 to 15 miles apart—were close enough to travel to and from in one day.

Slowly, as towns grew, these market meetings became more frequent until they became daily events. Eventually, a town would build a market hall to protect the sellers and buyers from the weather. Retail shops and warehouses developed so that the produce and wares did not have to be hauled back and forth to the farms each day.

This was a natural evolution of retail markets in the interior of Western Europe. The Middle East and the Mediterranean Sea coast cities had gone through these stages many centuries before. As soon as there was a sufficient surplus for trading beyond the town boundaries, wholesale markets in nonperishable commodites went through an evolution similar to that of the retail markets.

Industrialization forces more emphasis on marketing

During the Middle Ages, the roots of organized industry and specialization of labor were implanted. With the greater demand for goods, the old retail-handicraft method was no longer adequate. In the small village, journeymen and apprentices could produce goods that satisfied local preferences. But the great variety in design and quality was not satisfactory for large-scale trading in other areas. More standardized products were needed, and in larger quantities.

These needs were met by wholesale handicraftsmen, who supplied specifications and materials to workers paid by the piece. They were similar to some of our present subcontractors or small independent manufacturers, although their work usually was done in the homes of the workers.

In this system of production, workers became more dependent on production for the market. This work was profitable to the workers *as long as the goods were sold.* When the system did not function

---

[11] Herbert Heaton, *Economic History of Europe* (New York: Harper & Bros., 1948).

because of wars, famine, or other reasons, there was a natural reversion to village self-sufficiency.

Starting about 1700, the Industrial Revolution and the growth of the factory system increased productivity. Both new and old commodities were produced at lower prices. This offered new opportunities for trade, but it also meant that markets had to be found to absorb the greater output.

Adam Smith's *Wealth of Nations,* published in 1776, encouraged the development of free and unrestricted trade. Yet, in spite of the revived interest in trade, much of Europe's trading of this period took place – and, in fact, still takes place – in the original markets developed in the Middle Ages.

**Develop-
ment in
the United
States**

The development of trade in the United States parallels that of the Middle East and Europe. Some of the very early trade in America, especially in the southern colonies, was conducted by European trading companies operating under charters from their governments. Some of the early colonies were actually trading settlements established to gain a foothold in the New World. These colonies were supposed to provide a market for Europe's finished products and a source of raw materials for the mother country.

As settlers moved west, however, there was less and less dependence on England. As long as the majority of finished products came from Europe, the import-export firms pretty much controlled trading. But finished-goods production in the United States began to increase after the Revolutionary War and during and after the War of 1812, when imports declined. The canning industry, for example, developed during this period, and the meat-packing industry was started in 1818 in Cincinnati.

**The ports,
the rail-
roads, the
discount
houses**

Even before the development of a substantial American finished-goods industry, many of the larger retailers in the seacoast cities began buying from importers in large lots and servicing the smaller retailers, especially inland. Many of these large retailers switched entirely to wholesaling in the early 1800's.

These early wholesale centers usually were in waterfront towns, since transportation was still tied to the rivers, lakes, and oceans. By 1850, most of the major wholesale centers were well-established centers that have maintained their importance through the years, such as New York, Philadelphia, Baltimore, Boston, New Orleans, Detroit, Chicago, and the river towns of Pittsburgh, Cincinnati, Louisville, and St. Louis.[12]

The growth of railroads also opened new markets. After the Civil War, the number of manufacturing establishments grew rapidly, but the established wholesalers and retailers, while providing outlets for the many small farmers and manufacturers, easily dominated dis-

[12] T. N. Beckman and N. H. Engle, *Wholesaling – Principles and Practices* (rev. ed.; New York: Ronald Press Co., 1951), chap. v.

tribution. In the late 1800's, many manufacturers became dissatisfied with their distribution arrangements because they found that they could produce more goods than retailers and wholesalers wanted. Some manufacturers, discovering the value of aggressive sales and advertising efforts, began sending out their own salesmen and branding and advertising their products.

Retailers also responded to this outpouring of goods. Abandoning the general-store approach of the day, they began to specialize in various types of goods. Stores grew larger and larger. Today, we find a great variety of specialists in retailing, from small shops catering to special tastes to large discount houses offering lower prices to the masses.

The productivity of the American economy continued to grow at the rate of about 3 percent annually. Many progressive manufacturers sensed that more and more consumers were able to satisfy their basic needs and have something left for luxuries. They began to cater to the mass market rather than just the "carriage trade." In the early 1900's, for example, automobiles were already an important part of the American economy. The mass production of many thousands of varieties of "luxury" goods led to many dynamic and competitive changes in our economy. Mass advertising, personal selling, and newer and more complex forms of wholesaling and retailing have developed to adjust to this changing market.

From the production era to the marketing era

In recent years, an increasing number of producers, wholesalers, and retailers have recognized the importance of marketing. These companies have traveled the long evolutionary road from the days when the basic consideration was producing or stocking products. Now they focus their attention on the customer and try to integrate the company's total effort toward satisfying him.

Identifying the following three orientations should help clarify this evolution: (1) production or product, (2) sales, and (3) marketing.

Seldom has the story of this evolution been put so clearly and candidly as by R. T. Keith, the top executive of Pillsbury, Inc., a manufacturer of flour, cake mixes, and animal feeds.

Keith admitted that the marketing concept had been a long time coming for his company. Pillsbury was formed in 1869. It continued until about 1930 in what Keith called "the production era." This was a period when products were relatively scarce, and the most important function of the company was production. Beginning in 1930, the company went into the "sales era." It became conscious of the fact that it had to go out and get customers and that its dealers had other sources of supply. Promotion of the available products became extremely important, both to middlemen and for attracting their customers' customers.

The sales era continued until about 1950. By then, Pillsbury had developed new cake mixes, and the sales of these products were growing so rapidly that a coordinator became necessary to organize the efforts of production, research, procurement, and sales. As Pillsbury faced up to this task, Keith pointed out, the sales era was replaced by the "marketing department era." This meant a heavy emphasis on short-run policy planning.

The advertising department and the sales promotion department were dissolved into the one coordinating policy-making body. Obtaining people who were effective at short-run marketing policy making was difficult. Experienced men were relatively scarce. This led to a three- to four-year development period during which some of the marketing department's short-range planning was not fully effective. These marketing men were maturing, however, and learning how to translate ideas into products and products into profits.

In a relatively few years, Pillsbury had developed men with a marketing management approach, and in 1958, according to Keith, the company went into a new era — the "marketing company era." Now, in addition to short-run marketing planning, the *total company effort* is guided by the marketing concept, that is, that all the firm's activities should be organized to satisfy its customers. Long-range as well as short-range planning is involved. Pillsbury's marketing specialists now look and plan 3 to 10 years ahead.[13]

Much more is said about the marketing concept in the next chapter, but it is important to note here that the marketing concept is gaining enthusiastic acceptance in many progressive companies.

The overwhelming importance of the customer and a customer orientation in some firms is suggested by the following quotation *from a booklet distributed to production employees* by a large industrial organization.

What is a customer?

A customer is a person who brings us his wants. Our job is to fill them profitably — to him and to ourselves.

A customer expects value in what he buys from us. If we do not give him value, he will go elsewhere to find it.

A customer's good opinion of our company is the most valuable asset in the world. Whatever we can do to build that good opinion will eventually be to our advantage.

A customer's good opinion cannot be bought or stolen. However, it can be freely given in response to our gift of value.

A customer is never too far away to affect our jobs, no matter how remote from him our work may seem. One small slip or flaw in any department can lessen the value of our product or service in the customer's eyes.

A customer is the boss behind our boss. By serving him well, we serve ourselves as well.[14]

What is marketing?

We have deliberately avoided defining "marketing" until now, to allow you to develop some tentative definitions of your own.

From the historical discussion, for example, you may have based

---

[13] Robert J. Keith, "The Marketing Revolution," *Journal of Marketing*, January, 1960, pp. 35–38.

[14] *It Pays to Be Customer-Minded* (New York: Alumni Publications, Inc., 1955), p. 12.

your definition upon the exchange of surplus commodities. This certainly would have been appropriate for past times.

Or your tentative definition may have stressed the exchange of goods in a production-oriented economy. Such a definition would emphasize the production of goods by a family or a business, and exchange of those goods for other goods they were less able to produce for themselves.

A more modern definition, in tune with greatly expanded productive capacity, might emphasize the adaptation of production facilities to the market. Specifically, marketing might be defined as the response of businessmen to consumer demands through adjustments in production capabilities. Adjusting production capabilities would refer to the coordination of production, accounting, finance, and marketing in the light of the changing needs of consumers who are affluent enough to have varied buying choices.

Or, recognizing the growing interest in consumerism and the performance of our marketing system, you might have developed a definition which emphasized macro-marketing concerns, such as:

Marketing is concerned with designing an efficient (in terms of use of resources) and fair (in terms of distribution of output to all parties involved) system which will direct an economy's flow of goods and services from producers to consumers and accomplish the objectives of the society. We will make more use of this definition in Chapter 30, when we return to a macro-level discussion.

As the marketing manager knows, marketing directs!

For a more active view of marketing, however, we are going to look at it from the marketing manager's viewpoint – that is, the micro-level viewpoint.

The marketing manager is concerned with directing specific functions and activities (which encompass several functions). In this sense, the definition that emphasizes the need to adjust production capabilities might be too general. The marketing manager is concerned with specific activities, and he works toward specific results.

Within this micro-level framework, we can define marketing in the following way:

Marketing is the performance of business activities which direct the flow of goods and services from producer to consumer or user in order to satisfy customers and accomplish the company's objectives.

So that the student will realize the full importance and scope of micro-level marketing, let's examine the meaning of this definition by discussing its components.

Are the activities of product development, product design, packaging, credit and collection, transportation, warehousing, and price setting included in "marketing?"

There is little doubt that personal selling and advertising are marketing activities, and many business executives would limit the scope of marketing to them. They feel that the job of marketing is to "get rid of" the product which has been produced and priced by the production, accounting, and finance executives. This narrow view of marketing should obviously be rejected.

When we define marketing as those activities which *direct* the flow of goods and services, we mean just that: direct.

Marketing should begin with the customer, not with the production process. Marketing and not production should determine what products are to be made—including decisions about product development, design, and packaging; what prices are to be charged—credit and collection policies; and where and how the products are to be advertised and sold.

This does not mean that marketing should take over the traditional production, accounting, and financial activities, but merely that it provide direction for these activities.

After all, the purpose of business is to satisfy customer needs through the sale of products or services. It is *not* to supply products or services which *might* sell.

A factory can make products, and wholesalers and retailers can stock an assortment of goods, but it takes coordination of all the activities of a particular business to create profitable sales. In other words, we should see marketing as the coordinating force of the "total system" which is the business itself. And looking ahead a bit, it is possible that some firm within a larger "total system" comprised of producers and middlemen might provide this coordinating role. That is, a manufacturer, or a wholesaler, or a retailer might do the market-oriented thinking for its entire channel system.

Why study marketing?

Modern economies are "customer-oriented"

In our economy of abundance, businesses *must* cater to their customers. They cannot simply wait until customers "beat a path" to their doors, because most of us can get along quite well without the product offered by any particular manufacturer, wholesaler, or retailer. We need clothing, for example, but we do not need a particular clothing manufacturer's product. The same is true of food, housefurnishings, automobiles, sports equipment, and most other consumer goods. Likewise, manufacturers usually have several sources of supply for the components incorporated into their products.

The fact that customers do not depend on any one firm's product is partly responsible for our complex marketing structure. Take bread for example. It is normally available in bakeries, grocery stores, delicatessens, and sometimes even in drugstores. Since bread is bulky and perishable, several competing bakeries are usually located in or close to our cities. These factories handle their own distribution with their own drivers and trucks. This is a relatively expensive process, since only a few loaves are delivered to each store. But as long as prices are reasonable, it is unlikely that there will be much competition from bakeries out of the area.

Bread by air

Sometimes, however, consumer demand may create new opportunities and change the market situation. Certain customers may desire special products – specialty breads, for example – not being supplied by existing sources. To meet such demands, bread may be transported a much greater distance, at a correspondingly greater cost.

Such a situation did exist for some time when a New England baker flew bread products daily to the Chicago market. A number of Chicago consumers were willing to pay considerably higher prices for the products of this particular baker. Eventually, this market expanded to the point that the baker built a plant in Chicago. But other specialty breads are still shipped great distances. Breads made in Los Angeles and Washington State move all over the West Coast and to Hawaii. And frozen bread now is distributed all over the country and world.

The axiom, "The customer is always right," applies in these instances. It is, in fact, a guide to most marketing activities. The many and varied consumer demands often necessitate a more complex marketing structure to serve them. These varied demands also lead to marketing problems for individual businesses. But whatever the problems or opportunities, customers' needs must be served because, without sales, the firm cannot exist.

Almost half the consumer's dollar for marketing

A good share of the consumer's dollar goes for marketing activities.[15] Professor R. Cox estimated that 41.7 percent of this dollar is consumed by distribution activities. Other analysts, using other methods, have calculated figures up to 58.9 percent. Professor P. D. Converse estimated that the cost of marketing for 1929 through 1948 varied from 48 to 50.5 percent of the consumer's dollar.

An activity of this size and importance certainly requires study. If almost half the consumer's dollar is spent on marketing, it is probable that a similar percentage of the nation's work force is engaged in marketing activities. While the exact number of people employed in marketing has not been determined, it was estimated in 1950 that 407 persons were engaged in *commodity distribution* for each 1,000 engaged in *commodity production*. To this distribution group must be added the large number of people engaged in marketing services. Comparative figures from the late 1800's show the immense growth of U.S. marketing during less than 10 decades. In 1870, there were only 88 persons working in *commodity distribution* for every 1,000 in *commodity production*.[16]

[15] Reavis Cox, *Distribution in a High-Level Economy* (Englewood Cliffs, N.J.: Prentice-Hall, Inc., 1965), p. 149; Paul W. Stewart and J. Frederick Dewhurst, *Does Distribution Cost Too Much?* (New York: Twentieth Century Fund, 1939), pp. 117–18; and *Business Week*, January 12, 1952, p. 122.

[16] Harold Barger, *Distribution's Place in the American Economy Since 1869* (Princeton, N.J.: Princeton University Press, 1955), pp. 7–8.

Greater
opportunity
for youth

An equally important reason for a college student to study marketing
is the availability of many interesting and rewarding jobs in this area.
Even more important, marketing offers opportunities for rapid growth
and advancement.

A few years ago, an American Management Association official
predicted: "Every company president elected from 1965 on will be a
marketing man."[17] This was overstated, but it is true that young people
are welcomed and can move up fast in this dynamic field. Perhaps a sign
of what is coming is the fact that General Electric, the company that has
pioneered the acceptance of a marketing orientation, appointed a marketing man as its chief executive officer as early as 1963.[18]

In marketing, the compensation on the way up is very attractive.
Although some marketing jobs offer lower starting salaries than other
jobs, after 5 years the average earnings of those who started in marketing have matched or bettered those of other business groups—and
after 10 years they are ahead of all of them. One study (Table 1–1)
listed the average monthly salaries.

Table 1–1 Average monthly salaries in selected fields

Field	Five years after graduation	Ten years after graduation
Engineering	$970	$1,143
Accounting	959	1,191
Sales-marketing	964	1,212
General business	883	1,148

Source: Frank S. Endicott, "Trends in Employment of College and University Graduates
in Business and Industry," (Evanston, Ill.: Northwestern University, 1969) p. 70.

Further, employment opportunities hold up well—and sometimes
actually grow—when the economy becomes sluggish. In the first
quarter of 1970, for example, executive appointments dropped 4
percent below the previous quarter. But marketing appointments rose
24 percent.[19] A careful study of marketing will give the student a
better idea about business and where the best opportunities lie for a
career.

Marketing
encourages
innovation
and growth

There is an even more fundamental reason for studying marketing
Without sales, there can be no business. Marketing is a stimulus that
encourages innovation. Research effort and investment money are
attracted when customers are willing to pay for a new product or

[17] "Marketing Sold to the Company," *Business Week,*
July 27, 1959, pp. 78–83.

[18] "G. E. Shifts Herald Harder Consumer Sell," *Busi-*

ness Week, Ocotber 12, 1963, p. 88.

[19] "More Marketing Jobs," *Marketing Insights,*
May 4, 1970, p. 3.

service. When sales and profits justify it, companies press on to further innovations and improvements. In recent years, industries that have followed this pattern include business machines and electronics.

In general, where a well-organized market economy is operating, there are opportunities for new investment, and the level of business activity, employment, and so on, is high. But when marketing activities are neglected, the result is often slower growth or even stagnation.

Further, without an effective marketing system, the less developed countries may be doomed to what Professor Nurkse has called "a vicious circle of poverty."[20] By this, he means that no one will leave his subsistence way of life to produce for the market, because there is no market for any goods he might produce. And there are no buyers, because everyone else is engaged in producing for his own needs. Marketing institutions can provide the dynamic element for breaking this vicious circle.

In this sense, a study of marketing systems will not only improve our understanding of our present and future institutions but will also throw light on the problems of the less developed economies. A knowledge of these economies will be increasingly important as our interest in the world grows.

One management expert holds that marketing is the key to the growth of less developed countries. He states this idea as follows:

> Marketing occupies a critical role in respect to the development of such "growth areas." Indeed, marketing is the most important "multiplier" of such developments. It is in itself in every one of these areas, the least developed, the most backward part of the economic system. Its development, above all others, makes possible economic integration and the fullest utilization of whatever assets and productive capacity an economy already possesses. It mobilizes latent economic energy. It contributes to the greatest needs: that for the rapid development of entrepreneurs and managers, and at the same time it may be the easiest area of managerial work to get going.[21]

Conclusion

Marketing has its critics—both at the macro and the micro levels. Some of the complaints are justified; some are based primarily on theory or perhaps a few unfortunate run-ins with unscrupulous businessmen or exposures to offensive advertising. And some criticism is based on naïveté (or ignorance). Some consumers believe that marketing is a basically simple process of moving a finished product to an eager consumer. Farmers, especially, hold this idea. They look at marketing as a process for bringing their potatoes, tomatoes, eggs,

[20] Ragnar Nurkse, *Problems of Capital Formation in Underdeveloped Countries* (Oxford: Basil Blackwell, 1953), p. 4.

[21] Peter F. Drucker, "Marketing and Economic Development," *Journal of Marketing,* Vol. 22 (January, 1958), p. 253. Reprinted from the *Journal of Marketing,* national quarterly publication of the American Marketing Association.

and so on, into town where they are suddenly marked way up by mono-polistic distributors.

Some of the complaints ring true, but the student should not base his own conclusions on limited information. It's a good idea to take a thorough look at the facts and try to understand the problems, prac-tices, and objectives of those being criticized before reaching a judg-ment. Business has been given a vital role by society, just as have governments, schools, and churches. If business, and especially mar-keting, doesn't do the job right, another system, or a modification of the present system, may be needed.

Before trying to reach any conclusions, let's proceed with our analysis of marketing, recognizing that any economy requires a mar-keting system – and the more complex the economy, the more complex the marketing system may have to be. In this text, we will take the viewpoint of marketing managers – the actors on the marketing scene – to give you a better understanding of marketing systems and processes. Thus the primary focus will be on the micro view of mar-keting.

As we proceed, the role of marketing management will be em-phasized. However, running a strong second in emphasis will be an evaluation of the impact of consumer behavior and the firm's reac-tions on the economy.

At the end of the course, we will return to an evaluation of how well the macro-marketing process is working and can work in the future. This macro view is highly important because if consumers (and voters) decide that the process is not working well, they might decide to adopt some other system. There is no guarantee that the present system will be allowed to continue indefinitely; there is no mandate from heaven for business firms to operate the way they do. Each firm must con-tinue to earn the right to operate as part of the marketing process. It is only through the long-run satisfaction and acceptance of con-sumers that marketing management can justify its role in a free enter-prise system.

In more direct terms, even though central planners probably could not manage our economy (or any advanced economy) very efficiently, if the consumers and/or voters became disenchanted with the present system, they could opt for a centrally planned system, or at least a substantial modification of the present system. The current interest in consumerism, the legislation limiting cigarette promotion, and new automobile safety standards are simple illustrations of developments which could multiply. Some consumer-protection advocates, for example, have suggested that government standards should be es-tablished for new products. The logical next step would be specifying the price and perhaps even the quantities which could be produced and sold. Finally, bureaucrats – typically reactors, *not* actors – would be running the economy. This could happen in any free enterprise economy if businessmen do not meet the needs and demands of the consumer-voters.

1 It is fairly easy to see why people do not beat a path to the mousetrap manufacturer's door, but would they be similarly indifferent if some food processor developed a revolutionary new food product which would provide all necessary nutrients in small pills for about $100 a year per person?

2 Some critics feel that marketing costs too much. If this is true, who gets this "too much"? Be specific.

3 What costs are included in marketing costs? Which of these do you feel might be eliminated? How would our economy be changed if it were illegal to incur any marketing costs?

4 Distinguish between macro- and micro-marketing. Then explain how they are interrelated, if they are.

5 Explain why the same product may be bought and sold several times before it is finally sold to consumers at the retail store. Illustrate with a specific example in your answer.

6 Discuss the nature of marketing in a socialist economy. Would the development of wholesaling and retailing systems be any different?

7 Explain, in your own words, why the emphasis in this text will be on micro-marketing.

8 Discuss the kinds of marketing decisions that a socialist planner and a free enterprise entrepreneur have to make.

9 Contrast the importance of a market orientation for individual business firms in primitive economic systems and modern economies.

10 Explain in your own words the difference between the text's definitions of micro- and macro-marketing.

11 Why is the satisfaction of consumers apparently considered of equal importance with satisfying the firm's objectives in the text's definition of micro-marketing?

12 Define the marketing concept in your own words and then suggest how acceptance of this concept might affect the organization and operation of your college.

13 Describe a recent purchase you have made and indicate why that particular product was available at a store, and, in particular, at that store.

14 What kinds of problems is a new producer of cake mixes likely to encounter when beginning operations?

15 What does the text mean with respect to marketing as a "system of action" and "systems of action"?

...the underlying principle of the marketing concept is that
a firm should seek to meet the needs of customers at a profit
rather than placing the main emphasis on its own internal
activities and utilization of its resources.
...give the customer what he needs – this may seem so
obvious and logical that it is difficult to understand why
the marketing concept is considered such a breakthrough.
However, people haven't always done the logical and obvious.

2

Marketing management and marketing strategy planning

Marketing and marketing management play important roles in our society and in our business firms. As we saw in the previous chapter, marketing (the micro view) is concerned with those business activities which direct the flow of goods and services from producers to consumers. This occurs to satisfy the needs of consumers and accomplish either the economy's (the macro view) or the company's (the micro view) objectives.

To arrive at a better understanding of both macro- and micro-level marketing, we are going to study it from the point of view of the marketing manager – the man who makes the crucial company marketing decisions. In this chapter, we will look at the nature of the marketing function within a firm. We will also consider the importance of marketing strategy planning to the success of individual business firms and, in the aggregate, to the effective operation of the macro-marketing system.

The marketing concept—a new view of business

Modern management has evolved from a production-oriented to a sales-oriented and finally to a marketing-oriented view of business. The Pillsbury story in Chapter 1 was an outstanding example of this, but the same sort of evolution in thinking and organization has occurred in many companies.[1]

General Electric led the way

General Electric was the pacesetter in the movement toward marketing orientation, or what is formally called the "marketing concept." Rather than just a method of operation, this concept is really a new philosophy of business.

The underlying principle of the marketing concept is that a firm should seek to meet the needs of customers, at a profit, rather than placing its main emphasis on its own internal activities and utilization of its resources. These latter factors are also important, of course, but those who believe in the marketing concept feel that customers' needs should be the firm's primary focus and that resources should be organized to satisfy those needs.

A production-orientation is a major obstacle

Give the customer what he needs—this may seem so obvious and logical that it is difficult to understand why the marketing concept is considered such a breakthrough. However, people haven't always done the logical and obvious. In a typical company, production men thought mainly about getting the product out. Accountants were only interested in balancing the books. Financial people were absorbed in the company's cash position. And salesmen were mainly concerned with getting orders. No one was particularly concerned with whether the whole system made sense. As long as the company made a profit, each department went merrily on in its independent way, "doing its own thing." Unfortunately, they still do in the majority of companies today.

This typical lack of a unifying focus is called production orientation. But to be fair to production men, it also is seen in sales-oriented salesmen, advertising-oriented admen, finance-oriented finance men, and so on. We will use "production-orientation" to cover all such myopic orientations.

The difference between production orientation and marketing

---

[1] For further discussion on this, see Robert L. King, "The Marketing Concept," in George Schwartz (ed.), *Science in Marketing* (New York: John Wiley & Sons, Inc., 1965), pp. 70–97; Bernard J. LaLonde and Edward J. Morrison, "Marketing Management Concepts Yesterday and Today," *Journal of Marketing*, January, 1967, pp. 9–13; and Richard T. Hise, "Have Manufacturing Firms Adopted the Marketing Concept?" *Journal of Marketing*, July, 1965, pp. 9–12.

orientation in a company can be grasped better by viewing a business as a box which contains the various departments of the firm (see Figure 2-1a). Most firms have departments such as sales, accounting,

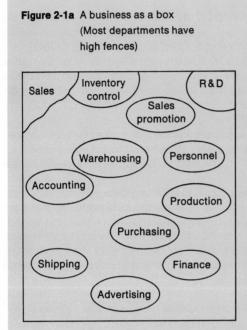

Figure 2-1a A business as a box (Most departments have high fences)

Figure 2-1b Total system view of a business (Implementing marketing concept; still have departments but all guided by what customer wants)

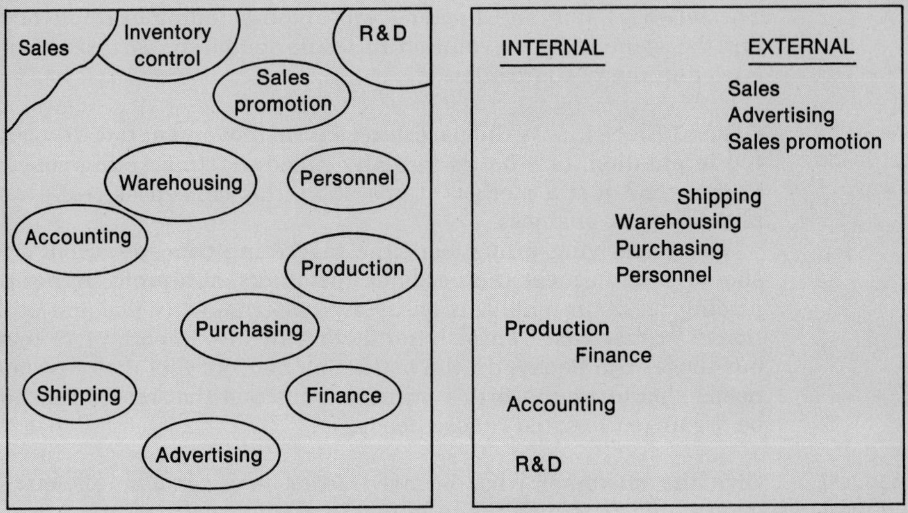

production, warehousing, finance, research and development, personnel, and so on. Often the managers of the various departments erect fences around their domains. Such businesses do not operate as a system. In such production-oriented operations, each department runs its own affairs for its own benefit. There may be coordinating committees to try to get them to work together, but usually each department head comes to such meetings with the idea of protecting his own interests (without seeming to appear too obstinate!).

Step across the line . . . do a better job

In a firm which has accepted the marketing concept, however, the fences tend to come down. There are still departments to be sure, but the total system's effort is guided by what customers want and what the firm can deliver, rather than what the various departments would like to do.

In such an environment, it might be more realistic to view the business as a box with both an internal and an external sector (see Figure 2-1b). Here, there are some internal departments primarily concerned with affairs inside the firm, such as production, accounting, and research and development (R&D). And there are external departments primarily concerned with outsiders, including sales, advertising, and sales promotion. Finally, there are departments that must be concerned with both the internal and the external sectors, such as warehousing, shipping, purchasing, finance, and personnel. The efforts of all of these departments, however, are directed to satisfying some market needs—at a profit, which measures the success of the operation.

As GE saw it, a logical implementation of the marketing concept would provide a systematic approach to managing the marketing process in any business, large or small.

This approach (1) insures that the manager knows what and where his markets are; (2) provides effective customer and product service; (3) puts the right product at the right place at the right price; (4) sells to the greatest possible number of customers through the most efficient sales and distribution channels; and (5) supports the product adequately with advertising and sales promotion.[2] This approach keys on the customer but also requires that all marketing activities focus on specific company objectives—profit, sales volume, and market share targets.

Where the marketing concept has been wholeheartedly accepted and implemented, it has led to substantial changes in the operation and often to significantly better results.

The typical executive in a production-oriented firm tends to view the company's operation from his own vantage point. He looks at the rest of the business as working around him. He often expects other executives to adjust themselves to his plans and activities. When all of a firm's executives follow this path, we sometimes see chaos, or at the very least a system with many malfunctions and little clear direction.

The marketing concept paves the way

The marketing concept provides direction to the "total system of action"[3] that each business firm needs. In the marketing-oriented firm, all planning is done with selected target markets in mind. And every aspect of the business is integrated to work together to accomplish the firm's objectives. Of course, someone has to be responsible for integrating this whole effort, and this is why our micro definition of marketing emphasized the word *direct*. Logically, this someone is the marketing manager, since he is the primary link between the firm and the customer.

EDP may help too

The move toward the marketing concept has also been aided by an important technological development—the computer. Departmental or functional "empires" may have been necessary when the flows of information between and among departments were slow. Now, however, with the growing use of data processing equipment, we see that

---

[2] Adapted from Edward S. McKay, "How to Plan and Set Up Your Marketing Program," *A Blueprint for an Effective Marketing Program* (Marketing Series No. 91 [New York: American Management Association, Inc., 1954]), p. 15.

[3] The need for tying all the parts of business together is presented in a new light in James W. Culliton, "Age of Synthesis," *Harvard Business Review*, September–October, 1962, pp. 36 ff.

the traditional departmental approach is not only unnecessary but may be quite inefficient. Furthermore, when the whole business is seen as a system, tasks that formerly seemed to require considerable management judgment can now be assumed by computers.

General Electric's system illustrates the possibilities of electronic data processing. It demonstrates why an internal business system should be seen as a system, crossing traditional functional lines wherever necessary.

Ask the computer, wait 15 seconds

General Electric has developed a computer-oriented system that ties together its widely dispersed manufacturing and distribution facilities. This computer system links together 65 customer service centers (sales offices) located in 49 states, 18 distribution warehouses in 11 states, and 40 product departments with 53 manufacturing plants in 21 states. If, for example, a customer wanted to place an order for a truckload of lamps *on the condition that shipment be made promptly*, he could call one of the GE local sales offices and place his order tentatively, assuming that GE could, in fact, meet his conditions.

If the customer telephoned the order to the local sales office, the salesman there could enter the required data into the GE computer system while the buyer was still on the phone. The computer system then would check to see if GE wanted to sell to this particular buyer (a credit check) and if the item were in stock at a convenient location. If the answer to both questions were yes, the computer would (*a*) issue an order to ship, (*b*) bill the customer, (*c*) update the inventory records, (*d*) generate the records that are reviewed periodically so that orders are issued automatically to factories to replenish inventory at the various distribution points, and (*e*) relay the message back to the GE salesman that the customer's order is on the way. And all of this would take less than 15 seconds!

No mourning for the passing of boundaries

The speed of this system is remarkable—but the most remarkable achievement is the integration of the system. What this means is that the computer now does a number of jobs that were formerly handled by separate departmental or line operations. These include credit checking, inventory control, production scheduling, shipping control, billing, order entry procedure, and all the bookkeeping that formerly kept many clerks busy.

This system also allows random inquiry for specific management information, and it regularly produces special reports for management.

Clearly, then, the traditional functional departmental boundaries make little sense in such an integrated system.[4]

[4]For more details on this system, see Clint De-Gabriell, "Design Criteria for an On-Line Nation-Wide Order Processing System," *Disc File Applications* (Detroit: American Data Processing, Inc., 1964), pp. 71–75. Westinghouse Electric has a similar system in operation. See *Systems*, April, 1965, p. 10. See also, E. J. McCarthy, J. A. McCarthy, and D. Humes, *Integrated Data Processing Systems* (New York: John Wiley & Sons, Inc., 1966).

The total system reaches out

The external as well as the internal affairs of any business should be viewed as part of a total system of action. The production-oriented businessman sometimes feels his job is done when the salesmen have somehow unloaded the company's products. But, we have seen, a firm must also operate and understand its role as part of a channel system. It will prosper only if the whole channel system functions well. Even so small a matter as a packing decision on the production line may have to be based on how wholesalers and retailers will handle the product in their warehouses and stores.

It may be annoying to those who would prefer to focus on their own problems, but total-system thinking is necessary for survival of entire companies in our competitive world. Competition is stiffening in many markets. The standardized, homogeneous products which production-oriented people like to turn out are often not profitable anymore in head-on competiton with similar products.

Marketing takes global view

A modern marketing-oriented firm is not limited to seeking customers merely in one region or even in one country. Increasingly, marketing-oriented companies are taking a broader view of potential markets. People all over the world are viewed as prospective customers, and multinational companies are being formed to serve them better. Throughout this text, we will take into account this global view of business and marketing.

More profits in world enterprises

The marketing concept is less well understood in foreign markets, and consequently there are great opportunities for those who know how to work with it and want to apply it abroad.

Some companies are expanding into worldwide operations. Sometimes they move from strictly domestic operations to exporting and licensing of foreign producers. Such operations are often treated as separate little departments, with resultant neglect. Increasingly, though, such companies are aggressively pursuing foreign market prospects, and often find foreign operations more profitable than domestic operations. As a result, they are paying more attention to worldwide markets. Domestic and foreign operations may even be integrated under one executive. Deere & Co., a farm machinery manufacturer, and Procter & Gamble, for example, have taken this step.

The involvement in international business may ultimately reach the point that the firm sees itself as a worldwide enterprise.[5] The chief executive of Abbott Laboratories, a pharmaceutical company with plants in 22 countries, said: "We are no longer just a U.S. company with interests abroad. Abbott is a world enterprise, and many major, fundamental decisions must be made on a global basis."

A Texas Instruments executive had a similar view: "When we

[5] "Multi-National Companies," *Business Week*, April 20, 1963, pp. 62–86.; "U.S., Europe Businessmen Adapt to Global Market Concept: de Windt," *Marketing Insights*, February 9, 1970, pp. 1 f; J. B. Quinn, "Technology Transfer by Multi-national Companies," *Harvard Business Review*, Vol. 47, No. 6 (November–December, 1969), pp. 147–61; and "The Multi-Nationals Ride a Rougher Road," *Business Week*, Dec. 19, 1970, pp. 57–146.

consider new opportunities and one is abroad and the other domestic, we can't afford to look upon the alternative here as an inherently superior business opportunity simply because it is in the U.S. We view an overseas market just as we do our market in, say, Arizona, as one more market in the world."

A General Motors executive sees this trend as: ". . . the emergence of the modern industrial corporation as an institution that is transcending national boundaries."

Marketing concept forces a sense of mission and integrated effort

Many other companies, following GE's lead, have emphasized marketing management and the central role marketing plays in their operations. In fact, it is hard nowadays to find a successful business in which the "customer-comes-first" idea has been ignored or flouted. This is because the marketing concept forces the company (1) to think through what it is doing, and why, and then (2) to develop a plan for accomplishing its goals. And, as we have seen, it encourages an integrated effort to achieve these goals.[6]

To illustrate, we can compare a very successful application of the marketing concept with an unsuccessful management effort. The Ford Motor Co. Mustang "sports" car *was* designed according to the marketing concept. Considerable marketing research was done *before* the product was designed or the marketing strategy developed. The strategy finally adopted took into consideration consumer research and company resources and objectives.[7] The outstanding success of the Mustang is well known.

Ford's earlier experience with the ill-fated Edsel is another story. While there was considerable consumer research on the Edsel, it tended to focus on promotional possibilities, because the automobile design itself and the basic marketing strategy were already fixed. Even though consumers expressed little enthusiasm for those parts of the plan to which they were exposed, their attitudes were not permitted to alter the basic plan. The research had come too late and was not used to help direct the whole effort.[8]

Too many companies, unfortunately, still are only paying lip serv-

[6]It can be argued that the integrating force of the marketing concept need not be limited to profit-oriented business. Any organization which is trying to satisfy needs probably would benefit by adopting the marketing concept. For more on this point, see P. Kotler and S. J. Levy, "Broadening the Concept of Marketing," *Journal of Marketing,* January, 1969, pp. 10–15; D. J. Luck, "Broadening the Concept of Marketing—Too Far," *Journal of Marketing,* July, 1969, pp. 53–55; P. Kotler and S. J. Levy, "A New Form of Marketing Myopia, Rejoinder to Professor Luck," *Journal of Marketing,* July, 1969,

pp. 55–57; J. W. Culliton, "A Marketing Analysis of Religion," *Business Horizons,* Spring, 1959; and Fedor V. Rocco, "Marketing in the Socialist Economy of Yugoslavia," *MSU Business Topics,* Summer, 1968, pp. 67–80.

[7]Talk by George Brown, Director of Marketing Research, Ford Motor Co., at Tri-State Marketing Teachers Meeting, May 8, 1965.

[8]Talk given by Paul Lazarsfeld at the University of Notre Dame in 1964.

ice to the marketing concept and the concept that the marketing system is supposed to satisfy consumers. This may be partly responsible for the rising voices of consumerities and politicians. We will say more about this as we discuss specific business decision areas.

The balance of this book will focus on the application of the marketing concept in a specific business firm — be it a manufacturer, farmer, miner, wholesaler, or retailer — selling goods *or* services.

The management job in marketing

Hitting the target customer

The marketing manager's job consists of trying to meet the needs of a particular group of customers (the target group) with a particular good or service. At the same time, he must work toward the firm's objectives and operate within its resources and other constraints.

The selection of the target group for a given product is an important part of the marketing manager's job. But it is only the beginning. Out of the almost infinite number of products offered to the consumer, the marketing manager wants to be sure that *his product* will succeed. How can he do this?

First, the marketing manager is a manager. It should be helpful, therefore, to look closely at the role of any manager.

Nature of the management job

Management generally has three basic tasks:

1. To set up a general plan or strategy for the business.
2. To direct the execution of this plan.
3. To evaluate, analyze, and control the plan in actual operation.

For simplicity, this might be condensed to planning, execution, and control. The three-cornered diagram in Figure 2–2 shows the interrelation of these three basic tasks. The relationship of the control and planning jobs is extremely important, since the feedback of information often leads to changes in the general plan or even a totally new plan. Thus the management job is *continuous*.

The *marketing* manager's job, then, consists of these basic management responsibilities. First, the marketing executive must evolve

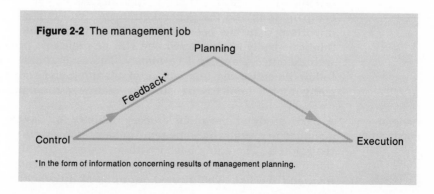

Figure 2-2 The management job

Planning

Feedback*

Control

Execution

*In the form of information concerning results of management planning.

a plan – or as we will call it, a "marketing strategy" – aimed at a given group of customers. How this group is selected will be discussed later in this chapter and beyond. The development of a marketing strategy is of primary importance. Without a well-defined master plan, there are no guidelines for execution or control.

Only after the basic strategy is developed can management concern itself with the implementation of that strategy (personnel selection, salary administration, dealer selection, commission rates, etc.). Implementation may, in fact, absorb a greater part of the manager's time, but it is not the major concern here. Detailed study of execution decisions must be left for your advanced work, after you have seen the "big picture," that is, when you have learned about planning marketing strategy.

We will emphasize control, too, since it provides the feedback that leads to the modification of marketing strategies. The tools most frequently used by the marketing manager to exert this control are electronic data processing, marketing research, and accounting.

All marketing jobs require planning and control

At first, it might appear that the planning and control responsibilities are only of concern to top management of large companies. This is not true. Even the smallest farmer, retailer, or wholesaler must plan his strategy. The salesman, however limited his territory, also must have a plan of attack. He may not have complete freedom, because of the master strategy already outlined for him, but he usually has some latitude. He develops his own special strategy in the light of his abilities and the problems of his particular territory.

Thus the material we will discuss throughout this chapter and text will be helpful to everyone engaged in the marketing process, whether they are top-level managers or are primarily involved in the execution of someone else's plan. You should find this information useful on your first, or even your present job.

Importance of marketing strategy planning

Most of our emphasis will be on the planning phase of the marketing manager's job, for a very good reason. The "one-time" planning decisions – the critical decisions that determine what business the company is in and the general strategy it will follow – may be more important than has been realized. In fact, an extremely good plan might be badly implemented and still be profitable, while a poor but well-executed plan can lose money. The several case histories that follow illustrate the importance of planning and show why we are going to be emphasizing strategy planning throughout this text.

General Foods study and General Foods hypothesis

A basic study of the retail grocery industry for General Foods was designed to reveal why some retail grocery stores were more profitable than others. The study began with an extensive evaluation of traditional internal company operating data such as turnover per square foot, and the like. This turned out to be of little help, but when the

34

study shifted its forcus to each company's planning decisions, new insights *were* developed. It became clear that original strategy decisions about (1) where a grocery store was placed in relation to competition and (2) how large it was compared to competition, were related to the profitability of individual stores.[9]

Within this framework, an analysis of operating effectiveness made sense. It was clear that some well-managed stores were doomed to poor profitability because of the initial planning decision. Conversely, some well-placed stores were doing very well, almost in spite of their operating management.

This leads to what we will call the *General Foods hypothesis:* Good strategy planning may be more important to the profitable operation of a business than good execution and control.

Gamble-Skogmo sought small-town markets

A practical application of this hypothesis can be seen in Gamble-Skogmo's effort to place relatively *large* discount stores in small midwestern towns. Importantly, this strategy reverses a general tendency for discounters to stay close to larger cities and markets. When asked why he was moving into small towns, the president of Gamble-Skogmo answered: "If you're first, you're apt to be alone. Most of the towns we're in won't take two stores of that size."[10]

Sears, Roebuck sought its own market

The General Foods hypothesis also helps to explain Sears, Roebuck's success since World War II. While other large retailers were concentrating downtown, Sears developed a new strategy – the development of stores with their own parking facilities in outlying and suburban areas where the population was growing fast. Some conventional retailers predicted dire results for Sears' new plan. But the company knew what it was doing. Sears placed its new units away from competition, provided ample parking space, and then built stores so large and well stocked that the customer could do all her shopping under one roof.

In short, instead of trying to meet competiton head on, Sears developed a strategy for reaching some target markets that had not previously been completely satisfied. At the same time, the market itself was shifting to those outlying areas.

U.S. Steel seeks new opportunities

As another example of the growing acceptance of the marketing concept and of the importance of strategic planning, U.S. Steel officials are developing long-run strategies. Rather than concentrating only on selling basic steel, U.S. Steel is designing steels that can be used in products of the future. A U.S. Steel vice president states: "The time to fight the market battle is in the design stage. We're confident that our salesmen will get our share of steel sold as a result."[11]

[9] *McKinsey–General Foods Study* (New York: General Foods Corp., 1963).
[10] "Small Town Greets the Discounters," *Business Week*, October 3, 1964, pp. 90–96.
[11] "How Steel Widens Its Targets," *Business Week*, March 27, 1965, pp. 119–23.

Henry
Ford's
strategy
worked

Henry Ford is remembered for his development of the mass production techniques that *enabled* a car to be produced for the mass market. His own recollection of his approach, however, suggests that mass production developed *because* of his basic strategy decision to build a car the mass market could buy. That is, he decided to depart from the then common practice of building cars for the wealthy, the sports drivers, and other specialty buyers, and to produce a car that would appeal to the majority of potential buyers. Ford felt that the low price necessary to appeal to so many buyers would stimulate the new production methods that would make the price possible.

As Henry saw it, the company set "a price so low as to force everybody in the place to the highest point of efficiency. The low price makes everybody dig for profits. We make more discoveries concerning manufacturing and selling under this forced method than by any method of leisurely investigation."[12]

Certainly, production innovations were required to implement Ford's mass-market strategy. But in terms of current thinking about marketing, it appears that the really critical decision was the initial market-oriented decision that there was a market for millions of cars in the $500 price range. Much of what followed was merely implementation.

General
Motors
found a
better
strategy

A great deal has been written about how and why General Motors has been such a spectacular success, but the focus has tended to be on its method of organization and financial arrangements. In his published memoirs, Alfred P. Sloan, Jr., the man who helped develop and guide General Motors Corp. to its position of dominance, adds new insights into General Motors' success. He claims that in the early stage of the reorganization of General Motors, he made only three really basic decisions. These concerned organization, financial controls, and product (product line). The balance of his tenure in the job was concerned with implementing those basic decisions. One of these three basic decisions was what we would call a marketing decision.

In the 1920's, Henry Ford, following his very successful strategy introduced many years earlier, was still offering a "mass-market" automobile in "any color you want as long as it's black."

Mr. Sloan and General Motors sensed that there was room for a new strategy. Their basic decision was to add new colors and styling, even if this required raising prices. They also hit upon the idea of looking at the market as having several segments (based on price and model types), and then offering a full line of cars with entries at the top of each of these price ranges. They planned to appeal to quality-conscious consumers, always offering good values.

Mr. Sloan acknowledges that the strategy was not immediately

[12] Henry Ford, *My Life and Work* (New York: Doubleday, Page & Co., 1923), pp. 146–47. See also Theodore Levitt, "Marketing Myopia," *Harvard Business Review*, July–August, 1960, p. 45.

successful and that there were many who felt that other strategies should be followed. But he persisted, and it is to this basic decision that Sloan gives credit for eventual success, even more than to the years of implementation.

As is now well known, General Motors persisted with its plan through the 1920's and slowly caught up with the unyielding Ford. Finally, in May, 1927, Ford closed down his assembly line and had to switch his own strategy to meet the new competition. He stopped producing the long-successful Model T and introduced the Model A. But General Motors already was well on its way to the commanding market position it now holds.[13]

General Motors and the replacement parts market

Thus far we have focused on success stories. But a failure may help demonstrate the General Foods hypothesis even more effectively. We have shown that General Motors' success was due, in great part, to a market-oriented decision. But it is important to note that while General Motors was successfully capturing a giant share of the automobile market, it was neglecting another very important market—the automobile replacement parts market. To be sure, parts were supplied—they had to be. But in those early days, supplying parts was viewed by the auto makers more as a supplemental service than an important business in itself. As a result, the market was left to many smaller suppliers, who were willing to move into this profitable market.

Even today, General Motors does not have the commanding position in the replacement parts market that it has in the car market. In other words, Mr. Sloan's successful strategy was concerned with automobiles, not with the broader concept of personal transportation and keeping the cars moving.

Good strategy planning pays off

The essence of all these examples is expressed by one author who has been arguing for longer-range thinking and innovation in marketing for some time. He says, "The real dough is in what economists call monopoly profits. I don't mean in a restrictive sense. I mean being first, the guy who skims the cream."[14]

These examples supporting the General Foods hypothesis show why we will emphasize marketing strategy planning in this text.

Marketing strategy planning

What is a marketing strategy?

Developing a marketing strategy involves two distinct and yet interrelated steps.

1. *Selection of the target market*—selecting particular groups of customers to whom a company wishes to appeal.

[13] Alfred P. Sloan, Jr., *My Years with General Motors* (New York: MacFadden Books, 1965), Introduction, chap. iv, and chap. ix.

[14] Theodore Levitt, in *Sales Management,* October 1, 1965, p. 32. See also Theodore Levitt, *Innovation in Marketing* (New York: McGraw-Hill Book Co., 1962).

2. *Development of a "marketing mix"* – choosing the elements which the company intends to combine in order to satisfy this target group.

Most of the balance of this chapter is devoted to explaining these two steps.

Decision framework – social, political, legal, etc.

Figure 2–3 illustrates the framework within which the marketing manager must operate. Those factors that he can control – the elements that make up the marketing mix – are shown around the customer Ⓒ. Surrounding these controllable factors are a number of uncontrollable factors that he must consider even though he cannot control them. Included are the cultural and social environment, political and legal environment, economic climate, existing competitive business situation, and resources and objectives of the firm. All of these uncontrollable factors are considered in detail in Chapter 3, but we cannot afford to overlook them here. To illustrate their importance, let's look at the factor of company objectives.

Objectives are extremely important to any manager and especially to the marketing manager. Since the objectives of the firm represent both goals and guidelines for him, he cannot begin to develop a workable marketing strategy until these are defined. Although ideally the

Figure 2-3 Marketing manager's framework

marketing manager should help set the objectives determined by top management, he does not always do so. And this fact may have an immediate bearing on marketing strategy planning.

Top management might decide, for example, that one of its objectives is to be the industry sales leader. This decision might exclude profitable but small target markets. In this situation, size might have to take precedence over profitability. Or the objective might be to dominate the low-price market, meaning a strategy of low prices combined with mass production and broad distribution.

But more about objectives in the next chapter. Here, we will focus on those variables the marketing manager *can* directly control.

Selecting target markets

Market grids help select target markets

Marketing management selects its target markets after analyzing the following: (1) potential customers; (2) marketing mixes; (3) its ability to provide these marketing mixes; (4) company objectives; and (5) other, often uncontrollable variables. When evaluating potential target markets, however, it should be realized that what is often considered as one market may actually be many smaller, more homogeneous markets. An analytical procedure that isolates all or at least most of the possible variations can certainly be useful here. The market grid approach provides such a technique.

The bull's-eye is a box

The market grid concept pictures a market as a box that is cross-hatched, like a checkerboard or grid, on the basis of relevant *market* characteristics. Each square in the large box represents a smaller, more homogeneous market (see Figure 2–4). Keep in mind that only

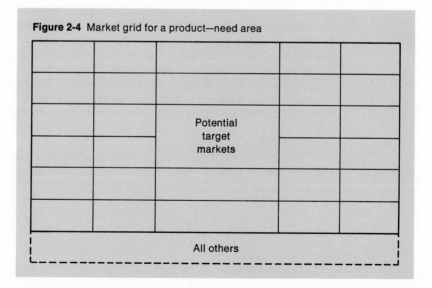

Figure 2-4 Market grid for a product—need area

Potential
target
markets

All others

potential customers are considered within the market grid that we draw.[15] On a grid concerned with men's clothing needs, for example, only characteristics pertaining to men would be considered. Children and women generally are not potential customers in this market. They could be indicated in a little area below the potential markets, perhaps surrounded by a dotted line as shown in Figure 2–4. But for practical purposes, such groups are not part of the potential market, and hereafter the dotted area will not be shown.

An example—the market grid for refrigeration

The refrigeration market is an excellent illustration for the market grid concept. Remember that in the following analysis we are talking about customers and their needs, not products that might satisfy them or that the company can produce. This is why we will discuss "re-frigera*tion*" rather than "refrigera*tors*."

Many consumers and businesses need refrigeration. It is used in homes, stores, institutions, and many other places, as shown in Figure 2–5. These customers do not all want the same product, nor are they equally accessible to the manufacturer. Some of these customer groups, indicated by the grid boxes, might be satisfied by electric refrigeration, while others would prefer gas refrigeration. Some would require large walk-in coolers and others would need compact units. Picnickers would prefer a small ice chest. Actually, to show all of the possible variations on a market grid would require more breakdowns than those in Figure 2–5.

In a more detailed breakdown, in Figure 2–6, the eastern food store market (shown with a large "X" in Figure 2–5) is analyzed. The food stores are listed by types: fruit and vegetable, dairy, fish, meat, and full-line grocery stores. These stores are of varying sizes, and this also may have a bearing on the type of refrigeration desired.

SIZE OF MARKET GRID BOXES NOT IMPORTANT INITIALLY The exact size of the markets represented by the boxes in Figure 2–5 and 2–6 need not concern us in this preliminary stage. Actually, it might take considerable market research to determine the potential sales volume in each of these boxes. But by developing a grid like this, the marketing manager is alerted to the existence of smaller, individualized markets. Perhaps many of these little markets can be satisfied by a single product. Before assuming this, however, it would pay to take a closer look, perhaps with some formal market research, to determine which if any of the many smaller markets can be merged and treated alike. This analysis is important, since *each unique target market requires a separate marketing mix.*

When the marketing manager first constructs a market grid, each box can reflect what he feels is the volume represented by each market. In Figure 2–6, for example, the boxes for small stores are drawn

---

[15] The general term *market grid* should be credited to Professor J. R. Malone, College of Business Administration, University of Notre Dame.

Figure 2-5 Market grid for refrigeration

East	Midwest	South	Mountain	Pacific	Region / Place of use
					Home
					Food stores
					Wholesalers
					Restaurants
					Hospitals
					Schools
					Military reservations
					Business offices
					Other institutions
					Trailers
					Picnics
					Planes
					Trains
					Ships

larger than for the medium and large stores because there are many more small stores. This should be done with care, however, because the manager's notions about the market may reflect past, not present or future conditions.

EACH LITTLE MARKET DIFFERENT Each of the small markets within the larger refrigeration market shown in Figure 2–5 represents a homogeneous group of potential customers with special needs. But some of these groups may be quite similar to others, and one manufacturer (or middleman) may go after several groups of customers or perhaps a whole row or column in the grid at the same time. In this particular case, it is unlikely that one manufacturer would cater

Figure 2-6 Market grid for refrigeration in eastern food store market

Large stores	Medium stores	Small stores	Size / Type
			Fruit and vegetables
			Dairy
			Fish
			Meat
			Full-line groceries

to a whole column represented in Figure 2–5, since the products desired would be quite different. Yet it is entirely feasible for some of the large consumer refrigerator manufacturers to sell successfully to the "Home" row in Figure 2–5, as Westinghouse, General Electric, and others do. And middlemen who can obtain their goods from various producers certainly have considerable freedom in deciding which groups to serve.

The same market might be served with different products, too. Gas and electric refrigerators of various types and sizes, and even old-fashioned iceboxes in some areas, would be suitable for the "Home" groups shown in Figure 2–5. This acceptability of substitutes will affect the competitive situation, of course.

Obviously, these boxes could be divided further to show the characteristics of *all* potential markets. Then, if there were no differences from box to box, they could be recombined.

If the variations in consumer demand from box to box are very great, or if some of the boxes are not very large, then it may be difficult or unprofitable for a particular firm to go after the business represented by these boxes. In such cases, a market may go unsupplied. Or it may not be completely satisfied until some firm sees its need and caters specifically to it.

Keep in mind that the market grid defines the characteristics and needs of *potential customers* for the type of product or service being considered — *not* the characteristics of present or possible products. For example, we would reject the traditional production-oriented approach used in the automobile industry, with its splitting of markets into compacts, foreign cars, low-price, medium-price, and luxury cars.

There is no magic formula for selecting the *right* grid dimensions. Rather, painstaking and systematic analysis of the thinking and characteristics of potential customers is required, while keeping in mind the company's own capabilities and objectives (to avoid excessive blue-sky thinking about markets that might be "nice," but impossible to serve). Insight may be aided by marketing research, but ultimately management judgment may have to enter, because this is an extremely important matter.

Selecting grid dimensions, and the resulting implications, are illustrated and discussed further in this chapter. Then grid analysis is treated in more detail in Chapters 6 through 9. It is important to note here, however, that this is *not* just a simple, mechanical process. Different dimensions may even be needed for different parts of the same general market grid, as will be illustrated later in the chapter. Be careful in gridding. Sloppy or too casual gridding can easily lead to bad strategies.

The lack of profit potential in some target markets helps explain why some customers are poorly serviced or dissatisfied with the products available to them. Or sometimes, due to changing consumer preferences, a new market has developed and has not yet been recognized. These grid boxes should not be seen as static markets, since they are in a constant state of flux.

Certain consumer group boxes may have so few "occupants" that mass production for them is not feasible. This presents an opportunity for smaller producers, wholesalers, or retailers to supply smaller volume and perhaps custom-fabricated products. A firm need not be small, though, to cater to the customers in small target markets. It merely has to be flexible enough to recognize and serve the needs of the customers in those markets.

Potential markets should be studied for new opportunities, not just to find places where existing products can be unloaded. There may be markets that are not satisfied with existing products, and this may represent a "breakthrough" opportunity for a particular firm.

A firm may find that its total market has customers in many boxes, although they may not all be adjacent to each other on the grid drawing. This is especially true if a large market is broken down geographically and then further subdivided. Even these differences may be important, however. The customers in various geographical markets — say, New York, Los Angeles, and Paris — may require different methods of distribution and, at the very least, will necessitate different wholesalers and retailers. Thus *each market grid box may require a unique marketing mix and should be thought of as a separate market.*

Developing marketing mixes

Many routes
to the
customer's
satisfaction

Developing a marketing mix must be an integral part of selecting a target market. That is, all the elements of a marketing strategy must be set simultaneously.

There are a large number of possible ways to satisfy the needs of target customers. A product can have many different characteristics, colors, and appearances. The package can be of various sizes, colors, or material; the brand names and trademarks can be changed; services and returned-goods privileges can be adjusted; various advertising media (newspapers, magazines, radio, television, billboards) may be used; a company's own salesmen and perhaps other sales specialists can be employed. Different prices can be charged; cash discounts and markups can be changed; a higher caliber of salesman may be hired or a different type of distributor may be used; intensity of sales effort may be varied from one locality to another; credit policies may be adjusted; and so on.

Each of these approaches can have many shades of differences, making the number of possible marketing mixes extremely large. With so many variables available, the question becomes: Is there any way of simplifying the selection of marketing mixes? And the answer is *yes*.

An analysis of the problems that face both large and small companies shows that it is possible to reduce the number of variables in the marketing mix to four basic ones:

Product

Place

Promotion

Price

It may help to think of the four major ingredients of a marketing mix as the "four P's." Figure 2–7 emphasizes their interrelationship

Figure 2-7

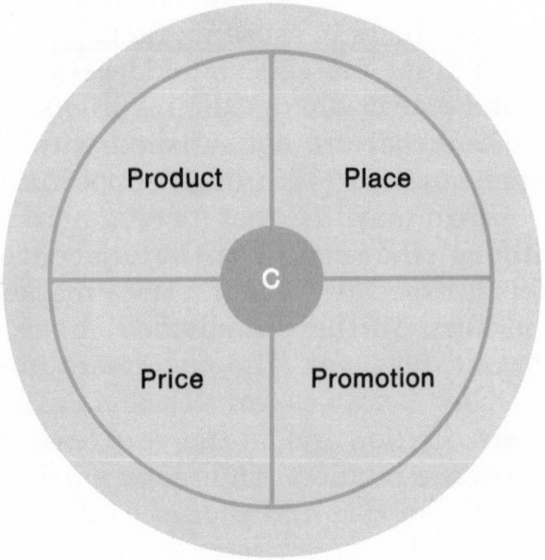

and their focus on customers Ⓒ. This text includes a set of chapters on each of the four P's, but for the present each is discussed briefly in the following paragraphs.

Product—the right one for the target

In Chapters 10 to 14, we will consider all the problems of developing the product or service that the company has decided to offer to each target market. Most of this text will be concerned with tangible products, but the principles in most cases also apply to services. It is important to keep this in mind, since the service side of our economy is growing.[16]

Under *Product,* we will specifically cover the problems of (1) selecting a product or product lines, (2) adding or dropping items in a product line, (3) branding, (4) packaging, and (5) standardization and grading. In short, the product area is concerned with *developing the right "product" for the target market.*[17]

Place—reaching the target

A product or service is not much good to a customer if it is not available when and where he wants it. We must consider where, when, and by whom the goods and services are to be offered for sale. Sometimes, for example, complicated channels of distribution are necessary, while at other times very simple methods are effective. Wholesaling, retailing, transportation, and storage play a part in the distribution of most goods and services.

In Chapters 15–19, then, we will consider under *Place* all the problems, functions, and institutions involved in *getting the right product to the target market.*

Promotion—telling and selling the customer

The third P, *Promotion,* is discussed in Chapters 20–22. It is concerned with any method that *communicates to the target market* about the right product to be sold in the right place at the right price. Promotion encompasses sales promotion, advertising, and personal selling. All are complementary methods of communicating with customers.

Price—making it right and fair

While the marketing manager is developing the right product, place, and promotion, he also must decide on the right *price,* one that will round out his marketing mix and make it as attractive as possible. In setting the price, he must consider the nature of competition in his target market as well as the existing practices on markups, discounts, and terms of sale. He also must consider legal restrictions affecting prices.

In short, Chapters 23–27 on *Price* are concerned with *determining*

---

[16] See Donald D. Parker, *The Marketing of Consumer Services* (Seattle: Bureau of Business Research, University of Washington, 1960); John M. Rathmell, "What is Meant by Services?" *Journal of Marketing,* October, 1966, pp. 32–36.

[17] It is tempting to use the terms *product mix, place*

mix, etc., to refer to all the aspects of each variable. But we will just use *Product, Place,* etc., in a broad sense. Finally, all four variables must be blended into one marketing mix, and concern with several *mixes* might lead to confusion with *the marketing mix.*

the "right" price to move the right product to the right place with the right promotion for the target market.

Relative
importance
of four P's

All four P's, we have seen, are essential to the marketing mix. In fact, they are interdependent. But is any one of them more important than the others? Generally speaking, the answer is no. When a marketing mix is selected, all decisions about the P's should be made at the same time. That is why, in the diagram, the four P's are arranged in Figure 2–7 around the Customer Ⓒ in a circle to indicate they are coequal.

Some sequence is needed in our discussion, however, and the following one has logical advantages. We develop a *Product* that we feel will satisfy the target customers. Then we find a way (*Place*) to reach our target customers. *Promotion* tells the target customers about the availability of the product that has been designed for them. Then the *Price* is established in the light of expected customer reaction to the total offering.

Strategy sets details of implementation

The needs of a target market virtually determine the nature of the marketing mix. Understanding the close interrelationship of market needs and the marketing mix is important, since it has a bearing on how the market gridding process is developed and the kinds of questions we ask about potential customers and their needs.

The objective of the gridding process is to find homogeneous sets of potential customers with needs which can be satisfied with the same marketing mix. Therefore, the dimensions of market grid boxes should be people-oriented dimensions. And if the needs of potential target markets are fully spelled out, then logical marketing mixes follow quickly. Such target market descriptions, however, may require imaginative combining of several market grid dimensions to more clearly summarize the needs and preferences, and maybe attitudes, of the people in each market grid box. Further, it would be helpful in estimating the size of each potential market if at least one of the relevant dimensions were linked to tangible characteristics for which we already have data, such as age, sex, income, geographic area, and so on. These ideas can be seen more clearly with two examples in the home-decorating market and the housing market.

A British
paint manu-
facturer
looks at the
home-
decorating
market

The experience of a paint manufacturer in England who followed the basic approach discussed above illustrates the strategic planning process and how basic "one-time" decisions determine subsequent implementation details.

First, this paint manufacturer's marketing manager interviewed many potential customers and analyzed the various needs for the products he could offer. By combining several catagories of customer needs and some available socioeconomic data, he came up with the view of the market shown in Figure 2–8. In the following description of these markets, note that useful marketing mixes come to mind immediately.

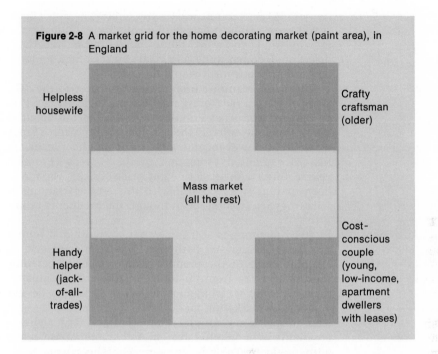

Figure 2-8 A market grid for the home decorating market (paint area), in England

Helpless housewife

Crafty craftsman (older)

Mass market (all the rest)

Cost-conscious couple (young, low-income, apartment dwellers with leases)

Handy helper (jack-of-all-trades)

There turned out to be a large mass market representing about 60 percent of the potential for all kinds of paint products. The manufacturer did not give much consideration to this market because he was not a large producer and he did not want to compete directly with the many companies already in the market. The other four markets, which he placed in the four corners of a market grid simply to show that they were different markets, were entitled Helpless Housewife, Handy Helper, Crafty Craftsman, and Cost-Conscious Couple.

The Helpless Housewife, the manufacturer found out, really did not know much about home decorating or specific products. She needed a helpful paint dealer who could supply not only paint and other supplies but also considerable advice. And the dealer who sold her the paint would want it to be of fairly good quality so that she would be satisfied with the results.

The Handy Helper was a jack-of-all-trades who knew a great deal about paint and painting. He wanted a good-quality product and was satisfied to buy from an old-fashioned hardware store or lumberyard, which sells primarily to men. Similarly, the Crafty Craftsman was willing to buy from a retailer who would *not* attract female customers.

In fact, this older man didn't want to buy paint at all, but pigments, oils, and other ingredients to mix his own paint.

Finally, the Cost-Conscious Couple was young, had low income, and leased an apartment. In England, an apartment dweller with a lease must paint the apartment during the course of the lease. This is an important factor for at least some tenants as they choose their paint. If you were a young apartment dweller with limited income, what sort of paint would you want? Some couples in England, the manufacturer discovered, do not want very good paint! In fact, something not much better than whitewash would do fine.

The paint manufacturer decided to cater to the "Cost-Conscious Couple" with a marketing mix flowing logically from the description of that market. That is, knowing what he did about their relevant dimensions, he offered them a low-quality paint (Product), made it available in lower-income apartment neighborhoods (Place), geared his price-oriented promotion to these areas (Promotion), and, of course, offered an attractive low price (Price). The manufacturer has been extremely successful with this strategy, giving his customers what they really want, even though the product is of low quality.

Apartment builders see different needs, too

Strategy planning is still somewhat of an art, and sometimes we will get faster results and better insights in market grid analysis if we examine some of the product-related needs of potential customers. This shift away from customer characteristics must be done with great care, but when applicable, it can speed the development of an appropriate marketing mix.

In this second example, the market grid for housing illustrates the possibility of combining customer characteristics (in summary form) with product-related housing needs. The customer characteristics shown in Figure 2–9, such as *swingers, sophisticates, newly married,* and so on, are summary descriptions of several simpler dimensions. For example, the swingers are young (in their 20's), unmarried, active, fun-loving and partygoing. The housing needs X'd in Figure 2–9 indicate what the swingers want. (It is interesting to note that they do *not* want "strong management." Most college students will probably understand why!)

A very successful appeal to the swingers in the Dallas, Texas, area includes a complex of apartments with a swimming pool, a putting green, a nightclub that offers jazz and other entertainment, poolside parties, receptions for new tenants, and so on. And to maintain their image, the management insists that tenants who get married move out shortly so that new swingers can be accomodated.

Descriptions of the other market segments are shown below Figure 2–9. Each of these segments required and was offered a different marketing mix, and as a result, apartment occupancy rates were extremely high in such buildings. At the same time, other builders were experiencing severe difficulties in filling their apartments, mostly because the units offered were hardly more than "little boxes" with few appealing characteristics. It is interesting to note, too, that the idea of building apartments to appeal to distinct target markets

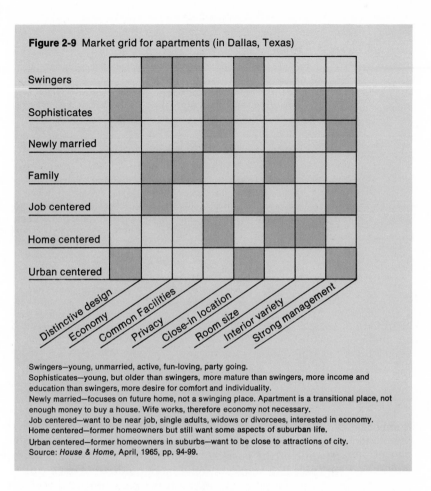

Figure 2-9 Market grid for apartments (in Dallas, Texas)

Swingers—young, unmarried, active, fun-loving, party going.
Sophisticates—young, but older than swingers, more mature than swingers, more income and education than swingers, more desire for comfort and individuality.
Newly married—focuses on future home, not a swinging place. Apartment is a transitional place, not enough money to buy a house. Wife works, therefore economy not necessary.
Job centered—want to be near job, single adults, widows or divorcees, interested in economy.
Home centered—former homeowners but still want some aspects of suburban life.
Urban centered—former homeowners in suburbs—want to be close to attractions of city.
Source: *House & Home*, April, 1965, pp. 94-99.

seems to be spreading. The swingers, especially, seem to be a group that attracts apartment developers.[18]

Market grid dimensions may set mix

The dimensions used in grid analysis are very important because they affect marketing mix planning. Therefore, informed judgment and care should be used in their choice.

Ideally, the grid box dimensions should be complete enough to guide marketing mix planning, within the constraints of the uncontrollable variables. More is said about planning the four P's in subsequent chapters, but the list of dimension characteristics and their probable affect on marketing decisions shown in Table 2–1 provides some perspective for what follows.

[18]"Singles Swing for Landlords," *Business Week*, March 5, 1966, pp. 38–40; "Catering to the Young for Fun and Profit," *Parade*, April 2, 1967, pp. 4–5; *Time*, August 26, 1966, p. 49; "Segmented Demand," *House & Home*, April, 1965, pp. 94–99;

"More Builders Prosper by Offering Tenants Organized Recreation," *Wall Street Journal*, January 22, 1969, p. 1; and "Single Life Goes Complex," *Seattle Post-Intelligencer*, August 3, 1969, pp. 1 f.

Table 2–1

Potential market grid dimensions	May affect these decision areas
1. Geographical location and other socioeconomic characteristics of potential customers.	Affects size of *Target Markets* (economic potential) and *Place* (where products should be made available) and *Promotion* (where and to whom to advertise).
2. Behavioral needs and how present and potential goods or services fit into customers' consumption patterns.	Affects *Product* (design, packaging, length or width of product line) and *Promotion* (what potential customers need and want to know about the product offering, and what appeals should be used).
3. Urgency to get need satisfied and desire and willingness to compare and shop.	Affects *Place* (how directly products are distributed from producer to consumer, how extensively they are made available, and the level of service needed) and *Price* (how much potential customers are willing to pay).

Number of potential dimensions is large

There are many potential market dimensions, and the obvious approach is to go after the more important ones. Table 2–2 suggests some of the possibilities for which published data *is* often available. Table 2–3 suggests some more qualitative ones which might develop out of marketing research or management's feel for the situation. These are *not* exhaustive lists.

Much more attention will be given in Chapters 6–9 to which dimensions might be appropriate, and when and where. However, take a look at what some of the potential market dimensions are, because you should have some feel for the kind of data that is available, before getting into the data details in later chapters.

If the more measurable kinds of information shown in Table 2–2 are relevant to potential customer buying behavior, then sales forecasting will be easier. The more qualitative dimensions may require considerable judgment to link them to measurable factors, but some linking is necessary if quantitative estimates of the size of market grid boxes are desired.

Finding the right dimensions may require research

One may get some insight concerning the relevant dimensions by placing himself, then friends, then very different kinds of people into a market grid and trying to invent descriptions which "explain" why you (they) do what you (they) do. If relevant market dimensions are difficult to pinpoint, then the marketing research procedures dis-

Table 2–2 Potential dimensions for market grid analysis for which data is usually available*

Data for:	Data for:
Households	Household heads
Geographic	Age
County size	Sex
Urban versus rural	Education
Region	Occupation
Age of children	Housewives
Family size	Age
Family income	Education
Home ownership	Employment
Dwelling characteristics	Business customers
Goods owned	Size of firm
Individuals	Dollar sales
Age	Number of employees
Sex	Geographic location
Education	Centralized versus decentralized
Marital status	purchasing
Occupation	Nature of target customers
Color	Nature of business (SIC codes)

*See William M. Weilbacher, "Standard Classification for Consumer Characteristics," *Journal of Marketing*, Vol. 31 (January, 1967), pp. 27–31, for finer breakdowns on these dimensions.

Table 2–3 Potential dimensions for market grid analysis for which data must be gathered or estimated

Needs for:	Desire for:
Status	Handiness
Affection	Durability
Privacy	Dependability
Convenience	Warmth
Distinctiveness	Softness
Economy	Speed
Variety	Activity
Newness	Movement
Security	Fun
	Excitement

cussed in Chapter 4 may have to be employed to get a better "feel" for the market.

Finally, it should be possible to narrow down the list of potential market grid dimensions to a workable few, perhaps through management judgment or a formal marketing research project. These market profiles can then be utilized in subsequent forecasting and marketing mix planning efforts.

Selecting the right dimensions for the firm's target market(s) is a dynamic circular process, however, requiring continuous analysis *and* judgment. After potentially relevant dimensions are determined, then the marketing manager must see if he can develop attractive and profitable mixes, within the uncontrollable constraints. In the process, he may discover new ways to segment the market. And he may find that some markets cannot be served profitably. He may return to looking at grid box dimensions, developing and evaluating potential mixes, refining the dimensions, and so on, many times. Finally, he will have to select the target market(s) and mix(es) which are "right" for his firm. This is not an easy job, and it is the subject of this whole text, not just this chapter.

Summary: the right box or boxes

Analyzing potential target markets using market grids requires considerable judgment and analysis of customers. But educated judgment and painstaking analysis are two of the major qualities expected of a marketing man. He must know his customers' needs, preferences, and desires. He should be expert in locating available data to add substance to the gridding process. He needs to be able to develop statistics as to the size and economic potential of possible target markets. As we said before, much more will be said on these topics in Chapters 6–9.

Hereafter, whenever we speak of target markets, we will mean customers in one or more grid boxes. Each box may require several dimensions, however, to fully describe the customers in it.

The market for a particular firm may consist of the customers in one or several of these boxes. At any one time, and for a specific product area, a particular customer probably would be in only one box. Markets are not static, however, so shifts must be anticipated, and marketing strategy planning must be adjusted accordingly.

In our increasingly affluent society, some customers may have different demands which might place them in two or more customer groupings simultaneously. Consider, for example, the large family with teen-agers. The family might need more than one car and desire quite different things in each car because of different uses. It is possible that these demands can only be satisfied by quite different products, perhaps from different producers, say, an Oldsmobile sedan, a VW sedan, and a Ford station wagon.

In general, each unique target market requires a unique marketing mix – which is why it is imperative to consider customer needs rather than product characteristics when planning marketing strategies. The latter is a hangover from the production-oriented era.

Our approach to strategy planning

Our general approach to strategy planning (as illustrated above) consists of two interrelated steps which are summarized briefly below – selecting the target market(s) and developing a marketing mix(es). They are elaborated on more fully in the balance of the text.

Selecting the target market(s)	First, we should define the area of the firm's interest. That is, the firm should define its objectives and determine what business it wants to be in. Otherwise, its search for market opportunities could be a shotgun approach with considerable waste of time and resources. The area of interest should not be too narrow (same old product and same old ideas), or so broad that the marketing manager has to evaluate ways of satisfying everybody.

Then, we should determine the needs in the area and relate them to demographic and socioeconomic characteristics, if possible, in order to estimate the size of potential market grid boxes. Here, formal or informal research may be needed to discover customer behavior and characteristics in the company's area of business. It might be helpful to identify *what* people are doing and *why*, and then relate this to characteristics such as age, income, etc., for which there is already published data. Or, if published data is not available for the relevant dimensions, then some original data may have to be collected to estimate the size of the various market grid boxes.

Developing the marketing mix(es)	Now, we should develop marketing mixes for promising market grid boxes and then select the one(s) we will offer to our target market(s). When the sizes of the market grid boxes are estimated, the profit potential of alternative marketing mixes geared for those customer groups can be calculated and compared. This would require, of course, an evaluation of market potential, the availability and cost of resources, and the probable impact of competition. More is said on this in Chapter 28.

Differentiating between strategy and tactics

Our primary emphasis in this text will be on strategy planning, but it should also be pointed out that a lot more than strategy planning is involved in successful marketing. Strategies work out as planned only when they are effectively carried out, and many decisions have to be made during these implementation efforts. These decisions are concerned with *tactics*.

Tactical decisions should be made within the guidelines set down during strategy planning. Product policies, place policies, etc., are established as part of strategy planning. Then, tactical decisions within these policies probably will be necessary while carrying out the basic strategy. It is important to realize, however, that as long as these tactical decisions stay within these guidelines, no change is being made in the basic strategy. If tactical decisions do not produce the desired results, however, it may be necessary to reevaluate the whole strategy decision rather than just "redoubling the effort" in a tactical decision area.[19]

[19] For more discussion of marketing policies, see *Formulating the Company's Marketing Policies* (Experiences in Marketing Management, No. 19 [New York: National Industrial Conference Board, 1968]).

It's easier to see the difference between strategy level policies and tactics if we illustrate these ideas using our paint manufacturer as an example. Possible four-P or basic strategy policies are shown in the left-hand column in Table 2–4, and likely tactical decisions are shown in the right-hand column.

Table 2–4 Relation of strategic policies to tactical decisions for paint manufacturer

Strategic policies	Likely tactical decisions
Product — Carry as limited a line of colors and sizes as will satisfy the target market prospects.	Add, change, or drop colors and/or can sizes as customer tastes and preferences dictate.
Place — Try to obtain distribution in every conceivable retail outlet which will handle this type of paint product in the areas where the target customers live or buy	If a new retailer opens for business in these market areas, immediately solicit his order.
Promotion — Promote the "low price" and "satisfactory quality" to meet the needs of the market's prospects.	Regularly change the point-of-purchase and advertising copy to produce a "fresh" image. Media changes may be necessary also. Salesmen have to be trained, motivated, etc.
Price — Maintain a low "one-price" policy without "specials" or other promotional deals.	If paint companies in other markets cut prices, do not follow.

It should be clear that some tactical decisions are made regularly, even daily, and such decisions should not be confused with strategic ones. Certainly, a great deal of effort is involved in all of these tactical decisions, and they might take up a good part of the time of a sales manager, advertising manager, and others. But they are not the strategic changes which will be our primary concern. In subsequent chapters, we will discuss the policies which provide the guidelines for such tactical changes. You should be alert to the importance of such guidelines, recognizing that additional thought and effort are required to put such policies into effect. These details of implementation are the subject of advanced texts and courses in marketing.

Specifying and selecting alternative strategies

Making choices is not easy

This text is concerned with developing and evaluating marketing strategies — primarily the analysis of target markets and the four P's.

The framework may appear simple enough, but the task of making choices within this framework is fairly complex. For one thing, each of the four P's has many potential variations, making the number of possible marketing mixes very large. For example, if there were 10 variations in each of the variables (10 prices, 10 products, etc.) there would be 10,000 possible marketing mixes. Yet 10 is a very small number of variations for each of these variables, and as the number of variations increases, the number of possible mixes increases geometrically.

No human mind can do it

It is obvious that no human mind is capable of accurately evaluating all possible mixes, but progressive elimination of the least desirable can reduce the problem to manageable proportions. And, fortunately, there are many combinations, not just a single combination, that can succeed, as target markets are continually changing in our dynamic markets.

Furthermore, some alternative marketing strategies are obviously inferior, and by the end of the text you will be able to spot these fairly quickly. Some strategies, on the other hand, are obviously better than others. These can be singled out for more careful analysis, with estimates of the probable effectiveness and success of each.

Then, if the firm is profit-oriented, it can assess the relative desirability of each strategy by calculating the expected profit. And assuming that the decision maker is willing to accept expected profit as the criterion, the strategy that is likely to produce the highest expected profit can be chosen. For example, in Table 2–5, strategy 3 would be

Table 2–5 Evaluation of various alternatives

Alternatives	Payoff (in dollars of profit)	Probability of occurrence	Expected profit
1	$ 100,000 or 0	.50 .50	$ 50,000
2	25,000 or 0	.90 .10	22,500
3	1,000,000 or 0	.20 .80	200,000
4	500,000 or 0	.30 .70	150,000

chosen. An extremely conservative decision maker, however, might select strategy 2 because of its seeming certainty.

Frequently the possible outcomes of the various strategies cannot be specified quite as clearly as suggested in Table 2–5. Managerial judgment must then come into play. It may also be that maximum profits are not the main objective of the firm. In this case, the evaluation of strategies may have to be even more subjective. More will be said about this in Chapter 28.

Organizing to implement the marketing concept

Pointing the company toward its goal

The first and most important step in applying the marketing concept is a wholehearted commitment to a customer orientation. Without acceptance of this concept, at least by top management, any change in the organizational structure will be purely mechanical. Such a commitment has been likened to a magnet applied to the bottom of a piece of paper sprinkled with iron filings; "The force of the magnet orients all of the filings toward the common point."[20]

Marketing is everybody's job

The degree of change which may be necessary is illustrated by the Worthington Corporation's experience.[21] Long a conservative manufacturer of custom-made heavy machinery, Worthington revamped its organization when it shifted its viewpoint from the factory to the marketplace. Worthington feels that the marketing concept is just a "bunch of words until it comes out in performance."

To get the desired performance, Worthington has followed a twofold approach: (1) a companywide reorganization along product lines, and (2) an educational program designed to sell the idea of marketing with all of its ramifications, to the company personnel from the top down to the foremen in the shop.

Worthington is trying hard to keep marketing from being only the marketing manager's job. The company wants every employee to feel that marketing is his job. To encourage this approach, the company has utilized task forces composed of men from various departments to solve developing problems. These groups frequently make many changes that go beyond the scope of the original problem; most of these changes are designed to serve their customers better.

According to the president, "Marketing is more a way of thinking than it is of organizing."

Some organization structure helps

After top management has accepted the marketing concept, some formal reorganization usually is desirable. The product planning function often is under the production or engineering departments; pricing is under the finance or accounting departments; and both sales and advertising often are separate departments. Sales forecasting and budgeting frequently is done in a separate department, or by the finance or accounting departments.

All of these activities involve the customer and should properly be under the direction and control of the marketing manager. The marketing manager normally should report directly to top management along with the heads of production, engineering, finance, and account-

---

[20]Robert E. Ringle, "The Marketing Concept in the Defense Industry," *Marketing Digest* (Southern California Chapter of American Marketing Association, June, 1961), p. 28. See also, "Why Marketing Gets Bogged Down," *Printers' Ink*, February 9, 1962, pp. 53–56.

[21]"Shifting the Stress to Marketing," *Business Week*,

October 4, 1958, pp. 57–60; and "Worthington Corporation Adopts New Marketing Philosophy, Builds Capacity for Growth," *Printers' Ink*, October 3, 1958, pp. 41–44; see also "Libby says 'aloha' to Old Marketing Life Style, Sells Hawaii Operation," *Marketing Insights*, February 2, 1970, p. 4.

ing. The exact arrangement of the marketing management department depends somewhat on the needs of a particular company and the personalities involved. Organization charts showing the structure in one company before and after adoption of the marketing concept are shown in Figure 2–10.[22]

Some companies have specific marketing activities delegated to specialized managers — such as product managers, pricing managers, distribution managers, promotion managers — in keeping with the four-P concept.

Marketing manager may reach outside his own firm's system

Marketing managers in some firms are beginning to realize that they are part of a total channel system and that it may be in their interests to cooperate with, or even direct, the activities of others in that larger "total system." It helps to think of the entire channel having a common strategy — focusing on the same market and then sharing the various marketing mix responsibilities in a logical way. More will be said on this concept in Chapters 15 and 19. Wholesalers and/or retailers might be leaders in these larger "total systems" and might even come to control such systems. But even if no one in such a larger system controlled it, all firms must develop marketing strategies. In fact, all firms have strategies, whether they realize it or not! "No strategy" is also a strategy!

Who should organize and run the total systems?

Top management is responsible for developing and running a total system of action, which is designed to meet the needs of target customers, for a profit. Ideally, the whole company becomes customer-oriented, and all the company departments pull together to reach its objectives. We will still have departments, because there are advantages in job specialization. But the former battles to protect "empire" boundaries are reduced because the total system is (or should be) supreme. To be sure, there may be disagreements over strategy. The production department might question whether the consumer really does want, and is willing to pay for, products which are practically custom-made. But rather than resort to an internal power struggle, a marketing-oriented system would do some marketing research, perhaps run some market tests, and calculate potential costs and company (not departmental) profits for alternate strategies. Then it would decide what is best for the firm (or channel), not just what is best for the strongest department or coalition of departments.

In such a system, the marketing manager would help develop this total system attitude within his firm and his channel system. He must work regularly with the external system as well as the internal system and is in an ideal position to keep the system working. In a sense, he is a coordinator and integrator — as well as a liaison man between the

[22]Eugene B. Mapel, "What is the 'Marketing Concept'?" Barrington Associates, New York; reprinted from *Sales Management*, July 5, 1957; for other examples of specific marketing jobs, see Henry Bund and James W. Carroll, *The Changing Role of the Marketing Function* (Chicago: American Marketing Association, 1957).

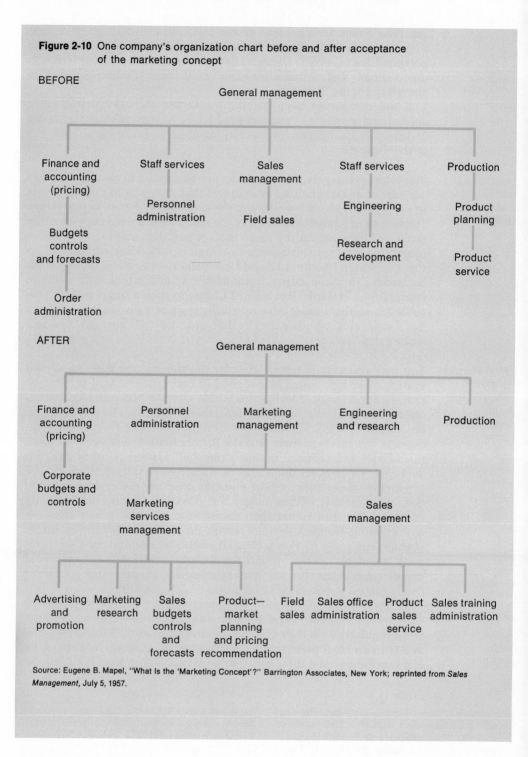

Figure 2-10 One company's organization chart before and after acceptance of the marketing concept

BEFORE

Source: Eugene B. Mapel, "What Is the 'Marketing Concept'?" Barrington Associates, New York; reprinted from *Sales Management*, July 5, 1957.

final customers of the channel system and the executives in his own company.

Who is suited to lead a marketing-oriented company? Many marketing managers probably will come from the ranks of sales management because they are more likely to be familiar with target customers. But this is not always the case. Some sales managers would make poor marketing managers because of allegiance to personal selling and their unwavering loyalty to the sales force. Similarly, an advertising manager may be so advertising-oriented that he believes almost any difficulty can be overcome with a larger advertising budget. Production managers, research and development engineers, and accounting and finance experts as well may be hindered by this sort of myopia.

Theoretically, at least, the marketing manager and the prospective marketing-oriented president could come from any specialty. In one cosmetic company, as might be expected in this type of business, the advertising and sales promotion manager gradually assumed major planning and coordinating responsibilities in the company's marketing organization. In another firm, however, which produced highly technical custom-built products, the production manager was the leader in the move toward the application of the marketing concept.

The most important consideration is that the prospective marketing manager and top manager accept the marketing concept — satisfying the customer, at a profit.

Conclusion

The job of marketing management, it should be clear, is one of continuous planning, execution, and control. The marketing manager must select target customers and design a marketing mix or mixes for them. But that is only the beginning of his task. He also must see that each strategy works successfully. If it does not, he must modify this strategy during the execution stage, or develop a new one.

Target customer groups can be divided and subdivided almost without end. Market grids can be used to segment potential markets. Then, possible marketing mixes can be considered for each of the grid boxes to evaluate their potential. Some may be likely markets. Others may actually subdivide into several markets, each requiring different mixes. And still others may not be worth bothering about when expense is weighed against potential profit.

To limit the problem of choosing a marketing mix, without oversimplifying the problem, we settled on the four P's — Product, Place, Promotion, and Price — to identify the main decision areas of the marketing manager. The problem, in brief, is to satisfy our target customers with the *right* product, available in the *right* place, promoted in the *right* way, and available at the *right* price.

For practical purposes, there is no "best" marketing mix because market conditions are in continual flux. Marketing management may have to estimate the probabilities of success of the alternative strategies and act accordingly. All of this will be accomplished with greater ease if the company has adopted the marketing concept, which may entail the development of a new organization structure.

The four P's give the manager a framework within which he can operate logically. His eventual success will be determined by the wisdom of his choices, his ability to modify his mix in the face of uncertainty and change, and his follow-through. To give you some picture of all the details a marketing manager must consider and what is to follow in the text, a checklist of marketing considerations is presented below. Do not try to memorize this list. It should be treated as a "list of considerations," to give you a feel for the many factors that the marketing manager must consider.

Checklist of marketing considerations[23]

1. Customers and Marketing Considerations
   A. *The Nature of the Market*
      Number of potential buyers – by region.
      Number of buyers – by region.
      Characteristics of buyers – age, income, occupation, education, sex, size of family, color, race – by region.
      Characteristics of users, if buyers and users are different – by region.
      Where buyers and users live – region, city size, urban and suburban.
      Where buyers buy – urban, suburban, rural; trading center, local; type of store.
      Size of purchase.
      When buyers buy – time of week, time of month, time of year, frequency of purchase.
      How buyers buy – brand specification or not; impulse or planned; personal inspection at counter; cash or credit.
      Why buyers buy – attitudes, motivation.
      Who influences buying decisions – type of product and brand.
      Uses for product.
      Unfavorable attitudes of buyers of brand.
      Indications of changes in buying habits.
   B. *The Structure of the Market*
      Number of competitors.
      Number of brands – national, regional, local.
      Share of market by brands, total, regional, city size, type of store.
      Characteristics of leading brands.
      Differentiation of own brand from leaders.
      Policies, the offer, methods and tools of principal competitors.
2. Product
   A. *The Product*
      Quality – materials, workmanship, design, method of manufacture.

[23] Adapted from: A. W. Frey, *The Effective Marketing Mix* (Hanover, N.H.: Amos Tuck School, Dartmouth College, 1956).

Models and sizes.

Essential or luxury.

Convenience or shopping.

B. *The Package*

Attributes of protection, convenience, attractiveness, identification, adaptability to type of retail outlet, and economy, through: material; size; shape; construction; label – design, color, copy; closure; competitive value.

C. *The Brand*

Adequacy with reference to memory value, suggestiveness, pleasingness, family expansion, legal protection, goodwill value.

D. *Service – Kind, Quality and Quantity*

Installation.

Education in use.

Repair.

Provision of accessory equipment.

Delivery.

Credit.

Returned goods.

3. Place

A. *Distribution Channels*

Total number of retailers, each type by region.

Total number of wholesalers, each type by region.

Percent retailers, each type, handling brand by region.

Degree of aggressive retailer cooperation, by region, store type and city size.

Indications of shift in relative importance of channels.

4. Promotion

A. *Personal Selling*

Recruiting and selection methods.

Training procedures.

Supervision procedures.

Stimulation devices.

Compensation plan.

B. *Advertising*

Size of space and time units – effectiveness.

Appeals and themes – effectiveness.

Use of black-and-white and color – effectiveness.

Methods of merchandising advertising.

C. *Sales Promotion*

Types of activity – deal, premiums, bulletins, portfolios, and so on.

Cooperative advertising arrangements.

D. *Publicity*

Volume and nature – releases, clippings, mentions.

5. Price

At factory.

To wholesalers, by type, size, and regions.

To retailers, by type, size, and regions.

Discounts – functional, quantity, cash, other.

Allowances and deals.

Service charges.

Price maintenance.

QUESTIONS AND PROBLEMS

1 Define the marketing concept in your own words, and then explain why the notion of profit is usually included in this definition.

2 Distinguish between "production orientation" and "marketing orientation," illustrating with local examples.

3 Explain why a firm should view its internal activities as part of a "total system of action." Illustrate your answer for (*a*) a large grocery products manufacturer, (*b*) a plumbing wholesaler, and (*c*) a department store chain.

4 Does the acceptance of the marketing concept almost require that a firm view itself as a "total system of action"?

5 Discuss the potential importance of a company information center to the marketing manager. In particular, would it be more helpful in his implementation efforts or in his planning efforts? Should he participate in the development of such a center, recognizing that usually he is already swamped with other responsibilities?

6 Explain the General Foods hypothesis. What is its relevance to marketing?

7 Distinguish clearly between a marketing strategy and a marketing mix. Use an example.

8 Explain why it may be desirable to define target markets and market grids in terms of *people's* needs rather than in terms of products. Further, explain why considerable ingenuity may be needed to develop market grids which clearly define market opportunities.

9 Why is the customer placed in the center of the four P's in the text diagram? Explain, using a specific example from your own experience.

10 Evaluate the text's contention that "a marketing strategy sets the details of implementation."

11 Distinguish between strategy and tactics, illustrating for a local retailer.

12 Develop a market grid for footwear in general, using as many customer needs and other characteristics as seem appropriate. Then discuss the many types and qualities of footwear which might appeal to the customers in your market grid boxes. Do not attempt to collect data.

13 Develop a market grid for the "automobile" market, using several customer-related dimensions—*not* product characteristics. Show where you are on the grid. Then, consider the products which are now available in the light of your breakdown and see if you can identify any unsatisfied target markets. Might they offer any substantial potential? Is your "ideal" available? Should it be?

14 Outline a marketing strategy for each of the following new products:
a) A radically new design for a haircomb.
b) A new fishing reel.
c) A new "wonder drug."
d) A new industrial stapling machine.

...as the role of business grows, the attitudes and reactions of the people, social critics, and government become increasingly important to the marketing manager.

...court interpretations and the growing success of the consumerism movement suggests that the ultimate criterion may be to protect the consumer, rather than to protect competition or competitors. Production-oriented businessmen...may find this new trend frustrating, but nevertheless...will have to adapt....

3

Uncontrollable variables affect marketing management

The marketing manager does not work in a vacuum. He must consider much more than the four P's and choosing target markets. As we noted in Chapter 2 (see Figure 2–2), the uncontrollable variables he must work with fall into the following categories:

1. Cultural and social environment.
2. Political and legal environment.
3. Economic environment.
4. Existing business structure.
5. Resources and objectives of the firm.

In the long run, the marketing manager's actions may affect some or all of these variables. This in turn would affect his future strategies.

But in the short run, we will consider these variables as uncontrollable *by the marketing manager.* Some of them, however, may be controllable by other people, either inside or outside the firm.

Since uncontrollable variables do affect the marketing manager's role, he cannot be concerned only with "marketing." He must understand how his firm, and other businesses, operate; he should have some knowledge of the social sciences, in order to anticipate future business and social trends.

He should be able to understand and relate the findings and analytical approaches of many other disciplines. For example, he should try to keep up with the newer work being done in the behavioral science areas of sociology, anthropology, psychology, and social psychology, in order to gain a better understanding of the cultural and social environment. He should learn about the traditional fields of political science, history, philosophy, law, and economics, to understand the political and legal environment. The fields of economics and business administration, as well as the natural sciences and engineering are relevant to an awareness of the economic environment. And business administration and economics are necessary for an understanding of existing business organizations and how they operate.

How important these variables are, and how they add to the complexity and challenge of marketing management, will be seen in this chapter.

Cultural and social environment

The cultural and social variable is beyond the control of the marketing manager—in the short run, at least. The traditions and values of various cultures and social classes are extremely relevant to marketing, and these tend to change very slowly. Obviously differences from country to country may come to mind quickly: Americans, for example, generally tend to accept and encourage change, while more tradition-bound societies are more resistant to innovators. But more subtle differences in customs, which can mean the difference between success and failure in marketing, are too often overlooked.

Friendliness and hush-puppies

Since customer behavior is given extensive treatment in Chapters 6–9, we will discuss it only briefly here. A few examples will suffice to emphasize the possible impact of customer behavior on marketing strategy planning.

Americans are often stereotyped as a friendly people, but actually this varies by regions. People on the West Coast, for example, tend to be more open and, at least superficially, more friendly. This is in part because many have moved west to find a new life and have left behind the more tradition-bound social structures of the smaller towns of the Midwest and the East. People on the West Coast also seem more willing to travel great distances. Some Californians, for example, think nothing of driving several hundred miles on a weekend, whereas this would be a major trip for a New Yorker. This has an effect on the location of retail facilities and loyalty to particular stores.

Eating habits vary to some extent among regions and within urban areas. For example, biscuits and hushpuppies are much more popular in the South, and Mexican food has long been favored in the Southwest. Within large metropolitan cities, we still find national and religious pockets that represent separate markets for some goods and services. Large midwestern and eastern metropolitan areas often have distinct neighborhoods of Irish, Italians, Poles, Jews, Puerto Ricans, and blacks. These urban areas have newspapers, radio stations, restaurants, grocery stores, and record shops which cater specifically to these culturally defined markets.

The melting pot is *not* homogenized

This great diversity within the American "melting pot" is ignored by the marketing manager only at his peril. Many foreign and American businessmen have tried to use the New York City market as a test of how products will be received in the United States. The idea is that since New York itself is such a big melting pot, it will reveal typical American consumer preferences. These businessmen have been badly misled. The New York metropolitan market is probably the most unusual market in the world; while it includes many ethnic and national groups it is, by its diversity, typical of no one market. The New York area has about as many Jews as Israel, about 30 percent of the world Jewish population. There are more Puerto Ricans in New York City than in San Juan, the largest city in Puerto Rico. But New York does not have as many Scandinavians as Chicago or Minneapolis–St. Paul, or as many Japanese as Los Angeles. It is no wonder that businessmen who ignore these obvious statistics fail to understand some of the subtleties discussed in Chapters 6–9.

Mañana is today some places

Besides differences in consumption behavior, we also must take into account cultural attitudes towards life and work, which are a reflection of religious, ethical, and moral values. It is evident that national attitudes have an effect on a country's rate of growth and the direction of its development.[1] This is an important consideration for students and companies thinking of going into international business or into areas of a country which may have quite distinctive attitudes, such as rural areas or inner-city ghettos.

Here we should generalize with care. For example, the _mañana_ attitude of Latin America is disappearing in some countries and especially in large urban areas. Venezuela is more eager than some of her neighbors to accept new technology, due probably to a large influx of Germans who long ago came to develop the mining enterprises and brought their North European attitudes.[2] And younger executives are

[1] David C. McClelland, "Business Drive and National Achievement," _Harvard Business Review_, July–August, 1962, pp. 99–112.

[2] Talk by Professor Edward Barnet, Tri-State Marketing Conference, Michigan State University, May, 1962.

changing the pace of business in Mexico.[3] In contrast, negative attitudes toward work and cooperation with others may be inhibiting growth in India and parts of Asia.[4]

Nationalism is limiting

Strong sentiments of nationality, along with the way people feel toward business institutions, also affect the work of some marketing managers. These feelings can inhibit sales or even block marketing activity in some areas. Oil and copper mining firms have felt such pressures in recent years, for example, in Latin America, Africa, and the Middle East.[5] The "Buy American" policy reflects similar attitudes in the United States.[6] And in the same vein, Philippine businessmen have tried to drive "excessively aggressive" Chinese merchants out of the Philippines. Africans have driven Indian merchants out of their countries. And some U.S. minority groups leaders have been urging their people to trade only with their own.

The prudent marketing manager seeks to understand these attitudes and adjust his marketing planning accordingly. If such attitudes are strong, the more practical course may be to adjust to them rather than try to fight or change them. This would be especially true if the firm had little to offer that was unique. On the other hand, an especially attractive marketing mix might win local acceptance, in spite of traditional attitudes, if it were uniquely innovative. And this fits with our emphasis on planning unique marketing strategies.

Is a business system desirable at all?

Some people have a negative attitude toward business itself — that is, they have doubts about the desirability or effectiveness of macro-marketing systems. In some countries, the word "earn" has the connotation of "outwit," and any business activity is suspect. The established businessman, no matter how wealthy and successful, sometimes is regarded with disdain, as an inferior kind of person. This was true in the time of Plato, it was true in Japan prior to the 19th century, and it is still true today in many countries, especially among certain intellectuals. Some of the support for the revived interest in consumerism which has been sweeping the United States, Canada, Western Europe, and Japan can be attributed to these basic attitudes. Where such attitudes are strong, they often affect the political and legal environment.

[3] "A New Business Beat Stirs Mexico City," *Business Week*, October 5, 1968, pp. 66–72; and "Business Shakes Up a Lotus Land," *Business Week*, January 13, 1968, pp. 88–92.

[4] "Asia's Emerging Industrial Revolution," *Business Week*, December 13, 1969, pp. 60–61; "Japan's Powerful Push Overseas," *Business Week*, August 19, 1967, pp. 92–106; "Japan Buys a Stake in Burgeoning Brazil," *Business Week*, September 14, 1968, pp. 168–72; "Indifferent India," *New Republic*, June 22, 1968, pp. 19–21; and "Asia — Soft State," *Time*, March 15, 1968, p. 24.

[5] "Why the Oil Giants Are under the Gun," *Business Week*, October 25, 1969, pp. 82–96; "Where the Yanqui Companies Are Feeling the Heat," *Business Week*, November 22, 1969, pp. 80–84; "Nationalism Sets Boundaries for Multinational Giants," *Business Week*, June 14, 1969, pp. 94–98; and "Nationalism Crimps the Spending Spree," *Business Week*, December 6, 1969, pp. 206–8.

[6] "Buy American Policy Touches Off a Fuss," *Business Week*, July 27, 1968, pp. 52–54.

Political environment

As the role of business grows in our society, the attitudes and reactions of the people, social critics, and governments become increasingly important to the marketing manager. In our discussion, we will separate political and legal questions, although in practice this separation is hard to maintain. A change in political environment often leads to changes in the legal environment or the administration of existing laws.

Political environment may limit marketing manager's freedom

The political arena is where people can sound off about the management of the whole economy. At one time, Americans expected their federal government to do relatively little for them. Today, more and more voters prefer greater government involvement in planning and controlling the economy. This trend can have a direct impact on the marketing manager, whether he operates solely within one economy or on the international scene. In fact, the political environment may be the most important factor to deal with for some multinational firms.

Consumerism cannot be ignored

Some social critics will never be satisfied, but others merely voice the growing frustration of some consumers with the quality and safety of products being offered by business. Consumer advocate Ralph Nader, for example, has done much to focus and organize consumer concern and to bring about the passage of specific legislation. His best seller, *Unsafe at Any Speed,* may have forced General Motors to remove its Corvair from the market. Nader is credited with the passage of major federal legislation designed to improve safety in automobiles, and to police the processing and distribution of some food products.[7]

Some of the complaints against business are certainly justified. Abuses by some firms – probably production- or sales-oriented ones – have long been deplored by conscientious businessmen and exposed by Better Business Bureaus. Government agencies and regulatory bodies also act to police and correct many of these abuses.

But a new mood seems to have developed among people. As the well-known business consultant, Peter Drucker, wrote: "We have been a very patient people by and large. Now people are fed up, and I do not blame them."[8] Some businessmen have recognized the new mood and are doing something about it. But more criticism can be expected, both in the United States and abroad.

This means that the marketing manager, as well as top management, will have to give serious consideration to consumer attitudes in marketing planning.[9] The alternative could be pretty drastic. Ralph

[7] "The U.S.'s Toughest Customer," *Time,* December 12, 1969, pp. 89–98.

[8] *Ibid.,* p. 92.

[9] "Listen to Demands of Public, Ford Tells American Business," *Detroit News,* December 3, 1969, p. 7-D; and "Pillsbury Eyes Basic Revamp of Consumer Stance," *Advertising Age,* September 16, 1968, pp. 1 f.

Nader wants General Motors broken up. Chartering of corporations by the federal rather than state government is another proposal. This might jeopardize a particular corporation's right to operate at all![10]

International action may be swift and/or far-reaching

Political climates are in constant change. Although long-run trends may be fairly discernible, short-run changes can be sudden and unexpected. For example, oil-rich countries will almost certainly grab for a greater share of oil profits or nationalize the industries, as was done recently in Libya and Algeria.[11] Or government administrators may arbitrarily change or apply tariffs and quotas to restrict the flow of particular items. Or they may tell importers to lower their prices, as they did recently in India on crude oil prices. Moreover, these companies were told that if they refused to "see reason," the government might take further action without consulting them.[12] In the same vein, Ford Motor Company and Coca-Cola suddenly were added to an Arab boycott list because they planned to establish plants in Israel.[13] Obviously, this economic warfare reflects the political environment, and the probable impact on individual companies cannot be underestimated.

Countries may choose to issue guidelines to foreign firms, as Canada did recently to encourage "good corporate behavior." These guidelines sometimes are supplemented with new laws or the threat of legislation. Laws were passed recently, for example, to restrict the flow of United States advertising and culture via television into the Canadian market.[14]

Such guidelines can be extremely important in both domestic and international business, because most businesses must get permission to operate in a foreign country. In some political environments, this is only a routine formality; in others, a lot of red tape is involved and personal influence is sometimes necessary.

Political environment may offer new opportunities

The political environment is not always a negative factor. Governments may decide that encouraging business and opening markets are constructive steps for their people. Japan recently decided to open its market more to foreign investors and competitors.[15] The United States and other highly developed countries may give industrial development a boost in Latin America, Africa, and Asia by allowing

[10] "Nader Asks G.M. Dissolution," (Lansing, Michigan) *State Journal*, December 9, 1969, p. A–10; "A Proposed Suit Aimed at Breaking Up GM Poses Perils for LBJ," *Wall Street Journal*, October 31, 1967, p. 1 f; and "Government Intercession Grows as Perils of Modern Life Proliferate," *Advertising Age*, January 20, 1969, p. 79.

[11] "Libya Nationalizes Service-Station Units," *The Wall Street Journal*, July 6, 1970, p. 3; "Algeria Extends Nationalization to Oil Producers," *Business Week*, June 20, 1970, p. 90; and "Oil—A Little Throat Cutting," *Time*, June 29, 1970, pp. 73–74.

[12] "India Tells Oil Men to Cut Crude Prices," *New York Times*, January 20, 1970, p. L 67.

[13] "Arabs Bar Coke, Ford," *Business Week*, November 26, 1966, p. 52.

[14] "Canadian Nationalism Vents Itself on U.S.," *Detroit Free Press*, June 2, 1970, p. 4–C; and "Ottawa Restricts U.S. Ads," *Business Week*, September 4, 1965, p. 36.

[15] "Detroit Gets Nod in Japan," *Business Week*, August 31, 1969, p. 58.

manufactured goods from those areas to be imported duty-free.[16] Another blow to political protectionism occurred when Common Market authorities rejected France's request to restrict the inflow of Italian electrical appliances.[17] Jamaica has offered tax holidays and other special treatment to companies that set up operations there.[18] In the United States, special programs and financial inducements have been developed to encourage urban redevelopment, employment and training of hard-core unemployed, and minority enterprises. State and local governments also try to attract and hold businesses, sometimes with tax incentives.

Legal environment

U.S. legislative developments: encouraging competition

American economic and legislative thinking has been based on the assumption that competition among many small firms will guide the economy with an "invisible hand." This idea became popular after the publication of Adam Smith's *Wealth of Nations* in 1776. Great Britain accepted this idea during the 1800's, in principle at least, and it was enshrined in common law there and in the United States. According to this concept, attempts to restrain or limit trade were held to be against the public interest and unenforceable. Practices tending to fix prices, limit markets, or in any other way control trade were considered undesirable.

This laissez-faire approach did not last long in Great Britain. England and the Commonwealth countries now permit (or at least tolerate) considerable restraint of trade, as do many other countries. But Americans have been especially reluctant to give up Adam Smith's free enterprise ideal. After the Civil War, however, industries began to grow larger, and some were consolidated into trusts, cartels, and monopolies by wealthy tycoons who were often called "robber barons." This led to a restraint of competition and hardships for smaller producers and consumers. As a result, there was a movement – especially among midwestern farmers – to curb monopolists.

Beginning in 1890, a series of laws were passed that were basically antimonopoly or procompetition. The names and dates of these laws are shown in Table 3–1.

The Sherman Act was aimed primarily at monopolists, or *conspiracies* to monopolize or restrain trade. The Clayton Act had the same intent, but was more specific. And the Federal Trade Commission (FTC) Act set up the Federal Trade Commission as a continuing body to serve as a watchdog for the public and to supplement the Justice Department's efforts to enforce the nations' laws affecting business. The FTC was to be concerned with "unfair methods of competition."

Besides supplementing the Sherman Act, the Clayton Act was

[16] "U.S. Lifts Bar to Trade Offer for the Have-Nots," *Business Week,* May 30, 1970, p. 71.

[17] *Business Week,* February 17, 1968, p. 145.

[18] "Industry's New Island in the Sun," *Business Week,* February 12, 1966, pp. 66 ff.

Table 3-1 Outline of federal legislation affecting competition in marketing

	Antimonopoly (Procompetition)	Anticompetition	Antispecific practices
1890	Sherman Act		
1914	Clayton Act		Clayton Act
	Federal Trade Commission Act		
1936	Robinson-Patman Act	Robinson-Patman Act	Robinson-Patman Act
1937		Miller-Tydings Act	
1938			Wheeler-Lea Amendment
1950			Antimerger Act
1952		McGuire Act	

aimed at several specific practices which the more general prohibitions of the Sherman Act did not cover—or did so in a manner that created confusion and ambiguities. The Clayton Act specifically tackled such practices as geographical price discrimination by manufacturers, exclusive dealer arrangements that limit a buyer's choice of suppliers, and tying contracts (contracts requiring that some goods have to be purchased in combination with others that the company controls, even if the former can be obtained more cheaply elsewhere). The intention of all this legislation was to protect and encourage competition, and to discourage monopolies.

The hardships of the depression of the 1930's, however, convinced many businessmen that too much competition had disadvantages. The pendulum swung the other way, and some of the resulting legislation was basically anticompetition, although it reads like the earlier procompetition legislation. The Robinson-Patman Act of 1936 was aimed at price discrimination and price cutting, especially that involving large price-competitive chains, such as A&P, which were hurting small competitors. Previous legislation had been directed at manufacturers, but the new threat was to small middlemen from the large-chain middlemen. Therefore, although the law was supposedly concerned with avoiding injury to "competition," it was often interpreted by the FTC and the courts to mean prohibiting injury to "competitors," especially small retailers. More is said about this in Chapter 27, when the impact of legislation on pricing is discussed.

Similarly, competitors were protected when price fixing was permitted by the Miller-Tydings Act, which was passed in 1937 and strengthened in 1952 by the McGuire Act. This legislation specifically exempted certain price fixers from the basic antitrust legislation, and reflected price-cutting problems for both brand-name manufacturers and for small retailers during the depression. It allows a manufacturer or wholesaler to sign a price-fixing contract with retailers, in states permitting such contracts.

The Wheeler-Lea Amendment to the FTC Act, passed in 1938, started a new trend—protection of the consumer. Under this law, unscrupulous advertisers were singled out. These firms had escaped prosecution under the earlier laws, which were concerned with injury to competition rather than the impact on individual consumers. Now it was possible to prosecute for deceptive advertising or sales practices without having to show that competition had been restricted. Such prosecutions have occupied much of the Federal Trade Commission's time and effort in the past two decades. The FTC regularly holds hearings and issues "cease and desist" orders against companies using deceptive practices. The companies can either obey these orders or appeal them to federal courts. FTC "guidelines," which will be discussed later in the text, have developed out of this judicial procedure.

The Antimerger Act of 1950, an amendment to the Clayton Act, is designed to make it easier for the FTC to regulate those mergers which might substantially lessen competition. The application of this law has led to tighter control over mergers, especially those which involve one firm buying out its competitors or those firms above or below it in a channel system. The issue generally is whether the merger will reduce competition in a market area. But this antimerger concept has now expanded to include acquisitions of noncompetitive firms by larger firms that might make it more difficult for the existing competitors to survive. Procter & Gamble, for example, was required to sell Clorox. And Bendix has been ordered to sell Fram, a manufacturer of filter products.[19] Finally, it is worth noting that foreign firms must abide by the U.S. merger laws, just as U.S. firms must obey the laws in host countries.

Let the seller beware

Traditional economic thinking with respect to buyer-seller relations is "Let the buyer beware," although some consumer protections are built into English and U.S. common law. A seller must tell the truth (if asked a direct question), fulfill contracts, and stand behind his product (to some reasonable extent). But beyond this, it is expected that vigorous competition in the marketplace will protect consumers, as long as they are wary.

Within this framework, the procompetition thrust of the antitrust laws is understandable. And the intention of both the Federal Trade Commission and the Justice Department has generally been to maintain competition in the marketplace.

But court interpretations and the growing success of the consumerism movement suggests that the ultimate criterion may be to protect the consumer, rather than to protect competition or competitors. Production-oriented businessmen and their "letter-of-the-law" advisors may find this new trend frustrating, but nevertheless they will

[19]"Bendix Ordered to Give Up Fram: Link Held Illegal," *Wall Street Journal*, June 26, 1970, p. 5.

have to adapt to the political and legal environment just as they have to learn to live with other uncontrollable variables.[20]

This growing concern for the consumer may have a special impact on manufacturers. They now are increasingly held liable for any injury their product causes—even injury caused by users' carelessness. Recently, for example, a manufacturer was held liable for damages that occurred when one of his vacuum cleaners was plugged into a 220-volt circuit and blew up. The label clearly stated that the product was to be used in 115-volt outlets, but the court concluded that the manufacturer failed to warn the customer that the consequences of plugging the unit into anything hotter would be disastrous.[21]

The law and marketing mix planning

The evolution of economic and business law in the United States has been sketched above, and specific application to the four-P's will be presented in subsequent chapters. To round out our discussion here, it will be helpful for you to know what the government must prove to obtain a conviction under each of the major laws and which of the four P's have been most affected by each law. Figure 3–1 provides such a summary, with a phrase following each of the laws to indicate what must be proved to obtain a conviction.

It is interesting to note how the wording of the laws leans progressively to the side of the consumer. And given the new emphasis on letting the seller beware, it is likely that future interpretations of the FTC and courts will be even more in favor of consumers.

Prosecution is a serious matter

The conduct of business is subject to both criminal and civil laws. Many business activities are regulated by civil laws, and penalties are limited to blocking or forcing certain actions, together with fines. Where criminal law applies, jail sentences can be imposed.

This is an important point to understand. Some business executives have gone to jail or received suspended jail sentences in recent years because they violated the criminal law provisions of antitrust legislation. Jail sentences are a relatively recent development and have added a new note of seriousness to the political and legal environment.

Laws about specific matters

Over the years, there have been a number of acts which have been designed to eliminate or regulate specific business practices. Probably the one most vigorously debated was the Pure Food and Drug Act of 1906, which was designed to prohibit the adulteration and misbranding of foods and drugs in interstate commerce. Colorful exposés[22]

[20] "A New Cry: Let the Seller Beware," *Chicago Today*, April 21, 1970, p. 4; "The Lengthening Reach of Liability," *Business Week*, September 16, 1967, pp. 100–108; "Nixon Administration Pushes for New Consumer Protection Legislation," *Marketing Insights*, February 9, 1970, p. 4; "New York Gets Strong Consumer Protection Act," *Marketing Insights*, February 9, 1970, p. 3; and "Business Responds to Consumerism," *Business Week*, September 6, 1969, pp. 94–108.

[21] "Business Responds to Consumerism," *Business Week* September 6, 1969, p. 95.

[22] See Upton Sinclair, *The Jungle* (Pasadena, Calif.: Upton Sinclair, 1920).

Figure 3–1 Focus (mostly prohibitions) of federal laws on four P's

	Product	Place	Promotion	Price
Sherman Act (1890) (Monopoly or conspiracy in restraint of trade)	Monopoly or conspiracy to control a product	Monopoly or conspiracy to control distribution channels		Monopoly or conspiracy to control prices
Clayton Act (1914) (Substantially lessen competition)	Forcing sale of some products with others—tying contracts	Exclusive dealing contracts (limiting buyers' sources)		Price discrimination by manufacturers, especially basing point systems
Federal Trade Commission Act (1914) (Unfair methods of competition)		Unfair policies	Deceptive ads	Deceptive pricing
Robinson-Patman Act (1936) (Tends to injure competition)		Prohibits paying allowances to "direct" buyers in lieu of middlemen costs (brokerage charges)	Prohibits "fake" advertising allowances or discrimination in help offered	Prohibits price discrimination on goods of "like grade and quality" without cost justification, and quantity discounts limited
Wheeler-Lea Amendment (1938) (Unfair or deceptive practices)	Deceptive packaging or branding		Deceptive ads or selling claims	Deceptive pricing
Antimerger Act (1950) (Lessen competition)	Buying competitors	Buying producers or distributors		
Miller-Tydings (1937) and *McGuire Acts* (1952) (Price-cutting retailers can be prosecuted)				Manufacturers or wholesalers can fix prices at retail level, in states which permit it

of meat-packing practices in the Chicago stockyards had fanned consumer interest in this act. Some loopholes in the original act were corrected in the 1938 Food, Drug, and Cosmetic Act. And the law was further tightened in 1962. Among other things, the law prohibits the shipment of unsanitary and poisonous food products and requires extensive testing of drugs.

The Food and Drug Administration attempts to police manufacturers of these products and to confiscate products which violate its regulations. It has drawn up regulations on branding and requires that food shipped in interstate commerce contain labels which correctly describe the ingredients. Habit-forming drugs must be marked "Warning—May Be Habit-Forming."

Other acts designed to be in the consumers' interest are: the Wool Products Labeling Act (1939), which provides for proper labeling of the kind and percentage of each type of wool; the Fur Products Labeling Act (1951), which provides that all furs show the true name of the animal from which they were produced; and the Flammable Fabrics Act (1953), which prohibits the shipment in interstate commerce of any wearing apparel or material which could be ignited easily.

Ralph Nader is given credit for some more recent legislation, including: the National Traffic and Motor Vehicle Safety Act of 1966, the Wholesome Meat Act of 1967, the Natural Gas Pipeline Safety Act of 1968, the Radiation Control for Health and Safety Act of 1968, the Wholesome Poultry Products Act of 1968, and the Federal Coal Mine Health and Safety Act of 1969.[23]

And we now have "Truth-in-Lending" legislation, which requires disclosure of the interest rates being charged for loans and credit; a Fair Packaging and Labeling Act for guidance in that area; and the Public Health Cigarette Smoking Act which restricts tobacco advertising on TV and radio after January 1, 1971.[24]

In summary, specific legislation to protect consumers seems to be increasing in volume, and more seems likely. The wise marketing manager might even find it desirable to cooperate with legislators who are trying to right "wrongs," to be sure that workable legislation is passed.

State and local regulations: Sunday laws, spreading disease

In addition to federal legislation which affects interstate commerce, marketers must be aware of state and local laws which concern intrastate commerce. Here legal advice and/or extensive knowledge of community or state politics is even more important. Some laws, for example, impose such harsh penalties that local prosecutors are reluctant to enforce them. For practical purposes, these particular laws are inoperative.

There are state and city laws regulating minimum prices and the setting of prices (to be discussed in Chapter 27); regulations for starting up a business (licenses, examinations, and even tax payments);

[23] Time, December 12, 1969, pp. 89–90.

[24] Journal of Marketing, October, 1970, p. 85; and Business Week, December 26, 1970, p. 21.

and in some communities, regulations prohibiting certain activities, such as door-to-door selling or selling on Sundays or during evenings. This latter problem has been prominent in recent years, as old "blue laws" have been rolled out by established retailers as a defense against discounters. Sunday selling is often offensive to religious groups as well.

Some states have regulations about movement or importation of agricultural commodities, ostensibly to protect product quality or to prevent the spread of animal or crop diseases. Some of these, of course, are justifiable, but others are simply a device to enable local producers to obtain higher prices. This has been especially true with respect to milk, some citrus products, and wine. This is also true of the buy-local and buy-American provisions of some government contracts.

Legislative developments abroad: trade for the common good

The English were pioneers in unrestrained competition, and then backed off when many of their businessmen decided they did not really want so much competition.[25]

The common law, based on statutes and court decisions, has generally been followed in English-speaking countries. But even within the English-speaking community, laws vary from country to country, and a specific knowledge of this legislation is necessary.

Even more study is required for non-English countries, where there are often special courts dealing only with business matters and specific laws replace the common-law system.

As we move from marketing within one country to multinational marketing, things become more complicated, especially within blocks of countries attempting to develop a common market.

The European Common Market – which consists of six countries in continental Europe (to be described in more detail in Chapter 7) – has approved some extremely tough antitrust legislation that is binding on all members and on all foreign businessmen who wish to sell their products within this Common Market. This legislation labels as illegal "any agreements which are likely to affect trade between member states which have as their object or result the prevention, restriction, or distortion of competition."

How this Common Market regulation will work out in practice has yet to be seen. Early decisions were encouraging, despite the traditional cartels and restrictive practices of continental European businessmen. Recently however, partly in response to aggressive U.S. and Japanese multinational firms, there has been growing interest in mergers. A Common Market panel recently proposed new legislation which would actually promote mergers, especially of small and medium-sized firms, to enable them to compete more effectively in the Common Market and elsewhere.[26]

[25]For more recent developments, see Richard C. Osborn, "Postwar Control of Restrictive Trade Practices in Great Britain," *Journal of Business,* October, 1962, pp. 367–85.

[26]"Europe Touts Mergers as Means to Face Increasing Competition in World Markets," *Wall Street Journal,* February 21, 1968, p. 32; and "Common Market Panel Proposes Company Law to Promote Mergers," *Wall Street Journal,* June 26, 1970, p. 4.

Know the
laws, follow
the courts

Because legislation must be interpreted by the courts, students should carefully study both legislative developments and the tenor of thinking of the courts. Often laws are vaguely phrased by legislators to convey intent but not specific detail. It is then up to the courts and administrative bodies to spell out the details. And good legal assistance is needed to keep up with these details.

If business students and businessmen had a better understanding of the intent of the makers and interpreters of the laws — legislators and jurists — there would be less conflict between business and government and fewer embarrassing mistakes. With such an understanding, businessmen might come to accept the political-legal environment as simply another framework within which business must function and develop its marketing strategies. After all, it is the consumers, through their governmental representatives, who determine the kind of economic system they want. Businesses cater to customers' needs and have to operate within the framework specified by these customers. This, of course, does not preclude businessmen from studying how and why an economic system should work and lobbying for the development of a more effective system.[27]

Economic environment

National
income
makes a
difference

An otherwise good marketing strategy may fail if a country goes through a depression or rapid business decline. For this reason, the marketing manager cannot ignore macroeconomics — the analysis of the behavior of whole economic systems.

The amount of new capital investment by the business community and spending by the government sector has a major impact on the overall level of the economy. Consumers' willingness to buy also has a bearing on economic prospects. These matters are discussed more fully in Chapter 5 with respect to sales forecasting.

During the U.S. recession of 1969–70, some firms were hurt badly while those offering lower-priced goods did very well. Retailers such as Kresge, J. C. Penney, and Woolworth had sales gains, as did sellers of used cars, camping equipment, wedding gown *rental* services, and

[27]In this regard, see E. T. Grether, "Business Responsibility towards the Market," *California Management Review*, Fall, 1969, pp. 33–42; E. T. Grether and R. J. Holloway, "Impact of Government upon the Market System," *Journal of Marketing*, April, 1967, pp. 1–5; Seymour Banks, "Commentary on 'Impact of Government upon the Market System.'" *Journal of Marketing*, April, 1967, pp. 5–7; "A Changing Balance of Power," *Business Week*, July 17, 1965, pp. 85–106; J. G. Van Cise, "Regulation — By Business or Government?" *Harvard Business Review*, March–April, 1966, pp. 53–63; Ray O. Werner, "Marketing and the United States Supreme Court," *Journal of Marketing*, January, 1967, pp. 4–8; J. F. Barron, "'Normal' Business Behavior and the Justice Department," *Journal of Marketing*, January, 1963, pp. 46–49; Wayne G. Broehl, Jr., "Insights into Business and Society," *Harvard Business Review*, May–June, 1966, pp. 6–37; Stanley C. Hollander, "Social Pressures and Retail Competition," *MSU Business Topics*, Winter, 1965, pp. 7–14; and Daniel J. Murphy, "The Federal Trade Commission of the 1960's," *Journal of Marketing*, April, 1963, pp. 1–5.

fabric for making one's own clothes.[28] In contrast, the gloom in the lumber and home-building industry was severe.[29]

It should be noted that when economic conditions for a particular industry or country turn sour, they may not improve for a long time, if ever. The world sugar industry has substantial excess capacity, and this has a severe impact on producers. The entire sugar industry of the Fiji Islands, supporting about 25 percent of the population, is "for sale" with no likely takers. If it is not sold, the island faces a major loss in income.[30]

Monetary and fiscal policies count, too

The way a country's money managers handle their affairs can directly affect both the domestic and international economy. Further, adjustments in the interest rates, money supply, and tax rates can affect the vigor of the domestic economy and particular industries.

A reduction in automobile excise taxes, for example, might be proposed to stimulate the automobile industry, and because of the industry's size, the economy as a whole. In such a situation, the marketing manager has to anticipate when the announcement is to be made and the probable customer reaction while the issue is being discussed. He might have to modify his marketing mix to inform target customers about the impact of the tax cut. If the cut is voted, he might have to reduce prices immediately or offer rebates, to keep the business moving and to avoid inventory pileups at both the retail and manufacturing levels.

A change in the value of a country's money in relation to other countries' money can also have an impact on business. When Britain devalued the pound, this immediately raised the price of foreign goods in England. The devaluation also led Japanese firms to fear British competition in the United States.[31] Similarly, when Canada decided to let its exchange rate be set by the marketplace, this immediately raised the price of Canadian goods and therefore made it more difficult for Canadians to compete in the world market.[32]

Inflation can change mixes

Inflation is a major factor in many economies, and the marketing manager has a big job keeping up with it, especially with respect to pricing. In South America, inflation has become almost a way of life, and it's a fairly big problem in the United States. Latin countries have experienced far more spectacular inflation, however, and it has profoundly influenced their economic thinking. Most people there now assume that prices will always go up, and they buy and sell accordingly. This behavior, of course, adds fuel to the inflationary fires. Some Latin

[28]"Dividends from the Drop," *Time*, July 8, 1970, p. 66.

[29]"The Boom in Wood that Busted," *Business Week*, October 25, 1969, p. 138.

[30]"Where Sugar May Turn Bitter," *Business Week*, April 25, 1970, pp. 46–47.

[31]"Britain's Devaluation Hurts Export-Based Economy of Asian Land," *Wall Street Journal*, December 4, 1967, p. 1.

[32]"The Floating Dollar Takes Its Toll," *Business Week*, June 13, 1970, p. 46.

countries have had from 25 to 100 percent inflation per year for many years. In contrast, the 6 to 8 percent level reached in the late 1960's and early 1970's in the United States was small. Nevertheless, this U.S. rate properly caused great anxiety about whether inflation was out of control and led to restrictive monetary policies which did reduce income and employment.

Obviously, the marketing manager has a big stake in the economic environment. In contrast to the legal and cultural environments, economic conditions change continuously; they can move rapidly up or down, requiring tactical and even strategic responses. Fortunately, various tools are available for economic forecasting. These are discussed in Chapter 5.

Technological developments offer new opportunities

Underlying any economic environment is the technological base, which affects the way the resources of the economy are converted to output. In tradition-bound societies, relatively little technology may be used, and the output may be correspondingly small. In modern economies, on the other hand, aggressive competitors tend to copy the best methods quickly and continually seek better ways of doing things. The marketing manager therefore should continually be on the alert for technological breakthroughs which may have application in his area. Early adoption may give him a competitive lead, while later adoption may be necessary just for survival.

Spectacular advances in technology have been made in the last 30 years. This is due in part to our newfound interest in and support of research and development. More technological developments probably can be expected. Some of these certainly will affect marketing, just as previous ones have had their impact.

The modern automobile, for example, has enabled farmers to come to town and urban people to go wherever they want, thereby destroying the local "monopolies" of some retailers and wholesalers. Modern trucks and airplanes have opened up many new markets and permitted production for national or international markets, with resulting competition and benefits for consumers. Electronic developments have permitted mass promotion via radio, TV, and telephone thereby reducing the relative importance of other media. And in time we may be able to shop in the home with a combination TV-computer system, eliminating the need for some retailers and wholesalers.

Computers have also permitted more sophisticated planning and control of businesses. Electronic equipment may permit us to return to custom production methods – but this time in automated factories which will enable the customer to decide more exactly what he wants and then obtain almost immediate delivery. This may cause drastic changes in our distribution structure, perhaps altering the roles played by middlemen. And it certainly would change internal company affairs, including sales forecasting, production scheduling, warehousing, and so on.

Such drastic changes are possible, because much of what we do is technology-bound – that is, we do the best we can given the present knowledge of how to organize our affairs to convert resources to products and services. As we move through the text, you should see that some of the major advances in business have come from creative and early recognition of new ways to do things. Additional breakthrough opportunities probably will arise as our technological base continues to change.

A marketing manager could help his firm see such opportunities by trying to understand the "why" of its present techniques, and what is keeping it from doing things more effectively. Then, as new developments come along, he will be sensitive to their possible application and be able to see how potential opportunities can be turned into profitable realities.

Further, he can make a contribution to his firm's effort by cultivating a sense of what technical developments would be acceptable to society. Given the growing concern about environmental pollution, the quality of life and working conditions, and so on, it is possible that some potentially attractive technological developments should be rejected because of their long-run implications. Perhaps what might be good for the firm and the economy's *economic* growth, might not fit with the cultural and social environment, and subsequently the political and legal environment. The marketing manager's closeness to the market could give him a better feel for what people are thinking and enable him to help the firm avoid blunders.

Existing business structure

When we talk about "existing business structure," we mean competition; the number and types of competitors the marketing manager must face in his various target markets, how rough their competition is, and the marketing strategies they use in the marketplace. This topic is a major concern of this text, as it is, of course, to the marketing manager. A few examples will show why.

The marketing manager can expect a great deal more competition, and probably much more emphasis on price, if the industry is composed of many small producers and retailers. For example, there are at least 650 boat builders and 4,000 engine and accessory manufacturers attempting to sell their products through more than 17,000 marine dealers and 3,500 marinas.[33] Competitive strategies in this industry are very different from those in the aluminum or computer industries, where there are relatively few competitors.

If all competitors in an industry are frantically offering two-for-one deals, stamps, games, or other promotional devices, a marketing manager may have to fight the competition at that level. Games were extremely popular among gas stations recently, for example. Although some of the major oil firms wanted to give them up, they were afraid of losing ground to competitors. In such cases, industry executives

[33]"From Back Yard Boats to Yachts," *Business Week,* August 28, 1965, pp. 28–29.

may even appeal to the government to ban such activities as unfair practices.[34]

The competitiveness of the businessman is also an attitude, and it varies from country to country. In France, the "individualistic" small retailer does everything in his power to avoid competition, particularly price competition. He joins a "syndicate" which determines strict rules for doing business and fixes prices – a seeming contradiction to his desire for individualism. Such groups seek to discourage competitors and innovations. Their counterparts can be found among producers, wholesalers, and retailers throughout the world.[35]

In this book, competition is viewed as uncontrollable by the marketing manager. But what he or his competitors do affects the competitive situation. Therefore, by intelligent analysis of what he might do in a particular situation – by putting himself in the competitors' shoes – the marketing manager should be able to make intelligent decisions for both existing and future business situations. More is said about these topics in Chapters 10, 14, 19, 26, and 27.

Resources and objectives of the firm

Two separate variables are involved here: resources and objectives. Top management establishes these variables, and they may impose real restrictions on short-run strategy planning. In the short run, the marketing manager must work within these constraints, but in the long run he will want to help shape the objectives and perhaps modify the resources of his firm.

Resources of the firm – find the unique strength

A smart marketing manager recognizes that his firm has unique resources. As a result of its own history, experiences, and personnel, it has strengths and weaknesses that distinguish it from other firms. A good marketing strategy makes extensive use of the firm's strong points. Various resources to consider when developing a marketing strategy include those discussed in the following pages.[36]

Financial strength

Industries such as steel, public utilities, oil refining, and chemicals require large amounts of capital to build efficient facilities. Smaller companies have little reason to consider these businesses. This is especially true because larger facilities in such industries may benefit from what are called "economies of scale." This means that the cost of production per unit decreases as the quantities produced increase. The smaller producer would be at great disadvantage if he tried to compete in these lines.

---

[34]"Why Gas Stations Keep Up Games," *Business Week*, September 21, 1968, pp. 62–66; and "End Gas Games, Atlantic Richfield Exec Urges FTC," *Advertising Age*, March 24, 1969, pp. 1, 114.

[35]*Experiment in Union: Latin America Broadens*

Its Market (New York: Vision, Inc., 1961), p. 21.

[36]Charles H. Kline, "The Strategy of Product Policy," *Harvard Business Review*, July–August, 1955, pp. 91–100.

Some industries, however, do not have economies of scale. In these lines, smaller, more flexible firms may be quite effective. This is why large companies often have difficulties when they enter low-investment-type businesses. In one situation, a large chemical processor, because it was producing the basic plastic sheets, attempted to make and sell decorated shower curtains. The firm lost heavily on the experiment, however, because the smaller shower curtain manufacturers and distributors could change their styles and policies more rapidly, meeting retailer demands for many product variations and styles.

Industries that require large amounts of capital to introduce products or to withstand cyclical instability are usually dominated by larger companies. The same is true of industries that require a great deal of basic or applied research. Middlemen, on the other hand, typically require lower financial investment, and these businesses provide good opportunities for those with smaller financial resources.

Raw material reserves

Firms that own or have assured access to basic raw material resources have a head start in businesses that require these resources. But companies, large or small, that are not in this position may find — especially in times of short supply — that they have difficulty even staying in business. Chemical and paper manufacturers usually attempt to control timber resources, and the large wallboard manufacturers often control sources of gypsum rock. Historically, the metals and petroleum companies have controlled their own resources.

For independent suppliers of raw materials, often it's a case of feast or famine. This is because most large processors use their own resources for the bulk of their needs and buy on the outside only during especially busy times. A smaller firm that requires these basic raw materials or intends to sell to larger integrated producers must be aware of the behavior of its potential customers and competitors.

The availability of raw materials has less relevance to retailers, wholesalers, and certain types of manufacturers, which are far removed from the processing of such raw materials. They would consider this factor, however, when selecting sources of supply for the finished goods they need.

Physical plant

Some lines of business require large aggregations of productive facilities. This is true in the steel, chemical, and railroad industries.

In other industries, much less physical plant is required, and it may be easy to acquire. Even renting or leasing, rather than buying, may be a possibility and facilitate entry of new firms. A trucker can rent a truck, warehouse, and office facilities. His roadbed is provided by the city or state, and repair facilities are available at most garages or truck manufacturers' branch offices. A wholesaler can rent a warehouse and delivery trucks. A retailer can rent a store and delivery truck, and used store fixtures are available. Even farms can be leased.

The existing physical plant may have considerable bearing on the development of a marketing strategy because one of the firm's objectives probably will be to use existing plant as fully as possible. Any logical strategy will attempt to make use of existing physical facilities, or provide for their disposal, so that the capital can be used more efficiently elsewhere.

Location

High transportation costs, product perishability, and demand variations in local markets may force the marketing manager to adopt a marketing strategy that emphasizes production for local or regional markets. Perishable food products, such as bread, potato chips, and dairy products, are produced and distributed in nearby markets. This presents great opportunities for smaller firms.

Sometimes the reverse is true. Being close to basic raw materials – hogs, in this case – a meat products firm, such as George A. Hormel Co., may produce certain kinds of meat products in one or several plants and then distribute over a wide area. But the marketing manager here is able to use an entirely different strategy with canned or smoked meat than with fresh meat, which must be sold much more rapidly.

Patents

Patents are of primary concern to manufacturers. A patent owner has a 17-year "monopoly" to develop and use his new product, process, or material as he sees fit. If a producer obtains a patent and is unwilling to license it, other manufacturers might have a tough time competing. If the patent covers a basic process, other producers may be forced to use second-rate processes, and their efforts may be doomed to failure. Many large firms attempt, through basic research, to protect their interests in their operating fields by securing patents covering most or all of the basic formulas and devices in these fields. Small producers, not engaged in this type of research, would be well advised to avoid direct competition with manufacturers who emphasize and are successful at basic research.

Public acceptance

If a large or small firm has developed a loyal following of customers – a "customer franchise" – for its product or service, others may have difficulty invading this market. A strong customer franchise is a valuable asset that the marketing manager should use in developing marketing strategy. Lack of such a franchise can be a real liability.

Sometimes a firm must test the strength of its own or a competitor's customer loyalty before knowing how to adjust its marketing strategy. In one case, a large manufacturer attempted to do this against a bakery product that had a strong customer franchise and had encountered little competition for more than 10 years. The large manufacturer found that his competitor's market strength could be overcome, but only at prohibitive cost. The big firm decided to develop another marketing strategy.

Personnel

Some organizations pay higher wages for skilled labor because trained workers may enable the marketing manager to develop a unique marketing strategy, with the emphasis on quality, service, or flexibility. A skilled sales force is also an asset, whereas lack of good salesmen may restrict strategy planning. Even if skilled production employees can produce a new product, the sales organization may not have the contacts or know-how to sell it. This is especially true when a firm moves from consumer goods to industrial products or vice versa.

Management attitudes

The attitude of top management is an important factor in company growth, especially as it affects the development and introduction of new products.

The president of a New England manufacturing company was enthusiastic about the prospects for a new product. But after evaluating the attitude of his company personnel, and especially his management people, he dropped his plans for the product. Why? He found that his employees had no ambition or interest in growth.

In another company, this one in the Midwest, it is unlikely that a new product ever will be accepted. Again, the reason is simple and sad. As the firm's top management expresses it, "Fortunately, not enough sensible ideas come along to cause us any trouble."

Objectives of the firm — getting there at a profit

It might have been best to treat the objectives of the firm first, perhaps even before marketing strategy was discussed, since the company's objectives shape the direction and operation of the entire business. But we have saved our discussion of objectives until this point because it is easier now to see how they can affect the development of marketing strategies.

Should set firm's course

A business organization should know where it is going or it is likely to fall into the trap expressed so well by the quotation: "Having lost sight of our objective, we redoubled our efforts."[37] In spite of their importance, studies of both large and small corporations show that objectives are seldom stated explicitly. In small businesses, they appear to be stated *after the fact!* And in some large businesses, there may be *several* implicit — but conflicting — objectives held by different executives. The relative importance of any of these objectives seems to depend upon the point of view of the man being interviewed.[38]

It would be convenient if a company could set one overriding objective, such as making a profit, and let that serve as a guide. Actually, however, setting objectives is much more complicated — which explains why it is done so poorly, or sometimes not at all.

Setting objectives that really guide the present and future development of the company is a soul-searching procedure that forces top management to take a systems view of the entire business, relate its

[37] Charles H. Granger, "The Hierarchy of Objectives," *Harvard Business Review,* May–June, 1964, p. 63.

[38] Robert F. Lanzillotti, "Pricing Objectives in Large Companies," *American Economic Review,* December, 1958, pp. 921–40. This was a continuation of the study by A. D. H. Kaplan, J. P. Dirlam, and R. F. Lanzillotti, *Pricing in Big Business* (Washington, D.C.: Brookings Institution, 1958); F. Parker Fowler, Jr., and E. W. Sandberg, *The Relation of Management Decision-Making to Small Business Growth* (Management Research Summary [Washington, D.C.: Small Business Administration, 1964]).

present needs and resources to the external environment, and then plot the broad outlines of the company's future course.

Taken together, the following three objectives provide a useful starting point and guideline for a particular firm. These three objectives could be phrased and made more specific in many ways. But these basic objectives should be sought together because, in the long run, a failure in even one of the three areas could lead to total failure of the enterprise.

1. Engage in some specific business activity that will perform a socially and economically useful function.
2. Develop an organization to perpetuate the enterprise and implement its strategies.
3. Achieve sufficient profitability to survive.[39]

Should be socially useful

The first objective suggests that the company should do something useful. This is more than a platitude. Businesses exist at the discretion of consumers, and if the activities of a business appear to be at variance with the consumer "good," business can be wiped out almost overnight by political or legal action or the customers' own negative response.

Should view business broadly as customer-satisfying activity

The first objective also implies that the firm should view its mission as satisfying customer needs rather than some more production-oriented objective such as using the company's resources, exploiting a patent, etc. The firm should define its efforts broadly, as we did in Chapter 2, when we focused on the refrigera*tion* market rather than the refrigera*tor* market. This should lead the company to "need-satisfying" goals rather than product-oriented goals. It could mean that the company will develop products or processes that will compete with, or even make obsolete, its present activities. But if the new offering will satisfy customers better (and probably would be discovered by other companies anyway), then developing it is certainly sensible.

Procter & Gamble produces many soap brands that compete with each other. The company feels that if there are markets which are not completely satisfied, Procter & Gamble may as well create new products to satisfy them, even if this means cutting into the sales of some of its existing products.

By following the need-satisfying approach, whole new businesses are born. Whirlpool Corp., a large manufacturer of refrigerators, views itself as being in the food preservation field, and this may lead

---

[39]These were adapted from Peter F. Drucker, "Business Objectives and Survival Needs: Notes on a Discipline of Business Enterprise," *Journal of Business,* April, 1958, pp. 81–90; and for a discussion of how objectives might develop, see Harper W. Boyd, Jr., and S. J. Levy, "What Kind of Corporate Objectives?" *Journal of Marketing,* October, 1966, pp. 53–58; see also, William D. Guth and Renato Tagiuri, "Personal Values and Corporate Strategies," *Harvard Business Review,* September–October, 1965, pp. 123–34; and Robert A. Howell, "A Fresh Look at Management by Objectives," *Business Horizons,* Fall, 1967, pp. 51–58.

them to abandon production of refrigerators. The reason for this seeming contradiction is that Whirlpool recently developed a process for reducing the oxygen, and therefore oxidation, in food storage containers. The new process has kept apples crisp and fresh for two years *without* refrigeration.[40]

The importance of a broad view should be obvious if objectives are supposed to help a company plan for the future. Too narrow a view may lead the company into a product area in which the product itself, because of changing customer needs, will soon be obsolete.[41]

Should organize to innovate

In a macro-marketing sense, consumers have granted businesses the right to operate and to make a profit if they can. But they do not expect them simply to exploit the status quo. Businesses are supposed to be dynamic — agents of change, adjusting their offerings to customers' needs. Competition is supposed to encourage innovation and efficiency, which is why we have antitrust laws and other legislation. Our patent system, plus the support of customers, rewards innovators and those who provide new and better services or perform old services more efficiently. Assuming that our society will continue this approach, a business firm should develop an organization that will insure that these consumer-assigned tasks are effectively carried out and that the firm itself continues to prosper.

Should achieve some profit

It is sometimes assumed that profit is the only objective of business. The traditional economic model of a firm assumes that firms do attempt to maximize profits, and it is certainly true that in the long run a firm must make profits to survive.

Yet simply stating that making a profit is a company objective does not constitute the whole of a modern business firm's objective-setting function. The time period involved in creating a profit also should be specified, since long-run profit maximization may require losing money during the first few years of the plan.

Further, setting an objective to maximize profit seems to imply that a firm will make good profits, but actually competition may be so fierce that poor results are almost inevitable. It might be more appropriate to set, as a target, some rate of profit return that would tend to guide the business into avenues having some possibility of such a return. Some firms probably should seek even higher rates of return than they are now achieving and more than is available in their *present* activities.[42]

Objectives probably should specify the degree of risk that management is willing to assume for larger returns. Very large profits might be possible in the oil prospecting business, for example, but the

[40] "Fresher Fruits, Vegetables on Way," *Detroit Free Press,* April 24, 1966, p. 12B.

[41] This point of view is discussed at much greater length in: Theodore Levitt, "Marketing Myopia," *Harvard Business Review,* July–August, 1960, p. 45 ff; Theodore Levitt, *Innovation in Marketing* (New York: McGraw-Hill Book Co., 1962); and T. Levitt, *The Marketing Mode* (New York: McGraw-Hill Book Co., 1969).

[42] Drucker, *op. cit.,* p. 87.

probability of success in that field might be quite low. If the business is to take a long-run view, if it intends to survive and be a useful member of the business community, it probably should include the costs of risk and potential losses in its calculations of long-run returns.

Both hands must work toward the same goal

Whatever objectives are selected by top management, they should be compatible with each other, or frustrations and even failure may result. The three broad objectives suggested above would help a firm avoid the blunder of working at cross-purposes with its various plans. But as these three guidelines are made more specific, care must be exercised. For example, management might choose to specify a 10 percent return on investment each year as one objective, while at the same time specifying that the current plant and equipment be utilized as fully as possible. Competition might be such that it would be impossible to use the resources fully and achieve this return, but the company managers might try to follow the resource-use objective through the course of the year and discover the incompatibility only at the end of the year!

Management myopia may straitjacket marketing

We are assuming that it is the marketing manager's job to work within the framework of objectives provided by the top executives. But some of these objectives may restrict marketing strategies, perhaps to the detriment of the entire business. This is why it is desirable for the marketing manager to help shape the company's objectives.

A few examples will help to illustrate how the marketing manager might have to choose undesirable strategies.

A quick return on investment is sometimes sought by top management. This might influence the marketing manager to select marketing strategies that would yield quick returns in the short run but kill his "customer franchise" in the long run.

Top management might decide on diversification. This might force the marketing manager to choose strategies that are poorly suited to the company's resources.

Perhaps for status or humanitarian reasons, top management might decide to serve certain target markets, without regard to the company's resources or market profitability. Some retailers trying to serve "inner-city" consumers, for example, seem to be following humanitarian objectives. In such situations, the marketing manager might still be expected to pursue profits, but less aggressively.

Some top managements want a large sales volume or larger market share for its own sake. This can lead to good profits – but this is not always the case, as we shall see later.

Another business objective is domination of a market for a particular commodity. Sometimes this objective is stated in terms of the rate of growth or share of a market; plans may call for doubling or tripling sales in five years, or increasing the share 10 percent each year. This objective places a tremendous burden on the marketing manager and may require an extremely aggressive marketing strategy. If the objectives are stated even more specifically, such as share of market within a particular geographical area or for particular products, the marketing manager's scope is even more limited. And the possibility of maximizing profits may be limited too.

Marketing manager may set sub-objectives	*The marketing manager may have no choice in determining the overall company objectives, but he can and should set subobjectives within the framework of these overall objectives.* In subsequent chapters, we will discuss Product, Place, Promotion, and Pricing objectives that should be developed within the larger framework, and the policies which, in turn, are developed to implement these narrower objectives.

Conclusion

This chapter has been concerned with the forces which, while beyond the marketing manager's control, profoundly affect the strategies and time-related plans he will develop. Some uncontrollable factors can change faster than others. But all can change, requiring adjustments in his plans. Ideally, likely changes would be considered in his planning.

As we have seen, he must develop marketing mixes appropriate to the customs of the people in his target markets. He must be aware, for example, that promotion which is appropriate in Gary, Indiana, may be offensive to citizens of New Orleans, Louisiana, or Yokohama, Japan.

The marketing manager also must be aware of the legal restrictions limiting his actions, and sensitive to changing political climates. The growing interest in consumerism may force many changes.

The economic environment—the chances of increased government spending, business cycle fluctuations, or spiraling inflation—also will affect his choice of strategies, and the marketing man must try to anticipate, understand, and deal with such changes.

Always mindful of these factors, he must also examine the existing business structure itself: How well entrenched are his competitors? What action can he expect them to take?

Finally, he must bear in mind the resources and objectives of his firm, for his strategies should be planned to gain those objectives within the constraints imposed by the firm's resources.

Developing good strategies is obviously a very complicated procedure. The marketing manager must be well informed. He can benefit by increased knowledge in the fields of sociology, anthropology, psychology, economics, political science, and history. Most important, he must know his own field thoroughly, for he will have to use the information he has drawn from all these sources in the formation of his strategies. Marketing management is clearly an integrating discipline. In the next chapter, on marketing research, we will begin to see how the marketing manager can find answers to the many problems facing him.

QUESTIONS AND PROBLEMS

1 For a new design of haircomb, or one of the items mentioned in Question 14 of Chapter 2, discuss the uncontrollable factors that the marketing manager will have to consider.

2 Discuss the relative importance of the uncontrollable variables, given the speed with which these variables move. If some must be neglected because of a shortage of executive time, which would you recommend for "neglect"?

3 Which way does the U.S. political and legal environment seem to be moving (with respect to business – related affairs)?

4 Why is it necessary to have so many laws regulating business? Why has Congress not just passed one set of laws to take care of business problems?

5 If the Federal Trade Commission is an arm of the government, why has it had difficulty in obtaining compliance with many of its rulings?

6 What and whom is the government attempting to protect in its effort to preserve and regulate competition?

7 For each of the *major* laws discussed in the text, indicate whether in the long run this law will promote or restrict competition (see Figure 3–1). As a consumer, without any financial interest in business, what is your reaction to each of these laws?

8 Discuss the impact of the economic environment on the marketing manager, illustrating with reference to very recent economic developments.

9 Discuss the probable impact on your hometown of a major technological breakthrough in air transportation which would permit foreign producers to ship into any U.S. market for about the same transportation cost that domestic producers must incur.

10 Specifically, how would various company objectives affect the development of a marketing mix for a new type of baby shoe? If this company were just being formed by a former shoemaker with limited financial resources, list the objectives he might have and then discuss how they will affect the development of his marketing strategy.

11 Discuss how a company's financial strength might have a bearing on the kinds of products it might produce. Will it have an impact on the other three P's as well? If so, how? Use an example in your answer.

...some marketing researchers see themselves at the center of an information system which works to integrate all activities of the company.

...marketing research is not a mysterious cult practiced by statisticians...it is a management tool that helps the manager make better decisions.

4

Gathering market information

Successful planning of marketing strategies obviously requires information—information about potential target markets and their responses to various marketing mixes, about competition and other uncontrollable factors.

It is the job of marketing research to help the marketing manager gather the information he needs to make wise decisions. This is not an easy job, because people and competitors are so unpredictable. It must be done, nevertheless. Without sound marketing information, the manager has to fly by the seat of his pants, and in our dynamic and highly competitive economy, this almost insures failure. Competitors would probably know more about such a manager's market and how he was doing in that market than he knew himself!

What is marketing research?

Marketing research is concerned with developing and analyzing the "facts" that help marketing managers do a better job of planning, executing, and controlling. Marketing research is much more than a bundle of techniques or a group of specialists in survey design or statistical techniques. Good marketing researchers must be both marketing- *and* management-oriented to assure that their research focuses on real problems on which action can be taken.

Some of the techniques of marketing research are as old as human history. The Children of Israel sent interviewers to sample the market and produce of Canaan. In medieval Europe, some merchant families prospered because their contacts throughout the world enabled them to get information before their competitors. Now, marketing planners – often isolated in company offices, far from their potential customers – must rely on research to be sure they know what is going on. This point cannot be overemphasized because it is all too easy for management to lose touch with its markets. One of the critical tasks of the marketing researcher is to help management get the "facts" and understand them. The many potential markets in the United States *and* abroad are not necessarily like the markets lived in by the typical middle-class suburban managers.

Is marketing research important for the marketing manager?

Marketing research details may come to be handled by staff or outside specialists, but the marketing manager must know how to plan and evaluate research projects. That is, he should be able to communicate with specialists in *their* language. He may only be a "consumer" of research, but he should be a knowledgeable consumer, perhaps regularly specifying what he wants to buy. For this reason, our treatment of marketing research will not focus on mechanics, but rather on how to plan and evaluate research. The marketing researcher must excel in these areas also, so in the following discussion we will take the marketing researcher's view, realizing that both of them should participate in the research process if the results are going to lead to action.

Investing money and faith

Marketing research as we know it today began around 1900 and grew as more companies became interested in regional and then national markets. The development of sampling techniques in the 1930's, the use of the psychological interview, and other attitude and opinion measurement techniques have expanded the field markedly.[1]

These and other refinements have increased the dependability of the findings and prompted businessmen to put more money and faith in research. In some consumer goods companies, no major decisions

[1] Lawrence C. Lockley, "Notes on the History of Marketing Research," *Journal of Marketing*, April, 1950, pp. 733–36.

are made without the support, and sometimes even the official approval, of the marketing research department. As a result, some marketing research directors rise to high levels in the organization. For example, at Pillsbury, this activity is headed by the Vice President of Growth and Technology.

Strategic planning framework can guide research

Marketing researchers often become involved with strategic as well as tactical planning. They also can be helpful in evaluating how strategies are working out — providing "feedback" and control which may lead to new plans. Thus research is a continuing process. Some marketing researchers see themselves at the center of an information system which works to integrate all activities of the company. In other words, this information system helps to plan and implement the total system of action which we discussed earlier.[2]

With such a wide range of potential responsibilities, it is important that the marketing researcher see clearly what kinds of problems he is being asked to work on and what types of information are actually needed to solve the problems. Strategic planning problems may require different techniques than simply checking the effectiveness of tactical efforts. An evaluation of potential target markets, for example, or how much a market's customers are willing to pay for products might require an in-depth survey or even a market test. On the other hand, if the sales manager wanted to be sure that each salesman was getting his share of the market in his area, he might want to analyze the company's own sales data in relation to industry data available from a trade association or commercial source.

The strategic planning framework introduced in Chapter 2 can be especially useful here — helping the researcher to see at what level the real problem lies. Do we really know enough about target markets? If so, do we know enough to work out all of the four P's? And so on down through tactical-level problems, such as how to motivate an older salesman or handle a price war in New York City or Tokyo.

The importance of understanding the nature of the problem and then trying to solve *that* problem can be seen more clearly in the following example of a manufacturer of a new easy-to-use baking mix. Top management had selected apartment dwellers, younger couples, and the too-busy-to-cook crowd as target markets — a logical market at first glance. Some modest research on the *size* of this market, *not* their interest in this product concept, indicated that if these consumers responded as expected, there were enough of them to create

[2] Conrad Berenson, "Marketing Information Systems," *Journal of Marketing*, October, 1969, pp. 16–23.

a profitable baking mix market. The company decided to cater to this market and developed a logical marketing mix.

During the first few months, sales results were disappointing. The manufacturer "guessed" that the product itself might be unacceptable, since the promotion seemed to be adequate. At this point, a consumer survey was undertaken – with surprising results. The product was apparently satisfactory, but the target consumers were just not interested – even simplified food preparation didn't particularly grab them. Instead, the best market turned out to be families who did their own cooking. They appreciated the convenience of the mix, especially when they needed a dish in a hurry.

In this case, the original strategy planning was done sloppily. The original choice of target markets was based on faulty executive guesswork. This led to an unsuitable strategy and wasted promotional expense. Preliminary research with a variety of consumers, about their needs and preferences, might have avoided this costly error. Both marketing research and management fumbled the ball by not studying the attitudes of the target market. Then, when sales results were poor, the company compounded the error by assuming that the product was at fault and overlooking consumers' real attitudes about the product. Fortunately, research finally uncovered the real problem, and the overall strategy was changed quickly.

The moral of this story is that the strategic planning framework which we introduced in Chapter 2 can be useful for guiding marketing research efforts. If the marketing manager has the facts on his potential target markets, then he can focus his research efforts on required marketing mix ingredients, their sensitivity to change, and the effectiveness of various tactics. Without such a framework, marketing researchers can get sidetracked into working on the wrong problems.

In our dynamic marketplace, marketing research often must try to provide answers to urgent questions – both strategic and tactical kinds. Sometimes answers are needed so urgently that quick-and-rough research work must be done. A little information may be better than total ignorance. Even though the most scientific approach is not feasible when time is short, researchers should attempt to use the best procedures possible. For this reason, we will begin our discussion of marketing research by using the scientific method to demonstrate that a logical approach to marketing problems is best. This scientific approach, combined with a strategic planning framework, can provide assured guidance in the typically chaotic and crisislike atmosphere of the business world.

It is clear that marketing research has wide application at various levels of management. Its scope is so wide, in fact, that it cannot be adequately covered in one chapter. We will therefore devote three chapters to this subject, with this chapter serving as a basic introduction. Sales forecasting will be treated in Chapter 5. The more control-oriented aspects of sales and cost analysis will be examined in Chapter 29, when we will have gained a better appreciation of what we want to control.

The scientific method and marketing research

In seeking to relate the scientific method to marketing research, we are not trying to cloak marketing research with scientific respectability. Businessmen want to make the best decisions possible, and this cannot be done consistently other than on a logical basis.

The scientific method is such an approach. In marketing, this logical method forces the analyst to follow certain procedures that reduce the possibilities of slipshod work or reliance on intuition.

The scientific method consists, basically, of four stages:

1. Observation.
2. Formulation of hypotheses.
3. Prediction of the future.
4. Testing of the hypotheses.

With this method, we seek to develop hypotheses (such as "There is no significant difference between Breads A and B"),[3] and then to test each hypothesis. The formulation of the hypothesis is extremely important. In fact, much exploratory research is aimed at getting information and suggesting testable hypotheses. But the research should always be decision-oriented, even if it is a question of whether to act or not.

Application of the scientific method helps the marketing manager develop and test the best hypotheses. It takes a commonsense but rigorous approach—formulation of hypotheses, testing, perhaps modifying, and testing again. The feedback principle is applied throughout the process.

The scientific approach to pain

To illustrate these stages in a simple nonmarketing case, consider a college student who develops a painful swollen ankle after a skiing accident. The ankle could be bruised, sprained, or broken. What should he do? If he goes to a doctor, he will probably find the doctor following the scientific method:

1. Observation:	Pain seems to increase if foot is twisted, but pain is not unbearable.
2. Formulation of an hypothesis:	Since a sprain would be more painful than this, the ankle is broken.
3. Prediction of the future:	Pain and swelling will reduce, but bone may heal improperly if not set.
4. Testing the hypothesis:	X-ray the ankle; don't wait to see if hypothesis is correct in this case.

[3] To those familiar with statistics, null hypotheses are developed and tested whenever appropriate.

Let us now use the same framework to show how a businessman might use this method.

The scientific approach to shirt wrappers

A manufacturer of men's shirts had no major immediate problems, but wanted to develop new opportunities. The approach he took is shown below:

1. Observation:	Notices some competitors' sales increasing and many competitors shifting to a new plastic wrapping.
2. Formulation of hypotheses:	Assumes (*a*) that plastic wrapping is sole cause of competitors' sales increases and (*b*) that his products are similar.
3. Prediction of the future:	His sales ought to increase if he shifts to the new wrapping.
4. Testing the hypotheses:	Produce some shirts in new package and test them in the market.

The market test revealed that his prediction was correct—sales did increase. But what if they had not increased? In the answer to this question lies one important benefit of the scientific approach. Through careful control (making certain that the test was correctly designed and run) and evaluation of results, we should be able to isolate the reason why a given test failed and pinpoint where the hypotheses were in error.

In this case, either one of the hypotheses could have been wrong. Either increased sales by competitors were *not* caused by the new wrapping, or this manufacturer's products were *not* similar.

Assuming that the first hypothesis was wrong, further research might show that competitors' sales were up simply because their promotion had been more effective. Or if the second hypothesis proved incorrect, it might be possible to identify ways the products differed and then to capitalize on these points, or modify the product.

Four-step approach to solving marketing problems

In marketing research, there is a four-step application of the scientific method: (1) definition of problem, (2) situation analysis, (3) informal investigation, and (4) formal research project.

Observation, the first stage in the scientific method, is used during the first three marketing research steps. Once the problem is defined, *formulation of hypotheses* takes place, perhaps during the situation analysis or informal investigation. *Prediction of the future* occurs any time before a formal research project is planned. And *testing the hypotheses* is completed in the formal research project unless, as frequently happens, informal investigation solves the problem.

Actually, then, the scientific method is a vital part of marketing research. Table 4-1 may help us see the relationships. The precise meaning of these terms is explained in the following pages.

It should be emphasized again that this orderly procedure helps us keep clear what we are doing. Mastery of this approach will greatly improve your ability to plan marketing research projects.

Table 4–1 Relation of scientific method to marketing research

Scientific method stages	Used during the following marketing research steps
Observation	Definition of problem Situation analysis Informal investigation Formal research
Formulation of hypotheses	Situation analysis Informal investigation Formal research (Planning)
Prediction of the future (Action implications)	Situation analysis Informal investigation Formal research (Planning)
Testing hypotheses	Formal research (Unless management is satisfied with an earlier but more intuitive solution.)

Definition of the problem

Defining the problem is the most important and often the most difficult job of the marketing analyst. It is slow work, requiring careful observation and sometimes taking up over half the time spent on a research project. But it is time well spent if the problem is precisely defined. The best research job on the wrong problem is wasted effort; it may even lead to more costly consequences, such as the introduction of a poor product or the use of an ineffective advertising approach.

Problem definition sounds simple, and therein lies the danger. It is easy to mistake identification of symptoms for the definition of the problem. For example, suppose that the continuing sales analysis that is part of the control function (to be discussed more fully in Chapters 5 and 29) shows that the company's sales are decreasing significantly in certain territories while sales expenses remain constant, with a resulting decline in profits. Will it help to define the problem by asking the simple question: How can we stop the sales decline? Probably not. This would be the equivalent of asking how to lower a patient's temperature instead of first trying to identify the cause of the fever.

We must discover *why* sales are declining – whether the cause is competitive activity, product deficiencies, inadequate support by company sales personnel, prices that are not competitive, inefficient advertising, or some other cause. If one or more of these factors can be isolated as the real problem, then the marketing executive is on the way to an effective solution.

The real problem may be very elusive. In the isolation of his office, the marketing manager may conceive of several likely problems he can investigate. He can start with the strategic planning framework, for example, and evaluate what he knows about the target market and the compatability of the marketing mix ingredients. If he has doubts about one or more of these factors, he can begin to focus on these likely problems. But without further investigation and evidence, he should not assume too quickly that he has defined the real problem. Instead, he should take his list of possible problems and then go on to the next step, trying to discover which is the fundamental cause of his trouble.

Situation analysis

When the marketing researcher feels that he has begun to focus on the problem, he can go on to this next step. He need not (and probably should not) commit himself completely to any particular problem as yet. Through this and the following steps, he should be prepared to revise or restate problems in the face of new facts. This reevaluation is continuous. Even after he has developed and tested an hypothesis by formal research, new factors can arise so that a new statement of the problem and a new hypothesis test may be necessary.

No talks with outsiders
In the situation analysis, the researcher first tries to size up the situation—but without talking to outsiders. He talks to informed executives within his own company, and studies and evaluates internal company records generated as part of the control function. He also searches libraries for all available published material.

This research is vital, since the analyst must be thoroughly familiar with the environment in which he must work. He analyzes information about his own company, its products, the industry, specific markets in which it is operating, dealers, its own promotion, and its competitors' activities. Libraries contain vast stores of information, but once the researcher has begun to narrow the scope of his problems, he can look for specific kinds of information.

Unless he knows what he is looking for, the researcher may be overwhelmed by the information available within his own company or in libraries. Let's take a closer look at the type of information we're talking about.

Secondary data sources
The data we are concerned with here is called *secondary data*. This is information which is already published. *Primary data* is gathered specifically to solve the current problem. Gathering primary data is discussed later, but it must be emphasized that too often researchers rush out to gather primary data when there is already a plentiful supply of secondary information. And this data may be available immediately, at little or no cost!

One of the first places a researcher should look for secondary data, after looking at internal data, is a good library. Familiarity with the references in the library's card catalog and bibliographies enables the researcher to pursue secondary sources more knowledgeably. Frequently your local library has the answer you need to a question.

Government sources

The federal and state governments publish data on almost every conceivable subject; therefore, it's difficult for even large libraries to maintain a complete and readily accessible library of government documents. The federal government publishes a monthly guide to its current publications, but it is more practical to refer to federal government summary publications to obtain leads to more detailed documents.

Three useful summaries, available from the U.S. Department of Commerce for less than $10 a year and also found in most libraries, are the *Statistical Abstract of the United States,* the *County and City Data Book,* and the *Survey of Current Business.*

The most useful of these summaries, the *Statistical Abstract of the United States,* is similar to an almanac. It is issued each year and lists more than 1,000 summary tables from work being published by the federal government as well as other groups. References to world markets are included. Detailed footnotes can guide a student to more specific detail on a topic. Each issue contains a "Bibliography of Sources and Statistics," about 40 pages in length, that lists all *Abstract* sources, classified by type of subject.

Every student should be familiar with the *Abstract* because it is probably the best starting point for locating statistical data. Marketing men must be experts on sources of information, and the time to start developing this expertise is *now.*

The *County and City Data Book,* published about once every three years, gives more local, geographical detail than the *Abstract.* It presents a selection of statistics for all counties and for cities of more than 25,000.

For more current data on a wide variety of subjects, monthly and quarterly statistics are published, without geographical detail, in the *Survey of Current Business.* Each issue of this monthly periodical also features articles on economic trends and other business subjects.

The U.S. Department of Commerce serves as a distribution agency for statistics compiled by all other federal departments. Commerce Department branch and field offices, located in major cities throughout the United States, are fertile sources of data. Staff members provide assistance and suggestions for locating specific data.

Some city and state governments have similar agencies that will provide leads for local data. University bureaus of business research may also prove helpful.

Private sources

Many private research organizations, advertising agencies, newspapers, and magazines regularly compile and publish data. A good business library is valuable here for good sources such as *Sales Management: The Marketing Magazine, Industrial Marketing,*

Advertising Age, Marketing/Communications, and the publications of the National Industrial Conference Board. Some of this information is available inexpensively as a customer service to clients of advertising agencies or buyers of advertising space or time. For example, J. Walter Thompson Co., an advertising agency, and the *Chicago Tribune* maintain continuing panels of housewives for consumer research purposes. These panels enable researchers to spot trends, an extension of market awareness not easily obtained in one-time surveys.

Research by subscription

There are a number of research firms whose exclusive business is supplying, by subscription, research data that will aid the marketing manager in situation analysis. Two of the better-known organizations specializing in continuing research are the Market Research Corporation of America (MRCA) and A. C. Nielsen Co. MRCA makes available information on product movements through certain grocery chains, using data from a customer panel of about 5,000 families located throughout the United States. These families record in diaries all food and drug items, plus other selected items, purchased each week. They list not only each item but its price and the store where it was purchased. This data is used by many large food and drug manufacturers to measure the rate of consumption of their products at the consumer level.

Similar reports are provided by A. C. Nielsen, which audits about 2,000 retail food stores and drugstores to measure movement at the retail level. These two services ought to provide roughly the same measure of movement of products at the consumer level. Nielsen, however, provides additional information about competitors' use of retail displays, 2 for 1 sales, and other activities. For this reason, some large companies subscribe to both services. They often find out more about the activity and sales of their smaller competitors than some of these competitors know about themselves. Nielson now offers similar services in 18 countries, including Canada, Mexico, Japan, and most Western European countries.

Trade associations can also be a good source of information about a particular industry. They not only compile data from and for their members but also publish magazines that focus on the problems and important topics in the industry.

Problem solving during the situation analysis

If the problem is clear-cut, it can sometimes be solved at this point without additional expense. Perhaps someone else already has done a study that answers almost exactly the same question.

The fact that further research *may* be reduced or eliminated is important. Too often researchers rush out a questionnaire to 100 or even several thousand persons or firms. This gives the impression that the analyst is "really doing his job." An effective situation analysis, unfortunately, usually is less impressive. If a supervisor asks the analyst what he is doing, about all he can say is, "I'm sizing up the situation" or "I'm studying the problem."

The fact of the matter is that the situation analyst is really trying to determine the exact nature of the situation and the problem. The man who rushes out all the questionnaires may be doing this too — although this fact may surprise him! The point is that when the results of his questionnaire come in, he may finally see the problem, but he still won't have the answer. He will still have to proceed to the next step in analysis, just the same as the more "scientific" researcher.

Informal investigation

During the informal investigation, the analyst is still attempting to define his problem and formulate hypotheses. But now the idea is to get outside the company and the library, and to talk to informed people, sometimes including customers. By informed people, we mean intelligent and efficient retailers, wholesalers, customers, and other knowledgeable people in the industry. No formal questionnaire is developed, as the analyst is not yet *testing* hypotheses, except intuitively.

When considering the development of machine tool products, for example, it would make sense to talk to a few machine operators, plant superintendents in more efficient factories, design engineers at independent research organizations or universities, and perhaps a few good industrial distributors who have close contact with potential customers.

Fast, informative, inexpensive

While these talks would be informal, they should help the analyst pinpoint his problem and hypotheses. By this time, he should have the problem area narrowed down. This is important, because asking informed people to discuss *general* problems will not be productive. Only specific questions will elicit specific answers.

The virtues of the informal investigation are that it takes little time and can be very informative. Moreover, it is inexpensive compared with a large-scale survey.

On the basis of the information gathered in a situation analysis and informal investigation, the analyst should now be formulating some specific hypotheses. Or he may be able to refine his hypotheses at this point, developing an answer to his problem without further research. This is especially likely in the industrial goods area, where the number of customers is limited and buying behavior is fairly predictable. Here, the views of a few well-informed people may be representative of the industry.

If management has to make a decision quickly — if it cannot wait for a formal test — then well-considered hypotheses may have to serve as the basis for an intuitive solution. Occasionally speed is more important than precision. In such cases, care in the preliminary steps may bear fruit far beyond the "extra" time and effort invested.

Planning the formal research project

If the analyst has failed to reach a solution to his problem by this time, his next step is to develop a formal research project to gather primary data. There are three basic methods that he can use: (1) the observation method, (2) the survey method, or (3) the experimental method.

Each method has its appropriate uses, and unless the problem is complex, only one method would be used in a single project. It is the analyst's responsibility to choose which method is best, according to problem characteristics as well as the time, funds, facilities, and personnel available to him.

The *observation method,* recognizing the possible pitfalls in direct questioning, avoids face-to-face interviews. Sometimes, however, asking questions cannot be sidestepped. Then, a survey may be helpful. The *experimental method* may use either or both of the preceding methods. Its distinguishing characteristic is a more rigorous procedure, which usually includes establishing control groups and applying advanced statistical techniques.

Observation method: not asking but watching

In pinpointing the problem, we have been using observation—asking ourselves what is happening inside and outside the firm. It makes sense to continue using observation in the research project. But this observation will now be focused on a specific, well-defined problem.

Here, the researcher avoids talking to the subjects. If a retailer or a bread manufacturer were interested in bread-buying behavior in supermarkets, for example, he could station a man at the bread counter to observe what takes place. This man could check the length of deliberation in the choice of a brand, the amount of label reading that takes place, or the extent of multiple purchases.

In other situations, films are made of consumers under varying situations. Their behavior can then be analyzed carefully by running the films at very slow speeds or actually analyzing each frame. This might be useful, for example, in studying product selection in a supermarket to decide how to package a product.

If, to help estimate the potential radius of his market, a supermarket operator were interested in the distance customers traveled to get to his store, he could take down license numbers in the parking lot and trace addresses. Traffic flowing by a particular location can be counted to provide an estimate of the potential for a shopping center.

Survey method: asking enough people the right questions

When researchers feel that they must talk directly to someone to get the right answers, they use the survey method. Sometimes surveys are conducted to test hypotheses, but they may merely be exploratory efforts to size up the situation before doing more research. Such an exploratory survey can provide the background data which, in another case, already would have been located during the situation analysis.

Usually some type of questionnarie is used in a survey. In some unstructured surveys, however, the researchers may only provide the interviewer with a series of questions intended as interview guidelines. Thereafter the interviewer "plays it by ear." The desirability of these various approaches will be discussed below.

By phone, mail, or face-to-face

There are basically three types of surveys: telephone, mail, and personal interview. Each has its advantages and disadvantages.

Telephone Surveys

Telephone interviews are effective for obtaining quick answers to short, simple questions, especially when it is not important to identify the respondent or to know any of the characteristics of the person or family. Yet if consumer characteristics – such as age, income, condition of personal belongings, household furnishings or family composition – have a bearing on the analysis, then another survey method may be more appropriate.

Telephone interviewing is relatively low in cost and is satisfactory where the researcher is primarily interested in people who are likely to own telephones. In some areas, however, 10 to 20 percent of the families do not have telephones, and excluding them may add bias to the results.

Mail surveys

The mail survey may be useful when the questionnaire is long. And it may be necessary for economy if potential respondents are widely scattered. With the mail questionnaire, the interviewer can take all the time he wishes to answer questions and may be more willing to fill in personal or family characteristics. Unfortunately, the response rate on mail questionnaires is not very high unless there is extensive follow-up or unless the questionnaire is especially interesting. From 1 to 10 percent may be considered a "good" response, by the researcher, but the respondents may not be at all representative. Those who respond may be entirely different kinds of people from those who do not, and the results can be very misleading.

Mail surveys are inexpensive if a large number of persons respond. Conversely, they may be quite expensive if the response rate is poor, as it typically is, or if extensive follow-up is required. And with mail questionnaires, it is difficult to probe for additional answers to questions or encourage respondents to elaborate on particular points.

Personal interview survey

The personal interview is used frequently because most people would rather talk than write. Each personal interview may be more expensive than each mail or telephone interview – but it offers the interviewer a chance to probe in depth certain questions.

The personal interview also enables the interviewer to develop new lines of thought that were not anticipated at the start. New hypotheses or even new problems might be covered in the personal interview. In addition, the interviewer has the opportunity to judge socioeconomic characteristics and to follow up with those people who are not at home the first time, perhaps reaching people who would not ordinarily answer mail questionnaires.

In this sense, the researcher using the personal interview has greater control over his sample, and the survey results may be more accurate because they are more "representative" of the researcher's target population.

Validity and reliability of surveys

When determining whether to use a survey, and in particular, which type of survey, it pays to question critically both the validity and reliability of the proposed survey—the same critical approach that should apply when evaluating any kind of research.

A survey is *valid* if it measures what it is supposed to measure. It is *reliable* if the results represent the entire market population accurately.

Validity

The important questions in testing for validity are, "What are we measuring?" "Does our research actually measure what we intend it to?" One sure way to get invalid findings is to ask consumers something they do not know. The main problem, however, is *not* that they don't know the answers. Respondents usually want to help. They may not even be aware that they do not know, but they are obliging and will give answers.

Sometimes the question arises whether a survey measures anything at all. In one case, a researcher wanted to obtain some direction for his company's activities. After much effort, an 18-page questionnaire was designed and sent to the company's *present list of customers*. They were, in effect, asked what other lines of business the company ought to go into. Many customers volunteered answers, but the answers were not useful because the respondents were not familiar with the company's particular resources or alternate target markets.

In this case, the problem was poorly defined, and questions were aimed in every direction. The respondents to whom the questionnaire was sent were not interested in the problem or even informed about it, and could not give useful answers. If, by some chance, the answers had made any sense at all, it is frightening to think how the company might have used the answers. Finally, after several months of work, the research project was dropped.

In evaluating the validity of surveys—indeed, all research—the researcher should continually seek to know: (1) whether the data was obtained from an informed source; and (2) if the problem has been answered with this data.

Reliability

The critical question in testing for reliability is, "Can we rely on these results as representative of the relevant population?" In most commercial research, it is economically and physically impossible to cover the total population in the research design. Even if you were interested in surveying all retailers, only a percentage could be interviewed on a practical basis. If the population were all college students, only some would be chosen. These are *samples*. Obviously the repre-

sentativeness of the sample has an important influence on the reliability of the research results.

If a sample is chosen in a random manner from a population, this
sample will *tend to* have the same characteristics and be representative of the population. The phrase, *tend to,* is important because it is
only a tendency. The possible deviation of sample results can be
predicted by sampling theory, *if* some random sampling technique
has been used.

The simplest random sampling technique is called *simple random
sampling.* Suppose that the total population to be sampled is all the
students at a college. Using the *simple random sampling* technique,
a list of all people in the college population is obtained; then the
sample is drawn so that each member of the population has an equal
chance of being included.

One of many possible variations of simple random sampling is
called *area sampling.* This approach may be used if it is not convenient or possible to develop a list of all people in the population.
Instead, researchers can list all of the blocks in a city, then select at
random some of the blocks to be sampled. Within each of these selected blocks, every household or some smaller number selected at
random could be interviewed.

STANDING ON THE CORNER IS HAPHAZARD In contrast, a *quota
sample* or a more *haphazard sample* might be drawn. In such samples, not everyone has an equal chance of being selected. The researcher may specify that 10 percent of the survey population should
consist of those with incomes over $10,000 a year, 20 percent in the
next lower income bracket, and so on. Further, he may specify that a
certain proportion of various age groups should be represented in
each income bracket.

These specifications may insure that the sample is more or less
representative of the population, *as far as those dimensions go.*
But if some controls are not imposed so that everyone has a reasonable
chance of entering the sample, the interviewers may reduce the
reliability by how they fill their quotas—for example, by talking to
people who pass through a railroad station or shop downtown on a
particular day. The limitations of this approach are obvious, but the
truth is that many samples are obtained in just this manner.

HOW TO DECREASE THE CONFIDENCE INTERVAL If a random sampling
technique has been used in designing the sample, methods are available for measuring and stating the degree of reliability of the data
obtained. These statements are in terms of "confidence intervals."
For example, if a sample of 100 were taken (using a strictly random
sample), and if it were found that 10 percent of the population preferred a new cake mix, the following statement could be made concerning your confidence in the 10 percent finding (with 95 percent
certainty): The true percentage preferring the new mix is between
4 and 16 percent of the population.

If this range of accuracy were not sufficient for management
action, then a larger sample could be used to narrow the confidence

interval. If a sample size of 1,000 were used and the same 10 percent preference were obtained, then the confidence interval would be approximately 8 to 12 percent instead of 4 to 16 percent.[3]

Will manage-ment have confidence in research?

Statistical reliability and confidence intervals should be seriously considered in planning the formal research project. This is especially important if the final results are to be presented to managers who understand statistical theory! If they do, obviously the confidence they place in the results will be affected by the width of the confidence intervals.

It is also important that both *validity* and *reliability* be considered in planning research. One study may be extremely valid but of ques-tionable reliability, while another study, using precise statistical techniques, may have only pseudo accuracy because it lacks validity. Failure in either area may lead to incorrect decisions.

When a nonrandom sampling method is used, it is technically wrong to compute confidence intervals. Even so, some researchers who use such samples are inclined to imply a great deal. The ma-jority of commercial research does use nonrandom sampling—because of the higher cost of selecting more reliable samples—and the results are somewhat suspect because of this.

Some researchers claim that with judgment and caution in inter-pretation, such nonrandom samples may produce good results at lower cost. This may be true in certain cases, especially in the in-dustrial field where the total number of customers may be relatively small.

But the marketing researcher who relies heavily on nonrandom sampling should not be surprised if the marketing manager is re-luctant to place much confidence in his results and relies on his own personal judgment instead.

Selecting the general approach to a survey

Two basically different approaches can be used for developing a sur-vey: the quantitative or the qualitative approach.

Quantitative approach

Here the researcher asks, "How many persons do certain things, how many products are purchased in certain quantities," and so on. Straightforward yes or no or multiple-choice questions are often used. This approach is characterized by rather large and perhaps statistically reliable samples varying from several hundred to several thousand respondents. If the solution of a problem requires straight-forward quantitative data, this approach can provide it. This kind of

---

[3] Detailed treatment of confidence intervals is be-yond the scope of this text and can be found in any introductory statistics book. Just to refresh mem-ories for those who have had statistics, however, the formula used here for a 95 percent certainty confidence interval is:

$$p \pm 2\sqrt{\frac{p \times q}{n}}.$$

In this formula p is the percent result; q is $100 - p$; and n is the sample size. For the 10 per-cent preference this yields:

$$10 \pm 2\sqrt{\frac{10 \times 90}{n}}.$$

Obviously, increasing n will decrease the con-fidence interval, as stated.

research sometimes helps management see what is happening in the market and, perhaps, begin to understand why it is happening.

Qualitative approach

The strictly quantitative approach is concerned with "facts" – with the *what, where,* and *when* rather than the *why.* But if a researcher is interested in what customers are going to do *in the future* or why they did something in the past, then qualitative *why* questions may be necessary.

BIBLE VERSUS BURLESQUE QUEEN Straightforward *why* questions, however, can be risky and reduce the validity of the research. Good judgment and careful design are vital in qualitative research, as the following case illustrates.

A research analyst, attempting to predict newsstand sales of pocket-sized books six months before they went on the market, asked a group of people what books they preferred. He got the usual answers – the Bible, Shakespeare, and so on. Then, at the end of the interview, he handed respondents a list of book titles. He said that he would like to send them a free book for their cooperation in the survey. All they had to do was pick out the title they wanted, by number. Included in the list were pocket-sized editions of the Bible, Shakespeare, and other classics as well as many of the titles that the company was considering. The favorite of the respondents was *Murder of a Burlesque Queen!*[4]

The moral is that when you ask someone a question, he may try to give you the answer he thinks you want. Or the one he thinks reflects the most credit on him. When given a choice of getting something free for himself, however, he reveals his true preferences.

There has been enough evidence of this kind of consumer reaction in applied research to convince researchers that special techniques are necessary when trying to determine consumers' real opinions and feelings.

MOTIVATION RESEARCH – A QUALITATIVE TOOL Motivation research applies the methods of the psychologist and sociologist, derived from clinical methods, to *why*-type problems. Rather than large samples, the motivation researcher works with relatively small samples – perhaps only 25 to 50 persons. And instead of one-, two-, or five-minute interviews, he may use depth interviews taking one to two hours.

The interviewer using motivational techniques attempts to probe the respondent's subconscious attitudes. The idea is to determine the basic motives of the person and to see how these inner motives are manifested in outward behavior when the person is faced with specific choices.

Technically trained interviewers must conduct these interviews. The results obtained are, in part, a function of the experience, training, and judgment of those who collect and analyze the data, as well as the attitudes and opinions of individual respondents.

[4]"Don't Believe All You Hear," (Louisville, Ky.) *Courier-Journal,* May 26, 1957.

EXPLAINING PRUNE PREFERENCES There is not much chance of quantifying the answers or developing an objective measure of the results of the qualitative approach. This is an important criticism, because results depend so heavily on the training of the research worker and his own point of view. This adds complications, since one study identified 39 different psychological schools of thought on human behavior.[5] *Yet only one group—the Freudians—*has been prominent in the motivation research movement.

To illustrate these complications, two of the top motivation research agencies in the country were employed independently by two different groups interested in why consumers bought so few prunes.

One agency interviewed a sample cross section of Americans and presented a 62-page report explaining, with statements such as the following, why people disliked prunes: "They are dried-out, worn-out symbols of old age. . . . The prune fails to give security. . . . It is a plebeian food without prestige. . . . The prune is a witch."

Based on these findings, the agency conducting this survey suggested that the California Prune Advisory Board "rename them black diamonds; surround prunes with an aura of preciousness and desirability; and take prunes out of the fruit family and put them in the same context as nuts."

At the same time, the other research agency presented a 61-page report which concluded that Americans have no emotional block about the prune's "laxative connotation." On the basis of this finding, the researcher suggested that the prune promoters "exploit the core of the prune market by advertising the laxative features—and don't pussyfoot about this angle, either."

If only one of these studies had been made, the prune producers would have had little difficulty in following the advice. But when two studies come up with such conflicting recommendations, there is reason to question the procedures.[6] Perhaps the results could be used for different target markets, but with the small samples used in this type of research it would be difficult to determine which specific markets had which views.

Now, interest in motivation research seems to be declining. As one researcher commented: "After all, Freud dealt with the abnormal personality, but the person we want to understand is the average consumer."[7]

Modified qualitative approach

Not all qualitative research is motivation research, although some

[5] Wroe Alderson, *Marketing Behavior and Executive Action* (Homewood, Ill.: Richard D. Irwin, Inc., 1957), p. 189.

[6] A good review of the arguments on both sides and the techniques involved can be found in Robert Ferber and Hugh G. Wales (eds.), *Motivation and Market Behavior* (Homewood, Ill.: Richard D. Irwin, Inc., 1958). Other sources are George H. Smith, *Motivation Research in Advertising and Marketing* (New York: McGraw-Hill Book Co., 1958); Robert J. Williams, "Is it True What They Say About Motivation Research?" *Journal of Marketing,* October, 1957, pp. 125–33; *Use of Motivation Research in Marketing* (Studies in Business Policy No. 97 [New York, National Industrial Conference Board, Inc.]); James U. McNeal, "The Disappearing Motivation," *Business Topics,* Autumn, 1964, pp. 30–36; and most basic marketing research texts.

[7] "New Way to Size Up How Consumers Behave," *Business Week,* July 22, 1961, p. 74.

motivation researchers have implied this, in the interest of promoting their own techniques or agencies. Any research that seeks subjective responses from people can be considered qualitative.

Some researchers have borrowed several of the more promising methods of the psychologist and sociologist, including motivation research techniques, and remodeled them for use with traditional quantitiative questionnaires. In this modified approach, respondents are given a better chance to express their feelings and attitudes.

Instead of giving respondents a flat yes or no choice of whether they plan to buy a product, the analyst might list five alternatives: "Definitely yes"; "I am pretty sure"; "I think so"; "I do not think so," and "Definitely no." Or open-end questions seeking short answers may be used. The answers are then categorized for quantitative tabulation.

To encourage responses to such questions, the interviewer may use cartoons with blank word balloons. The cartoon might depict a woman buying coffee in a supermarket. The respondent is asked to fill in the balloon explaining what the woman is saying to her friend. Or the balloon may be removed and the respondent asked merely to comment on her feelings about a woman buying instant coffee. These responses could then be categorized and tabulated in a quantitative manner.

Surfacing approach

Some analysts make effective use of motivation research techniques as background or preparation for more extensive quantitative studies. Here, motivation research may provide hypotheses that can be tested and substantiated with quantitative research.

The term *surfacing approach* is given to the method of gradually building up from subjective tests to objective ones. As its name implies, it means beginning at the subconscious level (pure motivation research) and working closer and closer toward the surface of awareness.[8]

Ideas plus "harder" measurements lead to action

Pure motivation research techniques, for example, might suggest that consumers would prefer real fruit flavor to artificial flavoring in a dessert being designed to compete with Jell-O gelatin dessert. Researchers using the surfacing approach might then put the identical product in each of two packages, indicating in some manner that one product was made with pure fruit flavor while the other was made with artificial flavoring. If consumers showed a strong preference for one or the other product after using it, there would be a quantitative measure of the importance of this claim—and the company and its advertising agency could act accordingly in developing the product and its promotion.

The appeal of the surfacing approach is that the strictly qualitative techniques provide ideas, while the quantitative techniques produce "harder" measurements that provide a firm base for action.

[8]C. Joseph Clawson, "The Coming Breakthroughs in Motivation Research," *Cost and Profit Outlook* (Philadelphia: Alderson Associates, Inc., May–June, 1958), p. 3.

Most marketing executives now feel that both qualitative and quantitative research have their uses.

Experimental method: watching, asking, and trying

The observation method avoids approaching the customer, while the survey method relies upon direct interview. The experimental method utilizes either or both of these methods.

The major difference, as the name implies, is that experiments are set up. Statistical controls may be used in a market test so that random variations can be factored out by statistical analysis. Or mathematical models, perhaps utilizing computers, can be developed for simulating customer behavior or total marketing system behavior.

While detailed discussion of these techniques is beyond the scope of this book, experimental techniques are becoming increasingly important in applied research. Again, note the growing sophistication of marketing management and the challenge this field offers.[9]

The experimental method is often used in traditional sales and customer use tests. In a sales test, a new product might be tried in one store, city, state, or region, while the marketing mix is held constant elsewhere. If a sales change takes place in all areas, only the net change in the trial territory will be attributed to the new factor. This method has been used by retailers to test packaging, displays, pricing, promotional plans, new products, and store equipment.

It's what's up front that sells

With this method, a bread manufacturer or retailer can check the effectiveness of display positions in different stores. Some bread deliverymen on commission have done this on their own initiative. They have discovered that a front position increases sales so much that they have been known to pay a store clerk—out of their own pockets—to walk over to the bread display occasionally and move their company's bread to the front.

In other situations, use tests may be developed. Potential customers are given the same or different products in different packages. Their response to the product's use is analyzed, using various statistic techniques.[10]

A method that holds promise is to have a representative group of consumers play experimental games in which various products, prices, or other alternatives are offered in turn. This is not fully realistic, but some interesting and encouraging results have been obtained.[11]

Little use now, but more later

There are four basic reasons why the experimental method is not used much at the present time:

[9]See Seymour Banks, *Experimentation in Marketing* (New York: McGraw-Hill Book Co., 1965); and Robert D. Buzzell, *A Basic Bibliography on Mathematical Methods in Marketing* (American Marketing Association Bibliography Series No. 7, 1962).

[10]Chi-square and analysis of variance tests, for example.

[11]Edgar A. Pessemier, *New-Product Decisions* (New York: McGraw-Hill Book Co., 1966); and L. K. Anderson, J. R. Taylor, and R. J. Holloway, "The Consumer and His Alternatives: An Experimental Approach," *Journal of Marketing Research*, February, 1966, pp. 62–67.

1. It is time-consuming, when most marketing decisions must be made quickly.
2. It is often more costly.
3. It may reveal plans prematurely to competitors.
4. Many market researchers do not have the statistical and mathematical training required to conduct such tests effectively.

This last factor is being overcome rapidly, and it is likely that this type of research will become more common as more trained researchers enter the field.

Execution and interpretation of the research project

How to organize and conduct formal research projects is beyond the scope of this text. This involves questionnaire and research design, training of field staff, tabulation, interpretation, and presentation of results, as well as the follow-through to make sure that results are utilized effectively. Such matters are explained in most *marketing research* texts and are specialized but highly important activities.[12]

Marketing manager and researcher should work in concert

The interpretation step is especially important for marketing management. While managers may not be research specialists, they have to evaluate the results of such research. The interpretation and presentation of the final results are a clue to the quality of the research and its planning.

If a report does not have action implications, for example, it may have little value to management and may suggest poor planning by the researcher. If confidence intervals are not specified, then the manager has no basis for evaluating statistical reliability. The width of the confidence interval depends on the size of the sample, as we have already seen. If the research method and the reliability of the data are not presented, the marketing manager must use even greater judgment in evaluating the data. In fact, if the researcher does not explain his methods and then suggest specific action, he should not be surprised if the marketing manager chooses to ignore his work.

The desirability of close working relationships between the marketing manager and the marketing researcher should be obvious. Both should put all their efforts into making the best decisions.[13]

Good research may require an integrated approach

Marketing analysts frequently must combine several steps to do an effective research job. These steps can be illustrated by an example of a company interested in expanding its market for interior decorating products.

[12]Harper W. Boyd, Jr., and Ralph Westfall, *Marketing Research: Text and Cases* (rev. ed.; Homewood, Ill.: Richard D. Irwin, Inc., 1964).

[13]J. G. Keane, "Some Observations on Marketing Research in Top Management Decision Making," *Journal of Marketing*, October, 1969, pp. 10–15.

The company wanted to increase its sales, but it did not know how many interior decorators there were in their market, or how much money consumers spent on the company's product type (*definition of the problem*). A review of U.S. *Census of Business* data indicated that there were approximately 1,300 interior decorators. According to their own sales records (*situation analysis*), this would not leave much room for expansion of sales volume with their present line. Management decided, tentatively, to branch out into other lines (*hypothesis* that business would improve in another market).

Before taking off on this tangent, the company decided to do additional research in their present market area. They interviewed the company's salesmen, checked the circulation data of an interior decorators' magazine (more *situation analysis*), talked with informed credit people (*informal investigation*), and made a limited mail survey to check on the size of the market (a *formal research project* to test an hypothesis that there were more potential customers).

This research revealed that there were actually 9,700 interior decorators who spent some $75 million on the company's type of product alone. For some reason, probably their small size, the decorators had not all been included in the published census data. It was clear at this point that the company's biggest and best market was the one which they were already selling.

In this case, no research at all, or a too sketchy situation analysis would have led to incorrect results. But further analysis, along with an informal investigation and a limited survey, obtained results that proved very satisfactory.[14] This type of research is within the reach of even small firms, and the student should now be able to understand and participate in such an effort.

Cost and organization of marketing research

Relatively little, perhaps too little, is spent on the typical marketing research department. Often the research department's budget is about 0.2 percent of sales or $100,000 for a company with a $50 million annual sales volume.[15] This is in contrast to research and development budgets that frequently run to 5 or 10 percent of sales. Unfortunately, this situation sometimes leads to the development of products with little or no market potential.

Shortcuts cut cost, add risk

Even on modest budgets, however, good research work can be done.[16] When a problem is carefully defined, formal research projects may *not* be necessary. This is especially true in industrial marketing research

[14]Arthur P. Felton, "Conditions of Marketing Leadership," *Harvard Business Review*, March–April, 1956, pp. 117–27.

[15]"Scouting the Trail for Marketers," *Business Week*, April 18, 1964, pp. 90–116.

[16]Donald F. Mulvihill, "Marketing Research for the Small Company," *Journal of Marketing*, October, 1951, pp. 179–82.

because of the relatively small number of industrial customers. But taking shortcuts increases the risk.

More dependable research can become expensive. A large-scale survey could easily cost from $10,000 to $100,000, and the continuing research available from companies such as A. C. Nielsen or MRCA can cost a company from $25,000 to $100,000 or more a year. But as noted, companies that are willing or able to pay the cost of *marketing* research may learn more about their competitors and their market than the competitors know themselves.

Who does the work?

Most larger companies have a separate commercial or marketing research department to plan and conduct research projects. Even these departments, however, frequently use outside specialists, such as interviewing or tabulating services, to handle particular assignments. This points up, again, the importance of good research planning because when part of the research job is sent out, it is imperative that it be fully described. Further, specialized marketing consultants and marketing research organizations may be called in on more difficult problems or in "frontier" research areas.

Few companies with sales of less than $2.5 million have separate market research departments, relying instead on sales personnel or top executives for what research they do conduct.[17]

How much research should be done?

No firm can afford to do without marketing research

Most companies do some marketing research even if it is not called by that name. The majority of marketing executives would agree with the manager of marketing research for Dow Chemical Co. who states:

> I feel that it is impossible to run a company today without market research, whether it is done by the president, the sales manager, or a separate group set up specifically to perform the function. Few companies are small enough to afford the luxury of having their market research done by the president. No company can afford not to do market research at all.[18]

What is the value of information?

The high cost of extremely valid and reliable research must be balanced against its probable value to management. You never get all the information you would like to have. Very sophisticated surveys or experiments may be "too good" or "too expensive" or "too late" if all that is needed is a rough sampling of dealer attitudes toward a new pricing plan by *tomorrow*. Further, no matter how good the research effort was, the findings are always out of date in that past behavior was stud-

[17]*The Role and Organization of Marketing Research*, (Experiences in Marketing Management, No. 20 [New York: National Industrial Conference Board, 1969]), 65 pp.

[18]William A. Marsteller, "Can You Afford a Market Research Department?" *Industrial Marketing*, March, 1951, pp. 36–37.

ied. It's the decision maker's job to evaluate beforehand whether the findings will still be relevant.

Marketing managers must take risks because of lack of complete information. That is part of their job and it always will be. They might like more data, but they must weigh the cost of getting it against its likely value. If the risk is not too great, then the cost of getting more or better information may be greater than the potential loss from a poor decision. A decision to expand into a new territory with the present marketing mix, for example, might be made with greater certainty of success after a $5,000 survey. But simply sending a salesman into the territory for a few weeks or a month to try to sell the potential customers would cost less than $5,000, and if he is successful, then the answer is in *and* so are some sales.

Faced with a continuous flow of risky decisions, the marketing manager seeks help from research only for problems where he feels the risk can be reduced substantially at reasonable cost.[19]

A framework helps the manager

Given a strategic planning framework and a scientific approach to solving marketing problems, the marketing manager has a better chance to recognize the real problems and get concrete results at as low a cost as possible. Similarly, the student should begin to develop this facility. At the very least, he should recognize the kinds of questions he should ask—starting with questions about the target market and then moving on to marketing mix ingredients.

There is much more to marketing research than the use of tools and techniques. In fact, a good marketing manager should be skilled in designing research projects, even though his command of tools is limited. Contrariwise, an extremely competent, tool-oriented person without a management framework can be very ineffective. The most sophisticated of tools applied to the wrong problems are useless. The student should be primarily concerned with developing an ability to define problems. Very often, great insight and even solutions to problems can be achieved by a situation analysis and an informal investigation, *without* a formal research project. This is especially fortunate because often there is just not the time nor money to take that final step in a dynamic world.

Conclusion

In this chapter, we have shown that marketing research is not a mysterious cult practiced by statisticians. In the best sense, it is a manage-

[19]For more discussion, see P. E. Green and D. S. Tull, *Research for Marketing Decisions* (Englewood Cliffs, N.J.: Prentice-Hall, Inc., 1966), pp. 454–59.

ment tool that helps the manager make better decisions. The manager should understand research procedures, and the researcher should understand management's problems of planning, executing, and controlling marketing strategies. Without such a close working relationship, the output of a marketing research department may be sterile, and the department may be relegated to a mere collector of data.

Marketing research tries to apply the scientific method to the solution of marketing problems. Some applications have been presented in this chapter, and many more will be shown in later chapters on Product, Place, Promotion, and Price. Where such applications are discussed, you should think through the process used by the researcher, to develop your own ability for stating problems and seeking solutions. You should concentrate on stating the problem—the real problem—since this is the most difficult aspect of any kind of research. The strategic planning framework introduced in Chapter 2 should be helpful here by providing a checklist of things a manager should know to be able to put together a strategy that works.

It should be stressed that there is more to marketing research than surveys. Surveys provide helpful information when they are needed, but there are many occasions when other methods provide better information at the same or lower cost. While the survey method is certainly glamorous—with all its possibilities for applying Freudian psychology, mingling with consumers and delving into personal preferences—it should be remembered that whenever people must be interviewed, there are chances of error. These errors are caused by the respondent himself, by the interviewer's bias and by nonrepresentative sampling.

Other research techniques are the observation and experimental methods, as well as the less formal approaches used in the situation analysis and informal investigation. Search for (and study of) available literature, together with an analysis of company data, provide interesting and unique ways to avoid the cost and pitfalls of a formal research project. Such a literature search and data analysis can help the marketing manager reach his basic goal of making better and faster decisions.

QUESTIONS AND PROBLEMS

1 Marketing research entails expense, sometimes a considerable expense. Why does the text recommend the use of marketing research even though a highly experienced marketing executive is available?

2 Explain the steps in the general scientific method and then show how the steps in marketing research are similar.

3 How is the situation analysis any different from the informal investigation? Could both these steps be done at the same time in order to obtain answers sooner? Is this wise?

4 Explain how you might use each of the research methods (observation, survey, and experimental) to forecast market reaction to a new kind of margarine which is to receive no promotion other than what the retailer will give it. Further, it should be assumed that the new margarine's name will not be associated with other known products. The product will be offered at competitive prices.

5 If a firm were interested in determining the distribution of income in the state of Ohio, how could it proceed? Be specific.

6 If a firm were interested in the sand and clay production in Georgia, how could it proceed? Be specific.

7 Explain the difference between validity and reliability of surveys. Would it be possible to have a survey with very high reliability and no validity? If not, why not? If so, suggest a situation.

8 Go to the library and find (in some government publication) three marketing-oriented "facts" which you did not know existed or were available. Record on one page and show sources.

5

...in the final analysis, the marketing manager must make forecasts for individual products or product lines.... In other words, the sales potential in the various market grid boxes is our forecasting goal.

...today's profit is no guarantee that you'll make money tomorrow...ignoring market analysis can lead not only to poor sales forecasting but to poor decisions in general.

5

Forecasting market opportunities

Good sales forecasts are vital for effective marketing management. The marketing manager is badly handicapped in his planning without a realistic estimate of future sales. But he cannot develop a forecast until he has some tentative plans. In other words, forecasting and marketing strategy planning are interdependent. Sales are not just "out there for the taking." Market opportunities may be out there, but they must be recognized and taken advantage of for actual sales to occur.

Market opportunities—actual and potential demands—may exist, but whether a particular firm converts these opportunities to sales depends upon which marketing strategy is selected. This strategy, therefore, should be incorporated into the sales forecasting process.

Sales forecasts are needed by others besides the marketing manager. Accountants and financial officers base their planning and budgeting work on these forecasts. Production schedules, purchasing plans, and manpower forecasts hinge on sales forecasts. Good forecasts are needed for control, too, since it is practically impossible to evaluate performance without a measure of expected achievement. In fact, a business organization is a system, and actual and anticipated sales keep the system going.

The main job is turning opportunities into sales

The balance of this chapter is concerned with various techniques for forecasting market opportunities. The term "market opportunities" is used sometimes rather than "sales," to emphasize that sales derive from opportunities. We must first estimate the opportunities before we can estimate what share of these opportunities a particular firm may be able to realize. Our primary focus will be on the prospects for a reasonable planning period, such as a year, for which we are developing marketing strategies, rather than long-run "blue-sky" estimates or very short-run forecasts to guide current operations. These forecasts require different techniques and are beyond our scope.

The forecasting to be discussed below would normally be the responsibility of marketing research, but in collaboration with others in various departments of the business. Forecasting is so important that it regularly receives top-level attention.

Two basic approaches to forecasting

Many techniques are used in sales forecasting, but they can be grouped under two basic approaches: (1) extending past behavior; and (2) anticipating future behavior. The profusion of techniques may seem confusing at first, but in fact this variety proves to be an advantage. Forecasts are so important that management often prefers to develop forecasts in two or three different ways and then reconcile the differences before preparing a final forecast.

Extending past behavior

When we forecast sales for existing company products, we usually have some historical data to go on. The basic approach is to project past sales experience into the future while making suitable adjustments for the many factors that have caused sales fluctuations in the past.

The first step in extending past sales behavior is to determine *why* sales fluctuate. This is a most difficult and time-consuming aspect of sales forecasting. Usually we can gather a lot of data about the product or market and about the economic environment. But unless the *why* of past sales fluctuations is known, it is difficult to predict in what direction and to what degree sales will move. Once we know why sales fluctuate, it generally is quite easy to develop a specific forecast — just as the execution function in marketing naturally follows from planning. Several techniques for extending past performance are discussed below.

Anticipating future behavior

When we try to anticipate what will happen in the future, rather than just extending the past, we have to use other methods and perhaps add a bit more judgment. These methods are discussed below also, and include what we will call "juries of executive opinion," salesmen's estimates, surveys, panels, and market tests. Each can be useful for estimating the sales potential in particular market grid boxes.[1]

Three levels of forecasts are useful

We are basically interested in forecasting sales in specific market grid boxes in order to guide marketing mix planning and implementation. To reach this goal, it helps to make several kinds of forecasts.

Some economic conditions affect the entire economy. Other economic factors may influence only one industry, and some may affect only a specific company or a particular product's sales potential. For this reason, a common approach to sales forecasting—and the approach we will follow—is to:

1. Develop an *economic forecast* for the whole economy and use this to . . .
2. Develop an *industry sales forecast*, which in turn is used to . . .
3. Develop a *specific company* or *product forecast*.

Developing national economy forecasts

Gross national product (GNP) is widely used as a measure of the economic health of an economy. GNP is an estimate of the market value of goods and services produced in a year and is roughly equal to the national income.[2] Sources for this and many other economic measures are discussed later in the chapter.

An estimate for GNP is a good starting point for developing industry and company sales forecasts, since sales curves usually rise when GNP goes up, and vice versa. In special situations—perhaps where a firm has developed an especially effective marketing strategy—sales by one firm may run counter to national trends. But in such cases, the firm is usually well aware of the situation and can make appropriate adjustments in the general forecasting procedures discussed below.

[1] For more discussion, see *Forecasting Sales* (Studies in Business Policy No. 106 [New York: National Industrial Conference Board, 1964]); Elmer C. Bratt, *Business Forecasting* (New York: McGraw-Hill Book Co., 1958); *Sales Forecasting, Uses, Techniques, and Trends* (New York: American Management Association, Inc., 1956); Delbert C. Hastings, *The Place of Forecasting in Basic Planning for Small Business* (Small Business Management Research Reports [Minneapolis: University of Minnesota, 1961]); and marketing research texts.

[2] Actually, national income is slightly less than GNP, but both are sometimes used as a measure of the aggregate activity of the economy. For a detailed discussion of these measures, see any beginning economics text.

The naïve approach — oversimplified analysis

The simplest approach to estimating GNP is to assume that next year's level will be the same as this year's. Or a slight refinement might adjust for the general upward trend in the economy — approximately 3 percent a year in the United States. This oversimple approach is widely used because it is easy and works reasonably well when the economy is stable or growing slowly. But it may be unreliable when the economy has been changing rapidly.

Trend extension — several years are better than one

The trend-extension approach seeks to project GNP into the future on the basis of several years of experience rather than on that of just one year. Here, historical data — say, GNP levels for the last 10 or 20 years — is plotted on a graph. From this we get what is called a scatter diagram (see Figure 5–1). By drawing a trend line through the scattered points on this diagram, the forecaster attempts to judge where the next point will fall.

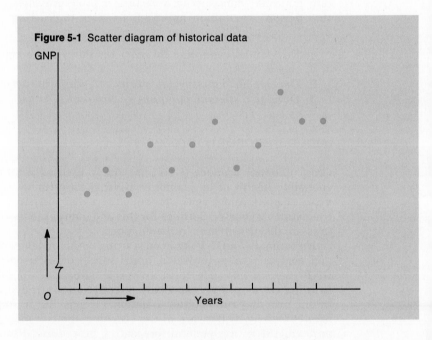

Figure 5-1 Scatter diagram of historical data

Depending on the location of the many points, either a curved or a straight line may be appropriate for summarizing past experience. A freehand line can be drawn, as in Figure 5–2, with a dotted line projecting into the future to show, hopefully, future values of the variable. Or the "least squares" statistical technique can be used to draw a straight line.[3]

[3] The goal here is to find a straight line such that the sum of the squared distances from each of the points to the straight line is a minimum. Readers unfamiliar with the least squares technique are referred to standard statistics texts. See, for example, Samuel B. Richmond, *Principles of Statistical Analysis* (New York: Ronald Press Co., 1957), chap. xviii; John Neter and William Wasserman,

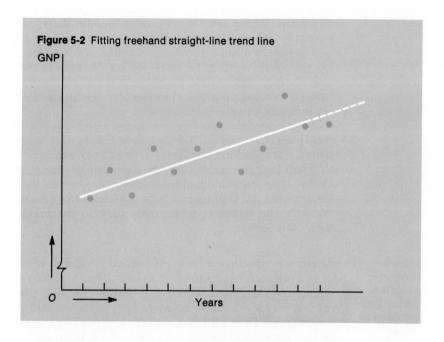

Figure 5-2 Fitting freehand straight-line trend line

A major limitation of the trend-extension method is that it assumes that conditions in the past will continue unchanged into the future, with the extension of the line (or curve) indicating future values. To be sure, trend extension often *is* accurate, since aggregates such as GNP and industry sales often change slowly. Most businesses, in fact, have little difficulty making forecasts when the economy is rising or declining at a steady rate.

But keep in mind that the future is not always like the past. The trend-extension approach usually will be wrong whenever there are important fluctuations.

Major business problems arise when economic conditions change quickly. If GNP rises rapidly, businesses may miss out on sales opportunities; but if it declines rapidly, they may be embarrassed with large inventories. For this reason, although they may use trend extension for one estimate, most forecasters seek another method to help them anticipate sharp economic changes.

Time series and leading series: up, down, staying ahead

Not all past economic behavior can be neatly extended with a straight line or even a simple curved line. Much economic activity is characterized by ups and downs. To cope with such variation, statisticians have developed time-series analysis techniques. A detailed discussion of these techniques is beyond the scope of this book, but it should be

Fundamental Statistics for Business and Economics (2d ed.; Boston: Allyn & Bacon, Inc., 1961), chaps. xiii and xv.

noted that there are techniques to handle daily, weekly, monthly, seasonal, and annual variations.[4]

The dream of all forecasters is to find accurate leading series. This is a time series which, for some reason, changes in the same direction *but ahead of* the series to be forecasted. Although we are interested here in forecasting national aggregates, leading series are sought also for industry and company sales.

No single series has yet been found that leads GNP, but the search continues. Lacking such series, most forecasters watch indices – statistical compilations of several series – in an effort to find some index that will lead the series they are attempting to forecast. Some indices of this type are published monthly by the Census Bureau of the U.S. Department of Commerce in a booklet, *Business Cycle Developments*.[5] And business magazines, such as *Business Week*, publish their own series.

Macro-economic models – seeing the whole as a whole

Another method used by many industry and government economists as a check on other methods is to look at the economy as an integrated whole and develop a model to describe this whole economy. These models include factors for consumer, business, and government expenditures.[6] They utilize data from surveys of consumers' intentions to buy, surveys of business plans to build plant and equipment, and the budgets of state, local, and federal governments. Some analysts merely add together the forecasts secured from various sources. Others use these data in developing mathematical equations for forecasting purposes.

Some mathematical model builders concentrate on estimating aggregates such as GNP, personal consumption expenditures, business investment, and the like. Others use input-output analysis, employing tables which look like market grids filled with data, to show the interaction of certain industries and producing and consuming sectors of the economy. This information is evaluated to determine how various parts of the economy will affect other parts and to indicate trends in the economy as a whole.

Aggregate forecasts from such models are available in business

---

[4]See most basic statistics textbooks under time-series analysis; and U.S. Bureau of the Census, *Estimating Trading Day Variation in Monthly Economic Time Series* (Technical Paper No. 12 [Washington, D.C.: U.S. Government Printing Office, 1965]).

[5]*Business Cycle Developments* also includes about 70 other indicators and about 350 series of various economic magnitudes. One or a combination of several of these might be more useful in a particular case than the aggregate measures, such as GNP, that are being discussed. This may require consider-

able analysis, but the general approach discussed above would be used. Some forecasters are also experimenting with combinations of series, called diffusion indices, which they hope will better describe the fluctuations in the economy. See *Diffusion Indices* (Technical Paper No. 13 [New York: National Industrial Conference Board, Inc., 1963]). NICB's diffusion indices are published weekly and monthly in its own publications.

[6]Students who have had economics may recognize a familiar equation which is used in such models: National income $= C + I + G$.

and government publications, so individual businessmen have little need for developing this type of forecast.[7]

Developing industry sales forecasts

Once the future course of the entire economy has been estimated, the next step is to make a forecast for industry sales. Since the two are often closely related, the trend-extension approach may be effective. Automobile sales, for example, reflect the level of national income, since auto sales normally go up as national income rises. But it would be most unusual for such a relationship to be direct, i.e., a 1 percent increase in some national aggregate seldom leads to a 1 percent increase in industry sales. Therefore, the idea is to determine the degree of relationship between two (or more) variables, assuming other possibly influencing factors will remain constant.

Trend extension is easy and risky

Plotting a scatter diagram is a simple approach for estimating the relationship between national economic figures and industry sales. Usually, however, more advanced time-series analysis techniques are used, including multiple regression.[8] Once the relationship is established, the forecast for the national figure, which usually is available earlier, is used to determine the industry forecast.

Simple trend extension is risky, as more sophisticated work with input-output analysis has demonstrated. A seemingly remote development in another part of the economy may have a direct impact on a particular industry, an effect which would not be anticipated by simple trend extension.

For example, a manufacturer of sulfuric acid, used in manufacturing paper pulp, can predict future industry sales of his product more accurately with an input-output analysis involving interactions such as the following: An additional $1 billion appropriated for federal aid to education would lead to a predictable increase in the number of textbooks used, which in turn would increase paper consumption and paper pulp manufacturing, which uses his firm's sulfuric acid. But if the manufacturer based his forecast only on past sales in the paper pulp business, his forecast might be seriously in error.

[7] "They Call It 'Instant Research'," *Business Week,* January 25, 1969; "Forecasters Turn to Group Guesswork," *Business Week,* March 14, 1970, pp. 130–34; "Rumania Starts Down Model Path," *Business Week,* October 25, 1969, p. 66; Clopper Almon, Jr., *The American Economy to 1975* (New York: Harper & Row, Publishers, 1966); for more details, see any elementary economics textbook, or E. F. Beach, *Economic Models* (New York: John Wiley & Sons, Inc., 1957); J. Tinbergen, *Econometrics* (Philadelphia: Blakiston Co., 1951); "Computers Take to Prophecy," *Business Week,* June 1, 1963, pp. 47–48; and "Planners Put Big Picture on a Grid," *Business Week,* September 23, 1967, pp. 63–65.

[8] Although space does not permit a detailed explanation of this approach, generally the least squares approach is extended. These topics are discussed in most statistics texts, and when mastered, become a highly useful tool of the marketing analyst.

Someone else may forecast

Each company should consider the probable economic activity of the national economy and its industry when forecasting its own future. But it need not do all this aggregate forecasting itself. Some basic economic and industry estimates are published regularly by government agencies, banks, trade associations, and business publications. Private firms also do forecasting for others at reasonable prices.

While a marketing manager doesn't have to gather all this data himself, he should know what is going on. Then he can use the forecasts properly at the next step—forecasting his own company and product sales—where less outside help is available, and his own and competitors' actions make forecasting more difficult.

What is your industry?

An industry forecast makes a lot of sense in industries such as steel, cement, plywood, and housing. It suggests the opportunities available to members of the industry. But since our emphasis in this text is on developing unique marketing strategies, we will play down emphasis on broad industry opportunities.

The more a firm tries to narrow its sights on some particular target market, the less attention it should pay to the overall opportunities of the industry. In the extreme, a firm might attempt to develop such a unique marketing strategy that it would, in effect, be creating its one-firm "industry." Then the firm would be more concerned with developing a forecast for the company and its specific products.

Developing company and product forecasts

Opportunities in market grids are the target

In the final analysis, the marketing manager and his firm must make forecasts for individual products or product lines, perhaps broken down by geographic areas. In other words, the sales potential in the various market grid boxes is our forecasting goal. This means determining the dimensions of those grid boxes and then estimating what the consumers with those dimensions will be willing to buy, from this company, given alternative marketing mixes.

Forecasting sales of new products is a tougher assignment than forecasting for established products, and also calls for slightly different techniques. Therefore, we'll discuss these two types of forecasting separately.

Forecasting sales for established products

Sales analysis shows what is going on

A detailed breakdown of a company's sales records can be very illuminating, especially the first time it is done. At the very least, the marketing manager ought to know what the market grid in his general area looks like, and what his company has done, to give him a solid basis for forecasting in the future. Then, a simple extension of past behavior would permit the marketing manager to make one forecast at least.

Too often, men who have moved into management positions are not aware of specific changes that have taken place in the field since they were out there. This is especially true of managers who have assistants to handle details. Yet the broad marketing decisions for which they are responsible are made on the basis of their knowledge of the business, however outdated or incomplete it may be.

Some managers resist sales analysis, or any analysis for that matter, because they do not fully appreciate how valuable it can be to them. One top executive in a large consumer products firm made no attempt to analyze his company's sales, even by geographical area. When asked why, he replied: "Why should we? We're making money!"

But today's profit is no guarantee that you'll make money tomorrow. In fact, ignoring market analysis can lead not only to poor sales forecasting but to poor decisions in general. One manufacturer did extensive national advertising on the premise that the firm was, in fact, selling all over the country. A simple sales analysis, however, revealed that the vast majority of his customers were within a 250-mile radius of the factory. In other words, the firm did not know who and where its customers were and was wasting most of the money it spent on national advertising.

But marketing manager must ask for it

Detailed sales analysis is only a possibility, however, unless management makes definite arrangements for gathering the data. Valuable sales information is regularly buried in sales invoice files after the usual accounting functions are completed. Manual analysis of such records is so lengthy and burdensome that it is seldom undertaken.

Today, with electronic data processing equipment, effective sales analysis can be done easily and at comparatively small cost – if marketing management makes up its mind to do it. In fact, the information desired can be obtained as a by-product of basic billing and accounts receivable procedures. The manager simply must be sure that identifying information on dimensions important to him, such as territory, salesman, etc., are recorded in machine-processable form. Then, sales analysis and sales projections can easily be run.

What to ask for varies

There is no one best way to analyze sales data. One or several information breakdowns may be appropriate, depending on the nature of the company, product, and which market grid dimensions are relevant. Typical breakdowns which are often useful include:

1. Geographical region – state, county, city, salesmen's territory.
2. Product, package size, grade, or color.
3. Customer size.
4. Customer type or class of trade.
5. Price or discount class.
6. Method of sale – mail, telephone, or direct salesman.
7. Financial arrangement – cash or charge.
8. Size of order.
9. Commission class.

While this information might be readily available on invoices, and useful for some types of analyses, relevant market grid dimensions might not be included. As we saw in Chapter 2, market grid dimensions are not always readily measurable. In these cases, extension of past sales data should be used with caution in forecasting. Sometimes this method may yield good forecasts, but at critical times such forecasts may go far astray. This is one reason why marketing managers typically like to use several techniques for sales forecasting.

Forecasting with trend extension can be useful

Despite the previous note of caution, trend extension of past relationships can be useful in forecasting sales for a company and its specific products, especially if market and economic conditions are reasonably stable.

One can simply project past sales behavior into the future, perhaps with adjustments for seasonal changes.

A more sophisticated trend-extension approach would find a relation between the company's sales and outside data which is readily available in detail and/or forecasted by others. This approach may yield more detailed and more accurate forecasts than would be possible with simple extension of the firm's own sales data.

The following example for a bread manufacturer shows how forecasts can be made for many geographical market grid boxes using available data. This general approach can be useful for any firm, be it a manufacturer, wholesaler, or retailer.

Analysis of past sales relationships may show that a particular bread manufacturer regularly achieved one half of 1 percent (0.005) of the total retail food sales in his target markets. Estimates of retail sales for the coming period in these areas, then, could be used by the firm to forecast its bread sales (by multiplying 0.005 times the expected retail food sales in each market).

Retail sales estimates can be based on past sales figures from sources such as *Sales Management* magazine. Figure 5–3 shows the kind of geographically detailed data available each year in a June issue of *Sales Management*.[9] Similar data is available for industrial markets.

This data is carefully updated year after year and has correlated with surprising accuracy with the U.S. censuses upon which it is based. Evanston, Illinois, for example, accounts for 0.0414 of the U.S. population, but has a much larger share, 0.0774, of effective buying income. The food sales dollar figure – $31,714,000 – is an estimate of last year's food sales in this city. Thus, by extending past trends, our bread manufacturer can estimate future food sales. Then, by finding his firm's usual share – 0.5 percent – he would have his own market estimate. Or if he planned an especially aggressive promotion campaign, he might increase his estimates by multiplying forecasted food sales by 0.0055 rather than 0.005, to provide for an expected sales increase of 10 percent.

[9] Look for the "Survey of Buying Power" issue. Similar current data are published by others. Standard Rate and Data Service, for example, provides less detailed monthly data of this type. *The Editor and Publisher Market Guide,* published annually by the Editor and Publisher Co., is another source. *Marketing/Communications* and *Industrial Marketing* magazines also publish annual data supplements.

Figure 5–3 Sample page from *Sales Management,* "Annual Survey of Buying Power," retail sales estimates

ILLINOIS COUNTIES CITIES	Met. Area Code	POPULATION ESTIMATES, 12/31/69 Total (thou-sands)	% of U.S.A.	House-holds (thou-sands)	EFFECTIVE BUYING INCOME ESTIMATES, 1969 Net Dollars (000)	% of U.S.A.	Per Hsld.	% Hslds. by Cash Income Groups: (A) $0-2,999; (B) $3,000-4,999; (C) $5,000-7,999; (D) $8,000-9,999; (E) $10,000 and Over — A	B	C	D	E	RETAIL SALES — SM ESTIMATES, 1969 Total Retail Sales (000)	% of U.S.A.	Food (000)	General Mdse. (000)	Furn.-House.-Appl. (000)	Auto-motive (000)	Drug (000)	Buying Power Index †
▲Champaign-Urbana		93.8	.0461	27.8	351,959	.0563	12,660	10.0	14.5	30.4	15.4	29.7	200,203	.0576	39,724	40,472	10,271	34,338	7,975	.0547
Rantoul		27.9	.0137	5.8	75,158	.0120	12,958	16.5	11.8	21.0	14.1	36.6	39,598	.0114	5,249	3,274	1,945	16,361	830	.0122
▲Urbana		31.1	.0153	9.7	114,302	.0183	11,784	21.0	13.3	22.5	15.7	27.5	48,023	.0138	10,041	11,126	2,381	3,151	1,704	.0164
Christian		35.9	.0176	11.7	104,663	.0167	8,946	26.6	16.3	20.7	14.6	21.8	82,581	.0238	15,695	6,129	2,911	14,022	1,867	.0190
Clark		15.8	.0078	5.5	43,878	.0070	7,978						24,649	.0070	4,905	685	300	3,157	501	.0071
Clay		15.1	.0074	5.2	41,517	.0066	7,984	23.8	14.9	24.4	16.1	20.8	22,166	.0064	4,088	1,485	911	3,777	430	.0067
Clinton		25.4	.0125	7.6	67,319	.0108	8,858	20.0	12.3	24.2	17.0	26.5	41,935	.0121	7,064	1,519	932	6,832	332	.0116
1Centralia																				
Coles		44.7	.0220	13.3	141,220	.0225	10,618	20.1	12.1	22.2	15.0	30.6	101,871	.0293	22,884	10,085	4,182	19,669	3,509	.0244
Mattoon		22.3	.0110	7.7	74,917	.0120	9,729	18.0	10.6	22.2	15.7	33.5	56,592	.0163	11,679	6,918	2,992	12,604	2,826	.0131
▲Cook	57	5,545.2	2.7251	1,780.0	22,041,606	3.5198	12,383	12.0	8.5	19.0	15.6	44.9	10,973,604	3.1550	2,227,304	2,599,917	518,937	1,673,776	458,245	3.2514
Arlington Heights		57.7	.0284	15.5	285,337	.0456	18,409	4.3	2.6	7.3	11.3	74.5	104,236	.0300	24,116	12,129	7,352	31,193	7,515	.0375
2Barrington		7.9	.0039	2.5	36,355	.0058	14,542	8.6	8.1	17.6	11.1	54.6	50,566	.0145	8,092	13,551	540	12,428	6,390	.0080
Bellwood		25.4	.0125	7.2	100,440	.0160	13,950	3.2	2.7	10.8	19.0	64.3	20,794	.0060	7,111	1,366	1,215	282	1,134	.0123
Berwyn		56.3	.0277	20.5	253,669	.0405	12,374	8.9	7.2	15.8	17.1	51.0	128,892	.0371	27,007	24,722	7,119	24,077	8,437	.0369
Blue Island		22.3	.0110	7.0	86,371	.0138	12,339	9.3	6.9	18.3	17.3	48.2	73,416	.0211	8,960	10,584	1,938	27,776	2,349	.0154
Brookfield		20.5	.0101	6.3	87,467	.0140	13,884	5.2	5.4	12.6	17.7	59.1	21,531	.0062	7,425	741	832	4,300	1,115	.0109
Calumet City		31.1	.0153	9.2	111,096	.0177	12,076	7.2	6.3	17.6	20.8	48.1	121,910	.0351	11,394	38,129	4,264	29,927	4,402	.0224
▲Chicago		3,506.1	1.7230	1,192.0	12,843,539	2.0510	10,775	15.0	10.5	21.9	15.5	37.1	6,685,781	1.9223	1,233,227	1,782,656	328,238	874,970	271,764	1.9468
Chicago Heights		39.9	.0196	11.7	140,525	.0224	12,011	9.5	7.1	19.0	17.7	46.7	132,658	.0381	25,868	25,357	9,130	37,194	5,416	.0266
Cicero		71.8	.0353	25.2	288,692	.0461	11,456	9.2	7.1	19.1	18.2	46.4	107,639	.0309	25,933	11,616	2,875	21,202	4,103	.0394
Des Plaines		59.4	.0292	17.2	256,656	.0410	14,922	4.5	3.6	10.7	16.0	65.2	170,907	.0491	42,623	14,527	2,446	56,608	8,305	.0411
3*Elgin																				
Elmwood Park		27.3	.0134	8.5	132,789	.0212	15,622	5.3	4.7	13.2	15.1	61.7	38,937	.0112	9,556	4,902	1,469	7,326	2,040	.0166
Evanston		84.2	.0414	28.5	484,537	.0774	17,001	11.1	7.1	15.0	12.0	54.8	185,772	.0534	31,714	30,299	11,443	61,292	5,705	.0630

1–Centralia is in Clinton and Marion counties.

2–Barrington is in Cook and Lake counties.

3*–Elgin is in Cook and Kane counties and is a satellite city.

†Buying Power Index (BPI) is a weighted average of each market's strength. Each market's share of U.S. population is multiplied (weighted) by 2. its income by 5. and its retail sales share by 3. The resulting sum is divided by 10 (the total weighting) to give the BPI.

Source: *Sales Management,* June 10, 1970, p. D–44. © 1970, Sales Management Survey of Buying Power; further reproduction is forbidden.

Forecasting sales with fast sales analysis by computer

Electronic data processing equipment enables more and more firms to analyze current sales data for individual items or product categories very quickly, and use this data for short-run forecasts. Food chains, discount houses, department stores, mail-order houses, and manufacturers are finding it both feasible and profitable to use computers to pick up and project sales trends.[10]

Fast analysis of sales data beyond a firm's boundaries may be helpful, too. Where there is a lag between consumer purchases and receipt of orders by manufacturers (because consumer purchases come out of retailers' and wholesalers' inventories), rapid analysis of retail sales is an aid in forecasting sales at both wholesaler and manufacturer levels.

Some wholesalers handling major appliances, for example, send in weekly reports of sales, by model, to guide the manufacturer and enable him to forecast sales trends. In this case, the wholesalers have agreed to accept shipments to replace units they have sold. This is an example of a total system of action which extends beyond a particular firm's boundaries. Rapid sales analysis is the feedback through the larger total system. It seems likely that more such total systems will develop in the future.

Jury of executive opinion

The methods discussed above make use of "hard" data, projecting past experience into the future on the assumption that the future will be somewhat like the past. But in dynamic markets, adding judgment to hard data is increasingly important. Further, competitors' and the firm's own marketing mixes affect both potential and current sales.

One of the oldest and simplest methods of forecasting—the "jury" approach—is an attempt to work in the opinions of several executives, perhaps from marketing, production, finance, purchasing, and top management. The idea here is to utilize as much seasoned management judgment as possible in combination with analysis of past data.

The main advantage of the jury approach is that it can be done quickly and easily. On the other hand, the results may not be spectacular, because they represent the concensus of a number of viewpoints. In addition, the jury method is most suitable for aggregate estimates, but what operating managers ultimately need is a more precise breakdown by products, time intervals, and specific geographic markets.[11]

Salesmen's estimates

This approach is similar to the jury approach, except that the opinions sought are those of sales personnel. This approach can be much more reliable where competition is dynamic.

The sales force is more likely than home office analysts to be familiar with customer reactions, to know what competitors are doing, and is, therefore, more able to anticipate changes. Salesmen's esti-

---

[10] "Where the Computers Care Too," *Business Week,* March 12, 1966, pp. 140–46; "Now Retailers Put It All on Tape," *Business Week,* January 16, 1965, pp. 30–31.

[11] For more discussion on this and other approaches and examples of their application, see *Forecasting Sales* (Studies in Business Policy No. 106 [New York: National Industrial Conference Board, 1964]).

mates are especially useful in industrial markets with a limited number of customers who are well known to the salesmen. But this approach is useful in any type of market. A good retail clerk has a feel for his market, and his observations should not be ignored.

Two qualifications concerning the use of salesmen's estimates, however, should be kept in mind.

First, salesmen normally are not familiar with anticipated changes in the national economic climate, nor even with proposed changes in the company's marketing mix. As a result, their estimates must often be adjusted by the home office in light of national and industry forecasts and other factors.

Second, sales force estimates must be used with care if there is high turnover in sales personnel and if the estimates are used for other purposes. If subsequent performance and compensation are based on estimates, for example, then the estimates may be low. Alternately, if the promotion money budgeted to each territory is based on sales prospects, then the estimates may be high. In these cases, it is only human for salesmen to tailor their forecasts to their own advantage.

Keeping these qualifications in mind, sales force estimates can provide another basis for comparison before final forecasts are developed.

Surveys, panels, and market tests
Instead of relying heavily upon salesmen to estimate customers' intentions, it may be desirable to use the marketing research techniques discussed in the preceding chapter. Special surveys of final buyers, retailers, and wholesalers can be illuminating, showing what is happening in different market segments. Some firms use panels of stores or final consumers to keep track of buying behavior and to determine when the use of simple trend-extension forecasting has become inadequate.

Survey techniques are sometimes combined with market tests when the company wants to estimate the reaction of customers to possible changes in the marketing mix. In one such market test, a product increased its share of the market by 10 percent when its price was dropped 1 cent below competition. Yet this extra business was quickly lost when the price increased 1 cent above competition.

Such market experiments enable the marketing manager to make realistic estimates of future sales when one or more of the four P's are changed.[12] And new statistical techniques, including factor analysis and cluster analysis, have been found effective in estimating market shares and giving insight to potential sales.[13]

[12] R. J. Weber, "The Relationship of Advertising to Pricing Policy," *Pricing and Prosperity* (Marketing for Executives Series No. 1 [Chicago: American Marketing Association, 1956]), pp. 16–17.

[13] These techniques are beyond our scope but it is important to recognize that new tools are continually becoming available to aid the marketing manager. See, for example, David H. Doehlert, "Similarity and Preference Mapping: A Color Example,"

Marketing and the New Science of Planning (Proceedings of the American Marketing Association, No. 28, 1969), p. 250; Lester A. Neidell, "The Use of Nonmetric Multidimensional Scaling in Marketing Analysis," *Journal of Marketing*, October, 1969, pp. 37–43; and Paul E. Green and Frank J. Carmone, *Multidimensional Scaling*, (Rockleigh, N. J.: Allyn & Bacon, Inc., 1970).

Forecasting sales for new products

Forecasting sales for new products is the most difficult task of all – and the most risky. If the product is really new, there is no relevant historical data that can be projected and no experience to indicate which leading series might be relevant. It is also unrealistic, as noted in Chapter 4, to expect potential customers or even salesmen to have valid opinions about things with which they are unacquainted.

The situation is not hopeless, however. The substitute method, need analysis, and market tests can be useful here. These techniques are discussed next.

Substitute method

Since few products are entirely new, careful analysis of the sales of products which the new one may displace can provide, at the least, an upper limit on potential sales. With imagination and research, a company can list most possible uses and determine the potential in the various target markets. Once the potential upper limits of the markets have been ascertained, these figures can be scaled down by market realities, including actual customer preferences at various price levels.

This procedure can be illustrated by the forecasting done by Du Pont for a plastic resin product.

The chemical company began by estimating the size of the various end-use markets – shown as the left series of boxes in Figure 5-4.

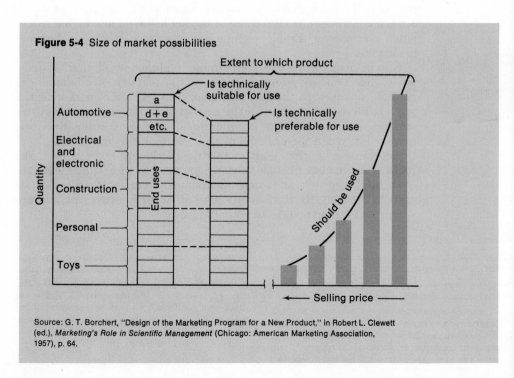

Figure 5-4 Size of market possibilities

Source: G. T. Borchert, "Design of the Marketing Program for a New Product," in Robert L. Clewett (ed.), *Marketing's Role in Scientific Management* (Chicago: American Marketing Association, 1957), p. 64.

These were markets where the resin product was technically suitable for use, including automotive, electrical, electronic, construction, personal, and toy products. The sum of the potential in all of these boxes indicated the upper limit on demand. Then a harder look at the suitability of the product in comparison with those currently being used indicated that one of the planned automotive and construction applications should be dropped.

The markets where the new product was technically preferable for use are shown in Figure 5–4, in the second bar from the left. These first two market-possibility bars, however, ignore potential selling prices which are realities in any market. So the potential demand at various selling prices was considered. The five right-hand bars in Figure 5–4 show the various quantities of the product that technically should be used at various price levels. The extreme right-hand bar indicates that if prices were low enough, all of the potential users would use the product.

Many potentials but one forecast

The data in Figure 5–4 are shown in a different way and with more detail in Figure 5–5.

Here the relation to the market grid concept and marketing strategy

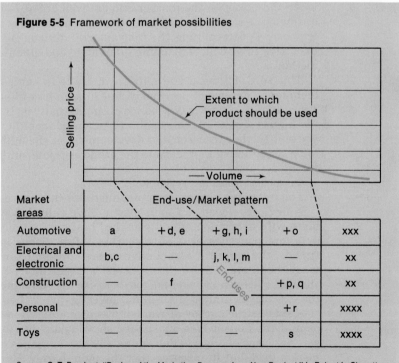

Figure 5-5 Framework of market possibilities

Market areas	End-use/Market pattern				
Automotive	a	+d, e	+g, h, i	+o	xxx
Electrical and electronic	b,c	—	j, k, l, m	—	xx
Construction	—	f		+p, q	xx
Personal	—	—	n	+r	xxxx
Toys	—	—	—	s	xxxx

Source: G. T. Borchert, "Design of the Marketing Program for a New Product," in Robert L. Clewett (ed.), *Marketing's Role in Scientific Management* (Chicago: American Marketing Association, 1957), p. 66.

planning becomes clearer. At a high selling price, interest would be shown by one of the potential automotive markets and by electrical and electronic users (markets a, b, and c). If the price were dropped slightly, additional automotive users (d and e) and a construction industry user (f) would add to the potential market. In other words, potential target markets are being specified as part of the sales forecasting procedure.

This approach, however, merely indicates market potentials. Determining a specific sales forecast requires a decision to go after particular target markets with the necessary marketing mixes. Many marketing strategy decisions—one for each potential target market—must be made. When all of these decisions are made and combined with judgments about the probability of achieving certain market shares, the sales forecast develops as a by-product.

Sales forecasting, it should be clear, is intimately linked with determining market strategy.

Need analysis in market grid boxes

If the product is so new that no present product markets can be used as a guide, the forecaster can try to determine who will be interested in the product—and not just who the company executives *think* are likely to be interested.

When potential target customers have been carefully described—when the boxes on the market grid are well defined—it is possible to estimate the size of each of the potential markets. But the major problem here is determining the relevant grid dimensions. Primary data may have to be collected, using qualitative and quantitative research methods.

This sort of forecasting may seem crude in comparison with the techniques described previously, but it is no less important. Careful analysis of this type may produce clear alternatives. It may show that the highest attainable sales volume for a product either is too small to warrant further research and development, or the outlook may prove to be so attractive that, despite the crude estimate, enthusiasm seems justified.

Calculations killed this slide rule

The following simple example illustrates this approach.

A firm developed a 5-inch plastic slide rule that would help the housewife determine which was the "best buy" among several products and packages at a supermarket. After discussion with a few friends, the company's executives were sure that some housewives would be interested. But how many? And which ones? Men probably should have been considered, too, because they do some shopping, but the executives limited their initial investigation to housewives.

A small-scale survey of women was discouraging, with only 5 percent of the housewives questioned showing any interest. The survey was not large enough to determine all characteristics on a housewife market grid, but it appeared that the more highly educated, younger housewives were the only ones who might be interested—and only if the retail price of the slide rule were under 70 cents.

The company then talked to retailers to see how they reacted to the product. Informal investigation with some retailers indicated a lack of enthusiasm, though some were willing to give it a try.

It looked as if the achievable potential would be quite low. Specific figures confirmed this. The 5 percent of the housewives who *might* be interested, multiplied by approximately 50 million American families, suggested an upper limit of 2.5 million units. When potential retail availability was considered, this potential upper limit was reduced to 100,000 units *or less*. In view of the fact that a premium price could not be obtained (the rule itself would cost about 25 cents to make), and that repeat sales were highly unlikely, the project was dropped.

Market tests — what will the S-curve look like?

Sometimes the only way to estimate the market potential of a new product is to actually try it in the market. Several test markets can be used, and assuming they are fairly representative (a very large assumption!), the results can be projected to a larger area.

Forecasting from market test results, however, can be misleading, since the very novelty of the product seems to attract some customers. This means that analysis of the sales pattern in the market test must consider what is called the "S-curve" effect. This refers to the phenomenon of sales shooting up just after the product is introduced and then declining quickly, leveling off, and then *perhaps* rising as a market of repeat customers develops.

Haste makes mistakes . . . or success

The major problem is estimating where the market will level off, not the initial peak. This may require continuing market research over several months or even a year or two, depending upon the product and the eventual repeat customer rate.

Some companies have been misled by the initial sales boom. Others have been misled by the early results *plus* their eagerness to market their product ahead of competition. Hurried testing (or none at all) may lead to costly mistakes — and the failure rate is very high on new products. But more extensive market testing may prove a luxury in our highly competitive markets, especially if more venturesome competitors are monitoring the test and then beat the innovator to national distribution. This has happened often enough to discourage some firms from testing new products.

Accuracy of forecasts

The accuracy of sales forecasts may vary considerably, depending upon the number of components in the magnitude being forecast. The more general the value being forecast, the more accurate the forecast is likely to be. This is because small errors in various components of the estimate tend to offset each other and make the aggregate estimate more accurate.

Annual forecasts of national aggregates, such as GNP, may be accurate within 5 percent. Industry sales forecasts, which tend to be more specific, are usually accurate within 10 percent, depending upon the inherent variability of the industry.

When estimates are made for individual products, there is even less chance of offsetting errors, except where errors from one salesman or territory offset those in another. Where style and innovation are important factors in an industry, forecast errors of 10 to 20 percent for *established products* are not uncommon. The accuracy of specific *new-product* forecasts is even lower. Many new products fail completely, while others are overwhelmingly successful.

We have focused on estimates for a reasonable planning period, such as a year. But when forecasts are made for shorter periods, say a week or a month, even greater error can be expected. This is unfortunate from a total systems viewpoint, because it is such short-run forecasts which would be most helpful for production scheduling and inventory control.[14]

Inaccuracy can happen easily

Data on the accuracy of specific product forecasts is not easy to obtain because individual forecasting departments are reluctant to admit errors. They tend to magnify their successes and hide their failures.

One forecaster of new consumer and industrial products claimed he had an excellent overall forecasting average for a particular year. He was off by only 2 percent on the average. His inaccuracy on specific product forecasts, however, was frightening. Many products did not sell at all—he missed by 100 percent, in other words—and others exceeded his expectations by 200 to 300 percent.[15]

Even less accuracy can be expected on sales forecasts in international markets. The data is poor; forecasters are less familiar with the markets; and the markets are less homogeneous due to inadequate transportation, natural barriers, illiteracy, and language differences. In Colombia, for example, the four major population centers are almost isolated from each other by high mountains. Each major city has a different climate, population makeup, dialect, and mode of living.[16] The market grid boxes there will be numerous and small, and as a result a forecast will be less accurate.

Conclusion

This chapter has discussed several approaches to forecasting market opportunities. The most common approach is to extend past behavior into the future. Where market conditions are fairly stable, reasonably

---

[14] Exponential smoothing techniques are helpful for such short-run forecasting. See production management texts for details.

[15] Checking the accuracy of forecasts is an intricate subject. For more detailed treatment, see Rex V. Brown, "Just How Credible Are Your Market Estimates?" *Journal of Marketing*, July, 1969, pp. 46–52; Robert J. Piersol, "Accuracy of Estimating Markets for Industrial Products by Size of Consuming Industry," *Journal of Marketing Research*, May, 1968, pp. 147–54; "How Good Are Consumer Polls?"

Business Week, November 8, 1969, pp. 108–10; Bratt, *op. cit.*, chap. xiii; *Sales Forecasting, Uses, Techniques, and Trends, op. cit.*, p. 148; and *Forecasting in Industry* (Studies in Business Policy No. 77 [New York: National Industrial Conference Board, 1956]).

[16] William Copulsky, "Forecasting Sales in Underdeveloped Countries," *Journal of Marketing*, July, 1959, pp. 37–38; and Henry Alderson, "Problems Peculiar to Export Sales Forecasting," *Journal of Marketing*, April, 1960, pp. 39–42.

good results may be obtained with this method. Unfortunately, projecting the past into the future is weak whenever sharp market changes occur—and it is precisely at those times that good forecasts are most needed. To compensate for this weakness, the manager must use his own experience and judgment. There are also several analytical approaches to guide executive judgment or gather new information that can lead to better forecasts.

A forecast should represent a goal that the company expects to achieve—with concentrated effort. A good forecast should take into account the expected impact of the company's proposed marketing strategies as well as competitors' strategies. In other words, *the forecast should estimate the effectiveness of the whole business as a single, integrated operating system in competition with other systems.*

Good forecasting obviously requires an understanding of the size and intensity of demand in various market grid boxes. Some market grid boxes offer great potential, while others may clearly be poor prospects if data is properly evaluated. This seems obvious, but some firms have gone into markets with high hopes for sales, unaware that the markets were not as large as they imagined. This is hard to believe, but production-oriented executives and firms have blundered badly for this reason.

One of the most effective tools the student can bring to the business world is a good knowledge of source materials about markets and what can be done with them. More will be said about this in Chapters 6–9 as we explore the nature of potential customer behavior more deeply. Following that analysis, we will go on to show how the needs in various market grid boxes affect the development of marketing mixes. At the end of the text, we will return to a discussion of tying together the whole business system so that it can consistently locate and capitalize on its opportunities.

In Chapter 29, we will look at the control function, returning to a discussion of forecasts and how they can be compared to actual results. We will see that performance analyses can be fed back into the planning function to help the marketing manager develop new and better strategies. This further emphasizes the circular nature of the marketing management function. The manager must be planning and controlling continually.

QUESTIONS AND PROBLEMS

1 Explain the difference between a forecast of market opportunities and a sales forecast.

2 Suggest a plausible explanation for sales fluctuations for (*a*) bicycles, (*b*) baby food, (*c*) motor boats, (*d*) baseball gloves, (*e*) wheat, (*f*) woodworking tools, and (*g*) latex for rubber-based paint.

3 Discuss the relative accuracy of the various forecasting techniques. Explain why some are more accurate than others.

4 Given the following annual sales data for a company which is not planning any spectacular marketing strategy changes, forecast sales for the coming year (7) and explain your method and reasoning.

a		b	
Year	Sales (in 000's)	Year	Sales (in 000's)
1	200	1	160
2	230	2	155
3	210	3	165
4	220	4	160
5	200	5	170
6	220	6	165

5 Discuss the impact of the following events on industry sales forecasts for automobiles: (*a*) a large tax cut for consumers; (*b*) a large increase in government expenditures without accompanying tax increases.

6 Discuss the relative market potential of Cicero and Evanston, Illinois, for: (*a*) prepared cereals, (*b*) automobiles, and (*c*) furniture.

7 Discuss how a General Motors market analyst might use the substitute method if the company were considering the potential for an electric car which might be suitable for salesmen, commuters, housewives, farmers, and perhaps other groups. The analyst is trying to consider the potential in terms of possible price levels – $1,000, $1,500, $2,000, $3,000, and $4,000 – and driving ranges – 10 miles, 20 miles, 50 miles, 100 miles, and 200 miles – which would typically be desired or needed before recharging. He is assuming that gasoline-powered vehicles would become illegal for use within the major urban cities. Further, it is expected that while personal gasoline-driven cars still would be used in rural and suburban areas, they would not be permitted within some suburban areas, especially around the major metropolitan areas.

6

…even though taxes have increased, and further increases are likely, we can nevertheless project continued growth of consumer spending power.

…the absence of guaranteed "captive demand" for necessities which are directly related to socioeconomic characteristics puts a heavy burden on marketing managers. They're constantly trying to sell specific products or services…to consumers whose preferences may be continually shifting.

6

Consumers: the American market

The *Customer* is the focal point of all business and marketing activity. Customers in the aggregate are markets – people with the ability (buying power) and willingness to spend their money to satisfy their needs.

The market grid concept leads us to think of any market as many smaller, more homogeneous submarkets. Unique and profitable marketing strategies may be discovered by more fully understanding the needs of some submarkets.

As we saw in Chapters 2 and 5, however, determining a market's relevant dimensions is not an easy task. Ideally, we want to find those dimensions which really make a difference, in terms of the needs, preferences, and attitudes of the potential customers. And we also would like to know how many think this way and where they are. Then we would be better able to plan attractive marketing strategies for them.

Three important questions should be answered regarding any potential market:

1. What are its relevant dimensions?
2. How big is it?
3. Where is it?

The first question—about relevant dimensions—is basic. Judgment—perhaps aided by analysis of existing data and new findings from marketing research—is needed in picking the right dimensions. To help build your judgment regarding consumer buying behavior, this and the following two chapters will discuss what we know about consumers.

Forget the Texas or New York stereotypes

The marketing manager should not fall into the trap of accepting common stereotypes about the size or potential of various markets, such as those illustrated in one artist's version of a New Yorker's and a Texan's view of the United States (Figure 6–1), which may be humorous but is of no real value.

When valid data is available, there is no excuse for decisions based on such misconceptions or regional propaganda. Data on *final consumers* will be presented in this and the following two chapters. In Chapter 9, we will present information for other types of customers: business, farmers, and government buyers.

Try to see this data in terms of estimating the potential in market grid boxes. Also, check your own assumptions against this data. Marketing decisions often must be made in a hurry, under pressure. Then, if you feel you really do know the relevant market dimensions, you may decide without even looking at the available data. Now is a good time to get the "facts" straight.

Population

Present population and its distribution

Table 6–1 shows the population by states for 1970. The first rank of California should sober the New Yorker and the Texan, and explain why some marketers are going after the West Coast market. On the other hand, the heavy concentration of population in New York and a few adjacent states—altogether twice as populous as the entire West Coast—does lend a certain validity to the New Yorker's view of the U.S. market. The population of Texas is large, but its partisans' views are based on area, not population, and now that Alaska has been admitted to the union, Texas is no longer even the biggest state.

Obviously, if numbers of people are important in a company's marketing strategy, the marketing manager should rely on the latest census statistics for market grid analysis rather than guesswork or some parochial view of the importance of a particular area.

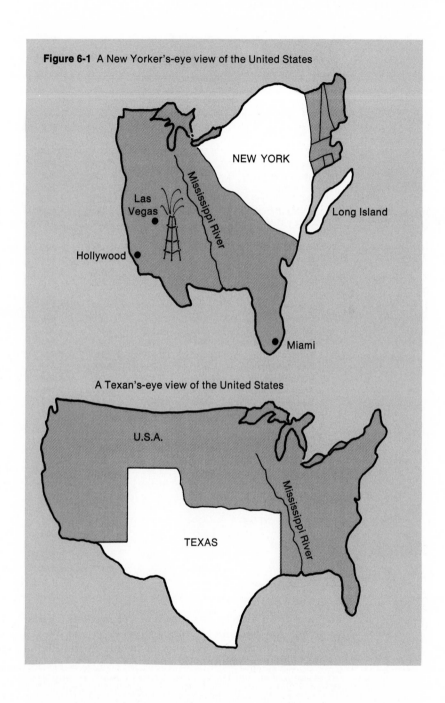

Figure 6-1 A New Yorker's-eye view of the United States

NEW YORK

Long Island

Las Vegas

Mississippi River

Hollywood

Miami

A Texan's-eye view of the United States

U.S.A.

Mississippi River

TEXAS

The map in Figure 6–2 emphasizes the concentration of population in various geographic regions. It shows the area of each state in proportion to its population. Notice the importance of the midwestern states and the southern states when viewed as a group. These regions,

Table 6–1 Population by states and for Puerto Rico: 1910 to 1970*

State or other areas	Population (1,000)				
	1910	1930	1950	1960	1970
United States	92,228	123,202	151,326	181,832	203,288
New England	6,553	8,166	9,314	10,509	11,678
Maine	742	797	914	969	977
New Hampshire	431	465	533	607	723
Vermont	356	360	378	390	438
Massachusetts	3,366	4,250	4,691	5,149	5,630
Rhode Island	543	687	792	859	922
Connecticut	1,115	1,607	2,007	2,535	2,988
Middle Atlantic	19,316	26,261	30,164	34,228	37,084†
New York	9,114	12,588	14,830	16,842	18,321
New Jersey	2,537	4,041	4,835	6,067	7,093
Pennsylvania	7,665	9,631	10,498	11,319	11,670
South Atlantic	12,195	15,794	21,182	25,972	30,057
Delaware	202	238	318	446	543
Maryland	1,295	1,632	2,343	3,101	3,875
Dist. of Columbia	331	487	802	764	746
Virginia	2,062	2,422	3,319	3,967	4,543
West Virginia	1,221	1,729	2,006	1,860	1,702
North Carolina	2,206	3,170	4,062	4,556	4,962
South Carolina	1,515	1,739	2,117	2,383	2,523
Georgia	2,609	2,909	3,445	3,943	4,492
Florida	753	1,468	2,771	4,952	6,671
East North Central	18,251	25,297	30,399	36,224	39,808
Ohio	4,767	6,647	7,947	9,706	10,542
Indiana	2,701	3,239	3,934	4,662	5,143
Illinois	5,639	7,631	8,712	10,081	10,978
Michigan	2,810	4,842	6,372	7,823	8,778
Wisconsin	2,334	2,939	3,435	3,952	4,367
East South Central	8,410	9,887	11,477	12,050	12,531
Kentucky	2,290	2,615	2,945	3,038	3,161
Tennessee	2,185	2,617	3,292	3,567	3,839
Alabama	2,138	2,646	3,062	3,267	3,373
Mississippi	1,797	2,010	2,179	2,178	2,158

too, are often viewed as unique target markets by marketers anxious to avoid the extremely competitive East and West Coast markets. Note, too, the relative scarcity of people in the Plains and Mountain states, which explains why some mass marketers pay less attention to these areas. Yet these states can provide an opportunity for an alert marketer who is looking for less competitive market situations.

Where are the people today and tomorrow?

Population figures for a single year fail to convey the dynamic aspects of markets. The U.S. population has been growing continuously since the founding of the country, more than doubling in the 60 years from 1910 to 1970. But – and this is important to marketers – the population

Table 6–1 — *Continued*

State or other areas	Population (1,000)				
	1910	1930	1950	1960	1970
West North Central	11,638	13,297	14,061	15,495	16,156
Minnesota	2,076	2,564	2,982	3,414	3,768
Iowa	2,225	2,471	2,621	2,758	2,790
Missouri	3,293	3,629	3,955	4,320	4,636
North Dakota	577	681	620	632	611
South Dakota	584	693	653	681	661
Nebraska	1,192	1,378	1,326	1,411	1,468
Kansas	1,691	1,881	1,905	2,179	2,222
West South Central	8,785	12,177	14,538	16,951	18,937
Arkansas	1,574	1,854	1,910	1,786	1,886
Louisiana	1,656	2,102	2,684	3,257	3,564
Oklahoma	1,657	2,396	2,233	2,328	2,498
Texas	3,897	5,825	7,711	9,580	10,989
Mountain	2,634	3,702	5,075	6,855	8,179
Montana	376	538	591	675	682
Idaho	326	445	589	667	698
Wyoming	146	226	291	330	329
Colorado	799	1,036	1,325	1,754	2,178
New Mexico	327	423	681	951	998
Arizona	204	436	750	1,302	1,752
Utah	373	508	689	891	1,060
Nevada	82	91	160	285	482
Pacific	4,449	8,622	15,115	21,198	26,168
Washington	1,142	1,563	2,379	2,853	3,353
Oregon	673	954	1,521	1,769	2,056
California	2,378	5,677	10,586	15,717	19,715
Alaska	64	59	129	226	295
Hawaii	192	368	500	633	749
Puerto Rico	1,118	1,544	2,211	2,350	2,690

*Insofar as possible, population shown is that of present area of state.
†1969 figure.
Source: *Statistical Abstract of the United States*, 1967, p. 12, and *1970 Census of Population* PC(P1)–(2–55).

did *not* double everywhere. Some states have seen very rapid growth, while others have grown only a little and at a slower rate (see Table 6–1).

These different rates of growth are especially important to marketing. For example, sudden growth in one area may create a demand for many new shopping centers, while existing facilities may be more than adequate in other areas. In fact, the introduction of new marketing facilities in slow-growing areas can create severe competitive problems for existing merchants, while in other areas demand may be growing so rapidly that even poorly planned and managed facilities can be profitable.

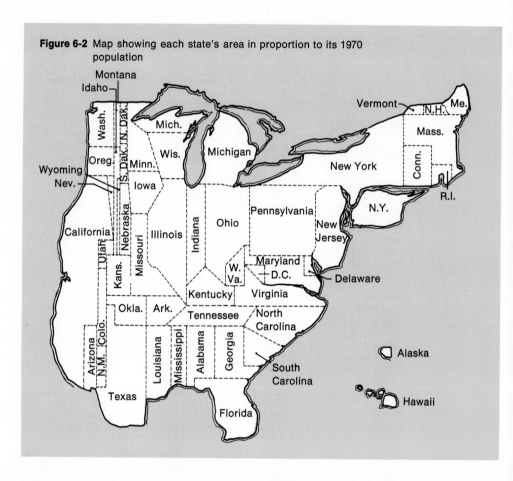

Figure 6-2 Map showing each state's area in proportion to its 1970 population

Population will keep growing	It seems certain that U.S. population will continue to grow.[1] The big questions are, "How much and how fast?" Although the birthrate is currently declining, the increasing number of young women and the pattern of earlier marriages suggest that population will continue to grow. A minimum of 10 percent growth in population from 1970 to 1980 is anticipated.[2]

These projections might be changed, however, by new attitudes towards marriage, family size, and family planning. These trends should be watched carefully by marketers, because they obviously have an impact on future market sizes. For the present, however, it is clear that population will continue to grow and that most of this population expansion will center in already crowded metropolitan areas.

---

[1] Detailed data on population growth and projections are available from the U.S. census. As a starting point, see the latest *Statistical Abstract*.

[2] "The Many More Faces of the Seventies," *Business*

Week, December 6, 1969, p. 83–86; "Is Long Decline in Birth Rate Ending?" *Business Week*, December 14, 1968, pp. 160–61.

Migration from rural to urban areas has been continuous in the United States since 1800, as Figure 6-3 shows. In fact, in the last few decades the migration may have been even faster than suggested in Figure 6-3 because many people classified as rural residents by the U.S. census do not live on farms. The old rural-urban definitions may be misleading because of new factories and suburban building in

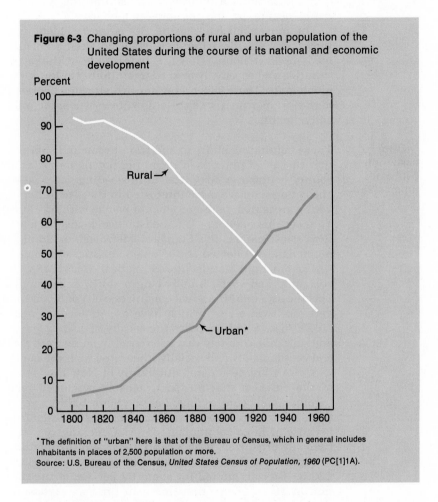

Figure 6-3 Changing proportions of rural and urban population of the United States during the course of its national and economic development

Percent

Rural →

← Urban*

1800 1820 1840 1860 1880 1900 1920 1940 1960

*The definition of "urban" here is that of the Bureau of Census, which in general includes inhabitants in places of 2,500 population or more.
Source: U.S. Bureau of the Census, *United States Census of Population, 1960* (PC[1]1A).

"rural" areas. About 5.2 percent of the U.S. population lived on farms in 1968 compared to about 15 percent in 1950. Clearly, we have become an industrialized society, and it seems that farming will eventually be dominated by corporate agricultural enterprises. This subject is explored further in Chapter 9.

Since World War II, there has been a veritable race to the suburbs. In 1970, more people were living in the suburbs than in the central cities. As people moved to the suburbs, retail and service businesses followed. And as middle-income people have moved out of the cities, lower-income consumers, often with different racial and national backgrounds, have moved in, thereby changing the nature of target markets in the center of the city.

A partial reversal of this trend seems possible, however. Some families have become disenchanted with the suburban dream, which they found to be a nightmare of commuting, yard and housework, rising local taxes, and gossiping neighbors.

The movement back to the city is most evident among older and sometimes wealthier families. Their children are usually married or ready to leave home. They feel hemmed in by the rapid expansion of suburbia and especially by the large number of lower-income families moving in. These older families are showing increased interest in high-rise apartments close to downtown shopping, recreational, and office facilities.

Developing a new concept of the urban area

These continuing shifts to and from urban and suburban areas mean that the usual practice of recording population by arbitrary city and county boundaries may lead to misleading descriptions of markets. Marketing men are more interested in the size of homogeneous marketing areas than in the number of people within political boundaries. To meet this need, the U.S. census has developed a separate population classification, the Standard Metropolitan Statistical Area, and much data is collected on the characteristics of people in these areas.

The Standard Metropolitan Statistical Area (SMSA) is an integrated economic and social unit having a fairly large population nucleus. Specifically, an SMSA must contain one city of 50,000 or more inhabitants, or "twin cities" which have a combined population of at least 50,000. The SMSA includes the county of such a central city or cities and adjacent counties that are found to be metropolitan in character and economically and socially integrated with the central city.

SMSA's are designated differently in New England because many of the cities in that compact, densely populated region are closer together, and counties must be split. Some SMSA's, especially those in the western part of the country, are exceptionally large geographically because of huge county boundaries. Generally, however, SMSA's are basically urbanized, with a central city and surrounding suburbs.

Figure 6–4 shows the location of the nation's biggest urban areas: 230 SMSA's accounted for about 67 percent of the country's population in 1970. Notice that this map further emphasizes the concentration of population in specific places—here, in SMSA's.

Big targets are easier

Some national marketing organizations are concerned solely with these metropolitan areas, in fact, only with certain ones among them, because of the large concentrations of population within easy reach of their major distribution facilities. Table 6–2 shows the size of the top 15 SMSA's in 1970.

These larger target markets also offer greater sales potential in dollars and cents than population alone would indicate, in part be-

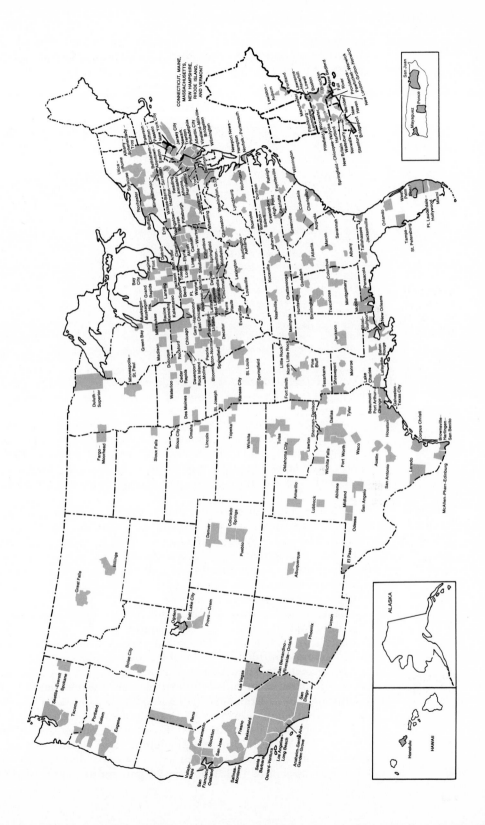

CONNECTICUT, MAINE,
MASSACHUSETTS,
NEW HAMPSHIRE,
RHODE ISLAND,
AND VERMONT

ALASKA

HAWAII

cause of generally higher wages in metropolitan areas and the concentration of higher paying occupations.

Table 6–2 Population and rank of top 15 Standard Metropolitan Statistical Areas in 1970

Rank	City	Population
1	New York	11,448,000
2	Los Angeles–Long Beach	6,974,000
3	Chicago	6,893,000
4	Philadelphia	4,777,000
5	Detroit	4,164,000
6	San Francisco–Oakland	3,070,000
7	Washington, D.C., Md., Va.	2,836,000
8	Boston	2,730,000
9	Pittsburgh	2,384,000
10	St. Louis, Mo.–Ill.	2,331,000
11	Baltimore	2,045,000
12	Cleveland	2,043,000
13	Houston	1,958,000
14	Newark	1,848,000
15	Minneapolis–St. Paul	1,805,000

Source: *Population of Standard Metropolitan Statistical Areas* PC (P3)–3, *1970 Census of Population*, U.S. Department of Commerce, Bureau of the Census.

The SMSA's should be considered as potential dimensions in market grid analysis. The farther customers are from major marketing centers, the more expensive they are to serve. Densely populated areas offer great opportunities – *if* the competition is not too great!

The age of the continuous city

Despite the return of some families to the central cities, the trend to the suburbs seems likely to continue. An expanding population must go somewhere, and the suburbs can combine pleasant neighborhoods with easy transportation to higher-paying jobs in the city. Further, the continuing decentralization of industry may move jobs closer to the suburbs than to the central city. Not only people but industries have been fleeing the old cities.

These sometimes rapid shifts into new communities can create overnight opportunities for alert marketers. Here, however, less reliance can be placed on the usual census data; it's too old. Both intuition and careful study of local trends are necessary.

This growth in suburban population may create a new kind of urban-suburban strip called "interurbia" or "megalopolis." J. Walter Thompson Co. – a large advertising agency that has done much work in projecting population growth in various areas – sees a 600-mile-long "city" stretching along the East Coast and joining the citizens of Boston, New York, Baltimore, Philadelphia, and Washington and their suburbs into one giant community. This particular interurbia constitutes 6 percent of U.S. land and 20 percent of the population (see

Figure 6–5). Other interurbia areas occur around the Great Lakes and adjoining areas in Pennsylvania, Ohio, and Missouri; in southern Florida; in the San Francisco Bay region; and in southern California.

Figure 6-5 Projected growth of "interurbias"

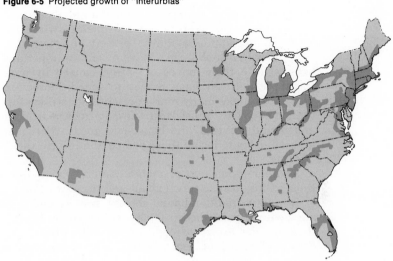

Source: J. Walter Thompson Co.

People who see the whole world becoming more urbanized look at these areas as laboratories of urban evolution.[3] The shaded parts in Figure 6–5 represent areas which are already fairly densely populated and can be expected to grow more.

It appears that the central cities in these interurbia areas will be rebuilt gradually and attractively as slum areas are cleared with the aid of federal funds. Some may become higher-income residential areas, drawing heavily from the suburbs.

The U.S. city of the past 70 or 80 years has been depicted as a series of concentric rings or bands ranging from low-income slums at the city center outward through progressively higher income areas to the wealthy suburban areas at the outer fringe. The city of tomorrow will probably be more heterogeneous with many small neighborhoods— some wealthy, some middle income, and some poor—intermingled throughout the area from the central city to the suburbs. This pattern of urban redevelopment already can be seen in the Los Angeles, Chicago, and Philadelphia areas. This new urban population structure

---

[3] For a detailed study of the Northeast area, see Jean Gottmann, *Megalopolis* (New York: Twentieth Century Fund, 1961); Wolf Von Eckardt, *The Chal-* *lenge of Megalopolis* (A Twentieth Century Fund Report based on the original study by Jean Gottmann [New York: Macmillan Co., 1964]).

will make the use of the market grid concept even more important. For example, retailers will have to find ways to serve various kinds of customers, to specify their target markets carefully and then develop marketing mixes specifically for the selected target markets. Aiming at the mass market may be fatal.

The mobile ones are an attractive market

It is important to remember that none of these population shifts is necessarily permanent. People move, stay awhile, and then move on again. In fact, approximately 20 percent of Americans move each year. It appears that mobile people represent an important economic market, because their moves are often caused by promotions and job transfers and they have money to spend. Moreover, it is clear that they must make many market-oriented decisions fairly quickly after their move. They must locate new sources of food, clothing, medical and dental services, and household goods. Alert marketers are well advised to try to locate these people and inform them of their market offering.[4]

Another dimension of mobile Americans should also be noted — their willingness to travel about and try new things.

In a very tradition-bound society, people tend to take one job and stick with it, partly because jobs are in short supply and partly because they are not aware of opportunities elsewhere. But in the United States, the idea of mobility has been a tradition dating from the 17th-century beginnings of this nation. Pioneering, homesteading, and prospecting — more recently, the cheap "tin lizzie," the Great Depression and wars — all have contributed to a feeling of mobility and impermanence.

The millions of military veterans who have traveled extensively during the wars of the past 30 years have expanded their horizons, and many have found new locations more attractive. The development of better highways since World War II has enabled workers to live at greater distances from their jobs. The increased popularity and availability of automobiles — brought about by the steadily rising prosperity of the 1950's and 1960's — has had a profound effect on the development of marketing institutions. Consider such developments as shopping centers in the metropolitan areas, and the retail facilities, marinas, and specialized services that cater to owners of second homes, vacation cabins, travel trailers, and boats.

[4] James E. Bell, Jr., "Mobiles — A Neglected Market Segment," *Journal of Marketing*, April, 1969, pp. 37–44; James E. Bell, Jr., *Selection of New Suppliers by the Mobile Family* (Bureau of Business & Economic Research, Michigan State University, 1969), 101 pp.; Alan R. Andreasen, "Geographic Mobility and Market Segmentation," *Journal of Marketing Research*, November, 1966, pp. 341–49. Also, the extensive studies that are now being conducted in connection with the development of road systems may be extremely useful for marketing decisions. Both location and mobility have a bearing, and considerable data is becoming available. See Henry K. Evans, "A Vast New Storehouse of Transportation and Marketing Data," *Journal of Marketing*, January, 1966, pp. 33–40. Several interesting applications are offered.

Income

So far we have been concerned primarily with demographic characteristics. It is obvious, however, that unless a person has money or the assurance of acquiring it, he cannot be regarded as a potential customer. The amount of money he can spend also will affect the type of goods he is likely to buy. For this reason, most marketing men study income data too.

Growth at least until the year 2000

Income is derived from producing and selling goods or services in the marketplace. As already noted, a widely available measure of the output and the growth of the economy is the gross national product, which represents the total market value of goods and services produced in a year. The GNP has increased at the rate of approximately 3 percent a year since 1880. This means that GNP doubles, on the average, every 20 years. If past trends continue, as is expected, the economy will probably continue to grow at about the same rate, that is, doubling every 20 years. And faster growth has been forecasted.[5] Even though taxes have increased, and further increases are likely, we can nevertheless project continued growth of consumer spending power. Some researchers see continued growth, with no serious drain on resources, until the year 2000.[6]

The income pyramid capsizes!

These aggregate figures are more meaningful when expressed in terms of family income and its distribution. Family income has been moving up, but even more important to marketing men is that the distribution of income has been changing drastically and will probably continue to change. Figure 6–6 shows that as recently as 1930 most families were bunched together in the lower income levels, and the distribution looked something like a pyramid. The data in Figure 6–6 is in terms of 1965 dollars, which means the effects of price inflation over the years have been removed.

By 1965, we see that the pyramid had turned over! Projections into the future indicate that real income will not only continue to grow but that more families will find themselves near or at the top of the income distribution.

Is $10,000 bare subsistence?

The importance of the income distribution data in Figure 6–6 cannot be stressed too much. Bad marketing strategy errors have been made by overestimating the amount of income available in various target markets. It is all too easy for businessmen to fall into such errors because of the natural tendency we all have of associating with others

---

[5]"Plotting the Fastest Growth Ever," *Business Week*, March 30, 1968, pp. 110–16.

[6]Hans H. Lansberg, *Natural Resources for U.S. Growth—A Look Ahead to the Year 2000* (Baltimore: Johns Hopkins Press, 1964); "Plenty of Re-

sources if We Use Them Right," *Business Week*, April 6, 1963, pp. 84–86. And the basic study: Hans H. Lansberg, Leonard L. Fischman, Joseph L. Fisher, *Resources in America's Future* (Baltimore: Johns Hopkins Press, 1963).

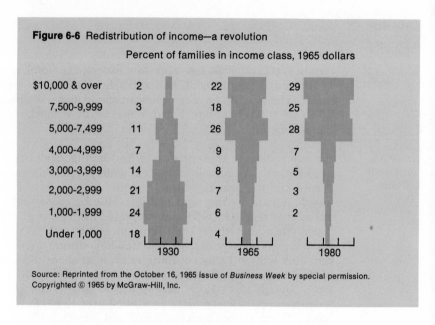

Figure 6-6 Redistribution of income—a revolution

Percent of families in income class, 1965 dollars

	1930	1965	1980
$10,000 & over	2	22	29
7,500-9,999	3	18	25
5,000-7,499	11	26	28
4,000-4,999	7	9	7
3,000-3,999	14	8	5
2,000-2,999	21	7	3
1,000-1,999	24	6	2
Under 1,000	18	4	

Source: Reprinted from the October 16, 1965 issue of *Business Week* by special permission. Copyrighted © 1965 by McGraw-Hill, Inc.

in similar circumstances and then assuming that almost everyone lives the same way. This was brought home most forcefully to the author when a group of students confronted him with what they felt was an error in a textbook. They questioned the statement in the book that many people made less than $5,000 a year. No one, they felt, could possibly survive on such a low income. They felt that $10,000 or more a year was necessary for "bare subsistence." This was in 1955. Figure 6-6 shows that 10 years later—1965—only 22 percent of the country's families made more than $10,000. Furthermore, 34 percent of the families were making less than $5,000 a year.[7]

The $10,000 income figure is a useful reference point, because a recent college graduate might earn almost this much (and a working couple together can easily go over this figure). This will seem like a lot in the initial flush of making money, but it is surprising how soon needs and expenses rise and adjust to available income. Before long it's difficult to see how anyone can live on less. Then, the fact that there *is* an income distribution and that some families must make do on much less should not be forgotten in marketing strategy planning.

On the positive side, income probably will continue to grow and the number of families at various income levels will continue to shift upward. One forcast expects real GNP in the 1970's to grow at a rate of 4.5 percent per annum, which will mean a real GNP of 1.5 trillion

[7]For a fuller discussion of the growth of the mass market and the implication for marketing strategy planning, see Walter Gross, "Income Flow Diffusion and Marketing Strategies," *MSU Business Topics*, Autumn, 1966, pp. 70-77; see also, "Cartier Opens Its Door Wider," *Business Week*, October 15, 1966, pp. 71-74; and Charles J. Collazzo, Jr., "Effects of Income upon Shopping Attitudes and Frustrations," *Journal of Retailing*, Spring, 1966, pp. 1-7.

dollars by 1980. Allowing for a 2.5 percent price inflation per year, this would produce a total GNP of 2 trillion dollars by 1980. This would indicate that 1 million families per year will move into the $10,000-a-year-plus income group. And by 1980, two out of every three families will have incomes of $10,000 a year or more.[8]

Consumer spending patterns related to population and income

Income, disposable income, discretionary income, and expenditures are different

We have been using the term *family* income because consumer budget studies suggest that most consumers spend their incomes as part of a family or household unit. If the wife or children work, they usually pool their income with the husband or father when planning family expenditures. Thus, most of our discussion will be on how households or families spend their income.

Disposable income is spendable income

It should be remembered, however, that families do not get to spend all of their income. Since governments are remote but "spending" members of each family, most consumers are able to spend only part of their income – the part called *disposable income*. Out of its disposable income – together with gifts, pensions, cash savings, or other assets – the family makes its expenditures. Some families do not spend all of their disposable income, saving part of it.[9] Therefore, we should distinguish between disposable income and actual expenditures when trying to estimate potential expenditures in market grid boxes.

Discretionary income is elusive

As we have already noted, peoples' incomes have been growing and probably will continue to grow. But not all of the growing income is uncommited. Most households allocate a goodly portion of their income to "necessities" – food, rent or house payments, car and housefurnishings payments, insurance, etc. – which are defined in various ways by different researchers and consumers. A family's purchase of "luxuries" comes from what's left, or what is called *discretionary income*.

Discretionary income is a rather elusive concept, because the definition of necessities varies from family to family and over a period of time. But it is also an important concept, because if consumers do not feel they have *any* discretionary purchasing power, they may stop buying certain luxuries altogether. Also, discretionary income may jump substantially with a small growth in income. One study, for example, shows that a family with $8,000 gross income may have almost four times the discretionary income of a family with $6,500

[8] Martin Gainsbrugh, NICB Chief Economist, in a speech before the National Industrial Conference Board's meeting on "The Consumer Market: The Coming Decade of Change," as reported in the *4 A News Letter,* American Association of Advertising Agencies, April 29, 1970, p. 10.

[9] Perhaps 6–7 percent. See "Consumers Bank More of Their Income, Often for No Special Reason," *Wall Street Journal, January 19,* 1968, p. 1 f.

gross income.[10] Again, much would depend on the attitudes of people in the target markets. A color television set might be purchased out of discretionary income by a lower-income family but be considered a necessity by a higher-income family.

People's needs for "necessities" also may continue to grow, outstripping their purchasing power. It was recently estimated that only "54 percent of American families can afford what is now perceived as a 'low moderate' life standard. And very few can afford the leisure-class life styles popularized by the spread of education and promoted by mass media."[11]

Expenditure data is useful and available

To avoid confusion regarding income-related measures of market potential, we will focus on expenditure data in the following discussion. Our major reason for emphasizing spending rather than income is that expenditure data shows what consumers actually have *spent* and much information is available here. Discretionary income data, on the other hand, is not as widely available, applies only to some purchases, and must be tailored to the needs of the individual situation.

Engel's laws show basic spending relationships

Before looking at hard expenditure data, some generalizations are possible about consumer spending patterns. These generalizations are commonly referred to as "Engel's laws" because they grew out of the work of a German statistician who published the first study of consumer spending patterns in 1857. Followers have rephrased these laws, until now they are stated in three parts:

1. As a family's income increases, the percentage spent on food will decrease.
2. As a family's income increases, the percentage spent on housing and household operations will be roughly constant (with the exception of fuel, light, and refrigeration, which will decrease).
3. As a family's income increases, the percentage spent on all other categories and the amount saved will increase (with the exception of medical care and personal care items, which are fairly constant).

Engel was primarily concerned with working-class families who spent *all* their income. This fits in with our emphasis on analyzing consumer *expenditures*. Note that it is implied in Engel's laws that as a family's income increases, *more money will be spent in total in all categories*. The decreases or increases occur as a percentage of the total.

Engel's laws are useful only for predicting the behavior of an individual family or groups of families moving from one income category to another. They should be used with care when it comes to predicting the spending pattern that develops in the whole economy when the

[10] Thomas T. Semon, "Family Income and Spending Capacity," *Journal of Marketing,* April, 1962, pp. 26–30.

[11] "Price of the Good Life Will Get Stiffer," *Business Week,* December 6, 1969, p. 197.

gross national product changes. Engel's laws were not based upon such movements, but rather on a comparison of the budgets of individual families. They can still be useful to marketing men, however. An established retailer, for example, might use Engel's laws to forecast how the expenditure patterns of his present customers would change if a new industrial plant coming into the community were likely to increase their incomes.

Expenditure data provides harder numbers

Generalizations such as Engel's laws are valuable when precise data is not available, but fortunately we do have some detailed information on consumer expenditure patterns. The National Industrial Conference Board (NICB) has developed an extremely comprehensive breakdown of data gathered by the Bureau of Labor Statistics as part of its project to revise its Consumer Price Index.

To make this revision, approximately 12,000 nonfarm families were interviewed during 1961–62 concerning their purchases of approximately 700 individual products and services. All of this data has been analyzed and cross-classified with 11 different family characteristics, and presented in detailed tables.[12] Some of this data will be presented in this chapter to show the variety of information that is available in most libraries, and how this information may be used in market gridding.

It must be understood that this data is somewhat dated now and incomes have since gone up. Nevertheless, the basic interrelationships probably still hold, and it is currently the most comprehensive and detailed data easily available. Some updating of the income distribution data from a source such as *Sales Management's* "Survey of Buying Power"[13] probably would be desirable if this data were to be used in a real business situation. But for our purposes we will discuss and illustrate the use of this basic information.

Why lower-income consumers may be ignored

Table 6–3 shows the average annual spending by households for major categories of expenditures, as developed in this study. These aggregate measures serve as bench marks, and as noted earlier, should keep you from making wild extimates based only on your own experience.

The data in Table 6–3 shows that those in the upper-income categories spend a large share of the total spent for goods and services. The families making over $7,500, for example, comprise only 30 percent of the population but account for almost half the expenditures. This may not be surprising information, but it does help to explain why some business organizations tend to ignore the lower-income consumers.

[12] Fabian Linden (ed.), *Expenditure Patterns of the American Family* (New York: National Industrial Conference Board, 1965).

[13] See Chapter 4.

Table 6–3 Average annual family expenditures by family income

Item	Total	Family income (before taxes)				
		Under $3,000	$3,000–$5,000	$5,000–$7,500	$7,500–$10,000	$10,000–$15,000	$15,000 and over
Percent distribution of:							
All families	100%	22.4%	20.8%	26.2%	16.1%	10.7%	3.7%
Total expenditures	100	8.9	15.6	27.1	21.2	18.0	9.1
Average family size	3.2	2.1	3.0	3.5	3.7	3.9	3.8
Expenditures for current consumption:	$5,152	$2,043	$3,859	$5,315	$6,788	$8,679	$12,687
Food	1,259	600	1,015	1,318	1,624	1,970	2,550
Alcoholic beverages	81	21	55	81	117	152	242
Tobacco	93	42	84	105	123	126	134
Housing and household operations	1,236	620	968	1,263	1,552	1,889	3,002
Housefurnishings and equipment	269	83	185	284	376	476	690
Clothing and accessories	525	145	348	528	720	1,001	1,550
Transportation	781	176	560	848	1,093	1,450	1,891
Medical care	342	174	269	350	425	539	771
Personal care	148	61	118	156	194	241	312
Recreation and equipment	205	48	133	201	291	419	597
Reading and education	100	26	55	88	126	215	440
Other expenditures	113	47	69	93	147	201	508

Source: Adapted from Fabian Linden (ed.), *Expenditure Patterns of the American Family* (New York: National Industrial Conference Board, 1965), p. 18.

Using
expenditure
data

To estimate dollars spent in major categories

Data such as that in Table 6–3 can help a marketing manager understand how his potential target markets spend their money. For example, if he is seriously considering consumers in the $15,000-and-over income bracket, he can analyze how families in this category distributed their expenditures. Then he can consider how they would have to rearrange their spending to purchase his product. A swimming pool manufacturer could calculate that such families spend about $600 a year on recreation and equipment. If his pool costs approximately $600 a year, including depreciation and maintainance, it follows that for the average family in this income category, such a purchase would necessitate a substantial realignment in its life style. Something would have to be substituted for something else – as we noted in Chapter 5 when we discussed the substitute method of forecasting.

Clearly, the data will not give the pool maker the answer that he seeks, but it may supply some of the raw materials he needs to make a sound decision. If he feels that he needs more information, he can use various marketing research techniques. For example, he might want to make a budget study on consumers who already have swimming pools to see how they adjusted their spending patterns. He might also want to incorporate differences in spending habits due to other factors for which data is available in the NICB study, such as age of household head, stage in the family life cycle, and so on. How these factors affect expenditure patterns is discussed later in the chapter.

To estimate size of product sales potential

The NICB study provides data not only on general categories but also on 700 products and services. Swimming pools are not such a category, but refrigerators are, and we will use them to illustrate the kind of detailed data which is available for the large number of items commonly purchased by consumers. To be more precise, we will look at the problem of a soft-goods department store manager who is thinking about adding refrigerators and similar large appliances.

The store manager knows that he is now serving a lower-income target market and wants to get an idea of the relative magnitude of their current refrigerator purchases. His credit records give him a good measure of the number and income of his regular customers. He finds that about half are in the under-$3,000-a-year family income bracket, while the other half are in the $3,000-to-$5,000 bracket.

One of the tables in the NICB study shows that while the average expenditure for refrigerators was $14.56, the lowest income category spent only $6.17 for refrigerators, and the $3,000-to-$5,000 income group spent only $12.90.[14]

As would be expected, the higher-income group spent more, probably reflecting both more frequent purchases and purchases of larger units. Data did show, nevertheless, that the lower-income consumers were buying refrigerators. By multiplying the average purchase per family times the number of families in each of the income groups, the department store manager was able to develop an estimate of the total purchases in his target market. By making similar calculations for the other major appliances he was considering, he could estimate the total spending for such commodities.[15]

The more the manager knows about his present target market, the more he can make use of the available data. For example, if his customers are mainly older people, the NICB data will show that their expenditures on refrigerators are below average for refrigerator buyers. If most of his customers have no children or are unskilled workers or have lower educational achievement levels, they will spend less on refrigeration.

Some of these characteristics are interrelated and will have to be used with care. Unfortunately, the data in this study and in most such studies is not cross-classified according to income *and* education *and* occupation *and* age and so on. Still, expenditure data is available to guide and supplement judgment on the behavior of alternative target markets.

After the department store manager has developed an estimate of

---

[14] Linden (ed.), *op. cit.*, pp. 70–75.

[15] The NICB study provides a variety of data, including information on the following appliances: refrigerators, home freezers, dishwashers, gas stoves, electric stoves, floor waxers, garbage disposal units, vacuum cleaners, washing machines, dryers, air conditioners, dehumidifiers, sewing machines, and ironers.

the expenditures of his target customers, he would then have to estimate the likelihood of his getting a share of this business. He would also have to evaluate the possibility of attracting other people, including those like his present customers, if he added appliances to his line. And before the final decision was made, the manager would have to consider competition and the relative profitability of appliance lines. At the start, however, the expenditure data would add hard facts to the analysis.

It should be clear that a manufacturer, a chain retailer, or other marketer could use the basic approach of our department store manager. First, he would have to select potential target markets. Then he could carry out the analysis in many more geographic areas. Much more judgment and greater care would be needed in such an analysis, because competition and local preferences would have to be considered. The local retailer might have a far better feel for this than someone in a headquarters office. This helps explain why some small retailers can compete very successfully with chain outlets that attempt to apply one marketing mix in differing areas.

Expenditure patterns vary
with other measurable factors

Income has a direct bearing on spending patterns, but there are other factors that should not be neglected in any careful analysis of market grids. Several of these factors and general relationships are discussed in the following pages.

Spend more on houses in town, food in the country

The location of a consumer's household, either inside or outside a metropolitan area, has a distinct bearing on the household's spending habits.

In Table 6–4, note especially that total expenditures are much lower outside metropolitan areas. This fits with our earlier comment about the importance of Standard Metropolitan Statistical Areas. But the detailed variations also are important. Note how the shares spent on major expenditure categories shift in several places, always remembering that a 1 percent share represents a lot of money. Consumers in central cities spend much less on transportation and much more on housing than those in outlying areas. And rural families spend a larger share on food, perhaps because there is less competition in rural areas for the grocery dollar. But incomes tend to be lower in rural areas, and Engel's laws may explain some of this. The more detailed NICB data that is available would have to be analyzed to answer specific questions.[16]

---

[16] See also, Donald F. Blankertz, "A Marketing Analysis of Suburban and Urban Expenditure Patterns," in Reavis Cox *et al.*, *Theory in Marketing* (Homewood, Ill.: Richard D. Irwin, Inc., 1964), pp. 289–309, re. Engel's laws.

Table 6-4 Average annual family expenditures by market location

| Item | Total | In metropolitan areas | | | Outside metropolitan areas | |
		Central cities	Urban fringe	Other areas	Urban	Rural
Percent distribution of:						
All families	100%	34.9%	26.5%	6.0%	16.1%	16.5%
Total expenditures	100	34.8	32.4	6.6	14.0	12.2
Average family size	3.2	2.9	3.4	3.7	3.1	3.3
Expenditures for current consumption:	$5,152	$5,132	$6,303	$5,665	$4,482	$3,813
Food	24%	25%	24%	23%	25%	26%
Alcoholic beverages	2	2	2	1	1	1
Tobacco	2	2	2	2	2	2
Housing and household operations	24	25	24	24	24	21
Housefurnishings and equipment	5	5	5	6	5	6
Clothing and accessories	10	11	10	10	10	9
Transportation	15	13	16	16	15	18
Medical care	7	7	6	7	7	7
Personal care	3	3	3	3	3	3
Recreation and equipment	4	4	4	4	4	4
Reading and education	2	2	2	2	2	2
Other expenditures	2	2	2	2	2	2

Source: Adapted from Fabian Linden (ed.), *Expenditure Patterns of the American Family* (New York: National Industrial Conference Board, 1965), p. 21.

Where do you live? What do you buy?

For the marketing man, geographical location is also relevant. Table 6-5 breaks the United States into four regions. As might be expected, total expenditures in the South are lower than in other regions because incomes there are lower. The important differences here, again, are in housing and transportation. As noted before, higher or lower expenditures in some categories change the whole budget pattern. These differences must be considered when evaluating the potential in various geographical target markets.

The young buy colored tissues

Two other dimensions of population — age and number of children — seem to have a direct bearing on consumption patterns and are therefore important to marketing men.

Age has a bearing on acceptance of new items. Younger people seem to be more receptive to new products. The under-35 group was the first to use cellulose sponges, fitted bed sheets, liquid detergents, and colored two-ply paper tissues. Then, too, younger families — usually with no children — are still accumulating durable goods such as automobiles and housefurnishings. They need less food. It is only as children begin to arrive and grow that the family emphasis shifts to soft goods and services such as education, medical and personal care. This tends to occur when the household head reaches the 35-to-44 age bracket.

Table 6–5 Average annual family expenditures by geographical region

Item	Total	North-east	North Central	South	West
Percent distribution of:					
All families	100%	26.9%	27.8%	28.9%	16.3%
Total expenditures	100	30.1	27.2	24.8	18.0
Average family size	3.2	3.2	3.2	3.2	3.2
Expenditures for current consumption:	$5,152	$5,761	$5,028	$4,410	$5,677
Food	24%	25%	24%	24%	24%
Alcoholic beverages	2	2	2	1	2
Tobacco	2	2	2	2	2
Housing and household operation	24	25	24	23	23
Housefurnishings and equipment	5	5	5	6	5
Clothing and accessories	10	10	10	10	10
Transportation	15	13	16	16	16
Medical care	7	6	7	7	7
Personal care	3	3	3	3	3
Recreation and equipment	4	4	4	4	5
Reading and education	2	2	2	2	2
Other expenditures	2	2	2	2	2

Source: Adapted from Fabian Linden (ed.), *Expenditure Patterns of the American Family* (New York: National Industrial Conference Board, 1965), p. 20

In the over-55 age bracket, there is more interest in medical care products, those that aid health, sleep, and digestion. These older families also have more interest in travel, recreation, and self-education.[17] Table 6–6 presents NICB findings concerning families in various stages of the life cycle along with their purchasing patterns. The relatively high expenditures by young families, especially those with older children, should be noted. These families are numerous, and their spending is especially high for food and clothing. Young families and families with young children are also good markets for homes and home improvements.

Reallocation for teen-agers

Much research on life cycles has been done because today's marketing man knows he must be familiar with the family characteristics of his market. It is fairly easy to obtain such data, since accurate information is available on births, marriages, and ages of children.

[17] S. G. Barton, "The Life Cycle and Buying Patterns," in Lincoln H. Clark (ed.), *Consumer Behavior* (New York: New York University Press, 1955), Vol. II, pp. 53–57. There are several other interesting articles in Vol. II on the relation of the life cycle to consumer behavior. See also, "Census-Eye View of Sales in '70's," *Business Week*, June 10, 1967, pp. 120–24.

Table 6–6 Average annual family expenditures by stage in life cycle

| Item | Total | Families with child under 6 | | 6 or over only | | No children | |
		Some under 6	All under 6	All 6 to 11	Any 12 or over	Hus-band–wife	Other
Percent distribution of:							
All families	100%	14.5%	12.7%	4.6%	25.7%	24.1%	18.4%
Total expenditures	100	17.1	13.3	5.4	33.4	21.3	9.5
Average family size	3.2	5.5	3.6	3.7	4.1	2.1	1.2
Expenditures for current consumption:	$5,152	$6,070	$5,406	$6,045	$6,710	$4,549	$2,664
Food	24%	27%	22%	24%	25%	23%	24%
Alcoholic beverages	2	1	1	2	2	2	2
Tobacco	2	2	2	2	2	2	2
Housing and household operation	24	24	26	23	21	25	31
Housefurnishings and equipment	5	5	7	5	5	6	4
Clothing and accessories	10	11	9	11	12	8	8
Transportation	15	14	16	15	15	16	12
Medical care	7	6	7	6	6	8	7
Personal care	3	3	3	3	3	3	3
Recreation and equipment	4	4	4	5	4	3	3
Reading and education	2	2	1	2	3	1	2
Other expenditures	2	2	1	2	3	2	2

Source: Adapted from Fabian Linden (ed), *Expenditure Patterns of the American Family* (New York: National Industrial Conference Board, 1965), p. 17.

Considerable attention, for example, has been directed to the babies born in the period from 1940 to 1960 and in general to those under 25 years of age. These people will make up key markets for decades (see Figure 6–7). Some are teen-agers who are eating more, beginning to wear more expensive clothes, and developing recreational and educational needs that are hard on the family budget. Their parents may be forced to reallocate their incomes to cover these expenses, spending less on durable goods such as appliances, automobiles, household goods, and houses. This, of course, would affect the producers of these goods.

As these teen-agers grow into young adults, we can expect a sharp increase in marriages, and perhaps a continuing baby boom. These young adults, in turn, will buy durable goods until their children be-

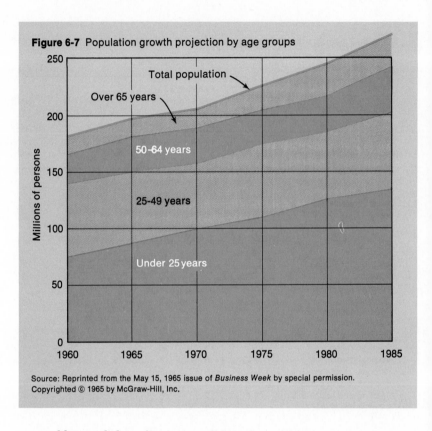

Figure 6-7 Population growth projection by age groups

Source: Reprinted from the May 15, 1965 issue of *Business Week* by special permission. Copyrighted © 1965 by McGraw-Hill, Inc.

come older, and then they, too, will have to reallocate their budgets to provide for food, clothing, education and recreation.[18]

Selling to the "empty nest"

There is an important group in the 50–64 age category that is sometimes called the "empty-nesters." Their children are grown, and they are now able to spend their money in other ways. It is an elusive group, however, because some people marry later and are still raising a family as they move into this age group. It is empty-nesters who move back into the smaller, more luxurious apartments in central cities. They may also be more interested in travel, small sports cars, and other things that have not been realistic possibilities for them until now.[19] Much depends on their income, of course.

[18] James U. McNeal, "The Child Consumer: A New Market," *Journal of Retailing*, Summer, 1969, pp. 15–22; "Teen-Age Income," *Business Week*, June 22, 1968, p. 58; "Grooving Shoe Sales to a Young Market," *Business Week*, April 27, 1968, pp. 78–81; "Youth Will Be Furnished," *Business Week*, April 27, 1968, pp. 36–37; Paul Gilkison, "What Influences the Buying Decisions of Teen-Agers?" *Journal of Retailing*, Fall, 1965, p. 33; "Young, Single Spenders

Pour It on the Market," *Business Week*, January 1, 1966, pp. 62–63; William D. Wells and George Gubar, "The Life Cycle Concept in Marketing Research," *Journal of Marketing Research*, November, 1966, pp. 355–64; and William H. Reynolds and James H. Myers, "Marketing and the American Family," *MSU Business Topics*, Spring, 1966, pp. 57–66.

[19] "When Offspring Fly the Coop," *Business Week*, July 11, 1964, pp. 52–62.

| Old folks are a new market | Finally, the "senior citizen" market is one that should not be neglected. The number of people over 65 is increasing rapidly because of modern medicine, improved sanitary conditions, and better nutrition. This group now constitutes 10 percent of the population. |

Although older people generally have reduced incomes, they represent a unique target market.[20] Many firms, in fact, are already catering to the senior citizen market. Special food products and diet supplements have been developed, and there are even housing developments designed especially to appeal to older persons.[21]

| More education means less for food and clothing | Education and occupation appear to have a bearing on consumption patterns, too. The NICB study provides data on both of these dimensions, but they are not presented here due to space limitations. Several observations are in order, however. |

If the household head is a college graduate, we find that he spends proportionately less on food and clothing than others. He spends more on household and automobile expenses. This study does not attempt to discover why, but when drawing market grids, these facts should be considered.

Since educational levels are rising, differences due to education will probably become increasingly important. More students are completing high school and college. In 1950, barely a third of the adult population had completed high school. By 1970, more than half will have had a high school education, and many will have had some exposure to college.

| Are savers spenders? | One factor logically related to consumers' ability and willingness to spend money is their asset position. It is reasonable to assume that if a consumer has a substantial bank account or a nest egg of savings bonds, he will be more willing to spend his current income and even go into debt. This concept has interested the Federal Reserve System, which has some control over credit policies, and it collects data on the subject. |

Table 6–7 indicates the kind of data available and shows that the majority of consumers have less than $1,000 in liquid assets. Companies planning to sell expensive products, homes for example, which would have to draw on savings should bear this in mind.[22]

| Nationality, race, and purchasing | America may be called the "melting pot," but there are still relatively distinct racial and nationality groups that require special consideration when the marketing man is dimensioning a market grid. This is obvious for some products, but there are other differences that may be ignored by the superficial observer. |

[20] "The Old in the Country of the Young," *Time*, August 3, 1970, pp. 49–54; John A. Reinecke, "The 'Older' Market – Fact or Fiction?" *Journal of Marketing*, January, 1964, pp. 60–64; and "The Family," *Time*, August 3, 1962, pp. 46–50.

[21] "Retirement City – Haven or Ghetto?" *Business Week*, April 11, 1964, pp. 128–30; and "How the Old Age Market Looks," *Business Week*, February 13, 1960, pp. 72–78.

[22] See also, a basic study: Robert J. Lampman, *The Share of Top Wealth-Holders in National Wealth* (Princeton, N.J.: Princeton University Press, 1962).

Table 6-7 Family units — percent distribution by liquid asset holdings, 1968

Asset size-class	1968
All family units	100
Own no assets	19
Own assets	81
$1 to $199	15
$200 to $499	12
$500 to $1,999	24
$2,000 to $4,999	13
$5,000 to $9,999	8
$10,000 and over	9
Median holdings	$660

Source: The University of Michigan, Survey Research Center; *Survey of Consumer Finances.*

In recent years, interest has been focused on differences in consumption patterns between blacks and whites, especially as the black consumer has become wealthier. Extensive analysis of available data has led one analyst to the following major conclusions:

1. Total consumption expenditures of Negroes are less than for comparable-income whites, that is, Negroes save more out of a given income than do whites with the same income.
2. Negro consumers spend more for clothing and nonautomobile transportation, and less for food, housing, medical care, and automobile transportation than do whites with comparable incomes.
3. Comparing Negroes and whites, there is no consistent difference in expenditures for either recreation and leisure or home furnishing and equipment at comparable income levels.

Differences of geography as well as race may have to be used together in a market grid, since the findings depend somewhat on when and where the differences were studied.[23] Several other observations are important here. The median age of U.S. Negroes is considerably lower than that of whites. This means that many more are in an earlier stage of the life cycle and therefore are a better market for certain goods, especially durable goods. Some Negroes seem to be striving for what they believe is the white middle-income standard in material goods; other Negroes have abandoned this goal in favor of identification with their own set of values. In either case, it probably would be desirable to treat this as an important dimension in market grid analy-

[23] Marcus Alexis, "Some Negro-White Differences in Consumption," *American Journal of Economics and Sociology,* January, 1962, pp. 11–28.

sis. Perhaps separate strategies should be developed for these markets, requiring only changes in place and promotion.[24]

When the wife earns, the family spends

A relatively new phenomenon in spending patterns that deserves attention is the growing number of married women who hold jobs. In 1967, about 17.5 million wives were on the nation's payrolls — more than double the number when employment of wives was at a high level during World War II.

In families where the wife works, about 40 percent of all the family spending power is derived from her income. Half of all U.S. families in the $10,000-to-$15,000 income bracket have achieved this income because the wife is working.

A study by the U.S. Department of Agriculture showed that while a wife's employment outside the home seems to have little effect on the nutritive value of her family's food, working wives do *spend more* for food and do choose more expensive types of food.

Families with working wives also spend more on clothing, alcohol and tobacco, housefurnishings and equipment, and automobiles.

In short, when a wife works, it has a very distinct effect on the spending habits of the family. This fact must be considered when developing market grids for certain types of products.[25]

Consumer behavior is multidimensional

So far in this chapter, we have tried to show that consumer expenditure patterns are closely related to various demographic and socioeconomic characteristics. Many specialized studies have shown such relationships. These analyses probably should be improved and made more precise, because it is obvious that consumers are multidimensional while the data we have been discussing is concerned primarily with one dimension at a time, for example, population *or* income *or* race.

Various socioeconomic characteristics can be very useful in evaluating the potential in market grid boxes. Population and income data, especially, are pertinent because there must be people in the box, and they must have income to be considered a market.

When several characteristics are evaluated together, we can get a much clearer picture of the individual's, or household's, life style and

[24] Raymond O. Oladipupo, *How Distinct Is the Negro Market?* (New York: Ogilvy & Mather, Inc., 1970); D. Parke Gibson, *The $30 Billion Negro* (New York: Macmillan Co., 1969): John B. Petrof, "Newspaper Advertising and the Negro Market," *Journal of Retailing*, Spring, 1970, pp. 20–32; "Why the Negro Market Counts," *Business Week*, September 2, 1967, pp. 64–77; and Raymond A. Bauer, "Negro Consumer Behavior," in J. Newman (ed.), *On Knowing the Consumer* (New York: John Wiley & Sons, Inc., 1966), pp. 161–66 and pp. 13–14.

[25] "More Moms on Payroll," *Business Week*, December 31, 1966, p. 59; *U.S. Department of Agriculture Food and Home Notes*, July 13, 1960; and Margaret S. Carroll, "The Working Wife and Her Family's Economic Position," *Monthly Labor Review*, April, 1962, pp. 366–74.

what he can afford, thus giving us a better insight into what he is able and likely to do in the future. Some marketing research may be necessary to obtain specifics, but experienced researchers and executives come to have a feel for how various kinds of consumers live and spend their money—thereby guiding their research efforts and decisions.

But do we know why anybody buys anything?

But now we must look at the other side of the story. Extensive studies using demographic and socioeconomic data have not been very successful in explaining why people buy *specific* products and *specific* brands. In fact, research results in this area have been very poor. These poor results can partly be explained by rising consumer incomes and the increasing importance of discretionary spending. It could even be argued that consumers have almost complete latitude in their choices and that almost all purchases are for nonnecessities, including most of our foods. One economist showed, for example, that in 1950 a person could have a nutritionally adequate diet for about $72 a year. To be sure, this was not a very attractive diet, as it consisted solely of wheat flour, evaporated milk, cabbage, spinach, and dried navy beans. However, the point is that purchasing a variety of foods, strictly speaking, may reflect emotional more than physiological needs. And the same probably applies to specific items of clothing, shelter, and many other things.

The absence of a guaranteed "captive demand" for necessities which are directly related to socioeconomic characteristics puts a heavy burden on marketing managers. They're constantly trying to sell specific products or services, in competition with many others, to consumers whose preferences may be continually shifting.

The factors discussed in this chapter can be very helpful in many market situations, but there are additional factors (sometimes hard to specify) which affect what an individual person or family will buy. Some of these dimensions are discussed in Chapter 8—and fortunately, they can be incorporated into the market gridding process.[26]

Conclusion

In our study of the American consumer, we have moved from the general to the particular. We first studied population data, dispelling various misconceptions about how our more than 200 million people are spread over the United States. In so doing, it became apparent

---

[26] For further discussion on the inadequacies of using socioeconomic characteristics only, see Ronald E. Frank, "Market Segmentation Research: Findings and Implications," in Frank M. Bass, *et al.*, *Applications of the Sciences in Marketing Management* (New York: John Wiley & Sons, Inc., 1968), pp. 38–68; James A. Carman, *Studies in the Demand for Consumer Household Equipment* (Berkeley, Calif.: Institute of Business and Eco-nomic Research, University of California, 1965); Newman, *op. cit.*, pp. 15–16 and 173–86; Steven C. Brandt, "Dissecting the Segmentation Syndrome," *Journal of Marketing*, October, 1966, pp. 22–27; and M. Alexis, L. Simon, and K. Smith, "Some Determinants of Food Buying Behavior," in M. Alexis *et al.*, *Empirical Foundations of Marketing: Research Findings in the Behavioral and Applied Sciences* (Skokie, Ill.: Rand McNally & Co., 1969).

that the potential of a given market cannot be determined by numbers alone. Income, stage in life cycle, geographic location, occupation, education, and other factors are important, too.

We also noted the growth of interurbia, such as the megalopolis of the Atlantic Seaboard. These urban-surburban systems suggest the shape of future growth in this country. It is also apparent that one of the outstanding characteristics of the American is his mobility. For this reason, even relatively new data is not foolproof. The wealth of available data can only aid judgment, not replace it.

Engel's so-called "laws" are useful generalizations about consumption patterns. They help predict individual and family buying behavior. But the American consumer is different from Engel's workingman in a very important respect, namely, he is the most affluent in the world, and this affluence affects his purchasing behavior. Beyond the necessities of life, he is able to buy a wide variety of products. In fact, it could be argued that little that he buys is an absolute necessity.

This is extremely important to a marketing manager because it means he must continually offer his target customers the top choice among many choices open to them. It also means that consumers can delay purchases for months or years, or shift them completely to more satisfying alternatives.

We saw that studying past consumer expenditure patterns can be very useful for estimating the market potential within market grids. We also saw that continual study of market behavior is necessary, and that, ultimately, management judgment must be applied to interpret trends and evaluate data. Judgment is especially important because, in spite of all the population, income, and other data related to past expenditures which is available, we still are not always able to predict what consumers are going to do.

In fact, the kind of data we studied in this chapter often does not fully explain actual customer behavior toward specific products. A fuller understanding of customer behavior may require more sophisticated and different kinds of analysis. More will be said on this in Chapter 8, where we discuss the decision-making behavior of individual consumers and of household groups. A knowledge of the American consumer's psychological and sociological makeup will help marketing men satisfy target customers more effectively and more often.

QUESTIONS AND PROBLEMS

1 Some socioeconomic characteristics are more important than others in determining market potential. For each of the following characteristics, identify two products for which this characteristic is *most* important: (a) size of geographic area, (b) population, (c) income, (d) stage of life cycle.

2 If a large new atomic research installation were being built in a formerly small and sleepy town, how could the local retailers use Engel's laws in planning for the influx of newcomers, first of construction crews and then scientists?

3 Name three specific examples (specific products or brands – not just product categories) illustrating how demand will differ by geographic location *and* market location, that is, with respect to size and location inside or outside a metropolitan market.

4 Explain how the continuing mobility of consumers as well as the development of "interurbia" areas should affect marketing strategy planning in the future. Be sure to consider the impact on the four P's.

5 Explain how the redistribution of income has affected marketing planning thus far and its likely impact in the future.

6 Explain why the concept of the Standard Metropolitan Statistical Areas was developed. Would it be the most useful breakdown for retailers?

7 With the growing homogeneity of the consumer market, does this mean that the market grid idea is less useful? Do you feel that all consumers of about equal income will probably spend their incomes similarly and demand similar products?

8 Specify which kinds of consumers would be most likely to buy a new type of haircomb selling for $1. Then estimate the number of potential customers. The factors which might be relevant in specifying the potential market are income, sex, stage in life cycle, and age. Use all of these factors which are relevant. State any assumptions you make and apply the data in the text.

9 If a recent college graduate is now earning between $10,000 and $15,000 a year before taxes, has some children under six, and is living in the western part of the United States in a surburban (urban fringe) area, how much would you expect him to be spending annually on (*a*) clothing and accessories, (*b*) transportation, and (*c*) housing and household operations? (Use the data in Tables 6–3, 6–4, 6–5, and 6–6 when developing your answer.)

...we may not have "one world" politically as yet, but business is rapidly moving in that direction – the old cliché, "trade follows the flag," might have to be revised to "the flag follows trade." ...the great variations in stages of economic development, income, population, literacy...mean that foreign markets must be treated as many separate target markets...Lumping foreign nations together [as] foreigners, or...assuming that they are just like U. S. customers is almost a guarantee of failure.

7

Consumers: international markets

Most Americans are proud of the United States' economic position in the world. This is understandable, for we are a rich country and enjoy a high standard of living. But this viewpoint may have given us myopia regarding the economic state of the rest of the world.

We hear our politicians, for example, speak of exporting our "free enterprise system" to aid the "less developed countries" of the world, and we know that our government spends billions of dollars annually on foreign aid programs. It is only natural that many Americans think of foreign countries as poor, with little market potential. While this may be true in some areas, such thinking ignores the fact that there are many opportunities in international markets. Some foreign consumers already have high standards of living, and markets in many countries are growing, some very rapidly.

Importance of world markets to the United States

As a nation grows, its trade grows

All countries trade to some extent, since we live in an interdependent world. But it may surprise Americans to know that the United States is the largest exporter and importer of goods in the world. Even the United Kingdom, which has built its growth on trade, exports, and imports, is below the United States.

Figure 7–1 shows that all types of nations – whether large or small, wealthy or poor – engage in trade. This figure shows the percentage of total world trade accounted for by the major trading nations of the world. It is easy to see that most of the largest traders are highly industrialized nations. Trade seems to expand, not contract, as a country grows and industrializes.

But while the United States is the biggest trading nation in the world, foreign trade does not dominate our economy. On a per capita basis, it is less important to us than it is to many other nations. This seeming paradox is explained by the larger size of our gross national product. Our foreign trade makes up a relatively smaller part of our GNP – less than 10 percent – but the smaller part is nevertheless greater in total dollars than in other major trading countries.

Favorable balance of trade supports government programs, but . . .

This large volume of trade has been a distinct asset to America's foreign policy. U.S. exports since World War II have consistently been greater than imports, leading to a favorable balance of trade. This surplus of exports over imports has been used primarily for foreign aid and the support of our troops stationed in foreign countries.

In recent years, however, our favorable balance of trade has been declining steadily as foreign competitors become more aggressive and also narrow the technological gap. Some foreign industries, (the Japanese steel industry, for example) have developed more advanced techniques than U.S. industry and also pay lower wage rates. This puts them in an excellent position to compete not only in world markets but in U.S. markets. Also, partly in self-defense, some U.S. manufacturers have set up production operations in other countries to compete in world markets *and* to supply domestic needs.

In the long run, these overseas developments could cause much difficulty for U.S. government planners and producers. We may even see a return to protectionism in the United States. Not only business but also labor unions may clamor for higher tariffs and quotas to restrict trade. A United Auto Workers' official, for example, recently criticized the practice of importing more and more small cars into the United States. And textile and shoe manufacturers have been pressing for additional controls over imports from Japan and Italy.[1]

[1] "Why the U.S. Must Sell More Overseas," *Business Week,* January 4, 1969, pp. 40–54; and William M. Roth, "Our Future Trade Policy," *Business Horizons,* February, 1968, pp. 81–85.

Figure 7-1 Map of the world showing each country's proportion of total foreign trade

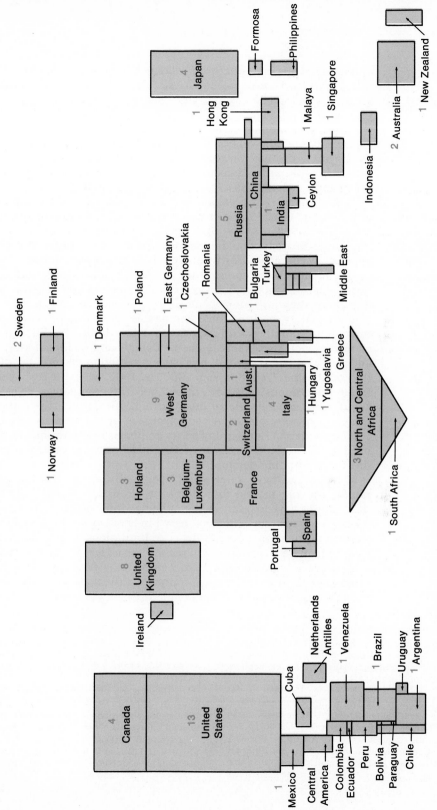

Source: *Clipper Cargo Horizons*, April, 1966. Drawn originally by Ing. G. Palacios Hardy, then rounded to nearest whole number by the author.

Multi-national marketing makes sense to some

Some American manufacturers, seeing the growing opportunities in world markets, have developed substantial stakes overseas. Companies such as Eastman Kodak, Warner-Lambert, Pfizer, Anaconda, Goodyear, Ford, IBM, IT&T, Corn Products, 3M, Standard Oil (N.J.), Mobil Oil, Gulf Oil, National Cash Register, Singer, Colgate-Palmolive, H.J. Heinz, Gillette, and others get over 30 percent of their total sales or profits abroad. Some companies, as already noted, now think of themselves as multinational operations and do not see producing and selling in foreign countries as a strange, separate entity.

U.S. companies are expanding worldwide, in part for profit, but also because of the force of competition and the problems of acting solely as exporters. At one time, foreign sales were handled by exporting domestic production, but exporting was a stepchild with little real support, encouraged only when domestic business was poor. Foreign agents or licensees representing the U.S. manufacturer were something of a nuisance and drain on the domestic plant—asking for information, drawings, new catalogs, special service, and so on.

Increasingly, multinational companies are finding it economically sensible to actually set up factories and distribution facilities in other countries, not just export to them. Capital and technical know-how and parts may be exported, but basic production often is handled in the country involved. Between 1960 and 1966, when the rush to set up foreign operations tailed off, over 2,400 U.S. companies invested in about 7,000 separate global business activities, primarily in the construction of new plants or the expansion of existing operations. In 1967, the rush to Europe slowed, as emphasis began to shift to oil and mining investments in Asia, Africa, and Latin America. But investment is continuing generally.[2]

We may not have "one world" politically as yet, but business is rapidly moving in that direction—the old cliché, "trade follows the flag," might have to be revised to "the flag follows trade." By the same token, we may have to develop new kinds of corporations and laws to govern multinational operations. The limitations of national boundaries in business and politics will make less and less sense in the future.[3]

A move toward international control may be accelerated by the rapid growth of multinational companies themselves. A well-known French businessman and politician, Jean Jacques Servan-Schreiber,

[2]"The Rush to Europe Slows to a Crawl," *Business Week*, August 3, 1968, pp. 82–84; "The Rewarding Strategies of Multinationalism," *Fortune*, September 15, 1968, p. 105; "U.S. Companies Keep Up the Pace," *Business Week*, August 15, 1970, p. 24; "World Markets Are Still a Lure," *Business Week*, August 7, 1965, pp. 26–27; "U.S. Business in the New Europe," *Business Week*, May 7, 1966, pp. 94–120; "Big, Bigger, Biggest—American Business Goes Global," *New Republic*, April 30, 1966, pp. 14–18; "How to Profit in Foreign Markets," *Printers' Ink*, June 5, 1964, p. 19 ff.; "Where the Cash Grows in Africa," *Business Week*, June 19, 1965, pp. 134–38; and "How Big Are Foreign Opportunities for Smaller U.S. Firms?" *Printers' Ink*, July 27, 1962, pp. 44–45.

[3]"The Helplessness of the Nation-State," *Business Week*, June 13, 1970; *Business Week*, August 8, 1970, p. 48; "International Incorporation Urged by Kendall," *Business Week*, March 22, 1969, p. 80; "Management Outlook," *Business Week*, February 17, 1968, p. 112; and C. P. Kindleberger, *American Business Abroad* (New Haven, Conn.: Yale University Press, 1969), chap vi.

predicts that within 15 years American industry in Europe will become the third most dominant power bloc – after the United States and the Soviet Union. Already, sales of U.S. subsidiaries located abroad are roughly six times U.S. exports, indicating not only growth in foreign sales but also a different kind of growth. Such economic power, of course, will certainly encourage countermovements. But some of these multinational operations may be difficult for nationalistic businessmen to stop, because they are no longer just importing. They live locally, employ local residents, build plants, and may even be jointly owned with local businessmen and politicians.[4]

The reason behind the development of multinational companies lies primarily in the economics of the situation. There are market opportunities all over the world, while production advantages exist only in certain places. But, blend the whole operation together into one total system of action, and you may have an effective multinational operation.

The complete blending of domestic and worldwide operations is illustrated by Bell & Howell. This firm:

1. Imports and sells a full line of cameras from Japan.
2. Manufactures and sells a line of cameras in Japan.
3. Purchases low-cost components from Japan for assembly in the United States.
4. Exports low-cost U.S. cameras to any foreign market.[5]

Real growth opportunities exist for these global enterprises. One important reason is that the marketing concept has *not* spread as rapidly to the rest of the world, which gives American businessmen a head start. Going after the world market puts an even greater burden on the marketing manager, but the opportunities are too great to ignore.

Will multi-national marketing make sense to host countries?

Multinational companies may have economic advantages working for them, but the rising tide of nationalism which we observed in Chapter 3 could inhibit or even block this development. At the worst, revived nationalism might even undo the progress made by these globally oriented firms, not all of which are U.S. companies. Time will tell, however, it should be observed that these firms are powerful organizations which have learned to cope with typical national tariff barriers and quotas – treating them simply as uncontrollable factors. And they may be able to handle the new restrictions raised by nationalistic political forces with equal ease.[6]

---

[4] "U.S., Europe Businessmen Adapting to Global Market Concept: de Windt," *Marketing Insights*, February 9, 1970, pp. 1–5.

[5] "How Big Are Foreign Opportunities for Smaller U.S. Firms?" *Printers' Ink*, July 27, 1962, pp. 44–45; See also, David S. R. Leighton, "The Internationalization of American Business – The Third Industrial Revolution," *Journal of Marketing*, July, 1970, pp. 3–6; and Robert D. Buzzell, "Can You Standardize Multinational Marketing?" *Harvard Business Review*, November–December, 1968, pp. 102–13.

[6] For further discussion on the development of world corporations, see *Saturday Review*, November 22, 1969, pp. 31–46.

Stages of economic development help define markets

International markets are so varied that it is impossible to generalize easily. Some foreign markets are much more advanced and/or growing more rapidly than others. Some countries or regions are at different stages of economic development, which means that their demands and even their marketing systems will vary. To get some perspective on the many possible differences in potential market grid boxes, we will look at six stages of economic development.

Stage 1 — agricultural self-supporting phase

In this phase, most people exist as subsistence farmers. There may be a simple marketing system — perhaps occasional weekly markets — but most of the people are not even in a money economy. Some parts of Africa and territories such as New Guinea are in this stage. In a practical marketing sense, these people do not represent a market, since they have no money to purchase goods.

Stage 2 — preindustrial or commercial phase

Some countries in Sub-Sahara Africa and the Middle East are in this second stage. During this phase of economic development, we see more market-oriented activity. Raw materials such as oil, tin, and copper are extracted and exported. Agricultural and forest crops such as sugar, rubber, and timber are grown and harvested for the market and exported. Often this is done with the aid of foreign technical skills and capital. A commercial economy may develop along with, but unrelated to, the subsistence economy. These activities may require the beginnings of a transportation system to link the extracting or growing areas to shipping points. A money economy functions at this stage.

In this phase, there are demands for imports of industrial machinery and equipment, and huge construction projects may require many specialized supplies. Buying for these needs may be handled by purchasing agents and engineers in industrial countries. There is also the need for imports, including luxury goods, to meet the requirements and living standards of technical and supervisory personnel; these may be handled by company stores rather than local retailers.

The relatively few large landowners and those who benefit by this commercial activity may develop expensive tastes. The few natives employed by these larger firms and the small businessmen who serve them may develop into a small, middle-income class. But the majority of the population is still in the first stage, for practical purposes not in the market. This total market may be so small that local importers can easily handle the demand, with little incentive for local manufacturers to attempt to supply it.

Stage 3 — primary manufacturing phase

In the third stage, there is some processing of metal ores or the agricultural products that formerly were shipped out of the country in raw form. Sugar and rubber, for example, are both produced and processed in Indonesia, and the same is true for sisal in Tanganyika and oil on the Persian Gulf. And multinational companies may set up factories to take advantage of low-cost labor, exporting most of the output but nevertheless stimulating local development. More local labor becomes involved at this stage, and a domestic market develops. Even small businesses are starting to handle some of the processing or to service larger firms.

Even though the local market expands in this third stage, a large segment of the population is still at the subsistence level and almost entirely outside the money economy. There may still be a large foreign population of professionals and technicians essential to the developing agricultural-industrial complex. The demands of this group and of the growing number of wealthy natives are still quite different from the needs of the lower class and the growing middle class. A domestic market among the local citizenry begins to develop, but local manufacturers still may have difficulty finding enough demand to justify operation.

Stage 4 — nondurable and semidurable consumer goods manufacturing phase

At this stage, small local manufacturing begins, especially in those lines requiring low capital investment relative to output. Often these industries are an outgrowth of small firms that developed to supply the primary manufacturers dominating the last phase. For example, plants making sulfuric acid and explosives for extracting mineral resources might expand into soap manufacturing. And recently, multinational firms have accelerated development of countries at this stage with infusions of capital where the opportunities were right.

Paint, drug, food and beverage, and textile industries develop in this phase. The textile industry is usually one of the first to develop. Clothing is a necessity, and the articles imported for the upper-income and foreign markets are too expensive for the majority of potential customers now entering the money economy. This early emphasis on the textile industry in developing nations is one reason the world textile market is so vigorously competitive.

Some of the small manufacturers become established members of the middle or even upper-income class, and help to expand the demand for imported goods. But as this market grows, local entrepreneurs begin to see sufficient volume to operate profitably. The heavy dependence on imports for nondurable and semidurable goods then declines, though consumer durables and capital goods are still imported.

Stage 5 — capital goods and consumer durable goods manufacturing phase

In this phase, the production of capital goods and consumer durable goods begins. These classes of goods include automobiles, refrigerators, and machinery for local industries. Such manufacturing in turn creates other demands — raw materials for the local factories, and food and fibers for clothing for the rural population entering the industrial labor force.

Full-fledged industrialization has begun. But the economy is still heavily dependent upon exports of raw materials, either wholly unprocessed or slightly processed.

It still may be necessary to import specialized heavy machinery and equipment to build the capital facilities needed at this stage. Imports of consumer durable goods may still compete with local products.

The foreign community and the status-conscious wealthy may prefer imports, and this demand can continue to provide an attractive market.

Stage 6 — exporting of manufactured products phase

Countries that have not progressed beyond the fifth phase are primarily engaged in exporting raw materials and in importing manufactured goods and equipment to build their industrial base. In the sixth stage, export of manufactured goods becomes dominant. The country may specialize in certain types of manufactured goods, such as iron and steel, watches, cameras, electronic equipment, and processed food. Large countries (Germany or Japan are examples) may have many specialities.

Opportunities for importing and exporting at this stage are great, since the countries have grown more affluent and have needs (and the purchasing power) for a great variety of products. In fact, countries in this stage often carry on a great deal of trade with each other, each trading those goods in which they have production advantages. In this phase, almost all consumers are in the money economy, and there may be a large middle-income class. The United States and many Western European countries are at this last stage today.[7]

What these stages mean

A good starting point for evaluating market potentials in a country is to estimate its present phase of economic development and whether and how fast it is moving to another stage. Actually, the speed of movement, if any, may be the most critical factor in whether market opportunities are there or are likely to open. But just identifying the country's present stage can be very useful in achieving perspective, to help one decide what to look at and whether there are likely prospects for what the firm can offer.

Suggest marketing possibilities

Manufacturers of automobiles, expensive cameras, or other consumer durable goods, for example, should not plan to set up a mass distribution system in a country that is in the preindustrial (stage 2) or even primary manufacturing (stage 3) phase. The market would be too limited.

Among the foreign population and the wealthy landowners, nevertheless, there may be a small but very attractive market for luxury models. A simple distribution system with one or a few distributors is usually quite adequate. The market for U.S. "necessities," however — items such as canned foods or drug products — may not yet be large. Large-scale selling of these consumer items requires a large base of

---

[7] This discussion is based on William Copulsky's, "Forecasting Sales in Underdeveloped Countries," *Journal of Marketing*, July, 1959, pp. 36–37; and *Aspects of Economic Development* (Freedom from Hunger Campaign Study No. 8 [United Nations, 1962]), pp. 4–7. Another set of stages is interesting although less marketing-oriented. See W. W. Rostow, *The Stages of Economic Growth — A Non-Communist Manifesto* (New York: Cambridge University Press, 1960).

cash or credit customers, and as yet too few are part of the money economy.

On the other hand, a country in the nondurable-goods manufacturing phase has more potential, especially for durable-goods producers. Incomes and the number of potential customers are growing, yet there is no domestic competition.

Opportunities might still be good for durable-goods imports in the fifth phase, while domestic producers are attempting to get started. But more likely, the local government would raise some restrictions to aid local industry. Then the foreign producer might have to start licensing local producers or building a local plant.

Pursuing that enticing inverted pyramid

Countries in the final phase often represent the biggest and most profitable markets. While there is obviously greater competition, there are many more customers with higher incomes. We have already seen how income distribution shifted in the United States from a pyramid to a more equal distribution, with a large middle-income mass market. This kind of development, which can be expected during the latter phases, makes mass marketing increasingly promising.

As incomes rise, we begin to see expenditure patterns somewhat similar to our own.[8] This can be seen developing in Western Europe, and it should not be surprising, since the original work on Engel's laws was done in Europe. The mass market is growing fast in increasingly affluent Japan, too.

Overview of world market dimensions

Markets, in the simplest of terms, are people with money and a willingness to spend. The market grid concept is even more valuable in world markets than in the American economy. This is because demands vary according to a country's stage of development and there is a wider range of different situations in the world economy.

While an entire chapter has been devoted to the American consumer, it is clearly impossible to cover all the characteristics of all the world markets in this chapter. On the other hand, we cannot ignore either the potential or the problems in world markets, and we would be foolish to be content with the stereotypes and half-truths that circulate about "foreigners." Therefore, we will sketch some of the dimensions of world markets and suggest some of the problems of working in this larger business environment.

[8] "How the British React to Affluence," *Business Week*, January 19, 1963, p. 44; "Sweden Goes All Out for the Leisure Boom," *Business Week*, September 7, 1963, pp. 32–33; "Three Europes, One Boom," *Business Week*, September 10, 1966, pp. 116–38; "Young Italy Spends Big," *Business Week*, May 13, 1967, p. 184; "Vive Les Teen-Agers!" *Business Week*, November 23, 1963, p. 49; and "Consumer's Day Dawns in Land of Rising Sun," *Business Week*, May 21, 1964, pp. 129–36.

Data, yes, but not always the best

Unfortunately, data sources for some areas abroad are not as numerous nor is information as accurate or as timely as that available for the United States. Foreign data may be unsatisfactory because the countries where it is compiled do not have the resources or facilities for frequent compilation of information. Brazil, for instance, started to take a census in 1950 and ran out of funds before the work was completed.

The *Statistical Abstract* and the U.S. Department of Commerce Bureau of International Commerce would be a good place to start locating current data. In its publication, *International Commerce,* the Department of Commerce issues a semiannual checklist of material it feels will be helpful to businessmen interested in the world market. The *Statistical Year Book* of the Statistical Office of the United Nations is also a good source of basic data.

The number of people in our world is staggering

Although you may be overwhelmed by the crowds of people you have to compete with in our urban areas, the over 200 million population of the United States is less than 5 percent of the world's population of over 4 billion.

Sheer numbers are important

Instead of a tedious breakdown of population statistics, let's look at a map showing area in proportion to population. Figure 7–2 reduces the United States to relative insignificance because of our small population in relation to land area. The same is true of Latin America and Africa. In contrast, Western Europe is considerably larger and Far Eastern countries are even bigger.

But people are not spread out evenly

There is a worldwide movement off the farm and into industrialized and urbanized areas. Shifts in population, combined with already dense populations, have led to extreme crowding in some parts of the world.

Figure 7–3 shows a map of the world emphasizing density of population. The darkest shading indicates areas with more than 250 persons per square mile.

The developing interurbias in the United States show up clearly as densely populated areas. Similar areas are found in Western Europe, along the Nile River valley in Egypt, and in many parts of Asia. In contrast, many parts of the world, like our western plains and mountain states, are sparsely populated.

Your own knowledge of the United States should help you avoid misreading a population density map. There are cities throughout the world, just as in the sparsely populated western United States, that are important markets even though surrounding areas have few people. These cities can be extremely important as markets if they serve as trading centers for a large region. Still, for locating large numbers of people, population density maps are invaluable.

Population densities are likely to increase in the foreseeable future. Birthrates in most parts of the world are high (higher in Africa, Latin America, Asia, and Oceania than in the United States), and death rates are declining as modern medicine is more widely accepted. Generally,

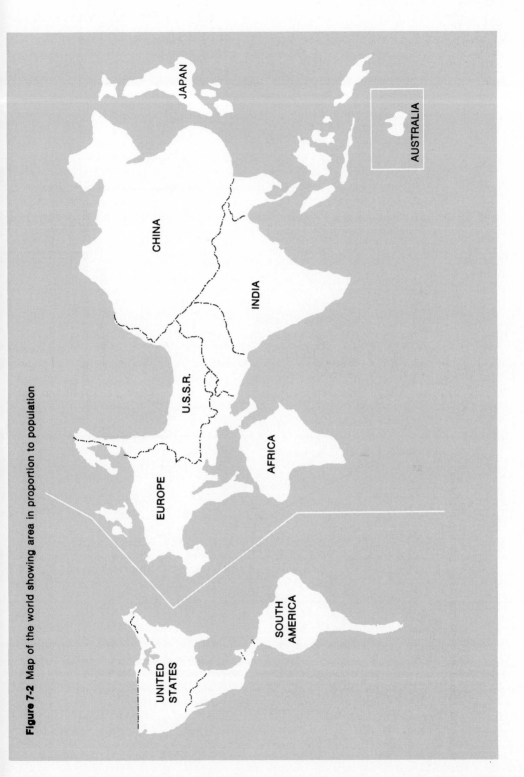

Figure 7-2 Map of the world showing area in proportion to population

175

Figure 7-3 Map of the world emphasizing density of population

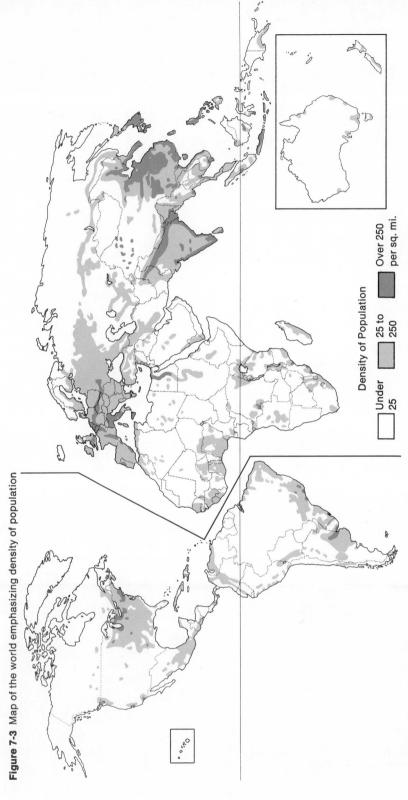

Density of Population

Under 25

25 to 250

Over 250 per sq. mi.

Adapted from *Atlas of Economic Development* by Norton Ginsburg by permission of the University of Chicago Press. © 1961 by The University of Chicago.

population growth is anticipated in most countries, but the big questions are, *How rapidly?*, and *Will output increase faster than population?* This has great relevance for marketing men because it determines how rapidly some economies evolve to higher stages of development and the kinds of goods that consumers have the income to buy.

You
must sell
where the
income is

Profitable markets require income as well as people. The best available measure of income in most countries is gross national product. Unfortunately, this may understate consumer well-being in many countries because the methods commonly used for calculating GNP may not be directly comparable for widely different cultures and economies. For instance, do-it-yourself activities, household services, and the growing of produce or meat by family members for their own consumption are not normally calculated as part of GNP. Since the activities of self-sufficient family units are not included, GNP can greatly underestimate economic well-being in less developed countries. The expenditures on fuel, heavier clothing, and more substantial housing needed in temperate climates add to GNP, yet no offsetting adjustment is made in tropical countries where such expenditures are not necessary and where the income available for other spending, therefore, is accordingly higher. Such expenditures may absorb 10 to 15 percent of consumer income in temperate climates.[9]

Gross national product, nevertheless, is useful and sometimes the only available measure of market potential in many countries. Table 7–1 shows the population and total GNP of major regions of the world, except for Soviet bloc countries and mainland China. It is quite clear

Table 7–1 Population and gross national product of major geographical regions of the world* (in 1965 prices)

Region	Population (millions)	Percent	GNP ($ millions)	Percent
North America	217.2	10	732,568	45
Latin America	235.6	11	90,926	6
Western Europe	354.4	16	508,437	32
Near East	88.5	4	23,304	1
South Asia	642.1	29	64,059	4
Far East	373.7	17	120,257	7
Oceania	17.5	1	28,722	2
Africa	264.3	12	40,637	3
	2,193.3	100	1,608,910	100

*Except Soviet bloc countries and mainland China.
Source: Reprinted with permission from the June 26, 1967, issue of *Advertising Age*. Copyright 1967 by Advertising Publications, Inc.

[9]Carl F. Shoup, *Principles of National Income Analysis* (New York: Houghton Mifflin Co., 1947), p. 13.

that the more developed industrial regions have the lion's share of the world's GNP. This is why so much trade takes place between these countries, and why they are viewed by many companies as the more important markets.

Income per capita can be more revealing

Since individuals and families rather than whole countries are buyers, GNP per capita may be a more relevant statistic. This is a commonly available figure – but it can be misleading regarding market potential. When GNP per capita is used for comparison, we assume that the wealth of each country is distributed evenly among all consumers. However, this rarely is the case, as we noted earlier. In an under-developed economy, 75 percent of the population may be supported by agriculture but receive 25 percent or less of the income.[10] And there may be unequal distribution along class or racial lines. In South Africa, for example, the average family income in 1970 for whites was $5,830, $2,352 for Asians, $1,411 for mulattos, and $538 for blacks, according to a market research survey.[11]

Purchasing power is where you find it

Don't assume in every case that the urban market is the best market. In tropical Africa, it is estimated that the extremely large population in the rural villages spends more in *total* than the relatively few but more prosperous consumers in the urban centers. Equally important, these two quite different markets have different demands.[12] The urban consumers, for instance, are more interested in imported "luxuries." Obviously, the market grid concept is needed here.

Income is not distributed equally *within* cities, either. For instance, a 1954 survey in Beirut, Lebanon, showed that only 30 percent of the estimated 35,000 native families had incomes exceeding $1,500 (U.S.) a year, the amount considered necessary to maintain a minimum standard of living. Only 4 percent of these families had incomes exceeding $8,000 (U.S.).

We usually find numerous foreigners even further up the income scale in such cities. For example, there are an estimated 2,500 Americans living in Beirut.[13] An entirely different way of life may exist in such foreign communities. Sometimes these "compounds" are supplied through company stores or purchasing facilities, but in other cases, local marketing units develop to serve these customers. The point is that foreign incomes help raise GNP estimates in a given nation and may give a false picture of the buying power of the masses in that nation.

To prove some bench marks, the GNP per capita for a variety of countries is presented in Table 7–2. The range is wide, from $45 (U.S.) per capita per year in Rwanda to $4,303 in the United States.

[10] Donald G. Halper, "The Environment for Marketing in Peru," *Journal of Marketing*, July 1966, pp. 42–46.

[11] (Lansing, Mich.) *State Journal*, February 10, 1970, p. D–7.

[12] Edward Marcus, "Selling the Tropical African Market," *Journal of Marketing*, July, 1961, p. 27.

[13] Charles F. Stewart, "The Changing Middle East Market," *Journal of Marketing*, January, 1961, pp. 47–49.

Table 7–2 Gross national product per capita for major regions of world* and selected countries (in 1968 U.S. dollars) and population (in millions in 1968)

	GNP/capita for countries	GNP/capita for regions	Population
North America		$4,160	225.0
United States	$4,303		201.2
Canada	3,182		20.8
Latin America		439	256.1
Argentina	724		23.6
Brazil	322		88.2
Haiti	65		5.0
Mexico	557		47.3
Western Europe		1,708	363.8
United Kingdom	1,862		55.3
France	2,536		49.9
Italy	1,418		52.8
Portugal	529		9.5
Sweden	3,316		7.9
Turkey	346		33.5
Near East		317	93.1
Israel	1,472		2.7
Egypt	183		31.3
South Asia		92	691.9
India	84		527.1
Far East		473	401.6
Indonesia	96		113.7
Japan	1,404		101.1
Philippines	203		35.9
Oceania		1,917	18.6
Australia	2,457		12.1
Africa (exc. Egypt)		180	293.0
Algeria	260		12.9
Ethiopia	63		24.2
Ghana	238		8.4
Kenya	125		10.2
Nigeria	120		50.1
South Africa	646		21.7
Rwanda	45		3.4

*Except Soviet bloc countries and mainland China.

Source: Reprinted with permission from the July 27, 1970, issue of *Advertising Age*. Copyright 1970 by Advertising Publications, Inc.

In the upper-income levels are the United States and Canada, most of Western Europe, Australia, and New Zealand. Near the bottom are most of Asia and the Far East, the Near Eastern countries and a few Latin American countries, though most of Latin America is at a considerably higher level than most of Asia and Africa. And Japan, while coming up rapidly, is still not up to the Western European average.

A business, and a human, opportunity

These data indicate that a large share of the world's population lives in extreme poverty. Many of these countries are in the early phases of economic development, with large parts of their population engaged in agriculture and living only barely within the money economy. More than one half of the world's active population is in agriculture, and these occupations typically bring only a small monetary return.[14]

These people, however, have needs, and many who have been exposed to Western ways are now anxious to better themselves. But they may not be able to raise their living standards without outside help. This presents a challenge and an opportunity to the industrialized nations and their business firms. There may be many opportunities for investments in basic industries, as well as in the marketing and transportation facilities needed in a modern nation. As we noted in Chapter 1, marketing institutions can speed economic development by helping to expand markets and develop opportunities for local producers.

Some companies, including American firms, are attempting to do something constructive for the people of less developed countries. Corporations such as Pillsbury, Corn Products, Monsanto, and Coca-Cola have developed nutritious foods that can be sold cheaply, but profitably, in poorer countries. One firm sells a milk-based drink with 10 grams of protein in the Middle East and the Caribbean area. Such a beverage can make an important contribution to some persons' diets, as poor residents in less developed lands typically obtain only 8–12 grams of protein per day in their normal diet.[15]

Reading, writing, and marketing problems

The ability of a country's people to read and write has a direct bearing on the development of the economy and on the marketing strategy planning of a firm planning to do business there. One research study showed the link between the literacy of a country's population and its economic development.[16] Certainly, the degree of literacy affects the communication of information – which in a marketing context means promotion.

An extensive analysis of literacy data in 136 countries showed that only 56 percent of the world's population is literate.[17] But this number must be interpreted with care. Most of this information is based on census materials that were compiled by asking the question, "Can you read and write?" A simple yes, as a second-grader might answer, would not pinpoint a person's literacy level.

The low literacy rates in some countries indicate that a large-scale, basic, and expensive educational job is required in these nations. Generally, there is a band of countries with low literacy rates extend-

---

[14] Norton Ginsberg, *Atlas of Economic Development* (Chicago: University of Chicago Press, 1961).

[15] *Wall Street Journal*, August 8, 1968, p. 1.

[16] The Indians in Latin America do not speak Spanish, for example, and as a result are more or less blocked from entering the money economy. See Douglas F. Lamont, "A Theory of Marketing Development: Mexico" (unpublished Ph.D. dissertation, University of Alabama, 1964). See also, Harry A. Lipson and Douglas F. Lamont, "Marketing Policy Decisions Facing International Marketers in the Less-Developed Countries," *Journal of Marketing*, October, 1969, p. 24.

[17] Ginsberg, *op. cit.*

ing from Latin America through Africa and the Near East to eastern Asia. At the other extreme, higher rates of literacy are found in Australia, Canada, United States, Western Europe, the Soviet bloc of Europe, and some Latin American countries.

Forty percent of the 136 countries for which data was available have literacy rates above the mean of 56 percent. These countries include almost the same percentage of the world's population. On the negative side, however, 43 percent of the countries have literacy rates of 25 percent or less—and they account for 31 percent of the world's population.

Beat the drums, draw a picture

To compound marketing difficulties, some countries are multilingual. For example, the low literacy in India—only 15 percent of the population is literate—makes national advertising as we know it practically impossible. Further, there are 51 dialects in India, and no single language is spoken by more than 50 million persons.[18]

Some imaginative Indian merchants hire "drummers" who walk through the streets beating a drum to get attention and stop periodically to give the merchant's message in the local dialect. Clothing merchants use a drummer when they receive a new shipment of goods or offer special price concessions.

Low literacy sometimes causes difficulties with product labels and with instructions for which we normally use words. In highly illiterate Africa, some manufacturers have found that placing a baby's picture on food packages is unwise, since illiterate natives believe that the product is just that—a ground-up baby! Singer Sewing Machine Co., met this lack of literacy with an instruction book which used no words.[19]

Even in Latin America, which has generally higher literacy rates than Africa or Asia, a substantial proportion of the population cannot read and write. Promotional programs have to use symbols, colors, and other nonverbal means of communication if they wish to reach the mass market.

In this situation, two promotional campaigns can be used—one for the literate and one for the illiterate. But even where the literacy rate supposedly is high, considerable care must be exercised. Literacy often means only that a person can read and write at a simple level. So it may be nearly as effective to develop one campaign for the illiterate, assuming that the literate are really not *very* literate.

New economic groups tumbling barriers
Some countries have a long way to go to achieve the high living standards we enjoy. But it also is obvious that dynamic and energetic people frequently have overcome natural obstacles and achieved much higher living standards. The Japanese economic miracle certainly

[18] Ralph Westfall and Harper W. Boyd, Jr., "Marketing in India," *Journal of Marketing*, October, 1960, p. 15.

[19] Edward Marcus, "Selling the Tropical African Market," *Journal of Marketing*, July, 1961, p. 30.

attests to the possibility of rapid growth without benefit of generous supplies of fertile land or natural resources.[20]

We also see nations banding together in cooperative groups to speed their mutual development. They have dared to abandon old ideas and nationalistic prejudices in favor of cooperative efforts to reduce tariffs and other restrictive arrangements.

Tariffs — taxes on incoming goods — vary, depending on whether the country is attempting to raise revenue or restrict trade. Restrictive tariffs often block all movement, but even revenue-producing tariffs lead to red tape and discourage free movement of goods such as we know in the United States.

Let's look at some of these economic arrangements, since they should be considered in any market grid analysis of worldwide markets. Where older arrangements have been superseded by broader organizations, it is important to realize the depth and strength of this cooperative effort in appraising the present economic situation.

Benelux

*Bel*gium, The *Net*herlands, and *Lux*embourg created the Benelux Customs Union in 1944. The participating countries formed a common market among themselves, abolished internal tariffs, and confronted the world with a common tariff system.

GATT

Until 1948, most countries in the world made bilateral arrangements on trade. Benelux probably paved the way for a more progressive system. In any case, most of the nations of the free world accepted the idea of multilateral negotiations in 1948, when they signed the General *A*greement on *T*ariffs and *T*rade (GATT). They agreed to meet every two years and negotiate for reductions in tariffs. This organization is still going strong, and through six major negotiation conferences has been very effective in lowering tariffs and encouraging greater trade.

This multilateral bargaining is especially important because most major trading nations use the "most-favored-nation" clause, which says that a significant tariff reduction offered to one nation immediately will be offered to all participating nations.

OEEC and OECD

Benelux showed the way to breaking down trade barriers in Europe. In 1948, 17 European nations signed the Convention for European Economic Cooperation, forming the Organization for European Economic Cooperation (OEEC). This group of nations agreed to work toward a common solution of their economic problems while retaining full national sovereignty.

In 1960, OEEC evolved into OECD (Organization for Economic Cooperation and Development). This organization now includes not only 18 European countries as full members, but also Japan, Canada,

---

[20] "Can Japan Maintain the Pace?" *Business Week*, December 19, 1964, pp. 71–82; and "Exports Spur Japan's Economy," *Clipper Cargo Horizons*, August, 1966, pp. 2–6.

and the United States. This is a consultant agency only, however, and has no binding power over its members.[21]

Coal and Steel Community

The first supranational economic institution developed in 1952 when Belgium, France, Germany, Italy, Luxembourg, and The Netherlands signed the Coal and Steel Community Pact. In this agreement, some national sovereignty was surrendered to the higher body for the purpose of establishing a free market for iron ore, steel scrap, coal, and steel.

The goal of the Coal and Steel Community was development of a regional, rather than national, pattern for the production and distribution of these products. Since none of these countries was self-sufficient in steel production, the agreement made considerable sense. It showed that economic integration, even without political integration, was possible when it was logical and desired by the countries involved.

The six nations in the Coal and Steel Community remained part of the OEEC, but were willing to go further than most of the members of that organization — to the extent of sacrificing some national sovereignty.

European Economic Community

As a result of the smooth functioning of the Coal and Steel Community, these same six nations met in Rome in 1957 to sign a treaty establishing a European Economic Community (EEC) and a European Atomic Energy Community. They were, in effect, applying the concept behind the Coal and Steel Community to their entire economic life. These six nations formed the nucleus of the European Common Market.

By the middle 1960's, it was obvious that this large free-trade market was breaking down old nationalistic and restrictionist attitudes, expanding employment and investment, reducing prices, and generally helping to raise the standard of living in these communities. So impressive are the advances made by the Common Market nations that a number of other nations are applying for or thinking about membership in the Common Market.

European Free Trade Association

Not all the original members of the OEEC, however, were willing to go this far toward political union. They wanted to cooperate and did not want to be left out completely, but still wished to retain control of their individual economies. Seven of these nations (Great Britain, Norway, Sweden, Denmark, Portugal, Switzerland, and Austria) organized a partially integrated economic organization in 1959. It was named the European Free Trade Association (EFTA). This group is working toward a reduction, and gradual elimination of tariffs and other restrictive measures among its members, but it does not have

[21] W. A. Hoellige, "International Business and OECD," *National Trade Review*, February, 1965, pp. 9–12.

common external tariffs, as does the EEC. Prior arrangements not directly affecting all the member countries were permitted to continue. For example, the Imperial Preference System used in the British Commonwealth is still permissible within EFTA.[22]

Latin American Free Trade Association and Central American Common Market

Organizations akin to the European Common Market also have developed in Latin America, where two groups have been formed. The Latin American Free Trade Association (LAFTA) was formed in 1960 and included Argentina, Brazil, Chile, Mexico, Paraguay, Peru, Uruguay, and later, Colombia and Ecuador. The second group, also formed in 1960, is known as the Central American Common Market and consists of El Salvador, Guatemala, Honduras, Nicaragua, and later, Costa Rica.

These groups have not had the same success as the European groups, what with a few border wars and strong nationalistic protectionist tendencies.[23]

In spite of some setbacks in the development of common markets elsewhere, the success of the European Common Market bodes well for the concept. The European Common Market approach may not be a panacea for all economic ills, but it has proved itself in its early years, and it should continue to foster economic growth in the future. It probably will encourage other cooperative arrangements as well, and long-range marketing plans should include the possibility of such developments.

Market grid concept vital

The opportunities in international marketing are exciting ones, but their diversity presents a real challenge to marketing management. Obviously, the market grid concept should find special application when a firm is considering these markets.

The grid concept is especially important since there often are subtleties that we would not pick up unless we were aggressively seeking out all the possibilities. Our neighbor, Canada, affords an excellent example.

Canadians
are different

Some Americans think of Canadians only as our northern neighbors and as being pretty much like themselves. Actually, however, the pro-

---

[22] This discussion is based upon George Donat and Lawrence Dowd, "Formation of the European Economic Community," in Lawrence P. Dowd, *The European Economic Community* (Michigan Business Reports No. 36 [Ann Arbor: Bureau of Business Research, University of Michigan, 1961]), pp. 1–12. See also, "In Europe, Economic Unity Becomes a Fact," *Business Week*, December 31, 1966, pp. 52–54.

[23] "Latin Trade Bloc Hits Crisis," *Business Week*, July 20, 1968, pp. 76–78; "Crisis Splits Central American Common Market," *Business Week*, October 25, 1969, p. 100; "Latins Give Up on Trade Group," *Business Week*, November 23, 1968, p. 106; and Harry A. Lipson and Douglas F. Lamont, "Marketing Policy Decisions Facing International Marketers in the Less-Developed Countries," *Journal of Marketing*, October, 1969, pp. 24–31.

vince of Quebec, which has 30 percent of Canada's population, is a unique market. Quebec is predominantly French in heritage and language. The French-Canadians of Quebec feel they have suffered at the hands of the English-speaking majority of Canada. There is a movement for the secession of Quebec and its establishment as a separate nation. This attitude finds its expression in the marketplace, where French Canadians support local producers, buying their goods in preference to those of firms from other parts of Canada or Great Britain or the United States.

The differences between the other Canadian provinces and the United States are less extreme. Even so, recent elections have shown there is considerable anti-U.S. feeling in Canada, caused by U.S. domination of the Canadian market in some industries. These differences in outlook, sometimes verging on hostility, must be given full consideration in market planning.[24]

If the French Canadians are individualistic, so are the French, and this national characteristic must be considered in market planning for France. A sales slogan such as "Everybody's buying it" might offend individualistic sentiments and cause sales of a product to drop in France, even though similar slogans are successful in the United States.

What are you drinking? Tastes differ across national boundaries. French Burgundy wine intended for Belgian export must have a higher sugar content than the Burgundy intended for consumption in France. Burgundy shipped to Sweden must have still another sugar concentration to be sold successfully there.

Even close neighbors in Europe have very different drinking habits. The average Frenchman in 1951, a fairly typical year, drank 137 quarts of wine and only 19 quarts of beer. In contrast, his Belgian neighbor drank 115 quarts of beer and only 9 quarts of wine. Coca-Cola has made such inroads in Spain that the Spanish wine producers have felt compelled to launch a rather defensive national campaign imploring Spaniards to "drink 10 percent more wine."[25]

Milk-drinking habits also differ substantially. Scandinavians consider milk a daily staple, while Latins feel that milk is only for children. A former French premier, Mendes-France, was able to get his picture on the front page of every Paris newspaper simply by drinking a glass of milk in public. Milk consumption figures are revealing. The Italians use 117 pounds per capita a year, while the French use 195.5 pounds, Americans 352 pounds, Swedes 487, and Norwegians 516 pounds per capita.[26]

[24] Bruce Mallen, "How Different Is the French-Canadian Market?" *The Business Quarterly*, Autumn, 1967, pp. 59–66; "Canada: New Boom, New Outlook," *Printers' Ink*, June 26, 1964, pp. 25–39; and "Canada: Growth and Headaches for the U.S. Marketing Man," *Printers' Ink*, May 11, 1962, pp. 21–32.

[25] "Three Europes, One Boom," *Business Week*, September 10, 1966, pp. 116–38.

[26] *The European Common Market* (Paris: Publicis S.A., 1958), pp. 21–22.

<table>
<tr><td>

Up with
hemlines,
out of
the café
</td><td>

The youth market seems to be growing in importance throughout Europe and the world. Young people adopted the "Mod Look" in London, and French youth are being attracted to foreign beers. But the impact of youth goes far wider and deeper than a current style in clothing and drink. The youth of the world no longer placidly accept traditional values and behavior patterns.[27]

The impact of television is quite significant, because people can now learn more quickly about how others are living. Many European consumers, especially younger ones, are becoming much more interested in style and are willing to discard things much sooner than their parents and grandparents.[28] Even the classic French café seems to be losing out to the living room TV set and the kitchen refrigerator, in which the Parisian can keep his wine, ice, and mixers to serve his friends in newfound elegance.[29]
</td></tr>
<tr><td>

Who wears
the makeup
in France?
</td><td>

Such diversity demands marketing research to ascertain the habits and preferences of the many market grid boxes. Prejudices and stereotypes will not do. The African market, for example, is not interested only in beads, trinkets, and beer, as suggested in some movies. Africans may not buy as much as others per capita, but they are extremely sophisticated and fussy about what they do buy.

The purchase of a fez — only a brimless, red, conical cap to most Americans — justifies careful shopping by an African. He will distinguish among the many shapes and color shadings, as well as the thickness and type of material and the extent and composition of the embroidery. He may have a strong loyalty to a brand that has proved satisfactory.[30]

The need for continuing marketing research can be dramatized even more by the following results from a large-scale survey of European Common Market adults:
</td></tr>
</table>

> The average Frenchman uses almost twice as many cosmetics and beauty aids as his wife.
> The Germans and the French eat more spaghetti than the Italians.
> French and Italian housewives are not as interested in cooking as their counterparts in Luxembourg and Belgium.[31]

Conclusion

The international market is large and keeps growing in population and income. New economic groupings such as the European Common

---

[27] "Beer Hops Old Frontiers," *Business Week,* February 7, 1970, pp. 40–41; and Dwight E. Robinson, "U.S. Style of Life Invades Europe," *Harvard Business Review,* September–October, 1968, pp. 140–47.

[28] "Three Europes, One Boom," *Business Week,* September 10, 1966, pp. 116–38.

[29] *Time,* March 31, 1967, p. 33.

[30] Edward Marcus, "Selling the Tropical African Market," *Journal of Marketing,* July, 1961, p. 27.

[31] Robert L. Brown, "The Common Market: What Its New Consumer Is Like," *Printers' Ink,* May 31, 1963, pp. 23–25.

Market are being developed in the hope of expanding output and income even more. Many American companies are becoming aware of the enormous opportunities open to alert and aggressive businessmen.

The great variations in stages of economic development, income, population, literacy, and other factors, however, mean that foreign markets must be treated as many separate target markets – and each studied carefully. Lumping foreign nations together under the common and vague heading of "foreigners" or, at the other extreme, assuming that they are just like U.S. customers, is almost a guarantee of failure. So is treating them like common movie sterotypes. It is clear that marketing management, marketing research, and the market grid concept all can play a significant role in international marketing.[32]

Much of what we will discover about American marketing in subsequent chapters will also apply in the world market. Actually, not too many adjustments are necessary to sell to the world market – *except* to realize that the all-important customer may behave differently from what we would expect or hope. International customers may require different marketing mixes. And marketing research may be needed to avoid errors.

The major stumbling block to success in multinational markets is an unwillingness to learn about and adjust to different peoples and cultures. To those who are willing to make these adjustments, the returns can be great.

---

[32] "U.S. Companies Find That Foreign Ventures Don't Always Succeed," *The Wall Street Journal*, August 20, 1968, p. 1 f; "Tighten Your Overseas Marketing Plan," *Marketing Insights*, February 9, 1970, pp. 6–7; and "The Multinationals Ride a Rougher Road," *Business Week*, December 19, 1970, pp. 57–146.

QUESTIONS AND PROBLEMS

1 Discuss the long-run prospects for (*a*) multinational marketing by U.S. firms producing in the United States only, and (*b*) multinational firms which are willing to operate anywhere.

2 Discuss the prospects for a Latin American entrepreneur who is considering building a factory to produce machines which would manufacture cans for the food industry. His country happens to be in stage 4 – the nondurable and semidurable consumer goods manufacturing phase. The country's population is approximately 20 million and there is some possibility of establishing sales contacts in a few nearby countries.

3 Discuss the value of gross national product per capita as a measure of market potential. Refer to specific data in your answer.

4 Discuss the possibility of a multinational marketer using essentially the same promotion campaign in the United States and in many international markets.

5 Evaluate the growth of "common markets" in relation to the phases of economic development of the members. Is this basically a movement among the developed countries which are seeking to "catch up"?

6 Discuss the kinds of products which you feel may become popular in Europe in the near future. Does the material on U.S. consumption behavior discussed in the last chapter have any relevance here?

7 Discuss the probable importance of the market grid concept within the European Common Market.

...no discipline can give us one theory to explain all human behavior.... Various disciplines...can offer useful insights and frameworks. Our job in marketing is to combine the various approaches and apply them...to marketing management. ...the present state of our knowledge about consumer behavior is such that we must still rely on intuition and judgment to develop useful descriptions of the "whys" of consumer behavior in various market grid boxes.

8

Consumers: a behavioral science view

How can marketing management predict which of a given group of products will be purchased by consumers? In what quantities? Why does a consumer select a particular product?

Basic data on population, income, and consumer expenditure patterns in U.S. and international markets were presented in the last two chapters. With such information, it is possible to predict basic trends in consumer expenditure patterns.

Unfortunately, when many firms sell similar products, the traditional socioeconomic analysis we discussed in the last two chapters is of relatively little value in predicting which *products* and *brands* will be purchased. Yet the question of whether its products and brands will be chosen, and to what extent, is extremely important to a firm.

To find better answers, we need a better understanding of people. For this reason, many marketing analysts have turned to the behavioral sciences for insight and help. The approaches and thinking in psychology, sociology, and the other behavioral disciplines are the topic of this chapter.

Our primary emphasis will be on psychology, sociology, and social psychology. Psychology is the study of *individual behavior*. Sociology is primarily concerned with the *behavior of groups*.[1] And social psychology is concerned with the *behavior of individuals as affected by groups*. Anthropology is also concerned with man—usually in the primitive state—but it, too, has something to offer to our understanding of how to bring consumers the goods they want and need.[2]

Buying in a black box

At the outset, we should be realistic about the prospects for fully understanding people and why they like, choose, buy, and use the products they do. The behavioral sciences are still at a relatively primitive stage, and their areas of interest overlap only occasionally with that of marketing. No discipline can give us one theory to explain all human behavior, and in fact, prominent men in the same discipline often disagree among themselves. Each discipline, nevertheless, can offer useful insights and frameworks.[3] Our job in marketing is to combine the various approaches and apply them, when relevant, to marketing management.[4]

A simplified way of summarizing the way various behavioral scientists understand consumer purchasing behavior is shown in Figure 8-1. We know that potential customers are subjected to various stimuli, including the marketing mixes of various competitors and an almost infinite number of other potentially influencing factors. Somehow, an individual person internalizes some or all of these stimuli (he is the "black box" in Figure 8-1), and then he might purchase some product or service of interest to the researcher.

This is the classical stimulus-response model of buyer behavior and was the model we were implicitly using in the last two chapters. There, we hoped to find some relationship between socioeconomic characteristics (of customers in the black box), products (stimulus), and the customer's purchasing behavior (response). We did find some relationships, but now we want to go even deeper. This will require a

[1] For more details, see Steven J. Shaw, "Behavioral Science Offers Fresh Insight on New Product Acceptance," *Journal of Marketing*, January, 1965, pp. 9–13; F. M. Nicosia, "Uses of Sociology in Studying 'Consumption' Behavior," *Journal of Marketing*, July, 1964, pp. 51–54; and Christen T. Jonassen, "Contributions of Sociology to Marketing," *Journal of Marketing*, October, 1959, pp. 29–35.

[2] Charles Winnick, "Anthropology's Contribution to Marketing," *Journal of Marketing*, July, 1961, pp. 53–60.

[3] Louis C. Wagner, "What Responding Behavioral Scientists Feel Their Disciplines Could Contribute to Certain Specialized Areas of Advertising," in William M. Stevens, *The Social Responsibilities of Marketing*, Proceedings of the American Marketing Association, 1962.

[4] William Lazer and Eugene J. Kelley, "Interdisciplinary Horizons in Marketing," *Journal of Marketing*, October, 1960, pp. 24–30. For a summary of current knowledge, see G. Steiner and B. Berelson, *Human Behavior: An Inventory of Scientific Findings* (New York: Harcourt, Brace & World, Inc., 1964).

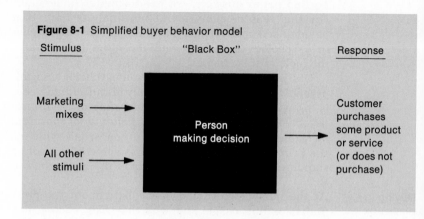

Figure 8-1 Simplified buyer behavior model

Stimulus   "Black Box"   Response

Marketing mixes   →

All other stimuli   →

Person making decision →

Customer purchases some product or service (or does not purchase)

better understanding of how the consumer decision-making process works.

There are many black boxes

Depending on a person's behavioral science training and the theories he subscribes to, we find many descriptions of how the black box works. These varying theories lead to different predictions about how consumers will react, so it helps considerably to have some feel for the various differences.

The economist, for example, typically assumes that consumers are "economic men," rationally evaluating alternatives in terms of cost and value received, in an effort to maximize their utility or satisfaction while spending their always scarce resources of time and money. Therefore, the economist collects and analyzes socioeconomic data when trying to predict consumer behavior. It was a logical extension of the economic man theory which led us to look carefully at socioeconomic characteristics in the last two chapters. Certainly, there is validity to this model, since consumers must at least have income to be in the market. But other behavioral scientists suggest that the black box works in a more complicated way than postulated by the economic-man model.

Some psychologists see consumers as "Freudian men," motivated by inner, subjective feelings which are difficult to define and measure. The motivation researchers discussed in Chapter 4 use Freudian concepts for their black-box model when they attempt to measure subconscious feelings with depth interviews. This view of how consumers make decisions sometimes focuses on sexual considerations, but basically it is concerned with complex inner drives which the person himself may not understand, but which nevertheless influence his buying behavior.[5]

And some social scientists have almost despaired of finding direct

[5] Philip Kotler, "Behavioral Models for Analyzing Buyers," *Journal of Marketing*, October, 1965, pp. 37–45.

relationships between external stimuli and peoples' actions. Instead they use the "probabilistic" or "stochastic man" model. They see man buffeted by many forces, producing a variety of decisions which can only be understood in probability terms. Some useful results have been obtained with this model, especially with frequently purchased, inexpensive items. Consumers do not always buy their favorite brand of candy or cigarettes, for example, but they seem to buy their "most favorite" brand or "most recently purchased" brand with higher probability than they purchase competing items, and this knowledge aids sales forecasting.[6]

Consumer is multidimensional

It should be clear by now that there is not one simple explanation of how all consumers behave. It should also be noted that to rely on one simple theory to explain how the black box works might be dangerous. You could make a forecast, but if these particular consumers did not behave as predicted, the forecast could be badly in error.

The marketing man's job is to attempt to understand and integrate the various behavioral theories, trying to apply the most useful model in the particular situation he must handle. Ideally, he would like to know *how* and *why* individual customers buy the way they do. Then he may be able to find homogeneous market segments to which he can offer unique marketing mixes. Because of the complexity of human behavior, just naming market segments may be difficult and require imagination. Multidimensional descriptions may be needed— such as "cost-conscious-couple." Underlying such descriptions of market grid boxes, however, would be models of how and why the consumers behave the way they do.

In the balance of this chapter, we will briefly review behavioral science thinking, with a view to integrating it into one model to help the marketing manager find promising submarkets for which he will know what to offer, and when and where.

To help your perspective in the following discussion, Figure 8–2 is presented. Note that the individual consumer decision maker— shown by the dot in the center of the diagram—is surrounded by many other influencing factors. Presumably he has his own needs and motivations. These in turn may be influenced by his family, social class, other reference groups, and the culture in which he lives. No man is an island. Yet ultimately the individual makes decisions, so we must understand both how he solves his problems and how his environment affects him. Markets are made up of many individuals. We may think of them and appeal to them as a group, but in the final analysis, we must sell to them one by one.

[6] David A. Aaker, "Using Buyer Behavior Models to Improve Marketing Decisions," *Journal of Marketing*, July, 1970, pp. 52–57; T. R. Rao, "Consumer's Purchase Decision Process: Stochastic Models," *Journal of Marketing Research*, August, 1969, pp. 321–29; Philip Kotler, "Mathematical Models of Individual Buyer Behavior," *Behavioral Science*, July, 1968, pp. 274–87; Donald G. Morrison, "A Stochastic Interpretation of the Heavy Half," *Journal of Marketing Research*, May, 1968, pp. 194–98; and R. J. Lawrence, "Patterns of Buyer Behavior: Time for a New Approach?" *Journal of Marketing Research*, May, 1969, pp. 137–45.

Figure 8-2 The individual decision maker (shown as a dot) is nestled
in an environment

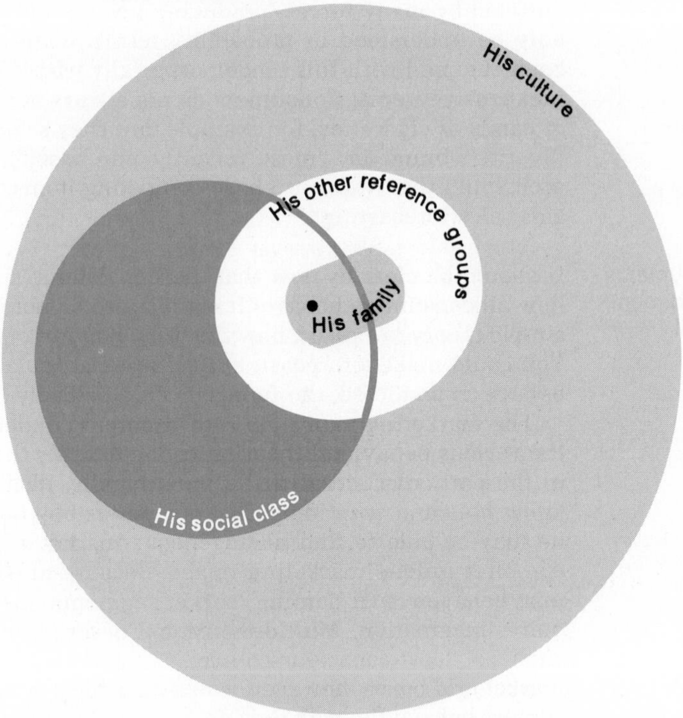

Consumers are problem solvers

It is generally agreed by behavioral scientists that people are problem
solvers; that individuals are motivated by drives or needs; that unsatisfied needs lead to tension and the desire to solve that problem.
How the individual solves his problem depends on his own makeup
and his environment. Nevertheless, given some needs, there does
seem to be a basic problem-solving process.

The basic process can be seen as consisting of five steps:

1. Becoming aware of or interested in the problem.
2. Gathering information about possible solutions.
3. Evaluating alternative solutions, perhaps trying some out.
4. Deciding on the appropriate solution.
5. Evaluating the decision.[7]

[7] Adapted from James H. Myers and William H.
Reynolds, *Consumer Behavior and Marketing
Management* (Boston: Houghton Mifflin Co., 1967),
p. 49.

Three levels of problem solving are useful	The basic problem-solving process indicates the steps a consumer might go through while trying to find a way to satisfy his needs, but it does not show how long he will take or how much thought he will give each step. Some individuals move quickly through certain steps, or may actually skip some, while others spend considerable time for each. This may be partly due to the nature of individuals, but it also is conditioned by how much and what kind of experience the person has had with solving this particular kind of problem. Some people have had much experience solving certain problems and can move quickly through some of the steps or almost directly to a decision.

It is helpful, therefore, to recognize three levels of problem solving: *extensive problem solving, limited problem solving,* and *routinized response behavior.*[8] These are problem-solving approaches which might be used for any kind of product or service.

When a need or a product or service is completely new to a person, then they may turn to extensive problem solving. It may take time to understand a newly felt need and to perceive how it can be satisfied. A new college student, for example, may have feelings of loneliness, a need for companionship, a need for achievement, and so on. It may take him some time to get his bearings on how and what he wants to do. After some initial decision making and experimentation, he should be able to fulfill these needs more quickly during the next few years. His need for companionship, for example, might be quickly solved by calling on or meeting with friends in familiar surroundings. A daily trip to the local "hangout" might become a routine answer to these problems. |
| Problem solving is a learning process | The reason problem solving becomes simpler with time is that people learn from experience – both positive and negative things. As a person approaches the problem-solving process, he brings with him attitudes, shaped by previous experiences and social training. Each new problem-solving process may then contribute to or modify this attitude set.

Learning theorists have isolated a number of steps in the learning process. They see a *drive* as a strong stimulus that motivates the individual to some *response* in an effort to satisfy the drive. The specific response chosen depends on the *cues* existing in his environment and, of course, his previous attitudes.

Reinforcement of the process occurs when the response is followed by satisfaction, that is, a reduction in the drive tension. Reinforcement strengthens the relationship between the environmental cue and the response and may lead to a similar response next time the drive occurs. Repeated reinforcement obviously would lead to the development of a habit, thereby making the decision process routine for the individual.

The learning process can be illustrated by a hungry person. The |

[8] John A. Howard and Jagdish N. Sheth, *The Theory of Buyer Behavior* (New York: John Wiley & Sons, Inc., 1969), pp. 46–48.

hunger drive could be satisfied by a McDonald's hamburger (response) if the person happened to be driving around and saw a McDonald's sign (cue) along the highway. If the experience were satisfactory, *reinforcement* would occur, and our friend might be quicker to satisfy this drive in the same way in the future. This also emphasizes the importance of developing good products which live up to the promises of the firm's advertising. Learning happens with negative experience also![9]

Adoption process is problem solving

Behavioral scientists especially interested in the process of accepting new ideas have identified the "adoption process," which explains how new ideas are learned and accepted. This process is similar to the problem-solving process, but makes clearer the role of learning and the potential contribution of promotion in a marketing mix.

The adoption process for individuals moves through some fairly definite stages, as follows:

1. Awareness – The potential customer comes to know about the product but lacks details. He may not even know how it works or what it will do.
2. Interest – *If* he becomes interested, he gathers general information and facts about the product.
3. Evaluation – He begins to make a mental trial, applying the product to his personal situation.
4. Trial – The customer may buy the product so that he can experiment with it in use. A product that is either too costly to try or cannot be obtained for trial may face severe difficulties in being adopted.
5. Decision – He decides on either adoption or rejection. A satisfactory evaluation and trial may lead to adoption of the product and regular use. According to psychological learning theory, reinforcement will lead to adoption.
6. Confirmation – The adopter continues to rethink his decision and searches for support for his decision – i.e., further reinforcement.

Selective processes facilitate problem solving

The searching that takes place during the awareness and interest stages may be facilitated by three selective processes. People seem to (1) seek out or read only some information sources (*selective exposure*), (2) screen out ideas, messages, and information not immediately relevant to solving their problems (*selective perception*), and (3) remember only what they want to remember (*selective retention*). This helps explain why certain people are not at all affected by some advertising, even offensive advertising – they just don't "see it."

---

[9] Gerald Zaltman, *Marketing: Contributions from the Behavioral Sciences* (New York: Harcourt Brace & World, Inc., 1965), pp. 20–21; and Peter D. Bennett and Robert M. Mandell, "Prepurchase Information Seeking Behavior of New Car Purchasers – The Learning Hypothesis," *Journal of Marketing Research*, November, 1969, pp. 430–33.

Riskiness may complicate decision making

The factor of risk also has a bearing. Trying a new candy bar does not involve much of a loss if it doesn't suit your taste. But trying a new car or clothing style involves a bigger risk, and a much more careful evaluation is called for.[10]

Dissonance may set in after the decision

After his decision has been made, a buyer may have second thoughts. He may have had to choose from among several attractive alternatives – weighing the pros and cons and finally making a decision. Subsequent doubts, however, may lead to "dissonance" – a form of tension arising out of uncertainty about the rightness of a decision. Dissonance may lead a buyer to search for additional information to confirm the wisdom of his decision and thereby reduce his tension. This points up the importance to the marketing manager of providing the information the consumer might seek at this stage. Without this confirmation, the adopter might buy something else next time and, further, would *not* give very positive comments to others.[11]

Several processes are related and relevant to strategy planning

The interrelation and interaction of the problem-solving process, the adoption process, and learning can be seen in Figure 8–3. It is important to see the interrelation of these processes and to note that they can be modified or accelerated by promotion, depending upon the nature of the individual and his social environment. Also note that the problem-solving behavior of a potential buyer would affect the design of distribution systems – if he is not willing to travel far to shop, then more facilities may be needed if you want his business. Similarly, his attitudes may help determine what price to charge. Clearly, a knowledge of how a target market handles these processes would facilitate marketing strategy planning.

The balance of this chapter will be concerned with discussion of some of the more important structures and findings from the various behavioral sciences which affect the basic problem-solving process. Our starting point will be the individual – how he sees needs and products – and the impact others have on his decision making.

---

[10] Charles W. King and John O. Summers, "Technology, Innovation, and Consumer Decision Making," in *Changing Marketing Systems* (American Marketing Association, 1967), pp. 63–68; and D. S. Cox and Stuart Rich, "Perceived Risk and Consumer Decision-Making," *Journal of Marketing Research*, November, 1964, pp. 32–39.

[11] For further discussion on perception and dissonance, see Myers and Reynolds, *op. cit.*; James F. Engel, David T. Kollat, and Roger D. Blackwell, *Consumer Behavior* (New York: Holt, Rinehart & Winston, Inc., 1968); Zaltman, *op. cit.*; L. Festinger, *A Theory of Cognitive Dissonance* (Evanston, Ill.: Row, Peterson & Co., 1957); Bruce C. Straits, "The Pursuit of the Dissonant Consumer," *Journal of Marketing*, July, 1964, pp. 62–66; James F. Engel, "Further Pursuit of the Dissonant Consumer: A

Comment," *Journal of Marketing*, April, 1965, pp. 33–34; Robert J. Holloway, "An Experiment on Consumer Dissonance," *Journal of Marketing*, January, 1967, pp. 39–43; S. Oshikawa, "Can Cognitive Dissonance Theory Explain Consumer Behavior?" *Journal of Marketing*, October, 1969, pp. 44–49; Joel B. Cohen and Marvin E. Goldberg, "The Dissonance Model in Post-Decision Product Evaluation," *Journal of Marketing Research*, August, 1970, pp. 315–21; Everett M. Rogers, *The Diffusion of Innovations* (New York: Free Press, 1962); E. M. Rogers with F. Schoemaker, *Communication of Innovation: A Cross-Cultural Approach* (New York: Free Press, 1968); and George M. Beal and Joe M. Bohlen, "The Diffusion Process" (Special Report No. 18 [Ames, Iowa: Iowa State University Press, 1962]).

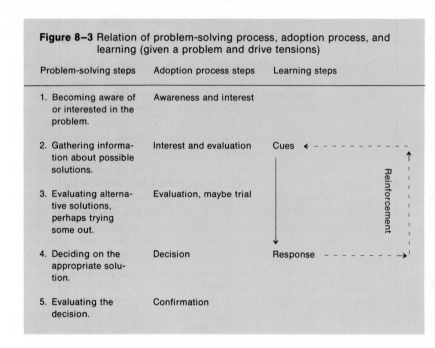

Figure 8–3 Relation of problem-solving process, adoption process, and learning (given a problem and drive tensions)

Problem-solving steps	Adoption process steps	Learning steps
1. Becoming aware of or interested in the problem.	Awareness and interest	
2. Gathering information about possible solutions.	Interest and evaluation	Cues
3. Evaluating alternative solutions, perhaps trying some out.	Evaluation, maybe trial	
4. Deciding on the appropriate solution.	Decision	Response
5. Evaluating the decision.	Confirmation	

How a person sees his needs and products

Needs lead to wants and purchasing decisions

Everybody has certain *needs* and *wants*. Some needs are physiological, concerned with a person's physical body. Examples are needs for food, drink, sex, and shelter. Other needs are psychological or sociological or cultural—they are concerned with the individual's view of himself and his relationships to others. Wants are less basic; these are learned during the course of the individual's life.

When a need or a want is not satisfied, it leads to a *drive*. The food need, for instance, leads to a hunger drive. The drive state is one of tension in which the individual tries to find ways of satisfying his drive. Drives are, in effect, the reasons or motives underlying certain behavior patterns. Drive tensions lead to behavior that will satisfy the need or want and thereby reduce the drive tension.

Needs— learned or innate?

Trying to separate learned from unlearned needs is not very useful and we will not try to do so here. But brief consideration of the idea is desirable because some critics feel that marketing creates and warps many needs.

It might be argued that all *basic* needs are innate in humans. A small child develops strong desires for "things," certainly before advertisers have had a chance to influence him. It is hard to believe that a small girl has "learned" all the feminine wiles she displays at the age of one and two.

Even the need for status, which some marketing critics feel is

related to the influence of advertising, is found among animals and in human societies where there is no such influence. Studies of birds show that there is a definite pecking order in flocks. In a study of jackdaws, for instance, it was found that the female, upon mating, acquires the status of her mate.[12] In the human realm, African villagers raise domesticated cattle and goats purely as signs of wealth and social status. For food, they hunt wild animals.[13]

Liking hamburger is learned behavior

Some needs may be culturally (or socially) determined, however. When a human baby is born, his needs are simple. But as he grows, he learns various and complex behavior patterns to satisfy the drives stemming from these needs. As his needs become more sophisticated and specific, they can be described as wants. The need for food, for instance, may lead to many specific food wants, depending on the experience of the person. The resulting hunger drive may be satisfied only by the specific food desired. The people of Western nations like beef, and our children learn to like it. In India, however, Hindus regard the cow as sacred and will not eat beef. Hindu children learn to eat and like other foods. Many foods, in other words, can satisfy the hunger drive—but in a particular culture, an individual might *want* a hamburger, and the hunger drive might not be fully satisfied until he has eaten one.

Primary versus selective motives

For marketing planning purposes, it is useful to distinguish between basic needs and some learned needs. Put another way, it makes sense to distinguish between *primary* and *selective* motives.

A primary motive involves some basic need that can be satisfied with a broad range of products and services. Food needs, for example, could be met with a wide variety of foods, served in different places. A person's learning experience in a particular cultural environment, however, might lead to his wanting his needs satisfied by a very particular product or even a specific brand, in a particular place. Cultivating such selective motives might be the job assigned to promotion, or to the whole marketing mix.

Are there hierarchies of motives?

Some schools of thought in psychology make distinctions between motives and drives.[14] Others dismiss motives as far too simple an explanation of consumer behavior. Some feel that a person may have several motives for buying as he does, and they see that person attempting to develop a balance between the forces driving him.

Still other psychologists portray motives in a hierarchy. Maslow,

[12] Robert Ardrey, *African Genesis* (New York: Atheneum Publishers, 1961), chap. iv.

[13] *U.S. News and World Report,* September 25, 1961, p. 78.

[14] Clifford T. Morgan, *Introduction to Psychology* (2d ed.; New York: McGraw-Hill Book Co., 1961), chap. iii; Ernest R. Hilgart, *Introduction to Psy-chology* (New York: Harcourt, Brace & Co., 1953), chaps. v–vi; Norman L. Munn, *Psychology—The Fundamentals of Human Adjustment* (2d ed.; Boston: Houghton Mifflin Co., 1951), chaps. x–xii; and S. H. Britt, *Social Psychology of Modern Life* (rev. ed.; New York: Rinehart & Co., Inc., 1949), chaps. vi–vii.

for example, proposed five levels of needs, in an ascending order of importance to the individual:

1. Physiological needs.
2. Safety needs.
3. Belongingness and love needs.
4. Esteem and status needs.
5. Self-actualization needs.

This concept sees consumers attempting to take care of certain needs before others, although they may be willing to satisfy the highest-priority ones only partially before going on to others. Food, for example, may have a high priority, but not all the consumer's expenditures will go for food. After an adequate supply of food has been assured, money may be allocated to satisfy "urgent" higher-order needs for housing, clothing, medical or beauty care, companionship, and education (satisfying the fourth- and/or fifth-level needs, in other words). But, clearly, one product might satisfy several needs at the same time in a modern society.[15]

Some social psychologists picture consumers as wanting to improve their self-image. In this view, a person has several selves: the way he really is, the way he sees himself, the way he would like to be, and the way he thinks others see him. To these psychologists, consumers continually try to create a better self-image, and it is obvious that products or services—a new car or suit, or a new hairdo—that help to achieve this goal have great appeal.[16]

Motives are numerous, overlapping, and sometimes mysterious

From a marketing standpoint, there are several problems in dealing with motives. Not all psychological theories have been thoroughly tested, nor are they all compatible with one another. Furthermore, as mentioned earlier, psychology tends to focus on the individual, while marketing often must be concerned with groups. Although one psychological theory might be more helpful in explaining a given consumer's behavior, another theory might be needed for his neighbor. This would be expected if one accepts the market grid concept, but it certainly does not simplify the marketer's task. In practice, considerable marketing research might be necessary to clearly define the motives and attitudes in various market grid boxes.

[15] A. H. Maslow, *Motivation and Personality* (New York: Harper & Bros., 1954); and B. Curtis Hamm and Edward W. Cundiff, "Self-Actualization and Product Perception," *Journal of Marketing Research*, November, 1969, pp. 470–72. See John McFall, "Priority Patterns and Consumer Behavior," *Journal of Marketing*, October, 1969, pp. 50–55, for an extension of this concept to the order in which consumers buy appliances.

[16] John Douglas, George A. Field, and Lawrence X. Tarpey, *Human Behavior in Marketing* (Columbus, Ohio: Charles E. Merrill Publishing Co., 1967,) pp. 64–67; Edward L. Grubb and Gregg Hupp, "Perception of Self, Generalized Stereotypes, and Brand Selection," *Journal of Marketing Research*, February, 1968, pp. 58–63; and Jospeh B. Mason and Morris L. Mayer, "The Problem of the Self-Concept in Store Image Studies," *Journal of Marketing*, April, 1970, pp. 67–69.

| Motives and | Another complication is that consumers may not be willing to discuss, |

Motives and degrees of awareness

Another complication is that consumers may not be willing to discuss, or even be aware of, the motives which drive them. At this point, it may be helpful to consider three *degrees of awareness* of motives on the part of consumers: *conscious, preconscious,* and *unconscious*.[17]

At the *conscious* level, the consumer is aware of his motivations and is willing to talk to others about them. At the *preconscious* level, however, he may be aware of the motives but would rather not discuss them with others; or perhaps he's not fully conscious why he behaves the way he does. A desire for status might be quite strong in an individual, but he might feel the need to rationalize a purchase in terms of its usefulness. Finally, at the *unconscious* level, a person is not even aware of what forces are driving him. A straightforward promotion appeal directed to such motives would not be effective.

Emotional motives drive many consumers

These levels of awareness are important because we do make emotional decisions. Americans, perhaps because of their cultural heritage, are generally reluctant to admit this fact, preferring to rationalize their actions in terms of economic necessity or other practical factors they are willing to talk about at the conscious level. People in other countries, for example, the Latin nations, are much less concerned about economic or practical justifications.

A marketing man's list of motives is thought provoking

The various psychological theories are useful because they help stimulate thinking. In the following pages, however, we will gloss over some of the distinctions given in the psychological theories discussed previously. In fact, we are going to lump together needs, wants, and drives, and refer to them all as *motives* — or the reasons why people buy. This is a simple but practical method. We will be working with eight basic types of motives, although some advertising agencies use checklists of hundreds of motives. Our list of motives, however, is a marketing man's approach to reasons for consumer behavior. It is not an all-inclusive list that explains all behavior, but simply a list to stimulate thinking and increased awareness of the reasons why people behave the way they do.[18]

Keep in mind that several motives may be operating on an individual at the same time, perhaps at different levels. In fact, a particular behavior system may be imbedded in a consumption system. That is, a consumer does not just eat a hamburger to satisfy a food need but may also buy several other products at the same time and in a particular place to satisfy needs for sociability, affection, or something else.[19] Further, it is important to recognize that similar behavior in two persons may be due to different motives.

[17] G. H. Smith, *Motivation Research in Advertising and Marketing* (New York: McGraw Hill Book Co., 1954), pp. 19–21.

[18] Francesco M. Nicosia, *Consumer Decision Processes* (Englewood Cliffs, N.J.: Prentice-Hall, Inc., 1966), p. 41.

[19] Harper W. Boyd, Jr., and Sidney J. Levy, "New Dimensions in Consumer Analysis," *Harvard Business Review*, November–December, 1963, pp. 129–40.

The motives we will discuss are arbitrarily classified as emotional and economic. This may be an oversimplification, but it's a useful one. These motives are not new but are the classical ones presented by Copeland in 1924.[20] More recent work has merely expanded the list or provided other organizational frameworks. These motives are useful in that they are thought provoking and help us see potential dimensions in market grid boxes.

Emotional motives are important

We will discuss emotional motives under the following eight categories:

1. Satisfaction of senses.
2. Preservation of species.
3. Fear.
4. Rest and recreation.

5. Pride.
6. Sociability.
7. Striving.
8. Curiosity or mystery.

SATISFACTION OF SENSES Satisfaction of the five senses—*touch, taste, sight, smell, and hearing*—is one of the most important motives. An appeal to this motive would emphasize the *enjoyment* or *satisfaction*, rather than nutritional values, that a person might get from food or drink Since most Americans live beyond the subsistence level, this motive obviously is more complex than simple hunger and thirst.

Advertisements illustrating a full meal or "a man's dinner" could appeal to this motive, but so could appeals involving *more subtle variations* sensed by the taste buds or the nostrils. An appeal to the sense of taste or smell might show a man inhaling perfume scents or a woman sampling a food delicacy.

This same motive would be concerned with eliminating unpleasant sights, smells, or noise and *avoiding discomfort or pain.* Particularly appealing here would be special kinds of mattresses, air conditioners, stomach aids, liniments, corn plasters, soft cashmere sweaters, creams which make your skin "nice to touch," and personal-care products to assure that you will be nice to be near—all day.

PRESERVATION OF SPECIES The drives of *courtship and mating* are strong in most humans. The subsequent *care of children* is also strong in most societies, though there are variations here. In some cultures, the father and older children as well as the mother join in the details of caring for the children in the family. In other cultures, children are primarily the mother's responsibility.

Marketing appeals to women (and especially young girls) are based on this motive when they mention the possibility of finding a mate through the purchase of pretty clothing, perfumes, and body-care products. Many products useful to newlyweds are presented in an aura of marriage and wedded bliss. Silverware, china, new furniture and appliances, honeymoon vacation trips, and even easy-to-follow cookbooks are in this category.

---

[20] For more details, see Melvin T. Copeland, *Principles of Merchandising* (New York: A. W. Shaw Co., 1924), chap. vi.

An appeal to this motive may be used to promote a variety of products for children – ranging from encyclopedias to cough syrup.

FEAR An appeal to *self-preservation,* or to *the protection of our family and friends,* may be emphasized here. For many people the uncertainties of the future, including the possibilities of accidents, sickness, and death, are of grave concern. Insurance, vitamins, and safety equipment in homes and automobiles may satisfy this motive.

REST AND RECREATION *Sleep* and *rest* are certainly basic needs, and flowing from these are desires to *lighten or eliminate work* and to *obtain greater leisure time.* More leisure time, in turn, creates needs for activities to fill it. Of appeal here would be sports, camping, travel, or indoor games, reading, television viewing, playing musical instruments, and spectator sports.

PRIDE Pride in *personal appearance* or the *appearance of one's property* appears to be a strong drive. Many people want to maintain their own dignity without regard to impressing others. Cleanliness, neatness, and personal appearance are related to this motive, and any product facilitating these ends, such as soaps, cleaning compounds, toothbrushes, washing machines, cosmetics, polishing waxes, and dust cloths, would be attractive. These can be sold more effectively by appealing to the *pride* motive rather than selling the items as ends in themselves.

Expression of artistic taste is another manifestation of pride. The consumer wants to have confidence in his own ability to choose esthetic articles for his own use or for others. The emphasis again is not on what others think about a person, but what he thinks about himself. Note that in making marketing plans, this *pride* motive should be distinguished from acts or motives concerned with impressing others.

SOCIABILITY Sociability is concerned with the individual's drive *to be a part of his group.* Belonging to clubs and organizations, especially those offering special drinking or dining opportunities, might satisfy this motive. Coca-Cola is often shown as part of a happy social situation. Pepsi-Cola has used the advertising theme: "Be Sociable – Have a Pepsi."

STRIVING The drive for *social achievement* can be very strong. Here the consumer may be concerned with achievement of success in social relationships by showing good sense in managing and participating in social affairs. Any products that help develop signs of good taste and manners can appeal to this motive.

Remember that striving can take various forms: Some people strive for their *own satisfaction,* or because they personally want to do a good job. Many strive for *distinctiveness* – that is, to do or have things which are not done or possessed by others. Others, by contrast, strive to *emulate* – to be the same as someone else. Different appeals would be needed for each group, and these appeals might have to change with time. What gives personal satisfaction now might have less appeal in 5 or 10 years. Today's distinctive product may be too popular tomorrow, and what is generally popular today may be passé next year.

Finally, some people desire to emulate others economically. Appeals to this motive might stress the offer of the very latest styles at budget prices.

CURIOSITY OR MYSTERY Some people just like to try new things. Others are romantic. Anything that grabs their sense of curiosity or mystery may be enticing. This includes anything *new, different, or exotic.*

Ocean trips or travel in general appeal to this motive. So would a new hot-weather drink or a salad dressing or herb cookery. An example of curiosity at work is the success of an "Around-the-World Shoppers' Club," an organization that sends knickknacks monthly from foreign lands. The main appeal to buyers is not the knickknacks themselves but the novelty of getting something unique from faraway places.

Economic motives can be important too

In contrast to emotional motives, economic motives are primarily concerned with making the most effective use of the customer's limited resources. A product that is easier to use or which will last longer, at lower cost, clearly accomplishes this purpose. These motives require less elaboration than the emotional motives. Eight categories are listed below.

1. Handiness.
2. Efficiency in operation or use.
3. Dependability in use.
4. Reliability of auxiliary service.
5. Durability.
6. Enhancement of earnings.
7. Enhancement of productivity of property.
8. Economy of purchase or use.

Here, more quantitative or specific appeals can be used — in contrast to the more subtle or descriptive appeals designed to reach emotional motives. Specific dollar savings, differences in weight, length of product life, and other such measurable factors can be emphasized.

Motives help market gridding, some

We have seen that motives may help explain why consumers might buy various kinds of products or product classes. But we know much less about why people buy specific products and specific brands. The consumers in different market grid boxes might buy them for a number of different reasons, depending on the needs they feel and the influence others have upon them.

A budget expert or production-oriented businessmen might feel that consumers should logically buy a particular product because it is the "best buy" economically. Based on economic considerations only, the experts could be right. But people have a wide range of different motives, and emotional motives may be stronger than economic ones in a particular case. This is implicit in the market grid concept, but it is important to note here that the same product may satisfy different motives and therefore become part of different mixes, aimed at different market grid boxes. And the relevant dimensions of these grid boxes may include both economic and emotional motives.

By understanding motives, a marketing manager may be able to develop a unique and very successful marketing strategy. Even using only his own insights about how some market segments behave and what they want, he may be able to develop a distinctive marketing mix far superior to the average mix developed by competitors for everyone. Our simple motive-oriented analysis of why people buy—especially if it is focused on unsatisfied needs—would carry the investigation of buying decisions farther than many firms ever go! Ideally, more powerful analytical tools would be desirable—and more approaches are discussed below—but motive analysis can be very useful.

So far we have been discussing insights which can be developed from psychology. Yet consumer behavior may be determined not only by a person's particular psyche and drives but also by his relations with others. We will turn to this subject now, to enrich your understanding of the buying process.

Impact of others on personal buying behavior

Social psychologists and sociologists see market behavior as a response to the attitudes and behavior of others. We will review this thinking in terms of the interaction of the individual with his family, social class, and reference groups.

An individual is not a completely free agent. Society provides a framework for an individual's judgments, and applies pressure to keep his decisions within the realm of socially acceptable behavior. Often he must consult his family. He certainly refers to his group's values. Some men, for example, would prefer to wear comfortable sports clothes to formal dances, rather than a constricting tuxedo and starched shirt—but custom rules otherwise. In the same way, many women who find a new fashion unattractive will still buy and wear it.

Family considerations may overwhelm personal ones

Most decisions are made within a framework developed by experience within the family. An individual may go through much of the thinking discussed above when developing his own preferences for various products and services. But this analysis may be only one of the influences in the final decision. Social processes—such as power, domination, and affection—may be involved, too. This decision-making behavior is often the result of much social learning.

A boat for father or a TV for mother

The interaction of various social forces can be illustrated by a choice between two products which appeal to rest and recreation motives—a television set and a boat with outboard motor.

The husband in a family might be particularly interested in the boat and motor for his camping and fishing trips. Weekend pleasure outings with the family would be only incidental. But in his arguments, he can present his preference in the desirable terms of *family wants and uses*. At the same time, his wife might prefer a new television set. It would enhance the beauty of her home and, secondarily, would be used as an entertainment medium for herself, her husband, and the children. She, too, could argue that this purchase is *for the family.*

The actual outcome in such a situation is unpredictable. It depends on the strength of the husband's and the wife's preferences; their individual degree of dominance of the family; who contributes the most money to the family's income; the need for affection; and the response of other family members.

Knowing how all these forces interact would be most helpful to the marketing manager. Unfortunately, each family behaves differently, and an overall marketing strategy usually has to deal with tendencies or averages. Yet an individual retail salesman in direct contact with the family might sense how the family operates and be able to adjust his marketing mix, especially his sales presentation, accordingly.

Who is the real customer?

Although one person in the family often makes the purchase, in planning strategy it is important to find out who is the real decision maker in the selection of a specific product or brand.

Traditionally, the housewife has been considered the family purchasing agent. She has normally been the one who had the time to shop and run the errands. As a result, most product promotion and advertising have been aimed at women. But the situation may be changing.[21] As more women work, and as night shopping and Sunday shopping become more popular, the housewife may be playing a less dominant role as family buyer and decision maker. One study found that 80 percent of the wives surveyed check with their husbands on any purchase of $50 or more, and nearly half consult him on smaller purchases.

Men now have more time for, and interest in, shopping, and they may make decisions involving large purchases or buy products of special interest to them, such as beer, liquor, automobiles, tires, life insurance, air conditioners, electric shavers, shaving creams, and outboard motors.[22]

Apparently the father is usually concerned with buying decisions that involve functional items. Of the two parents, he tends to be more concerned with matters external to the family. The mother is more likely to make those buying decisions that have expressive values, and she is more concerned with internal matters. These distinctions may apply even if the user of a purchased product is the other parent. For example, the wife may buy the husband's clothing accessories, while the husband might buy household appliances.

The husband and wife may work together where internal-functional or external-expressive matters are involved, because the husband-wife roles may overlap. Husbands and wives may share in home

[21]"Queen of the Family Purse—Or Is She?" *Business Week,* August 10, 1963, pp. 26–27; and *Printers' Ink,* December 13, 1957, pp. 40 ff.

[22]*Male vs. Female Influence on Purchase of Selected Products, an Exploratory Depth Interview Study with Husbands and Wives* (New York: Fawcett Publications, Inc., 1958), p. 6; and "Liquor Store Survey Uncorks Potent Data: Two-Fifths of the Customers Are Women," *Business Week,* May 13, 1967, p. 187.

improvements, for example, because they involve both functional and internal matters.[23]

The question of spending by the family is not limited to mothers and fathers. As the life-cycle stages of the family change, the children begin to handle and spend more money.[24]

In many cases, however, the person actually doing the shopping is merely acting as an agent for persons who may have specified which products should be bought. Small children may want specific kinds of cereals; the father may want a certain brand of cigarettes or golf balls.

We still need greater understanding to see why different families come to widely different decisions when faced with a choice among many available products. For one thing, it would be valuable to know the family's present and past experience and future expectations in relation to society's values and the family social class position. Social class is extremely important here, and is discussed next.

Social class affects buying of specifics

Up to now, we have been concerned with the individual and his relation to his family. Now let's consider how society looks at an individual and perhaps his family—in terms of social class.

The mere mention of class distinctions in the United States provokes a defensive reaction. We like to think of America as a land of equality. We have been brought up to revere the statement in the Declaration of Independence,"All men are created equal." Our class system is far less pronounced than those in European and Asiatic nations where the system is tied to religion, blood kinship, or landed wealth. Nevertheless, sociological research bears out the contention that a class structure *does* exist in this country.

In discussing class structure, we will use the traditional technical terms, "upper," "middle," and "lower." But a word of warning is needed. The choice of these terms, even though in general use, is unfortunate, because they have a connotation of superior and inferior. In sociological and marketing usage, however, no value judgment is implied. In fact, it is not possible to state that a particular class is "better" or "happier" than any other. Any such value judgment would be biased, as it could only be made from the vantage point of the individual making it, and his judgment would be colored by his own class values.

Some people strive to enter a "higher" class because they find the values of that class more admirable; others are comfortable with the standards of their own group and prefer to remain where they are.

[23] W. H. Reynolds and James H. Myers, "Marketing and the American Family," *Business Topics*, Spring, 1966, pp. 58–59; Harry L. Davis, "Dimensions of Marital Roles in Consumer Decision Making," *Journal of Marketing Research*, May, 1970, pp. 168–78; and E. A. Pessemier and D. J. Tigert, "Socio-Economic Status of the Family and Housewife, Personality, Life-Style and Opinion Factors," Paper No. 197, December, 1967, Krannert Graduate School of Industrial Administration, Purdue University.

[24] *The Dynamics of the Youth Explosion—A Look Ahead* (Los Angeles Chamber of Commerce, 1967), pp. 33–35; Lewis A. Berey and Richard W. Pollay, "The Influencing Role of the Child in Family Decision Making," *Journal of Marketing Research*, February, 1968, pp. 70–72.

The marketing man's goal should be learning the characteristics and typical behavior patterns of each class so that he will be better able to develop unique marketing strategies involving class differences.

Characteristics of American class system

The American class system is an individual and a family system. While a child is a member of a family, his social status will probably depend on the status of his family. But grown children often "join" a different class than their parents. This is especially the case when they attain higher educational levels or take up different occupations from those of their parents.

The U.S. class system appears to be a function of several dimensions: income, occupation, and housing arrangements. The early work on social class in the United States was done by Lloyd Warner, a social psychologist, who developed a class system for cities in the 10,000–25,000 population range. His class system is based on *income, occupation, house type,* and *residence area.* Warner's classifications, though widely used in sociology, had found little use in marketing until the *Chicago Tribune* undertook several studies with Warner's social class system to determine whether it had validity in larger metropolitan areas, especially concerning family buying patterns.[25]

After three years spent analyzing various marketing problems under the guidance of Warner, a population breakdown was derived for metropolitan Chicago, which is probably typical of a big industrial city. Many of the findings are interesting to marketing managers. Let us look at the *Chicago Tribune's* five class breakdowns first and then consider some of the findings.

1. *Upper Class* (0.9 percent of population). This was defined as old families (upper-upper class) and the socially prominent new rich (lower-upper class). This group has been the traditional leader in the American community. Most large manufacturers, bankers, and top marketing executives belong to it. It represents, however, less than 1 percent of the population. Being so small, the two upper classes were merged into one in this study. In some of the *Chicago Tribune* studies, these two classes are broken out separately, and a six-class breakdown is used.

2. *Upper-Middle Class* (7.2 percent of population). These are the successful businessmen, professionals and top salesmen. The advertising professional usually is part of this class, reflecting the tastes and codes of the first two groups. Yet, combined, groups 1 and 2 still represent only 8.1 percent of the population.

3. *Lower-Middle Class* (28.4 percent of population). These are the white-collar workers–small tradesmen, office workers, teachers, technicians, most salesmen. The American moral code and the

[25] Pierre Martineau, "The Pattern of Social Classes," in R. L. Clewett (ed.), *Marketing's Role in Scientific Management* (Chicago: American Marketing Association, 1957), pp. 233–49.

emphasis on hard work has come from this class. This is the most conforming, churchgoing, morally serious segment of society. We speak of America as a middle-class society, but the middle-class value system stops here. Two thirds of our society is *not* middle-class.

4. *Upper-Lower Class* (44.0 percent of population). These are the factory production workers, the union labor groups, the skilled workers, the service workers, and the local politicians and union leaders who would lose their power if they moved out of this class.

5. *Lower-Lower Class* (19.5 percent of population). This group includes unskilled laborers, racial immigrants, and people in non-respectable occupations.[26]

What do these classes mean?

The *Chicago Tribune* class studies suggest that an old economic maxim, "A rich man is simply a poor man with more money," may not hold true. While Engel's laws may still apply in general, it appears that a person belonging to the lower class, given the same income as a middle-class individual, handles himself and his money very differently. The various classes patronize different stores, would prefer different treatment from salesmen, buy different brands of products (even though their prices are approximately the same), and have different spending-saving attitudes.

The marketing implications of this and other studies are most interesting. Selection of media in advertising should be related to social class, for example. Customers in the lower classes would have little interest in *Fortune, Holiday, Vogue,* or *Ladies Home Journal,* while the middle and upper classes probably would have little desire to read *True Story.*

And the various classes might read quite different meanings into advertisements. One beer advertisement aimed at the lower classes, for example, was built around a fox hunter in full costume with scarlet coat, boots, and cap. Unhappily for the advertiser, the lower class had no feel for fox hunting. In fact, the advertisement repelled them because it seemed "snobbish." Similarly, lower-class women may eagerly read a busy, crowded, screaming "sale" advertisement which conveys a sense of urgency and potential bargains, while those in the middle or upper classes will ignore such ads because they interpret them to mean large crowds and low-quality merchandise.[27]

Class differences also have a bearing on product design, and the assortment carried by retailers. In a study[28] on lamps, furniture,

[26]Adapted from Pierre Martineau, *Motivation on Advertising* (New York: McGraw-Hill Book Co., 1957), p. 164.

[27]Sidney J. Levy, "Symbols by Which We Buy," a paper delivered at 41st National Conference, American Marketing Association, December 30, 1958. For a popular version about the class system, see Vance Packard, *The Status Seekers* (New York: David

McKay Co., Inc., 1959). See also, Richard P. Coleman, "The Significance of Social Stratification in Selling," in Martin L. Bell (ed.), *Marketing: A Maturing Discipline* (Chicago: American Marketing Association, 1961), pp. 171–84.

[28]Martineau, *Motivation in Advertising, op. cit.,* p. 168.

and home styles, for example, the lower-class half of the market selected completely different styles than did the top half. This lower group did not want the modern ranch homes and the two-story colonial homes, nor the severely plain, functional styling of furniture preferred by the higher classes. Instead, they preferred overstuffed and ornate furnishings (sometimes called "borax" goods) and conventional, less conspicuous one- or two-story homes.

Middle and lower classes compared

Several studies have been cited to illustrate the varying behavior of different classes. These findings are not "facts" about consumers, but are support for the idea of a social class system insofar as marketing is concerned. The summary in Table 8–1, comparing the attitudes and characteristics of the middle class to the lower class, accents general differences between classes as revealed in these and many other studies.

Once marketing men are aware of these differences, they can adjust their mixes. Understanding that lower classes are concerned about the present, for example, stores aiming at these classes frequently emphasize credit sales so that target consumers can satisfy their needs *now*. In such stores—such as credit jewelers and credit furniture stores—it is often difficult even to determine the total price of a product. Salesmen talk about the small down payment and easy monthly payments with little mention of the number of such payments. Furthermore, lower classes seem to be more concerned with financial security, and some stores offer insurance on the life of the breadwinner so that the housewife will not be left with a debt should her husband die.

Table 8–1 A comparison of attitudes and characteristics for two social classes

Middle class	Lower class
1. Pointed to the future.	1. Pointed to the present and past.
2. His viewpoint embraces a long expanse of time.	2. Lives and thinks in a short expanse of time.
3. More urban identification.	3. More rural identification.
4. Stresses rationality.	4. Nonrational essentially.
5. Has a well-structured sense of the universe.	5. Vague and unclear structuring.
6. Horizons vastly extended or not limited.	6. Horizons sharply defined and limited.
7. Greater sense of choice making.	7. Limited sense of choice making.
8. Self-confident, willing to take risks.	8. Very much concerned with security and insecurity.
9. Immaterial and abstract in his thinking (idea-minded).	9. Concrete and perceptive in his thinking (thing-minded).
10. Sees himself tied to national happenings.	10. World revolves around his family.

Source: P. Martineau, "The Pattern of Social Classes," in R. L. Clewett (ed.), *Marketing's Race in Scientific Management* (Chicago: American Marketing Association, 1957), pp. 246–47.

The lower classes seem to be confused by variety and apparently have difficulty in making choices. As a result, such buyers look on furniture salesmen, for example, as friends and advisors. The middle-class buyers are much more self-confident in contrast. They know what they want and prefer a furniture salesman to be an impersonal guide.[29]

The increasing affluence of the skilled worker (the upper-lower class) and his attitude that the world revolves around his family has led to a strong desire for home ownership in "respectable" city neighborhoods or suburban developments where other blue-collar people live. These people don't seek high-status neighborhoods, but simply want a good home for their families. They may look for certain types of retail facilities, too, such as discount stores.[30]

In contrast, the middle classes seem more concerned with selecting a house that has status value and might enable the family to rise in the social class structure. Housing location, and even social and political affiliations, may be chosen with a view to the family's social future.

From this review, it is obvious that social class cannot be ignored when analyzing market grids and developing marketing strategy.[31] Fortunately, it appears that some fairly objective and readily available data can be used for determining social class and estimating market sizes.[32] In particular, U.S. census measures of occupation, education, and expenditures on housing may be of service.

Reference groups have relevance too

A reference group is composed of people that the individual looks to when forming his opinions, attitudes, and beliefs. A person normally has several reference groups for various subjects.[33] Some he meets face-to-face, while others he may just aspire to emulate. In either case, he may take his values from "them" and make purchasing decisions based on what he feels they would accept. *Playboy* magazine, for instance, and the "in" people who presumably read it, might be a reference group for *Playboy* readers.

[29] *Advertising Age,* February 22, 1960, p. 63.

[30] David J. Rachman and Marvin Levine, "Blue Collar Workers Shape Suburban Markets," *Journal of Retailing,* Winter, 1966–67, pp. 5–13.

[31] For more discussion on this, see Joseph N. Fry and Frederick H. Siller, "A Comparison of House-wife Decision Making in Two Social Classes," *Journal of Marketing Research,* August, 1970, pp. 333–37. See also, William H. Peters, "Relative Occupational Class Income: A Significant Variable in the Marketing of Automobiles," *Journal of Marketing,* April, 1970, pp. 74–78; Chester R. Wasson, "Is It Time to Quit Thinking of Income Classes?" *Journal of Marketing,* April, 1969, pp. 54–56; S. U. Rich and S. C. Jain, "Social Class and Life Cycle as Predictors of Shopping Behavior," *Journal of Marketing Research,* February, 1968, pp. 41–49; H. Lee Mathews and John W. Slocum, Jr., "Social Class and Commercial Bank Credit Card Usage," *Journal of Marketing,* January, 1969, pp. 71–78; John W. Slocum, Jr., and H. Lee Mathews, "Social Class and Income as Predictors of Consumer Credit Behavior," *Journal of Marketing,* April, 1970, pp. 69–74; and Richard P. Coleman, *op. cit.*

[32] James A. Carman, *The Application of Social Class in Market Segmentation* (Berkeley, Calif.: Institute of Business and Economic Research, University of California, 1965). See also, William H. Peters, "Relative Occupational Class Income: A Significant Variable in the Marketing of Automobiles," *Journal of Marketing,* April, 1970, pp. 74–78.

[33] Zaltman, *op. cit.,* pp. 77–78.

The importance of reference groups depends somewhat on the nature of the product and on whether anyone else will be able to "see" which product and which brand is being used. Figure 8–4 suggests the interrelations here. For example, an individual may smoke cigarettes because his reference group smokes, and the group's preferences may even determine the brand he chooses. At the other extreme, most people in our society use soap, and which brand is not readily determinable. In this case, reference group influence may be negligible.

Figure 8-4 Reference-group influence

	Weak − [−]	Product	Strong + [+]	
Brand or type [+] [−]	Clothing Furniture Magazines Refrigerator (type) Toilet soap		Cars* Cigarettes* Beer (premium versus regular)* Drugs*	**Brand or type [+]** [−]
	Soap Canned peaches Laundry soap Refrigerator (brand) Radios		Air conditioners* Instant coffee* TV (black and white)	
	[−]	Product	[+]	

*Classification by the extent to which reference groups influence their purchase based on actual experimental evidence. Other products listed are classified speculatively on the basis of generalizations derived from the sum of research in this area and confirmed by the judgment of seminar participants.
Source: Bureau of Applied Social Research, Columbia University.

The reference-group concept has grown in importance in recent years as more people live and work together in today's larger corporations, schools, governments, communities, churches, and social action organizations. The large company employee – the "organization man" – seems to be especially responsive to group pressures and puts "getting along" with the group above other values.

This group consciousness has been described by Riesman as a sign of the transition from the "inner-directed" man to the "other-directed" man. The inner-directed man has his own value system and directs his own activities, whereas the other-directed person is the one whose character is formed chiefly by those around him. Other-directed people – a large proportion of our society according to Riesman – are led by each other, and consequently there is a strong tendency to conform.[34]

Reaching the leaders who are buyers

A trend toward other-directedness could have a profound effect on marketing through its effect on the way individuals and groups change their values and desires. Advertising, and promotion in general, might have to be more concerned with affecting trend leaders and whole groups rather than individuals.[35]

In this drive for conformity, some people are more effective than others as "opinion leaders" or "communicators." It is important to note that these communicators are not restricted to the higher-income people or the better educated. Rather, they are spread throughout all levels of society in varying proportions. Communicators on one subject are not necessarily communicators on another.

Housewives with larger families may be consulted for advice on cooking, while young girls may be leaders in new clothing styles and cosmetics. And all of this may take place within the various social classes, with different opinion leaders in the various classes.[36]

The influence of communicators and of group pressures to conform has been credited with great increases of sales of such post–World War II products as air conditioners, garbage and waste disposers, and automatic dishwashers. Apparently an unusual set of forces works within the group. The first adopters may be admired and copied if their innovations prove successful. Then a period of imitation by more members of the group follows, and finally the rest of the members may be dragged along for fear of offending the others because refusal to accept and buy the innovation can be interpreted as disapproval of the group's values. We will say much more about the "web of word of mouth" when we talk about promotion planning in Chapter 20.[37]

[34]David Riesman, N. Glaser, and R. Denney, *The Lonely Crowd* (Garden City, N.Y.: Doubleday & Co., Inc., 1950). For additional discussion on reference groups, see James H. Donnelly, Jr., "Social Character and Acceptance of New Products," *Journal of Marketing Research*, February, 1970, pp. 111–116; W. Bruce Weale and John R. Kerr, "Brand Choices of Teen-age 'In-group' versus 'Out-group,'" *Journal of Retailing*, Winter, 1969–70, pp. 30–35; and Robert E. Witt, "Informal Social Group Influence on Consumer Brand Choice," *Journal of Marketing Research*, November, 1969, pp. 473–75.

[35]Harold H. Kassarjian, "Social Character and Differential Preference for Mass Communication," *Journal of Marketing Research*, May, 1965, pp. 146–53.

[36]Carman, *op. cit.*, pp. 21 and 61; *Printers' Ink*, November 22, 1957, pp. 58 ff.; Elihu Katz and Paul E. Lazarsfeld, *Personal Influences* (Glencoe, Ill.: Free Press, 1955); and George Katona, *The Powerful Consumer* (New York: McGraw-Hill Book Co., 1960). For further discussion on opinion leadership, see John O. Summers, "The Identity of Women's Clothing Fashion Opinion Leaders," *Journal of Marketing Research*, May, 1970, pp. 178–86; Thomas S. Robertson and James N. Kennedy, "Prediction of Consumer Innovators: An Application of Multiple Discriminant Analysis," *Journal of Marketing Research*, February, 1968, pp. 64–69; Thomas R. Robertson and John G. Myers, "Personality Correlates of Opinion Leadership and Innovative Buying Behavior," *Journal of Marketing Research*, May, 1969, pp. 164–68; and Charles W. King and John O. Summers, "Over-lap of Opinion Leadership Across Consumer Product Categories," *Journal of Marketing Research*, February, 1970, pp. 43–50.

[37]William H. Whyte, Jr., "The Web of Word of Mouth," in Lincoln H. Clark (ed.), *Consumer Behavior*, (New York: New York University Press, 1955), Vol. II, pp. 113–22. Reprinted from *Fortune*, November, 1954. For additional examples of reference-group significance, see Zaltman, *op. cit.*, p. 93.

Culture
sets the
framework

The cultural environment was discussed briefly in Chapter 3 when uncontrollable variables were considered. Here, we are looking at culture in the same way, as encompassing the values and attitudes of the whole society within which the individual finds himself.

The American culture tends to encourage and reward hard work and achievement, while other societies seem less concerned about what they feel are materialistic values. Americans are willing to work, but they also want material rewards. This has led our economy to a concern for growth and physical output. In such an economy, an emphasis on producing and distributing goods logically follows, and much of our analysis of consumer behavior and decision making is within this cultural framework.

In another cultural situation, perhaps primary motives, and certainly selective motives, and social influences would be different. This basic impact of culture on the interaction of the other variables must be kept in mind when one ventures into the international environment.

It also might be useful to speculate on probable changes in the United States if the current interest in the "quality of life" leads to a desire for less materialistic solutions to drive tensions. Basic needs may be the same, but we may learn to satisfy them in different ways.

In some Latin societies, far greater stress is placed on leisure and the enjoyment of life. More holidays are built into the working year to permit more time to enjoy life, not things. The gross national product in such economies may not be quite as high as it could be, but the culture may not feel that it is suffering because of this lower physical output.

Regarding the possibility of changing the cultural environment, however, it is important to recognize that changes in basic attitudes come slowly. An individual firm could not hope to make big changes in the short run. Instead, it should identify which attitudes are and are not subject to change and work within these constraints.

Integrating the behavioral science approaches

We have been examining various approaches to explaining why individuals and families buy as they do. Hopefully, the decision processes within the consumer's "black box" are somewhat clearer. But we also have to acknowledge that the behavioral sciences have not answered all of the questions. It would be most desirable to have an integrating framework to relate the various influences on buying behavior and the theories about these influences. Unfortunately, we do *not* have such a framework. As of now, after the marketing manager has reviewed all of the behavioral data, he still has to rely on his own intuition and marketing research to help him estimate expected behavior in various market grid boxes.

Some integrating theories have been presented, however, and to try to tie all of this together we will discuss a recent effort which forces us to think beyond the typical stereotypes (or our own misconceptions) about consumer behavior. This model does not provide answers, but it presents a comprehensive view of what is happening in the black box.

Howard-Sheth model of buyer behavior

Figure 8–5 presents the Howard-Sheth theory of buyer behavior, with its many interactions. This is basically an elaboration of the stimulus ("black box") response model introduced in the beginning of the chapter.

On the left side of the diagram, we see the input or stimulus variables. The *significative stimuli* include the *physical* aspects of the firm's and competitors' marketing mixes, including the quality and price of the products, service offered, and availability of the product or service. The *symbolic stimuli* include the image-making information about the significative stimuli, for example the written or pictorial material available on packages or in advertising. Finally, the *social stimuli* include all information which a potential buyer would get from his family, reference groups, social class, and culture.

All of these stimuli then enter into the consumer's black box for processing. This is shown in Figure 8–5 as entering into the perceptual subsystem. How this information is processed, however, depends upon how much attention is given to these particular stimuli by the consumer, how clear the stimuli are, and the perceptual bias which is used by the individual in translating them.

The information, if any, which passes through the perceptual subsystem would then be processed by the learning subsystem. Here the individual's motives, his methods of making choices, attitudes, brand comprehension, confidence about making decisions, and intentions with regard to purchasing, all interact with his satisfaction, if any, with previous experiences of the type being evaluated.

The output of all of this information processing might be a purchase, shown at the right-hand side of the diagram. And depending on the satisfaction with this purchase, the buyer's intentions, attitudes, brand comprehension, and attention may be modified and in turn affect subsequent decision making.

Can aid marketing strategy planning

Such a framework is useful for estimating what form of problem-solving target customers are likely to use.

Extensive problem solving may be necessary if the information in a number of the boxes is inadequate and the consumer must develop such information on his own in order to make his decision. Routine buying behavior, on the other hand, could result if the consumer were quite familiar with the incoming stimuli, perceived them accurately (at least in his mind), and had already learned that a particular product would be very satisfactory.

Such a framework is also useful for the marketing manager – helping him to focus on what he does and does not know about his target customers' decision making. He may be willing to assume some things, while others will require some marketing research.

Figure 8-5 Theory of buyer behavior

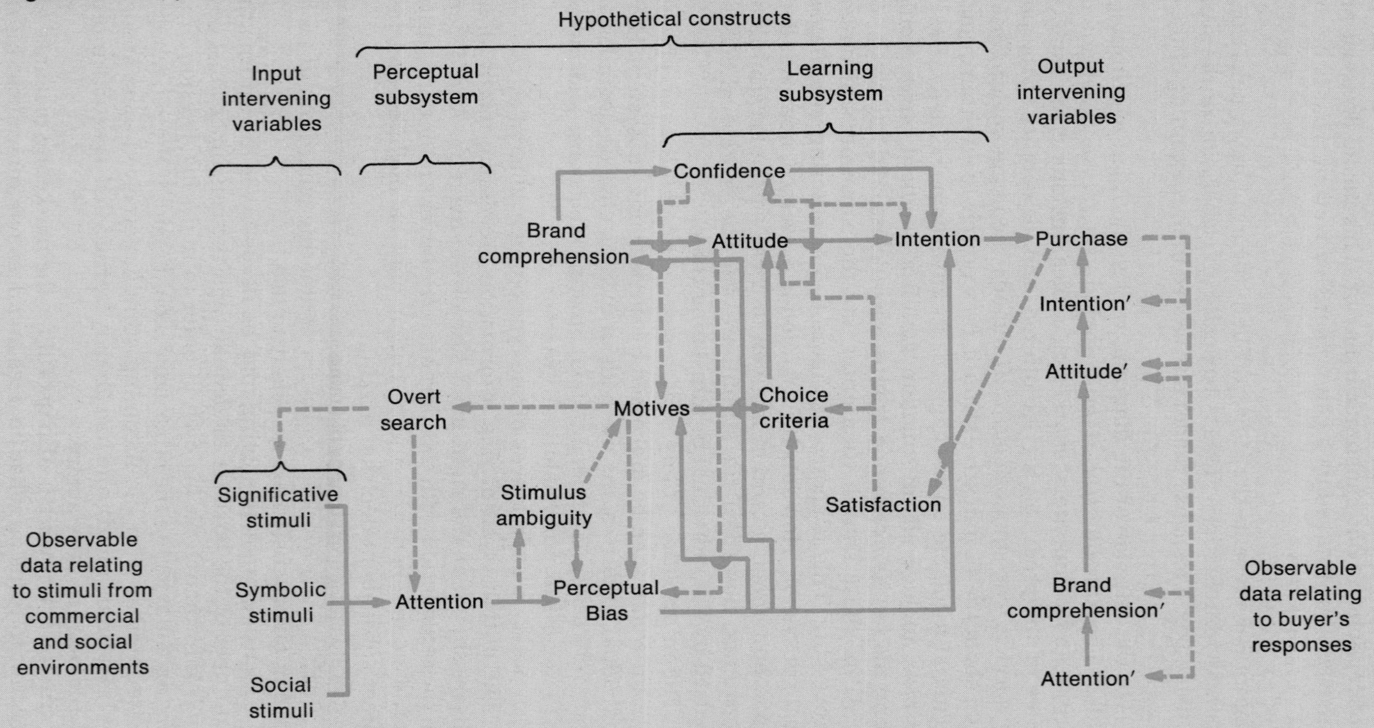

Source: John A. Howard and J. N. Sheth, *The Theory of Buyer Behavior* (New York: John Wiley & Sons, Inc., 1969), p. 54.

The model also indicates where his marketing plans might have some impact. If there is perceptual bias, for example, a promotional effort could be developed to clarify the information entering the buyer's "black box." Or if there is confusion about choice criteria, personal selling efforts could help potential customers evaluate various offerings. Or if the product's physical characteristics are not what the buyer perceives them to be, promotional effort could be directed to correcting this situation.

Can aid understanding of new research findings

Finally, this framework gives the marketing manager a chance to handle new research findings in a meaningful way. Instead of just saying, "Well, that's very interesting" (and wondering how it all fits), he can organize and classify his thoughts within this framework.

Suppose a marketing manager has to evaluate research data that suggests that men are buying many articles long purchased exclusively by women. He might reason, "This has some relation to family organization. Perhaps I should study male consumers to see which men are leading this trend since it may affect the 'social stimuli' area, which in turn may affect various parts of the perceptual and learning subsystems." He might ask himself additional pertinent questions: "Is the trend related to income? What occupations are involved? Is society likely to discourage this trend? Are the family roles changing? Does this trend seem to represent a basic change in consumer behavior? Will we have to discover what men think about our product and other competing products?" His next step might be to conduct research to get his answers. This framework would also provide guidance in the research design.[38]

Intuition and judgment still needed for marketing planning

The present state of our knowledge about consumer behavior is such that we still must rely on intuition and judgment to develop useful descriptions of the "whys" of consumer behavior in various market grid boxes. Socioeconomic characteristics help some. And behavioral theories provide insights too. But finally the marketing manager will have to mix in a dash of his own intuition and judgment to isolate homogenous groups of potential customers. This will often be the case because some of the determining dimensions may be either difficult or impossible to measure. Also, as we have already noted, consumer behavior is multidimensional, and it is very likely that the dimensions in seemingly "nearby" market grid boxes may be quite different. Income may be an extremely important dimension to lower-income consumers, for example, but among higher-income consumers, a social class or a status dimension may be critical.

[38] For a fuller discussion of the Howard-Sheth model, see John A. Howard and Jagdish N. Sheth, *The Theory of Buyer Behavior* (New York: John Wiley & Son, Inc., 1969; and J. U. Farley and L. W. Ring, "An Empirical Test of the Howard-Sheth Model of Buyer Behavior," *Journal of Marketing Research,* November, 1970, pp. 427–38. Also see, C. Glenn Walters and Gordon W. Paul, *Consumer Behavior: An Integrated Approach* (Homewood: Richard D. Irwin, Inc., 1970); and W. T. Tucker, *Foundations of a Theory of Consumer Behavior* (New York: Holt, Rinehart & Winston, Inc., 1967).

Clustering techniques may help

Some new techniques may be on the horizon to help the marketing manager in market gridding. Roughly called "clustering" techniques, they seek to do mechanically part of what previously required much intuition and judgment.

The basic approach of these techniques (which generally make use of a computer) is to try to find similar patterns within consumer attitudinal and purchasing behavior data. Realizing that several (yet to be determined) dimensions may be needed to describe the people in different market segments, the relevant consumer-related dimensions are not preset as they are in trend analysis (recall that we set the dimensions when we compared sales over time in Chapter 5 for forecasting).

Instead, a computer will search among all the data it is given for patterns – for clusters of homogeneous groups of people. When such clusters have been found, then the characteristics (dimensions) of the people in the groups must be analyzed by humans for insights into why the computer clustered them together. If the results make some sense – if they have face validity – then the consumer-related dimensions may suggest new or at least better marketing strategies.

An analysis of the "toothpaste market," for example, might show that there are several clusters of consumers, each seeking (or getting) quite different satisfactions. The relevant dimensions may have little to do with easy-to-measure socioeconomic characteristics, but may nevertheless suggest strategy implications. (And further research might determine the size of the markets.)

Some people buy toothpaste for its sensory satisfaction (the sensory segment), while others are concerned with the effect of clean teeth on their social image (the sociables). Others are worried about decay (the worriers), and some are strictly interested in the best value for their money (the economic men). Each of these market segments calls for a different marketing mix, although some of the four P's may be similar.

As more work of this kind is done, we may see similar kinds of clusters reoccurring in different product classes, for example (besides those mentioned above): the status seeker, the swinger, the conservative, and the inner-directed man. It should be clear, however, that these techniques only aid the manager. Judgment is still required to name the clusters and determine that they make market sense.[39]

[39] The details of these techniques are beyond our scope, but for more discussion, see Russell I. Haley, "Benefit Segmentation: A Decision-Oriented Research Tool," *Journal of Marketing*, July, 1968, pp. 30–35; Paul Green and Frank Carmone, *Multidimensional Scaling and Related Techniques in Marketing Analysis* (Boston: Allyn & Bacon, Inc., 1970); Paul E. Green and Frank J. Carmone, "Multidimensional Scaling: An Introduction and Comparison of Nonmetric Unfolding Techniques," *Journal of Marketing Research*, August, 1969, pp. 330–43; Henry Assael, "Segmenting Markets by Group Purchasing Behavior: An Application of the AID Technique," *Journal of Marketing Research*, May, 1970, pp. 153–59; Joseph M. Kamen, "Quick Clustering," *Journal of Marketing Research*, May, 1970, pp. 199–205; Lewis Alpert and Ronald Gatty, "Product Positioning by Behavioral Life-Styles," *Journal of Marketing*, April, 1969, pp. 65–69; Norman L. Barnett, "Beyond Market Segmentation," *Harvard Business Review*, January–February, 1969, pp. 152–66; and John G. Myers, *Consumer*

Why consumers select particular stores—patronage motives

We have talked about buying behavior in terms of why individuals or families make decisions about *products*. But why do they select particular stores? We will take up this topic now, following essentially the same line of discussion as above. In fact, it would be possible to consider a retailer's store as his "product," meaning that much of what we said above would apply directly. Some additional considerations and adjustments for stores are desirable however.

Economic motives— what is rational and irrational?

The motives listed below are similar to the economic motives for products and help explain why consumers buy at one store rather than another.

1. Convenience.
2. Variety or selection.
3. Quality of goods—freshness, purity, craftsmanship, etc.
4. Courtesy of sales personnel.
5. Integrity—reputation for fairness in dealings.
6. Services offered—delivery, credit, returned-goods privileges.
7. Value offered.

Customers patronize stores that offer the conveniences and services they want, at the lowest prices consistent with all the service they want. Some consumers want a great deal of service and are willing to pay for it. Others who do not care so much for service (or at least don't want to pay for it) often think of those who patronize such stores as irrational, citing their apparent disregard for higher prices. But are the service-minded customers really irrational? Perhaps they like these services and place a high value on their own time.

Emotional motives— where do you find prestige or comfort?

The conventional thinking in retailing tends to emphasize economic motives, especially the value offered or, more narrowly, low prices. But there may also be important emotional reasons for patronizing particular stores. The product motives of sociability, distinctiveness, pride, or emulation are relevant here.

Some people visit a store because they may meet their friends there. Others feel certain stores are distinctive and wear the labels of these institutions with pride. As a result, others may patronize these same stores to emulate the leaders. By contrast, they might not patronize another store because they would be embarrassed to carry home packages bearing the insignia of an obviously "inferior" store.

Social class seems to be especially important in consumers' selection of stores. In one study, it was found that the lower-class woman thinks that if she goes into a higher-class store, the clerks and the

Image and Attitude (IBER Special Publications [Berkeley: University of California, Graduate School of Business Administration, 1968]).

other customers in the store may "punish" her in various subtle ways. "The clerks treat you like a crumb," one woman said.[40]

Different stores do seem to attract different classes of customers. One study of two large Chicago furniture stores was quite revealing in this regard. Each store had a broad range of prices and felt it was catering to the mass market. Yet an analysis of their patrons revealed that each store appealed to quite different classes; one strongly to the upper-middle and upper classes and the other strongly to the lower-lower class.[41]

Ignorance about the relevant dimensions, including the social class dimensions, could obviously lead to serious errors in marketing strategy. There is no one "right" answer as to whom a store should appeal. In fact, not all stores have, or want, a distinct image. Some try to avoid creating a class image because they want to appeal to a wide audience. Macy's in New York, for example, tries to create a fairly universal appeal. John Wanamaker, in Philadelphia, thinks of itself as a family store with a friendly atmosphere; as a result, it (like Macy's) has departments that carry some very expensive merchandise and others that handle goods for the mass market. Carson Pirie Scott & Co., in Chicago, caters to the large middle majority. Its objective is to have a friendly family store that will satisfy the broad market, some of which might feel uncomfortable in a high-fashion outlet.

By contrast, Robert Hall Clothes, Inc., a national clothing chain, aims at the lower-class market. It tries to attract the average family who wants good clothing, not *high* fashion, and it emphasizes lower prices. At the other extreme, Lord & Taylor in New York and I. Magnin in San Francisco—as well as some of the shops in Marshall Field & Co. in Chicago—emphasize high-fashion merchandise and aim at the upper classes. The prestige of these stores enables them to hire sales personnel with the appropriate "company" attitudes. The personnel reinforce the image the management wishes to convey. Lord & Taylor says, "We try to have a well-bred store, run by well-bred people, for well-bred customers." But the store is quick to point out that this does not necessarily mean high prices: "There is no price tag on taste."[42]

Various kinds of stores may be needed

If consumers expect different things from stores, then perhaps different kinds of stores are needed. One sociologist classified shoppers into four categories: *economic shoppers, apathetic shoppers, personalizing shoppers,* and *ethical shoppers.* Each type might need a different type of store.

The largest group discovered in the study were the *economic shoppers,* the economists' "economic men." Middle-class shoppers tended to be in this group. They were primarily interested in price, quality,

[40] Martineau, "The Pattern of Social Classes," *op. cit.*, p. 234.

[41] Pierre Martineau, "The Personality of the Retail Store," *Harvard Business Review*, Vol. 36, No. 1 (January–February, 1958), p. 49.

[42] "What Makes a 'Favorite' Store?" *Business Week*, June 14, 1958, pp. 57–60. See also, H. Robert Dodge and Harry N. Summer, "Choosing Between Retail Stores," *Journal of Retailing*, Fall, 1969, pp. 11–21.

and variety, and looked with disfavor on practices (or salespeople) that inhibit or slow down their shopping.

The *apathetic shoppers,* a much smaller group, have practically no interest in shopping and are willing to patronize the most convenient store.

Personalizing shoppers seek stores in which they feel socially comfortable. They are inclined to rate stores in terms of the closeness of their relationship to the sales personnel. Sometimes such a shopper refers to the store she patronizes as "my store." These shoppers tend to be from the lower classes.

Ethical shoppers feel that they ought to support particular stores, especially neighborhood stores or small shops, because they sometimes appreciate their availability.[43]

It is obvious that if there were enough of each of these types of shoppers in a neighborhood, different kinds of stores could exist. More will be said about this in Chapter 16, on Retailing.

Clearly, the market grid concept has relevance in the consumer's selection of stores, and this should be noted by retailers because it means that consumers might develop loyalty to stores rather than products. It should also be noted by manufacturers and wholesalers because it points up the important role that particular retailers could play in reaching certain target markets. Some consumers may simply be more store-loyal than brand-loyal.

Conclusion

In this chapter we have analyzed the individual consumer, the consumer operating in a group, and the way individuals and groups view products and stores. We have stressed the fact that individual consumers behave very differently, sometimes motivated by economic and sometimes by emotional considerations, and often by a combination of the two. To assume that everyone behaves the way we do—or even the way our friends or families do—may lead to grave marketing errors.

Consumer buying behavior is the expression of the consumer's efforts to satisfy his needs and wants. We discussed some motives that suggest why consumers buy, but saw that consumer behavior cannot be explained by a list of motives. On the other hand, motives may be useful until a tested theory of consumer behavior is developed.

We also saw that our society is characterized by social classes, which does help explain some consumer behavior. Fortunately, it is possible to develop some estimates of the size of social classes, using

[43] Gregory P. Stone, "City Shoppers and Urban Identification: Observations on the Social Psychology of City Life," *American Journal of Sociology,* July, 1954, pp. 36–45.

readily available data on education, occupation, and housing expenditures.

A framework was presented in this chapter to help the student interpret and integrate the various approaches and data he might obtain from marketing research. As of now, the behavioral sciences can only offer insights and theories which the marketing manager must blend with his own intuition and judgment in developing his marketing strategies.

Marketing research may have to be used to answer specific questions. But if neither the money nor the time is available for research, then management will have to rely on the available description of present behavior and "guesstimates" about future behavior. You should study the popular magazines and the nation's leading newspapers carefully, for these publications often mirror the public's shifting preferences. You also should be familiar with the many studies concerning the changing consumer that are published regularly in the business and trade press. This material, added and related to the information in these last several chapters, will aid your own decision making.

Remember that the consumer, with all his likes and preferences, may be elusive—but not invisible. We have more data and understanding of consumer behavior than is generally used by businessmen.

QUESTIONS AND PROBLEMS

1 What is the behavioral science concept which underlies the "black-box" model of consumer behavior? Does this concept have operational relevance to the marketing manager, i.e., if it is a valid concept, can he make use of it?

2 Illustrate the three levels of problem solving with an example from your own personal experience.

3 What buying motives are being appealed to in the following statements?
a) "Don't hide your copper!" (Copper-bottomed cooking utensils.)
b) "Choose (our appliance) and welcome a tradition into your home . . . a tradition of quality. Because of it (our appliances) will serve you faithfully, year after year. And their classic beauty never dims. In fact, many are still in daily use today, after 20 or more years of service."
c) "Sign of good taste. Be really refreshed . . . have a (soft drink)!"
d) "America's best-selling honey. This honey is pure, clear, and golden as the sunshine. With a wonderfully mild, wholesome flavor created by Mother Nature—honey pure and delicious. Try it."

4 Cut out two recent advertisements: one full-page color ad from a magazine and one large display from a newspaper. Indicate which of the buying motives are being appealed to in each case.

5 What is the basic difference between emotional and economic motives? Is any use served by classifying motives into these two categories?

6 Illustrate the interaction of the individual and the family from your own personal experiences. Do you feel that other families behave in exactly the same way? Can some principle be developed out of this experience?

7 List three products for which the preferences of the actual user have no bearing on the purchasing decision.

8 How do society's values have an impact on purchasing behavior? Give two specific examples.

9 How should the social class structure affect the planning of a new restaurant in a large city? How might the four P's be adjusted?

10 What social class would you associate with each of the following phrases or items?

a) Sport cars.
b) *True Story, True Romances,* etc.
c) *New Yorker.*
d) *Life.*
e) Women listening to "soap operas."
f) TV bowling shows.
g) Families that serve Martinis, especially before dinner.
h) Families who dress formally for dinner regularly.
i) Families which are distrustful of banks (keep money in socks or mattress).
j) Owners of French poodles.

In each case, choose one class, if you can. If you are not able to choose one class, but rather feel that several classes are equally likely, then so indicate. In those cases where you feel that all classes would be equally interested or characterized by a particular item, choose all five classes.

11 Illustrate how the reference-group concept may apply in practice, by explaining how you personally are influenced by some reference group for some product. What are the implications of such behavior for marketing managers?

12 Explain how the patronage motives discussed in the text can be used to explain the success, or failure, of a local retail store.

13 What new status symbols are replacing the piano and automobile? Do these products have any characteristics in common? If they do, what are some possible status symbols of the future?

14 On the basis of the data and analysis presented in Chapters 6 and 8, what kind of buying behavior would you expect to find for the following products: (1) canned peas, (2) toothpaste, (3) ball-point pens, (4) baseball gloves, (5) sport coats, (6) dishwashers, (7) encyclopedias, (8) automobiles, and (9) motorboats? Set up a grid for your answer with products along the left-hand margin as the row headings and the following factors as headings for the columns: (1) how do you think consumers would shop for these products, (2) how far would they go, (3) would they buy by brand, (4) would they wish to compare with other products, and (5) any other factors which they should consider. Insert short answers—words or phrases are satisfactory—in the various grid boxes. Be prepared to discuss how the answers you put in the grid boxes would affect each product's marketing mix.

...most ultimate consumers probably would be startled to find
that the bulk of purchases are made, not by them, but by
intermediate customers...there are great marketing
opportunities in serving intermediate customers, and it is
quite probable that a college-level student will eventually
work in this area.

9

Intermediate customers and their buying behavior

The term *customer* is interpreted by most of us to mean the individual final consumer (or family). Yet most ultimate consumers probably would be startled to find that the bulk of purchases are made, not by them, but by intermediate customers.

This chapter will be devoted to these intermediate customers – who and where they are, and what their buying habits are. There are misconceptions about the nature and size of these "other" markets. In fact, there are great marketing opportunities in serving intermediate customers, and it is quite probable that a college-level student will eventually work in this area.

We want to show that the market grid concept may have even greater application here because of the great diversity of demand and types of intermediate customers. While we will limit our discussion to the United States to keep it specific, many of the ideas are applicable to the world market.

Who are intermediate customers?

There are many kinds of intermediate customers between producers of basic raw materials and final consumers. In Chapter 1, we introduced the concept of a macro-marketing system and showed a diagram of all the interrelations of the various producers, intermediate customers, and final consumers. Now, we will take a more careful look at *who* they are and *how* some of them buy.

The various types of intermediate customers and their numerical importance are shown in Table 9–1. Note that there are only about 11 million intermediate customers in the United States, compared to over 200 million final consumers. These intermediate customers may: (1) buy goods for resale to others; (2) buy materials or items that they incorporate into their own product for eventual resale to others; and

Table 9–1 Kind and number of intermediate customers in 1967

Agriculture, forestry, and fisheries	3,353,000
Service industries	2,174,000
Retailers	1,763,000
Contract construction	856,000
Wholesalers	311,000
Manufacturers	311,000
Governmental units	81,000
Others	1,702,000

Source: *Statistical Abstract of the United States,* 1970, pp. 405 and 468 and *1967 Census of Business.*

(3) buy plant and equipment that enable them to operate their businesses.

Farms, service, retailing

The most numerous intermediate customers are those engaged in *agriculture, forestry, and fishing.* While many of these are small farmers, each represents an individual decision-making unit and a potential customer. Farmers are given separate treatment in this chapter.

The *service industries* are the second largest group of intermediate customers. These include establishments such as restaurants, hotels, motels, barbershops, beauty shops, hospitals, medical clinics, and laundries and dry cleaners. Their great diversity and, frequently, small size make it difficult to generalize about their buying behavior. Labor is a big element in their operation, as opposed to materials, but the subject of labor relations is beyond our scope. Further, the owner's own labor may be the major cost.

We will not discuss service industries separately, but the way industrial customers (manufacturers) buy will probably be applicable to the purchasing methods for goods and services of service industries also. This is especially true where service industries are linked together into a chain or are part of a franchise operation.

Retailers are the next most numerous group of intermediate customers. Their buying behavior with respect to plant and equipment will be similar to that of industrial customers. Their buying of goods for resale, however, is so intimately linked to their selling activity that we will delay discussion of this until retailing is treated in Chapter 16.

Contract construction is the business of manufacturing homes, roads, buildings and other structures, and in this respect is similar to manufacturing in general. The two will be considered as similar in our discussion of manufacturers in this chapter.

Wholesalers, a somewhat smaller group, also behave like manufacturers in the purchase of plant and equipment. In buying for resale, however, they, like retailers, find their buying and selling policies closely related. We will delay this discussion until we treat wholesaling in Chapter 17.

Manufacturers, about equal in number to wholesalers, are discussed extensively in this chapter because their total volume of purchases is large and it is possible to generalize about their buying behavior.

A seemingly small group—*governmental units*—includes states, counties, cities, school districts, sanitary districts, and the federal government. But governments are growing in significance, especially for certain types of products. Our federal government is especially important, for it is the largest single buyer in the world. Governmental buyers will receive special treatment in this chapter.

A large number of firms fall into the "other" category—mining and quarrying, communications, and public utilities (all of which are basically manufacturing enterprises), *plus* transportation, finance, and real estate (all of which combine some aspects of manufacturing and the service industries). While the general principles we will discuss apply to these various enterprises, their specific needs, buying behavior, etc., are too specialized to be treated in this text.

Manufacturers are important customers

We will emphasize the buying behavior of manufacturers, first, because they are important (in sales volume) buyers and, second, because other intermediate buyers generally behave in the same fashion. This is especially true with respect to buying their plant and equipment and the goods and services they incorporate into their products.

How big are the targets?
One of the most striking facts about the industrial market is its small number of customers as compared to the final customer market, where we find over 200 million people in more than 60 million households. In the industrial market, there are about 311,000 manufacturing plants, and the majority of these plants are quite small, as indicated by the data in Table 9–2.

Table 9–2 Size distribution of manufacturing establishments, 1963

Number of employees	Number of establishments	Value added by manufacturing	Total number of employees	Percentage of firms	Percentage of value added	Percentage of employees
1–4	112,036	2,109,939	203,647	36.5	1.1	1.3
5–9	48,461	3,045,060	326,093	15.8	1.6	2.0
10–19	46,778	6,155,413	645,606	15.3	3.2	4.0
20–49	47,376	14,241,093	1,480,682	15.4	7.4	9.1
50–99	22,886	15,832,033	1,590,601	7.5	8.2	9.8
100–249	17,614	28,826,390	2,726,693	5.7	15.0	16.8
250–499	6,639	25,662,713	2,297,394	2.2	13.3	14.1
500–999	2,942	25,390,653	2,014,698	1.0	13.2	12.4
1,000–2,499	1,375	29,237,192	2,052,759	0.4	15.2	14.3
2,500 or over	544	41,819,313	2,898,617	0.2	21.7	23.0

Source: *1963 Census of Manufactures*, Vol III, *Area Statistics*, pp. 2–8, 2–9.

A relatively few large manufacturing plants employ the majority of workers and produce a substantial share of the value added by manufacture. For example, in 1963, 29,114 plants—about 9.5 percent of the total—employed 80.6 percent of the production employees and were responsible for 78.4 percent of the value added by manufacture.

Customers cluster

In addition to concentration by size, industrial markets are characterized by concentration in particular areas. Figure 9–1 is an industrial map of the United States showing the area of each state in proportion to the value of manufactured products in that state. The dominance of the Middle West and Middle Atlantic states is noteworthy.

As we discovered with final consumers, political boundaries leave something to be desired for describing industrial concentration. Big metropolitan areas are big industrial markets too. In 1963, the 212 SMSA's accounted for approximately 63 percent of the value added by manufacturing in the United States. Marketing managers can focus their attention on a relatively few clearly defined markets and be within reach of the majority of the business. This has a definite bearing on the number and type of wholesalers that manufacturers use and the kinds of wholesalers who develop, as we will see in subsequent chapters.

Concentration by industry

Not only do we see concentration by size of firm and geographical location but also by industry. Manufacturers of advanced electronics systems and instrumentation are concentrated in the Boston and New York areas and on the West Coast, for example. The steel industry is heavily concentrated in the Pittsburgh and Chicago areas. Other industries have similar concentrations based on the availability of natural or human resources.

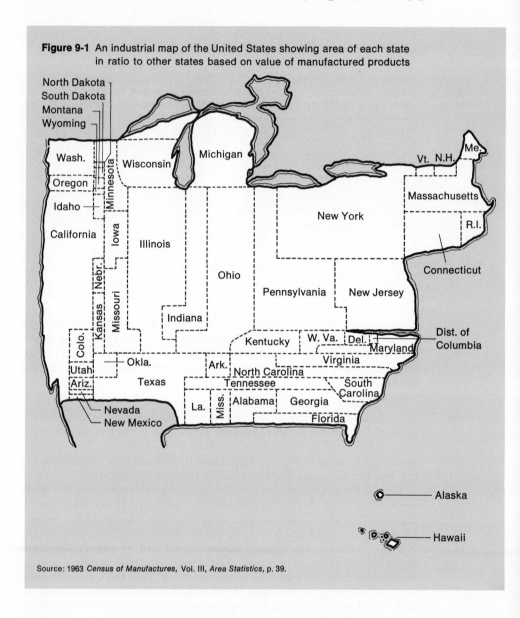

Figure 9-1 An industrial map of the United States showing area of each state in ratio to other states based on value of manufactured products

Source: 1963 *Census of Manufactures*, Vol. III, *Area Statistics*, p. 39.

Buyers are in metropolitan areas

The salesman's task of selling to some industries is made even easier because some large companies with multiple plants may do all of their buying from a central office which is usually located in one of the large metropolitan areas. One of the large building material manufacturers, for example, does the bulk of its buying for more than 50 plants from its Chicago office. In such a case, a salesman may be able to sell his products all over the country without leaving his home city.

This makes it not only easier for the salesman, but also for his competitors, and he may have to compete in an extremely competitive market. The selling job may be easier, but the marketing job may be much harder.

Much data is available on industrial markets by SIC code

The federal government regularly collects data on the number of establishments, their sales volumes, and number of employees of a large number of industry groups, broken down by county and SMSA. The data is reported for Standard Industrial Classification code industries (SIC codes). These codes greatly facilitate research by firms who can relate their own sales to their *customers'* type of activity. SIC code breakdowns start with such broad industry categories as food and kindred products (code 20), tobacco products (code 21), textile mill products (code 22), apparel (code 23), and so on.

Within each two-digit industry breakdown, much more detailed data may be available for three-digit and four-digit industries (that is, subindustries of the two- or three-digit industries). Within the apparel (23) industry, for example, the three-digit industry 232 — men's, youths', and boys' furnishings, work clothing and allied garments — contains the following four-digit industries: shirts, collars, and night wear (2321), underwear (2322), neckwear (2323), separate trousers (2327), work clothing (2328), and NEC (not elsewhere classified) (2329).

Four-digit detail is not available for all industries in every geographic area, of course, because industries do tend to concentrate. But as much specific data as possible is given, limited only by the U.S. Bureau of the Census' restriction that an individual firm's data cannot be disclosed. This often requires merging detailed data into higher-level industries, thereby losing interesting details in some geographic areas.

With all this detailed data available, it should be clear that some of the market gridding and the sales forecasting procedures discussed in Chapter 5 could be applied easily in the industrial area. It may be possible, for example, to use the number of employees in particular industries as a measure of potential in each geographic area. Or number of establishments or sales total might be useful.

The point is that a lot of good basic information is available. If companies aiming at industrial target markets can specify clearly who they are aiming at, readily available data organized by SIC codes may be extremely valuable. Besides the federal government, most trade associations and private organizations which gather data in the industrial area do so according to SIC code.[1]

It should be obvious that SIC code breakdowns may be an important dimension in market gridding for the industrial market. At the very least, SIC codes and geographic dimensions could serve as a starting point in gridding. Then, behavioral dimensions might have to be added as more was learned about each market segment.

[1] For more detail, see *Industry Profiles — 1958–1966* and *Facts for Marketers*, U.S. Department of Commerce, Business and Defense Services Administration.

Industrial buyers are problem solvers

Some people think of industrial buying as something entirely separate from consumer buying, but a deeper analysis of buying processes suggests that there may be more similarities than was once thought. In fact, it appears that the basic problem-solving framework which was introduced in Chapter 8 can be applied here. Similarly, the Howard-Sheth model may have general applicability.

A recent detailed analysis of the industrial buying process, however, shows that it may be desirable to break down the industrial buying process, within the previous general framework, to obtain a better understanding of the industrial market. These specifics are discussed below.

They use an eight-phase buying process

Based on an analysis of the behavior of 175 industrial marketing executives, it appears that companies pass through eight phases in their buying process. While some of these phases may occur simultaneously, they tend to follow in sequence:

Phase one – Anticipation or recognition of a problem (need) – realization that a problem exists and that it can be solved by buying a product or service.

Phase two – Determining the characteristics and quantity of the needed item – usually done within the firm, but outside sources may be helpful. In this phase, the process of narrowing down to a solution has begun.

Phase three – Description of the specific characteristics and quantity of the needed item – an extension of phase two.

Phase four – Seeking out and qualifying potential sources. This may involve selecting a supplier from a list or spending time investigating sources and suppliers.

Phase five – Getting and analyzing supplier proposals. This can be a routine step or involve a complicated series of proposals and counterproposals, running over several months.

Phase six – Evaluation of proposals and selection of suppliers – including analysis of offers and possible further negotiations on price, terms, delivery, and other details.

Phase seven – Selection of an order routine – includes both external and internal aspects. Among the former, preparation of purchase order and follow-up activities. Among the latter, reports to the using department and inventory management.

Phase eight – Performance feedback and evaluation – formal or informal, an evaluation of how well the product or service solved the problem, along with the performance of the supplier.[2]

---

[2] Patrick J. Robinson and Charles W. Faris, *Industrial Buying and Creative Marketing* (Boston: Allyn & Bacon, Inc., 1967), chap. ii.

Eight
phases are
compressed
into three
kinds of
buying

How quickly a firm moves through these phases and how important
each is depends somewhat on the nature of the company's need and
the experience the firm has had in satisfying the need. The same product might have to be handled in three different ways, depending upon
circumstances. To be specific, three buying processes might be necessary for the same product at different times and in different companies:
a *new-task buying* process, a *modified rebuy* process, or a *straight
rebuy*. These are similar to the extended, limited, and routine buying
we discussed in Chapter 8.

New-task buying

New-task buying would occur when a firm has a new need. In this
case, it must develop a great deal of information, and perhaps even set
up the criteria for selection. New-task buying can be quite important
because it establishes product specifications, sources of supply, and
an order routine which can be followed in the future if satisfactory
results are obtained.

Straight rebuy buying

A *straight rebuy* is a routine purchase which may have been made
many times before. Buyers probably would not bother looking for new
information or even new sources of supply. The majority of a company's purchases might be this type, but they would occupy a relatively small amount of the buyer's time.

Modified rebuy buying

The *modified rebuy* is the in-between process where some additional analysis or rethinking of the buying situation is done, but not
nearly as much effort is involved as in the new-task situation. Since
buyers may want additional information, this would provide an alert
marketing manager with an opportunity to fill the buyer's need. Also,
when appropriate, he might want to make the buyer conscious of new
information in order to convert a straight rebuy to a modified rebuy.

The fact that the identical product or service might be considered
in any of the three ways cannot be overemphasized. It points up the
importance of careful market grid analysis to determine how the
firm's products are accepted, and by whom. A new-task buy will take
much longer than a straight rebuy and provide considerably more
chance for promotional impact by the seller. This can be seen in Figure 9–2, which shows the time and the many influences involved in
the purchase of a special drill.

Industrial
buyers are
becoming
specialists

The size of some industrial operations has made the buying function
extremely important. Many have developed buying specialists, known
as purchasing agents. Some of these have banded together, forming
the National Association of Purchasing Agents in an effort to improve
the effectiveness and status of professional buyers. This is the knowledgeable modern-day buyer that confronts those who wish to sell to
the industrial market.

The industrial buyer, or purchasing agent, usually is the man all
salesmen must see first before contacting any other employee. The
buyer holds an important position and may take a dim view of sales-

Figure 9-2 Decision network diagram of the buying situations: special drill

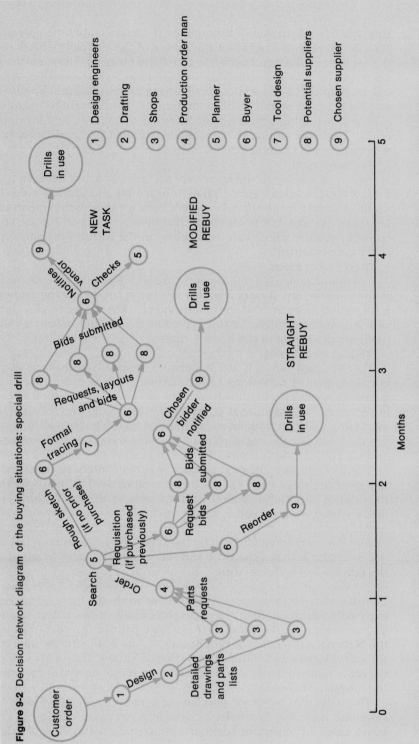

Source: Patrick J. Robinson and Charles W. Faris, *Industrial Buying and Creative Marketing* (Boston: Allyn & Bacon, Inc., 1967), p. 33. Reprinted by permission of the publisher.

men who attempt to bypass him. In large companies, he may even specialize by product area and be quite expert.

Rather than being "sold," these buyers expect precise and accurate information that will help them buy wisely. They appreciate assistance in buying as efficiently as possible. They like information on new products and services and tips on potential price changes, strikes, and other changes in business conditions. Most industrial buyers are serious, well-educated men, and salesmen should treat them accordingly.

Basic purchasing motives are economic

Industrial buyers are usually less emotional in their buying habits than final consumers. The basic objectives or motives of their purchasing can be stated as follows:

1. To maintain continuity of supply to support the manufacturing schedule.
2. To do so with a minimum investment in materials and inventory consistent with safety and economic advantage.
3. To avoid duplication, waste, and obsolescence of materials.
4. To maintain standards of quality and materials, based on suitability for use.
5. To procure materials at the lowest cost consistent with the quality and service required.
6. To maintain the company's competitive position in its industry and to conserve its profit position, where material costs are concerned.[3]

Specifically, buyers tend to look for certain product characteristics, including economy, both in original cost and in use, productivity, uniformity, purity, and ability to make the buyer's final product more suitable.[4]

In addition to product characteristics, buyers consider the reliability of the seller, his general cooperativeness, his ability to provide speedy maintenance and repair, past and present relationships (including previous favors), continuous supply under all conditions, and reliable fast delivery.

Emotional motives are relevant

Industrial purchasing does have some emotional overtones, too. There was a day, for example, when it might have been fair to characterize buyers by the following quotation:

> The typical buyer is a man past middle life, spare, wrinkled, intelligent, cold, passive, noncommital, with eyes like a codfish, polite in contacts, but at the same time unresponsive, cool, calm, and damnably composed as a concrete post or a plaster-of-paris cat; a human petrification with a heart of feldspar and without charms; or the friendly germ, minus passions or a sense of humor. Happily they never reproduce, and all of them finally go to hell.[5]

[3] Stuart F. Heinritz, *Purchasing: Principles and Application* (3d ed.; Englewood Cliffs, N.J.: Prentice-Hall, Inc., 1959).

[4] "Component Buyers Seek Tangible Savings," *Electronic Procurement*, May, 1962, pp. 26–29.

[5] Adapted slightly from Charles A. Koepke, *Plant Production Control* (2d ed.; New York: John Wiley & Sons, Inc., 1949), p. 104.

Such a view does not apply to a modern purchasing agent, who places less emphasis on price and more on value. He has a broader view of the purchasing function, usually has a sense of humor, and often can be approached in a lighter vein. International Minerals and Chemicals Co., a manufacturer of standardized chemicals, once even used a dramatic consumer-type promotion (including jets, rockets, and pretty models) for a trade-show presentation.[6]

Modern buyers, being human, want to have friendly relationships with suppliers.[7] Some buyers seem eager to emulate progressive competitors, even to be the first to try new products. In other words, the emotional product motives discussed in the last chapter may have some relevance here.

Survival is important, too

The buyer is generally concerned with helping his firm accomplish its goals, but he may also have some goals of his own, and these may be relevant to market gridding. One goal may be to protect his own position in the company, and dependability of sources may become vital. Most buyers, like people everywhere, seek to survive and improve their chances for promotion, without taking too many risks.

"Looking good" is an especially serious matter for purchasing executives. They often have to buy a wide variety of things from many sources. Perhaps more than other executives, they have to make decisions involving many factors beyond their control. A new component source may deliver low-quality materials, and the buyer may be blamed. And poor service or late delivery may reflect on his ability. Any product or service, therefore, that assures the buyer that he will look good to higher-ups has a definite appeal. In fact, this one factor might make the difference between a successful and an unsuccessful marketing mix.

Ideally, a marketing mix should satisfy both the buyer's company objectives and his individual goals. Therefore, it helps to be aware of some overlapping area where both can be satisfied. See Figure 9–3 for a graphic model of this concept.

Multiple buying influence may be important

Much of the work of the typical purchasing agent consists of placing orders to fill routine requisitions flowing from various production, warehouse, and office departments. Similar orders may have been placed many times before, and to obtain the goods, the purchasing agent can simply refer to his "source file" where he has recorded notes on his past relations with various sources of supply, their prices, and their dependability. For such routine items, he may place the order without further consultation with anyone.

---

[6] "Putting a Sales Idea into Orbit," *Business Week,* June 28, 1958, pp. 70–74.

[7] "How to Use Emotional Factors That Trigger Industrial Sales," *Steel,* April 6, 1959, for a motivational survey conducted in the metalworking industry by F. R. Shoaf of New York University. See also, Frederick E. Webster, Jr., "Modeling the Industrial Buying Process," *Journal of Marketing Research,* November, 1965, pp. 370–76, and Walter Gross, "Rational and Nonrational Appeals in Selling to Businessmen," *Georgia Business,* February, 1970, pp. 1–3.

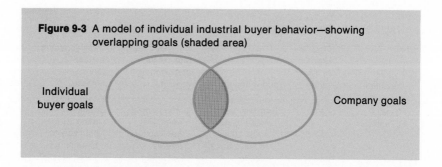

Figure 9-3 A model of individual industrial buyer behavior—showing overlapping goals (shaded area)

Individual buyer goals

Company goals

In other cases, the buyer is not the only company executive participating in the purchasing decision. In fact, sometimes five or more executives may be involved. The bigger and more important the purchase, the higher the level at which the decision will be reviewed, if not actually made. The more technical the decision, the more likely that technical employees will be involved, perhaps to the extent of writing specifications so that only one supplier can meet them.[8]

The nature of this multiple buying influence must be studied in each particular case. It can even be another dimension in the market grid for a particular product. Knowledgeable salesmen could probably help describe the nature of the multiple buying influence, though marketing research may be necessary in some cases. Table 9–3 shows how the Amercoat Corp. outlined its corrosion-control sales job. Although representing a specific case, the table should be studied carefully, since it shows the difference in outlook of various executive levels. A salesman might talk to every one of those possible "influencers," but he would take up different topics and stress different factors for each of them.

Sharing of buying decisions among a number of executives creates a relatively long selling period. Paper work must pass many desks. Approval of a routine order may take anywhere from a week to several months. On very important purchases – say the purchase of a new computer system, a new plant, or major equipment – the selling period may stretch out to a year or more.[9]

Basic methods and practices in industrial buying

Basic approaches for evaluating and buying

In various circumstances, industrial buyers (really, buyers of all types, including final consumers) use four basic approaches to evaluating and buying products: (1) inspection, (2) sampling, (3) description, and (4) negotiated contracts.

[8] For more detail, see John H. Platten, Jr., "How Industry Buys," *Scientific American*, September, 1950.

[9] Robert E. Weigand, "Why Studying the Purchasing Agent Is Not Enough," *Journal of Marketing*, January, 1968, pp. 41–45; and "Who Really Makes the Purchasing Decision?" *Industrial Marketing*, September, 1966, pp. 76–81.

Table 9–3 Analysis of customer buying behavior*

Key men	Contrib-utor factor rating	Job influence	Knowledge and interest in corrosion control	Knowledge and interest in control methods	Buying habits
General manager	"A"	Primarily interested in results. Likely to leave details to others.	Limited knowledge. May have active interest in obtaining better results.	Little knowledge. Interest likely to be in anticipated results only.	May make final decision. Likely to leave details to others.
Manufacturing director	"A" or "B"	Primarily interested in results. Likely to be important factor in obtaining action.	Knowledge likely to depend on size and nature of the company. Should have active interest if aware of own hazards.	Knowledge probably limited. Should have active interest in best methods.	May have authority to place or initiate order. Important factor in any case.
Plant manager or superintendent	"A" "B" or "C"	Degree of importance depends on size of company and operating practice.	If operating in place of manufacturing director, likely to have above average degree of knowledge and interest in both subjects. Otherwise, may be figurehead. His goodwill, however, is important.		Unlikely to have authority to buy. Recommendation or requisition may be important.
Maintenance or corrosion engineer	"B"	Important factor in companies where charged with responsibility for maintenance costs.	Likely to have both interest and knowledge particularly if operating as corrosion engineer.	Should have active interest and some knowledge. May be prejudiced regarding some methods of control.	Unlikely to have authority to place or initiate order, but recommendation important.
Purchasing agent	"C"	Negative rather than positive, but in many companies must be seen first.	Limited, if any.	Limited, if any.	Close buyers, but largely influenced by other department heads and by top management.

Inspection

The inspection method is used for products that are not standardized, and require examination. Here, each product is different, as in the case of some fruits and vegetables, and livestock. One-of-a-kind products, such as used buildings and cars, also must be inspected.

Table 9-3—Continued

Key men	Contributor factor rating	Job influence	Knowledge and interest in corrosion control	Knowledge and interest in control methods	Buying habits
Research department	"B"	Negative as regards operating costs. Positive as applied to products and testing.	Knowledge and interest may be purely "scientific," rather than from dollars and cents viewpoint.	Knowledge and interest likely to be "scientific" and possibly prejudiced.	Usually have no authority to place or initiate orders. Tests likely to be important.
Plant engineer	"B" or "C"	Degree of importance depends on size of company and operating practice	If operating in place of maintenance or corrosion engineer, likely to have most of his knowledge and interest in both subjects. Otherwise, important only from standpoint of goodwill.		May have authority to "requisition"; otherwise recommendation may carry some weight.
Paint foreman	"C"	Usually follows "line of least resistance." Interest and pride need to be stimulated, especially if new method involves extra effort.	Neither knowledge, nor interest except in rare cases.	Except in rare cases, no knowledge beyond methods now using and no active interest except in easier ways to do the job.	Usually have no authority to place or initiate orders. Goodwill and willingness to handle products properly are important.

* This table shows how Amercoat Corp. isolated the group of men who may exert buying influence on the corrosion-control plan they sell. Correlated paragraphs summarize each man's job influence, his knowledge and interest in corrosion control, his knowledge and interest in control methods, and his buying habits. The same technique can be used by any company that sells to the industrial market, working, of course, with its own key men.

Key to contributor factor rating:
  "A"—The men who must make the final buying decision and who have the authority to authorize the expenditure.
  "B"—The advisory, intermediate or subordinate men who must also be sold; otherwise the "A" men are likely to withhold approval.
  "C"—Other men who may influence the buying decision. As a rule, these men have no authority but can block the sale by direct opposition or a negative attitude.
Source: A. E. Turner, "Finding the Men Who Can Influence the Sale," *Sales Management*, September 15, 1953, p. 41.

Products that require inspection are often bought at auction, especially if there are several potential buyers. Auctions, for instance, are commonly found at the wholesale level. Potential buyers inspect the merchandise and then bid against competitors for the product. If there are too few buyers to make a good market at any one time, however, a price may be set by the seller. Even so, there may be bargaining before the final price is accepted by both parties. This would be true, for example, in the used building and machinery market.

Sampling

As products become more standardized, perhaps because of more careful grading and better quality control, buying by sample becomes feasible. The general price level may be set by the seller or determined by an auction-type market for standard grades. The price then may be adjusted from this level according to the quality of the specific sample.

In the grain market, for example, the general price level for standard grades is set by demand-and-supply factors. Then the price for a specific carload is the market price for the appropriate grade plus or minus an adjustment for quality variation based on a sample taken from the carload.

Description

Today, most manufactured items and many agricultural commodities can be subjected to more rigid quality control or grading. When quality almost can be guaranteed, buying by description – grade, brand, or specification – may be satisfactory, at least when there is mutual trust between buyers and sellers. In recent years, more wholesale and retail buyers have come to accept government grading standards for some fruits and vegetables. Now, much of this merchandise is packed in the fields and sold without any further inspection or sampling. This, of course, reduces the cost of buying and is used by buyers whenever practicable.

In modern economies, most products are purchased by description. Grocery, hardware, and dry goods items are examples, By contrast, in primitive economies, most buying is done by inspection or sampling, regardless of the products. The reason is skepticism and uncertainty about quality, or lack of faith in the seller.

Various pricing practices are used for products that can be bought by description. Some firms set fixed prices, and the buyer has little choice, especially if the seller has succeeded in developing a unique marketing mix. But if there is competition among several suppliers, then buyers may ask for bids and choose the seller with the lowest bid. This practice is formalized and made mandatory in much government buying. As an alternative, the buyers may negotiate for lower prices.

Negotiated contracts

The three methods discussed above are concerned with tangible products or products and services which can be described sufficiently well so that suppliers know what is wanted and can submit definite prices or bids. Usually a price is set for each shipment or order, or perhaps for a series of shipments against the same order. But a price is set for some fairly definite, agreed upon, product and marketing mix.

Sometimes, however, the buyer knows roughly what he wants but cannot describe it exactly. Perhaps he plans to change the specifications or total requirements as the job progresses, or maybe some of the details cannot be anticipated. This is found, for example, in research and development work and in the building of special-purpose machinery and large buildings. In such cases, the general project is described, and a basic price may be agreed upon, with provision for adjustments both upward and downward. Or a supplier may be willing to work under a contract that provides some type of incentive over coverage of costs, such as full coverage of costs plus a fixed fee, or full costs plus some percentage profit based on costs. The whole contract may even be subject to renegotiation as the work proceeds.

Supply sources must be dependable to win business

Many industrial products are produced and sold as branded items or to meet certain specifications. As long as suppliers at least meet these minimum specifications, buyers can safely concentrate on other factors, such as price, dependable service, delivery, and credit terms. But it is important that quality be maintained. The cost of a small item may have little to do with its importance. If it causes malfunctioning of a larger unit in which it is incorporated, it may cause a large loss completely out of proportion to its own value. Buyers are understandably concerned about consistent quality, and some even set up statistical quality control procedures to inspect all incoming lots.

Because of the importance of dependable product quality to industrial buyers, some producers deliberately seek to make products that are slightly better than required specifications, thereby giving a greater assurance of reliability and quality to the buyer. This is *the* important selling point for some firms. In effect, this "makes" their marketing mix.

The availability of this "better-than-needed" quality helps explain the behavior of some buyers who appear to favor certain suppliers. While several products may meet the minimum requirements, the buyer is inclined to choose suppliers of extra-quality products because his own future is involved in the buying decision.

Buyers may favor loyal suppliers

To be assured of dependable quality, a buyer may also develop loyalty to certain suppliers. This is especially important when buying nonstandardized products. When a friendly relationship is developed over the years, the supplier practically becomes a part of the buyer's organization – without the buyer assuming the additional cost of plant and working capital or the problems of management. This friendly, loyal relationship may be good business for all concerned. In an emergency, one can sometimes help the other through the crisis.

Most buyers have a sense of fair play, and when a salesman proposes a new idea that saves the buyer's company money, he usually attempts to reward that salesman with orders. This encourages future suggestions. In contrast, buyers who use a bid system exclusively – either by choice or necessity, as in some government and institutional purchasing – may not be offered much beyond the basic products or services. They are interested primarily in price. Marketing managers who have developed better products and technical or other assistance programs may not solicit such business, at least with their better mix.

But buyers must spread their risk

Even if a firm has developed the most ideal marketing mix possible, it probably will not get all of the business of its industrial customers. Purchasing agents usually seek several dependable sources of supply, to protect themselves from unpredictable events, such as strikes, fires, or floods in one of their suppliers' plants. But still, a good marketing mix is likely to win a larger share of the total business.

Buy EOQ quantities, especially if EDP is available

Some buyers in larger companies which have well-developed electronic data processing systems (EDP) have been able to delegate a considerable part of their routine order placing to computers. They develop decision rules that tell the computer how to order economic order quantities (EOQ) and then leave the details of following through to the computer. This is possible because there generally is a lowest-cost order quantity toward which the purchasing agent would aim, anyway.

The delivered cost of goods can be visualized as shown in Figure 9–4. This figure shows that cost per unit is high for very small quantity purchasing, declines as the quantity ordered increases, and then begins to rise again as greater quantities are ordered. Ideally, buyers will seek to purchase that quantity for which the unit cost is lowest.

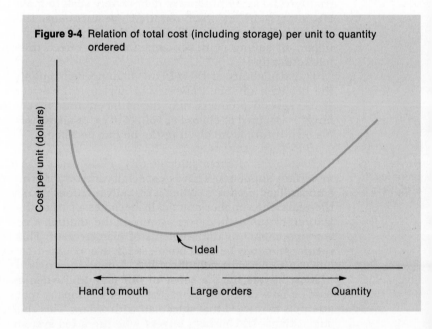

Figure 9-4 Relation of total cost (including storage) per unit to quantity ordered

Some factors that cause the curve in Figure 9–4 to decline as the quantity purchased increases are as follows:

1. Price discounts are sometimes given as quantity purchased increases.
2. Transportation costs are usually lower as the quantity shipped increases.
3. Purchasing costs may be relatively fixed per order, not per unit ordered. As quantity increases, therefore, the per unit ordering

costs decrease. An average purchase order may cost $5 to $10 regardless of the number of items ordered.[10]

The following factors cause the curve to rise and suggest the purchase of smaller quantities:

1. Interest, insurance, and taxes will be higher on larger quantities held in inventory.
2. Space costs will be higher, especially if additional warehouse space must be rented.
3. The risks of deterioration and obsolescence of inventory are increased as the quantity held in inventory is increased.

The costs of carrying inventory often are underestimated because some are intangible. Careful estimates, however, show that the total annual costs of carrying inventory range from 15 to 30 percent of the cost value of the average inventory.[11]

Some formulas have been developed to objectively relate all of the various factors in a particular buying situation and determine the EOQ's. These formulas are beyond the scope of this book, but the very fact that formulas and computers are used shows that buying is becoming increasingly analytical and that every effort is being made to reduce guesswork and intuition.[12]

Ideally, the buyer would appraise all of these factors on a continuing basis and adjust his economic order quantities accordingly. Actually, however, most buyers are faced with such a large number of items to purchase that they could not fully analyze all these factors all the time. When they have a computer system available, they tend to "delegate" as much as they can. Then they watch the general movement of economic conditions, and when conditions require, the buyers modify the basic formulas given to the computer. When nothing unusual happens, however, the computer system can continue to routinely rebuy as needs develop—printing out new purchase orders to the established suppliers.

It is extremely important, then, for a supplier to be one of those that the computer will consider. In such a situation, the critical thing is not whether a particular salesman will get a particular order, but whether he will be considered one of the major suppliers. Obviously, this is a much bigger "sale." It also is obvious that such a buyer might be more favorably impressed by an attractive marketing mix, perhaps for a whole line of products, rather than just a lower price for a particular order. It might be too costly and too much trouble to change his whole buying system just because somebody is offering a low price on a particular day.

---

[10] Actually, the curve would look more like a series of steps, depending on the relation of costs to quantity, but a curve is a fair approximation in most cases. A curve is assumed in the manipulation of mathematical formulas which are frequently used in determining the quantity to buy.

[11] T. M. Whitin, *The Theory of Inventory Management* (Princeton, N.J.: Princeton University Press, 1953).

[12] S. F. Heinritz, *Purchasing* (2d. ed.; Englewood Cliffs, N. J.: Prentice-Hall, Inc., 1951), pp. 177–95; Whitin, *op. cit.*; and Winston C. Dalleck and Robert B. Fetter, *Decision Models for Inventory Management* (Homewood, Ill.: Richard D. Irwin, Inc., 1961).

Inventory policy may determine purchases	Industrial firms generally try to maintain an adequate inventory – at least enough to insure that production lines keep moving. There is no greater calamity in a factory than to have a production line close down.

Adequate inventory often is expressed in terms of number of days' supply – for example, 60- or 90-days' supply. But what constitutes 60- or 90-days' supply depends upon the level of demand for the company's products. If the demand rises sharply, say by 10 percent, then total purchases will expand by more than 10 percent to maintain customary inventory levels *and* meet the new needs. On the other hand, if sales decrease by 10 percent, actual needs *and* inventory requirements decrease, and total purchases may decrease drastically while the inventory is being "worked off." During such a contraction, a seller would probably have little success with efforts to stimulate sales by reducing price or offering more favorable credit terms. The buyer is just not in the market at that time.

The buyer's first concern when his company's sales are shifting rapidly is to bring inventory into line with sales, preparing for either further declines or increases in sales. The severity in changes in buyer's demands in the market will depend in part on how rapidly the buyer insists upon adjusting his inventory. This in turn may depend on the firm's economic situation and the policies of its financial officers. Another factor is computer systems. We may see rapid buying swings upward or downward if a firm has moved its inventory control procedures to a computer, because it can react more quickly.

Value analysis improves buying

In recent years, some alert purchasing agents have expanded their concept of their job to include considering whether the product requisitioned should be purchased at all or if it is the most suitable one for the job. This broader approach is called *value analysis,* or sometimes *value engineering.* It requires that the purchasing agent become involved with areas outside his own department.

With this approach, perhaps 75 percent of the purchasing agents' effort will be required in *selling* new ideas and methods to engineering, manufacturing, and top management.[13]

A purchasing agent with such a broad view of his job would obviously be increasingly appreciative of suggestions and new ideas. Price, of course, is never ignored, but purchasing agents are coming to realize that the lowest price may not provide the best value.

Reciprocity helps sales, but . . .

Reciprocity implies that if "you buy from me, I'll buy from you." If a company's customers also can supply products which the firm purchases, then the sales departments of both buyer and seller may seek to "trade" sales for sales. Purchasing agents generally prefer to buy the required quality at the lowest prices consistent with dependable

[13] Burke B. Cochran, "Human Factors Important in Value Analysis," *Electronic Procurement,* July, 1962, pp. 24–27; see also, Lawrence P. Miles, *Techniques of Value Analysis and Engineering* (New York: McGraw-Hill Book Co., 1961); and "How Valuable Is Value Analysis?" *Business Week,* May 15, 1965, pp. 78–82.

quality, delivery, and so on. This leads them to resist reciprocity, but often it is forced upon them by their sales departments.

Reciprocal buying and selling is commonplace in some industries, particularly in paints, chemicals, and petroleum. Usually both prices and product qualities are competitive, and it becomes difficult to ignore the pressures of the sales departments involved. One chemical company brought purchasing under marketing to handle this problem.[14]

When prices and quality are competitive, an outside supplier seldom can break such a reciprocal relationship. He can only hope to become an alternate source of supply and wait for his competitors to let quality slip or prices rise. In this case, alert sellers provide a service to buyers who are not sympathetic with these reciprocal arrangements.

The U.S. Justice Department also frowns upon reciprocity. It has launched a program to block reciprocal buying on the grounds that it is an attempt to monopolize, restricting the normal operation of the free market. This may force those firms that place heavy reliance on reciprocal dealing to reevaluate their marketing strategies.[15]

Buying practices vary by product

These general buying habits and practices apply in the purchase of many industrial products. Specific habits and practices, however, vary according to the type of product, which is a subject covered in Chapter 13. These specifics, however, apply within the framework of our discussion of the geographical location and concentration of industrial customers, their basic purchasing motives and methods, the importance of the multiple buying influence, and other general considerations.

The farm market

Agriculture is fundamental to almost all economies. As we saw in Chapter 7, agriculture absorbs almost all of the work force in some countries. In the United States, however, the percentage of the population engaged in agriculture has been declining steadily, and even further decline is predicted (see Table 9–4).

American farmers have been progressive in the adoption of new equipment and farming techniques. In fact, output per man-hour in agriculture has gone up faster than manufacturing in the last 20 years. This high rate of productivity has caused some embarrassment in the farm market when surpluses (sometimes related to price supports) have continually depressed prices.

[14] "The Chemical Boom: Will New Stress on Marketing Make It Even Bigger?" *Printers' Ink,* November 17, 1961, pp. 22–28.

[15] "Suit Hits Two-way Buying," *Business Week,* March 11, 1967, pp. 162–64; see also Reed Moyer,

"Reciprocity: Retrospect and Prospect," *Journal of Marketing,* October 1970, pp. 47–54; and "Crackdown on Firms' Reciprocal Dealings Set by FTC," *Wall Street Journal* September 2, 1970, p. 5.

Table 9–4 Percent of U.S. labor force working on farms

1850	1900	1930	1960	1975 (estimated)
64%	38%	22%	9%	6%

Source: "Big Farms, Little Farms, in 1970," *Looking Ahead*, National Planning Association, May, 1962, p. 1.

The following discussion will emphasize the U.S. farm market, but it has wider application to foreign agricultural marketing.

Where are the farms and farmers going?

Farmers are the most numerous intermediate customers. Yet just as the percentage of the population engaged in agriculture is declining, so is the number of farms. In the 30-year period from 1940 to 1970, more than 3 million farm units disappeared, the total dropping from more than 6 million to less than 3 million farms. The remaining farms have absorbed some of this acreage, and from 1940 to 1970, the average farm increased in size from fewer than 200 acres to almost 400 acres.[16]

The degree of concentration is seen more clearly in that about a million and a half farmers produce almost 90 percent of the total farm output. More than one tenth of all farms in the United States exceed 500 acres, and it is the farmers of these larger, more productive tracts who have known how to work with and around agricultural subsidy programs. The idea of subsidy programs, justified politically and economically as supporting the small farmer's way of life, is dying hard. But many small farmers continue to leave the land, and more and more farming is being done by larger corporate farms.

The rapid decline in the number of farms is quite important to a marketing manager. It means he has fewer but larger potential farm customers. In addition to this, competition has changed. There has been a decline in the number of manufacturers catering to this market, a decline from a high of about 1,600 manufacturers in 1950 to something more than 700 in 1964.[17]

There also has been a similar decline among middlemen. The National Farm & Power Equipment Dealers' Association indicates that their membership declined from about 34,000 to 17,000 between 1940 and 1960.

Many middlemen who were in once rural areas have switched to lawn tools for the new suburbanites or to equipment for the new industrial plants which have moved out of the central cities. Other dealers have simply gone out of business.[18]

---

[16] U.S. Department of Agriculture.

[17] "The Farm Sees a New Revolution," *Business Week*, October 24, 1964, pp. 116–72.

[18] "Farm Tool Retailers Diversify to Lift Profit as Old Clients Dwindle," *Wall Street Journal*, November 30, 1962, p. 1.

Tailoring products to customers' specialization

Another important factor is that farmers are tending to specialize in one or a few products – such as wheat alone, or wheat plus oats and corn, or fruit and nuts, or poultry. These farmers are interested in only specific kinds of products.

A cotton farmer, for example, may have little interest in hen houses or antibiotics. Or a wheat farmer in the northern plains where hard wheat is grown would have different needs from those of a farmer further south where soft wheat is preferred.

Market grids for such different customers should be developed in great detail. Fortunately, much data is available from the U.S. Department of Agriculture.

Marketing mixes may have to be tailored for each individual farmer – and in some cases this is happening. Fertilizer producers have now moved far beyond selling an all-purpose bag of fertilizer. Now they are able to blend the exact type needed for each farm and load it directly onto fertilizer spreaders which do the job more economically than manual methods. Some producers, in fact, are working directly with farmers, providing a complete service – including fertilizing, weeding, and debugging – all tailored to each individual farmer's needs.[19]

Every farm dollar counts

Sheer numbers of farms, like sheer numbers of people, do not make markets. Customers must have buying power to be of interest to sellers. This part of the farm picture is not nearly so bright.

In 1964, more than one third of the commercial farms in the United States sold less than $5,000 worth of merchandise each, and less than a quarter of the farms sold more than $25,000 worth.[20] The number of larger farms has been increasing and small ones decreasing. But still there are many potential customers who are poor attractions from the market point of view.

In 1964, the average farm took in $15,869 in cash receipts from product sales. There are, however, many farms with sales far above this average, and they provide for an attractive market for farm equipment, new buildings, and consumer goods.[21] But from these receipts exceeding $15,000, various expenses must be subtracted for running the farm – and hopefully, supporting the house and family. It is easy to see that the average farmer does not have a great surplus to spend.

Groceries and feed in the station wagon

The income figures mentioned above make it easier to understand why farmers are often seen as conservative and slow to buy. Quite simply, many farmers do not have the money to buy much.

But the owner of the larger farm is another matter. He is just as questioning, but he is more knowledgeable and more receptive to change. He tends to run his farm as a business rather than a way of life, and consequently is susceptible to presentations stressing savings

[19] "Monsanto Moves into Farmers' Backyard," *Business Week*, February 6, 1965, pp. 60–62.

[20] Computed from data in *Statistical Abstract of the United States, 1969*, p. 592.

[21] "Farmer: A Market with New Status," *Printers' Ink*, March 15, 1963, pp. 21–26.

and increases in productivity. And he may have the assets to act on his decisions.

Some studies of farmer purchasing behavior, however, indicate that for some products, buying motivations are not much different from those for consumer goods.

Many farmers seem unwilling to shop around for the lowest price, preferring the convenience of patronizing the nearest farm implement or feed dealer. Some emulation is found, especially in the purchase of farm machinery. This is understandable when you consider that a farmer's home and place of business are the same. Some manufacturers take pride in office facilities and factories, and the same sort of motive may affect farmer purchasing behavior. Among owners of smaller farms, a new tractor may offer just as much status as a new car would to an urban resident. Moreover, the farmer's roles as a businessman and a final consumer sometimes overlap. For example, a station wagon might be used for carrying feed and the family's groceries. Thus the motives that drive both final consumers and businessmen may become intertwined.

Agriculture is becoming business

Another increasingly important factor is the tendency for farmers to engage in contract farming. Here, the farmer obtains his supplies and perhaps working capital from local dealers or manufacturers who agree to purchase his output, sometimes at guaranteed prices. This limits his buying freedom, since he becomes, in effect, an employee. Such arrangements are becoming more frequent, especially in raising chickens and turkeys and in growing fresh vegetables for commercial canning. These arrangements give stability to the agricultural structure but also limit the markets for sellers. It is all part of the move toward bigger and more businesslike agricultural enterprises – what has been called "agri-business."

In some parts of the country, we already see the development of corporate farms and closely integrated operations. Some large feed millers have moved into the poultry industry in order to assure an outlet for their feed. Some have integrated their operations all the way down to processing the broilers and eggs and then transporting them to retailers.

Where such contractual arrangements (or actual ownership) are common, marketing managers will have to adjust their marketing mixes. They may have to sell directly to large manufacturers or dealers who are handling the arrangements rather than to the farmer himself.[22]

In summary, the modern farmer is becoming more knowledgeable and more businesslike and seems willing to accept help and new ideas – but only when he feels sure they will help him improve production.

[22] L. R. Kohls, "The Farm Today," *Journal of Marketing,* October, 1959, pp. 59–62; "New Farm Market – Down in Customers, But Up in Money," *Printers' Ink,* March 16, 1962, pp. 23–28; *Wall Street Journal,* November 30, 1962, p. 1; and *Time,* November 9, 1962, p. 20.

The government market

Government is the largest customer in the United States. Approximately 33 percent of the gross national product is spent by various governmental units. These units buy almost every kind of commodity. They not only run schools, police departments, and military organizations but also supermarkets, public utilities, research laboratories, offices, hospitals, and liquor stores. And government expenditures for all these operations are growing constantly.

Spending by all government units totals more than $250 billion, and the federal government, the largest of all the governmental buyers, accounts for approximately 59 percent of the total. The states' share of this total is only 15 percent; local governments spend about 26 percent.[23] Expenditures of this magnitude cannot be ignored by an aggressive marketing manager.

Government
buying
methods

Bidding is common

Many government customers buy by description, using a mandatory bidding procedure which is open to public review. Often the government buyer is forced to accept the lowest bid. His biggest job, after deciding generally what he wants, is to correctly describe his need so that the description is unambiguous and complete. Otherwise, he may find sellers bidding on a product he does not want. By law, he might have to accept the low bid for an unwanted product.

Drawing specifications carefully is not an easy task, and buyers usually appreciate the help of knowledgeable salesmen. Legally, the buyer cannot draw the specifications so that only one supplier will be able to meet them (although this has been done!), but if all the relevant specifications are included, then the bidding must be on the items desired. The customer can then obtain the product he wants. And the knowledgeable salesman may get the business, even though his bid is not the lowest, because the lower bids do not meet the minimum specifications.

Not all of the items that governments buy, however, create specification difficulties. Many branded items or items for which there are widely accepted standards are routinely purchased through the conventional bidding procedures. School supplies, construction materials, and gasoline, for example, would fall into this category.

Negotiated contracts

For items that are not branded or easily described, or for products requiring research and development, or in cases in which there would be no effective competition, contracts may be negotiated directly. Depending on the government involved, the contract may be subject to audit and renegotiation, especially if the contractor makes a larger profit than was expected.

Negotiation often is necessary when there are many qualitative and

[23] *Statistical Abstract of the United States, 1969,*
p. 407.

intangible factors. Unfortunately, this is exactly where favoritism and "influence" can slip in. Such influence is not unknown, especially in city and state governments. Nevertheless, negotiation is an important buying method in government sales, and there is a definite need for a marketing mix that emphasizes more than just price.

Approximately 85 percent of the items purchased by the U.S. Defense Supply Agency are acquired through negotiation.[24] This has led USDSA to seek new ways of evaluating the total cost of buying. Techniques such as value analysis, discussed earlier, have been used. And elaborate cost accounting studies are being employed to determine what items *should* cost to produce, and use over their life. In other words, regular experimenting takes place with new approaches to buying that may replace the traditional low-bid practice and bring new dimensions into negotiated buying.[25]

Learning what government wants

Since most government contracts are advertised, the prospective supplier focuses on the government agency he wants to cater to and learns the bidding procedures of that particular agency or department. The marketing man can make a big contribution at this point, because there are so many different bidding procedures and possibilities.

The marketing man should be an expert on potential government target markets, using the assistance available from government directories. For example, the U.S. government offers a purchasing and sales directory that explains its procedures;[26] and various state and local governments also offer assistance. There are trade magazines and trade associations providing information on how to reach schools, hospitals, highway departments, park departments, and so on. These are unique target markets and must be treated as such when developing marketing strategy.

Why sell to government?

Selling to government sometimes involves costly red tape and even renegotiation of contracts. It also requires learning the idiosyncrasies of many new, and sometimes very competitive, markets. One might ask why firms go through all of this. The answer is that many of the government target markets are large, and offer good profits.

On some types of contracts, too, firms hope to gain valuable experience that will have later commercial application. In such cases, prospective suppliers actually may bid below their cost in order to get the opportunity of working on the project.

At one time, Bendix Corp. estimated that a research and development contract to develop a new radio device would cost approximately $500,000. They bid $300,000 in an effort to obtain the job. But a com-

[24] "DSA Is the Shopper for GI's Everywhere," *Business Week*, August 20, 1966, pp. 150–56.

[25] "Picking the Winners with a New System," *Business Week*, May 13, 1967, pp. 62–67; and "'Should-

Cost' Is the New Weapon to Test," *Business Week*, May 30, 1970, pp. 48–49.

[26] *U.S. Government Purchasing and Sales Directory.*

peting firm was so eager to obtain the experience that it bid $1 and won the contract.[27]

Competitive pressures may force firms to do business with government, at least on research and development work. And it is clear that marketing has a role to play in firms catering to government markets, and especially in the defense market where the competitors have traditionally been production-oriented.[28]

Conclusion

In this chapter we have considered the number, size, and buying habits and practices of various intermediate customers. We saw that intermediate customers – farmers, retailers, wholesalers, manufacturers, and others – do considerable buying and selling among themselves before products reach the final consumer. We saw that this buying is generally less emotional than that of final consumers but that the basic problem-solving models of buyer behavior introduced in Chapter 8 are applicable here, with modification. Intermediate customers may buy by inspection, sampling, description, and negotiated contracts, with the latter two methods becoming more popular.

We have concentrated our attention on manufacturers, farmers, and governmental units, postponing until later chapters the detailed discussion of wholesalers and retailers.

The first concern of modern industrial buyers is dependability of the supplier – dependability of quality, service, and delivery. Price is considered, but usually in relation to dependability and quality. In large companies, buying may be quite complex, with various people handling different products or exerting influence on final decisions. Reciprocity may be an important factor, too, especially in certain industries. Finally, there remains the human element – the personality of the purchasing agent, his need to protect his reputation, and his desire for good relationships with his suppliers. The successful salesman will not overlook these emotional needs.

As for the farm market, we have emphasized the rapid changes taking place there. The trend is toward fewer, larger, more productive farms. This trend will have a great impact on those who sell to the farm market and must adjust as the market changes.

Today's large commercial farmer is not only better off financially but is better informed and more progressive. He is willing to listen to new ideas, and to invest in machinery, fertilizers, and other products

[27]Malcolm P. Ferguson, "The Corporation as Supplier to the Government," *Business Topics*, Summer, 1961, pp. 37–50.

[28]Walter B. Wentz, "Aerospace Discovers Marketing," *Journal of Marketing*, April, 1967, pp. 27–30; William H. Reynolds, "The Marketing Concept and the Aerospace Business," *Journal of Marketing*, April, 1966, pp. 9–11; John J. Kennedy, "Defense-Aerospace Marketing: A Model For Effective Action," *Business Horizons*, Winter, 1965, pp. 67–74; and Leonard Marks, Jr., "The Aerospace Management Challenge," *Business Horizons*, Spring, 1966, pp. 19–24.

that he feels will increase his production. More and more, he tends to specialize. But the farm picture is not all bright. There are still many small, low-income farmers who offer little market potential.

Finally, we have seen that the government is a large market and an extremely complex one. Much government purchasing is done through prescribed bidding procedures. On nonstandardized goods and services, however, various types of negotiated contracts are used.

This review of intermediate customer buying habits and practices has tried to stress basic similarities. Actually, however, the practices among various buyers vary a great deal. Personal preferences and organizational setups cause differences. Furthermore, the nature of the specific products being purchased requires modification of the general principles. The nature of specific industrial products is discussed in Chapter 13. At that time, variations in buying behavior will be discussed by product category.

The need for specialized research on the buying habits and preferences of specific target customers should be obvious. The market grid concept clearly is needed when developing marketing strategies for intermediate customers.

QUESTIONS AND ANSWERS

1 Discuss the importance of applying the market grid concept when analyzing intermediate customer markets. Be sure to consider how easy it is to isolate homogeneous market segments.

2 Explain how SIC codes might be helpful in evaluating and understanding industrial markets.

3 Compare and contrast the problem-solving approaches used by final consumers and industrial buyers.

4 Describe the situations which would lead to the use of the three different buying processes for a particular product, such as computer tapes.

5 Compare and contrast the buying motives of final consumers and industrial buyers.

6 Distinguish among the four methods of evaluating and buying (inspection, sampling, etc.) and indicate which would probably be most suitable for furniture, baseball gloves, coal, and pencils, assuming that some intermediate customer is the buyer.

7 Discuss the advantages and disadvantages of reciprocity from the industrial buyer's point of view. Are the advantages and disadvantages merely reversed from the seller's point of view?

8 Is it always advisable to buy the highest-quality product?

9 How does the kind of industrial good affect manufacturers' buying habits and practices? Consider lumber for furniture, a lathe, nails for a box factory, and a sweeping compound.

10 Discuss the impact of value analysis on promotion.

11 Discuss the impact of the decline in number of commercial farmers on the marketing mixes of manufacturers and middlemen supplying this market. Also consider the impact on rural trading communities which have been meeting the needs of farmers.

12 The government market is obviously an extremely large one, yet it is often slighted or even ignored by many firms. "Red tape" is certainly one reason, but there are others. Discuss the situation and be sure to include the market grid concept in your analysis.

13 Based on your understanding of buying by (1) manufacturers, (2) farmers, and (3) governments, outline the basic ingredients of promotion to each type of customer. Use two products as examples for each type. Is the promotion job the same for each pair?

...the concept of product as potential customer satisfactions or benefits cannot be overstressed.

...the *total product* is more than just a physical product.... It can include accessories, installation, instruction on use, perhaps a brand name which fulfills some psychological needs, and the assurance that service facilities will be available.... It may not even include a *physical* product at all!

10

Product — introduction

Beginning in this chapter and continuing through the next several chapters, we will look at the demanding job of developing products and product lines to satisfy the ever changing desires of customers. This involves developing the right Product, which then can be put in the right Place, and sold with the right Promotion and Price.

Developing the right product is not an easy task. Not only are customer needs and preferences changing but competition also continually makes current products obsolete. In some lines of business, development of new products is so rapid that 50 percent or more of the products made by a given firm were not even in the planning stages 5 to 10 years earlier.

In addition to those in American firms, businessmen of other nations are realizing the importance of continually developing and improving products.

At a 1960 trade fair in Vienna, Russian and American tools were displayed side by side. Both functioned equally well, and although the Russian tools were priced lower, the U.S. tools sold more readily. Manufacturers attributed this to better industrial design, expressed in both function and appearance. Apparently the Russians did, too, since they sent delegates for the first time to the International Council of Societies of Industrial Design when it met the following year. It would seem that buyers throughout the world, even in developing nations, are interested, not just in any products, but in *better* products.[1]

In Chapter 10–14, we will consider the role of products in marketing strategy planning. This may have first-job relevance to you, because many companies have organized their production and marketing activities along product lines. Some multiple-product producers, for example, maintain separate sales forces for each of the company's product lines, and wholesalers and retailers frequently have salesmen and buyers who specialize along product lines.[2]

What is a product?

Customers buy satisfaction, not parts or ingredients

First, we must decide what we mean by a "product."

If we sell a washing machine, are we selling a certain number of nuts and bolts, some sheet metal, an electric motor, and a plastic agitator?

If we sell the detergent to be used in this washing machine, are we selling several chemical raw materials?

If we sell a delivery service, are we selling so much wear and tear on a delivery truck and so much operator fatigue?

The answer to all of these questions is *no*. Instead, what we are really *selling is the capacity to provide the satisfaction, use, or perhaps the profit desired by the customer.*

All the housewife asks is that her washing machine do a good job of washing and continues to run. She does not care how it was made. Furthermore, she wants to clean with her detergent, not analyze it. And when she orders something, she doesn't really care how much out of the way the driver had to go or where he has been. She just wants *her* package.

When producers and middlemen buy products, they are interested in the profit they will get from their purchase, through use and resale, not how the products were made.

The concept of product as potential customer satisfactions or benefits cannot be overstressed. Many business executives, trained in the production side of business, get wrapped up in the number of nuts and bolts, the tightness of the nuts, the fertilizer application per acre, and other technical problems. Middlemen, too, are often concerned with technical details. But while these are important to *them*, they

[1] "Reds Seek Better Product Design," *South Bend Tribune*, October 6, 1961, p. 24.

[2] Stanley C. Hollander, "Merchandise Classification and the Commodity Approach," *Journal of Marketing*, Vol. 2, No. 3, p. 275.

have little bearing on most customers' conceptions of the product. What is important to customers is how *they* perceive what is being offered – and these two views may be far apart.

Total product is physical product – plus – or maybe no physical product

The *total product* is more than just a physical product with its related functional and aesthetic features. It includes accessories, installation, instruction on use, the package, perhaps a brand name which fulfills some psychological needs, and the assurance that service facilities will be available to meet the customer's needs after the purchase.

In fact, the total product may be almost equivalent to the marketing mix of the firm, because each of the four P's contribute something to the whole which is offered to the consumer. We will try to focus on the Product aspects in the Product chapters, but inevitably there is some interaction. This problem was recognized in the Howard-Sheth model in Chapter 8 where the stimuli potentially affecting consumers were separated into significative (more tangible aspects of marketing mixes) and symbolic stimuli.

The *total product* may not even include a physical product at all! The product of a barber or hair stylist is the design, trimming or styling of your hair. A medical doctor may simply look at you, neither taking anything away or giving you anything tangible. Nevertheless, each satisfies needs, and therefore provides a product in the sense we will use "product" in this book.

This broader view of the product concept must be understood, because it is too easy to become overly occupied with producing and selling tangible products. Too many production-oriented people fall into this trap and neglect important opportunities for satisfying needs in other ways. Automobile manufacturers and dealers, for example, lost out on the rental car business, whose product is service rather than the sale of a physical product. Taking the auto example further, not all dealers want to *service* the cars they sell. They just want to sell them!

Defining a *product* as a physical entity and/or service which satisfies certain customer needs gives us considerable flexibility in marketing mix planning. It also fits with the marketing concept. That is, marketing mixes should be planned to satisfy customers' needs, whether they require a physical product or a service. Above all, a marketing mix should *not* be designed simply to *get rid of* products.

Within this broader concept of a product, we can also consider the total offering of a wholesaler or retailer as a total product. This will enable us to generalize about marketing strategy planning for any kind of a firm.

Treating services as products which satisfy needs is important for another reason. More than half of the work force in the United States is now involved in the service sector, and this trend is accelerating. An area of this magnitude certainly should not be ignored in favor of the more tangible products of our farms, mines, and factories.[3]

[3] See "The Service Economy Grows – But Does It?" *Business Week*, February 15, 1969, pp. 126–30; and Victor R. Fuchs, *The Service Economy* (New York: National Bureau of Economic Research, 1969).

Guarantees that satisfaction will continue

Customers want their needs satisfied. They want dependable products that will work, and prompt service if they do not. If a product breaks down easily and is difficult to repair or have serviced, it is of little use. And a life insurance customer would like to be sure that he is buying a policy that really does meet his needs, hopefully as economically as possible. The typical practice of trying to sell a technical and confusing piece of paper may not be wholly satisfying to some prospects and may account for the difficulty in selling insurance.[4]

Dependable quality and prompt service may be even more critical in the industrial sector. More than customer inconvenience is involved here, since a whole production line may be shut down when the total product is not satisfactory. Such malfunctioning is now formally considered in some industrial and government purchasing. That is, the cost of the product over its life rather than just the initial cost is considered in the buying decision.

To overcome customer objections, some market-oriented firms are designing more quality into their products and then offering longer and stronger guarantees or warranties. But even guarantees or warrantees may not keep the customer happy if they are limited to repairing or replacing the products. What is a customer supposed to do if an electric iron or electric shaver breaks down and cannot be repaired for two or three weeks? Must he have a second item in reserve for such contingencies? If the objective of the firm is to satisfy customer needs, these questions must be answered.

Some companies, such as Proctor Silex Corp. and Sears, Roebuck & Co., have met this problem by extending a one-year *replacement—* not just repair—guarantee on their appliances.

Although our approach to developing a total product that satisfies customer needs may seem logical, some production-oriented companies feel that service is not their business.[5] Automobile manufacturers and some appliance manufacturers, for instance, have passed on to wholesalers and retailers the job of guaranteeing that the physical product does work. *Sometimes* this work gets done, but production-oriented manufacturers don't seem to care.[6]

By contrast, other businessmen see very clearly that the customer wants more than just the physical product. General Electric, Whirlpool, and Maytag, for example, have developed manufacturer-owned or -franchised appliance service facilities to make sure that the total product *is* satisfactory. They see that this service is part of the product and must be provided as part of the marketing mix if they are to de-

[4] "Critics Say Practices of Industry Confuse Life Insurance Buyers," *Wall Street Journal*, September 5, 1967, pp. 1 f.

[5] "Guaranteeing More, Enjoying It Less," *Business Week*, January 26, 1963, pp. 46–48.

[6] "Detroit Guarantees Less," *Business Week*, September 30, 1967, p. 40; "Shorter Warranties Hit Some Car Owners in Their Pocketbooks," *Wall Street Journal*, December 19, 1969, p. 1; "Auto-Makers Blamed for Woes Resulting from Warranties," (Lansing, Michigan) *State Journal*, November 5, 1968, p. D–3; and "Detroit Tries a U-turn on Warranties," *Business Week*, July 25, 1970, pp. 44–48.

velop more attractive marketing strategies than their competitors.[7]

More businessmen will become aware of the wisdom of satisfying consumers' needs if the consumerism movement continues. If not, critics such as Ralph Nader, and the courts, may force more attention on this question. Actually, consumers now receive an implied warranty for products they buy. If they do not feel they have received full measure, they have the right to go to court and sue for damages. Already some "favorable-to-consumer" rulings have been observed and the move toward "class actions" may cause more legal suits. In a class action, lawyers bring suit for a group of consumers rather than a particular individual, thereby making the legal process more economical for consumers and potentially more costly for business firms.[8]

The best product is the total product

We have been emphasizing a single physical product and the related services that make up a single total product. But customer needs cannot always be satisfied by a single product. As we saw in Chapter 8, products may be used as part of a consumption system. Several foods, for example, are eaten at the same meal, and most sports require several pieces of equipment. Marketing managers may have to think in terms of an assortment of goods and services to satisfy customers' needs. The marketing manager may not have to provide all of them, but at least he should include these needs in his strategy planning.

Manufacturers and wholesalers may have to offer a complex total product to their intermediate customers. Likewise, retailers may have to offer a wide assortment in their total product. This may include the total assortment of goods they offer as well as related services. Good parking facilities, gift wrapping, elevators and escalators, charge accounts, and delivery services probably should be considered as part of the retailer's product—yet some retailers provide most of these related services only grudgingly.

In our discussion, we will focus mostly on a single product for convenience of exposition. But it should not be forgotten that several products *and*/or services might have to be combined to develop the most successful product as part of the most effective marketing strategy.

Products as seen by customers

How consumers see the Product has an important bearing on how much they are willing to pay for it, where it should be made available, and how eager they are to obtain it, if at all. Economists have been concerned for some time with how consumers see products because

[7]"Appliance Makers Seek to Teach Servicemen Tact as Well as Skills," *Wall Street Journal,* September 25, 1968, p. 1.

[8]David L. Rados, "Product Liability: Tougher Ground Rules," *Harvard Business Review,* July–August, 1969, pp. 144–52; George Fisk, "Guide-lines for Warranty Service After Sale," *Journal of Marketing,* January, 1970, pp. 63–67; and Jon G. Udell and Evan E. Anderson, "The Product Warranty as on Element of Competitive Strategy," *Journal of Marketing,* October, 1968, pp. 1–7.

this affects how they select among alternatives. Economists look at people as problem solvers, attempting to select what is best for them among many alternatives. As noted earlier, those economists who postulate the existence of "economic man" oversimplify the decision-making process of some people. Nevertheless, many consumers have economic motives, at least sometimes, and economists' analytical tools can be quite helpful to us in summarizing how customers view the total product. These summaries, in turn, can have a bearing on the firm's marketing strategy planning. The economic concepts reviewed in the following pages will also be useful in *several* subsequent chapters.

Individual customers choose among alternatives

Economics is sometimes called the "dismal" science because it shows that customers simply cannot buy everything they want. Since most customers have a limited income over any period of time, they must balance their needs and the costs of various products.

Economists usually assume that a customer has a fairly definite set of preferences. When he is given a set of alternatives, it is assumed that he evaluates these alternatives in terms of whether they will make him feel better (or worse) or in some way improve (or change) his situation.

But what exactly is the nature of the customer's desire for a particular product?

Usually the argument is presented in terms of the extra utility he can obtain by buying more of a particular product or how much utility would be lost were he to have less of the product. (Students who wish further discussion of this approach should refer to *indifference curve analysis* in any standard economics text.)

Utility is a conceptual framework. It may be easier to grasp this idea if we examine what happens when the price of one of the customer's usual purchases changes.

The law and potato prices

Suppose that a consumer were buying potatoes in 10-pound bags at the same time he bought other foods, such as meat and vegetables. If the consumer is basically interested in purchasing a certain number of calories, and the price of potatoes drops, it seems reasonable to expect that he will switch some of his food money to potatoes and away from some other foods. But if the price of potatoes rose, you would expect our consumer to buy fewer potatoes and more of other foods.

The general interaction of price and quantity illustrated by this example has been called "the law of diminishing demand." This law holds that *if the price of a commodity is raised, a smaller quantity will be demanded; conversely, if the price of a commodity is lowered, a greater quantity will be demanded.*

A group of customers make a market

When our hypothetical consumers are considered as a group, we have what is called a "market." It seems reasonable that many consumers in a market will behave in a similar way—that is, if price declines, the total quantity demanded will increase, and if the price rises, quantity demanded will decrease. Empirical data supports this reasoning, especially for broad product categories, or commodities such as potatoes.

The relationship between price and quantity demanded in a market is illustrated in Table 10-1. It is an example of what economists call

Table 10-1 Demand schedule for potatoes

	Price of potatoes per bag P (1)	Quantity demanded (bags per month) Q (2)	Total revenue per month $P \times Q = TR$ $(1) \times (2) = (3)$
A	$0.80	8,000,000	$6,400,000
B	0.65	9,000,000	
C	0.50	11,000,000	5,500,000
D	0.35	14,000,000	
E	0.20	19,000,000	

a "demand schedule." It should be noted that as the price decreases the quantity demanded increases. In the third column, total dollar sales or total revenue of the potato market is shown. Notice, however, that as prices go lower, the total *unit volume increases,* yet the *total revenue decreases.* It is suggested that you fill in the missing blanks and observe the behavior of total revenue — an important figure for the marketing manager.

The demand curve — usually down-sloping

If your sole interest is seeing at which price customers would be willing to pay the greatest total revenue, the demand schedule may be adequate. But in our subsequent analysis, it will help to think in terms of a "picture" of the relationship between price and quantity. When the demand schedule is graphed, the resulting curve is called a *demand curve.* Figure 10-1 shows the demand curve for potatoes, actually a plotting of the demand schedule. It shows how many potatoes would be demanded by potential customers at various possible prices. This is known as a *downsloping demand curve.*

Most demand curves have this downsloping appearance. A downsloping demand curve merely indicates that if price were decreased, the quantity that customers would demand would increase.

Note that the demand curve only shows how customers would react to various prices. Usually, in a market, we see only one price at a time, not all of these prices. The curve, however, shows what quantities will be sold, depending upon what price is set. It would seem that most businessmen would like to see the price set at a point where the resulting revenue was large.

Before discussing this, however, we should consider the demand schedule and curve for another commodity to get a more complete picture of what is involved in demand-curve analysis.

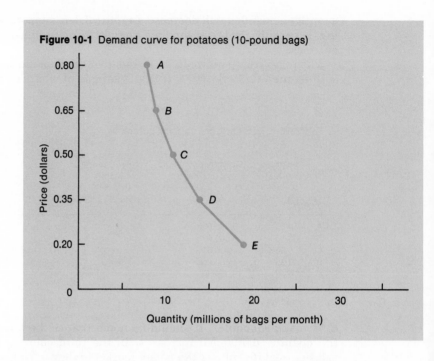

Figure 10-1 Demand curve for potatoes (10-pound bags)

Price (dollars) / Quantity (millions of bags per month)

Refrigerator demand curve looks different

A different demand schedule is the one for refrigerators shown in Table 10-2. Column 3 shows the total revenue that would be obtained at various possible prices and quantities. Again, as the price of refrigerators goes down, the quantity demanded goes up. But here, contrary to the potato example, total revenue increases—at least until the price drops to $150.

Table 10–2 Demand schedule for refrigerators

	Price per refrigerator P (1)	Quantity de-manded per year Q (2)	Total revenue per year $P \times Q = TR$ $(1) \times (2) = (3)$
A	$300	20,000	$ 6,000,000
B	250	70,000	17,500,000
C	200	130,000	26,000,000
D	150	210,000	31,500,000
E	100	310,000	31,000,000

Every market has demand curve, for some time period

These general demand relationships are characteristic of all products, but each product has its own demand schedule and curve *in each potential market*, no matter how small the market. In other words, a particular demand curve has meaning only with reference to a particular market. We can think of product demand curves for individuals, regions, and even countries. And the time period covered really should be specified, although this is often neglected as we think implicitly of monthly or yearly periods.

The
difference
between
elastic and
inelastic
demand

The demand curve for refrigerators (see Figure 10–2) is also down-sloping, but note that it is flatter than the curve for potatoes. It is quite important that we understand what this flatness means.

We will consider the flatness in terms of total revenue, since this is what interests businessmen.[9]

When you filled in the total revenue column for potatoes, you should have noticed that total revenue would decrease continually if the

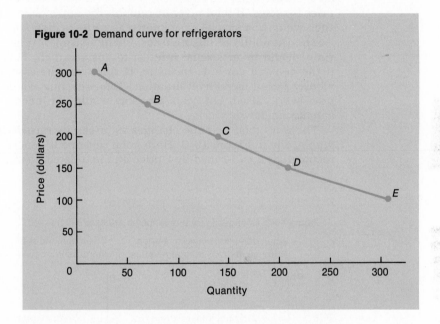

Figure 10-2 Demand curve for refrigerators

price were reduced. This looks undesirable from a businessman's point of view, and illustrates what is known as *inelastic demand*. This means that although the quantity demanded would increase if the price were decreased, the quantity demanded would not "stretch" enough—that is, it is not elastic enough—to increase total revenue.

In contrast, the quantity of refrigerators demanded would stretch enough—at least for a while—to increase total revenue as prices were dropped. *This part* of the refrigerator demand curve is an example of *elastic demand*.

Note that if the refrigerator price were dropped from $150 to $100, total revenue would *decrease*. It can be said, therefore, that when the

[9] Strictly speaking, two curves should not be compared for flatness if the graph scales are different, but for current purposes we will do so to illustrate the idea of "elasticity of demand." Actually, it would be more correct to compare two curves for one commodity—on the same graph. Then, both the shape of the demand curve and its position on the graph would be important.

price is less than $150, demand is inelastic—that is, total revenue would decrease if price were lowered.

Thus, elasticity can be defined in terms of changes in total revenue. *If total revenue would increase if price were lowered, then demand is said to be elastic. If total revenue would decrease if price were lowered, then demand is said to be inelastic.*

Total revenue may decrease if prices are raised!

A point that is often missed in discussions of demand is what happens when prices are raised instead of lowered. In an elastic demand situation, total revenue will *decrease* if the price is *raised,* while in an inelastic demand situation, total revenue would *increase* if the price is *raised.* If total revenue remains the same when prices change, then we have a special case known as *unitary elasticity of demand.*

The possibility of raising price and increasing revenue at the same time should be of special interest to businessmen. This only occurs if the demand curve is inelastic. If this were the case, it would obviously be an attractive situation. Total revenue would increase if price were raised, but costs probably would not increase and might actually go down.

The ways total revenue changes as prices are raised are illustrated graphically in Figure 10–3. Here, total revenue is conceived of as the rectangular area formed by a price and its related quantity.

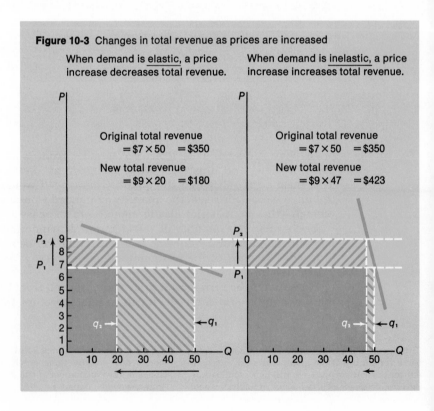

Figure 10-3 Changes in total revenue as prices are increased

When demand is <u>elastic</u>, a price increase decreases total revenue.

When demand is <u>inelastic</u>, a price increase increases total revenue.

Original total revenue
= $7 × 50 = $350

New total revenue
= $9 × 20 = $180

Original total revenue
= $7 × 50 = $350

New total revenue
= $9 × 47 = $423

P_1 is the original price here, and the total potential revenue associated with this original price is shown by the area with the diagonal lines slanted down from the left. The total revenue area associated with the new price, P_2, is shaded, with lines running diagonally upward from the left. In both cases, there is some overlap, so the important areas are those with only a single shading. Note that in the left-hand figure, where demand is elastic, the revenue added when price is increased is less than the revenue lost (compare only the single-shaded areas). When demand is inelastic, however, only a small single-shaded revenue area is given up for a much larger one when price is raised.[10]

An entire curve is *not* elastic or inelastic

It is important to note that is is *improper to refer to a whole demand curve as elastic or inelastic*. Rather, elasticity for a particular curve refers to the change in total revenue between two points on a curve and not along the entire curve. The change from elasticity to inelasticity can be seen in the refrigerator example. Generally, however, adjacent points are either elastic or inelastic, so it is common to refer to a whole curve by the degree of elasticity of the curve in the price range that normally is of interest — the *relevant range*.

Availability of substitutes, and urgency of need, helps explain elasticity of demand

At first, it may be difficult to visualize why one product should have an elastic and another an inelastic demand. Many factors, such as the availability of substitutes, the importance of the item in the customer's budget, and the urgency of the customer's need and its relation to other needs (recall our discussion of the many behavioral influences), influence demand for a particular product. By examining one of these factors, the availability of substitutes, we should better understand why demand elasticities vary.

Substitutes are goods or services that offer a choice or an alternative to the buyer. The greater the number of good substitutes available, the greater will be the elasticity of demand, the term "good" here referring to the degree of similarity or homogeneity that customers see. If they see the products as extremely different or heterogeneous, then a particular need cannot be satisfied by easily interchanging them, and the demand for the most satisfactory product may be quite inelastic.

As an example, if the price of hamburger is lowered (and other prices stand constant), the quantity demanded will increase considerably as will total revenue. The reason is that not only will regular hamburger users buy more hamburger, but those consumers who formerly bought hot dogs, steaks, or bacon probably will buy hamburger too. But if the price of hamburger rose, the quantity demanded would decrease, perhaps sharply. Consumers would still purchase some hamburger, depending on how much the price had risen, their

[10] It is possible to compute coefficients of elasticity of demand that will represent a numerical value for the degree of elasticity. We will not go into this here. Interested students should refer to any basic economics text under the topic "coefficient of elasticity of demand."

individual tastes, and what their guests expect (see Figure 10–4).

In contrast to a product which has many "substitutes," such as hamburger, consider a commodity with few or no substitutes. Its demand curve will tend to be inelastic. Salt is a good example. Salt is needed to flavor food. Yet no one person or family uses great quanti-

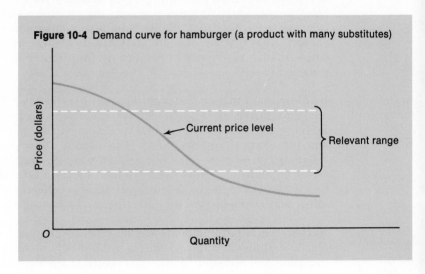

Figure 10-4 Demand curve for hamburger (a product with many substitutes)

ties of salt. And even with price changes *within a reasonable range,* it is not likely that the quantity of salt purchased would change much. Of course, if the price dropped to an extremely low level, manufacturers might buy more, say, for low-cost filler (Figure 10–5). Or, if the

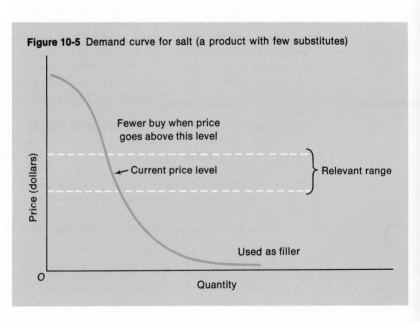

Figure 10-5 Demand curve for salt (a product with few substitutes)

price rose to a staggering figure, many people would have to do without. But these extremes are outside the relevant range.

Remember that the terms *elasticity* or *inelasticity* are applied only along a range of the demand curve somewhat above and below the normal price level—that is, within the relevant range. Further, remember that elasticity can be influenced not only by economic but also emotional motives and all the other behavioral considerations discussed in Chapters 8 and 9.

Product markets as seen by suppliers

Demand curves are introduced in the Product section of this text because the degree of elasticity of demand is a characteristic of a specific product in a particular market for a particular time period. It summarizes how potential customers feel about the total product, and especially, whether there are substitutes for the product.

Economists' thinking on demand was introduced to provide an insight into product-market situations. But to obtain a fuller understanding, we must continue this economic analysis.

Customers may want some product, but if suppliers are not willing to supply it, then there is no market. So we will study the economist's analysis of supply and then bring analysis of supply and demand together for a more complete understanding of product-market situations.

Economists often use the kind of analysis we are discussing here to explain pricing in the marketplace. This is *not* our intention. Here we are interested in product markets and the interaction of customers and potential suppliers. The discussion in this chapter does *not* explain how individual firms set prices or should set prices. That will come in the Price chapters.

Supply curves reflect supplier thinking

Generally speaking, suppliers' costs have a bearing on the quantity of products they are willing to offer in the market during any period. In other words, their costs affect their supply schedules and supply curves. While a demand curve shows the quantity of goods customers would be willing to buy at various prices, a supply curve shows the quantity of goods that will be supplied at various possible prices by all of the suppliers together (if we are thinking of a total market) or one supplier (if we are thinking of a single firm's situation). Eventually only one quantity of goods will be offered and purchased, and so a supply curve is really a hypothetical description of what would be offered at various prices. It is, however, a very important curve. Together with a demand curve, it summarizes the attitudes and probable behavior of buyers and sellers with respect to a particular product in a particular market.

Some supply curves are vertical

We usually assume that supply curves tend to slope upwards, that is, suppliers will be willing to offer greater quantities at higher prices. If a product's market price is very high, it seems only reasonable that producers will be anxious to produce more of the product and even put workers on overtime or perhaps hire additional workers in order to increase the quantity they can offer. To go further, it seems likely that producers of other products will switch their productive resources (farms, factories, men, or retail facilities) to the product that is in great demand.

Contrariwise, if a very low price is being offered for a particular commodity, it's reasonable to expect that producers will switch to other products, reducing supply. A supply schedule (Table 10–3) and a supply curve (Figure 10–6) for potatoes illustrates these ideas. This

Table 10–3 Supply schedule for potatoes

	Possible market price per 10-lb. bag	Number of bags sellers will supply per month at each possible market price
A	$0.80	17,000,000
B	0.65	14,000,000
C	0.50	11,000,000
D	0.35	8,000,000
E	0.20	3,000,000

supply curve shows how many potatoes would be produced and offered for sale at each possible market price in a given month.[11]

In the very short run (say, over a few hours, a day, or a week), a supplier may not be able to increase the supply at all. In this situation, we should see a vertical supply curve. This situation is frequently of practical significance in the market for fresh produce. Fresh strawberries, for example, continue to deteriorate, and a supplier must sell them quickly—preferably at a higher price—but in any event he must sell them. For less perishable commodities, he may set a minimum price floor and, if necessary, store his goods until market conditions are more favorable.

If the product is a service, it may not be easy to expand the supply in the short run, and there is no way to inventory it either. Additional barbers or medical doctors are not quickly trained and licensed, and they only have so much time to give each day. When the day is done, the unused "supply" is lost. Further, the prospect of much higher prices in the near future cannot readily expand the supply of many services. A good play, or an "in" restaurant or nightclub may be similarly limited in the amount of product it can offer at a particular time.

[11] This supply curve is for a month to emphasize that farmers might have some control over when they delivered their potatoes. There would be a different curve for each month.

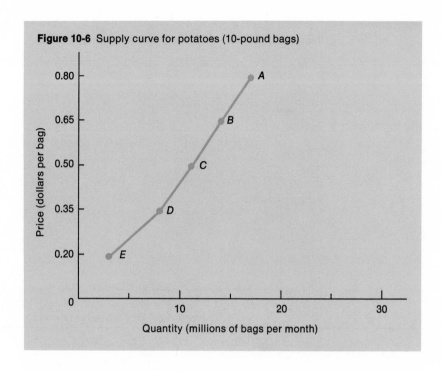

Figure 10-6 Supply curve for potatoes (10-pound bags)

Price (dollars per bag) / Quantity (millions of bags per month)

| Elasticity of supply | The term *elasticity* also is used to describe supply curves. An extremely steep or almost vertical supply curve, often found in the short run, is called *inelastic* because the quantity supplied does not stretch much (if at all) if the price is raised. A flatter curve is called *elastic* because it does stretch more. A slightly upsloping supply curve is characteristic of longer-run market situations. Given more time, suppliers have a chance to adjust their offerings and competitors may enter or leave the market. |

Demand and supply interaction establishes the size of the market and price level

We have treated market demand and supply forces separately. Now we must bring them together to show their interaction. The *intersection* of these two forces determines the size of the market and the market price, at which point the market is said to be in *equilibrium*.

The intersection of demand and supply is illustrated for the potato data discussed above. The demand curve for potatoes is now graphed against the supply curve presented in Figure 10-6 (see Figure 10-7).

In this potato market, the demand is inelastic; the total revenue of all the potato producers would be greater at higher prices. But the market price is at the equilibrium point, where the quantity and the price that sellers are willing to offer are equal to the quantity and price

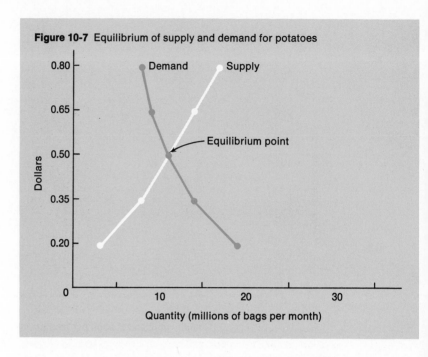

Figure 10-7 Equilibrium of supply and demand for potatoes

that buyers are willing to accept. The 50-cent equilibrium price for potatoes yields a smaller *total revenue* to potato producers than would a higher price. This lower equilibrium price comes about because the many producers are willing to supply enough potatoes at the lower price. *Demand is not the sole determiner of price level. Cost also must be considered, via the supply curve.*

Nature of product market situations

The elasticity of demand and supply, and the interaction of demand and supply curves, helps explain the nature of product-market situations. We will emphasize two kinds of market situations: pure competition and monopolistic competition. A third type, called monopoly, is encountered so infrequently that it will not be treated separately. Usually monopolies are controlled by local, state, or federal authorities. Where they are not, they can be treated as monopolistic competition, since monopolies are simply an extreme case of monopolistic competition.

Understanding these product-market situations is quite important because some situations considerably reduce the freedom of a marketing manager. For example, if the demand for a particular product of a firm is completely elastic—the demand curve is completely flat—the marketing manager would have no control whatever over price. It also would mean that his work with the other three P's would not be easy, since target customers apparently do not find his product different from others.

If his demand curve is inelastic, however, he may have much more freedom in varying the other three P's.

Pure
competition
is a
theoretical
limit

In pure competition, we find something like a perfectly flat demand curve for a particular firm. Each of our individual potato producers was in such a situation.

Pure competition develops in markets characterized by many buyers and many sellers offering very similar or homogeneous products. It is assumed here that all buyers and sellers have full knowledge of the market forces and that there is ease of entry for buyers and sellers—that is, new firms have little difficulty starting up in business and new customers can easily come into the market. This is more or less true in the potato industry, which is why we would call it a pure-competition situation.

Although the potato industry as a whole has a downsloping demand curve, each individual potato producer has a demand curve that is perfectly flat at the going market price—the equilibrium price.

To explain this in more concrete terms, let's look at the demand curve for the individual potato producer. Assume that the equilibrium price for the industry is 50 cents. This means he can sell as many potatoes as he chooses at 50 cents. The quantity he and all of his fellow producers choose to sell makes up the supply curve; but acting alone, he can do almost anything he wants to do.

If this individual farmer raises $\frac{1}{10,000}$th of the quantity offered in the market, for example, it is obvious that there will be little impact on the market whether he goes out of business or doubles his production.

The reason his demand curve is assumed to be flat in this example is that the farmer probably could not sell any potatoes above the market price, and there is no point in selling below 50 cents. (The subject of deciding the best quantity to offer is discussed in Chapter 25, where we cover pricing and output decisions.)

The relation between the industry demand-curve situation and the demand curve facing the individual farmer in pure competition is shown in Figure 10-8.

Not many markets can be characterized as purely competitive, where the competitors are facing a perfectly elastic demand curve. But there are enough markets with some of these characteristics to allow us to talk about extremely competitive situations in which the marketing manager may have to accept the going price.

Squeeze on the orange growers

Florida orange growers, for example, have essentially homogeneous products, and they have little control over price. When there is a very large supply, prices drop rapidly and are beyond the producers' control. When supplies are short, the reverse happens. The 1967 crop was 50 percent larger than the 1966 crop, and most operators sold their oranges below their costs. Oranges "on the tree" cost 75 cents a box to grow and sold for $1.25 in 1966. In 1967, they were selling for 35

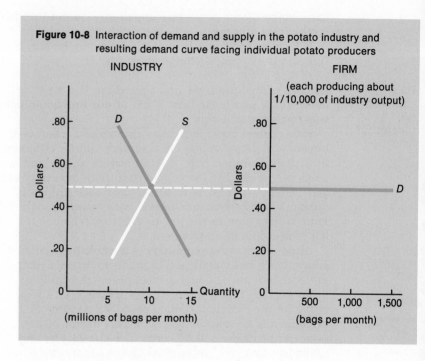

Figure 10-8 Interaction of demand and supply in the potato industry and resulting demand curve facing individual potato producers

cents a box. Supply turned around in 1968, however, and oranges were selling for $2.40–$2.60 a box.[12]

Similar situations are found with many agricultural commodities, and farmers often seek government help to "save" them from pure competition, especially if the industry demand is inelastic, as it often is. Agricultural parity programs are designed in part for this purpose, usually working to increase price by reducing supply. In 1961, the cling peach growers in California voted to destroy part of their crop in an effort to raise the market price.[13] And the Brazilian government, faced with a wholesale price drop for coffee from 95 cents a pound in 1954 to less than 35 cents in 1962, burned coffee trees to reduce supplies.[14]

Nor are such highly competitive situations restricted to agriculture. In any field where many competitors sell essentially homogeneous products—such as chemicals, plastics, lumber, coal, printing, and laundry services—the demand curve seen by *each producer* tends to be flat. Assuming no collusion among the firms, there is a tendency for each firm to expand production—and the action of all producers forces down the market price.

[12]*Business Week*, May 13, 1967, p. 187; "Orange Crush," *Time*, January 27, 1967, p. 67; and "Oranges Start Coming Up Roses," *Business Week*, May 4, 1968, pp. 127–30.

[13]*Wall Street Journal*, July 9, 1962, p. 2.
[14]*Wall Street Journal*, July 10, 1962, p. 1.

The impact of an extremely competitive situation can hit even a large firm such as Du Pont. Competitive activity among the producers of synthetic fibers has been extremely active in recent years. Major U.S. and world producers had been working for years to expand production capacity, and finally supply caught up and passed demand. Almost overnight many competitors were cutting prices drastically; Du Pont's profits declined, and their declining stock price even dragged down the Dow-Jones industrial stock average.[15]

Industries tend to become more competitive – that is, move towards pure competition. More competitors enter the market, the supply is increased, and the current equilibrium price is pushed downward. This tends to force profits down until some competitors are eliminated. Economists describe the final equilibrium position as that point at which there are no entrepreneurial profits, only sufficient return to keep the present competitors in the business.

On the way to this final equilibrium position, competition may become so vigorous that companies may actually lose money as the price goes below the equilibrium level and some firms are driven out of the market. It may take some time, however, before the industry price moves up to the equilibrium level so the remaining companies can survive. At the economist's final equilibrium point, however, none of the firms make a profit!

When competition is monopolistic

From the above discussion it is easy to see why firms would want to avoid pure-competition situations. A market in which they have more control would be preferable.

To avoid a purely competitive market, marketing managers seek to develop a differentiated or heterogeneous product, perhaps one of special interest to certain segments of a market grid. If these efforts are successful, the firm becomes, in effect, the "industry" for this product. Since target customers recognize the product as different, the firm does not have to share *this* industry demand with all competitors. Such a market situation is called *monopolistic competition*.[16]

The term *monopolistic* indicates that the firm is attempting to attain its own little monopoly, but the term *competition* means that there is still a competitive situation. The extremely vigorous – even cutthroat – competition of the purely competitive market is reduced, although there are still somewhat similar products (substitutes) to provide competition for the monopolistic competitor.

In monopolistic competition, the firm has its own downsloping demand curve, but the shape of the curve depends somewhat on

[15] "Sagging Du Pont Casts Shadow over Dow," *Business Week*, April 8, 1967, pp. 118–20; and "Du Pont Says Net in First Period Fell by 24 Per Cent from 1966," *Wall Street Journal*, April 11, 1967, p. 32.

[16] Sometimes it is called *heterogeneous* competition to emphasize that nonhomogeneous products are involved – to provide more contrast with pure competition where homogeneous products are characteristic.

competitors' actions. Each monopolistic competitor has freedom, but not complete freedom, in his own little "industry."

<table>
<tr><td>

Judging elasticity, if not shape, is helpful in strategy planning

</td><td>

Since the firm in monopolistic competition has its own downsloping demand curve, it must make a conscious price decision as part of its marketing mix. Here, the elasticity of the firm's own demand curve becomes extremely relevant. If it is highly inelastic, the firm may decide to raise prices to increase total revenue. But if demand is highly elastic, this may indicate many competitors with acceptable substitutes, and the company will have to focus attention on Product improvements, Place, and Promotion.

</td></tr>
</table>

The terms *elastic* and *inelastic,* used in relation to demand, give us a helpful shorthand for describing the nature of competition and demand facing a firm. The degree of elasticity is something the marketing manager can judge, even though he may not be able to specify the exact shape of the demand curve. This judgment can be very helpful in describing the nature of the market and can affect his overall strategy. (More is said on demand estimation in Chapter 25. For now, rough judgments will meet our need.)

Why are some products offered in pure competition?

Why would anyone compete in essentially profitless pure competition? The usual explanation is that the firm was either already in the industry, or enters without knowing what is happening or is going to happen, and then must stick it out until its resources are depleted. Production-oriented people seem more likely to make such a mistake than the market-oriented businessman. Avoiding pure competition seems advisable, and certainly fits with our emphasis on trying to develop unique marketing strategies, catering to unsatisfied target markets that will recognize the company's product as unique.

Despite their desire to avoid pure competition conditions, however, some firms find that (at least for part of their operation) they cannot do so. In some cases, production processes make this inevitable. For instance, in the chemical industry, caustic soda is produced as a by-product in the production of more profitable chlorine. At one time, the supply of caustic soda was so great that it was being dumped as waste into the Gulf of Mexico. Obviously, this had a depressing influence on the market and the nature of competition (to say nothing about the water)!

Some industries appear to be almost purely competitive, yet new firms keep entering, replacing the casualties, possibly because they might not have more attractive alternatives and can at least earn a living in the industry. Examples of such industries include small retailing and wholesaling, especially in less developed economies. Modern farmers continually attempt to shift their production to more profitable crops, but since there are many thousands of other farmers making similar choices, almost pure competition is inevitable.

Competition leads to standardization efforts

A marketing manager caught in nearly pure competition may, and often does, encourage or participate in an industry standardization program to reduce the variety of products he has to offer and thereby reduce his costs.

Standardization is the determination of specifications or grades to which manufactured goods must conform or into which the products of agriculture and extractive industries may be sorted. Standardization usually involves a reduction in the number of grades offered and agreement on which ones will be offered. Standards may be set by the government or by industry members.

Government standards usually are set up or suggested by an agency, such as the U.S. Department of Agriculture or the U.S. Bureau of Standards, a unit of the Department of Commerce. The standards are not established specifically for the products of any one firm but are applied generally to the grading and standardization of such commodities as wheat, corn, and apples; mechanical equipment; and nuts, bolts, and screws.

Industry standards are similar to government standards except that they are set by a trade association or group of firms. Examples are can and bottle sizes, and shoe and clothing sizes.

Standards may be based upon quantitative factors, such as weight per volume, or ingredients or performance. Standards also may be based on a variety of qualitative factors such as ripeness, color, flavor, taste, and texture.

Generally, quantitative standards are preferred because of ease of measurement. But for many products, strictly quantitative measures are not enough. Raw materials for paint manufacturing, for example, defy complete description, so paint buyers often specify "the same as the last satisfactory shipment" on purchase orders.

Standardization also facilitates marketing process

Standardization has been called a "facilitating" function, since it frequently simplifies trade. Uniform quality and a reduction in the number of grades make buying and selling easier, more economical, and frequently save time. Comparison between the selling prices of competitors is facilitated, and sales by sample or description become feasible.

For agricultural commodities, the use of standard grades facilitates sorting. Commodities can then be traded like quality-controlled manufactured products. Standardized grades permit the use of published market statistics and promote the development of a more competitive market.

If there are grades for which demand can be predicted, the producer has some assurance of product acceptance and a stable market, and he may be willing to lower prices. Standardization may also reduce the amount of promotion necessary on commonly accepted standard items.

For the consumer, standardization may lower prices and reduce buying risk for all of the reasons just enumerated.

Approaches for developing separate product markets

Product standardization efforts may make sense if it is obvious that the firm has to remain close to, or in, pure competition. But monopolistic competition is more attractive to a marketing manager than pure competition. The key to achieving monopolistic competition is to have a markedly different marketing mix. By differentiating its product, the firm may be able to "carve out" a separate market for itself.

Making a market

There are two basic ways to achieve some control of your market: market segmentation and product differentiation.

Market segmentation is the process of isolating previously unsatisfied target markets and designing a unique product for that part of the market grid. Here, the idea is to develop a uniquely different and more satisfying product.

When there are direct competitors for the customers in a particular market grid box, however, then it becomes necessary to stress product differences. This latter approach is called *product differentiation*. Sometimes a firm may be following both approaches at the same time. Its successful market segmentation efforts may attract competition and force it to rely on product differentiation too. These ideas are explained more fully below.

Product differentiation, not customer exclusion

Product differentiation seeks to direct consumer demand toward one manufacturer's or middleman's product even though it may be quite similar to the competitors' products.

In other words, the firm tried to shift its own demand curve to the right.

This approach, which often stresses promotion, also may involve physical product changes, including new packages or brands, new features, new flavors, or new novelties slipped into the box.

Even if physical changes are made, the intention is not to focus on the demand of separate target markets but to improve the company's position in many target markets, perhaps all the way across the market grid. The aim is to differentiate but not to become so unique that general appeal is lost. The theory here is that a firm should offer a better homogeneous product rather than a unique heterogeneous product desired by fewer consumers.

Some firms use promotion heavily in their product differentiation efforts because actual differences among competing products may be minor—but these minor differences nevertheless may be very important to some customers.

Some differences exist mainly in the eye of the beholder. If a woman truly believes that one cosmetic is more suited to her personality, she will use it. But different customers have different needs. Some women may be concerned with cleanliness, others with beauty, and others with glamour. A single cosmetic advertisement might appeal to all of them, but for different reasons.

Product differentiation is employed for most widely advertised products appealing to mass audiences—products such as soaps, cosmetics, foods, and automobiles. It also is seen in the industrial goods area, where firms try to meet generally accepted specifications but with improved products.

Control Data Corp., a small computer manufacturer competing with IBM, tries to make better and cheaper computer equipment, but all of it meshes with IBM's systems.[17] With product differentiation you want to be different—but not so different that you narrow your markets, excluding some customers. You may not satisfy anyone better than competitors can, but you hope your general appeal will be satisfying enough to a sufficient number of people to prove profitable.

Market segmentation to satisfy "very well" With market segmentation, we attempt to develop a special product to satisfy target customers in different market grid boxes. Here, more drastic changes, perhaps even in the physical product, may be made in the total product to appeal to smaller target markets. The result may be achievement of more inelastic demand curves in several different market segments.

A market segmentation approach recognizes that there may be different demand curves in different parts of the market grid. This focus on smaller markets tends to provide greater satisfaction to customers and therefore provides greater security for the marketing manager and his firm.

Although a product differentiation policy would attempt to satisfy a lot of people *pretty well*, market segmentation would attempt to satisfy a smaller number of people *very well*.[18] If done well, total sales could be greater with the same effort, because the market penetration in target market(s) would be much higher.

Market segmentation can lead to considerable product diversification and expansion of a manufactuer's line. There might be a special product for each market grid box, or even for each individual customer! Actually, this policy is seldom carried to its logical conclusion. Few customers' desires for different products are so strong that they will pay the higher costs that completely individualized products would entail. A market segmentation policy, nevertheless, can expand product lines markedly.

Thom McAn Shoe Co. has found it necessary to have 150 different styles, exclusive of different widths and lengths. Instead of trying to explain that one basic shoe model will fit every customer's personality, the company produces many different shoes to satisfy the varied demands.

Market segmentation may enable a small producer to move itself away from pure competition into monopolistic competition. For ex-

---

[17] "Poor Man's IBM," *Time*, August 14, 1964, pp. 62–63; and "Control Data Divides the Power," *Business Week*, April 25, 1970, p. 34.

[18] For the original and classic discussion on product differentiation and market segmentation, see Wendell R. Smith, "Product Differentiation and Market Segmentation as Alternative Marketing Strategies," *Journal of Marketing*, July, 1956, pp. 3–8.

ample, the Wolverine World Wide Co. came out with "Hush-Puppies," a casual, split-pigskin shoe, that enabled it to move into the extremely competitive U.S. shoe market with spectacular success while conventional small shoe manufacturers were existing in almost pure competition.[19]

The highly profitable operation of Volvo illustrates the possibility of a successful market segmentation policy in a fiercely competitive international market.[20] Volvo has stressed long life and performance in its cars and has not tried to compete head-on with the large producers aiming at the mass market. Similarly, Magnavox has fared well in the competitive U.S. television industry by aiming at the top of the market, not the whole market.[21] Zenith, appealing to the quality- and reliability-conscious, at several price levels, also has done well.[22]

Market segmentation combined with product differentiation

Even if a firm attempts a market segmentation policy, it probably will find that one or more competitors will quickly follow. Then it will have to shift emphasis to product differentiation.

The automobile industry has developed many different kinds of cars to appeal to different target markets. But the various companies and divisions within companies have quickly copied each other. Sometimes the car builders frankly admit that one car was designed to compete directly with another—for example, Chevrolet's Camaro with Ford's Mustang. Then the competitive focus tends to shift from the whole product to minor differences in features, trim, and accessories, together with psychological perceptions of the different products, styles, and brand names.

Even if a marketing manager preferred to follow a market segmentation policy, the extreme competition that most firms find in the marketplace might force him to use product differentiation along with market segmentation.

It's the intent that counts

It often is difficult for an outsider to tell which policy a firm is pursuing. As we have already seen, there is no simple, "correct" way to analyze market grids and precisely define the needs of different target markets. What one firm would recognize as a unique market, another might see as many markets and systematically design products and marketing mixes to satisfy only some of them. It might see itself following a market segmentation policy, while the first firm might understand its own and all the competitive efforts as product differentiation, aimed at the same larger market. Which firm wins would depend on how the market(s) respond(s) to the competing products and mixes. If there really are need differences which are correctly

[19] "This Little Pigskin Went to Market," *Business Week*, December 7, 1963, pp. 48–50.

[20] "Volvo Steers Course Around Giants," *Business Week*, September 21, 1968, pp. 140–41.

[21] "Only the Best," *Time*, January 20, 1967, pp. 76–78.

[22] Talk by Nelson Foote, General Electric Company, at Market Segmentation Conference sponsored by the American Marketing Association, Chicago, in February, 1967; and "Zenith Aims at the Top in Color TV," *Business Week*, September 11, 1965, pp. 128–34.

identified and satisfied, then the (perhaps more costly) market segmentation effort may be more profitable. But if the whole market really is more or less homogeneous, then the product differentiation effort may be just as successful, perhaps at lower cost.

As always, the customer decides what satisfies him best. A market segmentation policy tries harder, but it requires more careful analysis of the market and more risk. Product differentiation, on the other hand, tries to satisfy broader markets "pretty well." Given our present knowledge of consumer behavior analysis, this may be the safe path. But it will lead one into fairly direct competition from others following the same course. Safety may be purchased at the price of the attractive profits which usually accompany marketing breakthroughs. This "safe" "mass-market" route seems to be the one instinctively chosen by the production-oriented businessman, and then he wonders why his markets are so competitive!

Conclusion

This chapter has explored the concept of a *product* very broadly. The product may not even involve a physical product at all. It may be a service, or some combination of a product and a service. A product is the firm's offering which satisfies the needs of its target customers. In this sense, a retailer or wholesaler's offering can be thought of as a product, as can physicians' services, automobiles, appliances, wheat, or coal. By *product* we will mean the *total product*, which *may* include a physical product but also could involve a package, brand, installation, repair services, and so on—whatever it takes to meet the target customers' needs.

The economist's traditional demand and supply analysis provides us with useful tools for analyzing the nature of demand and product-market situations. It is important that you master the concepts of a demand curve and demand elasticity and their relationship to pure and monopolistic competition. A good marketer would try to avoid pure competition in favor of monopolistic competition. In pure competition, the individual firm faces a highly elastic demand curve and has little control over price, or the other three P's for that matter, since essentially homogeneous products are being offered by all competitors.

In an effort to achieve a monopolistic competition situation, a marketing manager may use either a product differentiation or market segmentation policy. A product differentiation policy seeks to adapt the firm's product to broad audiences by focusing on minor but still important differences. Promotion may be quite important when a product differentiation policy is followed.

Market segmentation, on the other hand, tries to satisfy fewer markets in depth; it often requires development of quite different products and/or services. The two policies are not incompatible, however, because competitors usually follow a firm's successful market segmentation quickly, and the marketing manager of that firm will have to resort to product differentiation.

Following either a product differentiation or a market segmentation policy, a marketing manager may be able to achieve relatively inelastic demand curves in one or many market grid boxes. He may operate more profitably than the many product-oriented firms that typically focus on lowering costs rather than satisfying customer needs and as a result find themselves in profitless pure competition.

QUESTIONS AND PROBLEMS

1 Define, in your own words, what a product is.

2 Explain how the addition of guarantees, service, and credit can improve a "total product." Cite a specific case where this has been done and explain how customers viewed this new "total product."

3 What "products" are being offered by an exclusive men's shop? By a nightclub? By a soda fountain? By a supermarket?

4 If the general market demand for men's shoes is fairly elastic, how does the demand for men's dress shoes compare to it? How does the demand curve for women's shoes compare to the demand curve for men's shoes?

5 If the demand for fountain pens were inelastic above and below the present price, should the price be raised? Why, or why not?

6 If the demand for steak is highly elastic below the present price, should the price be lowered?

7 What is the length of life of the typical demand curve? Illustrate your answer.

8 Discuss what factors lead to inelastic demand and supply curves. Are they likely to be found together in the same situation?

9 If a manufacturer's well-known product is sold at the same price by many retailers in the same community, is this an example of pure competition? When a community has many small grocery stores, are they in pure competition? Specify very carefully the characteristics of a purely competitive market.

10 Distinguish between product differentiation and market segmentation. Which policy is being followed if cold cream is offered in a new, more distinctively shaped jar? Which, if only the label is changed to gold foil for distinctiveness?

11 List three products which are sold in purely competitive markets and three in monopolistically competitive markets. Now list three products for which the sellers seem to be using product differentiation and three more where they appear to be using market segmentation. Do any of these products have anything in common? Can any generalizations be made about the relation between these approaches and market situations? Would it be expected that the marketing mix for any of these products would be similar? If so, which ones and how?

...about \$14 billion was spent on packaging *materials* alone in 1965.

...estimated at ☆19 billion in 1970.... For perspective, this is roughly equal to the total amount spent on advertising.

...in the grocery products area...there are approximately 38,000 brands....

...packaging and branding can create a new total product.

Variations in packaging can make a product salable in various target markets. Branding can be used by the marketer in creating and building a customer franchise for a given product.

11

Packaging and branding

A total product is much more than a physical product. But if a physical product is involved, it probably will need some packaging. Physical products *and* services probably should be branded to make sure that they are clearly identifiable. Moreover, brands, including corporate and store names, can carry much meaning for customers and potential customers.

In the same sense, there is much more to packaging and branding than just buying a cardboard box and sticking on the company's name. In some cases, the packaging and branding decisions may be more important than physical product decisions. They may enable a firm to differentiate its homogenous physical product or service and avoid pure competition.

Packaging and branding are discussed in this chapter. We will emphasize the decisions of manufacturers or the middlemen who must make packaging and branding decisions.

What is packaging?

Sometimes a distinction is made between packing and packaging — the former being concerned with protection and the latter with promotion. We will *not* make this distinction. The difference is seldom clear-cut. Modern packaging tries to do both jobs. It is important to note, however, that management conflicts may develop over the relative importance of these two packaging functions.

The production, shipping, and transportation departments of a manufacturer and the materials handling departments of middlemen and customers may be more interested in protection. The sales department may be more interested in promotion aspects. And final consumers may be more interested in the use characteristics of the package. All these interests must be balanced in developing a marketing strategy. The need for balance emphasizes the importance of having top management involved in this aspect of marketing strategy planning.

Growing importance of packaging

Amount spent large and rising

The importance of packaging is partially illustrated by its cost. About $14 billion was spent on packaging *materials* alone in 1965. This total was estimated at $19 billion in 1970 and is expected to continue rising in coming years.[1] For perspective, this is roughly equal to the total amount spent on advertising. And the actual cost of packaging might be twice as high, if all of the costs of handling, storing, and moving containers were included. These rising outlays for packaging are due in part to a shift from an earlier almost sole emphasis on protection to the current interest in protection *and* the promotional potential of the package — both in terms of greater convenience and the messages it can carry.

Higher corporate status for packaging

The purchasing agent used to be in charge of packaging in many companies when protection was the major function of the package. But now, some companies are establishing corporate packaging staffs. And in some the product manager or a specialist in packaging has taken over the job.[2]

General Foods Corp. appointed a manager of packaging development and procurement services when it reached the conclusion that packaging is an important tool of management. This manager coordinates packaging activities with the various product managers. The National

---

[1]*Modern Packaging Encyclopedia*, 1970 Issue, p. 17.

[2]David J. Luck, "Interfaces of a Product Manager," *Journal of Marketing*, October, 1969, pp. 32–36.

Biscuit Co. has a vice president of packaging acting as chairman of the packaging committee.[3]

This newfound status for packaging occurred in part because of the growing competitiveness in many markets. This status also reflects the costliness of packaging errors and the difficulty of correcting them. An advertising campaign, for instance, might prove ineffective and could be dropped. Its ineffectiveness might lead to a loss of money but have no impact on potential customers. In contrast, a poor package could have long-term effects, killing the product for customers who try it and creating ill will among middlemen. In other words, packaging can have great strategic importance.

Strategic importance of packaging

Marketing strategy planning tries to match target market needs and preferences to the marketing mix offered – and packaging is definitely a part of the mix. In some cases, it may be a vital part. A seemingly minor promotional change in packaging design, adding a more appealing illustration, may double sales, while another seemingly minor change might cut a brand's share of the market in half![4]

Clearly, packaging materials, sizes, and designs should be examined with a final target market(s) in mind. But in doing so, intermediate customer wants and preferences cannot be neglected either.

A new package can *make* a new strategy work, but it should be designed with consideration of the needs of all those who will buy or handle it.

When the package makes the product

A new package can become the major factor in a new marketing strategy by significantly improving the total product. A better box, wrapper, can, or bottle may even enable a relatively small, unknown firm to compete successfully with the established competitors. Carter Products Co., not previously in the men's toiletries field, introduced its first men's product, Rise shaving cream, in aerosol cans and was able to compete effectively. The normal tube and carton might not have been so successful.[5]

A package change often creates a "new" product by giving either the regular customers or new target markets the existing product in a new form or quantity that is more satisfactory. Packaging frozen vegetables in 1-pound packages instead of 10-ounce packages served larger families better. The small package held too little for them, while two packages held too much. Some producers are carving large turkeys into quarters to stimulate year-round sales. One such experiment expanded sales 200 percent.[6]

[3]"The New Power of Packaging: Management Takes Control," *Printers' Ink*, June 11, 1965, pp. 13–18.

[4]Dik Warren Twedt, "How Much Value Can Be Added Through Packaging?" *Journal of Marketing*, January, 1968, pp. 58–61.

[5]"New Packaging Concepts Sell, Resell, and Satisfy Customers," *Printers' Ink*, November 21, 1958, pp. 21–27; see also, "Packaging Brings a Sleeper to Life," *Printers' Ink*, March 22, 1963, pp. 48–49.

[6]*Ibid.* "Packaging Brings a Sleeper to Life."

Multiple packs can be the basis of a new marketing strategy, too. Consumer surveys showed that some customers were buying several units at a time of products such as soft drinks, beer, and frozen orange juice. This suggested an overlooked market grid box. Manufacturers tried multiple packaging of units in 4-, 6-, and 8-packs, and have gained wide acceptance, Such multiple packaging has advantages for both retailers and customers, for handling ease and lower cost. Multiple packs demonstrate why it is difficult (or wrong) to try to distinguish the protective and handling aspects from the promotional aspects of packaging.

Satisfy the wholesaler, help the retailer, *or else!*

Better protective packaging is especially important to intermediate customers, such as manufacturers and wholesalers, who may have to absorb the cost of goods damaged in transit. Sometimes the cost of such damage can be charged to the transportation agencies, but there still are costs for settling such claims – and getting them settled is a nuisance. Moreover, goods damaged in shipment may delay production and cause lost sales.

Packaging is vital to retailers. They benefit from both the protective and promotional aspects of packaging. Estimates are that better packaging could reduce supermarket handling costs by as much as 4.5 percent of total sales and increase sales 7.4 percent; the sales increase could total more than $3 billion a year, of which some $1 billion might be passed on to consumers in reduced prices.[7]

Packaging which provides better protection, supermarket operators claim, can reduce store costs by lessening breakage, shrinkage, and spoilage, preventing discoloration, and stopping pilferage. Packages that are easier to handle can cut costs by speeding price marking, improving handling and display, and saving space. And packaging can increase sales by such promotionally oriented moves as offering smaller or larger sizes, more multi-packs, better pictures of the product itself, illustrations of the product in use, and more effective use of color.

Food retailers attach such importance to packaging that they have formed supermarket industry committees to criticize manufacturers' packages and to encourage improved packaging. Retailers also make their feelings known individually. In South Bend, Indiana, for example, some supermarket operators refused to carry one manufacturer's gelatin products because he would not supply the products in larger cartons. The storekeepers maintained that the firm's small cartons, designed to serve small retailers, were a nuisance and cost too much to handle.

May be "better" than advertising

Packaged goods are regularly seen in retail stores and may actually be seen by many more potential customers than the company's advertising. An effective package sometimes gives a firm more promotional

[7]*Modern Packaging,* October, 1957, pp. 121 ff.; and "The Case of the Crumbled Cookie," *Printers' Ink,* January 13, 1967, p. 3.

impact than it could possibly afford with conventional advertising efforts.[8]

Packaging expenses as a percentage of the manufacturer's selling price vary widely, ranging from 1 to 70 percent. Low packaging expenses are found in such fields as office machines (1.4 percent), hardware (4.0 percent), cutlery (5.0 percent), and automotive parts (5.0 percent), where the primary job is protection and the value of products is relatively high. On the other hand, cost percentages are higher for candy (21), foods (21), drugs (26), and cosmetics and toiletries (36).[9] The really high percentages apply to soaps (50) and toothpaste (70).

May lower total distribution costs

Packaging costs money – but in many cases this expense may reduce total distribution costs by (1) providing more protection and ease in physical handling, thereby reducing damage and loss, and (2) providing more promotional impact than could be obtained in other ways for the same money and thereby increasing sales and turnover so that costs decline – that is, by cutting the cost of promotion and also achieving some of the economies of mass distribution.

The cost reducing value of protective packaging is clear. Some airlines have developed aluminum containers that can be loaded at the shipper's own plant, *sealed*, and delivered still sealed to the customer. This reduces costly packing and is reputed to be lossproof, weatherproof, and tamperproof. Similar containers have been developed for water shipments. The Volkswagen factory in West Germany, for instance, uses lightweight containers in shipments to its U.S. distributors. Each distributor's container holds several dealers' orders of prepackaged parts, which are ready to go on the shelf with minimum handling.[10]

Promotionally oriented packaging also may reduce the total distribution costs. An attractive package may speed turnover so that total costs will decline as a percentage of sales. While more will be said on this in subsequent chapters, rapid turnover is one of the important ingredients in the success of self-service retailing. Without packages that sell themselves, self-service retailing would not be possible.

Or . . . may raise total distribution costs

In other cases, total distribution costs may rise because of packaging – and yet *everyone may be satisfied* because the packaging improves the total product.

Consider sugar as an example. In 100-pound bags, the cost of packaging sugar is only 1 percent of the selling price; in 2- to 5-pound cartons, 25–30 percent; and for individual serving envelopes, 50 percent. Yet most housewives do not care to haul a 100-pound bag home, and are quite willing to pay the added costs for more convenient packages. Restaurants use one-serving envelopes of sugar, finding that they re-

[8]Twedt, *op. cit.*, p. 61.

[9]*Modern Packaging*, March, 1954, p. 127, and April, 1959, p. 146.

[10]"Hauling Freight by the Package," *Business Week*, September 16, 1961, pp. 84–86.

duce the cost of filling and washing sugar bowls and that customers prefer the more sanitary little packages. In both cases, packaging adds value to the total product – or more accurately, it creates new products and new marketing strategies.

What makes a good package design?

There are no easy rules-of-thumb for the marketer making packaging decisions. The right package depends upon such factors as:

1. Susceptibility of the product to damage.
2. The hazards to which the product *normally* will be exposed – in commercial packaging, it is too costly to protect against every possible hazard.
3. The length of time the product must remain in the package and still be in satisfactory condition.
4. The promotional role of the package.

Fortunately, much work has been done on package design research, and some specific techniques have been developed to aid marketing researchers in designing and evaluating packages, especially with regard to their promotional role. The problems of perception and learning are certainly involved here. Visibility on the shelf is also a problem, and instruments have been invented for measuring eye movements and depth perception. The seriousness of interest in this subject is due to the fact that there may be a wide "range in potential effectiveness among several designs offered by the same top-flight, professional designer in response to a given assignment."[11]

The right packaging, enough packaging

Experience shows that *a specific package must be developed for each specific product*. The package must safely transport its contents, serve in a specific climate (especially if the product is to be exported), and last for a specific time. To provide such packaging, the manufacturer must know his product, his customers, and how the product will be delivered to them. *Under*packaging costs money for damage claims or poor sales, but *over*packaging also costs money because dollars are spent but no gains are realized. Glassware, for example, needs to be protected from even relatively light blows that might smash it. Heavy-duty machinery seldom needs protection from blows but may need protection from corrosion caused by moisture.

Some of the factors a package designer must consider, perhaps with the help of marketing research, are detailed in Figure 11–1. To view packaging through the eyes of the designer or manufactuer, study this list in relation to a specific product, such as frozen peaches, table salt, women's sweaters, or television sets. When it is obvious that you do not know the answer (and the package designers probably would

[11]Twedt, *op. cit.*, p. 58.

Figure 11-1 Packaging considerations

A. *Package in the home or place of use:*
1. Package immediately destroyed?
2. Package used to store contents until used up? How long is this period?
3. Should package have a dispensing device?
4. What is average amount of contents used each time?
5. Is package designed for reuse?
6. Is package returnable?
7. Where is package stored? Before use? During use?
8. Where is the package used?
9. Is the package used later to store other material?
10. What effect does the foregoing have on size, color, material?

B. *Package in the store:*
1. What types of store will sell the package?
2. What class of customers do they serve?
3. Must the package do most of the selling?
4. Does the package form part of the display?
5. At what distance must package be identified?
6. How is identification of contents achieved?
7. What is the rate of turnover?
8. In what is package kept in the selling space?
9. How is package handled in the storeroom?
10. What can be done to simplify handling of packages?

C. *Package in transit:*
1. How is package shipped? What types of carriers?
2. Are standard cartons or crates used?
3. How do these factors affect dimensions?
4. What protective measures are required against temperature, moisture, shock, pilferage, vermin?
5. Have the carriers any recommendations or standards to be considered?

D. *Package in the warehouse:*
1. How is package stored?
2. How is it handled?
3. What are usual units of shipments?
4. How are inventories taken?
5. How long is package warehoused?
6. What protective measures are required?

E. *Package at plant:*
1. In what form is package received? Quantities?
2. Where are empties stored?
3. What are filling and labeling methods?
4. What types of machines are used?
5. What grades of employees are involved?

F. *Package and other design in promotion consideration:*
1. Are there trademarks? color? type face? or art work problems?
2. Are there established customs in the industry that affect packages?

G. *The package and the law:*
1. What government requirements exist as to size, description of contents, grades?
2. What trade customs exist within the industry?
3. What patent information is required?

Source: Adapted from Benjamin L. Webster, "First Steps in Package Design," *Distribution Age,* June, 1957.

not either) to a packaging problem, marketing research would be indicated before making major packaging decisions.

Consumers versus packaging

Despite all the time and money now spent on packaging, there is still much room for improvement. In one survey, 85 percent of the housewives interviewed told of having been hurt when opening a package. Women were especially vocal about having to use knives to open containers of frozen strawberries. Complaints were general about bottles that break, metal containers with sharp edges, reclosable baby-food jars that are practically unopenable, sardine tins without windup keys, sugar bags that are almost impossible to open, and flour bags that invariably spill.[12] The result is unsatisfied target markets.

Some consumers complain about partially filled packages. Others are confused by the many and varied sizes. Critics of business allege that some package designs are misleading, perhaps deliberately so. They feel that the great variety of package designs makes it difficult for consumers to make value comparisons readily.

Federal law tries to help   The concern of some consumers finally led to the passage of the Federal Fair Packaging and Labeling Act of 1966. This law basically requires that consumer goods be clearly labeled in understandable terms, in order to give the customer more information. The law also calls upon government agencies and industry to try to reduce the number of package sizes. The Food and Drug Administration is made responsible for foods, nonprescription drugs, and cosmetics. The Federal Trade Commission is responsible for nonfood items. And the Commerce Department is expected to seek voluntary agreements by industry groups with respect to package proliferation.

The results so far have been very disappointing to spokesmen for consumer groups, and it seems likely that more and perhaps tougher legislation is in the offing.[13] The fault may lie both with legislators (who did not appropriate enough to implement the legislation) and industry groups (some of whom feel that most consumers really aren't interested in value comparisons).

Some progress has been made, such as the reduction by industry groups of the number of toothpaste sizes from 57 to 5, and paper-towel packages from 33 to 8. But major problem areas still exist in the analgesics (aspirin and other pain-killers) and toiletry goods, such as hair spray, deodorants, mouthwashes, and aftershave lotions. The toilet goods people, for example, have not shown much interest because

[12] "The Perfect Package: It's Not Here Yet," *Business Week*, August 12, 1961, pp. 106–8; and "Cut Fingers in the Kitchen," *Time*, October 20, 1961, p. 56.

[13] "Consumer Forces Say Packaging Law Fails to Clear Up Confusion," *Wall Street Journal*, November 6, 1969, pp. 1 and 16; and David M. Gardner, "The Package, Legislation, and the Shopper," *Business Horizons*, Vol. 11, No. 5 (October, 1968), pp. 53–60.

they feel consumers are more concerned with how the products feel or smell or look than with value comparisons.

In spite of the difficulties of implementing the laws, and perhaps the inappropriateness of easily measurable standards such as weight and volume in some cases, it appears that more legislation may be coming. *Unit-pricing,* for example, is being tried in New York City and may become a federal requirement. This would require some indication of the cost per ounce, or some other standard measure which would facilitate comparison. The need may be urgent in some areas, due to the present confusion. How, for example, do you evaluate the best buy in toothpaste when faced with a "medium" size of Colgate, a "large" size of Crest, and a "giant" tube of Pepsodent, perhaps at various prices. The toothpaste may be different, but the package sizes are the same if you care to look hard enough! Situations such as this are not uncommon, which is why we will probably see more legislation to help simplify the consumer's buying efforts.

Packaging must fit into the strategy

Packaging certainly has strategic implications. Ideally, the needs and preferences of customers in various market grid boxes should be analyzed with respect to packaging. In addition, the needs and desires of intermediate customers should be considered in order to avoid such foul-ups as the packaging of a soft drink in an attractive new aluminum can that was fine for supermarket shelves but too tall for vending machines.[14]

In planning packaging, however, packaging is only part of a total marketing strategy. The marketing manager must be alert to make the packaging fit into the total strategy—and not vice versa.

Branding—why it developed

Use of brands evolved to meet economic needs

Brands are so numerous and commonplace that we are inclined to take their significance for granted. In the grocery products area alone, there are approximately 38,000 brands, even though the average supermarket can stock only about 6,500.[15] The following section discusses the importance of branding for individual firms and for the economy as a whole.

From our review of Western economic history, it will be recalled that production for the marketplace began early in recorded history, lapsed after the fall of Rome and during the Middle Ages, and expanded again as the feudal villages began to trade with each other. During this revival, craft guilds (similar to labor unions) and merchant guilds formed

[14]"RC Cola's Package 'Too Tall to Vend,'" *Printers' Ink,* May 12, 1967, pp. 56–57.

[15]*The Nielsen Researcher,* No. 1 (1967), p. 11.

to control the quantity and quality of production. One requirement was that each producer mark his goods so that output could be restricted when necessary. This also meant that inferior quality, which might reflect unfavorably on other guild products and discourage future trade, could be traced back to the offending producer. Early trademarks also were a protection to the buyer, who could now determine the source of the product.

Not restriction but identification

More recently, brands have been used primarily for identification rather than restriction of output.

The earliest and most aggressive brand promoters in America were the patent medicine manufacturers. They were joined by the food manufacturers, who grew in size after the Civil War. Some of the brands started in the 1860's and 1870's, and still going strong, are Dr. Lyon's Tooth Powder, Borden's Condensed Milk, Quaker Oats, Vaseline, Pillsbury's Best Flour, and Ivory Soap.[16]

Indians prefer sugar to chalk dust

Today, a good brand usually assures high or at least consistent quality and encourages repeat purchasing. This works where there is some trust of sellers by buyers and where the sellers can protect their brand. This is generally true in the United States, but much less so elsewhere. For example, in Formosa there are about a dozen red-and-white striped toothpaste packages of varying quality with brand names remarkably similar to Colgate — Coalgate, Goalgate, Goldkey, Goldcat, and Goldrat.[17]

Customers are willing to buy by brand rather than by inspection when there is some assurance of quality. In many countries, however, the consumer doesn't feel he has any such assurance. In India, inspecting the product is common because there is a complete lack of confidence in packaged goods and brands. This distrust has a solid foundation. In 1957, it was estimated that in Delhi, 25 percent of all food was adulterated. Sawdust, husks, colored earth, and ground seeds accounted for 10–50 percent of the weight of many products. As a result, Indian customers avoid buying packaged or prepared foods. They prefer to buy sugar in extremely coarse crystals, and grain rather than flour, because both fine-granulated sugar and flour can be adulterated easily with chalk dust.[18]

Soviets prefer brands

The importance of brands in a nation's economy can be seen clearly in the Soviet experience. The U.S.S.R. evolved toward an enthusiastic use of branding — after instances of economic disaster forced it upon them.

Several Russian factories were manufacturing supposedly identical 17-inch TV sets, but actually one of the plants was shipping "lemons." When customers became aware of this, they stopped buying all 17-inch

---

[16] Frank Presbrey, *The History and Development of Advertising* (New York: Doubleday & Co., Inc., 1929).

[17] *Time*, June 15, 1962, p. 83.

[18] Ralph Westfall and Harper W. Boyd, Jr., "Marketing in India," *Journal of Marketing*, October, 1960, p. 17.

sets, because they could not identify the bad ones. This obviously caused considerable inventory problems for the central planners. It also caused some public discontent with the Soviet system. Shortly thereafter, factory numbers on products were required to help the planners identify the production source. Subsequently, consumers discovered the factory numbers and plants that were producing poorer quality products began to have difficulties meeting their economic plans. Soviet consumers rather than planners forced the plants to pay more attention to quality. Interestingly, before long there were more than 25 state-sponsored advertising agencies to tell people about the "quality" of various factories. Now, advertising courses are even offered in Russian universities![19]

The important thing to note here is that the "brands" were created by the customers rather than the planners. The factory identification numbers had been added originally to help the planners – but the consumers quickly adapted them to their own use.

Why branding is advantageous to customers

Makes shopping feasible	Well-recognized brands make shopping feasible in a modern economy. Think of the consumer's dilemma in a grocery store, for example, if she had to consider seriously the advantages and disadvantages of each of 6,500 items every time she went shopping.
Assures regular satisfaction	Many customers are willing to buy new things, but having gambled and won, they like to buy a "sure thing" thereafter. The customer may even be willing to pay a premium for brands with which she has had favorable experience. And noneconomic considerations may enter here, too. A housewife considering a well-known brand versus a lower-priced and unknown brand of frozen peas, for instance, may evaluate the possible savings. She will also think hard about her embarrassment if her entire dinner is ruined because of hard or unappetizing peas.
Dependable guides to quality	There is considerable evidence that if the housewife used well-known brands rather than high prices as an indication of good quality, she might be further ahead. One study of grocery products found that the known brands usually had fairly consistent quality, but there was little assurance that a high price meant high quality.[20]

Branded drug products may also be better than unbranded ones which meet the same minimum specifications. This is an important political and social matter, because some branded drug products are prescribed by doctors and are priced substantially above unbranded

[19] T. Levitt, "Branding on Trial," *Harvard Business Review*, March-April, 1966, pp. 28–32.

[20] Robert H. Cole, "The Battle of Brands in Canned Goods," in S. H. Rewoldt (ed.), *Frontiers in Market-* *ing Thought* (Bloomington, Ind.: Bureau of Business Research, Indiana University, 1955), pp. 153–59.

ones in the same generic class. Business critics have been very vocal here. Industry representatives argue that there are differences, and some tests suggest that this is the case. In other cases, there is not even agreement over which test should be used, or if it is possible to measure effectiveness.[21]

Brands may give status

Lower-class housewives may buy well-recognized manufacturers' brands, not for status, but for assurance of quality within their more narrowly perceived range of choices.[22] Other customers, however, seem to be less concerned with the physical characteristics of the product and more concerned with the symbolic value. They seem to derive psychic satisfaction from the use of well-known branded articles, perhaps because they feel some of the status or prestige of the product may rub off on them. You may recall that both the physical and symbolic aspects of products were incorporated into the Howard-Sheth model.

Why branding is advantageous to branders

Encourages repeat buying

Brands obviously would not be used so aggressively by companies if target customers did not respond to them. Many of the advantages of brand promotion to the branders are a function of the advantages to customers. A good brand speeds up shopping for the customer, and so it reduces the marketer's selling time and effort. When a customer finds it convenient to repeat purchases by brand, promotion costs are reduced and sales volume is increased. A marketing manager who consistently attempts to provide a good buy and maintain quality can be assured of his reward by using brands.

May develop customer franchise

Another important advantage of successful branding is that the brander may be able to carve out a market for himself among loyal customers.[23] Whether the brander is a manufacturer, wholesaler, or retailer, this brand loyalty protects him from competition, because the brander, in effect, is given a customer franchise by the customers he is reaching. In other words, he achieves a monopolistic competition situation or even a little monopoly, and this gives him greater control in planning his marketing mix.

May help segment markets

A brander also can use various brands to segment markets and meet the needs of various intermediate customers. Instead of just selling "motor oil," for example, the marketing manager could offer three grades (and brands) to cater to final consumers' varying demands for

---

[21]"Just How Good?" *Time*, July 7, 1967, pp. 66–67; and "FDA Has Doubts on Generic Names," *Business Week*, January 13, 1968, p. 36.

[22] James A. Carman, *The Application of Social Class in Market Segmentation* (Berkeley: Institute of Business and Economic Research, University of California, 1965), p. 28.

[23] Ross M. Cunningham, "Brand Loyalty—What, Where, How Much?" *Harvard Business Review*, January–February, 1956, pp. 116–28.

oil quality. But if he were selling this oil to various competing whole-salers and retailers who did not want to compete directly with each other, he might offer them identical or almost identical products under different brand names. Such practices help explain why there are so many brands on the market.

Branding may return more than it costs

By offering customers what amounts to a "guarantee" of quality, branders may be able to obtain a price that is higher than the cost of giving this guarantee.[24] This is important because maintaining quality and providing a guarantee do, in fact, cost something. One study showed that customers were willing to spend approximately 13 per-cent more for well-known food brands.

But brands must be seen to be appreciated

Spending money on branding makes sense only if the customer who is going to make the buying decision will see the brand and be im-pressed by it.

Those who make items that are incorporated into other products, a car, for example, have a particularly difficult branding problem. Pro-ducers of automobile tires, spark plugs, and batteries have been suc-cessful branders, but makers of wheel bearings, door handles, radia-tors, and other such parts have not. Producers in the latter kinds of industries tend to face almost pure competition.

A good brand may build corporate image

Good brands can enhance the company's name, simplifying the intro-duction of additional products. Or the company may use its own name as a brand for many of its products. This is of special importance in the industrial goods area, where branding of individual products is more difficult. Here, it is really the company's total personality which it would like to project, positively.

The idea of improving the company's corporate image, as well as its brands, has been growing. When customers think a company is big and successful, they often have a better impression of it and its prod-ucts. The U.S. Steel Corp., with its many large subsidiaries, found that industrial customers who were aware of the relationship of U.S. Steel to its subsidiaries viewed the subsidiaries more favorably. This was important in their choice of supplier, especially when competing products were basically similar. For this reason, in 1958, U.S. Steel redesigned its trademark and began to identify all the subsidiaries with it.[25]

Growing acceptance of the idea that a good customer image is im-portant has led some companies to change their corporate name so that the name either is more descriptive of the firm's activity or is more inclusive of a variety of activities. Cities Service, for instance, took the name Citgo, and spent a lot of money popularizing the new

[24] J. O. Peckham, *Planning Your Marketing Opera-tions for 1959 . . . and the Years Ahead* (Chicago: A. C. Nielsen Co., 1958), p. 15; and "How A Small Packer Does Better than the Giants," *Business Week*, November 22, 1958, pp. 140–52.

[25] "What's Behind the New Look That U.S. Steel Is Sporting," *Business Week*, March 29, 1958, pp. 88–93.

name and the new symbol because the old name seemed inappropri-ate.[26] And U.S. Rubber, with its various foreign subsidiaries, adopted the Uniroyal name and trademark because it felt that the new name was a more accurate designation.[27]

Conditions favorable to branding

Most marketing managers accept branding as desirable and are pri-marily concerned with assuring the success of the brand name of the product(s) they are marketing.

The following conditions would be favorable to successful branding:

1. The demand for the general product class or in the selected tar-get market(s) should be large enough to support a profitable marketing plan.
2. The demand should be sufficiently strong so that the market price will offer a large enough margin over additional promotion cost to make the effort worthwhile.
3. It is best when there are economies of mass production. If the branding were really successful, the cost of production would decline with additional volume, thereby increasing profits.
4. The product quality being offered should be the best for the price in the market being served, and the quality should be easily maintained.
5. The product should be easily identifiable by a brand or trade-mark. This is easier said than done. Many products do not lend themselves easily to conspicuous marking. Few consumers would like to have a furniture manufacturer's label sewn con-spicuously on their sofa or lounge chair. But if the label or mark is inconspicuous, then much of the brand prestige value is lost.

   Some producers are ingenious in placing labels. Walnut and orange growers stamp their brand names directly on their prod-ucts; some coal producers color their coal; and large meat-packers place metal foil brand labels inside self-service meat packages.
6. Consistent and widespread availability is necessary. When a cus-tomer starts using a brand, she should be able to continue finding it in her stores.
7. Brand promotion will be more successful if the brander can be assured of favorable positioning of his products in the stores. For some manufacturers, this is just a hope or a goal for their sales-men. But when wholesalers and retailers brand their own prod-ucts, this is something they can control.

[26] "Cities Service Hangs New Shingle," *Business Week,* May 8, 1965, pp. 72–77.

[27] "One Name to Girdle the Globe," *Business Week,* August 1, 1964, pp. 74–75.

Achieving brand familiarity is not easy

There are
four levels
of familiarity

Our earlier discussion (in Chapter 8) of consumer buying behavior stressed that potential customers' awareness of brands is important. It also is clear that recognition and respect for a brand must be earned by means of a good product and persistent promotion. There are many brands which, for practical purposes, are valueless because they have no meaning to target customers.

Four degrees of brand familiarity are useful: (1) nonrecognition, (2) recognition, (3) preference, and (4) insistence. The closer a brand gets to the insistence stage, the more likely that routine problem solving would be used by the customer. At the other extreme, if a potential customer were unfamiliar with all of the brands in a product class, then extended problem solving might be required.

The degree of brand familiarity achieved by the brander (*and* his competitors) obviously affects the planning for the balance of the marketing mix, and especially influences decisions on where the product should be made available and what promotion is needed.

Nonrecognition of brand

Some products are seen as essentially homogeneous. Their brands are not recognized by final consumers at all. And they may never be, although middlemen may use the brand names for identification and inventory control and this may mislead production-oriented manufacturers. Examples here are: school supplies, novelties, inexpensive dinnerware, and similar goods found in variety stores and mass merchandising outlets.

Brand recognition

Brand recognition means that customers remember having seen or heard of the brand. This can be a significant achievement if there are many nondescript brands on the market. Potential customers could have either positive or negative feelings about a brand, of course, but here we will emphasize the positive aspects only.

Brand preference

Rather than just gaining brand *recognition,* some branders would prefer to reach the stage called "brand preference" in which target customers will choose the brand out of habit or past experience. At this stage, the firm may have achieved a favorable position in a monopolistic competition situation.

Brand insistence

"Brand insistence," a logical extension of brand preference, is the stage at which customers insist upon a product and would be willing to search extensively to find it. This stage is the goal of most product differentiation and market segmentation activities. Here, the firm has developed a strong customer franchise and may enjoy a very inelastic demand curve.

Knowing how well you're known may take research

While the degree of brand familiarity achieved will have an important bearing on the development of a marketing mix, marketing research may be necessary to determine exactly what the firm has achieved and in what target markets. Research on specific target markets may be needed because, in many situations, company executives feel their products have achieved a higher degree of brand familiarity than is really the case, and the firms develop their marketing mixes accordingly. This self-delusion can only lead to overburdening the other ingredients in the marketing mixes. Studies show that some brands do not reach even the brand recognition stage. One study, for example, revealed that two out of every five housewives could not even name the brand of furniture they owned.[28]

Choosing a brand name

In choosing a brand name, a firm may, (a) coin a name (Kodak), or (b) adapt and adopt words (Keen Kutter, or Perfection), or (c) use a name under license or agreement (Mickey Mouse).

It is difficult to pinpoint what constitutes a good brand name. The names of some products defy even the obvious rules, and yet the products are successful. Many of these items, however, got started when there was relatively little market competition. Where possible, a good brand name should be:

Short, simple, and easy to spell and read.
Easy to recognize and remember.
Pleasing when read and easy to pronounce.
Not disagreeable sounding.
Pronounceable in only one way.
Always timely (does not get out of date).
Adaptable to packaging or labeling requirements.
Available for use (not in use by another firm).
Pronounceable in all languages (for goods to be exported).
Not offensive, obscene, or negative.
A selling suggestion.
Adaptable to any advertising medium (especially billboards and TV).

Finding a good new brand name probably would require some marketing research. Computers have been used to screen long lists of potential names, once criteria for their selection have been determined. Finally, however, management judgment probably will be

[28] Business Week, February 20, 1960, p. 71; see also, Jagdish N. Sheth, "Measurement of Multidimensional Brand Loyalty of a Consumer," Journal of Marketing Research, August, 1970, pp. 348–54; James M. Carman, "Correlates of Brand Loyalty: Some Positive Results," Journal of Marketing Research, Vol. 7, (February, 1970), pp. 67–76; T. R. Rao, "Are Some Consumers More Prone to Purchase Private Brands?" Journal of Marketing Research, November, 1969, pp. 447–50; Y. Wind and R. E. Frank, "Interproduct Household Loyalty to Brands," Journal of Marketing Research, November, 1969, pp. 434–35; J. D. McConnell, "The Development of Brand Loyalty: An Experimental Study," Journal of Marketing Research, February, 1968, pp. 13–20; Dik W. Twedt, "How Does Brand Awareness-Attitude Affect Marketing Strategy?" Journal of Marketing, October, 1967, pp. 64–66; and "Women Flunk Identity Test," Business Week, April 6, 1965, pp. 50–52.

required to select among names which apparently fit with management's understanding of the target market's needs and preferences. Brand name selection is still largely an art.

What is a brand?

We have used the terms *branding, brand names,* and *trademarks* interchangeably so far, but it is important to distinguish among them because of the legal implications each term has.

Branding refers to the use of a name, a term, a symbol, or design (or a combination of these), to identify goods or services of one seller or a group of sellers and to distinguish them from those of competitors.[29] This is a broad term that includes the use of brand names, trademarks, and practically all other means of product identification.

Brand name has a narrower meaning. It is a word, letter, or a group of words or letters that can be spoken.

Trademark, however, is essentially a legal term and includes only those words, symbols, or marks that the law designates as trademarks.

The word *Buick* can be used to illustrate these distinctions. The Buick car is *branded* under the *brand name* "Buick," whether it is used orally or printed in any manner. When "Buick" is printed in a certain kind of script, however, it becomes a *trademark.* A trademark need not be attached to the product. It need not even be a word. A symbol can be used.

These distinctions may seem technical, but they are very important to business firms that spend much money to protect their brands.

Protecting brand names and trademarks

Common law assures the rights of the true originators and users of trademarks and brand names, stating that the ownership of brand names and trademarks is established by continued usage without abandonment. Clearly, by now Morton Salt, Coca-Cola, and Bon Ami are unmistakably identified with particular products.

The exact procedure for protecting trademarks and what could be protected were not clear, however, until the passage of the federal Lanham Act in 1946. This act specifies what types of marks (including brand names) can be protected by law, and it makes provision for registration records to facilitate their protection. It applies to goods shipped in interstate or foreign commerce.[30]

[29] "Report of the Definitions Committee," *Journal of Marketing,* October, 1948, p. 205.

[30] A detailed treatment of the requirements for trademark registration appears in *Printers' Ink,* December 19, 1947; see also, *Trademark Rules of Practice,* U.S. Department of Commerce, January, 1959.

No federal
tests or
policing

The Lanham Act does not make registration compulsory. Even getting onto the registration records does not establish ownership of a mark. It is still necessary to show that the firm was the first to use the particular trademark and that the trademarked product actually has been offered for sale on a continuing basis.

Registration under the Lanham Act merely gives public notice of a company's intention to use a particular trademark. Then, after a certain period of years, some marks – such as Morton Salt's little girl spilling salt – do become incontestably the property of the firm that has registered them.

Registration does not imply that the federal government endorses the product or that the product has passed any federal tests of quality. Neither does registration under the act with the U.S. Patent Office mean that the Patent Office will police the owner's rights to a mark. He himself still must bring suit against any infringers.

A principal reason for registering under the Lanham Act is to protect a trademark to be used in foreign commerce. Some countries require that a trademark be registered in its home country before it can be protected in that country. For this reason, the Lanham Act provides for two registers, the Principal Register, with rigorous requirements, and the Supplemental Register, more inclusive and basically a register for goods in foreign commerce.

Will Orlon
go the way
of shredded
wheat?

A legally valid trademark can be a real asset to a company. Every effort should be made to develop a trademark that will not become a common descriptive term for that kind of product. A unique product group may come to be known by its leading brand name rather than its common descriptive name. When this occurs, the brand name or trademark becomes public property, and the owner loses all his rights to it. This happened with the names *cellophane, aspirin, shredded wheat,* and *kerosene,* and there was concern that *Scotch Tape* and *Frigidaire* might become public property.

Companies with meaningful brands are careful in their promotion to indicate which of their product names are brand names and which are purely descriptive. Orlon is a brand name for acrylic fiber manufactured by Du Pont, which is very careful to require that all reference to Orlon indicate that it is a brand name and *not* a generic name for that type of acrylic fiber.

What kind of brand to use?

The old
established
family name

Branders who manufacture or handle more than one item must decide whether they are going to use the same brand name for all of their items – called a family brand – or individual brands for each item.

The use of the same brand for many products is sensible if all are essentially the same in nature and quality. The goodwill attached to one or two products may reflect on the others. This reduces the promotional overhead, tends to build a customer franchise for the family brand, and paves the way for the introduction of new products.

Examples of family brands are the Heinz "57" food products, A&P brands (Ann Page, Sultana, and Iona, each in different price classes), Sears, Roebuck's Kenmore appliances, and the Pittsburgh Plate Glass line of paints and other home products.

Use the family brand with care

But just because the company has an established name is no absolute assurance that products bearing this name will find customers with open arms. Much depends on the strength of the customer franchise and the nature of competition. Sunkist is a good example.

The owners of the Sunkist brand were late in entering the frozen citrus concentrate market. When they did get into it, they assumed that the brand name Sunkist would have the same appeal printed on frozen juice cans that it does stamped on fresh fruit. They were wrong. Sales were poor, and Sunkist had to fight for its share of the frozen concentrate market just like any other newcomer.

It is obvious that when a family brand name is used, it should be applied to approximately the same type and quality of product. Pillsbury, for example, uses its family name on baking mixes, refrigerator products, and farm feeds, all of which share some common point of origin as milled grain products. Pillsbury's president says: "The Pillsbury name should not mean everything to everybody. . . . If Pillsbury were to enter the appliance business, it shouldn't use the Pillsbury name for the same reason that a housewife probably wouldn't respond to a General Electric cake mix."[31]

Individual brands: outside and inside competition

Individual brands frequently are used by a manufacturer when his products are of varying quality or type. If the products are distinctly different, such as meat products and glue, individual brands are preferable. Or the quality and higher price of one of the company's well-known names may be protected while another brand (perhaps identifying a lower priced line) is used as a "fighting" brand to meet competition. Use of individual brands is preferred, too, if there is any risk of the failure of one product damaging the reputation of others.

The market grid concept and market segmentation — trying to aim straight for the right customer with exactly the right product — help explain why some large grocery products manufacturers, such as General Foods, Procter & Gamble, and Lever Brothers, follow a policy of individual branding for many of their lines.

Procter & Gamble has found that its brands appeal to different customers, who feel that they have very individualistic and definite needs. But sometimes these customers decide that a particular product no longer satisfies their needs and switch to another product with a different brand name. Frequently this will be one of P&G's other

[31] *Advertising Age*, September 15, 1958, pp. 2 ff.

products. If a family P&G brand name were used, however, and the customer specifically identified the product as a P&G item, it is possible that the disgruntled customer might switch to a product of Lever Bros. or some other competitor.

Sometimes firms use individual brands to stimulate competition *within* the organization. This is true, again, with P&G brands. Each brand is the responsibility of a different group; management feels that internal competition keeps everyone alert. The theory is that if anyone is going to take business away from a P&G brand, it ought to be another P&G brand. The same kind of competition is found among General Motors' brands, where Chevrolet, Pontiac, Oldsmobile, Buick, and even Cadillac compete with each other in some markets.

Who should do the branding?

Manufacturer brands versus dealer brands

Frequently wholesalers and retailers decide to use their own brands in preference to manufacturers' brands, commonly called "national brands," because of their promotion across the nation or in large regions. Such manufacturers' or national brands include Kellogg's, Stokely, RCA-Whirlpool, International Harvester, Sheetrock, and IBM.

The term *national* is not always an accurate designation, however, since many wholesalers' and retailers' brands have achieved national distribution and are advertised nationally, while some manufacturers' products have only regional distribution. Kroger, A&P, Sears, Roebuck, and Montgomery Ward brands, for example, are all advertised and distributed more widely than many so-called national brands.

For this reason, instead of the term "national brands," we will use *manufacturers' brands* to refer to this type—as contrasted to wholesalers' and retailers' brands. These latter brands frequently are called "private brands." But to reduce confusion, we will call the wholesalers' and retailers' brands *dealer brands*.[32]

Should a manufacturer make dealer brands?

Our major thrust in this book is on developing unique and profitable strategies which the firm controls. Making products for others—for example, dealer brands made to dealers' specifications at relatively low prices set in almost purely competitive markets—is not our main concern. Nevertheless, we must note that some manufacturers choose this strategy and others are forced into it by lack of resources (human and financial) to do the marketing job. Such firms have basically given up marketing and are dependent on the fortunes of their middlemen customers. They may receive enough profit to keep them in business, at least when economic conditions are good, but they are not likely to

---

[32] Thomas F. Schutte, "The Semantics of Branding," *Journal of Marketing*, Vol. 33, No. 2 (April, 1969), pp. 5–11.

achieve the profits earned by those who locate and satisfy new target markets.

Some manufacturers emphasize their own brands but produce dealer brands too. The main reason is to utilize capacity more fully. They realize that dealer branders will probably find someone to produce for them, so there is no point in worrying about increasing competition. This was a major concern of producers some years ago, but now most manufacturers will produce dealer brands if they feel it is profitable to them. They see the battle for sales in the market and plan to win their share there rather than by trying to restrict output. General Electric recently decided to make appliances for J. C. Penney. And RCA-Whirlpool does the same for Sears. These products usually are made to the dealers' specifications and become parts of different — and perhaps competing — marketing strategies.

Where basically homogenous products are packaged under both the manufacturer's and the dealer's brand, there may be problems with respect to the legality of pricing. We will say more about this matter when we discuss the Borden case in the pricing section. Here, we should note that dealer branders usually are able to buy from manufacturers at relatively low prices because they take over the entire marketing job.

Before launching a dealer brand

The chances of a dealer brand being successful are helped if a number of conditions exist:

1. If there are several manufacturers' brands, none should be strongly entrenched in the market.
2. A dependable quality and quantity of ingredients or raw materials for the dealer brand should be available at a reasonable price to insure a good margin in case the brand meets with acceptance.
3. It helps if manufacturers' brands are overpriced, so the dealer brand can be priced under them, yet with a larger-than-normal gross margin, to cover higher promotional costs.
4. Although the dealer's brand must be promoted, the promotion should not be so expensive as to use up the extra gross margin.
5. There should be an adequate, well-established market; dealers may find it expensive to pioneer the introduction of new products.
6. Product quality should be easily and economically determined by inspection or use — customers will be more willing to experiment if a dealer's brand does not present too much of a risk.
7. If the dealer brand is lower priced, depressed business conditions may help its sale — customers are more price conscious then.

Dealer brands in the food and drug lines usually are offered at slightly lower prices than manufacturers' brands. Dealer brands, however, are not always priced lower. Sometimes dealers, having analyzed their target market, choose to offer a prestige-laden, higher quality product and then price it even higher than major manufacturers' brands. Such decisions have sometimes been successful.

Advantages and disadvantages of branding for dealers

Our discussion of branding so far has applied to manufacturers as well as dealers, but branding has some special advantages and disadvantages for dealers.

Advantages of manufacturers' brands — more prestige, less inventory

The major advantage of selling a popular manufacturer's brand is that the product already is presold to some target customers. Furthermore, it may bring in new customers. It can encourage higher turnover with a reduced selling cost, and some of the prestige of the manufacturer's brand may rub off on the dealers. And in case the manufacturer doesn't maintain his quality, *he* receives the blame, not the dealer, and the customer can be shifted to another manufacturer's brand or a dealer brand. The dealer does not lose *his* customer.

Since manufacturers' brands usually are readily available at the wholesalers' or manufacturers' warehouses, the dealer needs to carry less inventory. Another major advantage for some retailers is that the retailer can advertise special prices on items which are carried in other stores and thereby call attention to his store as a source of bargains.

Disadvantages of manufacturers' brands — lost products, lost customers

The major disadvantage of manufacturers' brands is that manufacturers normally offer a lower gross margin than the dealer might be able to earn with his own brands. This, however, may be offset by higher turnover.

Another disadvantage is that the manufacturer still maintains control of his brand and may withdraw it from the dealer at any time. Wholesalers are especially vulnerable in this respect. If customers become loyal to a manufacturer's brand and the dealer does not or cannot carry the product, then the customers may go elsewhere. Here, loyalty may be tied to the brand rather than to the dealer.

Advantages of dealer brands — loyal salesmen, the best shelves

In some respects, the advantages of dealer brands are the converse of the disadvantages of manufacturers' brands. The dealer may be able to buy products at lower prices and so be able to obtain higher gross margins even with lower retail prices. He can have greater price flexibility with his own brands because price comparisons are not as easy as with manufacturer's brands and also because there is no manufacturer to dictate pricing policy.

Another advantage of dealer brands is that dealers easily can change from one supplier to another if any one firm can't offer the quality and price needed. By using their own brands, dealers may be able to protect themselves from the arbitrary action of manufacturers.

Wholesaler brands protect wholesalers from the defection of their salesmen — and the salesmen's customer following — to other wholesaling firms. Why? Wholesaler brands give the wholesaler, rather than his salesmen, a claim to customer loyalty.

Since the dealer's own brand ties customers to him, he may be able to estimate demand and buy more effectively. His salesmen can also control the point of sale and may be able to give their products special shelf position or displays.

Disadvantages of dealer brands — taking the blame, buying big quantities

The dealer must stimulate his own demand, and this may be costly, especially if turnover is typically slow in his lines. He must take the blame for inferior quality. He may have difficulty getting consistently good quality at low prices, especially during times of short supply such as wartime or inflationary periods. And the dealer must purchase in fairly large quantities from suppliers, assuming the risk and cost of carrying inventory.

The battle of the brands — who's winning?

Manufacturers and dealers have been vying with each other in what has been called the "battle of the brands." No criticism of branding is implied in the term battle. It is simply a question of whose brands are to be more popular and who is to be in control.

Some manufacturers and dealers do not recognize this competition, being so close to the competitive scene — but from a macro-marketing viewpoint it is clear that the various brands are competing for a share of the business.

Some motivation research findings suggest, for food products at least, that manufacturers' brands may be losing ground. In 1951, manufacturers' brands seemed to be preferred by a ratio of 2 or 3 to 1. Even higher prices were accepted. This strong preference has continued to decline, and in 1970 one survey showed that 45 percent of the consumers had shifted to dealer brands. And younger households may be leading here.[33]

This trend may continue. In another study, concerned with A&P's "Ann Page" brand, one respondent said: "You get a feeling that the whole personality of the store is behind each of its products, and when you buy you have a tendency to follow through on this pattern."

One of the reasons for this shift is that some of the manufacturers' brands have come to symbolize elegance and are regarded as a luxury, while the dealer-branded chain store products are seen as necessities.[34] The chains' dealer-branded products also seem to be more widely recognized and *are* more likely to be in stock. One consumer's statement may be revealing in this connection: "When something is highly advertised, I find it short in the supermarkets."[35]

The growth of dealer branding has been pushed by the established chain stores, who often use their brands as a competitive weapon against discount houses. But this in turn sometimes leads manufacturers to bring out lower-priced lines of their own.[36] Goodyear, for example, brought out a third-line nylon tire to compete with dealer-branded tires being sold at lower prices. Department stores, super-

[33] *Marketing Communications*, August, 1970, p. 13.

[34] E. Dichter, "Brand Loyalty and Motivation Research," *Food Business*, January and February, 1956; see also, *Printers' Ink*, March 1, 1963, p. 5.

[35] "Private Brands Score Well," *Printers' Ink*, May 12, 1967, p. 3.

[36] "A Wider Track for Tire Sales," *Business Week*, March 20, 1965, pp. 55–58; and *Business Week*, February 13, 1960, p. 80.

markets, service stations, clothiers, appliance dealers, and drugstores are all going more deeply into dealer branding.

Perhaps the end of dominance

The battle of the brands certainly is far from over, but the former dominance of manufacturers' brands may have ended. Some retailers are becoming so large that dealer brands frequently sell in large volume and are nationally advertised. Some wholesalers have developed extremely strong brands and have ties to regional chains with literally hundreds of stores.

Manufacturers may become only manufacturers

In the future, retailer-controlled brands may seek broader distribution among other retailers and perhaps wholesalers too. It seems logical that as retailers begin to advertise nationally but have only a limited number of sales outlets, they may find it profitable to permit others to carry their brands. This might be a serious challenge to manufacturers' brands.

If this trend continues, manufacturers could become just that— only the producers. Retailers and wholesalers might come to dominate marketing. Certainly, the latter are closer to final consumers and may have greater control of the final sale situation.[37]

Conclusion

Packaging and branding can create a new total product. Variations in packaging can make a product salable in various target markets. Branding can be used by the marketer in creating and building a customer franchise for a given product.

A specific package must be developed for each product. Both underpackaging and overpackaging can be expensive. Although the final customer remains the ultimate factor, the packager also must remember the needs of wholesalers and retailers. A small retailer might prefer the smaller package units that a supermarket operator would resist.

To customers, the main significance of brands is an assurance of quality. This confidence leads to repeat purchasing. For marketers, such "routine" buying means reduced promotion costs and increased sales.

Should brands be stressed? The decision depends on whether the costs of brand promotion and honoring the brand guarantee can be covered and made profitable by a higher price or more rapid turnover, or both. The cost of branding may reduce other costs by relieving pressure on the other three P's.

[37] "A&P's Own Brand of Consumerism," *Business Week*, April 11, 1970, p. 32; Victor J. Cook and T. F. Schutte, *Brand Policy Determination* (Boston: Allyn & Bacon, Inc., 1967); Victor J. Cook, "Private Brand Mismanagement by Misconceptions," *Business Horizons*, December, 1968, pp. 63-74; and H. W. Boyd, Jr., and R. E. Frank, "The Importance of Private Labels in Food Retailing," *Business Horizons*, Summer, 1966, pp. 81-90.

In recent years, the strength of manufacturers' brands has declined and dealer brands have become more important. The dealer-labeled products may win in the battle of the brands, perhaps because dealers are closer to customers and may choose to promote their own brands more aggressively.

Branding gives a marketing manager considerable latitude. He can add brands and use individual or family brands. Ultimately, however, customers express their approval or disapproval of the total product (including the brand). The degree of brand familiarity obtained is a test of management's ability to carve out a separate market, and has considerable impact on Place, Price, and Promotion decisions.

QUESTIONS AND PROBLEMS

1 Justify the increasing interest in packaging, not only for consumer goods but industrial goods. Is this likely to continue?

2 Suggest an example where packaging costs probably: (a) lower total distribution costs, and (b) raise total distribution costs.

3 Compare the kind of packages typically used for frozen peas and for phonograph records with respect to the considerations in Figure 11–1. Do these packages have anything in common? How are they dissimilar? Compare these packages to shoe packages. Why are they different?

4 Is there any difference between a brand name and a trademark? If so, why is this difference important?

5 Is a well-known brand valuable only to the owner of the brand?

6 Would it be profitable for a firm to expend large sums of money to establish a brand for any type product in any market situation? Why, or why not? If the answer is no, suggest examples.

7 Evaluate the suitability of the following brand names: (a) Star (sausage), (b) Pleasing (books), (c) Rugged (shoes), (d) Shiny (shoe polish), (e) Lord Jim (ties).

8 Explain family brands. Sears, Roebuck and A&P use family brands but they have several different family brands. If the idea is a good one, why don't they have just one brand?

9 What is the "battle of the brands"? Who do you think will win and why?

10 What does the degree of brand preference imply about previous promotion efforts and the future promotional task? Also, how does the degree of brand preference affect the Place and Price variables?

11 One of the larger furniture manufacturers in England recently embarked upon an aggressive promotional campaign stressing his brand name with the objective of obtaining between 40 and 50 percent of the English market. He started with about 3 to 4 percent of the market. What are his prospects?

12 If you have been operating a small supermarket with emphasis on manufacturers' brands and have barely been breaking even, how should you evaluate the proposal of a large wholesaler who offers a full line of dealer-branded groceries at substantially lower prices? Specify any assumptions necessary to obtain a definite answer.

...in our goods classification system,...goods can be
separated into four categories: convenience goods, shopping
goods, specialty goods, and unsought goods.
...these...categories...are arbitrary but workable. They
provide a framework for subsequent analyses.
...firsthand observations applied to this analytical framework
will speed the development of...''marketing sense.''

12

Consumer goods

Consumer goods are those goods and services destined for the ultimate consumer. These contrast with *industrial goods,* which are
those goods and services destined for use in producing other goods or
services.[1] All goods fit into one or the other of these two categories.

There are two major problems in discussing consumer goods. One
is that it is impossible to discuss the marketing process for thousands
of goods. The other is that some products usually considered consumer
goods also may be industrial goods, since they are destined for use by
intermediate customers.

The type of customer who will finally use the good determines

[1] *Marketing Definitions* (Chicago: American Marketing Association, 1960), pp. 11 and 14.

whether it should be classified as consumer or industrial. Although the same product may be involved, the two types of customers may need entirely different marketing mixes.

Many products and services can be either consumer or industrial goods, depending upon the final customer. Examples include typewriters, typing paper, rugs, decorators' services, lighting fixtures, brooms, and plumbing services.

A further breakdown for the consumer goods category is included in this chapter, and for the industrial goods category, in Chapter 13.

Need for a classification system

Fresh meat, canned salmon, and lettuce are all foods, yet all are marketed differently. Hosiery and women's party dresses are clothing items, but the marketing mixes for each are quite dissimilar. Hosiery is available in many different types of outlets and has a much simpler fitting problem. Hosiery has been successfully branded, but relatively few women's dress brands are widely known.

There are many other examples of apparently similar products with dissimilar marketing problems. The nature of the product has considerable bearing on how the four P's are combined in a marketing mix. To avoid treating every product as unique, we must try to develop sensible, if tentative, generalizations about how products are related to marketing mixes. If we can classify products this way, it can be highly useful as a starting point for developing marketing mixes for new products and evaluating present mixes.

A number of classification systems are conceivable. One type might be based on the kind of outlet through which the products are marketed. Another could be based on a division of all products into either of two categories: durable vs. nondurable, perishable vs. nonperishable, or necessities vs. luxuries. A third could be classification by the degree of demand elasticity. Each has its deficiencies.

A useful classification system

A particularly workable and useful product classification system would be one based on *the way people buy products.* Since the purpose of the marketing process is to satisfy customer needs, basing product classification on customer behavior makes the most sense.

Let the
buyer be
satisfied

The problem-solving approach discussed in Chapter 8 has relevance here. Some consumers regularly engage in extended problem solving to satisfy certain needs. They will spend a lot of time searching for the right product to satisfy those needs. At the other extreme, other consumers have found routine ways of fulfilling the same needs and therefore do not shop extensively. These problem-solving processes help us understand the goods classification system introduced here and applied throughout subsequent chapters.

In our goods classification system, which is based on customer buying behavior, goods can be separated into four categories: (1) convenience goods, (2) shopping goods, (3) specialty goods, and (4) unsought goods.

Convenience goods are those that customers want to buy immediately with minimum shopping effort, i.e., where the busy customer feels she stands to gain little from making price and quality comparisons. In other words, she wants to use routinized buying behavior.

Shopping goods are those goods for which customers do shop, comparing the price and quality of various brands by visiting several stores, studying performance evaluations, and reading advertisements. Here we might see either limited or extended problem-solving behavior.

Specialty goods are those that customers insist upon having, and are willing to search for until they find them. Here the consumer already has done extended problem solving and decided on a particular product as a solution. If the product's availability is unknown, she is willing to search for it. If only one place has it, as with some services, then she will only buy there.

Unsought goods are those items that potential customers don't want yet, or don't know they can buy, or aren't looking for. Here, the need has not yet arisen, or the consumer has not recognized that she has a problem, or that it can be solved with a particular good.

How much do people want what they buy?

Convenience and shopping goods are characterized by specific kinds of *shopping* behavior. In this sense, these goods are at the extremes of a customer shopping effort continuum. The amount of customer searching and comparison goes up as we move from shoestrings (a convenience good) to suits and dining room furniture (shopping goods).

Specialty and unsought goods are not on the same continuum of shopping effort. They are special cases. Unsought goods, of course, are not shopped for at all.

People are willing to travel extensively to find a particular specialty good because they already know what they want—but they are not shopping in the comparison sense. It is important to note that the customer looking for a specialty good may not have to look very far. Many retailers might carry such specialty goods, knowing that if they don't, they will lose the business of these highly motivated customers who will search out exactly what they want. Thus, evaluating the extent of searching that has been done for a product is *not* an accurate way of deciding whether a particular product is a specialty good. The customer's willingness to search is the determining measure.

Services are goods, too

In marketing, we have traditionally focused on physical goods almost to the exclusion of services. This reflects the production orientation of most manufacturers and the materials handling emphasis of most middlemen.

As we saw in Chapter 10, however, services represent a very important and growing share of total GNP. We certainly cannot ignore services, and at the same time, we do not want to treat them as greatly different from physical goods. Customer needs are satisfied not only by tangible products but also by services, or some combination of them. Indeed, one author has suggested that there are very few pure products or pure services. Most goods are a combination of both.[2]

An automobile without access to repair services, for example, is not a very useful product. The customer wants both the physical automobile and the maintenance and repair service to keep it running. To a consumer, the physical product and the service to keep it operative should not be separated—although this separation seems to exist in the minds of production-oriented businessmen.

In terms of their potential for satisfying customer needs, some services are even superior to physical goods. A rented car, for example, may be far more practical temporary transportation than an owned car.

We will not make a distinction between goods and services but will call them all goods or products. Where the intangibility of a service as contrasted to the physical nature of a product is of special significance, we *may* take some notice of the distinction. For the most part, however, we will focus on the similarities—based on customer buying habits and preferences—of various physical products and services. This is a sound method and is of great help in planning effective marketing strategies.

Product classifications help set strategy

The attitudes of a group of target customers who see a product in the same way pretty much determine what *their* "ideal" marketing mix would look like. That is, customer needs help determine the design of the product itself, help specify how much they will be willing to pay for it, and what they should be told about it. Moreover, when we know how strongly customers want the need satisfied, we get a better idea of their shopping behavior. This, in turn, helps show where goods should be made available, the promotion media that should be used, and how price-sensitive the target consumers will be.

The product classifications which we are discussing here are useful in summarizing how *some* target consumers view the product and therefore have immediate relevance for marketing mix planning. Thus this a practical approach which will provide a thread through the balance of the text. Research does support this approach, having found that customer behavior related product classifications are tied

[2] John M. Rathmell, "What Is Meant by Services?" *Journal of Marketing,* October, 1966, pp. 32–36; Robert C. Judd, "The Case for Redefining Services," *Journal of Marketing,* January, 1964, pp. 58–59; William J. Regan, "The Service Revoltuion," *Journal of Marketing,* July, 1963, pp. 57–62; and Dik W. Twedt, "What Is a 'Convenient Food'?" *Journal of Marketing,* January, 1967, pp. 67–68.

in with marketing mix planning.[3] Further validation is the clustering of retail stores according to goods classifications, especially those found in shopping centers. More will be said on this in Chapter 16 on Retailing.

Product classifications not automatic or unique

There is no simple, automatic classification for a particular good. While this may be bothersome, it means that there is no need to memorize a long list of products according to classifications. Yet the corollary of eliminating the list is that the manager must develop a theory about how different groups of customers on his market grid will regard his product—and proceed accordingly.

Different target markets sometimes react differently to the same service or physical product. For a particular product, two or more product classifications, combined into two or more marketing strategies might be needed to satisfy all potential customers.

A tale of three motels

Motels are a good example of a service that is viewed as three different kinds of goods. Some motorists — tired ones — are satisfied with the first motel they come to (a convenience good); other travelers shop for the best facilities at the best price (a shopping good); still others study their road guides and drive or phone ahead until they find a vacancy in a recommended motel (a specialty good).

Perhaps the same motel could satisfy all potential customers, but it would take some doing to produce a marketing mix attractive to everyone. Those looking for convenience would want easy access; the shopping tourists would want attractive appearance and comfort relative to price; specialty-goods travelers would require a listing in their touring guides.

The market grid for motels in one geographical area might appear as shown in Figure 12–1, with a very large convenience-goods market. This might suggest that motel owners should try harder to get convenient locations even if it meant skimping on facilities that would appeal to the shopping-goods travelers.

In other areas, the market grid might look more like Figure 12–2, which shows large shopping-goods and specialty-goods markets — which may be the best view of the motel market today. The newer

---

[3] Arno K. Kleinenhagen, "Shopping, Specialty, or Convenience Goods?" *Journal of Retailing*, Winter, 1966–67, pp. 32–39 ff; Louis P. Bucklin, "Testing Propensities to Shop," *Journal of Marketing*, January, 1966, pp. 22–27; William P. Dommermuth, "The Shopping Matrix and Marketing Strategy," *Journal of Marketing Research*, May, 1965, pp. 128–32; Gordon E. Miracle, "Product Characteristics and Marketing Strategy," *Journal of Marketing*, January, 1965, pp. 18–24; Richard H. Holton, "The Distinction Between Convenience Goods, Shopping Goods, and Specialty Goods," *Journal of Marketing*, July, 1958, pp. 53–56; and Leo V. Aspinwall, "The Characteristics of Goods Theory," in William Lazer and Eugene J. Kelley (eds.), *Managerial Marketing: Perspectives and Viewpoints* (rev. ed.; Homewood, Ill.: Richard D. Irwin, 1962), pp. 633–43; Perry Bliss, "Supply Considerations and Shopper Convenience," *Journal of Marketing*, July, 1966, pp. 43–45; S. Kaish, "Cognitive Dissonance and the Classification of Consumer Goods," and W. P. Dommermuth and E. W. Cundiff, "Shopping Goods, Shopping Centers, and Selling Strategies," *Journal of Marketing*, October, 1967, pp. 28–36.

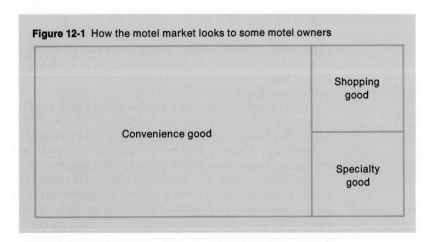

Figure 12-1 How the motel market looks to some motel owners

Convenience good

Shopping good

Specialty good

motels not only are conveniently located but also have rather sumptuous layouts and offer charge card and free reservation services to your next stop. Some are low-price oriented, while others are not.[4]

These motel examples show that if each marketing manager analyzed his own potential target markets in terms of these goods classifications, it would force him to clarify his thinking about consumers' behavior and marketing mixes. To better understand these goods classifications, let's look at them more carefully.

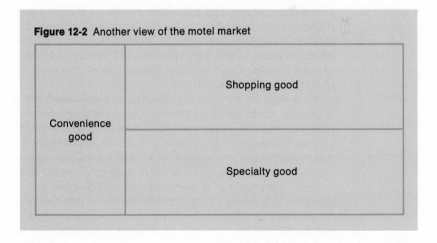

Figure 12-2 Another view of the motel market

Convenience good

Shopping good

Specialty good

[4] "A Motel Room at Bargain Rates," *Business Week,*
August 22, 1970, p. 20, and "Riches from Royal
Treatment," *Time,* November 16, 1970, p. 87.

Convenience goods

Convenience goods—those goods the customer wants but isn't willing to spend much time shopping for—include such items as cigarettes, soap, drugs, newspapers, magazines, chewing gum, candy, and most grocery products.

These products are bought frequently and readily, require little service or selling, are not very expensive, and may even be bought by habit. The classic cigarette slogan, "I'd walk a mile for a Camel," tried to imply that Camels were not a convenience good, but it is doubtful that many consumers think of their own cigarette brand in this light.

At the same time, you should also be careful about too readily classifying goods as convenience goods. Consider the attitudes of your target customers as they are influenced by income, wealth, and other factors. A 10-cent novelty might be a convenience good for most adults, but it might be a shopping good for a child with a 20-cent weekly allowance.

Convenience goods can be further classified into three subtypes, again primarily on the basis of how customers think about products and buy them, *not* of the characteristics of the products themselves. These subclassifications are (1) staples, (2) impulse goods, and (3) emergency goods.

Staples—as inevitable as death and taxes

The staple food and drug items used regularly in every household are usually bought frequently, and routinely, without much thought beyond the initial decision to buy. Here, branding becomes important because brand recognition helps the customer reduce shopping effort.

Staple items are offered for sale in such convenient places as food stores, drugstores, and hardware stores, as well as vending machines, because customers don't want to search far for them. Some customers, in fact, value convenience so highly that they prefer to have such goods as milk, bread, newspapers, and orange juice delivered directly to their homes. This may cost slightly more, but customers are willing to pay for the convenience.

Shopping for staples might not even be planned. Since many housewives do their meal planning while passing shelves in the supermarket, modern supermarkets have been laid out to facilitate this custom. Complementary goods such as strawberries and shortcake mix (biscuit mix) or sponge cake are sometimes placed next to each other. This encourages even more spontaneous buying.

Such purchasing of convenience goods does not mean that it is completely haphazard. One study did show that the purchase of about 50 percent of all grocery items might be classed as unplanned, but nearly 86 percent of these purchases were products and brands that had been bought before.[5]

[5] David T. Kollat and Ronald P. Willett, "Customer Impulse Purchasing Behavior," *Journal of Marketing Research,* February, 1967, pp. 21–31. See also: David T. Kollat and Ronald P. Willett, "Is Impulse Purchasing Really a Useful Concept for Marketing Decisions?" *Journal of Marketing,* January, 1969, pp. 79–83.

Unplanned purchasing of this kind is sometimes called "impulse buying," but this may be a misuse of the term. Rather, it would seem that some customers – especially experienced shoppers and those buying large quantities – are shifting their routine meal planning from the home to the store; this may be a very sensible way for them to buy.[6] This kind of buying should be analyzed carefully because it is *not* impulsive and some underlying patterns may exist, including buying by preferred brand. Further, the products may be used regularly as part of the consumer's consumption system, leading to even more routinized buying behavior.

Impulse goods – buy it now or never

Impulse goods are bought as unplanned purchases, but not in the same sense as are unplanned purchases of staples. Customers typically are not out shopping for impulse goods. True impulse goods are items that the customer decides to purchase on sight, probably has bought the same way many times before, and wants immediately.

If a housewife passes a street corner vendor, for example, and gets a sudden urge for ice cream and purchases an ice-cream bar, it would be considered an impulse good. The important distinction is that if the same housewife were to buy a box of ice-cream bars in the supermarket with the intention of using them for a family dessert, the bars would be regarded as staples because she was looking for desserts.

There is an important distinction between buying something to satisfy a *strongly felt current need* and buying to satisfy *ongoing needs,* perhaps for *subsequent use.* If the customer does not purchase an impulse good immediately, that need may disappear and no purchase will be made. Or, at least, *that* need will not be satisfied (at all or by a particular firm) and the opportunity for *that* sale is lost. But if the customer needs some desserts, she will eventually buy them.

This distinction is important because if affects Place and the whole marketing mix. Place is extremely important for impulse goods, because if the buyer doesn't happen across them at the "right" time, the potential sales may be lost forever. As a result, special methods have developed for selling impulse goods. Impulse-good specialists, such as ice cream vendors, specialize in putting these goods where they'll be bought. Department stores often place impulse goods on the first floor near main doors; supermarkets and drugstores put them near the checkout counter. Impulse goods sometimes achieve a strong brand preference – as in the case of Coca-Cola and some brands of candy bars.

Emergency goods – the price you're willing to pay

Emergency goods are purchased only when the need is urgent. The customer wants these products immediately; price and perhaps even quality are of small concern. The demand for such goods may be extremely inelastic.

Examples are ambulance services, umbrellas or raincoats during a rainstorm, and tire chains during a snowstorm.

[6] Kollat and Willett, "Customer Impulse Purchasing Behavior," *op. cit.,* p. 27.

Some retailers deliberately handle emergency goods to meet such needs. They know that many potential customers will face certain kinds of emergencies, and they set up their operations to help these customers solve their problems as easily as possible. Small gasoline stations in rural areas and big service stations on turnpikes carry tires to meet emergency needs. The buyer probably could get a tire at a lower price back home, but with a damaged tire on his car, he will pay what he has to.

Some small, neighborhood grocery stores meet the "fill-in" needs of customers who make only one major buying excursion to the super-market each week and need something else between trips. Usually these small stores charge higher prices for this service, but customers find it worthwhile because they take a different view of the products they buy there. One study found that almost 80 percent of the house-wives who were surveyed used such a "fill-in" store.[7]

Place is an important part of the marketing mix for emergency goods. Clearly, the marketing mix for emergency goods will be differ-ent from the one for staples, at least regarding where goods are placed.

Everything is becoming a con-venience

Convenience goods traditionally have been regarded as small, fre-quently purchased items. We accept this view, except that emergency goods are not purchased as often. But as consumers grow increasingly affluent, they seem to enjoy the luxury of treating more goods as con-venience goods, and even as impulse goods.

One marketing executive has taken the extreme position that "al-most anything that costs less than a new car is impulse purchased. Packaged goods, particularly, are bought on the fly today. There is far less thoughtful, considered buying than there used to be."[8]

In addition to foods, some consumers seem to be buying toys, jew-elry, cosmetics, some women's clothing, books, and phonograph records on impulse. The author has seen a $300 freezer bought with-out any comparison shopping – an isolated example, perhaps, but one that may become more common in the future.

You should watch the growing tendency to buy goods quickly, with little shopping, because this kind of buying may drastically alter mar-keting distribution patterns in the future. There seems to be a trend among neighborhood drugstores, variety stores, and grocery stores to carry increasingly high-priced goods that apparently are bought as convenience goods.

[7] M. Alexis, L. Simon, and K. Smith, "Some Determi-nants of Food Buying Behavior," in M. Alexis, R. Hancock, and R. J. Holloway, *Empirical Founda-tions of Marketing: Research Findings in the Behavioral and Applied Sciences* (Skokie, Ill.: Rand McNally & Co., 1969).

[8] E. J. Kelley, "The Importance of Convenience in Consumer Purchasing," *Journal of Marketing*, July, 1958, p. 33; see also, Hawkins Stern, "The Significance of Impulse Buying Today," *Journal of Marketing*, April, 1962, pp. 59–62.

Shopping goods

Shopping goods are those products that a customer feels are worth the time and effort to examine carefully and compare with competing products.[9] Extended problem solving is involved here.

Shopping goods can be divided into two classifications, depending on what customers are seeking: (1) homogeneous and (2) heterogeneous shopping goods.

Homogeneous shopping goods—the price must be right

Our earlier discussion of homogeneous products—those that consumers view as essentially similar—begins to bear fruit here. You will recall that when consumers view the various brands of a product as basically the same, each competitor has an almost perfectly elastic demand curve. Since a slight price cut on such products could substantially increase sales volume, we might expect vigorous price competition.

This, in fact, is the condition in many markets. Some consumers feel that certain sizes and types of refrigerators, television sets, washing machines, and even automobiles are essentially similar, and are primarily concerned about shopping for the best price.

Each manufacturer seeks to emphasize his differences, and every retailer tries to promote his "better service." But if the customers do not believe these differences are real, they will base their shopping decisions on the one variable they feel is or can be different—price.

This is particularly true in large urban areas where there are many firms selling the same physical product and similar services. In this situation, some customers on the market grid decide on the model they want, perhaps after seeing it advertised or talking to their neighbors, and then seek the best buy.

In a recent study of automobile purchasing behavior, about 56 percent of those interviewed wanted the "best price or deal," and about half of those interviewed did shop at more than one dealership.[10] And three out of four supermarket shoppers are reported to shop for advertised specials every week.[11]

Some consumers, interested only in price, try to simplify their search by attempting to obtain comparative prices by telephone. But some retailers refuse to give prices by telephone, feeling that they are selling more than the physical product—and want to be able to tell the customer face-to-face about their services.

It is this buyer emphasis on price, then, that helps explain the rise of certain types of discount houses.

---

[9] For a graphical approach to analyzing shopping behavior and its implications, see William P. Dommermuth, "The Shopping Matrix and Marketing Strategy," *Journal of Marketing Research*, May, 1965, pp. 128–32.

[10] L. P. Feldman, "Prediction of the Spatial Pattern of Shopping Behavior," *Journal of Retailing*, Spring, 1967, pp. 25–30 ff.

[11] "If You Don't Give the Lady What She Wants, She'll Go Elsewhere," *Marketing News*, January 1, 1968, p. 11.

Low-price items seen this way

Even some inexpensive items like butter, coffee, and other food items may be considered homogeneous shopping goods by some people. Some customers carefully read food store advertising for the lowest prices on these items, and then go from store to store getting the items—doing what is known as "cherry picking" in the grocery trade. Still, these customers may fill other needs while on their rounds, and this could enable the store to make profitable sales to offset the bargains they offer.

In some international markets where consumer incomes are low, homogeneous shopping goods are common. With limited buyer power, the consumers in these areas are unwilling to treat goods as convenience goods and prefer instead to shop extensively. One author reported, for example, that "virtually all goods are shopping goods" in Nigeria.[12]

Well-branded items too

Even if some manufacturers' branded products have achieved the brand preference stage, they still may be treated by some price-conscious consumers as homogeneous shopping goods when offered by several competing retailers who add nothing to the total product. Shopping for autos illustrates this. At the retail level, price may be all-important if everything else in the marketing mix seems equal to target customers.

Heterogeneous shopping goods—the product must be right

Heterogeneous shopping goods are products that the customer sees as nonstandardized and wants to inspect for quality and suitability. Examples are furniture, draperies, dishes, and clothing. Style is important, and price is secondary.

Even if an item costs only $5 or $10, consumers sometimes will seek it in three or four stores to be sure they have done a good job of shopping.

Price is not totally ignored in this kind of buying. But for nonstandardized merchandise, there are fewer bases for price comparison. Once the customer has found the right product, he may not be too worried about price, provided it is reasonable. That is, the demand for the product may be quite inelastic. The more close substitutes there are, the more elastic becomes the demand. But it does not approach the extreme elasticity found with homogeneous shopping goods.

Branding may be less important for heterogeneous goods. The more a consumer wants to make his own comparisons of price and quality, the less he relies on trade names and labels. These goods usually are branded, but often little effort is made to publicize them. While women's dresses have labels, they don't show. Style and quality usually are more important.

[12] Henry L. Munn, "Retailing in Nigeria," *Journal of Retailing*, Fall, 1966, p. 30.

When status sells

The fact that branding has not been common with heterogeneous shopping goods does not mean that they can't be branded effectively. Achieving the brand recognition stage might noticeably affect heterogeneous product choices. As with other types of products, if the customer is unsure about several apparently similar items, he may choose the brand he recognizes or which he thinks carries status. This status aspect may grow increasingly important if more consumers become other-directed. At the very least, a well-recognized brand may be more attractive for some parts of the market grid.

Service, please!

Often the buyer of heterogeneous shopping goods not only wants but expects some kind of help in buying, the kind and degree depending on the socioeconomic status or other relevent dimensions of the purchaser.

If the purchase is costly, the buyer may want expensive service, such as alterations of clothing or installation of appliances. For most customers, a sport shirt picked up on the run, as a convenience good, need not fit so precisely as a good suit—a heterogeneous shopping good.[13]

Specialty goods

Specialty goods are those consumer goods that a significant group of buyers want and will make a special effort to buy. The buyer knows he wants the product. Shopping for the specialty good doesn't mean comparing the product but merely finding it. If such goods are readily available, their purchase may look like routine staple buying.

Specialty goods usually are not product categories but specific branded products that have passed the brand preference stage and achieved brand insistence. Product differentiation and market segmentation efforts aim at creating specialty goods.

There are some instances in which a unique new product, even though not branded, also might be a specialty good. This could be true of a new drug or fertilizer, available only by generic name. Generally, however, a specific brand is involved.

Accept no substitutes!

Contrary to a common view, specialty goods need not be relatively expensive, durable items that are purchased infrequently. Any branded item that develops a strong customer franchise may achieve specialty-goods status. Consumers have been observed asking for a drug product by its brand name and, when offered a substitute (even though chemically identical), actually leaving the store in anger.

[13] For a basic study on shopping behavior in department stores, see Stuart U. Rich, *Shopping Behavior of Department Store Customers* (Boston: Harvard Graduate School of Business Administration, 1963).

As might be expected, the demand for specialty goods will be relatively inelastic, at least within reasonable price ranges, since target customers are willing to insist upon the product.

Ready availability of a product does not eliminate it as a specialty good. Although some customers might be willing to look hard to locate it, the following conditions in the competitive market structure might make extensive searching unnecessary:

1. If many retailers want to obtain a share of this specialty-goods market.
2. If the manufacturer, uncertain of his success in creating a specialty good, tries to obtain distribution in more outlets than really are needed to satisfy the specialty-goods market.
3. If the product is basically a staple convenience good and the major effort is directed at that target market.

As we noted earler, the same physical product might be classified in two or three ways, depending on how potential customers regard it. If different consumers view the product as a staple and a specialty good, the same Place facilities could serve both target markets. Yet the marketing manager would want to recognize the two distinct markets so that he could intelligently interpret research findings and comments from the field. He might, for example, be very pleased to find that some retailers are impressed with the apparent brand loyalty of those customers who continue to treat the product as a specialty good – but he should remember that the bulk of the market considers his product a staple.

Unsought goods

Unsought goods are those that potential customers do not yet want or know they can buy and, therefore, do not search for at all. In fact they probably would not buy these goods even if they came upon them unless additional promotion were used to show them the value of the goods or services. Needs or problems these goods might solve are not yet recognized.

There seem to be two types of unsought goods, and they can be called *new* unsought and *regularly* unsought.

New unsought goods

The *new* unsought goods are products offering *really new* concepts with which potential customers are not yet familiar. The concepts are such, however, that informative promotion can help convince consumers to accept or even seek out the product.

Regularly unsought goods

Regularly unsought goods are such products as life insurance, encyclopedias, and gravestones that may remain unsought but definitely not unbought forever. These products may represent some of the biggest expenditures a family ever makes, but few people would even drive around the block to find them.

New unsought goods— making dry shoes a conveneince

Not all new products are new unsought goods. There may be lots of good substitutes available already. Just another new brand of shoe polish, for instance, would not be an unsought good. Most customers probably would consider it a staple—as just another entry in the shoe polish market. The marketing manager's job would be to get distribution and hopefully some brand preference. Dow-Corning's Shoe-Saver, a silicone waterproofing product for shoes, was another matter, however. Dow-Corning fought an uphill battle to gain acceptance for Shoe-Saver. It was not a polish, and cost more than polishes. The marketing manager's job, here, was to end its unsought status by informing potential target markets that a new kind of product was available for shoe protection. Subsequently, Shoe-Saver was accepted by retailers and consumers as another convenience good.

Regularly unsought goods— selling to the guilt ridden

Regularly unsought goods are a different problem. There may be a need, but the potential customers are not motivated to satisfy it. Goods such as encyclopedias and life insurance must be promoted continually to achieve any sales. And there probably is little hope that they will move out of the unsought category for most consumers. For this type of challenge, greater stress is needed on Promotion, and it is likely that aggressive promotion will have to continue.

By imaginatively searching for unsatisfied customer needs, however, it may be possible to locate some target market that would find the unsought good so attractive that customers might go after it, or at least buy with enthusiasm. This would make demand fairly inelastic.

A producer of grave markers, for example, recently abandoned the not very productive approach of relying on a location close to cemeteries in the hope that customers would simply come in. Instead, he began using aggressive sales techniques.

He had considerable success with a TV advertising appeal, finding a good market particularly among guilt-ridden sons and daughters who long ago had buried their parents without a gravestone. Now, after years of uneasiness about the poorly marked grave(s) and with a newfound affluence, the heirs were willing to seek out the gravestone seller and discuss price and quality.

One product may be seen as several goods

We have been focusing on one good at a time, but let's also understand that the *same product* might be viewed as *different goods* by *different target markets* at the *same time.*

The marketing manager might find that his general market consists of several clusters of people each of whom has similar attitudes toward his product, as shown in Figure 12–3. This diagram clusters people in terms of their willingness to shop, and brand familiarity or preference—and is a simple way of summarizing our discussion of goods.

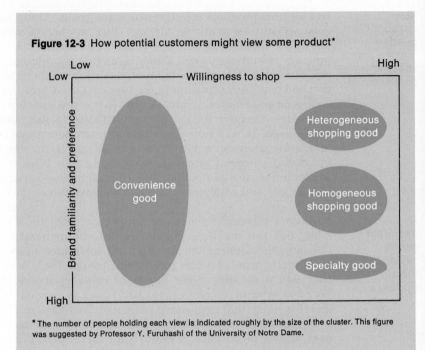

Figure 12-3 How potential customers might view some product*

* The number of people holding each view is indicated roughly by the size of the cluster. This figure was suggested by Professor Y. Furuhashi of the University of Notre Dame.

Each of these clusters might require a different marketing strategy. Or closer analysis of each might suggest the possibility for several profitable strategies, depending on how homogeneous the clusters are. Generally, we are looking for homogeneous market segments so we can design marketing mixes to satisfy each market grid box more exactly.

Clustering by goods classifications and then subdividing these clusters where necessary can be very revealing. Further, it is a commonsense approach which enables anyone with some market judgment to organize his thinking without extensive preliminary marketing research.

Need for consumer research to properly classify goods

Although the marketing manager can use his market judgment to classify a good, he probably could do a more reliable job by using marketing research. A formal research effort can uncover consumer attitudes and needs related to the product class and the company's particular product. Such an analysis might not only show the relevant dimensions for determining the appropriate goods class or classes but might also reveal useful ideas for designing the product and planning the promotion effort (including tactical decisions such as copy appeals).

The complexity of the buying process, especially with respect to selecting particular brands, was suggested in Chapter 8. Here, as we are attempting to identify classes of goods, perhaps for particular brands, let's recognize that although many factors may be involved for a particular product, the relative value of the various factors may be different for different customers. One exploratory study of gasoline purchasing behavior, for example, found 19 factors influencing the choice of particular brands.[14] To make such an analysis manageable, it is desirable to isolate two important classes of factors—the qualifying and the determining factors.

Qualifying and determining factors may make the difference

The *qualifying factors* affecting a product are those that are necessary for the consumer even to consider buying it. The *determining factors* carry the consumer a step farther, actually making him decide on a particular product. If the qualifying factors are about equal for a number of products, the determining factors, although they may seem minor, can become all-important in the final buying decision.

Fast service, clean rest rooms, and five shares at 46³⁄₈

The behavior of a female schoolteacher buying gasoline illustrates this process. The teacher always bought major brands of gasoline because she was afraid that cheap brands would ruin her car's engine. She bought several major brands at various times because she felt that all of them were quite similar. She never drove into a gas station unless it looked clean, and normally she patronized the stations nearest her home so that they would recognize her and be ready to give advice when she had mechanical problems. To her, therefore, the major brands were basically staple convenience goods.

From this description, it would appear that the qualifying factors here were experience, price, convenience, dealer's service, and prestige. Yet these factors did *not* determine her choice.

Her requirements were met by three major-brand service stations— Standard, Shell, and Mobil—located on different corners of the same intersection, one block from her house. Although the margin of choice seemed narrow, she stated that until recently she had been patronizing the Mobil station. After considerable questioning, she admitted she felt the Mobil station was larger than the others and had extensive repair facilities. The added weight of the dealer's service facilities appeared to be the determining factor.

But this was still not an absolute determinant, it turned out. Two months earlier, she had acquired some Standard Oil stock—and this ownership factor had caused her to switch her purchases to the Standard dealer. So a minor factor proved to be the determining one, although the qualifying factors were vital to the narrowing of her choice.

[14]William F. Brown, "The Determination of Factors Influencing Brand Choice," *Journal of Marketing*, April, 1950, pp. 699–706.

Fill 'er up
on staples

In general, the gasoline study showed that most gasoline buyers were favorably influenced by a standard group of *qualifying factors* — including prestige, advertising, and satisfactory experience — but in most cases the *preference for a particular brand of gasoline was weak*. The various *determining factors* were convenience, dealer services, salesmanship, and chance.

It would seem from this study that gasoline fits into the convenience-goods category. Once most consumers have evaluated the factors (at least subjectively), their judgment leads to rather consistent brand selection — or what might appear to be specialty-goods behavior. But it may be more accurate to say that this is a case of brand recognition or preference rather than insistence, and that gasoline producers would be better advised to consider their product a staple convenience good rather than a specialty good.

Even rough judgments will suggest strategy implications

The product classifications we have introduced may seem somewhat arbitrary, but they are workable. In developing marketing strategies, even rough judgments about how substantial groups of customers view products are helpful. Since we will use these goods classifications throughout the rest of this book, you should have a real understanding of them.

A new view
may suggest
break-
through op-
portunities

Looking at products the way customers do may create significant breakthrough opportunities for a firm. Too often production-oriented people in the factory or product-oriented people in the wholesale or retail firm see things very differently from their customers. As a result, they develop marketing mixes which are logical to them but not really satisfying to customers.

A simple illustration will help show that a "new view" may appear obvious *after* some one has had it, and that it also may be the key to getting ahead rapidly in business. The present chief executive of General Electric, Mr. Fred J. Borch, started out as an auditor in the lamp division in Cleveland. He moved quickly up through the marketing side of the business, however, after he developed a plan to sell light bulbs in grocery stores. At the time, the hardware store was virtually the only outlet for lamp bulbs because it was naturally assumed that light bulbs were shopped for specifically by men. Mr. Borch, however, regarded the light bulb as something that *housewives* would buy almost as an "impulse good," but these women were more likely to be found in *grocery stores* than in hardware stores.

Within our goods framework, he recognized that different segments of the market grid would buy light bulbs in different ways in different places and he built his marketing mixes accordingly. Light bulbs are now widely distributed because somebody had a new view and helped move his company in a new direction. These are the breakthrough opportunities which progressive firms seek. Hopefully, this goods framework will help stimulate your thinking and insight.[15]

For best results in planning actual marketing strategies, we should probably use marketing research to determine the goods classifications in various market grid boxes. In the following examples, however, we will use an intuitive approach to classifying products in order to clearly demonstrate what these goods classifications mean and their potential impact on strategy planning.

Prescription drugs . . . specialties and bargains

How should the drugs listed on a doctor's prescription be classified? The patient is seeking a specific product and will probably pay whatever price is charged. This has all the earmarks of a specialty good, yet the consumer has little or no choice of product, brand, or price.

In some areas, pharmacists would fill the prescription with similar products but at different prices. While it might be worthwhile for the patient to shop around, comparing prices is somewhat impractical and could be embarrassing to some customers because at each store they would have to ask the pharmacist to decipher the prescription and then quote his price. Besides, the customer buying a prescription usually wants his order filled as quickly and as conveniently as possible. Most consumers, therefore, probably think of prescriptions as convenience goods, either staples or emergency goods.

For an alert pharmacist, there is an opportunity in this situation. He could promote his establishment so effectively that consumers would have greater confidence in his products and his ability to fill prescriptions. If successful, he might turn his service into a specialty good. Other pharmacies have thought of their products as homogeneous shopping goods, emphasizing lower prices in their efforts to attract customers.

Saltine crackers — that's how the cracker crumbles

How are saltine crackers classified? Major commercial baking firms produce a number of well-advertised saltine cracker brands. Does this mean that these individual brands of soda crackers are specialty goods or close to it?

Researchers found that most consumers thought of a saltine as just a saltine – they saw little difference among brands and were not interested in investigating other crackers. This implied a staple convenience good, and attempts by the bakers to distinguish their crackers through promotion met with considerable indifference.

Additional research on saltines found, however, that consumers *did want* their crackers fresh and crisp. This led one firm to develop a new inner-seal package, enabling consumers to open only part of the package at a time, preserving the freshness and crispness of the other unopened crackers. This package modification, creating a "new" product, allowed the baker using it to differentiate his product for a time.

---

[15] "A New Team Rewires GE for the Future," *Business Week*, March 30, 1968, pp. 99–109.

This differentiation did not attract flocks of consumers. But the differentiation was strong enough to obtain some brand recognition and even brand preference for the product, even though it remained a convenience good.

Ski resorts make good snow

Ski resorts probably fit into the heterogeneous shopping-goods category. Skiers watch the snow reports carefully and go to the lodges where the snow is good. Their preference for a ski instructor and chalet accommodations may be qualifying factors but seldom overcome the one determining factor — snow.

In an effort to eliminate snow as a variable, some ski resorts have been installing snow-making machines. This puts an end to shopping for snow and has made it possible for some resorts to differentiate their service and to become specialty goods in the minds of some customers.

A mutual fund at Sears, Roebuck

How is a mutual fund classified, especially when it is sold by Sears, Roebuck? Sears has been selling various kinds of life insurance for years, both in its 1,500 stores and door-to-door. But now the company has moved into selling shares in the "Allstate Enterprises Stock Fund." Automobile insurance probably should be seen as a staple, especially in states where auto insurance is mandatory. But how do you classify shares in common stock?

Do Sears customers actively shop for such things? The feeling in the mutual fund industry is that they emphatically do not. Sears believes that its large existing sales force will be able to offer this new product to customers who pass by their sales booth and become curious. The strategy, as seen by a stockbroker, is that "Allstate is prospecting for people who wouldn't seek out an investment firm because they wouldn't know how they would be treated."[16]

In this case, for these customers, it would seem that the unsought-goods classification would be most appropriate. But the Sears name and reputation among its regular customers may give it an inside track and facilitate the introduction and sale of these unsought goods. Lesser-known mutual fund sales organizations, on the other hand, often have to go after customers with more aggressive sales promotion because many potential customers not only are not looking for mutual funds, but are completely unfamiliar with the concept.

Butter and other agricultural products

Butter is probably a homogeneous shopping good for many people. Why some consumers have focused so much attention on this product is not clear, but their practice of shopping for the lowest butter prices has made the retail butter market extremely competitive.

To escape from this extreme competition, Land-O'-Lakes Creameries, Inc., a producers' cooperative, branded its butter as "quality

[16] "Something New in Stock for Sears Shoppers," *Business Week*, April 25, 1970, pp. 120–22.

butter" and sought to promote Land-O'-Lakes butter to a specialty-goods status. Land-O'-Lakes has had some success in its efforts, as have the Idaho potato growers and the Sunkist orange growers in similar programs.

Brand preference and even insistence is so strong for products in *some* segments of the market that producers can command a slightly higher price, in addition to a substantial share of the market. Among some customers, these cooperatives may have achieved the specialty-goods status. Yet they continue to distribute these products as convenience goods because most customers probably see them this way.

Conclusion

A consumer product classification system based on consumers' buying habits and behavior has been introduced in this chapter. These classifications are workable and convenient. They will simplify our study of marketing and the development of marketing mixes because the attitudes of target customers almost determine the marketing mix which should be designed to serve them.

The four major categories of goods—convenience, shopping, specialty, and unsought—are arbitrary but workable. They provide a framework for subsequent analysis. They also relate to the concept of elasticity of demand. If customers do not give much thought to price when purchasing a product, as in the case of convenience goods, or if consumers have extremely strong brand insistence, as for specialty goods, then the demand for these products will be relatively inelastic. On the other hand, if consumers have a strong interest in comparing the products, as they do with shopping goods, then demand may be more elastic.

You should become familiar with these classifications and their subclassifications and begin to observe how marketing institutions handle specific products. Your firsthand observations applied to this analytical framework will speed the development of your "marketing sense."

The way customers in various market grid boxes view the same product may help explain how seemingly poor or irrational marketing mixes can become successful. Much of the diversity and complexity of the marketplace can be explained in terms of different product classifications in different market grid boxes.

QUESTIONS AND PROBLEMS

1 What kinds of goods are the following: (a) fountain pens, (b) men's shirts, (c) cosmetics? Explain your reasoning and draw a market grid in each case to help illustrate your thinking.

2 Some goods seem to be treated perpetually as "unsought goods" by their producers. Give an example and explain why.

3 Illustrate what is meant by the statement: "Convenience goods and shopping goods are at either ends of a continuum of customer shopping effort."

4 How would the marketing mix for a staple convenience good differ from the one for a homogeneous shopping good? How would the mix for a specialty good differ from the mix for a heterogeneous shopping good? Use examples.

5 Which of the P's would receive greatest emphasis in the marketing mix for an unsought good? Explain why, using an example.

6 Would the marketing mix for all convenience goods be essentially the same? Discuss, using an example for each type of convenience good.

7 In what types of stores would you expect to find: (*a*) convenience goods, (*b*) shopping goods, (*c*) specialty goods, and (*d*) unsought goods?

8 Draw market grid boxes showing your view of the relative sizes of the markets for the products discussed in the last few pages of the chapter, i.e., specifically (*a*) prescription drugs, (*b*) saltine crackers, (*c*) ski resort services, (*d*) a mutual fund, and (*e*) butter.

...the classification system we will use here is determined by
how buyers regard products and how the products are to be used.
...the salesman who fully understands and satisfies the needs of his
customers can get significantly better results. This
points up again the importance of careful market grid analysis
and the development of a marketing mix to fully satisfy
each target market. In the industrial goods area, this may require
treating each *buyer* as a separate target market...

13

Industrial goods

While a consumer goods classification system is useful for developing
effective marketing mixes, an industrial goods classification is even
more valuable. Over the years, industrial firms have developed a
rational system of buying that is related to the product classification
system we will discuss in this chapter. Before looking at the various
product *differences,* however, we will note some important product
similarities that have a direct impact on marketing strategy planning
for industrial goods.

General characteristics of industrial goods[1]

One demand derived from another

The outstanding characteristic of the industrial goods market is derived demand—i.e., the demand for industrial goods is derived from the demand for final consumer goods. There would be little need for fertilizer if there were no demand for food products. There wouldn't be much need for cans or canmaking machinery if consumers didn't want their food packed in cans.

Derived demand is clearly illustrated in the steel industry. Almost all forms of steel, such as beams, plate, and rods, are sold to manufacturers for the production of other products. About one fifth of all steel products goes to the automotive industry, which is highly dependent on final consumer demand. If a car manufacturer hopes to sell 50,000 cars of a particular model each month, then he will order enough steel to produce those automobiles. No amount of price cutting or other adjustments in the marketing mixes by the steelmakers will increase the total amount of steel demanded by this auto producer. Each steel producer may try to get a larger share of this total available business by developing a more attractive marketing mix, but the total amount demanded is limited by the expected final consumer sales.

The relationship between steel and automobiles is direct and fairly obvious. But the suppliers of bolts, screws, castings, textiles, and other industrial products find it is easy to forget that the need for their products is derived from the demand for final consumer products. As long as business is good and markets are growing, the derived nature of this demand does not seem very important. But it assumes great importance when final consumer preferences are shifting rapidly or in times of recession, when even the most efficient and aggressive companies lose sales because their customers cannot get business.

At such times, even a seemingly good marketing mix aimed at intermediate customers may not be very effective unless it has some impact on final consumer demand. Industrial goods producers sometimes advertise directly to consumers, in an effort to stimulate demands.[2] Cement and earthmoving equipment manufacturers, for example, have promoted road building to final consumers in an effort to build demand for *their* products.

Pay the going price, even if industry demand is inelastic

The fact that demand for most industrial goods is derived means that industry demand will be fairly inelastic. To satisfy final consumer needs, producers need a certain quantity of each of the components of their products, almost regardless of price. Since each of the components costs only a fraction of the total final cost of their product, the price behavior of any one item may have relatively little to do with

---

[1] Many of the ideas presented in this chapter are based on R. S. Alexander, "Goods for the Market: Industrial Goods," in C. F. Phillips (ed.), *Marketing by Manufacturers* (Homewood, Ill.: Richard D. Irwin, Inc., 1950), pp. 34–60.

[2] "Fundamental Differences between Industrial and Consumer Marketing," *Journal of Marketing*, October, 1954, p. 153; and "Carton Makers' Sales Slip, Adding to Evidence of Business Slow Down," *Wall Street Journal*, February 3, 1970, p. 1 f.

the quantity of that item purchased. The cost of the spice in a box of cake mix, for example, might represent only one half of 1 percent of the cake manufacturer's total cost. Even if the price of this spice were doubled and passed directly along to consumers, it would have relatively little impact on the cake producer's price or the quantity demanded by final consumers. Therefore the price increase might not reduce the quantity of spice purchased either.

Although the industry demand may be inelastic, the demand facing individual firms may be extremely elastic. This will be true if competitive products are essentially homogeneous, and there are many sellers – that is, if the market approaches pure competition.

In the case of the spice ingredients, if the spices available from all suppliers are basically similar and one spice supplier increases his price while his competitors do not, buyers probably will shift their purchases to the competition. Thus *there nearly may be pure competition among the suppliers of a product even though there is an inelastic industry demand.*

If the marketing manager faces an inelastic demand and has a unique product, perhaps protected by a patent, he may be in a very favorable position. Likewise, if there are only a few competitors and they have tacitly agreed not to emphasize price in their marketing mixes, then prices may tend to be higher than they would be in very competitive markets. (More is said on this in the Pricing chapters.)

An outstanding example of such a condition is the sale of labor services when a union has effectively organized the labor market. In effect, there is one seller, and wage rates may continue to rise in markets – such as the construction industry – where the workers are facing inelastic industry demand *in the short run.*

Interest in price may vary

As we saw in Chapter 9, industrial buying is generally less emotional than consumer buying. An industrial goods buyer usually knows fairly precisely what and how much he needs. If there are many sources for such a product – if competing products are homogeneous – then primary emphasis may be placed on price, assuming dependable quality and delivery, and other services. Price competition may be vigorous as the market moves close to pure competition.

When competing products are heterogeneous, however, more negotiation may be necessary. The multiple buying influences may become important, and emotional motives may figure more importantly in the buying decision. There may be much less interest in price, which will be reflected in the kind of marketing mixes developed for such products. Well-planned sales presentations, entertaining of customers, and more dependable delivery and after-sale service may become vital here.

Backward chain reactions can cause booms

Demand at the industrial goods level may fluctuate much more than demand at the final consumer level. This is true because demand for industrial goods, which may be several steps removed from the final consumer demand, reflects in part the expectations and buying practices of various middlemen and other producers. Intermediate customers attempt to: (1) anticipate price changes, (2) reduce costs by quantity buying, (3) anticipate demand, which may not materialize, and (4) place rush orders when their sales forecasts prove inadequate.

If intermediate customers believe prices are going to drop further, they may postpone all purchases. If they feel that prices are at their lowest point, they may buy in substantial quantities, anticipating future needs. Or firms may buy in large quantities to obtain quantity discounts and then work off the inventory as needed. On slow-moving items, this may mean that a firm will buy three to six months' inventory at one time to obtain a lower price.

Sales swings at the manufacturer level may be even more extreme when other intermediate customers try to anticipate growing demand. Home air conditioners are sold primarily when hot weather arrives. Orders for air-conditioner compressors may be heavy before the summer selling season. If really hot weather never comes, though, the retailers, wholesalers, and air-conditioner manufacturers may become overstocked, and the orders for compressors will stop completely. Yet if there is a prolonged heat wave, it can deplete retailers' air-conditioner stocks—and a chain reaction will start backward to component manufacturers.

In this situation, retailers and wholesalers may attempt to build inventories in advance of the season. This will drain producers' inventory and cause them to accelerate production, perhaps even going on overtime. The producers then place rush orders for compressors and the other components they need. This pattern can occur both in advance of and during the selling season.

If this sort of chain develops in an industry that is less seasonal than air conditioners, there may be pressures to expand the producer's plant capacity. Rush orders may develop for new plant and machinery, causing sudden boom conditions for these manufacturers.

These extreme but typical fluctuations have an impact on the nature of competition and the development of marketing mixes. Drastic changes in both price and promotion may be needed to handle these shifting conditions.

Paying taxes affects spending for equipment

How the cost of a particular purchase is handled on a firm's profit and loss statement may have a significant effect on the buyer. If, in computing profits, the cost of a large machine could be charged to the current year's expenses, the company executives might be more willing to buy it. Even though the cost of the equipment reduced current profits, it also would reduce tax liability and increase the company's assets. Typically, such purchases *cannot* be charged off in one year!

There are two general methods of charging costs: as capital and as expense items. Both are determined primarily by U.S. Internal Revenue Service regulations.

Capital items

Most large machinery and other durable, relatively long-lived items are treated as capital items. They are often called "capital goods." Internal Revenue regulations and accepted accounting procedure require that only a portion of the original cost be charged off or depreciated each year for a total depreciation period of 2 to 50 years, depending on the item. The depreciation rate usually is specified by the Internal Revenue Service.

In recent years the federal government has liberalized and then tightened depreciation rules to stimulate the economy and then later to cool an inflationary boom. These efforts have been effective, and it is clear that businessmen do look at capital investments differently from the way they view expense items.[3] The purchase of capital items is likely to lead to "new-task" purchasing because of its importance to the company, in the short run and the long run.

AN OPENING FOR EMOTIONS Businessmen generally are slow to buy capital items. The purchase of a capital item is, in effect, a long-term claim against future revenues. Yet management cannot predict exactly what the future holds. Since an error in judgment can have an influence for many years, company executives understandably are hesitant to make quick decisions. There seems to be little agreement on the best approach to capital expenditure decisions,[4] however, and this may offer opportunities for the marketer to introduce emotional considerations.

Expense items

In contrast to capital items, expense items are charged off as they are used—usually in the year of purchase. The potential value is more easily forecast and can be compared with the cost. Since the company is not putting a lien against its future when it buys expense items, it tends to be less concerned about these costs, especially if business is good. The multiple buying influence is likely to decline here, and straight rebuys may become more likely. If a firm's sales decline, however, some expense purchases may be cut back sharply or eliminated temporarily. There may also be a reversion to the modified rebuy process, as buyers are expected to reevaluate their sources of supply and the prices being offered to them.

Industrial goods classifications are used day by day

The non-shopper and the wily buyer

Industrial goods buyers do relatively little shopping, compared to consumer goods buyers. The accepted practice is for the seller to come to the buyer. This means that a product classification system based primarily on shopping behavior is not appropriate.

The classification system we will use here is determined by how buyers regard products and how the products are to be used. The categories of industrial goods are: (1) installations, (2) accessory

[3] "Orders for Rail Equipment Sag Sharply; Producers Blame Tax-Credit Suspension," *Wall Street Journal,* February 27, 1967, p. 26; "When Business Is Almost Too Good," *Business Week,* September 24, 1966, pp. 198–200; "Tax Credit Has Fans and Foes," *Business Week,* March 26, 1966, pp. 49–50; and "More Realism in Fiscal Policy," *Business Week,* March 18, 1967, p. 196.

[4] Donald F. Istvan, *Capital-Expenditure Decisions: How They Are Made in Large Corporations* (Indiana Business Report No. 33 [Bloomington: Indiana University, 1961]), p. 97.

equipment, (3) raw materials, (4) component parts and materials, (5) supplies, and (6) services.

While the consumer goods classification is tentative and perhaps arbitrary, the industrial goods classification is keyed directly to the way industrial purchasing departments and accounting control systems operate day to day. Buyers, for example, often specialize by product categories. And steel mills use categories similar to our industrial goods classifications for buying, maintenance, costing of orders, and control purposes.

The authority of certain plant executives to requisition and buy is limited frequently to one or more categories, either directly or by a dollar limit. Accessory expenditures, for example, might be limited to $10,000 an item to allow the department foreman some latitude in his requisitioning and, at the same time, to control expenditures. Yet by ingenuity an enterprising foreman can get around these controls. He might buy a large crane in pieces, including the bridge, $8,000; trolley, $4,500; two drums, $950 each; 800 feet of woven-wire cable, $3 a foot, etc. Under other control systems, perhaps the only items a plant foreman could buy without higher approval would be supplies, but it is remarkable what kinds of small machines and other accessories can be called supplies in this situation.

But these corruptions of organizational control procedures aside, our industrial goods classification system generally does make sense and is used extensively in the industrial goods market.

Installations, major capital items

Installations are large and expensive items that do not become a part of the final product but are expended, depleted, or worn out during years of use. All installations are *capital items*.

There are two major classifications of installations: *buildings and land rights*, and *major equipment*.

Buildings and land rights include assets such as factories, farms, stores, office buildings, mining deposits, and timber rights. Major equipment includes large items of machinery and production facilities such as diesel engines, tractors, papermaking machines, printing presses, and kilns.

Major equipment can be subdivided into two types: (1) custom-made and (2) standard.

Custom-made equipment is built to specification for a particular company. *Standard* installations are regular production items such as tractors, general-purpose diesel engines, lathes, and printing presses.

For our purposes in this text, *buildings* and *custom-made equipment* are treated alike, since both require special negotiations for each individual product. *Standard major equipment,* being more homogeneous, can be treated more routinely. All installations, however, are important enough to require high-level and even top-management consideration. New-task buying or modified rebuy buying will be involved here.

Size of market small at any time	Installations are long-lived goods, and the number of potential buyers at any particular time usually is small. For some custom-made machines, there may be only a half-dozen potential customers at any one time, compared to a thousand or more potential buyers for standard machines of similar type and capacity.

Potential customers generally are in the same or a related industry, permitting industry specialization by sales executives. Their plants are likely to be geographically concentrated. The automobile industry, for example, is heavily concentrated in and around Michigan, the tire industry in Ohio, copper mining in the western states, and the aircraft industry – from a global view – in the United States. |
| Multiple buying influence important | The importance of these items leads to considerable multiple buying influence. Negotiations can stretch over months or even years and often involve the top executives of the company, especially for buildings or custom-made products. This may complicate promotion, since these executives may be concerned with quite different problems than purchasing agents and may not use the same evaluation procedures. The top executive may be less concerned, for example, with the product's suitability for current needs than with its flexibility and possible usefulness in a new venture he is considering. The seller may need different sales approaches to cope with each of the possible influences. |
| Buying motives economic and emotional | Buying motives are essentially economic, and concerned with the projected performance of the installation over its expected life. After comparing expected performance to present costs and calculating interest, the expected return on capital can be calculated. Yet emotional motives, such as a desire for industry leadership and status, also may be involved. Emotion, for example, seems to have dictated some decisions to purchase computers. |
| Industry demand may be very inelastic, but . . . | The demand for a particular installation may be completely inelastic up to a certain price, especially if the firm badly needs expanded capacity. The potential return on the new investment may be so attractive that any reasonable price might be acceptable.

While demand can be very inelastic, however, the situation for sellers may be different. There may be many suppliers, such as building contractors, and so buyers of installations may be able to request bids and buy in a highly competitive market. |
| Installation industry, a "boom-or-bust" business | The installation industry has been described as a "boom-or-bust" business. During the upswing of a business cycle, businessmen want to expand production capacity rapidly and are willing to pay almost any reasonable price to do it. Competition is less vigorous, and profits are higher for the installation sellers. But during a downswing, buyers will have little or no need for new installations, and sales can fall off precipitously.

Installation manufacturers can even suffer a bust because con- |

sumer demand, although high, is no longer rising. At such times, the producers who previously needed additional installations to meet *rising* consumer demand are no longer in the market – except for replacements.

Installations may have to be leased or rented

Since installations are relatively expensive, the producer often will lease or rent the product rather than sell it outright. Examples are buildings and land rights and some specialized equipment, including electronic data processing machines.

Such lease or rental arrangements are attractive to some target markets because they shift the expenditure from a capital item to an expense item.[5]

Specialized services needed as part of the product

Since the expected return on an installation investment is based on efficient operation, the supplier may have to make service provisions to assure this efficiency. The sales contract may stipulate regular visits by servicemen; a serviceman may even be permanently attached to the company. Computer manufacturers sometimes station service personnel with the machines, and shopping center owners sometimes provide maintenance and even promotion services to their tenants. The cost is included in the price or rent.

The more homogeneous the installation, the more likely it is that the seller will try to differentiate his product by offering specialized services such as aid in installing his machine in the buyer's plant, training employees in its use, supplying repair service, and taking trade-ins on long-lived installations that a potential buyer already may have on hand.

Accessory equipment – important but short-lived

Accessory equipment, like installations, does not become a part of the buyer's final product. These products usually are less expensive and shorter-lived than installations and generally can be depreciated more quickly than installations, but are still *capital items*.

Accessory equipment is very similar to the smaller standard installations and includes tools and equipment that facilitate production or office activities. Examples include portable drills, sanding machines, electric lift trucks, typewriters, filing cases, accounting machines, wheelbarrows, hand trucks, and small lathes. Here, the modified rebuy process may be more typical, although sellers certainly will try to move their brands to straight rebuys. This might happen if a product is part of a "system," say, of office equipment or a production line, and the buyer wants to modify or expand his present facilities.

[5] "Can Leasing Make Ownership Obsolete?" *Business Week*, March 8, 1969, pp. 50–54.

Size of market may affect Place and Promotion decisions	Accessories are even more standardized than installations and are usually needed by more target markets. A large, special-purpose belt sanding machine, for example, might be produced as a custom-made installation for woodworking firms, but small sanding machines would be considered accessory equipment for general use in a variety of shops and factories. Since there is a larger number of target markets and less geographical concentration, different marketing mixes would be required for accessory equipment than for installations.
Multiple buying influences less important	Since these products cost less and last a shorter time than installation equipment, the multiple buying influence is less important. Operating personnel and purchasing agents rather than top-level executives may do the buying. Purchasing agents have more say in buying accessories as these become more standardized and are bought by brand or at least by widely recognized standards.

The nearer that accessory items come to being expense items, charged off in one year, the less the consideration given to these purchases by higher-level management. Some small accessories are treated as expense items, even if the Internal Revenue Service might prefer otherwise.

Leasing or renting accessories is attractive to some target markets because the costs can be treated as expenses. A manufacturer of electric lift trucks, for instance, was able to expand its sales by selling the basic truck outright but charging for the expensive battery system by the amount it was used. And these charges could be treated as operating expenses in some plants. This expanded sales because, as one of the company executives said: "Nobody worries about costs which are buried as an operating expense."[6]

Firm demand may be elastic	Essentially the same economic buying motives that would apply to standard installations apply here. But since accessories are purchased more frequently than installations and have less bearing on the quality and cost of the final product, reciprocity requests are more likely.

As accessory items become smaller and more standardized, the more likely it is that there will be competitive substitutes. Then, although buyers may have inelastic demands, they still are able to purchase in fairly competitive markets. And competition will be accentuated because when purchasing agents are buying less important items, they will be more willing to experiment with alternate suppliers.

Special services may be attractive	Ordinarily, engineering services or special advice is less important for accessory equipment because of its simpler operation. Yet some companies have managed to add attractive services to their accessories, as in the case of the office equipment firms that offer advice on office layouts and office systems.

[6] "Switching the Charge on Batteries," *Business Week*, March 13, 1965, pp. 132–34.

Raw materials — farm products and natural products

Raw materials are products that have been processed only as much as needed for safe, convenient, economical transport and handling.[7] Unlike installations and accessories, raw materials become part of a physical product.

Raw materials are *expense items* and may be purchased routinely — as straight rebuys — by purchasing agents. But top executives may take part in buying when certain raw materials represent a large part of the firm's costs, as with wheat in the flour milling business. Moreover, to assure sources of supply, top executives may help negotiate the annual contracts for some important raw materials.

It is useful to break raw materials into two broad categories: (1) farm products and (2) natural products. *Farm products* include crops, livestock, and other commodities such as cotton, wheat, strawberries, sugar cane, cattle, hogs, poultry, eggs, and milk. *Natural products* include animal, vegetable, and mineral products as they occur naturally, including, for example, fish and game, lumber and maple syrup, and copper, zinc, iron ore, oil and coal.

Some raw materials, such as fruits and vegetables, poultry, eggs, and milk, can be used directly by final consumers. In this text, we will treat raw materials sold directly to consumers or through middlemen for sale to consumers as consumer goods, not industrial goods.

The buying attitudes and practices of the various middlemen handling raw materials will be quite different. As we will see later, different middlemen may develop to handle raw materials when they are destined for consumer rather than industrial markets.

Farm products

The need for grading is one of the important factors distinguishing these products from other industrial goods. Nature produces what it will, and someone must sort and grade the wheat, corn, tobacco, cotton, and other similar products to satisfy various market segments. Some of the top grades of fruits and vegetables may find their way into the premium-quality consumer goods market, while the lower grades will be treated as industrial goods and be used in juices, sauces, and frozen pies.

Most farm products are produced seasonally, yet the demand for them is fairly constant throughout the year. As a result, storage and transportation are major activities in their marketing process.

As noted, buyers of industrial goods normally do not seek out suppliers. This is a complicating factor in marketing farm products, because the many small farm producers usually are widely scattered, sometimes far from potential buyers, and selling direct to final users would be difficult for them. Place and Promotion consequently are important factors in marketing mixes for these products.

Most buyers of farm products have specific uses in mind and generally prefer that products be sorted and graded. But since large buyers

[7] "Report of the Definitions Committee," *Journal of Marketing*, October, 1948, p. 213.

may have difficulty getting the quantities of the grades and types they want, contract production has developed. Here, the buyer deliberately seeks out potential sources of supply and makes contracts that assure the supplier a market for his goods. This has several effects. It tends to make the supplier a part of the buyer's operation and removes one more producer from the competitive market. This may be desirable from the suppliers' point of view, because it isolates him from a purely competitive market.

Firm demand is elastic

Most farm products have an inelastic market demand, even though the many small producers are in nearly pure competition. The market demand becomes more elastic when there are many substitutes (such as beef for pork or corn for wheat). But within the usual price ranges, the demand for agricultural products is generally inelastic, and so it helps agricultural producers to control output and prices, perhaps through U.S. Department of Agriculture programs.

Most attempts to control prices in the farm products market are frustrated by slow adjustment of supply and the difficulty of organizing the many producers. Once a crop is planted, the potential supply is more or less fixed (subject to weather, pests, etc.), and it is too late to change crop size that year. For some animal products, the planning cycle may be two or three years, and this further accentuates the problem of adjustment in supply.

At the end of a growing season, the quantity of available farm products is fixed. If this supply is large, the market price can be extremely low; if it is small, the price may be high. This can be seen in Figure 13–1 where vertical lines are used to show that in the short run, farmers would supply the same quantity regardless of the price.

This relatively long planning period has led to some peculiar cycles in production and prices. The poultry farmers in the Delaware, Mary-

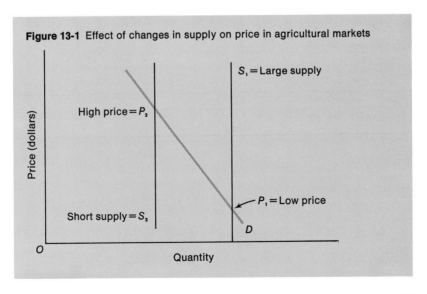

Figure 13-1 Effect of changes in supply on price in agricultural markets

$S_1 =$ Large supply

High price $= P_2$

Price (dollars)

$P_1 =$ Low price

Short supply $= S_2$

D

O

Quantity

land, and Virginia area traditionally went through boom-and-bust periods on an annual basis. High poultry prices one year attracted many growers the following year, who then overproduced, driving prices down below cost. This caused many small producers to leave the market, creating an inadequate supply and again raising price to a high level. Recently, however, the entry of a few large producers with better control over supply has reduced this seesawing of supply and prices.

Natural products

In contrast to the farm products market, with its many producers, natural products are produced by fewer and larger companies. There are some exceptions, of course, such as the coal and lumber industries.

In general, the total supply of natural products is limited and cannot be expanded readily. But the supply harvested or mined in any one year *is* adjustable.

Most of the products are bulky and pose transportation problems. But storage is less important, since fewer are perishable and some can be produced year-round. Major exceptions are fish and game, which have runs or seasons and resemble farm animal products more than forest or mineral products in their marketing patterns.

Buying motives

As with farm products, buyers of natural products usually need specific grades and dependable supply sources to assure continued production in their own plants. Large buyers, therefore, often seek to buy, or at least control, their sources of supply. This is easier than with farm products because fewer and larger production facilities are involved.

One way to control supply sources is *vertical integration* – ownership of the natural product producer by the user. Examples are synthetic fiber and paper manufacturers who control timber resources, oil refiners who control crude oil sources, and tire manufacturers who control rubber plantations. Probably the best known are the steel producers who control not only iron ore and coal deposits but also the ships and trains to carry ore and coal.

When a great deal of integration has taken place in a given industry, there may be an erratic or spotty open market. This is because buyers and sellers will come into the market only when their own captive sources are producing too much or too little or the wrong quality.

Sellers in markets who do not formally integrate with users normally find that their customers buy in large quantities and are interested in assuring themselves dependable sources of supply. This usually is done through contracts or "understandings," perhaps negotiated by top-level executives and referring to standard grades or specifications for products.

Firm demand may be inelastic or elastic

The industry demand is derived and basically inelastic. The large producers of natural products are quite responsive to market demands and are inclined to limit supply to maintain stable prices. In the coal and lumber industries, however, where there are many producers, there is close to pure competition.

Component parts and materials —
the sum is no better than . . .

Like raw materials, component parts and materials become a part of a finished product. Both are treated as *expense items*. Component parts, however, undergo more processing than is required for raw materials and may require different marketing mixes. All three buying processes may be seen here.

Component parts include those items that are (*a*) finished and ready for assembly or (*b*) nearly finished, requiring only minor additional processing (such as grinding or polishing) before being assembled into the final product.

In the parts category are automobile batteries, small motors, tires, and forgings or castings, all of which are incorporated directly into a finished product. It also includes other items, such as automobile jacks, that are sold with the product but not physically attached to it or incorporated into it.

Component materials are items such as wire, paper, textiles, or cement. They have already been processed but must be processed further before becoming part of the final product.

Multiple buying influences

Some component parts are custom-made and much negotiation may be necessary between the engineering staffs of both buyer and seller to arrive at the proper specifications. If the price of the item is very high or if it is an extremely important component of the final product, top-level executives may become involved, as with raw materials. New-task buying is found here to help set the specifications and sources.

Other component parts and materials are more likely to be processed to commonly accepted standards or specifications and produced in quantity. For such items, engineering or production people in the buying firm may specify quality. The purchasing agent will do the actual buying. Modified rebuys and straight rebuys are seen here.

Buying motives are more economic

As with other types of industrial goods, the motives involved in buying components are basically economic and concern price, availability, quality, and suitability. Assurances of availability and prompt delivery are most important. A purchasing agent must do everything in his power to avoid a plant shutdown caused by unavailability of materials. Moreover, an assured source of supply will enable the buyer to reduce his inventory, reducing both his inventory investment and the risk of damage to, and obsolescence of, goods in stock.

Since components are incorporated in the firm's own product, quality is extremely important, too. The buyer's own name and whole marketing mix are at stake. Quality may be less important for component parts, however, if they are well branded — such as a tire or spark plug — and the blame for a defective product can fall upon the component supplier. Generally, however, a progressive buyer would attempt to buy from component sources that would help assure a satisfactory product to the final customers.

Firm
demand
may be
elastic

Although the industry and individual firms' demand may be fairly inelastic for components, there usually are many possible suppliers, enabling buyers to purchase in a fairly competitive market. In fact, the market for many component parts and materials is extremely competitive. There are several reasons for this competition.

1. Most component buyers want to have several sources of supply, and encourage new suppliers.
2. There usually are many small producers – small tool-and-die shops, machine shops, and foundries – with general-purpose machinery that can produce a great variety of component parts.
3. There often are many suppliers of component materials willing to produce to widely accepted specifications or standards.

Design
services
may help

Design services may be important for some components, and this enables an alert seller to achieve an inelastic demand curve. Or if the seller has obtained some design patents or in some way developed a particularly unique (heterogeneous) product, he may achieve an extremely inelastic demand curve.

Replace-
ment
markets
may develop

Since component parts are incorporated in a finished product, a replacement market often develops. This market can be both large and very profitable, as in the case of automotive tires and batteries.

This replacement market may involve new target markets. The part originally may have been considered a component part when it was sold in the OEM (original equipment market), but as a replacement the same product might become a consumer good. The target markets are different, and probably different marketing mixes will be necessary.

Some component parts suppliers may be eager to have their parts used in the OEM market because the "after" market composed of final consumers is attractive.

The Mallory Battery Co. worked hard to get its small batteries installed as original components in cameras, watches, hearing aids, and dictating equipment because marketing research had told them that half of all final consumer battery buyers don't know what kind of battery powers their equipment. They simply walk into a store and say, "Gimme one just like this."

Mallory coordinated its efforts in both markets – the components and final consumer markets – and achieved a 50 percent increase in profits.[8]

---

[8] "Will Tiny Cells Power Big Sales," *Business Week,*
January 14, 1967, pp. 60–64.

Supplies—everybody wants them but how much?

Firms consume supplies currently, just as they do raw materials and component parts and materials. Supplies are, therefore, *expense items*. But unlike raw materials and components, *supplies do not become a part of a physical product*. Although they are necessary, most supplies are not as vital as the products in the first four classifications—and when a firm economizes, orders for supplies may be the first to go.

Supplies can be divided into three categories: (1) maintenance, (2) repair, and (3) operating supplies, giving them their common designation, MRO items.

Maintenance items include such things as paint, nails, light bulbs, sweeping compounds, brooms, and window-cleaning equipment. *Repair items* are nuts and bolts or parts needed to repair existing equipment. *Operating supplies* include lubricating oils and greases, grinding compounds, coal, typing paper, ink, pencils, and paper clips.

Most supply items are used by industry in general and are similar to the kinds of items purchased by final consumers in hardware stores. Some supplies are more important than others, as noted below.

Important operating supplies

Some operating supplies needed regularly and in large amounts receive special treatment from buyers. Some companies buy coal and fuel oil in carload or tank-car quantities. Usually there are several sources for such homogeneous products, and large volumes may be purchased in highly competitive markets. Or contracts may be negotiated, perhaps by high-level executives. Such contracts have several advantages. Subsequent purchase requisitions may be drawn routinely against them—as straight rebuys. They sometimes assure lower prices, and they eliminate the buyer's concern about a dependable source for these important operating supplies.

When several dependable sources are available and orders are large, reciprocity may become important. If quality and price are roughly the same, it becomes more difficult to refuse the sales department's request for reciprocity relationships. Purchasing departments usually resist such overtures, but this is one place where the sales department's arguments are strong.

Maintenance and small operating supplies

These items are similar to consumer's convenience goods and are so numerous that a purchasing agent cannot possibly be an expert in buying all of them. There usually is little multiple buying influence. They may not even justify modified rebuying.

Each requisition for maintenance and small operating supplies may be for a relatively few items. The purchase requisitions can amount to only $1 to $2. Although the cost of handling a purchase order may be from $5 to $10, the item will be ordered, because it is needed, but as simply as possible.

Branding may become important for such products. It makes product identification and buying of such "nuisance" items easier.

Industry demand for supplies is fairly inelastic, and sellers may see pretty inelastic demand curves, too. Since only small amounts of money are involved and shopping around for bargains would hardly be worth the time, a purchasing agent might find several dependable sources of supply and patronize them for the bulk of such items.

A new company offering only one supply item might have trouble entering such a market. The job of buying these many small items is difficult enough, and buyers usually don't have time to review the small advantages of some new product or supplier. The purchasing agent wouldn't be as interested in price for such items – the breadth of assortment and dependability of the source are of utmost important in buying supply items. Yet a characteristic of a dependable source of supply is that it offers good values, and a skilled purchasing agent continually shops for good value. The threat of losing a substantial amount of business from one buyer tends to keep the various suppliers' prices in line.

Repair items	The original supplier of installation or accessory equipment may be the only source of supply for repairs and parts. The cost of repairs relative to the cost of disrupted production may be so small that buyers are willing to pay the price charged – whatever it is.

Demand for repair items is quite inelastic. But if the demand for such items is large and steady – say, for truck mufflers or power transmission belts – there may be many suppliers. The market then may become quite competitive even though each buyer's demand is relatively inelastic.

Services – you pay for what you get

Services supplied by specialists frequently are valuable in supporting the operations of a firm.[9] Engineering or management consulting services can improve the plant layout or the organization of the company. Design services can supply designs for the physical plant, products, and graphic materials. Outside maintenance services can handle window cleaning, painting, or general housekeeping services. Other organizations can supply in-plant lunches and piped-in music to improve employee morale and production.

All these services are considered *expense items*. The cost of buying them outside the firm is compared with the cost of having company personnel provide them. For special skills needed only irregularly,

[9]For a discussion of the marketing problems associated with technical services, see James G. Hauk, *Technical Service in the American Economy: A Problem in Marketing Management* (Michigan Business Studies, Vol. 31, No. 1 [Ann Arbor: University of Michigan, 1962]). For further discussion of the opportunities and problems of marketing services, see E. B. Turner, "Marketing Professional Services," *Journal of Marketing*, October, 1969, pp. 56–61; "Here's a Company That's Cleaning Up," *Business Week*, October 26, 1968, pp. 176–80; "A Builder 'Packages Everything,'" *Business Week*, November 2, 1968, pp. 146–48; "Ship Line Charts New Courses," *Business Week*, February 8, 1969, pp. 106–12; "Business Knowhow Fertilizes the Farm," *Business Week*, September 14, 1968, pp. 64–74; "A New Industry's Wild Ride" (computer services) *Business Week*, May 24, 1969, pp. 64–78; and "Management Seminars Fade Fast in Popularity as the Economy Slows," *Wall Street Journal*, June 18, 1970, pp. 1 f.

an outsider can be the best source. Specialists are proliferating in our increasingly complex economy.

The demand for special services is often inelastic if the supplier has a unique product. And the supply may be fairly inelastic, too. The suppliers may consider themselves professionals and charge accordingly. For example, engineers, architects, and medical doctors have commonly accepted fee schedules, and the competition among them is not based on price but on quality of service.[10]

Industrial goods classes and buying behavior are related

The previous focus on kinds of goods may not seem very exciting, but it is important because the nature of goods has an effect on how the buyers will accept and buy them. And this obviously has a direct bearing on the planning of marketing mixes. But it is all too easy to focus on goods, when we are actually using these goods as a shorthand description of how customers behave.

Don't forget that an individual buyer may behave differently toward different kinds of goods. Or in a larger company, there may be specialists buying the various goods. This can both simplify and complicate the selling process. Buying specialists may be easier to deal with—at least they are more expert and therefore require less education about technical points. On the other hand, if there are many buying specialists in a company, then a salesman cannot casually conclude that he is calling on the entire company just because he calls on one man.

Each buyer of each type of good should be treated as an entirely separate customer (as though he were in a different firm). He may behave and think quite differently when he is buying different products, or than his buying colleagues do. He may not feel any obligation to give a salesman any special consideration just because he happens to sell another buyer in the company. In fact, this might even be a handicap, in that the two buyers might have quite different philosophies about purchasing. Being able to get along with one might not be viewed as an asset by the other.

A firm with many buyers, specializing by product

The organization of buyers in a large purchasing department may help illustrate these ideas. Figure 13–2 shows the layout of a centralized purchasing department for a large manufacturer, with plants throughout the country. Seventeen men work under a vice president of purchasing. Some of these buyers (shown by rectangles in the figure) report to group supervisors (shown in offices along the left edge

---

[10]Warren J. Wittreich, "How to Buy/Sell Professional Services," *Harvard Business Review*, March–April, 1966, pp. 127–38.

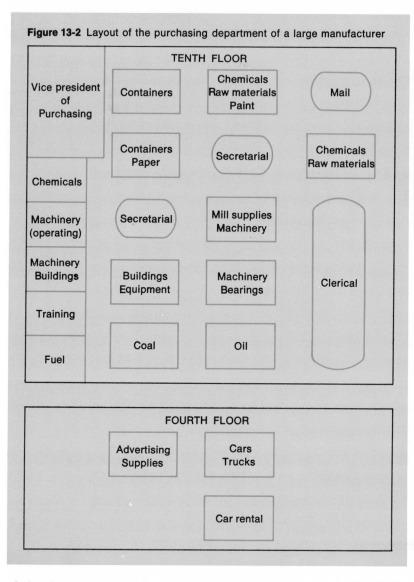

Figure 13-2 Layout of the purchasing department of a large manufacturer

of the figure), who also do some buying and report directly to the vice president.

Coal and oil buyers

As you can see in the figure, each of the buyers specializes in certain kinds of goods, and some are quite specialized. The coal and oil buyers are limited to these operating supplies because the manufacturer is a major fuel user. They are supervised by a man who is responsible for all fuel purchases. Considerable time is spent by all three in locating sources of supply and negotiating long-term contracts. All types of purchasing are involved: new-task buying when a new plant is opened and new sources of supply must be developed; modified rebuys when contracts are renewed; and then straight rebuys, mainly issuing purchase orders against established contracts.

Installation and accessory buyers

Sitting just in front of the fuel buyers are two men and their supervisor who specialize in installations and accessories for new plants and major replacements for existing plants. One of these buyers, however, also purchases bearings (repair items) because they are quite important in this business and justify special treatment. On the supply side, bearings are important enough so that there are bearing specialists. These buyers, also, are involved in all three types of purchasing.

Accessories and supplies buyers

In front of this group is a man who specializes in mill supplies and machinery. His supervisor concentrates on accessories and standard installations, which are used as replacements for currently operating equipment. These men might buy from the same sources used by the previous buyers, but here much less emphasis is placed on consultation with the engineering department and those concerned with new facilities. Here, the multiple buying influence, if any, would come from the plant managers in individual plants. Thus machinery purchases here would tend to be modified rebuys. The mill supplies purchases consist of the full range of MRO items needed to keep the factories going. This buyer has several dependable sources of supply with whom he routinely places the large flow of requisitions for mill supplies. Getting rid of these requisitions leaves him more time to focus on larger, more important machinery purchases.

Raw materials, components, and more supplies

The supervisor of chemical purchases presides over four buyers of an assortment of raw materials, components, and supplies. The containers buyer in the upper left-hand corner of Figure 13-2 specializes in cans for paint and other products. Behind him is another container buyer, in this case, of boxes. This man also purchases large rolls of paper which are used in the production processes. Next to the first container man is the buyer of various raw materials and component materials which are used in the production process. He also is assigned to buying paint for maintenance purposes, perhaps because the kinds of chemicals and raw materials he buys are also used in paint. And behind him and to his left is another buyer of chemicals and raw materials. But these are quite different products, and generally not available from the same sources as those bought by the previous buyer. All four of these buyers regularly engage in each of the three buying processes, although here some of the new task negotiation is done by the supervisor because of the magnitude of these purchases.

Supplies and automotive needs

Due to lack of space on the tenth floor, three buyers are located on the fourth floor. One specializes in renting cars for the sales force. Another purchases cars and trucks for any use. And another man buys advertising specialties, point-of-purchase materials, salesmen's portfolios, and anything else (supplies) which no one else wants to buy! These "nuisance" requisitions are handled in the same way that the mill supplies buyer handles requisitions for factory supplies!

Requisition-
ing and
ordering in
practice

Requisitioning before ordering

The basic ordering process used by this firm is as follows. Whenever a department or plant wants to buy anything, it fills out a requisition which, after approval by some operating supervisor, is forwarded to the centralized purchasing department for placement with the "best" vendor. The requisitions flow in large numbers to the mail desk and then are sorted to the various buyers by a clerical supervisor in the clerical pool. The nature of the product facilitates this sorting to buyers. The requisitions have already been approved, and now the buyer is responsible for placing a purchase order and obtaining delivery by the date requested on the requisition.

Ordering may be routine

The requisitions are converted to purchase orders as quickly as possible. Straight rebuys are usually made the day the requisition is received, while new task and modified rebuys take longer. If time is important, the buyer may place the order by telephone, and then a confirming purchase order is typed in the clerical pool and sent out. More routine straight rebuys would consist of the buyer (1) deciding which of his several vendors would get this order, (2) filling in the vendor's name and other details on the face of the requisition, and (3) forwarding it to the clerical pool for typing into a purchase order and mailing.

It pays to know the buyer

Notice the importance of being one of the regular sources of supply. The buyers do not even call potential sources for straight rebuys. Vendors' salesmen regularly call on these buyers, typically *not* to sell a particular item but to cement relations, or to become a source, and/or to point out new developments which might cause the buyer to re-evaluate his present "straight rebuy" procedure and give more favorable attention to the salesman's company.

The fact that buyers do specialize by product, and that a considerable amount of buying is of the "straight rebuy" type, points up the vital importance of treating each buyer as a separate target market and understanding how and why he works the way he does. It also shows us the importance of being on the buyer's list of potential vendors. The salesman cannot always be there exactly when the requisitions come in, and the buyer may not consult all potential sources before placing his orders.

It also makes sense to recognize the potential advantage to a salesman of the buyer having a favorable image of him. Unless a definite percentage share of the business is to be allocated to each of several sources, it is likely that a favored source might achieve a slightly larger share than he would otherwise get. Moving from a 20 percent to a 30 percent share may not seem like much from the buyer's point of view, but for the salesman it represents a 50 percent increase in his sales!

The salesman who fully understands and satisfies the needs and preferences of his customers clearly can get significantly better results. This points up again the importance of careful market grid analysis and the development of a marketing mix to fully satisfy the needs of *each* target market. In the industrial goods area, this may require treating each *buyer* as a separate target market. Within larger companies, this may mean treating each individual man as a separate target market.

The buyers discussed above in relation to Figure 13–2 are all individuals, and each has slightly different goals and ways of approaching buying problems. None of them would be particularly impressed with the fact that a vendor had succeeded in selling one of his colleagues. Each has to be sold as an individual—an individual with his own goals who is also operating within the constraints of the objectives provided by the organization. The goods classes are a great help in summarizing how and why they behave as they do, but it is still necessary to understand each individual buyer as well.

Conclusion

The industrial goods classification system developed in this chapter is considerably easier to use than the one for consumers' goods because it starts with products and the way they are used. Customer buying behavior and product-market competition are related to the product classifications.

You should have a thorough understanding of the various kinds of products and their distinguishing characteristics, since this has a significant bearing on where and how these products are distributed, promoted, and priced.

It also is important to distinguish between consumer and industrial goods. The same physical product may belong in both categories but require quite different marketing mixes.

A vital characteristic of industrial goods is that demand is derived from demand for consumer goods. Further, *industry demand for industrial goods tends to be inelastic, but because of competition among suppliers, the demand facing any one industrial goods seller may be quite elastic.* Derived demand and industrial buying practices also may lead to violent and hard-to-forecast fluctuations in sales. Capital-goods producers, in particular, experience boom-and-bust cycles, because of changes in final consumer buying patterns.

In contrast to consumer buying, which may be emotionally motivated, industrial purchasing of all categories of goods is more concerned with economic factors. Multiple buying influence may be important too. Some industrial goods even warrant top-level decisions.

While consumer goods classifications are somewhat arbitrary, those for industrial goods are not. Industrial purchasing and accounting systems use similar classifications, and areas of purchasing responsibility are frequently assigned according to these product classifications.

The following chapters will begin to use these product classifications to bring order out of a complex marketing structure. Before reading these chapters, you will profit by a serious consideration of what kinds of marketing institutions might develop to distribute specific products and the functions which they would provide. This will enable you to better appreciate why certain marketing specialists have developed and why they use certain marketing practices.

Industrial goods, 13

QUESTIONS AND PROBLEMS

1 Present two examples of industrial goods which require a substantial amount of service in order to make them useful "products."

2 Would you expect to find any wholesalers selling the various types of industrial goods? Are retail stores required (or something like retail stores)?

3 What kinds of goods are the following?
a) Nails and screws.
b) Paint.
c) Dust-collecting and ventilating systems.
d) An electric lift truck.
Explain your reasoning.

4 What impact does the fact that demand for industrial goods is derived and fairly inelastic have upon the development of industrial goods marketing mixes? Use examples.

5 How do farm product raw materials differ from other raw materials or other industrial goods? Do the differences have any impact on their marketing mixes? If so, what, specifically?

6 How would an Internal Revenue Service relaxation of depreciation regulations affect the marketing mixes of industrial goods? Would it affect all of them equally?

7 Discuss the kinds of wholesalers and retailers you might expect to find in the sale of farm-produced raw materials. Specifically what activities would you expect each to provide and why?

8 Consider how much latitude an industrial buyer has in selecting the specific brand and the specific source of supply for that product, once a product has been requisitioned by some production department? Consider this question with specific reference to pencils, paint for the offices, plastic materials for the production line, a new factory, and a large printing press. How should the buyer's attitude affect the seller's marketing mix?

9 For the kinds of goods described in this chapter, complete the following table (use one or a few *well-chosen* words).

Goods	1	2	3
Installations			
Buildings and			
land rights			
Major equipment			
Standard			
Custom-made			
Accessory			
equipment			
Raw materials			
Farm products			
Natural products			
Components			
Parts			
Materials			
Supplies			
Operating supplies			
Maintenance and			
small operating			
supplies			
Services			

1–Kind of distribution facility(ies) needed and functions they will provide.
2–Caliber of salesmen required.
3–Kind of advertising required.

...following the marketing concept, customers' needs and
wants should dominate product development.

...the product life-cycle concept is especially important to
marketing strategy planning because it shows that different
marketing mixes, and even strategies, are needed as a
product moves throughout its cycle.

...new products are so important to the survival of firms...
that some organized method for developing them is needed.

14

Product planning

So far in our discussion of Product, we have been concerned primarily
with describing and classifying the various types of products and suggesting implications for marketing strategy planning. At various
places, we have noted that product markets are dynamic. To satisfy
customers and meet competition, marketing managers must be interested in the development of new products. We will now discuss
product planning and new-product development.

Need for product planning

Products are not commodities	Some production-oriented businessmen think of their company's product as the natural result of the production process. They see no need for product planning. Yet this view is at the root of many new-product failures and weak marketing strategies.[1]

Long ago, when economies were much simpler, most products were commodities — more or less homogeneous products that were in general demand. They were the natural result of the simple production processes available then. And middlemen tended to specialize by the available commodity lines. The idea of planning products to satisfy specific customers' demands was not very prevalent.

Today's more aggressive competitors, including even agricultural producers, strive to satisfy specific markets. Modern production processes permit a growing number of choices. Farmers are offered not just one type of seed, but many types of carefully bred hybrid seeds. In the same way, a variety of foods, fibers, raw materials, services, and manufactured products compete with each other for the customer's favor.

The customer seldom has to get by with a basic commodity. Usually there are many competitive products vying to satisfy the need which used to be met by a commodity. Therefore, product planning is necessary if the firm is to avoid selling its products as homogeneous commodities in purely competitive markets.

Product markets are dynamic and innovative	Another factor that stimulates product planning is the extreme competitiveness and innovativeness of most product markets. New ideas can be copied quickly and made obsolete by better ones. Some progressive companies are planning 5 and 10 years ahead, and some even further. Westinghouse Electric Corp., for example, has planners working ahead to the year 2000 on developments in 21 different technological fields.[2]

Products have life cycles

Since products, like consumers, have life cycles, it is essential that a company concentrate on the product-planning activity. We will discuss this product life-cycle concept, since it is extremely important and underlies ideas to be found later in the text.

The life of a product can be divided into four major stages: product introduction, market growth, market maturity, and sales decline. A

---

[1] "NICB Discusses New-Product Failures," *Printers' Ink*, April 14, 1967, p. 57.

[2] "Setting a Time Table," *Business Week*, May 27, 1967, pp. 52–61.

product's marketing mix must change during these stages, because: (1) customers' attitudes may change through the course of the product's life cycle; (2) entirely different target markets may be appealed to at different stages in the life cycle; and (3) the nature of competition moves toward pure competition.

In addition, the sales history of the product varies in each of its four stages, and more importantly, the profit picture changes. It is significant that the two do not necessarily move together. Profits may decline while sales rise. Their general relationships can be seen in Figure 14–1.

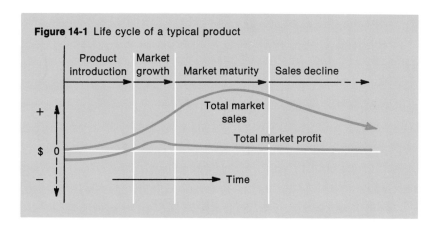

Figure 14-1 Life cycle of a typical product

Introduction — investing in the future

In the introduction stage, a company needs promotion to *pioneer* the acceptance of the product, since it is not sought out by customers. Potential target customers must be told about the existence, advantages, and uses of the new product.

Even though a firm has successfully carved out a new market for itself, the product may not be an immediate success. This introductory stage usually is characterized by losses, with much money spent for promotion and product and place development. Funds, in effect, are being invested with the expectation of future profits.

Market growth — many competing products and better profits

In the market growth stage, the innovator usually begins to make substantial profits. Competitors start coming into the market, and each tries to develop the best product design. There is much product variety. Some competitors copy the most successful products. Monopolistic competition with downsloping demand curves is characteristic of both the period of product introduction and of market growth.

During this stage, the sales of the total industry are rising fairly rapidly as more and more customers enter the market. This second stage may last from several days to several years, depending on whether the product is hula hoops, credit card service, or color television sets. This is the time of peak profitability — *and* also the beginning of the decline of profits.

Market
maturity—
competition
up, profits
down

By the market maturity stage, many competitors have entered the market. (In some cases, entry is not as easy, and the market behaves differently. If there are only a few large competitors and products are homogeneous, the situation is called oligopoly. This is discussed in detail in Chapter 26.)

In this stage, competition is rougher, with declining profits. Promotion emphasizes the advantages of particular brands, but products actually differ only slightly because most of the companies have discovered the most effective appeals to the market, and there is a tendency to copy competing features. Dealer brands and manufacturers' "fighting" brands often are introduced in this stage, adding further to the competition.

This market, still characterized by monopolistic competition, is becoming much more competitive on product, price, and promotion. Basic product similarities cause firms to resort to product differentiation. At this time, emotional appeals become more common — they are the only remaining way to add value to the product.

Industry profits decline throughout the market maturity stage because promotion costs climb, and some competitors begin to cut prices to attract business. Although each firm may still have its own demand curve, the curves are becoming increasingly elastic as the various products become almost homogeneous. Prices may be cut even as total industry volume is rising. This was the case recently in the fields of semiconductors, tiny computers, and the computer time-sharing industry, for example.[3] And the retail banking industry in New York frantically competed for new deposits using extravagant giveaways such as TV sets and watches, until new regulations stopped this competition.[4]

At about the same time, the fast-food franchising boom collapsed, as some markets became saturated and too many competitors were vying with similar franchise offerings.[5]

In the United States, the markets for most automobiles,[6] boats,[7] many household appliances, most groceries, television sets,[8] and tobacco products are in the market maturity stage.

[3] "A European Glut in Semiconductors," *Business Week*, August 22, 1970, p. 18; "Where Time Moves at a Dizzying Pace," *Business Week*, April 20, 1968, pp. 174–82; "Tiny Computers Lead a Price Decline," *Business Week*, May 11, 1968, pp. 108–14; and "Outlook," *Computer Decisions*, May, 1970, p. 8.

[4] "Business Bulletin," *Wall Street Journal*, February 26, 1970, p. 1.

[5] "Many Franchise Firms Fall on Hard Times after a 15-Year Boom," *Wall Street Journal*, May 29, 1970, pp. 1 f.

[6] R. J. Holloway, "Which Automobiles Will Be Here Tomorrow?" *Journal of Marketing*, January, 1961, pp. 35–36.

[7] *Wall Street Journal*, July 19, 1962, p. 1.

[8] William E. Bell, "The Maturing TV Industry," *Journal of Marketing*, April, 1966, pp. 12–15; "A Case of TV Nerves," *Business Week*, November 19, 1966, p. 48; and "Curtis Mathes Reports 3rd Period Loss; Firm Had Year-Earlier Profit," *Wall Street Journal*, April 10, 1967, p. 8; "Color TV's Rainbow Fades a Bit," *Business Week*, February 1, 1969, pp. 38–41; "Color TV Sales Are Looking Bluer," *Business Week*, November 8, 1969, pp. 36–38; "Color TV Makers Hit by Slump in Sales in 4th Quarter: '69 Total Seen Trailing '68," *Wall Street Journal*, December 15, 1969, p. 34; "RCA Cuts Inventories of Small Color TV's: Sluggish Sales Are Seen Continuing into '70," *Wall Street Journal*, October 28, 1969, p. 2; "Color TV Set Sales Fall 26% in 1st Period; Shake-out Seen In Tube Making Industry,"

The market maturity period may continue many years until a basically new product idea comes along to completely change the market. Gasoline-powered automobiles, for example, replaced horse-drawn carriages, and eventually may be replaced by some other method of transportation, such as electric autos and high-speed mass transit. Note the possible competition between physical products and services.

Sales decline

In the fourth and final stage of the life cycle, new products replace the old. Price competition from dying products may become more vigorous, but products with strong customer franchises may make profits almost till the end. These firms will have downsloping demand curves because they have successfully differentiated their products.

As the new products go through the introductory stage, the old ones may retain some sales by appealing to the most loyal target customers, perhaps older people or those who found unique satisfactions.

Our earlier discussion of consumer behavior showed that some customers accept new ideas more readily than others. The former would "discover" the new product; more conservative buyers might switch later, smoothing the sales decline.

The early bird makes the profit

The total length of the cycle may vary from 90 days, as in the case of hula hoops, to possibly 90 years for automobiles. The probable length of the cycle should figure in strategy planning, to assure that realistic plans are made for the latter stages. Technical progress, the passage of time, and changing customer preferences seem to make a sales decline inevitable for any product. Few products that originated 100 years ago have escaped substantial change – if, indeed, they are still sold at all.

Product life cycles also seem to be shortening in the face of growing competition. One research study found the cycle for grocery products declining from about 36 months for those starting in 1962 to 18 months for starters in 1964.[9]

Du Pont's top executive says: "Lead time is gone. . . . There's no company so outstanding technically today that it can expect a long lead time in a new discovery."[10] Du Pont had nylon to itself for 15 years, but in just 2 years a major competitor, Celanese Corp., came out with something very competitive to Delrin, another synthetic fiber discovery that Du Pont considered potentially as important as nylon.

In 1970, Du Pont also had developed an office copier with some technical advantages, but the company was not certain that it would

Wall Street Journal, April 20, 1970, p. 4; "Motorola Closes Plant Making Color TV Tubes," *Wall Street Journal,* April 7, 1970, p. 2; and "For Motorola, a Chance to Unload," *Business Week,* April 11, 1970, pp. 24–25.

[9]Reported in a special presentation to an American Marketing Association Conference on Market Segmentation by A. C. Nielsen, Jr., president, A. C. Nielsen Co., February 24, 1967. See also: William E. Cox, Jr., "Product Life Cycles as Marketing Models," *Journal of Business,* October, 1970, pp. 375–84; "The 'Life Cycle' of Grocery Brands," *Nielsen Researcher,* No. 1 (1968); and Robert D. Buzzell and Robert E. Nourse, *Product Innovation In Food Processing: 1954-1964,* (Boston: Division of Research, Harvard Business School, 1967).

[10]"The Short Happy Life," *Time,* March 29, 1963, p. 83.

be offered for sale. The director of the development department said: "We may just be too late. Perhaps we should have moved faster."[11]

Six months after U.S. Steel came out with a new economical "thin tin" plate, competitors were out with even better products. Electric skillets, electric can openers, and electric toothbrushes also experienced the fast rise of competition.

Even copying of products is not unknown, and this speeds up the cycle. Westinghouse found a company copying its new hair dryer *and* instruction book almost exactly.[12] Even patent protection may not be enough, since the product's life may be over before a case would get through the courts. What this means is that the modern firm must be developing new products continually and must seek to have a marketing mix (and not just a product) that will make the most of the early stages of the life cycle when profits are highest.

How to meet or beat competitive forces

Clearly, a succession of new products is needed to offset the impact of competition and the product life cycle. Yet new or improved products do not just happen. Ideas for new products must be translated into salable form, and existing products may have to be improved or dropped. More is said on this later in the chapter.

A company does not have to sit by in frustration and watch its product go through the complete product life cycle, however. It can either significantly improve the product and let it start off on a new cycle, or withdraw it before it completes the cycle (Figure 14–2).

Market needs are related to product life cycles

The product life-cycle concept is very useful for explaining how competition evolves in the market for a particular product or product class. But great care should be taken to avoid adopting a production-oriented view which focuses too much on the tangible aspects of products. A product must satisfy some market needs, and the market being served should be implicit, at least, in any consideration of the product life cycle.

Market should be identified

Ideally, to fully understand the *why* of a product life cycle, we should be aware of what market needs are being satisfied. Market needs may be enduring, and the particular product being evaluated may be simply a current way of satisfying these needs. If there are many potential substitutes, and/or if consumers are faddish, a new product's life cycle may move *very* quickly. Likewise, if the product is defined very narrowly, then it may also have a short life cycle as improved products come along to replace it.

[11] "Du Pont's Troubled Dynasty," *Time*, January 5, 1970, pp. 50–51.

[12] *Time*, March 29, 1963, p. 83.

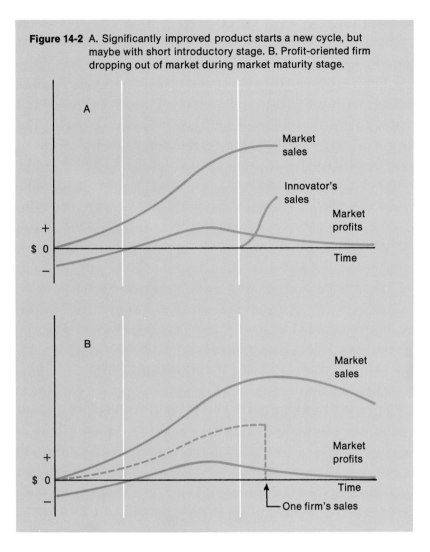

Figure 14-2 A. Significantly improved product starts a new cycle, but maybe with short introductory stage. B. Profit-oriented firm dropping out of market during market maturity stage.

Two views may be useful

There may be an ongoing general market demand for copies of letters, term papers, and book pages, for example. If we add the annual sales of all the copying machines which have come on the market during the last few decades and treat them as the sales of one product, it probably would appear to be in the market growth stage. If we think of individual kinds of machines applying different technical principles, however, we see relatively short life cycles as new generations of machines come along.[13] If this narrower view is taken, some of the

[13] "Xerox Unveils First of 'New Generation' of Copying Machines," *Wall Street Journal*, May 20, 1970, p. 11.

earlier machines have already gone through the sales decline stage and have disappeared from the market. Both views can be useful.

Another illustration can be seen in the boating industry, which has moved from wood and aluminum construction to fiberglass. Consumer needs may be described in terms of the "fun of boating" and "pride in ownership" of boats, and the total market is growing—indicating the market growth stage. But some suppliers may see the world and their product life-cycle position in terms of physical products and their methods of construction and materials used, especially if their resources limit them to certain designs and materials, and they cannot readily change. With the growing preference for fiberglass, for example, wood-oriented boat producers are locked in the sales decline stage, while more diversified producers are focusing on boating needs and see a market characterized by market growth.[14]

Each market segment has its own product life cycle

The way we define a market is quite relevant to the way we see product life cycles, and who we have as competitors. This is definitely related to our earlier discussion of the relevant market dimensions in market gridding. If a businessman produces or sells exercise machines, he can focus on the "exercise machine market," but it really makes more sense to sell to the "fitness market." Then he competes not only with other exercise machine makers but with health clubs, and suppliers of jogging suits, athletic shoes, and other sporting goods as well. In this case, he has two product life cycles to work with—the exercise machine and the fitness markets. The growth patterns in both might or might *not* be closely related.[15]

Note, too, that if all competitors see a market's needs the same way, they may try to satisfy them in the same fashion. This is what leads to market maturity. But if there is another way to look at the same market needs, a new product may achieve a quick breakthrough. If car manufacturers focus on price levels, horsepower, and weight, for example, they may miss the determining dimension for some people. This would leave room for a more perceptive competitor who might succeed in spite of his ignoring the usual dimensions. In effect, he is carving out a separate market for himself and starting another product life cycle.

These qualifying comments should emphasize that the product life-cycle concept is useful but must be applied with care to realize full benefit. Ongoing market needs might be stable (as for food) or growing (as for copying), and particular product efforts to satisfy these needs would go through their own product life cycles. Depending on the number of competitors (as in the fitness market) and the fickleness of consumers, these particular product life cycles can be relatively short.

The moral here is that market needs being satisfied by a general

---

[14] "Boating Charts a Merger Course," *Business Week,* February 1, 1969, pp. 20–21 and "Boatbuilders Adjust to Winds of Fashion," *Business Week,* July 13, 1968, pp. 60–61.

[15] "Getting Fat by Making Others Slim," *Business Week,* March 22, 1969, pp. 140–44.

product class as well as a particular product should be stated explicitly in order to derive the maximum understanding and benefit from use of the product life-cycle concept.

Style and fashion cycles

The concept of the product life cycle applies generally to most products, but a special kind—a fashion cycle—can be seen clearly in markets where style or fashion are important to consumers. A whole category of consumer goods—the heterogenous shopping goods—exists, in part, because of the importance of style or fashion. Usually these goods must be examined to determine their suitability. For instance, women must try on, feel, and look at hats, shoes, and dresses to appraise subtle variations in style or fashion.

The short happy life of fads

The words "style" or "fashion" commonly are used synonymously by consumers. Technically, however, they should be differentiated.

Style is a "characteristic or distinctive mode or method of expression, presentation, or conception in the field of art."[16] Various residential architectural styles such as colonial, Cape Cod, ranch, and modern have come to popularity during certain periods of history.

Fashion, however, refers to the *currently* accepted or popular style in a given field. A particular style of house such as a ranch house or A-frame may be in fashion for a time and then lose its popularity. Or a certain color and style of women's dresses, such as mini style, may be in fashion one year, then outdated the next. It is still a style but no longer a fashion.

A *fad* is a particular fashion that seems fashionable only to certain groups who are enthusiastic about it but so fickle that it is short-lived as a fashion. Some teen-agers' music tastes can be called fads. And chlorophyll, which deodorizes cigarettes, socks, and soap and makes toothpastes, mouthwashes, and even vitamins smell good, has been labeled a fad.[17]

Fashion cycles have stages, too

Consumer acceptance of fashions usually goes through a cycle closely related to consumer buying motives. A fashion cycle is commonly composed of three stages: the *distinctiveness, emulation,* and *economic emulation* stages, which roughly parallel the product life-cycle stages.

In the *distinctiveness* stage, some consumers seeking new styles are especially interested in, and willing to pay for, products that are different from those possessed by the majority. They have products custom-made or patronize manufacturers or distributors who offer goods in small quantities.

[16] P. H. Nystrom, *Economics of Fashion* (New York: Ronald Press Co., 1958), p. 3.

[17] "The Death of a Fad: Chlorophyll Vanishes from Most Products," *Wall Street Journal*, February 9, 1970, p. 1.

If a particular style catches on with a number of style leaders, then other consumers, because of their desire to emulate, may copy them. *Emulation* may come easier as manufacturers begin to make larger quantities of the products that seem to be catching on. This stage can be likened to the early market growth stage of the product life cycle.

Then, if it seems assured that a fashion is going to be popular with a large segment of the population, the product moves into a third stage, *economic emulation.* Manufacturers mass-produce large quantities of the product at low cost, and we move quickly through the market growth stage and maybe through the market maturity stage into sales decline.

Perhaps in the second stage, and certainly in the third stage, the style that began as the private fling of the few becomes less attractive to these original style leaders. They already are trying other styles — which eventually may become fashions and run through another cycle.[18]

How a particular fashion gets started is not well understood. Most present fashions are adaptations or resurrections of previously popular styles. Designers and entrepreneurs continually seek styles that will suit those consumers who want distinctiveness. The results may be exaggerations of earlier styles or perhaps new adaptations of styles from Japan, India, or Egypt.

Predicting what will sell is not easy. Fortunes can be lost in the fashion business by guessing wrong about consumer behavior. Ambrose Bierce once wrote, "Fashion is a despot whom the wise ridicule — and obey." And Thoreau commented, "Every generation laughs at the old fashions but follows religiously the new."[19]

Despite the chancy nature of any fashion-oriented enterprise, businessmen keep trying to find new fashions.[20] It is mostly "trial and error," but there are a few generalizations which are relevant to marketing.

1. Fashions cannot be forced, but many styles can be presented, and when one becomes fashionable, its cycle may be accelerated by aggressive promotion.
2. A higher standard of living and greater mobility encourage a greater interest in fashions.
3. The speed of communication affects the rate of change or acceptance of fashions.
4. Speed in change of fashions increases the cost of producing and marketing products. There are losses due to trial and error in finding acceptable styles, then producing them on a limited basis because of uncertainty about the length of the cycle. These increased costs are not always charged directly to the consumer,

[18] M. T. Copeland, *Principles of Merchandising* (New York: A. W. Shaw Co., 1924), p. 167.

[19] Alfred H. Daniels, "Fashion Merchandising," *Harvard Business Review,* May, 1951, pp. 51–60. See also, Chester R. Wasson, "How Predictable Are Fashion and Other Product Life Cycles?" *Journal of Marketing,* July 1968, pp. 36–43.

[20] "Marketing: Latest Thing in Fashions," *Printers' Ink,* April 26, 1963, pp. 25–30.

since some firms lose their investment and go out of business. But in the aggregate, fashion changes cost consumers money. This added cost resulting from consumer desire and preference for change should not be considered as the "fault" of marketing or business.

Need for product objectives

Guidelines are needed for the whole product-planning process. This is the function of product objectives, which are extensions and elaborations of company objectives. If company objectives are specific with respect to products, there may be no need for product objectives. But if company objectives are very general and are concerned with such matters as sales growth and the possible future direction of the firm, then the marketing manager may have more latitude in his product planning.

To guide his planning, the manager should set down his product objectives. These objectives should apply to his whole program and not just to new products, since he is probably responsible for some established (and perhaps even declining) products, too. But product objectives cannot be conceived in a vacuum. They must flow from overall company objectives and be compatible with the Place, Promotion, and Pricing objectives.

Ideally, product objectives are customer-oriented. But in practical terms, the marketing manager is limited by company resources. The company's productive and executive resources must be considered in developing product objectives, and in fact, wise use of resources might become a product objective. What happens when this kind of objective is adopted is illustrated by the experience of the paper industry in the 1960's. The industry was searching aggressively for new *paper products* to keep the mills going. Yet the emphasis was not on what paper products customers wanted but on what products they wanted that could be made out of paper.[21]

Take more shelves, ship by boxcar

While no one list of product objectives will suit all businesses, here are a few which suggest the range of possibilities.

1. One marketing manager might want to develop a line of products to satisfy not only several consumer markets but also to keep the wholesalers and retailers he supplies happy. He might want to offer a brand at the "top" of his line that would add prestige to the whole line even if the brand itself did not sell well. He might want to develop a "fighting" brand to give his retailers a low-priced brand to meet discount house competition.

[21] "Mills Step Up Research on New Products, Hope to Utilize Idle Capacity," *Wall Street Journal,* December 1, 1961, p. 1.

2. Another marketing manager might want to offer a full line so that he could achieve more shelf space and reinforce his in-store image by increasing the "faces" before the consumer. And the full line might attract enough volume to warrant truckload or rail-carload-size orders, thereby reducing his delivery costs.

3. Another marketing manager might want to practice as much market segmentation as possible. This would have a direct impact on both the new-product planning function and the production department. Such an objective probably would have to be cleared with the production department to avoid later conflicts over the size of production runs. This illustrates, again, why a business system should be considered as a total system.

Need for product policies

Product objectives serve as guides for writing explicit product policies. These policies provide quick answers to routine questions. Consider the marketing manager who is constantly being badgered with salesmen's requests to add new products to the line.

If he has specific policies about adding new products, the answer can be fast and simple. If he doesn't, every request may force him to reevaluate objectives or to give quick answers that he may regret later.

Product policies may actually be determined by specific product objectives or company objectives. For instance, if top management were only interested in selling current products, then one product policy would be definite. All requests to add new products would be refused.

Policies for telling "very good" from "very poor"

As with product objectives, there is no set list of product policies. Generally, however, policies are more specific statements than the objectives and usually they cover recurring problem areas. The product policies of one large manufacturer illustrates some possibilities. This firm developed nine statements of product policy on the following topics:[22]

1. Sales volume.
2. Type and number of competitors.
3. Technical opportunity.
4. Patent protection.
5. Raw materials required.
6. Production load.
7. Value added.
8. Similarity to major business
9. Effect on other products.

[22] Charles H. Kline, "The Strategy of Product Policy," *Harvard Business Review,* July–August, 1955, pp. 91–100.

To illustrate what policy might be written on each topic, three statements are paraphrased from the policy definition of the manufacturer:

1. *Sales volume.* Each product line should have a large potential volume of sales. It should be useful in a number of different applications and salable to a large number of customers.
4. *Patent protection.* Each line should be well protected by patents arising from the company's own discoveries or acquired by purchase or other means.
9. *Effect on other products.* Each line should improve the company's overall sales and profit position, helping to promote the sales of the company's other products. If, however, any new line would hinder the sales of other company products, it should have a greater potential long-range profit than the products in conflict with it.[23]

Such product policies can be used in evaluating present products or selecting new ones. These topics could be used as a checklist. Each present or prospective product could be rated, for example, from "very poor" through "very good."

Table 14–1 shows the evaluation of two proposed products by this same manufacturer. In neither case were all the ratings "very good." But while the product in Case A was different from the present products, it looked very favorable – and it actually developed into a major new business for the company. Case B, however, showed a generally unfavorable pattern, with too many low ratings, and it was not considered further by the company.

Apply product policies to established products, too

When product policies are developed, they should be applied to old products as well as new. A regular procedure should be developed for reviewing established products. Conditions in and out of the company change, and what was wise years ago may prove less desirable now.

Some product lines may have become obsolete, or considerable effort may be devoted to low-volume, relatively unprofitable products.

If the company has only one major line, review may be easy. When sales of White sewing machines were seriously challenged by competition from low-priced Japanese machines, the need for the White Sewing Machine Co. to adjust its product policy became clear. In evaluating its resources, White realized it had no special production strong points – but it did have strength in its marketing organization. White adjusted its product policy accordingly, buying machines from Japan and distributing them under the White name in the United States. The company successfully capitalized on its resources of financial strength, public acceptance of the brand name, and sales and management experience.

For the company with many products and product lines, review of products and policies may be more difficult. A clear understanding of

[23] *Ibid.*

Table 14-1 Examples of summary product appraisals by a large materials processor

Case A: A generally favorable pattern	Rating				
	Very good	Good	Fair	Poor	Very poor
Sales volume	x				
Type and number of competitors	x				
Technical opportunity	x				
Patent protection		x			
Raw materials		x			
Production load		x			
Value added		x			
Similarity to major business				x	
Effect on present products			x		

Case B: A generally unfavorable pattern	Rating				
	Very good	Good	Fair	Poor	Very poor
Sales volume	x				
Type and number of competitors					x
Technical opportunity				x	
Patent protection					x
Raw materials		x			
Production load			x		
Value added		x			
Similarity to major business	x				
Effect on present products	x				

Source: Charles H. Kline, "The Strategy of Product Policy," *Harvard Business Review*, July–August, 1955, pp. 91–100.

the company's whole strategy is important. Over the years, the sales department usually presses for expanding the product line, paying less attention to balancing or reducing the line. But the whole line may be the company's "product." Some seemingly unprofitable items may be very important to some target customers, and dropping them might lead to the loss of very profitable volume in other parts of the line. Understanding the company's overall strategy, therefore, is essential. If the marketing manager knows whom he is aiming at and what they want, then he can correctly define and evaluate the whole "product."[24]

[24] For a good selection of readings on product strategy, see Thomas L. Berg and Abe Shuchman, *Product Strategy and Management* (New York: Holt, Rinehart & Winston, Inc., 1963).

Pruning sick products for better profits	A careful appraisal of the company's product policies plus detailed sales and cost analysis (to be discussed in Chapter 29) may show points at which substantial savings can be made and profits increased. One company with an annual sales volume of $40 million increased the sales volume 50 percent and its profits 20 times during a three-year period by eliminating from its line 16 products with a total volume of $3.3 million. This product pruning not only eliminated unprofitable products but enabled the company to spend more time on the profitable ones.[25]

Need for product managers

	Product managers[26] have evolved to do the job of product planning as well as the continuing management of established products. Product managers are especially common in large companies producing many kinds of products. Sometimes they are responsible for the profitable operation of the whole marketing effort for a particular product. In this capacity, they usually have to coordinate their efforts with those of other executives, including the sales manager, advertising manager, and production and research people.

Whether there is a product manager or not, however, it is obvious that someone must manage Product. The balance of this chapter will cover the special problems of designing and developing new products.

Designing new products

What is a new product— lemons!?	Since there is no consensus on what constitutes a new product, a company should define what *it* means by the term. A simple technical change made by the engineering department might turn out to have an impact on the whole marketing mix or even the marketing strategy if new target markets were attracted by the change, or old markets were repelled!

The market grid concept is relevant here again. The needs and preferences of the customers in the selected market grid box should determine the product design for that target market. The company's present products may have to be modified to satisfy a new market's

[25] Kline, *op. cit.* For further case histories on savings achieved by line simplification or product elimination, see Charles H. Sevin, *How Manufacturers Reduce Their Distribution Costs* (Economic Series No. 72, U.S. Department of Commerce [Washington, D.C.: U.S. Government Printing Office, 1951]). See also, R. S. Alexander, "The Death and Burial of 'Sick' Products," *Journal of Marketing*, April, 1964, pp. 1–7; "Steel Checking Out of the 'Supermarket'," *Business Week*, March 14, 1970, pp. 34–36; Conrad Berenson, "Pruning the Product Line," *Business Horizons*, Summer, 1963, pp. 63–70;

S. A. Greyser, "The Case of the Unproductive Products," *Harvard Business Review*, July–August, 1964, pp. 20–48; and P. Kotler, "Phasing Out Weak Products," *Harvard Business Review*, March–April, 1965, pp. 107–18.

[26] Sometimes they are called brand managers or merchandise managers. See also, David J. Luck and T. Nowak, "Product Management—Vision Unfulfilled," *Harvard Business Review*, May–June, 1965, pp. 143–57.

needs (or the changing needs of present markets). Or the product might not be changed, but perhaps it still should be treated as a "new" product if it is part of a new mix aimed at old or new markets.

In this text, we will consider a product as new if it is *new in any way* for the company concerned. To be considered new, there need not even be a physical change in the product, package, or brand—if different target markets are sought. Lemons illustrate the point.

In the marketing of lemons by one organization, no physical changes were made, but extensive promotion and consumer education created many "new" products. The same old lemons were promoted successfully for lemonade, mixed drinks, diet supplements, cold remedies, lemon cream pies, a salad condiment, dressing for fish, and many other culinary uses. For each of these markets, the product had to go through the early stages of the product life cycle.[27]

A product can be called new for only a limited time. Six months is the maximum time that a product should be called new, according to the Federal Trade Commission. To be called new, says the FTC, a product must be entirely new or changed in "a functionally significant or substantial respect."[28] While six months may seem a very short time for production-oriented businessmen, it may be reasonable in the light of our earlier discussion of the length of product life cycles.

Give the customer the right color

Following the marketing concept, customers' needs or wants should dominate product development. The final choice and design of the product should be compatible with a company's overall objectives and also provide for effective use of resources. But it may be a costly mistake if production-oriented considerations are given precedence over customer wishes.

Customer-oriented decisions must be more than good intentions, however, which is where marketing research comes in. A survey by Rubbermaid, Inc., of Wooster, Ohio showed that the firm's current customers preferred gray or neutral shades for its rubber drainer trays, dish racks, and sink basins. Rubbermaid, however, had been using color to "brighten the home," turning out products in bright blues, reds, yellows, greens. Rubbermaid's president noted, "We get all wrapped up with ourselves out at the plant, sometimes, and when I bring home a new product, my wife will often say, 'Who dreamed that up?'"[29]

Color generally is becoming more important, however, not only for final consumer products but industrial goods too. Black typewriters in perfect condition were retired by some businesses when the colored machines arrived. And more color is being used in industrial machinery and plant design.[30]

[27] See Chester R. Wasson, "What Is 'New' about New Products?" *Journal of Marketing*, July, 1960, pp. 52–56.

[28] *Business Week*, April 22, 1967, p. 120.

[29] *Business Week*, March 21, 1959, p. 92.

[30] Ernest Dichter, "Color Can Stimulate Sales" (Small Marketers Aids No. 85, Small Business Administration, November, 1962).

The product
design must
fit customer
needs

The importance of marketing research in aiding product development
is seen even more clearly in the context of world markets. Variations
from one nation to another in taste and expectations emphasize the
need for finding out what the target customer wants and needs.

The Japanese are designing their own "Western style" furniture
because Japanese customers find copies of Western designs uncomfortable.[31] Picks, shovels, and even tractor seats designed for sale in
Africa must be made smaller than those sold in Western countries,
because potential users are smaller in size.[32]

To help assure good product design, the internationally minded
management of one firm checks the factors listed in Table 14-2. These
factors are general, and the answers might vary from target market to
target market—but if any is found relevant, the implications for marketing mix planning are obvious.

Table 14-2 Considerations and their implications in designing for world
markets

Considerations	Implications
Level of technical skills	Product simplification
Level of labor cost	Automation or manualization of product
Level of literacy	Remarking and simplification of product
Level of income	Quality and price change
Level of interest rates	Quality and price change (investment in high quality might not be financially desirable)
Level of maintenance	Change in tolerances
Climatic differences	Product adaptation
Isolation (heavy repair diffi- cult and expensive)	Product simplification and reliability improvement
Differences in standards	Recalibration of product and resizing
Availability of other products	Greater or lesser product integration
Availability of materials	Change in product structure and fuel
Power availability	Resizing of product
Special conditions	Product redesign or invention

Source: Reprinted from the *Journal of Marketing,* national quarterly publication of the American
Marketing Association. Richard D. Robinson, "The Challenge of the Underdeveloped Market,"
Journal of Marketing, October, 1961, Vol. 25, p. 22.

An example involving one of these factors, *level of maintenance,*
shows why it is essential to know each market.

An African government purchased hand-operated dusters for applying pesticides to cotton fields. The product supplied by the American manufacturer was a finely machined device that turned more

[31] "Japan's Newest Quest for Quality," *Business
Week,* July 28, 1962, pp. 98–100.

[32] Edward Marcus, "Selling the Tropical African
Market," *Journal of Marketing,* July, 1961, p. 27; see
also "Some Firms Simplify Products for Markets in
Poorer Countries," *Wall Street Journal,* May 27,
1969, pp. 1 f; and "More New Products Now Are
Designed with User in Mind," *Wall Street Journal,*
September 24, 1968, pp. 1 f.

easily than competing equipment but required regular oiling for good care. Used in the African cotton fields, however, the duster seldom was oiled properly, and it quickly broke down. The government went back to an older French duster which didn't work as well but also didn't need regular oiling and so lasted longer. In this market, the French product was superior because it met the target customers' needs.[33]

Keeping score on product design

Market research alone, however, cannot assure good product design. Some management judgement must be used. Consumers have been notoriously unreliable in predicting what they will like.

Since some judgment and risk will probably always be involved, the checklist in Figure 14–3 may help management to narrow the areas in which judgment is necessary.[34] This checklist is useful because it usually is safer to make 12 separate small judgments than one large "yes" or "no" judgment.

On this checklist, a score of "yes" on 11 or 12 questions would indicate a good design; 9 or 10 points, a fair design (with "no" answers indicating weak spots to be corrected); and below 9 points, a poor

Figure 14–3

Good design: Does your product have it?	Yes	No
1. Does the product's present design reflect quality?	——	——
2. Is the present design economical to manufacture?	——	——
3. Is the design well accepted by wholesalers, retailers, salesmen and customers?	——	——
√ 4. Is the design in tune with current design trends?	——	——
5. Does the design have a comparatively long life?	——	——
√ 6. Are the details of the product well designed?	——	——
7. Does the design contribute to the product's usefulness, safety, and convenience?	——	——
8. Are the materials used practical for product's end use?	——	——
9. Is the color right for use and environment?	——	——
10. Is the size right for best use?	——	——
11. Is the weight right for best use?	——	——
12. Does the design stand up well with competition?	——	——

design, probably indicating that profits will be reduced through lost sales and possibly through high manufacturing costs. This list is suitable for all manufactured products except high-fashion women's apparel—which is a world of its own. Adaptions must be made for services.

---

[33] Richard D. Robinson, "The Challenge of the Underdeveloped Market," *Journal of Marketing*, October, 1961, p. 21.

[34] Victor Petertil, "Is Your Product Designed to Sell?" *Management Methods*, July, 1958, p. 48.

To see how this list could be helpful, try it on some product you bought recently.

Designing for market segmentation or product differentiation

The product design selected by a firm may depend on whether it is following a policy of market segmentation or product differentiation. Market segmentation would suggest designing a product precisely to meet the needs of some unique target market.

Product differentiation might mean building several features into a product to make it more appealing to more people. For example, extra features might be added to a camera *without* making it too complicated for amateurs. This would enable the camera manufacturer to appeal to more buyers with the same product. This approach might appeal to production-oriented people because it might allow longer production runs, offsetting the added cost of adding extra features. Decisions about a step like this, however, should be made only after a careful analysis of the potential target markets. Adding more features to a camera might make it look more complicated and scare off more customers than it attracted.

Safety should be considered in design too

The marketing concept would certainly lead to the design of safety into products, if potential customers want it. But, as already noted, the consumerism movement is focusing greater attention on this subject and finding fertile ground in some places. Apparently, production-oriented businessmen have not always paid as much attention to this matter as might be desirable. Some people have been seriously injured due to design failures.

Large court settlements for defective designs have increased business' interest in safety. But consumers' newfound interest in safety is worth noting also. Early efforts (in the late 1940's and early 1950's) to "sell" seat belts to American motorists were not successful. The Ford Motor Company backed off from its efforts to sell safety when it found that consumers were not too concerned about needs which they personally did not feel. Now, a change in the social environment has caused much more interest in the matter by both politicians and businessmen.[35]

For the intermediate customer, new pop, better sales help

All people who handle, sell, or use a product must be considered when developing a product. Manufacturers' marketing managers have to look at their products through the eyes of intermediate customers as well as final consumers. For example, retailers or wholesalers might need a wider product line than a manufacturer is currently providing. Coca-Cola added several new products to its line – Fanta, Sprite, Tab, Fresca, and even orange juice – to satisfy bottler and consumer demands. Yet the company moved too slowly for some of its bottler

---

[35] "Detroit Presses Drive to Reduce the Number of Defects in Autos," *Wall Street Journal,* September 24, 1968, pp. 1 f; "The Pressure Is on for Safer Products," *Business Week,* July 4, 1970, pp. 36–44; "America the Inefficient," *Time,* March 23, 1970, pp. 72–80; and "New Agency Strives to Make Life Safer in and around Home," *Wall Street Journal,* May 12, 1969, pp. 1 f.

customers, and they had begun promoting their own lemon-lime soda, "Veep."[36]

The trend to self-service in some retail outlets has forced product designers to make many product changes. Multi-packs may help the retailer as well as the consumer. And good product instructions and sizing aids for clothes may have to be built into the product to compensate for the lack of personal selling effort. One firm that sells its sleeper-suit pajamas through self-service outlets prints a size formula on the package. The customer can estimate the correct size without the help of a clerk. In fact, the information on the package may be even more helpful in selecting these clothes than the typical clerk.

New-product development: a total company effort

Some organization helps

A new-product development department or committee helps assure that new ideas for products are carefully evaluated and good ones profitably marketed. Delays may lead to late test marketing or market introduction and give competition a head start in the product life cycle. A delay of even six months may make the difference between a product's success or failure in a competitive market.

A well-organized development procedure might even enable a firm to copy others' attractive innovations quickly and profitably. This possibility should not be overlooked. No one company can hope to be first always, with the best.[37]

Top-level support vital

New-product development must have the enthusiastic support of top management. New products tend to disrupt the old routines that managers of established products may try in subtle but effective ways to maintain. So someone should be responsible for this effort. The organizational arrangement may not be too important, as long as new-product development has top-level support.[38]

Complicated integrated effort needed

Developing new products should be a total company effort, as Figure 14-4 shows. Here, we see that the whole process is a sequential activity involving personnel in management, research, production, promotion, packaging, and branding. The process moves from an early exploration of ideas and concepts (see Figure 14-4) to a development of the product and product-related concepts. Technical development

[36]"Coke Tries New Ways to Refresh," *Business Week*, August 24, 1963, pp. 100–110; and *Printers' Ink*, February 10, 1961, p. 5.

[37]See T. Levitt, "Innovative Imitation," *Harvard Business Review*, September–October, 1966, pp. 63–70.

[38]William A. Bours, III, "Imagination Wears Many Hats," *Journal of Marketing*, October, 1966, pp. 59–61; John H. Murphy, "New Products Need Special Management," *Journal of Marketing*, October,

1962, pp. 46–49; S. C. Johnson and Conrad Jones, "How to Organize for New Products," *Harvard Business Review*, May–June, 1957; E. J. McCarthy, "Organization for New Product Development?" *Journal of Business of the University of Chicago*, April, 1959, pp. 128–32; and James H. Wolter, "An Analysis of the Process of New Product Idea Evaluation for Consumer Goods" (unpublished Ph.D. dissertation, Indiana University, 1960).

Figure 14-4 New-product market development sequence

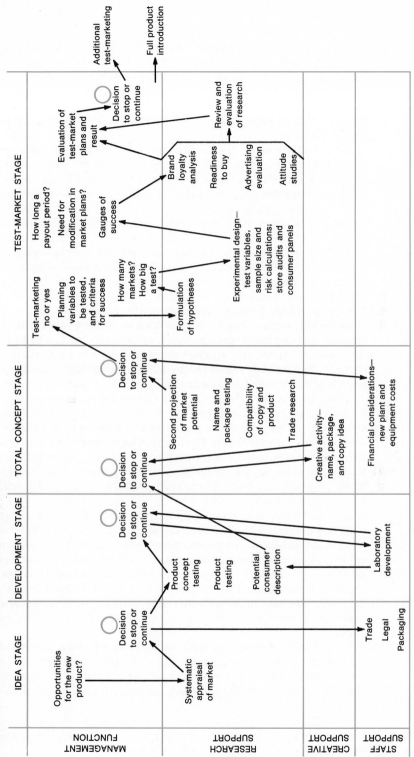

Source: Benton & Bowles Research and *Printers' Ink*, April 13, 1962, pp. 22-23.

of the product itself is not the first step in new-product development. Concept appraisal comes first. Many items can be produced—even a Rube Goldberg device can be developed, but who wants it?

After the product and related concepts have been developed, the total concept—really, the total marketing mix—is developed and matched against the company's resources to see whether the product looks profitable.

If the answer is yes, then management must make another decision: Does it want to test-market, before a full-scale market introduction? This is not a trivial decision, because, as noted in Chapter 4, although test marketing may test out ideas, it also may tip the company's hand to competition. After seeing the speed of product life cycles, we can better understand why some managements are reluctant to test-market.

The role of marketing management and top management in product development is shown in Figure 14-4. Management has the power to push or veto development, but to keep it going it must commit more funds. These sequential decisions become more difficult as the process proceeds because the costs are increasing.

Some of the many marketing research techniques applicable in new product development are indicated in Figure 14-4. Yet even with these careful plans and studies many new products *do* fail—about 50 percent of all those marketed by larger companies. And the rate is even higher for smaller companies.[39]

The rejection rate for new ideas during this new-product development process is even higher. One study of 80 companies found that only 1 out of 40 new ideas survived the kind of organized development process we have just discussed. The rate of rejection, however, varies; an especially conservative organization, for example, might have even more rejects. A well-known investment firm found that of 2,100 new-product propositions studied, only 17 had real merit.[40]

Flowcharts point the way

Some marketing managers and analysts find it helpful to draw flowcharts or diagrams of all of the interrelated tasks that must be accomplished on schedule. In recent years, some firms have successfully applied such flowcharting techniques as CPM (critical path method) or PERT (program evaluation and review technique). These techniques were originally developed as part of the United States' space program (NASA) to insure that the various contractors and subcontractors' efforts would stay on schedule and reach their goals as planned.

The detailed flowcharts used in these approaches describe which marketing activities must be done in sequence and which can be done concurrently. These charts also show the time allotments needed for various activities. By totaling the time allotments along the various

[39] *Management of the New Products* (Chicago: Booz-Allen & Hamilton, 1960), p. 14.

[40] Paul Stillson and E. Leonard Arnoff, "Product Search and Evaluation," *Journal of Marketing,* July, 1957, p. 33.

chart paths, the most critical (the longest) path, as well as the most desirable starting and ending dates for the various activities within the project will be shown.

The flowchart approach is credited with helping Diamond Alkali Co. avoid a difficult situation when introducing a new product. By spending a few days flowcharting their plans for this product, Diamond Alkali found that they would spend about 76 weeks introducing it—although their predetermined schedule had allotted only 36 weeks for the introduction. By rearranging their plans with the aid of the flowchart technique, they were able to squeeze the effort into 36 weeks. Now the use of flowcharts is mandatory for all Diamond Alkali new-product introductions.

Basically, a flowcharting effort follows a number of logical steps. First, a marketing strategy is needed. Then the various elements of the strategy which must be implemented over a period of time must be listed. Each of these elements, in turn, must be broken down into subelements or activities. A basic element such as sales promotion probably would include "Preparing a Sales Brochure." But this, in turn, would require detailed activities such as preparing performance charts and graphs, preparing rough copy, agency preparation of preliminary copy and layouts, and so on.

These activities are then flowcharted to pinpoint the bottlenecks.

The Diamond Alkali analysts isolated 105 activities, some of which could be done concurrently, but others which had to be done sequentially. Figure 14-5 shows the complete diagram drawn by Diamond Alkali analysts, with a heavier line drawn through the critical path which would have delayed the product introduction and very likely reduced its total profitability.

It should be noted that this charting is *not* unduly complicated. The Diamond Alkali chart took two men only about two days. Basically what it requires is that all of the activities which will have to be performed anyway be identified ahead of time and their probable duration and sequence shown on one diagram. (Nothing more than addition and subtraction is used.) Working with such information should be part of the planning function, anyway. Then the chart can be extremely useful for guiding implementation and control.

Outside testing organizations may improve product planning

Some firms that are not strongly market-oriented may be nudged by outside testing organizations into a more careful consideration of the customer during the product development process. The work of these testing organizations affects the market in two ways:

Provide customer-accepted research reports

Private testing laboratories may do testing for firms that do not have their own laboratories. But even more important, they can give their seal of approval to products, and this in itself may improve a product's chance for success.

Some of the organizations that evaluate products and allow use of their own brands, seals, or trademarks as an additional guarantee of the quality of the product are: the Underwriters Laboratories, the

Figure 14-5 How diamond alkali diagrams the critical path for new-product introduction

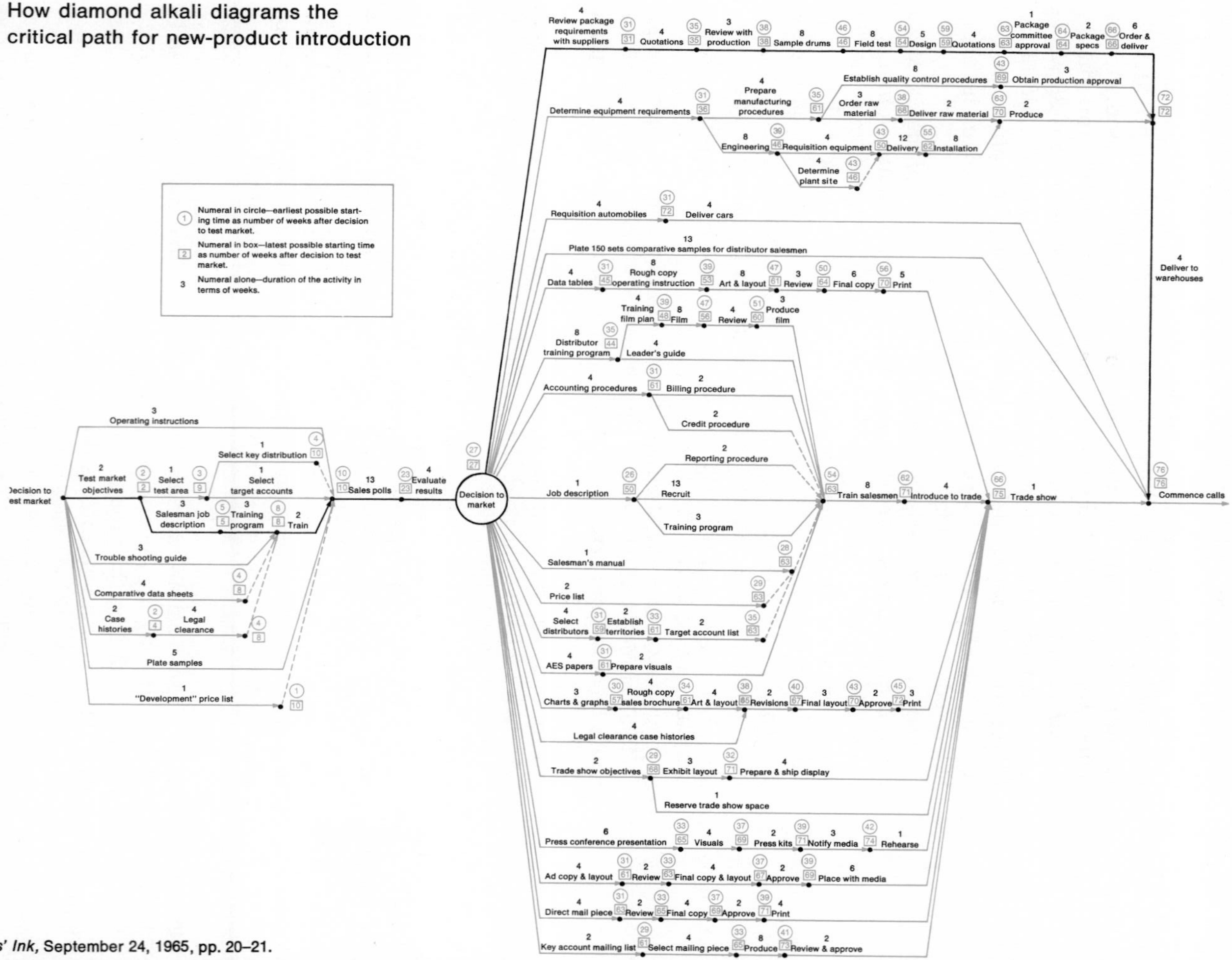

Source: *Printers' Ink*, September 24, 1965, pp. 20–21.

American Gas Association, the American Institute of Laundering, *Good Housekeeping, Parent's* magazine, *McCall's,* U.S. Testing Co., and the York Research Corp. (associated with *Reader's Digest*).[41]

Forces customer orientation

Two consumer-sponsored rating organizations in the United States report on and evaluate a wide variety of products in their own monthly magazines. High ratings in *Consumer Reports* and *Consumers Research* have been known to increase sales, while low ratings have prompted product changes.[42]

Similar testing abroad by members of the International Association of Consumer Unions has been similarly effective. An unfavorable report about an automatic washer in a German consumer publication caused the washer maker's market share to drop from 38 to 20 percent. Another manufacturer of spin driers lost his contract with a large mail-order company because of unfavorable ratings.

Evaluation of product planning

"Planned obsolescence" can't be all bad
Deliberately developing new products, sometimes only slightly updating them in the hopes of replacing older but still serviceable models has roused the ire of some critics of marketing. Such "planned obsolescence," as it is called by its critics, is especially common in the automobile, appliance, and clothing industries, where new styles or fashions are introduced at least once each year. The critics are concerned, among other reasons, because products that are not yet worn out may be discarded by some consumers.

Some marketers see this so-called "planned obsolescence" as simply new-product planning. Regular introduction of such new products certainly has advantages for some producers and middlemen, since new models may help them out of the market maturity stage of a product life cycle and back into the more profitable market growth stage. The effectiveness of this approach may depend on which part of the market grid is the target. Volkswagen customers seem satisfied with little change from year to year, while many others are attracted by yearly model changes.

Much of the continued innovation that is manifested in new-model introductions seems to have been forced upon producers by the demands of some market segments and competitive pressures. Continued novelty seems to satisfy some consumer needs. Marketing research sometimes shows that customers truly prefer a face-lifted model to the old model simply because it is new, perhaps for prestige reasons. Recall our discussion of the early stage of the fashion cycle. Catering to such needs can even be seen as a policy of market segmen-

---

[41] For a description of testing techniques, see "Testing the Product," *Industrial Design,* November, 1960, pp. 41–51.

[42] *Wall Street Journal,* March 15, 1962, p. 1.

tation. Without this continued newness, these innovation-minded segments of the market would not be truly satisfied.[43]

It can be argued further that planned obsolescence not only satisfies many customers but also encourages research and investment, helping to maintain high levels of employment.

"Old" products, moreover, are not always wasted. There is a large secondhand market in those markets where innovation and product changes are more rapid. In fact, a strong secondhand market seems to encourage change, making it less costly and economically more feasible for more customers. In the automobile market, for example, there is a ready secondhand market. A car may be sold several times before it is finally junked. The furniture market, on the other hand, has no organized secondhand market, and furniture is not replaced nearly as rapidly, to the sorrow of many housewives.

"Obsolescence" or "planning," it keeps customers supplied

Further support for aggressive and continuing product differentiation and market segmentation comes from an unexpected source.

The earlier Soviet practice of producing only homogeneous products was not successful. And so, responding to consumer wishes, Soviet production agencies have been expanding product variety. The Soviet radio-TV industry offers 30 to 40 different brands of radios and phonographs and about 20 types of television sets.

In fact, Soviet interest in product variety has even spread to laundry soap and detergents, important areas of product differentiation in the United States.[44] Witnessing this development, one American specialist on Soviet economic affairs feels that many American critics of marketing may have underestimated the advantages of our present economic system and ought to reevaluate their thinking.

Clearly, what the critics call "planned obsolescence" and the marketing practitioners call "product planning," may have a number of desirable characteristics. In any case, these practices seem to be responses to some customer demands in a competitive marketplace.

Conclusion

Product planning is an increasingly vital activity in a modern economy because it is no longer very profitable to sell just "commodities." And product planning must be continuous to meet the dynamic and innovating competition which is causing product life cycles to shorten.

The product life-cycle concept is especially important to marketing strategy planning because it shows that different marketing mixes, and even strategies, are needed as a product moves through its cycle. This is an important point because profits change during the cycle, with most of the profits going to the innovators or fast copiers.

[43] See, for example, H. M. Case, "Designed Decay," *Harvard Business Review,* January–February, 1966, pp. 126–31.

[44] Marshall I. Goldman, "A New Perspective on Product Differentiation and Advertising: The Soviet View," *Business Review,* Boston University, Spring, 1962, pp. 3–12.

It is clear that effective management of Product is important, and this led us to a consideration of product objectives and policies, and of new-product development.

Once a company has decided on its overall objectives, it is wise to specify product objectives. These are simply more specific statements of the implications of the overall objectives with respect to products. Specifically, there might be statements about the type of products to be offered, the width of product line, and how much newness should be worked into new products.

Within the limits of company and product objectives, it is desirable to set down written product policies. These may be rewordings of the product objectives, but they should offer definite answers to recurring problems. If one objective is to cater to the mass market, then a product policy might state that all new products should satisfy this market (and by implication all products not aimed at this market would be rejected).

Possible product objectives and policies were suggested, although there is no single list applying to all situations.

We pointed out that a new product is not limited to physical newness. We will call a product "new" if it is new in any way — to any target market.

New products are so important to the survival of firms in our competitive economy that some organized method for developing them is needed. A general approach was discussed, but it is obvious that it must be a total company effort to be successful.

The failure rate of new products is high, but it is considerably lower for larger and better-managed firms that have recognized product planning as a vital function in the business process. Some firms have appointed product managers to manage individual product lines and new-product committees to assure that the process is carried out successfully. And some use flowcharting techniques to plan and control the new product development and introduction process. It is clear that modern product planning can help improve marketing strategy planning in a competitive world where more and more products are being demanded and offered.

QUESTIONS AND PROBLEMS

1 Cite two examples of products which you feel are currently in each of the product life-cycle stages.

2 Explain how different conclusions might be reached with respect to the correct product life-cycle stage(s) in the automobile market, especially if the market grid concept is used.

3 Discuss the life cycle of a product in terms of its probable impact on a manufacturer's marketing mix. Illustrate, using battery-operated toothbrushes.

4 If product differentiation or market segmentation efforts are especially successful, some people feel that this will accelerate the trend toward similar products. They point to the refrigerator market as an example. Comment on the idea of "success breeding its own downfall."

5 Distinguish among a fad, style, and fashion. How should a retailer adapt to them? Some people maintain that fads or fashions can be created by businessmen. Can you give an example of any business firm that has *consistently* created successful fads or fashions? *Consistently* is important, because anyone can be lucky a few times; the successes are publicized but the failures are not.

6 What overall objectives and product objectives might a recent business college graduate set for himself if he has a desire to go into a business of his own. He has already had some electronics sales experience and has $30,000 to invest. After setting the objectives, what product policies logically flow from it? In answering this question, "product" must be considered broadly to include the services he may contribute to this enterprise.

7 A farmer has discovered a large deposit of sand just below his topsoil and is considering going into the sand and gravel business. After all, he feels, "I already have my product ready-made." Evaluate his thinking. Should he go into this business? Specify any assumptions necessary to obtain a definite answer.

8 Explain why product policies should be written.

9 Should there be different product policies for new and for established products?

10 Discuss what is a new product and why it is important to make this distinction.

11 Discuss the thinking which should go into the design of washing machines for the Latin American market, using the checklist in Table 14–2.

12 Discuss how the checklist "Good design: Does your product have it?" (Figure 14–3) could be used to evaluate: (*a*) a can opener, (*b*) a baby stroller, (*c*) men's hats (fedoras), (*d*) a coffeemaker.

13 Explain the importance of an organized new-product development process and illustrate how it might be used for: (*a*) an improved phonograph, (*b*) new frozen-food items, (*c*) a new children's toy.

14 Some persons criticize planned obsolescence as it encourages the disposal of goods which are not yet completely worn out. What assumptions are they making about consumer preferences and behavior? Are these assumptions valid?

15 Discuss the social value of planned obsolescence policies, especially when they encourage people to discard products which are not "all worn out." Is this an economic waste? How worn out is "all worn out"? Must a shirt have holes in it? How big?

...what is the importance of time and place utility? How much satisfaction would a Chicago consumer derive from owning a pound of coffee in Brazil? How happy would a coed be if her date brought her a certificate showing that she owned one orchid in Hawaii?

...look at Place in terms of supply and demand.... Here the job of marketing is to match supply capabilities to the demands of the many target markets, moving goods wherever they are needed.

15

Place — introduction

Your product may be the best in the world, but it will be of little use to the customer if it is not *where* he wants it *when* he wants it. In the next five chapters, we will take a look at all of the activities and institutions needed to provide "Place." For simplicity, we will use the term *place* to refer to all of the factors that go into providing the time, and place, and possession utilities needed to satisfy target customers, just as we use *Product* to mean the "total product" offered.

Place decisions are concerned with the location of marketing facilities and the selection and use of marketing specialists, including transportation and storage agencies, wholesalers, and retailers. Some of the material we will discuss may seem theoretical and descriptive, but it is extremely important that the marketing manager understand the *why* and *what* of present distribution methods so that he can effectively plan for the future.

In our dynamic economy, marketing facilities are in such a constant state of flux that the marketing manager must continually evaluate his own (and his competitor's) current and possible place offerings. He should be constantly alert to market shifts that provide new opportunities or cause new problems. Established place facilities may grow inefficient and need to be changed, or unfilled needs might offer an opportunity for a marketing "breakthrough."

Place decisions hard to change

Place doesn't just happen, contrary to the feelings of some production-oriented businessmen. To be sure, there are lots of wholesalers and retailers around. And there are many wholesale and retail facilities for rent to prospective middlemen. But are they the right place facilities?

The marketing manager's decisions on Place may be the most important ones he makes because they have long-range implications and are harder to change than Product, Price, and Promotion decisions. It is difficult to move retail and wholesale facilities once leases have been signed and customer movement patterns have been established. Cordial working arrangements with middlemen can take several years and a good deal of money to develop. Place decisions are likely to be the *one-time strategic decisions* whose importance we discussed in Chapter 2.

Place is so important and yet so poorly understood that we will examine the subject carefully, beginning with a theoretical discussion and then building our understanding on this solid foundation.

Place provides time, place, and possession utility

Economists usually define four kinds of utility: form, time, place, and possession. So far we have considered only the creation of form utility — the development of a product. But the other three utilities are equally important. A customer can use a product only if it is in his *possession* at the right *time*. And to possess a product it must be in a *place* convenient to him.

The idea of possessing a product is understood easily when physical products are considered, but the same basic idea applies to pure services. They are just perishable "products" which cannot be stored. And place is still important. Customers would prefer to have services available where and when they want them, too.

In the following discussion, we will emphasize the place problems of physical products because they may require special handling, storing, and transporting. But most of the concepts are equally applicable to the marketing of pure services. Location, for example, is often of great importance for goods *and* services.

There's an awful lot of coffee in Brazil—and Chicago

We sometimes overlook why we can get a cup of coffee or a rubber tire or a woolen suit, apart from the fact that we have the money to buy them.

One of the functions of marketing is to provide a product possessing form utility with time and place utility.[1] Only when this is done can the customer plunk down his 15 cents and enjoy possession utility of a cup of coffee.

What is the importance of time and place utility? How much satisfaction would a Chicago consumer derive from owning a pound of coffee in Brazil? How happy would a coed be if her date brought her a certificate showing that she owned one orchid in Hawaii? Or consider the value of tire chains at the factory during a snowstorm or electric fans in the warehouse during a heat wave.

Look at Place in terms of supply and demand. Producers are willing to supply products and consumers may be demanding them, yet no transactions take place unless the buyers and sellers get together. Here, the job of marketing is to match supply capabilities to the demands of the many target markets, moving goods wherever they are needed.

Markets develop to facilitate exchange

The historical development of organizations specializing in providing time and place utility, which we call simply *Place,* was sketched in Chapter 1. You will recall that marketing was not necessary when families existed as self-sufficient units. As these family units developed surpluses and became interested in bartering for other products, Place became relevant. The products had to be brought together before they could be exchanged.

We assumed in our earlier discussion that this trade would be mutually beneficial. Now we must see why and how, for the marketing manager who understands the advantage of such exchange may find new and better ways to accomplish it.

Begin by asking why central markets have developed. Suppose a group of five families found that each has some special skill for producing some item. After meeting basic subsistence needs, each family might decide to specialize. This decision would be very practical. It is easier for one family to make two pots and another to make two baskets than it is for either to make one pot and one basket. Specialization makes labor more efficient and more productive.

If these five families specialize in one product apiece, they will have to trade with each other. As Figure 15–1 shows, it would take the five families 10 separate trips and exchanges to obtain some of each

---

[1] Wroe Alderson, *Marketing Behavior and Executive Action* (Homewood, Ill.: Richard D. Irwin, Inc., 1957), p. 199. See also, Wroe Alderson, "The Analytical Framework for Marketing," in Perry Bliss, *Marketing and the Behavioral Sciences* (Boston: Allyn & Bacon, Inc., 1963), pp. 25–43.

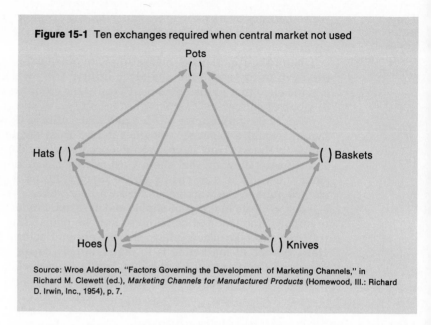

Figure 15-1 Ten exchanges required when central market not used

Pots

Hats

Baskets

Hoes

Knives

Source: Wroe Alderson, "Factors Governing the Development of Marketing Channels," in Richard M. Clewett (ed.), *Marketing Channels for Manufactured Products* (Homewood, Ill.: Richard D. Irwin, Inc., 1954), p. 7.

of the products. If the families live near each other, the exchange process would be relatively simple. But if they are far apart, travel back and forth will be time-consuming. And who would do the traveling and when?

Faced with this problem, the families can agree to come to a central market and trade on a certain day. Then, each family would need to make only one trip into the market to trade with all the others, reducing the total number of trips to five. The reason for the development of central markets is clear. They facilitated exchange, left more time for production, and also served as social gatherings.

Modern economies are well beyond this simple example, but the principle still holds. The fundamental purpose of markets is to facilitate exchange and allow greater time for production or other activities, including leisure.

Money system speeds trading

But while a central meeting place would simplify exchange, all of the individual bartering transactions would still take much time. Bartering takes another party who wants what you have and vice versa. Each trader must find others who have products of approximately equal value. After trading with one group, a family might find itself with a collection of hats, knives, and pots, and then it would have to find others who were willing to trade for these products.

A money system would change all of this. A seller would merely find a buyer who can either use or sell his product, negotiate the price, and be free to spend his money to buy whatever he wants.

Specialists facilitate trade even more

Even though a money system simplifies the trading, considerable time and effort are needed to complete all transactions among the families. And once they were using money, each family head might have to open (and pay for) a stall at the market, while other family members shopped at other parts of the market.

Enter the middleman   The exchange process can be facilitated by the appearance of a dealer who is willing to trade with the families for *all* of their surpluses in exchange for what they need (see Figure 15–2).

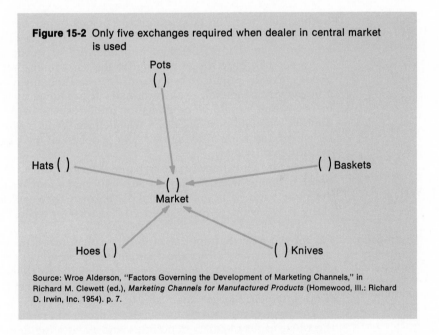

Figure 15-2 Only five exchanges required when dealer in central market is used

Source: Wroe Alderson, "Factors Governing the Development of Marketing Channels," in Richard M. Clewett (ed.), *Marketing Channels for Manufactured Products* (Homewood, Ill.: Richard D. Irwin, Inc. 1954). p. 7.

In our simple example, using the services of a dealer at a central market, the 10 exchanges needed previously are now reduced to 5. Such a dealer would make a charge for this service, but if the time saved were considerable, each family might have more time for production at home and visiting at the market. Each family could specialize in production and let the dealer specialize in trading.

Such dealers, offering permanent trading facilities, are known today as wholesalers and retailers. The advantages of working with a dealer become substantial as the number of producers and customers, their distance apart, and the number and variety of competing products increase. That is why there are so many wholesalers and retailers in more complex economies.[2]

Discrepancies of quantity and assortment must be adjusted

Marketing managers must continually adjust supply to demand. The process is somewhat more complicated than the simple supply and demand analysis we discussed earlier, however, because there are (1) so many different demands on the market grid for a general type of product and (2) many different kinds of middlemen and producers with different costs and objectives. To simplify our introductory discussion, we will consider the discrepancies between producers and final users or consumers.

Discrepancies typically occur

Rather than wanting large quantities of one item, customers usually are more interested in an assortment of products to serve some specific purpose. The assortment and quantity of goods wanted by a customer has little direct relation to the assortment and quantity of goods normally produced by a manufacturer. Probably no two products a housewife needs for a cake are made or produced by the same firm or farm; flour would be produced by millers specializing in flour production who had purchased the wheat from farmers who specialized in wheat (or from middlemen who specialized in handling larger quantities of wheat).

It is clear that there are discrepancies both of *quantity* and *assortment* between what producers normally make and what consumers normally want. It is important to distinguish between the two, especially if we want to understand why marketing specialists develop.

Discrepancy of quantity— don't put all your golf balls in one place

Earlier we saw that specialization by a firm often makes economic sense. A company offers those products (or services) that it can produce most efficiently, given its resources and objectives. Rather than offering small quantities of many items, most producers now specialize in producing larger quantities of a few items.

The large quantities that specialized production makes possible are the cause of discrepancy of quantity and a major factor in the development of specialists. Few customers have such large demands for specific items that they can consume a big part of the producer's output. If a customer did need a large quantity of an item, it might be more economical for him to make it himself.

Consider the movement of golf balls from manufacturers to golfers

[2] One author has developed a ratio of advantage that demonstrates clearly how the advantages offered by middlemen grow fast as the size of the market grows. See Wroe Alderson, "Factors Governing the Development of Marketing Channels," Richard M. Clewett (ed.), *Marketing Channels for Manufactured Products* (Homewood, Ill.: Richard D. Irwin, Inc., 1954), pp. 7–9, for further elaboration.

as shown in Figure 15-3. Most manufacturers of golf balls produce in large quantities, such as 200,000, 400,000, or 500,000, in a given time period. The average golfer, however, is interested only in a few balls at a time—say 1 to 12 balls for this same time period.

For a golf ball manufacturer to deal directly with thousands of golfers—perhaps more than 100,000 in all—would be a Herculean task. For one thing, it would be necessary to use cash to avoid a costly

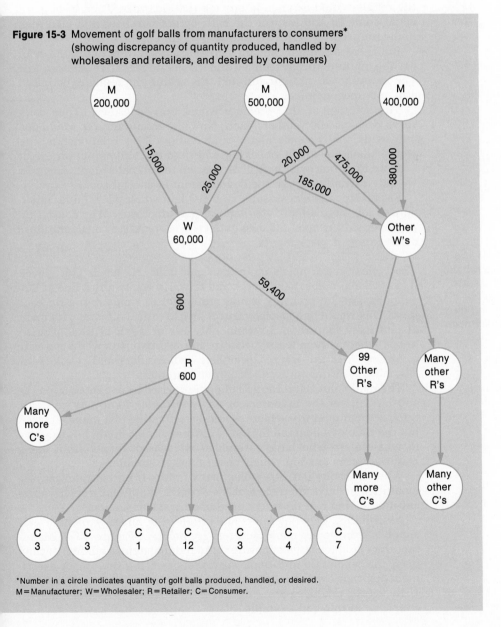

Figure 15-3 Movement of golf balls from manufacturers to consumers*
(showing discrepancy of quantity produced, handled by
wholesalers and retailers, and desired by consumers)

*Number in a circle indicates quantity of golf balls produced, handled, or desired.
M = Manufacturer; W = Wholesaler; R = Retailer; C = Consumer.

investigation of each potential customer's credit rating, even though requiring cash would annoy many customers. And each individual order would have to be mailed to the customer's home, unless the manufacturer opened thousands of his own retail stores handling only golf balls.

A local specialist—a retailer—might develop to fill the obvious need of all these individual consumers for a product. If the demands from golfers in the locality totaled, say, 600 balls for a specific time period, the retailer could arrange to provide that quantity. Then each golfer could come in and inspect the balls before purchase and take them home immediately. This retailer also might extend credit.

But there still might remain a great discrepancy between the quantity the manufacturer produced and the quantity each retailer wanted. The manufacturer might still find this selling the retailers both difficult and uneconomical.

The solution of this problem would be wholesalers. They could serve perhaps 100 retailers each. Now the manufacturer would deal only with a few wholesalers, establishing closer relationships that would facilitate credit checking and quantity shipments on credit.

If we limit our hypothetical discussion to golf balls alone, however, we only partially explain the development of specialists.

For instance, why can some independent wholesalers and retailers do this job more effectively than the manufacturer? Why doesn't the producer simply open his own outlets? This requires consideration of discrepancy of assortments.

Discrepancy of assortments— giving the customer a choice

The typical golfer needs more than golf balls. He needs golf gloves, hats, jackets, clubs, bags, carts, and tees. He wants a full line of golf supplies, and he probably would prefer *not* to shop around for each item. This would be especially true if he had to deal directly with many distant manufacturers. He wants only *one or a few* of each of many items, whereas producers specialize in making one or a few items in *quantity*. It is the job of specialists—wholesalers and retailers—to assemble assortments for their target customers.

The total value of all the golf supplies carried by one retailer may be substantial, yet the inventory of any *particular* item may be small. Such a small quantity seldom would be attractive to a manufacturer, but the retailer's demand for *many* different items might be attractive to wholesalers who have assembled wide assortments from many manufacturers to supply their target market—retailers.

When a wholesaler assembles many orders from his retailers, the quantities he buys from each of his supplier-manufacturers becomes substantial and can represent an economical transaction.

Assembling, by wholesalers and retailers, of an assortment of golf supplies from many manufacturers is shown in Figure 15-4. Manufacturers produce large quantities of individual items and then depend upon the wholesale and retail specialists to bring the proper assortments to their own retailer and final customers.

In actual practice, bringing goods to customers is not quite so simple as in this golf example.

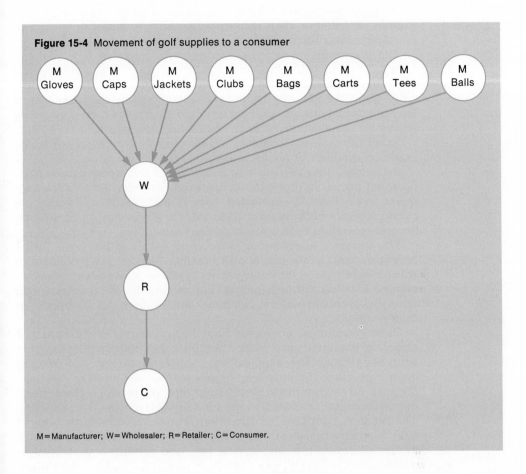

Figure 15-4 Movement of golf supplies to a consumer

M=Manufacturer; W=Wholesaler; R=Retailer; C=Consumer.

A retailer may buy golf supplies from many wholesalers, not just one, especially if they carry different brands. It is likely that both the wholesaler and retailer would carry more than golf supplies. The retailer might be a general sporting goods dealer, carrying golfing items only as a minor part of his line. In addition, there are wholesalers who supply other wholesalers, not retailers. These complications will be discussed later.

The point to remember is that discrepancies in quantity or assortment or both may cause specialists to develop.

Why discrepancies happen and how they are adjusted

Quantity dis- *Collecting* substantial supplies of homogeneous products – the *accu-*
crepancies *mulation process* – creates the first discrepancy of quantity. In a
– cutting factory, the products that pass inspection are accumulated over a
costs if day or a week for shipment in economic lots. In agricultural commodi-
possible ties, specialists (wholesalers) typically accumulate the production of a

379

number of farmers, then ship these products in larger quantities to locations nearer the market.

The accumulation process is commonly practiced to obtain the lowest possible transportation rate by accumulating and shipping goods in truckload or carload lots. Transportation will be discussed in a subsequent chapter, but it should be noted here that the possibility of lowering transportation charges on larger shipments is one important reason for the existence of many marketing specialists.

Small farmers, for instance, seldom produce enough of particular grades or qualities of products to ship at the lowest rate.

Collecting, however, must be done with an eye to the needs of the potential target market because the qualities collected affect subsequent levels. Here, the expanded "total system" mentioned earlier becomes relevant because once collected, the goods may move through several specialists before reaching final consumers.

The Burmese government found it necessary to intervene in the collecting process for rice because farmers and even wholesalers in Burma were mixing different strains of rice to amass quantities large enough for economical handling. The mixing did cut transportation costs, but it caused milling problems—and lowered the quality of the final product.[3]

Once economical quantities have been accumulated and moved closer to potential customers, then *breaking bulk*—the *allocation process*—begins. The homogeneous supply is broken into smaller quantities, since the next level or group of customers have less need for such large quantities. Depending upon the product, wholesalers may sell smaller quantities to other wholesalers or directly to retailers. The retailers continue the allocation process, as they in turn break bulk for their customers. In a sense, the housewife even participates in the allocation process, buying food and serving it in individual portions.

Assortment discrepancies—get the customer what he wants

Discrepancy of assortment can be caused by the necessary process of using established standards to grade the heterogeneous production of farms, mines, forests, and factories into more homogeneous lots. This is called *sorting-out*. The quality control operations of manufacturers are an example of the sorting-out process. So is grading of agricultural products, such as apples, oranges, or wheat, by a grower or wholesaler.

Sorting-out may create assortments that are undesirable but exist because of the inherent variability of the production process. These assortments may create additional opportunities or headaches for marketing managers.

There can be headaches if some of the output does not fit into a product line and must be distributed to entirely different target markets than originally planned. Minor defects in clothing, tires, appli-

[3] J. C. Abbott, *Marketing Problems and Improvement Programs* (Rome: Food and Agriculture Organization of the United Nations, 1958), p. 188.

ances, sporting goods, and musical instruments may require the marketing manager to offer them, perhaps at little profit, as "seconds" in regular or even special outlets.

Or assortments may be created deliberately—to create a product line. This approach, called the *assorting process,* means putting together a line of heterogeneous products to give a target market what it wants. This usually is done by those closer to the final consumer or user, that is, retailers or wholesalers who are attempting to supply a wide assortment of products for the convenience of their customers.

An electrical goods wholesaler may take on a line of lawnmowers or even garden products for the convenience of his hardware retailer-customers. Even manufacturers participate in the assorting process when they attempt to develop a new product line to satisfy their customers.

The last member of the assorting chain is the final consumer or user, who assembles products from many different sellers—retailers, wholesalers, or manufacturers. Seldom does a single retailer or wholesaler satisfy all of the needs of final consumers.

Marketing opportunities come from spotting badly handled discrepancies

We have seen that marketing specialists may develop to facilitate exchange and to make adjustments for discrepancies in both quantity and assortment. These discrepancies may result from both the nature of the production process and customer demands. To overcome discrepancies of quantity and assortment, it may be necessary to use "regrouping" activities: accumulation (collecting), allocating (breaking bulk), sorting-out, and assorting (developing assortments). When one or more of these activities is required, a marketing specialist might develop and fill this need.

Sometimes discrepancies are adjusted badly, especially when there have been rapid shifts in buying habits and preferences. Here, new firms are given a chance to fill these needs. In other cases, breakthrough opportunities may occur when some marketing specialist takes a big-picture view of what he or some other specialists are doing.

A metal wholesaler, for instance, regularly had been supplying aluminum ingots in rather large quantities to aluminum fabricators. His major activity seemed to be adjusting the discrepancy in quantity between the aluminum ingot manufacturer from whom he bought the ingots and his aluminum fabricator customers. On more careful analysis, he found that some customers were regularly melting down the ingots almost as quickly as he delivered them, while the ingot manufacturer-supplier had to cool the aluminum to supply it in ingot form.

Since there was no substantial discrepancy of quantity in this case, the wholesaler bought a specially designed truck to haul molten aluminum directly from the ingot manufacturer to the fabricators. This wholesaler recognized the big picture and developed a unique marketing mix to serve his customers better.

Specialists should develop to adjust discrepancies, if they must be adjusted, but there is no point in having intermediaries just because "that's the way it has always been done." The specialist must provide a real service, as most of them do. But in a dynamic economy, we see the development of new needs and the evaporation of old ones, while some producers and marketing specialists continue offering the same marketing mixes. Clearly, there always is an opportunity for the marketing manager who has an understanding of his customers' needs and how they can best be served.

Place objectives suggest what is "ideal"

All detailed objectives, including Place objectives, should be compatible with the company's overall goals. And, of course, all four P's of the marketing mix must work together. This need for compatibility of the components in a marketing system is really an aid rather than an obstacle, however, especially when developing Place.

When we have selected some potential target markets, it is likely that these customers have similar attitudes toward our product or products. The goods classifications summarize our judgment on the nature of the product, including what the target customers think of it, their willingness to shop for it, and the amount of service desired.

These factors all have a bearing on the ideal Place objectives. Ideally, the Place facilities we should supply are related to customers' needs and preferences. For example, if some target customers think of several different grocery products as staples, it follows that Place should be handled similarly for all of them.

Figure 15–5 suggests ideal Place objectives for our consumer and industrial goods classifications. These ideal objectives are based on the interaction of customer behavior and the nature of the products. Before studying this figure—and it should be studied carefully—it will be fruitful for you to consider what would be ideal for each type of product.

Several Place objectives may be ideal for appliances

Place objectives should be studied carefully, since they set the framework for developing the whole Place setup. But remember that different target markets' differing views of the same physical product can influence the development of Place. If some target customers think of a particular appliance as an heterogeneous shopping good, there is no need for a manufacturer's marketing manager to distribute in every store in the country. It would be enough to distribute where other shopping goods are displayed, because these target customers are willing to shop around. Yet if the same appliance was an impulse good to other target markets, more outlets should be sought, particularly ones that would give preferred display positions.

Just as there are no automatic classifications of products, we cannot automatically determine the best Place arrangement. Place selection depends on what customers like best and what various channel members can provide profitably.

Figure 15–5 Place objectives

Consumer goods

1. *Convenience goods*
   a) *Staples* — need maximum exposure — need widespread distribution at low cost.
   b) *Impulse goods* — need maximum exposure — need widespread distribution but with assurance of preferred display or counter position.
   c) *Emergency goods* — need widespread distribution near probable point of use.

2. *Shopping goods*
   a) *Homogeneous* — need enough exposure to facilitate price comparison.
   b) *Heterogeneous* — need adequate representation in major shopping districts or large shopping centers near other, similar shopping goods.

3. *Specialty goods* — can have limited availability, but in general should be treated as a convenience or shopping good (in whichever category product would normally be included), to reach persons not yet sold on its specialty-goods status.

4. *Unsought goods* — need attention directed to product and aggressive promotion in outlets — or must be available in places where similar products would be sought.

Industrial goods

1. *Installations*
   a) *Buildings* (*used*) *and land rights* — need widespread and/or knowledgeable contacts, depending upon specialized nature of product.
   b) *Buildings* (*new*) — need technical and experienced personal contact, probably at top-management level (multiple buying influence).
   c) *Major equipment*
      1. *Custom-made* — need technical (design) contacts by man able to visualize and design applications, and present to high-level and technical management.
      2. *Standard* — need experienced (not necessarily highly technical) contacts by man able to visualize applications and present to high-level and technical management.

2. *Accessory Equipment* — needs fairly widespread and numerous contacts by experienced and sometimes technically trained personnel.

3. *Raw Materials*
   a) *Farm products* — need contacts with many small farmer producers and fairly widespread contact with users.
   b) *Natural products* — need fairly widespread contacts with users.

4. *Component Parts and Materials* — need technical contacts to determine specifications required — widespread contacts usually not necessary.

5. *Supplies*
   a) *Maintenance* — need very widespread distribution for prompt delivery.
   b) *Repairs* — need widespread distribution for some, and prompt service from factory for others (depends on customers' preferences).
   c) *Operating supplies* — need fair to widespread distribution for prompt delivery.

6. *Services* — most need very widespread availability.

Channels of distribution do marketing functions

Goods and services do not flow from producers to consumers automatically. They move through channels of distribution where a great deal of marketing work is done. Channel members may or may not handle the goods. Some may own them and transfer title, provide return and repair services, store and transport them, and transmit money and information. In other words, a number of things besides goods flow through a channel, both ways. Marketing functions get done there.

Any sequence of marketing institutions, from producer to final user of consumer, including any number of (or perhaps no) middlemen, is called a *channel of distribution*. A channel of distribution is an example of the larger total system mentioned earlier.

Sometimes a channel system is quite simple (short), perhaps running directly from a producer to the final user or consumer. Often it is much more complex (long). In Figure 15–6, four basic channels for consumer goods are presented: (1) direct from manufacturer or

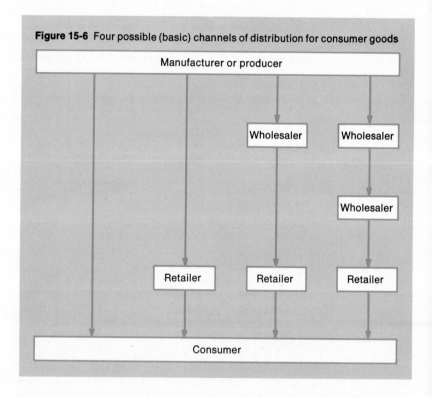

Figure 15-6 Four possible (basic) channels of distribution for consumer goods

producer to consumer, (2) to a retailer, (3) through a wholesaler and then a retailer, and (4) through two levels of wholesalers (who provide a different set of marketing functions) to a retailer and then to a final consumer. The same kinds of alternatives are possible for industrial goods, except that retailers are omitted. By definition, retailers do not sell industrial goods, but some types of wholesale facilities look like those of retailers.

These four channels only suggest the possibilities. Actually, there may be many different kinds of retailers, which will expand the number of possible channels. There are many different kinds of wholesalers, too. Some provide only a few functions, such as promotion or transfer of title, while others actually handle the goods and provide varied services. The many variations of middlemen are discussed in later chapters.

Alternate channels may serve different target markets

The many possible variations should not be seen as competitive channels. Each should be considered a separate "possible" channel. A marketing manager may have many different target markets in mind, and this might require him to use several channels at *the same time* to reach the different parts of his market grid. It is important to think of these different channel systems as different entities. Each potentially is part of, and may require, a different marketing mix.

The marketing manager and competing channels

While one channel may be best for reaching a particular target market, it also may serve other markets for which other channels are stronger. If the various channels consist of independent businessmen, it is only logical to expect these men to seek opportunities wherever they can. Yet this can lead to considerable interchannel rivalry. And if it leads to open price warfare, especially on well-known and branded merchandise, considerable ill will can result, all along the channel. The management of competing channels of distribution is a continuing and difficult problem for marketing managers.[4]

Different channel, different package, same product

The complexity that can develop in actual markets is illustrated in Figures 15–7 and 15–8, involving both consumer and industrial goods. Although these figures appear somewhat complex, they actually are simplified pictures of what is happening in the real world.

Note that each set of lines represents a channel consisting of many individual firms, each with its own peculiarities. In addition, each of these channels may require a separate marketing mix. Sometimes a manufacturer not only will use a separate sales force for each channel, but supply his product with different packaging, pricing and advertising.

Figure 15–7 shows the 10 separate channels used by one manufacturer of a wide line of wire and cable to reach its various target markets. But note that several channels are aimed at the same target markets. This, as pointed out, can lead to competitive problems.

Figure 15–8 shows the many channels used by manufacturers of household, cartridge, and auto fuses. It should be noted that household fuses go through grocery, drug, variety, and hardware wholesalers, all of which supply goods to retailers who are accustomed to different gross margins. Among such channels, there is a great deal of opportunity for competition, including price competition.

[4]For more discussion on this point, see Martin R. Warshaw, "Pricing to Gain Wholesalers' Selling Support," *Journal of Marketing*, July, 1962, pp. 50–54.

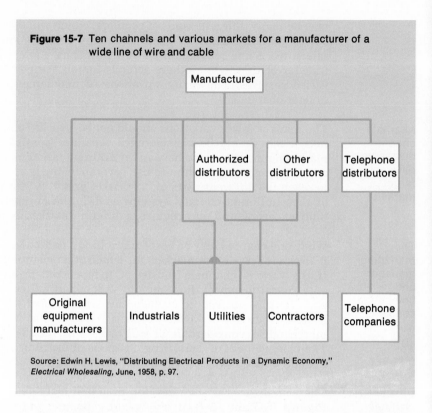

Figure 15-7 Ten channels and various markets for a manufacturer of a wide line of wire and cable

Source: Edwin H. Lewis, "Distributing Electrical Products in a Dynamic Economy," *Electrical Wholesaling*, June, 1958, p. 97.

Sometimes there are no middlemen

These examples seem to suggest that there are plenty of middlemen around to form almost any kind of a channel of distribution. This is not always the case. Sometimes there is only one key middleman serving a market, and he may have a virtual monopoly. To reach the markets he serves, small producers may have no choice but to use him.

Sometimes there are just no middlemen at all, and a producer has to go directly to target customers. One large U.S. apparel maker described this kind of situation as follows: "There is a production super-highway and a retailing super-highway, but a cowpath in between." This manufacturer found it necessary to set up his own retail chain, building a channel directly from producer to the retail level.[5]

This U.S. apparel maker's problem is typical outside the United States, especially when aggressive, marketing-minded middlemen are needed. Such middlemen are scarce in Europe, for example.

Following the Treaty of Rome, which led to the European Common Market, many European manufacturers rapidly expanded manufacturing capacity without paying any attention to distribution facilities. Now, many are forced to use their own controlled retail and wholesale outlets. This may be their only solution for years to come.

[5] "Apparel Maker Sets Up Own Discount Chain," *Business Week*, September 16, 1961, pp. 70–75.

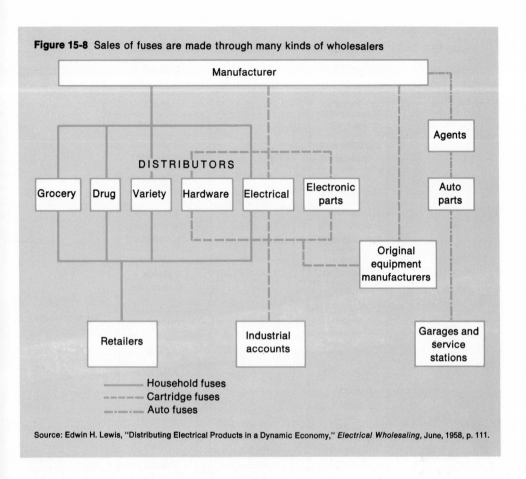

Figure 15-8 Sales of fuses are made through many kinds of wholesalers

Manufacturer

Agents

DISTRIBUTORS

Grocery | Drug | Variety | Hardware | Electrical | Electronic parts

Auto parts

Original equipment manufacturers

Retailers

Industrial accounts

Garages and service stations

———— Household fuses
- - - - - Cartridge fuses
—·—·— Auto fuses

Source: Edwin H. Lewis, "Distributing Electrical Products in a Dynamic Economy," *Electrical Wholesaling*, June, 1958, p. 111.

Channel system may shift and share functions

Ultimately the channel system must deliver the goods and services desired by target customers. Regardless of whether the marketing manager uses long or short channels, the channels must provide all the functions of marketing. Some buying and selling are required. Transporting, storing, grading or sorting, financing, and risk-taking are necessary in all channels. These functions can be shifted and shared, but not eliminated. Note that the customer can participate in this shifting and sharing too.

Figure 15–9 shows how the marketing functions were shifted and shared differently in two channels for auto parts. Note in Channel 1 that the *manufacturer* spent more time and money on marketing and so charged a higher price. But because of the manufacturer's activities the distributor had less to do, and so the price to retailers was the same in Channel 1 as in Channel 2, where the manufacturer's price was lower but the distributor had more responsibility.

If a manufacturer has been extremely successful in differentiating

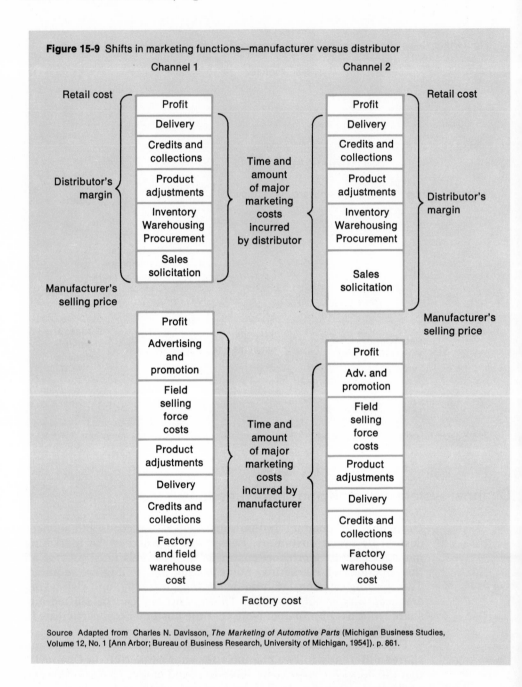

Figure 15-9 Shifts in marketing functions—manufacturer versus distributor

Channel 1

Channel 2

Retail cost

Retail cost

| Profit |
| Delivery |
| Credits and collections |
| Product adjustments |
| Inventory Warehousing Procurement |
| Sales solicitation |

Distributor's margin

Time and amount of major marketing costs incurred by distributor

| Profit |
| Delivery |
| Credits and collections |
| Product adjustments |
| Inventory Warehousing Procurement |
| Sales solicitation |

Distributor's margin

Manufacturer's selling price

| Profit |
| Advertising and promotion |
| Field selling force costs |
| Product adjustments |
| Delivery |
| Credits and collections |
| Factory and field warehouse cost |

Time and amount of major marketing costs incurred by manufacturer

Manufacturer's selling price

| Profit |
| Adv. and promotion |
| Field selling force costs |
| Product adjustments |
| Delivery |
| Credits and collections |
| Factory warehouse cost |

Factory cost

Source Adapted from Charles N. Davisson, *The Marketing of Automotive Parts* (Michigan Business Studies, Volume 12, No. 1 [Ann Arbor; Bureau of Business Research, University of Michigan, 1954]). p. 861.

his product in the minds of customers, there may not be much for other channel members to contribute, and the manufacturer might not have to offer channel members very attractive returns for their efforts. Auto and appliance manufacturers, for instance, offer dealers a lower margin on fast-selling, lower-priced models than on less popular, top-of-the-line models.

Even if a producer takes goods directly to the user, the channel functions are not eliminated. The direct-to-user route may reduce the number of times the functions are performed—but it does not eliminate them, and it may *or may not* reduce the cost.

Channel captain needed to guide channel planning

Until now, we have considered the individual marketing manager as the integrating force in marketing planning. But now we see that there may be several firms and managers in a single distribution channel. If we follow the systems concept, we see that each *channel* should act as a unit, directed by someone we can call a "channel captain." The question is, which marketing manager should be the captain?

The concept of a single channel captain is useful, but we must recognize that some channels may not have an acknowledged captain, since the various firms are not acting as a system. The reason may be lack of leadership or lack of understanding that members of the system are interrelated. Many businessmen, more concerned with those firms immediately above and below them, seem almost unaware that they are part of a channel.[6]

But, like it or not, firms are interrelated, even if poorly, by their policies. It would seem to make a lot more economic sense to make a whole channel work efficiently.

It should be remembered, however, that the role of channel captain is earned by leadership and market power, not by the fiat of an ambitious businessman.

In the middle and on top
In the United States, manufacturers frequently take the initiative in channel relations. Middlemen wait to see what the manufacturer intends to do and what he wants done. After the manufacturer sets his pricing, promotion, and place policies, middlemen decide whether their roles will be profitable and whether they want to participate in the manufacturer's plans. Middlemen may not play an active role in building the channel, but they must be considered by manufacturers in their planning, if only because they (middlemen) have the power to say no. The marketing mix offered to them must be appealing if they are to become active members of the channel team.

There are large or strategically located middlemen who do take the initiative, especially in foreign markets where there are fewer large manufacturers. Such middlemen may determine the types of products their customers want and then seek out manufacturers—perhaps small ones—who can provide products at reasonable prices.

[6] Phillip McVey, "Are Channels of Distribution What the Textbooks Say?" *Journal of Marketing*, January, 1960, pp. 61–65.

Such middlemen may develop their own dealer brands. Or they may handle manufacturers' brands, but on their own terms. These strong middlemen can even become, in effect, manufacturers. They specify the whole marketing mix for a product and merely delegate production to a factory.

Large middlemen are closer to the final user or consumer and are in an ideal position to assume the channel captain role. Some students of marketing have even suggested that middlemen, especially retailers, may dominate the marketing structure of the future.[7]

Our captain, the producer

We cannot overemphasize the importance of a whole channel system seeing itself in competition with other systems. Without this self-conception by members of the channel, one firm might adopt policies that clearly would be unfavorable to another member of his own system. In the short run, a stronger firm might succeed in forcing its policies by sheer weight of market power. Yet in the long run this might lead to the failure, not only of a weaker channel member but of the whole team.

A good example of how *not* to act as channel captain is the manufacturer who loads his retailers with excessive inventory. He may make money in the short run, but he will not be welcomed back by the overloaded firms.

Clearly, the person or firm that helps direct an integrated system of action is the leader. We will consider him our channel captain. His identity may change from time to time — depending on the success of product development or promotional programs, financial reserves, and management personalities — but this does not change the concept or its impact on marketing.

For convenience, we will assume in the following discussion that the channel captain is a producer. Remember, though, that a middleman may play this role too.[8]

Direct or indirect channels may be best

Direct channel systems

Many producers would prefer to handle the whole distribution job themselves. Perhaps they have a desire to control large organizations, or perhaps it is simply a case of, "If you want a job done right, do it

[7]David R. Craig and Werner K. Gabler, "The Competitive Struggle for Market Control," reprinted from *Annals of the American Academy of Political and Social Science*, May, 1940, pp. 84 ff., in J. H. Westing, *Readings in Marketing* (New York: Prentice-Hall, Inc., 1953), pp. 46–57; and Donald F. Dixon, "The Emergence of Marketing Systems," in G. Fisk and D. F. Dixon, *Theories for Marketing System Analysis* (New York: Harper & Row, Publishers, 1967), pp. 61–65.

[8]For further discussion on the idea of channel control, see Robert W. Little, "The Marketing Channel: Who Should Lead This Extra-corporate Organiza-

tion?" *Journal of Marketing*, January, 1970, pp. 31–38; Louis W. Stern, "The Concept of Channel Control," *Journal of Retailing*, Summer, 1967, pp. 14–20 f.; Bruce Mallen, "Conflict and Cooperation in Marketing Channels," in L. G. Smith (ed.), *Reflections on Progress in Marketing* (Chicago: American Marketing Association, 1965), pp. 65–85; and Valentine P. Ridgeway, "Administration of Manufacturer-Dealer Systems," in S. C. Hollander (ed.), *Explorations in Retailing* (East Lansing: Michigan State University Bureau of Business and Economic Research, 1959), pp. 250 ff.

yourself." In any event, there are genuine advantages in selling directly to the final user or consumer.

When the producer is close to his target customers, marketing research is easier. He is more sensitive to changes in customer attitudes and preferences and is in a better position to promptly adjust his marketing mix. If aggressive selling effort or special technical service are needed, he can be sure that his sales force receives the necessary training and motivation.

Naturally short channels

Some products typically have short channels of distribution, and a direct-to-user channel is not uncommon. For example, many industrial products are sold to a relatively few target customers, making a direct channel system logical. Or if the product is "used up" by the first customers, as in the case of machinery, or if it otherwise loses its identity so that no marketing effort is needed farther along in the channel, then a direct channel system may be sensible.

The typical channels used for various kinds of products are discussed and explained in Chapter 19; we will not elaborate on them here. The important point here is that a direct manufacturer-to-final-user channel is typical for some products in certain situations. It is not always necessary to use middlemen.

Corporate integration of typically longer channel systems

Some channels normally contain several firms, but we also find integrated firms developing full-channel systems. With corporate ownership ranged all along the channel, we can say that the firm is going direct, but actually it may be handling manufacturing, wholesaling, *and* retailing. This is more activity than usually is implied when we refer to direct distribution.

Integration usually refers to the acquisition of other firms, though a company can reach the same goal through internal expansion. Internal expansion is less likely to bring about government intervention because it is controlled only by antimonopoly laws, while integration by acquisition is subject to specific antimerger legislation. There has been considerable government restrictive and punitive activity in this area in recent years.

At first, it might seem that *horizontal integration* – the acquisition of firms at the same level of activity – would have little to do with channels of distribution, which are usually depicted as vertical. But discrepancies of quantity and assortment must be considered, too, and it is for these reasons that horizontal integration can make sense.

To integrate vertically, a firm might have to integrate horizontally or expand its horizontal operations by internal expansion. Woolworth's, Kresge's, A&P, National Tea Co., Safeway Stores, Kroger, Florsheim Shoes, Genesco, and J. C. Penney have expanded or integrated horizontally at the retail level. General Motors Corp. and U.S. Steel Corp. are integrated horizontally at the producer level.[9]

[9]"How Far Can a Producer Retail?" *Business Week,* January 21, 1961, pp. 77–84; and *Time,* November 23, 1962, p. 76.

In *vertical integration,* control is expanded to two or more successive stages of production or distribution. A retailer might go into wholesaling and perhaps even manufacturing. Some companies are integrated both horizontally and vertically. A&P, Kroger, Genesco, Florsheim Shoes, and J. C. Penney are wholesalers or manufacturers as well as retailers. A&P, for example, has fish-canning plants. Genesco and Florsheim make their own shoes, and J. C. Penney controls textile plants. Firestone Tire and Rubber Co. has rubber plantations in Liberia, tire plants in Akron, Ohio, and Firestone label wholesale and retail outlets all over the United States.

There are many advantages to vertical integration, such as stability of operations, assurance of materials and supplies, better control of distribution, better quality control of products, an opportunity for larger research facilities, greater buying power, and reduction in executive overhead expense.

The economies of vertical integration may benefit the consumer, too, through lower prices and better products. Vertical integration brings smooth, routine operation of the traditional marketing functions and can cut costs. The business transactions that once required negotiations between separate firms now are routine requisitions, acknowledgements, and internal accounting transactions.

In conclusion, we can see that vertical integration is a method for assuring exclusive arrangements in a channel. Provided that the discrepancy of quantity and assortment is not too great at each level in a channel—that is, the firms fit together well—vertical integration may be extremely efficient and profitable.[10]

Indirect channel systems

Indirect channel systems seem to be most effective for certain kinds of products. There are various types of indirect channel systems, and the survival of a firm may depend on what type it joins or develops.

Traditional channel systems

We have noted already that there are operating advantages in corporately integrated channel systems, but there is a great deal less freedom of decision making at each level, too. On the other hand, in a traditional channel system, the separate firms (often with highly individualistic managers) have their independence, but the channel may be inefficient because of it.

In some highly independent channels, buyers may even prefer to wait until sellers desperately need to sell, hoping to force the price down. This leads to erratic production, inventory, and employment patterns that can only increase total costs.[11] More will be said about such businessmen in later chapters, but here it can be pointed out

[10] This discussion is based on the advantages and disadvantages discussed in Nugent Wedding (ed.), *Vertical Integration in Marketing* (Bulletin 74 [Urbana: Bureau of Economic and Business Research, University of Illinois, 1952]), pp. 11–12, 30.

[11] For more discussion on this interaction, see Jay Forrester, "Industrial Dynamics—A Major Break-Through for Decision-Makers," *Harvard Business Review,* July–August, 1958, pp. 37–66.

that such channels are declining in importance, and with good reason. They are still typical in some industries, however.

Administered channel systems

The inherent advantages of an integrated system have been understood by some progressive businessmen. But instead of integrating corporately, they have tried to develop formal and informal relationships with others in the channel system. Some have achieved the advantages of corporate integration while retaining some of the flexibility of the traditional system.

Norge Division of Borg-Warner Corp., for example, has an arrangement with its independent distributors to provide them automatically and continually with a six weeks' inventory of appliances, based on current inventory and sales, plus projected sales. Every week, Norge makes a thorough item-by-item analysis of 125,000 – 130,000 major appliance units valued at around $18 million. These units are located in many warehouses operated by 87 distributors throughout the country. Each week, all of this data is analyzed by the president and his managers of distribution, sales, and marketing research (as well as his manufacturing heads), and plans for production and sales activities for the following week and weeks are established.

Similar systems have been developed and coordinated by middlemen in the grocery, hardware, and drug industries. In fact, a retailer in these lines almost has to be a member of such a system to survive.

Channel systems — new wave in the marketplace

In addition to their other virtues, smoothly operating channel systems also appear to be competitively superior.

In the consumer goods field, corporate chains that are at least partially vertically integrated account for about 26 percent of total retail sales; firms aligned with various administered systems account for an additional 37½ percent. This gives vertical systems in the consumer goods area a healthy majority of retail sales. Importantly, it appears that such systems will continue to increase their share in the future.[12] The inevitable conclusion is that vertical marketing systems are becoming the principal competitive units in the U.S. distribution system.[13]

This trend toward the development of vertical marketing systems suggests that both new and established firms should give serious consideration to becoming a part of such a channel system.

One reason for the movement toward integrated systems is that once channel captains see what must be done to spur sales and growth, they may have difficulty accomplishing it with their traditionally independent channel members. General Electric and Westinghouse

---

[12]Bert C. McCammon, Jr., "Vertical Marketing Systems: An Exploratory Analysis," a paper presented at the 9th Annual Paul D. Converse Awards Symposium, University of Illinois, April 13, 1967.

[13]Bert C. McCammon, Jr., "The Emergence and Growth of Contractually Integrated Channels in the American Economy," a paper presented at the Fall Conference of the American Association, Washington, D.C., September 2, 1965.

may be moving in the direction of direct distribution of major appliances for this reason. The small retailers may not be completely eliminated, but some of their functions may be assumed, including stocking, delivery, installation, and service.[14]

Today, every independent firm should decide what kind of a channel system it wishes to be a part of. In the next several chapters, we will discuss the components of channel systems. Then, in Chapter 19, we will discuss how these components can be combined into effective systems.

Place functions are done in different kinds of central places

We already have seen the valuable functions performed by central markets and dealers when producers and the potential transactions among them are multiplying. It is only logical that marketing specialists would tend to congregate where they can conveniently serve more customers—in cities. Cities are not all the same, however, and do not play the same kind of role in marketing. And we do *not* find marketing specialists evenly distributed purely on the basis of population. This fact is important to any marketing manager who must work with and through specialists.

An understanding of the role of cities is vital to the marketing manager because this role may be changing in the future. For example, what will happen when computers can talk to computers and handle the buying and selling functions automatically? And what will happen when salesmen can call on customers with Phone-vision? Will we need the kinds of cities we have now with their towers of offices and square blocks of warehouses? After seeing what cities do, perhaps you can decide what the future city will look like.[15]

What do the cities do?

Retailing and service operations are important functions of many cities. But none of the world's major cities has grown large purely as a

---

[14] "Building a Faster Track from Factory to Home," *Business Week*, February 16, 1963, pp. 45–46; "Westinghouse Retail Outlet Will Double as Microscope to Scan the Consumer," *Business Week*, February 16, 1963, p. 50; E. B. Weiss, "Will Manufacturers Go into Retailing?" *Advertising Age*, December 31, 1962, p. 35; and "Has G.E. Taken Another Step Toward Retailing?" *Advertising Age*, September 3, 1962, p. 52.

[15] For further discussion on the evolution of cities, see "Rethinking Cities," *Time*, June 1, 1970, pp. 64–65; "If Only Cities Were Like London," *Business Week*, May 30, 1970, pp. 64–67; "Staving Off Auto Paralysis," *Business Week*, February 28, 1970, pp. 54–58; "What Makes A City Great?" *Time*, November 14, 1969, pp. 47–48; "Office Boom Changes the Scene," *Business Week*, October 7, 1967, pp. 167–72; "Italy's Chaotic Capital Exemplifies Ultimate in Urban-Area Problems," *Wall Street Journal*, December 11, 1969, pp. 1 f; "A Daring Look at City Ills," *Business Week*, June 14, 1969, pp. 142–46; "Railroads Spur Urban Renewal," *Business Week*, April 12, 1969, pp. 153–60; and "Sao Paulo in Brazil Wrestles Woes Facing Continent's Big Cities," *Wall Street Journal*, November 21, 1968, pp. 1 f.

retail or personal service center. Most retail business is a service to the people who live and work in the community.[16]

Basic employment is fundamental to the growth of cities. It is employment in activities that serve people outside the local community, and therefore is a kind of "export." Through basic employment, the city earns the revenue to pay for its "imports" from other areas. Detroit builds automobiles for customers throughout the world. Some are produced for Detroit residents, but only the cars sold outside of Detroit contribute to *basic* employment.

The remainder of the work done in the city is *service employment* — that is, "taking in each other's washing." But this service employment is not trivial. In most American cities, about three persons are employed in service employment for every two persons engaged in basic employment.

The major contributors to city growth are commerce and manufacturing. The term *commerce* refers to all the activities of trade between regions, including transportation, warehousing, wholesaling, and financing. The term *manufacturing* means factory production.

Commerce not only causes the major growth of cities but also attracts manufacturing. As a country's economy becomes more interdependent and trade becomes more important, greater volumes of goods must be traded in and through these cities. A commercial city might even grow rapidly without the added stimulus of manufacturing growth.

San Francisco is a good example of a U.S. city that is largely based on commerce. It services the far western part of the United States. As the volume of goods handled has increased, the San Francisco metropolitan area has grown at a much faster rate than the total population in the region it serves. Other examples of such cities include New Orleans, Chicago, Philadelphia, New York, London, Hamburg, Rotterdam, Amsterdam, Tokyo-Yokohama, and Manila.

By contrast, cities that are chiefly noncommercial — including smaller manufacturing towns and rural trading centers — generally have reached a certain size, then stopped growing. Their size depends on the growth and health of the particular manufacturers who happen to locate there, or the number and prosperity of farmers in the immediate trading area.

[16]The following discussion is based on Richard L. Nelson, *The Selection of Retail Locations* (New York: F. W. Dodge Corp., 1958), pp. 5–18; see also, Brian J. L. Berry, *Geography of Market Centers and Retail Distribution* (Englewood Cliffs, N.J.: Prentice-Hall, Inc., 1967); Wolf Von Eckert, *A Place to Live: A Crisis of the Cities* (New York: Delacorte Press, 1967); Peter Scott, *Geography and Retailing* (Chicago: Aldine Publishing Co., 1970); C. McLaughlin Green, *American Cities in the Growth of the Nation* (New York: Harper & Row, Publishers, 1965); W. R. Bishop, Jr., and E. H. Brown, "An Analysis of Spatial Shopping Behavior," *Journal of Retailing*, Summer, 1969, pp. 23–30; Percy Johnson-Marshall, *Rebuilding Cities* (Chicago: Aldine Publishing Co., 1966), pp. 374; Morris L. Sweet, "History of Municipal Markets," *Journal of Housing*, June, 1961; Morris L. Sweet and Finn B. Jensen, "The Planned Community," *National Civic Review*, May, 1962, pp. 251–56; Raymond Vernon, *The Changing Economic Function of the Central City*, January, 1959; and Robert C. Wood, *Metropolis Against Itself* (New York: Committee for Economic Development, March, 1959).

As the larger cities become more efficient at commerce, the growing interdependence of the economy actually may decrease the regrouping activities provided by the noncommercial areas. Remember that the advantage of dealers in central markets grows as the size of the market increases.

Cities house different marketing specialists

The marketing manager should recognize the qualitative differences among cities because marketing facilities and institutions differ from city to city. The following breakdown of U.S. cities into four basic types explains some of these differences more specifically:

1. The big commercial city, called "Commerce City."
2. The industrial city, called "Centertown."
3. The rural trading center, called "Countyville."
4. The dormitory suburb, called "Forest Lake,"[17]

Most cities fit into one of these categories or are making a transition from one to another. The marketing manager should look for such transitions, for it is during this stage that present institutions may become inadequate to meet marketing needs. Note these city types carefully because they will be referred to later in our discussion of specific retailing and wholesaling institutions.

Commerce City

Most Commerce Cities have a population exceeding a half million and are located at transportation centers and on waterways. In Commerce Cities, wholesaling, warehousing, finance, and transportation usually are more important activities than manufacturing as the source of basic employment.

Often the downtown district has grown up along a river, lake, or ocean because the early development of the city depended upon the use of the waterfront. Expansion since that time has fanned out from the downtown area. Today the city, surrounded by suburbs, has difficulty expanding geographically.

The population of the city itself may have ceased to grow because of lack of room. Or it actually may be declining, as the 1970 census showed. But the dormitory suburbs in the city's metropolitan area are expanding. The suburban areas that first developed by stringing out along the railroads, now are filling between the rail lines as population grows and as automobiles and superhighways make commuting more acceptable to more people.

Nearly all highways and railroads radiate from the city center, a downtown area with multistoried department stores, tall office buildings, and well-defined sub-areas, such as financial, retailing, and entertainment sections.

On the major streets leading out from the downtown area are a

[17]Nelson, *op. cit.*, pp. 5–18.

number of large shopping districts, perhaps centered about one or two large department stores that are branches of the big stores downtown. Throughout the city, along major streets, there are strips of stores selling convenience-type goods in the grocery, drug, hardware, and liquor categories. A series of these stores may be repeated every three or four blocks, or in densely populated areas they may line solidly along the major business streets. Out in the suburbs, there are large shopping centers.

Commerce Cities usually have large warehouses and extensive shipping facilities, both rail and truck, and sometimes barge or ship. They are also the headquarters for large corporations with their buying offices. As already indicated, this makes it convenient for sellers to reach many important buyers. There are large advertising agencies, banks, management consultants, and others providing services in these cities. Commerce Cities often are the homes of large distribution centers for the major mail-order companies. They may also be the homes of important dealer branders, who maintain their central offices and warehouses there.

Large manufacturers may find it desirable to maintain substantial warehouses in Commerce Cities rather than in the more numerous Centertowns because this enables them to reduce their total inventory. More is said on this later, but for now, note that centralization of marketing facilities often provides economies similar to those achieved in centralized, mass production factories. This centralization of marketing activities takes place in Commerce Cities.

Centertown   Centertown is likely to be a manufacturing-oriented community. It is called Centertown because most of the activities are in the center of the town. The downtown area is a concentration of stores and service facilities. In a larger Centertown, the downtown stores may emphasize shopping goods, while the downtowns of smaller Centertowns will consist of stores selling both convenience and shopping goods.

Sometimes retail facilities are concentrated together in one or two blocks, but frequently they are wedged in among other service and civic facilities. Even industrial suppliers for local industry may be found downtown.

In one study of Centertowns, more than 20 percent of the cities studied had a downtown street called "Main Street." It was or still is the main street through town, although there is a tendency for state and federal highways to avoid Main Street in favor of a faster, safer bypass. The retail stores usually originated at the intersection of Main Street and the railroad, or at the intersection of an important crossroad. But as newer buildings have been built, the center of downtown has often moved a little farther out along the main street, generally toward the area of largest population growth.

The outward growth most often takes the form of subdivisions similar to the suburbs of Commerce Cities. But these areas have few, if any, shopping facilities of their own, except strips of stores carrying convenience goods. The major retail shopping facilities are downtown, including the majority of stores carrying shopping goods and specialty goods. But in some of the larger Centertowns, outlying discount stores and shopping centers are developing.

Depending on the proximity of Commerce Cities, there may be some wholesale and commercial facilities in Centertown. But the emphasis is on manufacturing (or education, medical facilities, or some other noncommercial activity), and goods may be shipped directly to Commerce Cities for regrouping activities.

Countyville   Countyville is a small, rural trading center. It frequently is built around a courthouse square or along a railroad. There usually is no suburban shopping center of any kind, and usually the majority of the commercial buildings are old and obsolete by modern retailing standards. There may be some limited shopping-goods facilities, depending upon the proximity to a Centertown or Commerce City.

The major function of a Countyville is to serve the agricultural market. Its role as an agricultural market may include the accumulation of enough volume of farm products from the region to achieve the most economical transportation rate and permit the commodities to be handled as a standard unit in subsequent markets. For example, the common unit in the wheat market is a rail carload.

If the Countyville middlemen who sell to farmers do a good job, they need not fear competition from Centertown businesses, which are oriented more toward manufacturing. The same may be true for those who buy the farmers' output.

But with the decline in the number of small farmers, many Countyvilles are having difficulties. The larger farmers who are becoming more important in U.S. agriculture may be able to deal directly with buyers in Commerce Cities or may make contracts with manufacturers either in Countyvilles or Centertowns. They also may search farther for their supplies. And because more farm families have money and can travel superhighways into distant cities, the limited shopping-goods retail facilities in these towns are having troubles.

Forest Lake   Forest Lake is a dormitory suburb. Most people who live in this suburb work in Commerce City or the sprawling plants that are moving to the edge of the city. Many commute by train or car via high-speed highways. The majority of retail stores sell convenience goods, and there is little or no wholesaling or other commercial activity.

Many suburban towns are overgrown rural trading centers which happened to be within convenient commuting distance of large cities. Some are just large housing developments with little community identity. The majority of residents do their buying of shopping goods and specialty goods in Commerce City or in the large outlying shopping centers that are developing to serve several Forest Lakes.

Conclusion

This chapter has discussed the role of Place in an economic system. The development of a satisfactory product provides *form* utility, but this is of little value unless it is combined with *time* and *place* utility to permit *possession* utility.

Possession utility can be achieved only when products are exchanged—usually in markets. We found that markets and marketing specialists facilitate exchange and help adjust discrepancies of quantity and assortment.

Discrepancies of quantity occur when there is a difference between the quantity produced by individual producers and the quantity demanded by individual customers. They also occur when the output of many small producers, especially farmers, must be accumulated to obtain the most economical transportation rate.

Discrepancies of assortment occur because producers tend to specialize in a few products although individual customers want variety. One of the roles of marketing is to help match these differences between supply and demand.

Discrepancies of assortment are likely to occur for pure services, while discrepancies of quantity are less likely for services because they tend to be produced and delivered at the same time.

The concept of a channel of distribution was introduced and defined. Many different channels are possible—in fact, each target market may require a slightly different one. All channels must provide the same basic functions, although channels may shift and share the functions in different ways. A channel captain can be helpful in planning and coordinating channel effort.

"Ideal" Place objectives were outlined, based on the nature of customer demand as reflected in the goods classifications. These ideal objectives can be achieved with either direct or indirect channels of distribution.

We have seen that a decision to use a direct-to-final-consumer or -user channel might encourage vertical or horizontal integration, or both. Decisions to integrate, however, must be made carefully, because mergers may be subject to review and reversal in the federal courts, especially if they seem to threaten smaller competitors.

Administered channel systems made up of cooperating independent businessmen may achieve some of the same economies characteristic of corporate vertical systems. Such vertical marketing systems must have some inherent advantages because they are coming to dominate the marketing scene.

Finally, we discussed where place functions are done. We saw that cities have different modes of existence and house different kinds of marketing specialists. The roles of the various city types are important in marketing strategy planning because certain marketing specialists are more likely to congregate in certain kinds of cities than others. In some, adequate marketing specialists may not be available at all, providing an opportunity for a marketing manager to offer a unique marketing mix to his target markets.

Now we will go beyond some of these theoretical considerations and look carefully at the various kinds of specialists that have developed and are part of some channel systems. In particular, we will look next at retailing and the many kinds of retailers which might be part of a channel system or actually dominate it as channel captains. Then, in Chapter 17, we will look at wholesalers and wholesaling. In Chapter 18, we will study the specialists who handle storing and transporting – the physical distribution activities. Finally, in Chapter 19, we will return to the development and management of channel systems, after we have a fuller understanding of what components are available and can be combined into channel systems.

QUESTIONS AND PROBLEMS

1 Explain the differences among time, place, and possession utility. For the following products, describe the kinds of business effort required to provide these utilities and the nature of business firms which could provide them (describe these firms in general – do not try to name specific types):
a) Beefsteaks.
b) Men's shoes.
c) A drill press (for industry).
d) A diamond ring.

2 Describe what the economic organization of your college town or city would be like if there were no organizations specializing in providing place utility (that is, explain the kind of economic activities in which each of the members of the community would participate).

3 Explain "discrepancies of quantity and assortment" using the clothing business as an example. How does the application of the concept of discrepancies change when coal for sale to the steel industry is considered rather than clothing? What impact does this have on the number and kinds of marketing specialists required?

4 Explain the four steps in the regrouping process with an example drawn from the building supply industry (nails, paint, flooring, plumbing fixtures, etc.). Would you expect many specialists to develop in this industry or would the manufacturers handle the job themselves? What kind of marketing channels would you expect to find in this industry and what functions would be provided by various channel members?

5 In view of the Place objectives suggested for convenience goods, what kinds of specialized marketing institutions would the manufacturer hope to find when he went into the market to implement the objectives? What kinds for shopping goods? For unsought goods? For industrial goods? (In your answer, don't be concerned with whether there are any such institutions, just indicate ideally what you would like to find.)

6 Discuss the Place objectives and distribution arrangements which might be appropriate for the following products (indicate any special assumptions required to obtain a definite answer):
a) A postal scale for products weighing up to two pounds.
b) Children's toys: (1) electric train sets costing $20 or more, (2) balloons.
c) Pneumatic nut tighteners for factory production lines.
d) Caustic soda used in making paper.

7 Distinguish between channels of distribution and middlemen.

8 Why are there so many channels of distribution for electrical goods? Would you expect so many different channels in the sale of a perishable agricultural product like oranges? Why, or why not?

9 If a manufacturer has five different markets to reach, how many channels is he likely to use? If only one, why? If more than one, what sort of problems will this raise?

10 Find an example of horizontal integration within the confines of your city. Do there appear to be any particular advantages from this horizontal integration? If so, what are they? If there are no such advantages, how do you explain the integration?

11 Explain how a "channel captain" could help independent firms compete with integrated ones.

12 Discuss the possibility of retailer-organized integrated channels (either formally integrated or administered) dominating consumer goods marketing.

13 Why have Commerce Cities tended to grow more rapidly than the country as a whole? Is this trend likely to continue? Why, or why not?

14 Many Countyvilles and Forest Lakes are of approximately the same size. Which of these two would be a better market? For what kinds of goods?

...the function of retailing will continue to be needed, but the role of individual retailers, and even the concept of a retail store, may have to undergo considerable change.

...changes appear to be evolutionary, not revolutionary, and usually reflect changes at the consumer level.... When very rapid changes do occur, it is usually because orthodox retailers have not recognized, or made adjustment to, changes in consumer behavior.

16

Retailing

Retailing is a vital part of the marketing process for consumer goods. For these goods, Place decisions at the retail level may determine the success or failure of a particular product or service.

Retailing involves the sale of goods to the *ultimate* consumer. It is not concerned with industrial goods nor the sale of consumer goods to retailers or wholesalers.

Retailing consists primarily of buying a satisfying assortment of goods for some market segments, making these goods available at a reasonable price, and often convincing the target customers that the goods will satisfy them.

Retailers often use the term *merchandising* to cover all these activities. For established retailers, this means developing a marketing strategy, adjusting all four P's – perhaps excepting the store location, which usually is fixed.

Marketing managers of consumer goods at all channel levels, not just retailers, must understand retailing, since retailers eventually handle most consumer goods. If the retailing effort is not effective, the goods may not be sold, and *all* members of the channel will suffer. The kinds of retailers in a channel may make the difference between a product's success or failure.

Understanding retailing today is not simple, because many different types of retailers have developed in recent years. Most retailers used to display goods, give credit, and deliver. Now, some announce proudly that they do none of these! Why? And is this the trend of the future?

In this chapter, we will consider the nature and development of retail facilities and will discuss retailers' methods of operation and trends that are now modifying these operations. We will *not* cover, in this chapter, the promotional and pricing aspects of retailing. These problems are similar for all firms and are discussed in the Promotion and Price chapters.

The customer's-eye view of retail facilities

Different target markets may have different images of the same store, as noted in Chapter 8. Individual retailers should be aware of these attitudes and so should the other channel members who may sell through their stores. If the target customers do not think a store is going to satisfy their needs, they won't shop there, and obviously will have no exposure to the products there.

Building on our earlier discussion of consumer behavior and the goods classifications, we can classify three types of stores: convenience stores, shopping stores, and specialty stores. There is no point in discussing unsought stores. They have no image at all. They cannot last long unless they do acquire an image in the eyes of some market segments.

These labels do not limit any store to one type of merchandise. A convenience store might stock specialty goods. Rather, the classification refers to the customers' image of the store.

A centrally located or neighborhood *convenience store,* for example, might draw many customers simply because it is convenient. They would go first to this store even for shopping goods.

Certain other stores seem to be favored by consumers shopping for such items as clothes, furniture, and household appliances. These stores carry all types of merchandise, but their attraction is the width and depth of their assortments. Such stores are classified as *shopping stores.*

Finally, a customer may develop an extremely strong allegiance to a particular store. Whatever his reasons – service, selection, or store reputation – the customer consistently will buy convenience, shopping, and specialty goods at this store. It would be classified as a *specialty store.*

Store type
affects
retailer and
channel
strategies

A retailer's planning must allow for customers' attitudes toward both the products and the store – that is, the planners must view product and patronage motives together. Classifying stores by type of goods, as shown in Figure 16–1, is a good way to understand this complete view.

Figure 16–1 How customers view store-product combinations*

Product type \ Store type	Convenience	Shopping	Specialty
Convenience	Will buy any brand at most accessible store.	Shop around to find better service and/or lower prices.	Prefer store. Brand may be important.
Shopping	Want some selection, but will settle for assortment at most accessible store.	Want to compare both products and store mixes.	Prefer store but insist on adequate assortment.
Specialty	Prefer particular product but like place convenience, too.	Prefer particular product but still seeking best total product and mix.	Prefer both store and product.

*For more discussion of these ideas, see Louis Bucklin, "Retail Strategy and the Classification of Consumer Goods," *Journal of Marketing*, January, 1963, pp. 50–55.

A retailer can better understand his potential market and competition by estimating the relative size of each of the market grid boxes, shown in Figure 16–1, and then identifying which retailers are satisfying which boxes. He may find that he and his competitors are all charging head on for certain kinds of customers, and completely missing a substantial number of others.

When the retailer sees more clearly what he is doing, he may continue his present marketing strategy more vigorously or he may alter it. The manager of a shopping store, for instance, would be wise to add something to the physical products he carries. And if he succeeds in making his store a specialty store, he might even become the channel captain in his geographical area.

A decision on store types should be part of a retailer's overall strategy; it affects a retailer's whole marketing mix. Type-of-store classification also is important to the strategies of manufacturers and wholesalers. If, for example, the majority of a manufacturer's target customers patronize convenience stores, widespread distribution may be necessary.

Store type could be used as another dimension on a multidimensional market grid to provide greater understanding of the needs, preferences, and behavior of customers. A dealer-branded product might be no better than a manufacturer's brand, but if the dealer's store is a specialty store for such products for some target customers, then the product may sell well despite its lack of superiority. An example involves Sears, Roebuck's washing machines, which are similar to competing manufacturers' brands. Some target customers seem to view Sears as a specialty store, and Sears' share of the home-laundry business regularly has been over 25 percent.

To determine store type takes detailed evaluations of individual retailers. Since implementation efforts are beyond our scope, we will de-emphasize store types in this chapter and continue to stress the goods classifications introduced earlier. But remember that a store's entire offering of goods and services can be described as its Product. Thus many of the concepts discussed below with respect to products would be directly applicable to retail store planning and management.

Number and size of actual facilities available

Since retailers sell to final consumers, they usually are nearer to people than to production facilities. Retailers also are much more numerous than manufacturers because customers are widely dispersed and have greatly varied wants. In 1967, there were almost 1.8 million retailers compared to about 310,000 wholesalers and 310,000 manufacturers.[1]

Retailing: many small businesses

The large number of retailers might suggest that retailing is a field of small businesses. To an extent, this is true. In 1967, for instance, 34.9 percent of the nation's retailers accounted for only 2.7 percent of total retail sales, grossing less than $30,000 each annually.

Yet in the aggregate, retailing is big business. Retail sales in 1967 totaled $310 billion, making retailing a key element in the U.S. economy. The larger retail stores – those selling more than $1 million in goods or services annually, such as supermarkets – do most of this business. Only 3.0 percent of the retail stores fell in this bracket, yet they accounted for more than 44 percent of all retail sales. Table 16–1 gives details on the number of retailers and the sales volume by various sales classes.

The many small retailers, however, cannot be ignored, especially because they frequently cause the marketing manager difficult problems. Their large number and relatively small sales volume make it expensive to work with them, and they often require additional mar-

[1] U.S. Bureau of Census.

Table 16–1 Retail trade, 1967 – United States, sales by size of establishment

Sales size of establishments	Establishments			Sales volume		
	Number (000)	Percent	Cumulative percent	Sales ($000,000)	Percent	Cumulative percent
Total, all establishments	1,763			$310,214		
Establishments operated entire year, total	1,671	100.0		299,430	100.0	
With annual sales of:						
$1,000,000 or more	50	3.0	3.0	132,876	44.4	44.4
$500,000–999,999	55	3.3	6.3	38,464	12.9	57.3
$300–499,999	74	4.4	10.7	28,110	9.4	66.7
$100,000–299,999	359	21.5	32.2	60,290	20.1	86.8
$50,000–99,999	323	19.3	51.5	22,888	7.6	94.4
$30,000–49,999	227	13.6	65.1	8,769	2.9	97.3
$29,999 or less	583	34.9	100.0	8,033	2.7	100.0

Source: *U.S. Census of Business, 1967*, Vol. I

keting mixes. Yet these stores reach many consumers and often are invaluable channel members for some products and target markets.

Evolution of present retailing facilities

In the following section tracing the development of retailing institutions, we will try to get a better understanding of why there are so many stores – and especially so many small stores. We will focus on "pure" types for clarity, but note that an actual retail operation may be a hybrid of several types.

House-to-house retailers

House-to-house selling in the United States today is a relatively insignificant form of retailing, but it was an important step in the development of retailing. Its greatest advantage is that it offers marketing managers an opportunity to control their whole channel of distribution. It may be especially useful during the introductory stage of the life cycle of a product, for sales of unsought goods, or during a recession when goods need a special push. It is an old but still effective method inherited from the Yankee peddler.

The total number of house-to-house salesmen has increased over the years, but their share of total retail sales has declined to less than 1 percent. In 1967, about 78,000 house-to-house organizations were enumerated by the census. Most of these were one-man organizations. Only about 7,000 were large enough to employ salesmen, and many of these larger organizations were milk or bread distributors.

This is an expensive method of selling. True, overhead costs are lower because the house-to-house retailer has no store, but travel is costly and the number of personal contacts possible in a day is limited. Markups range from 30 to 50 percent, and often are higher.

Success can be achieved with this method, however, if it meets the needs of certain segments of the market grid. Vacuum cleaners may be an unsought good for some housewives, for example, and therefore no store type will reach them. If a demonstration is needed to show how a vacuum cleaner will meet the housewife's needs, then door-to-door selling may be indicated. Electrolux has sold vacuum cleaners door-to-door since its introduction from Sweden decades ago. And it still claims the top position in the vacuum cleaner business selling all of its cleaners at list price! The same kind of success has been seen by the Avon ladies who sell cosmetics directly to housewives.[2] And Fuller Brush, Tupperware, and most encyclopedia companies use this approach successfully.

Trading posts — general stores

Historically, trading posts or general stores sold anything the local consumers would buy in sufficient volume to justify carrying it. Before the Civil War, they were the main type of retail outlet in this country.

The main advantage of the general store is its convenient location for some target customers. It sometimes serves, too, as a social center and a collecting point for agricultural produce.

Such stores are still found at rural crossroads and sometimes in small Countyvilles, carrying mainly food and other convenience goods, but there are so few now that the U.S. Bureau of Census no longer reports them as a separate category.

Single-line, limited-line stores

Single-line stores became common after the Civil War, when the continuing expansion in the volume and variety of consumer goods began to make it possible for the general store to offer depth and breadth in all its traditional lines. Some stores began specializing in certain lines such as dry goods, apparel, furniture, or groceries. Some stores not only specialize in a single line, such as food, but in a limited-line within the category — in the food classification: meat, staples, fresh produce, or bakery goods. The modern convenience food store is a limited-line store in that it limits its assortment to meet particular needs.

Most retail stores are single- and limited-line stores — specializing in groceries, or hardware, or gasoline, or clothing, or sporting goods — and this probably will continue to be true as long as customer demands are numerous and varied. The main advantage of a single-line, and especially a limited-line, store is that it can satisfy some target markets better, perhaps achieving a specialty-store status, by adjusting its marketing mix — including store hours, credit, and product assortment — to suit certain customers. Several stores, catering to various parts of the market grid, can satisfy the whole market.

Such stores face a major disadvantage in having to stock some items in depth that are slow-moving but must be carried to satisfy the

[2] See also: "Apparel Salesmen Take Samples to the Party," *Business Week*, July 15, 1967, pp. 148–52.

store's target market. Further, many of these stores have the disadvantage of being small, with high expenses relative to sales.

There are some extremely large single-line and limited-line stores – supermarkets and furniture stores, for example – especially in larger Centertowns and Commerce Cities. But a manufacturer's or a wholesaler's marketing manager must remember that there are many more small stores in *both* large cities and small towns and adjust his strategies accordingly.

Specialty shops

The specialty shop is a type of limited-line store found in downtown areas, fashionable shopping districts, and large shopping centers. It usually is small, has a distinct personality, and aims at a carefully defined market segment by offering a unique product assortment, knowledgeable salesmen, and better service.

Usually the specialty-shop designation is reserved for stores dealing in special types of shopping goods, such as high-quality sporting goods, men's exclusive ties, high-fashion dresses, clothes in special sizes, and women's shoes.[3] Boutiques are examples of specialty shops.

Using the term "specialty" should not cause us to confuse specialty *shops,* specialty *stores,* and specialty *goods.* A successful specialty shop might achieve the specialty-store status, discussed earlier in the chapter, among a small group of target customers, but the owner probably would be more satisfied to be well known among a larger group for the distinctiveness of its line and the special services offered. Similarly, a specialty shop might carry specialty goods, but only if they fit into its narrow line and they could benefit by the additional service and display the specialty shop offers.

The specialty shop's major advantage is that it caters to certain types of customers whom the management and salespeople come to know well. This familiarity simplifies buying, and the resulting quicker turnover cuts the costs due to obsolescence and style changes.

Specialty shops probably will continue to be a part of the retailing scene as long as customers continue to have such varied tastes and the money to satisfy them.

Department stores

Department stores handle a *wide* variety of goods, such as women's ready-to-wear and accessories, men's and boys' wear, piece goods, housewares, and housefurnishings.

The distinguishing characteristic of department stores is that they are organized into separate departments like limited-line stores and specialty shops – for purposes of promotion, service, and control. They normally are large stores.

Some specialty shops, grown large and departmentalized, appear to

---

[3] See, for instance, a description of the operation of a sporting goods retailer of this type (Abercrombie & Fitch), "Caterer to the Outdoor Man," *Business Week,* December 16, 1961, pp. 84–89; see also, "Boutiques Rack Up Big Sales," *Business Week,* October 12, 1968, pp. 90–97; "Like Wow Montgomery Ward?" *Business Week,* March 28, 1970, p. 47–48; "Where Shopping Is Child's Play," *Business Week,* March 8, 1969, pp. 88–90.

be department stores, and we will treat them as such. As a rule, however, specialty shops do not carry complete lines. They frequently omit housewares, housefurnishings, and furniture, and prefer instead to emphasize depth of line and distinctivenesss in the lines they do choose to carry. Neiman-Marcus in Dallas, for example, is departmentalized, but insists it is a specialty shop.[4]

Department stores generally try to cater to customers seeking shopping goods. Originally they were located in downtown districts close to other department stores and convenient to many potential customers. Historically, this close grouping developed to facilitate shopping at the junctions of major railroad and streetcar routes, the principal forms of urban public transportation in the 19th century, when the major U.S. department stores began.

Since World War II, many downtown department stores have opened suburban branches in shopping centers to serve the middle- and higher-income groups who have moved to the suburbs, especially around the large Commerce Cities. The big J. L. Hudson store in Detroit was a leader in the movement toward building shopping centers around a large branch department store.

Some downtown department stores now are making efforts to renew the appeal of their traditional downtown locations by (1) carrying wide lines in the major shopping-goods items for which they have long been famous; (2) attracting the trade of conventioneers and tourists; and (3) appealing to low-income groups remaining in the residential neighborhoods near the downtown area. New urban trends, including downtown apartment units and urban redevelopment, may provide new markets for the big downtown stores.[5]

Department stores are often looked to as the retailing leaders in a community. Leaders, first, because they seem to be so generous in giving the customer services he can't get elsewhere—credit, merchandise return,[6] delivery, fashion shows, and Christmas displays. And leaders also because of their size. In 1967, the annual sales volume of U.S. department stores averaged more than $5 million, compared to about $175,000 for the average retail store. The biggest—Macy's, Field's, and Hudson's—each top $100 million in sales annually. Although department stores account for about one third of 1 percent (5,792) of the total number of retail stores, they accounted for over 10 percent of total retail sales in 1967.

Certain department stores have a strong grip on their market. Some market grid segments can be reached *only* through particular department stores. These stores have achieved a strong specialty-

---

[4] "The Merchant Prince of Dallas," *Business Week,* October 21, 1967, pp. 115–18 f; and "The Showdown at Post Oak," *Business Week,* February 28, 1970, pp. 124–25.

[5] Louis H. Grossman, "Merchandising Strategies of a Department Store Facing Change," *MSU Business Topics,* Winter, 1970, pp. 31–42; "Store on the Move," (London) *Sunday Times,* August 27, 1967,

p. 20; "Venerable Store Begins to Swing," *Business Week,* September 9, 1967, pp. 74–81; "Secret Shop for Little Spenders," *Business Week,* December 21, 1968, pp. 52–54.

[6] "In Atlanta Everyone Goes to Rich's Store—to Take Back Things," *Wall Street Journal,* August 28, 1969, p. 1.

store status, and their buyers can make it tough on suppliers. In other words, instead of playing the role of channel captain because of their strength, they simply demand all of the concessions they can get. These might include restricting suppliers from selling preferred lines to their direct retail competitors.[7]

Catalog retailers

Catalog retailing—usually done by mail—should not be ignored by marketing managers. It may be useful for reaching widely scattered markets with products that otherwise might be unsought. A mail-order house in Los Angeles successfully sells products "people really don't need but can't live without," such as electric back-scratchers and invisible thread for mending multicolored materials.[8] Some mail-order houses aim at narrow target markets, selling only electronic components, or phonograph records, or health foods. Others, such as the big mail-order houses, offer both convenience and shopping goods.

Some of the early mail-order houses, including Sears, Roebuck and Montgomery Ward, were started shortly after the Civil War, as railroads and postal service expanded. They were so successful with their low prices and wide variety that some conventional retailers sought legislation to restrict their operations.

Yet catalog selling today isn't like catalog selling a century ago. The emphasis is no longer solely on low-price selling by mail. The kitchen hardware and coveralls are still there, but there is an increasing emphasis on high-fashion women's and girls' wear, sporting goods, and luxury items. Product assortments and quality have grown. And some companies offer catalog stores, telephone service, convenient pickup depots, and delivery, to make catalog buying easier. The big mail-order houses started this practice, but now department stores and limited-line stores are seeing the profit possibilities and are becoming catalog retailers too.

To appeal even more strongly to customers, most catalog sellers have strong merchandise guarantees and liberal return policies. Because they can handle this part of their business in warehouse-type buildings and need limited sales help, they can offer wider selections at lower prices than conventional retailers. Sears' mail-order and catalog operation typically undersells its own retail stores by about 10 percent, and Europe's largest mail-order firm, Die Quelle, keeps its prices 15–20 percent below those of other retailers.[9]

Mail-order houses have continued to grow with the U.S. economy, numbering almost 6,000 establishments in 1967. Yet they have never achieved more than 1.3 percent of total U.S. retail sales, and in 1967, they were down to about 1 percent.

Mail-order houses seem to be making greater headway in Europe, where conventional retailers may be less effective and customers may want the convenience of ordering by mail as well as the lower prices.

[7]"Anti-Trust Verdict Rocks the Stores," *Business Week,* July 26, 1969, p. 29.

[8]"When the Needless Is Essential," *Business Week,*

December 15, 1962, pp. 50–52.

[9]*Time,* April 19, 1963, p. 110.

Mail-order sales accounted for 4.5 percent of all retail sales volume in Britain in 1966.[10] This may be a hint of things to come in the U.S. if our cities continue to grow and visiting stores in person becomes even less convenient. More is said on this under "Trends In Retailing," near the end of the chapter.

Vending machines

Although vending machines are the newest revolution in marketing methods, and their growth has been spectacular, automatic vending still represents less than 2 percent of total U.S. retail sales. But in certain lines, the vending machine is an important factor – 16 percent of all cigarettes sold in the United States, 20 percent of the candy bars, and 25 percent of the bottled soft drinks are sold through machines.[11]

The largest part of the vending-machine business (about 40 percent) is in cigarettes, and the next largest share is from hot and cold beverages (36 percent). For some target markets, clearly, the marketing manager cannot ignore this retailing method.

The major stumbling block in vending is high cost of operation. The machines are relatively expensive for the volume they sell, and they require much stocking time and repair labor. Mass marketers of similar, nonvended products can operate profitably on a margin of about 20 percent; the vending industry seems to require about 41 percent, and so usually must charge higher prices.[12] If costs come down and consumers' income and desire for convenience rises, perhaps we will see more growth in this method of retailing.

Planned shopping centers

The planned shopping centers that have grown rapidly in the last 15 years can be viewed as both a new development and a variation of old marketing institutions. Shopping centers' forerunners were the early villages and country fairs, and department stores composed of many individual shops leased to merchants who operated them as limited-line and specialty shops within one large building.[13] The new shopping centers also are similar to the old shopping districts in larger cities, except shopping centers are planned as a unit.

Shopping centers may be planned by a real estate developer to facilitate one-stop shopping. But the developer's job is to lease space, and centers are not always planned with a specific target in mind. In fact, many markets may be considered or perhaps just the mass market. Usually there are substantial parking facilities, and some are

[10] "Europeans Take Fancy to Buying by Book," *Business Week*, June 3, 1967, pp. 87–92.

[11] "Vendors Pull Out All Stops," *Business Week*, August 15, 1970, pp. 52–54; "Vending in 1964, and Vending in 1961," National Automatic Merchandising Association, Chicago, Ill.; and Malcolm L. Morris, "Growth Parameters for Automatic Vending," *Journal of Retailing*, Fall, 1968, pp. 31–45.

[12] Douglas J. Dalrymple, "Will Automatic Vending

Topple Retail Precedence?" *Journal of Retailing*, Spring, 1963, pp. 27–31; See also, *Starting and Managing a Small Automatic Vending Business*, (Starting and Managing Series, Vol. 13 [Washington, D.C.: Small Business Administration, 1967]).

[13] Paul E. Smith, "Prescription for a Successful Shopping Center," *Business Topics*, Autumn, 1966, p. 17.

pleasantly landscaped. Although the centers are composed of independent merchants, they sometimes act together for promotional purposes.

Shopping centers have been classified into three basic categories based on the type of tenant and the size of the market they must serve to be profitable: (1) the neighborhood center, (2) the community center, and (3) the regional center.

Neighborhood shopping centers

These centers, similar to the many "strips" of convenience stores found in most Commerce Cities and Centertowns, usually include a supermarket, drugstore, hardware store, beauty shop and barbershop, laundry, dry cleaners, gas stations, and others, such as a bakery or appliance shop. They normally serve 7,500 to 40,000 people living within 6 to 10 minutes' driving distance. There were more than 6,000 such shopping centers in 1966.

Community shopping centers

These larger operations usually include a variety store or a small department store in addition to the stores found in the neighborhood center. There is more emphasis here on shopping goods (apparel and home furnishings), but the bulk of sales are of convenience goods. These centers must serve 40,000–150,000 people within a radius of 3 to 4 miles. They are quite common around Forest Lakes and are found around larger Centertowns. There were more than 500 such community centers in 1966.

Regional centers

These are much larger units. They include one or two large department stores and as many as 100 smaller stores. Most of these emphasize shopping goods; in fact, the stores that emphasize convenience goods often are at the edge of the center, where they will not interfere with customers primarily interested in shopping.

Regional centers must serve 150,000 or more persons within a radius of 5 or 6 miles. They closely resemble downtown shopping districts of Centertowns or even some small Commerce Cities, and usually are close to the Forest Lakes near large Commerce Cities. In 1966, there were about 250 regional centers in the United States out of a total of about 7,000 shopping centers.[14]

One aspect of shopping center development, important to manufacturer and wholesaler marketing managers, is that the financial requirements of shopping center developers often have barred small independent stores from the centers in favor of national chain stores.

[14] *Ibid.*, pp. 17–26; "Shopping Centers and New York State's Retail Economy," *New York State Commerce Review*, September, 1958, p. 2; and "Specialty Fashion Center in Santa Ana Will Make 'Shopping Around' Easier," *Business Week*, March 8, 1958, p. 51. For a detailed list of available shopping centers, see annual *Directory of Shopping Centers in the United States and Canada* (Chicago, National Research Bureau, Inc.); "Factors in Considering Shopping Center Location," (*Small Marketers Aids, No. 143* [Washington, D.C.: Small Business Administration, May, 1970]); "Big Shopping Centers Are Becoming the Focus of Life in the Suburbs," *Wall Street Journal*, February 20, 1959, pp. 1 f.

This sometimes has blocked manufacturers' brands from these important centers, since some chains tend to emphasize their own dealer brands.[15]

Mass marketing methods

Mass marketers see things differently from conventional retailers

So far we have been describing retail institutions primarily in terms of the number of lines carried and their physical facilities. This is the traditional or conventional way of thinking about retailing. But there are some important retail institutions that cannot be adequately described this way. Supermarkets and discount houses, for instance, could have been shoved into our previous classifications. But by so doing, we would have missed their essence, just as some conventional retailers did when these stores first developed.

Mass marketers reject the conventional retailer's notion of a fixed demand for a territory and also the "buy-low-and-sell-high philosophy." The mass marketer's approach is to offer lower prices to achieve faster turnover and substantial sales volumes by appealing to larger markets. Some mass marketing institutions were started by nonretailers who were willing to depart from the conventional wisdom of existing retailers. Their success is history now.

Some conventional retailers have adopted mass marketing methods and prospered. Other retailers missed the boat and are out of business today. And others have ignored mass marketing and continue to operate, perhaps because they satisfy different segments of the market grid. To understand more fully what mass marketing is, we will discuss its evolution from the development of supermarkets and discounters to the mass merchandisers.

Supermarkets started move to mass marketing

A supermarket is essentially a large store specializing in groceries. As late as 1930, most food stores were relatively small single- or limited-line operations. In the early depression years, some innovators felt that price appeals could move merchandise in volume. Their early experiments in vacant warehouses proved an immediate success. Conventional retailers, both independents and chains, quickly copied the innovators—emphasizing lower prices and self-service.

According to the Super Market Institute, $1 million is considered the minimum annual sales volume for a store to be classified as a supermarket. In 1969 there were 23,480 supermarkets meeting this definition, and they handled about 62 percent of total grocery sales. Today with supermarkets continuing to multiply, it appears they are beginning to reach the saturation level, yet new ones still do well when they

---

[15] "Small Concerns Are Frozen Out of Shopping Centers, Panel Is Told," *Wall Street Journal*, December 19, 1961, p. 28; and E. B. Weiss, "Retailing by Treaty," *Advertising Age*, March 11, 1963, p. 94.

are wisely located.[16] Supermarkets are growing in popularity all over the world, with several thousand in Europe alone.[17]

Supermarkets sell convenience goods, but in quantity. Their target customers don't want to shop for groceries every day as was common in pre-supermarket times. To facilitate quantity buying, supermarkets generally offer free parking facilities.

Present-day supermarkets are planned for maximum efficiency; some carefully analyze the sales and profit of each item, and allocate space accordingly. This approach helps sell more merchandise in less time, reduces the investment in inventory, makes stocking easier, and reduces the cost of handling goods.[18] Such efficiency is essential. Grocery competition is keen, and net profits after taxes in grocery supermarkets usually run a thin 1 percent of sales.

Discount selling preceded mass merchandisers

Discount selling has become quite popular since World War II, but price cutting or discounting goes back to the earliest days of marketing. Bargaining has always been the way to get a better price. And clergymen, teachers, members of labor unions, and members of various social groups have long received discounts in certain stores.[19]

Some discounting has been done through brokers and in "open showrooms" where furniture and similar bulky items ostensibly are shown only to wholesalers or retailers but actually are shown to anyone. The details of these arrangements vary. Sometimes retailers act as brokers between the consumer and the wholesaler. Usually these showroom operations are not well publicized, account for only a small portion of retail sales, and might better be described as discount selling.

Discount houses upset some conventional retailers

Discount houses are fast-turnover, price-cutting operations that have expanded beyond discount selling. The term was originally associated with retailers selling hard goods such as appliances, cameras and jewelry, and furniture.

The early post–World War II discount houses formally adopted a policy of low-margin selling and were much more open about their operations than those retailers who were simply offering discounts to selected customers. To get the lower prices, the discount house customer would have to go to the discounter's low-rent facilities, pay cash, and take care of service and repair problems himself, because the

---

[16] *Progressive Grocer,* April 1970, p. 53; "The Grocery Business – Maybe the Stockholders Should Be Picketing Instead," *Forbes,* November 1, 1969; Brian Thompson, "Intraurban Retail Structure: The Supermarket Sector," *Journal of Retailing,* Fall, 1969, pp. 69–80; Ben L. Schapker, "Behavior Patterns of Supermarket Shoppers," *Journal of Marketing,* October, 1966, pp. 46–49.

[17] *Business Week,* September 10, 1966, p. 132; "Europe Goes Shopping," *Business Week,* May 18, 1963, pp. 58–72; "Supermarts on the Seine," *Time,* April 12, 1963, pp. 95–96; and "Supermarkets in Siberia," *Chain Store Age,* November 1960, pp. 144 ff.

[18] For further discussion on this, see "How Super Valu Study Was Used to Lay Out Motts' New Super," *Progressive Grocer,* an updated reprint.

[19] Discount selling and discount houses have been discussed extensively in the literature. See a special-interest bibliography compiled by S. C. Hollander, *Discount Selling, Retail Price-cutting, and Resale Price Controls* (Chicago: American Marketing Association, 1956).

lower prices didn't cover such extras (although manufacturers' guarantees were available on some items).

Word-of-mouth advertising made the discount houses well known, and eventually some advertised through local media. Such steps were taken very cautiously, however. Sales and profits were growing, and the discounters did not wish to antagonize their manufacturer-brand suppliers or conventional competitors for fear that they might—as in fact they eventually did—put pressure on their sources to cut off the discounter's supplies.

In the early 1950's, with war shortages finally ended, goods became more plentiful, and a buyers' market developed. Discount houses became more attractive to suppliers, and the discounters themselves became more aggressive. Earlier they had emphasized products that had been bought cheaply but often with little regard to assortments. Now they were able to offer full assortments.[20]

At this stage, many discounters sought respectability, moving to better locations and offering more services and guarantees. They began to act more like regular retailers, but kept their prices lower than conventional outlets to keep turnover high.[21]

Discount houses are a new approach to retailing. In the face of discount house competition, some conventional retailers have resorted to price cutting on highly competitive items. But these purely defensive tactics are just that—price cutting—while discounters make a standard practice of selling all of their goods with small markups.

More than price cutting is involved, however. Careful buying with the firm's target markets in mind is essential, to assure high turnover. A major discounter's first venture into apparel sales flopped, for instance, because its buyers were appliance experts and knew little about fashions. The discount approach worked only after they hired experienced buyers from department stores.

Mass merchandisers are more than discounters

Unlike the early discount houses—which emphasized manufacturer-branded hard goods, such as appliances and TV sets, where it was easier to show that discounts were being given—the mass merchandisers tend to emphasize soft goods and, more recently, groceries. These "discount" stores are a force to reckon with. They are selling more food (among other things) per store than the chain supermarkets![22]

The mass merchandisers are simply large, departmentalized stores that are more *super* than the supermarkets and follow the discount

---

[20] For a description of a discount house that has gone through these stages—Polk Brothers in Chicago—see "Chicago's Red Hot Merchandiser," *Fortune,* September, 1955, pp. 130–54; and Edward M. Barnet, "A Showdown in the Marketplace," *Harvard Business Review,* July–August, 1956, p. 89.

[21] *Time,* September 15, 1961, p. 100.

[22] "Discounters Sell More Food than Chain Markets," *Detroit Free Press,* February 26, 1967, p. 15C; see also, R. J. Minichiello, "The Real Challenge of Food Discounters," *Journal of Marketing,* April, 1967, pp. 37–42.

house's philosophy of emphasizing lower margins to win faster turn-over. They offer a wider range of goods than some supermarkets and discount houses, stress lower prices and self-service and, inevitably, are bigger.

In 1967, there were almost 3,000 such outlets. By definition their minimum floor space is 10,000 square feet, but the average mass merchandiser has over 60,000 square feet – three to four times the size of the average supermarket.[23]

Mass merchandisers typically are fully committed to a self-service operation, with checkout counters in the front of the store and little or no sales help on the floor. This is in contrast to more conventional retailers, such as Sears and Penney's, who still offer some service and have sales stations and cash registers throughout the store. The more conventional retailer may attempt to replenish sizes and stocks in lines it carries, whereas some mass merchandisers make little effort in this regard. They want to move merchandise – quickly, they hope – and are less concerned with continuity of lines and assortment.

The mass merchandisers are usually operated as chains. Some were started by relative newcomers to retailing. Two important competitors, however, are Kresge with its K-Marts and F. W. Woolworth with its Woolco stores. The K-Marts are 100,000-square-foot, full-line department stores that sell top-quality manufacturers' and dealer brands at moderate prices. Kresge also has a slightly lower-price operation – the Jupiter Stores.

Are today's innovators tomorrow's retailers?

Mass merchandisers, especially in the food line, can be understood better if seen as following a marketing strategy in which primary emphasis is on a price appeal to broader markets, with secondary emphasis given to in-store promotion, services, trading stamps, and give-aways – things conventional retailers have stressed more.[24] The success of this strategy indicates that at least some customers in the market grid were not fully satisfied with the conventional strategies.

Mass merchandisers already have made some dent in the market, accounting for about 4 percent of total grocery sales, 14 percent of health and beauty aids sales, and a larger but more difficult to estimate share of some general merchandise lines. Clearly, there is a demand for this kind of operation, and it is likely that the mass merchandisers will continue to use their present methods, because they see these methods as "conventional" for their type of operation. Others may come to see this approach as desirable, too. By 1970, the majority of supermarket chains had switched to price-oriented mixes to meet the competition of supermarket discounters and mass merchandisers.[25] Is this a good move for all of them?

[23] "A New Measure of Mass Merchandisers," Nielsen Researcher No. 1 (1969), pp. 4–10 and No. 3 (1966), pp. 3–11.

[24] Minichiello, op. cit., p. 42.
[25] "Discounting: A Good Chain Reaction," Business Week, September 26, 1970, pp. 44–46.

Will scrambled merchandising continue?

Who's
selling what
to whom?

Current retailing might be called "scrambled merchandising." Variety stores (the old 5-and-10-cent stores) are almost indistinguishable nowadays from department stores and some discount houses. Department stores are offering houses, and mass merchandisers are selling groceries. Some discount houses are becoming department stores and want to be called "promotional department stores." Supermarkets are selling anything they can move in volume, including appliances, drugs, general merchandise, and clothing. Catalog houses are selling through supermarkets. Drugstores, seeing the loss of many health and beauty aid sales to supermarkets and mass merchandisers, are moving into movie cameras, costume jewelry, electric shavers, clocks, and watches. Camera and jewelry stores, in turn, are affected by these moves.

The Wheel
of Retailing,
the ladder
of success

What is behind this scrambled merchandising? According to the "Wheel of Retailing" hypothesis, new types of retailers enter the market as low-status, low-margin, low-price operators. If successful, they evolve into more elaborate establishments and offer more services, with resulting higher operating costs and higher prices. They are then vulnerable to new low-status, low-margin, low-price outlets—and the wheel turns again.

Early department stores began this way, then became higher priced and built basement departments to serve the more price-conscious customers. The 5-and-10-cent store and the mail-order house were developed on a price basis, as were the food chains, economy apparel chains, drug chains, and the automotive accessory chains which developed during the 1920's. The supermarket, in turn, was started with low prices and little service.[26]

Today, conventional retailers are concerned about the competition offered by discount houses and the growing mass merchandisers. But some of these mass marketers are already offering more services and raising their prices. Perhaps they in turn will open the door to a new type of retailer.

But why should various types of retailers repeatedly go through this cycle from low cost and prices to higher costs and prices?

There are several possibilities. The original innovators may relax their vigilance and control as they acquire age and wealth. Or their successors may be less competent or aggressive than they were. Or they may simply want to trade up as some of their original customers grow affluent with age, leaving to others the younger, lower-income customers. Or these firms simply may feel they have to add the addi-

[26]William R. Davidson and Alton F. Doody, "The Future of Discounting," *Journal of Marketing*, January, 1963, pp. 36–37.

tional services to remain competitive as the product (the retailers' whole offering) life cycle moves along.[27]

It's all in hearing the knock, perhaps

The wheel theory, however, does not explain all major retailing developments. Vending machines entered retailing as high-cost, high-margin operations. The branch trend of the department stores and the development of shopping centers have not been low-price oriented. On the contrary, they sometimes have even been high-price operations. Nor have all innovations been immediate successes. Some of the first department stores failed, while vending-machine history is filled with failures.

The probable cause of these crosscurrents has been summarized very well by Hollander:

> . . . retailers are constantly probing the empty sectors of competitive strategy with many failures until someone uses exactly the right technique at the right time. In at least some cases, the merchant prince's skill may have been in judging opportunities rather than in originating techniques.[28]

Or the market grid concept may help

A clearer view of the present retailing scene can be achieved by building on the market grid concept. Figure 16–2 is a simplified view of the market which suggests that three consumer-oriented dimensions affect the types of retail facilities customers choose. These dimensions are: (1) width of assortment desired; (2) depth of assortment desired, and (3) a price/service combination. Within this three-dimensional market grid it is possible to position most of the retail facilities now operating.

Figure 16–2, for example, suggests the *why* of vending machines. Some people – in the front upper left-hand corner – have a pressing need for a specific item and are not interested in the width of assortment, the depth of assortment, *or* the price.

On the other hand, some people have very specific needs in mind and would like to be able to select from a very deep assortment and a range of price alternatives as well. Various kinds of specialty shops have been developed to fill these needs. This market can be seen in the lower left front corner of Figure 16–2.

At another extreme, if a customer wanted to shop for a broad assortment of items with reasonable depth, he might choose a large department store or a mass merchandiser, depending upon his price/service preferences.

Drawing a three-dimensional grid is relatively easy, but it does not guarantee that all parts of the grid have equal quantities of market needs to be satisfied. In fact, it is quite possible that certain grid boxes would be almost empty. This emphasizes the importance to retailers

---

[27] Alton F. Doody, "Historical Pattern of Marketing Innovations," in William F. Decker, *Emerging Concepts in Marketing, Proceedings of the Winter Conference of the American Marketing Association, December, 1962* (Chicago, American Marketing Association), pp. 245–56.

[28] Stanley C. Hollander, "Retailing: Cause or Effect?" in Decker, *ibid.*, pp. 220–30.

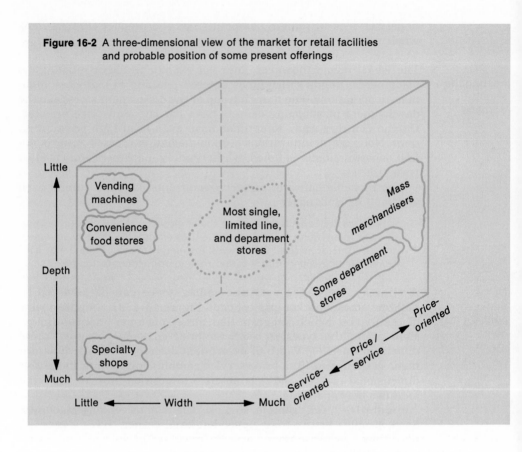

Figure 16-2 A three-dimensional view of the market for retail facilities and probable position of some present offerings

of focusing on market needs *before* developing their offerings. Blindly "scrambling" is unlikely to yield profits. In fact, it may so scramble the firm's image that potential customers will become confused – and the new image may be worse than the old.

Product life-cycle concept helps too

The market grid concept helps explain why a variety of marketing institutions can develop, and this line of thinking is consistent with our emphasis on strategy planning and locating new opportunities. The degree of competitiveness which develops in some markets, however, leads us to apply the product life-cycle concept to retail institutions to understand fully the evolutionary process. The merchant prince may exploit new opportunities for a while, but if his judgment is correct, he can count on fairly prompt imitation and a squeeze on his innovator's profits.

Some conventional retailers are far along in their cycle, some have already declined, while current innovators are still in the market growth stage. It seems that some conventional retailers have not recognized the critical importance of focusing on certain market segments. They simply shoot for everybody.

As long as all competing retailers do the same, and the markets are large enough to accommodate everyone, then they manage to survive fairly well. But as the market maturity stage comes, profits are squeezed. These product-oriented retailers have been too involved with their internal problems, rather than studying market needs. They don't really know what's going on in the market or how to react when more innovative competitors start catering to submarkets all around the market grid.

It is not surprising to find that some modern success stories in retailing are among firms which aim at needs along the edges of the market grid shown in Figure 16–2. The convenience food store chains, for example, don't just sell food, but deliberately sell a particular assortment-service combination to meet a special need. The same can be said for certain specialty-shop and boutique chains as well as some of the mass merchandisers and department store chains.[29]

Will retailers keep scrambling for profits?

Scrambled merchandising may continue into the future. There are still many inflexibilities and rigidities in our marketing system, including the inflexibility of the traditional retailers' pricing policies. Pricing will be discussed in detail later, but it should be noted here that many retailers have traditionally used fixed percentage markups for *all* items, regardless of the rate of turnover. The fast-moving items contributed nicely to profit, while the slow-moving items tended to reduce profits. If a firm were looking for opportunities, it would sell these fast-moving, high-profit items. And it is exactly these items that are crossing traditional lines and appearing in unexpected places.

Table 16–2 shows the ranges of gross margins conventional retailers have found necessary, to assure staying in business and making *some* profit. *Some* is emphasized because typically the net profit – the difference between a seemingly big gross margin and apparently necessary expenses – is only 1 or a few percent.

Mass merchandisers and discounters like to operate on gross margins and markups of 15 to 25 percent but, as shown in this table, conventional retailers usually require much higher percentages. This table should give you a better idea of the *why* of scrambled merchandising and suggest possible directions it will take. This table shows,

[29] For more discussion on gridding of retail markets, see H. Robert Dodge and Harry N. Summer, "Choosing between Retail Stores," *Journal of Retailing*, Fall, 1969, pp. 11–21; Fred C. Allvine, "The Supermarket Challenged!" *Business Horizons*, October, 1968, pp. 61–72; David L. Appel, "Market Segmentation – A Response to Retail Innovation," *Journal of Marketing*, April, 1970, pp. 64–67; John Farley, "Dimensions of Supermarket Choice Patterns," *Journal of Marketing Research*, May, 1968, pp. 206–8; Charles T. Moore and Joseph B. Mason, "A Research Note on Major Retail Center Patronage," *Journal of Marketing*, July, 1969, pp. 61–64; P. Ronald Stephenson, "Identifying Determinants of Retail Patronage," *Journal of Marketing*, July, 1969, pp. 57–61; Steven R. Flaster, "A Consumer Approach to the Specialty Store," *Journal of Retailing*, Spring, 1969, pp. 21–31; Leonard L. Berry, "The Components of Department Store Image: A Theoretical and Empirical Analysis," *Journal of Retailing*, Spring, 1969, pp. 3–20; A. Coskun Samli, "Segmentation and Carving a Niche in the Market Place," *Journal of Retailing*, Summer, 1968, pp. 35–49; R. J. Minichiello, "Comparative Assortments of Discount Food Stores and Conventional Supermarkets," *Journal of Retailing*, Winter, 1968, pp. 29–43; and H. L. Green, "The Structure of Outlying Retail Centers: Where Do Retail Functions Belong?" *Journal of Retailing*, Winter, 1968, pp. 54–60.

Table 16–2 Gross margins in selected retail trades for recent years

Gross margin ranges	Retail trades
50 percent or more	Custom tailors, monuments, florists and nurseries, bakery shops, furs.
40 to 50 percent	Garages, jewelry, restaurants, eating places, furniture, and undertaking.
35 to 40 percent	Musical instruments, housefurnishings, dairy and poultry products, gifts, novelties, souvenirs, books, furniture, drinking places, taverns, bars, office equipment and supplies, floor coverings, shoes (family stores), electric and gas household appliances.
30 to 35 percent	Paint, wallpaper, glass, confectionery, drugs, women's accessory and specialty stores, men's clothing, stationery, men's furnishings, women's ready-to-wear, limited-price variety, automobile accessories and parts, family clothing, coal and other fuel.
20 to 30 percent	Hardware, sporting goods, dry goods, general merchandise, lumber, cigar stores and stands, filling stations, meats, hardware and farm implements.
Below 20 percent	Alcoholic beverage package stores, farm implements, motor vehicles, groceries and meats, groceries.

Source: Dun & Bradstreet.

for example, why scramblers want to sell bakery goods, jewelry, appliances, refreshments, and gifts. Try to analyze why some of the conventional retailers have such high gross margins and why other types of retailers can operate more economically.

Size and channel system thinking

As already noted, mass production is not the only source of economies related to larger size. A few specific comments on how the advantages and disadvantages of larger size apply to retailing will help show why some retailers have grown and why channel system thinking is vital.

The large
and small
advantages

The small independent retailer may satisfy his own psychic needs by being his own boss, and he can be very helpful to some target customers because of his flexibility. But his shop may only *seem* profitable because some of the costs of doing business are ignored. He may not be allowing for depreciation or for family members clerking or keeping books without pay. Sometimes he can keep the doors open only because he operates the store and has a full-time job elsewhere. As we noted already, about 580,000 small retailers gross less than $30,000 of sales annually, which, after expenses, leaves hardly enough to support one person.

Even the average retail store is too small to gain economies of size.

Annual sales for the average store of only $175,000 is not very impressive, especially considering that net profits as a percentage of sales range from 1 to 5 percent. We gain some perspective on size when we realize that a grocery supermarket sells more than $1 million worth of goods per year!

Retailing is easy to enter, and the mortality rate is predictably high. The new small storekeeper must be expert in almost all phases of the business immediately. In a larger organization, on the other hand, specialists take care of buying, accounting, taxes, and building maintenance.

But although larger organizations can buy in quantity at lower prices, take advantage of mass advertising, and hire specialists, larger size alone does not guarantee more efficient operation. It merely gives management an extra opportunity for efficiency.

Large-scale retailing can have economic advantages. Department stores, for example, achieve some of the advantages of horizontal integration, whether the store was formed by merging several limited-line stores or by internal expansion. As a single larger unit, the department store may be able to attract more customers through storewide advertising. Once customers are in a store, they can cross departmental lines and buy on impulse.

But size does not automatically confer advantages. A large department store may be made up of many small-scale specialty shops and limited-line stores that require special management skills. Leasing of some departments – optical goods, hats, restaurants – may be necessary if specialized skill is required to operate them. Moreover, the departments in a department store might not be any larger than independent limited-line stores, and so there may be little or no possibility for volume buying.

There's strength in numbers

The disadvantages of small size, even among large department stores, has led to chain operations to achieve the benefits of large-scale operations.

Chains grew slowly until after World War I, then spurted ahead during the 1920's. The first Census of Distribution in 1929, designed in part to determine the importance of chains, found that more than 7,000 chain organizations controlled about 21 percent of all retail sales and a much larger share in certain lines. This discovery caused a number of states to pass antichain store legislation. The Robinson-Patman Act of 1936 was intended, in part, to stop certain chain store practices, especially demanding and getting lower prices because of their size.

This legislative reaction may have inhibited some managements. Chains did continue to grow, but at a less dramatic rate. In 1948, 23 percent, and in 1969 about 29 percent, of the country's retail sales were made by chain stores.

Chains have done even better in certain lines. Variety store chains have 80 percent of sales in that field. Department store chains are an important factor across the nation in selling general merchandise. Such chains as Sears, Montgomery Ward, and J. C. Penney are in this category.

In the general merchandise field, chains of four or more establishments handled 86 percent of sales in 1963, compared to only 60 percent of the volume in 1954. Grocery chains of four or more outlets have expanded from 39 percent to 49 percent of the market during the 1954–63 period. And those with 11 or more stores had 52 percent of the market in 1969.

Independents form chains too

One of the reasons chain store sales have been climbing recently is that chain management is paying more attention to achieving the economies of scale in distribution, either corporately or through administered systems. We already have mentioned corporate chains, but here we must note the development of cooperative and voluntary chains.

Retailer-owned *cooperative chains* are formed by independent retailers in their efforts to compete with chains. They band together to set up their own wholesaling organization, and cooperation in such groups has enabled many "independents" to meet chain competition effectively. Sales of cooperative chains have been rising.

Wholesaler-sponsored *voluntary chains*, operating similarly to cooperative chains except that they are sponsored by wholesalers, also have been most helpful to the "independent" retailers. Some are linked together by contracts specifying common operating procedures and the use of common storefront design, store name, and joint promotional efforts.[30]

Franchising is similar

Franchise operations – such as McDonald's Carry-Out Restaurants and Colonel Sander's fried chicken shops – are similar to voluntary chains. Someone has developed a good marketing strategy, and the members of the group carry it out. The voluntary chains have tended to work with existing retailers, whereas franchisors like to work with newcomers whom they train and get started. Sometimes they will locate the site, as well as supervise building and the initial promotion and opening.[31]

Cooperatives are something else

Cooperative and voluntary chains should not be confused with *consumer cooperatives*, which are groups of *consumers* who have banded together into voluntary buying associations and normally operate on a nonprofit basis with voluntary or poorly paid management. These

---

[30] "Cooperatives Give Independent Retailers More Marketing Muscle," *Marketing Insights*, November 7, 1966, p. 20. "Prescribing for the Drug Stores," *Business Week*, September 10, 1966, pp. 149–52; "A Supermarket Chain That Isn't a Chain," *Business Week*, August 22, 1964, pp. 81–84, has a description of Super Valu, a Midwest food wholesaler running a voluntary group; and Russell L. Childress, "Trends in Affiliated Wholesale-Retail Food Operations," *Management Research Summary* (Washington, D.C.: Small Business Administration, 1963).

[31] E. H. Lewis and R. Hancock, *The Franchise System of Distribution* (Minneapolis: University of Minnesota Press, 1963). See also, the special issue on franchising in the *Journal of Retailing*, Winter, 1968–69; and Robert J. Mockler and H. E. Easop, "The Art of Managing a Franchise," *Business Horizons*, August, 1968, pp. 27–36.

consumer cooperatives have never been sizable in the United States, their high point being 1 percent of retail sales in 1954.[32]

Such cooperatives have been more successful in Europe where most retailers apparently have been high priced and inefficient. Most U.S. markets, on the other hand, have been so competitive that the cooperative patronage dividends, basic to co-op customer loyalty, have not been attractive enough to keep the customers coming to the typically out-of-the-way store for the (sometimes) unknown or co-op dealer brands.

The fate of consumer cooperatives is further evidence that size or goodwill alone do not make an efficient channel system. Economies of scale may be possible, but it takes some hardheaded business decisions to link the members of a channel system efficiently. As always, the final test is customer approval. Some large horizontal and vertical linked systems seem to be getting this approval.

How retailers operate

Retailing includes so many different kinds of operations that it is difficult to find generalizations that cover the behavior of both the small independent store operator and the highly specialized buyer in large integrated systems. Still, retailers do share many common characteristics, so we will consider *what* goods retailers choose; *how* they choose and handle the goods; *when* they buy; and *who* does this buying.

Retailer must buy for both his customers and himself

Most retail buyers see themselves as purchasing agents for their target customers, remembering the old retailing maxim: "Goods well bought are half sold." Typically, they do *not* see themselves as sales agents for manufacturers. Retailers have a selfish interest in serving their customers well—namely, their own survival and profit—and this takes priority over helping manufacturers sell their products.

Some retailers emphasize manufacturers' brands, then attempt to evaluate various manufacturers' promotional programs to anticipate future customer demands, both generally and week by week. Other retailers, in contrast, have a deliberate and successful policy of promoting their own dealer brands.

There is no sure way to determine what items a retailer should stock. He should try to develop a marketing mix that includes an attractive product assortment for his target customers. This assortment will vary according to his customers and the kind of store (convenience, shopping, or specialty) he operates. Even in a large chain operation such as Sears, the particular location determines what a particular store carries. The assortment offered in each of the Sears

[32] H. G. Canoyer and E. F. Cheit, "Consumer Cooperatives in Minnesota," *Business News Notes*, School of Business Administration, University of Minnesota, November, 1952.

retail stores in the Chicago area depends on the neighborhood in which the store is located. And as many as half of the items carried by a grocery chain may be specifically ordered for particular neighborhoods with the remainder being standard for all stores.[33]

The price policies of the channel also may affect the choice of products. Some retailers, especially druggists, have encouraged resale price maintenance and refused to carry merchandise not protected under the fair trade laws. Here, because they feel unprotected prices will not be favorable to them, the retailers refuse to carry products that might be favorably priced for their customers—a slight twisting of the concept that the retailer is the purchasing agent for the consumer.

How retailers buy and why

Although most retailers carry a large number of items—drugstores up to 12,000 items, hardware stores from 3,000 to 25,000, and grocery stores up to 8,000 items—they do not often carry a large inventory of any single item. Instead, modern retailers seek to stock their shelves, perhaps keep some reserve stock, and depend on a continual flow through the channel. The size of their inventory depends on how efficiently and dependably the channel operates. To help simplify buying, most retailers limit their buying to only a few wholesalers, especially if they are affiliated with voluntary or cooperative chains.

Often retail buyers are annoyed by the number of wholesalers' and manufacturers' representatives who call on them. These retailers feel that their sales of each item are so small that they cannot afford to spend much time choosing each product. The manufacturer's marketing manager should understand this attitude in developing his promotion. His marketing mix may be more successful if his salesmen emphasize display and shelf arrangement—things that help the retailer directly—and not worry as much about product features.

As the retailer's sales volume expands, he can justify spending more time buying individual items. Buyers may begin to specialize in certain goods; some large chains buy such large lots that they can assign buyers to find additional and lower cost sources of supply. This is necessary, of course, when they go into dealer branding.

Buyers must read the signs—and computer too

Retail buyers must constantly decide how much of which products to stock and restock. One aid to the buyer is a form, the want slip, that salespeople, perhaps working directly for the buyer, make out to show customers' unfilled requests. Many retailers, however, can't afford to wait until wants materialize. They must anticipate them. To do this, they review trade papers, listen to ideas and plans of salesmen, and watch the sales of their competitors, especially the leaders in retailing. Often they look to New York City or nearby Commerce Cities for the latest trends.

Buyers are not completely in the dark when they make their selec-

[33] "Coming: Customized Assortments," *Chain Store Age*, November, 1966, p. 69.

tions. Fads and fashions may come and go, but consumers always need suits, dresses, sugar, nails, and safety pins. Their sizes, appetites, and other needs don't change appreciably from year to year, and routine sales analysis and sales forecasting can be very helpful in anticipating future needs.

Retail buyers may be in charge of inventory control. To keep a close tab on stock on hand, most retailers – and especially the modern mass merchandisers – maintain detailed inventory controls. Some firms even use computers to monitor the turnover of individual items. Inventory records are maintained on a dollar basis, unit basis, or both.

Dollar inventory control aggregates records for many products. Departments keep records in dollar terms on sales, gross margins, inventories, markups, markdowns, returns to sellers, and returns by customers. This kind of analysis shows general tendencies.

Unit control uses records of actual units – by types, sizes, styles, prices, colors, etc. These more detailed records help reveal best sellers, slow sellers, and any imbalance of stocks. Such close control makes it easier to buy intelligently and tends to make buying more routine.

Mass merchandisers are using unit control increasingly to quickly pinpoint sales of every product on their shelves. As one discounter put it, "We are not satisfied to know what we are selling in a thousand-foot area – we want to know quickly what we are selling on each table."

Over a given time period, such detailed data from the various stores in a chain can be used to identify trends and direct buying.[34]

Remember his ego, his invoice, his business

In conventional retailing operations, however, much still depends on the buyer's judgment. Each buyer usually has a fairly strict budget. This is a miniature profit-and-loss statement for each department or merchandise line. In an effort to make a profit, the buyer attempts to forecast sales, merchandise costs, and expenses. The figure for "cost of merchandise" is the amount the buyer has to spend over the period of the budget. If he has not yet spent it all, he is "open to buy." *The buyer, therefore, does have considerable latitude to exercise his judgment.*

The buyer can be an important figure in a channel system.[35] He must be sold before the final consumer even has a chance to inspect the merchandise. His ego needs boosting just like an industrial buyer's. He is concerned about his future and buys accordingly. Nor are these trivial considerations. In most retailing operations, each buyer runs his own department and his decision is final. Special efforts may be needed to satisfy each one, even if this means invoicing in a certain way, packaging different assortments, and so on. In the extreme, each buyer may require a separate marketing mix.

---

[34] "What's the Sales Potential of Those Products Taking Up Space on a Store's Valuable Shelves," *Systems Management*, January, 1962, pp. 35 ff.

[35] For discussions of the importance of buyers, see E. J. Gross, "Bureaucracy, the 'Gatekeeper' Concept, and Consumer Innovation," *Journal of Retailing*, Spring, 1967, pp. 9–16, 64; "Prestige Store Grows Without Losing Gloss," *Business Week*, April 9, 1966, pp. 58–62.

When they buy — on Monday or in April

Proximity to sources of supply and speed of turnover help determine how often, and how far in advance, retailers place orders. Many retailers don't buy more than a week ahead, because their wholesalers are nearby. Grocery supermarket buyers count on a continual flow from wholesalers and manufacturers and may place their orders every week. In grocery retailing, rapid turnover dictates frequent ordering.

Women's ready-to-wear retailers, on the other hand, may have to order well in advance of actual sale to assure delivery because some manufacturers may not make up the goods until they are sure of orders. Lead time, however, also depends on how far the retailer is located from the central market. Dress buyers in New York City may buy several times a week; buyers in Pocatello, Idaho, may place their large orders only four times a year.

When a channel system has been developed, the retailers might be expected to place orders on a more regular and predictable schedule to smooth the flow of goods from manufacturer to wholesaler to retailer. This may change the retailer's ordering patterns somewhat, and perhaps increase or decrease inventory levels. But it all would be done to improve the efficiency of the whole channel. This system might be supplemented by a direct telephone link between the retailer's store and the wholesaler's computer for urgent orders.[36]

Buyers are people who like to satisfy

The buyers in small stores usually are the owners or managers, since there is a very close relationship between buying and selling. In larger stores, buyers tend to specialize in certain lines. But usually those buyers sell as well as supervise the salesclerks who will sell the new merchandise. These buyers, therefore, are in close contact with their customers, *and* with their salespeople, who are sensitive to the effectiveness of the buyer's efforts — especially when they are on commission. A buyer may even buy some items to satisfy the preferences of his salespeople.

As sales volumes rise, a buyer may specialize in buying only and have no responsibility for sales. Sears, for example, has a buying department of more than 3,000, supported by a staff department exceeding 1,400. There are 44 buying departments located in Sears' headquarters city, Chicago, with 6 in New York and smaller buying offices in Los Angeles, Dallas, Kansas City, Minneapolis, Atlanta, London, Brussels, Paris, Milan, Frankfurt, and Tokyo.

Departments in Chicago and New York concentrate on a narrow assortment of items. Each is set up as an independent unit under a supervisor with a controller, a mail-order sales manager, a retail sales manager, and the buyers and assistant buyers.[37]

---

[36] "Hardware Retailers Order Supplies Via Touch-Tone," *Data Systems News,* March 25, 1968, p. 11.
[37] "Why Sears Stays the No. 1 Retailer," *Business Week,* January 20, 1968, pp. 65–73; "The Buying Story," reprinted from *1956 Report to Stockholders,* Sears, Roebuck & Co., pp. 4, 5; "Inside Sears, Roebuck," *Printers' Ink,* October 22, 1965, pp. 15–30.

Resident buyers

Many department stores, and ready-to-wear clothing chains handling fashion merchandise, work with independent buying agents, called *resident buyers,* in the central markets of New York, Chicago, Los Angeles, and San Francisco. They cover new styles and fashions on the spot, and buy fill-in items as the retailers run out of stock during the year. Some resident buying organizations buy everything except furniture, shoes, and food for their stores. Some resident buyers have hundreds of employees and buy more than $1-billion worth of goods a year.

Resident buying organizations fill a retailer's need to reach the many small manufacturers who cannot afford large selling organizations. Resident buyers' usually are paid an annual fee based on their purchases. The store's regular buyers often use the resident buyer's offices as headquarters on their regular buying trips to the central markets for fashion merchandise.

Committee buying and multiple buying influences

In some large chain store organizations, especially in grocery and variety lines, the major decisions—to add or drop lines or change buying policies—may be delegated to a committee. The seller still will contact the buyer, but the buyer does not have final responsibility. In some organizations, the buyer prepares forms summarizing proposals for new products. The seller completes these forms but may not get to present his story in person to the buying committee.

This rational, almost cold-blooded, approach reduces the impact of the persuasive salesmen, but it has become necessary because of the flood of new products. In an average week, 150 to 250 new items are presented for consideration to the buying offices of the larger food chains. If all were accepted, 10,000 new items would be added during a single year, more than their present stock! Obviously, buyers must be hardheaded and impersonal. About 90 percent of the new items presented to food stores are rejected.

Wholesalers' and manufacturers' marketing managers must develop good marketing mixes when buying becomes so sophisticated and competitive. This approach is likely to become more common as computers facilitate sales and inventory analysis.[38]

What does the future look like?

The changes in retailing in the last 30 years have been extremely rapid. No end to this pace seems to be in sight. Scrambled merchandising may become more scrambled. Some analysts are forecasting larger stores while others are predicting smaller ones.

[38] E. B. Weiss, *The Decline of the Store Buyer* (New York: Doyle-Dane, Bernbach, Inc., 1961).

The new age of servoselling

Any effort to forecast trends in such a situation is extremely risky, but the market grid approach can be helpful. Those who suggest bigger and bigger supermarkets and discount houses may be primarily concerned with the mass market. Those who look for more small stores and specialty shops may be anticipating more small but increasingly affluent target markets which are able to afford higher prices for different total products.

To serve these smaller but affluent markets, small, convenience-type grocery stores may continue to spread, and sales by vending machines — even with their higher operating costs and prices — may grow steadily. Certainly, some customers are getting tired of the large supermarkets that take so much of their time. Logically, convenience goods should be offered at the customer's, rather than the retailer's convenience, as has been the case. Some retailers still fight night and weekend hours, for example, when it is most convenient for many families to shop.

Telephone shopping is another possibility. The catalog houses and department stores already find phone business effective. Telephone supermarkets, now a reality, sell only by phone and deliver all orders. Linking the phone to closed-circuit TV would enable the customer to see the goods at home while hearing well-prepared sales presentations. Then the customer could place an order through a small computer system or through a telephone system and have the billing and delivery arranged automatically. One catalog company, Gamble Alden, has experimented with a system whereby customers throughout the country can call their Chicago headquarters any time of the day or night and order merchandise. And using a computer-oriented system similar to the GE system discussed in Chapter 2, it can process the order in about eight minutes — keeping track of the order, inventory, credit, and billing, and arranging for immediate shipment.[39] Some prophets are even talking about delivery systems directly into the home, just as gas and oil are delivered now.[40]

With present electronic and servomechanism capabilities, there seems to be no reason why the customer couldn't shop from his home instead of traipsing up and down the aisles of larger and larger shopping facilities.

Such an advanced form of automated retailing — perhaps the equipment involved would warrant the name "servoselling" — could take over a large share of the convenience-good and homogeneous shopping-good business.

[39] "New Shopping Methods Coming," (Lansing, Mich.) *State Journal,* December 1, 1967, p. D–5.

[40] E. B. Weiss, "What Will Retailing Be Like in 1975?" *Marketing Insights,* November 7, 1966, pp. 14–16; A. F. Doody and W. R. Davidson, "Next Revolution in Retailing," *Harvard Business Review,* June, 1967, pp. 4–21; "Retailing in the 1980's," *Marketing Insights,* November 18, 1968, pp. 10–12; "Dial-ing for the Groceries," *Business Week,* March 28, 1970, pp. 110–16; "Computers Reach the Checkout Counter," *Business Week,* June 13, 1970, p. 86; "Computerized System to Cut Checkout Lines at Markets Unveiled," *Wall Street Journal,* August 7, 1970, p. 22; and "G.E. Builds a Robot Cashier," *Business Week,* May 10, 1969, p. 70.

| If shopping centers are too conventional | Shopping centers may continue to grow but may feel increasing competition from mass merchandisers who were not able to or not interested in obtaining space in the planned centers. If these shopping centers turn out to be strong-holds for conventional retailers but don't meet the needs of today's target customers, then shopping centers may be forced to change their methods – or take the consequences. The branches of some department stores, for example, entered shopping centers with relatively high prices but then had to drop them. |

| Retailers becoming manufacturers and vice versa | We also may see more horizontally and vertically administered channel systems. One prophet foresees perhaps 50 giant corporate chains, together with perhaps 100 giant chains of independents, controlling most of the nation's retail sales.[41] These chains probably would integrate vertically as well, or at the very least work closely with their suppliers and perhaps become the channel captains. |

This would have a major impact on present manufacturers who already see retailers developing their own brands and using manufacturers primarily as production arms. The large manufacturers themselves may go into retailing in the future for self-protection.

General Electric and Westinghouse, as noted earlier, are experimenting along this line. But they would not be the first, since Rexall Corp., Sherwin Williams, B. F. Goodrich, Van Heusen, and others already control or own retail outlets.[42]

The function of retailing clearly will continue to be needed, but the role of individual retailers, and even the concept of a retail store, may have to undergo considerable change. There will always be customers' needs and they will probably want to satisfy these needs with combinations of goods and services. But retail stores are not necessarily the best way of accomplishing this in all cases.

| Different product assortments may be needed | Just as builders of tract homes shifted some home appliance sales from retailers, the builders of new cities may sell completely furnished homes and eliminate the need for retail home furnishing stores. And catering to the mobile young, apartment builders may rent furnished apartments or offer assortments of furniture for rent from a selection owned by the management. This may fit the needs more precisely of a mobile population less interested in the possession of goods. But it will also have a direct impact on present retailers. Many may just not be needed at all![43] |

[41] "Independent Retailing: New Outlook," *Printers' Ink*, April 5, 1963, pp. 53–54.

[42] "Westinghouse Tries Its Hand at Appliance Retailing in Deal with West Coast Chain," *Business Week*, August 5, 1967, p. 57; and "Burlington to Turn Retailer," and "A Giant Tries Home Building," *Business Week*, August 27, 1969, p. 34; E. B. Weiss, "Will Manufacturers Go into Retailing?" *Advertising Age*, December 31, 1962, pp. 35–36; "Has G. E. Taken Another Step Toward Retailing?" *Advertising Age*, September 3, 1962, p. 52; and "The Coming Crisis in Mass Retailing," *Advertising Age*, January 28, 1963, pp. 78–80.

[43] E. B. Weiss, "The Retail Store Won't Last Forever," *Marketing Insights*, November 18, 1968, pp. 12–13.

A selection of opportunities and problems

One thing is certain – change in retailing is inevitable. For years, traditional retailers' profits have declined. Even some of the newer discounters and shopping centers have had disappointing records. Department stores and food and drug chains have experienced profit declines. The old variety stores have fared even worse. Some are shifting into mass merchandising operations, but this may only make that picture less attractive.

A few firms, among them Sears and J. C. Penney, have avoided this general profit squeeze. But generally, declining profits have helped cause the sometimes desperate moves into scrambled merchandising. Where it will all end is not yet clear, but it is safe to say that the imaginative marketing manager will find opportunities as well as problems in this unsettled situation.

Conclusion

There are many crosscurrents in today's retailing. Many new developments are resulting from changing customer preferences, rising incomes, aggressive action by competitors, and technical innovations.

But retailing is not completely chaotic. Some generalizations about the development of retailing institutions are possible. These can be summarized as follows:

1. Certain types of retailing facilities are extremely stable. It is likely that in every city in the country there are stores with ancient Roman counterparts, such as limited-line food and clothing stores.
2. Although the development of new retailers has frequently been viewed with alarm by conventional retailers, these newcomers have tended (a) to become a stable part of the retailing system, and (b) now account for only a relatively small percentage of retail sales. Sometimes the newcomers have encouraged changes – the traditional retailers have been forced into modifications – but they have not eliminated all the former leaders. This has been true for the department store chains, mail-order houses, and most recently, discount houses.
3. Changes in retail institutions appear to be evolutionary, not revolutionary, and usually reflect changes at the consumer level. Even changes caused by uncontrollable variables – the laws passed in the political environment, for instance – may be traced to the consumer. When very rapid changes do occur, it is usually because orthodox retailers have not recognized, or made adjustment to, changes in consumer behavior. Unmet demands open the door to innovators, and then conventional retailers may have to make swift and dramatic modifications to catch up. Such a situation very well may be in the making now.

Emphasizing the evolutionary nature of retailing does not mean that all competitors evolve at equal speed or with comparable success.

Many do not see the portents of change until it is too late, or worse, attempt to ignore or resist them. Others simply do not have the resources to change their marketing strategy substantially.

It is vital that the marketing manager foresee these coming changes and estimate their impact on the existing retail structure and his own channels. The successful marketing manager will be the one who correctly anticipates – or at least meets – these changing customer demands by adjusting his place policies and marketing strategies accordingly.

QUESTIONS AND PROBLEMS

1 Identify a specialty store selling convenience goods in your city. Explain why you feel it is that kind of a store and why an awareness of this status would be important to a manufacturer. Does it give the retailer any particular advantage? If so, with whom?

2 Try to estimate the return to the owner and the profitability of a retail grocery store grossing about $150,000 in sales a year. First, compute the average daily sales volume needed to achieve this annual sales figure (assuming a six-day week). Then estimate the cost of help, rent, utilities, etc., that would be needed to handle this sales volume. Assume that competition would force him to operate at about a 20 percent gross margin. Briefly contrast the economics of this situation with that of the average supermarket.

3 What sort of a "Product" are specialty shops offering? What are the prospects for organizing a chain of specialty shops?

4 A department store consists of many departments. Is this horizontal integration? Are all of the advantages of horizontal integration achieved in a department store operation?

5 Many department stores have a bargain basement. Does the basement represent just another department, like the hat department or the luggage department for example, or is some whole new concept involved?

6 Distinguish between voluntary and cooperative chains. Which is likely to be most effective in competing with corporate chains? Why?

7 Distinguish among discount houses, discount selling, and mass merchandising. Forecast the future of low-price selling in food, clothing, and appliances.

8 In view of the wide range of gross margins (and expenses) in various lines of trade, suggest what the supermarket or scrambled merchandising outlet of the future may be like. Use care here. Are products with high gross margins necessarily highly profitable?

9 List five products which seem suitable for automatic vending and yet are not normally sold in this manner. Generally, what characteristics are required?

10 Considering the nature of retail buying, outline the basic ingredients of promotion to retail buyers. Does it make any difference what kinds of products are involved? Are any other factors relevant?

11 How is the increasing professionalism of grocery chainstore buyers going to affect food processors' marketing mixes in the future?

12 Apply the "Wheel of Retailing" hypothesis to your local community. What changes seem likely? Does it seem likely that established retailers will see the need for change or will entirely new firms have to develop?

13 Discuss the kinds of markets served by the three types of shopping centers. Are they directly competitive? Do they contain the same kinds of stores? Is the long-run outlook for all of them similar?

14 Explain the growth and decline of various types of retailers in your own community, using the market grid and product life-cycle concepts and treating the retailers' total offering as a "Product."

...in this text we are emphasizing the evolutionary character of change in our economy. This concept applies fully to wholesaling.

...despite various predictions of the demise of wholesalers, they continue to exist, and the more progressive have adapted to a changing economic environment. No such revolutions as we saw in retailing have yet taken place in wholesaling and none seem likely.

17

Wholesaling

Wholesaling is extremely important in the marketing process. Wholesalers are a vital link in many channel systems. To understand their role better, you should look at wholesalers primarily as members of channels rather than separate entities. You should ask how wholesalers fit into various channels, why they are used, and what effect they have on the marketing mixes of both manufacturers and retailers.

How to tell a wholesaler from a retailer

Precisely what is a "wholesaler?" What does he do?

These questions are hard to answer precisely, but one way to get at these definitions is to find out why a given firm wants to be considered a wholesaler rather than a retailer. There are several reasons why he might seek this classification.

First, in some channels, manufacturers permit only wholesalers to buy directly from them. The wholesalers, in turn, are expected to sell only to retailers. Exactly which firms will be permitted to buy from the manufacturer depends on how the manufacturer defines what a wholesaler is.

Second, and related to the first point, is the amount of discount granted. If retailers in a certain line normally expect a 30 percent discount off the suggested retail list price, then the wholesalers supplying them may be given a 45 percent discount off retail list. They, in turn, are expected to pass on a 30 percent discount to their retailers. In practice, this can be much more complicated.

Some manufacturers set up a scale of wholesale discounts depending on the size of the wholesaler and the services he offers. Called "trade discounts," these are discussed further in the Pricing chapters. Correctly determining which firms are entitled to what trade discounts is especially important to manufacturers because of the provisions of the Robinson-Patman Act, prohibiting price discrimination and discriminatory discounts.

Third, some cities and states have retail sales taxes or taxes on inventories or gross receipts that apply only to retailers. These levies require record keeping and occasionally out-of-pocket costs when the retailer fails to collect the tax from the consumer. It is natural, therefore, that some firms should try to avoid classification as a retailer.

Fourth, fair-trade laws usually are binding only on retailer sales to consumers. Some discount houses have sold below the fair-trade price to consumers who were buying as "wholesalers." Being a member of a buying group—such as a labor union, church group, or local business concern—was sufficient rationalization for the purpose. Interestingly, some discount houses, although operating as wholesalers to avoid the manufacturer's ire, have not wished to risk prosecution by state taxing units and have charged a retail sales tax on these "wholesale" sales.

Any of these four points explains why a firm might wish to be labeled a wholesaler rather than a retailer. The *fifth* point operates in reverse. Retailers, but not wholesalers, are generally exempt from federal minimum-wage legislation, including the requirement that overtime be paid for more than 40 hours' labor a week.[1]

Somebody has to do the wholesaling job

Despite the apparent difficulty in writing a single, hard definition of wholesaling, the *main* source of confusion is not simply semantic, but rather the wide variation in how wholesale firms operate—the functions performed, the cost of operations, and the operating policies followed.

Many wholesalers perform more functions than we traditionally associate with the term. Some wholesalers engage in all four of the

---

[1] For a detailed discussion of the definition of wholesaling and the operation and management of a wholesale business, see T. N. Beckman, N. H. Engle, and R. D. Buzzell, *Wholesaling* (3rd ed.; New York: Ronald Press Co., 1959). See also, Charles B. Saunders and John D. Logsdon, "Retailing—What's That?" *Journal of Retailing,* Fall, 1969, pp. 46–54 f.

regrouping steps, and some of their sorting-out and accumulation activities may even seem like manufacturing. As a result, we find some firms calling themselves manufacturer and jobber, or manufacturer and dealer. In addition, some use general terms such as merchant, dealer, distributor, or jobber because their actual operations are flexible, and they do not wish to be narrowly classified.

To avoid a prolonged technical and semantic discussion, we will use the U.S. Bureau of Census definition, the essence of which is:

Wholesaling is concerned with the activities of those persons or establishments which sell to retailers and other merchants, and/or to industrial, institutional, and commercial users, but who do not sell in significant amounts to ultimate consumers.[2]

It should be noted that producers who take over wholesaling functions are not considered wholesalers. However, if separate establishments, such as branch warehouses, are set up, those facilities are counted as wholesalers by the U.S. Bureau of Census.

Wholesaling is a middleman activity. When a manufacturer goes direct, he still must assume the marketing functions that an independent wholesaler might provide. This is important from a channel standpoint. Wholesaling functions usually must be performed by some channel member, whether a wholesaler or the manufacturer himself.

Possible wholesaling functions

Wholesalers may perform certain functions for both their own customers and their suppliers – in short, for those above and below them in a channel. These wholesaling tasks really are elaborations of the basic marketing functions – buying, selling, grading, storing, transporting, financing, risk-taking, and gathering market information. These wholesaling functions are basic to the subsequent discussion and should be studied carefully now. But *keep in mind that these functions may be provided by some, but not all, wholesalers.*

What a wholesaler might do for his customers

1. *Anticipate needs.* As a purchasing agent for his customers, the wholesaler forecasts his customers' demands and buys accordingly.

2. *Regroup goods.* The wholesaler provides at least one and sometimes all four of the regrouping steps in an effort to provide the assortment wanted by his customers at the lowest possible cost.

3. *Carry stocks.* The wholesaler carries inventory, relieving his customers of the necessity to carry a full inventory.

4. *Deliver goods.* The wholesaler frequently has transportation facilities and can provide prompt delivery service at low cost. Speed may be essential to keep factory production lines rolling or to satisfy a retailer's customers.

---

[2] Similar to definition in "Report of the Definitions Committee," *Journal of Marketing*, October, 1948, p. 217.

5. *Grant credit.* The wholesaler has traditionally extended credit to many of his customers, sometimes for several months. This financing function may be especially important to small customers and is sometimes the reason why they buy through wholesalers rather than directly from the manufacturer. Generally, the smaller the customer, the more financially dependent he is on wholesalers.

6. *Provide information and advisory service.* The wholesaler and his salesmen may be specialists in the products in which they deal. They are in a position to provide price and technical information as well as suggestions on how to install and sell products.

7. *Provide part of buying function.* Many customers appreciate the wholesaler having salesmen call on them. This relieves customers of the responsibility of looking for supply sources – that is, it simplifies *their* buying function. They have only to evaluate the worth of the various products offered.

8. *Own and transfer title to goods.* Ownership of inventory permits a wholesaler and his customer to complete a sale without benefit of other intermediaries (such as a manufacturer or broker), thus facilitating the whole transaction.

What a wholesaler might do for his producer-suppliers

1. *Provide part of producer's selling function.* The wholesaler sometimes seeks out supply sources, decreasing the number of salesmen the producer needs. The wholesaler also may participate in the producer's advertising and sales promotion programs.

2. *Store inventory.* The classic wholesaling function of storing reduces a manufacturer's need for carrying large stocks, reducing his warehousing expenses.

3. *Help finance by owning stocks.* Some producers, especially small ones, need financial assistance. When the wholesaler carries inventory, this reduces the producer's need for working capital.

4. *Reduce credit risk.* A producer's customers – retailers and other producers – may be numerous, and some may be poor credit risks. It is expensive for a small producer, especially one far distant, to evaluate all of these potential credit risks when selling only one or a few products. The wholesaler who sells these customers many products is in a better position to evaluate their credit status. And if the wholesaler is a source of supply of many products, the customer may be more likely to pay him than to pay a manufacturer from whom he may not reorder.

5. *Provide market information.* The wholesaler is closer to the consumer and is in a better position to evaluate customer reactions. As an informed buyer and seller, he may reduce the producer's need for market research.

Kinds and costs of available wholesale facilities

Table 17–1 lists the types, number, sales volume, and operating expenses of wholesalers operating in 1967. The differences in operating expenses suggest that each of these types performs or does not perform certain wholesaling functions. But which ones and why?

Why, for example, do manufacturers use merchant wholesalers costing 13.8 percent of sales when manufacturers' branches with stock cost only 11.3 percent?

Why use either when brokers cost only 3.2 percent?

Table 17-1 Wholesale trade, 1967, United States, by type of operation

Type of operation	Establish-ments (number)	Sales (000,000)	Operating expenses (including payroll) percent of sales
United States, total	311,464	$459,476	
Merchant wholesalers' total	212,993	206,055	13.8%
Wholesale merchants' distributors	204,783	181,776	14.8
Importers	5,171	10,354	10.3
Exporters	2,272	9,508	4.1
Terminal grain elevators	767	4,418	4.5
Manufacturer's sales offices, sales branches, total:	30,679	157,097	7.2
Manufacturers' sales branches (with stock)	16,709	67,175	11.3
Manufacturers' sales offices (without stock)	13,970	89,922	4.1
Petroleum bulk plants, terminals, LP gas facilities, total	30,229	24,822	0.3
Merchandise agents, brokers, total	26,462	61,347	4.0
Auction companies	1,594	4,792	2.9
Merchandise brokers	4,373	14,030	3.2
Commission merchants	5,425	14,068	3.4
Import agents	270	1,791	2.2
Export agents	548	3,372	1.9
Manufacturers' agents	12,106	15,257	6.4
Selling agents	1,891	6,890	4.2
Purchasing agents and resident buyers	255	1,147	3.6
Assemblers of farm products, total	11,101	10,156	8.6

Source: 1967 *Census of Business.*

Is the use of wholesalers with higher operating expenses the reason why marketing costs are high—if, in fact, they are?

Historical background will help answer these questions.

Each wholesaler found his niche

In this text, we are emphasizing the evolutionary character of change in our economy. This concept applies fully to wholesaling. America has transformed itself from colonial territory, dependent on the mother country for its finished goods in exchange for its raw materials, into a prime industrial nation. As output grew, so did the need for middlemen to handle it.

To serve the retail general stores of earlier times, early wholesalers carried a wide line of merchandise. They were called "general merchandise" wholesalers because their merchandise was so varied. We already have seen that the general store developed into a single- or limited-line store as towns grew and more goods became available. To serve these stores, "single-line" wholesalers evolved; those specializing in very narrow lines were called "specialty" wholesalers. Single-line wholesalers were well established in the eastern grocery and dry goods fields by the early 1800's. This same evolution took place a little later in the markets farther west.

Since wholesaling developed to distribute the greater production of the factories to an expanding population, wholesalers served not only retailers and final consumers but also manufacturers. Many manufacturers were so small that it was hard for them to contact the growing number of wholesalers or other manufacturer customers, and special wholesalers—called agents and brokers—developed to make these contacts. In general, specialized needs arose, and specialized wholesaling institutions developed to meet them.

Learn the pure to understand the real

To get a clear understanding of wholesaling, we will identify and analyze as pure types several specific kinds of wholesalers. Actually, however, it is difficult to find examples of pure types in wholesaling. No two wholesalers operate exactly alike. Rather, they are a blend of the basic types presented here. And it becomes even more difficult to identify the type by the name commonly used in a particular trade. Some so-called "brokers" actually behave as limited-function wholesalers, and some so-called "manufacturers' agents" operate as full-service wholesalers.

This casual use of terminology in the business world makes it important that you be thoroughly familiar with the pure types before trying to understand the hybrids. A manufacturer's or retailer's marketing manager should understand these differences *and* clearly specify *his* place objectives before trying to select suitable wholesalers.

In the following pages we will discuss the major types of wholesalers which have been identified by the U.S. Bureau of Census to guide its data collection. There are difficulties with any definitional scheme, but this one is workable and data is available.

In international markets, we find the same kinds of wholesalers as we have in the United States, although good data may be lacking. In addition, in foreign markets, different terms may be used, and this again emphasizes the importance of understanding the "pure" types.

Finally, of course, each firm must be evaluated individually. This is especially true if a firm is trying to build a channel system and distribute the channel functions in an effective manner. Not all wholesalers do the same things, and not all of them who supposedly perform the same functions do them equally well.

437

Merchant wholesalers are the most numerous

Merchant wholesalers are the most numerous of all wholesalers. In 1967, they consitituted about 68 percent of wholesaling establishments—but handled only 45 percent of wholesale sales.

Their major distinguishing characteristic is that they take title; they assume the ownership of the goods they handle. They also provide some of all of the wholesaling functions. The two basic types of merchant wholesalers are: (1) service, sometimes called full-service, wholesalers, and (2) limited-function or limited-service wholesalers. Their labels are suggestive of their difference.

Service wholesalers provide all the functions

Service wholesalers normally provide all of the functions discussed previously. Within this basic group are three main subtypes: (1) *general merchandise,* (2) *single line,* and (3) *specialty.*

General merchandise service wholesalers

General merchandise service wholesalers handle a broad variety of nonperishable staple items such as hardware, electrical supplies, plumbing supplies, furniture, drugs, cosmetics, and automobile equipment. With this broad line of convenience and shopping goods, they serve general stores, hardware stores, drugstores, electric appliance shops, and small department stores. In the industrial goods field, the mill supply house (or distributor) operates in a similar way. Somewhat like a hardware store, the industrial supply house carries a broad variety of accessories and supplies.

Single-line or general-line wholesalers

This type of wholesaler differs from general merchandise wholesalers or mill supply distributors in restricting himself to a narrower line—and sometimes to a specific line—such as dry goods, groceries, wearing apparel, paint, hardware, or certain types of industrial tools or supplies. In consumer goods, he services the limited-line stores. In industrial goods, he covers a wider geographical area and offers more specialized service.

Specialty wholesalers

This type of wholesaler stocks only a narrow range of products. A *consumer goods* specialty wholesaler might carry only health foods or Oriental foods, rather than a full line of groceries. Or the specialty house might carry only automotive items, selling exclusively to mass merchandisers. One wholesaler, for example, is willing to arrange and stock his mass merchandisers' shelves, an important service to these retailers because their customers' behavior seems to vary according to geography. Final consumers in northern Indiana, for instance, respond to different shelf arrangements and products from those in southern Indiana.

The specialty wholesaler's task is to learn these differences, and adjust stocks and displays accordingly. In this effort, he goes further than most merchant wholesalers—providing some of his customers' selling functions, since displays do most of the selling in mass merchandising outlets.

For industrial goods, a specialty wholesaler might limit himself to fields requiring technical knowledge or service, perhaps electronics or plastics.

The Cadillac Plastic and Chemical Co., in Detroit, became a specialty wholesaler serving the needs of plastics makers and users alike because neither the large plastics manufacturers nor the merchant wholesalers with wide lines were in a position to give individual advice to the many users (who often have little knowledge of which product would be best for them). Cadillac now carries 10,000 items and sells to 25,000 customers, ranging in size from the very small firms to General Motors.

Limited-function wholesalers provide only certain functions

The limited-function wholesaler, as the name implies, usually provides only certain wholesaling functions. The full-service wholesaler frequently operates at higher cost because he provides all of these services. Still, some customers do not want all services, and some of the service wholesaler's policies do not exactly fit some customers' needs.

Rather than change or adjust policies for each customer, some wholesalers have set up separate departments or subsidiaries to give each customer the special assortment of services he wants. This usually means dropping one or more of the wholesaling functions discussed previously. Some full-service wholesalers have been slow to give the customer what he wants, however, and perceptive innovators have entered the market to supply the customer what he wants at the price he wants to pay.

Table 17–2 outlines the services typically provided by the various limited-function merchant wholesalers. It shows what services are, and are not provided by each general type.

In the following paragraphs, the main distinguishing characteristics of each of the limited-function wholesalers will be discussed. Wholesalers operating solely or principally as limited-function wholesalers are not numerous; in fact, they are not itemized separately in the 1967 Census of Business. Limited-function wholesalers are, nevertheless, important in some trades. You should be able to identify the various pure types of wholesalers so that you will be able to understand more fully the roles (and thus the operating costs) of the middlemen actually at work in the marketplace today. Cash-and-carry wholesalers, for example, might have operating costs of about 9 percent of sales, while mail-order wholesalers might operate for as little as 4 or 5 percent of sales.

Cash-and-carry wholesaler

Many small retailers, especially small grocers and garages, are too small to be served profitably by a service wholesaler. Discovering this fact, wholesalers establish a minimum charge or, in some cases, merely refuse to handle certain customers' business. Or they may establish cash-and-carry subsidiaries to give the small retailer the products he needs in exchange for cash on the counter. This works like a retail store, but for small retailers; it can operate at lower cost because the

Table 17–2 Functions provided by limited-function merchant wholesalers

	Limited-function or limited-service merchant wholesalers					
	Cash-and-carry	Drop shipper (desk jobber)	Wagon or truck	Mail order	Coopera-tives	Rack jobbers
Functions for customer:						
Anticipates needs	X		X	X	X	X
"Regroups" goods (one or more of 4 steps)	X		X	X	X	X
Carries stocks	X		X	X	X	X
Delivers goods			X		X	X
Grants credit		X	Maybe	Maybe	Maybe	Consignment (in some cases)
Provides information and advisory services		X	Some	Some	X	
Provides buying function		X	X	X	Some	X
Owns and transfers title to goods	X	X	X	X	X	X
Functions for producers:						
Provides producer's selling function	X	X	X	X	X	X
Stores inventory	X		X	X	X	X
Helps finance by owning stocks	X		X	X	X	X
Reduces credit risk	X	X	X	X	X	X
Provides market information	X	X	Some	X	X	Some

retailer provides many of the wholesaling functions himself. And using cash-and-carry outlets may enable the small retailer to stay in business.

Drop-shipper (or desk jobber)

A drop-shipper obtains orders from wholesalers, retailers, or industrial users, then passes these orders on to producers, telling them to ship directly to these customers. He takes title and technically owns the goods, but he does not physically handle, stock, or deliver them. This lowers his operating costs.

Drop-shippers most commonly deal in products that are so bulky that additional handling would be expensive and possibly damaging. Or the quantities may be so large that there is little need for regrouping, as with rail carload shipments of coal, lumber, oil, or chemical products.

The drop-shipper's major function is selling, but he does have to locate supplies, arrange for transportation, finance customer purchases, and assume some of the risks that go with taking title to goods.

Wagon or truck wholesaler

This wholesaler is always on the go, selling his stock from a wagon or truck. Handling perishable commodities in general demand, such as tobacco, candy, potato chips, and salad dressings, the truck jobber may provide almost the same functions as a full-service wholesaler. His major contribution is delivery of perishable lines that regular wholesalers prefer not to carry because of the special problems involved.

Truck wholesalers sometimes supply small service stations and back-alley garages with local delivery of the many small items they often forget to pick up from the service wholesaler. Truck wholesaler operating cost ratios are relatively high because they do a lot for the little they sell.

Mail-order wholesaler

We discussed catalog selling in the chapter on retailing. Wholesale mail-order houses operate in much the same way. In fact, many wholesale mail-order houses also will sell to *final* consumers who may, in some way, have access to their wholesale catalogs. To bona fide retailers, however, wholesalers give special discounts for ordering larger quantities. Otherwise, all the advantages and disadvantages of of mail-order selling apply here. These houses operate in the hardware, jewelry, sporting goods, and general merchandise lines, often catering to small outlying stores.

Producers' cooperative

Producers' cooperatives are also limited-function wholesalers, although they frequently attempt to give the same service as service wholesalers. Here, the "profits" go to the cooperative's customer-members – in the form of patronage dividends.

The successful producers' cooperatives have emphasized the sorting-out process – to improve the quality of farm products offered to the market. They have also branded these improved products and then promoted the brands. These farmers' cooperatives sometimes have had success in restricting output and increasing price by taking advantage of the normally inelastic demand for agricultural commodities.

Examples of such organizations are the California Fruit Growers Exchange (citrus fruits), Sunmaid Raisin Growers Association, The California Almond Exchange, and Land O'Lakes Creameries, Inc.

Aside from demand stimulation and supply restriction activities, the cooperatives operate basically as service wholesalers.

Rack jobber – sells nonfoods in food stores

The rack jobber is a relatively new type of wholesaler, catering mainly to food stores and especially to supermarkets. He specializes in products, such as housewares, hardware items, and health and beauty aids, that frequently are displayed on wire racks he provides.

Many grocers don't want to bother with reordering and maintaining displays of nonfood items, since it involves small quantities of so many different kinds of goods. Regular wholesalers who were handling such items were not too interested in this business either, because opening up this new channel might jeopardize relations with their present customers. While many wholesalers specialize by product line, the rack jobber must handle a scrambled assortment because this is what consumers want.

The rack jobber is practically a service wholesaler, except that he usually is paid cash for the amount of stock sold or delivered. This is a relatively expensive operation, with operating costs calculated at 18.3 percent of sales in 1958, but sales have grown impressively because this way of selling offers convenience to some target customers.[3] Although the large volume of nonfood sales from these racks has prompted some large chains to experiment with handling such items themselves, it appears now that rack jobbers can provide this service as effectively as (or more effectively than) the supermarket chains.

Wholesalers specialize by product and customer

One of a merchant wholesaler's principal assets is his customer list. He attempts to offer a unique service to certain customers and may be the only one who does this particular job. The manufacturer who wishes to reach the market segments served by this wholesaler may have to use him.

Most wholesalers specialize by product or product line—an important fact for channel planners, and especially manufacturers who usually are product-oriented. The U.S. Bureau of Census uses 59 categories, basically SIC groups, to enumerate the kinds of businesses engaged in by merchant wholesalers. These categories reflect product classifications rather than methods of operation.

Detailed data is available from the U.S. Bureau of Census on these various types of wholesalers. This data is not presented here, but for channel planning purposes it is important to know that such detailed information is available, roughly by product categories.

The detailed census data also is categorized geographically. This enables a marketing manager to determine if there are potential channel members in his target areas.

Finally, however, a marketing manager must become intimately acquainted with those specific firms which might be blended into a channel system. He must know what functions he wants done, and then seek out those who can perform them most effectively. Specific wholesalers might place different emphasis on various marketing functions. Some might be classed as full-service wholesalers but also have flourishing separate departments providing limited functions. For this reason, it is useful to look at each geographic territory as a separate channel-building problem. And this might lead to quite different channels of distribution in different areas.

Manufacturers' sales branches provide wholesaling functions

The drive toward economic integration that began in the late 1880's had its effect in wholesaling, too. Many manufacturers set up their own sales branches whenever the sales volume or the nature of their

---

[3] James J. Sheeran, "The Role of the Rack Jobber," *Journal of Marketing*, July, 1961, pp. 15–21; and John D. Horn, "Merchandising Non-Food Items through Supermarkets," *Journal of Marketing*, April, 1954, p. 380.

products warranted it. By 1967, less than 10 percent of wholesale establishments were manufacturers' sales branches, but they handled 34 percent of the total wholesale sales.

One reason for this disproportion is that these branches are usually placed in the most fertile market territories. This helps explain why their operating costs often are lower. But cost comparisons between alternate channels can be misleading, since cost allocation methods may differ. Sometimes the cost of selling is not charged to the branch but to the manufacturer's sales expenses. If all expenses were allocated similarly, it is likely that manufacturers' sales branches would prove more costly than they appear to be.

The U.S. Bureau of Census collects extensive data showing the number, kind, location, and operating expenses of manufacturers' sales branches. Such data can help manufacturers determine competitors' distribution systems and probable costs. If many competitors are going direct, it may mean that there are no good specialists available – or at least none who can provide the functions desired.

Petroleum bulk plants, terminals, and LP gas facilities

Another major census bureau wholesale classification (see Table 17-1) covers wholesale petroleum product distribution. These specialized wholesalers work closely with the major oil companies. We will not treat them in detail here, since their major contribution to the marketing process is providing storage and handling facilities that are not generally applicable to other marketing management problems.

Agents and brokers are strong on selling

They do
not take
title

All merchant wholesalers at least take title to the goods, even when they do not actually handle them. These are the middlemen that most people picture when thinking of wholesalers. Yet there is another important group of middlemen – the merchandise agents and brokers – who do *not* take title. Their main service is to facilitate the buying and selling functions. They normally provide even fewer functions than the limited-function merchant wholesalers. In certain trades, however, their contribution is extermely valuable, and they may operate at relatively low cost, say 2 to 6 percent of selling price.

Agents and brokers, like merchant wholesalers, generally specialize by customer type and by product or product lines, and so it is extremely important to determine exactly what each agent or broker does.

In the following paragraphs, only the most important points about each type of agent or broker will be stressed. For details on the functions provided by each, see Table 17–3, which continues the scheme used for merchant wholesalers, based on functions performed. It is obvious from the large number of vacant spaces in Table 17–3 that agents and brokers provide fewer functions than merchant wholesalers.

443

Auction companies— just a shed down by the tracks

Auction companies provide a place where buyers and sellers can come together and complete a transaction. Auction companies are not numerous (see Table 17–1), but they are extremely important in certain lines such as fruit, livestock, fur, tobacco, and used-car markets.[4] For these products, demand and supply conditions change rapidly, and the product must be seen to be evaluated. Buyers and sellers, therefore, are brought together by the auction company, and demand and supply interact to determine price while the goods are being inspected.

Facilities can be plain, keeping overhead costs low. Frequently, auction sheds are close to transportation facilities so that the commodities

Table 17–3 Functions of agents and brokers

Functions	Auction companies	Brokers	Commission merchants	Manufacturers' agents	Selling agents
Functions for customers:					
Anticipates needs		Some		Sometimes	
"Regroups" goods (one or more of four stages)	X		X	Some	
Carries stocks	Sometimes		X	Sometimes	
Delivers goods			X	Sometimes	
Grants credit	Some		Sometimes		X
Provides information and advisory services		X	X	X	X
Provides buying function	X	Some	X	X	X
Owns and transfers title to goods	Transfers only		Transfers only		
For producer:					
Provides selling function	X	Some	X	X	X
Stores inventory	X		X	Sometimes	
Helps finance by owning stocks					
Reduces credit risk	Some				X
Provides market information		X	X	X	X

can be reshipped quickly. The auction company charges a set fee or commission for the use of its facilities and services.

Brokers— helpful guide in a strange land

The broker's principal function is to bring buyers and sellers together but, unlike the auction company, his facilities are not crucial. He may not even have a separate office but may operate out of his home, perhaps with the aid of an answering service. His "product" is information about what buyers need and what supplies are available. He aids

[4]"Dealing Out Used-car Dealers," *Business Week,* October 26, 1969, pp. 76–80.

in buyer-seller negotiation and if the transaction is completed, earns a commission from whichever party engaged him.

Usually, some kind of broker will develop whenever and wherever market information is inadequate. Brokers are especially useful for selling seasonally produced products. For example, they could represent a small food canner during the canning season, then go on to other activities. Some have expanded their operations, still calling themselves "food brokers," but operating more like manufacturers' agents. They are discussed later.

Brokers also are active in used machinery, real estate, and even ships.[5] These products are dissimilar, but the marketing functions needed are not. In each case, buyers come into the market infrequently, and someone with extensive knowledge of available products is needed to help both buyers and sellers complete the transaction quickly and inexpensively.

| Commission merchants — to sell in absentia | Commission merchants are common in agricultural markets. When a producer does not use a local auction to sell his output, he may ship it to a big-city central market. There he needs someone to handle the goods as well as selling them for him, since it is obviously not practical to accompany every shipment. |

Commission merchants have grown up to meet this need. They are especially common in markets for livestock and grain, both commodities that buyers want to inspect and if they so choose, buy immediately. Commission merchants, although they do not take title, are generally permitted to sell goods at the market price or the best price obtainable above some stipulated minimum. They usually are numerous in central markets, each competing with the others and trying to get the highest price for his producer-sellers. Since prices in these markets usually are a matter of public record, the producer-seller has a check on the performance of his commission merchant. Usually costs are low because commission merchants handle large volumes of goods and buyers usually come to their central market location.

A commission merchant is similar to a broker, except that he actually handles goods, completes transactions, and remits the selling price (less his commission) to the seller.

Commission merchants sometimes are used in other trades, too, such as textiles, where many small producers wish to reach buyers in a central market without having to maintain their own sales forces.

| Manufacturers' agents — free-wheeling salesmen | A manufacturers' agent works for several manufacturers almost as if he were each company's own salesman. He may cover one city or several states. If the sales potential of an area is low, he may be used in lieu of a company's own salesmen. Or a small firm may have to use agents everywhere because sales volume is inadequate to support a sales force. |

[5] "Dealers in Ships, New and Old," *Business Week,*
January 13, 1962, pp. 114–16.

Manufacturers' agents can be useful in any field where many small manufacturers need representation. They are used frequently in the sale of machinery and equipment, dry goods, electrical goods, automotive products, clothing and apparel accessories, furniture, and some food products.

Manufacturers' agents usually know their own territory quite well and handle the noncompeting lines of several manufacturers. They work on commission and often can operate profitably in situations where a producer's sales force cannot. This is mainly because they have well-established contacts, detailed knowledge of an industry, and a wide line of goods obtained by representing several companies. This wide product line enables them to spread fixed selling costs over many products.

As with a manufacturer's salesman, the agent's main job is to call on wholesalers or industrial customers or both. Orders picked up are sent to the producer, or the customer sends them directly to the producer, but in either case the agent is credited with the sale. Agents seldom have any voice in setting prices or determining the producer's policies.

As a service to customers, manufacturers' agents sometimes stock goods and make deliveries, but the majority concentrate on sales calls. The producer delivers the merchandise and bills the customers.

The distinguishing characteristic of manufacturers' agents is a rather freewheeling, independent, and aggressive approach to selling – especially in the sale of new products. They become specialists in certain lines and can be more effective than the producer's own sales force because of their wider experience and their good contacts with key customers.

When practicing their specialty of developing markets for new products, manufacturers' agents charge a healthy 10 to 15 percent commission. By contrast, their commission for large-volume established goods may be quite low – perhaps only 2 percent. The higher rates often come to be the agent's major disadvantage, from the manufacturer's point of view. The original commission rate may have seemed small when the product was new and sales volume was low, but once the product is selling well and large commissions are going to the agent, the agreed rate may seem high. At about this time, the firm often begins using its own salesmen, and the manufacturers' agent must look for another new product to develop.[6]

Food brokers – successful filling of a gap

Food brokers, operating like manufacturers' agents, have become extremely important in grocery distribution. More than half the processed goods sold by grocery stores is sold to them by these brokers.

Food brokers call on grocery wholesalers for their manufacturer clients. Some aggressive food brokers have become more involved

---

[6] For a description of this situation in the electronic components industry, see "Easing the Squeeze on the Sales Rep," *Business Week*, July 13, 1963, pp. 130–31.

with their client's marketing strategy than the typical manufacturers' agent. They may even work closely with the producer's advertising agency and marketing manager in planning overall strategy.[7] They are consulted for this role because they are so intimately familiar with their territory.

For the usual commission of 5 percent of sales, these firms may take over the entire selling function for a manufacturer. Some even suggest what prices and advertising allowances should be offered to particular retailers. For a small manufacturer, they can perform a vital service; for large firms with many small divisions they can be equally helpful.

Each food broker organization specializes in a given territory. Most manufacturers can achieve national distribution with between 70 and 100 food brokers.

The food broker fills a gap in the sales efforts of many manufacturers. The brokers generally have an effective sales force because they pay their salesmen well and keep them in the field. In contrast, manufacturers often use their sales territories as training grounds, and promote their good salesmen to larger territories or home offices as soon as (and sometimes before) they have really become effective in their sales areas.

Selling agents — in effect, marketing managers

The selling agent operates somewhat like the manufacturers' agent, only he may handle competing lines. He usually takes over the whole *marketing* job nationally — not just the *sales* contacts in one area. He handles the entire output of one or more producers and has almost complete control of pricing, selling, and advertising. In effect, he becomes each producer's marketing manager.

Financial trouble is one of the main reasons a producer calls in a selling agent. The selling agent may provide working capital, but in turn he may take over the affairs of the business.

These agents have been especially common in highly competitive fields such as textiles and coal, and they also have been used for marketing lumber, certain food products, clothing items, and some metal products. In all these industries, marketing is much more important than production for the survival of firms. The selling agent provides the necessary financial assistance and marketing know-how.

International marketing is not so different

We find agents in international trade, too. Most operate much like those just described. *Export* or *import agents* are basically manufacturers' agents. *Export* or *import commission houses* and *export* or *import brokers* are really brokers. A *combination export manager*

[7]"Food Brokers: A Comprehensive Study of Their Growing Role in Marketing," in *Grocery Manufacture* (magazine), December, 1969, also available from the National Food Brokers Association, 1916 M Street, N.W., Washington, D.C. 20036; "How Food Brokers Help Small Manufacturers" (Management Aids for Small Manufacturers, No. 63, [Washington D.C. Small Business Administration, n.d.]); "Food Brokers: New Force in Grocery Marketing," *Printers' Ink,* December 1, 1961, pp. 20–27; "Food Brokers Thrive on Local Sales Push," *Business Week,* June 17, 1961, pp. 55–62; and Frank Johnson, "Census Distortions of Food Broker Sales," *Journal of Marketing,* July, 1963, pp. 67–69.

serves as a blend of a manufacturers' agent and a selling agent, handling the entire export function for a number of manufacturers of allied but noncompetitive lines.[8]

As with domestic agents, it is necessary to determine exactly what functions each institution provides before deciding to use it in a channel system. Agents are more common in international trade because of the critical problem of financing in that field. Many markets include only a few well-financed merchant wholesalers. The best many manufacturers can do is obtain local representation through agents and then arrange for financing directly, often through banks with specialized services and facilities in international trade.

Assemblers of farm products help farmers *and* others in channel

Assemblers are specialists in agricultural products. As already indicated, there are many small producers in the agricultural market. Output must be accumulated and sorted to ship it to market in the most economical quantities. Once accumulation and sorting are completed, the wholesalers already described may handle these commodities.

The specialists who do the sorting and accumulation are assemblers. They also usually handle transportation, storage, grading, and financing, taking the risks these functions involve. The assembler's costs may be relatively modest, but for perishable items such as fresh fruits and vegetables, operating expenses may exceed 25 percent of sales. Such high handling costs help explain why farmers sometimes receive only 10 to 25 percent of the retail price for some agricultural commodities.

Other specialized middlemen fill unique roles

Factors —
hiring a
credit
department

Factors are important specialists in financing. In effect, they are wholesalers of credit. They buy their clients' accounts receivables. Usually they specialize in certain lines of trade and are willing to extend credit for longer periods than commercial banks. Sometimes factors provide management advice or assistance and almost become selling agents. In fact, some are former selling agents who have concentrated on financing rather than selling. Like selling agents, factors are especially common in the highly competitive textile industry.

In buying accounts receivables, factors provide their clients with

[8]To see the role some play, see "Japan's Giant Web of World Traders," *Business Week,* January 8, 1966, pp. 76–78; and "Decking the Halls with Imports," *Business Week,* December 17, 1966, pp. 134–38.

working capital. The factor's lending charge varies from 6 to 18 percent, depending on whether he has any recourse to the seller for collection in case of nonpayment. He may charge extra for his advice in customer selection and collection, and these additional charges may be 1 to 3 percent of the invoice face value. In effect, the factor may assume the function of a credit department, relieving his client of this expense.

Usually factors have many clients in a given line, such as textiles, and so are able to spread their risks over many customers. By specializing in a certain line, they get to know most of the buyers in the trade and are better able to evaluate the credit risks. One result is that while a buyer, for example, might be willing to delay payment to a single seller, he might not run a similar risk when he owes money to a factor. The factor might seriously hurt his credit rating or even cut off all future credit.

Field ware-housemen — goods on hand are money from the bank

Another specialist in financing is the field warehousing organization. If a firm has accounts receivable, it can use a factor or even borrow at a bank. But if it has financial problems and its goods are not yet sold, then borrowing may be more difficult. One solution to this problem is to move the goods to a public warehouse and obtain a warehouse receipt, which can then be used as collateral for borrowing at a bank. But moving goods can be expensive.

In field warehousing, the selling company's own warehouse is used, but a portion is formally segregated by the field warehouseman. The seller retains title to his goods, but control of them passes to the field warehouseman. He in turn issues a warehouse receipt, as collateral in borrowing. These field warehousing organizations usually know capital sources and may be able to arrange loans at lower cost than obtainable locally.

Using this method, large stocks may be maintained at various distribution points in anticipation of future needs. Or economical production runs can be made and then stored at the factory against future needs.

Sales finance companies — you sell what they own

Sales finance companies normally deal only in consumer credit, but a number have become interested in financing inventories for middlemen, especially auto and appliance dealers. This type of financing is called "floor planning." Many auto dealers, for example, do not own outright any of the cars on their display floors. They may have only a 10 percent interest in each of them, the other 90 percent belonging to a sales finance company. The auto dealer has physical possession, but the finance company owns the cars, and the proceeds from sales may go directly to it.

In effect, these companies are providing part of the dealer's financing function. But because the goods are usually well branded, and therefore easily resold, there is relatively little risk. The charge to the dealer for these services may be as low as 6 percent a year, depending on the finance company's cost of borrowing money in the capital markets.

449

Geographical distribution of wholesalers

Different
wholesalers
are found
in different
places

Wholesalers, like retailers, must consider both the location and preferences of their target customers when deciding on their own locations. And where they are located affects the jobs of other channel members, too. Some wholesalers, such as petroleum distributors whose customers are widely distributed geographically, are widely dispersed. Likewise, assemblers of farm products do most of their work close to the farm, often in Countyvilles.

Despite this dispersion, however, almost 49 percent of all wholesale sales in 1967 were made in the 15 largest Standard Metropolitan Statistical Areas.

This heavy concentration of wholesale sales in large cities is caused, in part, by the concentration of manufacturers' sales offices and branches plus agents and brokers in Commerce Cities, where there are more wholesalers and industrial buyers. Some large manufacturers buy for many plants through one purchasing department located in the general offices in those cities. And large general merchandise wholesalers often are located in these transportation and commerce hubs.

The prominent role played by the New York City area should be especially noted – 13 percent of all wholesale sales. This results partly from the concentration of much of the U.S. wholesale clothing and jewelry industries in this one market. But it also points up the important role played by all large Commerce Cities in the nation's trade.

Methods of operation of merchant wholesalers

Now that we know what the various kinds of wholesalers are like, let's see how they operate. This is especially important to manufacturers' marketing managers because they must know how wholesalers operate in order to deal with them. It is also important to retailers in that they should know what to expect from their wholesaler suppliers. Taking a broader view, we must know how wholesalers operate in order to plan effective channel systems.

This section will be concerned with *what* and *for whom* wholesalers buy, *how* they buy, *when* they buy, and *who* in the organization is responsible for buying. For the sake of clarity, we will limit our discussion to merchant wholesalers, since they are the most numerous and provide so many wholesaling functions.[9] The foregoing descriptions of the other wholesaler types are suggestive of their methods of operation.

[9] Much of this material is based upon R. S. Alexander and James Snitzler, "Wholesale Buying and Merchandising," *Journal of Marketing*, September, 1949, pp. 178–91. The *average* wholesaler has not changed too much since then.

That popular retailing philosophy, "Goods well bought are half sold," is equally appropriate for merchant wholesalers. Their main function is obtaining the products of many manufacturers and distributing them in smaller quantities to customers — that is, adjusting discrepancies of quantity and assortment.

The merchant wholesaler is not expected to judge the desirability of products but simply to get his target customers the products they want.

He is not in a position to educate consumers either, although some wholesalers have conducted limited consumer research in an effort to help their customers operate their businesses more profitably.[10] Few merchant wholesalers make such efforts but rely instead on their own judgment, their salesmen, and manufacturers' research.

Most wholesalers handle so many items that they cannot give continual individual attention to each one of them. A grocery wholesaler may stock up to 20,000 items; a drug wholesaler, up to 125,000; and a dry-goods wholesaler, up to 250,000 items.

Understandably, most wholesalers buy the bulk of their products on a routine, automatic reorder basis, once the initial decision to stock these products has been made. Most wholesalers try to maintain two months' inventory on most items, except faster moving items. They carry two weeks' to a month's inventory of these items and watch them more closely, so that there is time to reorder before supplies are too low.

Most dry-goods firms order standard items, such as sheets, pillowcases, and towels, on this basis. Drug wholesalers, hardware wholesalers, electrical wholesalers, and industrial distributors follow the same procedure for their standard items.

Careful maintenance of inventory records makes routine buying practical. Only a minority of wholesalers keep perpetual inventory records on all of their items, but most do keep records on the fast-moving or high-unit-value items. One drug wholesaler, for example, maintains a perpetual inventory record on 800 items that are extremely important to his operation.

Modern record-keeping systems — including Robot Kardex equipment, punched card accounting machines, and computers — enable progressive wholesalers to maintain perpetual inventory on all of their items, often at little or no increase in cost. One New York drug wholesaler modernized his inventory record system and expanded sales volume 6.9 percent while lowering administrative costs.[11] A plumbing-heating wholesaler adopted Robot Kardex equipment and now maintains a perpetual inventory on 13,000 items. This system so speeds pricing and other activities, thereby cutting his other costs,

---

[10] See, for example, "Streamlining the Middleman," *Business Week*, July 21, 1962, pp. 64–67.

[11] "Saving Money Is Fine; Making More Is Even Better," *Systems Management*, January, 1962, pp. 30 ff.

that this inventory control system operates "for free."[12] This helps explain why more wholesalers are adopting such systems.

Companies lacking this timesaving equipment usually control inventory by taking a monthly count of all items and a biweekly count of fast-moving items. Assuming a normal two months' inventory, this procedure may be satisfactory. For the small firm, more accurate control might be too expensive compared to the cost of carrying a little extra inventory.[13]

Some wholesalers rely on the order pickers in the warehouse to assure maintenance of at least minimum stocks. But this procedure obviously depends on the reliability of the warehouse help.

Whatever the method of inventory control, some procedure must be developed for deciding how much to carry and when to reorder. Mathematicians and statisticians have been working with the problem of optimum inventory, and wholesalers are beginning to use their statistical techniques.

The previously mentioned wholesaler who adopted the Robot Kardex system uses a probability system for setting stock levels. He found it unprofitable to have every single item in stock at all times. Inventory levels, therefore, are set so that supplies of some items probably will be exhausted occasionally. Being willing to be out of stock on any item once in five years enabled this wholesaler to reduce the investment required to carry inventory. This wholesaler not only is willing to be out once in five years—he *plans* to be out that often. Using monthly sales and purchase records accumulated over several years, it is not difficult to adjust stock levels when items do not run out as planned.[14]

In addition to the routine buying, some wholesalers buy products on seasonal or annual contracts. Among products that may be bought in this way are antifreeze, blankets, rubber footwear, suntan lotion, cough syrups, lawnmowers, fans, heaters, garden hose. Seasonal or annual contracts assure the wholesaler of an adequate supply and also enable the manufacturer to plan his production, thereby reducing manufacturing costs. Channel system thinking can be seen in action here.

Seasonal items are sometimes bought 6 to 10 months before they are sold; such advance stocking adds to the cost of wholesaling. Some wholesalers attempt to reduce or avoid it when possible. They may insist that the material merely be *consigned* to them—they receive but do not own or pay for it—or they ask manufacturers to "forward-date" their invoices so that payment is not due until a later date, perhaps during the actual selling season. In addition, a wholesaler may require that manufacturers guarantee the price of the goods they

[12]"Aaron Company's Total Inventory Control of 13,000 Items," *Supply House Times,* February, 1959, pp. 48–70.

[13]Donald F. Mulvihill, "Inventory Control for Small Wholesalers," *Management Research Summary,* [Washington, D.C.: Small Business Administration,

1963]; and *Controlling Inventory in Small Wholesale Firms,* (Small Marketer's Aids, No. 122, [Washington, D.C.: Small Business Administration, September, 1966]).

[14]"Aaron Company's Total Inventory Control of 13,000 Items," *op. cit.,* p. 53.

take in stock and even permit the return of merchandise if new or better products are brought out before the selling season.

It is obvious, then, that most wholesalers order rather routinely once the original decision to stock an item has been made. The next questions are: who makes the initial buying decision and how is this decision reached?

Who buys — and how can they do it for less?

Clerks handle much of routine wholesale buying by simply reordering the items that the inventory control procedure shows to be out of stock. Unless the company has modern data processing equipment, the sheer bulk of paper work on so many items precludes extensive analysis of what products are selling best, which ought to be dropped, or what new items ought to be added.

Most wholesalers are reluctant to drop items, because they feel obligated to provide service to their customers. Under these circumstances, the manufacturer's major hurdle is to get his product onto the wholesaler's buying list in the first place. Since wholesale buyers seldom seek new supply sources, it is easy to understand why manufacturers must employ salesmen or agents to reach wholesalers.

In a small firm, the owners, partners, or general manager will make the decision to add or eliminate items. In larger firms, the buying decisions may be made by a committee including the president, general manager, or a vice president in charge of buying. Some firms include the sales manager in buying talks because of the interdependence of purchasing and sales in wholesaling businesses. In fact, some businessmen feel that the two activities should not be separated at all, and they use "merchandise managers" to direct and control both buying and selling in specific lines.

In larger companies, merchandise managers handle certain lines of goods. Reporting to them are buyers who are even more specialized in the items they buy but often have no control over the selling function. All of this is similar to the specialization we saw in retail buying.

The degree of buyer specialization depends on the size of the company and the variety of goods handled. A large grocery house in the Middle West employs nine buyers, some of whom buy as many as 50 types of articles. A medium-sized hardware house employs four buyers, specializing in garden tools and supplies, electrical appliances, general tools, and miscellaneous items. A large firm in the hardware field divides its buying work among 13 buyers, each specializing in one of the following lines of goods.

Mechanical and industrial supplies
Plumbing and heating
Farm and garden supplies
Sporting goods
Builders' hardware
Painters' supplies and drapery fixtures
Industrial supplies
Heavy hardware
Housewares and gifts

Major appliances
Electrical supplies
Guns and ammunition
Cutlery, toys, and wheel goods

At the other end of the scale is the small house which has two buyers, one purchasing builders' hardware and the other buying all other items.[15] Yet, regardless of the buyer's title or scope, the wholesale buyer is basically economic in his choices – but he, like industrial and retail buyers, is susceptible to ego boosting and other appeals.

Some use resident buyers

Some wholesale firms, dispersed geographically, delegate some buying to independent purchasing agents or resident buyers who are located in central markets, such as New York or Chicago. Such agents maintain continuous contact with manufacturers on behalf of many wholesalers. These organizations are especially helpful to the smaller wholesaler, allowing him, in effect, to shift some of his buying responsibility to a specialist who can buy efficiently at minimum cost. Some wholesalers use these outside buyers for standard and routine items, handling the nonstandard and fashion items themselves.

Such outside buying groups are working for the buyer (the wholesaler, in this case) and not the seller. These buyers usually make a commission charge to the buyer; since the passage of the Robinson-Patman Act, their connections with the buyer preclude their obtaining additional discounts from the seller that are not justified by cost savings. Their existence depends upon providing additional information and better buying for less money than it would cost the wholesaler to do the job himself.

Comeback and future of the wholesaler

In the 1800's, the wholesaler held a dominant position in marketing. The many small producers and small retailers needed his services. As producers became larger, some bypassed the wholesaler by setting up their own sales organizations or by selling directly to industrial customers. When retailers also began to grow larger – and especially during the 1920's, when chain stores began to spread rapidly – many predicted a dire future for the wholesaler. Chain stores normally assume the wholesaling functions, and it was thought that the days of the independent wholesaler were numbered.

Not fat and lazy, but enduring

Some analysts and critics felt that the decline of the wholesaler might be desirable from the social point of view, for many wholesalers had apparently grown "fat and lazy," contributing little more than breaking bulk. Their salesmen often were only order takers; the selling function was neglected; high-caliber management was not attracted

---

[15] Alexander and Snitzler, *op. cit.*, p. 179.

to the wholesaling industry, and it became a domain of vested interests which many persons felt should be eliminated.

Our review here, however, has shown that wholesaling functions *are* necessary, and wholesalers have not been eliminated. True, their sales volume declined from 1929 to 1939, but wholesalers have since made a comeback. By 1954, they had regained the same relative importance they had in 1929,[16] and they have continued to hold their own since then.[17]

Producing profits, not chasing orders

Wholesalers have held their own, in part, because of new management and new techniques. To be sure, there are still many operating in the old ways, and wholesaling has had nothing comparable to the rapid changes in retailing. Yet progressive wholesale firms have become more concerned with their customers and with channel systems. Some are offering more services to their independent customers, and others are developing voluntary chains, as noted in Chapter 17, that bind them more closely to their customers. Some of this ordering is done routinely by mail or telephone, or directly by telephone to computer.

Today's *progressive* wholesaler is no longer a passive order taker. As part of the new look in wholesaling, not only have many salesmen been eliminated, but in place of the old order takers wholesalers are now using order slips similar to those used between a chain warehouse and chain retail stores.

Some modern wholesalers no longer require all customers to pay for services simply because certain customers use them. This traditional practice had the effect of encouraging limited-function wholesalers and direct channels. Now, some wholesalers are making a basic service available at a minimum cost, then charging additional fees for any special services required. In the grocery field, for instance, the basic servicing of a store might cost the store 3 to 4 percent of wholesale sales. Then promotional assistance and other extra aids are offered at extra cost.

Modern wholesalers also are becoming more selective in picking customers, as cost analysis shows them that many of their smaller customers are clearly unprofitable. With these less desirable customers gone, the wholesaler can give even more attention to preferred customers. In this way, he is helping to promote healthy retailers who are able to compete in any market. The larger, more profitable customers receive the best service the wholesaler can give. As one executive said: "We try to train our people to evaluate profits beforehand, not just to chase after orders."[18]

Some wholesalers have renamed their salesmen "store advisers" or

[16] Paul D. Converse, "Twenty-Five Years in Wholesaling: A Revolution in Food Wholesaling," *Journal of Marketing,* July, 1957, pp. 40–41.

[17] Richard S. Lopata, "Faster Pace in Wholesaling," *Harvard Business Review,* July–August, 1969, pp. 130–43.

[18] "The Changing Anatomy of Industrial Sales Distribution," *Dun's Review & Modern Industry,* January, 1963, pp. 37 ff.

"supervisors" to reflect their new roles. These representatives provide many management advisory services, including location analysis; store design and modernization; legal assistance on new leases or adjustments in old leases; store-opening services; and sales training and merchandising assistance, and advertising help. Such salesmen, really acting as management consultants, must be more competent that the mere order takers of other days.

The end of overloaded shelves

Training a modern wholesaler's salesmen is not an easy task, and it is sometimes beyond the capacity of management in small wholesale firms. In some fields, such as the plumbing industry, wholesaler trade associations have taken the problem in hand. They organize training schools designed to show wholesaler salesmen how they, in turn, can help retailers manage their businesses and promote sales. These schools may give instruction in bookkeeping, figuring a markup, collecting accounts receivable, advertising, and sales planning—all in an effort to train salesmen to improve retailers' effectiveness as channel members.[19]

We have noted that some wholesalers are now using electronic data processing systems, and in the next chapter, we will see what some wholesalers are doing to modernize their warehouses and physical handling facilities.

Some wholesalers are offering central bookkeeping facilities for their retailers, realizing that their own survival is linked to their customers' survival. In this sense, some wholesalers are becoming more channel system minded, no longer trying to overload retailers' shelves but now trying to clear the merchandise *off* the retailers' shelves.[20] They follow the adage, "Nothing is really sold until it is sold at retail."

Perhaps goodbye to some

Despite these changes, however, not all wholesalers today are progressive. Many still follow outmoded practices; some of the smaller, less efficient ones may have difficulty in the future. While the average operating expense ratio is 13.8 percent for merchant wholesalers, some small wholesalers have expense ratios of 20 to 30 percent.

Low cost, however, is not the only criterion for success. The higher operating expenses for some smaller wholesalers may be a reflection of the special services they offer to some segments on a market grid. Truck distributors are usually small and have high operating costs, yet some customers are willing to pay the higher cost of this service. Some of the apparently expensive, older, full-service wholesalers probably will continue operating because they offer the services and contacts needed by some small manufacturers. And, of course, some goods and some markets traditionally have slow turnover; wholesalers

---

[19]*Dealer Development Institute Progress Report* (Chicago: Central Supply Association, August 27, 1958).

[20]For further discussion of these ideas, see E. H. Lewis, "Comeback of the Wholesaler," *Harvard Business Review*, November–December, 1955, pp. 115–25; E. B. Weiss, "The Independent Druggist Gets More Tranquilizer Pills," *Advertising Age,* June 3, 1963, pp. 88–90; and Robert L. Bull, "Counselling Affiliated Food Retailers," *Management Research Summary,* (Washington, D. C.: Small Business Administration, 1963).

may be the best choice here even though they have high operating expenses.

Even making these allowances, though, it is clear that the smaller wholesalers and the larger, less progressive ones face future difficulty unless each has carved out a specific market for itself. Profit margins are not large in wholesaling, typically ranging from less than 1 percent to 2 percent. And they have been declining in recent years as the competitive squeeze has become tighter.

In short, the institution of wholesaling certainly will survive, but weaker, less aggressive wholesale firms may not. Retailers and industrial customers are motivated basically by economics. They will patronize those middlemen who help them most. They are concerned with their own success and with the efficiency of their channel, not with the success or failure of a particular wholesaling firm.

Conclusion

Wholesalers can provide functions for those both above and below them in a channel of distribution. These services are closely related to the basic marketing functions. There are many types of wholesalers. Some provide all the wholesaling functions while others specialize in only a few. Eliminating wholesalers would not eliminate the need for the functions they provide, and we cannot assume that direct channels will be more efficient.

Merchant wholesalers are the most numerous and account for a sizable share, although not the majority, of wholesale sales. Their distinguishing characteristic is that they take title and often physical possession of goods. Agents and brokers, on the other hand, act more like salesmen for sellers or representatives for buyers, and usually they do not take title or possession.

Despite various predictions of the demise of wholesalers, they continue to exist, and the more progressive have adapted to a changing economic environment. No such revolutions as we saw in retailing have yet taken place in the wholesaling area and none seem likely. But it is probable that some smaller and less progressive wholesalers will fail.

We have seen that some modern wholesalers are acting more like channel captains or at least close advisers to their associated retailers, especially when they are a part of voluntary or cooperative chains. Others are adopting modern data processing and materials handling methods, and trying to improve their position in the channel.

Independent wholesalers are still vital to some smaller manufacturers, retailers, and industrial customers, but some producers and retailers are big enough to handle the wholesaling functions themselves and do so when it is economically desirable.

Some wholesalers find competition not only from other wholesalers but from producers and retailers as well. As a result, profit margins are not large in wholesaling. Looking at this from a macro point of view, we see progressive wholesalers providing useful functions very economically in many channels of distribution. Clearly, they contribute significantly to the effective operation of our marketing and economic system.

QUESTIONS AND PROBLEMS

1 Discuss the evolution of wholesaling in relation to the evolution of retailing.

2 What risks do merchant wholesalers assume by taking title to goods? Is the size of this risk about constant for all merchant wholesalers?

3 Why would a manufacturer set up his own sales branches if established wholesalers were already available?

4 What is an agent middleman's marketing mix? Why don't manufacturers use their own salesmen instead of agent middlemen?

5 Explain the concentration of merchant wholesalers in Commerce Cities. Is this true of all wholesalers? Is this concentration likely to become more pronounced in the future? What impact will the continued development of Interurbia have on the location of wholesalers?

6 Discuss the future growth and nature of wholesaling if low-margin retailing and scrambled merchandising become more important. How will wholesalers have to adjust their mixes if retail establishments become larger and the retail managers more professional? Might the wholesalers be eliminated? If not, what wholesaling functions would be most important? Are there any particular lines of trade where wholesalers may have increasing difficulty?

7 Which types of wholesalers would be most appropriate for the following products? If more than one type of wholesaler could be used, provide the specifications for the situation in each case. For example, if size or financial strength of a company has a bearing, then so indicate. If several wholesalers could be used in this same channel, explain this also.
a) Fresh tomatoes.
b) Paper-stapling machines.
c) Auto mechanics' tools.
d) Canned tomatoes.
e) Men's shoes.
f) An industrial accessory machine.
g) Ball-point pens.
h) Shoelaces.

8 If you were operating a small grocery store (say, $50,000 annual sales volume) in a Forest Lake where several large grocery chains were operating, would it be desirable to affiliate with a voluntary or cooperative chain? (Make any necessary assumptions about your product policy, etc., to obtain a specific answer.)

9 In view of the large size of many manufacturers and retailers, how can the existence of wholesalers be explained? It would seem that these large firms could buy and sell in quantity directly from each other.

10 Would a drop-shipper be most suitable for the following products: coal, lumber, iron ore, sand and gravel, steel, furniture, or tractors? Why, or why not? What channels might be used for each of these products if drop-shippers were not used?

11 Explain how factors differ from commercial banks and why factors developed.

12 Explain how field warehousing could help a marketing manager.

13 Which types of wholesalers are likely to become more important in the next 25 years? Why?

...today marketing-oriented firms are giving more attention to physical distribution....

...separation of storage and transportation from the rest of marketing is anachronistic. We recognize now that these functions must be seen together as physical distribution and that this, in turn, must be treated as part of a total system.

18

Physical distribution

Physical distribution is the handling and moving of physical goods within individual firms and through channel systems. It is very important within firms *and* the macro-marketing system. Nearly half of the cost of marketing is spent on physical distribution.

Goods in the factory or on the farm are somewhat like the "sound" of the fallen tree in the deserted forest. They really have no "use" at all. Possession utility is not possible until Time and Place utility have been provided. This usually requires the transporting and storing functions that are part of physical distribution.

Knowing who will haul and store is essential

As any marketing manager develops the Place part of his strategies, he should consider how transporting and storing functions can and should be divided within the channel. Who will store and transport the goods, and who will pay for these services? Merely deciding to use certain types of wholesalers or retailers does not automatically or completely answer these questions. A wholesaler may use his own trucks to haul goods from a producer to his warehouse and from there to retailers, but only because the manufacturer gives him a transportation allowance. Another wholesaler may want the goods delivered to him.

When developing a marketing strategy, the marketing manager must determine precisely how these functions are to be shared, since this will affect the other three P's, and especially Pricing.

The truth is, however, that there is no ideal sharing arrangement. Physical distribution can be varied endlessly in a marketing mix and in a channel system. To appreciate the possibilities, we need to know more about transporting and storing functions and the specialists who handle these functions.

In this chapter, we will discuss these subjects and also some important new developments in physical distribution, including the distribution center, the total cost approach, and the physical distribution manager.

Remember that physical distribution is an important, though often neglected, activity. It has even been called the "other half" of marketing.

Today, marketing-oriented firms are giving more attention to physical distribution. This chapter deserves careful study.

The transporting function

From back-pack to cargo planes

Freight transportation, so vital to an interdependent society, now accounts for about 9 percent of the U.S. gross national product.[1] Without transportation there could be no mass distribution with its regrouping activities, or any urban life as we know it today. We understand this most clearly during a major rail or truck strike.

Before powered vehicles, when the movement of goods was limited to what a man could carry on his back or haul in a wagon, transportation was so difficult, expensive, and time-consuming that most people didn't try to transport much. They lived where the goods were, on self-sufficient farms. They traded their surpluses in nearby markets. Such inadequate transporting facilities still exist in many less developed countries and inhibit economic development.

Early societies developed along seacoasts or rivers partly because transportation of goods by water was easier than by land. Yet most commercial river transportation was still one way – downstream – until the development of steamboats in the early 1800's. Then major river valleys such as the Ohio and Mississippi prospered. Cincinnati, for example, became a great wholesale and meat-packing center after the steamboats began plying the Ohio in both directions.

The introduction of the first practical steam locomotive in 1829

[1] D. J. Bowersox, E. W. Smykay, and B. J. La Londe, *Physical Distribution Management* (rev. ed.; New York: Macmillan Co., 1968), p. 125.

opened up a whole new era for inland transportation. In the United States, rail transport made it possible to ship midwestern farm produce to the eastern industrial area, lowering food prices there considerably. Later, motor trucks and highways brought even small towns and remote farms closer to the markets.

Air transport has not had as spectacular an impact on marketing as other modes; the reason is its higher cost. For higher-value items, though, shipping by air is of growing importance.

The availability of air transport, ironically, may have an unfortunate side effect in less developed countries. It may discourage the development of more basic transportation facilities in areas such as Central and South America, and some parts of Africa, where air transportation is developing rapidly—but at the expense of other methods. Ultimately, dependence on air transportation could severely limit trade in and among these countries.

Can you afford to get to the target?

The cost of shipping an average product by rail is about 5 percent of wholesale cost.[2] For many bulky or low-value products, however, the percentage of cost is much higher. Transporting sand and gravel, for example, costs about 55 percent of its value; bituminous coal, 42 percent; cabbage, 38 percent; watermelons, 38 percent; and iron ore, 20 percent. At the other extreme are lighter or more valuable commodities, such as copper ore and copper concentrates and business and office machines, at less than 1 percent of wholesale cost; cigarettes, and butter, less than 2 percent.[3]

Transportation costs may limit the target markets that a producer's or middleman's marketing manager can consider. Shipping costs increase delivered cost, and this is what really interests the customer. High costs for goods in outlying areas, caused by higher transportation costs, encourage local production. The high costs of shipping sand and gravel dictate that these materials be sold in the limited geographical areas near the pits where they are extracted.

If a product is unique in some way, however, customers who really want it will have to bear the transportation costs. A unique clay product selling for only $12.50 a ton in Georgia costs an additional $12 a ton to ship to an Ohio paint factory. A unique paint ingredient, pyrophyllite, costs only $20 a ton in the Carolinas but another $21 a ton to transport to a California paint plant.

How transportation costs are decided

The transportation rates we have been referring to are those charged by *common carriers,* such as the railroads and major truck lines. These carriers, given a franchise by a government regulatory body, must accept merchandise from any shipper and maintain regular service. They usually must obtain permission to discontinue service or change their rates.

---

[2] D. Philip Locklin, *Economics of Transportation* (4th ed.; Homewood, Ill.: Richard D. Irwin, Inc., 1954), p. 35.

[3] D. Philip Locklin, *Economics of Transportation* (6th ed.; Homewood, Ill.: Richard D. Irwin, Inc., 1966), p. 35.

In contrast to common carriers are *contract carriers,* who are less strictly regulated and do not maintain regular schedules. They make up a more freewheeling group. They can work for anyone for an agreed sum and for any length of time. Like agents and brokers, they appear wherever needed.

In the following discussion of transportation rates, we will concentrate on *rail common carrier rates,* since they set a competitive standard. Most other transportation rate structures have similar characteristics.

The development of the railroad rate structure was guided by governmental regulatory commissions. The underlying rationale of the rate structure was that the railways could carry the heavy and bulky items — such as sand and gravel — at a relatively low charge per ton; carry the more valuable, less bulky items at higher rates per ton; and then balance the low charges against the high charges to show a profit. As we will see, however, this has not worked out as planned. The railroads have been carrying the heavy bulky items at low rates, but trucks and airlines have been taking the high-rate business.

There are three basic types of rates: (1) class, (2) commodity, and (3) exception. These three kinds of rates are quoted for carloads (CL, 60,000–100,000 lbs.), truckloads (TL, 15,000 lbs. or more), less than carloads (LCL), and less than truckloads (LTL).

Rates on less than full carloads or truckloads vary but are often twice as high as those on full loads. These rate differentials are one reason for the development of wholesalers, who buy in larger quantities than most users need, to get the advantage of full-load rates and then sell in the smaller quantities the users *do* need.

Bear in mind that there is nothing final about the present rate structure; since it is man-made, it could be changed. If it were changed, it might lead to a vastly different, and perhaps more efficient or more equitable, transportation system. In some other countries, for instance, these rate differentials are much smaller or nonexistent. As a consequence, goods are shipped in much smaller quantities, freight cars are smaller, and wholesalers and retailers handle smaller quantities.

Class rates — higher rates for smaller volume

The railroads handle so many different products that they have had to develop a freight classification system covering more than 10,000 different articles or groups of articles. Each class is assigned rates based on the cost and value of the service, the size of the shipment, and the distance shipped.

Most of the goods shipped under class rates are general manufactured products that are shipped in volumes too small to justify much negotiation by shippers. Between 2 and 4 percent of the volume shipped by rail comes under these rates, and these are the rates which were supposed to offset the low rates on bulky, low-value items.

Commodity rates — lower rates for big bulk

In many instances, there is no provision within the 10,000 class-rate classifications for the specific characteristics of certain commodities, especially bulky or low-value items. Commodity rates are set for transporting specific commodities, usually between specific points or over specific routes. These rates frequently develop out of negotiation between shippers and railroads.

There are special commodity rates for most bulky items, such as wheat, iron ore, coal, lumber, or any products shipped regularly in substantial volume. Some of the negotiated commodity rates are called "blanket rates," because the same rate applies over a large geographical area regardless of the distance between specific points within that area. Fresh fruits and vegetables, for example, can be shipped from the West Coast to almost any place on the East Coast for the same rate. Approximately 90 percent of the rail carload traffic moves under commodity rates.

Exception rates—special rates for special conditions

If a certain producer needs lower rates so that he can compete in other markets, or if competition from other methods of transportation is especially strong, the carriers sometimes are forced to reconsider their costs and set special rates.

Railways have been forced to grant "exception rates" on many items to meet truck competition in certain territories. But less than 10 percent of carload traffic moves under these rates.[4]

Correct rate not easy to determine

The large number of rate classes, and the many exceptions, makes traffic management a difficult job. A freight agent frequently charges a higher rate when a lower rate should apply. Some companies find it profitable to audit all freight bills before payment. There are even private firms specializing in this kind of work, earning a share of the savings.

It is not that carriers are deliberately overcharging, but rather that the agents who determine the appropriate rates must choose from a vast number of possible routes, rates, and rate combinations. Determining the best routing for the lowest rate gets more complex each year, since more than 150,000 rate changes are made annually.[5] And the basic rate books do not show cross-references to all of these new rates. For this reason, some channel members prefer to have prices quoted on a delivered basis.

Marketing manager may affect rates

The previous discussion has been concerned primarily with how to operate within the existing rate structure. Yet, as noted previously,

[4] F. M. Cushman, *Transportation for Management* (New York: Prentice-Hall, Inc., 1953), pp. 173–74; Locklin, *op. cit.* (6th ed.), p. 164; and Heskett, *op. cit.*, pp. 91–103.

[5] C. A. Taff, *Traffic Management* (3d ed.; Homewood, Ill.: Richard D. Irwin, Inc., 1964), p. 248.

the rate structure is not *permanently fixed*. Carriers can and do initiate changes, and if no one objects, the new rates usually go into effect. Rate changes can be made relatively quickly (1 to 30 days) and easily, as indicated by those 150,000 changes made each year.

Be aggressive, buy for less

Most rates are based originally on supply considerations; that is, the cost of providing necessary services — loading, product liability, regular scheduled service even though it is not used, special equipment such as refrigerated cars, and so on.[6] But supply factors are not the final determinants of transport rates. Rather, they determine the rate the carrier *would like to charge*. The rates actually charged are determined by competition among the various carriers and alternate methods of transportation. It is by capitalizing on these factors that an aggressive marketing manager can influence the cost of the transporting function.

Carriers are usually interested in stimulating business in their areas. If the marketing manager can show that he could expand his business if lower rates were granted into certain territories, the carriers may be willing to grant these lower rates. In fact, distance traveled and total transportation costs often do not vary in the same ratio.

On shipments to western points, New England railroads for many years have charged the same rates from New England as from New York, enabling New England firms to compete on equal terms with those in New York. When the textile industry developed in the South, the carriers serving the southern mills reduced their rates on finished cotton goods so that these mills could sell in northern territories in competition with New England mills.[7] Note the behavior of competing channel systems, again, with the railroads as part of the channel.

The creative marketing manager and channel captain can capitalize on the opportunity to bargain for rate changes. Whoever can provide the transporting function most economically and effectively is most likely to develop an effective channel team. And this is the kind of team that individual companies will be eager to be part of.

When buying goods from other channel members, for example, a channel captain might provide a valuable service to them by helping with the transporting function. He could specify the best routes, determine the rates, negotiate with the transportation agencies, if necessary, and check their invoices. When selling to others in the channel, he could sell on a delivered basis and assume the same functions.

Some manufacturers and middlemen maintain traffic departments staffed by 10 or more employees to provide these services. This is another area of specialization in distribution activities that may be well worth the cost.

[6] Locklin, *op. cit.* (6th ed.), pp. 410–17, 434–47.
[7] Locklin, *op. cit.* (6th ed.), pp. 54.

The marketing manager generally has several carriers in one or more modes competing for his transportation business. There are five basic modes of freight movement: railroads, motor vehicles, waterways, pipelines, and airplanes.

Table 18–1 shows the annual volume of intercity freight moved in the United States by each mode. Ton-miles carried is the most common method of measuring the importance of various methods of

Table 18–1 The intercity freight movement in the United States

	Ton-miles carried in 1968	
	Billions	Percent of total
Railways	768.5	42.0
Motor Vehicles	396.0	21.5
Inland Waterways	287.0	15.5
Pipelines	391.0	21.0
Airways	3.0	
Total	1,845.5	100.0

Source: *Statistical Abstract of the United States, 1970*, p. 535.

transportation. A ton-mile represents the movement of a ton of goods one mile. If, for example, 10 tons of sand were carried 10 miles, the total movement would be 100 ton-miles.

Using this measure makes it obvious that railways are the backbone of the U.S. transportation system. Following in consecutive importance are trucks, oil pipelines, and barges. Relatively speaking, airplanes do not yet move a significant volume of freight.

The numbers in the table do not tell the whole story, however. They show total ton-miles, but do not identify the mass of goods shipped by trucks, but only for short distances. Information on this subject is sketchy, but it is likely that at least 75 percent of all freight moves by trucks, at least part of the way, from producer to user. Railroads may carry goods for long distances, but trucks haul the bulk of the short-haul movement. The trucking industry slogan, "If you have it, it came by truck," is certainly accurate for consumer goods, although many industrial goods are still delivered by railroads or other transportation modes.

Railroads—
workhorse
of the
nation

The railroad, the workhorse of U.S. transportation, has been important mainly for carrying heavy and bulky freight such as coal, sand, and steel. By handling large quantities of such commodities, according to standardized methods and in a variety of standardized car types, the railroads are able to transport at relatively low cost. But railroads have had profit difficulties in recent years, in part because trucking firms have set their rates low enough to compete for the more profitable, less bulky items that the railroads were counting on to offset the low rates on the bulky commodities.

The railroads have taken various steps to bring their profits up. Computerization and automation of rail facilities has helped. Catering more specifically to the needs of some target customers has helped, too. By introducing an efficient triple-deck carrier for automobiles, the rails were able to win back from trucks a substantial share of the new-car transport. And now a specially designed railcar can carry 30 minicars – twice as many as the triple-deck carriers – by stacking them vertically rather than horizontally. And the design of special refrigerator cars, tank cars, hopper cars, and cars especially suited for loading and unloading livestock has helped attract and hold business from firms that are willing to pay extra for services tailored to their needs.[8]

Other such services, designed to offset some of the railroads' natural disadvantages and to attract customers, include those discussed in the following paragraphs.

Piggyback service

Operating with the apparent philosophy, "If you can't beat them, haul them," railroads have offered more flexible service by loading truck trailers onto specially designed flatcars and hauling them "piggyback." The trailers are picked up at the producer's location, loaded onto rail flatcars, hauled as close to the customer as rail lines run, then picked up by a truck tractor and delivered to the buyer's door. Such service provides all the flexibility of trucking, and on some routes it costs even less. A loaded truck trailer can be shipped piggyback from the Midwest to the West Coast for approximately half the cost of sending it over the highways.

Fast freight

Many of the goods shipped by rail are not particularly perishable or in urgent demand, and as a result, much railroad freight moves more slowly, for example, than truck shipments. But when speed is needed, a train can really move.

Some railroads have instituted a "fast freight" service for perishable or high-value items. Such trains, highballing at 60 m.p.h. and stopping only to change crews and load water and ice, can be competitive in speed with trucks, provided shippers and receivers are located near rail lines.

Pool cars

Railroads are most efficient at handling full carloads of goods. Less-than-carload (LCL) shipments take a considerable amount of

---

[8] "Railcars Haul Vegas Vertically," *Detroit Free Press*, August 6, 1970, p. 8-D; "High-Mountain Railroad with Profits to Match," *Business Week*, June 10, 1967, pp. 174–80; "Doubling the Freight Car's Work-Day," *Business Week*, December 18, 1965, pp. 122–26; and *Railroads Unlimited!* (Washington, D.C.: Association of American Railroads, no date).

handling and rehandling. They usually move slowly, and at a higher price per 100 pounds than carload shipments.

To counter the shortcomings of low speed and high cost and still encourage the business of small shippers, some railroads encourage groups of shippers to cooperate and pool their shipments as a full car. This service enables one producer to ship to several buyers in a single area at greater speed and under the lower carload rates. If the buyers of these goods are not located in the same area, the goods may be shipped in a pool car at the carload rate to the first buyer and then broken up for further shipment at LCL rates.

Sometimes local retailers buying from a single area, such as New York City, consolidate their shipments in single cars. Local truckers deliver the goods when they arrive. When various commodities are shipped in the same car, it is called a "mixed car" rather than a "pool car," and the highest rate for any of the commodities applies to the whole shipment.

Diversion in transit

Some railroads allow redirection of carloads already in transit. A carload of California oranges could be shipped toward Chicago or simply eastward toward no specific destination, and as market demand and supply conditions changed, the shipper could change or specify the destination. The railroad would then reroute the car for a small fee.

This service lets a marketing manager get his goods rolling but still stay flexible in his final target market selection.

Transit privilege

Some agricultural or industrial raw materials must be shipped from their original source to a processing plant and then to users. To facilitate this regrouping and processing, some railroads permit shippers to ship commodities away from the source, stop along the way for processing, and then reship them toward the final destination at the "through" rate—as long as the same general direction is maintained. This privilege is especially important in the flour milling industry, where the procedure is called "milling in transit."

Transloading privilege

A more recent innovation, the transloading privilege, speeds delivery of parts of an original carload shipment to two or more destinations. When goods are to be shipped in a car cross-country to customers at several destinations, the railroad does not pull the car from city to city, unloading it bit by bit, here and there. Instead, it moves a full carload of goods to the single point that is closest to the various customers, then reloads parts of the shipment into other cars for the remaining distance to destinations in different directions. Since the transloading privilege makes LCL size deliveries feasible, customers can maintain smaller inventory, shifting the storage function back to the manufacturer or wholesaler. Like other privileges, transloading gives channel members more latitude in planning marketing strategies and sharing channel functions.

Trucks are flexible

The flexibility of trucks makes them especially suitable for moving small lots of goods short distances. They can travel on almost any road, can serve broad areas without unloading and reloading, and give extremely fast service. Trucks also cause less breakage and rough handling than rails, an important factor because it may permit a reduction in packaging cost.

For short distances and for higher valued commodities, trucks may charge rates that are the same as (or lower than) railroad rates, yet provide much faster service. The way truckers compete with railroads for these high-charge items is somewhat like the way retailers compete in "scrambled merchandising." Going after such business is logical for the truckers because it is these smaller high-charge items that trucks are best equipped to handle.

Trucking has opened many new markets and permitted a considerable amount of decentralization by bringing fast, dependable transport to outlying urban areas, smaller towns, and rural areas. Whatever the truth may be about charges that trucks congest traffic and damage highways, it *is* a fact that trucks are indispensable to our present economic and marketing system.[9]

Waterways are slow but inexpensive

Barges on the internal waterways are used chiefly for bulky, nonperishable products such as iron ore, grain, steel, petroleum products, cement, gravel, sand, coal, and coke. Water transportation is the lowest-cost method, but it is also the slowest and most seasonal. When winter ice closes fresh water harbors, alternate transportation must be used. Some shippers, such as those dealing in iron ore, ship their total annual supply during the summer months and store it near their production facilities for winter use. Here, low-cost transportation combined with storage reduces *total cost*.

The availability of ocean transport to the vast industrial and agricultural regions of the inland United States was made possible in 1959 by the completion of the St. Lawrence Waterway System. This 2,342-mile-long waterway opened the Great Lakes to 80 percent of all ocean vessels. Only the very largest ships are excluded.

A recent advance in coastal and transoceanic shipping is the redesign of ships to handle large standard-size containers or "containerized freight," and truck trailers. Now ships combined with trucks can offer a "fishyback" service similar to rail piggyback handling of truck trailers. Door-to-door service is now being offered between the U.S. and European cities.[10]

Pipelines keep moving

In the United States, pipelines are used primarily by the petroleum industry to move petroleum liquids and natural gas. Extensive lines in the Southwest bring oil from the fields to refineries. From there, the

---

[9] "Tank Truckers Thrive on Diversified Fare," *Business Week*, December 7, 1968, pp. 84–88.

[10] "Roll-on Ships Gather More Cargo," *Business Week*, May 10, 1969, pp. 74–76; "Speeding the Schedule for Seagoing Cargo," *Business Week*, August 26, 1967, pp. 124–26; and "Europe's Ports Fight for New Riches," *Business Week*, October 19, 1968, pp. 99–103; "Containers Widen Their World," *Business Week*, January 7, 1967, pp. 88–90.

more flexible railroads, trucks, and ships usually transport refined products to customers.

Ships can transport petroleum products from Texas to the large eastern seaboard markets at less cost than pipelines, but during World War II, two pipelines were built to serve the East Coast because German submarines were sinking the oil tankers. After the war, this traffic returned to the more economical ships, and the pipelines are used today for natural gas.

Airways are fast and expensive

The most expensive means of cargo transportation yet developed is airfreight — but it also is fast! Trucks took the cream of the railroads' traffic. Now airways are taking the cream of the cream. They also are creating new transportation business by carrying across continents and oceans perishable commodities that simply could not be moved before. Tropical flowers from Hawaii, for example, now are jet-flown to points all over the United States. And California's strawberries are flown to the Midwest and East all through the winter. French bread comes into Detroit daily from Paris. Brazilian manufacturers sell goods throughout South America by air. And Italian retailers fly samples and goods from all over the world when time is important, as with seasonal merchandise.

The bulk of airfreight so far has been fashions, perishable commodities, and high-value industrial parts for the electronics and metal-working industries.

Airfreight rates normally are at least twice as high as trucking rates, but the greater speed may more than justify the added cost. Although airfreight still is only a small percentage of all freight, the volume of airfreight has been increasing yearly and a real breakthrough may come when the huge flying boxcars, developed originally for the military, become available for civilian service. Some members of the airfreight industry, perhaps optimists, expect these larger planes to be able to compete with trucks over long distances.[11]

But may cut total cost

An important advantage of air transport is that the cost of packing, unpackaging, and preparing the goods for sale may be reduced or eliminated when goods are shipped by air. One Los Angeles manufacturer of electronic products who makes all his deliveries beyond 150 miles by airfreight, merely wraps the complex 600-pound machines in heavy wrapping paper. His increased transportation costs are more than offset by the reduction in packaging costs, and he is now competing for business nationally. The speedy service at lower costs has improved the company's marketing mix *and* market position.

Although the *transportation cost* of air shipments may be higher, the *total cost of distribution* for a firm using airfreight may be lower.

[11] Charles W. Foreman, "The Hidden Benefits of Air Freight," *Business Horizons*, December, 1968, pp. 27–34; and David H. Reeher, "Air Freight Has Problems on the Ground," *Business Horizons*, February, 1968, pp. 33–38; "Air Space Cargo Sees a Higher Ceiling," *Business Week*, May 13, 1967, pp. 106–10 and 116–20.

Airfreight may enable a firm to reduce its inventory costs by eliminating outlying warehouses. One eastern company had maintained a central warehouse on the West Coast, shipping across the country by rail and then reshipping from the warehouse. Then the company discovered it could save $60,000 annually by doing away with the warehouse and shipping everything direct by airfreight.[12]

Finally, valuable by-products of air transport's speed are the reduction of spoilage, pilferage, and damage. With less time from shipper to customer, goods are exposed to fewer hazards.

Freight forwarders are transportation wholesalers

Many marketing managers use freight forwarders to make optimum use of available transportation facilities, especially for the many small shipments that may have to move by varied transportation services.

Freight forwarders do not own their own transportation facilities, except perhaps for pickup and delivery trucks. Rather, they wholesale air, ship, railroad, and truck space. Accumulating small shipments from many shippers, they reship in larger quantities to obtain lower transportation rates. Their profits mainly come out of the difference in freight rates between small- and large-quantity shipments, though they sometimes make special service charges.

Freight forwarders can help the marketing manager who ships many small shipments in many directions. They handle an estimated 75 percent of the general cargo shipped from U.S. ports to foreign countries. More than 90 percent of all exporters, including companies with large shipping departments, use their services; a decisive reason is that the forwarders are located right at the exporting point and can more easily process all the complicated paper work necessary in overseas shipments.[13]

Should you do it yourself?

To cut transportation costs, some marketing managers provide their own transportation facilities rather than buy from specialists. Trucking has made it easier for a businessman to use do-it-yourself transport. Some large manufacturers own thousands of cars and trucks, and there are iron ore, gypsum rock, and petroleum producers who have their own ships.

Most wholesalers and retailers do at least some of their transporting with their own trucks. A large midwestern grain exporter arranged to

[12] For more examples of the advantages to be obtained from shipping by air, see H. T. Lewis and J. W. Culliton, *The Role of Air-Freight in Physical Distribution* (Boston: Graduate School of Business Administration, Harvard University, 1956); and *The Role of Air-Freight in Determining Company*

Policy (a report prepared for Emergy Air Freight Corporation by Stanford Research Institute, no date).
[13] Paul V. Horn and Henry Gomez, *International Trade Principles and Practices* (4th ed.; Englewood Cliffs, N.J.: Prentice-Hall, Inc., 1959), p. 521.

rent a freight train from the Illinois Central to haul its grain to the Gulf Coast.[14]

This drink
and driving
did mix
The concept of discrepancy of quantity applies here. If there is a great difference between the quantity a firm normally ships and the quantity that carriers find most economical, the firm may have to ship via common carrier or freight forwarder. But if a company normally ships in the same quantities that common carriers find economical, it may save money by using its own trucks and avoiding the cost that common carriers must charge for maintaining a regular schedule or contract carriers must charge against future uncertainties.

If a marketing manager is fairly certain of his future plans, do-it-yourself transportation may be good business. One wholesale wine distributor in New Orleans found that he was paying considerably more to ship wine by rail from California than if he rented a tank truck and hired his own driver for the California run. Because this was a regular and frequent shipment, he bought a truck and operated it himself at a large saving. While negotiations with a railroad might have led to a rate reduction, railroads can't always amend their rates, and then "doing it yourself" may be the only answer.[15]

Which is the best transportation alternative?

It should be apparent by now that picking the lowest-cost transportation depends on the commodities, the distances, and the peculiarities of rate structures. But by careful tabulation of the costs of alternate methods, it is possible to evaluate the alternatives, using graphs similar to Figure 18–1. This shows the costs for 400- to 1,000-mile shipments of a particular commodity. These cost patterns are found for many commodities.

Here, it appears that rail is the best alternative, if large shipments are involved. But note that in Figure 18–1 the cost per 100 pounds overlaps for motor and rail shipments of 15,000 to 20,000 pounds — the full truckload range — and that rail rates do not drop precipitously thereafter. This means that if speed or flexibility in delivery were important for this commodity, trucks might win the business, and goods would move in truckload quantities. If speed were *extremely* important and quantities to be shipped were small, perhaps air shipments would be superior, and that cost structure properly would be shown above the others on the graph.

Lowest transportation cost is not the only criterion that should be used in selecting the best method. Without any analysis we know waterways probably would be least expensive, rail next least expen-

---

[14] "Rent Your Own Freight Train," *Business Week*, October 26, 1968, pp. 104–8.

[15] For a fuller discussion of the advantages and disadvantages of a do-it-yourself approach, see "A Creative Approach to the Question of Private Carriage," *Handling & Shipping*, December, 1962, pp. 38–41.

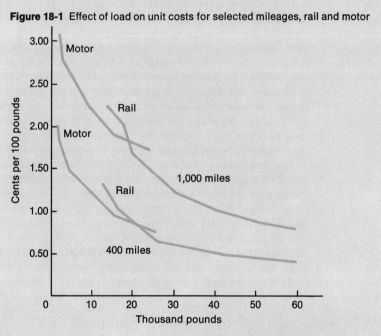

Figure 18-1 Effect of load on unit costs for selected mileages, rail and motor

Source: Reprinted with permission of the publisher from p. 53 of *Physical Distribution Management,* by E. W. Smykay, D. J. Bowersox, and F. H. Mossman. Copyright 1961 by the Macmillan Co.

sive, and so on. We must also allow for the services needed, and specify the quantities expected to be shipped.

As in buying other services, getting the best transportation requires that someone in the firm (big companies have specialists) first make a critical appraisal of all his firm's needs and then evaluate the available combinations against these needs. More is said on this later in the chapter.

The storing function

Store it and make money

Storing is the marketing function of holding physical goods between the time of production and the time of final use. It provides time utility.

Storing is necessary because production does not always match consumption. Some products, such as agricultural commodities, are produced seasonally though they are in demand year-round. If crops could not be stored when they matured or ripened, all the crop would be thrown onto the market at one time, and prices might drop sharply. The consumer might benefit temporarily from this surplus, but later in the year, when supplies were scarce and prices high, he would suffer. Storage, therefore, permits price stabilization throughout the consuming period, although prices usually do rise slightly over time to cover storage costs.

Unlike agricultural commodities, some goods—such as film and beachwear—are produced regularly throughout the year in anticipation of demand peaks. Until these goods are consumed, they must be stored somewhere. In contrast, however, to the refrigerated, vermin-proof storage needed for some food, warehousing for these items does not necessarily increase total costs. In fact, storage of seasonal, non-perishable items may make it practicable for factories to run at a regular rate yearlong, thereby lowering production costs and more than offsetting storage costs.

The practice of storing and therefore withholding products from the market to get better prices is the basic principle behind the U.S. Department of Agriculture's parity program and the occasional stockpiling of commodities such as rubber, coffee, and cocoa beans in other countries. Our federal government has stockpiled metals not only for defense but also to maintain prices. Storing, we can see, may be intimately related to Price as well as to Place.

Planning to use storage, some buyers purchase in large enough quantities to get quantity discounts. Goods also are sometimes stored as a hedge against future price rises, strikes, shipping interruptions, and other disruptions.

Finally, storing goods enables manufacturers and middlemen to keep stocks at convenient locations, ready to meet customers' needs. In fact, storing is one of the major activities of some middlemen.

Remember the rats

In spite of the advantages of storing, these benefits cannot always be achieved, especially in foreign countries where adequate storage facilities are not available. We in the United States tend to take our storage facilities for granted—for example, the huge grain elevators throughout the Middle West and at our port cities. In other countries, storage often is inadequate or even nonexistent. Grain, for example, may be stored on the ground or in open sheds. India completed its first grain storage elevator in 1957!

Lack of capital is one reason for the lack of storage facilities. And a poor understanding of the potential savings from storing is another. But there also are cultural differences in outlook regarding storage. When that Indian grain elevator was completed in 1957, an observer stated that it would protect the grain from rats. An unimpressed Indian official replied: "We look at it differently. We think the rats also have to eat."[16]

Storing varies the channel system

Most channel members provide the storing function for varying lengths of time. Even final consumers store some things for their future needs. Since storing can be provided anywhere along the channel, the storage function offers several ways to vary a firm's marketing mix and its channel system by: (1) adjusting the time goods

[16]Ralph Westfall and Harper W. Boyd, Jr., "Marketing in India," *Journal of Marketing*, October, 1960, p. 16.

are held, (2) sharing the storage costs, and (3) delegating the job to a specialized storage facility. This latter variation would mean adding another member to the distribution channel.

Which channel members store the product and for how long affects the behavior of all channel members. If a manufacturer of groceries were to maintain a large local stock, wholesalers probably would maintain smaller inventories, since they would be assured of dependable local supplies. Hawaiian food retailers, for example, maintain four to six weeks' inventory on the items they must receive from the mainland, but they stock only one week's inventory of those goods that are kept in stock locally by a manufacturer or wholesaler. Some manufacturers maintain their own stocks in Hawaii to woo wholesalers and retailers from competitors. Others provide storage allowances to encourage Hawaiian wholesalers to maintain stocks beyond their normal needs. This assures adequate local stocks and protects the manufacturers' customer franchises, especially during shipping interruptions.

Specialized storage — collateral for a loan, age for the bourbon

Private or branch warehouses

Private warehouses are those that are owned by individual companies for their own use. Most manufacturers, wholesalers, and retailers have some kind of storage facilities, either in their main buildings or in a warehouse district, often in a Commerce City. Management of a manufacturer's finished-goods warehouse often is the responsibility of a sales manager, especially at sales branches located away from the factory. In retailing, storage is so closely tied to selling that the buyers may control this function.

Private warehouses are used when a large volume of goods must be stored regularly. Owning warehouse space, however, can be expensive, since it is a fixed cost and may limit flexibility in the company's operations. If sales should fall and warehouse stocks decline, the extra space may be hard or impossible to lease, and costs may remain constant while revenue declines.

Public or commercial warehouses

The company that does not need permanent warehouse space may find public warehouses useful. The customer pays only for the space he uses and may, if he wishes, purchase a variety of additional services.[17] Public warehouses are useful to manufacturers who must maintain stocks in many areas, including foreign countries.[18]

Some public warehouses provide all the services that could be obtained in the company's own branch warehouse or from most wholesalers. These warehouses will receive goods in carload quantities, unload and store them, and later reship them in any size lots ordered

---

[17] For more details on public warehouses see *Distribution Age,* September, 1962, pp. 53–55; December, 1961, pp. 35–41; February, 1960, pp. 24 ff.; and April, 1960, pp. 52 ff.

[18] "Firm Tells How to Place U.S. Merchandise Closer to the European Consumer," *International Commerce,* July 8, 1963, pp. 14–16.

by the company or its customers. They will inspect goods, package them, and even invoice customers. They will participate in the financing function by issuing warehouse receipts that can be used as collateral when borrowing from banks. Some public warehouses will provide desk space and telephone service for a company's salesmen. And the public warehouse is responsible for the risk of damage or the loss of the product in the warehouse.

Public warehouses are located in all major metropolitan areas and many smaller cities. Rural areas also have public warehouses for locally produced agricultural commodities.

General merchandise warehouses store almost every kind of manufactured goods. A special form of warehouse is the *bonded* warehouse used for storing imported goods or other goods, such as liquors or cigarettes, on which a tax must be paid before the goods are released for sale. If a long storage period is needed, say to age liquor, then these warehouses may lower costs by delaying payment of taxes or duties until the goods are removed. Private bonded warehouses also can provide this latter feature.

Commodity warehouses and *cold-storage* warehouses are designed specifically for storing perishable or easily spoiled products such as apples, butter, and furs. Grain is stored in huge elevators.

New warehousing is switched on

The cost of physical handling is a major storage cost. The goods must be handled once when put into storage and again when removed to be sold. Particularly in older, multistoried warehouses, located in congested districts, these operations take many man-hours of high-cost labor. Difficult parking, crowded storage areas, and slow freight elevators all delay the process, increasing the cost of distribution.

Today, one-story modern structures are replacing the old multistoried buildings. These new single-level designs eliminate the need for elevators and permit use of power-operated lift trucks, battery-operated motor scooters, roller-skating order pickers, electric hoists for heavy items, and hydraulic ramps to facilitate loading and unloading. Some grocery warehouses even have radio-controlled tractors that order pickers drive by remote control. Most of these new warehouses use lift trucks and pallets (wooden "trays" which carry many cases) for vertical storage and better use of cube space.

One Los Angeles drug wholesaler, through careful planning and use of electronic controls, has now almost eliminated physical handling for most of his repeat business — covering 1,800 items. The system of controls and conveyor belts now assembles in a few seconds the kind of order that an experienced stock clerk formerly spent 20 minutes putting together.[19]

[19] "Automation Gets It Wholesale," *Business Week,* March 15, 1958, pp. 157–60.

Distribution-center concept asks: Is storing really needed?

Storage is justifiable only if it helps achieve time utility. Storage is *not* necessary just because there is some discrepancy of quantity or assortment between one channel level and another. If there is a discrepancy *and* time must be used, then it can make economic sense to regroup and store at the same time. But if time is not needed, then no storage should be provided. This leads us to a whole new idea – the distribution-center concept.

Don't store it, distribute it

A distribution center is a special kind of warehouse designed, *not* to stock goods, but to *speed* the flow of goods and eliminate unnecessary storage.[20] It is a breaking-bulk operation. Turnover is increased, and the cost of carrying inventory is reduced (such cost may run as high as 25 percent a year of the value of the average inventory).

The concept underlying the distribution center is the same one that led to the development of discount houses and mass merchandisers: *Reducing costs and increasing turnover will lead to bigger profits.*

There are many variations of the distribution center. The two following illustrations will help clarify this concept. Both show distribution centers in an integrated operation – and are similar in concept to the General Electric system described in Chapter 2. Some public warehouses are gearing for this approach, too. It may be possible for a manufacturer eventually to use only 10 or 15 such public warehouse centers and still service the country efficiently and at lower cost than with present methods.[21]

A clothing chain develops 45-minute warehousing

One chain of 124 stores handling women's and children's clothing is trying to reduce its storage operation. This company feels that some warehousing is required, but only because of the inability of industry to balance production with sales. Yet, because clothing styles change rapidly, it is essential to keep storage time to a minimum.

How can this be done? The chain is trying to make the warehouse an integral part of the whole marketing operation, not just a storage place. To speed distribution, this company uses a complicated conveyor system that enables it to receive goods from its 5,000 suppliers, route them to the appropriate "storage" areas in its warehouse, and from there move the goods out to trucks which take them to each of the firm's 124 stores. Total time: 45 minutes. Final result: Prices are lower, and retail stores get the newest styles sooner.[22]

---

[20] See Bowersox, Smykay, and LaLonde, *op. cit.,* chap. x.

[21] "Distribution Center – Texas Style," *Distribution Age,* May, 1962, pp. 44–46 ff; Howard E. Way, Jr., "The Role of the Public Warehouse in the Future," *Transportation and Distribution Management,* December, 1962, pp. 20–24.

[22] "In and Out of a Warehouse in 45 minutes," *Business Week,* July 6, 1957, pp. 64–70. For a description of a trucker who has developed a somewhat similar system serving many manufacturers and retailers, see "Trucker Tries for Something Extra," *Business Week,* March 4, 1967, pp. 112–18.

The Pillsbury Co., a large manufacturer of baking mixes and flour, used to move its products in carload lots directly from factory to wholesaler or large retailer. Plants were as near to customers as possible, and each plant, initially, was equipped to produce the whole Pillsbury line. As lines were expanded, however, it became apparent that no plant could produce all the various products. When customers began to ask for mixed carload shipments and faster delivery, Pillsbury found itself adding warehouse space and hauling goods from plant to plant. By 1955, Pillsbury had set up 100 branch warehouses, controlled by 33 sales offices. Each sales office had its own accounting, credit, and other processing operations.

Later, one Pillsbury official was to say of this old system: "Turnover was slow, warehousing costs were high, and there was no effective control over inventories." It was then taking the company one week *just to process an order.*[23]

Today, Pillsbury guarantees its customers "third morning delivery" anywhere in the United States. To make this dramatic advance in efficiency, Pillsbury appointed a director of distribution, equal in rank to the heads of manufacturing and marketing, and established multiple distribution centers. Now, each manufacturing plant specializes in a few product lines, and this permits longer runs. They ship carload lots directly to distribution centers, virtually eliminating warehousing at the factories. The distribution centers themselves are controlled by four regional data processing centers.

The field sales organization at Pillsbury no longer handles physical distribution or inventory. Sales is its only activity, and it has been able to expand its branches from 33 to 52. Sales orders are routed to one of the data processing centers, which immediately determines where and when the goods are to be shipped for that "third morning delivery." Centralized accounting speeds invoices to customers, resulting in quicker payment. And because each distribution center always has adequate supplies, it is possible to route and ship orders directly from that point, by the most economical means.

Before these changes at Pillsbury, neither the production nor sales departments had precise responsibility for what happened to goods between manufacture and sale. Now the entire physical distribution effort is treated as one system.

Pillsbury salesmen now have something extra to sell—better and faster service. Costs have been reduced and profits increased. Over a four-year period, the new system is credited with boosting the company's ratio of pretax income to sales from 2.9 percent to 4.9 percent.

Clearly creative use of physical distribution can improve, and perhaps even "make" a marketing mix.

[23]"New-fangled Routes Deliver the Goods—Faster and Cheaper," *Business Week*, November 4, 1959, pp. 108–10.

Physical distribution concept focuses on total system

We have been looking at the transporting and storing functions as separate activities, partly because this simplifies discussion but also because it is the traditional approach. In recent years, however, attention has turned to the *whole* physical distribution function, not just warehousing and transportation. This sometimes affects production planning, too, since the business should work as one unit. We just saw this in the Pillsbury case.

Physical distribution, a new idea whose time may come

According to the physical distribution (PD) concept, a relatively new business theory, all physical handling activities of a business and a channel system should be thought of as part of one system. It may be hard to see this as a startling development, but until just a few years ago, even the most progressive companies treated these various functions as separate and quite unrelated activities. Many firms still do.

In some firms, the production department is responsible for warehousing and shipping, and it builds inventories that are related to its production activities rather than market needs. In other companies, inventory may be a separate activity. If those in charge of inventory put little faith in sales forecasts, they may simply adjust stocks according to their own expectations.

Progressive firms, however, are beginning to integrate all their activities, often with the aid of electronic data processing equipment.[24] Although the majority of firms give little evidence of applying the physical distribution concept, considerable interest now surrounds this approach, and it is likely that great strides will be made to implement it in the near future.[25] Certainly the literature has been growing rapidly and shows the way.[26]

[24] For a discussion and examples of how individual firms have and others might integrate, see E. J. McCarthy, J. A. McCarthy, and D. Humes, *Integrated Data Processing Systems* (New York: John Wiley & Sons, Inc., 1966), chaps. ii and xxiii.

[25] D. J. Bowersox, "Physical Distribution Development, Current Status and Potential," *Journal of Marketing*, January, 1969, pp. 63–70; Alan H. Gepfert, "Business Logistics for Better Profit Performance," *Harvard Business Review*, November–December, 1968, pp. 75–84; R. P. Neuschel, "Physical Distribution–Forgotten Frontier," *Harvard Business Review*, April, 1967, pp. 125–34; J. L. Heskett, "A Missing Link in Physical Distribution Systems Design," *Journal of Marketing*, October, 1966, pp. 37–41; W. M. Stewart, "Physical Distribution: Key to Improved Volume and Profits," *Journal of Marketing*, January, 1965, pp. 65–70; R. E. McGarrah, "Logistics for the International Manufac-

turer," *Harvard Business Review*, March–April, 1966, pp. 154–66.

[26] Bowersox, Smykay, and LaLonde, *op. cit.*; J. L. Heskett, "Ferment in Marketing's Oldest Area," *Journal of Marketing*, October, 1962, pp. 40–45; J. L. Heskett, R. M. Ivie, and N. A. Glaskowsky, Jr., *Business Logistics* (New York: Ronald Press Co., 1964); J. A. Constantin, *Principles of Logistics Management* (New York: Appleton-Century-Crofts, 1966). See the periodical issues of *Transportation and Distribution Management*, and *Handling & Shipping*. See in particular the "Presidential Issue," Fall, 1969, compiled by the editors of *Handling & Shipping*.

Evaluate PD systems with total cost approach

The early interest in, and concepts about, physical distribution can be traced to the military supply forces responsible for getting the right men and material to the right places at the right time. The armed forces were not directly concerned with cost, but they were concerned with an optimum allocation of resources. Transferred to the business world, the military approach leads to lower costs.

Early stress was on reducing total cost

The early efforts to apply logistics to business focused on trying to reduce the cost of physical movement while giving essentially the same level of service. Determining the best, most economical method of physical distribution required comparison of complicated alternatives. To focus on the total cost of the various alternatives was quite logical.

The tools of the cost accountant and economist were applied to this problem. Sometimes the total cost analyses revealed that unconventional physical distribution methods might yield service as good as or better than conventional means, and at lower cost. The following simple examples illustrate the approaches that have been used.

Evaluating rail/warehouse versus airfreight

Table 18-2 shows the result of a comparative cost analysis of two alternatives: airfreight with no warehouse versus rail freight with warehouse. The comparison was based on the distribution of 1,000 tons of a particular commodity during a definite period of time.

Table 18-2 Comparative costs of airfreight versus rail and warehouse

	Total cost	Cost per ton
Rail and Warehouse		
(2) Interest on inventory, 30-day cycle, 360-day interest year at 6% on $1,500,000 of inventory	$ 90,000.00	$ 90.00
(2) Taxes on inventory	40,000.00	40.00
(2) Warehouse cost	55,200.00	55.20
(1) Transport expense (rail carload)	58,000.00	58.00
Cost via rail and warehouse	$243,200.00	$243.20
Airfreight		
(2) Interest on investment in inventory, 10-day cycle, 360-day interest year at 6% on $500,000 inventory	$ 30,000.00	$ 30.00
(1) Airfreight	120,000.00	120.00
(1) Local delivery	10,000.00	10.00
Cost via airfreight	$160,000.00	$160.00

Note: Total sales = 1,000,000 units or 1,000 tons

(2) indicates fixed and variable expense; (1) indicates variable expense only.

Source: Reprinted with permission of the publisher from p. 76 of *Physical Distribution Management* by E. W. Smykay, D. J. Bowersox, and F. H. Mossman. Copyright 1961 by the Macmillan Co.

Comparing the final totals showed that using airfreight would be less expensive than the rail-warehouse combination, even though airfreight itself was considerably more costly than rail.

Comparison of five alternatives

Figure 18–2 presents another cost analysis, this time with five alternatives:

 I. Airfreight.
 II. Motor common carrier.
 III. Direct rail.
 IV. Rail-warehouse.
 V. Branch plant.

Here, a more sophisticated approach is shown. Instead of calculating the total cost of two alternatives at one volume level, the total (PD) cost of supplying a market at all feasible volume levels for each alternative is calculated and then converted to a per-ton basis. This permits a more complete understanding of the cost of using the five alternatives. The figure shows clearly that the best alternative depends on the expected sales volume. If the company's sales volume will not exceed 20,000 tons during the given period, then the airfreight system will yield the lowest unit cost. If a 20,000- to 40,000-ton volume is expected, however, the motor freight alternative becomes more economical, and so on.

In any total cost analysis of this kind, all practical alternatives

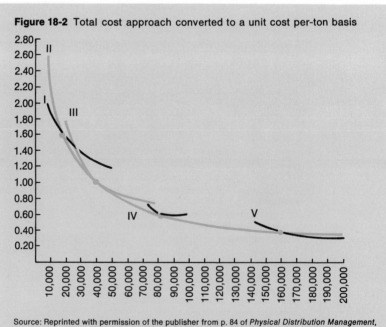

Figure 18-2 Total cost approach converted to a unit cost per-ton basis

Source: Reprinted with permission of the publisher from p. 84 of *Physical Distribution Management,* by E. W. Smykay, D. J. Bowersox, and F. H. Mossman. Copyright 1961 by the Macmillan Co.

should be evaluated and compared. The easiest course is to do things as they always have been done. Yet this could lead to the death of the firm in our competitive economy. It is imperative that all practical alternatives be evaluated and compared.

Sometimes alternatives are so numerous or complicated that advanced mathematical and statistical techniques, and perhaps a computer, are needed for their analysis.[27] For evaluating many alternatives, some companies have found it desirable to use a new approach: simulation with a computer. In simulation, the characteristics and costs of the many alternatives are described as carefully as possible, and then the computer tests the alternatives, using a trial-and-error technique.[28] For many applications, however, the straightforward total cost analysis discussed previously is practicable and will show whether there is need for a more sophisticated analytical approach.

PD man may increase service levels

Physical distribution not just cost-oriented

Although cost reduction was the main focus of early physical distribution efforts, more attention is being directed now toward integrating physical distribution planning into the company's strategy planning. Perhaps by increasing physical distribution costs somewhat, service levels can be increased so that, in effect, a new marketing mix has been created. Larger and broader inventories might be carried to assure prompt delivery *and* adequate supply. Improved packaging and physical handling might cut damages and repairs. This would reduce the time and effort needed for adjusting claims.

In extremely competitive situations, simply increasing the service levels – perhaps through faster delivery or wider stocks – can enable a firm to make significant headway in a market without altering prices or promotion – two changes that are often noticed and easily copied by competitors. In fact, improved service levels can put a marketing mix across, and competitors may not fully realize what has happened. As noted earlier in our discussion about industrial buying practices, an industrial buyer usually must have several sources of supply, but he does have some option as to how to distribute the shares to each. Superior delivery service might prompt a buyer to forget about splitting orders equally among three vendors in order to reward a more dependable supplier with half of the business – a 50 percent increase in sales for the favored supplier![29]

Physical distribution specialists are also interested now in the possible impact of packing and packaging changes on total cost throughout the whole channel of distribution. They are interested, too, in ma-

[27] Stanley S. Stasch, "Distribution Systems Analysis: Methods and Problems," *The Logistics Review*, March–April, 1968, pp. 7–34; see also, Bowersox, Smykay, and LaLonde, *op. cit.*

[28] For a discussion of this approach, see Harvey N. Shycon and Richard B. Maffei, "Simulation – Tools for Better Distribution," *Harvard Business Review*, November–December, 1960, pp. 65–75.

[29] See also, P. Ronald Stephenson and Ronald P. Willett, "Selling With Physical Distribution Service," *Business Horizons*, December, 1968, pp. 75–85.

terials handling methods and in the development of new transportation facilities that will make the whole physical distribution process more effective. While it is true that the traditional specialists in storing and transporting have shared these interests, the physical distribution man adds a desire to integrate all these factors not only within his firm but all along the channel system.

Need for physical distribution manager

Basic company reorganization may be necessary for full acceptance and exploitation of the physical distribution concept. Just adding an executive called a "distribution manager" or a "manager of physical distribution," or simply giving the traffic manager or warehouse manager a new title will not in itself do the job. This would only be paying lip service to the concept of integrating physical distribution activities unless the whole organization also accepted the idea that new methods of production, warehousing, shipping, promotion, and sales were necessary to achieve this total integration.[30]

For the real item, a big job

These far-reaching changes may be a long time coming. Many sales and marketing executives still have not recognized their responsibility for physical distribution.

One survey found that fewer than 10 percent of top marketing executives were fully responsible for transportation decisions, and only a slightly greater percentage, 10.95 percent, were fully responsible for warehousing. What is worse, in 43 percent of the firms the top marketing executive did not assume any responsibility for physical distribution, and in 35 percent of the firms he did not participate in the discussions concerning this important phase of marketing.[31]

Such separation of storage and transportation from the rest of marketing activities is anachronistic. We recognize now that these functions must be seen together as physical distribution and that this, in turn, must be treated as part of the total marketing system.

A true physical distribution manager would have a big job. He would be concerned not only with physical product flows but also with the location of Place facilities through which the flows would move. He might have to become directly involved in the selection of plant locations, warehouses, and retail facilities. In some companies, it might be a good idea to have a separate distribution manager or controller, coequal with the marketing manager, with centralized control of all physical distribution activities. There is much ferment and controversy in this area, because how best to organize a "total system" is involved. But it is clear that major changes will be required in many companies if the marketing concept and the physical distribution concept are wholeheartedly adopted.

---

[30] For further discussion, see John F. Stolle, "How to Manage Physical Distribution," *Harvard Business Review*, July–August, 1967, pp. 93–100.

[31] Robert E. Weigand, *Business Topics*, Summer, 1962, pp. 70–71.

Future physical distribution problems and opportunities

The marketing system of the future, responding to new living patterns and technology, may change drastically in some urban areas. Urban redevelopment programs may cause even more significant shifts of population than we have seen so far. With mounting population pressure, radical new regulations might be introduced, such as the exclusion of private automobiles from city streets, either by ordinance or by prohibitively high taxation.

Getting ready for an age of planning and people

New approaches must be found to mass transportation and urban living. Already, the federal government is subsidizing urban mass transportation systems. There are some limited attempts at developing new residential and commercial building arrangements. France and Sweden have experimented with communities combining residential, working, and recreation facilities in the same center.

Adjustments in transportation rate structures may lead to drastic changes in physical movement patterns. The railroads have seen more and more of their most profitable business go to competitors; if this situation were to be adjusted on a grand scale, the changes in transport might have a profound impact on the whole economy.

Suppose, for example, that the low rail rates charged on bulk commodities such as lumber and coal were raised sharply. This probably would force some producers to relocate nearer their supplies. It might force others to manufacture or use substitutes.

A lumber company in the Northwest, for example, might suffer if rail rates for lumber rose. Contractors might shift to other types of building materials. Such a rate increase might even force the whole construction industry to revamp its methods and materials.

Planes may race trucks for business

Transportation is not one problem but many problems. Any major changes in the existing rate structure will affect manufacturers, wholesalers, retailers, and consumers. So far these adjustments have been made on a piecemeal basis, but a national transportation policy may be coming. The recent formation of a separate U.S. Department of Transportation could bring solutions to some of the problems, but change comes slowly and is resisted by vested interests and the sheer magnitude of the problem. The number of people, cars, trucks, and airplanes continue to grow, and no one wants to be restricted.[32]

Finally, technological developments, including new materials handling equipment and electronic computers, no doubt will encourage changes in physical distribution. We already have discussed the distribution-center concept and the activities of some progressive

[32] "When Traffic Jams Stall the Nation," *Business Week*, December 6, 1969, pp. 186–92; "Is There Too Much Regulation?" *Business Week*, November 2, 1968, pp. 55–56; "Off on the Wrong Track," *Business Week*, June 24, 1967, p. 39; and John A. Volpe, "To Build a Truly Integrated . . . System," "Presidential Issue," *Handling & Shipping*, Fall, 1969, p. 12; and "Homing in on the Airport Crisis," *Business Week*, November 18, 1967, pp. 115–18.

wholesalers. It also appears that larger and more automated rail facilities will be built. Trucks may travel as large multiunits and be able to handle heavy, bulky loads as railroads do.[33] Larger airplanes may be able to compete with trucks on a cost basis.

Such developments may further reduce the cost of overcoming the barriers of time and distance and enable interested firms to expand their operations. Multinational firms seem to see possibilities in more integrated production and distribution systems and may continue to grow and prosper if they are permitted to continue to capitalize on these opportunities.

As always, the marketing manager who has been able to carve out a target market today will still have to be alert if he wishes to keep it tomorrow.

Conclusion

This chapter has dealt with providing Time and Place utility. We have discussed the various means of transportation and their comparative costs at some length, and also examined the advantages and disadvantages each presents. The railroad rate structure, particularly, seems in need of a drastic overhauling, and this might have a marked impact on our present marketing system.

Storage, the second aspect of physical distribution, was considered, together with the types of warehousing now available. Examples were given of modern techniques which can cut storage and physical handling costs.

Although we discussed transportation and storage separately, it was emphasized that both are related. The distribution center, a new approach in this area, is an attempt to integrate these two activities for the purpose of speeding turnover and lowering handling and storage costs.

The physical distribution concept is concerned with integrating all the physical handling, storing, and transporting activities into a smoothly working system. The total cost approach has been helpful in selecting the most effective physical distribution alternatives. But it focuses on costs, when management often wants to improve service and may select a higher cost alternative to improve its marketing mix. Or the total cost approach might reveal that it is possible *both* to reduce costs and to improve service, perhaps by eliminating warehouses and using airfreight to speed delivery.

Finally, physical distribution can contribute greatly to a marketing mix, for example by raising service levels, perhaps without increasing costs. New organizational structures may be needed within the firm to achieve the potential benefits of integrating physical distribution activities. In addition, new thinking may be indicated if these activi-

[33] "What Shippers Will Be Using in 1973," *Handling & Shipping*, December, 1962, pp. 17–36.

ties are to be shared within a channel system. Here the channel captain may have to take the lead. It should also go without saying that the specialized transporting and storing institutions could also contribute to this effort, by adopting the marketing concept themselves and showing how they can contribute to the better operation of channel systems.

QUESTIONS AND PROBLEMS

1 Discuss the relative advantages and disadvantages of railroads, trucks, and airlines as transporting methods.

2 What method of transportation would probably be most suitable for the following products (specify any assumptions necessary to obtain a definite answer):
a) Hogs.
b) Apples.
c) Diamond rings.
d) Large tractors or other agricultural machinery.
e) Coal.
f) Television sets.

3 Describe how your college town would be changed if there were no incoming or outgoing transportation except by foot, horseback, or horse-drawn covered wagon.

4 Distinguish between common carriers and contract carriers. What role do the contract carriers play in our economic system? How would our economy be different if there were no common carriers?

5 Distinguish among the following types of railroad rates: class, commodity, and exception rates. If all three rates might apply in a particular situation, which one would probably be the lowest?

6 Explain which transportation method would probably be most suitable for shipment of goods to a large Chicago department store:
a) A 10,000-lb. shipment of dishes from Japan.
b) 15 lbs. of screwdrivers from New York.
c) Three couches from High Point, N.C.
d) 500 high-fashion dresses from the garment district in New York City.
e) 300 lbs. of Maine lobsters.
f) 60,000 lbs. of various appliances from Evansville, Indiana.
How would your answers change if this department store were the only one in a Centertown in Ohio?

7 Indicate the nearest location where you would expect to find substantial storage facilities. What kinds of products would be stored there and why are they stored there instead of some other place?

8 Indicate when a producer or middleman would find it desirable to use a public warehouse rather than a private warehouse. Illustrate, using a specific product or situation.

9 Discuss the distribution center concept. Is this likely to eliminate the storing function of conventional wholesalers? Is it applicable to all products? If not, cite several examples.

10 Clearly differentiate between a warehouse and a distribution center. Explain how a specific product would be handled differently by these marketing insitutions.

11 Explain the total cost approach and why it may be necessary to have a physical distribution manager to implement the concept.

12 How would a distribution manager differ from a transportation manager? Would he really be any different than a marketing manager?

...the marketing manager not only must get involved with the needs and wants and problems of his target customers but also with the needs, wants, and problems of his cooperating channel members.

...in the final analysis, it is channel systems that compete with each other. The "battle of the brands," for example, can be seen in a broader context as only a skirmish in the battle between various channel systems.

19

Development and management of channel systems

Channel systems don't just happen. They are developed by someone, and then continue to evolve. We have called the person or firm who develops and coordinates a channel system the *channel captain*. The captain may be a producer, wholesaler, or retailer. Some channels, of course, don't have captains, since they're made up of firms that haven't yet been shown the advantages of mutual cooperation by a channel captain.

Most producers probably would prefer to handle the whole distribution job themselves. But, as we will see, this is not always possible or even desirable. It may not be possible because vital middlemen control the end of the channel, having satisfied certain market segments for some time. And it may not be desirable because it is so uneconomic. Where indirect channels clearly are indicated, the answer to the question of who becomes channel captain depends in part on the relative strength of the various channel members. In this chapter, for convenience of exposition, we will assume that the producer is the channel captain. But this is for convenience only. Middlemen are already dominant in some channels and may be the typical channel captains in the future.

Don't mem-
orize what;
understand
why

By now you should have a general knowledge of the various types of marketing specialists who have evolved and how they might be combined in channel systems.

We will be specific here about the dominant channels for various kinds of products. You must remember, however, that there may be more than one effective (workable) channel for one kind of product or one target market. You should *not* try to memorize *what is done;* rather, you should try to understand *why* many alternative channels can and do develop. Your job is to try to anticipate what channels will or should look like in the future, and what role you might play in them.

The best channel system is the one that works best

It may seem trite to say so, but the best channel system is the one that works best in the strategy that the marketing manager selects. An extension of the total cost approach, discussed in Chapter 18, to the whole channel system can be helpful in analyzing the cost of alternative channel systems, but the lowest-cost system is not necessarily the best. Ideally, we would like to select the lowest-cost channel that does the job. This may turn out to be a relatively high-cost system, but if the customers are satisfied with what it does, then the channel system and the strategy may be profitable.

The market grid concept is applicable here. Some parts of a market might want many services that only an expensive channel system could provide. Some gourmet food customers, for example, might want personal service and a large assortment, but they would still buy only in very small quantities. They might be served very well by a high-cost, high-price system composed of manufacturers who sell through small wholesalers to small retailers. Supermarket customers, on the other hand, demand less service, and the volume moving through that channel system allows lower prices. Yet both channel systems may exist side by side and be good channel systems for the different target markets.

Planned channel systems may be best

Since the costs of alternate channel systems can be calculated, they may show that some systems have significant cost advantages over others. This may suggest that prices will drop significantly, if they have not already, or that some channel systems are doomed to failure and will disappear when their plant and equipment wear out and must be replaced.

An analysis of egg production-marketing systems, for instance, showed that when small farmers produce Grade-A large eggs and then move them through the usual middlemen channels to a medium-sized retailer, the cost is about 64 cents a dozen. But when production and distribution are handled through an integrated production-marketing system to large supermarkets, the cost is only about 36 cents a dozen, which is closer to the market price.[1]

This study clearly shows why there has been a movement toward larger integrated production-marketing systems for eggs and why there are similar movements in other agricultural products. Similar cost analyses of other channel systems probably would help explain the trend towards vertical integration and administered channel systems we noted in Chapter 15.

Lower cost, however, may not be the only reason an integrated channel works well. There could be a better flow of information along an integrated or administered channel, permitting it to function better and sell more.[2]

More basically, better performance may be due to the fact that the whole channel system is able to focus on satisfying certain needs and organizes itself to do this job effectively. In other words, the General Foods hypothesis may apply here: the whole channel system (not just the firm) develops a superior strategy.

Product-market commitment can guide channel strategy planning

The idea of a channelwide strategy is intriguing. It is also a reality, as we saw in Chapter 15 when we discussed the development of administered and corporately run channel systems. Here, at this point, it helps to think of the members of such a channel system having a *product-market commitment,* with all members focusing on the same target market at the end of the channel, and sharing the various functions in appropriate ways.

A channel strategy can be visualized in the circular diagram of the four P's surrounding target customers, which we used to describe a firm's own strategy in Chapter 2. The job of the channel captain is to arrange for the performance of the necessary functions in the optimum way. This might be done as shown in Figure 19–1 in a manufacturer-dominated channel system. Here, the manufacturer has selected the target market and developed the product, set the price structure, done some mass promotion and promotion in the channels, and developed the place setup. Middlemen are then expected to finish the promotion job in their respective places.

In a middleman-dominated channel system, we would see quite different diagrams. In the extreme, in a channel similar to that dominated by Sears, Roebuck, the middleman circle would be almost completely shaded for some products, and manufacturers would be almost

[1] E. J. McCarthy and R. J. Williams, "Simulation of Production-Marketing Channels," in Raymond M. Haas (ed.), *Science, Technology, and Marketing* (Chicago: American Marketing Association, 1967), pp. 335–46.

[2] Walter Gross, "Profitable Listening for Manufacturers and Dealers," *Business Horizons,* December, 1968, pp. 35–44.

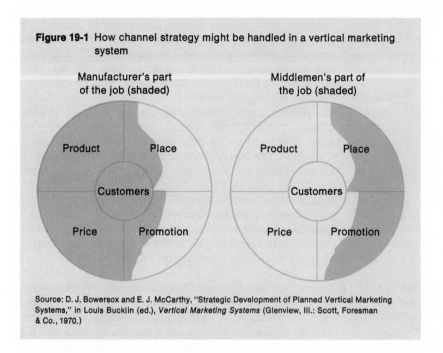

Figure 19-1 How channel strategy might be handled in a vertical marketing system

Manufacturer's part of the job (shaded)

Middlemen's part of the job (shaded)

Product | Place
Customers
Price | Promotion

Product | Place
Customers
Price | Promotion

Source: D. J. Bowersox and E. J. McCarthy, "Strategic Development of Planned Vertical Marketing Systems," in Louis Bucklin (ed.), *Vertical Marketing Systems* (Glenview, Ill.: Scott, Foresman & Co., 1970.)

solely concerned with manufacturing the product and perhaps designing it to meet the specifications set by Sears.[3]

New and better ways of organizing channel systems might evolve out of this way of thinking. By rearranging who does what functions, unnecessary and costly duplication may be avoided and information and physical goods flows smoothed and speeded. Just because a merchant wholesaler "controls" a market, for example, doesn't mean that obviously he should provide his normal functions in all cases. Perhaps everyone would be as well or better off if he just did the selling and billing and left the physical distribution functions to the manufacturer. Creative channel system planning offers great opportunities.

A good channel system can help everyone

A channel system where the various members have accepted a common product-market commitment can function very well, even though not everyone in the channel system is strongly market-oriented. As long as someone, say, the channel captain, is market-conscious, it should be possible for him to win the confidence and support of production-oriented firms and make the whole channel work effectively. He can convince his channel partners that he knows what he is doing and that a commitment to mutual cooperation is well worth their while.

[3] D. J. Bowersox and E. J. McCarthy, "Strategic Development of Planned Vertical Marketing Systems," in Louis Bucklin (ed.), *Vertical Marketing Systems* (Glenview, Ill.: Scott, Foresman and Co., 1970).

Small production-oriented producers in Japan or Hong Kong, for example, may become part of an effective channel reaching the U.S. market if there is a middleman who correctly diagnoses market needs and relays them clearly to his producers. The producers may not even know where their products are going, but the system still can be competitive with other systems.

Franchising organizations, and voluntary and cooperative wholesalers, are also illustrations of channel systems in which the members have made the same product-market commitment. In the fast food franchising industry, for example, a successful franchiser who really knows what he is doing will have a training program for prospective franchise holders and carefully instructs them in how to carry out this strategy effectively. The importance of not deviating from the basic strategy may be stressed, or even required by contract. If the franchiser knows his business and expects to share profits with the franchise holder, then he will feel even more strongly about the franchisee carrying out the channel strategy.[4]

Don't let stodgy George do it!

In ideal terms, a whole channel system of marketing-oriented firms, fully aware of what is happening, would be preferable to a marketing-oriented producer working through stodgy middlemen. This, unfortunately, is the position many progressive manufacturers find themselves in, and it is why some have chosen to take over more and more of the distribution job themselves.[5] Remember—the best channel system is the one that satisfies customers' wants *and* meets the needs of the various channel members.

The best channel system should achieve ideal market exposure

The best Place system does not happen automatically. Someone must plan the system, and the Place objectives introduced in Chapter 15 suggest the kind of system that should be developed. But then someone must make specific decisions about how many facilities should be in a geographic area and how the various marketing facilities should be linked together.

Although it might seem that all marketing managers would want their products to have maximum exposure to potential customers, we have seen in our earlier discussion of Place objectives that while some products need widespread distribution, others need only limited distribution. The question, then, is what degree of market exposure should be sought?

[4] "McDonald's Makes Franchising Sizzle," *Business Week*, June 15, 1968, pp. 102–110; and A. M. Rothenberg, "A Fresh Look at Franchising," *Journal of Marketing*, July, 1967, pp. 52–54.

[5] For further discussion on this point, see E. J. McCarthy, "Are Effective Marketing Institutions Necessary and Sufficient Conditions for Economic Development?" in S. A. Greyser (ed.), *Toward Scientific Marketing* (Chicago: American Marketing Association, 1964), pp. 393–404.

Generally, the ideal market exposure should meet target customers' needs and preferences—but not exceed them. Excessive exposure would merely increase the number and kinds of outlets, the work involved, and probably the total marketing cost.

Three degrees of market exposure may be ideal

We will discuss three degrees of market exposure: *intensive distribution, selective distribution*, and *exclusive distribution*. As we move from intensive to exclusive distribution, we give up exposure in return for some other advantage—including, but not limited to, cost reduction.

Intensive distribution is the sale of a product through any responsible and suitable wholesaler or retailer who will stock and/or sell the product. *Selective distribution*, as the name implies, refers to the choice or selection of only those middlemen who will do a good job with the product. *Exclusive distribution* is the choice of only one middleman in a particular geographic area.

In practice, this means that cigarettes are handled, through *intensive distribution,* by at least a million U.S. outlets, while Rolls Royces or expensive chinaware products are handled through *exclusive distribution,* by only a limited number of middlemen across the country.

A more detailed explanation of each of the three degrees of market exposure will clarify the differences.

Intensive distribution—sell it where they buy it

Intensive distribution is commonly needed for convenience goods and for industrial supplies—such as pencils, paper clips, and typing paper—used by all plants or offices. Customers want such goods nearby.

Manufacturers of "new" unsought goods that must compete with convenience goods want to achieve intensive distribution. They may not be able to get this degree of exposure, because customers aren't demanding their products and the channel consequently isn't willing to carry them; nevertheless, these manufacturers have an intensive distribution policy.

The seller's intent is important here. Intensive distribution refers to the *desire* to sell through *all* responsible and suitable outlets. What this means depends on customer habits and preferences. If target customers normally buy a certain product at a certain type of outlet, then ideally we would specify this type of outlet in one of our Place policies. If customers prefer to buy hardware items only at hardware stores, we would solicit all hardware stores to achieve intensive distribution. If, however, as it seems today, many customers will buy certain hardware items at any convenient outlet, including drugstores and food stores, an intensive distribution policy logically requires use of these outlets—using more than one channel to reach one target market.

Selective distribution—sell it where it sells best

Selective distribution covers the broad band of market exposure between intensive and exclusive distribution. It may be suitable for all categories of products. Only the better middlemen, chosen on some predetermined basis, are used here. The usual purpose in going to selective distribution is to gain some of the advantages of exclusive distribution while still achieving fairly widespread market coverage.

A selective policy might be used to avoid selling to wholesalers or retailers who (1) have a poor credit rating, (2) have a reputation for making too many returns or requesting too much service, (3) place orders that are too small to justify making calls or providing service, or (4) are not in position, for any other reason, to do a satisfactory marketing job.

Selective distribution is growing in popularity over intensive distribution as firms decide it no longer is necessary to obtain 100 percent coverage of the market in order to justify or support national advertising. Often, the majority of sales come from a relatively few customers, while a large number are clearly unprofitable to serve. A study by one manufacturer for instance, showed that 41 percent of its wholesaler customers accounted for only 7 percent of its sales. Most of them gradually were dropped, and after four years of aggressively cultivating the remaining customers, sales increased 76 percent. Marketing expenses were reduced from 22.8 to 11.5 percent of this larger sales volume, and a net loss of 2.9 percent of sales was converted into a net profit of 15 percent.[6]

Selective distribution may produce greater profits for all channel members because of the closer cooperation among them. Here, the systems concept is relevant. Transactions become more routine, requiring less negotiation in the buying and selling process. Wholesalers and retailers may be more willing to give aggressive promotion to products if they know they are going to obtain the majority of sales produced through their own efforts. They may carry more stock, wider lines, do more promotion, and provide more service, all of which contribute to increased sales.

Selective distribution makes sense for shopping and specialty goods, and for those industrial goods that require special effort from channel members. If the channel captain selects only "good" members for his team, this reduces interchannel competition and gives each of the members a greater opportunity to profit if they do a good job.

When selective distribution is used by manufacturers, fewer sales contacts have to be made, and fewer wholesalers may be needed. In fact, as in the garment industry, a manufacturer may be able to contact retailers directly if selective distribution is suitable at the retail level.

In the early part of the life cycle of a new unsought good, a manufacturer's marketing manager may have to use selective distribution to encourage enough distributors to handle his product. He wants to get his product out of the unsought category as soon as possible, but he can't as long as it lacks distribution. Well-known middlemen may have the power to get a product introduced — but sometimes on their

[6] Charles H. Sevin, *How Manufacturers Reduce Their Distribution Costs* (Economic Series No. 72 [Washington, D.C.: U.S. Government Printing Office, 1948]), p. 13. This text presents a large number of case studies showing similar results.

own terms, which often includes limiting the number of competing wholesalers and retailers.

Exclusive
distribution
— if your mix
will permit
or requires it

Exclusive distribution arrangements usually entail a verbal or written agreement stating that channel members will buy all or most of a given kind of product or product line from a particular firm. In return, these middlemen are granted the exclusive rights to that product in their territory. Many dealers are so anxious to get a manufacturer's exclusive franchise that they will do practically anything to satisfy the manufacturer's demands. In effect, the dealer becomes a part of the manufacturer's organization. The dealer supplies the capital and local management, but the major policy decisions are made by the manufacturer.[7]

Exclusive distribution may be satisfactory for some shopping goods and the more expensive specialty goods. It may also be practical for many industrial products — including installations, larger accessory equipment, some raw materials, and component materials — that have limited markets and require special selling effort. When a middleman has a monopoly in an area, he is more likely to sell aggressively when he knows all the fruits of his efforts will come to him.

Exclusive distribution is often used when it is necessary for middlemen to carry large inventories to provide adequate service, as in sales of industrial machines, major household appliances, and some lines of men's suits. It also may be useful when extensive installation or repair services are needed, as in sales of automobiles and heating equipment.

Unsought-goods manufacturers may have to adopt an exclusive distribution policy if they cannot get distribution without granting exclusive rights to some middlemen. This must be done with care, however, especially if the product should have wider distribution. All channel members should thoroughly understand the arrangement, and how long it will last. An exclusive middleman may agree to help move a product through the introductory stage only if attractive terms are offered, because he knows that when the product has achieved greater customer acceptance, the producer will want to change to a selective or intensive distribution policy.

Exclusive distribution sometimes is used by manufacturers as a device to help control prices and the services offered in a channel. For years, Magnavox Corp. maintained its list prices and service standards by selling only through 3,000 exclusive franchise dealers.[8]

Exclusive distribution also may help to build a channel team. A producer is assured of reliable contact with target customers; this protects the goodwill developed by his advertising and product quality control. Since the producer using exclusive distributors doesn't have

---

[7] For a good discussion of exclusive dealing, see K. J. Curran, "Exclusive Dealing and Public Policy," *Journal of Marketing,* October, 1950, pp. 133–44; and Leonard J. Konopa, "Exclusive Dealing Arrangements in Marketing," Michigan State University *Business Topics,* Summer, 1964, pp. 63–72.

[8] *Advertising Age,* May 6, 1963, p. 26.

to do as much aggressive selling in the channels, his selling expenses are cut, and this permits more emphasis on assisting the exclusive middlemen. Furthermore, the producer using exclusive distribution can expect better feedback to aid his planning and control. These assured outlets also protect the producer against the activities of competitors, at least in "his" outlets, because the exclusive arrangement bars those outlets to his competition.

But is it legal?

Marketing managers must operate within the law, and any consideration of Place must raise the question of the legality of limiting market exposure.

Exclusive distribution, per se, is not illegal. But current interpretation of the various antimonopoly laws gives the impression that almost any exclusive-dealing arrangement could be interpreted as an injury to some competitor somewhere. For example, horizontal arrangements among competing retailers, wholesalers, and/or manufacturers to limit sales by customer or territory are illegal, as shown by recent decisions of the Supreme Court in the Sealy mattress case and the General Motors case. Similarly, the Supreme Court decision in the Schwinn case discourages vertical relationships that would limit territories.[9] And a recent case involving a large retailer who allegedly blocked sales of certain manufacturers' lines to nearby competitors may tend to limit the power of some large retailers.[10] The matter of conspiracy and its impact on competition is important in all these cases.

In general, it would seem that companies should be cautious about entering into any exclusive-dealing arrangements. Apparently the law would allow some exclusive arrangements in order to permit the introduction of a new product or to enable a new company to enter a market, but these arrangements probably should be restricted to less than three years.[11] The same cautions probably apply to selective distribution; here, however, less formal and binding arrangements are typical and the possible impact on competition more remote.

Market exposure versus brand familiarity, when to cater to the lowest common denominator

We have related the ideal market exposure to our goods classifications, but the exposure needed is also related to the degree of brand familiarity achieved by Product and Promotion efforts. If a product has attained only the brand recognition stage, it probably should be distributed as widely as consistent with its goods classification. Potential customers obviously won't search for it.

When a product reaches the brand preference stage, more thought can be given to selective distribution, although this degree of buyer interest still cannot override the goods classification. But if selective

[9] S. Powell Bridges, "The Schwinn Case: A Landmark Decision," *Business Horizons*, August, 1968, pp. 77–85; "Are Supermarkets for Autos Next?" *Business Week*, May 7, 1966, p. 33; "Is the Franchise System Legal?" *Business Week*, April 3, 1965, pp. 66–68; "High Court Hits Sealy-Schwinn Franchise Plans," *Advertising Age*, June 19, 1967, pp. 1 ff.

[10] "Antitrust Verdict Rocks the Stores," *Business Week*, July 26, 1969, p. 29.

[11] *Business Week*, July 2, 1966, p. 30.

distribution were indicated before, perhaps an even more selective policy would be possible now.

Finally, when the brand insistence stage is reached, selective distribution and perhaps even exclusive distribution become feasible.

Even though a product seems to have achieved the brand insistence stage with *some* market segments, the marketing manager still may not go all the way to exclusive distribution because new potential customers may be coming into the market all the time. In terms of the market grid concept, some target customers may insist on the brand, while others have not yet reached the brand recognition stage. In such situations, marketing managers probably would prefer to cater to the lowest common denominator—those who have not yet learned to recognize the brand.

Brand familiarity may not be as important with respect to exclusive distribution. An exclusive distribution policy (or an extremely selective one) usually is chosen for other reasons besides the level of brand familiarity. The aim may be to control price or to achieve a greater selling effort, but the degree of brand familiarity achieved cannot be neglected.

Realities affect channel system(s) used

Each marketing manager must reconcile the ideal Place objectives of each channel system with various market realities, including the nature of the target market, special characteristics of the product, the market structure, and his own firm's capabilities and limitations. Often the marketing manager must settle for a channel that is less than ideal. His company may even have to join a channel that is controlled by another firm.

It will be useful to see how some of these market realities might affect channel decisions. While we examine some of these situations, keep in mind that although a direct channel system has advantages, it also forces the company to incur some more or less fixed overhead expenses (such as the costs of salesmen, office staff salaries, and the expenses of office facilities and warehouses). If the sales potential is not at least large enough to cover these costs, then some kind of *indirect* channel system is clearly indicated.

Not all targets look the same

Size and geographical dispersion affect sales contacts needed

If the sales potential of the target market selected by the marketing manager is large enough, it may be possible for him to go directly to retailers, consumers, or users. This is especially true if the potential target customers are highly concentrated, as are the customers for many industrial goods. For final consumer goods, however, potential customers usually are numerous and widely dispersed, and buy in small quantities. Although the total market may be relatively large, it might be split up into small geographical segments, with too little demand in each market grid box to support a direct approach.

Geographical dispersion is a decisive factor in international marketing. Here, middlemen become almost indispensable. Even if world demand is great, direct distribution to individual markets is seldom feasible because of the distance between the producer and the many separate markets.

Value of item and frequency and regularity of purchases

Even low-priced items such as groceries may be handled directly if they are purchased frequently and the cumulative volume is large – as in the case of home-delivered milk and bread. But for products purchased seldom and irregularly – even though purchases are substantial – specialized agencies such as commission merchants, agents, brokers, and other middlemen may be useful. A critical factor is the cost of regularly providing the needed marketing functions in relation to the sales obtained over several months or a year's time.

Customers view some products differently

We have stressed many times that the same physical product may be viewed differently by different target customers. This leads to a different goods classification and, as we would expect, a different channel system might be appropriate. An example from the building materials industry illustrates the point – but also shows that inter-channel problems can develop when channels overlap.

Before World War II, most homes were built by small contractors who sold them completely unfurnished. Today, the vast majority of houses are put up by large tract builders who may install washers, dryers, and dishwashers as part of their total product. These large appliances formerly were sold as consumer goods, going from wholesaler to retailer to final consumer. The large tract builders, on the other hand, consider such major appliances as components – that is, industrial goods – and want to buy in quantity at lower prices.

DUAL DISTRIBUTION MAY DEVELOP To serve this builder market, some manufacturers have attempted to make adjustments within their present channels.

Others have handled this business directly because their consumer goods distributors were too small to serve the big tract builders; and the manufacturers did not want to disrupt all of the policies they had established for reaching and serving the retail market.

Not unnaturally, this latter approach, sometimes called *dual distribution,* was resented by some of the established middlemen because they saw substantial sales volumes going to competing channels – and in this case, channels set up by their own sources of supply.[12]

Dual distribution is a regular problem for manufacturer's and wholesaler's marketing managers as markets (or the firm's plans) change or their present channel members become inadequate. The present middlemen may be needed to some extent, or past loyalties

---

[12] "The Builder's the Hot Market," *Business Week,* February, 4, 1961, p. 82.

may encourage continued relations. But often the manager must recruit new middlemen who will compete with the established middlemen, or even compete directly himself, to get the job done.

Customer preferences

Customer preferences vary even within the same goods classification. Some target customers, especially some industrial customers, have a bias against dealing with middlemen, and even though they may want only small quantities, they may prefer to buy directly from manufacturers. This may be a nuisance to the manufacturer, but he may tolerate it because the customers occasionally may buy larger quantities.

Other buyers, however, may prefer the convenience of buying through a middleman because they can telephone orders and get immediate action from a local source. Two quite different marketing mixes handled through two channel systems, therefore, could be needed to fully satisfy both types of customers.

Not all products are the same
Some goods, because of their technical nature, perishability, or bulkiness, require more direct distribution than is implied by their goods classification.

Technical products

Complicated products, such as conveyor systems and electronic data processing equipment, call for a high degree of technical selling knowledge and expert installation and servicing. Wholesalers usually do not wish, nor are they equipped, to provide all these required services.

Perishability

Perishable items, such as cut flowers, milk, and fresh seafood, may have to be handled directly if produced on a small scale, perhaps in an isolated town or in a less developed economic environment. But if many small producers are clustered together, specialists may develop to handle transportation, refrigeration, and storage. Complicated terminal markets, such as those dealing in fresh produce, may develop, along with a host of specialized commission merchants, brokers, merchant wholesalers, and truck wholesalers.

High-fashion items also are perishable, and more direct distribution may be sensible to speed the flow to retailers. Sometimes retailers and final consumers even go directly to the producers to see the latest fashion showings, say in New York and Paris.

Bulkiness

Transportation, handling, and storage costs mount when bulky products are moved about, making it difficult for middlemen to operate. If a producer is unable to make an adequate number of sales contacts when selling bulky items direct, he may decide to use brokers, manufacturers' agents, and especially drop-shippers, to make sales contacts and then ship the goods himself directly to the customer. This is another example of function shifting and sharing in a channel system, required in this case because of the nature of the product.

Availability of suitable and cooperative middlemen

The kinds of specialists the marketing manager would like to use may not even be available or willing to cooperate, especially if the company is a late entrant in the field and his competitors already have tied up the best middlemen, perhaps as part of a selective or exclusive distribution policy. It is important to realize that *aggressive* market-oriented middlemen usually are not readily available and waiting for someone to pick them up. They *may be* receptive to good proposals, but just another "me too" mix may have trouble.

The specific customers already being reached by each proposed specialist are extremely important. If these do not include the marketing manager's target markets, then that middleman doesn't have much to offer. A wholesaler specializing in groceries would have a valuable customer list for the food business, but it would not be of much value in distributing electronic machinery.

While this example is obvious, errors often are made in more subtle cases. To expand his sales, a manufacturer of industrial steam traps was considering the appointment of additional distributors in outlying territories. The company assumed that its outlets in large cities were adequate to maintain the present level of sales and that further sales increases in large cities were unlikely. Yet a more careful analysis of its present distributors' customer lists revealed that more wholesalers *were* needed in the cities. The reason: While the steam traps had been handled by distributors catering to the mechanical industries, other distributors were needed to contact the paper and chemical industries where a large share of the potential business was centered. The additional distributors were added, and sales were tripled in a short time.[13]

Strength of traditional arrangements

The market structure may be dominated by traditional arrangements. There may be long-established, highly successful "home-owned" retailers or wholesaler-retailer links based on family or nationality ties. This kind of traditional arrangement is seen in its extreme in tropical Africa, where channels are divided by race and target markets. Large European-owned firms import goods and export domestic production. These Europeans sell to some smaller wholesalers and retailers, but generally Levantines in West Africa and Indians in East Africa serve as middlemen to small retailers who typically are Africans.

There are exceptions to these generalizations, and breakthroughs can happen for those who deviate from the traditional arrangements. But in international markets, the traditional roles of the various groups are long standing and firmly rooted.[14]

The rather freewheeling competition we see in the United States is not typical of international markets. Because of this, the traditional

---

[13] R. E. Sessions, "Effective Use of Marketing Channels," in R. M. Clewett (ed.) *Marketing Channels for Manufactured Products* (Homewood, Ill.: Richard D. Irwin, Inc., 1954), p. 415.

[14] Edward Marcus, "Selling the Tropical African Market," *Journal of Marketing*, July, 1961, pp. 27–28; and Alice G. Dewey, *Peasant Marketing in Java* (New York: Free Press 1962).

channels of distribution may be the only practicable ones for a new-comer. Innovators may be punished by social sanctions or even legis-lative restraints aimed specifically at them.[15]

Uniformity of market coverage of available specialists

The middlemen available in large metropolitan centers may be highly effective there, but may not cover outlying areas. This may re-quire two channels to reach both areas. But it may also lead to a dual distribution problem because the middlemen who might be suitable for outlying areas may also cover the large metropolitan areas, but not as well. Everyone likes to work where sales are plentiful and easy to make.

Nor does distribution through national or international companies guarantee uniform coverage. For example, A&P has a much larger share of the retail grocery market in the East than in the Middle West. Sears, Roebuck has been relatively stronger in the Middle West and West than in other sections. This uneven coverage of marketing spe-cialists simply means that, in practice, every channel for every target market must be tailor-made. In this context, geographic dimensions may greatly expand the number of market grid boxes which must be treated separately.

Financing required in channel system

Adequate credit may be critical in smoothing the flow through a channel system. Some wholesalers enter a channel mainly because they can give financial assistance to the members.

We already have mentioned the role of factors, but some merchant wholesalers also hold a secure position in a channel because of their strong financial condition and ability to meet the financial needs of other channel members. This is especially true in international mar-kets.

In some African markets, the credit cycle from sale to final pay-ment may extend over three years. Since few African businessmen have this much working capital, well-financed European and Chinese importing and exporting firms have been attracted to Africa.[16]

Political and legal environment

Each geographical target market must be studied carefully for special legal or tax requirements that may affect channels. We already have mentioned the controls on exclusive distribution and the anti-merger legislation in the United States. Outside of the United States there are fewer controls of this type, but there are important tax con-siderations.

In Europe, a major portion of the tax income is collected from sales or "turnover" taxes that are assessed every time title passes from one level of distribution to the next. Partly because of turnover taxes — which may run as high as 25 percent — many European manufacturers

---

[15] Bert C. McCammon, Jr. "Alternative Explanations of Institutional Change and Channel Evaluation," in S. A. Greyser (ed.), *Towards Scientific Marketing* (Chicago: American Marketing Association, 1964),

pp. 477–90.

[16] Marcus, *op. cit.*, p. 31.

sell directly to retailers or users. When they cannot or do not wish to sell directly, they use commission merchants, who make the contacts and sales but avoid taking title.[17] This avoids the turnover tax, but using commission merchants who are intended for other purposes may reduce the effectiveness of the whole channel system.

Nature of company itself—is it big, rich, and un-prejudiced?

In deciding how to work with a channel system, each marketing manager—be he manufacturer, wholesaler, or retailer—must evaluate his own company's capabilities, needs, and potential contributions to a channel. If he is realistic, he may find that his best course is to join a strong system rather than try to play the role of channel captain himself.

Size of company and width of product line

A company's own size has an important bearing on its place in a channel system because it affects discrepancies of quantity and assortment.[18] A large firm already handling a wide line of food or soap products, for example, may be in a good position to take on an additional product of the same type and handle it the same way, perhaps directly. In contrast, a smaller company or one with narrower lines might suffer from a discrepancy of quantity or discrepancy of assortment or both, and would probably find middlemen more practical. Similarly, a large company going into a completely unrelated line would lose its size advantage, since it would be functioning as the small producer of a new line.[19]

Some industrial goods producers sell enough to overcome the discrepancy-of-quantity problem in *some* of their major markets. There they can use their own branches and warehouses. But the same producer may find middlemen more attractive where markets are smaller or scattered.

Financial strength

A company's financial strength can also be important if its customers need financial assistance. Firms not in a position to provide this financing may find specialized middlemen useful. Selling agents, factors, merchant wholesalers, or large retailers, may be in a position to finance a producer or channel members, including users or final consumers. In fact, a channel captain's dominance may depend heavily on his financing capacity.

Executive prejudices

Although the prejudices of company executives should not be a dominant factor, executives are a company resource, and their attitudes may influence channel selection or even be incorporated into company objectives. Some "old-time" sales managers, for example, have strong anti-chain store attitudes which color their thinking.

---

[17] Stewart C. Dalrymple, "Major Pitfalls in Sales and Distribution Methods in the Common Market," *International Trade Review,* January, 1963, pp. 12–13.

[18] Robert E. Weigand, "The Marketing Organization, Channels, and Firm Size," *Journal of Business,* April, 1963, pp. 228–36.

[19] For a description of Philip Morris' distribution system, see "A Machine That Will Sell Anything," *Business Week,* March 14, 1967, pp. 92–104.

Likewise, some sales managers prefer to control their own sales force rather than work with independent manufacturers' agents who may resist strict direction.

Currently dominant channels by product type

We have discussed (*a*) how an ideal channel system might look and perform, (*b*) factors that should be considered in developing or selecting a channel, and (*c*) the kinds of specialists available. Now we will tie this together in a description of how and why various products typically are distributed.

This discussion, in effect, will be a review, but now we will be using the names of specialists, not the general term *middlemen* in our description. You will want to see whether the material we will discuss jibes with your previous thinking. If it does not, try to determine why not. It may be that you have in mind different target markets, a different size firm, and so on. Or it may be that you have thought of a new system—perhaps a "breakthrough" opportunity for you.

In the following discussion, we will merely describe the *dominant* or *typical* channels. What follows should not be considered "right" but rather typical.

Conven-
ience goods
—get them
where the
customers
are

Staples

Middlemen of various types are commonly employed to handle convenience goods, and especially staples. The wide dispersion of target customers and the typically small size of each purchase encourage the use of several middlemen, especially merchant wholesalers and retailers. Furthermore, there are discrepancies of quantity and assortment between most manufacturers and final consumers. Setting up their own retail outlets would be impractical for the manufacturers, even if they had the financial resources to do so. Finally, most convenience goods are relatively uncomplicated items. They seldom require installation, service, or even much personal selling, and so direct marketing is unnecessary.

Intensive distribution at the retail level is appropriate for most convenience goods. This may also require intensive distribution at the wholesale level because each wholesaler has his own customer list and the only way to reach all retailers might be to work through nearly all wholesalers. If a producer promotes his product adequately, the merchant wholesalers and retailers may not have to do much more except handle, break bulk, and store the appropriate assortment until needed. Such middlemen usually are available.

The producer may be able to arrange for promotional displays by giving promotional allowances to retailers and/or wholesalers, or having special salesmen call on retailers for this purpose. Food manufacturers often send their own salesmen into supermarkets to set up promotional displays. Any orders obtained by these salesmen while working on promotion are turned over to the firms in the channel.

Food brokers also may be used to promote products in the channels.

Impulse goods

The promotional support for impulse goods must be more aggressive. The manufacturer may have to go directly to retailers with his own salesmen unless aggressive middlemen, such as food brokers, are available. But the need for intensive distribution at retail is obvious.

Emergency goods

Emergency goods must have wide distribution and must be available at times when regular distribution channels might not be open for business. A wide assortment is not necessary. In an emergency, anything that will do the job is acceptable. A variety of outlets cater to emergency business—all-night service stations, open-till-midnight grocers, and vending machines. Intensive distribution to these outlets is indicated, and this could require intensive distribution to wholesalers to reach these outlets, again because of the lack of overlap of wholesalers' customer lists.

Shopping goods—the direct route if necessary

Target customers for shopping goods, like the customers for convenience goods, are widely dispersed, but shopping-goods customers are willing to make more of an effort to satisfy their needs. The producer needs fewer outlets, and direct-to-retail distribution is feasible. Producer-to-consumer selling is unlikely, however, because consumers generally want to compare shopping goods. Retailers play a key role here.

Homogenous shopping goods

Homogenous shopping goods do not require attractive surroundings or knowledgeable sales personnel. For well-known manufacturers' brands of appliances, for instance, price is important to some consumers on the market grid, and they are willing to patronize back-alley discount houses, if necessary, to buy them. Or unbranded soft goods, such as towels and children's clothing, may be dumped into bins and customers will paw through them for the lowest-priced items.

A manufacturer of homogenous shopping goods might decide that it is too difficult or even impossible to upgrade the consumer image of his product, especially if it is in the last stages of the product life cycle. He may then abandon selective distribution efforts and attempt to gain intensive distribution through as many wholesale and retail outlets as possible. Some appliance producers have done just this, encouraging even more scrambled merchandising. Some soft-goods producers realize that some consumers are willing to do their shopping for such goods in one large mass merchandising outlet, and therefore attempt to achieve distribution in every such outlet.

Heterogeneous shopping goods

These goods require more retail display and often more personal selling both to final consumers and to middlemen. Producers frequently prefer to bypass wholesalers because, in any event, they *must* tell the sales story to retailers, sometimes including technical information that must be explained, directly to the retail clerks. Since producers must make the sales calls anyway, they feel they might as well take the orders and deliver the goods themselves.

Fairly direct channels are also encouraged by the willingness of retail buyers to make regular trips to central markets, say for furniture and clothing. Resident buyers in such cities as New York, Chicago, Dallas, or Los Angeles also facilitate the movement of these goods, especially in the style- and fashion-goods markets where new offerings are presented continuously.

If the potential sales volume is fairly large, as in clothing and shoes, large producers may begin to integrate down to the retail level or large retailers might integrate backwards, as we already have seen. This process is further encouraged in the case of these products because larger inventories or specialized services may be necessary. Home appliances are an example. If General Electric should move into retailing as prophesied by some marketing analysts, the reason, at least in part, would be GE's desire to do an effective selling job for heterogeneous shopping goods and to keep these goods from being viewed as homogeneous shopping goods.

Specialty goods — ready to handle a plum

Specialty goods normally are distributed through the same channels as those convenience or shopping goods they most nearly resemble. The best middlemen usually are happy to handle them because of the favored position of these goods with consumers.

Promotion in these channels will probably continue however, to assure good relations and favorable display and selling support.

Unsought goods — need some extra push

A large, established firm just introducing an unsought good (but one similar to the firm's other products) may be able to use the rest of its line and its customer franchise to obtain distribution for the new product. A well-known cake mix manufacturer, for instance, felt that on the basis of its reputation it could sell a million cases of a new mix containing only sawdust — just once, of course!

The position of such a manufacturer may enable it to use its typical channels to place the product where similar products are sought. The producer may still have to pay for or supply all promotion, but it *is* able to get distribution — an important and sometimes difficult feat in these days of expanding product lines.

A smaller producer, or a larger one going into a new line might not be so fortunate. It may have to resort to the use of less efficient middlemen, mail-order selling, or aggressive house-to-house selling. Established middlemen sometimes refuse to handle unsought goods until they have achieved some market acceptance. Or they may demand exclusive rights in their territories. Manufacturers' agents and merchant wholesalers, for example, might insist on exclusive rights before they would take on a new product or firm.

Installations — president may turn salesman

Brokers frequently handle sales of used buildings and land rights, since buyers and sellers are only in the market irregularly. These specialized middlemen have a knowledge of the market and can provide a useful service.

New installations normally are sold directly by the contractor's or manufacturer's own saleman, since (1) customers are relatively few and geographically concentrated, (2) the potential sales volume is large, and (3) there is a need for design, technical assistance, and service of a kind that middlemen don't normally provide. Even smaller companies may sell directly, since they are normally in a position to provide the sales and technical assistance required for this type of product. In these companies, the president or executive officers often serve as the sales personnel.

Accessory equipment— middlemen often needed

Since technical assistance is required for some accessories, direct selling by the producer is common. For other accessories, however, potential customers are widespread and need frequent contact by experienced sales personnel. For such products, large firms use manufacturers' agents or brokers in less populous areas, and smaller firms use them throughout the country. These agents provide continuous contact, and there is no cost to the producer except when a sale is completed. Since the cost of the agents' regular sales calls is spread over a number of products, the producer can obtain sales coverage without the high overhead sales cost he would incur doing this job for himself for only one line.

If good agents or brokers are not available, then merchant wholesalers — such as mill supply houses or oil field supply houses — may be used. Relatively little sales effort, however, can be expected from them. They may simply list the items in a catalog and sell them if customers ask about them. They may want exclusive rights in the territory, but not do much for the producer. Typically, the salesmen are not specialists and cannot be expected to provide a technical sales job or service. Furthermore, some merchant wholesalers will not even stock such items, serving more as agents, although they may insist upon the normal merchant wholesaler margin.

Raw materials— many small farmers, few big producers

Farm products

The large number of small farmers creates a real discrepancy of quantity and perhaps of assortment. It also makes practical the development of many specialized middlemen. Assemblers are used to gather farm products in rural areas, and commission merchants and merchant wholesalers handle these products in the terminal markets as the products are brought closer to users.

Natural products

These are being produced by fewer and larger firms. There is little or no need for assemblers. Users are not numerous, at least not compared to final consumers. The result is that many of these producers handle distribution themselves, although smaller producers may use brokers or drop-shippers. The smaller firms need practically the same market coverage as the larger firms but have less to sell and, consequently, a smaller sales volume to cover selling costs.

The concept of ideal degree of market exposure is not too relevant for farm products or natural products because they are essentially homogenous products sold in the open market at market prices. Whoever sells them, however, may try to reach as many potential customers as possible.

<table>
<tr><td>

Component parts and materials — dealing face-to-face

</td><td>

Most components producers are specialized and cater to a relatively small, concentrated group of users. Since technical and design assistance may be required, these producers normally deal directly with their target customers. The executive officers of these smaller producers may do the direct selling, as in the case of installations. If potential customers are numerous and widespread, however, agents may help locate and service new business. And they may be granted exclusive territories to encourage selling effort.

</td></tr>
<tr><td>

Supplies — middlemen rank high here

</td><td>

Maintenance items

Maintenance items are used widely and are similar in many respects to convenience goods. Customers are fairly widely dispersed, their purchases of each item are relatively small, and little technical assistance or service is required. Since this is an ideal situation for middlemen, merchant wholesalers are common in this field. Mill supply houses and office and stationery supply stores often serve as middlemen for maintenance items. They are contacted directly by the larger producers in the more populous areas and by manufacturers' agents in other areas. The smaller producer may use manufacturers' agents exclusively for his contacts with these merchant wholesalers. The agents may be given exclusive rights in territories, but the manufacturer must do this with care. The agents may call only on certain merchant wholesalers, whereas the manufacturer might be looking for intensive distribution at the merchant wholesaler level.

Repair items

Repair items are used widely and, with some exceptions, may be distributed in the same way as maintenance items. Large customers might have complete repair facilities and prefer to buy repair parts directly; smaller manufacturers and contractors more often prefer to have wholesalers carry the parts inventory and perhaps handle the repair service, too.

Operating supply items

Operating supply items, with few exceptions, are similar to maintenance items and are distributed in the same way. The exceptions are some bulky items, such as coal, lubricants, and fuel oil. Direct distribution of these supplies by the producer may be advisable because of technical service considerations (as for lubricants) or the large volume of sales (fuel oil). Drop-shippers commonly act as middlemen for the many small coal producers.

</td></tr>
</table>

Channel systems evolve — management must be dynamic

We have been trying to stress the importance of what should and could be in channel systems. This will be your main concern in the future.

If a company has been using the same channel system for more than a few years, the chances are good that it needs to make some changes. Perhaps a new channel should be added, or an existing channel replaced, or specific wholesalers or retailers changed. Perhaps the firm's own retail stores, sales branches, and/or warehouses should be expanded or modified in line with the modern trend to distribution centers.

To make all this more concrete and show how change might work its way through an industry, we will return to the discussion of the channels in the electrical goods industry which we began in Chapter 15. For a better appreciation of why channel management is a continuing problem, we will investigate how all the variety in that industry developed.

When agents become distributors

Traditionally, merchant wholesalers – called electrical distributors – handled a large share of the business in the electrical goods industry. As product lines increased, however, many manufacturers found that to obtain adequate promotion they had to go direct or establish agents to assist the wholesalers. Some of the manufacturers set up field stocks under their own control or under the control of agents. This ostensibly was to aid the distributors, but in fact the agents made many direct sales. The ready availability of these field stocks also encouraged some small distributors to use drop shipments. This enabled them to cut price because they did not have the cost of handling the goods.

Some manufacturers resorted to the use of brokers because it was the only way they could reach some industrial customers. But these brokers usually would sell only the fast-moving items, on a price basis. This made the market even more competitive. Furthermore, some manufacturers put pressure on agents to obtain business for new lines or less popular lines that distributors would not stock. As a result, some agents assumed the role of distributors and began to solicit all types of orders directly – although these agents dealt in narrower lines than those traditionally handled by the electrical distributors[20]

No bemoaning, please

All this is very much like the scrambled merchandising we observed in retailing. Here, small, probably production-oriented producers of narrow lines had to resort to various expedients because they could not get complete distribution of their lines through the traditional full-function merchant wholesalers.

While there is room for doubt as to whether this complexity actually improves the efficiency of electrical supply distribution, this becomes an academic point. This situation typically develops when there are many small, production-oriented manufacturers competing in the

[20] E. H. Lewis, "Distributing Electrical Products in a Dynamic Economy," *Electrical Wholesaling*, June, 1958, pp. 83–95.

latter stages of the product life cycle. Dual distribution, at least, and much competition can be expected.

Rather than bemoan his fate, a good marketing manager, faced with stiff competition, should try to find ways to differentiate his product and his channel system. This might require the kind of innovative thinking we have been trying to encourage. At the very least, he should attempt to develop or become a part of a smoothly flowing channel. This would enable him to reduce his costs as much as possible and obtain a share of whatever profits are possible at his stage in the product life cycle.[21]

Pushing or pulling through the channel system

A producer has a special challenge with respect to channel systems: How to win channel cooperation to insure that his product reaches the end of the channel. Middlemen, and especially retailers, don't have this problem, since they already control that end of the channel.

The two basic methods of achieving channel cooperation are *pushing* and *pulling*.

Pushing policy — get a hand from the boys in the channel

Pushing a product through the channels means using normal promotional effort — personal salesmen and advertising — to help sell the whole marketing mix to possible channel members. This method is common, since these sales transactions are between rational, presumably profit-oriented businessmen. The approach emphasizes the importance of building a channel and securing the wholehearted cooperation of prospective channel members in a total system of action. The channel captain, in effect, tries to develop a team that will work well together to get the product to the user.

Pulling policy — make them reach for it out there

By contrast, a manufacturer pulls a product through the channels when he tries to develop channel support by making consumers want his product. This entails highly aggressive promotion to final consumers or users, perhaps using coupons or samples, and temporary bypassing of middlemen. If the promotion works, the middlemen are forced to carry the product to satisfy their customers.

This method, familiar in the soap industry, may be necessary if many products are competing already in all of the desired outlets, and the channel members are reluctant to handle a new product. They may be told about the promotion beforehand so that they can anticipate demands if the promotion is successful.

Regardless of how channel cooperation is won, potential channel members must be convinced that the channel captain knows what he

[21] For further discussion on the dynamics in channel systems, see William R. Davidson, "Changes in Distributive Institutions," *Journal of Marketing*, January, 1970, pp. 7–10; "Trans-shippers — Keep the Hell Out of my Markets!" *Dealerscope Magazine*, October, 1969, or *Marketing Insights*, January, 1970, pp. 10–13; and "Dealers Feel Shortchanged," *Business Week*, January 24, 1970, pp. 33–34 (Autos).

is trying to accomplish and why. The marketing manager's salesmen must be able to tell prospective channel members what is expected of them and how much competition they may get from other channels. And it may be a good idea to spell out how the firm and channel will react to probable competitive marketing mixes. In other words, Place policies must be integrated with the rest of the marketing mix if implementation is to be effective.

Implementation of the channel plan

We have not said much about the selection of individual firms for a channel system and the relations among them. Implementation details of this kind are beyond our scope, but a few general comments are in order. Continuous management of channels is extremely important and may consume a big portion of a marketing manager's or a channel captain's time. Often, however, channel management is done poorly, if at all. The job may not be assigned to anyone specifically. Presumably the salesmen work in the channels, but if channel planning and administration are not given explicit recognition in the firm's strategic plans, then these important jobs may be neglected or ignored.

In our general discussion, we will look at the problems of channel systems composed of two or more independent firms, for purposes of simplicity and clarity. We will view the problem first as it develops when a producer plays the channel captain role, and then when a middleman has this dominant position.

Producers look down the channel

Channel relations are extremely important to a producer because middlemen are the ones who eventually sell his products, and if this job is not done well, he may go out of business. For this reason, producers often attempt to play the channel captain role.

Before approaching prospective channel members, the marketing manager for a producer should have carefully planned his own marketing strategy. Part of this strategy should include his distribution plans. While developing his marketing mix, he should take into account how prospective channel members may react. His mix should provide sufficient incentive to make all members want to "play the game—hard."

Selecting prospective channel members requires considerable field experience. Marketing research can be useful.[22] A research analyst could determine the availability, size, and market coverage of potential channel members. Market coverage is especially important here because a middleman's customers are his major asset, but it cannot be assumed that he reaches everyone—recall the example of the "trap" manufacturer. By interviewing their customers, competitors, and suppliers, the analyst could get a good picture of the reputation

[22] See Martin D. Steinberg, "Predicting Dealer Success," *Journal of Marketing*, April, 1962, pp. 75–76.

and past behavior of these specialists. Experienced sales executives would then interview likely prospects to determine present and probable future sales capacity.

But caution is required here, with checks and double checks.

A middleman's good reputation may be based on the past performance of salesmen who are now older and less aggressive. Or the good salesmen may have left the company. Investigating the proposed specialist's facilities and talking with his top executives and salesmen can be invaluable.

Once the marketing manager has decided to use a particular firm, he must explain and sell his whole marketing mix, not just to the top executives but to the whole organization. He should make clear exactly what he will do for them and what they in turn will be expected to do for him. It is important that everyone understand at the outset how the team is to operate and how each member will be compensated for his efforts.

It is not enough to sell the channel members initially. They must remain sold. This continuing job, often neglected because it is time-consuming and takes considerable effort, is extremely important in maintaining effective distribution channels. By obtaining and evaluating feedback about the channel, the marketing manager can adjust policies whenever necessary and replace or assist less effective channel members. *The marketing manager and channel captain must be not only an imaginative planner of marketing strategies, but a skillful negotiator and salesman as well.*[23]

Middlemen may dominate rather than coordinate

Middlemen sometimes don't see themselves as sales arms of producers. Instead, they may follow their own strategies, perhaps including dealer branding.

Strong middlemen often are the channel captains because of the strength of their market position in a particular geographic area. But they might not choose to exercise the coordinating function we are assigning to the channel captain. Instead, they could exert their influence by being more demanding of producers. They may seek lower prices, larger advertising allowances, local manufacturer stocks, fast shipments on small orders, and other conditions that enable *them* to operate more effectively.

Some large, strategically located retailers behave this way and some large wholesalers do, too. Their behavior adds weight to the belief of some observers that middlemen may come to dominate marketing.

Other large middlemen, including some large cooperative and voluntary wholesale chains, recognize that there are advantages in the whole channel system working together. They have developed more cordial relations with their producer-suppliers. It should be clear,

[23] For further discussions, see *Selecting and Evaluating Distributors* (Studies in Business Policy, No. 116 [New York: National Industrial Conference Board, 1965]).

nevertheless, that when a strong middleman, such as Sears, Roebuck, specifies what, when, and how much is to be produced, where it is to be shipped, and what label is to be put on it, then the producer has become *just* that and nothing more – a *producer.*

Most of the important marketing decisions are being made *for* such a producer, and he is now concerned primarily with production problems. This is not necessarily bad from the standpoint of developing efficient channel systems. But it does mean that there may be less need for a marketing manager in such a firm, unless the company is also catering to other target markets. And the firm should not expect the rewards which typically go to innovators, if it is simply producing for someone who is making all of the marketing strategy decisions and assuming the risk that they will turn out right.

Conclusion

This chapter has been concerned with the development of channel systems intended to get the right Product to the target customer – always, of course, at the right Price, with the right Promotion. We have stressed that because each channel system must compete with other channels, a marketing manager of a particular firm must not only consider his own firm's needs and goals but also the needs of others in his channel system.

Although we generally assume that a producer would prefer to sell his product directly to final users or consumers, it is often much more sensible and profitable to use the specialized marketing institutions that are available to do this job. This leads to the possibility of a large number of alternative channel systems and interchannel rivalry.

The most appropriate channel for a given marketing job at any particular time depends upon a great many factors – the nature of the product, the market exposure desired, the target market, competitive activity, the size and resources of the company, and others.

What may be the right channel for one company may be completely impractical for another. Sometimes a single company must use several channels to reach different target markets most effectively.

It is clear that the development of Place policies, while closely related to Place objectives, also must be consistent with the other three P's of the individual marketing manager's firm. The Place policies also must be compatible with the needs and goals of other members of the channel system. We now see that the marketing manager not only must get involved with the needs and wants and problems of his target customers but also the needs, wants, and problems of his cooperating channel members.

Taking a broader view of channel systems, a marketing manager or a channel captain might conceive of a channelwide strategy which would center around a product-market commitment to which all of the members of the channel system would contribute. In the final analysis, it is channel systems which compete with each other. The "battle of the brands," for example, can be seen in a broader context as only a skirmish in the battle between various channel systems. Finally, it should be emphasized that producers are not necessarily channel captains. Often, middlemen control or even dominate channels of distribution.

QUESTIONS AND PROBLEMS

1 Cite a local example of a firm which seems to be implementing a channel strategy. Is there a channel captain in this system? If so, who is it? Also, identify competing channel systems and indicate which one of all these systems seems to have the advantage over the others.

2 Relate the nature of the product to the degree of market exposure desired.

3 Why would middlemen seek to be exclusive distributors for a product? Why would producers seek exclusive distributors? Would middlemen be equally anxious to obtain exclusive distribution for any type of product? Why or why not? Explain with reference to the following products: cornflakes, razor blades, golf clubs, golf balls, steak knives, hi-fi equipment, and industrial woodworking machinery.

4 Explain the present legal status of exclusive distribution. Describe a situation where exclusive distribution is almost assured to be legal. Describe the nature and size of competitors and the industry, as well as the nature of the exclusive-dealing arrangement. Would the exclusive dealing arrangement so described be of any value to the producer or distributor?

5 Would a direct or some type of indirect channel be most appropriate for the following products? (Utilize the general factors discussed in this chapter and make any assumptions necessary to obtain a definite answer.)
a) Hedge clippers
b) Fly swatters
c) Earthmoving machinery
d) Fingernail clippers
e) Motor scooters
f) Grass seed
g) Picture frames
h) Trucks
i) Fresh apple cider

6 For those products in the previous question where indirect distribution was the answer (in light of the assumptions), indicate specifically the kinds of channels which might develop.

7 How would the distribution channels for building materials be changed in 1985 if by that time all new buildings were prefabricated at factories and merely assembled on the job by factory crews?

8 Discuss the competitive situation in the electrical goods industry. Would it be desirable from the consumer viewpoint to legislate against the development of competitive channels? If so, which channels should be eliminated by law?

9 Describe how an electrical tool manufacturer (drills, sanders, etc.) might go about selecting an exclusive distributor in one city. Why might he want to do this?

10 Discuss the promotion a grocery products manufacturer would need in order to develop appropriate channels and move goods through these channels. Would the nature of this job change at all for a dress manufacturer? How about for a small producer of installations?

11 Many persons think of direct sale from the producer to the consumer as "obviously" the most efficient. Why then do we find such complicated channels? Why doesn't everyone buy directly from the farmer or factory and save?

12 Although wholesalers are normally supposed to provide a selling function for the producer, many producers find it necessary to have salesmen call upon the wholesalers' customers. Why? In these cases why doesn't the producer bypass the wholesaler as long as he must provide salesmen anyway? Are these producers' salesmen necessary for all products? If not, why not?

13 Discuss the development of a marketing strategy by a truck gardener who lives within 25 miles of a large northern Commerce City. Would the mix change for a farmer capable of growing essentially similar products but located 150 miles from the nearest Centertown or Commerce City?

14 Discuss the advantages and disadvantages of either a pushing or pulling policy for a very small manufacturer who is just getting into the candy business with a line of inexpensive candy bars. Which policy would probably be most appropriate for him? State any assumptions you need in order to obtain a definite answer.

...the marketing manager's job is to combine all the possible promotion ingredients into a blend which tells target customers that the right product is available at the right place at the right price. ... we will stress this *blending* of promotion ingredients throughout our discussion of promotion.

...we will discuss basic promotion objectives, methods of implementing these objectives, and ways in which these methods can be blended for effective promotion.

20

Promotion — introduction

Promotion is communication between seller and buyer. It is one of the four major variables with which the marketing manager works. Some people believe that marketing begins and ends with promotion but, as we will see, although promotion is a vitally important part of marketing, it is not the whole pie. Nor are advertising and personal selling the whole of promotion. The marketing manager also has the tools of publicity, public relations, and various other forms of promotion.

What should be communicated is basically determined when the target customers' needs and preferences are known. In this context, setting promotion is clearly only a part of strategy planning. But it is an important part because it is what gets your customer's attention, tells him what you have to sell, and hopefully convinces him that you have the product he's looking for.

The marketing manager's job is to combine all of the possible promotion ingredients into a blend which tells target customers that the right product is available at the right place at the right price.

The big push from factory to consumer

We will stress this *blending* of promotion ingredients throughout our discussion of promotion. We will see why one product may need heavy accent on personal selling — encyclopedias are an example. But another, such as gum, might be sold primarily by advertising and sales promotion, with little or no special effort by the salesman at the candy counter. Other products will require a mixture between these extremes. In addition, we will see that some products may require different blends of mass and personal selling (1) at different levels of the channel system as they move from factory to consumer, and (2) as their product life cycles move along.

In this chapter, we will discuss basic promotion objectives, methods of implementing these objectives, and ways in which these methods can be blended for effective promotion. The next two chapters will be devoted to personal selling and mass selling, the two basic approaches to promotion.

Basic promotion objectives

Informing, persuading, reminding

The basic, broad objectives of promotion are to *inform, persuade,* or *remind* target customers about the company's marketing mix and the company itself. Agreeing on and defining promotion objectives is critical if the firm's promotion is to be effective, because the right blend depends on what is to be accomplished.

A specific set of promotion objectives would state exactly what and why we want to inform, persuade, or remind. For example, a firm might want to convince customers of its products' virtues in order to create brand preference among target customers — a preference for Brand *A* over both Brands *B* and *C*.

Promotion objectives are set with marketing strategy

Promotion objectives should be established as part of the overall marketing strategy, taking into account the needs and preferences of the target market. In other words, the strategy should include specifics on *what* should be accomplished by the promotion effort.

Specific objectives would guide tactical promotion planning and implementation efforts. Some specific promotion methods for implementing such clear-cut specific objectives will be discussed in this and the next two chapters. But specific promotion objectives are unique to each company's strategy, and we do not have the space in this text to handle the subject in such detail. Instead, we will work with the more general objectives—informing, persuading and re-minding—and discuss why these are our objectives and how we might reach them.

May need a blend from shout to soft sell

The firm with a distinctly new product may not have to do anything but *inform* consumers about its offering and show them how it works better than all existing products. A peddler in a primitive market might rely on a loud voice to attract attention. In a more complicated society, the firm may have to send out salesmen or advertise to get its message across. But newness and uniqueness in a product can simp-lify the process and may even get free publicity for the seller.

When others offer similar products, as is usually the case, the firm must not only inform customers that a product is available but also persuade them to buy its product. This is really two different jobs. You cannot persuade potential customers if they have never heard of your product or you. As population continues shifting geographically; as changes occur in the age, educational, and occupational character-istics of the population; and as more and more competitive products come into the market, reaching and talking to target customers be-comes more difficult and expensive. To solve this problem, the firm may place greater reliance on advertising, which may be more eco-nomical for telling a large number of potential customers about the firm's total product.

But even after customers have been attracted and sold once, they are still subject to competitive influences which force the firm to continue persuading and reminding. As the number of competitors and competitive products have multiplied, this has become simul-taneously more necessary and more difficult. Usually a firm must use several promotion methods, all at the same time, to inform, persuade, and remind.

May need a blend for each market grid box

It should be clear that each unique market grid box may need a sepa-rate marketing mix, with each perhaps requiring a different promotion blend. This is mentioned here because some specialists in promotion have missed this point, and think mainly in "mass-market" terms. A product differentiation approach to the "mass market" may be needed in some situations, but unfortunately, promotion aimed at everyone can end up hitting no one. In promotion, we should be especially cautious about slipping into a "shotgun" approach when what we really need is a "rifle" approach with more careful aiming.

Basic promotion methods which are available

The marketing manager may have to work with several promotion objectives at the same time. For the same market grid box, for ex-ample, he may want to do both informing and persuading. He might also be implementing several strategies at the same time and there-fore have to plan to get across many different messages to different target customers. Normally, he uses a blend of three basic promotional methods: personal selling, mass selling, and sales promotion.

Personal selling—flexibility is the biggest asset

Personal selling involves *direct face-to-face relationships between sellers and potential customers.* A salesman is often a very important part of a marketing mix because he can adapt the company's marketing mix to the needs and circumstances of each little target market and, in the extreme, to each potential customer. Moreover, face-to-face selling provides an immediate feedback, which helps the salesman to adapt effectively.

The flexibility offered by personal selling is absolutely necessary for certain products. As we saw earlier when we discussed customer behavior, the needs and preferences of individuals vary greatly. There are group influences, too, and market conditions vary. Adjusting to all these target market differences often requires the skills of an individual salesman.

Mass selling—reaching millions at a price or even free

Mass selling is designed to *communicate with large numbers of customers at the same time.* Obviously, such a method has less flexibility than personal selling, which can use *immediate* feedback to adjust the presentation for *each* prospect. When the target market is large and dispersed, however, mass selling may be much less expensive than personal selling.

Advertising is the main form of mass selling. *Advertising is any paid form of nonpersonal presentation of ideas, goods, or services, by an identified sponsor.* It involves the use of such media as the following:

Magazines and newspapers
Outdoor posters, signs, skywriting, etc.
Novelties (calendars, blotters)
Cards (bus, train)
Programs and menus
Motion pictures
Direct mail
Store signs
Radio and television
Catalogs, directories, and references
Circulars

Advertising must be paid for by the advertiser. There is, however, another form of mass selling which is "free," and that is publicity.

Effective publicity and public relations efforts can contribute to mass selling at relatively low cost. In some cases, it can be more effective than advertising. Advertising expenditures may create a favorable climate for publicity. Trade magazines, for instance, may write or carry articles featuring the products of regular advertisers. And this publicity may generate far more inquiries than the company's advertising. These mass selling efforts are too specialized for coverage here, but they can make an important contribution to the promotion effort and probably will become more important in the future as more attention is focused on smaller and more clearly defined target markets.[1]

Sales promotion — tell the customer, show him, sell him

Sales promotion specialists complement the efforts of salesmen and advertising men. *Sales promotion* is one tool of promotion. It refers to specific activities (such as point-of-purchase displays, booklets and leaflets, direct mailings, etc.) which can make both personal and mass selling more effective, by coordinating and supplementing both efforts.

Sales promotion personnel may design and arrange for distribution of novelties, point-of-purchase material and premiums, store signs, catalogs, directory references, and circulars. They assist in the development of displays, sales demonstrations, and trade-show exhibits. Trade shows are well established and important in domestic and international marketing.

Sales promotion men often prepare training materials and sales portfolios for the company's own sales force and its customers' salesmen. They may develop "jackpot" or "sweepstake" contests and coupons designed to get customers to try the product — perhaps as part of a pulling policy.

It is difficult to generalize about sales promotion efforts because they are custom-designed and often nonrecurring. They can be very effective, but making them work is a learned skill and not a sideline for amateurs. Consequently, specialists in sales promotion have developed within companies and as consulting firms.[2]

Promotion requires effective communication

Promotion obviously must get the attention of the target audience or it is wasted effort. What is obvious, however, is not always easily accomplished. Much promotion does not really communicate. Recent behavioral science studies indicate that the communication process may be more complicated than we imagine.

That body is not a corpse!

Researchers have demonstrated that the audience evaluates not only the message but also the source of the message in terms of trustworthiness and credibility. These studies have also shown that some persons are more easily persuaded than others. Persuasibility seems to be related to feelings of inadequacy and social inhibitions. While women

[1] See "The World of PR: More Firms Build Big Public Relations Staffs: Bloopers Still Occur," *Wall Street Journal,* November 19, 1962, pp. 1 ff; and "Public Relations Abroad Puts Diplomacy in Marketing," *Printers' Ink,* January 26, 1962, pp. 59–60.

[2] For more discussion on sales promotion activities, see Alfred Gross, *Sales Promotion* (2d ed.; New York: Ronald Press Co., 1961); A. W. Frey, *The Role of Sales Promotion* (Hanover, N.H.: Dartmouth College, 1957), p. 8.

seem to be more open to persuasion than men, persuasibility does not seem to be related to the level of general intelligence.[3]

Different audiences may perceive the same message in different ways and interpret the same words differently. Such differences are often obvious and to be expected in international marketing, where there are translation problems. General Motors' "Body by Fisher" came out as "Corpse by Fisher" in Flemish.[4]

Semantic problems in the *same* language may not be so obvious, and yet they must be recognized and solved to avoid giving offense. For instance, a large food company recently discovered that potential female customers didn't like being called "consumers" because they thought the word was too impersonal. They preferred "customers" or "homemakers," and married women, specifically, preferred the term "housewife."[5] These might seem like small differences, but it is just such subtleties that can make the target audience tune out a message, wasting the whole promotion effort.

Talk in circles to be understood

The communication process can be seen more clearly with the aid of a diagram (Figure 20-1). The relation to the stimulus-response model of consumer behavior which was discussed in Chapter 8 should be noted here. But the critical importance of some feedback to direct the process should also be understood.

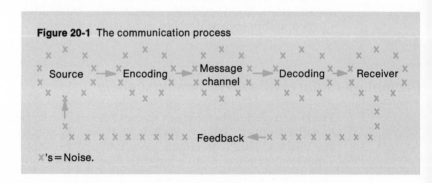

Figure 20-1 The communication process

The source shown here is attempting to deliver a message to a receiver, perhaps a potential customer. The source can deliver his message in many ways. The personal salesman does it with his voice and actions, while advertising must do it with mass media, such as magazines, newspapers, handbills, posters, radio, and TV.

[3] Abe Shuchman and Michael Perry, "Self-Confidence and Persuasibility in Marketing: A Reappraisal," *Journal of Marketing Research*, May, 1969, pp. 146–55. Carl I. Hovland and Irving L. Janis (eds.), *Personality and Persuasibility* (New Haven, Conn.: Yale University Press, 1959), pp. 229–40. See also, other volumes in the Yale Studies of Attitude and Communications: Carl I. Hovland (ed.), *The Order of Presentation in Persuasion; Attitude Organization and Change: An Analysis of Consistency among Attitude Components;* and *Social Judgment: Simulation and Contrast in Communication and Attitude Change.*

[4] *Time,* September 20, 1963, p. 93.

[5] *Management Review,* June, 1961, pp. 4 ff.

A major advantage of personal selling is that the source – the seller – may receive immediate feedback from the receivers. He can judge how his message is being received and adjust the balance of his message accordingly. This gives a real edge to the personal salesman. Mass sellers must rely on marketing research or aggregate sales results to measure what the salesman can see and feel.

The "noise" shown in Figure 20-1 refers to many factors which reduce the effectiveness of the communication process. Perhaps the source cannot agree on what should be said and how, and compromises with a general message. Or the receiver, a housewife, for example, may be distracted by children when the message comes out of her radio. Or other advertisers or salesmen may be saying essentially the same thing, and the receiver may become confused or ignore everyone. And the feedback process (including the salesman's interpretations and research results) may be filled with "noise."

The fundamental difficulty in the communication process occurs during encoding and decoding. The source must decide what it wants to say and then try to translate it into terms that will be decoded with the same meaning by the target audience. This can be very tricky because the meanings attached to various words and symbols may differ depending on the frames of reference and experience of the two groups. This can be seen in Figure 20-2. If there is no overlap, communication may be bad or impossible.

The average car driver, for example, might think of the Ford Mustang as a sports car; if he constitutes the target audience, then sports car terminology should be used in the message. Auto engineers and

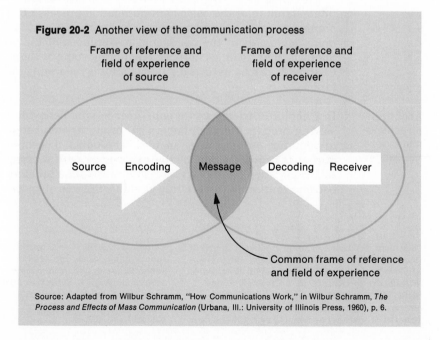

Figure 20-2 Another view of the communication process

Frame of reference and field of experience of source

Frame of reference and field of experience of receiver

Source Encoding Message Decoding Receiver

Common frame of reference and field of experience

Source: Adapted from Wilbur Schramm, "How Communications Work," in Wilbur Schramm, *The Process and Effects of Mass Communication* (Urbana, Ill.: University of Illinois Press, 1960), p. 6.

sports car buffs, however, do not consider the Mustang a true sports car, and when specifying, writing, or approving copy, they might encode the message in regular "small-car" terms, while their average-driver audience wants to hear about ease of handling, acceleration, and racing symbols such as wide tires. Errors could be minimized by knowing the relevant market grid dimensions, in terms of the needs and preferences of potential customers. This data should be available for strategy planning anyway, and here it would be especially useful.

Too frequently, the source – which is familiar with the technical details about a product – is inclined to talk about them and ignore the characteristics the target audience wants to know about. The result is relatively little effective communication.

Further complicating the communications process is the receiver's awareness that the message is not only coming from a sender but that it is coming via some media. Consciously or subconsciously, the receiver may ascribe more virtue to a product if its message comes in a well-respected newspaper or magazine, just as the president of a company might seem more impressive than a junior salesman.

Whether the message should emphasize only the positive features (one-sided arguments) or perhaps both positive and negative features (two-sided arguments) depends on the attitudes of the target market. Sometimes accenting the positive is desirable, since it's less confusing. But if the potential customers already know something of the pros and cons, it may be desirable to use a two-sided approach. Research on this and other topics with respect to putting together a message are beyond our scope, but it is important to realize that such matters may affect the effectiveness of communication.

The findings of the behavioral sciences are valuable for a general understanding of the basic communication process.[6] But in planning promotion for a particular product in a particular situation, we need more details about the needs and preferences of the target market. Some of their findings, however, including some of those discussed in Chapter 8, can be used as a guide to strategy planning and implementation.

Adoption is an achievement, not a happening

In Chapter 8, we discussed consumer buying behavior as a problem-solving process in which buyers go through several steps on the way to adopting (or rejecting) an idea or product. Learning takes place during this process, and if the experience with a certain product is satisfying, then habits may form and subsequent problem solving may become routine. This certainly could be the role of specific promotion

---

[6] For more discussion of basic studies in the communications area, see David K. Berlo, *The Process of Communication* (New York: Holt, Rinehart & Winston, Inc., 1960); Carl I. Hovland, Irving L. Janis, and Harold H. Kelley, *Communication and Persuasion Effects of Mass Communications* (Urbana, Ill.: University of Illinois Press, 1954); Edgar Crane, *Marketing Communications* (New York: John Wiley & Sons, Inc., 1965); S. H. Britt, *Consumer Behavior and the Behavioral Sciences* (New York: John Wiley & Sons, Inc., 1966); Gerald Zaltman, *Marketing: Contributions from the Behavioral Sciences* (New York: Harcourt, Brace & World, Inc., 1965).

efforts — that is, to bring a product to the brand insistence or preference stage, where promotion would only remind the customer about the product, and where it can be obtained.

In our earlier discussion of the adoption process, we isolated six stages in this process: awareness, interest, evaluation, trial, decision, and confirmation. These stages in the adoption process dovetail very neatly with an action-oriented framework — called AIDA — which we will use in this and the following chapters to guide our discussion.

The AIDA framework consists of four fundamental and interrelated promotion tasks which have been recognized for many years: (1) to get *attention*, (2) to hold *interest*, (3) to arouse *desire*, and (4) to obtain *action*.[7] (As a memory aid, note that the initial letters of each key word spell out the four-letter word, AIDA, the well-known opera.)

The relationship of the stages of the adoption process to the AIDA promotion tasks can readily be seen:

Obtaining *attention* is obviously necessary if the potential customer is to become *aware* of the company's offering. Holding *interest* gives the communication a chance to really build the prospect's *interest*. Arousing *desire* favorably affects the *evaluation* process. And obtaining *action* includes encouraging *trial* and subsequent *adoption*. Continuing promotion is needed to *confirm* the adoption and assure continuing *action*.

These interrelations can be seen better in Figure 20–3. This action-oriented AIDA framework will guide our subsequent discussion. But

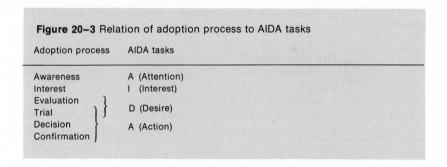

Figure 20–3 Relation of adoption process to AIDA tasks

Adoption process	AIDA tasks
Awareness	A (Attention)
Interest	I (Interest)
Evaluation	
Trial	D (Desire)
Decision	A (Action)
Confirmation	

it should be noted that this framework does not solve our problems. Most marketing managers deal not only with individuals going through the adoption process but with whole markets. Different promotional blends may be needed for different parts of the market. Some prospects may already have become aware of the product and developed considerable interest, while others have never heard of it. Still others might have adopted the product but want confirmation.

[7] M. S. Heidingsfield and A. B. Blankenship, *Marketing* (New York: Barnes & Noble, Inc., 1957), p. 149.

Good communication varies promotional blends along adoption curve

The communication and adoption processes discussed above concern individuals. This focus on individuals is important in order to understand the process. But it also helps to see markets in the aggregate and to understand that different customers within a market may behave differently — with some taking the lead in accepting products and, in turn, influencing others. Awareness of this phenomena, along with the fact that individual customers may be at different stages in their adoption process, complicates promotion planning; at the same time, it forces the manager to seek better methods of promotion and communication.

Research on how markets accept new ideas has led to the development of the adoption-curve concept, which is oriented to markets and not just to individuals. The adoption curve shows how and when different groups accept ideas, and points up the need for varying the promotional effort as time passes. It also emphasizes the interrelations within groups, showing that some groups act as leaders in accepting a new idea. The adoption-curve concept is similar to the product life-cycle concept — both are concerned with the rate of acceptance of innovations.

Promotion for innovators leaves laggards behind

The adoption curve for a typical successful product or idea is shown in Figure 20–4. Some of the important characteristics of each of these potential customer groups are discussed below. Before describing each of these groups, let's remember that not all can be reached by the same promotion blend, and certain groups and individuals may resist any messages. Moreover, not all potential customers in a market grid can be expected to adopt a new idea, at least within a reasonable time period.

Innovators — 3 to 5 percent of the market

The innovators are the first to adopt. They tend to be young and, at the same time, high in social and economic status. They are cosmopolites, with many contacts outside their own social group and community. Coupled with this is mobility and apparent creativeness.

Business firms in the innovator class usually are large and rather specialized.

For promotion purposes, an important characteristic of innovators is that they tend to rely on impersonal and scientific information sources or other innovators rather than personal salesmen. They often read articles in technical publications or informative advertisements in "respectable" sources to get information.

Early adopters — 10 to 15 percent of the market

This group is likely to be relatively high in social status, probably being opinion leaders. They may be younger, more mobile, and more creative than later adopters. But their social relationships are confined to their local group.

Business firms in this category also tend to be specialized.

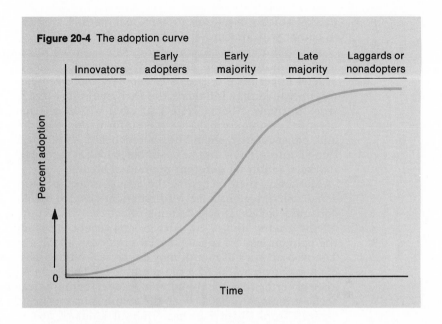

Figure 20-4 The adoption curve

Innovators | Early adopters | Early majority | Late majority | Laggards or nonadopters

Percent adoption

0

Time

This group tends to have the greatest contact, of all the groups, with salesmen. Mass media are important information sources, too.

Early majority — about 34 percent of the market

This group consists of those with above average social status. They usually will not consider an innovation until many early adopters have tried it. A long period may elapse between trial and adoption.

Average-sized business firms with less specialization would fit in this category.

The early majority have considerable contact with mass media and salesmen *and* early adopters.

Late majority — 34 percent of the market

People in this group tend to be below average in social status and income. They are less likely to follow opinion leaders and early adopters. In fact, some social pressure from their own group may be required before they try the product, but then adoption may follow quickly.

Business firms in this group tend to be smaller-sized firms with little specialization.

The late majority make little use of mass media and of salesmen. They tend to be oriented more to other late adopters than to outside sources of information.

Laggards or nonadopters — 5 to 16 percent of the market

This group has the lowest social status and income, and tends to be tradition-bound.

The smallest businesses with the least specialization are often in this category.

The main source of information for laggards is other laggards, which certainly bodes ill for marketers who want to reach the whole market quickly or use one promotional method. In fact, it may not pay to bother with this group.[8]

Adoption-curve research reinforces our earlier discussion in Chapter 8 on communicators and the "web of word of mouth." It shows the crucial importance of the early adopters (not necessarily the innovators) because they influence the early majority—and help spread the word to many others.[9] Note that even within *one* market grid box, potential customers may seek their information from different sources, and, consequently, should be approached in different ways in promotion planning. Or, it may be desirable to look at these as different target markets, requiring different promotion blends.

Marketing men recognize the prime importance of these interpersonal conversations and recommendations by opinion leaders, for consumer goods. If early groups reject the product, it may never get off the ground. But if the early groups accept the product, then what the opinion leaders in each social group say about it may be critical. The web of word of mouth may do the real selling job long before the customer ever walks into the retail store. This points up the importance of trying to reach the opinion leaders (communicators) in various social groups. And because all the communicators are hard to identify —recall from Chapter 8 that different kinds of people may be communicators for different products—mass media can play an important role in getting the message to them.[10]

Less is known about the adoption process in industrial goods markets. It seems likely that the same general process is at work, but one study suggests that there is little word-of-mouth communication in these markets. This points up the importance of both personal selling and mass selling in communicating with industrial buyers *and* the multiple buying influencers.[11]

[8] For further discussion, see Zaltman, *op. cit.*, pp. 45–56 and 23–37; Everett M. Rogers, *The Diffusion of Innovations* (New York: Free Press, 1962); E. M. Rogers with F. Schoemaker, *Communication of Innovation: A Cross-Cultural Approach* (New York: Free Press, 1968); and George M. Beal and Joe M. Bohlen, "The Diffusion Process" (Special Report No. 18 [Ames, Iowa: Iowa State University Press, 1962]); Norman Kangun, "Advertisers Use Learning Theory," *Business Horizons*, April, 1968, pp. 29–40; Kenneth Uhl, Roman Andrus, and Lance Poulsen, "How Are Laggards Different? An Empirical Inquiry," *Journal of Marketing Research*, February, 1970, pp. 51–54.

[9] Extensive research has been done on the adoption curve. The results of over 1,000 studies have been content analyzed at the Diffusion Documents Center in the Department of Communications at Michigan State University. This information is stored in an information retrieval system which facilitates research.

[10] C. W. King and J. O. Summers, "Overlap of Opinion Leadership across Consumer Product Categories," *Journal of Marketing Research*, February, 1970, pp. 43–50; Thomas S. Robertson and James N. Kennedy, "Prediction of Consumer Innovators: Application of Multiple Discriminant Analysis," *Journal of Marketing Research*, February, 1968, pp. 64–69; James S. Engel, R. J. Kegerreis, and Roger D. Blackwell, "Word-of-Mouth Communication by the Innovator," *Journal of Marketing*, July 1969, pp. 15–20; and Joseph R. Mancuso, "Why Not Create Opinion Leaders for New Product Introductions?" *Journal of Marketing*, July 1969, pp. 20–25; Frederick E. Webster, Jr., "New Product Adoption in Industrial Markets: A Framework for Analysis," *Journal of Marketing*, July, 1969, pp. 35–40; W. H. Whyte, Jr., "The Web of Word of Mouth," *Fortune*, November, 1962, p. 208; Ernest Dichter, "How Word-of-Mouth Advertising Works," *Harvard Business Review*, November–December, 1966, pp. 147–167; and Thomas S. Robertson, "The Process of Innovation and the Diffusion of Innovation," *Journal of Marketing*, January, 1967, pp. 14–19.

[11] Frederick E. Webster, Jr., "Informal Communica-

Successful promotion may be an economical blend

Once promotion objectives for a product have been established, a marketing manager may decide to use a blend of promotion methods, since certain jobs can be done more economically one way than another. This can be illustrated most clearly in the industrial goods market. The same arguments apply, also, to promotion in the channels for most goods.

While personal selling dominates most industrial goods promotion budgets, mass selling is necessary, too. A blend usually is desirable. A personal salesman nearly always has to complete the sale, but it is seldom practical for him to carry the entire promotion load. In 1970, the average cost of a manufacturer's salesman's call was estimated at over $40, and this figure is rising.[12] This relatively high cost comes from the fact that a salesman has only limited time, and much of what he does is expended on nonselling activities – 34 percent of his time is spent traveling and waiting; 20 percent on reports, paper work, and attending sales meetings; and 5 percent on strictly service calls. Only 42 percent of his time is available for face-to-face selling.

The job of reaching all the buying influences is made more costly and difficult by the continuing turnover of buyers and influencers. An analysis of the circulation records of McGraw-Hill industrial magazines showed that out of every 1,000 paid subscribers in a 12-month period, 304 are replaced, 56 change titles due to promotions and reorganizations, 141 are transferred to different locations with the same or similar type company, and only 499 stay in the same jobs.[13]

An industrial salesman may be responsible for several hundred customers and prospects, with about four buying influencers per company. Clearly, he does not have enough time to get the company's whole message across to every potential customer. The problem was depicted by a McGraw-Hill advertisement that showed a salesman facing an industrial buyer and the buyer's thoughts run:

I don't know who you are.
I don't know your company.
I don't know your company's product.
I don't know what your company stands for.
I don't know your company's customers.
I don't know your company's record.
I don't know your company's reputation.
Now – what was it you wanted to sell me?

As the ad suggests, too much has been invested in a salesman to use his time and skill to answer questions that could be better handled through mass selling. Mass selling can do the general spadework; the salesman should concentrate on answering specific questions and

---

[12]*Wall Street Journal,* April 16, 1970, p. 1.

tion in Industrial Markets," *Journal of Marketing Research,* May, 1970, pp. 186–90.

[13]*The Mathematics of Selling* (New York: McGraw-Hill Publishing Co., Inc., no date).

clinching the sale. These mass selling "sales calls" can be made at a fraction of the cost of a personal call. One McGraw-Hill study found a mass selling "call" costing $0.0094 per call; a personal call, $22.[14]

Not all these mass selling calls are effective. Some advertisements will not even be read by the target audiences. When actual audience size decreases, the cost of an effective mass selling call increases. Yet some mass selling can be very economical, reaching the elusive multiple buying influencers and giving potential customers a better image of the firm, or at least an awareness of its existence. Personal selling has to carry much of the promotion load, but mass selling helps a lot.

Although similar studies about the costs of reaching final consumers are not available, it seems only logical that mass selling and sales promotion would be relatively more effective with final consumers than with intermediate customers. As expected, mass selling tends to be relatively more important in such promotion blends.[15]

Factors affecting selection of a promotion blend

Most business firms develop a promotion blend of some kind, because the various methods complement each other. But what blend is right in a particular situation?

Wholesalers invariably rely on personal selling, perhaps with good reason. Some retailers do, too, although other retailers may advertise aggressively.

At the same time, a food products manufacturer may develop a promotion blend composed of 10 parts advertising to 1 part personal selling, although some of this advertising money may be allocated to help his channel system retailers advertise. A lawn seed producer might emphasize advertising 4 to 1, while a paint manufacturer might reverse the ratio. Is there some logical pattern underlying these differences?

Each promotion blend is designed to accomplish the firm's overall objectives. But the particular blend selected depends on a number of factors, including (1) the promotion budget available, (2) stage of product in its life cycle, (3) target of the promotion, (4) nature of the market situation, and (5) nature of the product.

Size of promotion budget affects promotion efficiency

There are some economies of size in Promotion. Network radio or television may reach more people more economically than local media. Local radio, TV, and newspapers may be more economical than neighborhood media or direct personal contact. But the minimum charge for some alternatives may force smaller firms, or those with small promotion budgets, to use the less economical alternative, in terms of

---

[14] *Ibid.*

[15] For discussion on the lack of availability of research in this area, see J. B. Haskins, and W. C. Hugli, Jr., "Evaluating the Effects of Company Promotional Activities: A Neglected Area for Research and Management Attention," *Journal of Marketing,* October, 1969, pp. 66–68.

cost per contact. For example, a small retailer might like to use local television, but all he can reasonably afford are handbills and perhaps ads in neighborhood newspapers, together with church and school bulletins.

Some smaller manufacturers, out of necessity rather than choice, use personal selling as their major method of promotion. A personal salesman can be hired for $10,000 a year plus expenses. Sponsorship of a single hour of network television can cost from $50,000 to $100,000. The TV show might bring the firm's message to more people for less per person, but its total one-lump cost might be too high for a small firm.

A small budget, however, need not limit a firm to personal selling. Sales promotion, public relations, and direct mail are attractive possibilities. A small tire manufacturer who wanted to tell potential dealers about his product and was not in a position to compete with the big tiremakers' promotion programs decided instead to use direct mail. His carefully targeted campaign was extremely successful, yielding $196 in new business for every dollar invested.[16] A direct-mail expenditure of $1,861 brought in 101 new dealers and more than $360,000 of new business.

Stage of product in its life cycle

A new product seldom becomes a spectacular success overnight. The adoption curve discussed earlier in the chapter helps explain why. Usually the product must go through the several stages described in Chapter 14 — introduction, market growth, market maturity, and sales decline. During these stages, promotion blends may be changed to achieve changing promotion objectives, including reaching different groups at varying stages of their adoption process.

Introduction stage — color TV sets and dishwashers are good

During the introduction stage, the basic objective is to inform. If the product contains an entirely new idea, that idea must be sold — and not just the company's version of it. The promotion must pioneer acceptance of the product idea — not just the company's own brand.

The purpose of this emphasis is to stimulate *primary demand,* a job which may be long and costly. Color TV, portable dishwashers, and skillets with detachable electric units in the handles are examples of new products which required long introductory periods because they were new concepts.

There may be few potential "innovators" during the introductory stage. Personal selling can be very useful, especially for industrial products. Salesmen certainly are needed to select good channel members and then persuade them to carry the new product. Sales promotion may help draw attention to the product.

Since there are few competitors at this stage, mass selling can con-

---

[16] "Direct Mail Puts Jack with Giants," *Printers' Ink,* November 10, 1961, pp. 49–50.

centrate on the basic informing job. Initial advertisements might be designed to draw inquiries and uncover new uses. Documented case histories can be used, as this is often a very persuasive type of advertising.

Market growth stage—our color TV and dishwasher are best

In the market growth stage, competitors begin entering the market, and promotional emphasis must shift from stimulating primary demand to stimulating *selective* demand for the company's own brand. The main job is to persuade customers to buy and stay with the company's own product.

Now that more potential customers are trying and adopting the product, mass selling may become more economical. But personal salesmen must still work in the channels, expanding distribution.

Market maturity stage—you must not miss our color TV

In the market maturity stage, additional competitors have entered the market. Products differ only slightly now because most manufacturers have settled on similar methods of production and have a clear idea of the most attractive form for the product. By now, producers are copying competing features; promotion, beginning to emphasize minor or psychological differences, becomes increasingly persuasive rather than informative.

At this stage, mass selling may dominate the promotion blends of consumer products manufacturers. Industrial products might require more aggressive personal selling, perhaps complemented by more advertising. The total dollars allocated to the promotion blend may rise as the competitive frenzy rises.

Firms which have achieved a strong customer franchise are able to use reminder-type advertising, the type that seeks only to remind the customer of the product name and may be considerably less expensive than more persuasive efforts.

Sales decline stage—let's find those who still want our product

During the sales decline stage, the total amount spent on promotion may decrease as firms attempt to cut costs and remain profitable. Since the product may still be acceptable to some target markets, more specific promotion might be needed to reach these remaining customers. Personal selling can help. The mass selling media must be aimed more carefully. Firms with a strong customer franchise may use reminder-type promotion.

Closely related to the product life cycle is the nature of competition in the target market.

Nature of market situation requires different promotion

Firms in monopolistic competition may favor mass selling because they have differentiated their product somewhat and apparently have something to talk about. Mass selling can be more economical, especially if they are trying to reach broad audiences.

As the market tends toward pure competition, it is difficult to generalize about what will happen. Competitors in some markets aggressively seek to outpromote each other, using mass or personal selling or both. The only way for a competitor to stay in such a market is to match rivals' promotional efforts—unless, of course, his whole marketing mix can be improved in some other way. We see such competitive advertising in our daily newspapers all the time.

In markets that are drifting toward pure competition, some companies may resort to price cutting. This will divert funds from promotion and drag price levels down faster. In such a situation, the cash revenues flowing into the business may decline, and all promotion will have to be cut back.

Once a firm is in pure competition, there is less reason to promote the product. But someone has to get the business, and using persuasive personal salesmen can be the way to get it. For the customer's part, he must buy needed products someplace, and often prefers to buy from friendly salesmen who call regularly.

This condition also exists in oligopoly situations (discussed in Chapter 27). Only here, there may be sales revenue to support promotional efforts such as entertaining and business gift giving.

Target of promotion helps set the blend

Promotion can be directed to four different groups: final consumers, industrial customers, retailers, and wholesalers. The right promotion blend for each group can be slightly different.

Promotion to final consumers

The vast number of potential customers practically forces consumer goods manufacturers and retailers to use mass selling in their promotion blends. Mars Candies uses outdoor billboards and magazines to reach as many people as possible, since they estimate that over a one-month period, almost every person over three years of age eats at least one candy bar.[17]

The traditional belief that some personal selling was needed in retailing to make the final sale has given way today to the recognition that for some products, mass selling can establish brand preference to such an extent that little personal selling may be needed. Self-service and discount operations attest to this.

It appears that some consumers do seek information about goods they consider buying. Mass communication may be the way to provide the information. We noted earlier that there are innovators and early adopters, and communicators within social groups, to whom others look for guidance and suggestions. Mass selling is necessary to reach these communicators because they are widely dispersed and it is not possible to identify or approach each one individually.

The predominance of mass selling in promoting to final consumers, however, should not obscure the spectacular success of some blends which emphasize personal selling. Although some retail salesclerks and door-to-door salesmen can perform effectively, this kind of personal salesman usually is hard to find and more expensive. As a result, aggressive personal selling to final consumers usually is found only in relatively expensive channel systems (though a less costly system might not succeed at all).

[17] "Mars Candy: The Limitless Market," *Printers' Ink,* July 12, 1963, pp. 40–42.

Promotion to industrial customers

Industrial customers are much less numerous than final consumers, and there is more justification for a promotion blend emphasizing personal selling to such customers. Industrial customers may have specific questions or might need adjustments in the total product. A manufacturer's or wholesaler's personal salesman can be more flexible in adjusting his company's appeals to suit each customer. He is also able to call back later and provide the confirmation and additional information that often are necessary in bigger industrial sales. Personal selling becomes more practical as the size of each purchase increases, and larger unit purchases are more typical in the industrial goods field.

Although personal selling dominates industrial goods promotion blends, mass selling *is* used for some jobs. The McGraw-Hill studies showing the economic feasibility of mass selling helps explain why.

Promotion to retailers

As with industrial buyers, the relatively small number of retailers makes it feasible for manufacturers and wholesalers to emphasize personal selling. Sales promotion activities and some mass selling in trade magazines and newspapers are valuable, but the bulk of the promotion effort is by personal salesmen—who can answer retailers' questions about what promotion will be directed toward the final consumer, the retailers' own part in selling the product, and important details concerning price, markups, and promotional assistance and allowances.

In other words, promotion to retailers is primarily informative. But since the manufacturer's or wholesaler's salesman cannot *guarantee* the retailer a profit, promotion to retailers must also be persuasive.

The salesman must persuade the retailer that demand for the product exists and that making a profit will be easy. Sometimes persuasion takes the form of extra services—management advice, promotional aids, and demonstrators—special price concessions, advertising allowances, free goods, or some other "extra" that makes the offer more attractive.

Another reason personal selling is so important in dealing with retailers is that marketing mixes may have to be adjusted drastically from one geographical territory to another to meet competitive situations. The mixes in highly competitive urban areas, for example, may emphasize price more than those in outlying areas. Personal salesmen can judge these conditions. We already have seen the development of a specialist—the food broker—to assist producers' salesmen in the extremely competitive grocery industry.

Personal selling is also important in a promotion blend aimed at retailers because part of the selling job is to establish and maintain good channel relationships. The retailer must be shown that the manufacturer or wholesaler has his interest at heart. A channel is a human system and depends on the mutual trust and understanding of channel members which can be built only by personal relations.

Promotion to wholesalers

Promotion to wholesalers is very similar to promotion to retailers except that wholesalers are less numerous and perhaps even more conscious of demand and cost. They respond to economic arguments. They are most interested in the promotion which the producer intends to direct at retailers and final consumers.

Mass selling may play some role here because some wholesalers seem to be impressed by a company which advertises in prestigious national media. In fact, for just this reason, manufacturers may place ads in consumer magazines, such as *Life*, and then distribute copies of the ads among present and prospective channel members.

Yet, in the end, personal salesmen are still needed to cement the relationship between producer and wholesaler.

Nature of product makes a big difference

The customers' view of the product is the common theme tying together all the variables that must be combined into a marketing mix. Their view of the product affects the promotion blend, too. This was implicit in our discussion of Place objectives in Chapter 15 and of typical channels in Chapter 19.

Later we will discuss typical promotion blends for the various goods categories. Here, however, we will consider the impact of some general product characteristics on promotion blends.

Technical nature of product

An extremely technical industrial product may require a heavier emphasis on personal selling, preferably by technically trained salesmen. This is the only sure way to make the product understood and obtain feedback on how industry can use it. The technical salesman can meet with engineers, plant people, purchasing agents, and top executives, and can adjust the sales message to the needs and wants of these various influencers within the target market.

Mass selling, on the other hand, is feasible for many consumer goods because there is no technical story to be told. Or, if there are some technical factors—for example, with cars or appliances—they can be offered where there is demonstrated customer interest in them, perhaps in booklets at the dealer's showroom.

Degree of brand familiarity

If the product has already won a strong brand preference, perhaps after years of satisfactory service in the market, there may be no need for aggressive personal selling. Reminder-type advertising is usually adequate. Indeed, Hershey Chocolate long prided itself on not having to do any advertising! Recently, however, it did begin some advertising and sales promotion to counter increasing competition in the United States. But in Canada, where it is not well established, Hershey has advertised aggressively.[18]

If a manufacturer has not differentiated its product, and does not plan to invest in building a brand name—perhaps because its product is not different—then much heavier emphasis on personal selling is

---

[18] "Hershey's Sweet Tooth Starts Aching," *Business Week*, February 7, 1970, pp. 98–104; and "Big Chocolate Maker, Beset by Profit Slide, Gets More Aggressive," *Wall Street Journal*, February 18, 1970, pp. 1 f.

sensible. The major goals then should be building good channel relations and getting distribution in as many outlets as possible. Rather than spending—perhaps fruitlessly—to build a brand name, the firm could invest in Place development.

Typical promotion blends

Many factors affect the selection of a promotion blend, as we have seen. To summarize the interrelation of all these factors, we will tie them to the goods classifications that we have been using throughout the text. As we do so, try to see the "why" of typical blends rather than memorizing "right" answers.

Although the blends shown here are typical, this does not mean they are right for all situations. Some very profitable promotion blends and marketing mixes have departed from the typical to satisfy some target market better.

For the consumer, print it, say it, deliver it

Convenience goods

Staples are often in the market maturity stage, with large potential target markets. A manufacturer's promotion blend, therefore, usually emphasizes mass selling. Brand recognition or brand preference might have been achieved already, but continuing mass selling efforts are needed to reach newcomers and those who regularly switch from brand to brand. The majority of food and drug items are in this category, where much of the total of consumer advertising dollars is spent.

Retailers usually will not voluntarily provide displays or special promotion aids except for their own dealer brands. Consequently, producers and wholesalers' salesmen have to promote each product to wholesalers and retailers and to provide any store displays which are required.

Manufacturers' sales promotion departments generally prepare in-store displays and point-of-purchase aids, expecting their own or wholesalers' personal salesmen to make sure they are used to the best advantage in the retail store. Unfortunately, large amounts of such material are wasted because of inadequate followthrough by personal salesmen, perhaps because the promotion blend was poorly planned.

Impulse goods need well-placed displays. They usually require highly persuasive personal selling to the retailer. Consumer advertising may not be essential unless several similar goods are competing in the channels. Then a producer may have to promote his product to final consumers to impress retailers and wholesalers that his product is the best impulse item available.

Retailers can also use local informative advertising by mail or telephone, to encourage impulse buying. Basically, however, promotion of impulse goods is aimed at the channels, relying mainly on personal selling.

Emergency goods are regarded as necessities for special circumstances. Little consumer promotion is needed, except that which is

532

necessary to remind buyers of its availability when an emergency occurs.

The main promotion job for these goods is in the channels – to obtain distribution. An especially persuasive personal selling job may be needed if competitive products are available. Again, as with impulse goods, mass selling can be used to impress channel members with the firm's offering. Direct mail might develop leads for new outlets, but inquiries probably will have to be followed by personal salesmen. The manufacturer's sales promotion department might develop effective storage racks, posters, or displays for emergency items.

Mass selling to consumers could be used if a producer wanted to move a product from the emergency goods category – where brands are less important – to another category. Antifreeze manufacturers, for example, advertise to try to get motorists to install *their* brand early in the fall to avoid the last-minute rush. For quite a few years, the major antifreeze makers have been trying to differentiate their product, stressing their brand identity. But despite their efforts, many drivers still wait until the first freeze warning and then pour anything that's available into the radiator. At this point, having widespread distribution is all-important to the producer and wholesalers.

Shopping goods

Homogeneous shopping goods are compared primarily on price, and consumers may feel little need for retail salesmen to help them. The retailer might still use personal selling to try to get potential customers to see that his total product offers more than just low price. Others, such as the mass merchandisers, have gone to self-service and checkout counters for such goods.

But manufacturers and wholesalers may still use aggressive personal selling to gain distribution at the retail level. And manufacturers and some retailers continue to use mass selling, focused on particular products, to meet competitors' promotion. Growing promotion budgets, however, may result in diminishing profits as these products move into the market maturity stage. This could result in a decline in mass selling, as both manufacturers and retailers recognize how consumers see these goods and conclude that it may be fruitless to try to change their views.

Some retailers of homogeneous shopping goods, mass merchandisers, for example, may continue to advertise them – emphasizing low prices – to project a low-price image for *all* their goods. Here the objective is to sell the store, not just particular items.

Heterogeneous shopping goods are compared by consumers in a broader light than price alone. Mass selling may be used by manufacturers or retailers to inform customers about the different characteristics of these goods. Consumers searching for the best values often read such ads carefully. Here, advertising can affect consumer understanding of quality, either directly or through opinion leaders – *if* it doesn't contradict the thinking of the various reference groups.

Mass selling by manufacturers can impress middlemen by adding luster to the manufacturer's name and brand. Copies of national advertisements may be distributed to retailers and displayed by them to show customers that they offer nationally advertised products.

Generally, brand promotion is less important for these goods. Some manufacturers do little or no advertising for clothing and house-furnishings because consumers want to compare products in the store. Manufacturers may rely more heavily on informed retail clerks. Retail sales personnel may be paid financial incentives, such as a $5 bonus for each new mattress sold. Personal contacts in the channels, stressing economic arguments and demonstrating effective selling techniques, are essential here.

Specialty goods

Retailers advertising these products may use mass media, such as billboards or newspaper advertisements, simply to remind customers where they are for sale. The favored status of these products makes it relatively easy to promote them to wholesalers and retailers on the basis of profit potential. Even so, the producer's story must be told and told again in the channel. And the manufacturer's and wholesaler's personal salesmen often offer sales promotion aids to retailers to assist their reminder efforts.

Despite their preferred status, specialty goods might require continued mass selling by the manufacturer. Consumers are notoriously fickle. If similar products are being promoted aggressively, the manufacturer would not want to risk losing his customer franchise. New customers are continually entering the market and must be convinced that the product is a specialty good. This mass selling by producers also helps assure middlemen of continued customer acceptance.

Unsought goods

These goods are in the introductory stage of their life cycle. All potential customers must be fully informed about them. Mass selling may be used by the manufacturer to reach final consumers, but wholesalers and retailers will need to be convinced of the profit potential of these goods. If they aren't convinced, the goods might not even reach the retail level. This channel promotion job is becoming increasingly difficult every year as more and more products vie for distribution.

Aggressive and persuasive personal selling are needed to put these products across, especially in the channels. But to impress the channel members, it may have to be supported by mass selling — and even a pulling policy. Manufacturer's or wholesaler's salesmen may be needed to give demonstrations and set up displays and point-of-purchase materials. Perhaps the company will need to offer promotional pricing deals. Again, personal salesmen may have to adapt a company's marketing mix to each individual situation.

For the industrial buyer, a handshake and confidence

Unlike final consumers, industrial buyers usually do not seek out the goods they will need. By accepted practice, they wait for the seller to present products or ideas. Routine orders may be sent to regular suppliers, but industrial buyers still expect sellers to contact them in person or by telephone.

Mass selling may be used to locate prospects (through inquiry requests) or to develop a well-known brand name. This simplifies the salesman's task. But the promotion blends of both producers and middlemen, for most industrial goods, emphasize personal selling because the market is relatively limited and concentrated and the selling job is often technical. The specific promotion blend, as with consumer goods, varies with the product.

Installations

Some installations — specific buildings or pieces of property, or custom-made machines — are unique and have special technical characteristics. Promotion must inform target customers about these products and persuade them of the advantages.

Usually personal selling is the most effective method. Advertising can locate prospects and help presell them, but it takes personal selling to complete the sale. Moreover, many of the products in this category remain in the introductory stage indefinitely because of continuous technical improvements.

For some products in this category, however, the buyer has his own specifications or plans, and many competitors may have the capacity to satisfy the demand. Then, personal persuasion becomes even more important.

Accessory equipment

A basic promotion task here is to impart technical information. Mass selling can play a role in achieving some degree of brand familiarity and in locating prospects, but personal selling is paramount to convince users (or channel members, if they exist) of the merits of buying one company's product rather than another's.

Raw materials

Most of these products have reached the market maturity or even sales decline stages and tend to be standardized. Prices, which usually are widely disseminated, are competitive. Promotion is not unimportant, however. Buyers still must decide from whom they will buy. There are opportunities for considerable persuasive personal selling. The personality of the particular salesman and the company image which he conveys can, in fact, be the deciding factors. Other things being equal, a buyer would prefer to deal with a salesman who is pleasant to deal with and who can assure good quality and prompt delivery.

Component parts and materials

Promotion for these products must inform the prospective buyer about technical details as well as price, quality, and delivery dependability.

Personal selling is the chief means of promoting component parts and materials. Some components are custom-made for specific applications, and salesmen are vital to assure that both buyer and seller are aware of each other's needs and capabilities. Salesmen also are important because many competitors can offer the same technical service or even identical products, and much personal persuasion is needed. Again, given essentially homogeneous products and price, the competence and personality of the salesman play an important role.

Supplies

MAINTENANCE AND OPERATING SUPPLIES For these goods, the producer's main promotion job is personal selling in the channel.

So many essentially homogeneous products are available in this category that the chief differences the industrial buyer sees are in price and ready availability. Since industrial buyers are likely to telephone their local wholesalers, or wait for their calls, a manufacturer's main problem with these goods is to get distribution. Well-known brands and some mass selling to users is sometimes desirable to encourage wholesalers to stock his product. But personal selling is vital to actually get the business.

The wholesaler's job is to inform and persuade his potential customers to patronize his outlet because of the availability of all necessary products at reasonable prices. Personal salesmanship, perhaps including business lunches and entertaining, are important to build friendly relationships.

Most of these products are in the market maturity stage. For a new product requiring some pioneering, the normal channels may not be able to promote the product adequately. The producer then might have to resort to direct-to-user promotion to do the job properly, using both mass and personal selling.

REPAIRS Since most repair parts come directly from the original manufacturer, the main promotional task is to inform buyers of their availability. This is especially true if branch outlets have been established to offer better service. These products have a "captive market," and persuasion is not necessary. However, if the market is large enough to attract competitors, as in the automotive and electrical goods fields, then persuasion must be used, too. The main promotional appeals are faster, more dependable service. Mass selling might be adequate to tell this story, but personal selling may have to be used anyway, to meet competition.

Services

Since most service businesses have relatively undifferentiated products, their promotional task usually is persuasive in nature. The emphasis is on personal selling.

When a service is new, information about price, availability, and dependability is important. But competitors usually enter a profitable field quickly, and personal persuasion is then needed to hold customers. Persuasion will continue to be necessary even as prices are forced down by competition and profits are squeezed. This situation is seen in the highly competitive industrial towel and cleaning service markets.

How some promotion budgets have been allocated

There is no right promotion blend for all situations. Each must be developed as part of a total marketing mix. But to round out our discussion of typical blends, it will help to see how various manufacturers have allocated their promotion budgets. Typically, wholesalers use personal selling almost exclusively. Retailers' blends, however, might vary as widely as the ones discussed below for manufacturers. No comparable study is available, however.

Figure 20–5 shows the variation observed in one careful study of promotion blends. The lines show the variation in ratios of advertising expenditures (including sales promotion) to personal selling. Do *not* read the lines as measures of total expenditures. A short line merely means that the expenditures for advertising and personal selling were roughly equal.[19]

Figure 20–5 shows that the ratio of advertising to personal selling varied from over 10 to 1, to 1 to 10. The 10-plus-to-1 ratio for one food product represented an instance in which the company was selling a staple convenience good with heavy emphasis on brand identification. Practically no personal selling was done, even in the distribution channels. In this case, strong brand preference pulls the product through the channel.

A lawn seed producer used a ratio of 3 or 4 to 1 in favor of advertising. The lawn seed was a well-recognized brand, and considerable emphasis was placed on brand promotion. But it had not achieved the strength of the food product, so some personal selling was necessary in the channels. In contrast, the promotion blend for bulk lawn seed was almost the reverse. The manufacturer had chosen not to build a brand name, but instead to win cooperation in the channels. So most of the promotional effort was directed through personal salesmen to channel members to assure distribution and dealer support. Basically different strategies are involved here.

Heavier emphasis on brand advertising to mass consumer markets can be seen for malt beverages, grocery products, and some consumer flour products. Some personal selling would be necessary in the channels, but in today's competitive markets, at least some brand recognition must be won through mass selling in order to win wholesaler and retailer support.

Note that when flour is sold as a consumer good, one type of promotion blend is needed, but when it is sold in large quantities as bakery flour, another blend is used. Basically, the nature of the product has changed—it is now an industrial component material, and logically, there is greater emphasis on personal selling. The bakery flour market is extremely price competitive, with trading in standard grades which most competitors can supply. The main promotional job is persuading customers to buy from a particular company on a service or friendship basis.

Most of the other products cited in Figure 20–5 are industrial products, and heavier emphasis on personal selling would be expected there. The manufacturer would either sell directly to the users or have his salesmen call directly on wholesalers, who in turn would go after the industrial buyers.

Two of the three remaining consumer products, bedding and wear-

[19] Edwin H. Lewis, "Sales Promotion Decisions," *Business News Notes* (Minneapolis: School of Business Administration, University of Minnesota, November, 1954), p. 2.

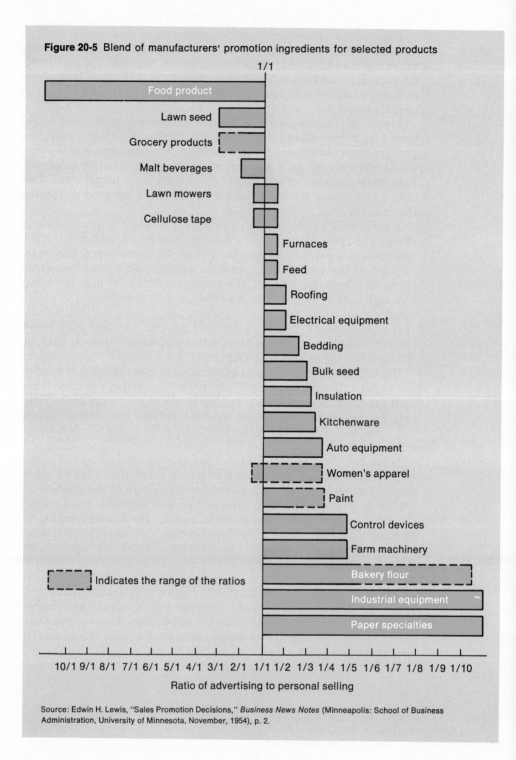

Figure 20-5 Blend of manufacturers' promotion ingredients for selected products

1/1

Food product	
Lawn seed	
Grocery products	
Malt beverages	
Lawn mowers	
Cellulose tape	
	Furnaces
	Feed
	Roofing
	Electrical equipment
	Bedding
	Bulk seed
	Insulation
	Kitchenware
	Auto equipment
	Women's apparel
	Paint
	Control devices
	Farm machinery
	Bakery flour
	Industrial equipment
	Paper specialties

Indicates the range of the ratios

10/1 9/1 8/1 7/1 6/1 5/1 4/1 3/1 2/1 1/1 1/2 1/3 1/4 1/5 1/6 1/7 1/8 1/9 1/10

Ratio of advertising to personal selling

Source: Edwin H. Lewis, "Sales Promotion Decisions," *Business News Notes* (Minneapolis: School of Business Administration, University of Minnesota, November, 1954), p. 2.

ing apparel, are heterogeneous shopping goods. Here again, we would expect greater stress on personal selling because the major promotion job is to get retailer cooperation. In the sale of kitchenware, personal selling also dominated at the time of this study. There were many small competitors in this industry, and aggressive brand promotion to final consumers had not yet been undertaken by any of them. The stress instead had been on getting widespread distribution through personal selling, because many of these items are probably purchased as impulse goods anyway.

Two companies cited in Figure 20–5, one a manufacturer of lawn mowers and the other of cellulose tape, had advertising-to-personal-selling ratios of 1 to 1. The reason is that these companies have a wide range of both consumer and industrial products and target markets. Heavier advertising emphasis on the consumer products tends to be offset by heavier personal selling on the industrial products.

Someone must plan and manage promotion blend

Good
blending
takes
judgment

The selection of a promotion blend is a strategic-level decision which should jibe with the rest of the marketing strategy. The whole should be greater than the sum of the parts. Once the basic outlines of the promotion blend are set, then more detailed plans for the parts of the blend must be developed and implemented, perhaps by specialists such as the sales and advertising managers.

Deciding on the appropriate promotion blend is obviously difficult, dependent as it is on fitting together with the rest of a marketing strategy. Conceptually, this can be seen as a problem of balancing the alternative use of scarce resources among the various elements of a marketing mix, trying to balance the amounts allocated to each to achieve the maximum return. This still requires considerable judgment and experience and is why we show it as a job for the marketing manager.

Once the basic allocations of tasks and of budgets are made to the various promotional methods, then more quantitative tools are available to guide decision making. More will be said on this in the next two chapters.[20]

Sales
manager
manages
salesmen

Personal selling usually is the responsibility of a sales manager. Since most sales managers have been personal salesmen, they usually place great confidence in the power of personal contact.

The sales manager may be responsible for implementing Place policies, especially building good distribution channels, and in smaller companies, he often acts as the marketing manager.

[20] See David B. Montgomery and Glen L. Urban, *Management Science in Marketing* (Englewood Cliffs, N.J.: Prentice-Hall, Inc., 1969), especially chaps. iii and vi.

Advertising manager works with ads and admen	An advertising manager, on the other hand, is concerned with mass selling effort via television, newspapers, magazines, billboards, and other media. His job is choosing the appropriate media for each purpose and developing the ads. He may implement this effort in an advertising department within his firm, especially if he is in retailing, or through an independent outside advertising agency.[21]
Sales promotion manager, a jack of all promotion	The sales promotion manager often fills the gaps between the sales and advertising managers, enhancing their effectiveness. Nearly everything the sales promotion department does could be done by either the sales or advertising departments. But sales promotion activities are so varied that specialists tend to develop. In some companies, the sales promotion manager works for the sales manager; in others, he is moving toward independent status with responsibility only to the marketing manager.
Marketing manager, talks to all, blends all	Because of differences in outlook and experience, the advertising, sales, and sales promotion managers may have difficulty working with each other as partners or equals, especially when each feels that his approach is the most important. In some companies, they are hardly on speaking terms. It remains the marketing manager's job to weigh the pros and cons of the various approaches and come up with an effective promotion blend, fitting the various departments and personalities into it and coordinating their efforts.[22] All of these jobs might have to be carried by one man in a smaller company, perhaps with the title of sales manager. In this case, *he* is responsible for developing an effective promotion blend.

Conclusion

Promotion is a vital factor in any marketing mix. Most consumers and intermediate customers can choose from among many products. To be successful, a manufacturer must not only offer a good product at a reasonable price but also must tell potential customers about his product and where it can be purchased. The producer must tell wholesalers and retailers in the channel about his product and his marketing mix. These middlemen, in turn, must use promotion to reach their customers.

The nature of the promotion job should fit logically into the strategy which is being developed to satisfy the needs and preferences of some target market. *What* should be communicated to them should be stated explicitly as part of the strategy planning.

Basic promotion objectives might include informing, persuading, or reminding.

Various promotion methods can be used to reach these objectives.

---

[21] "The Role of the Advertising Manager," *Printers' Ink*, April 14, 1967, pp. 41–45.
[22] See also, R. Clifton Andersen and Edward W. Cundiff, "Patterns of Communications in Marketing Organizations," *Journal of Marketing*, July, 1965, pp. 30–34.

Among them are personal selling, mass selling, and sales promotion. Personal selling is done face-to-face. Mass selling primarily involves advertising. Sales promotion activities consist of many special-purpose and nonrecurring promotional activities, such as the design and distribution of novelties, store signs and catalogs, and the development of displays for trade shows and international expositions.

How the promotion methods are combined and used to achieve effective communication can be guided by some behavioral science findings. In particular, we know more now about the communications process, how individuals adopt new ideas, and how groups react.

An action-oriented framework called AIDA will help guide strategic planning of promotion blends, but finally the marketing manager is responsible for blending the alternative promotion methods into one promotion effort for each marketing mix. Special considerations which may affect the promotion blend are the size of the promotion budget, stage of product in its life cycle, the particular target customers who must be reached, the nature of the market situation, and the nature of the product.

In this chapter, we have considered some typical promotion blends. In the next two chapters we will treat personal and mass selling in greater depth.

QUESTIONS AND PROBLEMS

1 Relate the three basic promotion objectives to the four tasks (AIDA) of the promotion job, using a specific example.

2 Discuss the communication process in relation to a manufacturer's promotion of an accessory good, say a portable air hammer used for breaking up concrete pavement.

3 Explain how an understanding of the way individuals adopt new ideas or products (the adoption process) would be helpful in developing a promotion blend. In particular, explain how it might be desirable to change a promotion blend during the course of the adoption process. To make this more concrete, discuss it in relation to the acceptance of a new sport-coat style.

4 Discuss how our understanding of the adoption curve should be applied to planning the promotion blend(s) for a new, small (personal) electric car.

5 Discuss the nature of the promotion job in relation to the life cycle of a product. Illustrate, using household dishwashing machines.

6 Promotion has been the target of considerable criticism. What specific types of promotion are probably the object of this criticism?

7 Might promotion be successful in expanding the general demand for: (*a*) oranges, (*b*) automobiles, (*c*) tennis rackets, (*d*) cashmere sweaters, (*e*) iron ore, (*f*) steel, (*g*) cement? Explain why or why not in each case.

8 Indicate the promotion blend which might be most appropriate for manufacturers of the following established products (assume average- to large-sized firms in each case) and support your answer:
a) Candy bars.
b) Men's T shirts.
c) Castings for automobile engines.
d) Car batteries.
e) Industrial fire insurance.
f) Inexpensive plastic raincoats.
g) A camera which has achieved a specialty-goods status.
h) A completely new home permanent-wave concept packaged in a convenient kit.
i) A contracting service, capable of bidding on projects up to large dams.
j) Lumber.
k) Production tools for finishing furniture.
l) Glass for window repair.

9 Discuss the potential conflict among the various promotion managers.

...we are seeing the development of a new kind of salesman.
...the day of the grinning glad-hander is passing in favor of the specialist who is ingenious, knowledgeable, and highly trained.
...the sales manager is becoming a real manager of men, not just an older salesman.

21

Personal selling

Promotion is communication with potential customers. What needs to be communicated would be specified by the marketing strategy and promotion objectives, as discussed in Chapter 20.

Often a personal presentation is the best way to do the communicating. While face-to-face with the prospect, a salesman can get more attention than an advertisement or a display. He can adjust the presentation as he goes along, stay in tune with prospect feedback, and if (and when) the prospect indicates that "this might be a good idea," the salesman is there to close the sale and take the order.

In this chapter, we will discuss the nature of the personal selling job and the sales management decisions that are needed to make it an effective part of a promotion blend and a marketing mix.

Importance of personal selling

We already have seen that personal selling is important in some promotion blends and vital in others. Some of its supporters feel that personal selling is the dynamic element which keeps our economy going.

Without question, our economy does need and use many salesmen. Census Bureau statistics show that almost 10 percent of the total U.S. labor force is in sales work. Keeping in mind that the Bureau is inclined to place many persons who are primarily personal salesmen into other classifications, it is likely that *at least* 10 percent of the nation's labor force, or over 7 million people, are engaged in personal selling. Contrast this with less than half a million people working in advertising. Any activity that engages so many people and is so important to the economy deserves study.

Death of a salesman? Personal selling is vital to the survival of most businesses, but the role of the personal salesman has come in for considerable criticism. The aggressive and sometimes sharp practices of some salesmen, especially door-to-door peddlers, and the hucksters involved in county or street fairs, have soured some prospective personal salesmen. And the grinning glad-hander by the name of Willie Loman in the play *Death of a Salesman* established a pathetic stereotype for salesmen in some peoples' minds. There also has been criticism about the personal salesman's effectiveness, especially at the retail level. Many people have had experience with incompetent retail clerks who couldn't care less about the customer and her needs.

The poor image of personal selling in some peoples' minds, coupled with the ineffectiveness of many sales personnel, led some prophets to predict that personal selling would decline in importance. And this has happened to some extent in retailing, resulting in an increase in self-service.

Rebirth of the salesman The personal salesman is far from dead. His role is simply being redefined and upgraded. Obviously, some kinds of personal selling are absolutely vital for the survival of many businesses. Until something is sold to the wholesaler, the retailer, and ultimately to the consumer, those who work in manufacturing, agriculture, mining, etc., cannot depend on a job or an income.

But different types of sales tasks are required. And modern sales and marketing management have gone far toward redefining what needs to be done and then selecting, training, and motivating salesmen to perform effectively—while also providing them with personal satisfaction. In some cases, sales work is taking on the characteristics of a profession. Many high-caliber salesmen believe in the importance and value of personal selling, and often subscribe to codes of ethics.

This "new breed" of salesmen see their customers' satisfaction as a better test of their accomplishments than volume of sales or personal income. Some are engaged in what is called *systems selling*. Here

543

they emphasize selling, not just products, but whole systems to satisfy needs or solve problems. Office equipment manufacturers' salesmen, for example, try to show how offices can be redesigned for more effective work flows. Then they sell the equipment needed to accomplish this goal, but only after the basic concept of a redesigned work space is sold. Or, a wholesaler's salesman, calling on retailers, might try to sell the complete service provided by his organization rather than individual products.

In short, we are seeing the development of a new kind of salesman. In the following paragraphs, we will focus on the nature of selling jobs and show how and why the new breed of salesman is developing and why he is needed.[1]

Nature of the selling job

Good salesmen are taught, not born

The idea that good salesmen are born has some truth in it, but it is far from the whole story. A *born* salesman – if that term refers to a gregarious, aggressive kind of individual – may not do nearly as well when the going gets rough as his less extroverted colleague who has had solid, specialized training. Experiments have shown that it is possible to train any alert person to be a good salesman. Much of this training is grounded on basic steps that each salesman should follow. These include:

1. Search out or meet prospective buyers.
2. Select appeals especially adapted to the particular buyer.
3. Help him to make a selection – that is, help him to buy.
4. Give the prospect advice.
5. Answer individual questions and objections.
6. Assure buyers when they have doubts about a particular point.
7. Show samples and demonstrate the use of the product.
8. Help indecisive buyers to make up their minds.
9. Close the sale – that is, ask for the order.
10. Make suggestions for additional or complementary items.
11. Follow up with buyer after sale to assure satisfaction.

These steps may seem logical and even obvious, but what is obvious in theory may not always be practiced. Many salesmen fail, or are mediocre in performance, because they don't apply the fundamental rules. Others have never even been taught them in the first place. And many orders are lost simply because the salesman does not have enough information about the product or doesn't ask for the order.

New salesmen often are hired and immediately sent out on the road or the retail selling floor with no grounding in the basic steps and no

---

[1] Carl Rieser, "The Salesman Isn't Dead – He's Different," *Fortune,* November, 1962, pp. 124–27 ff; "How To Raise the Prestige of Salesmanship: Keep It Professional, or Recognize Everybody," *Printers' Ink,* May 4, 1962, pp. 56 ff; Leslie M. Dawson, "Towards a New Concept of Sales Management," *Journal of Marketing,* April, 1970, pp. 33–38.

information about the product or the customer—just a price list and a pat on the back. This isn't enough.

It is up to sales and marketing management to be sure that the salesmen have adequate training.

It's more than "get rid of the product"

In discussing some of the fundamentals of selling, from the standpoint of marketing management, we will assume that the rest of the marketing mix the salesman is to sell is reasonably good.[2] But in fairness to salesmen and salesmanship, this is not always the case, and a salesman should not be expected to compensate completely for his firm's failings. Production-oriented businessmen often feel that it is the salesman's job to "get rid of the product," whether it is good or not. But if the salesman can see that he doesn't have much to sell, it is easy to understand why his morale might slip and the whole promotion job suffer.

Finding prospects— the big buyer who wasn't there

Finding prospective buyers is not as easy as reading census reports. While there are over 200 million final consumers and 11 million intermediate customers in the United States, only a fraction of these are "live" prospects—prospective buyers for a particular product at any one time. What the salesman needs are methods to locate prospects.

The market analysis techniques discussed earlier can be helpful. The market grid concept is useful, too, since making a cold call on John Smith is expensive. Even on industrial calls, when it is known that a company needs a product, it may be difficult to locate the specific person who would be the prospective buyer or who will influence the purchase. One study found that 64 percent of industrial calls are made on the wrong person.[3] Another showed that retail organizations frequently rearrange their organizational structure and buying responsibilities. Therefore, continuous and detailed customer analysis is needed at the retail level, too.

Three kinds of sales presentations may be useful

Once a prospective buyer has been found, the salesman must make a sales presentation. Usually he follows the procedures listed on page 544, at least roughly. However, some of these steps may have to be abbreviated or even skipped if the selling situation is relatively simple —that is, if the customer does not want to spend much time in discussion.

The nature of the selling job depends on the situation, and generally speaking, this would be determined by the marketing strategy. The marketing manager should know the needs and preferences of poten-

[2] The details of salesmanship are beyond the scope of this book. For more detailed treatment, see C. A. Pederson and M. D. Wright, *Salesmanship: Principles and Methods* (4th ed.: Homewood, Ill.: Richard D. Irwin, Inc., 1966); F. A. Russell, F. H. Beach, and R. Buskirk, *Textbook of Salesmanship* (7th ed.; New York: McGraw-Hill Book Co., 1963); P. H. Nystrom, *Marketing Handbook* (New York: Ronald Press Co., 1958), Section 18; and Steven J. Shaw and Joseph W. Thomson (eds.), *Salesmanship— Modern Viewpoints on Personal Communication* (New York: Holt, Rinehart & Winston, Inc., 1960).

[3] "64 Per Cent of Industrial Calls Are on the Wrong Man," *Sales Management*, February 6, 1959, pp. 53–56.

tial buyers, and then choose and train salesmen accordingly. He can choose among three basically different sales presentation theories in his planning: the *stimulus-response* theory, the *selling formula* theory, and the *need-satisfaction* theory. Each of these approaches has its place, and is discussed below.

Stimulus-response theory

The basic stimulus-response model discussed in Chapter 8 applies here. Presumably, a customer faced with a particular stimulus will give the desired response – say, a yes answer to the salesman's request for an order. In applying this theory, however, the salesman usually does not have a very good idea about what goes on in the consumer's mind, and so he tries various appeals, one after another, hoping to get the desired response. This is shown in Figure 21–1. Basically, the salesman does most of the talking, only occasionally letting the customer talk when he attempts to close. If one closing attempt does not work, he goes on with another standard presentation until he makes another try at closing. This procedure could go on for some time, until either the salesman runs out of material or the customer buys or decides to leave.

This theory can be effective and practical when the prospective sale is low in value and the time which can be economically devoted

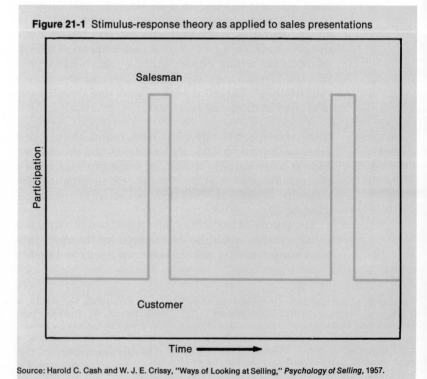

Figure 21-1 Stimulus-response theory as applied to sales presentations

Source: Harold C. Cash and W. J. E. Crissy, "Ways of Looking at Selling," *Psychology of Selling*, 1957.

to selling is short. This would be true for many convenience goods in food stores, drugstores, and department stores. The presentation might be as simple as: "That's very nice, can I wrap it up?" or "That looks nice on you, would you like to take one?" or "Would you like to try it on?" or "Would you like a carton instead of a package?" or "Shall I fill'er up?" Each can be effective for some customers and thus all the situation demands.

This theory treats all potential target markets the same. It may work for some and not for others, and the salesman probably will not know why. Moreover, he doesn't really improve his performance as a result of experience, because he is just mechanically trying standardized presentations. This approach may be suitable for simple selling situations but is no longer considered good selling for more complicated selling situations.

Selling formula theory

This theory also builds on the stimulus-response model, but it assumes that we know something about the customer and his needs and preferences and can therefore take him through some logical steps to the final close.

This approach is illustrated in Figure 21–2, where we see that the salesman does most of the talking at the beginning of the presentation,

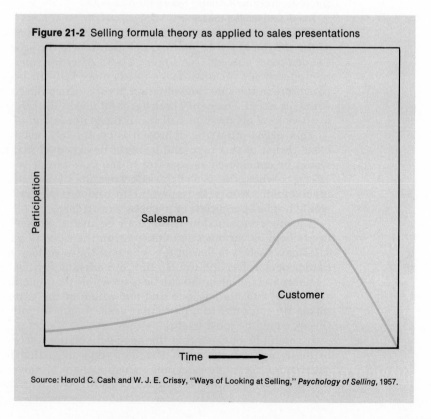

Figure 21-2 Selling formula theory as applied to sales presentations

Source: Harold C. Cash and W. J. E. Crissy, "Ways of Looking at Selling," *Psychology of Selling,* 1957.

because he knows what he wants to say to implement the strategy. As the sales presentation moves along, he brings the customer into the discussion to help clarify exactly what needs this customer has. Then he comes back to dominate the conversation in an effort to show how his product satisfies these needs and to close the sale.

This approach is sometimes associated with the AIDA approach, which has sometimes been used mechanically by sales managers who felt themselves responsible for getting rid of products. They had their salesmen memorize canned AIDA-type speeches which worked fairly well. At least some product information was presented. Certainly, such an approach would be better than no preparation at all, which is often the case. But it is less effective when the customer wants a question answered out of the sequence being followed by the salesman, or if the customer doesn't want to hear the whole story. If the salesman does not perceive these individual differences, he may go ahead with his presentation after the potential customer has already tuned him out.

This approach may be useful for situations where potential customers are quite similar in terms of their needs and preferences and relatively untrained salesmen (perhaps because of high turnover) must be used. It can be likened to using mass selling – where one general presentation must be tailored to a large audience – only here the presentation is being made face-to-face.

Need-satisfaction theory

With this approach, the saleman leads the customer into doing most of the talking at the beginning, in order to help the salesman pinpoint the customer's needs (see Figure 21–3). After the salesman feels that he understands the customer's needs more fully, he begins to participate more in the sales presentation, trying to help the customer understand his needs. Once they both agree on needs, the salesman attempts to show how his product will fulfill these needs and to close the sale.

This needs-satisfying approach is completely consistent with the basic thrust of this text, and it might be expected that this approach would be considered as superior to the first two. It is certainly more effective where the size of the sale warrants such customer-salesman involvement. But it is important to understand that this approach would *not* be appropriate or necessary in all cases.

The need-satisfaction theory can be useful if there are different needs held by various customers within the same target market. The salesman's job is to determine which of these various needs this particular person has and to help him to understand what his needs are.

Alternately, a salesman can be responsible for implementing several strategies, and his job is to find out which of the various marketing mixes he can offer in a particular case. Again, the need-satisfaction theory would be most useful.

It should be obvious that the need-satisfaction theory is applicable in most higher-level sales jobs. This type of selling provides great satisfaction for some salesmen, causing them to move toward a professional status. Some become so deeply involved with satisfying their

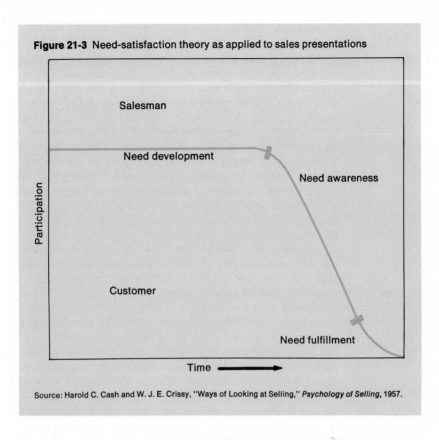

Figure 21-3 Need-satisfaction theory as applied to sales presentations

Salesman

Need development

Need awareness

Participation

Customer

Need fulfillment

Time ➡

Source: Harold C. Cash and W. J. E. Crissy, "Ways of Looking at Selling," *Psychology of Selling,* 1957.

customers' needs that they see themselves as representatives of their *customers* in dealings with their own firms.[4]

Using AIDA to plan sales presentations

If the marketing strategy has determined basic promotion objectives and has outlined the selling job and even the appropriate sales presentation, then the content of the sales presentation can be guided by the AIDA framework.

Each presentation (except for some simple stimulus-response types), would tend to follow the AIDA sequence. The time spent with each of the steps might vary depending upon the situation and the selling theory being applied, but it is still necessary to begin a presentation by getting the prospect's *attention* and, hopefully, moving him to *action* through a close. The ways in which these steps might unfold are discussed in the following paragraphs.

---

[4]The diagrams in the figures accompanying this discussion should be credited to Harold C. Cash and W. J. E. Crissy, "Ways of Looking at Selling," *Psychology of Selling,* 1957, pp. 9–20.

Attention

There is no sure way to get a prospect's attention. Much depends on the salesman's instincts and his originality, as well as his knowledge of his customers. If a salesman calls on the same customers frequently, he will want to use a new approach each time. If each call is on a new prospect, a few successful attention-getters will suffice.

At the first stage of his meeting with a customer, the salesman's main purpose is to distract the potential customer from his current thoughts and begin a conversation. He might do this by just introducing himself or saying, "Hello, can I help you?" as a retail clerk might. Or a statement about the plans of the prospect's competitors might get attention. Other attention-getting devices can range from a movie or slide projector to a model of the product or even a colorful hat or necktie.[5]

Whatever method is used, the attention-getter should be casual, not elaborate, so that the salesman can move quickly, naturally, and logically into the next step — creating interest. Otherwise, attention may be followed by a letdown.

Interest

Creating interest takes more time. The best way is to probe for the prospect's basic needs or problems, especially those which the salesman might be able to solve. A furniture store salesman should not make a prepared speech about rugs every time a customer comes in — some might want lamps, sofas, and so on. Getting the customer to talk begins a dialogue and gives the salesman the all-important feedback which guides his subsequent effort. Theoretically, he should select prospects from among the target customers of the marketing strategy or strategies he is implementing. Therefore, he should know roughly what they want and have a marketing mix that has been designed specifically for them. His job is to show how and why it fits their needs, in order to close the sale.

If the salesman has correctly selected his prospect, he may be able to use some visual aids specifically designed to hold interest and avoid having the presentation cut short. A slide or movie projector might communicate what the salesman's company sells or does. Or to appeal to his senses, the potential customer might be given a product or model to handle, or in the case of food, a sample to taste.

Desire

Arousing desire requires an even more persuasive effort. At this stage, the salesman definitely has to determine exactly what his prospect's problems are. This enables the salesman to show how his product fits the need, counter any objections, and prepare for closing the sale. This feedback is vital to his sales presentation and is an important advantage of personal selling.

Knowing the prospect's specific needs, the salesman can explain

---

[5]"Opening the Door with an 8mm Film," *Sales Management*, April 5, 1963, pp. 73–75.

specifically how the product could be used in the customer's factory or how it would be purchased by the buyer's customers.

One goal at this stage is to encourage the prospect to make a mental trial of the product to see how it could fit in with his needs. For example, the salesman might show a grocer statistics and testimonials on the success of the product in other stores.

Action

Finally, the salesman will try to summarize the important points he has made, tailor his arguments to the customer's needs and interests, and try to close the sale. It is interesting to note that one of the most frequent reasons for the loss of a sale is that the salesman never *asks* for the order. Perhaps this is because he does not want to be refused. He's afraid that a direct request for the order is all too easily answered with a no.

There are ways, however, to avoid this awful word. The experienced salesman knows how to avoid a direct confrontation with human inertia and reluctance to make a decision. Without asking for a direct yes or no, he may begin to write up the order or ask which of various delivery dates would be preferable. He may inquire about the quantity the customer would like to try in a new display. This may lead the customer into taking action without consciously having to make a direct decision — a difficult step for some people.

The name of the game is PAID–A

A good salesman must not only be able to make a good sales presentation but also must be able to locate live prospects. Effective prospecting can be more important than making a good presentation, especially if the company's marketing mix is basically strong. Follow-up may be critical, also, to be sure customers are satisfied. Satisfied customers are not only good word-of-mouth promoters but also a source of new prospects; thus follow-up can finish one selling cycle and start the next. All of the promotion tasks are important in selling, and it is helpful to think of selling as a circular process, requiring PAID–A — Prospecting and AIDA.[6]

Helping to buy is good selling

Increasingly, good salesmen don't try to *sell* the customers, rather they try to *help him buy* by presenting both the advantages and disadvantages of their products and showing how they will satisfy his needs. They find that this helpfulness results in satisfied customers and long-term relationships. This new approach recognizes the growing sophistication of buyers, especially industrial buyers.

The old-line salesman with the funny story and the engaging grin is being replaced by the salesman who has something concrete to contribute. The smiling "bag of wind" with the big expense account is headed toward extinction. Many such salesmen are still around, but it is difficult for them to compete against the modern breed. Purchasing agents may still be civil to them, but more and more the people

---

[6] This idea should be attributed to Professor F. Mauser of Wayne State University.

in purchasing are placing their orders with those salesmen who can see a way to apply the right product in the right way and get results for the buyer.

Salesman represents the whole company

Increasingly, the salesman is recognized as a representative of the whole company, responsible for explaining its total effort to target customers, rather than just moving products. As evidence of this change in thinking, some companies now give their salesmen such titles as field manager, market specialist, sales representative, or sales engineer.

The sales-man is both transmitter and receiver

A salesman is expected to do much more than just bring in new business, though this certainly is an important part of his job. But in terms of the communication process discussed earlier, he must both get action – the adoption of the product – and then continue to work with customers to help them confirm their decision and continue buying. This may take the form of regular follow-up calls to be sure the customer is satisfied with his last purchase.

At the same time, the salesman may gather feedback data to enable the company to do a better job in its subsequent planning. Recall that a feedback function is an integral part of both the communications process *and* the basic management process of planning, executing, and controlling.

The modern salesman, in other words, not only communicates the company's story to customers but also feeds back customer reaction to the company. He is a vital link both in the communication and marketing processes.

Defining the sales job with specifications

One of the difficulties of discussing selling is that each sales job is different. While the engineer or accountant can look forward to fairly specific duties, the salesman's job is constantly changing. He does far more than merely talk to interested customers, play golf, and go to lunch.

No small-time operator

Two salesman's job descriptions prepared by the management of two companies illustrate the variations in salesman's duties.

The first covers the activities of a retail salesman for the Scott Paper Co., the well-known paper products manufacturer. These products – convenience goods requiring intensive distribution – are sold through wholesalers to retail outlets. The retail salesman's job is to call directly on retailers, less to sell than to assure continued co-operation, especially regarding good merchandise display. Scott cannot depend on the wholesaler's salesman to accomplish this objective. As is customary in this business however, any orders obtained by the retail salesman are filled by the normal wholesale channels.

Analysis of Scott retail salesman's job[7]

I. *Making the sale on Scott products*
   A. Sells new orders to retail outlets.
   B. Sells repeat orders to retail outlets.

II. *Service on Scott products*
   A. Renders merchandising advice and assistance to retail outlets.
      1. Builds displays.
      2. Plans and conducts demonstrations.
      3. Distributes dealer helps related to Scott products (including visual aids such as special display stands, price cards, and folders).
      4. Delivers merchandise where required.
   B. Secures newspaper and handbill advertising and other tie-in promotions from indirect customers (coordinates trade features with company advertising campaigns).
   C. Counsels with retail customers on most advantageous Scott resale prices. (Those that produce profits yet largest possible volume of repeat business).

III. *Routine duties*
   A. Records daily calls and results, and mails this report to divisional office daily.
   B. Maintains selective selling records on our products and on leading competitive brands, and summarizes these periodically, upon completion of each route coverage.
   C. Sends orders to divisional office daily.

IV. *Executive*
   A. Plans his daily and long-range work program.
   B. Helps in training of younger retail salesmen.
   C. Observes facts in his territory that have a bearing on the sale of his products.
   D. Works out new ideas and mails suggestions to superiors.
   E. Studies and keeps abreast of merchandising and marketing in other fields. Discusses some of these problems with other salesmen and his superiors.

V. *Creating goodwill toward himself and his company*
   A. Sells Scott Paper Co., its concepts and policies to retail dealers.
   B. Offers retail dealers constructive merchandising ideas not related to Scott products.
   C. Distributes dealer helps not specifically related to Scott products.
   D. Continually strives to maintain and improve friendly relationship with retail customers.

The second illustration of a salesman's job description is from an industrial goods manufacturer who sells record control systems. This firm not only sells machines and devices for processing a firm's paper work but also the specialized forms used by the machines. While the company is primarily interested in the sale of the forms, the whole system – including the machines – must be sold initially. This amounts to selling two products: a systems installation, plus supplies on a continuing basis. Note the concept of "systems selling" used here. This

[7]D. M. Phelps, *Sales Management Policies and Procedures* (Homewood, Ill.: Richard D. Irwin, Inc., 1953), pp. 545–46.

broader view of the sales job is what makes professionals out of some salesmen and gives them greater satisfaction as well.

The company describes the tasks the salesmen are to perform as follows:

Job description for salesmen of record control systems[8]

1. Must deal with executive-type personnel.
2. Prepares approach material by gathering, through various sources, information as complete as possible about prospects concerned before calling. Selects proper sales tools for making the first call.
3. Makes a detailed survey of a selected system or group of systems presently in use by the prospect.
4. Flowcharts all procedures in present system.
5. Applies principles of work simplification to improve present procedures. Designs . . . Company business forms to fit the revised procedure.
6. Prepares written proposal to present to prospect.
7. Explains proposals and flowcharts quite often to a group of executives in prospective concerns.
8. Communicates details of the orders to the home office and draws copy for the business forms as they are to be printed.
9. Arranges and holds clinics for executives from different companies, or for executives within one company, on the subject of work simplification as applied to office paper work.
10. Maintains three different types of personal sales records.
11. Must be familiar with principles and mechanical specifications of 20 or more different business machines.
12. Must be thoroughly familiar with printing specifications.
13. Spends 20 percent of his time in personal selling. Eighty percent of his time is devoted to methods study, office work, detail work.
14. Calls on customers for soliciting repeat order business where the question is largely that of handling the details in writing up orders and specification sheets.

Clearly, there is more to selling than talking. The salesman must bring to each selling job an overall yet detailed view of what his company offers and what his customer needs. This requires planning, continuous prospecting, and follow-through as well as effective sales presentations.

The industrial salesman's job is neither simple nor limited. The salesman today, in effect, must play the role of manager in his own territory or in his own retail department. Some beginning salesmen, especially those working for manufacturers or wholesalers, are responsible for larger sales volumes than are achieved by average or even large-sized retail stores.

Basic sales tasks may be split

Selling is divided into three parts
Not only is every salesman's job unique but the tasks of any salesman continually change. These tasks vary with company objectives, with

[8] *Ibid.*, pp. 546–47.

market conditions, and not the least, with the preferences of each individual customer.

There are, however, three basic sales tasks that are found in any sales *organization*. Although one salesman may have to do all three tasks, management must recognize that these essentially different activities are performed by one man. Among other things, the method of compensating salesmen should be based on the blend of these three sales tasks.

These tasks are: (1) *order getting*, (2) *order taking*, and (3) *supporting*. For convenience we will designate salesmen by these terms, referring to their primary task.

As the names imply, order getters and order takers are order-oriented. They are specifically interested in obtaining orders for their company. In contrast, supporting salesmen are not directly interested in orders. Their function is to help the order-oriented salesmen.

While it is true that specific individuals with certain abilities, interests, and training may be best suited for specific jobs, note that there is a place in personal selling for nearly everyone.

Order getters develop new business

Order getting is concerned with developing new business. *Order getting, sometimes called "creative selling," means seeking out potential buyers aggressively with a well-organized sales presentation designed to sell a product, service, or idea.*

Order getters may sell complete lines or only a single line, in which case they may be called specialty salesmen. They may be interested in selling the advantages of buying from one company rather than from another, or shifting the share of purchases from others to the salesman's company, or finding completely new customers and even entirely new markets.

An order getter must have complete confidence in his abilities, his company, and his product, since his attitude shows through to customers. He must be patient with the potential customer's employees, doing a thorough selling job throughout the potential customer's organization. The order getter must be a teacher and counselor, not just a contact man, and must inspire confidence by his manner and performance. But most important, he must be aggressive and confident – ready, willing, and able to face (and control) new faces and new situations.

Order-getting salesmen work for manufacturers, wholesalers, and retailers.

Manufacturers' order-getting salesmen

Manufacturers of all kinds of goods, but especially industrial goods, have a great need for order getters. They are needed to locate new prospects, open new accounts, visualize new opportunities, and help establish and build channel relationships.

High-caliber order getters are essential in sales of installations and accessory equipment, where substantial sums are involved and top-level management participates in the buying decision. Such salesmen must be especially knowledgeable and persuasive, but not extremely aggresive in the manner of the typical door-to-door consumer goods salesmen.

Top-level customers are more interested in ways to save or make more money than in technical details, and a good order getter caters to this interest. He sells concepts and ideas rather than physical products. The products are merely the means of achieving the ends desired by the customer.

In selling other industrial goods—such as raw materials, components, supplies, and services—skilled order getters also are necessary. Yet in these fields they may be required only for initial contacts. Since many competitors offer nearly the same product in this area, the salesman's crucial selling job here is getting his company's name "on the list." Persuasion of the highest order and sometimes deliberate social cultivation of top-executive prospects may be necessary, perhaps at the local country club.[9]

Industrial goods order getters may be required to help solve the customers' problems which continually arise in the course of production. To supply themselves with technically competent order-getting salesmen, firms often give special technical training to business-trained college graduates. Such salesmen then can deal intelligently with their specialist customers. In fact, they may be more technically competent in their narrow specialty than anyone they are likely to encounter and so may be able to provide a unique service.

"WORMS," SAID THE SALESMAN The crucial need for technical training and an interest in service and problem solving can be seen in an incident in the career of a young salesman who was selling Ralston-Purina hog feed, (a component material) to hog raisers. This salesman had worked at Ralston Purina Co.'s huge (26,000 animals) experimental farm, which that firm uses as a training school for its salesmen. After training at this school, a salesman knows about the care and feeding of animals because he has fed and weighed many animals and recorded their gains in weight.

One day he called on a hog raiser—one of the biggest buyers of hog feed in that part of the state. The farmer was not interested in Purina products. While our young salesman was talking with him, one of his hogs lay down and died in the mud right in front of them. "Worms," said the salesman. "No such thing!" said the farmer. *"I'v had my hogs tested for worms and they don't have any."* "Give me a sharp knife and let's see," suggested the newly graduated youngster. So he performed an autopsy on that porker and revealed that it was full of worms.

His next step was an offer of *service.* He said, "Now let's de-worm the rest of your hogs before you lose any more of them. I'll hang around and help you do it." He spent the best part of three days helping with this rather unpleasant chore, then made bold to suggest that the farmer would be wise to put a solid floor on his pens so that the hogs could live under cleaner

[9] For a story of how one top-level order getter deliberately cultivated the acquaintance of a railroad executive, see "The Personal Touch Clinched the Sale," *Printers' Ink,* March 27, 1959, p. 70.

conditions. By this time, the hog raiser was somewhat humbled and genuinely grateful; so he promised to make this improvement. Then, without being asked, he same across with the startling proposition: "Young fellow, you know hogs. You know things that I had never learned. I'd like your advice on how I should feed my hogs."

Of course, he became one of the biggest buyers of Purina hog feed and, through his influence, almost an assistant salesman to our young friend.[10]

HE MUST KNOW OTHER MEN'S BUSINESS Business training also is important to enable the manufacturer's salesman to visualize the needs and potentials of particular prospects and to discuss prices and long-run business conditions with purchasing agents.

The Kaiser Aluminum Co. expects its industrial salesmen to know "financial rating and background, raw-materials usage, plant locations, names of key persons, policies as to buying and use of aluminum, status of company's orders, delivery schedule, pattern of aluminum buying, and developments which might involve the use of aluminum."[11]

Manufacturers need order getters to make at least the initial contacts with wholesalers and retailers and to convince prospective channel members that they should take a chance with a new product or new line.

In recruiting channel members, the manufacturer's order getter ought to know how they should be running their business, how his product will help them, and what objections they may have to his product. He must be extremely self-confident, sure of the proposition he is offering and able to radiate this mood to his prospects.

Order getting is a big job, and manufacturers' order getters normally are well paid. Many earn more than $25,000 a year.

Wholesalers' order-getting salesmen — hand it to the customer, almost

We have seen already that progressive wholesalers are developing into counselors and store advisers rather than just order takers. In some situations, routine orders are simply handled by mail or telephone, with wholesalers' salesmen functioning as "partners" of retailers in the job of moving merchandise from the wholesale warehouse through the retail store to consumers.

The emphasis here is on *through*. Modern wholesalers attempt to cooperate with retailers rather than merely stocking them. The idea here is that nothing is really sold until the final consumer or user buys it.

These salesmen truly are in the order-getting class. Many have found it much more profitable to do an extremely good job with few accounts rather than wearing themselves out with large numbers of retailers, but selling little to each of them. These order getters practically become a part of the retailer's staff, helping to check stock, write

[10] F. A. Russell and F. H. Beach, *Textbook of Salesmanship* (6th ed.; New York: McGraw-Hill Book Co., 1951), pp. 113–14.

[11] *Ibid.*, p. 59.

orders, conduct demonstrations, and plan advertising, special promotions, and other retailing activities.

Wholesalers probably would employ more order getters if so many small retailers didn't seem to shun help. The more aggressive wholesalers avoid dealing with such retailers, as evidenced in this statement by a successful wholesale salesman: "I can't afford to waste my time calling on the grippers and the men who do nothing to help themselves. There are too many other retailers with whom I can work . . . merchants, not storekeepers. Men who want to improve their stores and their sales . . . who have open minds, not closed minds."[12]

Agent middlemen often are order getters, particularly the more aggressive manufacturers' agents and brokers. They face the same tasks as manufacturers' order getters.

Retail order-getting salesmen — visionaries at the storm window

Order getters are necessary for unsought goods and desirable for some shopping goods.

UNSOUGHT GOODS Convincing customers of the merits of products they have not seriously considered takes a high degree of personal salesmanship. Encyclopedia salesmen, for example, must convince prospects that $300 or $400 is a small price for a lifetime of literacy and happiness.

Order getters may have to visualize how a particular product will satisfy existing needs now being filled by something else. Early salesmen for aluminum storm windows and other aluminum and plastic home improvements faced the difficult task of convincing skeptical prospects that these materials were not only durable but would save money and require less maintenance in the long run. Similar problems were faced by early refrigerator salesmen in the 1920's and air-conditioning salesmen in the 1930's, but encyclopedia salesmen will probably face them from now until doomsday.

Without order-getting salesmen, many of the products we now accept as part of our standard of living — such as refrigerators and window air conditioners — might have died in the introductory stage. Most people reject or wait for others to accept new ideas. It is the visionary order getter who helps bring products out of the introductory stage into the market growth and market maturity stages. It is the order getter who sells enough customers to get the web-of-word-of-mouth going. Without sales and profits in the early stages, the product may fail and never be offered again.[13]

LOW-PRESSURE KEEPS THE FOOT OUT OF THE DOOR Some order getters selling unsought goods are the high-pressure, born salesmen, who give certain aspects of selling a bad name. Low-priced appliances, especially washing machines, are now being introduced aggressively in Britain by such salesmen.[14] But some of today's companies have

---

[12] "The Salesman's Changing Role," *Hardware Retailer,* May, 1958, p. 35.

[13] Robert C. Brooks, Jr., "Relating the Selling Effort to Patterns of Purchase Behavior," *Business Topics,* Winter, 1963, pp. 73–79.

[14] "Good Show — But Is It Cricket?" *Business Week,* January 5, 1963, pp. 42–44.

found it more desirable to use a lower-pressure approach with better-trained and more mannerly salemen. Some firms even apply the need-satisfaction theory in their sales training, rejecting the stimulus-response and the selling formula approaches. For these companies, customers are responding favorably, and in some lines, house-to-house selling is attaining a new respectability.

GIVE HER THE INSTRUCTIONS Order-getting salesmen are desirable for selling *heterogeneous* shopping goods. Consumers shop for many of these items on the basis of price *and* quality, and they welcome useful information. Automobiles, furniture and furnishings, power tools, cameras and photographic supplies, paints, and fashion items can be sold effectively by an aggressive, helpful order-getting salesman. Friendly advice, based on thorough knowledge of the product and its alternatives, may help consumers and bring profits to the salesman and retailers through the trade it attracts.

Many specialty shops and limited-line stores have developed a following because of the assistance offered by the stores' salesmen. Some retail salesmen notify their regular customers when they have special offerings. They frequently will advise a customer *not* to buy a particular product because it will not fit his needs, even though they do not have a suitable substitute. The store may lose an immediate sale, but this type of assistance in buying is profitable to retailers seeking loyal customers and repeat business.

Well-trained order-getting salesmen can help retailers compete with low-markup mass sellers. A pet shop owner, for instance, emphasizes that customers ask his advice on what pet to select, how to feed it, and how to care for it. If a customer wanted "just a parakeet," she could buy it at department stores, variety stores, or even discount houses at about half the pet shop price.

This retailer feels he is selling not just birds, but pets *plus* the instructions and supplies to care for them properly—just as the good industrial salesman sells more than nuts, bolts, and castings.[15]

Order takers — keep the business coming

Order takers complete the bulk of all sales transactions. After the customer acquires an interest in the products of a specific firm—either by an order-getting salesman, a supporting salesman, or through advertising or sales promotion—an order taker may be necessary to answer any final questions and complete the sale.

Order taking, which is defined as the routine completion of sales made regularly to the same or similar customers, accounts for much personal selling. Most wholesaling and retailing transactions require some order taking. Higher-caliber order takers may use need-satisfaction selling, but in other cases the simple stimulus-response model may be quite adequate and appropriate.

The term "order taker" should not be considered derogatory. Sometimes sales managers or customers will use the term in a snide way when referring to unaggressive salesmen, but such usage is often

[15] *The Pet Dealer,* March, 1961, p. 39.

inaccurate and highly colored with prejudice. A salesman may perform so poorly that criticism of him is justified. But it is a mistake to downgrade the *function* of order taking. Order taking is extremely important whether handled by human hands or machines.

The order-taking function *can* sometimes be reduced to taking money mechanically and delivering the product, as by vending machine. Computers may take over many routine buying and selling transactions in the channel and in the industrial goods area; companies can now buy supplies in this way.[16] But there are many aspects of order taking that demand the human touch.

Manufacturers' order takers — sales by the carload

After order getters open up industrial, wholesale, or retail accounts, a day-in and day-out follow-up is necessary. Someone has to explain details, make adjustments, handle complaints, and keep customers informed on new developments. In selling certain products to manufacturers, it may be necessary to train the company's employees to use machines or products. In sales to dealers, it may be necessary to train the wholesalers' or retailers' salesmen. These activities are part of the order taker's job.

Usually these salesmen have a regular route with many calls, which they may make at fixed times. To handle these calls well, they must have considerable physical energy, persistence, enthusiasm, and a friendly personality that wears well over time.

Many times the order taker must set up displays, or place the company's sales promotion materials. He must continually explain the company's marketing mix to his customers. As it changes, he has to negotiate new prices, allowances, guarantees, credit terms, cooperative advertising, and other aspects of the mix.

Sometimes jobs that are basically order-taking tasks are used to train potential order getters and managers, since they may offer order-getting possibilities. This can be seen in the following description of his job by a young Colgate salesman, who moved rapidly into the ranks of sales management:

> Over many months, I worked carefully with Gromer's Super Market in Hammond, Ill. It was an aggressive young store. After a few calls, I felt I had built up a warm friendship with the store personnel. They came to trust me and, more frequently than not, after I straightened shelves, checked out-of-stocks and did the usual dusting and rearranging, I gave them an order blank already filled in.
>
> It got to be a joke with big, husky Paul Gromer, the owner, and his hardworking manager-brother. They kept asking, "Well, what did we buy today?" and they signed the order book without checking.
>
> Naturally, I worked at the order like it was my own business, making certain that they were never stuck with dead stock or over-orders. They were making continual progress, though nothing sensational.

[16]"The Computer," *Sales Management*, April 5, 1963, pp. 44–46; and "Electronic Salesman at Customer's Elbow," *Systems Management*, March, 1963, pp. 14–15.

Finally, Colgate came out with a good deal. I knew it was right for Gromer's and I thought the store ought to double its weekly order to 400 cases. I talked to Paul Gromer about it and, without any reason that I'm able to think of today, I said, "Paul, this is a hot deal and I think you're ready for a carload order."

He looked at me for just a moment. I braced myself for an argument. Then he said, "Sure, why not? You've always been right before. Just ship it."

It was the biggest order of soap Gromer's had ever taken—and the store soon became a regular carload buyer.[17]

Normally, order takers don't have to be as aggressive as the order getters who open accounts. But this type of job does offer considerable challenge and is satisfying to many men. While not nearly as wearing on the physical and nervous system, it can yield very satisfactory financial returns.

Wholesalers' order takers—not getting orders, but keeping them

While manufacturers' order-taking salemen handle relatively few items and sometimes even a single item, wholesalers' order takers may handle 125,000 items or more. Here, they obviously cannot be much more than order takers in the narrow sense of the word. In fact, the term often applies specifically to wholesalers' salesmen.

Most order takers just sell out of their catalog. They have so many items that they cannot possibly give aggressive sales effort to very many of them, except perhaps newer or more profitable items. But once a new product has been featured, it is unlikely that the order taker will give it much attention for some time, if ever. He just has too many items to single any out for special attention. The order taker's strength is his wide assortment rather than detailed knowledge of individual products. Even if shown that he could expand sales of particular items substantially, he probably would not do it.

To show wholesalers' order takers that the market potential for a small accessory tool was worth pursuing, a manufacturers' agent spent one week in one city and personally sold more tools than were sold by all the merchant wholesalers in the surrounding six-state area during the previous three-months' period. This performance did not change the methods of the order takers, however, nor should it have. This kind of selling should be handled by a different kind of salesman and a different kind of wholesaler.

The wholesale order taker's main function is to keep in close contact with his customers, perhaps once a week, and fill any needs that have developed. Sometimes the salesman gets very close to industrial customers or retailers. Some retailers permit him to take inventory and write up his own order like the Colgate soap salesman. Obviously, this position of trust cannot be abused. After writing up the order, this salesman normally checks to be sure his company fills the order promptly and accurately. He also handles any adjustments or com-

[17] Michael F. Lennon, "Don't Limit Customer's Horizon," *Printers' Ink,* June 30, 1961, p. 43.

plaints and generally acts as a liaison between his company and his customers.

Such salesmen are usually of the low-pressure type, friendly and easygoing. Usually these jobs are not as high paying as the order-getting variety but are attractive to many because they are not as physically taxing. Relatively little traveling is required, and there is little or no pressure to develop new accounts.

Retail order takers—often they are poor clerks

Order taking is most mechanical at the retail level. Here, the customer may not want to spend much time hearing a sales presentation, and the straightforward stimulus-response approach is quite appropriate. A grocery checkout clerk's simple question, "Is there anything else?" or "Do you need milk?" may greatly increase sales of easy-to-forget staples or impulse goods at the checkout counter. Similarly, the gas station attendant's: "Shall I fill 'er up?" may greatly increase gasoline sales.

Workable, short sales presentations often are provided for retail clerks. In spite of this, most retail clerks selling convenience and specialty goods (and sometimes, unfortunately, even heterogeneous shopping goods) are poor order takers. They are compensated accordingly, and it is sometimes difficult to know which came first, the low salary or poor order taking.

For most convenience goods and for specialty goods which have already been thoroughly presold, not much needs to be done except to fill the customer's order, wrap it, and make change. As a result, retail clerks often are expected to concentrate on setting up and arranging stock—and sometimes they seem to be annoyed by having to complete sales. Many are downright rude.

One survey of customers of retail outlets, selling both convenience goods and shopping goods, indicated overwhelmingly that:

Most salesclerks are indifferent to customers.

Very few clerks know much about the merchandise they are selling, and many are of no help at all to the customers seeking information.

Most salespeople apparently assume a customer is presold.

If a store doesn't have an item a customer asks about, rarely does the salesman try to sell the prospective buyer anything else.

The ratio was 1 alert, interested clerk to every 10 who were lackadaisical and unconcerned.

This survey, and others like it, suggests that many retail order-taker salesmen are not good at their basic function.[18] It is understandable that more and more merchants are turning to self-service selling. This

---

[18] "Crisis in Selling: What Can Salesmen Do to Win Back Discouraged Customers?" *Printers' Ink,* August 1, 1958, p. 22; "Retailers: Weak Link in Marketing?" *Printers' Ink,* March 9, 1962, pp. 51–53; Allen F. Jung, "Are Retail Salesmen Selling?" *Journal of Retailing,* Summer, 1962; and "Unhappy Customers," *Wall Street Journal,* December 4, 1961, pp. 1 ff.

reduces the need for order takers but increases the need for other types of promotion.

It would appear that although many retail order getters and order takers are needed, there may be far fewer such jobs in the future as manufacturers and wholesalers make adjustments in promotion to offset poor sales personnel at the retail level.

Supporting salesmen — inform and help the source of business

There are two types of salesmen who *support and assist the order-oriented salesmen, but do not themselves try to secure orders.* These two types are *missionary salesmen and technical specialists.* Their activities, naturally, are directed toward obtaining sales, at least in the long run. For the short run, however, they are ambassadors of goodwill who provide specialized services. Almost all supporting salesmen work for manufacturers or are middlemen specialists who do this supporting work for manufacturers.

Missionary salesmen

A missionary salesman is employed by a manufacturer to work with his distributors and his distributors' customers. His usual purpose is to develop goodwill and stimulate demand, help or induce the distributor to promote sales of his employer's goods, help the distributor train his salesmen to do so, and often take orders for delivery by such distributors.[19]

Sometimes missionary salesmen are called *merchandising salesmen.* They are especially useful, and sometimes absolutely necessary, if the manufacturer uses merchant wholesalers to obtain widespread distribution and yet requires aggressive personal selling. They may be used to give an occasional shot in the arm to the company's regular wholesalers and retailers.

Usually these jobs do not require order-getting talents, but often men with such talents do this work when the position is used as a training ground for new salesmen. Normally, missionary selling takes less imagination than order getting, and the missionary salesman may get a good deal of supervision.

A special kind of missionary salesman is the *detail man.* He is used in the drug industry to call on doctors, dentists, pharmacists, and nurses, as well as drug wholesalers and retailers. Men who have had some science training frequently hold these jobs, since they must be able to talk to the professional people both knowledgeably and convincingly. They leave professional samples and explain possible uses for new products. They are normally selling the reputation of the company and the quality of its products rather than any particular product. The goal is to encourage professional people to recommend or use the

---

[19] "Report of the Definitions Committee," *Journal of Marketing,* October, 1948, p. 211, and *Marketing Definitions* (Chicago: American Marketing Association, 1960), p. 17.

company's products and, in the case of doctors, to write prescriptions specifying the company's brand names.

Technical specialists

These men are usually scientists or engineers who have relatively little interest in sales. Instead, they have technical competence, plus the ability to explain the advantages of the company's product. Since they normally talk to the customer's technical people, there is little need for a high order of salesmanship. Prior to the specialist's visit, an order getter probably has stimulated interest. Then the technical specialist can provide the details.

Frequently, it is the order getter's job to get past the purchasing agent or other company executives who serve as a screen for the company's engineering or technical personnel. The order getter locates a problem and suggests that his technical people can solve it. Then it is up to the technical specialist. The order getter probably will consummate the sale, but only after the customer's technical people give at least tentative approval. Some of these technical specialists eventually become fine order-getting salesmen, but the majority are more interested in establishing the technical excellence of their product than working closely with people to persuade them to buy it.

Most selling takes the right blend of all three

We have isolated and described three sales tasks — order getting, order taking, and supporting. You should understand, however, that a particular salesman might be given at least two of these tasks and perhaps all three. Ten percent of a particular salesman's job may be order getting, 80 percent order taking, and the additional 10 percent supporting. Another salesman may have the same title but a far different blend of sales tasks.

The type of man required for a given sales position and the level of compensation will depend largely on which sales tasks are required and in what combination. This is why job descriptions for salesmen's positions are so important.

A careful job description should be written for each sales job as part of the marketing strategy planning effort. This, in turn, can guide implementation.

To see this more clearly, turn back to the two job descriptions presented earlier in the chapter and try to determine which of the three sales tasks, or what combination of the three, is needed for each of these jobs. You will see that these job descriptions provide fairly clear guide-lines to the kind of salesmen who should be selected, the amount and kind of training needed, how much they will have to be paid, and how they should be paid. These matters are discussed below.

Sales management must be planned, too

Marketing strategy planning must include some consideration of how the personal selling job will be carried out — in particular, how the job of selecting, training, compensating, and controlling salesmen will be handled. Otherwise, planning may be unrealistic. We will not cover in detail the sales management function, but we will discuss briefly the sales manager's major tasks.[20]

Hiring by
blood lines
or psycho-
logical tests

It is extremely important to obtain *good, competent* salesmen. But since these descriptive terms mean different things to different companies, a careful job analysis and job description should be used as the basis for the selection process.

The selection of salesmen in most companies is a hit-or-miss affair, normally attempted without any job analysis or serious thought about exactly what kind of man is needed. Friends and relations or people who are available may be used because many people feel that the only qualifications for sales jobs are friendliness and a presentable appearance. This approach has contributed to poor sales and high personnel turnover for many companies.

Progressive companies have attempted to use more scientific procedures in hiring, including multiple interviews with various executives, and psychological tests. The personality and characteristics of an applicant may be compared with those of successful salesmen in the job.

Unfortunately, none of these techniques can guarantee success — but experiments have shown that using some kind of selection method brings in better personnel than using no selection aids at all. Psychological tests particularly have caused a great deal of controversy; as in the case of motivation research, many proponents have oversold the technique. But used with care, such tests can be valuable aids to management judgment.

The market grid concept may have to be given greater recognition in the selection of salesmen. Behavioral science research seems to indicate that the effectiveness of salesmen depends upon the kinds and personalities of the company's customers. Insurance salesmen, for example, seem to be more successful when dealing with individuals similar to them in age, height, income, religious affiliation, education, politics, and even smoking habits.[21]

Logically, this would mean that the sales manager should know as much as possible about his various target markets before selecting salesmen. He may need to hire a wide variety of men to meet different kinds of customers. Insurance companies, for example, probably make a mistake when they hire only college graduate athletes from middle-class backgrounds to sell for them. The former athlete may be very good for some potential customers but totally inappropriate for

[20] For further treatment, see W. J. Stanton and R. H. Buskirk, *Management of the Sales Force* (3d ed.; Homewood, Ill.: Richard D. Irwin, Inc., 1969); and D. M. Phelps and J. Howard Westing, *Marketing Management* (3d ed.; Homewood, Ill.: Richard D. Irwin, Inc., 1968).

[21] Franklin B. Evans, "Selling Is a Dyadic Relationship—A New Approach," *American Behavioral Scientist*, May, 1963, p. 79. Frederick W. Webster,

Jr., "Interpersonal Communication and Salesman Effectiveness," *Journal of Marketing*, July 1968, pp. 7–13; Charles W. King and John O. Summers, *Dynamics of Interpersonal Communication: The Interaction Dyad* (Reprint Series, No. 272, Institute for Research in the Behavioral, Economic and Management Sciences, Krannert Graduate School of Industrial Administration, Purdue University).

others. As applied psychology and sociology are developed further, firms probably will be able to select and manage their sales forces more scientifically.[22]

A sales organization can't be successful unless its salesmen know how to reach the goals of the organization. This information can be imparted in a sales training program. Such a program should cover the following fundamental areas: (1) company policies and practices, (2) product information, and (3) selling techniques.

Company policies and practices

Since the salesman may be the only company representative that a customer ever sees, he ought to be thoroughly familiar with the company's policies on credit, size of orders, dating of invoices, delivery, transportation costs, returned-goods privileges, and pricing. He should thoroughly understand his firm's requirements concerning reports expected of him, expenses and their control, and attendance at sales meetings. And he should understand internal procedure so that he can assist his customers in expediting orders, securing adjustments, and generally making it easier for them to deal with his company.

Product information

The amount of product information a salesman needs depends on the type of sales job he has and the complexity of the product line. We have discussed these matters already in Chapter 20 and in other sections of this text that deal with the classification of products and customer buying motives and habits. The important thing is that the salesman have enough information to be able to satisfy his customers —considerable information for some accessory and shopping goods, for example, but less for convenience goods.

Selling techniques

The ability to handle a selling situation is basic.

As we saw above, some companies find it more profitable to train salesmen in the specific selling methods they wish them to use. They rely less upon the old-fashioned born salesman, because he frequently does not do well when competition gets tough.

More progressive companies are learning that salesmanship can be taught effectively by observing senior salesmen, making trial demonstrations and sales presentations, and by analyzing why present customers buy from the company, why former customers now buy from competitors, and why some prospects remain only prospects. This training is started in the classroom and often supplemented by on-

---

[22] For more discussion on this, see G. Zaltman, *Marketing: Contributions from the Behavioral Sciences* (New York: Harcourt, Brace & World, Inc., 1965), pp. 116–21; S. M. Stevens, "The Application of Social Science Findings to Selling and the Salesman," in S. H. Britt and H. W. Boyd, Jr., *Marketing Management and Administrative Action* (New York: McGraw-Hill Book Co., 1963), pp. 601–10; M. S. Gadel, "Concentration by Salesmen on Congenial Prospects," *Journal of Marketing*, April, 1964, pp. 64–66; and James E. Stafford and Thomas V. Greer, "Consumer Preferences for Types of Salesmen: A Study of Independence-Dependence Characteristics," *Journal of Retailing*, Summer, 1965, pp. 27–33 ff.; and J. A. Belasco, "The Salesman's Role Revisited," *Journal of Marketing*, April, 1966, pp. 6–8.

the-job coaching by sales managers. Time for this training must be included in the promotion blend, or the whole promotion effort may suffer.

Length of training period

Some sales training programs last as long as three years, though most last only a few weeks. The length of the initial training period should be in almost direct proportion to the difficulty of the salesman's task as shown by the job description.

Sales training, as such, however, should go on indefinitely. For this ongoing training, many companies use weekly sales meetings, annual or semiannual conventions, regular weekly or biweekly newsletters, and a regular program of sales supervision. Many salesmen tend to get set in their ways and can profit greatly from additional training. This training also provides additional opportunities for evaluating and selecting men for greater responsibilities.[23]

Compensating and motivating

While it is true that public recognition, sales contests, and simple personal recognition for a job well done may be highly effective in stimulating greater sales effort, most companies use monetary spurs to sales personnel.[24] Our primary emphasis here, too, will be upon monetary stimulation.

Two basic decisions must be made in developing a compensation plan: (1) determine the level of compensation and (2) establish the method of payment.

Level of compensation

The job description makes possible a careful appraisal of the sales-man's role in the total marketing mix. This description shows whether any special skills or responsibilities are required that suggest higher pay levels.

To make sure that it can afford a given type of salesman with a certain set of responsibilities, the company should estimate, at the time this description is being written, how valuable such a salesman will be. A good order getter might be worth over $50,000 a year to one corporation, but only $5,000 to another company, simply because the firm does not have enough to sell. In the latter case, the company probably will have to redraft its job specifications or completely re-shape its promotion plans, since the going compensation level for such salesmen is far higher than $5,000 a year.

To attract and retain men, most companies must at least meet the going market wage for salesmen of a particular caliber. Order getters are paid more than order takers. Some retail store clerks, basically

---

[23] For a description of a sales training program in an industrial goods company, see Joseph W. Thompson and William W. Evans, "Behavioral Approach to Industrial Selling," *Harvard Business Review*, March-April, 1969, pp. 137–51.

[24] "The Sales Incentive: Booster or Fringe Benefit?" *Sales Management*, September 21, 1962, Part 1 of two parts, p. 41; Some organizations, such as Ma-ritz, Inc., in St. Louis, have specialized in sales force motivation problems and have grown to over 1,000 employees. Such firms can be a real help in improving salesmen's attitudes and thus better implementing marketing plans.

low-level order takers, may not even be paid the federal minimum wage.

If there are particularly difficult aspects to a job, such as extensive traveling, aggressive pioneering, or contacts with less pleasant kinds of customers, the compensation may have to be increased. The salesmen's compensation level should correspond at least roughly with the pay scale of the rest of the firm, normally running higher than the compensation of the office or production force but seldom exceeding that of the executives who supervise them.

Method of payment

Once the general level of compensation has been determined, then method of payment must be set. There are three basic methods of payment: (1) *straight salary,* (2) *straight commission,* or (3) *a combination plan.*

Straight salary normally supplies the maximum security for the salesman and straight commission, the maximum incentive. Because these two represent extremes, and most companies want to offer their salesmen some balance between incentive and security, the most popular method of payment is a combination plan which includes some salary and some commission. Bonuses and other goal-directed incentives are becoming more popular, too. Pensions, insurance, and other fringe benefits may be included, too, but straight salary and straight commission methods are basic to most combination plans.[25]

What determines the choice of the pay plan? Four standards should be applied: control, incentive, flexibility, and simplicity.

CONTROL A sales manager's control over a salesman tends to vary directly with the proportion of the compensation which is in the form of salary. The straight-salary plan permits the maximum amount of supervision, while the man on commission tends to be his own boss. The salesman on straight salary earns the same amount regardless of how he spends his time or which products he pushes. If the sales manager wishes the salesman to spend substantial time on order taking, supporting sales activities, repair work, or delivery services, then the salaried salesman can be expected to do these activities without complaining. The company is paying for the use of his services for a set period of time, and he should expect to work as needed.

Since the sales manager must give more supervision when there is a straight salary or large salary element in the compensation plan, a compensation plan which included some commission or even a straight commission with built-in direction should be used if such personal supervision would be difficult.

A poorly designed commission plan can lead to lack of control. A manufacturer of industrial fabrics which paid its salesmen a straight commission on sales volume found his plant was swamped with a large quantity of small-yardage orders. Furthermore, the plant was

[25] For further discussion, see *The Conference Board, Incentives for Salesmen* (Experiences in Marketing Management, No. 14 [New York: National Industrial Conference Board, 1967]); and Richard C. Smyth, "Financial Incentives for Salesmen," *Harvard Business Review,* January-February, 1968, pp. 109–17.

continually receiving requests for bids on highly competitive low-margin items. This was unsatisfactory, since the company's objective was the development of new markets, rather than obtaining immediate business. In this case, the sales compensation plan was directing the salesmen toward the wrong objective.[26]

INCENTIVE An incentive plan can range anywhere from an indirect incentive (a modest sharing of company profits) to a direct incentive, where a salesman's income is strictly a commission on his sales. The incentive should be large only if there is a direct relationship between the salesman's effort and results. If the relationship is less direct, as when a number of people are involved in the sale – engineers, top management, or supporting salesmen – then each one's contribution to the total results is less clear-cut and greater emphasis on salary may be appropriate.

Strong incentives are normally offered order-getting salesmen when a company wants to expand sales rapidly. Strong incentives may be used, too, when the company's objectives are shifting or varied. In this way, the salesman's activities and efforts can be directed and shifted as needed. One trucking company, for example, has a sales incentive plan that pays commissions on business required to balance the freight movement, depending on how heavily traffic has been moving in one direction or another. At any one time, commissions are paid only on traffic moving in one direction.

FLEXIBILITY Flexibility is probably the most difficult standard to maintain in the pay plan. One major reason that combination plans have become more popular than straight salary or commission plans is that they offer a way to meet varying situations. Four major kinds of flexibility will be considered.

1. Flexibility in selling costs. This is important for most small companies. With their limited working capital and uncertain markets, small companies like the fixed selling costs (as a percent of sales) aspect of straight commission, or at least combination plans with a large commission element. When sales drop off, costs do, too. This feature is often overriding in selecting a method of sales compensation.

2. Flexibility among territories. Different sales territories present different potentials. Unless the pay plan allows for this fact, the salesman in a growing territory might have rapidly increasing earnings for the same amount of work, while the salesman in a poor area has little to show for his effort. Such a situation is not fair and can lead to considerable dissatisfaction and high salesman turnover. The star salesman may be the one who through luck or a family relationship has managed to obtain the best territory.

3. Flexibility among men. Most companies use salesmen at varying

[26] D. J. Wilson, "Common Characteristics of Compensation Plans for Industrial Salesmen," in R. L. Clewett (ed.), *Marketing's Role in Scientific Management* (Chicago: American Marketing Association, 1957), p. 168.

stages of their professional development. Trainees and new salesmen usually require a special pay plan with considerable emphasis on salary.
4. Flexibility among products. Most companies sell several different products which have different profit potentials. Unless this
fact is recognized, the salesmen may emphasize the sale of those
products which sell easiest without respect to the overall company profit. A flexible commission system may more readily
adjust to changing profit potentials as demand conditions warrant.

SIMPLICITY A final consideration is the need for simplicity as a
standard to be maintained in the pay plan. Complicated plans are hard
for salesmen to understand and costly for the accounting department
to administer. Considerable dissatisfaction may result if salesmen
cannot see a direct relationship between their effort and their income.

Simplicity is best achieved with straight commission. A predetermined commission is paid on the amount of the sale. There is no need
to adjust salary levels for the age and experience of salesmen, the
changes in demand and supply conditions in the personnel market,
the size and potentials of the various territories, and so on.

It is also true, however, that in practice it usually is better to sacrifice some simplicity to gain some flexibility, incentive, or control. The
actual combination of these factors must depend on the job description, the marketing mix, and the company's objectives.[27]

**Sales man-
agement
must coor-
dinate with
marketing
manage-
ment**

There are, unfortunately, no easy answers to the compensation
problem. A strong incentive compensation plan might have been
suitable when a company was small and growing and had a great need
for order getters. But this plan might be entirely unsuitable just a few
years later when there is more need for order *takers*.[28]

The sales manager in cooperation with the marketing manager
must develop a good compensation plan. The sales manager's efforts
must coordinate with the whole marketing plan because he can accomplish his goals only if adequate funds are allocated to this task. As
already noted, it is the marketing manager's job to balance the promotion blend. The expected cost and performance of the sales force is
only one of the many variables he must consider in making the final
decision. To make these judgments, the marketing manager must
know what a sales force should consist of, what its goals should be,
and what it should cost.

Once the sales manager's basic plan and budget have been accepted,
his job becomes one of implementing the plan, including directing and

[27] For more discussion, see F. E. Webster, Jr., "Rationalizing Salesmen's Compensation Plans," *Journal of Marketing*, January, 1966, pp. 55–58; and R.
L. Day and P. D. Bennett, "Should Salesmen's Compensation Be Geared to Profits?" *Jouranl of Marketing*, October, 1962, pp. 6–9.

[28] Kenneth R. Davis, "Salesmen's Compensation:
Two Basic Problems," *Management Aids for Small
Manufacturers* (Washington, D.C.: Small Business
Administration, September, 1958).

controlling the sales force. This would include determining and assigning sales territories, and the evaluation of performance.

More is said on this in Chapter 29, but it should be noted that the sales manager has more to do than fly about the country entertaining customers. A sales manager is deeply involved with the basic management tasks of planning and control, as well as the ongoing execution of the personal selling effort.[29]

Conclusion

In this chapter, we have discussed the importance and nature of personal selling. Basically different sales jobs are required for different products and situations and perhaps different approaches to the sales presentation may be indicated. Obviously, the communications process, adoption process, and AIDA approaches discussed in Chapter 20 are applicable here in guiding the planning of the personal selling element of a promotion blend.

The vital role of personal selling was shown, but it should also be emphasized that almost any person can fit into some personal selling job. In fact, many starting jobs in marketing are in personal selling. This can be an extremely rewarding experience if the full marketing process is understood.

We noted that some personal selling is achieving a new almost professional status, because of the competence and degree of personal responsibility required. The day of the grinning glad-hander is passing in favor of the specialist who is ingenious, industrious, persuasive, knowledgeable, and highly trained. Many companies now have training programs that last several weeks or months, during which time the salesman does no productive work except preparing to serve the company's customers.

Salesmen of this caliber are usually welcome at a buyer's office because they are in a position to help the buyer. This type of salesman always has been, and probably always will be, in short supply. And the demand for high-caliber salesmen is continually growing.

The first step in determining the type of salesman required in a particular situation is to develop a detailed job description. Three *basic* kinds of sales tasks were isolated: (1) order getting, (2) order taking, and (3) supporting. Most sales jobs are a combination of at least two of these three tasks, and the nature of the job (and the level and method of compensation) depends in large part on the blend of these tasks.

[29] Leslie M. Dawson, "Towards a New Concept of Sales Management," *Journal of Marketing*, April, 1970, pp. 33–39; Derek A. Newton, "Get the Most Out of Your Sales Force," *Harvard Business Review*, September–October 1969, pp. 130–43; R. O. Loen, "Sales Managers Must Manage," *Harvard Business Review*, May–June, 1964, pp. 107–14; "A Sales Chief's Week Is Whirl of Jets, Calls and Sheer Exhaustion," *Wall Street Journal*, April 7, 1969, pp. 1 f; and *The First-Line Sales Supervisor* (Experiences in Marketing Management, No. 17 [New York: National Industrial Conference Board, Inc., 1968]).

There is a real challenge to sales management to select, train, compensate, and control this growing army of salesmen. Sales efforts in the past too often have been poor or even slipshod, in part because the need for salesmen was so pressing and sales management was not always the best. This situation is changing rapidly as marketing and sales management improves its techniques and adapts the tools and findings of cost accounting, statistics, economics, psychology, and sociology.

The sales manager is becoming a real manager of men, not just an older salesman. His efforts, however, still must be part of a promotion blend as well as a total marketing mix.

QUESTIONS AND PROBLEMS

1 Cite three actual local examples of the three kinds of sales presentations discussed in the chapter. Explain for each situation whether a different type of presentation would have been better.

2 Describe a need-satisfaction theory sales presentation which you have experienced recently and explain how it might have been improved by fuller use of the AIDA framework.

3 Write a job description for a college textbook salesman. Does it make any difference whether the salesman knows anything about the material in the books he is selling? What kind of a salesman is he?

4 What kind of salesman is required to sell the following products? If there are several selling jobs in the channel for each product, then indicate the kinds of salesmen required (specify any assumptions necessary to give definite answers):
a) Soya bean oil
b) Costume jewelry
c) Nuts and bolts
d) Handkerchiefs
e) Mattresses
f) Corn
g) Cigarettes

5 Distinguish among the jobs of manufacturers', wholesalers', and retailers' order-getting salesmen. If one order getter is needed, must all the salesmen in a channel be order getters? Illustrate.

6 Distinguish between merchants and shopkeepers as far as promotion is concerned. Are there any other differences? Illustrate.

7 Refer to the two detailed job descriptions in the chapter, and estimate what proportion of each salesman's time would be expended for order getting, order taking, and supporting activities (estimate in minutes for one day and then convert to proportions, making any assumptions necessary). Which of the two would probably receive the higher compensation and why? What compensation plan would be most appropriate for each job? Where might such salesmen be recruited and how should they be selected? What type and how much training would seem appropriate?

8 Explain how a straight commission system might provide flexibility in the sale of a line of women's clothing products which continually varied in profitability.

9 Explain how a compensation system could be developed to provide incentives for older salesman and yet make some provision for trainees who have not yet learned their job.

10 Discuss the role of the manufacturers' agent in the marketing manager's promotion plans. What kind of salesman is he?

11 Discuss the future of the specialty shop if manufacturers place greater emphasis on mass selling because of the inadequacy of retail order taking.

12 Describe the operation of our economy if personal salesmen were outlawed. Could the economy work? If so, how; if not, what is the minimum personal selling effort necessary? Could this minimum personal selling effort be controlled effectively by law?

...every advertisement and advertising campaign should seek clearly defined objectives.

...until more effective advertising research tools are developed,...the present method of carefully defining specific advertising objectives, testing plans, and then evaluating the results of actual advertisements, would seem most productive....

22

Mass selling

Mass selling facilitates mass distribution. Although a marketing manager might prefer to use personal selling exclusively, it can be expensive on a per-contact and a per-sale basis. Mass selling is a way around this roadblock. It is not as pinpointed as personal selling, but it does permit the communication of ideas or information to large numbers of potential customers at the same time. Today, most promotion blends contain both personal and mass selling.

Primary emphasis in this chapter will be on the use of advertising as a mass selling tool. The need for advertising objectives, reaching target customers (via media), and communicating with target customers (with messages) will receive extensive treatment. The management and control of advertising also will be discussed.

Importance of advertising

**By the bi-
centennial,
$30 billion
in ads**

We saw in Chapter 20 that advertising can get results in a promotion blend. It may help a marketing manager differentiate his product or even carve out a separate little target market for his firm. It may even help obtain product and brand familiarity to the point that customers will willingly pay substantial price premiums for advertised brands.

Good advertising results are obtained at a cost, of course. Expenditures in the U.S. for advertising have been growing continuously since World War II, and more growth is expected. In 1946, they were slightly more than $3 billion; by 1969, they topped $18 billion – and it is predicted that by 1976 the total annual advertising expenditure will be $30 billion.[1]

**It's all done
by less than
half a million**

While total advertising expenditures are large, the advertising industry itself employs relatively few people. The major expense is for media time and space. And in the United States, the largest share of this – almost 30 percent – goes for newspaper space. Television takes about 17 percent of the total and direct mail, about 15 percent.[2]

Fewer than 500,000 people work directly in the U.S. advertising industry. This would include all people who help create or sell advertising for advertising media, such as radio and television stations, newspapers, and magazines, as well as those in advertising agencies and those working for retailers, wholesalers, and manufacturers who handle their own advertising. The sometimes glamorous and often maligned 4,800 U.S. advertising agencies, however, employ only about 200,000 persons. Among these, not many are large, most employing fewer than 10 persons and they are highly concentrated in New York and Chicago.[3]

**Advertisers
aren't really
spending
that much**

U.S. corporations invest an average of only about $1\frac{1}{2}$ percent of their sales dollar in advertising. This is relatively small compared to the aggregate cost of marketing – perhaps 50 percent of the consumer's dollar – and the 20 to 50 percent gross margins with which we have been dealing at various channel levels.

In reviewing overall U.S. advertising expenditures, however, it is important to note that the figures reported as totals and averages may be misleading. Some industries spend a considerably larger percentage of sales for advertising than the average of $1\frac{1}{2}$ percent. One study

[1] "TV Will Need Finer Tuning," *Business Week*, December 6, 1969, pp. 200–201; Jules Backman, "Advertising in the 1970's," *Business Horizons*, April, 1968, pp. 7–14; and *Advertising Age*, September 18, 1967, p. 2; and Jules Backman, *Advertising and Competition* (New York: New York University Press, 1967), p. 179.

[2] *Ibid.*, p. 188.

[3] Exact data on this industry is elusive. For the most recent estimates available from a good industry source, see "How Many People Work in Advertising?" *Printers' Ink* December 6, 1957, p. 88. See also, John J. Humpal and H. G. Meyer-Oertel, "Measuring Change in the Advertising Agency Business," *Journal of Marketing*, January, 1967, pp. 56–59; "Advertising: A Career of Action and Variety for Exceptional Men and Women," (New York: American Association of Advertising Agencies, 1969); and and 4A *Newsletter* (New York: American Association of Advertising Agencies, November 10, 1969,) p. 1.

showed that soap and related products manufacturers spent 14.2 percent, drug manufacturers 11.05 percent, and tobacco manufacturers 6.06 percent. At the other extreme, coal mining companies spent only 0.09 percent, construction companies 0.10 percent, dyers and finishers of textiles 0.15 percent, men's and boys' clothing 0.11 percent, aircraft manufacturers 0.13 percent and wholesalers and retailers in the aggregate 1.05 percent.[4]

Likewise, advertising expenditure figures must be read carefully because the amount spent by a particular firm or industry may not show the total amount of advertising in a product. The reason is that many firms sell to others who advertise farther along in the channel. And when this channel advertising is included, the total channel bill is somewhat higher. In 1966, total advertising expenditures accounted for 2.24 percent of gross national product and 3.56 percent of personal consumption expenditures.[5]

Clearly, advertising is an important factor in certain markets, especially the consumer goods markets. Nevertheless, we must keep in mind that in the aggregate it costs much less than personal selling.

Advertising objectives tied to marketing strategy

We have emphasized throughout this text the importance of setting and following specific objectives, including overall company, marketing, and promotion objectives.

You get what you ask for

Every advertisement and advertising campaign should seek clearly defined objectives. But we have also noted that objectives frequently are not stated explicitly, if at all. As a result, it is not surprising to find that many advertisers merely turn this task over to their advertising agency with instructions to "promote the product," having no idea themselves exactly what they want done. The agency then must shift for itself, but the "noise" added to the communication process may lead to poor results.

The agency may face-lift the previous campaign or develop what appears to be reasonable objectives. Or they may develop objectives which, although reasonable, allow the agency to experiment with new approaches or to plan campaigns that *will win awards within the advertising industry.*

Progressive advertisers realize that without clearly defined objectives, preparing an advertising campaign is guesswork, and measuring the effectiveness of the advertising is difficult or impossible. They are beginning to state their objectives more specifically. This provides standards for measuring performance.

Some firms—and their agencies—are most eager to evaluate advertising effectiveness. The Campbell Soup Co. and its agency have

[4]*Advertising Age*, September 18, 1967, pp. 77–78.
[5]Backman, *op. cit.*, p. 182.

even agreed to tests by a third party to help evaluate how effectively the advertising agency's plans will accomplish the objectives set by Campbell advertising executives. This approach has a useful by-product. It forces both the company and the agency to specify very clearly their objectives.[6]

If you want half the market, say so!

Advertising objectives should be extremely specific, probably much more specific than personal selling objectives. One of the advantages of personal selling is that the salesman can shift his presentation to meet customers' needs. Each advertisement, however, is a specific communication that must be effective, not just for one customer, but for thousands or millions of target customers. Moreover, each advertisement in a continuing advertising campaign may seek to accomplish different objectives. It is essential, therefore, to specify not only the objectives of the whole campaign but of each individual advertisement.

Specific advertising objectives should include, (1) the customer reaction sought by the campaign or individual advertisement and (2) the role played by the campaign or advertisement in the overall promotion blend – and in the larger framework, as part of the marketing mix.

More specifically, an advertisement or advertising campaign might work toward the following *advertising objectives:*

1. Aid in the introduction of new products to specific target markets.
2. Assist in the expansion or maintenance of market share.
3. Help obtain desirable dealer outlets.
4. Prepare the way for salesmen by presenting the company's name and the merits of its products.
5. Tell about the availability of new products and the possible uses of other products.
6. Provide contact with the target customers even when the salesman is not available.
7. Sell the company "brand image."
8. Obtain immediate buying action.
9. Help a buyer confirm his purchasing decision.
10. Develop goodwill for the company itself.

Even these objectives, however, are not specific enough as a basis for measuring the effectiveness of advertising. An advertisement which sought (as in number 5) to tell about the availability of a new product could, for example, be judged successful if market research results showed that *any* customers were now aware of the existence of the new product. But would a 1 percent awareness be impressive? Not if the advertiser had been hoping for a 50 percent awareness!

[6]"Getting the Most Ad for the Money," *Printers' Ink,* September 27, 1963, pp. 27–30; and "Ad Roles Shifting for Agencies and Clients," *Business Week,* December 8, 1962, pp. 53–56.

Two examples show the interrelation of specifying goals and measuring results.

1. Rather than just telling about the availability of a particular new product, the specific advertising objective might be "to increase the awareness of Product X by 20 percent, over a one-year period, among housewives between the ages of 25 and 40 years in the 230 U.S. Standard Metropolitan Statistical Areas."

This objective would give the advertising agency something to work toward. It clearly specifies some actions and eliminates others. For example, it is clear that no effort is needed to increase awareness in rural areas. Also a test of *current* awareness would be needed as a bench mark, to be able to measure the *increase* in awareness.

2. A general promotional objective, "To assist in the expansion of market share," could be rephrased more specifically, "To increase traffic in our cooperating retailer outlets by 25 percent during the next three months."

Such a specific objective obviously has an impact on implementation plans. Advertising that might be right for building a good image among communicators might be entirely wrong for getting customers into the retailers' stores. Here we might use contests or tie-in sales. And the media used would be pinpointed to help particular dealers, perhaps including local newspapers and billboards rather than national consumer magazines.[7]

Objectives determine kinds of advertising needed

The advertising objectives selected will largely determine which of two basic types of advertising to use—*product* or *institutional*.

Product advertising, as the name implies, is concerned with *informing about and selling a product.* It may be aimed at final users or consumers, or to channel members.

Institutional advertising, on the other hand, does not involve a product but rather a company or even an industry. It is intended primarily to *develop goodwill toward the company or industry.* The long-run goal is to improve sales and relations with the various publics with whom the company deals. This includes not only consumers but current and prospective channel members or component suppliers, shareholders, etc.

Product advertising falls into three categories: pioneering, competitive, and reminder advertising.

Pioneering advertising—builds primary demand

Pioneering advertising is aimed at developing primary demand for a product category rather than a specific brand. It is needed in the early

[7]For further discussion on this, see Russell H. Colley, *Defining Advertising Goals for Measured Advertising Results* (New York: Association of National Advertisers, Inc., 1961), Part 2, and *Setting Advertising Objectives* (Studies in Business Policy, No. 118 [New York: National Industrial Conference Board, 1966]).

stages of the adoption process to inform potential customers about a new product or concept.

Pioneering advertising is used in the introductory stage in the product life cycle and can be used with several advertising objectives (numbers 1, 3, 4, and 5, for example). Its basic job is to inform, not persuade.

Pioneering advertising doesn't have to mention the brand or specific company at all. The California olive industry promoted olives as olives, not certain brands. This was so successful that after only five years of promotion, the industry's surplusses had become shortages, and it diverted promotional funds to horticultural research to increase production.[8]

Competitive advertising — emphasizes selective demand

Competitive advertising stimulates selective demand by selling a specific brand rather than a general product category. A firm can be forced into competitive advertising as the product life cycle moves along, to hold its own against competitors' products and promotion. Hershey Chocolate Co., a long holdout against advertising, finally began competitive advertising in 1969 as its profits declined in the face of tougher competition.[9] The United Fruit Company gave up a two-decade pioneering effort to promote bananas in favor of advertising its own "Chiquita" brand. It launched a nationwide advertising campaign with the theme, "We've put a seal on our peel." The reason for the change was simple. While United Fruit was single-handedly promoting bananas, it slowly lost market share to competitors. The competitive advertising program was launched to avoid further inroads.[10]

Competitive advertising is useful when the product has reached the market growth, and especially the market maturity, stage. It can work well with a product differentiation policy — stressing physical or psychological differences.

Competitive advertising may be either direct or indirect.

The *direct type* is aimed at immediate buying action. The *indirect type* is intended to point out product virtues so that when the customer is ready to buy, he will buy *that* product.

Much airline advertising is of the competitive variety. The various airlines are bidding for patronage, either immediately — in which case the ads are of the direct-action type with prices, timetables, and phone numbers to call for reservations — or eventually, in which case

[8]*Business Week,* November 17, 1962, p. 68.

[9]"Hershey's Sweet Tooth Starts Aching," *Business Week,* February 7, 1970, pp. 98–104; and "Big Chocolate Maker, Beset by Profit Slide, Gets More Aggressive," *Wall Street Journal,* February 18, 1970, pp. 1 f.

[10]"Chiquita, United Fruit's 'Banana Girl,' to Narrow Her Field of Sales," *Business Week,* May 25, 1963, p. 108.

the ads are of the indirect-action type, suggesting that you mention their name when talking to your travel agent.[11]

Reminder advertising — reinforces earlier promotion

Reminder advertising may be useful when the product has achieved a favored status, probably in the market maturity or sales decline stage. The advertiser mainly wants to keep his product's name before the public and will use soft-sell ads that merely mention the name as a reminder. Much traditional Coca-Cola advertising has been of this variety.

Institutional advertising — remember our name in St. Louis, Seattle, Charleston . . .

Institutional advertising focuses only on the name and prestige of a company or industry. It may seek to inform, persuade, or remind. A well-known Texas retailer, Neiman-Marcus, uses institutional ads that have reminder aspects. It does not expect the majority of its ads to pay for themselves immediately, but rather to maintain its image.

A persuading kind of promotion is sometimes used by large companies with several divisions. General Motors Corp., for example, does considerable institutional advertising of the GM name, emphasizing the quality and research behind *all* GM products. These are often keyed to GM's "Mark of Excellence."

Some large companies, such as General Motors and Du Pont, use institutional ads to emphasize the value of large corporations. Their ultimate goal is developing a favorable political and legal environment in which to work.

Sometimes an advertising campaign may have both product and institutional aspects because the federal government has taken an increasingly dim view of institutional advertising. The Internal Revenue Service has limited tax deductions on institutional advertising. And defense contractors are specifically barred from including advertising expenditures as a cost of doing business with the government.[12]

Put your money where it buys more — cooperatively

The discussion above might suggest that only producers do product or institutional advertising. This is not true, of course, but producers can affect the advertising done by others. Sometimes a manufacturer knows what promotion job or advertising job he wants done but finds that it can be done more effectively or more economically by someone further along in the channel. In this case, he may offer *advertising allowances* to buy the promotion he feels is needed by the channel system. In other cases, he advances only part of the

---

[11]For an extensive analysis of competitive advertising in the cigarette industry see: Neil E. Beckwith, "Competitive Advertising," Paper No. 225, January, 1969, Krannert Graduate School of Industrial Administration, Purdue University, Lafayette, Ind.

[12]"Will Defense-Contractor Ads Run into New Snags in Washington?" *Printers' Ink,* January 4, 1963, p. 7; and Nugent Wedding, "Advertising Mass Communication, and Tax Deduction," *Journal of Marketing,* April, 1960, pp. 17–22.

money, and the middlemen are expected to add the balance — this is called *cooperative advertising*.

Cooperative advertising helps the manufacturer get more promotion for his advertising dollar because media rate structures usually are set up to give local advertisers lower rates than national firms. In addition, the retailer is more likely to follow through where he is paying a share of the cost. Such cooperative efforts encourage more local effort from salesmen or salesclerks.[13]

Cooperative ad allowances are subject to abuse, however, because allowances can be given to retailers with little expectation that they will be used for ad purposes. This may become a disguised price concession and result in price discrimination. The Federal Trade Commission has recently become more interested in this problem, and some manufactures have pulled back from cooperative advertising. To avoid this, intelligent producers insist on advertising tearsheets and other proof of use.

Media reach target customers

For effective promotion, specific customers on the market grid must be reached. Unfortunately, not all potential customers read all newspapers, magazines, or other printed media, or listen to all radio and television programs. So not all media are equally effective.

What is the best medium for fur coats and pediatricians?

There is no simple answer to the question, "What is the best medium?" Effectiveness depends upon (1) the promotion objectives, (2) the funds available to accomplish the objectives, (3) the target markets, (4) the market coverage of each medium, (5) the life of messages in each medium, and (6) the environment in which the ads will appear.

Relatively little would be gained by advertising women's fur coats in the humor magazine of an all-male university. The use of men's magazines such as *Esquire* and *True* to reach doctors would be highly inefficient. Medical journals and direct mail are the most effective advertising media for telling doctors about new drugs.[14] And if the product is for children, a specialized journal such as *Pediatrics* might be the best medium.

On the other hand, if the mass market is the target — including women fur-coat buyers, men, doctors, etc., etc. — then the mass media such as network radio and television and *Life* magazine can be most economical.

The need for comparing different types of media — such as magazines, which are read, with radio and television, which are heard and seen — makes the selection task even harder.

[13]"Co-op Ad Allowances," *Marketing Insights*, January 19, 1970, pp. 1 f; R. L. Hicks, "Can You Buy Distribution with Your Cooperative Advertising?" *Sales Management*, September 5, 1958, p. 58.

[14]*Advertising Age*, February 28, 1958, p. 24.

Figure the
cost per
something

To guarantee good media selection, the advertiser first must *clearly* specify his target markets, a step necessary for all our marketing strategy planning. Next, media must be chosen that are heard, read, or seen by these target customers (including, perhaps, all the purchase influencers).

This is the major stumbling block to effective media selection, because it is not always certain who sees or hears what. To be sure, most of the major media have used marketing research to develop profiles of the people who buy their publications or live in their broadcasting area. Some have broken down their "audience" by sex, age, income, education, occupation, place of residence (such as farm or nonfarm), ownership of various appliances or automobiles, and ownership of homes or other articles of particular relevance.

But they cannot be as definite about who actually reads each page or sees or hears each show. And, they seldom tailor their marketing research to gather information on the market grid dimensions which *each* advertiser may deem important. Generally, media research focuses on socioeconomic characteristics. But what if the really important dimensions are concerned with behavioral needs or attitudes which are difficult to measure or unique to a particular product or market?[15]

Furthermore, there has been little standardization of audience measurement among competing media, and some media buyers distrust media research, expecting bias. In most foreign countries, even these audience profiles are usually not available.

In the face of all these subjective uncertainties, there is one measure that is not subjective—cost. Until better audience data becomes available, media buyers will probably continue to evaluate media in terms of *cost per something*. Media buyers typically choose media they think may do the needed job and then compare the costs of alternative media.

Newspapers—inch by inch

Most media costs are expressed as cost per unit—per line, per page, or per minute. Newspapers, for example, quote their rates in terms of a line $\frac{1}{4}$-inch deep and one column wide; usually there is a minimum allowable linage.

But these line rates tell little about the value offered by a particular paper. A high rate per line might be a good buy in a large-circulation publication, a poor one in a smaller medium. To make allowance for this, a special yardstick is applied to newspaper rates. This yardstick, "milline rate" is computed as follows:

$$\text{Milline rate} = \frac{\text{Line rate} \times 1,000,000}{\text{Circulation}}$$

The milline rate converts the cost per line to a common standard—the cost per line per 1 million circulation. Using milline rates instead of actual line rates frequently reveals that the seemingly higher cost

---

[15]"TV Will Need Finer Tuning," *op. cit.*, pp. 200–201.

paper actually offers a significantly lower cost because of its larger circulation.

Magazines—page by page

Magazines also charge by space and circulation size. Their rates usually are quoted by the page or fraction of a page. Their yardstick is a cost per page per thousand circulation or more commonly, "cost per thousand." This formula is:

$$\text{Cost per thousand} = \frac{\text{Page rate} \times 1,000}{\text{Circulation}}$$

To compare media effectiveness if the target market were teen-agers or upper-income families, the total circulation figures in the formulas can be replaced with the total for the groups in question. Or if the pass-along audience were significant to the advertiser, it might be better to insert total number of *readers* rather than circulation.

Outdoor advertising—you have to see it to believe it

The audience for outdoor advertising, including billboards, posters, and car cards in transit vehicles, is measured on a slightly different basis, namely, the number of cars passing the billboards or the number of people riding on the vehicles. These measures, too, are subject to criticism concerning how many and what types of customers actually do see and receive the message.

Radio and television—minute by minute

Radio and television are sold on a time basis. An advertiser can buy time on a number of specific stations or cover the entire nation by paying for network time.

It is possible to compute a cost per commercial minute per thousand viewers or listeners for TV or radio. The weak link in such computations, however, is the figure for audience size. At present, there are relatively few reliable measures of audience size. There are too many variations by time of day, program, audience, etc., because it is so easy to use the on-off switch and tuning dial.[16]

New media selection methods may force better perspective

In view of the difficulty of evaluating competing media, it is easy to see why a media analyst resorts to the use of whatever objective measures are available, and especially measures of the milline or cost-per-thousand variety. Yet this may result in cost, and only cost, becoming the overriding concern of the analyst and lead him into ignoring the varying characteristics of his target markets. He may even become mesmerized by the relatively low cost per something of a mass medium when, in fact, a more specialized medium might be a much better buy, since its readers might have more interest in the product, or more money to spend, or more willingness to buy, etc.[17]

While it is impossible to evaluate fully all the potential media that

[16]G. J. Goodhardt and A. F. C. Ehrenberg, "Duplication of Television Viewing between and within Channels," *Journal of Marketing Research*, May, 1969, pp. 169–78; E. Crane, A. Talbott, and R. Hume, "Time Use Profiles and Program Strategy," *Journal of Broadcasting*, Fall, 1961, pp. 335–43.

[17]"The Cost per Thousand Home Worshippers and the Error of Their Ways," *Advertising Age*, April 1, 1963, pp. 86–87.

might be considered, some mathematical approaches are now being used to aid in media selection. With linear programming and computers, it is possible for a media analyst to evaluate possibilities and pick the best media to reach the objective. The major obstacle here has been the poor quality of, or lack of, sound audience data. But some agencies and firms have found these methods useful, especially in the consumer goods markets. And a way of extending them to the industrial goods market has been suggested.[18]

As greater use is made of these potentially powerful tools, the media will be forced to supply better audience descriptions. Marketing managers and agencies, in their turn, will have to specify their target markets more carefully.

The growing acceptance of a more analytical approach to media selection will not replace the human media analyst. But it certainly will force him (or more typically, "her") to be more analytical and more efficient. The idea that everyone is our market is certainly not always true, and more advertisers and media buyers are recognising this fact.[19]

Specialized media help zero-in on target markets

According to the market grid concept, any market can consist of many smaller markets. We find attention directed increasingly to reaching smaller target markets. Many magazines now offer regional editions to meet special needs. *Life* magazine offers 26 regional markets and 20 SPOT city markets. *Time* offers not only seven regional editions and eight metropolitan editions but also has special editions for college students, educators, doctors, and businessmen.

Many magazines serve only special-interest groups, such as fishermen, radio and television enthusiasts, homemakers, religious groups, and professional groups. In fact, the most profitable magazines seem to be the ones which are aiming at clearly defined markets, while the mass magazines are experiencing difficulties. *Life* and *Look*, for example, have faced profit squeezes and *Saturday Evening Post* went out of business, while magazines such as *Playboy, Car Craft, Skiing, Bride's Magazine,* and *Southern Living* have been doing well.[20]

---

[18] Various advertising agencies have their own versions of these methods, and the *Chicago Sun-Times/Chicago Daily News* newspaper combination has developed one, too. For more discussion, see Robert D. Buzzell, *Mathematical Models and Marketing Management* (Boston: Graduate School of Business Administration, Harvard University, 1964), chap. v; David B. Montgomery and Glen L. Urban, *Management Science in Marketing* (Englewood Cliffs, N. J.: Prentice-Hall, Inc., 1969), pp. 137–53; Douglas B. Brown, "A Practical Method for Media Selection." *Journal of Marketing Research*, August, 1967, pp. 262–69; Robert J. Schreiber, "A Practical Procedure for Media Selection: Comments," *Journal of Marketing Research,* May 1968, pp. 221–24; and Harper W. Boyd, Jr., Henry J. Claycamp, and Charles W. McClelland, "Media Models for the Industrial Goods Advertiser – A Do-It-Yourself Opportunity," *Journal of Marketing*, April, 1970, pp. 23–29.

[19] Media selection models are not panaceas, however. See F. M. Bass and R. T. Lonsdale, "An Exploration of Linear Programming in Media Selection," *Journal of Marketing Research*, May, 1966, pp. 170–88.

[20] "The Hot Magazines Aim at Special Targets," *Business Week*, May 2, 1970, pp. 64–74; and "More Magazines offer a Chance to Aim Ads at a Specific Group," *Wall Street Journal*, March 17, 1970, pp. 1 f.

Many trade associations and labor unions have their own magazine or newspaper, and there may be a number for each trade or line of business. There are trade magazines in countless fields, such as chemical engineering, electrical wholesaling, farming, and the defense market. *Standard Rate and Data* provides a guide to the thousands of magazine media available. For those especially interested in the industrial market, *Industrial Marketing* magazine publishes the *Media Market Planning Guide.*

Radio suffered at first from the inroads of television. But now, like a number of magazines and newspapers, it has become a more specialized medium. Some stations cater to particular nationality, racial, and religious groups, such as Puerto Ricans, Negroes, Catholics, etc., while others emphasize Western, popular, or classical music.

Perhaps the most specific medium is direct-mail advertising. The purpose of this medium is to go directly to the reader via his mailbox. The method is to send a specific message to a carefully selected list of names. There are organizations that specialize in providing these names in the form of mailing lists, ranging in number from hundreds to millions of names. The diversity of these lists is shown in Table 22–1 and indicates the importance of knowing specifically the firm's target market or markets.[21]

Table 22–1

Quantity of names	Name of list
425	Small Business Advisors
40,000	Social Register of Canada
5,000	Society of American Bacteriologists
500	South Carolina Engineering Society
2,000	South Dakota State Pharmaceutical Association
250	Southern California Academy of Science
12,000	Texas Manufacturing Executives
720	Trailer Coach Association
1,200	United Community Funds of America
50,000	University of Utah Alumni
19,000	Veterinarians

Messages carry the message

Some messages communicate poorly

Once the objectives of the advertising campaign determine generally what is to be communicated, the key problem is how to develop messages—both copy and illustrations—to communicate it.

Advertising must use general appeals, which is one source of difficulty. It must communicate with large numbers of target custo-

[21] Available from Walter Drey, Inc., New York and Chicago, and Zeller-Letica, Inc., New York.

mers who constantly change their attitudes, outlooks, and desires. Our understanding of the communication process helps guide message planning, but adapting specific messages to the many potential target markets is not easy. As we saw in Chapter 20, common frames of reference and experience are desirable for good communication.

Some advertisers realize the complexity of the communication process and use research to help them as much as possible. Others rely almost exclusively on their own "creative genius." This is at the root of many poor campaigns. Some are brilliant and others are miserable failures. Sometimes copywriters feel their audience is much more sophisticated than it is; at other times, they talk down to it.

Much advertising emanates from agencies in New York City, and one advertising manager has deplored advertising "conditioned by our New York sophistication." His experience has taught him that "New York's price of being New York is loss of perspective; New York is not America."[22]

A study by the American Association of Advertising Agencies indicated that the majority of consumers felt advertisers considered them "stupid," and almost half chose the work "gullible." Interestingly, however, the consumers did not seem to be particularly offended by being talked down to or considered stupid. They just ignored or discounted advertising which did this.[23]

Bottoms up in New York, thumbs down in L.A.

Advertising innovators find that successful ad approaches are copied quickly by competitors, just as products are copied. Whether this makes competitive sense has not been demonstrated. Perhaps it simply shows that there are few really creative people. In any case, some advertisers feel that if you can't beat competition, you should at least meet it.

There are relatively few tried-and-true rules in message construction. Everything we see and every new way we see it changes us in some way. An idea that may have worked a year ago can fail today. A highly successful advertising program that sold much beer in the New York area flopped in Los Angeles.[24] And one industrial advertiser received more inquiries as it *reduced* the size of its ads.[25]

Let AIDA help guide message planning

How should we plan messages to assure access to the customer's eye, ear and, hopefully, pocketbook?

Basically, the overall marketing strategy should determine *what* should be said in the message. Then marketing research can be helpful in determining how this content can be decoded in order to have it

[22] *Advertising Age,* May 27, 1963, p. 90.

[23] "Advertising: Its Own Worst Enemy," *Sales Management,* May 17, 1963, pp. 19–20.

[24] "More Than Ads Sell Rheingold," *Business Week,* September 21, 1957, p. 70.

[25] "How to Advertise *Not* by The Book," *Printers' Ink,* September 6, 1963, pp. 47–48.

encoded as intended. As a guide to message planning, however, we can make additional use of the AIDA concept: getting Attention, holding Interest, arousing Desire, and obtaining Action. This approach is general, but these four steps can be a framework within which we can discuss the important problem areas requiring specific research.

Attention

Getting attention is the basic job of an advertisement. If this is not done, it doesn't matter how many people can or do see it. Many readers leaf through magazines and newspapers without paying attention to any of the advertisements. Many listeners or viewers run errands or get snacks during commercials on radio and television.

The devices for catching the customer's attention are numerous. A large headline, newsy or shocking statements, pictures of pretty girls, babies, cartoon characters—or anything that is "different" or eye-catching—may do the trick. But . . . the attention-getting device must not distract from the next step—holding interest.[26]

Interest

Holding interest is another matter. A pretty girl may get attention, but once you've seen her, then what? A man will pause to appreciate her, women will look at her. But if there is no relation between the girl and the product, observers of both sexes will move on.

More is known about holding interest than getting attention. The tone and language of the advertisement must be compatible with the field of experience and attitudes of target customers and their reference groups. A food advertisement featuring persons in riding costumes, for example, might be noted but passed over by many potential customers who do not ride to the hounds. An ad aimed at farm families using obviously city-bred models and city language could not expect to hold as much interest among farmers, especially those with lower incomes.

The need to consider the cultural training of the target market is vital. Perfume has long been considered feminine, but male cosmetics makers, by carefully avoiding feminine appeals and stressing the "maleness" of their products, have been successful. Shaving lotion would have the same utility if it contained only its base material, alcohol. But by adding perfume and coloring, the manufacturers have satisfied emotional needs and developed a profitable product. The words and ideas used in shaving lotion advertising are entirely different from those used in female perfume advertising.[27]

In addition to speaking the target customer's language, the advertising layouts should look right to the customer. The illustrations and copy should be arranged so that the eye is encouraged to move smoothly through the ad, perhaps from the upper left-hand corner to the signature or brand name at the lower right-hand corner. Advertisements

[26] Alfred Politz, "The Dilemma of Creative Advertising," *Journal of Marketing*, October, 1960, pp. 1–6.

[27] I. S. White, "The Functions of Advertising in a Culture," *Journal of Marketing*, July, 1959, pp. 10, 12.

having this natural flowing characteristic are said to encourage *gaze motion.*[28]

Desire

Arousing desire to own or use a particular product is one of the most difficult jobs of an advertisement. It requires that the advertiser be successful in communicating with the customer. To communicate effectively, the advertiser should understand how his target customers think, behave, and make decisions.

To be successful, an advertisement must convince the customer that the product can meet his needs. *Pioneering* advertising may be useful to develop primary demand and show how the whole product class would satisfy latent wants. Later, in the market growth and market maturity stages, *competitive* advertising can show how a particular brand satisfies particular wants.

An advertisement may also have the function, especially during the market growth and market maturity stages, of supplying words that the customer can use for rationalizing his desire to buy. Although products may satisfy certain emotional wants, in our society many consumers find it necessary to justify their purchases on an economic or even moral basis. Desire may develop around emotional motives, but economic motives must also be reinforced.

Action

Getting action is the final requirement, and not an easy one. We now know, from communications research, that the potential customer should be encouraged to try the product before he adopts it. The prospective customer must be led beyond considering how the product might fit into his life to actually trying it or letting the company's salesman come in and show him how it works.

Getting action with advertising is especially difficult because it must appeal to broader audiences than a personal salesman can.

Strongly felt customer needs might be pinpointed in the ads to communicate more effectively. Careful research on the attitudes and wants in the various market grid boxes may help uncover such strongly felt unsatisfied needs.

Appealing to these needs can get more action and also provide the kind of information the actual buyer seeks to confirm his decision. We are beginning to see that this approach may be one of the important roles of advertising. Some customers seem to read more advertising *after* the purchase than before. What is communicated to them may be very important if customers are to start or keep the web of word of mouth going. The ad may supply the words they use to tell others about the product.

---

[28] Advertising practitioners have found many rules useful for holding interest. While these are beyond our scope, many textbooks are devoted to these matters. See Otto Kleppner, *Advertising Procedure* (5th ed, New York: Prentice-Hall, Inc., 1966); C. H. Sandage and V. Fryburger, *Advertising Theory and Practice* (8th ed.; Homewood, Ill.: Richard D. Irwin, Inc., 1971); and H. G. Wales, D. L. Gentry, and M. Wales, *Advertising Copy, Layout and Typography* (New York: Ronald Press Co., 1958).

Advertising manager directs mass selling

Most companies have an advertising manager identified either by title or function. His job is to develop the advertising campaign within the framework of the promotion blend and the overall marketing mix.

Many advertising managers, especially those working for retailers, have their own advertising departments that plan the specific advertising campaigns and carry out the details, including copy and artwork preparation, purchase of artwork and printing, hiring of radio and television talent, production of programs and commercials, media selection, preparation of advertising schedules (timing of placement), space and time buying, and many details of shipping ad materials to media, issuing direct-mail items, and monitoring presentation of ads by media.

Considerable technical skill is involved in handling all these details, and largely for this reason, many advertising managers delegate much of the advertising task to specialists – the advertising agencies.

Advertising agencies often do the work

Evolution of agencies

Advertising agencies are specialists in handling the mass selling details we have been discussing. Agencies play a useful role because they are independent of the advertiser and have an outside viewpoint. They bring broad experience to bear on the individual client's problems because they work for many other clients with different products who sell in different markets and use other channels of distribution and media. In addition, agencies become specialists in the various phases of technical preparation and placement of advertising, and often can perform these functions more economically than a company's own department. Agency discounts in the media rate structure also help cover some or all of the costs of their services for national advertisers (a term used to distinguish this class of advertisers from *local* advertisers who pay lower rates).

Historically, advertising agencies started as space salesmen (brokers) working for a commission *from the media.* The amount of the commission paid to space salesmen has varied, but until recently it was about 15 percent of the charge paid by national advertisers.

In the early days, space salesmen earned their income by selling empty time or space. As competition grew, these salesmen helped their customers fill this time or space by writing the advertisements. In time, the advertisers became even more demanding, and the original space or time salesmen have moved closer to customers than to media. Nevertheless, the commission system has continued. It is ironic to note that many media now find it necessary to hire salesmen to call on the advertising agencies, who ostensibly are selling space for them.

As they moved closer to the space buyers, advertising agencies took on more and more functions. Agencies sometimes handle overall marketing strategy planning as well as marketing research, product and package development, and the development of sales promotion aids. Some agencies make good marketing partners and almost assume the role of the firm's marketing department.[29]

One of the ad agency's virtues is that the advertiser is free at any time to cancel the arrangement. This provides extreme flexibility for the advertiser. Some companies even use their advertising agency as a scapegoat. Whenever anything goes wrong, it's the advertising agency's fault, and the advertiser shops around for a new one. But a more fundamental advantage of the agency is that it is normally able to use specialists more effectively and continuously than individual advertisers. For this reason, it may be able to do a better job at less cost.

Loyalties may be divided

A major deficiency of advertising agencies is related to the way their commission compensation system has evolved. Generally, agencies get most of their income from selling advertising time and space. There is a natural temptation to recommend maximum expenditures on time and space, while limiting other activities for which they frequently do *not* receive any extra income, such as research, other supporting services, and sales promotion.

It's the way they are paid

The major users of advertising agencies are manufacturers or national distributors, because of the media rate structure in the industry. Normally, media have two prices: one for national advertisers and another, lower one for local advertisers, such as retailers. The agencies earn their discount, usually 15 percent, only when time or space is purchased at the higher national rate. National distributors or manufacturers have a real incentive to use advertising agencies because the 15 percent discount is allowed to any authorized agency they choose, but it is not available to them. Retailers, who are entitled to the lower local rates, seldom use agencies.

There is a growing resistance to the present method of agency compensation. The chief complaints are that the agencies receive the flat 15 percent commission, regardless of work performed, and also that the commission system makes it hard for the agencies to be completely objective about low-cost media or promotional campaigns that use little advertising space or time.

Not all agencies are satisfied with the present arrangement, either. Some would like to charge additional fees as they see rising costs and advertisers demanding more services.

The commission system is most favored by those accounts, such as producers of industrial goods, that require extensive service but buy relatively little advertising. These are the firms the agencies would like to, and sometimes do, charge additional fees.

The commission system is generally opposed by very large consumer goods advertisers who do much of their own research and planning, and require only basic services from their agencies. Some of these accounts can be very profitable for agencies, and naturally these agencies would prefer the fixed-commission system.

[29] "Why Ad Agencies Make Good Marketing Partners," *Printers' Ink,* November 11, 1960, pp. 68–69.

Fifteen percent no longer mandatory

The Federal Trade Commission worked for many years to change the method of advertising agency compensation. Finally, in 1956, the American Association of Advertising Agencies signed a consent decree with the Justice Department, indicating that by joint action they would no longer require the maintenance of the 15 percent commission system. This opened the way to discounts and fee increases, and other changes in compensation methods.[30]

Agency arrangements are changing

The dissatisfaction on the part of certain advertisers and agencies has led to many changes in the last few years. Some advertisers have set up or bought their own agencies.[31] Independent buying services compete with and supplement the services of in-agency media departments, forcing some of them to become more effective.[32] Some agencies specialize only in the creative functions. Some agency people predict the end of the present system and the development of a wholly new kind of agency which would focus on planning and getting promotion projects done, and not just getting out the advertising for a company.[33]

Much of the criticism of the present agency system and the changes which have occurred probably can be traced to the work of less efficient agencies who, under the umbrella of the 15 percent commission, were able to obtain and maintain business primarily through social contacts rather than business ability. Advertising is no business for incompetents with good contacts. Many of the large agencies have grown large because they truly do a better job for their clients. These agencies understand marketing and seek to improve their clients' marketing mixes. Some of these agencies provide complete marketing services for clients, assisting in developing strategy, preparing sales promotion as well as advertising, and even helping implement the detailed plan. They probably will continue to play an even larger role in the future, adapting to new situations as needed.

Some of the current ferment in the advertising business, however, is due to an internal struggle between the creative and the business types. This tension has been there for years, but a drop in revenues in 1967 forced the advertising business into thinking as much about cost accounting as creativity. As profits declined drastically in some agencies, tensions increased—especially as employees were laid off and the

---

[30] "Fee Is Pay for Actual Services: Elliott to 4A's," *Advertising Age*, November 11, 1963, pp. 1 and 77; and "How Should Agencies Be Paid for Test-Marketing Programs?" *Printers' Ink*, September 6, 1963, p. 8.

[31] "Advertisers Do It Themselves," *Business Week*, July 18, 1970, p. 66.

[32] "Middlemen Put Squeeze on Ad Men," *Business Week*, October 18, 1969, pp. 80–84; "Media Services Aid Client, Agency: It's Station Which Pays," *Advertising Age*, June 15, 1970, pp. 1 f; and "Buying Services Alter, but They're Changing Media Scene, Reps Say," *Advertising Age*, August 17, 1970, pp. 1 f.

[33] "It's Time for Major Revamp of Out Dated Agency System," *Advertising Age*, April 13, 1970, pp. 98–100.

high salaries which had been paid to some creative "stars" were cut sharply.[34]

At the root of some of the tension is the fact that the advertiser's product manager or brand manager may be personally responsible for the success of a particular product and feels, therefore, that he has some right to direct and even veto the work of the creative people. This has resulted in confrontations in which the agency often loses, because the advertiser is paying the bills. One agency woman turned client said she had lost patience with the "ego-dominated creative type who is blindly in love with his own efforts." She feels the yardstick of successful advertising is whether advertising communicates what it's supposed to communicate to its target audience.[35] It is advertisers such as this woman who pay the bills and who have been partly responsible for the changes which are occurring in the agency business.

FTC interested in agencies — and deceptive advertising

Advertising agencies face a challenge from another direction. The growing indignation over deceptive advertising, a reaction encouraged by the consumerism movement, has affected agencies. According to a recent Federal Trade Commission opinion, agencies would share equal responsibility with the client for advertising which is false, misleading, or unfair. This is of special interest to agencies and advertisers because of the possibility of large financial penalties. The FTC, for example, recently turned over a case to the Justice Department involving a suit of $1 million in penalties against an advertiser and its agency.[36]

Advertisers and their agencies probably will have to give greater attention to the issue of deceptive advertising. Legally, the Wheeler-Lea Amendment (passed in 1938) gives the FTC the responsibility of controlling deceptive advertising. But the consumerism movement is creating a new interest in what is deceptive, which is not always easy to define. Some advertising leaders are calling for a new outlook, including more honesty. They feel that some of their clients will have to learn that "dressing up a parity claim so that it sounds like a superiority claim just isn't kosher."[37] This has obvious implications for

---

[34] "Ad Agencies Have New Campaign — Efficiency," *Business Week,* April 20, 1968, pp. 144–54; "Ad Men Shiver as Profits Melt," *Business Week,* December 23, 1967, p. 36–37; "Agency Creative Stars Are Fading Away," *Marketing/Communications,* July, 1970, pp. 42–46; and "Boutique, Not Account Exec, is Doomed, Kurtz Tells AAF," *Advertising Age,* May 11, 1970, p. 10.

[35] Helen Van Slyke, Vice President, Advertising, Sales Promotion, and Public Relations, Helena Rubenstein, Inc., New York, "You Can't Make an Omlette Without Breaking Egos," a speech to the April 25, 1970, meeting of the American Association of Advertising Agencies.

[36] "The Darkening Drug Mood," *Time,* August 10, 1970, p. 60; and Dorothy Cohen, "The Federal Trade Commission and the Regulation of Advertising in the Consumer Interest," *Journal of Marketing,* January, 1969, pp. 40–44.

[37] "Frankfurt Sees End of Ad Hyperbole: Wipe Out Phony Advertisers, Cone Urges," *Advertising Age,* April 20, 1970, p. 2; E. John Kottman, "Truth and the Image of Advertising," *Journal of Marketing,* October 1969, pp. 64–66; and Boris W. Becker, "The Image of Advertising Truth: Is Being Truthful Enough?" *Journal of Marketing,* July 1970, pp. 67–68.

marketing mix planning. Advertising should not be counted on for embellishing a poor or just average marketing mix, a not uncommon practice, especially in production-oriented firms.

Measuring advertising effectiveness is not easy

Total sales results, the sum of all parts of the mix

It would be convenient if we could measure the results of advertising by a simple analysis of sales. Unfortunately, this is not possible. The total marketing mix, not just promotion generally or advertising specifically, is responsible for the sales result. The one exception to this rule, as it concerns advertising, is direct-mail advertising. If it doesn't produce immediate results, it is considered a failure.

Still, advertising literature is filled with success stories that "prove" advertising has increased sales.[38] Sometimes statistical analysis of sales over time in relation to advertising seem to show that advertising is more or less directly related to sales.[39] But these general approaches tend to give all the credit for improved performance to advertising, when the total marketing mix is involved.

Creative men say it's great— but will it communicate and sell?

Ideally, management should pretest advertising before it is run rather than relying solely on the judgment of creative people or advertising "experts," who too frequently judge solely on the basis of originality or cleverness of the copy and illustrations. Management people may be no better, if as good, at divining how good an ad will be.

Some progressive advertisers now demand laboratory or market tests to evaluate the effectiveness of ads. In addition, before ads are run, opinion and attitude research is sometimes used. Researchers try to evaluate consumers' reactions to particular advertisements or parts of advertisements, using the basic marketing research techniques discussed earlier as well as psychological and sociological scaling procedures and laboratory-type devices which measure skin moisture or eye reaction.[40]

Hindsight may lead us to foresight

After the advertisements have been run, researchers may attempt to measure how much is recalled about specific products or advertisements. Inquiries from customers may be used as a measure of the effectiveness of particular ads.

The response to radio or television commercials or magazine read-

---

[38] The pages of *Printers' Ink* (now *Marketing/Communications*) regularly carry such stories. See, for example, "Proving Business Papers Produce," *Printers' Ink,* June 29, 1962, pp. 29–36.

[39] "More Proof that Ads Build Sales," *Printers' Ink,* May 25, 1962, pp. 25–50; and "Westinghouse: Too Little Advertising," *Printers' Ink,* June 21, 1963, pp. 21–25.

[40] "Research Must Predict Ad's Effects, Says Coulson—And He Cites Examples of How It's Done," *Advertising Age,* September 30, 1963, pp. 89–98; and "Burnett Men Get Fast Test Results via Busy Creative Workshop," *Advertising Age,* September 10, 1962.

ership can be estimated using various survey techniques to check the size and composition of audiences (the Hooper, Crosley, Nielsen, and Starch reports are produced routinely) with implicit assumptions that larger audiences lead directly to greater purchases.

These specific measurements are relevant only when the advertiser knows what measurable level of performance he is trying to reach. When detailed advertising objectives are set, research can provide feedback on the effectiveness of the advertising.

While such advertising research techniques are far from foolproof, they are probably far superior to reliance on pure judgment by advertising experts.

Until more effective advertising research tools are developed, moreover, the present method of carefully defining specific advertising objectives, choosing media and messages to accomplish these objectives, testing plans, and then evaluating results of actual advertisements, would seem most productive.[41] The traditional marketing research techniques — applied with imagination — can be very helpful in this process.

Conclusion

Theoretically, it is relatively simple to develop a mass selling campaign. The target customers must be selected and advertising objectives set. Then media must be picked and messages must be developed.

Yet this is no simple process. There are many complications, and specialists — advertising agencies — have evolved to handle some of these tasks. Specific objectives must be set, or the advertising may have little direction and will be almost impossible to evaluate. Media and message planning may need to rely on considerable marketing research. When specific tasks are outlined in this way, it is much easier to measure the effectiveness of the advertising effort and to compare the actual performance against goals.

Ultimately, effective advertising should affect sales. But the whole marketing mix affects sales, and the results of advertising cannot be measured by sales changes alone. Advertising is only a part of promotion, and promotion is only a part of the total marketing mix that the marketing manager must develop to satisfy target customers.

[41] Roy H. Campbell, *Measuring the Sales and Profit Results of Advertising: A Managerial Approach* (New York: The Association of National Advertisers, Inc., 1969); David A. Schwartz, "Measuring the Effectiveness of Your Company's Advertising," *Journal of Marketing*, April, 1969, pp. 20–25; John E. Morrill, "Industrial Advertising Pays Off," *Harvard Business Review*, March–April, 1970, pp. 4–14 f; D. B. Lucas and S. H. Britt, *Measuring Advertising Effectiveness* (New York: McGraw-Hill Book Co., 1963); H. D. Wolfe, J. K. Brown, and G. C. Thompson, *Measuring Advertising Results* (Studies in Business Policy, No. 102 [New York: National Industrial Conference Board, 1962]); Harry D. Wolfe *et al.*, *Pretesting Advertising* (Studies in Business Policy, No. 109 [New York: National Industrial Conference Board, 1963]); and Howard L. Gordon, "Yes, Virginia, Research Helps Make Better Advertisements," *Journal of Marketing*, January, 1967, pp. 64–66.

QUESTIONS AND PROBLEMS

1 Discuss the relation of advertising objectives to marketing strategy planning and the kinds of advertising actually needed. Illustrate.

2 Present three examples where advertising to middlemen might be necessary. What would be the objective(s) of such moves?

3 What does it mean to say that "money is invested in advertising"? Is all advertising an investment? Illustrate.

4 Find advertisements to final consumers which illustrate the following types of advertising: (*a*) institutional, (*b*) pioneering, (*c*) competitive, (*d*) reminder. What objective(s) does each of these ads have? List the emotional and economic motives utilized in each of these advertisements.

5 A movie producer was comparing the cost of advertising in two magazines. He was planning to purchase a full-page ad in either one of the two magazines. The page rate in the first magazine was $2,000 and in the second magazine, $9,500. The circulation of the first magazine was 1 million in total and 300,000 teen-agers. The second magazine had a circulation of 5 million persons in total and 1 million teen-agers. Which would be the better buy? Which would be the better buy if the objective were to reach teenagers only? Would these magazines appear to be a good buy in view of this latter objective?

6 List the mass selling media which might be utilized by the advertising department of a large department store in a Commerce City. Then list the media which might be utilized by a small specialty shop in the same city. Would your answers be any different if these stores were located in a relatively small Centertown?

7 Describe the type of media which might be most suitable for promoting: (*a*) tomato soup, (*b*) greeting cards, (*c*) an industrial component material, (*d*) playground equipment. Specify any assumptions necessary to obtain a definite answer.

8 Discuss the use of testimonials in advertising. Which of the four AIDA steps might testimonials accomplish? Would they be suitable for all types of products? If not, for which types would they be most suitable?

9 Find an advertisement which seeks to accomplish all four AIDA steps and explain how you feel this advertisement is accomplishing each of these steps.

10 Discuss the future of independent advertising agencies now that the 15 percent commission system is not required.

11 Discuss the importance of advertising objectives to an advertiser and advertising agency seeking to avoid deceptive advertising.

12 Does mass selling cost too much? How can this be measured?

13 How would retailing promotion be affected if all local advertising via mass media such as radio, television, and newspapers were prohibited? Would there be any impact on total sales? If so, would it probably affect all goods and stores equally?

...Price can never be ignored in a marketing mix....the marketing
manager can have considerable latitude in pricing, but price
still must be compatible with the rest of the marketing strategy....
...in the long run, profits are squeezed until there is just
enough profit to encourage enough efficient firms to stay
in business.... Contrary to common belief, a profit
maximization objective may be desirable from a social
viewpoint....

23

Price and pricing objectives

Price is one of the four major variables that the marketing manager
controls. His Price decisions affect both the firm's sales and profits.

Uniqueness of the product, creative promotion, or simple availability may be more important than Price in some cases. But Price can
never be ignored when developing a marketing mix. Although customers sometimes behave as though they were ignoring Price – on
impulse items, for example – price always is a consideration. Many
customers treat a 39-cent bag of potato chips as an impulse item. They
want it and casually put down the money. But price that bag at $1 or $2,
and not many people will buy so casually. For purchases such as these,
price may not be the *determining* factor, but it is a *qualifying* factor,
since the price must remain within a reasonable range.

We reviewed demand and supply analysis in Chapter 10, but we did not define Price nor discuss price determination. In the following five chapters, we will discuss these matters together with the development of pricing objectives and policies and the impact of legislation on these policies. We will see that the marketing manager can have considerable latitude on pricing, but price still must be compatible with the rest of the marketing strategy. In this context, the needs and preferences of each target market will suggest or even establish certain price policies.

What is price?

Everyone has had experience with prices, so the answer to this question may seem obvious. In Chapter 10, we casually referred to "market price" and "equilibrium price" as these terms are traditionally used by the economist. Yet it is not quite so easy to define Price in real-life situations. Price, as we shall see, has many dimensions. It gives the alert marketing manager another opportunity to tailor his marketing mix to his target markets.

I'll tell you what I'm gonna do . . .

If you were offered a current model Ford station wagon for $1,000, would this be a good price for an automobile that normally sells for over $3,000? Or if you were offered bananas at a penny a pound that normally sell for 15 cents a pound in the supermarkets, would this be a good price? Or if you were offered a 21-inch television set for $100 when they normally sell for $200, would this be a good buy?

In each case, the first reaction would be an enthusiastic "Yes!" But wait a minute. It might be wiser to investigate further. The $1,000 for the Ford station wagon might be the price of a wreck worth only a few hundred dollars at the scrap yard. The penny-a-pound for bananas might be the price of bananas in large bunches – green bunches hanging on trees in South America, rather than at your local supermarket.

The $100 for the TV set might be a reasonable price for all its components in a parts bin at the factory. If you wanted these assembled, you would have to pay $25 extra. If you were interested in buying the cabinet, it would be an additional $25. But if you wanted a quality guarantee, there might be an added charge of $50.

The price equation: Price equals something

These examples emphasize that when a price is quoted, it is related to *some* assortment of goods and/or services. *Any transaction in our modern economy can be thought of as an exchange of money – the money being the price – for Something.*

This *Something* can be a physical product in various stages of completion, with or without the services normally provided with such products; with or without quality guarantees; with or without installation and instruction services and the assurance of repair facilities; and with or without packaging. And this "product" may or may not be conveniently available to you.

If the product is made available to channel members instead of final users or consumers, the price may be set so that each of the channel members has a chance to cover his costs and make a profit when he sells it at a higher price.

The nature and extent of this *Something* will determine the amount of money to be exchanged. Final consumers or users may pay the suggested "list price," or they may be able to obtain significant discounts or allowances because something is *not* provided. The possible variations are summarized in Figure 23–1 for consumers or users and in

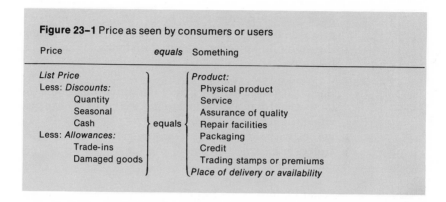

Figure 23–1 Price as seen by consumers or users

Price	equals	Something

List Price
Less: *Discounts:*
    Quantity
    Seasonal
    Cash
Less: *Allowances:*
    Trade-ins
    Damaged goods
	equals	*Product:*
		    Physical product
		    Service
		    Assurance of quality
		    Repair facilities
		    Packaging
		    Credit
		    Trading stamps or premiums
		Place of delivery or availability

Figure 23–2 for channel members. Some of these variations are discussed in the following pages to help make the point that price is a multidimensional variable.

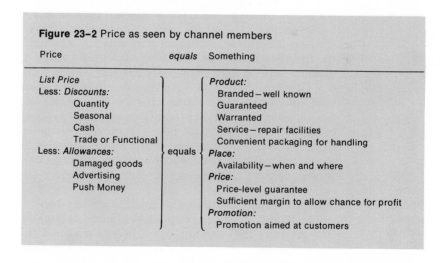

Figure 23–2 Price as seen by channel members

Price	equals	Something

List Price
Less: *Discounts:*
    Quantity
    Seasonal
    Cash
    Trade or Functional
Less: *Allowances:*
    Damaged goods
    Advertising
    Push Money
	equals	*Product:*
		    Branded—well known
		    Guaranteed
		    Warranted
		    Service—repair facilities
		    Convenient packaging for handling
		Place:
		    Availability—when and where
		Price:
		    Price-level guarantee
		    Sufficient margin to allow chance for profit
		Promotion:
		    Promotion aimed at customers

Some consumers get the surplus

First, however, we should note that not everyone gets merely his money's worth in a sales transaction. The price we are talking about is an equilibrium price related to demand and supply forces. You will recall that the demand curve which we discussed in Chapter 10 was generally downsloping and that some of the demand curve was above the equilibrium price. This is simply a graphic way of showing that *some* customers would be willing to pay more than the equilibrium price if they had to. In effect, some of them are getting a "bargain" by being able to buy at the equilibrium price. Economists have traditionally called these bargains the "consumer surplus."

There may be several list prices

Most price structures are built around *list prices*. How these list prices come to be determined is the subject of Chapters 24 and 25. For the moment, however, we must understand that there may be several list prices.

Basic list prices

Basic list prices are the prices that final consumers (or industrial customers) normally are asked to pay for goods. These prices may change when the firm decides to change its price level. But here, we are concerned with the list price structure, not with these price-level changes. Unless otherwise specified, the term "list price" here will refer to "basic list price."

Unchanging list prices— an administrative convenience

Some list prices are not changed over a period of time and may have little relation to market prices. They might have been set years ago with the expectation that continual adjustment would be needed. When price changes must be made, the add-ons or discounts are simply changed. The new current prices are calculated by adding or subtracting specific dollar or percentage amounts from the unchanging list prices. Since this method of changing prices avoids constant catalog revisions, it is often used in industries where frequent price changes are necessary. Rather than printing a complete new catalog, the firm can simply publish a new list of discounts or increases, applicable item by item or by broad product categories.

This method of changing prices does *not* give the marketing manager another way of varying his mix. It is merely an administrative device to reduce the cost of announcing price changes. It is important to know about such "list" prices, however, because firms may offer extremely impressive discounts from these so-called list prices. These prices are the ones some discount house customers are shown as the "costs" below which prices cannot be cut!

Phony list prices for bargain hunters

Sometimes, especially at the final consumer level, what might be called *phony list prices* are published so that customers can be shown that the price they are to pay has been discounted from "list."[1] Most businessmen, Better Business Bureaus, and government agencies

[1] The FTC has suggested that automobile prices are of this type. See "Do Auto Prices Mean What They Say?" *Business Week,* September 6, 1969, pp. 60–65.

frown upon this practice. But many customers, by equating discounts with value and savings, have encouraged the use of these jacked-up list prices. Some customers, in fact, seem more interested in the size of the purported discount than the price itself, and they can wind up paying more than the competitive market price.

List price may depend on who pays transportation costs

Retail list prices often include free delivery. Or free delivery may be offered to some customers as an aid to closing the sale. In short, what is included (or not included) in the retail list price may not be formally published. This helps the retailer adjust his marketing mix, depending on the needs and preferences (and interest or bargaining ability) of each customer.

Deciding who is going to pay the freight is more important on sales to intermediate customers than to final consumers, because more money may be involved. Usually purchase orders specify place, time, method of delivery, freight costs, insurance, handling, and other incidental charges. There are many possible variations here for an imaginative marketing manager, and a number of specialized terms have developed. A few are discussed in the following paragraphs:

F.O.B. the customer's doorstep

F.O.B. is a commonly used term regarding transportation. It means "free on board" some vehicle at some place, and typically is used in conjunction with *some named point,* that is, the location of the seller's factory or warehouse, as in "F.O.B." Detroit," "F.O.B. Chicago," etc. It means that the seller pays the cost of loading the merchandise onto some vehicle, usually a common carrier such as a truck, railroad car, or ship. At the point of loading, title to the goods passes to the buyer, who pays the freight and assumes responsibility for damage in transit, except as covered by the transportation agency.

Variations are made easily, however, by changing the *some named point* part of the terms. If the marketing manager wanted to pay the freight for the convenience of his customer, he could use: "F.O.B. delivered" or "F.O.B. buyer's factory" (or warehouse). In this case, title would not pass until the goods were delivered. If he did want title to pass immediately—but still wanted to pay the freight bill (and then include it in the invoice)—he could use: "F.O.B. seller's factory—freight prepaid."

In international marketing, terms must be specified even more carefully. Commercial practices vary among countries, and even competing carriers' rates can vary, so it is desirable to specify which carrier is to be used, how the shipment is to be routed, what the seller's and buyer's responsibilities are, and where they begin and end. The main objective here is to avoid misunderstanding and dispute, because

599

this could lead to long and costly litigation and damage to the commercial relationship.[2]

These terms help clarify the "something" that is being offered for the quoted list price. If the buyer pays the freight, the quoted price can be lower. If the buyer is to be responsible for damage in shipment—or at least for negotiations with the transportation agency in case of damage—then the seller's marketing manager can offer lower prices. Some marketing managers have strengthened their marketing mix by adjusting these terms to the wants of their target markets. By offering customers their preferred terms, the profit per unit might be increased, in addition to which total sales volume could be increased if more potential customers were more satisfied with this offering.

List price may depend on currency

The currency used in a price quotation in international trade is an important but technical matter that is beyond the scope of this text.[3] The problem is complex, since not all currencies are convertible to all others without restriction. Moreover, exchange rates fluctuate continually. A U.S. firm's price quotation of $100 in U.S. currency may mean a Canadian firm will have to pay $110 in Canadian currency one day and $109.50 the second day later. Thus, just a change in the exchange rate between U.S. and Canadian dollars may change the product's price in Canada and affect sales. Alternately, the U.S. firm could quote prices in Canadian dollars and expect varying dollar returns, depending on the exchange rate.

Quoting prices in U.S. dollars may be easier and advisable if the buyer's government will release dollars, but quoting in the local currency and three-way or barter arrangements may bring in sales that would be lost otherwise. Here is another opportunity for the imaginative businessman.

Some customers get discounts off list

Discounts are reductions from the list price that are granted by a seller to a buyer who either *foregoes some marketing function* or *provides the function for himself*. Discounts can be highly useful tools in marketing strategy planning.

In the following discussion, consider what function the buyer is foregoing or providing for himself when he obtains each of these discounts.

---

[2] For more extensive details on terms in foreign shipments, see Paul V. Horn and Henry Gomez, *International Trade Principles and Practices* (4th ed.; Englewood Cliffs, N.J.: Prentice-Hall, Inc., 1959), chaps. xxi–xxiv; Ronald Kramer, *International Marketing* (3d ed.; Cincinnati: South-Western Publishing Co., 1970), chap. viii; *Ex-* porter's Encyclopedia (annual; New York: Dun and Bradstreet); and *Revised American Foreign Trade Definitions* (National Foreign Trade Council, 1951).

[3] See Horn and Gomez, *op. cit.*, chaps. xiv, xxi, and xxii; Kramer, *op. cit.*, chap. viii; and A. O. Stanley, *Handbook of International Marketing* (New York: McGraw-Hill Book Co., 1963), chap. xi.

Sellers offer quantity discounts to *induce customers to purchase in larger quantities.* This enables the seller to get more of a buyer's business or shift some of the storing function to the buyer or reduce shipping and selling costs, or all of these. These discounts are of two kinds: cumulative and noncumulative.

Cumulative discounts apply to purchases over a given period— such as a year—and normally increase as the quantity purchased increases. Cumulative discounts are intended to encourage buying from a single company by reducing the price for additional purchases.

Noncumulative discounts are quantity discounts that apply to individual shipments or orders only. Such discounts encourage larger orders but do not tie a buyer to the seller beyond that one purchase.

Quantity discounts may be given in a number of ways. Some common methods are:

1. Based on the *dollar value* of the entire order. Orders over $50 might be allowed a 10 percent discount, and over $100 the discount might rise to 15 percent.
2. Based on *number of units purchased.* Men's shirts are sometimes sold at three for $10 or $4 each. One manufacturer of materials handling equipment quotes prices subject to the following discounts:

Units	Discounts
1–24	45 percent off list price.
25–49	48 percent off list price.
50 or more	51 percent off list price.

3. Based on the *size of the package purchased.* One drug wholesaler offers retailers a 40 percent discount when purchase is made in "shippers" (shipping cartons), but only 36 percent discount when purchases are made in less than "shippers." This encourages orders that permit the wholesaler to reship in original containers.

Quantity discounts usually are given in money—a reduction in the price—but sometimes they are given as free or bonus goods. In this case, customers receive one or more units "free" with the purchase of a specified quantity.

Quantity discounts can be a very useful variable for the marketing manager. Customers are eager to get them. But marketing managers must use quantity discounts, and especially cumulative quantity discounts, with care to avoid price discrimination. The Robinson-Patman Act states that quantity discounts must be based on actual cost savings to the seller, yet it is sometimes difficult to show these cost savings to the satisfaction of government officials. The impact of legislation on pricing is discussed more fully in Chapter 27.

Seasonal discounts are especially important within channels. They induce buyers to stock earlier than immediate demand would necessitate. This discount tends to shift the storing function farther along in the channel. The discount also tends to smooth out sales during the year and therefore permit year-round operation. If seasonal discounts are substantial, channel members may pass them along to their customers. In coal sales, seasonal discounts are given in the spring and summer all the way through the channel to final consumers and users.

Besides shifting the storing function, seasonal discounts may gain new business by tapping additional target markets during slack periods. By using seasonal discounts to win new business, even at a lower price, the marketing manager can help pay the overhead when business is slow. *Family Circle* magazine recently lowered off-season advertising rates by 10–15 percent to attract business to normally thin issues. And TV time salesmen regularly cut rates in the post-Christmas and summer months when audience viewing drops off.[4]

Seasonal discounts are given to offset a reduction in the something offered the buyer. Where physical goods are involved, a seasonal discount may mean that the buyer has to absorb the cost of carrying inventory. Many firms now try to shift the storing function because of the high cost of carrying inventory. There is also the risk of price changes during the longer storage period. Seasonal discounts often run to 5 to 10 percent of the usual list price to offset the burden being assumed by the buyer.

The special price reductions (or "free" goods) offered by grocery stores, gasoline stations, and department stores during their slow periods are a type of seasonal discount. Many businesses find a distinct seasonal pattern within each week, month, and the year. Although such price reductions may not be announced as seasonal discounts, the concept is the same. The marketing manager is attempting to make more effective use of his fixed facilities.

Final consumers often delay payment at a cost

Cash
discounts
should
encourage
prompt
payment

Most retail transactions, at least those involving small nondurable items, are on a cash or credit (with no charge) basis; no discounts for prompt payment are given. Such charge accounts are usually payable in full each month. Charge accounts often are provided as a convenience so that customers will not have to carry cash.

For major purchases of, say, clothing or expensive durable goods which last for several years, the regular monthly payment charge account with all payments due in 30 days is less practical. To pay for a new Easter outfit, a new car, or a living room furniture suite in one month is out of the question for many customers. Many merchants and sales finance companies, therefore, have set up plans to make it easier for consumers to buy more costly items. Payments, usually due monthly, may be stretched to 36 months at interest rates of 6 to 8 percent or more per annum on the *initial* balance. Since the balance owed declines as the payments are made, the effective rate of interest amounts to 12 to 16 percent or more.

These seemingly high rates are needed to cover the cost of borrowing money and the collection and repossession process. For some mer-

---

[4]*Business Week*, October 19, 1968, p. 92.

chants, granting credit can be a profitable business, perhaps more so than their basic business. Clearly, customers get a substantial discount by paying immediately or within the 30-day "free" period.

How cash discount terms look to channel members

Most sales to channel members and final users are made on credit. The seller issues an invoice, and the buyer sends it through his accounting department for payment. Many channel members come to depend on other members for temporary working capital, and therefore it is extremely important for both sides to clearly specify the terms of payment, including the availability of cash discounts. The following terms of payment frequently are used:

Net means that payment for the face value of the invoice is due immediately. These terms are sometimes altered to "net 10" or "net 30," which mean payment is due within 10 or 30 days of the date of the invoice.

1/10 net 30 means that 1 percent discount off the face value of the invoice is permitted if the invoice is paid within 10 days. Otherwise, the full face value is due within 30 days. And it usually is implied that an interest charge will be made after the expiration of that 30-day free credit period.

The due date for payment usually is based on the date of the invoice. This often is the date the goods are shipped, but a convenient alternate way for the seller to offer additional credit without changing his basic terms is to *advance* the date of the invoice. This practice is called "forward dating" and is sometimes used in extremely competitive situations. If a firm frequently forward dates its invoices, this practice may be formalized by stating the additional terms discussed below. All these special terms could be used in conjunction with basic terms such as *net 30* or *1/10 net 30.*

E.o.m. means end of month and gives free credit to the end of the month, when other terms apply. The terms 2/10 net 30 e.o.m. would mean that the invoice should be treated as though it were dated the first of the month following the date on the face of the invoice. In other words, if some goods were purchased on January 7, the invoice date might be January 7, but the 2 percent cash discount could be taken until February 10, more than a month after purchase.

Another type of special dating terms is *r.o.g.* or *a.o.g.* (receipt of goods, or arrival of goods). Under these terms, the discount period begins the day the purchaser receives the goods. These terms would also be in conjunction with basic terms, such as 2/10 net 30 *r.o.g.*

R.o.g. terms are especially useful when a marketing manager attempts to sell throughout a large geographical area because the terms could meet the objections of distant purchasers who don't want to pay for goods before they are received.

Why cash discounts are given and should be taken

A marketing manager may use cash discounts to obtain his money more quickly, to reduce his credit risk, or to reduce his credit and collection staff.

Cash discounts are used chiefly to encourage buyers to pay their bills promptly, and smart buyers take advantage of them. A discount of 2/10, net 30 may not look like very much, but any company that passes it up is missing a good financial opportunity because it would be money ahead to borrow at a bank to pay such invoices.

The 2 percent discount is earned for paying the invoice just 20 days sooner than it would have to be paid anyway. And if it is not taken, the company in effect is borrowing at an annual rate of 36 percent. That is, assuming a 360-day year and dividing by 20 days, there are 18 periods during which the firm could earn 2 percent – and 18 times 2 equals 36 percent a year.

In some trades, the cash discount is even more attractive and may run as high as 10 percent if the bill is paid within 10 days. These extremely attractive cash discounts are more like price cuts, since they probably cannot be justified for encouraging prompt payment.

While the marketing manager can use the cash discount as a marketing variable, in some cases a specific cash discount may be so firmly established in his industry that he cannot change or use it to suit his needs. He must grant the customary terms, even if he has no need for cash. Purchasing agents are aware of the attractiveness of cash discounts and will insist that the marketing manager offer the same terms normally offered by his competitors. In fact, some buyers automatically will deduct the accepted cash discount from their invoices regardless of the seller's invoice terms.

Cash terms are different in international trade

Financial resources usually are in shorter supply outside the United States, and you might expect to find more use of cash discounts abroad. This is not the case. Sellers in foreign countries are more concerned about collecting than prompt payment. They may be willing to extend credit up to 180 days for normal shipments, but usually will make financial arrangements through domestic and foreign banks to insure payment. On shipments requiring even longer credit terms, the marketing manager may seek a government guarantee against nonpayment or expropriation.[5]

Trade or functional discounts make channels work

A trade or functional discount is a list price reduction given to channel members in anticipation of a job they are going to perform.

A manufacturer, for example, might allow his retailers a 30 percent trade discount from the suggested retail list price to cover the cost of their retailing function and their profit. Similarly, the manufacturer might allow wholesalers a *chain discount* of 30 percent and 10 percent off the retail price. In this case, the wholesalers would be expected to pass the 30 percent discount on to retailers.

As an example, suppose the suggested retail price were $100. The wholesaler's selling price would be $70 (70 percent of $100), and the manufacturer's selling price would be $63 (90 percent of $70).

The wholesaler, according to our percentages, would be allowed

[5]Clarence J. Ruethling, *Financing Export Sales,* Management Aids for Small Manufacturers No. 149, February, 1963.

only $37 off the retail list price. It is important to note that a chain discount of 30 and 10 percent is not the same as a 40 percent discount, just as a chain discount of 50 percent and 50 percent does not represent 100 percent but, rather, 75 percent off the retail list price.

Trade discounts offered to wholesalers and retailers vary by trades, but they are based roughly on the operating expenses of each particular trade. The usual turnover rate of the specific merchandise and the required selling effort are important factors. One drug manufacturer gives 30, 10, 5, and 4 percent discounts to his wholesale customers – 30 percent for the retailers, and the rest for the wholesaler involved as follows: 10 percent for handling costs and 5 percent for profit, and 4 percent for selling effort.

Trade discounts might seem to offer a manufacturer or wholesaler's marketing manager great flexibility in varying his marketing mix, but in fact they may limit him greatly. The customary trade discount can be so well established that he has to accept it in setting his prices. More will be said about this in the next chapter.[6]

Some customers get allowances off list

Allowances are similar to discounts. They are given to final consumers or users for accepting less of "something," or adjusting for variations. Or they are given to channel members for providing a service, perhaps additional selling effort.

Bring in the old, ring up the new – with trade-ins

Trade-ins give the marketing manager a convenient way to reduce his price to the customer without reducing list price. An automobile buyer may be able to get a substantial discount by trading in his old car. But although he pays less than the list price for his new car, the "something" has varied. Once the deal is completed, he no longer has his old car.

Proper handling of trade-ins is especially important for the marketing manager who is selling durable goods, both to final consumers and intermediate customers. Customers buying machinery or buildings, for example, buy long-term satisfaction in terms of more manufacturing capacity. If the list price less the trade-in discount and the old equipment does not offer greater satisfaction or value – as the customer sees it – then no sales will be made.

Many firms replace machinery slowly, perhaps too slowly, because they value their old equipment more highly than the firm selling the new equipment. This same situation seems to apply to new cars. Customers want higher trade-ins for their old cars than their current market valuation. This prompts the use of high, perhaps "phony," list prices so that high trade-in allowances can be given.

---

[6]This discussion on discounts is based on G. E. Larson and M. N. Poteat, *Selling the United States Market* (Domestic Commerce Series, No. 29 [Washington, D.C.: U.S. Government Printing Office, 1951), pp. 73–76.

Damaged-goods allowances —less for less	Frequently, prices to both final consumers and intermediate customers are reduced because the goods they have bought or wish to buy were delivered soiled or damaged. To complete the transaction, the marketing manager makes a damaged-goods allowance, since the *something* is not as originally specified. (A damaged-goods allowance should be distinguished from a lower price offered on goods known to be "seconds." Such lower prices for seconds are offered as the original list price for an entirely different marketing mix.)

Advertising allowances —something for something	Manufacturers frequently give price reductions to firms farther along in a channel to encourage them to advertise, display, or otherwise promote goods locally. Channel system thinking is involved here. General Electric has given a 1.5 percent allowance to its distributors of housewares and radios who, in return, are expected to provide something—in this case, local advertising. Often manufacturers expect the middlemen to match their allowance in a joint effort called *cooperative advertising* (see Chapter 22, pp. 579–80).

P.M.'s— push for cash	Push Money or Prize Money allowances are similar to advertising allowances. They are given to retailers by manufacturers or wholesalers to pass on to the retailers' salesmen in return for aggressively selling particular items or lines. The P.M. allowances usually are reserved for new merchandise, slower moving items, or higher margin items, and are especially common in the furniture and clothing industries. A salesman, for example, might earn an additional $5 for each mattress of a new type sold.

Brokerage allowances —may be illegal	While brokerage allowances probably should be included under trade or functional discounts, they are treated separately because of their special legal status. Brokers normally are allowed a trade discount for their services. But sometimes large organizations, such as grocery chains, act as their own brokers and request the broker's trade discount in the form of a brokerage allowance. Under the Robinson-Patman Act, such brokerage allowances for buyers or buyers' representatives are now illegal. In highly competitive fields, however, the marketing manager may feel he has to grant such an allowance, perhaps calling it an advertising allowance but without any expectation of obtaining additional promotion. In effect, competitive pressures are pushing prices downward. This has been seen in the low-profit-margin grocery retailing industry where the buyer's ability to win extra allowances and favorable cash discounts may make the difference between profit and loss for the whole business.

The "something" obtained by final consumers may vary

The "something" in our price equation really consists of the rest of the marketing mix—all of the nonprice aspects. This something varies from one marketing strategy to another. So far we have discussed the major variables in the marketing mix, noting how interrelated they are. But there is one factor we have not yet examined – trading stamps.

Trading stamps may add that important "something" for some customers

Trading stamps frequently are used in lieu of price competition. For this reason, although they are sometimes considered an addition to the product or a promotional device, we will discuss trading stamps under pricing.

Retailers usually buy trading stamps from trading-stamp companies or set up their own plans and distribute stamps to customers at a cost of about 2 to 3 percent of the retail sales dollar. Customers can then redeem stamps for merchandise premiums or cash or goods at the merchant's own store.

Saving stamps has become almost a rite for many consumers, who feel they are getting something for nothing. It may be more accurate to say that they are getting something, but they *are* paying for it. In one test of customers' preferences for stamps in connection with gasoline purchases, about half of the customers preferred stamps, while the other half preferred cheaper gas.[7] Obviously, market grid awareness is important here. What should a retailer do if approximately half of his target market likes stamps and the other half does not?

Do stamps work?

There has been much controversy about the value and desirability of stamp plans, particularly concerning their effect on prices. It is difficult to generalize about this subject, since so many factors are involved, including the degree of competition and past market history.

Stamps have been very popular recently in grocery retailing, where the net profit margin is approximately 1 to 2 percent of sales. A stamp plan costing the retailer 2 to 3 percent of his sales would seem inevitably to push prices up. Yet this is not always the case. The increased cost of the stamps may be offset by reduced promotional expenditures or by a substantial increase in sales – both resulting from customers' eagerness to buy goods and get stamps. In the food business, however, it usually is necessary for sales to increase 10 to 15 percent before a stamp plan begins to be profitable.[8]

The early users of stamps in a community seem to gain a competitive advantage, but when competitors also start offering stamps, as some feel they must to meet competition, the advantage may be canceled. This is similar to competition in the product life cycle where innovators are copied and profits are squeezed.

Trading stamps have been spreading to other countries, too, and are received with mixed feelings by some businessmen abroad just as in the United States.

Many small businessmen, such as some filling station operators in the United States and some small shopkeepers in Britain, are vigor-

[7] "Buyer's Choice: Stamps or Savings," *Business Week*, February 7, 1970, p. 106.

[8] Albert Haring and Wallace O. Yoder (eds.), *Trading Stamps Practice and Pricing Policy* (Indiana Business Report, No. 27, Bureau of Business Research [Bloomington: Indiana University, 1958]), p. 301.

ously opposed to using stamps. The executive secretary of the Petroleum Congress (U.S.) calls giving stamps "a cancerous business practice."[9] And a spokesman for the 12,000-store Multiple Grocers Association in Britain says, "We have had the advantage of seeing what happened with stamps in the U.S. You have an initial competitive advantage; then your rivals have stamps and you lose the advantage. But you're stuck with the stamps."[10]

Stamps probably here to stay

There have been efforts to outlaw stamps, just as there are continuing efforts to outlaw various other promotional devices and certain kinds of advertising. It seems, however, that the larger and stronger stamp companies will likely continue for many years to come. The oldest one has operated since 1896.[11]

It appears that the rapid growth in the use of stamps is over, however. In grocery retailing, a drop in use has already occurred, in part because of the major inroads made by the food discounters. Now that some of the initial enthusiasm for stamp plans is subsiding, perhaps they can be seen in perspective as a potential addition to a marketing mix, perhaps in lieu of a price reduction. In some situations, stamp plans may be very effective, especially if half of the mass market would like stamps. Perhaps there will be room for both stamp and nonstamp stores in the future.[12]

The "something" for channel members may vary, too

The something offered channel members by the channel captain, perhaps the manufacturer, is the opportunity to participate in the implementation of a channel strategy. That is, the producer or channel captain should have in mind a product-market commitment and attempt to offer a marketing mix which will be attractive to potential channel members.

For channel members, it's the whole mix

For the money they pay, channel members receive a product, perhaps well branded, guaranteed, and specially packaged for easy handling. They may receive service or repair facilities. There may be promotional assistance from others in the channel, most often the producer.

[9] *Time,* October 26, 1962, p. 64.

[10] *Time,* May 17, 1963, p. 114.

[11] "Trading Stamps Start to Look More Like Money," *Business Week,* April 1, 1967, p. 68; "Are Trading Stamps Losing Their Punch?" *Business Week,* September 4, 1965, pp. 66–68.

[12] "Green Stamps Get the St. Louis Blues," *Business Week,* April 25, 1970, p. 32; "Supermarket Use of Trading Stamps Declines from 55% a Year Ago to 46% This Year," *Business Week,* June 1, 1968, p. 82; (reporting further declines in use) *Advertising Age,* May 11, 1970, p. 4; Fred C. Allvine, "The Future of

Trading Stamps and Games," *Journal of Marketing,* January, 1969, pp. 45–52; Bernard J. LaLonde and Jerome Herniter, "The Effect of a Trading Stamp Discontinuance on Supermarket Performance: A Panel Approach," *Journal of Marketing Research,* May, 1970, pp. 205–10; F. E. Brown and Alfred R. Oxenfeldt, "Price and Quality Comparisons between Stamps and Nonstamp Food Stores," *Journal of Retailing,* Fall, 1969, pp. 3–10; and F. E. Brown, "Price Movement Following the Discontinuance of Trading Stamps," *Journal of Retailing,* Fall, 1967, pp. 1–16.

Channel members may be offered national or regional advertising support, plus an advertising allowance for local promotion. And the channel captain should offer a price structure with enough margin to give each channel member an opportunity for profit.

Although pricing considerations are only part of the total mix, they are an important part. Much more is said about pricing in the following chapters, but here two additions to the "something" for channel members will be covered: price guarantees and profit guarantees. Both can be useful to a marketing manager.

A price is a promise

Manufacturers' marketing managers or channel captains sometimes give assurances to other channel members that their price structure will not change in the near future. Such assurances, called price guarantees, free other channel members from one of the risks of distribution.

Price guarantees are especially valuable to middlemen who, to provide their function effectively, must buy goods six months to a year in advance of sale. If they normally operate on a margin of 1 or 2 percent profit on sales, then any price decrease can quickly lead to losses—especially if competitors get supplies at the new lower prices. If there is any possibility of imminent price reductions, middlemen may balk at carrying out their normal accumulating function, and movement through the channel is slowed. A manufacturer's marketing manager may be able to improve the operation of a whole channel by giving a price guarantee.

Sometimes price guarantees take the form of an assurance that goods can be returned at their original prices or that rebates will be made if prices decrease. No such problem arises if prices increase. In this case, inventory stocks appreciate in value.

Guarantees against price decreases, however, are not always completely satisfactory. Once the granter announces such a guarantee, he may hold his list prices constant while market prices are declining. He avoids making good on a guarantee, even though the channel's competitors are cutting their prices and he is losing any goodwill he had achieved. Generally, though, a price guarantee would be valued by channel members and could be a very useful addition to a marketing mix.

A profit you can bank on

A variation on the price guarantee is the profit guarantee. This may take the form of an assurance that a certain volume will be sold at a given markup—or the channel member will be paid an equivalent profit.

A quality frozen-food manufacturer guaranteed profits to grocery stores that agreed to buy at regular prices and display practically its full line of products for a 90-day trial period. The manufacturer's purpose was to get distribution of his full line without giving special price concessions. Instead, he guaranteed certain minimum financial returns.

Pricing objectives should guide pricing

Pricing has many facets, and pricing objectives should be clearly specified to guide pricing policies and price determination. This sounds quite logical, but the setting of pricing objectives and related policies is actually neglected in many companies. In fact, a thorough understanding of price determination is comparatively rare. Some firms simply take the market price. Others use rather mechanical cost-plus pricing procedures accepted in the industry, seeing little opportunity for creative use of Price.[13]

Pricing objectives may be somewhat different from the other three-P objectives in that they flow more directly from company-level objectives. In fact, company-level objectives may constrain pricing by the marketing manager. This provides additional difficulties, because company objectives often are not stated or are so general as to be platitudes. Or they may not be compatible with each other. One study of 20 of the largest corporations in the United States found that although many did *not* have *written* pricing objectives, they did have pricing objectives—and sometimes several at the same time. Multiple and sometimes conflicting objectives were found by interviewing different executives! The relative importance of any one objective depended on the point of view of the man interviewed![14]

This seeming confusion about pricing objectives and pricing policies should emphasize the importance of careful study of price. Price is one of the marketing manager's four major variables, and haphazard or unimaginative handling of this variable is not likely to lead to maximum profits or any other specific objective—except by dumb luck.

Generally, pricing objectives should flow from overall company objectives. Indeed, the two may be synonymous, depending on how specifically the overall objectives are stated. For our purposes, we will not try to distinguish between the two. Rather, we will discuss some objectives that have definite pricing implications under three headings: profit-oriented objectives, sales-oriented objectives, and status quo objectives. This introductory discussion on pricing objectives is intended to be just that—an introduction to what pricing policies and pricing methods might seek to accomplish. The next two chapters will get into methods before we return to show the relation among methods, policies, and objectives.

The pricing objectives of the 20 large corporations mentioned earlier are presented in Table 23–1 and used below to make our dis-

---

[13] J. E. Anderson and E. C. Gassenheimer, *Pricing Arithmetic for Small Business Managers* (Management Aids for Small Manufacturers, No. 100 [Washington, D.C.: Small Business Administration, February, 1959]), p. 1.

[14] Robert F. Lanzillotti, "Pricing Objectives in Large Companies," *American Economic Review,* December, 1958, pp. 921–40. This was a continuation of the study by A. D. M. Kaplan, J. P. Dirlam, and R. F. Lanzillotti, *Pricing in Big Business* (Washington, D.C.: Brookings Institution, 1958).

cussion more concrete. Most of the following discussion will center around the objectives of larger companies because this is the only area where formal research has been done. Still, the evidence is scanty even here, since the companies that have specified objectives consider them private and have no reason to publish this information.

Profit-oriented objectives

By their
target
returns
know them

Seeking a target return is a common objective. The target may be a certain percentage return on sales or on investment or a fixed dollar amount of profit. The new target may be equal to or slightly above last year's return. Targets may be set for the short or long run.

The size of the desired short-run target return depends partly on industry or market practice, and partly on competition. Some companies deliberately set a relatively moderate objective to discourage potential competitors. But if little competition is expected, the company may set extremely high targets for the short run. The style or novelty of goods may be a factor in such a case.

In relatively stable or slowly expanding markets, a target return objective can have the desirable effect of leading to stable or slowly growing profits. A firm may select a target return that is consistent from year to year. If its competitors have similar objectives and use similar methods of price determination, then all may obtain their objectives. Their profits will tend to be stable through the years unless demand shifts markedly. When all the firms in a market have this objective, both profits and prices may be stable, and there will be little price competition. Instead, competition may shift to the other three P's.

Long-run targets are used by companies that have carved out markets for themselves or that are, at least, leaders in their fields, such as Alcoa, Du Pont, General Motors, International Harvester, and U.S. Steel.

For such companies, a long-run target return objective makes considerable sense. These companies might be considered public utilities. They are well aware that the public and the government are keeping an eye on them. They frequently play the role of price leaders and wage setters, and the public seems to expect them to follow a policy that is popularly referred to as being "in the public interest."

The pricing practices of large companies after World War II gave clear evidence of long-run target return pricing and a consciousness of public reaction. The large pent-up demand for goods coupled with the inadequate supply easily could have led to extremely high prices on products such as steel, building materials, and automobiles. The automobile manufacturers did raise prices, but not nearly so much as demand might have permitted. It was, instead, individual new- and used-car dealers who took advantage of the situation. Some raised prices considerably, often with mandatory extras. Some new-car dealers funneled new cars to "used-car" dealers who could obtain even higher prices without incurring the wrath of the manufacturers.

Table 23–1 Pricing goals of 20 large industrial corporations

Company	Principal pricing goal	Collateral pricing goals	Rate of return on investment (after taxes) 1947–55 average	range
Alcoa	20% on investment (before taxes); higher on new products (about 10% effective rate after taxes)	(a) "Promotive" policy on new products (b) Price stabilization	13.8	7.8–18.7
American Can	Maintenance of market share	(a) "Meeting" competition (using cost of substitute product to determine price) (b) Price stabilization	11.6	9.6–14.7
A & P	Increasing market share	"General promotive" (low-margin policy)	13.0	9.7–18.8
Du Pont	Target return on investment—no specific figure given	(a) Charging what traffic will bear over long run (b) Maximum return for new products—"life cycle" pricing	25.9	19.6–34.1
Esso	"Fair-return" target—no specific figure given	(a) Maintenance market share (b) Price stabilization	16.0	12.9–18.9
General Electric	20% on investment (after taxes); 7% on sales (after taxes)	(a) Promotive policy on new products (b) Price stabilization on nationally advertised products	21.4	18.4–26.6
General Foods	33⅓% gross margin: "⅓ to make, ⅓ to sell and ⅓ for profit"); expectation of realizing target only on new products	(a) Full line of food products and novelties (b) Maintaining market share	12.2	8.9–15.7
General Motors	20% on investment (after taxes)	Maintaining market share	26.0	19.9–37.0
Goodyear	"Meeting competitors"	(a) Maintain "position" (b) Price stabilization	13.3	9.2–16.1
Gulf	Follow price of most important marketer in each area	(a) Maintain market share (b) Price stabilization	12.6	10.7–16.7

Stay out of the courts and in business

The size of target returns varies considerably, as can be seen in Table 23–1. The average of the targets was 14 percent, after taxes. Only one was below 10 percent, and the highest was 20 percent.

The most frequent justifications for seeking a particular return were (1) fair or reasonable return in relation to risk—the public utility concept applied using past price and volume relationships, (2) desire to equal or better the previous returns, (3) desire to get what they thought they could get in the long run, something close to maximum profit, and (4) a means of stabilizing industry prices—if competing

Table 23–1 (*continued*)

Company	Principal pricing goal	Collateral pricing goals	Rate of return on investment (after taxes) 1947–55 average range	
International Harvester	10% on investment (after taxes)	Market share: ceiling of "Less than a dominant share of any market"	8.9	4.9–11.9
Johns-Manville	Return on investment greater than last 15-year average (about 15% after taxes); higher target for new products	(a) Market share not greater than 20% (b) Stabilization of prices	14.9	10.7–19.6
Kennecott	Stabilization of prices		16.0	9.3–20.9
Kroger	Maintaining market share	Target return of 20% on investment before taxes	12.1	9.7–16.1
National Steel	Matching the market— price follower	Increase market share	12.1	7.0–17.4
Sears, Roebuck	Increasing market share (8–10% regarded as satisfactory share)	(a) Realization of traditional return on investment of 10–15% (after taxes) (b) General promotive (low margin) policy	5.4	1.6–10.7
Standard Oil (Ind.)	Maintain market share	(a) Stabilize prices (b) Target return on investment (none specified)	10.4	7.9–14.4
Swift	Maintenance of market share in livestock buying and meatpacking		6.9	3.9–11.1
Union Carbide	Target return on investment	Promotive policy on new products; "life cycle" pricing on chemicals generally	19.2	13.5–24.3
U.S. Steel	8% on investment (after taxes)	(a) Target market share of 30% (b) Stable price (c) Stable margin	10.3	7.6–14.8

Source: Robert F. Lanzillotti, "Pricing Objectives in Large Companies," *American Economic Review*, Vol. 48, No. 5 (December, 1958), pp. 921–40.

firms have a similar target return objective, this may lead to essentially the same prices and a condition of stability.[15]

A target return objective has another advantage in a large company. It simplifies measuring and controlling the performance of the many divisions and departments, all of which are using capital. Some companies will eliminate divisions or drop products not yielding a certain predetermined rate of return on investment. Naturally, then, man-

[15] Much of this section is based upon Lanzillotti, *ibid.*

agers use target return pricing, trying to hit this desired figure. It isn't easy. Too large a return may invite government action. Too small a return may put the division out of business.

Profit maxi-
mization
has its
supporters

Does high morality mean low profits?

Objectives seeking to maximize profits might be stated as a desire to achieve profit growth and rapid return on investment or, more bluntly, "all the traffic will bear."

Profit maximization objectives seem to be found more frequently among smaller firms, especially small merchants and manufacturers who are out of the public limelight or who have successfully carved out their own market.[16]

One small industrial tool manufacturer, for example, is well aware that the demand for his product is highly inelastic, and he acts accordingly. He gives attractive margins to channel members and sets his own price to allow for substantially more than a 100 percent markup on his production cost. But such profits may lead to competition, as the small tool manufacturer now knows. Even though he has fairly strong patent protection on his basic product, the company has had to improve it continually and use aggressive promotion to maintain its profit position among the many competitors its success has attracted. Examples such as this one make some economists feel that profit seeking and the resulting competition encourage a dynamic economy and economic growth.

Some business executives seem reluctant to admit that they hold a profit maximization objective. Not all hold the strong beliefs of the president of Cummins Engine Company, who says: "The idea that the highest morality brings the lowest profit does not necessarily apply. If we concentrate on giving the consumer what he needs at a price favorable to him, profits roll in as a by-product."[17]

High profits need not mean high prices

The public, and many businessmen, have come to associate a profit maximization objective with high prices and monopolies. Many people feel that anyone attempting to maximize profits is operating contrary to the public interest. In the United States, public fear of a profit maximization objective probably has its origins historically in the pricing behavior of some companies who obtained a public utility type of monopoly during the late 1800's. Railroads, in particular, are frequently cited.

Economic theory, however, does not support this reaction. Profit maximization does not necessarily lead to high prices. True, if competition cannot offer effective substitutes, then demand and supply *may* bring extremely high prices. But this happens *if, and only if,*

[16]W. Warren Haynes, *Pricing Decisions in Small Business* (Lexington: University of Kentucky Press, 1962).

[17]*Time,* September 29, 1961, p. 86.

demand is highly inelastic. If demand is highly elastic, it might be in a monopolist's interest to charge relatively low prices so that sales will be expanded.

Most markets with extremely inelastic demand curves have been regulated, as in the case of the transport systems and utilities. Aside from these, relatively few monopolies exist today. Most firms have direct competitors within their own industry, and industry and target market boundaries are not rigidly fixed. Other firms are always trying to offer substitutes. Even steel, often cited as a near-monopoly, has intraindustry competition, both domestic and foreign, and also interindustry competition from substitute materials such as aluminum and plastics.

Please do squeeze the profits

Profit maximization can have desirable results for both business and consumers. Profit can be viewed as a return for efficiency. If the customer is served poorly, there might be no profit at all. If he is served more adequately, profit may be larger. A firm should be allowed to reap the benefits of its efficiency. Competitors will see the company's high profits and want to emulate it. In this way, competition—even the monopolistic competition variety—will eventually reduce profits (and probably prices, too).

In the long run, profits are squeezed until there is just enough profit to encourage enough efficient firms to stay in the business. We saw this process at work in Chapter 14 in the rise and fall of profits during the life cycle of a product. Contrary to common belief, a profit maximization objective may be desirable from a social viewpoint.[18] Much of our discussion on price determination will be aimed at implementing this objective.

After the entre-preneurs, just satisfaction

Although the pricing study just cited did not find any firms admitting that their goal was *satisfactory* profits, some management theorists maintain that this is the level of profit sought by some businessmen today. To be sure, they work for profits, but they aren't nearly as aggressive as they might be if they were seeking maximum profits. They do want to convince stockholders of their competence and assure the firm's survival, but as long as profits are *satisfactory* for these purposes, they will have achieved their ends.

"Satisficing" may be a characteristic of present-day administrators as distinct from the original entrepreneurs of the business world.[19] It is clear that the administrator whose goal is satisfactory profits might find it easier to pursue several pricing objectives than the administrator who is seeking a specific target return or maximum profits. Perhaps the study of pricing objectives in large companies was based primarily on interviews with "satisficers!"

---

[18] For a more extensive discussion of these ideas, see Claude Robinson, *Understanding Profits* (Princeton, N.J.: D. Van Nostrand Co., Inc., 1962).

[19] For more discussion of the behavior of satisficers, see Herbert A. Simon, *Administrative Behavior* (2d ed.; New York: Macmillan Co., 1961).

Sales-oriented objectives

Does big growth mean big profit?

Some business executives seem more concerned about growth in sales than in profits. One economist states that "the typical large corporation in the United States seeks to maximize not its profits but its total revenues, which a businessman calls his sales."[20]

One reason advanced for the popularity of the sales growth objective is the tendency to equate growth with profitability. Yet the two are not always corollaries. Since World War II, major corporations have faced a continuing profit squeeze while sales have grown. Average returns on investments have dropped to the 5 to 10 percent level, depending on the industry and line of trade. Excessive emphasis on sales growth has been partly responsible. More recently, however, this fallacy has been recognized, and some companies now are trying to determine whether growth does, in fact, lead to more profit.

Another explanation of the popularity of growth-oriented objectives is that the administrator's salary may be more closely related to sales than to profits.[21] As noted in Chapter 21, compensation systems should be used to get desired results. Here it seems that compensation systems may have had a bearing on the selection of corporate objectives rather than vice versa.

Getting your share, getting enough

Maintaining market share—the percentage of the market you are "entitled" to because of your size and reputation—seems to be extremely important to some business executives. Maintaining market share is such an important objective to certain larger companies, especially grocery manufacturers, that they seem willing to forego other objectives to reach this highly measurable goal.

It is fairly easy to determine by surveys whether a company has maintained its percentage of the market. This is much easier to measure than whether profits are being maximized. Consequently, as long as some profit is returned, managers seem to prefer emphasizing market share instead, especially if job promotions are based on market share performance!

Don't rile the government— do be on the offensive

Note, however, that some large companies do not want more than a certain percentage of the market. Why? The reasons vary among firms.

Some companies don't want to rile or arouse government officials. Some observers feel that General Motors is not as aggressive as it could be in certain markets because it doesn't want to get substantially more than 50 percent of the market. One GM executive, commenting on his corporation's share of the market, stated: "Yes, it's a little

---

[20] W. J. Baumol, "On the Theory of Oligopoly," *Economica*, August, 1958, p. 187.

[21] Joseph W. McGuire, John S. Y. Chiu, and Alvar O. Elving, "Executive Incomes, Sales and Profits," *American Economic Review*, September, 1962, pp. 753–61; "For the Chief, Sales Sets the Pay," *Business Week*, September 30, 1967, p. 174.

better. Our market penetration in March was under 53 percent. In February, you remember, we took more than 57 percent."[22]

Viewed from another standpoint, some managers want only a relatively small percentage of a market because they would rather be on the offensive, trying to gain an additional share or maintain their share, than to achieve a temporary success and then be on the defensive. Johns-Manville and General Electric officials indicate that, for this reason, they would prefer to have 20 to 25 percent of a market than 50 percent.[23] This is like the rationale leading to the sales expansion objectives and may result from the compensation system used.

Aggressive and especially smaller companies often emphasize an objective of *increasing* their market share or even dominating a market. In some businesses, economies of scale can be gained by larger operations, and a firm may work both to increase market share and maximize profits. In other cases, however, firms blindly follow the market expansion goal, and this leads to pricing goods practically at cost in order to get more of the market. These growth preferences sometimes lead to profitless prosperity, where slight miscalculations may lead to bankruptcy.

Status quo objectives

More time for golf or action elsewhere

These can be described as *don't-rock-the-boat* objectives. The purpose of these objectives is stated variously as "meeting competition," or "avoiding competition," or "stabilizing prices."

Often a status quo objective is held by a conservative management that wishes to minimize the risk of loss, preferring instead a comfortable way of life and some assurance of profit. Maintaining stable prices may forestall competition and eliminate the need for hard decisions, and managers may have more time for golf.

On the other hand, status quo pricing objectives can be part of an extremely aggressive marketing strategy. The *pricing* objective may seem conservative, but the intention could be to avoid price competition in favor of aggressive action on one or more of the other P's. If a company chooses to hold a status quo objective regarding pricing, it should have either aggressive objectives in one or more of the other P's or an extremely strong customer franchise. Otherwise, the continuing pressure of time along the product life cycle will lead to poor results. A firm may de-emphasize price in its marketing mix, but it cannot de-emphasize marketing generally and hope to survive.

A number of the large firms listed in Table 23–1 admitted to status quo objectives, yet they are aggressive in other respects. Examples include American Can, Esso, General Electric, Goodyear, Gulf, Johns-Manville, Kroger, Standard Oil (Ind.), and U.S. Steel.

[22]*Wall Street Journal*, April 18, 1962, p. 1.
[23]Lanzillotti, *op. cit.*

Conclusion

The Price variable has many facets and offers an alert marketing manager many possibilities for varying marketing mixes.

Most price structures have a basic list price from which varying discounts and allowances are subtracted. Among the discounts discussed in this chapter are quantity, seasonal, cash, and trade or functional discounts. We also discussed trade-ins, and damage, advertising, and brokerage allowances. Special terms, such as F.O.B., specify more clearly the nature of the Something; which party is to assume the freight and other charges, and where and when the title is to pass.

The Something that is offered for a price really represents the total marketing mix (except Price) being developed for a particular target market. It may even include such things as trading stamps or profit guarantees.

How prices are set and which prices are set depends on pricing objectives. We examined profit-oriented, sales-oriented and status quo-oriented objectives. We saw that some companies have multiple objectives, perhaps because different executives hold different objectives. Ideally, objectives should be clearly stated and *written*, because they provide direction for subsequent pricing policies.

Pricing objectives should be consistent with the company's overall objectives. A company might choose rather conservative status quo pricing objectives while following a very aggressive marketing strategy. The purpose would be to de-emphasize the highly visible and easily imitated price variable in favor of other elements of a marketing mix.

Throughout this chapter, we have assumed that a list price had already been established. We have placed primary emphasis on what may be included (or specifically excluded) in the "something" and what objectives a firm might have to guide its pricing policies. The critical matter of price determination itself was not discussed. We will cover this in the next two chapters, showing ways of implementing the various pricing objectives.

QUESTIONS AND PROBLEMS

1 Indicate what the final consumer really obtains when he (she) pays the list price for the following "products": (a) an automobile, (b) a portable radio, (c) a package of frozen peas, (d) a lipstick in a jeweled case.

2 Explain what the retailer gets for the products in Question 1 when paying the wholesale price. Explain what the wholesaler obtains from the manufacturer when paying the manufacturer's price for the same products.

3 Explain how a marketing manager might change his F.O.B. terms to make his otherwise competitive marketing mix more attractive.

4 Some critics have suggested that the manufacturer ought to be responsible for all guarantees and warranties on his products and include the cost of this service in his price. How would this affect our marketing structure? What role would wholesalers and retailers play in such a system? Would promotion be more or less important? What would happen to prices?

5 Are seasonal discounts appropriate in agricultural businesses (which are certainly seasonal)?

6 What are the "effective" annual interest rates on the following cash discount terms: (a) 1/10 net 60, (b) 1/5 net 10, (c) net 30, (d) 1/10 net 30 e.o.m. for goods bought on November 20, (e) 3/10 net 30 r.o.g. (goods shipped on November 15 and received on December 15).

7 What is the manufacturer's selling price if he grants trade discounts of 30, 20, and 10 percent off a list price of $200 per unit? What might these discounts be allowed for?

8 Evaluate the use of trading stamps. In what lines or in what situations would they be most appropriate? Would they have any value for use among middlemen? Why or why not?

9 How might a company's pricing objectives vary depending on the point of view of the price maker? Consider the objectives which might be held by the: production manager, controller, and sales manager.

10 If Alcoa's pricing objective is a 10 percent return on investment after taxes, how can its average return of 13.8 percent for the period 1947–55 be explained? Note that its range during this period was from 7.8 to 18.7 percent.

11 In view of A&P's policy of low-margin selling, how can a return on investment after taxes of 13 percent be explained, when Kroger, a company which has not pursued a low-margin policy, had a rate of return of only 12.1 percent during the same period (1947–55)?

12 Which of the 20 large corporations seem to be consciously following a profit maximization policy?

13 Discuss the implementation of General Food's objectives.

14 How would the acceptance of a profit-oriented, or a sales-oriented, or a status quo-oriented pricing objective affect the development of a company's marketing strategy?

...cost-oriented pricing is not as simple or foolproof as it
might seem at first glance....

...cost-oriented pricing frequently yields a price that is "too
high." This causes slow turnover and low profits or even
losses....

...although the break-even approach can bring various
prices into the analysis, it can also lead to less than optimum
results unless the prices used are related to demand.

24

Price determination — cost-oriented

In the previous chapter, we accepted the fact that a list price can be
established in a number of ways. Now we will go on to see how a list
price might be set by an individual firm.

Although in practice there are many ways of arriving at a price,
these can be reduced, for simplicity, to two basic methods: (1) cost-
oriented and (2) demand-oriented price determination. We will discuss the cost-oriented approach in this chapter and the demand-
oriented approach in Chapter 25.

Neither
simple nor
foolproof

Cost-oriented pricing is quite commonly used because most accounting systems accumulate the costs of doing particualr tasks, and
profit-and-loss statements show very clearly that all costs must be
covered. Costs provide a floor below which prices cannot go (for long,

anyway), and it is only logical that prices should be built on seemingly precise cost data.

As we will see, however, cost-oriented pricing is not as simple or foolproof as it might seem at first glance. We will begin our discussion by examining how retailers, wholesalers, and producers set cost-oriented prices.

Pricing by wholesalers and retailers

A case can be made for tradition

Most retail and wholesale prices are determined by a cost-oriented markup approach, using the traditional markups taken in those trades. The markup is normally the trade or functional discount allowed by the previous channel members. Using this method, the retailer or wholesaler adds a markup to the delivered cost of his goods.

Generally, the trade discounts or traditional markups are applied rather mechanically. Some retailers or wholesalers, in fact, use the same markup for all of their goods – which, if nothing else, certainly simplifies their pricing procedure. Other retailers (and sometimes wholesalers) may take a higher markup on some items because of their apparent quality or their slow turnover. Or they may take a lower markup to meet competitive prices or because they feel consumers will not accept the price set by using the traditional markups.

In general, though, wholesalers and retailers use the traditional markups. This is true especially in larger firms where management may be reluctant to delegate pricing to a large number of retail clerks who may have relatively little experience.

Considering the large number of items the average retailer and wholesaler carries and the small sales volume of any one item, this cost-oriented markup approach to pricing seems both reasonable and practical. Spending the time and effort to determine the best price to charge on every item in stock, day to day or week to week, probably would not pay for itself.

It will be helpful to understand how retailers usually determine a selling price, and a discussion of this follows. Wholesalers follow essentially the same procedure.

There are two kinds of markups

Suppose a retailer buys an article for $1. To make a profit the retailer obviously must sell this article for more than its cost. If the retailer adds 50 cents to the selling price of the article to cover his operating costs and provide a profit, we say that he is marking up the item 50 cents.

Markups, however, generally are expressed as percentages rather than dollar amounts. And this is where the difficulty begins. Is a markup of 50 cents on a cost of $1 a markup of 50 percent? Or should the markup be computed as a percentage of the selling price – $1.50 – and therefore be 33⅓ percent? A clear definition is necessary.

We will use the following definition: Unless otherwise specified, *markup means "percentage of selling price."* By this definition, the 50-cent markup on the $1.50 selling price is a markup of 33⅓ percent.

Markups are related to selling price for convenience. For one thing, the markup on selling price is roughly equivalent to the gross margin,[1] which is computed in relation to total sales. Most businessmen have a full appreciation of the concept of gross margin because they continually see gross margin data on their profit-and-loss statements. They know that unless there is an adequate gross margin, there will not be any profits left at the end of the period. For this reason, businessmen readily accept traditional markups that are close to their gross margins.

Relating markups to the selling price also is consistent with our emphasis on the consumer rather than internal considerations, such as cost. There is nothing wrong, however, with the concept of markup on cost. The essential thing is to clearly indicate which markup we are using, to avoid confusion. Some retailers use the term *mark-on* to indicate a markup based on cost, but this is by no means common. In the everyday world, the terms are often interchanged rather haphazardly.

Some retailers frequently need to convert a markup on cost to one based on selling price, or vice versa. Conversion tables have been developed for this purpose, but they are not essential because the calculations are simple.[2]

Markup chain may be used in channel pricing

A chain of markups can set the price structure in a whole channel. A markup is figured on the selling price at each level of the channel—by producers (if they use this approach to pricing), wholesalers, and retailers. The producer's marked up selling price to the wholesaler becomes the wholesaler's cost; the wholesaler's marked up selling price to the retailer becomes the retailer's cost; and his marked up cost becomes the retail selling price. Each markup is expected to cover the expenses of selling and administration and to leave a profit. Figure 24–1 shows how a markup might be used at each level of a channel system.

This illustration starts with a production cost (factory cost) of $21.60. In this case, the producer is taking a 10 percent markup and sells the goods for $24. The markup is 10 percent of $24 or $2.40. The producer's selling price now becomes the wholesaler's cost—$24. If the wholesaler is accustomed to taking a 20 percent markup on selling price, his markup is $6, and his selling price becomes $30. The wholesaler's selling price of $30 now becomes the retailer's cost. And if the retailer is accustomed to a 40 percent markup, he adds $20 and the retail selling price becomes $50.

Fallacy of high markups

Final consumers often are shocked by a retail markup of 50 or 60 percent. They immediately think of this as "price gouging" which creates exorbitant profits. Yet some retailers and wholesalers strive in

---

[1] This includes all costs beyond the product itself: the ratio of sales and administrative expenses plus profit to net sales—usually expressed as a percent. See Appendix on Marketing Arithmetic at the end of the book.

[2] See "Markup Conversion," in the Appendix on Marketing Arithmetic.

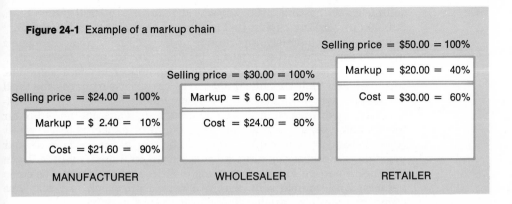

Figure 24-1 Example of a markup chain

MANUFACTURER

Selling price = $24.00 = 100%

Markup = $ 2.40 = 10%

Cost = $21.60 = 90%

WHOLESALER

Selling price = $30.00 = 100%

Markup = $ 6.00 = 20%

Cost = $24.00 = 80%

RETAILER

Selling price = $50.00 = 100%

Markup = $20.00 = 40%

Cost = $30.00 = 60%

vain for larger profits with higher markups. Instead, if they were primarily concerned with increasing their total profit or return on investment, they probably should be more concerned about the profit achievable with various markups than about the size of the markup itself. Full appreciation and use of this idea helps account for the spectacular success of the mass marketers. Why?

The fallacy of seeking high profits through high markups can be seen by an extreme example. A 90 percent markup on selling price may not be nearly as profitable as a 10 percent markup on selling price! This apparent paradox is easy to understand if we assume an extreme condition in which no units are sold at the high markup, but a very large number are sold at the low one. The key is *turnover*. You cannot earn much if you don't sell much, regardless of the size of the markup. Nevertheless, many retailers and wholesalers seem more concerned with the size of their markup than with their total profit.

Markups varied, turnover faster, profits up

Not *all* retailers and wholesalers, however, are enamored with the traditional markups. Some are concerned with speeding turnover to increase profit, even if this means reducing the markup. They see themselves running an ongoing system that is incurring costs of operation as a function of time and the volume of goods handled. If they can sell a much greater volume of goods in the same time period, they may be able to take a lower markup on such items and still have a higher profit at the end of the time period.

An important concept in this connection is the *stockturn rate* – the number of times the average inventory is sold in a given time period, such as a year. Various methods of computing a stockturn rate are used, but they are all involved with how many times the average inventory is sold.[3] If the stockturn rate is low, this may be undesirable for profits.

At the very least, a slow stockturn will increase cost by tying up working capital. If the stockturn were 1 (once per year) rather than 5,

[3] See "Computing the Stockturn Rate," in the Appendix on Marketing Arithmetic.

selling goods costing $100,000 would require $100,000 rather than $20,000 in working capital just to carry the necessary inventory.

Turnover is obviously important in profit and financial planning and may determine whether a particular firm can afford to operate in a certain line. Newcomers to retailing often appear not to understand turnover, and their lack of capital forces narrow assortments and then bankruptcy when the goods fail to move quickly.

What constitutes high or low stockturn depends on the industry. For instance, an annual rate of 1 or 2 might be expected in the retail jewelry industry, while 40 to 50 would be typical for fresh fruits and vegetables. Comparison among firms within an industry will indicate whether a particular firm is turning over its stock as rapidly as competitors. And comparisons within a firm, from week to week, and month to month, by product line can help spot troubles.

Living too high on the markup hurts the image

The use of high, inflexible markups can have a damaging impact on the image and subsequently on the profits in an industry. Hardware retailers, for example, have been especially inflexible about markups and this has led to real difficulties.

A study by the National Retail Hardware Association, a trade association of hardware retailers, found that fewer than 100 items in the average hardware store were bought on the basis of price. Since many hardware retailers traditionally have marked up all items 50 percent *on cost*, consumers have felt that hardware stores were high priced and have traded there only to get items unobtainable elsewhere. This has meant relatively low total profits for hardware retailers. For thousands of their items, the turnover is so low that even the normal 50 percent markup yields no profit.

To convince its members of the cause-effect relation of turnover and profit, the National Retail Hardware Association has developed a *Turnover Handbook* which strongly urges the abandonment of the practice of marking up all goods by 50 percent of cost. Instead, it suggests classifying about 5,000 different items into six categories, on the basis of demand sensitivity.

In the "A" category are goods that should be sold competitively. The markup for these items vary from a 45 percent markup in a small town to only 10 percent in a large city where there is greater competition. The "A" category includes only a relatively small number of items but involves the store image; it is important that the store be competitive on these items.

The *Handbook* suggests that goods in the other five categories be marked up progressively, the last group to more than 100 percent of cost. The items for which the highest markups are suggested are (1) those carried as a community service—low-priced items with a low turnover—and (2) high-priced items that require extensive product knowledge to sell.[4]

---

[4] "Handbook Teaches Dealers How to Sell," *Printers' Ink,* March 27, 1959, pp. 65–69.

| Grocers run a fast company | Grocery supermarket operators have shown that they understand the importance of turnover. They have been more flexible than the hardware retailers and many smaller grocers, too. The big grocers put only small markups on fast-selling items such as sugar, shortening, soaps and detergents, canned milk, soups, desserts, beverages, baby foods, pet foods, bleaches, flour, and canned vegetables. Sugar, for example, may carry a margin of 8 percent; shortening, 9 to 10 percent; soaps and detergents, 10 or 11 percent. |

Since supermarket expenses run 16–18 percent of sales, some people feel that many of these items are carried at a loss. But since such figures are storewide averages, this need not be true.

Fast-moving goods generally are less expensive to stock and sell. They occupy valuable space for shorter periods, are damaged less, and tie up less working capital. Lower markups will cover the costs of these items and make a profit too. With lower markups, the goods may turn even faster, and a small profit per unit will be earned more frequently.

These fast-moving goods may be more profitable per item, in spite of the low margins, because of the higher turnover. The average turnover in the grocery department in one study was 14 times a year. Yet sugar turned over 31 times, beverages 28 times, shortening 23 times, and soups 21 times.

It should be noted here that the high-margin items were not necessarily unprofitable. They simply were not as profitable *per item* as some of the low-margin items.[5]

| Discounters are running faster | The modern food discounters and mass merchandisers carry the fast-turnover concept of the supermarket even further. By pricing even lower and attracting customers from wider areas who purchase in substantial quantities (perhaps the economic shopper), they are able to operate profitably on even smaller margins. The same argument can be used to explain why discount houses were able to operate on so much lower margins than the traditional department stores. They picked the product lines which they felt they could move in large volume, cut the prices (and perhaps services), and sold two or more times the volume of goods per square foot of selling space.[6] |

| Varied markups may imply demand consideration | The use of varied markups and careful attention to stockturn rates seems to imply that the retailer has an interest in demand. Nevertheless, most of the retailers and wholesalers using varied markups do so from custom or habit, not because they have analyzed the demands of their target markets.[7] Firms which are using varied markups and have a full recognition of demand seem to be the exceptions, not the rule. |

[5] *Super-Valu Study* (New York: *Progressive Grocer*, 1957), p. S–4–7.

[6] See a study of A&P's customers by *Progressive Grocer* as referred to in "Discount Grocery Shopping," *Detroit Free Press*, August 18, 1970, p. 4–B.

[7] "Colorado Seedsmen Admonished for Obsolete Pricing Methods," *Western Feed & Seed*, January, 1963, p. 37; and "Pricing Practices of American Enterprise," *Business Record*, September, 1958.

Some small firms seem to be less rigidly tied to cost-oriented pricing than larger firms.[8] And some department stores have been using sales and cost analysis procedures (to be discussed more carefully in Chapter 29) to determine the prospective profit contribution of any *item* of merchandise, given various markups. This, however, is difficult to do in a large retail establishment handling many items; as an alternative, some stores have developed cost patterns for *groups of* similar products.[9]

Pricing by producers

It's up to the captain to set the list price

Some markups eventually become customary in a particular trade whether retailers and wholesalers use a common markup for all items or whether they vary their markups. Most of the channel members will tend to follow a similar markup process, adding a certain percentage to the previous price. Who determines price in the first place?

The basic list price usually is determined by the channel captain—a large retailer, a large wholesaler, or most often the producer. Here we are concerned with the pricing approach of such firms, and for convenience we will call them "producers."

Producers commonly use some cost-oriented approach. They may start with a dollar-cost-per-unit figure and add a markup, perhaps a customary percentage, to obtain the selling price. They may be guided by a rule-of-thumb formula such as: *production cost × 3 = selling price*. In the electronics industry, a customary formula is: *price = material cost + direct labor cost + 100 percent of direct labor for overhead + 120 to 180 percent of direct labor for all other costs*.[10]

Each producer usually develops his own rules and markups in the light of his own costs and objectives. Yet even the single step of selecting the appropriate cost per unit to build on is no simple matter. So we must discuss several approaches to see how cost-oriented price determination really works.

The cost-plus method

Naïve, simple, and dangerous

One simple and common approach to price determination—the naïve cost-plus method—consists of adding a "reasonable" markup to the cost per unit. The cost per unit is found by assuming that all the inventory has been sold during a specific period, such as the past

[8]W. Warren Haynes, *Pricing Decisions in Small Business* (Lexington: University of Kentucky Press, 1962), p. 152.

[9]See a special issue of the *Journal of Retailing* devoted exclusively to merchandise management accounting, Spring, 1958; and "Pinning Down Retailing Costs," *Business Week* October 19, 1957, pp. 134–38.

[10]"Management Problems in the Electronics Industry," *Management Research Summary*, Small Business Administration, November, 1962, p. 3.

month, then taking the total cost for that period and dividing this figure by the number of units produced and sold in the same period.

If the total cost of the latest month were $5,000 for labor and materials and $5,000 for fixed overhead expenses (such as selling expenses, rent, and executive salaries), then total cost would be $10,000. If the company produced 10,000 items in the previous month, the average cost was $1 a unit. To get the price, the producer decides how much profit markup per unit seems "reasonable," then adds this figure to the cost per unit. If 10 cents were considered a reasonable profit for each unit (perhaps they had a target return of $1,000 a month), the new price would be set at $1.10.

The chief merit of this approach is its simplicity. This is also its weakness. To see why, we will observe this firm further.

If, in the next month, only 5,000 units are produced and sold, the firm may be in trouble. Five thousand units sold at $1.10 each would yield a total revenue of $5,500. The overhead would still be fixed at $5,000, and material and labor costs probably would amount to $2,500, for a total of $7,500. This would mean a loss of $2,000 or 40 cents a unit. The method that seemed to allow for a profit of 10 cents a unit instead would cause a loss of 40 cents a unit.

It is apparent that this naïve cost-plus method does not adjust for cost variations at different levels of output. Since all costs do not behave the same way as sales expand or contract, the average cost per unit may change considerably as output rises or falls. The following paragraphs explain these variations.

Many costs make one price

One reason the naïve cost-plus approach fails is that total cost includes a variety of costs, and each of these changes in a different way as output changes. Any method that uses costs as the basis for determining prices must make allowance for these variations. The more realistic approach described below does so.

To fully understand this method, however, it will be desirable first to define and illustrate six types of cost. An understanding of the differences among these costs is important because these differences are at the root of the problems many companies have with pricing.

Total fixed cost is the sum of those costs that are fixed in total regardless of output level. Among these fixed costs are rent, depreciation, executive salaries, property taxes, and insurance. Such costs must be paid even if production stops temporarily. Over a period of years, fixed costs can change—the factory may be expanded or sold; new executives may be hired or fired. But in the short run, total fixed cost is set.

Total variable cost, on the other hand, is the sum of those variable expenses that are closely related to output level—expenses for components, wages paid to workers, packaging materials, outgoing freight, and sales commissions.

At zero output, total variable cost is zero. As output increases, so do variable costs. If a dress manufacturer doubles his output of dresses in a year, his *total* cost of cloth would also roughly double (ignoring quantity discounts), although the cost of cloth *per dress* would remain about the same.[11]

Total cost is the sum of total fixed and total variable costs. The rate of growth of total cost depends upon the increase in total variable cost, since total fixed cost, by definition, is already set.

Average costs are not equal to total costs

The pricing executive usually is more interested in cost per unit than total cost because prices in the marketplace usually are quoted per unit. Costs per unit are called "average" costs, and there are several types.

Average cost per unit is obtained by dividing total cost by the related quantity (i.e., the total quantity produced which led to the total costs).

Average fixed cost is obtained by dividing total fixed cost by the related quantity.

Average variable cost is obtained by dividing total variable cost by the related quantity. We commonly assume that average variable cost is *constant per unit* over a short production range. Actually, average variable cost usually decreases as a firm gains some economies of scale, levels out for a while, and then it begins to rise again at still higher levels of output if the firm must use less efficient machines or workers, pay overtime wage rates, or pay higher prices for materials when expanded sales cause shortages.

The assumption that average variable cost is constant for short ranges is reasonable only in certain cases — but when appropriate, it simplifies analysis. This assumption is used in the following example.

A cost structure example illustrates relations

In Table 24–1, typical cost data is presented for one firm; it is based on the assumption that average variable cost is constant for each unit. Notice how average fixed cost decreases steadily as the quantity increases, and how, although the average variable cost remains constant, total variable cost increases when quantity increases. Average cost decreases continually. This is because average variable cost is constant and average fixed cost is decreasing. Figure 24–2 graphs the behavior of the three average-cost curves.

The average-cost method

Average-cost-curve pricing commonly used

The pricing executive could set prices using a graph such as that in Figure 24–2. Assuming that the average-cost curve includes a provision for profit (either a fixed total amount included in total fixed cost or a fixed amount per unit included in average variable cost), then all he has to do is decide how many units the firm is going to sell. If he

---

[11] Some expenditures have both fixed and variable components and are called semifixed or semivariable costs. To simplify this discussion we will omit this refinement. For more discussion on the nature of costs, see Robert N. Anthony, "What Should 'Cost' Mean?" *Harvard Business Review,* May-June 1970, pp. 121–131; and F. E. Brown and A. R. Oxenfeldt, "Should Prices Depend on Cost?" *MSU Business Topics,* Autumn, 1968, pp. 73–78.

Table 24–1 Cost structure of a firm

Quantity	Total fixed costs (TFC)	Average fixed costs (AFC)	Average variable costs (AVC)	Total variable costs (TVC)	Total cost (TC)	Average cost (AC)
0	$30,000	$	$ 0	$ 0	$ 30,000	$
10,000	30,000	3.00	0.80	8,000	38,000	3.80
20,000	30,000	1.50	0.80	16,000	46,000	2.30
30,000	30,000	1.00	0.80	24,000	54,000	1.80
40,000	30,000	0.75	0.80	32,000	62,000	1.51
50,000	30,000	0.60	0.80	40,000	70,000	1.40
60,000	30,000	0.50	0.80	48,000	78,000	1.30
70,000	30,000	0.43	0.80	56,000	86,000	1.23
80,000	30,000	0.38	0.80	64,000	94,000	1.18
90,000	30,000	0.33	0.80	72,000	102,000	1.13
100,000	30,000	0.30	0.80	80,000	110,000	1.10

expects to sell 50,000 units, then by referring to the average-cost curve shown here, the price could be determined. It woud be $1.40. If he plans to sell 80,000 units, the price suggested by the average-cost curve would be $1.18.

Those using this approach often estimate the quantity to be sold by

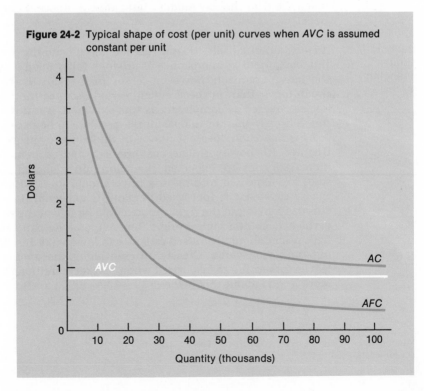

Figure 24-2 Typical shape of cost (per unit) curves when *AVC* is assumed constant per unit

assuming that next period's sales will approximate the volume of the last period.

Assuming the firm will sell a quantity similar to past sales, the average-cost method works easily. The "average-cost" price is found along the AC curve at that previous quantity. This seems to assure that all the fixed costs will be covered. The fixed costs covered by each unit are easily calculated. And it is an easy next step to develop pricing formulas to insure that on each item that amount of fixed cost is covered.

Various cost-oriented pricing formulas might be invented but the intent would be the same—to cover all the costs. The formulas suggested earlier in the chapter illustrate the possibilities.

Get all the figures, get them right

Cost-oriented pricing of this type is used in calculating bid prices for industrial goods and for government business. The major task is assembling all the costs, including the variable costs and the fixed costs that should apply to each order. This may sound relatively straightforward, but in actual practice thousands of cost components may have to go into a complicated bid.

Thousands or even millions of dollars have been spent just developing cost-oriented bids for large industrial or government orders. To assure that all costs are included in a given order, computers often are used to help accumulate the costs.[12] Great care is essential in developing such bid prices. The omission of an important cost item might make the firm the low bidder—but cause it to lose money on the contract.

But how about a changing market?

As long as actual sales do not vary too much from the previous period, this cost-oriented approach will produce fairly good results. As with the naïve approach, however, losses may result if actual sales are much *lower* than in the previous period because the fixed costs will not be covered as completely as was expected. But if actual sales are much *higher* than in the past, then profits will be excellent.

This approach does not jibe with the demand theory discussed in Chapter 10, however. The cost-oriented approach indicates that if increased sales are expected, the selling price should go down. Or if sales are expected to drop, the price should go up. But the demand theory says that if increased demand is expected (i.e., the demand curve is moving to the right), more could be sold at the same price and perhaps even at a higher price. Depending on demand elasticity, perhaps prices should be raised rather than lowered if demand is expanding—and vice versa. Clearly, pricing along the average-cost curve leaves something to be desired when market conditions are changing. More is said about this below.

[12] "Estimating Bids by Computer," *Business Week*, November 23, 1963.

The target return method

Target return pricing, seeking a target return objective, has become popular in recent years. With this approach, the price setter seeks to obtain (1) a percentage return (say 10 percent per year) on his investment or (2) a specific total dollar return.

The method is basically the same as the average-cost method described previously, since the desired target return is added into total cost. An example illustrates the method: 12,000 units were sold last year, and it is hoped the same quantity will be sold this year.

Executive salaries, general administrative overhead, and other fixed expenses total $600,000.

Total investment is $300,000.

Target return is a 10 percent return on investment.

Therefore . . . *total fixed cost* – including the 10 percent target return – is $630,000.

This total, divided by 12,000 units, yields a fixed cost and target return per unit figure of $52.50. If the variable cost per unit is $40, the price that apparently should be set to bring a 10 percent return on investment is $92.50.

This approach suffers from the same deficiency as the average-cost approach. If the quantity that actually is sold in a given period is less than the quantity used in setting the price, then the target return is not achieved, even though it seems to be an integral part of the price structure. To see more clearly how this happens, look at the results when either 10,000 or 20,000 units are sold (see Table 24-2).

Table 24–2 Results of target return pricing

	10,000 units sold		20,000 units sold	
Total revenue		$ 925,000		$1,850,000
Total cost				
Total fixed cost	$600,000		$600,000	
Total variable cost	400,000		800,000	
		1,000,000		1,400,000
Profit (loss)		($75,000)		$ 450,000
Return on investment	$\left\{\dfrac{-75,000}{300,000}\right\} = -25\%$		$\left\{\dfrac{450,000}{300,000}\right\} = 150\%$	

If only 10,000 units are sold, there is a 25 percent *loss* on investment instead of a 10 percent return. If 20,000 units are sold, there is a 150 percent return on investment instead of only a 10 percent target return. Target return pricing clearly does not guarantee that the target objective will be achieved.

The long-run target return method

<table>
<tr>
<td>

Hitting the target in the long run

</td>
<td>

Executives in some larger and more stable firms, wanting to achieve long-run target return objectives, perhaps covering five or more years, have adopted another cost-oriented approach. Instead of estimating the quantity they expect to produce in any one year, they assume that during several years' time their plants will produce at, say, 80 percent of capacity. They use that quantity in their pricing.

No reference at all is made to current demand when setting current prices. Demand was estimated when the plant was built. Some demand and cost factors had to be considered at that time, and in reality it was the decision to build a plant of a certain size that determined subsequent prices.

Companies taking this longer run view assume that there will be recession years when sales drop below 80 percent of capacity, and the target return won't be earned, but also there will be other years when the plant operates at a higher level and betters the target return. Over the long run, the target return will be achieved. If business is consistently good, it would be expected that such firms would consistently earn higher than their target figure. Of the large companies whose objectives we discussed in the last chapter, those with target return objectives made profits in the prosperous 1947–55 period that were higher than their target levels for that period.

This long-run approach to target return pricing sounds simple. But like pricing in general, it cannot be approached mechanically. For example, "capacity" is a rather flexible concept, perhaps referring to a five-day, single-shift operation or to a seven-day, three-shift operation.

Long-run target return pricing, consequently, need not lead to a unique price or a stable price. Typically, however, companies using long-run target return pricing tend to have more stable prices.

</td>
</tr>
</table>

The break-even method

<table>
<tr>
<td>

Break-even analysis may be helpful in seeing profitability of possible prices

</td>
<td>

Some businessmen use break-even analysis in an attempt to bring prospective revenue (and perhaps demand) into pricing.

Break-even analysis is especially useful for considering the relation of revenue and cost. A break-even chart can be drawn showing the total revenue which would be received at various levels of operation when selling *at an assumed price*. This total revenue curve can then be related to the total cost curve to find where the company would break even. This intersection is called the break-even point (*BEP*).

At this point, total revenue and total cost are equal; beyond it, at a greater output level, the company will begin to make a profit on each unit; below it, the company incurs a loss. Figure 24–3, a break-even chart, shows these profit and loss areas.

In most break-even analysis, *average variable cost is assumed to be constant per unit. Total cost is segregated into fixed and variable costs. And a single price is assumed when drawing the total revenue curve.*

</td>
</tr>
</table>

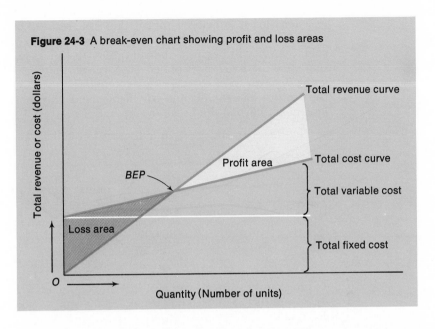

Figure 24-3 A break-even chart showing profit and loss areas

Total revenue or cost (dollars)

Total revenue curve

Profit area

BEP

Total cost curve

Total variable cost

Loss area

Total fixed cost

O ⟶

Quantity (Number of units)

In a situation that is correctly described by break-even analysis, th obvious conclusion is to try to sell as many units as possible. The big question is: Will break-even analysis help find the right price? Before answering this question, let us look at the details of this analysis.

Computation of break-even point

The *BEP* may be computed in terms of units or dollar value of units. In units, the *BEP* can be found by using the following formula:

$$BEP \text{ (in units)} = \frac{TFC}{FC \text{ contribution per unit}}$$

The *fixed-cost contribution per unit* is equal to the selling price per unit minus the variable cost per unit. Variable cost *should* be covered on each item or there is no point in producing the item. Total fixed cost, however, does *not* have to be covered (in the short run) because it would continue even if the company were temporarily shut down. In fact, it is sometimes better to continue operation for a time, even without a profit, if all the variable costs and at least some of the fixed costs can be covered.

To illustrate the formula, let us use the cost data for the firm in Table 24–1, and assume a selling price per unit of $1.20. Using the following values:

Total fixed cost	=	$30,000
Variable cost per unit	=	$0.80
FC contribution ($1.20 − $.80) =		$0.40

and substituting in the formula:

$$BEP = \frac{30,000}{0.40} = 75,000 \text{ units}$$

From this it is evident that if this firm sells 75,000 units, it will cover exactly all its fixed and variable costs. If even one more unit is sold, then it will begin to show a profit—in this case, 40 cents. Note that once the fixed costs are covered, the portion of revenue formerly going to cover fixed costs now goes completely to profits. This is where the profit grows rapidly and why firms using this method are so anxious to get beyond the break-even point.

The *BEP* can also be figured in terms of dollar value:

$$BEP \text{ (in dollars)} = \frac{TFC}{1 - \dfrac{VC/\text{Unit}}{\text{Selling price/Unit}}}$$

Using the figures above, we obtain:

$$\frac{\$30,000}{1 - \dfrac{\$0.80}{\$1.20}} = \$90,000$$

To check our result, we can multiply the selling price ($1.20) times the *BEP* in units (75,000): $1.20 times 75,000 equals $90,000, the *BEP* in dollars.[13]

The results of the foregoing analyses can be graphed as shown in Figure 24–4. The definiteness of this graph and the probable growth of profits beyond the break-even point certainly make it appear that the pricing problem is solved, at least if we are sure of being able to sell more than the break-even quantity. It appears that the more optimistic we are about exceeding the break-even point, the more satisfaction we can feel, since profits will grow as volume expands.

Helpful, yes—but not a pricing solution

Break-even analysis is useful for comparing pricing alternatives. The break-even points of various assumed prices can be calculated and evaluated to see how reasonable they are—that is, is it likely the *BEP*'s will be exceeded? The assumed prices might come from other cost-oriented approaches, and a check of their respective *BEP*'s might quickly eliminate some of them.

Yet, helpful as it is for evaluating the impact of various *assumed* price levels, break-even analysis does *not* solve the pricing problem. Break-even analysis can be done without relating the assumed price to potential demand. In fact, many assumed prices can be analyzed in break-even analysis without any relation to market reality.

Although the graph, with its straight-line total revenue curve, makes it appear that any quantity might be sold at the assumed price, this usually is unrealistic. This is equivalent to assuming the existence of

[13] Students familiar with algebra may find the following approach more meaningful. Where x equals *BEP* in quantity, and we solve for the intersection of the *TR* and *TC* lines.

(Price) $(x) = TFC + VC\,(x)$

$1.20x = 30,000 + .80x$
$.40x = 30,000$
$x = 75,000$ units
and $1.20\,(75,000) = \$90,000 = BEP$ in dollars.

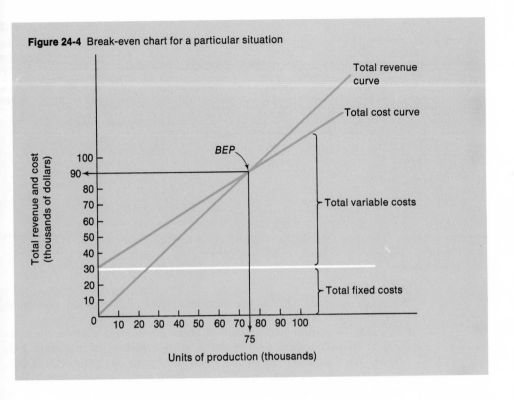

Figure 24-4 Break-even chart for a particular situation

a perfectly horizontal demand curve at that price; if demand is perfectly elastic, there is no need for pricing analysis because the pricing executive would have no pricing decision to make.

At the end of this chapter, we will evaluate the effectiveness of break-even analysis, along with other cost-oriented approaches. For now, though, we can see that our pricing problem is not solved.

The marginal cost method

The cost of just one more may help in special cases

By now we know that various kinds of costs behave differently and that there is no single type of cost that should be the basis for setting the price in all situations.

In some special pricing situations, however, there is another cost that may be useful. This is *marginal cost — the change in total cost that results from producing an extra unit.*

The subject of marginal cost will become especially important in the next chapter on demand-oriented pricing. In anticipation of this use, we will introduce a new set of cost data to illustrate the concept of marginal cost (see Table 24–3).

According to the marginal cost concept, if it costs $275 to produce 9 units of a product and $280 to produce 10 units, then marginal cost is $5 for the 10th unit. In other words, marginal cost contrasted to

Table 24–3 Cost structure for individual firm

Quan-tity Q (1)	Total fixed cost TFC (2)	Average fixed costs AFC (3)	Total variable cost TVC (4)	Average variable cost AVC (5)	Total cost (TFC + TVC = TC) TC (6)	Average cost (AC = TC ÷ Q) AC (7)	Marginal cost (per unit) MC (8)
0	$200	$ 0	$ 0	$ 0	$200	Infinity	
1	200	200	96	96	296	$296	$96
2	200	100	116	58	316		20
3	200				331	110.33	
4	200	50			344		
5	200	40	155	31		71	11
6	200		168			61.33	13
7			183				15
8			223				
9			307		507	56.33	
10		20	510	51	710	71	203

average cost per unit is the additional cost of producing one more *specific unit,* while average cost is the average for *all units.*

Table 24–3 indicates how all of these costs could vary for an individual firm. You should fill in the missing numbers on this table. Notice that variable cost no longer is assumed constant per unit in Table 24–3. In this situation, we use the more realistic assumption that variable costs will decline for a while and then rise.

In Table 24–3, several important points should be noted. *First,* total fixed costs do not change over the entire range of output, but total variable costs increase continually as more and more units are produced. It is obvious, then, that total costs—the sum of total fixed costs and total variable costs—will increase as total quantity increases.

Second, average costs will decrease over most of the range of production, since average costs are the sum of average fixed costs and average variable costs, and total fixed costs are divided by more and more units as output mounts. Given a total fixed cost of $200 at a production level of four units, the average fixed cost is $50; at a production level of five units, the average fixed cost is $40 and average fixed cost continues to decline.

Third, average costs in this table start rising for the last two units because average variable costs have been increasing faster than average fixed costs have been decreasing. The firm may have been forced to use less efficient facilities and workers, go into overtime work or pay higher prices for the materials it needed. This turn-up of the average cost curve happens frequently.

How little can keep us in business?

The *marginal cost* column in Table 24–3 is the most important column for our purposes. It shows specifically what each extra unit costs, and therefore indicates the minimum extra revenue we should get for each additional unit. Like average cost, marginal cost drops, but it begins to rise again at a lower level of output than average cost.

Total fixed costs do *not* affect marginal cost computations. Although average cost per unit is going down over most of the quantity range, marginal cost *starts up earlier* at five units. Figure 24–5 shows the behavior of the *average cost, average variable cost,* and *marginal cost* curves. Note that the marginal cost curve intersects the average variable cost and average cost curves from below *at their low points,* and then rises rapidly thereafter. This is how this curve typically behaves.

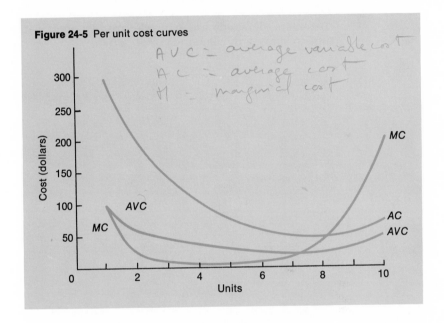

Figure 24-5 Per unit cost curves

The marginal cost curve shows the *extra* cost of producing and selling each extra unit. This cost curve can be extremely important to a marketing manager who is trying to find a way to keep operating in depressed times and still not lose money out-of-pocket. A wholesaler or retailer, for example, would certainly not want to offer goods or services below their marginal cost. Similarly, a producer would not want to produce additional goods if he could not cover the direct out-of-pocket cost. (Note: If the goods have already been produced or purchased, however, then he might want to think of these as fixed costs and be willing to sell them even below their original cost if the alternative is not to sell them at all!)

Marginal cost thinking might be useful when setting a price on a promotional item which will be used to attract business to other parts of the company's line. And marginal cost pricing is often used during short-term price wars, or to attract business a company would not ordinarily get, or for other short-run objectives.

637

Cost-oriented price determination has major deficiencies

If a company is to base its pricing on costs, it must be able to make some estimate of the quantity to be sold in the coming period. But unless this estimated quantity is related to price – that is, unless demand is considered – the pricing executive may set a price that either does not maximize profits or, worse, does not even cover total costs. Such a possible predicament can be seen in a simple illustration of a firm with a total fixed cost of $90,000 and a variable cost of $40 per unit. This firm's demand curve is shown in Figure 24-6. Remember – customers' demands are still relevant, whether management takes time to analyze the demand curve or not.

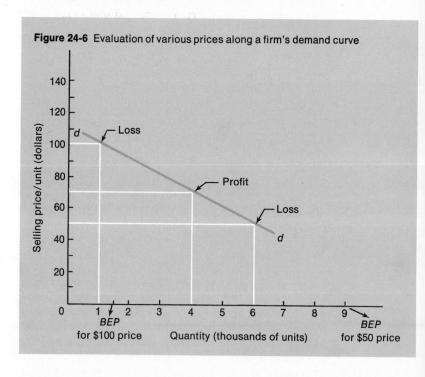

Figure 24-6 Evaluation of various prices along a firm's demand curve

Simple in theory, crude in practice

In this example, whether management sets the price at a high $100 ($60 markup) or a low $50 ($10 markup), it will incur a loss. At $100, 1,000 units will be sold, but the BEP is 1,500 units. At $50, 6,000 will be sold but the BEP is 9,000 units! In both instances, the firm has a loss.

If management made some attempt to estimate the demand curve, however crudely, the price probably would be set in an intermediate range, say at $70, where the BEP is 3,000 units. At this price, 4,000 units would be sold at a profit of $30,000, that is, $280,000 less $160,000 TVC less $90,000 TFC equals $30,000 profit.

In short, a cost-oriented approach to price determination is simple in theory but often very crude in practice. In static situations, prices set in this manner may yield profits—but not necessarily maximum profits. And interestingly, such prices may be higher than the price that would maximize the firm's profit, as shown in Figure 24–6.

First the
customer,
then the
price

Typically, demand is ignored in cost-oriented approaches to pricing. To be sure, some estimate of quantity may be included in the calculations, but this quantity may set a price that may be far higher than customers will pay for that quantity.

It has become almost axiomatic in this book that the *customer must be considered before anything is done.* This certainly applies to pricing. It means that when management is setting the price, it must consider the prices customers will be willing to pay.

In the next chapter, we will discuss methods of estimating demand curves and demand-oriented pricing.

Conclusion

In this chapter, we considered various methods of cost-oriented price determination. Generally, retailers and wholesalers use traditional markups that they feel will yield a reasonable rate of profit. Some retailers and wholesalers use the same markup on all of their items; others have found that varying their markups may increase turnover and profit. And demand may enter here implicitly!

Cost-oriented pricing seems to make sense for retailers and wholesalers because they handle small quantities of many items. Perhaps they are not maximizing profit on each item, but the extra cost of more analysis might actually reduce total profit.

We found that it is less desirable for a producer or channel captain to use traditional markups. A common alternative, the naïve cost-plus approach, ignores demand completely and is not the answer. A more realistic cost-plus approach using average-cost curves requires some forecast of sales. Such a forecast often amounts to assuming that sales in the next period will be roughly the same as in the last period.

Given such an assumption, the average-cost pricing method enables the pricing executive to determine a price. But this price *may or may not* cover all costs and yield the desired rate of profit. It depends on how accurately the pricing executive has estimated the quantity which will be sold. Estimating sales is the crux of the problem in the average-cost and target return methods of pricing. Using these methods, the quantity estimate may be set without regard to the price, although in fact the quantity demanded by customers *varies* with the price. This can be seen on a demand curve.

Cost-oriented pricing frequently yields a price that is "too high." This causes slow turnover and low profit or even losses. The first concern of too many businessmen is an "adequate" margin. They do not like to take the risk of lower prices in anticipation of increased sales and possibly greater profits. Their reluctance results both from their cost orientation and an absence of demand analysis.

Although the break-even approach can bring various prices into the analysis, it can also lead to less than optimum results unless the prices used in the analysis are related to demand.

Chapter 25 shows that it is possible to bring demand into price determination.

QUESTIONS AND PROBLEMS

1 Many retailers mark up their goods by more than their gross margin. Explain how this can be if the gross margin is the difference between selling price and the cost of the goods.

2 Why do department stores seek a markup of about 40 percent when some discount houses operate on a 20 percent markup?

3 A manufacturer was selling an item for $120. What would be the final price to the consumer if the wholesaler took a markup of 20 percent and the retailer took a markup of 40 percent?

4 A buyer for a department store was computing the price he should charge for an item that cost him $72. In order to cover his expenses of 36 percent and still secure a profit of 4 percent, what retail price should be placed on the item?

5 A manufacturer of household appliances distributed its products through wholesalers and retailers. The retail selling price was $250, and the manufacturing cost to the company was $100. The retail markup was 40 percent and the wholesale markup 25 percent.
a) What was the cost to the wholesaler? Retailer?
b) What percentage markup did the manufacturer take?

6 Does it make any difference in which order a chain of markups is taken? Illustrate your answer.

7 Relate the concept of stock turnover to the rise of discounters. Use a simple example in your answer.

8 If total fixed costs are $100,000 and total variable costs are $200,000 at an output of 10,000 units, what are the probable total fixed costs and total variable costs at an output of 20,000 units? What are the average fixed costs, average variable costs, and average costs at these two output levels? Determine the price which should be charged. (Make any simplifying assumptions necessary to obtain a definite answer.)

9 Explain how target return pricing differs from average cost pricing.

10 Construct an example showing that mechanical use of a very large or very small markup might still lead to unprofitable operation while some intermediate price would be profitable. Draw a graph and show the break-even point(s).

11 The Apex Company's fixed costs for the year are estimated at $100,000, the variable costs are usually about 70 percent of sales. Sales for the coming year are expected to reach $380,000. What is the break-even point? Expected profit? If sales were forecast at only $200,000, should the Apex Co. shut down operations? Why?

...now we will bring demand into pricing, explicitly.

...flexible break-even analysis and traditional supply and demand analysis provide tools that enable the marketing manager to develop the *most profitable* price per unit....

...it is clear that the marketing manager should make use of the analytical tools at his disposal to estimate customer demand, because the firm's demand curve does not cease to exist simply because it is ignored....

25

Price determination — demand-oriented

The marketing concept stresses the importance of the customer, and nowhere should the customer be in sharper focus nor more carefully scrutinized than at the point of determining price.

The previous chapter showed the difficulty of trying to set prices without recognizing potential customer demand. In this chapter, we will bring demand explicitly into the analysis, discussing several demand-oriented approaches to pricing and several ways of estimating demand curves.

Flexible break-even analysis considers demand

Demand *can* be brought into the pricing picture through the use of break-even charts. Instead of using only one straight-line total revenue

(TR) curve at a time as we did in the previous chapter, many such total revenue curves can be used. Each of these total revenue curves may be arbitrary, of course, since they are based on *assumed* prices. If high prices are assumed, the total revenue curves are sharply upsloping. If lower prices are assumed, the total revenue lines become flatter. (See Figure 25–1 for an illustration of five such *TR* lines for various prices.)

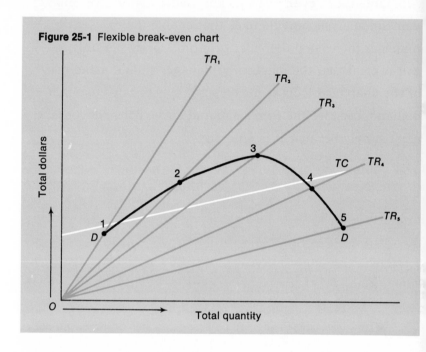

Figure 25-1 Flexible break-even chart

Each of these hypothetical total revenue lines, however, still has no connection with potential demand. This demand factor is considered when the exact quantity that customers would demand at each of the assumed prices is determined and plotted on each of the total revenue curves. These quantities are assumed to be the points D^1, D^2, D^3, D^4, D^5, in Figure 25–1. Connecting these points develops a potential total revenue curve (like a demand curve). This is not a demand curve in the usual sense, however, since it indicates the *total revenue* that will be received at various prices and quantities.

More common way to find the best price

The most profitable output is indicated by the point on the potential total revenue curve that is at the greatest vertical distance above the total cost curve. Of the five prices represented on this figure, the most profitable price would be the one which was used to draw line TR_3. Clearly, the quantity which will be sold at this most profitable price is greater than the related *BEP*—that is, the quantity indicated at the intersection of TR_3 and *TC*.

Management men who are accustomed to using break-even analysis can easily understand this flexible approach. For this reason, a marketing manager might choose this approach to illustrate how potential demand could and should be considered in price determination.

But the more common method of finding the most profitable price uses demand and supply curves to show price and cost *per unit* rather than as totals. Greater insight into the behavior of revenue and cost curves and effective price determination is gained with this approach.

The balance of this chapter follows this more traditional method. Remember, however, that the flexible break-even approach and the following approach are similar except in method of graphic presentation.[1]

Traditional demand and supply analysis shows how to maximize profits

In Chapter 10, we saw that most demand curves are downsloping and most supply curves are upsloping. The intersection of these demand and supply curves would seem to determine price and, therefore, take care of demand-oriented pricing for the firm. Unfortunately, reality is not quite that simple.

Although such analysis may be appropriate for whole industries, some refinements are necessary in applying it to the individual firm seeking to maximize profits.

Not just profit but the biggest profit

In the following pages, we will discuss these refinements, concentrating on price determination in the large majority of situations in which demand curves are downsloping—that is, monopolistic competition situations. In these situations, the firm has carved out a little market for itself and does have a pricing decision to make. By contrast, in the pure or nearly pure competition situation, the marketing manager has little difficulty with the pricing decision. He simply uses the market price.

Our discussion also will focus on how to maximize profits, not just seek some profits. This has been the traditional approach of economic analysis, and it is a reasonable one. If you know how to make the biggest profit, you can always adjust to pursue other objectives while knowing how much profit you are giving up!

Is selling just one more really worth it?

Most monopolistic competitors—and these apparently constitute the vast majority of business firms[2]—have a downsloping demand curve. The marketing manager must pick a price on that curve, and generally must offer that price to all potential buyers (to avoid price discrimina-

[1] This idea was developed by E. R. Hawkins. See Edward R. Hawkins, "Price Policies and Theory," *Journal of Marketing,* January, 1954, p. 234; see also, Bill R. Darden, "An Operational Approach to Product Pricing," *Journal of Marketing,* April, 1968, pp. 29–33.

[2] W. Warren Haynes, *Pricing Decisions in Small Business* (Lexington: University of Kentucky Press, 1962), p. 152.

tion under the Robinson-Patman Act). Therefore, he must consider the effect on total revenue of the alternative prices he is considering.

If he chooses a lower price, the demand curve shows that he will sell additional units, but *all* his customers would be offered this lower price, and he should calculate the impact on total revenue. Or if he chooses a higher price, he must expect to sell less. What will be the impact on revenue, both total and marginal? The important point to see here is that the marketing manager usually does *not* have the option of selling individual items at different prices, but instead must make one decision about price and quantity, and then live with it for the length of the plan, or until a new plan is set. Marginal analysis helps him evaluate the attractiveness of various prices and quantities, by focusing on the last unit which would be sold. But keep in mind that this kind of analysis is not ignoring the previous units.

Marginal revenue helps decide

Marginal revenue is the change in total revenue which results from the sale of one additional unit of product. Since the firm's demand curve is downsloping, this extra unit can be sold only by reducing the price of all items. The total revenue that would be obtained if price were cut might still be positive, but the marginal revenue—that is, the extra revenue gained—might be negative.

Table 25–1 indicates the relationship between price, quantity, total revenue, and marginal revenue in a hypothetical situation with roughly a straight-line downsloping demand curve.

Table 25–1 Marginal revenue and price

Quantity q (1)	Price p (2)	Total revenue (1) × (2) = TR (3)	Marginal revenue MR (4)
0	$150	$ 0	
1	140	140	$140
2	130	260	120
3	117	351	91
4	105	420	69
5	92	460	40
6	79	474	14
7	66	462	−12
8	53	424	−38
9	42	378	−46
10	31	310	−68

If four units could be sold for $420 and five units for $460, then marginal revenue for the fifth unit is $40. Considering only revenue, it would be desirable to sell this extra unit. But Table 25–1 shows that negative marginal revenues may occur at lower price levels. Obviously, the way in which marginal revenue changes may be relevant to pricing.

The marginal revenue curve is always below a downsloping demand curve, as can be seen in Figure 25–2 where the data in Table 25–1 is plotted. The fact that the demand curve and the marginal revenue curve are different in monopolistic competition is quite significant. We will use both of them when finding the best price and quantity, but for different purposes.[3]

Make the marginal cost curve the supply curve

We introduced the marginal cost curve in the previous chapter because we were considering cost-oriented ideas, and marginal cost has special applications there. It is even more useful here, however, in relation to maximizing profits because it reflects what is happening to costs the manager can control. As we saw in the previous chapter, the marginal cost curve might be going up while the average-cost curve was going down at larger quantities. Clearly, we should not plan to increase the quantity we will offer unless the sales return will at least cover the extra costs we will incur. The marginal cost curve shows these costs.

Computing most profitable price and quantity

We see now that a firm should not supply additional units unless it can obtain at least a marginal revenue equal to the marginal cost of those extra units. From this we can derive the following rule for maximizing profit: *The firm should produce that output where marginal cost is just less than or equal to marginal revenue.*[4]

The selling price for this optimum quantity is determined by referring to the demand curve, which shows what price customers are willing to pay for the optimum quantity. The optimum price is *not* found on the marginal revenue curve.

This method of finding the most profitable price and quantity is a useful tool for the marketing manager. To assure full understanding of the approach, we will illustrate its application. To make doubly sure that this approach is fully explained, we will calculate the most profitable price and quantity using total revenue and total cost curves first, and then show that the same answer is obtained with marginal curves. This will give us a check of the method as well as perspective on how the marginal revenue–marginal cost method works.

[3] The data for drawing a marginal revenue curve always can be derived by calculating changes in the total revenue curve, but a simple graphical shortcut is available if straight-line demand curves are being used. Although the demand curve within the relevant range normally may not extend all the way to the horizontal and vertical axes, it can be extended to these axes. The marginal revenue curve is then obtained by drawing a line running from the intersection of the demand curve with the vertical (price) axis down to the point on the quantity axis bisecting the segment from 0 to the point where the demand curve extension intersects that axis. This marginal revenue curve also can be extended below the quantity axis to obtain the negative marginal revenue values. The only relevant part of the marginal revenue curve is that part directly below the relevant range of the demand curve.

When working with curved demand curves, tangents to the curve can be drawn at several places to obtain the general shape of the MR curve. Readers familiar with calculus probably will recognize that the marginal revenue curve is simply the derivative of the total revenue curve, and they can use this approach in finding the marginal revenue curve.

[4] This rule applies in the typical situations where the curves are shaped similarly to those discussed here. Technically, however, we should add the following to the rule for maximizing profit: *The marginal cost must be increasing at a greater rate or decreasing at a lesser rate than marginal revenue.*

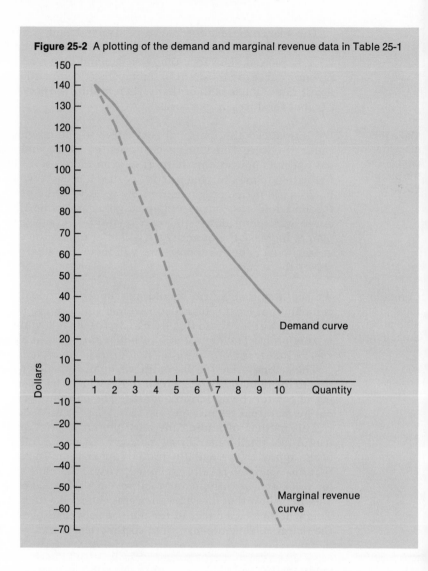

Figure 25-2 A plotting of the demand and marginal revenue data in Table 25-1

(Demand curve; Marginal revenue curve; Dollars on vertical axis; Quantity on horizontal axis)

Profit maximization with total revenue and total cost curves

Table 25–2 provides illustrative data on total revenue, total cost, and total profit for this firm. Figure 25–3 simply graphs the total revenue, total cost, and total profit relationships. It is clear from the graph of the total profit curve that the most profitable quantity is six—this is the quantity where we find the greatest vertical distance between the TR curve and the TC curve. Table 25–2 shows that the most profitable price is $79 and a quantity of six will be sold.

The similarity of this approach to the flexible break-even analysis should be obvious. The TR line is similar to the curved total revenue curve we saw there. The total cost curve, however, is curving and more

Table 25–2 Revenue, cost, and profit for individual firm

Quan-tity q (1)	Price p (2)	Total revenue TR (3)	Total cost TC (4)	Profit $(TR-TC)$ (5)	Marginal revenue MR (6)	Marginal cost MC (7)	Marginal profit $(MR-MC)$ (8)
0	$150	$ 0	$200	$−200			
1	140	140	296	−156	$140	$ 96	$+ 44
2	130	260	316	− 56	120	20	+100
3	117	351	331	+ 20	91	15	+ 76
4	105	420	344	+ 76	69	13	+ 56
5	92	460	355	+105	40	11	+ 29
6	79	474	368	+106	14	13	+ 1
7	66	462	383	+ 79	− 12	15	− 27
8	53	424	423	+ 1	− 38	40	− 78
9	42	378	507	−129	− 46	84	−130
10	31	310	710	−400	− 68	203	−271

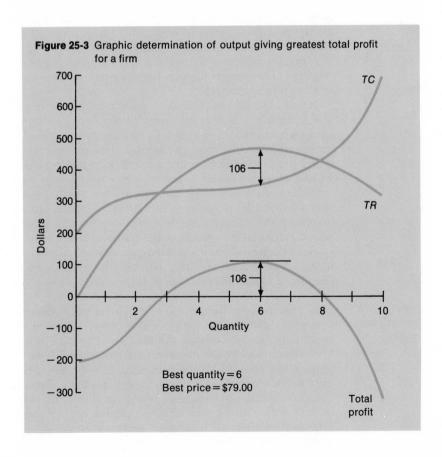

Figure 25-3 Graphic determination of output giving greatest total profit for a firm

Best quantity = 6
Best price = $79.00

accurately reflects the nature of fixed and variable costs. It is clear that beyond a quantity of six, the total profit curve declines; the marketing manager would not be interested in selling more than this number. This is *not* apparent with a simple break-even analysis. In fact, as already noted, simple break-even analysis often suggests that profits will grow and grow beyond the break-even point!

Profit maximization using marginal curves

Now we can apply the rule we developed earlier for maximizing profit using marginal curves. The same best quantity and price are obtained, as is shown in Figure 25–3 based on the data for marginal revenue and marginal cost in Table 25–2.

In Figure 25–4, the intersection of the marginal cost and marginal revenue curves occurs at a quantity of six. This is the most profitable quantity. But the best price must be obtained by going up to the demand curve. It is *not* at the $MR - MC$ intersection. Again, the best price is $79.

The graphic interpretation is supported by the data in Table 25–2. At a quantity of six, marginal revenue equals $14 and marginal cost is $13. There is a marginal profit of $1, and this suggests that it might be profitable to offer seven rather than six units. This is not the case, however. The marginal cost of the seventh unit is $15 while its marginal revenue is actually negative. Offering to sell seven units (instead of only six)will reduce profit by $27.

It is important to realize that marginal revenue can actually become negative. This simply means that the *total* revenue curve is declining, as shown in Figure 25–3.

It also is important to realize that *total* profit is *not* near zero when MR equals MC. *Marginal profit* (the extra profit on the last unit) is near zero, but that is exactly why the quantity obtained at the $MR - MC$ intersection is the most profitable. Marginal analysis indicates that when the firm is determining the best price to charge, it should be willing to increase the quantity it will sell as long as the last unit it considers offering will yield *extra* profits. Again, the marketing manager finally will choose only *one* price. Marginal analysis is useful in helping him to determine the best price to charge for all that he will sell. It might help to think of the demand curve as in "iffy" curve – *if* a price is selected, *then* a related quantity will be sold. Before the price is set, all these *if-then* combinations can be evaluated for profitability. But once a particular price is set, the results follow.

How to lose less, if you must

This approach to determining the most profitable output also will determine that output which will be least unprofitable when market conditions are so poor that the firm must operate at a loss.

If sales are slow, the marketing manager may even have to consider suspending operation. When making this decision, he should ignore fixed costs, since these will continue regardless. Some fixed costs may even involve items that are so "sunk" in the business that they cannot be sold for anything near the cost shown on the company's records. The special-purpose buildings and machines of an unsuccessful company might be next to worthless to anyone else.

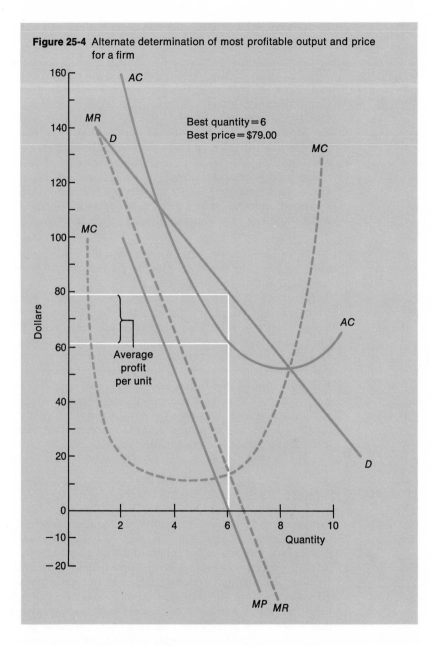

Figure 25-4 Alternate determination of most profitable output and price for a firm

Best quantity = 6
Best price = $79.00

Marginal costs are another matter. If the firm cannot recover marginal costs, it should suspend operations temporarily or go out of business. The only exceptions are mitigating social or humanitarian considerations, or the fact that the marginal costs of closing temporarily are high and stronger demand is expected *soon*. But if marginal costs can be covered in the short run, even thought fixed costs are not, the firm should remain in operation, at least until fixed facilities

649

such as plant and machinery wear out. This will earn at least some contribution to fixed costs.

Getting the most in pure competition

The marketing manager caught in a pure-competition situation also can apply the methods just discussed. He does not have a price decision, but he does have an output decision. The demand curve facing him is flat, and this means that the marginal revenue curve is also flat at the same level. He could equate that marginal revenue curve, therefore, with his own unique marginal cost curve to determine his most profitable (or least unprofitable) output level. A little experimentation will show that the marginal cost approach might lead to a different output decision than the average-cost approach. In general, a marginal approach is the most dependable if you are seeking to maximize profits or, if it is necessary, to minimize losses.

A profit range is reassuring

We have been seeking the most profitable price and quantity, but in a dynamic world this is an elusive goal. Fortunately, this optimum is surrounded by a profitable range.

Note that in Figure 25–3 there are *two* break-even points rather than a single point, which was the case when we were discussing break-even analysis. The second break-even point falls farther out because total costs turn up and total revenue is turning down.

These two break-even points are important to note because they define the range of profitable operations. Although we are seeking to find the point of maximum profit, we know that this point is an ideal goal rather than a realistic possibility. What is essential is that the marketing manager knows there is a range of profit around the optimum—it is not just a lone point. This should provide greater assurance that pursuing the optimum is a wise policy.

How some businessmen see demand curves

For the firm interested in profits, demand-oriented pricing obviously makes considerable sense. The use of marginal analysis provides a convenient technique for incorporating demand into a profit-oriented pricing procedure. Yet relatively few firms use this approach. Why? In part because demand estimation is not a simple task. A demand curve represents the summation of a considerable number of variables, including potential customers' reactions to the firm's planned marketing mix. It is easy to imagine but harder to pin down.

Yet we do find businessmen setting prices as though they believe certain types of demand curves are present. And pricing research indicates they are. It is clear that some prestige, odd-even, psychological, and market segmentation pricing efforts do consider demand. Even some retailers appear to be involved—a fact that manufacturers working through them must recognize in their own pricing. In addition, as we will see later, methods are available for estimating demand curves—and some firms are using them.

Prestige pricing — make it high and not too low

To some target customers, relatively high prices seem to mean high quality or high status. If prices are dropped a little bit, these customers may see a bargain. But if the prices begin to appear cheap, they start worrying about quality and may stop buying.[5]

Such target customers present the marketing manager with an unusual demand curve. Instead of a normal downslope, the curve slopes down for a while, and then bends back to the left again (see Figure 25–5). The marginal revenue curve for such a demand curve would drop sharply and show minus marginal revenues over most of the course.

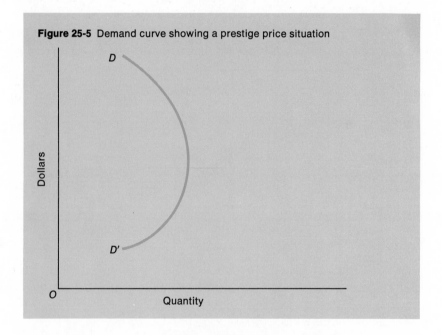

Figure 25-5 Demand curve showing a prestige price situation

Marketing managers dealing with this kind of demand — such as jewelry and fur retailers and nightclub owners — typically set high prices, sometimes called "prestige prices."

Odd-even pricing — it's $5.95. . .

Some marketing men also feel that the notion of a smooth demand curve oversimplifies the case. They feel that consumers will react more favorably to prices ending in certain numbers, usually the odd

---

[5] For more discussion on the relation between price and quantity, see D. S. Tull, R. A. Boring, and H. M. Gonsior, "A Note on the Relationship of Price and Imputed Quality," *Journal of Business*, April, 1964, pp. 186–91; James E. Stafford and Ben M. Enis, "The Price-Quality Relationship: An Extension," *Journal of Marketing Research*, November, 1969, pp. 456–58; F. E. Brown, "Price Image Versus Price Reality," *Journal of Marketing Research*, May, 1969, pp. 185–191; and David M. Gardner, "An Experimental Investigation of the Price/Quality Relationship," *Journal of Retailing*, Fall 1970, pp. 25–41.

numbers. Retail studies show that merchants *do use* certain prices more frequently than others.[6]

For merchandise selling under $50, prices ending with 95—such as $5.95, $6.95, and so on—are common. In general, prices ending in nine are most popular followed by prices ending in five and three.[7] For merchandise selling over $50, prices that are $1 or $2 below the even-dollar figure are the most popular.[8]

Marketing men using these prices seem to assume that they have a rather jagged demand curve; that consumers will buy less for a while as prices are lowered and then more as each "magic" price is approached. This kind of demand curve is shown in Figure 25–6.

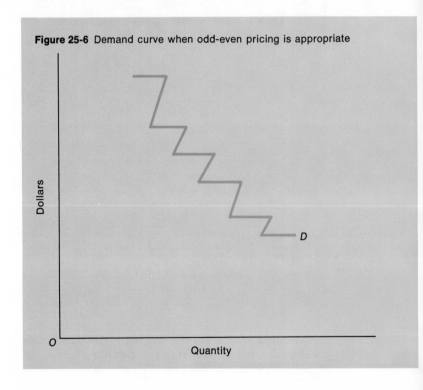

Figure 25-6 Demand curve when odd-even pricing is appropriate

It is debatable whether these odd prices are effective. They apparently were adopted by some retailers to force their clerks to make change. Then they would have to record the sale, and could not pocket the money. Today, however, it is not always clear why these odd prices are used and whether they are effective. Perhaps consumers have been conditioned to expect more favorable offers at certain prices

[6]See Eli Ginsberg, "Customary Prices," *American Economic Review*, May, 1936, p. 296.

[7]Dik W. Twedt, "Does the '9 Fixation' in Retailing Really Promote Sales?" *Journal of Marketing*,

October, 1965, pp. 54–55.

[8]H. J. Rudolph, "Pricing for Today's Market," *Printers' Ink*, May 29, 1954, pp. 22–24.

and they do work. Or perhaps it is done simply because "everyone else does it"; if so, it may lead to rigidities in the price structure that actually may reduce profits.

Psychological pricing— some prices just seem right

So-called psychological pricing has no real basis in psychological research. Some businessmen simply feel that certain prices for certain products are psychologically appealing. Between these prices are whole ranges where customers perceive prices as roughly equivalent. Price cuts in these ranges would not increase the quantity sold. Below such a range, customers would buy more for a while, and then the quantity demanded would remain constant.

The kind of demand curve that seems appropriate in this case is shown in Figure 25-7. Vertical drops mark the price ranges which

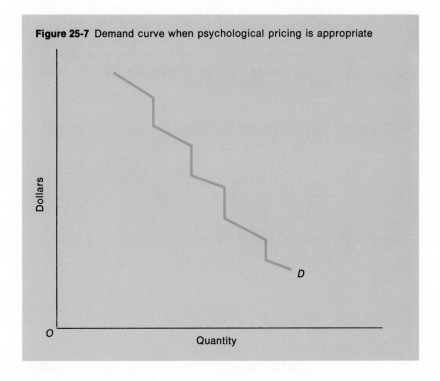

Figure 25-7 Demand curve when psychological pricing is appropriate

customers see as equivalent. Some pricing research indicates that there do seem to be such demand curves.[9]

Pricing neckties at various levels—say, $1.50, $2.50, $3.50, and $5—may be an attempt to price as nearly as possible to the top of such

[9] E. R. Hawkins, "Price Policies and Theory," *Journal of Marketing*, January, 1954, p. 236; see also, B. P. Shapiro, "The Psychology of Pricing," *Harvard Business Review*, July–August, 1968, pp. 14–25.

ranges. This conception of demand underlies the price-lining policy we will discuss more fully in the next chapter.

Throughout this text, we have discussed various approaches to segmenting markets. We have assumed that each such market had its own demand curve, and often this is the case, especially if distinctly different needs have been isolated. In other cases, however, businessmen seem to see a general demand curve for a product type and then develop slightly different qualities for different segments of the market. We already have noted that appliance and car manufacturers, for example, may develop a prestige product for the top of the market, a mass market product, and a "fighting" brand at lower prices.

The demand-oriented thinking behind such moves can be seen as an effort to segment a general demand curve into three distinct segments, as shown in Figure 25–8. Actually, the segments may not be so neatly separated; it may be possible, for instance, to "trade up" a customer from one segment to the other. But it does add clarity to our marketing strategy planning to think of each market as having different demand curves.

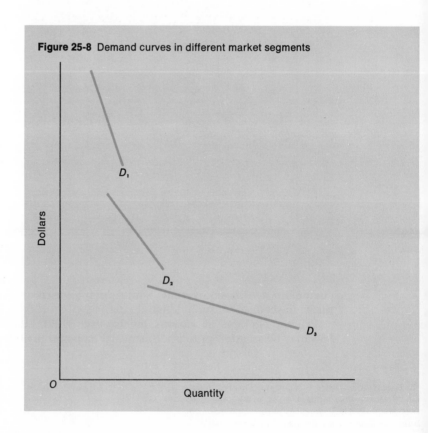

Figure 25-8 Demand curves in different market segments

How to estimate demand curves

Businessmen obviously have some knowledge of the demand in their target markets and often seem to behave accordingly. Sometimes they may make only rough judgments, but even these may be better than nothing. As we saw earlier, even rough estimates of the elasticity of demand may be helpful in estimating the nature of the market situation and sometimes even the direction that price changes should take.

Ideally, we would like to have a quantitative estimate of the demand curve because this would enable us to use marginal analysis. Let's consider some of the ways we can derive demand curves.[10]

Demand analysis using equal profit curves

This easy-to-use approach is suitable only for products with which the marketing manager has had recent experience. Basically, he attempts to determine whether demand has changed enough since the last period so that a new price would lead to a greater profit. This approach seeks only to *improve* his profit position and not necessarily to maximize profits. In other words, if the marketing manager knows what quantity he sold recently (for example, last year) at a particular price and expects future conditions to be somewhat similar, he can think of that price and quantity as one point on his unknown demand curve. The question then is, should he use the same price again – or is there a more profitable price?

First, the marketing manager must construct an equal profit curve showing the various prices which could be charged and the quantities which would have to be sold to make the same profit he made during last period. Figure 25–9 shows an equal profit curve. It shows that the profit obtained last period, when 20,000 units were sold at $4 each, also could have been obtained if he had sold 30,000 units at $2.75, 50,000 units at $2, and so forth.

Given an equal profit curve, the marketing manager might ask others intimately familiar with the market whether they think the company can sell more than 20,000 units at $4 each. There might be similar questions about sales at less and more than $4, but still along the equal profit curve. In other words, could he sell more than 25,000 units at $3.50 and more than 17,000 units at $4.50? If mixed Yes and No answers are obtained to several such questions, the equal profit curve probably would be a reasonable approximation of the demand curve. This would mean that any price along this curve would be equally profitable, and there probably would be little reason to change the $4 price.

If, however, very emphatic Yes or No answers are obtained, the demand curve would be either above or below the equal profit curve. The course of action should be clear. For instance, if it appears that

---

[10] For additional discussion, see Edward R. Hawkins, "Methods of Estimating Demand," *Journal of Marketing*, April, 1957, pp. 428–38.

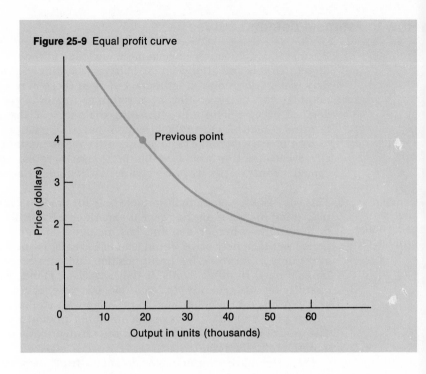

Figure 25-9 Equal profit curve

the demand curve would be somewhere above the equal profit curve at lower prices, then it might be desirable for the firm to drop its price to increase profit. Such a demand curve is illustrated in Figure 25–10. How far prices should be lowered would depend in part on the strength of the pricing executive's feelings about the shape of the curve.

As noted earlier, this procedure does not assure profit maximization, but it is certainly better than ignoring demand. It brings management judgment regarding demand to bear on pricing decisions.[11] And price changes suggested by the analysis should increase profit and thus tend toward maximum profit.

Asking-curve approach estimates whole demand curves

It is possible to "guesstimate" where a whole demand curve is with the asking-curve approach. The marketing manager (or other executives knowledgeable about the probable reaction of the market to price changes) can answer questions using his educated judgment. And these answers can lead to rough-and-ready, yet quantitative, demand curve estimates.

Here we want a whole demand curve, not just the small portion above and below the current price level which we sought with the equal profit curve approach. When we are seeking the most profitable

---

[11] This analysis is developed in Wilford J. Eiteman's, *Price Discrimination in Oligopolistic and Monopolistic Situations* (Michigan Business Reports, No. 33 [Ann Arbor: Bureau of Business Research, University of Michigan, 1960]).

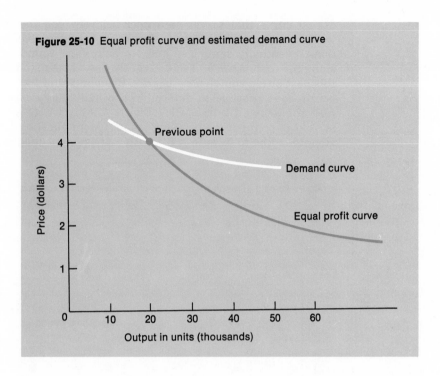

Figure 25-10 Equal profit curve and estimated demand curve

price, substantial price shifts may be necessary, and the equal profit curve approach is not suitable. Concern with small changes may be very useful in fairly static situations, but it also can be misleading because it often gives the impression that demand is inelastic around current prices—probably because of the inertia of customers' attitudes and habits. The asking-curve approach, which attempts to estimate a whole demand curve, gets around this difficulty.

Just a simple Yes or No

The asking-curve approach to estimating demand curves is similar to the equal profit curve approach. Managers are asked questions about whether they expect they would be able to sell more than certain quantities at specific prices. They are *not* asked to make specific numerical estimates. Only Yes or No responses are required. For most people, it is easier to say Yes or No to a suggested price than to conceive their own numbers.[12] Despite their interest in prices, people seem to have little exact knowledge of them.

The approach is to ask experienced executives: "Could you sell more than (a specific quantity) at (a specific price)?" The specific quantities and prices that are asked about are along a cost-per-unit

[12] This approach is somewhat similar to Schlaifer's use of questions about different "bets" to extract subjective probability distributions from businessmen. See R. Schlaifer, *Probability and Statistics for Business Decisions* (New York: McGraw-Hill Book Co., 1959), chaps. i and ii; and for an example of the use of subjective probabilities in pricing strategy, see Paul E. Green, "Bayesian Decision Theory in Pricing Strategy," *Journal of Marketing*, January, 1963, pp. 5–14.

asking curve that serves as a floor below which the firm probably would not want to sell anyway. By asking the executives several questions, eventually some Yes and No points are found in succession along the cost curve, and this suggests that the demand curve crosses this cost curve somewhere nearby. By connecting two such crossing points, it is possible to determine a workable approximation to the relevant demand curve. (See Figure 25-11, where a straight line is used to connect the crossing points.) More questions can be asked along this line to be sure it fits with management judgment.

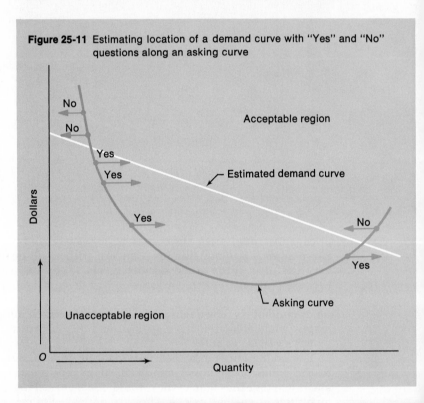

Figure 25-11 Estimating location of a demand curve with "Yes" and "No" questions along an asking curve

This subjective approach to quantifying management's feelings about demand appears to get the pricing executives within striking distance of the best price and quantity. It gives them a quantitative summarization of their attitudes—a demand curve—and if the price obtained through marginal analysis differs from their intuitive feel of the price they should charge, it may force them to recheck their thinking and subsequently to change their pricing decision.

In one case, for example, marginal analysis following the development of such a demand curve indicated that the producer's retail price should be 42 cents. The current price level was about 39 cents. At this time, the producer was the industry price leader. He was seriously considering a price cut in reaction to price dealing and free goods being given away by his competitors.

When marginal analysis indicated that he should raise his price rather than lower it, this industry leader decided to hold his general price level constant, while meeting the price cutting in extremely competitive areas. Further marginal analysis showed that selective price cuts in some areas would actually help cover overhead rather than lose money—as his accountants had figured with average cost analysis! This led to the development of different strategies for different target markets.[13]

Experimental methods of demand estimation

Various methods discussed in Chapter 4 ("Gathering Marketing Information") can be used for estimating demand. Surveys, for example, can be used, but with care. Questions such as: "What would you pay if . . . ?" must be interpreted cautiously. But if survey results suggest little interest in price—perhaps because of strong brand loyalty or simple indifference—it may be reasonable to conclude that demand is inelastic. Then, perhaps, prices can be raised substantially.

Industrial goods buyers may be more aware of prices and the impact costs have on their firms' operations. Their answers about possible reactions to price changes may be quite meaningful.

Market tests also may be useful, either in trial areas or as general experiments. Two classic cases of market tests are worth noting.

The long-play phonograph record industry long resisted price reductions. At last, one price cut was tried, and demand was found to be quite elastic. This brought about greatly increased sales and profits for all members of the industry.

Henry Ford's Model T was another famous experiment. He cut prices dramatically because he anticipated a much larger consumer demand, and in so doing, established the basis for great expansion of the automobile industry.[14]

Historical analysis and its dangers

Historical sales data can be and has been subjected to statistical techniques to estimate demand. This approach is less valuable to us, however, because historical records are available only for essentially homogeneous commodities, such as farm, mine, and forest products, and these usually are sold in almost purely competitive markets anyway.

The real need for demand estimates is in markets where conditions are shifting and where products are continually changing. As seen in our discussion of product life cycles, changing conditions are inevitable. Analysis of historical data not only may be difficult but dangerous

[13] For further discussion on this method, see "Determining a Subjective Demand Curve," in E. J. McCarthy, *Basic Marketing: A Managerial Approach* (rev. ed.; Homewood, Ill.: Richard D. Irwin, Inc., 1964), pp. 799–804. For a discussion on estimating probabilities for use in price bidding, see A. W. Walker, "How to Price Industrial Products," *Harvard Business Review*, September-October, 1967, pp. 125–32.

[14] For further discussion on experiments, see Ray G. Stout, "Developing Data to Estimate Price-Quantity Relationships," *Journal of Marketing*, April, 1969, pp. 34–36; E. A. Pessemier, "An Experimental Method for Estimating Demand," *Journal of Business*, October, 1960, pp. 373–83; and William D. Barclay, "Factorial Design in a Pricing Experiment," *Journal of Marketing Research*. November, 1969, pp. 427–29.

in these situations. Entirely different market situations may exist at different points in time, while statistical analysis of historical data must work with homogeneous data—and mechanical misuse of these methods may lead to invalid estimates. Statistical techniques are most useful for developing industry demand estimates for commodities, rather than the differentiated products with which we are most concerned in this text.[15]

Conclusion

Flexible break-even analysis and traditional supply and demand analysis provide tools that enable a marketing manager to develop the *most profitable* price per unit. "Most profitable" is emphasized because cost-oriented pricing often will yield a profit but *not* necessarily the maximum profit. Sometimes, in fact, even with a high unit price, cost-oriented pricing will result in losses.

Demand and supply analysis utilizes the concepts of marginal revenue and marginal cost in the determination of the *most profitable quantity to produce.* The most profitable quantity is found graphically at the intersection of the marginal revenue and marginal-cost curves. To determine the *most profitable price,* the pricing executive takes his most profitable quantity to the firm's demand curve to determine what price target customers will be willing to pay for this quantity.

The major difficulty in using marginal analysis is determining a demand curve. It is clear from observing the behavior of businessmen that they do have opinions about demand. This is reflected in prestige, odd-even, and psychological pricing.

Several ways of estimating demand were presented. The equal profit curve approach is useful when the marketing manager has had recent experience with the product and when market conditions are fairly stable. Using the previous price as a starting point, he tries to determine whether prices should be changed to increase profit.

The asking-curve approach uses Yes or No questions to estimate a complete demand curve. These questions should be asked of someone who is intimately familiar with the market and can predict probable reaction to the planned marketing mix. Market tests or other marketing research techniques also can be used to estimate demand.

Our discussion of price determination has been intentionally critical of cost-oriented approaches. Too many firms seem to ignore demand and depend almost blindly on cost-oriented pricing. This is often the case in firms where pricing is controlled by financial or accounting officers who have not yet accepted the importance of customers.

Deriving demand curves is not easy nor will estimated curves be perfectly accurate. Nevertheless, experienced executives—aided perhaps by marketing research—should make estimates of the nature

---

[15] For more details on estimating with this approach—basically a "least squares" approach—see Richard S. Watt, *A Method of Analyzing Demand for* *General Commodities, A Case Study of Salt* (U.S. Department of the Interior, Bureau of Mines, Information Circular 8057, 1962), p. 35.

of demand for their product. Such estimates, even if they are inexact, are useful, since prices are usually changed in discrete steps anyway, and an estimated demand curve would probably get one in the right "ball park." Sometimes, when all that is needed is a decision about raising or lowering a price, demand estimates can be very revealing.

It is clear that the marketing manager should make use of the analytical tools at his disposal to estimate customer demand, because the firm's demand curve does not cease to exist simply because it is ignored. Some information is better than none at all.

QUESTIONS AND PROBLEMS

1 Explain the difference between a flexible break-even chart and a regular break-even chart. Relate flexible break-even analysis to demand and supply analysis.

2 Distinguish among marginal revenue, average revenue, and price.

3 Draw a graph showing a demand and cost situation where marginal analysis would correctly indicate that the firm should continue producing even though the profit and loss statement shows a loss.

4 How would a prestige pricing policy fit into a marketing mix? Would exclusive distribution be necessary?

5 Cite a local example of the use of odd-even pricing and then evaluate whether you feel it makes sense.

6 Cite a local example of the use of psychological pricing and then evaluate whether you feel it makes sense.

7 Cite a local example where the manufacturer or retailer seems to be attempting to segment the market and offer class, mass, and fighting brands with appropriate prices. Does the approach seem to be working? Why, or why not?

8 Explain the basic difference between estimating demand curves using equal profit curves and asking curves.

9 Discuss the idea of drawing separate demand curves for different market segments. It seems logical because each target market should have its own marketing mix. But won't this lead to a considerable number of demand curves and possibly prices? And what will this mean with respect to functional discounts and varying prices in the marketplace? Would this be legal? Would it be practical?

10 Evergreen Pea Co. has been enjoying a profitable year. Their product sells to wholesalers for 20 cents a can. After careful study, it has been decided that a 60 percent gross margin should be maintained. Their manufacturing costs are divided in this manner: material, 50 percent of cost; labor, 40 percent of cost; and 10 percent of cost goes for overhead. Both material and labor costs experienced a 10 percent increase. Determine the new price per can based on their present pricing methods. Is it wise to hold fast to a 60 percent margin, if *a price increase* would mean lost customers? Answer using graphs and *MC-MR* analysis. Show a situation where it would be most profitable to (1) raise price, (2) leave price alone, (3) reduce price.

...pricing policies should state specifically: how flexible prices will be, at what level they will be set, how pricing will be handled during the course of the product life cycle, what will be the relation of prices for a single product to those for a whole product line, and how transportation costs will be handled....Specific pricing policies are vital for any firm....Otherwise, the marketing manager has to reexamine his strategy every time a customer asks for a price....

26

Pricing policies

A company's pricing objectives, as we pointed out in Chapter 24, can serve as a general guide for determining prices. The cost- and demand-oriented approaches to price determination discussed in the last two chapters show how prices can be set to accomplish those objectives. Moreover, the marketing strategy a firm develops may suggest or even determine its pricing policies.

Finally, however, a marketing manager must develop a precise set of pricing policies. He must spell out what pricing situations the firm will face and how it will handle them. These policies should state specifically: (1) how flexible his prices will be, (2) at what level they will be set, (3) how pricing will be handled during the course of the product life cycle, (4) what will be the relation of prices for a single product to those for a whole product line, and (5) how transportation costs will be handled.

Specific pricing policies are vital for any firm, and especially for producers and channel captains. Otherwise, the marketing manager has to reexamine his strategy every time a customer asks for a price. This not only would be a drain on executive time, but customer goodwill easily could be lost if quoted prices did not appear to follow a logical pattern.

They don't leave prices to market forces, they administer them

Specific price policies must be established by firms, either implicitly or explicitly. Even where government or industry forces discourage active price competition, pricing policies are needed to solve recurring problems. These policies should lead to consciously set prices aimed at reaching the firm's objectives. In other words, rather than let daily market forces determine their prices, most firms (including *all* those in monopolistic competition) set their own prices, sometimes holding them steady for long periods of time. For this reason, most prices are called *administered prices*.

The various pricing policy decisions which a marketing manager must make, regardless of his objectives or his price determination methods, are the subject of the balance of this chapter.

Price flexibility policies

One of the first decisions any marketing manager has to make is to choose between one price and flexible prices.

One-price policy

A one-price policy consists of offering the *same price to all customers* who purchase goods under essentially the same conditions and in the same quantities. A majority of U.S. producers adopt a one-price policy, mainly for administrative convenience and to maintain goodwill among customers. Most food stores, department stores, and even the modern discount houses and mass merchandisers use a one-price policy, too.

A marketing manager could change his price every day and still be following a one-price policy, because the frequency of change is not involved here. Neither is the question of whether the price is at the right level. The policy simply means that the same price is offered to all customers at the same time.

A one-price policy may make pricing easier for the seller, but the marketing manager must be careful to avoid rigid adherence to a one-price policy. Such a policy could amount to broadcasting a price which his more aggressive competitors could undercut—especially if his prices were somewhat high. One reason for the growth of discount houses is that conventional retailers applied traditional margins and rigidly stuck to them.

Flexible-price policy

Under a flexible-price policy, the same products and quantities are offered to *different customers at different prices,* depending on their bargaining ability, family relationship, or other factors.[1]

Flexible pricing was most common when businesses were small, products were not standardized, and bargaining was traditional. These conditions still exist in most foreign countries. But in the United States, the one-price policy is more common, especially at the retail level, since it facilitates mass selling efforts.

Flexible pricing does have advantages, however, and is often used in the channels, in direct sales of industrial goods, and at retail for more expensive items and homogeneous shopping goods. It allows a salesman to make adjustments for competitive conditions rather than having to turn down an order. An aggressive salesman might first emphasize the quality of his product rather than its price. He may charge a higher price to those customers who will pay it and cut the price for those who won't. Some firms grant discounts or make adjustments for "salesmen's errors" when competitive conditions require it or when highly elastic demand conditions exist in certain segments of the market grid.

Flexible prices can also enable a marketing manager to adjust more readily to the different jobs required in various channels of distribution or in different territories. In some places, his products may be well accepted; in others, he might have to "buy" distribution by offering lower prices.[2]

These flexible-pricing advantages really occur because the firm modifies its marketing mix for different market grid boxes – that is, it creates new strategies. If this approach is properly handled and based on an intimate knowledge of the needs and preferences of different market grid boxes, it can be both profitable and acceptable to customers.

The use of flexible prices can cause legal difficulties for manufacturers and wholesalers, however. Although they might attempt to reach different target markets with their flexible prices, some of their middlemen customers may be competing with each other in the same markets. This might make the firm's flexible prices illegal under the Robinson-Patman Act, since this act prohibits charging different prices to *competing* buyers for the same goods under the same conditions, unless the prices are necessary to *meet competition.* In practice, this last clause *encourages* a considerable amount of price flexibility, at least for small companies.

A flexible pricing policy has other disadvantages, too. The customer who finds that others have obtained lower prices for what he feels is the same marketing mix is not going to be happy. The time needed for bargaining may increase, and the cost of selling may rise as buyers become aware that this could be profitable to them. Finally, some sales-

[1] For an interesting discussion of the many variations from a one-price system in retailing, see Stanley C. Hollander, "The 'One-Price' System – Fact or Fiction?" *Journal of Retailing,* Fall, 1955, pp. 127–44.

[2] Martin R. Warshaw, "Pricing to Gain Wholesalers' Selling Support," *Journal of Marketing,* July, 1962, pp. 50–54.

men may let the practice of offering price cuts become a habit. This could eliminate price as a competitive tool and lead, instead, to a new and lower price level.

Price-level policies

When a marketing manager administers his prices—as most do—he must consciously make another policy decision: Will his prices be set below the market, at the same level as competition, or above the market? If the firm is in pure competition, of course, no policy is really necessary; to offer goods above or below the market price would be foolish. We will be concerned, therefore, with those less than purely competitive situations in which the marketing manager does have a choice. Strictly speaking, if a firm used marginal analysis in an effort to maximize its profits, it would not have to make a specific decision on price level. The price level would be set by the data analysis. However, in the process of estimating the appropriate demand curves in various markets, the ideas reflected in the following discussion would be relevant. Basically, every price setter must consider not only the needs and preferences of his target markets and their likely reaction to his whole mix (not just the product), but also the probable reactions of his direct competitors, if any, when establishing his prices.

Below the market—but perhaps not really below Retail discounters and mass merchandisers of both soft and hard goods, and more recently of foods,[3] have consistently offered goods below the prices charged by conventional retailers. Even some conventional retailers use this approach. R. H. Macy & Co., in its main midtown Manhattan store *only*, has followed a policy of always selling below competitors' prices. Obviously, this policy successfully appeals to certain target markets—perhaps the economic shoppers.

Some manufacturers emphasize below-the-market prices in their marketing mixes. This is most effective when the firm is not large in relation to the total industry, making competitive retaliation less likely. It helps, too, if the firm or product has a reputation for dependable quality which, at a lower price, makes for a good value.

The Elkhart (Ind.) Paint Co., a small industrial paint supplier, recently held its prices steady when its large competitors raised theirs. A company official observed that Elkhart paint customers charged fixed prices for their own products and "We feel they will appreciate our stand and favor us as their paint supplier so long as we continue to give them good products at a good price and good service."

A major example of a large company attempting to price under the market is Volkswagen with its "beetle," which has consistently sold at lower prices than U.S. small cars, compacts, and minicars. The com-

[3] E. W. Cundiff and R. C. Anderson, "Competitive Food Pricing of Discounters," *Journal of Retailing*, Spring, 1963, pp. 15–17; and "Discounting: A Food Chain Reaction," *Business Week*, September 26, 1970, pp. 44–46.

pany's strategy has been successful for many years, as VW has expanded its share of the market and built an increasingly powerful dealer organization. A critical question here, however, is whether potential customers recognize the various cars in the market as direct competitors. Or, more basically, is there such a thing as the *automobile market*? Or does this market consist of many market grid boxes?

The important point here is that if some customers *do* perceive differences in the physical product, or in convenience of location, or in the whole marketing mix, then what we really are talking about are different marketing strategies, not different price levels. Seemingly lower prices are merely lower prices in different marketing mixes. This raises the question: Are any prices truly below the market? Ultimately, the answer depends on the attitudes of the various target customers. The same price might be seen as below the market in some market grid boxes and merely "the price that is needed to make a good mix" in other boxes.

Meeting competition — sense for a few nuts

A firm with a unique marketing strategy might not have to worry much about meeting competition. It might even be difficult to define exactly what the competition is. Most firms, however, must set their prices within a range determined by the prices of nearly direct competitors and substitutes. They have some latitude in their pricing — but not complete freedom.

Meeting competition to avoid price competition

A meet-competition policy could be used in any market situation by a busy executive who did not wish to disturb the pricing status quo, either in his own company or among competitors. Prices are highly visible competitive weapons and are more easily matched by competitors than any of the other marketing mix components.

Meeting competition in very competitive situations

In highly competitive markets, all firms must of necessity meet competition — at the market price. Even the large oil companies, such as Standard Oil Co. of New Jersey and Standard Oil Co. of Indiana have to meet competition. They might attempt to set prices to get a target return on investment, but there are usually so many competitors, both large and small, that they are not able to rely strictly on cost-based pricing.

Smaller firms often will sell at any price above variable cost, especially when the market becomes flooded. Then larger firms must meet competition whether they like it or not. As one Citgo official said: "We would not have this situation (price cuts) if a few nuts got some sense into their heads."[4]

Meeting competition in oligopoly situations

Meeting competition may be the only sensible policy — following either a target return or profit maximization objective — in *oligopoly* situations.

[4] *Time*, October 6, 1961, p. 82.

Oligopoly situations are special market situations which develop when a market has several basic characteristics. In oligopoly situations there are:

1. Essentially homogeneous products, such as basic industrial chemicals or gasoline.
2. Usually relatively few sellers, or a few large firms and perhaps many smaller ones who follow the lead of the large ones.
3. Usually fairly inelastic *industry* demand.

The marketing manager knows that cutting prices under such oligopolistic conditions may lead to ruinous competition, and raising prices could be pointless, since there is no assurance that competitors will follow.

When demand goes kinky

The demand curve for each firm is particularly interesting in an oligopoly situation. Although the industry demand curve can be inelastic throughout the relevant range, the demand curve facing each individual oligopolistic competitor looks "kinked," as shown in Figure 26-1. The current market price is at the kink.

Each marketing manager must expect that raising his price above the market for such a homogeneous product would cause a substantial loss of sales. His demand curve would be relatively flat above the market price, since few, if any, competitors would follow his price increase. But if he lowers his price, he must expect competitors to

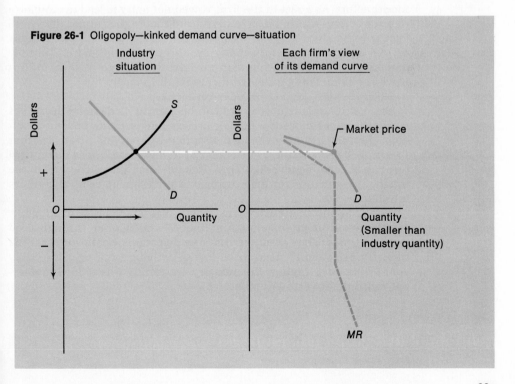

Figure 26-1 Oligopoly—kinked demand curve—situation

follow. Therefore, given inelastic industry demand, his own demand curve would be inelastic at lower prices. Since lowering price along such a curve is clearly an unprofitable move, he probably would not do so. He would leave his price at the kink—the market price.

The dashed marginal revenue line in Figure 26–1 shows that marginal revenue drops precipitously at the kinked point. This means that if the supply curve crosses the MR curve any place along this drop, the firm should hold its price at the kinked price level. Reducing price below the kink would actually reduce total revenue and profit.

Prices may move—with difficulty

Most of the firms in an oligopoly situation are aware of the economics of the situation, at least intuitively. A price leader usually sets a price, perhaps to maximize profits or to get a certain target return on investment. Then, without any collusion, other members of the industry follow, and the price may be maintained for a long period or at least as long as all members of the industry continue making a reasonable profit.

The price leader might try to lead others to higher levels if basic industry conditions seem to warrant, perhaps if labor costs have increased. Or the leader might try to get the market price back up to former levels after an extended period of price cutting. But this must be done carefully. The competitors may not play the game, and the leader may lose substantially before being forced to retreat. The National Gypsum Co., for example, recently tried to return industry price levels to list price levels and was "chopped up" during its two-month effort. As a result, the firm vowed not to try to lead the industry in price actions again. Its executives said that in the future, they were "going to be absolutely convinced in the marketplace by the actions of our competitors before doing anything." Furthermore, "If they demonstrate statesmanship, our participation will go with them. But if we see them being cute, we will react differently."[5]

Either you need sulfur or you don't—at our price

Price adjustments downward can be painful. If demand decreases considerably, as in a recession, or if large new supplies become available, the industry may readjust its price by trial and error. Another firm might become the price leader or at least lead prices downward until an acceptable level is found. In some cases, if prices are cut too much, a dominant firm may resort to a price war to bring the others into line.

The U.S. sulfur industry was long a classic oligopoly example. A few large sulfur producers maintained a similar price through good and bad times. They assumed that demand was inelastic and that the industry price didn't need to be lower. Although the price probably could have been higher, the industry apparently was following a target-return-on-investment objective.

[5] "National Gypsum Vows Not to Lead Industry Again in Price Actions," *Wall Street Journal*, July 17, 1970, p. 11; and "Gypsum Makers Move to Stop Sharp Discounts," *Wall Street Journal*, December 3, 1969, p. 6.

Then a major new source of supply, Mexican sulfur, became available at lower prices. This upset the kinked-demand-curve situation and set off a round of price cuts. Certain industry members deplored the price cutting and pointed to the inelastic demand situation. They said, "The price cut won't cause increased consumption. Either a person uses sulfur or he doesn't."[6] Yet prices stayed at a lower level, and profits decreased—as would be expected.

Usually oligopoly situations are fairly stable as long as all competitors' prices remain close to the leader's price, and competitors do not change market shares too much by other marketing tactics. But when the market is upset, as it was by the lower-priced Mexican sulfur, the situation can degenerate into a price war.

More recently, world demand for sulfur increased significantly and prices moved up, with prices of all U.S. producers going up at about the same time as would be expected in an oligopoly situation. Next, new suppliers were attracted to this market and prices began to decline, again with the various producers moving together.[7]

Oligopoly fairly common—often leads to price cutting

In recent years, we have witnessed price cutting and price wars among oligopolists in electrical equipment, aluminum, steel, copper, zinc, synthetic fibers, and TV picture tubes. Sometimes the price cuts are drastic, such as Du Pont's "Dacron" price cut of 25 percent on one occasion. This was caused, in part, by production capacity that already exceeded demand and that was scheduled for further expansion.[8]

A common local example of oligopoly is in retail gasoline marketing, at a major intersection or along a busy highway. Enough final consumers think of gasoline as homogeneous to create oligopoly conditions, and oligopoly-type price wars are common.

These usually start when some dealer-brand price discounter successfully attracts "too much" business, perhaps by price cutting 1 cent a gallon below his usual price. The war proceeds for a time, until one of the dealers calls a meeting and suggests that they all "get a little sense." Sometimes these price wars will end immediately after such a meeting, with prices returning to a "reasonable and proper" level. Usually this is a level where all costs are covered and *some* profits are earned, although in gasoline retailing, profits traditionally have not been too attractive.[9]

[6] "Sulphur Heads into Price War," *Business Week*, September 18, 1957, p. 50.

[7] "Price of Sulphur is Cut $2 a Ton by Texas Gulf," *Wall Street Journal*, January 21, 1969, p. 3; "Freeport Sulphur Joins Texas Gulf in Cutting Price," *Wall Street Journal*, January 22, 1969, p. 2; "Sulphur Market Scraps Price List as Prices Tumble," *Business Week*, November 8, 1969, p. 22; and "Unlocking a Rich Store of Sulphur," *Business Week*, April 22, 1967, pp. 60–66; and "Price Wrangle Approaches a Climax," *Business Week*, June 18, 1966, pp. 126–30.

[8] *Business Week*, June 24, 1967, p. 85.

[9] For further discussion of the economics of gasoline price wars, see Dan E. Schendel and Pietro Balastra, "Rational Behavior and Gasoline Price Wars," *Applied Economics*, Vol. 1 (1969), pp. 89–101; and G. A. Churchill, Jr., Neil M. Ford, and U. B. Ozanne, "An Analysis of Price Aggressiveness in Gasoline Marketing," *Journal of Marketing Research*, February, 1970, pp. 36–43; and J. M. Kamen and R. J. Toman, "Psychophysics of Prices," *Journal of Marketing Research*, February, 1970, pp. 27–35. For further discussion on oligopolistic pricing, see Robert L. Knox, "Competitive Oligopolistic Pricing," *Journal of Marketing*, July, 1966, pp. 47–51.

Above the
market — but
above may
not be above

Unless they offer a better product or better service, marketing managers cannot consistently or for long periods charge prices that are above the market. Vigorous promotion may enable a firm to obtain a premium price above those for essentially similar physical products, perhaps because of implied or stated product guarantees or the greater psychic satisfaction that customers receive because of the advertising. But here a new product has been created, and its price might not really be above the market. Actually, a new price is set for a new marketing mix or even a new marketing strategy. Note that the market grid concept is relevant here.

Even top management may not clearly understand the concept that a different price would be required, or at least be possible, for a different marketing mix or marketing strategy. Zenith Radio Corp. executives proudly claim that their prices start well above those of competing models and that one of the reasons for their outstanding success in recent years is that while other companies cut prices and skimped on quality, Zenith consistently maintained high quality. In marketing strategy terms, however, Zenith prices were not above the market, but rather were higher prices for higher quality. Some customers want high quality more than they want low price, and Zenith benefited by satisfying these target markets.

Pricing over the product life cycle

When the original price level for a new product is established, the product life-cycle concept must be considered. The initial strategy decision should take into account the impact of this pricing decision on subsequent pricing decisions as the product life cycle moves along. Strategies have to be implemented over a period of time, and if conditions change, new strategies may be needed.

You will recall that profits generally rise during the early stage of a product's life and then decline as competitive products enter the market. In the early stages, the firm is more likely to have a strong monopolistic competition situation. Later in the product life cycle, its market situation may tend toward pure competition. Here meeting competition is more critical, but even when pricing is handled correctly profits will tend to decline.

To skim or
penetrate

The price policy a firm adopts will significantly affect how fast the product moves through the cycle. The initial price can be especially important. A high price, for example, tends to encourage competitors because they will see more opportunity for profit at this price level.

The specific prices used will depend somewhat on the company's pricing objectives, but there are two extremes that should be considered in pricing a new product. Should the firm use a *skimming* or a *penetration* price? Both elasticity of demand in the target market(s) and competition affect this decision.

Skimming pricing – feeling out demand at a good price	A skimming policy is aimed at getting the "cream" of the market (the top of the demand curve) at a high price before catering to the more price-sensitive segments of the market. Skimming frequently is practiced to maximize profits on new products – particularly in the product introductory stage when demand is fairly inelastic, at least in the upper price ranges.

Skimming is useful for feeling out demand – for getting a better understanding of the shape of the demand curve. It is easier to start with a high price that customers can refuse and then reduce it, than to start with a low price and then try to raise it. When the top of the market is insensitive to price and willing to pay what is asked – when the demand curve is inelastic – a skimming policy will produce more income in the early stages of the product life cycle. This produces funds for expansion into new markets and for repaying research and development costs quickly.

A skimming policy can lead to a slow reduction of the price in a step-down or "cascading" process. This helps the marketing manager to get information about the shape of the demand curve that he can use in setting the best price for the mass market. The step-down technique, however, is part of a dynamic process. As the prices are lowered, new target markets are sought. New place and promotion policies may be needed, too. In short, a skimming pricing policy may involve changing prices through a succession of marketing strategies during the course of the product life cycle.

Penetration pricing – get the business even at a loss	A penetration policy is the opposite of a skimming policy. The intention is to try to sell the whole market at one price, that is, a low price on the firm's demand curve where the quantity demanded is larger. This policy might be indicated where there is no "elite" market – that is, where the whole demand curve is fairly elastic, even in the early stages of the product life cycle.

A penetration policy will be even more attractive if, as volume expands, substantial economies of scale reduce costs, or if the firm seriously expects strong competition *very soon* after introduction. A *low* penetration price may be called a "stay-out" price, since it is intended to discourage large competitors from entering the market.

A penetration price might slow down the speed of the product life cycle and enable the firm to hold the same price for a longer time. The firm might have to accept some losses in the early stages, however, while the product is gaining customer acceptance.[10]

Introductory price dealing – okay, get in there and fight!	Outright price cuts do attract customers. Retailers or producers offering new products, therefore, often use *temporary* price cuts to speed their entry into a market. These temporary price cuts should be distinguished from low-penetration prices, however, because the intention is to raise prices as soon as the introductory offer is over.

[10] Joel Dean, *How to Price a New Product* (Management Aids for Small Manufacturers, No. 62 [Washington, D.C.: Small Business Administration, April, 1955]), pp. 1 and 2; and "Pricing Policies for New Products," *Harvard Business Review*, November, 1950, pp. 45–53.

Established competitors often choose not to meet this introductory price dealing, as long as the introductory period is not too long or too successful. But realizing that customers may shift their loyalties if they try competitors' products, some aggressive competitors do meet such introductory price cuts, perhaps with a price cut of their own or combination offers such as a "free" toothbrush with toothpaste at the regular toothpaste price.

Once price dealing gets started in a market, it may continue for some time — perhaps with "cents-off" offers — especially if the basic product type is late in the market growth stage or in the market maturity stage. Profits could be declining at the same time that new-comers are trying to enter the market with price deals. Some firms associate the dealing with their declining profits and retaliate, thereby contributing to the vigorous competition which is typical as the life cycle moves on.

Clearly, when a marketing manager sets pricing policies, he must have a full appreciation for the product life-cycle concept, understanding how long his product's cycle is likely to run and where his product is in the cycle.[11]

Pricing a full line or total product

Our emphasis has been — and will continue to be — on the problems of pricing a single item, mainly because this simplifies our discussion. But most marketing managers actually are responsible for more than one product. In fact, their product may be the whole company line. Therefore, some discussion of full-line pricing and price lining is necessary.

Full-line pricing — market or firm oriented?

Many companies offer a complete line (or assortment) of products and have to price this full line. But the correct pricing approach depends on which of two basically different strategies the firm follows. In one case, all products in the company's line may be aimed at the same general target market, which makes it important for all prices to be somewhat related to one another.

In other cases, the different products in the line might be aimed at entirely different target markets. Here, there doesn't have to be any relation between the various prices, although production-oriented firms might look at it as a full-line pricing problem. A chemical manufacturer of a wide variety of organic compounds with a variety of target markets, for example, probably should price each product separately, in light of the needs and preferences in each market seg-

---

[11] For more discussion on price dealing, see Charles L. Hinkle, "The Strategy of Price Deals," *Harvard Business Review*, July–August, 1965, pp. 75–85; H. J. Claycamp, "Dynamic Effects of Short Duration Price Differentials on Retail Gasoline Prices," *Journal of Marketing Research*, May, 1966, pp. 175–78; and W. F. Massy and R. E. Frank, "Short Term Price and Dealing Effects in Selected Market Segments," *Journal of Marketing Research*, May, 1965, pp. 171–85.

ment. To use a full-line pricing approach here might lead needlessly to under-pricing some products and over-pricing others.

Examples of a full line being offered to the same target market are a TV manufacturer selling an entire line to retailers, or a forklift truck producer offering various sizes to large manufacturers, or a grocery retailer with his thousands of items. Here the firm *must* consider the customers' reaction to its full line of prices.

Usually the marketing manager attempts to price products in the line so that the prices will appear logically related and make sense to potential customers. Most customers, especially industrial customers, feel that prices should be related to cost, and this must be considered in developing prices. Customers usually realize that small production runs or handling small quantities is likely to cost more, and they may be willing to pay higher prices for items which they know have a small market.

Further, the various prices in the line should be set with competition in mind. A few out-of-line prices may project a high-price image which will carry over to other items on which comparison is more difficult, if not impossible. Price competition on some lines often comes from rivals who offer low prices to offset their lack of a complete line. The full-line competitor's approach in such a case should be to meet the competition by lowering prices where necessary and raising prices on items facing less competition.

A well-publicized example of full-line pricing involves IBM computer systems. Under pressure from antitrust authorities who were concerned about stimulating competition, IBM announced separate prices for its various computers, auxiliary equipment, and special services. Previously, whole systems, including the training of operators and programs to make the machines work, were included in a single price.

The new "unbundled" pricing system could make it easier for some smaller competitors to compete for part of this business, but it may also hurt others. Leasing organizations, for example, which formerly bought machines and then leased them to users, may see this part of the business dry up as IBM's new pricing policy makes it more attractive to rent a machine than to purchase it or lease it from a third party. Perhaps other parts of IBM's unbundled package will turn out to be appealing to short-line competitors, but IBM marketing executives probably will try to price each part of the line competitively so that no business is given to competitors by default.[12]

Cost not much help in full-line pricing

The marketing manager must try to recover all of his costs on the whole line, perhaps by pricing quite low on competitive items and much higher on less competitive items. But costs are not much help to the marketing manager in full-line pricing. There is no single cor-

---

[12] "IBM Programs Another Winner," *Business Week,* August 22, 1970, pp. 19–20; "The Wide-Open Market that IBM Unbundled," *Business Week,* May 2, 1970, pp. 84–88; "IBM Rewrites the Price Book," *Business Week,* June 28, 1969, pp. 102–4; and John L. Wilson, "Separate Pricing for Computer Support Services," *Business Horizons,* June, 1970, pp. 79–85.

rect way to allocate a company's total fixed costs to each of the products. Many methods are tried in practice, but all are arbitrary. And if a certain method is carried through without regard to demand, it may lead to extremely unrealistic prices. The marketing manager has to be able to judge demand for the whole line as well as demand for each individual product in each target market in order to avoid mistakes.

As an aid to full-line pricing, the marketing manager can assemble directly variable costs on the many items in his line for calculating a floor under which he won't lower his price. To this he can add a "reasonable" markup based on his assessment of the quality of the product, the strength of the demand for the product, and the degree of competition he faces. Marginal analysis obviously could be used here if desired. But finally, the image projected by the entire line must be evaluated.

Price lining — a few prices cover the field

Price lining is similar to full-line pricing in that prices are developed for more than one product at a time. But here the focus is on prices at the retail level.

Price lining is an application of the concept of psychological pricing discussed in Chapter 25. It is the policy of setting a few price levels for given classes or lines of merchandise and then marking all items at one of these established prices. There are no prices at the intermediate points. Exactly how does price lining work?

It would be reasonable to assume that most men will pay between $1.50 and $5 for a necktie. In price lining, there will *not* be many prices in this range; there will be only a few. Ties will *not* be priced at $1.50, $1.65, $1.70, $1.75, $1.95, $2.05, etc. They will be priced in perhaps four levels at $1.50, $2.50, $3.50 and $5.

The main advantage of pricing lining is that for both clerks and customers it lessens the confusion caused by a multiplicity of prices. Some customers may consider goods in only one price category. The major decision then becomes *which* item to choose at that price. Price no longer is a question unless the goods at that price are unsatisfactory. Then perhaps the salesclerk can trade the customer up to the next price level.

For the retailer, price lining has several advantages. Sales may increase because he can offer a larger assortment in each price line and because it is easier to get customers to make decisions within one price line. Stock planning is simpler because demand is larger at the relatively few prices. Price lining also can reduce expenses because total stock requirements are lessened even though ample stocks are carried in each line. Price lining results in greater turnover rates, fewer markdowns, quicker sales, and simplified buying procedures.

Care must be taken with price lining for shopping goods. Most such items cover a wide price range, often making it difficult for a retailer to "trade up" the customer, because each jump means a sizable increase. If the price lines for men's slacks are set at $10, $15, and $20, the customer who is considering a pair at $10 may not be willing to jump all the way to $15. But if more lines are available, say at $12.50 and $17.50, he might be moved up one level. When the jump is too great, the customer may look elsewhere, and the retailer could lose a sale.

Another potential price-lining difficulty is the adjustment of prices when costs are raised or lowered. Consider the retailer carrying two price lines, perhaps $9.95 and $13.50, with costs of $5.89 and $8.00 respectively. A 10 percent wholesale price rise would be a problem for the retailer. His costs on the $9.95 retail line would rise to $6.48, but a $13.50 retail price would be too high to be competitive. Yet if he kept the goods at $9.95 retail, his gross profit would fall from $4.06 to $3.47.

One solution to this problem would be to establish a new price line. But as other price changes followed, this could confuse customers and even destroy the image of the store.

This problem often can be prevented in the first place by manufacturers who know their retail market. When manufacturing costs increase, instead of increasing their price, the firms reduce the size of the package or cheapen the product so that established prices can be maintained. In other words, these producers use demand-backward pricing.

Demand-backward pricing facilitates price lining

Demand-backward pricing is commonly used by producers of final consumer goods, especially shopping goods, such as women's and children's clothing and shoes, and other things like toys or gifts for which the customer will spend a specific amount because he is seeking "a two-dollar or a five-dollar gift." Here, a sort of reverse cost-plus pricing process is used, inspired by the availability of demand at various price levels. This process has been called "market-minus" pricing.

The producer starts with the retail price for a particular price line and then works backward, subtracting the typical margins which channel members expect. This gives him the approximate price he should charge. Then, he deducts from this price his average or planned marketing expenses to determine the allocation for the production cost of each item. The kind of a product he can offer at this price depends on the nature of his cost structure and the expected sales volume.

Obviously, demand estimates are necessary if demand-backward pricing is to be done effectively. Since competitors can be expected to make the best product possible, marginal analysis can be helpful to determine the optimum amount to be spent on manufacturing costs. By increasing marginal costs slightly, the product might be so improved in consumers' eyes that the firm would sell many more units. But if consumers are not quality conscious, but only seeking novelty, additional quality might not increase the quantity demanded and therefore should not be offered.

Price lining does not solve retailer pricing problems

Some retailers seem to feel that adopting commonly used price lines eliminates the need for pricing decisions. This is not true.

The retailer must first decide which price lines will appeal most to his customers. Then he must decide what quality of goods to buy for these price lines.

Theoretically, the more a retailer pays for an item to be sold in a particular price line, the greater the quantity he should sell. That is,

675

the better the value he offers his customers, the greater his turnover should be. The question is: How small a margin should he take to increase his turnover and profit? This is a profit-maximizing process requiring serious consideration of prices – both his own and competitors' – and costs.[13]

Some pricing policies have promotional impact

A marketing mix consists of four hard-to-separate variables. Now we will look at several possible pricing policies which also have promotional value.

Multiple-unit pricing – sell more, pay more, use more

Multiple-unit pricing is primarily a consumer goods phenomenon. It is something like a quantity discount, designed to increase sales. Three units, a six-pack, or a case of any item may be offered at a lower price per unit. Multiple packs of soft drinks and other beverages appeal to many customers, mainly because of their convenience but sometimes also because of a lower price. Not all multiple packs are sold at a unit discount, however.

Some customers – note the market grid concept again – seem to be impulsive quantity buyers. Others need larger quantities and probably expect that they will not be penalized by quantity purchases. As a result, multiple-unit offerings, even at *higher* prices, may actually sell better than cheaper single units. For example, when a manufacturer's brand of apricots regularly selling at 29 cents a can was offered at 3/89 cents, the stockturn rate improved rapidly. Some consumerists feel, probably correctly, that such pricing is deceptive, in that it takes advantage of a reasonable assumption which some consumers would make to routinize their buying. Mandatory "unit-pricing" legislation would seek to discourage this sort of multiple-unit pricing.

Multiple-unit offerings may be merely "borrowing" sales from the future, but in some cases they do seem to increase consumption, especially if the size of the pack fits in with typical consumer usage patterns. Few families buy or use one soft drink at a time, for example, and a multiple-pack offer may actually increase sales of the product because availability at the point of consumption may encourage greater consumption – to "finish off" the carton.

Leader pricing – boost sales but don't play football

Leader pricing is commonly used to get customers into retail stores. Certain products are picked for their promotional value and priced low. In food stores, the leader prices are the "specials" that are run and advertised regularly to communicate an image of low prices. Large stocks of these low-priced items are sold.

The leader-priced items are bona fide bargains priced very low for the sole purpose of getting customers into the store. Leader pricing

[13] For a fuller discussion of product-line pricing, see A. R. Oxenfeldt, "Product Line Pricing," *Harvard Business Review,* July–August, 1966, pp. 137–44.

usually is restricted to well-known, widely used, branded items on which customers will recognize a bona fide price cut. Ideally, the leader item should be chosen from items that are reasonably expensive, so that customers have something to gain, but not so expensive that they would have limited appeal. A 40 percent cut on a candy bar, from 5 cents to 3 cents, might not seem important enough to customers to bother with. On the other hand, 40 per cent off a $15 or $18 Virginia ham might still yield a higher price than many customers would want to pay.

Leader pricing usually is restricted to goods that customers don't stock heavily — butter, coffee, cigarettes, and similar items. The idea is to attract customers, not sell large quantites of the leaders. And to avoid hurting the firm's own profits, it may be desirable to use items that are not directly competitive with major lines, as in the sale of bargain-priced cigarettes at a gasoline station.

Leader items usually are sold above cost but below the normal price level. For consumers, leader pricing is desirable, since money that might have been spent on promotion is used to cut prices. For manufacturers, leader pricing can mean something else.

Some manufacturers become very unhappy when retailers choose their product as a price leader. They feel their product becomes a "price football" that customers will only buy at a discount. They also fear that established channel relationships will suffer and that eventually the sales of their product will decrease. For well-known brands of established quality, however, this fear seems exaggerated, unless the low price were maintained for a considerable length of time. Generally, it is not. The novelty and promotional value of a price cut is quickly lost, and most drugstores and grocery stores that regularly use leader pricing switch continually from one item to another. They want to attract business, not lower some manufacturer's price level.

Bait pricing — offer for a pittance, but sell under protest

Bait pricing, like leader pricing, is used to attract business. But unlike leader pricing, the seller *does not* plan to sell much merchandise at the low price.

This procedure is commonly used in the retail furniture trade. To attract customers, an extremely low price is offered on an item which the trade considers "nailed down." Then, once customers are in the store, the salesmen are expected to point out the disadvantages of the lower-quality item and to switch customers to higher-quality and more expensive products. Customers can buy the bait item, but only with great difficulty.

This policy attempts to attract bargain hunters, or customers on the very low end of the demand curve who are not normally part of the market. If bait pricing is successful, customers may be traded up, and the demand for higher-quality products will expand. But extremely aggressive and sometimes deceptive bait-pricing advertising has brought this method into disrepute. The Federal Trade Commission considers bait pricing a deceptive act and has prohibited its use in interstate commerce. Still, some retailers who operate solely within one state continue to advertise bait prices.

Pricing policies that affect geographic size of firm's market

A major pricing policy decision that a marketing manager must make concerns who is to pay the freight or how it is to be split between buyer and seller. The firm's objectives or target market may help establish this policy, often by requiring that some of the freight be absorbed by the seller in order to reach a larger market. But a poor decision on freight policy might block any chance for satisfying certain segments of the target market and for reaching the firm's objectives.

In Chapter 23, we discussed the commonly accepted terms used in geographic pricing, such as F.O.B. In Chapter 18, we explained that an alert marketing manager or channel captain might maintain a traffic department to help suppliers and customers ship most economically, and thereby improve his own channel position. But now we must look more carefully at the meaning of these terms and their potential impact on marketing strategy planning.

F.O.B. pricing — the closer, the cheaper

F.O.B. shipping point pricing simplifies the seller's pricing but may unduly narrow his market. Since the delivered cost of his goods will vary depending on the buyer's location, a customer located at a greater distance from the seller must pay more for his goods and might be inclined to buy from nearby suppliers.

F.O.B. pricing has an added difficulty since it may limit the potential *buyer's* market. That is, after he has purchased goods from a seller who prefers to use F.O.B. pricing, a remote buyer might have difficulty incorporating the higher-cost product into his finished product and then shipping it back for sale near the original seller's plant. This problem has had an impact on the location of some producers. It is one reason why so many producers operate plants near their basic raw material suppliers. Industries which use large quantities of steel, for example, are concentrated in Milwaukee, Chicago, Detroit, Cleveland, Pittsburgh, and Philadelphia, near the biggest steel mills. A location close to his basic material suppliers enables a manufacturer of a final product to compete over a wider area.

Zone pricing smoothes delivered prices

Zone pricing is designed to reduce the wide variation in delivered prices which result from an F.O.B. shipping point pricing policy. It also simplifies the charging for transportation.

Under zone pricing, an average freight charge is made to all buyers within certain geographical areas. The seller pays the actual freight charges and then bills the customer for an average charge. The United States might be divided into five zones, for example, and all buyers within each zone would pay the same freight charge. Buyers nearer to the shipping point really would be subsidizing those farther away, but if freight charges are not too high, it makes little difference to the buyers.

Zone pricing also may tend to stabilize prices within an area, since all buyers will pay the same basic price before quantity or other discounts. Such stabilized prices can be especially important when there is pricing rivalry between middlemen in adjacent geographic territories.

The zone approach often is used by manufacturers of hardware and food items, both to minimize the possibility of price competition in the channels and to simplify the computation of transportation charges they would have to make for the thousands of wholesalers and retailers they serve.

Uniform delivered pricing – one price to all

Uniform delivered pricing – sometimes called "postage stamp pricing" – is simply an extension of zone pricing. An entire country may be considered one zone, and the average cost of delivery is included in the price. It is most often used when transportation costs are relatively low and the seller wishes to sell his product in all geographic areas at one price, perhaps one which is nationally advertised.

Freight absorption pricing – competing on equal ground in another territory

When all the firms in an industry use F.O.B. shipping point pricing, a firm tends to do well near its plant or shipping point but not so well farther away. As salesmen solicit business at greater distances, delivered prices rise, and they find themselves priced out of the market.

This situation does not always benefit either the consumer or business firms. Since competitors have difficulty competing in someone else's home market, the home-market seller is faced with less competition and may raise his own price. Without competition, the home-territory seller may also let quality or service slip.

Freight-absorption pricing enables manufacturers and wholesalers to compete in larger territories – which on the whole increases competition. When a marketing manager decides to penetrate a new territory, he generally absorbs freight cost so that his delivered price will meet the nearest competitor's. This amounts to cutting his price to appeal to new market grid segments.

With freight absorption pricing, the only limit on the size of his marketing territory is the amount of freight cost a marketing manager is willing to absorb. These absorbed costs cut net return on each sale, but the new business may raise total profit.

Freight absorption pricing is commonly used when firms have high fixed costs and low variable costs. These conditions dictate that the company achieve good volume. Actually, a company could absorb freight costs until its net return was barely above variable cost.

Basing-point pricing

Basing-point pricing policies benefit a company uniquely by reducing or eliminating the need for freight absorption. Here, competitors recognize the same shipping points – basing-points – as places from which to figure the cost of transportation, regardless of the actual shipping point. Basing-point pricing grows out of the competition in a dynamic marketplace.

To understand how basing-point pricing might develop, assume that all plants in a new industry are located together and have the same production costs. Each producer might start out selling F.O.B. his plant. Delivered prices in distant markets would be considerably higher than near the home market, and these higher prices would encourage competitive plants to develop in outlying markets. When they did, how would you determine what prices would be charged in these markets?

Single-basing-point system

This was precisely the situation during the early days of the steel industry. Steel offers the outstanding example of a single basing-point system.

Originally steel was produced in the United States in the Pittsburgh area and sold F.O.B. Pittsburgh. As additional plants developed in Cleveland and Chicago, there was the question of what price to set. If the Chicago producer had identical production costs and set his price F.O.B. Chicago, then he might eliminate Pittsburgh sellers from the Chicago market and other markets where he had a freight advantage. Pittsburgh sellers could absorb freight cost, but this would reduce their profits.

To solve this problem, the steel industry leaders decided that all steel in the country would be sold, regardless of where it had been produced, *as if it had come from Pittsburgh* — the single basing point for prices.

The advantage to the Pittsburgh sellers was obvious, but why did the Chicago area sellers agree? The answer is simple: it was extremely profitable for them.

Their total sales might be reduced by Pittsburgh competition, but in return, the system permitted them to charge their Chicago customers freight from Pittsburgh. If the basic steel price were $50 a ton in either Pittsburgh or Chicago, and the transportation charge from Pittsburgh to Chicago were $10 a ton, then the Chicago producer collected a $10 "phantom freight" charge on all steel sold in the Chicago area. (See Figure 26–2 for a pictorial view of how basing-point pricing works.)

Basing-point pricing systems have been found in basic industries — such as steel, cement, and building materials — that are characterized by oligopoly, high transportation costs relative to the goods' price, and high fixed costs relative to variable costs. In such situations, it is desirable to expand sales volume, yet inelastic demand has made this difficult. A basing-point plan was an industry's reaction to a difficult market situation.

Basing-point pricing, however, was so obviously at variance with the consumer interest that the Federal Trade Commission, as early as 1921, took action against the U.S. Steel Corp. and other steel companies. As a result of this FTC action, the steel industry, beginning in 1924, shifted to a multiple-basing-point system which was not nearly as detrimental to the consumer. This system used several steel production centers as basing points. But since not all steel centers were considered basing points, some phantom freight still was being charged. The FTC opposed this multiple-basing-point system too, and

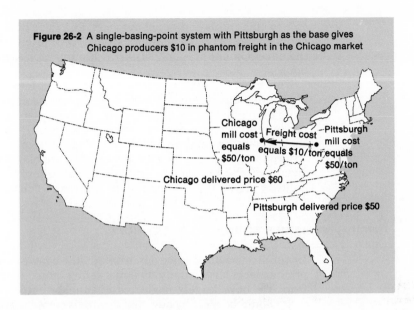

Figure 26-2 A single-basing-point system with Pittsburgh as the base gives Chicago producers $10 in phantom freight in the Chicago market

Chicago mill cost equals $50/ton

Freight cost equals $10/ton

Pittsburgh mill cost equals $50/ton

Chicago delivered price $60

Pittsburgh delivered price $50

finally, in 1945 and 1948, the U.S. Supreme Court ruled against *any* industrywide system involving phantom freight.[14]

Multiple basing points

Something resembling basing-point pricing is still used in some industries. Now, however, all the major producing points usually are considered basing points. The practical result is that all competitors set their prices to compete with the nearest producing point, absorbing whatever freight cost is necessary.

Under these conditions, alert purchasing agents continually look for new or closer producers. When they find one, they exert pressure on their suppliers to treat this new source as a basing point, too, and so there is little likelihood of phantom freight charges lasting for long.

Present legal status of geographical pricing

There are two points of view on what constitutes geographical price discrimination under the Robinson-Patman Act. According to one view, the delivered price should be the same to all buyers. According to the other, the factory price should be the same to all buyers.

The first view would permit a considerable amount of freight cost absorption to enable the seller to broaden his territory, perhaps allowing him to expand his factory and operate at a more efficient level — assuming that economies of scale are possible.

The second view, by contrast, insists on F.O.B. pricing, on the assumption that it is improper for outlying customers to pay less than the "full cost." But without freight absorption, sellers might not be

---

[14] In cases against Corn Products Refining Co. and A. E. Staley Co. in 1945 and against the Cement Institute in 1948.

able to obtain this additional business, and their basic costs and prices could actually rise. In addition, strict F.O.B. pricing might encourage the development of monopoly areas around each firm's plant or warehouse.

This view is a logical extension of antitrust legislation designed to block price discrimination which would force some customers to pay more than others. This second view has long been favored by the FTC and is gaining acceptance in the courts. Currently, however, although basing-point systems involving phantom freight are illegal, freight absorption systems which are designed to enable firms to reach more distant markets are not considered illegal unless the members of an industry arrive at a common method through conspiracy.[15]

Pricing to make a channel system work

In our discussion of price determination, we have concentrated on the pricing decisions an individual marketing manager must make for his firm. We have largely neglected channel-oriented pricing decisions.

It should be clear by now that channels compete with channels, and that the prices set by competing channels should be competitive – or at least their marketing mixes should be competitive. If we view a channel as a unit, then all the analytical tools and policies discussed above could be applied to the channel as a unit.

If a channel captain wanted to maximize profits for the entire channel, he could use marginal analysis. The channel captain might use the demand curve facing the whole channel to derive the channel's marginal revenue curve. He could obtain the channel's marginal cost by adding the marginal costs of the various middlemen to the marginal cost of production. Then, equating marginal revenue and marginal cost would enable him to calculate the optimum quantity to move through the channel at the optimum list price.

This approach would maximize profits for the channel as a whole, but how would the profits be shared among the channel members? Presently, the best answer is through negotiation. This could be a delicate matter, far more difficult than setting prices within an individual firm, which itself is not an easy matter.

Pricing hits the channel where it lives

The problem of setting prices within the channel is similar to determining costs as a product moves from one factory department or operating division to the next. There is no single right answer. Intrafirm pricing may be determined arbitrarily by an executive or committee; the whole issue can be avoided by transferring products at their direct or variable costs; or if there are comparable market prices, these can be used.

[15] For a more extensive discussion of geographical pricing policies, see Jules Backman, *Price Practices and Price Policies* (New York: Ronald Press Co., 1953), pp. 174–208; and E. F. Pegrum, "The Present Status of Geographic Pricing," *Journal of Marketing*, April, 1951, p. 425.

Pricing within a firm is a serious matter, sometimes leading to heated arguments. The profitability of various departments may determine the bonuses or salary increases in those departments, and profitability *is* affected by how costs are allocated.

The same stresses apply to channels composed of independent members. The way in which channel prices are determined directly affects the profits of each individual business! The channel captain may set prices or negotiate prices with various members, but this only underlines the fact that each situation must be resolved separately. The only rules are those which flow from the supply and demand of the particular situation.

Be a strategist, be a salesman

It is the job of the channel captain to try to insure that everyone feels adequately rewarded. In the absence of a clearly superior way to allocate potential profits, it is easy to understand the middlemen's attachment to the traditional markups and long-established channel arrangements, including trade discounts. The channel captain must try to lead them, remembering that they have the option to quit (or not join) his channel. But if a channel captain develops a drastically new approach, it behooves all channel members to reassess how profits are shared—remembering that faster turnover, not just high markups, affects profitability.

A successful marketing manager and channel captain must be both strategist and salesman, able to develop good strategies and to sell them to his prospective colleagues in the channel system.

Conclusion

In this chapter, we have considered the many pricing policies that the marketing manager must establish, guided by the framework of the company's overall objectives and specific pricing objectives. We have seen that the marketing manager must be concerned with decisions about price flexibility—will the firm use one price or flexible prices? And price levels—will they be below, at, or above the market?

Product life cycles move on and may require different pricing policies at different stages. For new products in particular, the marketing manager must decide whether he is going to "skim the cream of the market" or use a penetration policy to ward off competition and perhaps lengthen the life cycle.

Companies having more than one product must make a decision with respect to full-line pricing. Retailers see this in terms of price lining; producers serving such retailers often use demand-backward pricing to facilitate price lining.

Direct price cuts obviously have promotional value, but other pricing policies have promotional impact, such as multiple-unit, leader, and bait pricing, and introductory dealing.

In all cases, a decision must be made about who will pay transportation charges and from what point. We discussed various possible geographical pricing policies and evaluated their present legal status.

683

Finally, we considered the problem of pricing within a channel system. Clearly, a channel can operate as a unit in competing with other channels, perhaps using marginal analysis if the objective of the channel is to maximize profits. Traditional margins may or may not be adequate, or prove workable. Enlightened self-interest among members in a system probably should guide negotiations on how jobs, costs, and potential profits should be shared, remembering that the marketing mix of their channel system must compete with the mixes of other systems.

QUESTIONS AND PROBLEMS

1 Distinguish between one-price and flexible-price policies. Which would be most appropriate for a supermarket? Why?

2 Cite a local example of an oligopoly. Discuss how stable price has been in this oligopoly.

3 Cite two examples of continuously selling above the market price. Describe the situations.

4 Explain the types of market situations which might lead to a "meeting competition" price policy.

5 Is a full-line pricing policy available only to producers? Cite local examples of full-line pricing. Why is full-line pricing important?

6 Distinguish between leader pricing and bait pricing. What do they have in common? How can their use affect a marketing mix?

7 What pricing objective(s) would a skimming pricing policy most likely be implementing? Could the same be true for a penetration pricing policy? Which policy would probably be most appropriate for each of the following products:
a) A new type of home lawn-sprinkling system.
b) A new low-cost meat substitute.
c) A new type of children's toy.
d) A faster computer.

8 What type of geographical pricing policy would seem most appropriate for the following products (specify any assumptions necessary to obtain a definite answer)?
a) A chemical by-product (no fixed costs charged to it).
b) Nationally advertised candy bars.
c) Rebuilt auto parts.
d) Tricycles.

9 Explain how the prohibition of freight absorption (that is, requiring F.O.B. factory pricing) might affect a producer with substantial economies of scale in production.

10 Specifically, what basic pricing decisions are required when a producer selling to middlemen is developing a price structure?

11 Idential items often can be purchased at lower cost out of a Sears, Roebuck catalog than from one of its own retail stores. The difference amounts to about 10 percent. Is a flexible pricing policy being used?

...if a marketing manager has succeeded in developing a unique marketing strategy, he may not have to worry about the legality of his pricing or other decisions. Legal problems arise out of the failure to develop and maintain a differentiated strategy.

...the marketing manager has latitude but not license in manipulating the price variable. The more he caters to distinct target markets and differentiates his marketing mixes, the less attention he needs to pay to competitors' prices.

27

Influence of legislation on pricing and marketing strategy planning

From our general discussion of legislation in Chapter 3, you might have gotten the impression that companies have little latitude in pricing or may even need government approval for their prices. Generally speaking, this is *not* the case. As long as businessmen don't conspire with their competitors or discriminate against some of their customers, they can charge what they want, even "outrageously high" prices.

Pricing legislation may focus on whole strategy

There *are* restrictions on pricing, which we will discuss later in this chapter. But first, it is important to understand that U.S. legislation generally counts on the forces of competition to keep prices *and* other competitive weapons in line. In fact, pricing is only one of the four P's; although some legislation tends to focus on prices, this is simply because they are tangible and highly visible – they are what customers must pay for the whole marketing mix. Difficulties with pricing, and perhaps violation of price legislation, usually occur only when competing marketing mixes are quite similar. When the success of an entire marketing strategy depends upon price, there is pressure (and temptation) to conspire with competitors or discriminate among customers.

Although the legality of a particular pricing action may be spotlighted in a particular business situation or court case, the more meaningful approach usually is to broaden the scope of the discussion to the marketing mix or marketing strategy level. Is the rest of the mix really similar? And are the same target markets involved? These are important matters which are often involved in antitrust and pricing cases and partly explain why price legislation is a complex field.

There are few neat answers that apply entirely to all similar situations, and you should not be discouraged by apparent ambiguities. Even legal authorities cannot assure their clients of clear-cut advice in all legal matters, including pricing cases. In part this is because no two situations are ever exactly alike and in part because several of the most important U.S. Supreme Court decisions have been almost evenly divided.[1]

Get a feeling for pricing legislation

Your primary concern in this chapter should be to get a feeling for how pricing legislation, and antitrust legislation in general, affects pricing and marketing strategy planning. We sketched the broad outlines in Chapter 3, and in subsequent chapters made specific applications to Product, Place, and Promotion. Now we must focus on Price.

The first step is to try to understand the thinking of legislators and the courts. Ideally, they attempt to design and administer laws which will help the economy perform more effectively in the consumers' interest. In practice, this does not always work out as neatly as planned. But generally their intentions are good, and if we take this view, we may get a better idea of the "why" of some legislation. And this helps us to anticipate and evaluate future rulings in an ever changing field. We will stress U.S. legislation here so that we can be specific, but other countries have similar legislative constraints on business.[2]

After a review of the impact of legislation on pricing policy, we will broaden the discussion to show the impact on marketing strategy planning. In particular, we will examine the pricing policies available to the marketing manager within the context of two basic approaches: (1) de-emphasizing price in the marketing mix, and (2) using price as an active variable. In both cases, the other three P's are relevant to the selection of the appropriate marketing mix and strategy.

[1] W. David Robbins, "A Marketing Appraisal of the Robinson-Patman Act," *Journal of Marketing*, July, 1959, p. 15.

[2] For further discussion, see Sumner Marcus, "Antitrust in Practice," *Business Horizons*, Fall, 1967, pp. 59–66; Ray O. Werner, "Marketing and the United States Supreme Court, 1965–68," *Journal of Marketing*, January, 1969, pp. 16–23; and for discussion concerning European countries, see *Market Power and the Law* (Washington, D.C.: Organization for Economic Cooperation and Development Publication Center, 1970), 206 pp.

It should be noted here that if a marketing manager has succeeded in developing a unique marketing strategy, he may not have to worry about the legality of his pricing or other decisions. Typically, legal problems arise out of the failure to develop and maintain a differentiated strategy and not out of normal business operations.

Understanding this point as you study this chapter will give you a better insight into why legislation is needed and how law violations can be avoided. As noted in Chapter 3, a note of realism has been introduced now that some business executives have gone to jail for violating business legislation!

How legislation affects pricing policy

Unfair trade practice acts contol some minimum prices

The "unfair trade practice acts" which have been passed in more than half the states are designed to put a floor under prices, especially at the wholesale and retail levels. Wholesalers and retailers are normally required to take a certain minimum percentage markup over their merchandise-plus-transportation costs. The most common markup figures are 6 percent at retail and 2 percent at wholesale. The specific provisions of these state laws and the strictness of their enforcement will vary from state to state and from time to time.

If a specific wholesaler or retailer can show that his operating costs are lower than the minimum required figure, he may be permitted to offer merchandise at lower prices. But he must prove conclusively that he does have lower costs, and this usually is quite difficult if any fixed costs are involved. As we have already seen, several kinds of costs—average cost, average variable cost, and marginal cost—can be used as a basis for pricing. The various state control boards normally require the use of average cost, allocating fixed cost over all the items handled or sold.

The practical effect of these laws is to protect certain limited-line food retailers, such as dairy stores, from the kind of "ruinous" competition that full-line stores might offer if they chose to sell milk as a leader, offering it below cost for a lengthy period. For other than food lines, however, the 2 or 6 percent markup is so low that significant price reductions from normal levels could be made without approach-this floor, and therefore the laws are of little importance.

Most of these laws were enacted during the 1930's, when the distressed economic conditions caused a considerable amount of variable-cost pricing. Unless we have another depression, it is unlikely that these laws will again become important. Even the most vigorous discounters know enough about their costs to seek larger markups than these minimums.

Antitrust legislation permits some price fixing

Price fixing is generally prohibited under the Sherman Act and more specifically under the Federal Trade Commission Act. There are special cases, however, in which collusion and price fixing are specifically permitted by law.

"Fair trade" (or "resale price maintenance")laws permit price fixing by manufacturers or wholesalers *who choose to do so*. These state laws, for example, would permit a manufacturer to sue retailers for not adhering to the 79-cent retail price set by the maker for a tube of toothpaste.

Too much competition for small retailers

These price-fixing laws were a product, again, of the depression of the 1930's. The mass migration of low-income families into California made price cutting an attractive sales stimulant. In an effort to control this sometimes drastic price cutting, California passed an act in 1931 to permit manufacturers or wholesalers to set retail prices for trade-marked goods – the ones commonly discounted – by signing price-fixing contracts with their retailer customers.

This act was not particularly effective at first, since it did not bind nonsigners. But this was changed in 1933 with the passage of a "non-signer's clause." This clause bound all retailers in the state if one retailer signed a price-fixing contract.

Wholesalers and retailers in other states, seeing the success of the California law, lobbied for such legislation, and eventually 45 states passed them. In fact, the legislators in seven states – Arizona, Iowa, Louisiana, New Jersey, New York, Pennsylvania, and Tennessee – were so responsive to this prodding that in their haste they incorporated in their legislation a stenographic error from the original California act that made one part of the original and all its imitators meaningless.[3]

Fair trade is basically a state-by-state matter

All of this legislation was alike in being limited to *intra*state trade. The question remained whether price-fixing agreements in *inter*state commerce were legal. In 1937, the Miller-Tydings Act was passed by the U.S. Congress, allowing branders in interstate commerce to make such agreements in states which had fair-trade laws, without violating federal antitrust legislation. This was an *enabling* act, since it permitted such agreements only in states that had such laws.

The Miller-Tydings Act, however, did not specifically contain a provision for the nonsigner's clause. In a court test of this loophole, precipitated by Schwegmann Brothers, a large supermarket chain in New Orleans, the U.S. Supreme Court ruled (1951) that the Miller-Tydings Act applied only to signers. This decision led to a rash of price cuts on fair-traded merchandise throughout the country. The following year, 1952, Congress passed the McGuire Act, which said in effect that Congress had intended the nonsigner's clause to be in the Miller-Tydings Act.

With the previous ambiguity cleared up, fair trade became effective again in those states having such laws. Schwegmann Brothers again violated the law as a test case and lost, and the Supreme Court refused to review a lower court's decision against the New Orleans firm. Fair

[3] Jules Backman, *Price Practices and Price Policies* (New York: Ronald Press Co., 1953), p. 420.

traders have not had free sailing, however, since some states have repealed their laws. About half still have such legislation.

The tide moved against fair trade on a large scale when General Electric capitulated to the discounters in 1958. General Electric had staunchly adhered to fair trade on small appliances, even though aggressive discounters in New York and other markets made this practice extremely difficult. Finally, when Masters, Inc., of New York, a discounter, won a court fight with General Electric over the right to sell by mail in fair-traded New York from nonfair-traded Washington, D.C., General Electric gave up. A wave of price cutting began on GE appliances – and other appliance manufacturers abandoned fair trade, too.[4]

Fair-trade supporters continue to offer fair-trade bills in various state legislatures, but in recent years they have not had much success.

A new approach for accomplishing roughly the same objective as fair trade is known as "quality stabilization." Proponents of quality stabilization legislation supposedly are trying to insure that consumers are offered quality products – but *at fixed prices.* So far, these efforts have not succeeded, but supporters probably will continue to press for a federal law requiring price fixing rather than relying on the Miller-Tydings Act, which only permits price fixing where individual states take action.

Fair trade can be a useful managerial tool

Fair trade has been used effectively for well-differentiated products with relatively inelastic demands and with manufacturing costs that represent a small percentage of the price. Drug and cosmetics products are examples.

For drug items such as aspirin, there is relatively little relationship between production cost and retail price. Yet significant price reductions would create little expansion in demand and would therefore decrease total revenue.

Retail druggists have found fair trade an effective managerial device to maximize profits on inelastic demand curves – the very thing that some large companies are discouraged from doing by the current legal and political environment. Druggists, however, have been able to keep their fair-trade prices. Why?

One reason is that they have been able to maintain their position legally, in part because druggists are numerous and have considerable influence in state legislatures. Another factor is that consumers have not been too concerned because each fair-traded item represents only a relatively small part of their total expenditure.[5]

Advocates of fair trade sometimes argue that such laws are in the consumer interest because, they say, (1) without fair trade, small retailers would go out of business, and consumers would not have the

[4] "Bargain Hunters Have a Heyday as G.E. Gives Up on 'Fair Trade,'" *Business Week,* March 18, 1958, pp. 26–28.

[5] For a comprehensive examination of the history and effects of resale price fixing, see E. T. Grether, *Price Control under Fair Trade Legislation* (New York: Oxford University Press, Inc., 1939); also E. R. Corey, "Fair Trade Pricing: A Reappraisal," *Harvard Business Review,* September–October, 1952, pp. 47–62.

convenience of nearby stores, (2) consumers would be further penalized without fair trade because price cutters would have to make up for lost margins by raising prices on other items, and (3) consumers might be inconvenienced when seeking items that discounters have used as price leaders – because some small retailers drop the items.

To the retailer and wholesaler who is fair-trade minded, these laws make sense because they help assure a "fair" percentage of the price to cover costs. They feel they are entitled to this percentage, and if they do not get it, they will refuse to become a member of the channel team.

To the manufacturer, fair trade sometimes makes sense because discounters frequently will provide a place for a product and emphasize price but ignore promotion. They use only three of the four P's, skimming the cream by dealing only with customers who are presold or easily sold, and ignoring the balance of the market.[6]

But it might not make economic sense

Although fair trade has some attractive features, 90 to 95 percent of all retail goods have never been fair traded because manufacturers, wholesalers, and some retailers realized that such activity would merely provide a price umbrella and that short-run profits would encourage competition from more retailers and manufacturers.

From the consumer viewpoint, there is probably little justification for fair trade. Its main purpose is to stabilize or increase the price level. The exact effect has been subject to considerable controversy, but "most disinterested consumers seem to believe that fair trade has tended to narrow the range and raise the average level of prices."[7]

One analyst has concluded that the breakdown of fair trade results more from economic factors than legal setbacks.[8] If the retailer's task costs only 15 to 20 percent of the retail price, then trade discounts larger than this will encourage price cuts by discounters. Many so-called ethical or legitimate sellers have not recognized changing conditions in retailing. They are still geared to give their normal service in return for relatively high 30 to 40 percent margins – even though manufacturers no longer require nor do all consumers really want such a selling job.

Another factor contributing to the decline of fair trade is that legislation is normally permissive rather than mandatory. A manufacturer does not have to use fair-trade pricing, but if he chooses to, then the burden of policing is on him. Yet effective policing can be expensive.

[6] For further discussion see Louis W. Stern, "Economic Factors Influencing Manufacturers' Decisions Concerning Price Maintenance," *Journal of Retailing*, Spring, 1965, pp. 30–37, 55.

[7] Stanley C. Hollander, *Retail Price Policies* (East Lansing: Bureau of Business and Economic Research, Michigan State University, 1958), p. 5; also, M. Frankel, "The Effects of Fair Trade: Fact and Fiction in the Statistical Findings," *Journal of Business*, July, 1955, pp. 182–94; S. M. Lee, "The Impact of Fair Trade Laws on Retailing," *Journal of*

Retailing, Spring, 1965, pp. 1–6; and Charles J. Stewart, "Mandatory Resale Price Maintenance of Distilled Spirits in California," *Journal of Marketing*, April, 1954, p. 370.

[8] Stanley C. Hollander, "Is Fair Trade Finished?" *Challenge*, June–July, 1958, pp. 48–52; see also, S. C. Hollander's discussion of the U.S. Fair Trade movement in B. S. Yamey, *Resale Price Maintenance* (Chicago: Aldine Publishing Co., 1966), pp. 65–100. The experience in other countries is also discussed in this text.

It involves court cases, and often there is difficulty in securing prompt injunctions against discounters. And the relatively small penalties awarded to the producer together with the ill will generated among channel members concerned in the dispute may overbalance the benefits of fair-trade pricing.

On balance, it is easy to see why a relatively small share of consumer goods have been fair traded and why fair trading has declined in importance. Modern marketing men are finding much more imaginative and more positive approaches to improving the effectiveness of their marketing mixes. Now, they adopt offensive rather than defensive tactics. That is, they are becoming actors, not reactors. Instead of inhibiting competitive activity, they initiate new approaches—generating even more competition, but competition on all four P's, not just price. Examples here include more targeted marketing strategies by manufacturers and middlemen, and the development of aggressive voluntary and cooperative chains.

Antitrust legislation prohibits price discrimination unless . . .

The legislative concern about price discrimination culminating in the Robinson-Patman Act of 1936 was discussed in Chapter 3. You will recall that the Robinson-Patman Act makes unlawful, in interstate commerce, any price discrimination between different purchasers of "commodities of like grade and quality" which may *tend to injure competition*. This law does permit some price differentials, but they must be based on cost differences or the need to "meet competition." Both buyers and sellers are liable to prosecution if they knowingly enter into discriminatory arrangements.

How many Robinson-Patman Acts are there?

The major difficulty with this potentially powerful law is that it is confusing, to say the least. As the U.S. Supreme Court observed, "Precision of expression is not an outstanding characteristic of the Robinson-Patman Act."[9] While one chairman of the FTC felt that "its substance is both sound and clear," a respected legal authority called it "an extremely poorly drafted statute."[10]

Although the wording of the original act has not changed, W. David Robbins feels that because of changing interpretations of the courts and the FTC, there has been, in effect, three different Robinson-Patman Acts.

The first "act" was applied during the period of limited enforcement from 1936 until the middle of the 1940's. In the middle and late 1940's, there was another "act" marked by enforcement ranging from strict to radical. Practically all price differentials were illegal during this period. During the 1950's, the courts and the Commission became more temperate in their interpretation of the act, reverting back to "injury to competition" as opposed to "injury to competitors."[11]

[9] 346 U.S. 6173 Supreme Court 1017.

[10] "Robinson-Patman Act: It Demands a Close Look Now," *Printers' Ink*, October 20, 1961, pp. 22–27.

[11] Robbins, *op. cit.*, p. 15.

A later analyst felt Robbins was being too optimistic in his depiction of increasing clarity and temperance of Robinson-Patman enforcement.[12] Currently the Robinson-Patman situation is still not absolutely clear.[13]

Lack of criteria for investigation certainly is obvious. As Lowell Mason, a former FTC commissioner says, "Nowhere is institutional whim more apparent and more deadly than in the choice of defendants the FTC sues under the Robinson-Patman Act."[14]

Unfortunately for businessmen, the FTC is responsible not only for investigation but for enforcement. It is not only investigator and prosecutor, but judge. The FTC's rulings, however, can be, and often are, appealed to the federal courts and finally to the U.S. Supreme Court. Litigation is often extensive, with one court reversing the other, sometimes on close votes.

What does "like grade and quality" mean?

The Robinson-Patman Act permits a marketing manager to charge different prices for similar products if the products are not of like grade and quality.

It might seem that many price differentials for products could be justified by offering a different *something,* even if the same physical product were involved. If customers feel this something makes a difference and are willing to pay for it, then there is a difference.

The FTC position is that if the physical characteristics of a product are similar, then they are of like grade and quality.

The FTC view was upheld in a 1966 U.S. Supreme Court ruling against the Borden Co. The court held that a well-known label *alone* does not make a product different from one with an unknown label. The issue was rather clear-cut in the *Borden* case because the company acknowledged that the physical characteristics of the canned milk it sold at different prices under different labels were essentially the same.

The FTC's "victory" in the *Borden* case was not complete, however. Although the Supreme Court agreed with the FTC in the *Borden* case with respect to like grade and quality, it sent the case back to a U.S. Court of Appeals to determine whether the price difference injured competition. In 1967 this court found no evidence of injury and further noted that there could be no injury unless Borden's price differen-

[12] Brian Dixon, *Price Discrimination in Marketing Management* (Michigan Business Studies, Vol. 15, No. 1 [Ann Arbor: University of Michigan, 1960]), pp. 98–99.

[13] See Charles C. Slater and Frank H. Mossman, "Positive Robinson-Patman Pricing," *Journal of Marketing,* April, 1967, pp. 8–14; Daniel J. Murphy, "The Federal Trade Commission of the 1960's," *Journal of Marketing,* April, 1963, pp. 1–2; and Lawrence X. Tarpey, Sr., "Who Is a Competing Customer?" *Journal of Retailing,* Spring, 1969, pp. 46–58.

[14] "Robinson-Patman Act: It Demands a Closer Look Now," *Printers' Ink,* October 20, 1961, p. 24. For a more extensive discussion, see Robert C. Brooks, Jr., "Businessmen's Concepts of 'Injury to Competition'," *California Management Review,* Summer, 1961, pp. 89–101; Lawrence X. Tarpey, "What About the Good-Faith Defense?" *Journal of Marketing,* July, 1960, pp. 62–65; "Indirect Price Discrimination and Robinson-Patman," *Journal of Marketing,* January, 1963, pp. 68–71; and Earl W. Kintner, "Avoiding Price Discrimination," *Business Topics,* Winter, 1962, pp. 18–28.

tial exceeded the "recognized consumer appeal of the Borden label." How "consumer appeal" is to be measured was not spelled out and may lead to additional litigation.[15]

Eventually, what the consumer thinks about the product may be the determining factor. For now, however, it would appear safer for producers who want to sell several brands or dealer brands at lower prices than their main brand to offer actual and genuine physical differences. It also seems advisable to make differences that are genuinely useful to various buyers, not merely decorative or trivial. Another possibility for differentiation that has won some support in the courts is packaging differences.[16]

Can cost analysis justify price differentials?

The Robinson-Patman Act supposedly allows price differentials if there are cost differences. Justifying cost differentials is a difficult task, however, since fixed costs usually must be allocated to several products, and perhaps arbitrarily. It is easy, then, to raise objections to whatever allocation method is used. The Federal Trade Commission successfully won a quantity discount case against the Morton Salt Co. for this reason. Morton had to change its quantity discount schedule, partly because it was not able to justify its case on the basis of cost, but probably more because of the possible injurious effect on competitors.[17]

If a firm planned to use the cost defense, it would make sense to segregate its marketing costs to show that the cost of selling and servicing different target markets did, in fact, differ. The availability of computers could help here. But it is still a difficult and expensive task, and the courts may decide that the way the costs are determined and allocated is not detailed enough. In the extreme, each receiving point of each customer might have to be treated separately, and the cost of doing this could be more expensive than it would be worth.[18]

Even when cost differentials can be shown, quantity discounts might only be allowed to a certain extent. The FTC has sought to control the size of quantity discounts on the grounds that big discounts, although justified on a cost basis, may be unfair to small competitors.

The FTC ruled against Thompson Products, Inc., for selling certain replacement parts to the Big Three automobile makers—for their own use and resale to car dealers—at prices lower than Thompson's own distributors were being charged. Thompson argued, unsuccessfully,

[15]Morris L. Mayer, Joseph B. Mason, and E. A. Orbeck, "The Borden Case—A Legal Basis for Private Brand Price Discrimination," *MSU Business Topics*, Winter, 1970, pp. 56–63; Jacky Knopp, Jr., "What Are 'Commodities of Like Grade and Quality'?" *Journal of Marketing*, July, 1963, p. 63; and Frederick D. Buggie, "Lawful Discrimination in Marketing," *Journal of Marketing*, April, 1962, p. 1; "Price Differentials on Brands Upheld," *Business Week*, July 29, 1967.

[16]T. F. Schutte, V. J. Cook, Jr., and R. Hemsley, "What Management Can Learn from the Borden Case," *Business Horizons*, Winter, 1966, pp. 23–30.

[17]Peter G. Peterson, "Quantity Discounts in the Morton Salt Case," *Journal of Business of the University of Chicago*, April, 1952, pp. 109–20.

[18]Robert A. Lynn, *Price Policies and Marketing Management* (Homewood, Ill.: Richard D. Irwin, Inc., 1967), pp. 262–64; "Is the Cost Defense Workable," *Journal of Marketing*, January, 1965, pp. 37–42; and *Business Week*, December 14, 1968, p. 48.

that it was able to produce the large orders in special production runs and ship without warehousing.[19] The possible injurious impact on distributors' ability to compete was seen as more important.

How do you legally meet competition?

"Meeting competition" is permitted as a defense in price-discrimination situations under the Robinson-Patman Act, although the FTC normally has taken a rather dim view of this argument.

In a significant 5–4 decision in 1956, the U.S. Supreme Court said that "meeting competition" in "good faith" is a permissible defense if it can be shown that the price discrimination occurred as a *defensive* rather than an offensive action. The dissenting justices saw the implications and suggested that this ruling "crippled the enforcement of the act." They added that if price cutting should begin generally, the majority decision could permit a great deal of price cutting — *perhaps to the detriment of less efficient outlets.*[20]

A major objective of antitrust legislation is to protect competition, not competitors, and "meeting competition" in "good faith" still seems to be acceptable, even if it is large firms which meet the lower prices of small firms. This issue was temporarily in doubt recently, in the *Utah Pie Co.* case. Here, a small local company had entered an established market with a low-price appeal, and its success led to a downward spiral of prices, including sales below cost by the larger national companies. In 1967, the Supreme Court ruled 6 to 2 that regional price cutting by a national manufacturer was illegal where it involved "persistent sales below cost." Subsequent litigation, however, has clarified the matter and absolved the larger companies' price cutting. It was the smaller firm which started the price cutting, and the 10th Circuit Court of Appeals in Denver ruled that Utah Pie lacked sufficient evidence of injury. Actually, the market share it won by price cutting declined from 66 percent to 45 percent only because it was challenged by lower prices. Probably it will continue to be all right to meet competition as long as consumers seem to benefit, and smaller competitors are not hurt too much.[21]

Are functional discounts discriminatory?

Can functional discounts be considered price discrimination? Legislation is not completely clear on this issue, but court decisions appear to have settled the matter with emphasis on functions provided.[22] At the root of the situation is the distinction between wholesalers and retailers, since wholesalers are entitled to certain discounts from producers to provide wholesaling functions.

Generally, the courts have felt that the identification of a firm as a wholesaler or a retailer depends, not on the quantity he buys or handles, but on the nature of the service he provides. A producer could legally refuse to give a wholesale discount to a large retail grocery chain, al-

[19] *Business Week,* April 26, 1958, p. 57.

[20] *Business Week,* February 1, 1958, p. 53.

[21] "Utah Pie Review Denied," *Wall Street Journal,* October 15, 1968, p. 2; "Court Raps Price Cuts,"

Business Week, April 29, 1967, p. 50; and *Journal of Marketing,* October, 1967, p. 74.

[22] *FTC* v. *The Mennen Company,* and *National Biscuit Company* v. *FTC.*

though the chain might handle a much larger volume than small wholesalers. The justification is that functional discounts are imperative for the small wholesaler if he is to cover his costs and still sell to retailers at prices low enough to permit the retailers to be competitive.

A chain probably would not have to pay the same price offered a small retailer, however. A special functional discount could be set up for chain stores. As long as a functional discount seems to reflect the nature of the job required in the channel, the courts probably would consider it legal.

Special allowances might not be allowed

Some firms have violated the Robinson-Patman Act by providing P.M.'s (Push Money), demonstrators, advertising allowances, or other promotional aids to certain customers and not others. The act specifically prohibits such special allowances unless they are made available to all customers on "proportionately equal" terms. No proof of injury to competition is necessary, and the FTC has been fairly successful in prosecuting such cases.

The need for such a rule is clear, once price regulation begins. Allowances for promotional aid could be granted to retailers or wholesalers without expectation that any promotion would actually be undertaken. This plainly would be price discrimination in disguise.

The provision does work hardships, since it sometimes is difficult to provide allowances on "proportionately equal" terms to both large and small customers. The Robinson-Patman Act does not state clearly whether a small store should be allowed the same dollar advertising allowance as a large one or an allowance in proportion to sales. The latter probably would not buy the same promotional impact.

It may also be difficult to determine exactly who are competing customers. The FTC might define a relevant list of competitors much more broadly than either the seller or the competing buyers. Supermarket operators might only be concerned about other supermarkets and the new food discounters, while the FTC might feel small drugstores were competitors on health and beauty aids.[23]

In 1969, the FTC issued some new guidelines for advertising and promotional allowances, including more stringent requirements for informing all competitive customers that deals were available. The early results seem to indicate a trend away from cooperative advertising, and perhaps promotional allowances in general.[24]

"Equal price" equals no wrath

In general, the FTC seems more concerned about the protection of small competitors, regardless of cost to consumers or variations in total marketing mixes. The Commission is following what has been called the "equal price theory" — that all competitors should obtain equal prices. This tends to guarantee that small middlemen will have

[23] Lawrence X. Tarpey, Sr., "Who Is a Competing Customer?" *Journal of Retailing,* Spring, 1969, pp. 46–58; and John R. Davidson, "FTC, Robinson-Patman and Cooperative Promotional Activities," *Journal of Marketing,* January, 1968, pp. 14–18.

[24] "Lower Ad Allowances Effected by FTC Rule Starting to Pinch, Retailers Say," *Marketing Insights,* January, 1970, pp. 1 f.

a place in the channel even though larger firms could be served at lower cost.

An alternate approach, called the "equal profit theory," would require price differentials to reflect cost differences – to avoid price discrimination. This might lead to substantially lower prices to some customers, especially larger customers, who could be much more economical to serve.

Distribution cost accountants have the ability to implement this theory and suggest that its use could substantially reduce the economy's total distribution costs.[25] For now, however, any considerable deviation from the "equal price" approach is likely to incur the FTC's wrath.

How to avoid discriminating

One way to avoid discriminating is to avoid price differentials. Until this potentially powerful but confusing law is clarified, many business executives probably will continue to think it wise to de-emphasize price as a marketing variable. They have concluded that the safest course is to offer few or no quantity discounts, and to offer the same cost-based prices to *all* customers.

As long as the FTC appears to favor "equal" prices, marketing managers probably will try to avoid active price competition. This shifts competition to areas that are more difficult both to measure and to copy. It also can lead to other activities condemned by the FTC, such as conscious parallel action, which we will discuss later.

It is obvious that today many companies carefully avoid active price competition. It would be unfortunate if all price competition were eliminated, ostensibly in the public interest but actually more to the benefit of individual competitors. Prices probably would rise, as would the total cost of distribution because of the restriction on the free operation of the economy.[26]

Government may discourage price increases

Strictly speaking, there is no legislative rule against price increases. But in recent years, concern about inflation has led to wage-price guideposts developed by the President and his advisors. Compliance has been encouraged by sometimes not-so-veiled threats of antitrust investigations.[27]

The Nixon administration was more inclined to follow a "hands-off" policy. Nevertheless, it intervened directly in a lumber market situation where the government was at the same time a big buyer and owned the land on which the timber stood. Federal pressure on prices can also be applied, by shifting sources, where the government is a major buyer. And the potential threat of sales from

[25] See Slater and Mossman, *op. cit.*

[26] For further discussion, see Corwin D. Edwards, *Maintaining Competition* (New York: McGraw-Hill Book Co., 1949), pp. 161–62; and Dixon, *op. cit.*, pp. 107–16.

[27] Charles A. Bliss, "Flaw in the Wage-Price Guide-

posts," *Harvard Business Review*, May–June, 1966, pp. 73–78; Michael C. Jensen, "Gamesmanship with the Guideposts," *Harvard Business Review*, November–December, 1966, pp. 168–83; and "Oilmen Get the Word on Prices," *Business Week*, February 25, 1967, p. 142.

stockpiles or the adjustment of import and export curbs and quotas serve as deterring influences.[28]

The potential impact of the federal government on Price re-emphasizes the importance of continual study of the political and legal environment.

Deceptive pricing — when the price isn't the price

The Federal Trade Commission and others maintain that some prices are deceptive and only lead to price confusion. Examples include: phony "preticketed" prices, "factory" or "wholesale" prices, and half-price, 50-percent-off, "two-for-one," and 1-cent sales which are commonly seen at the retail level and in consumer goods advertising. The FTC has sought to control such deceptive pricing under the Wheeler-Lea Amendment of 1938, which prohibits "unfair or deceptive acts in commerce." It has had some success, but deception is sometimes difficult to define. Some consumers are so eager for price discounts that they encourage this sort of pricing and advertising. But are they really deceived?

In the late 1950's, deceptive pricing was used commonly as a competitive device, not only by back-alley discount houses but by major retailers. Television sets advertised at $309.95 would be placed "on sale" for $249.95, but might be available elsewhere for a nonadvertised price of $215.

The situation worsened as regular retailers attempted to compete with discounters. Soon, few advertisers' prices made any sense at all. Yet Better Business Bureaus found that all the blame for tricky practices could not be placed on retailers. The vice president of the Chicago Better Business Bureau said, "The customer wants to think he drove a hard bargain. The retailer helps the customer kid himself. And the retailer and the manufacturer get together to back up their inflated price."[29]

In 1958, the FTC finally stepped into the chaos caused by these phony prices and established its "Guides Against Deceptive Pricing." These were clarified in 1964 to protect advertisers, especially national advertisers, from being responsible for what happened in the channels, beyond their control.

The FTC guides said that manufacturers, distributors, and retailers "must in every case act honestly and in good faith on advertising a list price, and not with the intention of establishing a basis . . . for a deceptive comparison in any local . . . trade area." This was designed to reduce collusion on pricing along the channel. At the retail level, it is expected that the retailer will have a good grasp of competitive prices and not advertise so as to create a false impression of the value being offered.[30]

The Better Business Bureaus encouraged compliance with the FTC

[28] "How Government Wields Its Pricing Power," *Business Week*, March 29, 1969, p. 46.

[29] *Time*, November 10, 1958, p. 78.

[30] "War on Phony Bargain Prices," *Business Week*, October 18, 1958, p. 34; or "Guides Against Deceptive Pricing," Federal Trade Commission, October 10, 1958, and January 8, 1964.

guides. Many manufacturers were also willing and anxious to go along, since it enabled them to stop practices which they felt forced into by competitive action.

Nevertheless, we still see what some call "deceptive pricing." Some customers on the market grid apparently are quite price conscious, and sellers find it effective to appeal to them with price-oriented promotion. Whether the customers are really deceived, however, may be another matter. Are the list prices from which discounts are offered on automobiles deceptive? The FTC thinks so, but auto industry executives feel that consumers understand the nature of the sticker price as a ceiling price or a starting point from which to begin bargaining.

To be sure, some customers may pay different prices than others at the same or different times, but this could be a legitimate aspect of an extremely competitive market. Many retailers, including automobile dealers, would be happy to be out from under such price competition. But as long as we have competition without price control, we will see price competition in some markets. And if cutting list prices for some buyers is considered deceptive pricing, then we probably will continue to have deceptive pricing.[31]

Legislation and marketing strategy planning

In the preceding paragraphs, we have examined the impact of legislation on pricing, recognizing that price is only one of the four major variables with which the marketing manager works. It should be clear by now, however, that a marketing manager must keep in mind the political and legal environment when developing not only price policies but also whole marketing strategies.

To summarize our discussion of the impact of legislation on pricing policies and marketing strategy planning with a focus on action implications, we will consider two extremes: (1) de-emphasizing price in a marketing mix, and (2) using price as an active variable.

De-emphasizing price in a marketing mix

The three basic ways of de-emphasizing price in a marketing mix are (1) nonprice competiton, (2) price control via legal or administrative devices, and (3) price leadership.

Nonprice competition

Nonprice competition involves the conscious use of the other three variables—Product, Place, and Promotion—so that the marketing manager can carve out a market for himself and escape a competitive price situation. This requires careful analysis of the market grid and the selection of marketing mixes which appeal to distinct target markets.

Through product differentiation or market segmentation, the marketing manager can attempt to obtain his own downsloping de-

---

[31]"Auto Pricing Is Deceptive, FTC Says," *Detroit Free Press*, September 17, 1969, p. 16–C.

mand curve. Ideally, he would like demand curves that are as far to the right and as inelastic as possible. But as long as he serves somewhat separate markets, he may be able to maintain an extremely profitable position without worrying too much about others' prices.

Under these conditions, because of the uniqueness of his marketing strategies, there is less need for direct price competition. Prices, nevertheless, cannot deviate too far from those of similar products because few products are truly without substitutes. The marketing manager has latitude but not license in manipulating the pricing variable. The more he caters to distinct target markets and differentiates his marketing mixes, the less attention he needs to pay to competitors' prices.

Over the years, nonprice competition can lead to rising prices as more costly improvements are added. This has been true in the automobile industry, where more powerful engines, better suspension systems and brakes, new power accessories, and varied safety features have caused a steady rise in the total dollar price of cars.

But nonprice competition—or at least competition where price is not considered an important variable—can lead to lower prices, too, as the product moves through the product life cycle and some of the economies of mass production are achieved. Examples are the falling prices of refrigerators, television sets, and other appliances.

In nonprice competition, the marketing manager does have to set prices. Every marketing mix contains a price. The major point is that in nonprice competition, a marketing manager does not rely on a lower price to carry his mix. Instead he, and perhaps his competitors, carefully avoid aggressive pricing moves to avoid provoking others to follow. Each competitor may price near the "competitive" level and then do his best to bring out a better product at this price level, advertise more effectively, build better relations within his channels, and so on. These moves are harder to copy—a major advantage of nonprice competition to good marketers.

No collusion need be involved. Each of the competitors simply wants to avoid direct price competition, since Price is so easily and quickly copied, and price competition can hit profits hard.

Each competitor is well aware that a price war may lead to lower price levels, squeezing margins and profits to the extent that there will be little money later to pay the cost of nonprice competition. Then, the only remaining course may be additional price cuts. The product may be doomed to a profitless future, unless the market expands greatly at the lower prices or competitors grow discouraged and leave the field.

Price control

As a firm's market situation approaches pure competition or oligopoly, the marketing manager may have real problems controlling price, especially if firms in his own or in competing channels place heavy emphasis on price in their marketing mixes.

One of the following approaches may be useful, however, depending on the situation.

Fair trade, or resale price maintenance, may effectively control retail prices in states where use of this tool is legal. If the retail price is fixed, this can lead to less pricing ferment in a channel and among competing producers. Then emphasis can shift to nonprice competition.

This approach may be useful in the short run, but not as good over the long haul, as it encourages the development of new dealer brands and new manufacturers' brands. The price fixing applies only to each manufacturer's product. Although the manufacturer may be able to fix *his* prices, he must consider the prices of substitute products that may become available at substantially lower prices. In effect, his higher fair-trade prices may provide a price umbrella for the dealer branders, assuring them of no price competition. And the higher price may provide the retailers carrying lower priced dealer brands with an easy way to show that they provide good values.

Exclusive or selective distribution might be used, choosing distributors and retailers who can be relied on to maintain prices. When small-appliance fair-trade pricing collapsed in 1958, for example, the Sunbeam Corp. and the Dormeyer Corp. drastically reduced the number of wholesalers and retailers handling their lines in an effort to obtain price stability.[32] This effort to establish closer relationships with a smaller number of channel members is a logical step if a producer wants to control prices in the channel. Wholesalers are in an ideal position to offer substantial discounts to final consumers because they have been granted both the wholesale and retail functional discounts. Given that they are independent businessmen, technically the manufacturer has no control over them, except to select "reliable" middlemen who can be counted on to perform their functions, perhaps including the maintenance of prices.

Careful planning of functional discount structures by the producer or channel captain avoids price cutting by leaving no room for the cuts. Each job in the channel is carefully defined. A discount is offered that should cover the cost of providing that function plus the necessary profit.

Such tight planning is basic to effective, smoothly operating channel systems. It is especially important when there are many target markets, and some channels serve the same, as well as different, markets. Different channels may have different requirements and need different discounts, but if too large a discount is allowed at some point, it is likely to lead to price cutting at the most competitive points of the competing channel systems.

Tight planning is possible, however, only if the company offers something unique that a good middleman will be eager to handle. As we have noted already, middlemen do not always see themselves as the selling arms of those above them in the channels. In addition, many are tradition-bound and may insist on the traditional markups. Any effort to change the system might be resisted.

Leasing rather than selling the product to customers may enable a

---

[32]*Business Week,* June 28, 1958, p. 76.

producer to retain control over price because all *contracts* then are directly between the producer and the final customer. Middlemen can be used to handle local selling, as, for example, in car leasing. But prices and terms of the lease would be specified by the producer.

Leasing also may change the marketing mix to such a degree that price is de-emphasized. When a computer is leased, for example, its high purchase price is not too relevant. Neither is its operative life-span, if the supplier has agreed to replace it when a new model is available. In such cases, price in relation to basic hardware characteristics becomes less relevant than the service it will provide, availability for delivery, and sales and service backup.

Leasing tends to change the purchase from a capital to an expense item, and as we have already seen, this tends to change the buying procedure.

In part for these reasons, some of the office equipment manufacturers, including IBM and Xerox, have set their prices to encourage leasing rather than buying.

Consignment selling consists of selling the product to the final user or consumer only. The manufacturer retains ownership of the goods until the final transaction, and channel members act merely as agents in arranging the transaction.

Consignment selling has been used in the distribution of electrical conduit, plumbing piping, caskets, bicycles, electric light bulbs, bread, magazines, and newspapers. It is a rather complicated procedure, usually requiring that the seller have considerable financial resources — unless rapid turnover minimizes inventory problems, as in the case of bread, newspapers, and magazines.

Consignment selling may gain new attractiveness following a 1967 Supreme Court ruling involving Arnold Schwinn & Co., the bicycle maker. The Court held that while companies should not impose restraints on dealers who buy their products outright, they may — as Schwinn was doing — set conditions for sales made on consignment.[33]

Price fixing by collusion is mentioned as a method here only because some businessmen have conspired to fix prices, often in desperation. Aside from fair trading, all price fixing is illegal. In highly competitive and oligopolistic situations, some marketing managers have been so unsuccessful in differentiating their marketing mixes that the only remaining variable left is pricing. Yet price cutting can lead to ruinous competition.

It is interesting to note that the industries in which price fixing actually or allegedly has arisen have been primarily in the industrial goods market where product differentiation and branding are difficult and consequently less developed. These industries include drugs, carbon dioxide, railroad wheels, pipe flanges, steel rings, brazing alloys, carbon sheet steel, toilets, bathtubs, sinks, aluminum cable,

---

[33] "High Court Hits a Softer Tone," *Business Week*, June 17, 1967, p. 40; "G. E. Challenged on Bulb Prices," *Business Week*, October 1, 1966, p. 50.

asphalt, salt, and electrical equipment.[34] In the famous electrical equipment industry price-fixing case, some executives went to jail for their violations of the law.[35]

The predisposing conditions for the development of price fixing should be understood. Price fixing can develop if a marketing manager has failed to differentiate his product effectively or has been unduly hamstrung by company objectives or other company policies. It may be that he is not even a marketing manager in the full sense of the word, having little control over any company policies *except* selling and prices, but with the requirement that he meet unit and dollar sales goals, and perhaps profit goals as well. If he fails, he may be fired! But the market situation may be such that he cannot achieve these goals without collusion.

Regardless of the pertinent circumstances or excuses, however, price fixing is illegal in the United States. An interesting question, though, is, who should go to jail for it?

Should it be the sales manager who actually conducts collusive activities or should he share the guilt with (1) the production and financial executives who should have been well aware of the market situation and what the sales manager had to do to keep the plant working and the revenue flowing in, or (2) the top executives who presumably are integrating the firm's whole business system?

In world markets, price fixing is viewed quite differently. Price fixing and cartel arrangements are more common and may become more so as production capacities grow.[36] Price fixing is sanctioned or even encouraged by some foreign governments. And the U.S. government permits U.S. firms, when operating in the foreign trade, to engage in price-fixing, market sharing and other activities which would be illegal in domestic trade, to enable them to compete successfully.[37]

Mergers can reduce competition by eliminating competitors. Reducing competition would seem to be an attractive way to control prices, but this is one of the very reasons for federal antimerger legislation in 1950. And since the federal government may prohibit or undo mergers, this no longer can be thought of as an effective way to control prices.

---

[34]"Drug Makers Offer to Settle," *Business Week,* February 15, 1969, p. 34; *Wall Street Journal,* May 5, 1969, p. 6; January 17, 1969, p. 2; and November 15, 1961, p. 3; February 1, 1967, p. 1; *Business Week,* October 15, 1966, p. 43; September 25, 1965, p. 38; October 9, 1965, p. 42; April 6, 1963, p. 36; and December 9, 1961, p. 38; and the (Lansing, Michigan) *State Journal,* March 11, 1967, p. 1.

[35]*Time,* February 17, 1961, pp. 84–85; *Business Week,* April 20, 1961, p. 28; *Wall Street Journal,* September 26, 1962, p. 6, January 10, 12, and 13, 1961, pp. 1 ff. and January 2, 1962, p. 1. For a general discussion of price fixing, see Walter Jensen,

Jr., and Harold A. Wolf, "A Legal and Economic Note on Price-Fixing," *Business Topics,* Spring, 1962, pp. 55–65; "Climbing Toll for the Price-Fixers," *Business Week,* August 29, 1964, pp. 96–102.

[36]*Business Week,* March 30, 1962, p. 50, June 8, 1963, p. 62 and April 6, 1963, pp. 96–99; and Norman B. Obbard, "The Common Market and Its Relationship to the United States Steel Industry," *Iron and Steel Engineer,* December, 1962.

[37]Under the Webb-Pomerene Law, passed in 1918, or under specific commodity agreements.

Procter & Gamble was required by the federal government (in a 1967 Supreme Court ruling) to sell Clorox Chemical Co., which it acquired in 1957. The U.S. Justice Department decided that P&G's great marketing and advertising power—it is one of the largest advertisers—would upset the competitive balance in the laundry-bleach field, and probably lessen competition. The P&G dissolution did not even involve a competitor buying out a direct competitor, but rather a large firm buying into another industry.[38] Unfortunately, the final court ruling came 10 years after the merger, which is one reason companies planning mergers often seek a preliminary Justice Department opinion.

FTC's message with regard to mergers should be clear, however, following some guidelines issued in 1968. The FTC is no longer concerned only with mergers between companies manufacturing the same products but also those between companies in consumer markets where advertising and promotion strength are important to success. A large company such as Procter & Gamble has sufficient marketing muscle to have a large impact in any market it chooses. Here, the FTC is concerned with all aspects of competition, not just price competition. The Commission recently required P&G to sell part of the assets of a coffee company (Folger's) it purchased as a condition for keeping the rest. But as part of the agreement, the coffee division is forbidden to share in the marketing efficiencies of other P&G divisions. It cannot engage in joint promotions with other P&G products or benefit by media discounts which P&G gains. The intent here clearly is to simulate a competitive market composed of many small firms.[39]

Price leadership

In oligopoly situations, a marketing manager may be able to assume the role of price leader and discourage active use of price. We have noted that each individual firm sees a kinked-demand-curve situation and generally is not eager to cut price. So the best way of avoiding active price competition is to be sure that the price at the kink is suitable for all potential competitors. This does not mean that all competitors must make equal profits but that they should make reasonably acceptable profits. This requires careful analysis of the price leader's own cost structure, estimation of his competitors' cost structures and pricing objectives, and analysis of industry demand.

Setting too high a price also may lead to difficulty. Additional competitors may be attracted into the market by the high price. This often leads to trouble later, when capacity has expanded, unless demand keeps growing.

Setting too low a price, on the other hand, can lead to action from

---

[38] "P&G Is Told It Must Sell Clorox," *Business Week,* December 21, 1963; *Detroit News,* April 13, 1967.

[39] "FTC Sets Merger Rules," *Business Week,* May 18,

1968, p. 46; and *Business Week,* February 25, 1967, p. 46.

antitrust officials who become concerned about the plight of small competitors.

An optimum price may be one which is just high enough to support the marginal firm – the least efficient company whose production would be needed to meet peak long-run demands.[40]

Whatever analytical approach is used, if the price leader chooses a price that others can accept profitably, they may follow without any necessity for agreement. This is called "conscious parallel action." It is a policy the FTC and the Justice Department deplore, but it still has not been declared illegal. Indeed, it is hard to see how it could be, because each firm must administer its prices and it certainly is legal to choose to meet competition. In fact, essentially the same behavior is observed in pure competition. So long as conspiracy is avoided, meeting competition in any market situation probably will continue to be acceptable.

The price leader must take his responsibility seriously. If the followers are not able to make a reasonable profit at the market price, then they may try secret price cuts to expand sales without incurring retaliation. If very much of this activity takes place, the price leader will lose a considerable volume of business, and the situation may degenerate into a violent price war. Or there may be a temptation to collude, as we have seen. Lacking an effective leader, the market may be unstable, and severe price cutting can be a continual threat.

Using Price for all it's worth

Although some marketing managers de-emphasize the pricing variable, others find pricing useful in their marketing mixes. They may rely on product development and promotion programs to help make their marketing mixes as attractive as possible and, in this way, shift the demand curve to the right and make it more inelastic than it might be otherwise. Then these managers can use price actively by (1) making fuller use of demand in market grid boxes, and (2) price changing along the present demand curve.

Full use of demand in market grid boxes

Leader and bait pricing attempt to draw in customers and, in effect, expand the demand for the total line. For the retailer, this involves all of the products of a store. These policies are related to full-line pricing and price lining in that they are intended to affect both the demand for individual products in the line and the full line itself.

With full-line pricing, there usually are "fighting brands" at the bottom of the producer's line. These low-priced items can be promoted as leaders to get the business at the low end of the market where the demand curve may be quite elastic. Higher-priced items appeal to

[40]For more extensive discussion, see J. Howard Westing and Jon G. Udell, "Pricing and the Anti-Trust Laws," *Michigan Business Review*, November, 1962, pp. 6–11; Marcus Alexis, "Marketing Laws and Marketing Strategy," *Journal of Marketing*, October, 1962, pp. 67–70; John J. Scanlon, "How Much Should a Corporation Earn?" *Harvard Business Review*, January-February, 1967, pp. 4-21; and J. G. Van Cise, "Regulation – By Business or Government?" *Harvard Business Review*, March–April, 1966, pp. 53–63.

other target markets that may offer less elastic demand curves. Or a marketing manager may add prestige products to the top of the line simply to attract customers who might not want to buy these premium-priced items, but who do want to buy from a firm that offers them.

In short, by selling several items in a line, the firm attempts to satisfy various segments of the market grid. Each of these may have a demand curve with different demand elasticities.

Except for leader pricing and bait pricing, active pricing does not necessarily mean emphasizing low prices. Certainly, pricing a full line to take advantage of the different demands in different market grid boxes is not a low-price policy. Neither is a skimming policy. Odd-even and psychological pricing policies do not always yield low prices. Even leader and bait pricing use low prices merely to draw potential customers to a wider assortment of items.

Price changing along the present demand curve

Straight price changes, either increases or decreases, take the demand curve as given and try to make the best of it. Here, we are concerned with price changes on established products. New-product prices should be set to minimize the need for correction. But if conditions change, the prices may have to be changed, too.

Price increases are not easy to make unless the firm's marketing mix is significantly better than the competition's. Customers don't like price increases and may temporarily stop buying or look for new sources. But if the firm's marketing mix is truly unique and if its demand curve is inelastic upward from the present prices, a price increase probably will increase profits once customers have adjusted to the new price.

If a firm has to worry about competitive reaction, and has recently faced raw material or labor cost increases, it can attempt to play the price leader role by publicly announcing why it is increasing prices. This might attract followers if the industry demand is inelastic.

Price cuts are easier to make, either as offensive moves or in an effort to relieve pressure on the other three P's — especially Promotion. Both simple price cutting and a conscious below-the-market price policy are efforts to expand sales by moving down the demand curve that already exists for the product.

In highly competitive markets, price cutting is frequently used as an active variable. The tendency, of course, is to slowly push the price level down, and then down again. As the price level drops, the original cutters may achieve some short-run gains, although in the long run all the industry members may be in worse condition.

Industry price cutting may be effective only if the general demand for the product is fairly elastic, because then total revenue will increase if the price is cut. Price cutting can be useful in a marketing mix, but it must be used only after careful analysis of demand and cost. At the extreme lower end of a demand curve, demand still might be expandable, but costs may begin to rise, and further price cutting could be unprofitable.

Conclusion

In this chapter, we have discussed the legal framework within which the marketing manager sets prices and develops his marketing strategies. Legislation and legal cases often focus on pricing matters, because prices are tangible and highly visible. This does *not* mean that the marketing manager is entirely limited, however. Generally, he can set any price he wants as long as he avoids collusion and price discrimination.

Pricing legislation becomes especially important when the marketing manager has not been able to differentiate his marketing mix and the bulk of competition is based on price. Then he may have to become more interested in methods for controlling price. There is legislation which controls minimum prices at the wholesale and retail level which might be relevant. Also, in some states, it is permissible to fix prices under fair trade. And some customers may be anxious for special prices, a situation which will require a marketing manager to be familiar with the price-discrimination laws.

Operating within the political and legal environment is sometimes difficult and confusing. Although most legislation, including that covering pricing, ostensibly was designed to protect competition and consumers, "competition" often has been narrowly interpreted as meaning "competitors." Although the guidelines laid down by legislation and court cases are sometimes dim and uncertain, there are good reasons for the marketing manager to heed them. Some business executives have gone to jail and others have received heavy fines. As in other legal areas, ignorance is no excuse. A good marketing man should understand the legal environment and know how to work within it.

Finally, the marketing manager must develop a set of price policies as part of each marketing mix. Two basic approaches were isolated (1) de-emphasizing Price, and (2) treating Price as an active variable.

Pricing can be de-emphasized by stressing nonprice competition. Various price control measures can also be useful, such as fair trading, exclusive or selective distribution, planned functional discount structures, leasing and consignment selling. Pricing can be further de-emphasized by statesmanlike price leadership which considers the welfare of the rest of the industry and the dangers of a too-low or too-high price.

Using Price as an active variable involves catering to different target markets on the market grid and then pricing in line with the demand and cost situations in each of the market grid boxes. Or straight price cuts can be used to expand the quantity demanded along a demand curve.

Whether Price is used actively or de-emphasized, Price is one of the four major variables the marketing manager works with. It should be based on well-defined policies. Lack of policy really is a form of policy, too. It would seem more desirable to set policies consciously, in the light of the competitive and legal environment in each target market.

1 Discuss unfair trade practices acts. To whom are they "unfair"?

2 Discuss the thinking behind fair trade laws. To whom are they "fair"?

3 How would our marketing structure be changed if manufacturers were required to specify fair trade prices on *all* products sold at retail and *all* retailers were required to use these prices? Would this place greater or lesser importance on the development of the manufacturer's marketing mix? What kind of an operation would retailing be in this situation? Would consumers receive more or less service?

4 Would it be price discrimination if a large oil company sold gasoline to taxicab associations for resale to individual taxicab operators for $2\frac{1}{2}$ cents a gallon less than charged to retail service stations? What happens if the cab associations resell gasoline not only to taxicab operators, but to the general public as well?

5 Discuss the economic forces or situations which might lead to deceptive pricing. Why might some marketing organizations include deceptive pricing in their marketing mixes? In what lines of trade or for what types of products would such pricing be more likely?

6 If a company did not wish to use Price as an active variable, what policy (or policies) might be appropriate to minimize or eliminate price competition for each of the following products? (Specify any necessary assumptions in order to obtain a definite answer.)
a) Cough syrup
b) Lipstick
c) Men's ties
d) Electric shavers
e) Cuff links
f) Industrial paint products
g) Nickel
h) Electronic measuring instruments for paper production
i) Automobiles
j) Passenger tires

7 Why is active price competition always a possibility, even in oligopoly situations? Illustrate why active price competition might be attractive to a marketing manager. Would active price competition seem to be in the public interest? If so, why is it frequently looked upon with disfavor by the courts and legislatures?

8 Discuss the problem of granting P.M.'s and other promotional allowances within the provisions of the Robinson-Patman Act. How can these allowances be made on "proportionately equal terms" when stores are of varying size and importance to the producer or wholesaler? Should all retailers be allowed a sufficient allowance to run the same size advertisement or should it be on some basis such as percentage of sales? In the latter case, would the small retailer make as effective use of such allowances in view of the fact that there are substantial economies in purchasing large blocks of advertising?

9 In view of downsloping demand curves, price cutting at the retail level would mean expanded sales volume for producers. Why then do some manufacturers support fair-trade legislation?

...an individual firm should see each of its internal activities as well as its relations with outsiders as part of a total system of action.

...important as organizing the total system is, organization as such is not enough to guarantee success in our increasingly competitive marketplace....The system must be innovative. That is why total commitment to the marketing concept is essential.

28

Integrating a marketing program

In recent years, an increasing number of producers, wholesalers, and retailers have adopted the marketing concept and have seen the parallel importance of viewing a business as a total system of action.

These companies have traveled the long, evolutionary road from the days when the overwhelming consideration of manufacturers and middlemen was producing or stocking products. We discussed this process in the early chapters and have seen its application throughout this text. Now we will round out our discussion and show why an individual firm should see each of its internal activities as well as its relations with outsiders as part of a total system of action.

Our major stress so far has been on developing parts of, and whole, marketing strategies, but usually in terms of one product or market at a time. Now we will see that a marketing manager must develop a marketing program—a set of marketing strategies and plans which seek to reach the firm's goals by making the most effective possible use of the firm's resources.

Need for a total system view

In Chapters 1 and 2, we discussed the growing acceptance of the marketing concept and why a deep commitment by top management *and* the whole organization is so vital. Some company reorganization may be necessary (and sometimes is essential) to implement the marketing concept and effectively run a total system of action. But without the enthusiastic support of top management, organizational changes may be only window dressing.

Must organize for strategy and tactics

Our basic focus has been on planning strategy, while realizing that considerable tactical planning is needed also. The policies established within a strategy, however, set the framework for tactical efforts. This guiding influence of the strategy emphasizes again the importance of care in strategic planning.

Both tactical efforts (the execution or implementation efforts) and controlling activities are important to the success of a firm, of course. All of these activities are necessary for it to operate effectively as a dynamic total system of action. At any time during the execution phase, it should be possible to revise the strategic plan and embark on a new one. For this reason, it is vital that a permanent information system be set up as part of the controlling process to help keep the total system alert and management on its toes.

As we saw in Chapter 2, the marketing manager should help develop this total system attitude within his firm and his channel system. And in his role as both a planner and implementer, he is in an ideal position to keep the system working, serving as a liaison man between final customers in the channel system and executives in his own company.[1]

Need for innovative strategy planning

Important as organizing the total system is, organization as such is not enough to guarantee success in our increasingly competitive marketplace. Competent execution of poor or obsolete strategies can lead to poor results. The system must be innovative. This is why total commitment to the marketing concept is essential.

Too many businesses are worried about maintaining or increasing

[1]Matthew F. Tuite, "Merging Marketing Strategy Selection and Production Scheduling: A Higher Order Optimum," *Journal of Industrial Engineering,* February, 1968, pp. 76–84; Harry A. Lipson and Fred D. Reynolds, "The Concept of the Marketing Mix: Its Development, Uses, and Applications," *MSU Business Topics,* Winter, 1970, pp. 73–79; and Peter F. Drucker, "Management's New Role," *Harvard Business Review,* November–December, 1969, pp. 49 ff.

their share of their *current* market, rather than trying to find new markets or expanding the current market. *They are essentially competitive rather than innovative* – getting by with yesterday's strategies, *not* creating more effective and satisfying ones. This accounts in part for the declining profit rates we see in some industries and firms.

Make it new, make it better, or you may not make it

Although investments in plant and equipment have been growing, it appears that profits no longer can be bought simply by spending more money on hardware. Moreover, domestic and foreign competition threatens those who do not create more satisfying goods and services. New markets, new customers, and new ways of doing things must be found if companies are to operate profitably in the future.[2]

The importance of aggressive, imaginative marketing strategy planning was discussed in Chapter 2 and summarized in the General Foods hypothesis. The intervening chapters should have given you greater perspective on the implications of this hypothesis. In particular, it may mean that less attention should be paid to finding ways to use a company's present resources – a typical production-oriented approach – and more attention given to locating wholly new market opportunities which may obsolete your own or competitors' strategies.

Market grids are revealing

A company can find tremendous new opportunities while trying to locate unsatisfied target markets. Research in the watch industry, for instance, showed that there were three distinct groups of watch customers but that only one was being catered to by present strategies.

Consumers in the first two groups were primarily motivated by economic factors. The first group wanted to pay the lowest price possible for a watch that worked reasonably well. Consumers in the second segment were willing to pay higher prices for product features that added longer life, greater durability and accuracy, or more attractive styling. Consumers in the third segment, on the other hand, were turned on by emotional values. They usually purchased a watch as a gift and wanted it to have symbolic or sentimental value.

The research showed that 23 percent of the market was in the first segment – the low-price buyers; 46 percent was in the second – those who want durability and general excellence; and 31 percent was in the third segment – those who buy a symbol for some important occasion. It was clear that the better-known watch companies were aiming at the third segment almost exclusively. They produced primarily expensive watches and stressed the symbolic appeal in advertising. Their promotion was heavily concentrated in the gift-buying seasons of Christmas and graduation time.

[2] David S. R. Leighton, "The Internationalization of American Business – the Third Industrial Revolution," *Journal of Marketing*, July, 1970, pp. 3–6; W. Jack Butler and John Dearden, "Managing a Worldwide Business," *Harvard Business Review*, May–June, 1965, pp. 93–102; Peter G. Peterson, "Conventional Wisdom and the Sixties," *Journal of Marketing*, April, 1962, pp. 63–67; and J. B. McKitterick, "Needed: New Thinking on Market Strategy and Investment," *Advertising Age*, July 23, 1962, pp. 73–76.

<table>
<tr><td>Find a
market, sell
to it</td><td>This commonly accepted strategy of the major watch companies left the first two segments unsatisfied. But then the U.S. Time Co. successfully filled this void with its "Timex" watches. This "market segmentation" strategy has made the U.S. Time Co. the world's largest watch company.[3]</td></tr>
</table>

It is interesting to note that the major companies had been trying to compete with lower-priced foreign competition, but all competitors were using essentially the same marketing mixes. U.S. Time completely upset the watch industry, both foreign and domestic, by not only offering a good product (with a one-year unconditional guarantee) at a lower price but also by using new channels of distribution. Its watches are widely available in department stores, drugstores, discount houses, and nearly any other retail outlet which will carry them.

Such drastic shifts in strategy may be startling to the conventional production-oriented businessman. But they are becoming much more frequent in industries where some or all of the firms have accepted the marketing concept. Such new marketing strategies often cannot be met by competitors through a simple price cut. In effect, the innovators carve out their own market. This search for unsatisfied target markets is not only socially desirable but absolutely necessary for survival in a marketing-oriented age.

<table>
<tr><td>A systematic
approach
helps</td><td>In Chapter 2, we introduced a two-step approach to strategic planning to help organize and guide this vital process. You may recall that this involved: (1) selecting a target market – that is, defining the area of the firm's interest, determining dimensions of consumer need, and tying them to socioeconomic characteristics, if possible, in order to estimate the size of potential market grid boxes; and (2) developing a marketing mix – that is, determining what the firm can do most profitably for promising looking market grid boxes.</td></tr>
</table>

This approach helps insure that a company maintains a constant search for new opportunities by expanding its marketing vision, but at the same time does not waste time and effort trying to figure out ways to satisfy all human needs.

Note that the initial focus is on *all* the customers' needs in a product-market area. A watch manufacturer, for example, should *not* think only of his customer's need to keep track of the time; he should also be aware of consumer desires for gifts, status, ego boosting, pride in personal possessions, styling, and economy. This broader view of the market would suggest many more possibilities, yet would limit analysis to those markets which can be served by the firm, perhaps even with its present resources. An example of the results of such an analysis is the experience, reported earlier, of U.S. Time Co. with its "Timex" watches.

---

[3] Daniel Yankelovich, "Psychological Market Segmentation," in Jack Z. Sissors (ed.), *Some Bold New Theories of Advertising in Marketing* (Evanston, Ill.: Northwestern University, Jack Z. Sissors, 1963), pp. 23–25.

The Tramisol Story

Another recent example of the application of this systematic approach, emphasizing interrelations and the need for continuing analysis, is "The Tramisol Story."

The story behind the development of Tramisol, Cyanamid's new broad-spectrum cattle wormer, began with the "Farmerized Marketing Concept," a management philosophy based on the customer's need.

Harry W. Jamison, Jr., manager of marketing research for Cyanamid's Agricultural Division, explains the concept this way: "First, we determine the farmer's need. Then we ask Research and Development to come up with a new product to satisfy the need. Once a product is developed, we prod manufacturing to produce it at reasonable cost."

Market strategy

The next step is development of market strategy – defining the target market and designing a marketing mix to reach it. The marketing mix consists of four P's – Product, Price, Place and Promotion – supported by continuous market research on all four ingredients.

In the Tramisol case, Cyanamid began with the farmer's need to control cattle worms that reduce weight gains and result in poor animal health and uneconomic production.

Market research people had been monitoring the increasing use of anthelmintics by farmers for years. The research was broad enough to keep track of the use of anthelmintics across all species of livestock and poultry.

At the same time, research and development efforts included a search for chemical compounds that had activity against worms. When Tramisol was found to have a high marginal utility over existing products used to worm beef cattle, the initial target market was narrowed to this area.

Look at product characteristics

"To develop the marketing mix, we first examined Product," Jamison states. "Outside research services helped us determine the volume of each existing branded product being sold by farm supply stores, veterinarians and other dispensers for the worming of cattle. We checked package sizes and product formulations.

"In terms of Price, we measured the farmer's valuation of available products to control ruminant worms by what he was willing to pay. This amount seemed reasonable when measured against total cost of producing beef cattle and the losses from worms.

"In terms of Place, we analyzed product purchases by feedlots and through outlets such as farm stores and veterinarians. We charted sales by geographic regions and forecast potential shifts in beef cattle population."

Jamison also looked at use by season of year. In keeping with the Farmerized Marketing Concept, he believes seasonality of product movement should determine manufacturing activity. "Manufacturing should be timed to meet the farmer's need, not the manufacturer's convenience," he adds.

Importance of awareness

Once the first three P's were taken care of, Promotion became important. With Tramisol, a major translation from market research for promotional purposes was the high awareness of cattlemen to the worm problem. Cyanamid's studies showed that 85 percent of cattlemen knew about worming products, 70 percent could describe and name specific products, and 2/3 had used one or more wormers.

Roger B. Clark, Cyanamid's advertising manager for animal health products, and E. H. Brown Advertising Agency translated this information into a copy platform aimed at selling product rather than educating cattlemen on the need to worm. But this covered only the established market.

marketplace. Some companies already have recognized this by keeping one set of books for tax purposes and another to reflect more realistically what is happening in the business.

Planning for a changing strategy

Figure 28–1 indicates why it might be desirable to develop a strategic plan to cover the product's life cycle. Typically, marketing variables should change throughout the product life cycle.

This figure should be an instructive review. For example, you will see that as the product life cycle moves on, the marketing manager should *expect* to find more products entering "his" market and pushing the market situation closer to pure competition. At the same time, he might want to shift from a selective to an intensive distribution policy *and* move from a skimming to a penetration pricing policy.

His original plan for implementing his strategy should include these likely adjustments and the probable timing involved. If it is likely that the cycle will move very quickly, then he may have to select a less-than-optimal plan early in the product life cycle, knowing that

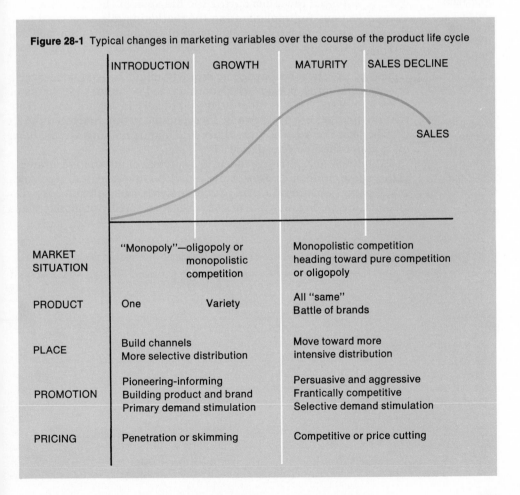

Figure 28-1 Typical changes in marketing variables over the course of the product life cycle

	INTRODUCTION	GROWTH	MATURITY	SALES DECLINE
MARKET SITUATION	"Monopoly"—oligopoly or monopolistic competition		Monopolistic competition heading toward pure competition or oligopoly	
PRODUCT	One	Variety	All "same" Battle of brands	
PLACE	Build channels More selective distribution		Move toward more intensive distribution	
PROMOTION	Pioneering-informing Building product and brand Primary demand stimulation		Persuasive and aggressive Frantically competitive Selective demand stimulation	
PRICING	Penetration or skimming		Competitive or price cutting	

he will not be able to change the plan fast enough later. Regarding his distribution structure, for example, he might choose intensive rather than selective distribution because he knows this will be necessary in a year's time.

Whole plans should be compared

A highly detailed strategic plan can be developed for one year, perhaps to conform to company planning practices. But when it comes to evaluating alternative plans, it may make more sense to project their economic potential over a more logical planning period. If a product life cycle is likely to last three years, for example, then a good strategy may not produce profitable results during the first six months to a year. But examine the plan over the projected three-year life-span, and it might look like a winner. When evaluating the potential of alternative strategic plans, it is important to evaluate like things — i.e., *whole* strategic plans.

Total profit approach can help evaluate alternative plans

The total profit approach to evaluating strategic plans requires forecasts of potential revenues during the life-span of the plan as well as cost projections for implementing the marketing mix associated with the plan. This is basically an extension of the total cost approach discussed in Chapter 18, only here expected costs are subtracted from forecasted sales.

The prospects for a particular strategy might be evaluated over a five-year planning period, with monthly and/or annual estimates of sales and costs. This is illustrated graphically in Figure 28–2. Note that the product life cycle can be incorporated in this analysis through the shape of the sales and cost curves. There is nothing sacred, however, about the five-year period.

In addition to evaluating the profit potential of alternative strategic plans, some companies project the return on investment of resources required to implement a plan. Such analyses can be useful for discriminating among alternative plans because equally profitable plans

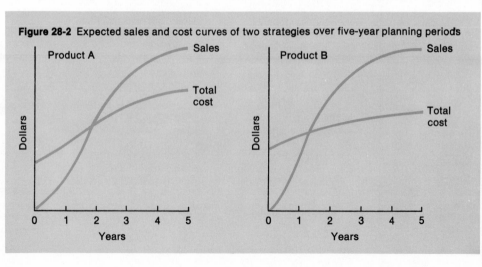

Figure 28-2 Expected sales and cost curves of two strategies over five-year planning periods

may require vastly different resources and offer different rates of return on investment. Such analyses can also show that some plans are riskier than others or will tie up resources for a longer time period, thereby reducing flexibility.[5]

Finally, if many alternative plans must be evaluated for each potential strategy, putting them in graphic terms may be helpful. The tree diagram in Figure 28–3 shows several alternatives clearly. At the end of each branch, a measure of effectiveness, such as total profit, can be shown for comparison. If the success of any of the plans is uncertain, the expected values can be estimated and compared, as shown in Chapter 2.[6]

Companies plan and implement marketing programs

Most companies implement more than one strategic plan at the same time. Typically, they aim at several target markets and prepare quite different marketing mixes for each one. Each of these plans, therefore, must be merged into a total *marketing program,* which then becomes the responsibility of the entire company, working as a total system of action.

A dynamic example

The dynamics of this ongoing planning and implementation effort is well illustrated in the activities of the Agricultural Division of American Cyanamid Company, which has thoroughly adopted the marketing concept. This division alone (there are 10 other operating divisions in the company) markets more than 300 different agricultural products, including drugs, pharmaceuticals, fertilizer products, insecticides, fumigants, weed killers, industrial nitrogen products, and chemicals for the food industry—all industrial goods. It realizes that agriculture is not a single industry but a collection of dozens of heterogeneous subindustries, each with its own market grid.

Each of the division's marketing mixes contains the four P's as ingredients. But because of the complexity of the agricultural market and the wide product line offered, the marketing mixes vary from sales territory to sales territory and from product to product. This diversity of mixes is well described by the Agricultural Division's director of marketing:

There are times when we use across-the-board national media and promotion, but usually our programs are pin-pointed to individual agricultural

[5] Leon Winer, "Are You Really Planning Your Marketing?" *Journal of Marketing,* January, 1965, pp. 1–8; Robert J. Mockler, "Theory and Practice of Planning," *Harvard Business Review,* March–April, 1970, pp. 148–69; T. A. Andersen, "Coordinating Strategic and Operational Planning," *Business Horizons,* Summer, 1965, pp. 49–58; Donald J. Smalter, "Anatomy of a Long Range Plan," in *Long Range Planning,* Proceedings of the American Marketing Association Meeting in Cleveland, Ohio, March 31–April 1, 1966, pp. 28–49; and W. Dickerson Hogue, "What Should Market Planning Cost?" *Business Horizons,* April, 1970, pp. 61–72.

[6] If the plan covers more than one year, it may be desirable to compute the *present value* of future returns. For more discussion on this approach, see John F. Magee, "Decision Trees for Decision Making," *Harvard Business Review,* July–August, 1964, pp. 126–38.

Figure 28-3 Decision tree for evaluation of alternative one-year plans, given that target market and product have already been selected and one-year plans are realistic

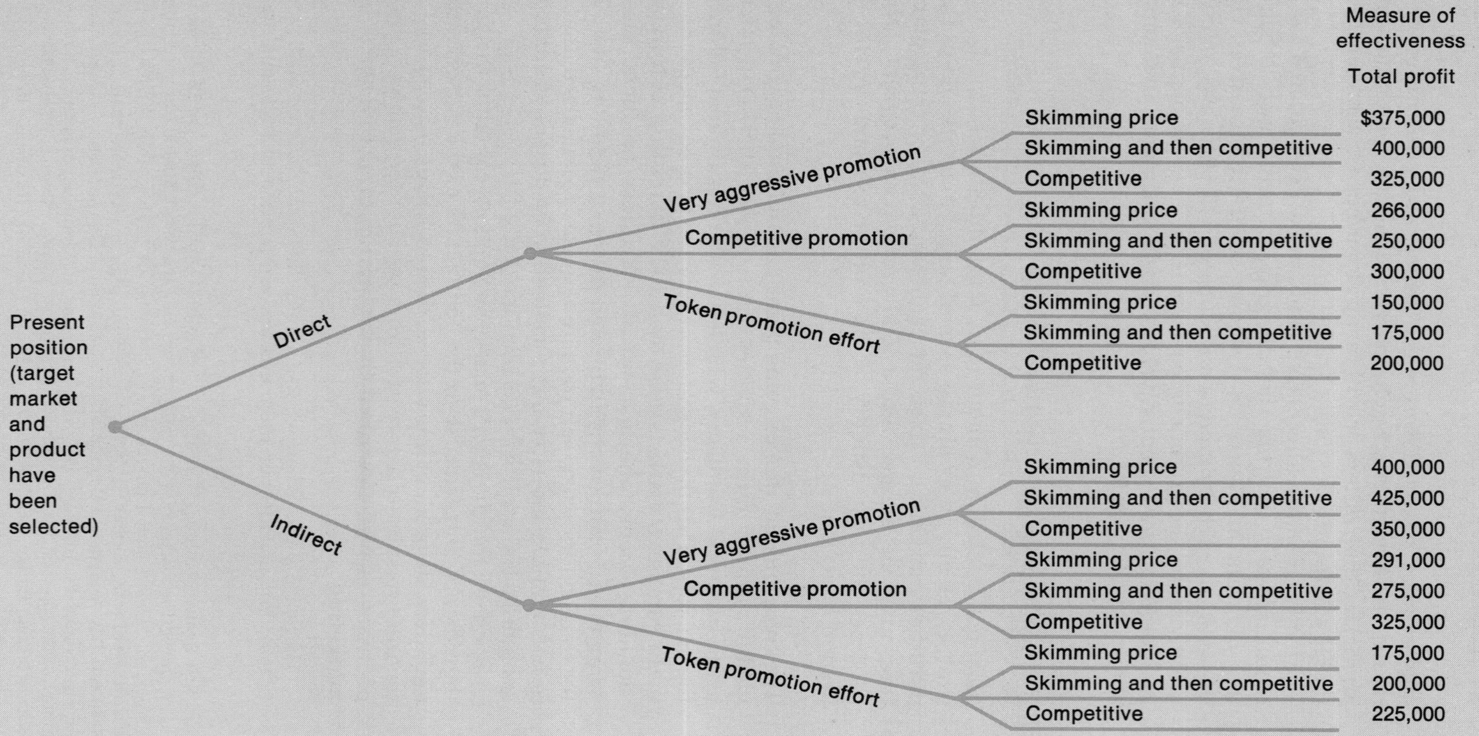

	Measure of effectiveness
	Total profit

Present position (target market and product have been selected)

Direct

Very aggressive promotion
- Skimming price — $375,000
- Skimming and then competitive — 400,000
- Competitive — 325,000

Competitive promotion
- Skimming price — 266,000
- Skimming and then competitive — 250,000
- Competitive — 300,000

Token promotion effort
- Skimming price — 150,000
- Skimming and then competitive — 175,000
- Competitive — 200,000

Indirect

Very aggressive promotion
- Skimming price — 400,000
- Skimming and then competitive — 425,000
- Competitive — 350,000

Competitive promotion
- Skimming price — 291,000
- Skimming and then competitive — 275,000
- Competitive — 325,000

Token promotion effort
- Skimming price — 175,000
- Skimming and then competitive — 200,000
- Competitive — 225,000

industries and areas. A case in point would be our TV Farm Newsreel which was carried on more than 50 television stations in high income farm areas. During the past year all the commercial messages have been tailored to local needs. The majority of our print advertising is directed to specific segments of the agricultural industry through schedules in specialized horizontal publications serving the feed milling industry, veterinarians, cattle growers, broiler producers or various other agricultural sub-industries. We also run heavy schedules in state and local publications and on local radio and television stations. Our promotions (sales promotions) are also tailored to individual agricultural industries or geographic areas.

Aurofac needs technical sales

We have no pat marketing mix formula. I will use four of our products and product lines as examples of how our marketing mixes vary. First come our *Aurofac* animal feed supplements. These are various strengths and formulations of *Aureomycin* which are used as ingredient products by feed manufacturers in their feed products. *Aurofac* maintains livestock health and promotes livestock growth. The *Aurofac* marketing mix primarily depends on a large technically trained sales force and sharing the top position in the *Aurofac* marketing mix is our technical service by scientists. These scientists, working in close relationship with the technically trained sales force, provide research and consultation on feeding problems. They prepare and supply to the trade highly specialized bulletins on the use of *Aurofac* in feeding problems. They conduct field trials and demonstrations using the most advanced methods of statistical control. In conjunction with professional motion picture producers, these scientists have prepared and are continually enlarging an extensive library of films which in simple language document the benefits of *Aurofac* to animal health and growth – animal industry by animal industry.

Next in importance are advertising and public relations. Our *Aurofac* trade advertising is for the purpose of supporting our technically trained sales force and our scientists in their relationship with feed manufacturers. It tells the feed manufacturer how *Aureomycin* will benefit him and benefit his customers. Our *Aurofac* advertising to the livestock grower is designed to support the feed manufacturer in the sale of his products containing *Aureomycin*. Our advertising to the farmer tells him that having *Aureomycin* in his feeds is profitable and insures against disease loss and promotes animal growth. To the farmer we sell a concept. To the feed manufacturer we sell a product.

Packaging and promotion come next. Good packaging is necessary, but it is not of primary importance. Our *Aurofac* promotion is not extensive and here again its purpose is to make it easier for the feed manufacturer to sell his products containing *Aureomycin*.

Aureomycin needs channel sales

The next example is *Aureomycin* Mastitis Suspension which cures mastitis, a high incidence disease among dairy cows. Although this product's basic ingredient is chlortetracycline, which is also the basis of *Aurofac,* the two marketing mixes are substantially different. In this case, primary emphasis goes to a large sales force trained in merchandising. *Aureomycin* Mastitis is sold through many types of wholesalers and distributors and about 25,000 farm supply outlets. Getting and holding distribution, controlling inventories, displaying the merchandise and educating the trade are the salesmen's primary tasks. Sharing top position in its marketing mix are advertising, promotion and packaging. Here our advertising sells *our* specific product. Special promotions are utilized at three distinct links in the marketing chain, namely, the wholesale, retail and ultimate user levels.

Our packaging must include identification, imagery and impulse appeals not too unlike those of a convenience goods manufacturer, but it must also educate the user and make it easier for him to utilize the product in a highly specialized use situation.

Technical service by scientists occupies a subordinate position in the marketing mix mainly because we do not have to send a scientist with every order as is sometimes the case with *Aurofac*. This product was developed for a specific mass market so the vast majority of technical problems was licked in the development stage. Our scientists, however, supply research and consultation where needed, technical bulletins, educational films, and are continually running field trials and demonstrations. The scientists take second place in the marketing of this product.

Fertilizers need technical sales and good place

Then come our Phosphate and Nitrogen Products which fall roughly into two groups. One group consists of ingredient concentrates which are sold to fertilizer manufacturers who formulate them into finished fertilizer products. The second group compromises finished fertilizer products which we sell through farm supply channels. The most important part of our phosphate and nitrogen fertilizer marketing mix is a special technically trained sales force. Again, as in the case of *Aurofac,* the sales force works in close cooperation with our technical service men. The second ingredient in our fertilizer marketing mix is an item which ordinarily would not be considered part of a marketing mix but because fertilizers are heavy tonnage, relatively low priced products, the location of our production facilities is very important in the marketing mix. Strategic advertising, public relations, and promotion are used, but not nearly to the extent that they are in the majority of products in our line.

Cotton defoliant needs place timing

The fourth example is our Cyanamid Special Grade Defoliant, a product based on our original Cyanamid compound which was developed 51 years ago. This product defoliates cotton prior to mechanical picking. It is a packaged item and is sold through farm supply channels. Defoliants are used by cotton farmers only when there has been rainfall just before picking time. This rainfall causes fresh new growth and the resulting green leaves stain the cotton when it is mechanically picked if they are not removed prior to picking. Since the product is useful only when there is fresh new growth, the most important ingredient in Cyanamid Special Grade Defoliant's marketing mix is availability when and if needed. The hardest job is to have it on hand at the right time, the right place and in the right quantity. Advertising, public relations, promotion and packaging are relatively unimportant for this product. The advertising we do is highly localized and conveys the message that the defoliants are available in the locality.

I mentioned earlier that our total product line is a long one. We don't have a distinctly different marketing mix for every product in this line, but we do have several dozen product sub-groups with significantly different marketing mix requirements. Add to this the variations in marketing mix caused by geographic differences and special area problems, and I believe you will see why we say we have no pat formula for developing marketing mixes.[7]

[7] Adapted slightly from Burton S. Bowman, "The Utility of Marketing Tools and the Accomplishment of Marketing Objectives," speech to the 41st National Conference of the American Marketing Association, Chicago, December 29, 1958.

Marketing programs must be planned, but flexible	Clearly, a marketing manager must be flexible in creating, executing, and then reshaping strategic plans within a program. He must be willing to change his plans as shifting uncontrollable variables, or market or customer needs, direct. Many tactical changes are certainly possible within the framework of individual plans and the program, but if a basic plan goes awry, then the marketing manager must have the good sense and the courage to change it.

Also, a company's resources are always limited, so the marketing manager cannot launch a plan to pursue every promising opportunity he sees. Instead, limited resources always force him to make hard decisions among alternative plans while developing his program.

Match potential and resources— by trial and error	How do you find the best program? There is no one best way of comparing various plans. A great deal of reliance must be placed on management judgment. Yet some calculations are helpful, too. If a five-year planning horizon seems to be realistic for the firm's product markets, then expected profits over the five-year period can be compared for each plan.

Assuming the company had a profit-oriented objective, the more profitable plans could be looked at first, both in terms of potential profit and resources required. Also, the impact on the entire program should be evaluated. One profitable-looking alternative might be a poor first choice because it will eat up all the company's resources and side-track several plans which together would be more profitable.

Some juggling among the various plans in relation to profitability versus resources needed and available tends to move the company toward the *most profitable* program.

This trial-and-error approach can be aided with a computer program if a great number of alternatives have to be evaluated. Actually, however, the computer would merely perform the same function— trying to match potential revenues and profits against available resources.[8]

---

[8] For further discussion on evaluating and selecting alternate plans, see W. I. Little, "The Integrated Management Approach to Marketing," *Journal of Marketing*, April, 1967, pp. 32–36; and Leon Winer, "A Profit-Oriented Decision System," *Journal of Marketing*, April, 1966, pp. 38–44. This latter reference discusses discounting the future flow of profits to provide a more realistic appraisal of the value of alternate plans. This procedure can be used for equating the profit flows for different time periods, that is, a five-year profit flow would be compared with a 10-year profit flow by discounting all the future flows to their present value. See also, S. C. Brandt, "Dissecting the Segmentation Syndrome," *Journal of Marketing*, October, 1966, pp. 22–27; F. H. Mossman and M. L. Worrel, Jr.,

"Analytical Methods of Measuring Marketing Profitability," *MSU Business Topics*, Autumn, 1966, pp. 35–45; and W. J. E. Crissy and R. M. Kaplan, "Matrix Models for Marketing Planning," *MSU Business Topics*, Summer, 1963, pp. 48–66.

In attempting to develop more profitable programs, some firms may find it useful to use computer simulations of their own and competitors' potential strategies to evaluate the attractiveness of various plans. For more discussion on simulation, see Harold Weitz, "The Promise of Simulation in Marketing," *Journal of Marketing*, July, 1967, pp. 28–33; and P. Kotler, "The Competitive Marketing Simulator—A New Management Tool," *California Management Review*, Spring, 1965.

Allocating budgets for marketing programs

Once the overall marketing program and five-year (or whatever) plans have been set, shorter-term plans also must be worked out. Typically, companies use annual budgets both to plan what they are going to do and to provide control over various functions. Each department may be allowed to spend its budgeted amount, perhaps by months, for each of their departmental functions. As long as departments stay within their budgets, they are allowed considerable (or complete) autonomy. But spending over the budget is considered a deviation from the general plan and requires a lot of discussion and clearance at a higher level.

Budgeting for marketing? – 50%, 30%, or 10% is better than nothing

The most common method of budgeting for marketing expenditures is to compute them as a percentage of either past or forcasted sales. The virtue of this method is its simplicity. A similar percentage can be used rather automatically each year, eliminating the need to repeatedly evaluate the kind and amount of marketing effort that is needed and its probable cost. It enables those executives who are not too tuned into the marketing concept to "write off" a certain percentage or number of dollars, and at the same time control the amount spent. When a company's top executives have this attitude, they often get what they expect from their marketing activities – something less than the best results.

Some marketing executives find this percentage-of-sales approach convenient. It assures them of a reasonable budget. It should be clear, however, that the believers in this approach do not fully understand the relation between effort and results.

Find the task, budget for it

Mechanically budgeting a certain percentage of past or forecasted sales leads, ironically, to expanding marketing expenditures when business is good and sales are rising, and contracting them when business is poor. It may, in fact, be desirable to increase marketing expenditures when business is good, though it is questionable whether this should be in a direct ratio. But when business is poor, the most sensible approach may be to be *more*, not less, aggressive!

There are other methods of budgeting for marketing expenditures. Some of these are as follows:

1. Match expenditures with competitors.
2. Set the budget as a certain number of cents or dollars per sales unit (by case, by thousand, or by ton), using the past year or estimated year ahead as a base for computation.
3. Set aside all uncommitted revenue, perhaps including budgeted profits. Companies willing to sacrifice some or all of current profits for future sales may use this approach, i.e., *invest* in marketing.
4. Base the budget on the number of new customers desired or the amount required to reach a predetermined sales goal, as when

entering new territories, increasing volume, or seeking other objectives. This method is frequently called the "task method."

In the light of our continuing discussion about marketing strategy and its part in a total system of action, the most sensible approach to budgeting marketing expenditures would seem to be this last approach, the *task method*.

The amount budgeted using this method can be expressed ultimately as a percentage of sales, but developing this shorthand description would be much more involved than picking up a past percentage. It would require a careful review of the five-year plans discussed previously and the specific tasks to be accomplished this year as part of each of these five-year plans. The costs of these tasks then would be totaled to determine how much should be budgeted for marketing and the other business functions provided for in the one- and five-year plans. If a careful five-year planning procedure has been used and accepted by top management, then the budget should be assembled directly from these detailed plans, rather than from historical patterns or ratios.

Spending without agony

After the marketing department has received its budget for the year, it could, presumably, spend its money any way it saw fit. But if the previous planning-budgeting procedure has been followed, it would make sense to continue allocating expenditures within the marketing function according to the plans in the program.

Again, everyone in the marketing department and in the business should view the company as a system of action and plan accordingly. If this is done, it will be possible to eliminate some of the traditional planning-budgeting decisions which have been so agonizing because, in the nature of things, one executive often was pitted against another and one department against another.[9]

Decisions still must be made

Our discussion of an organized planning-budgeting process using the task method makes budgeting for marketing sound simple. In fact, however, it is not. The procedures we have been describing set the framework, but considerable management judgment and marketing research still have to be employed to weigh the relative effectiveness of the four P's in various target markets. Marginal analysis of the

[9] For more discussion on budget allocation, see C. E. Eldridge, "The Marketing Budget and Its Allocation," *Printers' Ink,* May 12, 1967, pp. 35–44; David Novick, "Long-Range Planning through Program Budgeting," *Business Horizons,* February, 1969, pp. 59–66; Stanley D. Henrici, "Eyeing the ROI," *Harvard Business Review,* May–June, 1968. pp. 88–97; Alfred Rappaport, "A Capital Budgeting Approach to Divisional Planning and Control," *Financial Executive,* October, 1968, pp. 1–9; Joseph S. Moag and Eugene M. Lerner, "Capital Budgeting Decisions under Imperfect Market Conditions – A Systems Framework," *Journal of Finance,* September, 1969, pp. 613–21; and *Managing the Budget Function* (Studies in Business Policy, No. 131, [New York: National Industrial Conference Board, 1970]), 88 pp.

potential effectiveness of alternative variables often is useful. And new techniques are being tried and applied by progressive companies as soon as they are effective.[10]

Because he's out on the breakthrough frontier

The procedures we have discussed can be helpful as guides, but the ultimate responsibility for developing a profitable marketing program rests with management. And typically, much judgment is required, because future market conditions must be forecasted. This is why we stressed earlier the importance of looking for breakthrough opportunities rather than merely trying to patch up or improve present marketing strategies. It is relatively easy to decide between one strategy that probably will yield a 30 percent return on investment in the next two years and one that will yield only 10 percent during the next year. Finding a new strategy that will return 50 percent the first year is more difficult but makes strategy selection even easier.

As we see it, one of the marketing manager's important roles is helping to find such opportunities. And this role falls to him especially because such opportunities are more likely to be found in the marketplace, by locating unsatisfied customer needs, than through cost savings in the plant, warehouse, or store.

Coordinating marketing programs

We have assigned the role of coordinating the whole marketing program to the marketing manager. The title of the executive responsible for this function, however, may differ from company to company. The point is that *someone* in each firm must be responsible for planning and then implementing an integrated marketing program.

Many of the topics we have discussed in this book are helpful for both integrating the marketing effort and carrying it out. Overall company goals and specific Product, Place, Promotion, and Pricing objectives determine what is to be accomplished. Job specifications, advertising campaign plans, pricing policies, and so on, should be designed to guide the tactical decision making and to meet specific problems as they arise during the course of implementation.

Flowcharts point the way

Some marketing managers have found flowcharts helpful for diagraming all the interrelated tasks in each marketing plan and the total program. Flowchart techniques, similar to the critical path or PERT methods discussed in Chapter 14, can also be useful here.

Each week or month in an ongoing 12-month plan, for example,

---

[10] For a more detailed discussion of how to spend or budget parts of the total marketing budget more effectively, see R. L. Mela, "Sales Budgeting for Controlled Growth Objectives," *Journal of Marketing Research*, May, 1965, pp. 133–40; Joel Dean, "Does Advertising Belong in the Capital Budget?" *Journal of Marketing*, October, 1966, pp. 15–21; J. S. Schiff and M. Schiff, "New Sales Management Tools: ROAM," *Harvard Business Review*, July-August 1967, pp. 59–66; M. Schiff, "The Use of ROI in Sales Management," *Journal of Marketing*, July, 1963, pp. 70–73; J. L. Simon, "A Simple Model for

could be graphed horizontally. The timing of each activity could then be seen. If it was clearly impossible to accomplish some of the tasks in the time allotted, this fact would become clear during the flowcharting process and adjustments could be made. Basically, this is similar to the scheduling by production planners, where wall-sized graphic aids are often used.

Knowing must come before deciding

Unfortunately, marketing managers often make decisions based almost totally on their judgment and on very little hard information. Yet when data is or could be available, it is pointless to take the risks that such blind-flying decisions entail.

To improve the quality and quantity of decision-related information, progressive firms are expanding the role assigned to their marketing research departments, turning them into marketing *information* centers. In other companies, this new function may be separated into a new department because management, regarding the information process as extremely important, wants to make sure that it does not get buried in the ongoing activities of the marketing research department.

Careful analysis of data already available to the company could lead to more effective planning and implementation, helping the marketing manager in his coordinating role. Routine sales analysis, for example, can be organized to determine whether the firm's various target markets are really buying the product.

If management has made its plans carefully, it ought to be able to test continuously whether these plans are working out and the firm is moving toward its objectives. This control activity is discussed at greater length in the next chapter, but here it should be noted that the control activity can do much more than merely assure that the various functional activities will stay within their budgets.

Finding new customers, feeding back data

Routine sales analysis can also reveal surprising new opportunities, perhaps showing that although the original target market is not buying, new and better markets have shown interest.

At Ford Motor Co., sales analysis indicated that more doctors bought Thunderbirds than men in any other profession. Although doctors had typically driven larger and more formal cars – by tradition, a dark-colored Buick – sales results showed they were switching to the Thunderbird, a sporty personal car. As a result, another strategy was devised. Special promotion was aimed directly at the medical profession, with good results.

At the very least, a marketing information system would provide

Determining Advertising Appropriations," *Journal of Marketing Research*, August, 1965, pp. 285–92; P. E. Green, P. J. Robinson, and P. T. Fitzroy, "Advertising Expenditure Models: State of the Art and Prospects," *Business Horizons*, Summer, 1966, pp. 73–80; Joel Dean, "How Much to Spend on Advertising," *Harvard Business Review*, January–February, 1951, pp. 65–74; W. J. Semlow, "How Many Salesmen Do You Need?" *Harvard Business Review*, May–June, 1959, pp. 126–32.

the data needed to control the whole marketing program and the feedback which helps management plan new programs. More is said on this in the next chapter.[11]

Conclusion

In this chapter, we have emphasized the role of marketing management as an integrating force in company management. The marketing concept says that *all* the activities of a company should be directed toward satisfying customers – at a profit. This may require eliminating conflicting departmental "empires" often found within a company.

Throughout this text, we have stressed marketing strategy planing. In this chapter, we have seen that a marketing manager should develop a plan for carrying out each strategy and then, in turn, coordinate a set of plans into a marketing program. If the planning has been effective, the allocation of budgets to particular functions should be relatively simple.

The development of a marketing program can make use of the total cost and total profit approaches for evaluating alternate opportunities. Evaluation should not be limited to one year at a time, however, but should cover some reasonable time period, depending primarily upon the length of the product life cycle and the nature of competition in the firm's target markets. In some extremely competitive markets, a few months may be a reasonable planning cycle. In other markets, 5 to 20 years might be appropriate.

Finally, it is the marketing manager's job to coordinate the whole marketing program and provide liaison within his firm, and between his firm, the channel system, and target customers.

[11] For more discussion on these ideas, see Arnold E. Amstutz, "Market Oriented Management Systems: The Current Status," *Journal of Marketing Research,* November, 1969, pp. 481–496; "Litton's Electronic Information Machine," *Business Week,* March 28, 1970, pp. 158–62; Victor J. Cook and Jerome E. Herniter, "A Manager's Guide to Model Based Information Systems in Marketing," in *Marketing in a Changing World,* American Marketing Association, June, 1969, pp. 121–28; Stanley F. Stasch, "Systems Analysis for Controlling and Improving Marketing Performance," *Journal of Marketing,* April, 1969, pp. 12–19; and D. F. Cox and R. E. Good, "How to Build a Marketing Information System," *Harvard Business Review,* June, 1967, pp. 145–54.

QUESTIONS AND PROBLEMS

1 Distinguish clearly between (*a*) strategy and tactics, (*b*) strategic planning and tactical efforts, and (*c*) strategic plans and marketing programs.

2 Consider how the job of the marketing manager becomes more complex as he must develop and plan *several* strategies as part of his marketing program. Be sure to discuss how he might have to handle different strategies at different stages in the product life cycle. To make this more concrete, consider the job of a marketing manager for a sporting-goods manufacturer.

3 Discuss how a marketing manager could go about choosing among several possible marketing plans, given that he must because of limited resources. Do you feel that the job would be easier in the consumer goods or in the industrial goods areas? Why?

4 Illustrate how you would go about seeking new and potentially profitable opportunities in your local community if you had $10,000 to $15,000 to invest, your present knowledge and training, and a willingness to work. Become quite specific about how you would proceed, steps you would take, data you would look for, whom you would talk to, and so on.

5 Explain why the budgeting procedure is typically such an agonizing procedure, usually consisting of extending past budgets, perhaps with small modifications for current plans. How would the budgeting procedure be changed if the marketing program planning procedure discussed in the chapter were implemented?

6 Explain how flowcharting might be helpful to a marketing manager in coordinating his implementation efforts. In particular, explain how flowcharts might be used to help him plan the implementation of his strategies on a week-by-week and month-by-month basis. Sketch what one such flowchart might look like.

7 When we view a channel as a "total system of action," is there any company executive at any level in the channel who should obviously be considered for the channel captain role? Is it a role which logically falls to someone or some company? Is it a role which could be sought?

8 The marketing concept seeks to satisfy customers, but does this mean that marketing management should seek to satisfy the customer in all respects if this entails a reduction in profit? What should guide the efforts of the marketing manger in this respect?

9 Who might be expected to lead the movement toward the marketing concept in manufacturing organizations producing the following products?
a) Dog food
b) Garden tractors
c) Shovels
d) Cake mixes
e) Electronic machinery controls
f) Industrial conveying machinery
g) Industrial lift trucks
Why?

10 Explain why the marketing concept may be even more important to a firm as it expands into worldwide operations. Would such an expansion seem desirable? Or should it be thought of as a necessity? Does it make any difference what products the company is making?

...it is clear that a marketing program must be controlled. Good control helps the marketing manager locate and correct weak spots, while at the same time finding strengths which he may be able to turn to his own advantage and apply throughout his marketing program. Control works hand in hand with planning in a total system of action.

29

Controlling marketing programs

So far, our main emphasis has been on marketing strategy *planning* — with good reason, as we discussed in Chapter 2. Better results can be achieved by finding unsatisfied target markets and developing good marketing mixes for them.

In fact, if you can do something unique, you may not have to worry too much about how effectively you do it. For this reason, we have de-emphasized the details of implementation and of control. Now, however, we want to show that attention to control is very important, both for running an ongoing business system and for discovering new opportunities.

In this chapter, we will discuss methods and techniques for evaluating whether our strategies are being carried out effectively — or if they are even good strategies. In particular, we will focus on sales analysis, performance analysis, and cost analysis.

Control requires feedback

The basic management process consists of planning, execution, and control. For effective management, the executive must receive feedback on how his plans are working. Sales and cost analyses help provide this feedback by showing results achieved and comparing them with what the manager expected would happen.

If extreme discrepancies are found, they are reported back to management as exception reports. This not only permits control of the ongoing process, but also aids in planning for the future. A good manager wants to know more than which products' sales are highest. He wants to know why, and whether the products are profitable, so that he can base his judgment on hard facts in developing better plans for the future.

Sales analysis shows what is going on

As indicated in Chapter 5, when we discussed sales analysis and sales forecasting, a detailed breakdown of a company's sales records can be very illuminating, especially the first time it is done. Detailed data can quickly update marketing executives who have been out of touch with what is happening in the field. In addition, routine sales analyses prepared each week, month, or year may show trends. These analyses also permit members of management to check their hypotheses, assumptions, and "gut feelings" about how, for example, various market grid customers respond to certain products, package sizes, and stores. Opportunities for new strategies may be revealed, as discussed in Chapter 28 when we saw how the Ford Motor Company quickly added another strategy when it discovered that doctors were buying Thunderbirds.[1]

It is hard to overstate the value of continuous sales analysis—not only to marketing executives but also to the total system. Most of the major auto manufacturers, for example, have installed large-scale electronic computers to analyze daily sales by style and model, because slow analysis of sales could have severe repercussions on production planning and on profit. One day's overrun of fenders may cause a loss of at least $10,000. In the days before production was closely tied to sales analysis, overruns of several days and sometimes several weeks were common.

Enough reports can drown a manager

While some sales data is better than none or getting data too late for action, extremely detailed sales breakdowns can easily "drown" a manager in reports. Computers can now print out at over one thousand lines per minute, which is far faster than any manager can read.

[1] Russell I. Haley and Ronald Gatty, "Moniter Your Markets Continuously," *Harvard Business Review*, May–June, 1968, pp. 65–69.

To avoid having to cope with mountains of data, much of which may be irrelevant, most managers move on to a slightly more sophisticated type of analysis, called *performance analysis*.

Performance analysis looks for differences

Performance analysis seeks exceptions or variations from planned performance. In simple sales analysis, the facts and figures are merely listed, with no attempt to measure them against standards. In performance analysis, however, comparisons are made. One territory might be compared against another, against the same territory's performance last year, or against the expected performance based on a sales forecast in the marketing plan.

The purpose of performance analysis is to improve operations. The salesman, territory, or other factors showing poor performance can be identified and singled out for detailed analysis and remedial action. Or especially outstanding performances can be analyzed to see whether the successes can be explained and made the general rule.

Performance analysis need not be limited to sales. Other data can be analyzed and compared, too. This data might include miles traveled, number of calls made, number of orders, or the cost of various tasks.

Some performance analyses use non-dollar units, such as tons or numbers of units shipped, or numbers of salesmen, because the continual fluctuation of prices and costs may make analysis of dollar data misleading. In the meat-packing industry, for example, tonnage shipped is a more significant variable than dollars worth of meat products shipped, because market price levels fluctuate continuously.

How to organize a flood

Much of our discussion of strategy planning was concerned with setting objectives, policies, and tasks to be accomplished. If a firm has expressed these in specific terms, performance analysis can be used routinely to determine whether plans are being carried out.

Salesmen's call reports contain a great deal of timely and often vital information. But they continue to flood into the home office, and frequently their sheer bulk makes them useless unless the data is quickly transferred into machine-processible form *and* processed. This information may be quite revealing of differences, as is evident in the following example of performance analysis.

Straight performance analysis—an illustration

A manufacturer of industrial products sold to wholesalers through five salesmen, each serving a separate territory. Total net sales for the year amounted to $1,193,000. Compensation and expenses of salesmen came to $99,000. This yielded a direct-selling expense ratio of 8.3 percent—that is, $99,000 divided by $1,193,000, times 100.

This information, drawn from a profit and loss statement, was interesting but did not explain what was actually taking place from one territory to another. To obtain a clearer picture, the analyst segregated and compared the sales results with other data from each territory (see Tables 29-1 and 29-2).

The salesmen in sales areas D and E obviously were not doing well. Sales were low, and marketing costs were high. Perhaps salesmen with more "push" could have done a better job, but the number of customers suggests that the potential might be low. Perhaps the whole plan needs revision.

Table 29-1 Comparative performance of salesmen

Sales area	Total calls	Total orders	Sale–call ratio	Sales by salesman	Average salesman order	Total cus-tomers
A	1,900	1,140	60.0%	$ 456,000	$400	195
B	1,500	1,000	66.7	360,000	360	160
C	1,400	700	50.0	280,000	400	140
D	1,030	279	27.1	66,000	239	60
E	820	165	20.1	31,000	187	50
	6,650	3,784	44.8	$1,193,000	$317	605

Source: Charles H. Sevin, "Analyzing Your Cost of Marketing," *Management Aids for Small Manufacturers* (Washington, D.C.: Small Business Administration, June, 1957), p. 2.

Table 29-2 Comparative cost of salesmen

Sales area	Annual compen-sation	Expense pay-ments	Total salesman cost	Sales produced	Cost–sales ratio
A	$11,400	$ 5,600	$17,000	$ 456,000	3.7%
B	10,800	7,200	18,000	360,000	5.0
C	10,200	5,800	16,000	280,000	5.7
D	9,600	12,400	22,000	66,000	33.3
E	10,000	16,000	26,000	31,000	83.8
	$52,000	$47,000	$99,000	$1,193,000	8.3%

Source: Charles H. Sevin, "Analyzing Your Cost of Marketing," *Management Aids for Small Manufacturers* (Washington, D.C.: Small Business Administration, June, 1957), p. 2.

The figures themselves, of course, do not provide the answers — but they do reveal the areas that need remedial action.[2] This is the main value of performance analysis. It is up to sales management to provide the remedy — either to revise tactics or to change the strategic plan.

[2] Charles H. Sevin, "Analyzing Your Cost of Marketing," *Management Aids for Small Manufacturers* (Washington, D.C.: Small Business Administration, June, 1957), p. 2.

With a straight performance analysis report, the marketing manager can personally evaluate the variations among salesmen in an effort to explain the "why." This is time-consuming, however, and sometimes the truth is that "poor" performances really are not so bad as the bare figures seem to indicate. There may be adverse uncontrollable factors in a particular territory which automatically lower the sales potential. Or it may be found that a territory did not have good potential to begin with.

A better check on the effectiveness of performance is obtained using performance indices. With this approach, the marketing manager compares what "ought to have happened" with what did happen. At first, this may seem akin to looking into a crystal ball, but it need not be.

When the marketing manager develops his plans and forecasts, he should break them down into their components so that when the figures are in, he can compare actual performance against expected performance. If the regular planning procedure does not require such detailed breakdowns, it may be helpful to prepare them anyway. As the basis for such breakdowns, he can use such measures as population in each salesman's territory, the number of last year's orders, or other logical quantitative measurements.

When the company is selling a product that should appeal to all consumers, for example, the size of population in each territory can be useful for estimating what "ought to" happen in each territory. But if the marketing mix is directed to very specific target markets, their particular dimensions should be used as discussed in Chapters 2–9.

How are the salesmen batting?

When standards have been developed—that is, quantitative measures of what "ought to happen"—it is then a relatively simple matter to develop a *performance index*. This is merely a number, such as a baseball batting average, which shows the relation of one value to another.

Baseball batting averages are computed by dividing the actual number of hits by the number of times at bat (the possible number of times the batter could have had a hit). A sales performance index is computed by dividing actual sales by expected sales for an area (or salesman, product, etc.) and then multiplying this figure by 100 to eliminate decimal points. If a salesman is "batting" 82 percent, the index is 82.

Now, that's where the problem is

The development of a performance index is illustrated in the following problem, which assumes that population provides an adequate measure of sales potential.

In Table 29–3, the population of the United States is broken down by regions as a percentage of the total population. The regions in this case are the Eastern, Southern, Midwestern, Mountain, and Western.

This firm already has achieved $1 million in sales and now wants to evaluate performance in each region. The actual sales of $1 million, broken down in proportion to the population in the five regions, are shown in column 2. This is how sales should have been distributed

Table 29–3 Development of a measure of sales performance (by regions)

Regions	Population as percent of U.S. (Col. 1)	Expected distribution of sales based on population (Col. 2)	Actual sales (Col. 3)	Performance index (Col. 4)
Eastern	25	$ 250,000	$ 150,000	60
Southern	20	200,000	250,000	125
Midwestern	25	250,000	300,000	120
Mountain	10	100,000	100,000	100
Western	20	200,000	200,000	100
Total	100	$1,000,000	$1,000,000	

if population were a good measure of future performance. The third column in Table 29-3 shows the actual sales for the year for each region. The fourth column shows measures of performance (performance indices), which are column 3 divided by column 2, multiplied by 100.

Note that population in the Eastern region was 25 percent of the population, and expected sales (based on population) were $250,000. Actual sales, however, were only $150,000. This means that the Eastern region's performance index was only 60 – actual sales were much lower than would be expected on the basis of population.

If population is a sound basis for measuring expected sales (an important *if*), the explanation for poor sales performance will have to be traced further. Perhaps salesmen in the Eastern region are not doing as well as they should. Perhaps promotion there is not as effective as elsewhere. Or competitive products may have entered the market in this region.

Whatever the cause, it should be understood that performance analysis does not solve problems. It pinpoints problems – and it does this well.

A series of performance analyses may find the real problem

Performance analysis enables a marketing manager to probe and discover whether the firm's marketing activities are working properly and, if not, to correct the problems. But this may require a series of performance analyses as shown in the following example.

To get an impression of the passage of time, follow this example carefully, one table at a time. Try to anticipate the marketing manager's decision.

The case of Stereo, Inc.

Stereo's sales manager found that sales for the Pacific Coast region were $130,000 below the quota of $14,500,000 (that is, actual sales were $14,370,000) for the January-June, 1970, period. The quota was based on forecasted sales of the various types of stereophonic sound equipment which the company manufactures. Specifically, the quota was based on forecasts for each product type in each store in each salesman's territory.

The sales manager felt this discrepancy was not too large (1.52 percent) and was inclined to forget the matter, especially since forecasts usually err to some extent. He thought about sending a letter, however, to all salesmen and district supervisors in the region — a letter aimed at stimulating sales effort.

The overall story of what was happening to Stereo's sales on the Pacific Coast is shown in Table 29-4. What do you think the manager should do?

Table 29-4 Sales performance — Pacific Coast region, January–June, 1970 (in thousands of dollars)

District	Quota	Actual	Plus or minus	Performance to quota
Los Angeles	$ 4,675	$ 4,765	Plus $ 90	102%
San Francisco	3,625	3,675	Plus 50	101
Portland	3,000	2,800	Minus 200	93
Seattle	3,200	3,130	Minus 70	98
	$14,500	$14,370	Minus $130	99%

Portland district had the poorest performance, but it wasn't too bad. Before writing a "let's get with it, fellas" letter to Portland, and then relaxing, the sales manager decided to analyze the performance of the four salesmen in the Portland district. A breakdown of the Portland figures by salesmen is shown in Table 29-5. What conclusion or action is suggested now?

Table 29-5 Sales performance — Portland district, January–June, 1970 (in thousands of dollars)

Salesmen	Quota	Actual	Plus or minus	Performance to quota
Johnson	$ 750	$ 780	Plus $ 30	104%
Smith	800	550	Minus 250	69
Jones	790	840	Plus 50	106
Carson	660	630	Minus 30	95
	$3,000	$2,800	Minus $200	93%

Since Smith previously had been the top salesman, the sales manager wondered if Smith were having trouble with some of his larger accounts. Before making a drastic move, he obtained an analysis of Smith's sales to five large accounts (see Table 29-6). What action could the sales manager take now? Should Smith be fired?

Table 29–6 Sales performance—selected stores of Mr. Smith in Portland district, January–June, 1970 (in thousands of dollars)

Stores	Quota	Actual	Plus or minus	Perform-ance to quota
1	$140	$ 65	Minus $ 75	46%
2	110	70	Minus 40	69
3	105	60	Minus 45	57
4	130	65	Minus 65	50
5	205	150	Minus 55	73
Others	110	140	Plus 30	127
	$800	$550	Minus $250	69%

Smith's sales in all the large stores were down significantly, although his sales in many small stores were holding up well. It would seem that Smith's problem was general. Perhaps he was simply not working. One other aspect which the sales manager decided to investigate was Smith's sales of the four major products. The data in Table 29–7 was obtained. What action is indicated now?

Table 29–7 Sales performance—Mr. Smith in Portland district, January–June, 1970 (in thousands of dollars)

Product	Quota	Actual	Plus or minus	Perform-ance to quota
Tape recorders	$ 70	$ 80	Plus $ 10	114%
Portable phonographs	430	160	Minus 270	37
Console phonographs	150	150	0	100
Speakers	100	110	Plus 10	110
Others	50	50	0	100
	$800	$550	Minus $250	69%

Smith was having real trouble with portable phonographs. Was the problem Smith or the phonographs?

Further analysis by product for the whole region indicated that everyone on the Pacific Coast was having trouble with portable phonographs because a regional competitor was cutting prices. But higher sales on other products had obscured this fact. Since phonograph sales had been doing all right nationally, this problem was only now coming to light. Clearly, this is *the* major problem.

Since overall company sales were going fairly well, many sales executives would not have bothered with this analysis. They might or might not have traced the problem to Smith. But without detailed sales records and performance analysis, the natural human reaction of a Smith would be to blame business conditions or aggressive competition or to seek some other handy excuse.

Stay home and use the computer

This case shows that aggregate figures can be deceiving. Marketing managers should not jump on the first plane or reach for the telephone until they have all the facts. The home office should have the records and facilities to isolate problem areas, then rely on the field staff for explanations and assistance in locating the precise problem. The field sales force and those in charge of execution may not be familiar with all details. A salesman may know only generally what products are ordered by his customers, especially if the customers send orders directly to the company. Even if the salesman gets copies of the invoices, it is not a simple task to summarize mentally all details on many invoices and to draw accurate conclusions.

Even worse than rushing to the scene would be a rash judgment based on inadequate information. Some students have wanted to fire Smith after the store-by-store data (Table 29–6) was given to them. Continuing detailed analysis usually gives us better insights into problems, as this case shows. With EDP equipment, this can be done routinely and in great detail, *provided marketing management requests it.*

The "iceberg" principle	One of the most interesting conclusions to be drawn out of the Stereo illustration is the iceberg principle.[3] Icebergs, as you probably know, show only about 10 percent of their mass above water level, with the other 90 percent below water level – and not directly below, either. The submerged portion almost seems to be searching out ships that come too near.

The same is true of much business and marketing data. Since sales volume may be large and overall company activities varied, difficulties or problems in one area may be submerged below the surface. All may appear to be calm and peaceful, yet a more careful analysis may reveal jagged edges which can severely damage or even "sink" the business. The idea is that averaging and summarizing data can be helpful to the business executive, but he had better be wary that his summaries do not hide more than they reveal.[4]

Marketing-cost analysis

So far we have emphasized sales analysis. But sales cost money. And costs can and should be analyzed and controlled.

Detailed cost analysis has been highly useful in the factory, but

[3] Richard D. Crisp, *Marketing Research* (New York: McGraw-Hill Book Co., 1957), p. 144.

[4] For further discussion on these matters, see John Dearden, "Appraising Profit Center Managers," *Harvard Business Review,* May–June, 1968, pp. 80–87; Paul H. Thompson and Gene W. Dalton, "Performance Appraisal: Manager Beware," *Harvard Business Review,* January–February, 1970, pp. 149–57; and Richard A. Feder, "How to Measure Marketing Performance," *Harvard Business Review,* May–June, 1965, pp. 132–42; Allan Easton, "A Forward Step in Performance Evaluation," *Journal of Marketing,* July, 1966, pp. 26–32; *Sales Analysis* (Studies in Business Policies, No. 113 [New York: National Industrial Conference Board, 1965]); and *Measuring Salesmen's Performance* (Studies in Business Policies, No. 114 [New York: National Industrial Conference Board, 1965]).

much less has been done with marketing cost accounting.[5] Many accountants, unfortunately, have shown little interest in the marketing process. Many think of salesmen as swingers who wine-and-dine the customers, play golf all afternoon, and occasionally pick up orders. In this situation, they feel it is impossible to allocate the wide-ranging costs of selling to particular products or customers. Many accountants feel, too, that advertising is almost a complete waste of money—that there is no way of relating it to particular sales. They wind up treating it as a general overhead cost, then forget about it.

Marketing costs have a purpose

Careful analysis of most marketing expenditures, however, shows that the money is spent to accomplish a specific purpose—either to prepare or promote a *particular product* or to serve *particular customers*. It is reasonable, then, to seek ways to allocate costs to specific customers or to specific products. Expected costs then can be compared to actual costs, and performance indices can be computed as we did with sales data.

There are two basic approaches to cost analysis—the full-cost approach and the contribution-margin approach. We will discuss each of these in turn.

First, however, let's note that marketing cost analysis usually requires a new way of classifying accounting data. We want to use functional accounts rather than natural accounts.

Natural versus functional accounts

Natural accounts are the categories to which various costs are charged in the normal accounting cycle. These accounts include salaries, wages, social security, taxes, supplies, raw materials, auto, gas and oil expenses, advertising, and other such categories. These accounts are called "natural" because they bear the names of their expense categories.

This is not the approach to cost analysis used in factories, however, and it is not the one we will use. In the factory, functional accounts are set up to indicate the *purpose* for which the expenditures are made. Factory functional accounts include shearing, milling, grinding, floor cleaning, maintenance, and so on. Frequently, factory cost accounting records are so organized that the cost of particular products or jobs can be calculated from them.

Various marketing jobs are done for specific purposes, too. With some foresight and analysis, the costs of marketing also can be allocated to specific categories, such as customers and products. Then their profitability can be calculated.

---

[5] See "Norton Helps Distributors in Cost Analysis," *Industrial Marketing*, March, 1958; "15,800 More Sales Calls per Year," *Sales Management*, December 5, 1958, pp. 48–55; Donald R. Longman and Michael Schiff, *Practical Distribution Cost Analysis* (Homewood, Ill.: Richard D. Irwin, Inc., 1955), and J. Brooks Heckert and Robert B. Miner, *Distribution Costs* (2d ed.; New York: Ronald Press Co., 1953).

First, get costs into functional accounts

The first step in marketing cost analysis is to reclassify all the dollar cost entries in the natural accounts into functional cost accounts. The many cost items in the natural *salary* account might be allocated to functional accounts with the following names: storage, inventory control, order assembly, packing and shipping, transportation, selling, advertising, order entry, billing, credit extension, and accounts receivable. Similarly, the entries in the natural *supplies* account would be allocated to the functional accounts for which those supply expenditures were made. The same would be true for rent, depreciation, heat, light, power, and other natural accounts.

The method of reallocating natural to functional accounts is not fixed. It depends on the method of operation of the particular firm. If a company were making only one product and selling its entire output to a single customer, it could assign all of its marketing costs to that product or customer. But since most companies serve a diverse market with a large number of products, a more detailed reallocation of costs is necessary.

After the firm's method of operation has been studied, specific cost items can be distributed to functional cost groups by means of time studies, space measurements, actual counts, and managerial estimates.

Then reallocate to evaluate profitability

The next step is to reallocate the functional costs to those items or customers for which the costs were incurred. The most common reallocation of functional costs is to products and to customers. After all of the costs are allocated to each product and each customer, these detailed totals can be recombined in any way desired – for example, by product or customer class, region, and so on.

The costs allocated to the functional accounts would equal in total those in the natural accounts. They are merely organized in a different way. But instead of being used just to show total company profitability, they can now be arranged to show the profitability of territories, products, customers, salesmen, price classes, order sizes, methods of distribution, methods of sale, or any other breakdown desired. Each unit, in effect, can be treated as a profit center.

Illustrative example

These ideas can be seen more clearly in the following hypothetical example. In this case, the usual accounting approach – with natural accounts – showed that the company made a profit of $938 last month (Table 29–8). When a question is raised about the profitability of the company's three customers, the profit and loss statement is of no help. The marketing manager decides to use marketing cost analysis because he wants to know whether a change in marketing methods might improve profit.

First, the costs in the five natural accounts are distributed to four functional accounts – sales, packaging, advertising, and billing and collection (see Table 29–9) – according to the functional reason for incurring the expenses. Specifically, $1,000 of the total salary cost was for salesmen who seldom even come into the office, since their

Table 29-8 Profit and loss statement

Sales		$17,000
Cost of goods sold		11,900
Gross Margin		5,100
Expenses		
Salaries	$2,500	
Rent	500	
Wrapping supplies	1,012	
Stationery and stamps	50	
Office equipment	100	
		4,162
Net Profit		$ 938

function is to call on customers; $900 of the salary cost was for packaging labor; and $600 was for office help. Figure that the office force split its time about evenly between addressing and mailing advertising and other material, and the billing and collection function. So the $600 is split evenly into these two functional accounts.

The $500 for rent was for the entire building, but 80 percent of the floor space was used for packaging and 20 percent for the office. Thus $400 is allocated to the packaging account. The remaining $100 is divided evenly between the advertising and billing accounts because these functions used the office space about equally. Stationery, stamps

Table 29-9 Spreading natural accounts to functional accounts

		Functional accounts			
Natural accounts		Sales	Packaging	Advertising	Billing and collection
Salaries	$2,500	$1,000	$ 900	$300	$300
Rent	500		400	50	50
Wrapping supplies	1,012		1,012		
Stationery and stamps	50			25	25
Office equipment	100			50	50
	$4,162	$1,000	$2,312	$425	$425

and office equipment charges are allocated equally to the latter two accounts for the same reason. Charges for wrapping supplies are allocated to the packaging account because these supplies were used in packaging. In another situation, different allocations and even different accounts might be appropriate, but these are workable here.

Now we are in a better position to calculate the profitability of the company's three customers. But we need additional information before we can allocate these functional accounts to customers or products. It is presented in tabular form in Table 29–10 for convenient reference.

Table 29–10 shows that the company's three products vary in cost, selling price, and sales volume. The products also have different "bulks," and so the packaging costs are unrelated to the selling price. For example, product C is six times bulkier than A. When packaging costs are allocated to products, this must be considered. This is accomplished by computing a new measure – a packaging unit – which is used to allocate the costs in the packaging account. Packaging units take into consideration relative bulk and the number of each type of product sold. While only 10 units of product C are sold, it is bulky and requires 10 times 6, or 60 packaging units. This will cause relatively more of the costs in the packaging account to be allocated to each unit of product C.

Table 29–10 Basic data for cost and profit analysis example

A. PRODUCTS

Products	Cost/Unit	Selling price/Unit	No. units sold in period	Sales volume in period	Relative "bulk" per unit	Packaging "units"
A	$ 7	$ 10	1,000	$10,000	1	1,000
B	35	50	100	5,000	3	300
C	140	200	10	2,000	6	60
			1,110	$17,000		1,360

B. CUSTOMERS

Customers	No. of sales calls in period	No. of orders placed in period	No. of each product ordered in period A	B	C
Smith	30	30	900	30	0
Jones	40	3	90	30	3
Brown	30	1	10	40	7
	100	34	1,000	100	10

Table 29–10 also shows that the three customers require different amounts of sales effort, place different numbers of orders, and buy different product combinations.

Jones requires more sales calls. Smith places many orders which must be processed in the office, with increased billing expense. Brown seems to be a great customer, since he placed only one order – but that order accounted for 70 percent of the sales of high-valued product C.

The basic computations for allocating the functional account amounts to the three customers are shown in Table 29–11. There were 100 sales calls in the period. Assuming that all calls took the same amount of time, it is logical to derive the average cost per call by dividing the $1,000 sales cost by 100 calls, giving an average cost of $10. Similar reasoning is used in breaking down the billing and packaging account totals. Advertising during this period was for the benefit of product C only, and this cost is split among the units of C sold.

Table 29–11 Functional cost account allocations

Sales calls =	$1,000/100 calls	= $10/call
Billing =	$425/34 orders	= $12.50/order
Packaging units costs =	$2,312/1,360 packaging units	= $1.70/packaging unit or
		$ 1.70 for product A
		$ 5.10 for product B
		$10.20 for product C
Advertising =	$425/10 units of C	= $42.50/unit of C

Now we can compute a profit and loss statement for each customer, combining his purchases and the cost of serving him. This is done in Table 29–12. A statement is developed for each customer, and of course the sum of each of the four major components (sales, cost of goods sold, expenses, and profit) is the same as on the original statement. We have merely rearranged and renamed the data, for analysis purposes.

The procedure is explained for customer Smith's statement in Table 29–12. Smith bought 900 units of A at $10 each and 30 units of B at $50 each for the respective sales totals ($9,000 and $1,500) shown in Table 29–12. Cost of goods sold is computed on the same basis. Thirty sales calls at an average of $10 each were made on Smith. Total sales calls cost $300. He placed 30 orders (at an average cost of $12.50 each) for a total ordering cost of $375. Total packaging costs amounted to $1,530 for A (900 units purchased times $1.70 per unit) and $153 for B (30 units purchased times $5.10 per unit). There were no packaging costs for C because Smith did not buy any of product C. Neither were any advertising costs charged to Smith, since all costs were spent promoting product C, which he did not buy.

We see now that Smith was the most profitable customer – yielding over 75 percent of the net profit.

This analysis shows that Brown was profitable, too, but not as profitable as Smith, because Smith bought three times as much. Jones was unprofitable because he didn't buy very much and received one third more sales calls.

It is clear that the "iceberg" principle is operating again here. Although the company as a whole is profitable, customer Jones is not profitable. Before taking any drastic action, however, the marketing manager should study his figures and methods of operation very carefully. Perhaps Jones should be contacted less frequently, or maybe he will grow into a profitable account. The marketing manager may also

Table 29–12 Profit and loss statements for customers

	Smith	Jones	Brown	Whole company
Sales				
A	$9,000	$ 900	$ 100	
B	1,500	1,500	2,000	
C		600	1,400	
Total Sales	$10,500	$3,000	$3,500	$17,000
Cost of goods sold				
A	$6,300	$ 630	$ 70	
B	1,050	1,050	1,400	
C		420	980	
Total Cost of Goods Sold	$ 7,350	$2,100	$2,450	$11,900
Gross Margin	$ 3,150	$ 900	$1,050	$ 5,100
Expenses				
Sales calls ($10 each)	$ 300	$ 400.00	$ 300.00	
Order costs ($12.50 ea.)	375	37.50	12.50	
Packaging costs				
A	1,530	153.00	17.00	
B	153	153.00	204.00	
C		30.60	71.40	
Advertising	—	127.50	297.50	
	2,358	901.60	902.40	4,162
Net Profit (or Loss)	$ 792	$ (1.60)	$ 147.60	$ 938

want to analyze his advertising costs against results, since this is a heavy expense against each unit of product C. Perhaps his strategic plans should be revised.

Cost analysis is not performance analysis

Such an analysis is not performance analysis, of course. If the marketing manager had budgeted various costs to various tasks, it would be possible to extend the analysis to a performance analysis. This would be a logical and perhaps a desirable extension, but few companies have moved this far as yet.

As the cost of computer record keeping drops, we may see more companies accumulating detailed data on the cost of servicing customers. They could then compute fairly realistic profit and loss statements for individual customers, just as some factory cost accounting systems develop realistic cost estimates for products, and advertising agencies monitor the profitability of their clients.

Cost analysis can be quite sophisticated

It is clear that cost analysis can help spot trouble—if management is willing to reallocate costs from natural to functional accounts, and then to products and customers. Our simple example emphasizes the concepts. A more realistic example would involve much more detail, but the ideas and approach are the same.

To show the detail that might be needed in a real situation, the 12 functional accounts used by one company are presented in Table 29–13 together with the bases for allocating the functional account totals to products and customers.

Note that some cost groups show bases of allocation to both products and customers. Obviously, a functional cost group will not be allocated to both at the same time. If the analysis is by products, all the expenses that logically can be allocated directly to specific products will be carried there. The remainder of the functional cost groups will be allocated to *all* products on some sensible basis, such as dollars of sales or numbers of units.

If the analysis is by customers, all the functional costs are allocated to customers, if possible. Others would be allocated to products. Then these product-oriented costs can be charged to customers on the basis of the volumes of each product sold to each customer.

We have discussed the general principles, but the matter of allocating costs is a sticky one. Some costs are likely to be fixed for the near future, regardless of what decision is made. And some costs are likely to be *common* to several products or customers, making allocation difficult.

There are two basic approaches to handling this difficult problem — the full-cost approach and the contribution-margin approach.

Full-cost approach — everything costs something

In the full-cost approach, all functional costs are allocated to products, customers, or other categories. Even fixed costs (those that do not vary in the short run) are allocated in some way, as are common costs.

The full-cost approach usually requires that some costs that are

743

difficult to allocate be apportioned on some, perhaps arbitrary, basis such as dollars of sales or numbers of units.

The assumption here is that the services provided for those costs are equally beneficial to customers, to products, or to whatever group they are allocated. Sometimes this is done mechanically, but often logical reasoning can support the allocation if we accept the idea that marketing costs are incurred for a purpose. Advertising costs, for example, that are not directly related to specific customers or products, *might* be allocated to all customers on the basis of their purchases. The theory is that advertising has helped bring in the sales.

Table 29–13 Functional cost groups and possible bases of allocation to products and customers

| | Bases of allocation | |
Functional cost groups	To products	To customers
1. Investment in finished goods	Average inventory value.	(Not allocated)
2. Storage of finished goods	Floor space occupied.	(Not allocated)
3. Inventory control, finished goods	No. of invoice lines.	(Not allocated)
4. Order assembly (handling)	No. of standard handling units.	No. of invoice lines.
5. Packing and shipping	Weight or no. of shipping units.	Weight or number of shipping units.
6. Transportation	Weight or no. of shipping units.	Weight or no. of shipping units.
7. Selling	Time studies.	No. of sales calls.
8. Advertising	Cost of space, etc., of specific product.	Cost of space, etc. of specific customer advertising.
9. Order entry	No. of invoice lines.	No. of orders.
10. Billing	No. of invoice lines.	No. of invoice lines.
11. Credit extension	(Not allocated)	Average amount outstanding.
12. Accounts receivable	(Not allocated)	No. of invoices posted.

Source: Charles H. Sevin, "Analyzing Your Cost of Marketing," *Management Aids for Small Manufacturers* (Washington, D.C.: Small Business Administration, June, 1957), p. 3.

Full cost finds a poor strategy

The full-cost approach allocates all costs, so it is possible to relate costs to income for various "profit centers" and determine each one's profitability. An evaluation of this profitability and the effort expended may help determine the effectiveness of various strategies and lead to the development of new ones.

These ideas are illustrated in the following example and the data in

Table 29-14. A detailed cost allocation approach of the kind shown in Table 29-13 was used in this case.

When product "I" was added to the company's line, it was promoted vigorously because of its high gross margin. Many businessmen automatically associate a high gross margin with a high net profit!

The company's sales executives were enthusiastic about the new product because they felt it could be added to a family of products at little additional cost. A subsequent analysis, however, indicated that the new item was not really in the same product family. There were differences in physical characteristics, handling, and volume per sale. But more important, the new product appealed more strongly to a different target market.

Table 29-14 Margins, distribution costs, and profits, by product groups during one year's operations

Product group	Gross margin per unit of product	Distribu-tion cost per unit of product	Profit or loss per unit of product	Volume per item percent of average	Volume per sales call percent of average
A	$0.46	$0.43	$0.03	178	219
B	0.45	0.53	−0.08	119	109
C	0.24	0.42	−0.18	186	150
D	0.99	0.64	0.35	52	56
E	1.08	0.58	0.50	77	82
F	0.76	0.42	0.34	158	151
G	0.71	0.79	−0.08	63	56
H	0.96	0.72	0.24	52	56
I	1.31	1.25	0.06	15	21
Averages or Totals, Entire Business	$0.74	$0.65	$0.09	100	100

Source: Charles H. Sevin, *How Manufacturers Reduce Their Distribution Costs* (Economic Series No. 72, U.S. Department of Commerce), Case 44.

The company found that product "I" was contributing a small profit but far less than was expected from its high gross margin. More detailed analysis indicated that the product was sold and consumed in small quantities, and found its largest market in small stores (which are generally more expensive to serve). It appeared that it would be difficult to change customers' buying habits. Demand was quite elastic, but because of the relatively high expense of serving this target market, a price cut did not seem profitable.

To solve this problem, the firm switched promotional effort away from product "I" to the faster moving products. In one year, the marketing costs for the firm's average unit had dropped from 65 cents to 59 cents and the profit per unit had climbed from 9 to 17 cents. The cost of distributing product "I" had declined so that its profitability was about average. It appeared that this new strategy would be continued until better use could be made of the company's resources.[6]

Contribu-
tion margin
ignores
some costs
to get
results

When we use the contribution-margin approach, it is not necessary to consider all costs in *all* situations. Why?

When various alternatives are being compared, management may find it more meaningful to consider only the costs which are directly related to particular alternatives. Variable costs are particularly relevant here, as we saw when we discussed break-even analysis in Chapter 24.

The contribution-margin approach focuses management attention on variable costs rather than on total costs, which may include some fixed costs, which do not change in the short run and can safely be ignored, or some common costs, which are more difficult to allocate.[7]

The distinction between the full-cost approach and the contribution-margin approach is *not* academic. Different decisions may be suggested by the two approaches. These are contrasted in the following example. Table 29–15 shows a profit and loss statement, using the full-cost approach, for a department store with three operating departments.

Table 29–15 Profit and loss statement by department for the year 197X

	Totals	Depart- ment 1	Depart- ment 2	Depart- ment 3
Sales	$100,000	$50,000	$30,000	$20,000
Cost of goods sold	80,000	45,000	25,000	10,000
Gross margin	$ 20,000	$ 5,000	$ 5,000	$10,000
Other expenses				
Selling expenses	5,000	2,500	1,500	1,000
Administrative expenses	6,000	3,000	1,800	1,200
Total Other Expenses	$ 11,000	$ 5,500	$ 3,300	$ 2,200
Net Profit or (Loss)	$ 9,000	$ (500)	$ 1,700	$ 7,800

Source: Robert K. Jaedicke, "A Method for Making Product Combination Decisions," *Business News Notes* (Minneapolis: University of Minnesota, April, 1958), pp. 1–2.

The administrative expenses, which represent the only fixed cost in this particular case, have been allocated to departments on the basis of percentage of sales volume of each department—a typical method of allocation. In this case, some executives argued that Department 1

[6] Charles H. Sevin, *How Manufacturers Reduce Their Distribution Costs* (Economic Series No. 72, U.S. Department of Commerce), Case 44.

[7] Technically, a distinction should be made between variable and direct costs, but we will use these terms interchangeably. Similarly, not all common costs are fixed costs and vice versa, but the important point here is to recognize that some costs are fairly easy to allocate, and other costs are not.

was clearly unprofitable and should be eliminated because it showed a net loss of $500. Were they correct?

To find out, see Table 29–16 which shows what would happen if Department 1 were eliminated.

Table 29–16 Profit and loss statement by department for the year 197X if Department 1 were eliminated

	Totals	Department 2	Department 3
Sales	$50,000	$30,000	$20,000
Cost of goods sold	35,000	25,000	10,000
Gross margin	$15,000	$ 5,000	$10,000
Other expenses			
Selling expenses	2,500	1,500	1,000
Administrative expenses	6,000	3,600	2,400
Total Other Expenses	$ 8,500	$ 5,100	$ 3,400
Net Profit or (Loss)	$ 6,500	$ (100)	$ 6,600

Several facts immediately become clear. The overall profit of the store would be reduced if Department 1 were dropped. Fixed costs amounting to $3,000, now being charged to Department 1, would have to be allocated to the other departments; this would reduce net profit $2,500, since Department 1 previously covered $2,500 of the $3,000 fixed costs charged. This shifting of costs would then make Department 2 unprofitable!

A contribution-margin income statement for the department store is shown in Table 29–17. Note that each department has a positive contribution margin. Here the Department 1 contribution of $2,500 is obvious. This actually is the amount that would be lost if Department 1 were dropped. (This example assumes that the fixed adminis-

Table 29–17 Contribution-margin statement by departments for the year 197X

	Totals	Dept. 1	Dept. 2	Dept. 3
Sales	$100,000	$50,000	$30,000	$20,000
Variable costs				
Cost of goods sold	80,000	45,000	25,000	10,000
Selling expenses	5,000	2,500	1,500	1,000
Total variable costs	$ 85,000	$47,500	$26,500	$11,000
Contribution margin	15,000	2,500	3,500	9,000
Fixed costs				
Administrative expenses	6,000			
Net Profit	$ 9,000			

Source: Robert K. Jaedicke, "A Method for Making Product-Combination Decisions," *Business News Notes* (Minneapolis: University of Minnesota, April, 1958), pp. 1–2.

trative expenses are *truly* fixed—that none of them would be eliminated if this department were eliminated.)

A contribution-margin income statement shows the contribution of each department more clearly, including its contribution to both fixed costs and profit. As long as a department or other unit has some contribution margin—and as long as there are no better alternative uses for the resources invested in it—the department or salesman or product or other variable in the particular analysis should be retained.

Contribution margin versus full cost—choose your side

The full-cost approach often leads to controversy within the company. Any one method of allocation tends to make some products or customers appear less profitable than another allocation method.

Assigning all common advertising costs to customers, based on their purchases, can be supported logically. But it also can be criticized on the grounds that it may make large-volume customers appear less profitable than they actually are, especially if the marketing mix which is aimed at the larger customers focuses more on price than on advertising.

Those in the company who want the smaller customers to look more profitable will argue for this allocation method on the grounds that general advertising helps "build" good customers because it affects the overall image of the company and its products.

In one sense, such arguments are futile, since the only goal of allocation is to clearly identify expenses and their sources and to give the firm a better picture of its operations.

The argument about allocation methods may be deadly serious, however, because the method used may reflect on the performance of various company executives and, subsequently, their salaries and bonuses. The product managers, for example, would be vitally interested in how the various fixed and common costs were allocated to products. Each, in turn, might like to have costs shifted to his colleagues' products.

Arbitrary allocation of costs also may have a direct impact on salesmen morale. If salesmen see their variable costs loaded with additional common or fixed costs over which they have no control, they may decide, "What's the use?"

To avoid this problem, the contribution-margin approach is frequently used. It avoids many of the problems of arbitrarily allocating fixed or common costs. It is especially useful for evaluating alternatives, and also for showing operating executives and salesmen how they are performing. The contribution-margin approach shows what they have actually contributed to general overhead and profit.

Top management, on the other hand, often finds full-cost analysis more useful. In the long run, some products, departments, or customers must bear the fixed costs. Full-cost analysis has its place here.[8]

---

[8] For further discussion on these methods, see Michael S. Morton and Andrew M. McCosh, "Terminal Costing for Better Decisions," *Harvard Business Review,* May–June, 1968, pp. 147–56;

Planning and control combined

We have been treating sales and cost analyses separately up to this point. But management often will combine them to keep a running check on its activities – to be sure that the plans are materializing or to see when and where new strategies are needed.

**Sales +
costs +
everybody
helps =
$8,150**

Let's see how this works at the XYZ Hardware Co., a typical hardware retailer.

This firm netted $7,750 last year. Expecting no basic change in the competitive situation and slightly better local business conditions, the manager set this year's profit goal at $8,150, an increase of about 5 percent.

Next, he began developing tentative plans to show how this hither profit could be made. He estimated the sales volumes, gross margins, and expenses – broken down by months and by departments in his store – necessary to net $8,150.

Table 29-18 is a planning and control chart which the XYZ manager developed to show the contribution which each department should make each month. At the bottom of Table 29-18, the plan for the year is summarized. Notice that space is provided to insert the actual performance and a measure of variation, allowing both planning and control functions to be implemented with this table.

Table 29-18 shows that XYZ's manager is focusing on the monthly contribution by each department. The purpose of monthly estimates is to get more frequent feedback and to enable faster adjustment of plans. Generally, the shorter the planning and review period, the easier it is to correct problems before they become emergencies.

In this example, a modified contribution-margin approach is being used, since some of the fixed costs can be allocated logically to particular departments. On this chart, the balance left after direct fixed and variable costs are charged to departments is called "Contribution to Store." The idea is that each department will contribute to covering *general* store expenses, such as top-management salaries and Christmas decorations, and to net profits.

In Table 29-18, we see that the whole operation is brought together when the monthly operating profit is computed. The contribution from each of the four departments is totaled, then general store expenses are subtracted to obtain the operating profit for each month.

Frank H. Mossman, *Differential Cost and Revenue Analysis* (MTA Paper No. 10 [East Lansing: Bureau of Business & Economic Research, Michigan State University, 1962]); Charles H. Sevin, *Marketing Productivity Analysis* (New York: McGraw-Hill Book Co., 1965); R. D. Buzzell *et al., Product Profitability Measurement and Merchandising Decisions* (Boston: Division of Research, Graduate School of Business Administration, Harvard University, 1965); *Cost Analysis for Product Line-Decisions* (Management Services Technical Study No. 1 [New York: American Institute of Certified Public Accountants, 1965]); *Cost Analysis for Pricing and Distribution Policies* (Management Services Technical Study No. 2 [New York: American Institute of Certified Public Accountants, 1965]); C. G. Baumes, *Allocating Corporate Expenses* (Business Policy Study No. 108 [New York: National Industrial Conference Board, 1963]); and J. L. Goldstucker, "Allocating Costs in International Operations," *Business Horizons*, Winter, 1965, pp. 75–84.

Table 29–18 XYZ Hardware Company planning and control chart

1970	Contribution to store				Total	Store expense	Operating profit	Cumulative operating profit
	Dept. A	Dept. B	Dept. C	Dept. D*				
January								
Planned	1,350	450	200	−50	1,950	1,200	750	750
Actual								
Variation								
February								
Planned	1,000	325	125	−50	1,400	1,200	200	950
Actual								
Variation								
November								
Planned	1,600	375	125	0	2,100	1,200	900	5,325
Actual								
Variation								
December								
Planned	3,150	625	200	450	4,025	1,200	2,825	8,150
Actual								
Variation								
1970								
Planned	15,800	3,500	3,450	−200	22,550	14,400	8,150	8,150
Actual								
Variation								

*The goal of minus $200 for this department was established on the same basis as the goals for the other departments, i.e., it represents the same percentage gain over 1959, when Department D's loss was $210. Plans call for discontinuance of the department unless it shows marked improvement by the end of the year.

Each department must plan and control too

Table 29–19 shows a similar planning and control chart for a single XYZ department, Department B. In this table, actual results have been entered for the month of January. An unfavorable deviation is revealed between planned and actual sales performance (−$700), and gross profit (−$85).

Now, the marketing manager must determine why actual sales were less than projected, with a view to making new plans. Possible hypotheses are that: (1) Prices were too high; (2) promotion was ineffective; (3) the product selection was not satisfying the target customers; and (4) errors might have been made in marking the prices or in tallying sales.

Corrective action could take either of two courses; namely, improving tactics (or their implementation) or developing new, more realistic strategies.

Table 29–19 XYZ Hardware Company planning and control chart—
Department B

| 1970 | Sales | Gross profit | Direct expense | | | Contribution to store | Cumulative contribution to store |
			Total	Fixed	Variable		
January							
Planned	3,000	900	450	300	150	450	450
Actual	2,300	815	415	300	115	400	400
Variation	−700	−85	35	0	35	−50	−50
February							
Planned	2,500	750	425	300	125	325	775
Actual							
Variation							
~~							
November							
Planned	3,500	1,050	675	500	175	375	2,875
Actual							
Variation							
December							
Planned	4,500	1,350	725	500	225	625	3,500
Actual							
Variation							
1970							
Planned	30,000	9,000	5,500	4,000	1,500	3,500	3,500
Actual							
Variation							

Source: Wallace O. Yoder and Clarence E. Vincent, "Control Methods for Hardware Dealers," *Management Research Summary* (Washington, D.C.: Small Business Administration, May, 1961), pp. 2–3.

Implementing the control process

All of this analysis can be implemented by manual methods, which may be best for small or nonrecurring jobs. But when the sales volume and complexity of the business have grown, mechanical methods not only may be faster and more accurate but may be the only way to handle the control procedure.

A crucial capture by the marketing manager

Electronic data processing systems are commonly used for data analysis in larger companies. Increasingly, smaller companies have access to computing capabilities through time-sharing systems offered by computer manufacturers and service bureaus.

But this kind of analysis is not possible unless the sales and other performance data is in machine processible form, so it can be sorted and analyzed rapidly. At this point, the marketing manager can play a crucial role, by insisting that the data he wants is collected. If the data he wishes to analyze is not captured as it comes in, information will be difficult if not impossible to obtain later.

Practically, the only limitation on more effective and revealing data analysis is the imagination of the marketing manager, now that machines can handle the drudgery. But he must see the interrelation of the planning and control process, and be sure the data he wants to use will be available when needed. Then he can confidently ask the data processors to produce the reports he needs.[9]

Analysis crosses company boundaries

Continuous data analysis may even go beyond analyzing the firm's own data. As we have seen earlier, some manufacturers and wholesalers, trying to develop a smoother flow through the channel system, are currently keeping inventory records for some of their wholesalers or retailers. With the growing capabilities of electronic data processing, we may see much more of this.[10]

The marketing audit

While crises pop, marketing goes on

The analyses we have discussed so far are designed to help a marketing manager plan and control his own operations. They can help him do a better job. Often, however, the control process tends to focus on only a few critical elements — such as sales variations by product in different territories — and it misses such items as the appropriateness of various marketing strategies and the possible effectiveness of alternative mixes.

The marketing manager usually is responsible for the day-to-day execution function as well as planning and control functions, and he seldom has the leisure to casually contemplate the effectiveness of his efforts. Sometimes, crises are popping in several places at the same time, and a good deal of his concern must be focused on adjusting marketing mixes or shifting strategies in the short run.

To insure that the whole marketing program is properly evaluated, therefore, marketing specialists have developed a new concept — the marketing audit. It is similar to the accounting audit or the personnel audit, both of which have been accepted by business for some time.

The marketing audit has been defined as "A systematic, critical, and unbiased review and appraisal of the basic objectives and policies of the marketing function and of the organization, methods, procedures, and personnel employed to implement the policies and achieve the objectives."[11]

---

[9] For further discussion on the development of data processing systems, see E. J. McCarthy, J. A. McCarthy, and D. Humes, *Integrated Data Processing Systems* (New York: John Wiley & Sons, Inc., 1966).

[10] See Felix Kaufman, "Data Systems that Cross Company Boundaries," *Harvard Business Review*.

January–February, 1966, pp. 141–55.

[11] A. R. Oxenfeldt, "The Marketing Audit as a Total Evaluation Program," in *Analyzing and Improving Marketing Performance: Marketing Audits in Theory and Practice* (New York: American Management Association, 1959), p. 26.

It shouldn't
be neces-
sary A marketing audit would take a big view of the business and evaluate the whole marketing program. It might be conducted by a separate department within the company. Or to avoid bias, it might be desirable to have it conducted by an outside organization such as a management consulting firm.

Ideally, a marketing audit should not be necessary. A good manager does his very best in planning, executing, and controlling and should continually attempt to evaluate the effectiveness of his operation.

In practice, however, managers often become identified with certain strategies and pursue them persistently when alternate courses might be more effective. Since an outside view may give needed perspective, we may see greater use of the marketing audit in the future.

Conclusion

In this chapter, we have tried to show how sales and cost analysis can help a marketing manager control his marketing program, and that control procedures can be useful in his planning. Controls lead to feedback that can be incorporated into subsequent planning.

Simple sales analysis merely gives a picture of what has happened. But when sales forecasts or other data showing expected results are brought into the analysis, it is possible to evaluate performance, using performance indices.

Cost analysis also can be useful, providing costs are reallocated from natural to functional accounts and then to customers and products. There are two basic approaches to cost analysis – full cost and contribution margin. Using the full-cost approach, all costs are allocated in some way; using the contribution-margin approach, only the variable or direct costs are allocated. Both methods have their advantages and special uses.

Ideally, the marketing manager should arrange for a continual flow of data that can be analyzed routinely, preferably by machine, to enable him to control and subsequently plan new strategies. A marketing audit may assist him in this ongoing evaluation. Either a separate department within the company or an outside, objective organization might conduct this audit.

Whichever evaluation procedure is used, however, it is clear that a marketing program must be controlled. Good control helps the marketing manager locate and correct weak spots, while at the same time finding strengths which he may be able to turn to his own advantage and apply throughout his marketing program. Control works hand in hand with planning in a total system of action.

QUESTIONS AND PROBLEMS

1 Various breakdowns of sales are suggested for sales analysis in certain situations, depending upon the nature of the company and its product. Describe a situation (one for each) where each of the following breakdowns would yield useful information. Explain why.
a) By geographical region.
b) By product.
c) By customer.
d) By size of order.
e) By size of salesman's commission allowed (on each product or product group.)

2 Explain carefully what the "iceberg principle" should mean to the marketing manager.

3 Explain the meaning of the comparative performance and comparative cost data in Tables 29–2 and 29–3. Why does it appear that eliminating sales areas D and E would be profitable?

4 Most sales forecasting is subject to some error (perhaps 5 to 10 percent). Is it proper to conclude then that variations in sales performance of 5 or 10 percent above or below quota are to be expected? If so, how should such variations be treated in evaluating performance?

5 Develop appropriate functional cost accounts for a house-to-house selling organization. First, list logical natural expenses and show how they would be allocated to functional accounts. It is planned to allocate the costs in these functional accounts to various customer types in an effort to determine the profitability of calling on different kinds of customers. (Specify any assumptions necessary to obtain a definite answer.) To make this more concrete, assume the company is selling encyclopedias at $150 a set. This distributor is involved in hiring and training salesmen as well as making sales calls on his own. He must make out supervisory and progress reports as well as keep records on his own customers. He receives commissions on his sales as well as override commissions on the sales of his salesmen. Credit, billing, and commissions are all handled by the home office, but the distributor has enough clerical work to justify a full-time secretary. He has rented office facilities and occasionally rents halls for training and recruiting purposes. He does no advertising, except to recruit salesmen, but may set up displays at educational meetings, and so on. Finally, assume that his primary interest in this cost analysis is to make his own personal selling efforts more effective. If he is successful in this regard, then he might pass on what he learns to his own salesmen and his supervisors.

6 Explain why there is a controversy between the advocates of the "net profit approach" and the "contribution margin" approach to cost analysis.

7 The profit and loss statement for June for the Brown Bag Co. is as follows:

	Retailers	Hospitals and schools	Total
Sales			
80,000 units at $0.70	$56,000		$56,000
20,000 units at $0.60		$12,000	12,000
Total	$56,000	$12,000	$68,000
Cost of goods sold	40,000	10,000	50,000
Gross margin	$16,000	$ 2,000	$18,000
Sales and adminis. expenses			
Variable	$ 6,000	$ 1,500	$ 7,500
Fixed	5,600	900	6,500
Total	$11,600	$ 2,400	$14,000
Net profit (loss)	$ 4,400	$ (400)	$ 4,000

If competitive conditions make price increases impossible, and management has cut costs as much as possible, should the Brown Bag Co. stop selling to hospitals and schools? Why?

8 Explain why it is so important for the marketing manager to be directly involved in the planning of control procedures.

9 Explain why a marketing audit might be desirable even in a well run company. Discuss who or what kind of an organization would be the best one to conduct a marketing audit. Would a marketing research firm be good? Would the present C.P.A. firms be most suitable?

...now that you have a better appreciation of what the marketing manager does and how he can contribute to the *macro*-marketing process, you should be able to give thoughtful consideration to whether marketing costs too much.

...your answer is extremely important. Your own business career and the economy in which you live will be affected by your answer.

30

Does marketing cost too much? — an evaluation

Does marketing cost too much? Again, we return to this fundamental question.

Many people feel strongly that marketing costs too much — that it is a waste of resources which would be better used elsewhere. This may be partly because it is human to look for quick and easy solutions to pervasive problems, such as unemployment, rising prices, and unsatisfactory product quality. Marketing activities are especially vulnerable to public criticism. They are continuously exposed to the public, and people react emotionally when their pocketbooks are hurt.

In Chapter 1 and at various times throughout the text, we referred to criticisms of marketing and to the possible effects of business practices on consumer welfare. But we have *not* attempted to answer the underlying question of whether marketing costs too much — believing that you needed background information before developing your own answer.

We have attempted to provide this necessary background in this book. The focus has been primarily on the *micro* view of marketing — that is, marketing as seen through the eyes of the marketing manager. Now that you have a better appreciation of what the marketing manager does and how he can contribute to the *macro*-marketing process, you should be able to give thoughtful consideration to whether marketing costs too much.

Your answer is extremely important. Your own business career and the economy in which you will live will be affected by your answer.

In this chapter, we will try to reach some conclusions regarding the effectiveness of marketing, particularly in the American economy.

What to measure and how?

The question is, which marketing?

As we saw in Chapter 1, it is useful to distinguish two levels of marketing: the *macro* level and the *micro* level. Therefore, when evaluating the question of whether marketing costs too much, we must treat each of these levels separately.

Some complaints against marketing are aimed at only one of these levels at a time, while in other cases the criticism seems to be directed to one level but actually is aimed at the other. Some critics of specific advertisements, for example, probably would not be satisfied with *any* advertising.

To clarify our thinking, we gave two definitions of marketing.

The macro-level definition is: *Marketing is concerned with designing an efficient* (in terms of use of resources) *and fair* (in terms of distribution of output to all parties involved) *system which will direct an economy's flow of goods and services from producers to consumers and accomplish the objectives of the society.* This is clearly concerned with the whole economic system.

In contrast, the micro-level definition of marketing is: *Marketing is the performance of business activities which direct the flow of goods and services from producer to consumer or user in order to satisfy customers and accomplish the firm's objectives.*

Evaluating these two different levels of marketing requires different techniques. It also requires some agreement on the purpose of our economic system. Unless we agree on the purpose of our society, little can be accomplished through dialogue.

Why we let the buyer be the chooser

We have emphasized the importance of the customer in planning marketing strategies because we have assumed that *the basic objective of our economic system is meeting consumers' needs as they, the consumers, see them.* Thus, the consumer is the focal point in both of our definitions of marketing. This is an acknowledgment in economic terms that in a free society, free men have a right to live as they choose.

This is no place for an extensive discussion of the merits of this objective. Philosophers, politicians, and others can (and should) explore this subject. Perhaps, eventually, such dialogue will lead to a change in our economic goals.

It is sufficient here to note that different economies have different objectives. Dictatorships, for example, may be concerned mainly with satisfying the needs of the society as seen by the political elite. In a socialist state, the objective might be to satisfy needs as defined by social planners—perhaps the equal division of wealth. In still other economies, the goal may be to build up the country militarily or economically, perhaps for the long-term benefit of all consumers (the people), but as seen by the state planners.

A marketing system would be required in all of these economies, but it might operate quite differently according to the various objectives.

In the following paragraphs, our basic concern will be evaluating the operation of marketing in the American economy where the objective is to satisfy consumers' needs, *as consumers see them*. This is the essence of our system, and the business firm that ignores this fact does so at its own peril.

| What do you measure to get the measure? | Since consumer satisfaction is our goal, the efficiency of marketing must be measured by *the extent of this satisfaction*. Unfortunately, however, we cannot measure this satisfaction quantitatively and, therefore, provide a precise measure of marketing effectiveness. While there are a number of approaches to such measurement, none is fully satisfactory. |

Measuring macro-marketing

The macro-marketing definition refers to *efficiency* (in terms of use of resources) and *fairness* (in terms of distribution of output to all parties involved), as well as accomplishing the society's objectives.

Efficiency is concerned with the ratio of input to output. Given an economy's resources (and its state of technology), it would be possible to evaluate alternate ways of combining the inputs to increase the output, as measured, say, by GNP. For a particular year, the combination which yielded the highest GNP might be considered the most efficient.

The combination of resources which seems most efficient may not be considered "fair" by some people, however. The way resources are allocated in a society has a bearing on the fairness of the distribution of income and, therefore, output. Very efficient use of productive machinery, or richly endowed land, for example, together with low-cost labor might maximize the total GNP attainable but still seem unfair to some people because of inequitable returns to the factors of production.

Furthermore, efficient use of resources and fairness in allocating work roles (and therefore the distribution of income) are matters primarily related to "production," and *not* to how satisfied consumers are with the results of the production process. Input costs may be equated with output value – as is done with the *value-added* approach – but this does not really do the job because costs of production and distribution may have little relationship to consumer satisfaction.

However, there is no quantitative way of measuring aggregate consumer satisfaction, so our evaluation of macro-marketing effectiveness will have to be subjective with the realization that ultimately the macro-marketing system must satisfy consumer/voters or they might decide to vote to modify the system or change to an entirely new system. Let's remember that, in our economy, it is the consumers' votes in the marketplace, and in the ballot box, which finally decide whether the macro-marketing system costs too much.

Measuring micro-marketing

Measuring micro-marketing effectiveness is also difficult, but here the relative cost or profitability of alternative ways of doing specific things could be used. The cost of alternative physical distribution plans or advertising campaigns designed to accomplish the same specific objective, for example, could be compared. Presumably the lowest-cost alternative would be "best." Care must be used when evaluating only costs, however, because using the lowest-cost method for one part of a system may not lead to lowest cost for the whole system. We saw this when we discussed physical distribution, and the same concept applies to a firm's complete effort. Low-cost "efficient" production might require high marketing costs and not be efficient for the whole business – total costs might be high and profits low.

It is generally more practical to think of marketing and business as synonymous for the current purpose, and evaluate the profitability of whole firms or profit centers, rather than only parts of a business system.

In the final analysis, every company uses slightly different marketing strategies, and it is up to each customer to decide how effectively individual firms satisfy his needs. Generally speaking, customers are willing to pay higher prices or buy more of those goods which best satisfy them. Thus, efficient marketing plans can increase the profits needed to attract investment, provide jobs, and pay for research to develop new or better products. Profits are not only the goal of most businesses, but they can be used as a rough measure of a firm's efficiency in satisfying customers. In this sense, a firm's own interests and society's interests are not at odds.

Not gospel, but arguments

In view of the difficulty of measuring consumer satisfaction and, therefore, the effectiveness of micro- and macro-marketing, it is easy to see why reasonable men might have different views on the subject. If the objective of the economy is clearly defined, however, and the argument is stripped of emotion, the broad question of marketing effectiveness and value probably can be answered.

In this chapter we will argue that micro-marketing (how individual firms and channels operate) *frequently does cost too much, but that macro-marketing* (how the whole marketing system operates), *does not cost too much, given the present objective of the American economy – consumer satisfaction.* These views should not be accepted as "gospel" but rather as arguments. In the end, you, the student of marketing, will have to make your own decision.[1]

Micro-marketing often *does* cost too much

Many new products, old businesses fail

Our focus throughout the text has been on what marketing managers should or could do to run a business more efficiently. But it must be acknowledged that the majority of firms are still production-oriented.

Many firms are not nearly as efficient as they might be. We have noted already that at least four out of five new products fail. New and old businesses fail regularly, too. The main reason for such failure is poor management or just plain managerial incompetence. One survey of 15,782 failures found that more than 90 percent were caused directly by incompetent or inexperienced management. Other surveys have shown similar results.[2]

Incompetence and bad management lead to higher costs of operation and tend to reduce the effectiveness of the business system in general. Generally speaking, business inefficiencies are due to one or more of three reasons:

1. Lack of interest in, or understanding of, the sometimes capricious customer.
2. Improper blending of the four P's, caused in part by an overemphasis on production and/or internal problems as contrasted with a customer orientation.
3. Lack of understanding of, or adjustment to, uncontrollable factors.

The company can get in the way of the customer

Serving the customer is plainly the function of business, yet some business managers seem to feel that customers avidly await any product they turn out. So they turn instead to internal problems. They do not understand a business as a "total system" responsible for satisfying customer needs.

The production manager, for example, may be primarily interested in designing products that are easy to make or can be made readily on the company's present machines. But he might be less worried about quality control. It is estimated that only 20–30 percent of U.S. manufacturers have quality control procedures.[3] And this in turn may lead

---

[1] For an extensive discussion of the problems and mechanics of measuring the efficiency of marketing, see R. S. Vaile, E. T. Grether, and R. Cox, *Marketing in the American Economy* (New York: Ronald Press Co., 1952), chaps. xxxii and xxxiii; and T. N. Beckman, H. H. Maynard, W. R. Davidson, *Principles of Marketing* (6th ed.; New York: Ronald Press Co., 1957), chap. xxxv; Stanley C. Hollander, "Measuring the Cost and Value of Marketing," *Business Topics*, Summer, 1961, pp. 17–26; and Reavis Cox, *Distribution in a High-Level*

Economy (Englewood Cliffs, N.J.: Prentice-Hall, Inc., 1965).

[2] B. Charles Ames, "Trappings vs. Substance in Industrial Marketing, *Harvard Business Review*, July–August, 1970, pp. 93–102; *Time*, June 21, 1963, p. 86; and Merchant's Service, National Cash Register Co., *Establishing a Retail Store*, p. 3.

[3] "Government Crackdown on Unsafe Goods," *Detroit Free Press*, October 7, 1968, p. 9–B.

to consumer dissatisfaction, or injury. Furthermore, it is costly and annoying to retailers and wholesalers who must try to repair the goods or return them to the manufacturer. Approximately $130 million worth of apparel alone is returned to manufacturers each year for repairs or replacement.[4]

Production people usually like long production runs of standardized products since this helps to lower costs. Sometimes the production department emphasizes low-cost production mainly because it "sells" its products to the sales department at a fixed price, and therefore can make a good showing with sizable, low-cost runs. Yet this may create the need for costly promotion in an effort to move large quantities of less desirable goods.

Middlemen, too, often get tied up in their own internal problems. Goods may be stocked where it is convenient for the retailer to handle them, rather than for consumers to find them—for example, by handling characteristics rather than with complementary goods which meet similar needs. And fast-moving, hard-to-handle goods may not be stocked at all because "They are too much trouble" or "We're always running out."

In the same fashion, accounting or financial departments in all kinds of businesses may try to cut costs by reducing raw material or finished-product inventory, even though this may not serve customers well. It may require more expensive hand-to-mouth buying, or cause loss of sales because of lack of stock.

The high cost of poor marketing mixes

Perhaps lack of concern for the customer is most noticeable in the ways the four P's are combined—or sometimes are forced—into a marketing mix. This can happen in many ways, as the following discussion shows.

Product—forget the customer, full speed ahead!

Some production-oriented executives develop a company's product not to meet the needs of certain target customers but rather to satisfy some pet concept held by themselves or their friends. They sometimes produce products too high or too low in quality, or too complicated for many target markets. Then, to compound these errors, the packaging people frequently put this ill-conceived product in a container that is easy to make and fill but not really protective or appealing to the customer.

These poorly designed, poorly packaged products then are turned over to the sales department for unloading on the market. Sometimes these products cannot be moved off the counter or can be moved only with overly aggressive (or even fraudulent) promotion. Middlemen may participate in this aggressive selling if they are given high enough markups, or additional advertising or promotion allowances. This sort of promotion can be expensive and may become more common unless businesses become more customer-oriented.

[4]"Retailers Fret Over Poorly Made Goods, Loose Inspection Practices," *Wall Street Journal,* October 30, 1969, p. 1.

A study of more than 22,000 salesmen from 1960 to 1966 showed that their attitude toward the products they sell dropped from an 86 percent favorable rating in 1960 to 63 percent in 1966. Unless quality improves, it is likely that this pattern of decline will continue, inevitably leading to poor performance and costly turnover of salesmen.[5]

Place—don't rock the boat, or sell to chains

Sales managers seldom make adjustments in channels as frequently as might be desirable, partly because of their personal relationships in their channel and partly because, being human, they prefer not to rock the boat. Yet such inflexibility can be extremely costly, especially in view of the "scrambling" we saw in the distribution structure.

Some old-timer salesmen are so tied to the idea of small independent wholesalers and retailers that they even refuse to sell to chain stores or large organizations. Their personal relationships with their old customers may make business more pleasant, but do not necessarily contribute to efficiency and profits. The continued use of obsolete and overly expensive channels may give substance to the charge of "too many" wholesalers and retailers.

Price—pick a price, any high price

Prices frequently are set on a cost-plus basis. This method of pricing may ignore customer demand and lead to unnecessarily high (and less profitable) prices. Many businessmen consider both margin and expected volume in pricing goods, but margins are definite, while volume is only predictable. These businessmen, therefore, choose high margins, which may lead to high prices and reduced volume. Firms faced with elastic demands, however, probably should set lower prices, since they would be appreciated by the customer—and might be more profitable for the seller, depending on the cost structure.

Promotion—in spite of the advertising geniuses and star salesmen

If a product is poorly or improperly designed, or if inadequate channels are employed, or if cost-plus pricing is used, it is easy to see why promotion may be costly. Aggressive selling may be needed to overcome previous miscalculations or errors. Perhaps it is understandable that some sales and advertising managers feel they have to resort to tricks (including unethical ones) to sell goods.

Even if a good job is done on the other three P's, however, Promotion is sometimes inefficient and costly. As already noted, the sales manager and the advertising manager may not cooperate, each feeling that his own technique is most effective and does not need the support of the other. In some companies, the advertising manager and sales manager do not communicate at all.

Until recently, only lip service was paid to the value of customer research in some firms. Some advertising executives still feel that all a promotional campaign needs is their creative genius. And the diffi-

---

[5] "Salesmen's Product Faith Down," (*Lansing, Michigan*) *State Journal*, June 20, 1966, p. C–4.

culty of checking advertising results makes it hard to tell whether ad men are talking to the customers or to themselves.

Sales management also has its problems. There are many types of sales jobs. Recruiting the right person for each is difficult. Furthermore, the very nature of the sales job makes it difficult to measure sales performance.

Careful analysis and management are necessary to build a productive sales force at a reasonable cost. Unfortunately, many sales managers, although former "star" salesmen, are not up to this management task.

Company objectives may force higher cost operation

Top-management decisions on compnay objectives significantly affect the cost of marketing. A decision to pursue growth for growth's sake, for example, might mean big spending for promotion. Or trying to expand market share—again for its own sake—might be accomplished only by aggressive, costly promotion.

Diversification for diversification's sake could require development of costly new arrangements for Place. Or if the established firms already had developed and protected basic ideas, perhaps through obtaining solid customer franchises, the firm might be forced to turn out second-rate products. And even if the company *had* a competitive physical product, the Place and Promotion tasks might be overwhelming.

For these reasons, it is imperative that the marketing manager both be alert to the possibility of such pitfalls and participate fully in shaping the firm's objectives. Recognizing the importance of marketing, many progressive firms have given marketing management a greater voice—and sometimes the dominant voice—in determining company objectives. Unfortunately, though, in many more firms, marketing is still looked upon as the department that "gets rid of" the product.

But the customer is coming into view

It appears that marketing does cost too much in many firms. However, the waste comes from misdirected effort, not some fallacy in the marketing concept. Marketing mixes often are put together by departments and executives who have interests other than serving customers. The customer, in effect, is the last factor considered in some company planning.

But all business firms and marketers should not be criticized out of hand. An increasing number *are* becoming customer-oriented. And the Better Business Bureau, the Chamber of Commerce, the U.S. Department of Commerce, the American Marketing Association, the American Management Association, and other trade associations have developed programs which encourage emphasis on satisfying consumers. Some organizations have developed "codes of ethics" to guide members' behavior with respect to customers. Some of these developments are responses to the consumerism movement, but others reflect long-established commitments. More industry groups might be willing to get together to discuss how to do a better job (with good intentions and perhaps subsequent results) but are inhibited from doing so because of possible criticism for collusion.[6]

There is also a trend toward improved marketing strategy planning and elimination of unnecessary costs, through more effective business management. Distribution channels are continually shifting as new ways are found for doing the marketing job more effectively. Limited-function wholesalers have developed in many lines. Discount houses have eliminated many small, conventional retail stores which did not recognize changing customer demands. Wholesalers who have not adopted the new methods of storing and transporting have been bypassed.

One encouraging sign is the end of the notion that practically anybody can run a business successfully. This never was true, and today the growing complexity of business is drawing more and more professionals into business. This includes not only professional business managers but psychologists, sociologists, statisticians, and economists.

The professional business managers who adopt the marketing concept as a way of business life will do a better job. This concept provides that all the activities of the business will be integrated into one "total system of action" oriented toward the one objective of serving the customer, at a profit. If this is done effectively, both businesses and customers will benefit. Then *micro-marketing* will *not* cost too much.

Macro-marketing *does not* cost too much

Many criticisms of marketing take aim at the operation of the macro-marketing system. These criticisms suggest that advertising and promotion in general are socially undesirable; that the macro-marketing system causes an improper allocation of resources, restricts income and employment, and leads to an improper distribution of income. Most of these complaints imply that some micro-marketing activities should not be permitted; that because they are allowed, macro-marketing costs too much or yields poor results.

Much of this criticism is expressed by those who have their own version of the ideal way to run an economy. Some of the most severe critics of our marketing system are theoretical economists who use the pure-competition model as their ideal. They would give consumers free choice in the market but are critical of the way the present market operates. Other critics would take free choice away from consumers, or at least some of them, and substitute their own values for those of individual consumers. These divergent viewpoints should be kept in mind when evaluating criticism.

[6] "U.S. Chamber Enters Lists to Do Battle for Consumers," *Advertising Age,* March 9, 1970, p. 1, 74; "Look Around, Local Consumer Protection Activity is Popping," *Washington Report,* American Advertising Federation, April 14, 1970; and "AMA Code of Ethics Voted by Directors" (American Marketing Association), *Marketing News,* Mid-July, 1970, p. 3.

In the following discussion, the word *business* probably could be substituted for *marketing* in most instances. Marketing is the most exposed arm of business, but it is nearly impossible to separate this arm from the rest of the body. A criticism of marketing at the macro level usually implies a criticism of our entire market-directed economic system as it now exists and suggests that some modification or an entirely different system would be more effective. Let's look at some of these positions so we can evaluate whether or not our macro-marketing system does cost too much.

Is pure competition the welfare ideal?

A major criticism of our macro-marketing system is that it permits or even encourages the allocation of unduly large share of resources for marketing activities and that this may actually reduce consumer "welfare." This argument is concerned with how the economy's resources (land, labor, and captial) are allocated for producing and distributing goods. These critics usually maintain that scarce resources could be better spent on producing goods than on marketing them. The foundation for this viewpoint is the assumption that marketing activities are unnecessary and do not create value, or more technically, that pure competition is the ideal for maximizing consumer welfare.

The pure-competition economists see little need for advertising, except perhaps for purely informative ads which would advise their "economic men" about the availability of products. In pure competition the assumption is that consumers are well informed about all available offerings and will choose rationally among the alternatives to maximize their own welfare. Therefore, these critics feel that emotional or persuasive advertising discourages the economic comparison required for their ideal pure-competition economy and further is wasteful because society does not need it.

Theoretical economic analysis can show convincingly that pure competition will provide greater consumer welfare than monopolistic competition—provided all of the conditions and assumptions of pure competition are met. It is for this reason that pure-competition proponents feel that advertising, personal selling, and marketing in general—any activities causing deviations from pure competition—should be condemned on welfare grounds.

It is important that we evaluate this view.

Different people want different things

At the outset, we can say that our present knowledge of the complexity of human behavior and peoples' desire for different products pretty well demolishes the economists' "economic man" assumption, and therefore the pure-competition ideal.[7] A pioneer in monopolistic competition analysis, E. H. Chamberlin, also argues logically against

---

[7] F. M. Nicosia, *Consumer Decision Processes* (Englewood Cliffs, N.J.: Prentice-Hall, Inc., 1966), p. 39.

the pure-competition ideal. He observes that people, in fact, are different and that they do have different demands. He translates these differences into demands for different products. Given this type of demand (downsloping demand curves), monopoly elements naturally develop. He concludes that "monopoly is necessarily a part of the welfare ideal. . . ."[8]

Once it is acknowledged that not all consumers know everything and that they have varied demands, the need for a variety of micro-marketing activities becomes clear.

It is certainly true that micro-marketing activities can lead to a different allocation of resources than would be found in a pure-competition economy. It takes more time and effort to satisfy varied demands. But this allocation of resources probably results in greater consumer welfare. People are getting what they want.

Advertising, for example, can make both the micro- and macro-marketing processes work better. It can cut promotion costs for a firm. And at the macro level, it can, says another economist, be a powerful influence in eliminating ignorance and disseminating price information, making the whole searching process more economical.[9]

Creating demand does not misallocate resources

It would seem, then, that simply satisfying customers' demands certainly does not lead to a misallocation of resources. Giving individuals what they want, after all, is the purpose of our market-directed economic system. But there is still another issue that concerns certain critics. They ask, "Is it right to influence consumers' demands?"

We already have seen that psychologists view consumers as a bundle of needs and drives, some of which are innate, but most of which are learned. Some critics feel that promotion not only stimulates people's needs and drives toward a particular product, but often teaches entirely new wants – and that this violates, if only subtly, the individual's control of his own actions.

Behavioral scientists find that it *is* possible to change attitudes and behavior. But an important question is: How basic are the needs which might be created? If we think of promotion for a new recreational gadget as "creating new demands," there can be no argument. Promotion can do this job. But to state broadly that promotion can create a wish for (or pleasure in) recreation, distinctiveness, or emulation, is another matter. It is likely that the human being already has learned these needs in other ways or from other sources.

Take the midi, for example

It is difficult to think of any new product for which an entirely new set of basic needs or drives had to be created. Even the exaggerated, up-again-down-again styles of women's clothing meet some women's need to be distinctive, to be style leaders. Yet some new feminine

---

[8] E. H. Chamberlin, "Product Heterogeneity and Public Policy," *American Economic Review,* May, 1950, p. 86.

[9] George J. Stigler, "The Economics of Information," *Journal of Political Economy,* June, 1961, p. 213.

styles do not sell well even with extensive publicity. Consider the midi and topless bathing suits, for most women.[10]

Don't be pigheaded — swim downstream!

Rather than seeking to create entirely new basic needs, which would be extremely difficult and expensive, business firms seek to stimulate or direct those needs or drives which already are held. They find it is "easier to swim with the current than against it."[11] Marketing research is used to test the current.

Marketing research helps management discover what target customers want or would like, so that the four P's can be tailored to their desires. Instead of just "guessing" what might be wanted, then working at expensive hit-or-miss development of new products, the modern marketing man seeks to assure maximum customer satisfaction by analyzing the customers' needs, drives, and likely behavior.

Once this data is known, marketing follows an intelligent course — not a selfish, pigheaded, or diabolical one. It gives the customer what he wants. In return, customers give the company what it wants: profits. This customer-oriented procedure also reduces the need to rely on heavy promotion to differentiate a product or try to create basically new demands.

"False" standards according to whom?

Promotion also has been criticized for creating and serving "false" standards, and thereby leading to an improper allocation of resources. But this standard has never been precisely defined. What is "false" apparently depends on the critic's point of view.

One critic of the two-car-family advertising which started in 1959 was a New York television critic who found even *one* car an inconvenience in crowded New York City.[12] To the suburban housewife, however, who perhaps is marooned miles from public transportation while her husband has *the* car, the advertisers are not creating any need at all. She has been thinking about this need for some time. The historical truth is that the two-car ad campaign came *after* the fact. It grew out of consumer research showing that many suburban families, especially those with teen-agers, already were developing into two-car and in some cases, three-car families.

Certain critics of "false" standards are either unwilling to accept the idea or are truly unaware that other people may prefer standards different from those the critics hold. They see judgment or taste measured on an absolute scale, ranging from "good" at the top — where they exist — to "bad" at the bottom, and they do not want the lower end of the scale served.

Regarding the serving of "false tastes," a well-known economist, George Stigler, said:

The marketplace responds to the tastes of consumers with the goods and

---

[10] "Moribund Midi — Woeful Retailers Say the Lower the Hem, the Lower the Sales," *Wall Street Journal*, Oct. 2, 1970, pp. 1 f, and "The Long Way Out," *Time*, Oct. 26, 1970, p. 80.

[11] George Katona, in a seminar at the University of Notre Dame during 1962.

[12] John Crosby, "One-Car Captivity Now Brand of Poor," *South Bend Tribune*, April 17, 1959, p. 51.

services that are salable, whether the tastes are elevated or depraved. It is unfair to criticize the marketplace for fulfilling these desires, when clearly the defects lie in the popular tastes themselves. I consider it a cowardly concession to a false extension of the idea of democracy to make sub rosa attacks on public tastes by denouncing the people who serve them. It is like blaming the waiters in restaurants for obesity.[13]

Sometimes it's the little things that count

Criticism of promotion which focuses on minor product differences has been common, especially among the very "rational." Sociological and psychological research, however, indicates that promotion actually may create *new* values for these products—new psychological values that may be of greater value to the buyer than the physical product itself.

How does this value-creation process work? Consider an extreme example, the placebo or sugar pill that a doctor uses for his hypochondriac patients to give reassurance that, yes, they are being medicated. The doctor's advice (promotion) that the pill will do some good frequently gets very desirable results when, in fact, the only value of the pill is psychological, not medicinal.

In a similar way, promotion sometimes enables marketers to satisfy better the many varied demands of consumers without an expensive physical variation of the product. With a little help from an ad copywriter, women can imagine all sorts of desirable consequences of using a particular perfume or lipstick—and if they believe it, it may come true. (Value has been added!)

Micro-marketing efforts expand macro output through innovation

Some critics feel that marketing helps create monopoly, or at least monopolistic competition, and that this in turn leads to higher prices, restriction of output, and reduction in the national income and employment.

Behind this criticism is economic analysis showing that profit-maximizing firms in monopolistic competition should choose a lower level of output and higher price than would prevail in pure competition. This criticism is valid if pure competition is, in fact, the ideal economic situation. But again the critics miss the main point—that consumers differ. As long as this is true, there will be demand for varied products; and this will lead to downsloping demand curves and monopolistic competition, as described previously.

Monopolistic competition brings innovation, innovation brings barnacles

Given the monopolistic competition situation, it is quite true that use of the Product, Place, and Promotion variables does cause a shifting of demand curves and in some cases even makes demand curves inelastic. The exact effect of this on output and prices, however, is indefinite. It depends on the shape of the cost curves and the extent to which the demand curves are shifted. If the new curves are extremely elastic, prices might be lower with output increased considerably. But

---

[13] "Intellectuals Should Re-Examine the Marketplace; It Supports Them, Helps Keep Them Free; Prof. Stigler," *Advertising Age,* January 28, 1963; see also, E. T. Grether, "Galbraith versus the Market: A Review Article," *Journal of Marketing,* Jan. 1968, pp. 9–14.

it is not possible to generalize on the effect of marketing activities for all situations.[14]

There is no arguing that firms in a market-directed economy make a real effort to carve out separate monopolistic markets for themselves. This approach may have the short-run effect of restricting output (depending upon the shape of the new demand and supply curves) and raising prices on *that particular new product*.

Customers are not taken advantage of in the short run, however. They do not have to buy the new product unless they feel it is a better value. The old products are still available. Ironically, the prices may even be lower on the old products to meet the new competition, and yet their sales may decline because customers shift to the new product.

Over several years, the profits of the innovator may rise – but the rising profits also act as a spur to further innovation by competitors. This leads to new investments, which contribute to economic growth, raising the level of national income and employment.

Here, the increasing profits attract competition. The profits then begin to drop as competitors enter and begin producing somewhat similar products. Recall the rise and fall of industry profit during the product life cycle.

Monopolistic competition, it is clear, provides a dynamic element in the economy and breeds its own competition. The innovators also pave the way for the coming of the "barnacle" brands, so called because they attach themselves to the successful market established by the innovators. They are offered at lower prices and for this reason are accepted in the latter stages of the product life cycle.[15]

Output pie not fixed in size

Some critics argue that there is only a certain amount of income to be spent and that higher prices, which sometimes accompany effective market segmentation or product differentiation, could lead to a reduction in the level of income or employment. Most economists consider this a naïve view of the economy. The economic pie is not fixed in size. The levels of income and employment appear to be more directly related to the level of expenditures of consumers, business, and the government.[16]

Advertising didn't concentrate them

Certain critics are concerned that promotion leads to greater concentration of industry – that is, a few large firms dominating each industry – and, as a result, a reduction in competition. This seems an illogical objection, since there was much concentration of industry before promotion became widespread in the 1920's and 1930's.

The most recent analysis of the available statistical data shows that industrial concentration was not caused by advertising, but rather by the availability of economies through large-scale production and distribution and the potential for financial advantage in larger units.

[14] E. H. Chamberlin, *The Theory of Monopolistic Competition* (Cambridge, Mass.: Harvard University Press, 1936), pp. 166–67.

[15] Jules Backman, *Advertising and Competition* (New York: New York University Press, 1967), p. 44.

[16] See Chapter 5 on national income forecasting.

There appears to be no relationship between the intensity of advertising and the trend to concentration.[17]

Large firms are vigorous, customers are benefiting

Another objection to micro-marketing activities is that supposedly they aid the growth of large organizations, thus further restricting market entry and reducing competition, output, and employment. In recent years, though, the reverse seems to be true. Many firms have grown quite large, but this growth has been primarily because of diversification into many different fields.

In many industries, competition (using all four P's) is extremely vigorous among a number of large, well-diversified organizations. They have the money to undertake basic research, resulting in true innovation. These firms can afford the extensive market research and careful planning of marketing mixes needed to compete effectively with their large competitors. They can underwrite and carry a new product until volume permits economies of scale and lower prices.[18]

These large firms may compete aggressively, true, but out of this may come better service to the public than is offered by small firms which take refuge in guildlike behavior, following the "accepted customs of the trade."[19]

A well-known economist, John Maurice Clark, cites the home-building industry and small retailing as illustrations of areas in which the existence of many small firms has not led to especially good results. He concluded that consumer interests often are best served by companies that are strong and well financed.[20]

Protecting small competitors may push prices up

Many small retailers have lobbied for laws ostensibly designed to protect competition. Some of these laws, as we have discussed, were not designed to protect competition but to protect competitors. Sometimes there is a vast difference between the two.

To protect an inefficient competitor may be injurious to competition. Yet certain aspects of the Robinson-Patman Act, the Miller-Tydings and McGuire Acts, some state unfair practices acts, and certain court decisions concerning the Sherman Act seem intended to protect competitors. It is obvious that the state anti–chain store laws are designed more to hamstring competitors than protect price competition, since most surveys indicate that the large chain stores already offer goods at low or the lowest prices.[21]

Legal restrictions that protect the small or inefficient firm naturally

[17] Backman, *op. cit.*, pp. 113–14

[18] J. B. McKitterick, "What Is the Marketing Management Concept?" in Frank M. Bass (ed.), *The Frontiers of Marketing Thought and Science* (Chicago: American Marketing Association, 1957), pp. 71–82.

[19] Backman, *op. cit.*, pp. 79–81 and 112–14; see also, Dean A. Worcester, Jr., *Monopoly, Big Business, and Welfare in the Postwar United States* (Seattle: University of Washington Press, 1968).

[20] "How U.S. 'Giants' Compete," *Business Week*, February 3, 1962, pp. 104–5; and John Maurice Clark, *Competition as a Dynamic Process* (Washington, D.C.: Brookings Institution, 1961).

[21] Werner Z. Hirsch, "Grocery Chain Store Prices — A Case Study," *Journal of Marketing*, July, 1956, p. 9; and Charles F. Stewart, "Mandatory Resale Price Maintenance of Distilled Spirits in California," *Journal of Marketing*, April, 1954, p. 70.

have their effect on total marketing costs. That effect probably is to increase them, because it is difficult to adjust efficiently when the guidelines are so vague and confusing.

Concerning legislation on competition, a well-known economist, Professor Kenneth E. Boulding, once said, "Mr. Bumble's ass seems to have developed a remarkable ability to ride off in several directions at once. The A&P is condemned for being too competitive; the tobacco and cement companies are condemned for not being competitive enough."[22]

Marketing men get their fair share of income

The main concern about distribution of income is that a market-directed economic system may divert a large share of the national income to marketing people because of the greater profitability of firms which have successfully sold their products. Such criticism does not seem justified, however, if the purpose of a free economy is to satisfy consumers and if market-oriented firms do that job successfully. Logically, the marketing segment of the economy should then be entitled to its higher incomes and higher profits.

Incomes in marketing *are* high for certain types of jobs, especially order-getting salesmen and certain advertising and sales promotion people. But it also is true that many of the order takers, especially retail salespeople, have low incomes – in many cases below the federal minimum wage. These salaries probably reflect fairly accurately the contribution of each to the economy.

Market system is automatic and effective

Our market system provides for a fairly automatic operation of the economy. Many competitors in a relatively free market serve the needs of millions of consumers far better than central economic planning could serve them.

In the planned Soviet economy, it usually has been necessary to tolerate a gray or black market and free-economy-type brokers to make the economy work. Now the Soviets are coming to see that product differentiation, branding, and advertising actually may help to facilitate the operation of a planned economy. They find that when customers recognize products by advertised brand, this permits self-service, speeds selling, and cuts cost. Requiring that each plant succeed in the market with its own brand acts as an automatic control on quality. Bureaucratic control, using standards and inspectors, would be increasingly difficult or impossible to accomplish now that the economy of the U.S.S.R. is offering more heterogeneous products.[23]

Consumers ask for it, consumers pay for it

Certainly we do not now have the economists' "ideal" – pure competition. But the monopolistic competition situation that is typical of our economy is the result of customer preferences, not manipulation of markets by businessmen. Monopolistic competition may seem costly

[22] "A Pricing System that Works Only One Way – Up," *Business Week,* June 15, 1957, p. 190.

[23] "Making the Soviet Future Work," *Business Week,* June 10, 1967, pp. 128–34; and Marshall I. Goldman,

"A New Perspective of Product Differentiation and Advertising: The Soviet View," *Business Review,* Boston University, Spring, 1962, pp. 3–12.

at times – when we look at micro-level situations, but it seems to work fairly well at the macro level – in serving the welfare of consumers who have many and varied demands.

Many consumers, for example, use material possessions as a means of differentiating themselves from their fellows. The newness of products is one measure of their distinction, and consumers may insist upon frequent product changes for this reason alone.

Many consumers want extensive services, such as credit, returned-goods privileges, and delivery services.

Many wish extensive product variety and immediate service at retail outlets. Large numbers may want this service at the same time of the day or week, and may be particularly insistent on service at Thanksgiving, Christmas, or Easter. But in the middle of the week or the middle of the summer, these consumers might leave the required facilities almost idle.

All of these demands add to the cost of satisfying consumers. Certainly, the total cost is larger than it would be if spartan, undifferentiated products were offered at the factory door on a take-it-or-leave-it basis to long lines of buyers.

But if the role of the marketing system is to serve the consumer, then the cost of whatever services he demands cannot be considered excessive. It is merely the cost of serving the consumer in the manner he wants to be served.

Should the consumer be king?

Some critics sincerely question the doctrine of *consumer sovereignty*, which allows each consumer to choose what he wants to buy for himself. They don't think that some consumers are able to make correct choices for themselves.

Those who take the consumer's side agree that some people do not use their income wisely by others' standards; but at the same time, they argue that we do not yet have (*a*) ways of measuring consumer satisfaction, or (*b*) mechanisms for allowing one citizen to impose his choice of "correct" purchases on another citizen.

Planners often make such choices in totalitarian or socialist states. But it is axiomatic in democracies with market-directed economies that individual consumers *are* the best judges of what will satisfy them most. This system has its deficiencies and some consumers make mistakes, but it is generally considered to be better than letting someone else decide for you. A college student might appreciate this idea better by reflecting on whether he would rather have someone else – his parents, for example – make all of his decisions for *him*.

Does marketing cost enough?

The question, "Does marketing cost too much?" has been answered by one well-known financial expert with another question, "Does distribution cost enough?"[24] His analysis demonstrated that marketing is an important and integral part of our economic system. And he sug-

---

[24] Paul M. Mazur, "Does Distribution Cost Enough?"
Fortune, November, 1947.

gested that perhaps even more should be spent on marketing, since "distribution is the delivery of a standard of living" – that is, the satisfaction of consumers' basic needs and wants.

The role of marketing and business in our market-directed economy is to satisfy consumers. Production cannot do this job alone, nor can marketing. It makes little sense to think of production and marketing as truly separate entities. They are different sides of the same coin.

Mass production requires mass distribution and our macro-marketing system helps make the whole market-directed economic system work well. In this sense, then, macro-marketing does not cost too much. Some of the activities of individual business firms may cost too much, and if these micro-level activities are improved, the performance of the macro system probably will improve. But regardless, our macro-marketing system performs a vital role in our economic system.

What is needed to satisfy critics?

We have suggested that our macro-marketing system does not cost too much, given the present objective of our economy, while acknowledging that the micro-level performance of many business firms leaves a lot to be desired. At this point, it should be worth our while to suggest what may be needed to meet the rising tide of consumerism. Should anything be done in this area, and if so, what?

Would need better performance at micro level

It is obvious that many firms do not satisfy enough consumers profitably, and, as a result, they go out of business. But others somehow get along without satisfying consumers very well, because their production-oriented competitors perform no better than they do. These firms mechanically follow long-accepted industry practices, and, perhaps, are limited by technological processes. In any case, their primary focus is on internal problems.

Greater acceptance of the marketing concept can help here – that is, guiding firms to determining what consumers want and *then* satisfying *this* demand, rather than simply trying to persuade them that what the firm has *is* what they want.

Furthermore, by knowing more about consumers' needs and preferences, the firm's promotion could help communicate the essence of what the firm has to offer.

It should be obvious that such things as fraud, deception, collusion, and other unethical or illegal practices should be avoided.

Beyond this, it makes sense to follow the "spirit" rather than the "letter" of business law. Consumer/citizens want their needs satisfied and are probably willing to be tolerant and understanding of a business firm's occasional errors if that firm seems to be trying to provide a legitimate product or service.

Effective legislation is difficult to write and administer, and if business firms insist on pursuing the "letter" – trying to find loopholes—they may provoke consumers into adopting specific, hard-to-work-with legislation which will hurt business *and* consumers. In an effort to stop deliberately deceptive advertising, for example, all advertising might be tightly restricted or prohibited.

Some business firms seem to feel that in a free-market economy, they should be completely "free." They don't understand the idea that ours is a market-directed system and that—in the long-run anyway—the needs of consumer/citizens must be served.

A smart business executive puts himself in the consumer's position, even when making manufacturing decisions. A useful rule to follow might be: "Do unto others at you would have others do unto you." At the operational level, this would mean developing satisfying marketing mixes for specific target markets.

Low-quality, short-lived products might be quite suitable in certain circumstances, as long as the target market understood what it was getting. Recall our cost-conscious couple in the paint market in Chapter 2. Low-cost paint might be seen as a "good value" by certain market segments. In other markets, an entirely different marketing mix could be required to offer "good value."

Production-oriented businessmen often neglect this market-oriented rule and thus provide ammunition for the critics. It often is difficult, or impossible, to determine what grade or quality is being offered at various prices. Labels, salesmen, and advertising may offer no help at all. Furthermore, the producer himself may not know, because no specific customer-related quality has been built into the product. The producer may feel it is better, because higher-cost components were installed. But although the higher costs may result in higher prices, these higher-cost components may or may not contribute to consumer satisfaction. Also, *some* components may be superior to other components, but what does this do for the consumer when the weakest component breaks down? He is concerned with the use of the product, not its components.

The job of satisfying customers' needs becomes increasingly difficult as these needs become more varied, as products become more complicated, and as consumers expect more from technology. But, clearly, more attention must be paid to learning precisely what customers want and then satisfying *those* needs, rather than doing what the firm might like to do and then trying to use promotion to convince the customer that his needs are being met.

It is understandable why some promotion men faced with production-oriented bosses would resort to extremely aggressive, or even deceptive and fraudulent, promotion to get "rid of the goods." But it seems doubtful that this approach will work very well in the future.

In other words, the typical production-oriented businessman may truly be forced to accept the marketing concept to survive and prosper in the future. The "lip-service" acceptance of the past or plain production-orientedness will not do. A good share of the concerns of the consumerism movement seem to be due to the failure of businessmen to put the marketing concept into practice.

A wholehearted endorsement of the marketing concept will require considerable change within some organizations, to assure acceptable marketing strategies. Research, product design, and promotion may have to work together more closely, because what consumers consider "acceptable" and "reasonable" in product quality may change with time. This, in turn, will affect future consumerism activity, along with court and out-of-court settlements.

Business firms may also have to help educate consumers, because almost any product has potential disadvantages. Anything which uses power, for example, could be potentially dangerous. A manufacturer of gas and electrical appliances argues, "It's not feasible to design a product so that it's foolproof." Citing the case of an oven, he says: "If it were cool on all sides, it would be either too small inside to cook a turkey, or too big outside to fit in the kitchen."[25]

Clearly, more communication with consumers about the advantages and disadvantages of various alternatives in relation to their needs is needed.

Would need better performance at macro level

One of the advantages of a market-directed economic system is that its operation is relatively automatic. But in our version of this system, consumer/citizens provide certain constraints (laws). And at any time, these constraints can be strengthened or modified.

Before piling on too many new or different constraints, however, it probably would be wise to apply and vigorously enforce the ones we have. The antitrust laws, for example, have often been applied to protect competitors from each other when in fact they were intended to protect competition. Refocusing present constraints could make a big difference, as we may soon see, since, in 1970, the FTC seemed to be shifting to a consumer-oriented emphasis.[26] Congress and local authorities also are taking stronger stands.[27]

The results of vigorous enforcement of present constraints could be far-reaching if more price fixers, fraudulent or deceptive advertisers, and others who are obviously violating existing legislation – and thereby affecting the performance of the macro-marketing system – were sent to jail or given heavy fines. A quick and basic change in attitudes might occur if members of the board of directors and top management, who plan business strategy, were prosecuted, rather

---

[25] "The Pressure Is On for Safer Products," *Business Week,* July 4, 1970, pp. 36–39.

[26] "The FTC Gets Tough," *Time,* October 19, 1970, p. 80; "Coca-Cola's Ads for Hi-C Drinks Assailed by FTC," *Wall Street Journal,* September 29, 1970, p. 34; "FTC Chief Says Agency Seeks to Regulate Cars' Quality, Performance Only, Not Price," *Wall Street Journal,* March 11, 1970, p. 6; and "FTC Calls Autos 'Public Utility,' Urges Car Quality Control Law," *Advertising Age,* February 23, 1970, pp. 1 f.

[27] "Consumer Power Grows in Congress," *Business Week,* July 11, 1970, p. 20; "New York City Fights Shady Merchandisers with New Legal Curbs," *Wall Street Journal,* January 9, 1970, pp. 1 f; "FDA Unveils Unit Price Plan to Deal with Deceptive Packaging," *Advertising Age,* May 25, 1970, pp. 1 f; and Maurice H. Stans (U.S. Secretary of Commerce), "Marketing and Consumer Interests," *Marketing News,* First-of-January, 1970, p. 3; and Michael Pertschuk (Chief Counsel, Senate Commerce Committee), "The New Consumerism," a paper given for the annual meeting of the American Association of Advertising Agencies, 1970.

than the salesman or advertisers who are required to "deliver" on weak or undifferentiated strategies "or else" (lose their jobs).

In other words, if the government made it clear that it was serious about improving the performance of our economic system, much could be achieved within the present system, *without* adding new constraints or trying to "patch up" the present ones.

Further, it probably would be desirable for business leaders to expand their understanding of, and efforts to improve, our macro system. That is, take the offensive, not the defensive. More dialogue with legislators, government administrators, and consumer advocates could increase awareness of each others' problems, perceptions, and even use of terminology. Confusion or differences regarding the meaning of words such as: competition, product, market, consumer needs, rationality, and information can be crucial.[28]

And some changes may be desirable, to help potential customers choose among the bewildering array of goods and services on the market. Legislation to insure that consumers do have grounds for comparing products (for example, life expectancy of light bulbs and appliances) would be useful. And consumer education programs designed to teach people how to buy more effectively could be helpful.

But great care must be exercised here, so that the consumer's free choice *really* is preserved. If only those characteristics which are easily measurable are used, consumers might be encouraged or even trained to use quantitative criteria, when in fact qualitative characteristics (for example, style, taste, freshness, and fun in use) may be more important for many of them.

Moreover, arbitrarily restricting the kinds of offerings that can be made would be inadvisable, because this would restrict innovation. Besides, from a pragmatic viewpoint, it is difficult to draw other than minimum specifications for some products. As noted, the Soviets have discovered this fact the hard way.[29]

We may need a new macro-marketing system

Some marketing critics are just not happy with the idea of the consumer as king. In part, this is because they see the consumer becoming too "materialistic" and deplore this trend. They would rather limit personal consumption in some way—especially for the middle- and upper-income groups—and redistribute resources to others, either in this country or elsewhere.

Some critics question whether continued growth of GNP really is a desirable goal for the economy, because such growth equates more goods and services with more satisfaction for consumers. These ob-

---

[28] R. Bauer and S. Greyser, "The Dialogue that Never Happens," *Harvard Business Review*, November–December, 1967, pp. 2–12 and 186–90; and T. Levitt, "Why Business Always Loses," *Harvard Business Review*, March–April, 1968, pp. 81–89.

[29] Louis L. Stern, "Consumer Protection via Increased Information," *Journal of Marketing*, April, 1967, pp. 48–52.

servers feel that greater satisfaction would be achieved by less aggressive pursuit of material growth or even redirecting our goals.[30]

This is not the place to discuss this issue extensively. Instead, let's note that some critics, while ostensibly focusing on the faults of individual firms or micro-level activities, would really like to remedy the ills they see through basic changes in our macro-marketing system.

Such basic changes *might* be accomplished by *seemingly minor* modifications in our present system. Therefore, consumer/citizens should be careful to distinguish between proposed changes designed simply to modify our system and those which are designed to change it, perhaps drastically. In either case, the consumer/citizen should have the opportunity of making the decision (through his elected representatives). But it *is* his responsibility to recognize the difference and support the representatives and changes he really wants.

Regardless of the changes which might be voted by consumer/citizens, however, some kind of a marketing system would be needed. And market-oriented businessmen probably would be needed to help define and satisfy any "new needs." In fact, if satisfying more subtle needs, such as the "good life," becomes the goal, it could be even more vital to have market-oriented firms. And the market grid concept might be especially important. It may be necessary, for example, not only to define individual's needs, but also collective needs, for a "better neighborhood" or "more enriching social experiences," and so on. As one goes beyond tangible physical goods into more sophisticated need-satisfying blends of goods and services, the trial-and-error approach of the typical production-oriented businessman becomes even more inappropriate.

Macro-marketing system must keep satisfying customers, micro-marketers can help

Once again, macro-marketing does *not* cost too much. Business firms, in the aggregate, have been assigned the role, by consumers, of satisfying their needs. Consumers find it satisfactory, and even desirable to permit businessmen to cater to them and even to stimulate wants. As long as consumers are satisfied, macro-marketing will not cost too much, and business firms will be permitted to continue as profit-making entities.

[30] "Pollution and the Profit Motive," *Business Week,* April 11, 1970, pp. 82–86; "The Trade-Off for a Better Environment," *Business Week,* April 11, 1970, pp. 63–78; "We're Headed Down the Drain unless We Solve Urban, Pollution Crises Soon, Hauser, *Advertising Age,* May 18, 1970, pp. 59–62; Richard F. America, Jr., "What Do You People Want?" *Harvard Business Review,* March–April, 1969, pp. 103–12; "Human Needs Gain the Top Priority," *Business Week,* December 6, 1969, pp. 150–54; Andrew Hacker, *The End of the American Era,* (New York: Atheneum Publishers, 1970); Staffan B. Linder, *The Harried Leisure Class* (New York: Columbia University Press, 1970); E. J. Mishan. *Technology and Growth,* New York:(Frederick A. Praeger, Inc., 1970); William Lazer, "Marketing's Changing Social Relationships," *Journal of Marketing,* January 1969, pp. 3–9; and George C. Lodge, "Top Priority: Renovating Our Ideology," *Harvard Business Review,* September–October, 1970, pp. 43–55.

Market-oriented business firms can help make this system work better by pinpointing consumers' needs more accurately and then developing marketing mixes to satisfy them more effectively. In other words, aggressive, market-oriented businessmen can make a difference. They can provide a dynamic element to the macro-marketing system. They can insure that new and evolving consumer needs will be satisfied.

Yet make no mistake. Business in a free economy enjoys no special privilege. Its role is neither God-given nor royally sanctioned nor bureaucratically protected. The right to do business is a right given by individuals in their capacities as consumers, through continued patronage, and as citizens, through their votes. At any time the right to engage in business can be revoked by the consumer/citizen. Many businesses fail for lack of customers. More drastically, consumers may revoke private business's right to operate, and turn the activity over to public authorities.

This has happened in such cases as power plants taken over by municipalities; establishment of the postal service, TVA, and school systems; and government operation of defense plants.[31]

It must always be remembered that business exists at the consumers' discretion, and it is only by satisfying the consumer that a particular business firm and our private enterprise system can justify its existence and hope to perpetuate itself.[32]

Conclusion

Our macro-marketing system certainly *does not* cost too much. It provides a necessary function in our economy, which is keyed to serving the consumer. By the decisions of many consumers and businesses, rather than a few planners, the needs and desires of consumers are satisfied.

In carrying out this role granted by consumers, however, the activities of business firms are not always as effective as they might be.

[31] James W. Culliton, "A Marketing Analysis of Religion," *Business Horizons*, Spring, 1959.

[32] Marketing men are paying much more attention to the issue of social responsibility in marketing and the performance of the macro-marketing system. See Robert J. Lavidge, "The Growing Responsibility of Marketing," *Journal of Marketing*, January 1970, pp. 25–28; C. Merle Crawford, "Attitudes of Marketing Executives toward Ethics in Marketing Variable," *Journal of Marketing*, April, 1970, pp. 46–53; Albert Z. Carr, "Can an Executive Afford a Conscience?" *Harvard Business Review*, July–August, 1970, pp. 58–64; David W. Cravens and Gerald E. Hills, "Consumerism: A Perspective for Business," *Business Horizons*, August, 1970, pp. 22–28; George S. Day and David A. Aaker, "A Guide to Consumerism," *Journal of Marketing*, July, 1970, pp. 12–19; E. T. Grether, "Business Responsibility toward the Market," *California Management Review*, Fall, 1969, pp. 33–41; J. T. Hackett, "Corporate Citizenship," *Business Horizons*, October, 1969, p. 69; Theodore Levitt, "Why Business Always Loses," *Harvard Business Review*, March–April, 1968, pp. 81–89; Louis W. Stern, "Perspective on Public Policy: Comments on the 'Great Debate,'" *Journal of Marketing*, January, 1969, pp. 32–39; Louis L. Allen, "Making Capitalism Work in the Ghettos," *Harvard Business Review*, May–June, 1969, pp. 83–92; Charles S. Goodman, "Do the Poor Pay More?" *Journal of Marketing*, January, 1968, pp. 18–25; Frederick D. Sturdivant, "Better Deal for Ghetto Shoppers," *Harvard Business Review*, March–April, 1968, pp. 130–39.

Many businessmen do not understand the marketing concept nor the roles that either marketing or business play in our way of life. Furthermore, many businessmen are not as competent as they should be. In this sense, micro-marketing does cost too much. This situation is being improved, however, as training for business expands and as more competent people are attracted to marketing and business generally.

The efficiency of business and marketing would be increased greatly if more business managers understood and accepted the marketing concept—that the primary purpose of the whole business operation is to satisfy the customer. Acceptance of this philosophy forces an integration of all the activities of a business into a total system of action. This integration and the direction of all activities toward a specific goal can only lead to more effective business management.

The techniques and philosophy presented in this book indicate how acceptance of the marketing concept would encourage more efficient operation of business as well as whole economies, both underdeveloped and advanced.[33]

[33] For a more thorough discussion of this point, see J. P. Austin, "World Marketing as a New Force for Peace," *Journal of Marketing,* January, 1966, pp. 1–3; Peter F. Drucker, "Marketing and Economic Development," *Journal of Marketing,* January, 1958, pp. 252–59; E. J. McCarthy, "Are Effective Marketing Institutions Necessary and Sufficient Conditions for Economic Development?" and J. C. Abbott, "Marketing Studies, Organization, Methods and Services of Development and Settlement Areas," in *Proceedings* of 1963 Winter Conference of the American Marketing Association.

QUESTIONS AND PROBLEMS

1 What distinction can be made between marketing and production? Of what use is this distinction?

2 It appears that competition sometimes leads to inefficiency in the operation of the economic system in the short run. Many people argue for monopoly in order to eliminate this inefficiency. Discuss this solution to the problem of inefficiency.

3 How would officially granted monopolies affect the operation of our economic system? Specifically, consider the effect on allocation of resources, the level of income and employment, and the distribution of income? Is the effect any different than if a monopoly were obtained through winning out in a competitive market?

4 Discuss the merits of various economic system objectives. Is the objective of the American economic system sensible? Do you feel more consumer satisfaction might be achieved by permitting some sociologists or some public officials to determine how the needs of the lower-income or less-educated members of the society should be satisfied? If you approve of this latter suggestion, what educational or income level should be required before an individual is granted free choice by the social planners?

5 Discuss the conflict of interests among production, finance, accounting, and marketing executives. How does this conflict contribute to the operation of an individual business? Of the economic system? Why does this conflict exist?

6 Why does the text indicate that the adoption of the marketing concept will encourage more efficient operation of an individual business? Be specific about the impact of the marketing concept on the various departments of a firm.

7 What impact does legislation have on the efficiency or inefficiency of micro- and macro-marketing?

8 Should the goal of our economy be maximum efficiency? If your answer is yes, efficiency in what? If not, what should the goal be?

9 Cite an example of a critic using his own value system when evaluating marketing.

10 Is there any possibility of a pure competition economy evolving naturally? Could legislation force a pure competition economy?

11 Comment on the following statement: "Ultimately, the high cost of marketing is due only to consumers."

12 Should the consumer be king? How should we decide this issue?

Appendix: Marketing arithmetic

The beginning business student must become familiar with the essentials of the "language of business." Businessmen commonly use accounting terminology when discussing costs, prices, and profit. So it is essential for the student to have an understanding of this terminology if the use of accounting data is to become a practical tool in analyzing marketing problems.

The following discussion introduces the basic ideas underlying the operating statement, some commonly used ratios relating to the operating statement, markups, and the markdown ratio which is frequently used in retailing. Other analytical techniques are introduced at various parts in the text and so are not treated separately here.

The operating statement

An operating statement for a wholesale or retail business, commonly referred to as a profit and loss statement, is presented in Figure 1. A complete and detailed statement is presented so you will see the framework throughout the discussion, but the amount of detail on an operating statement is by no means standardized. Many companies present financial statements in considerably less detail than that shown. Their emphasis is placed on clarity and readability, rather than detail. To understand an operating statement, however, one must be aware of the items of which it is composed.

The operating statement is, in fact, only a simple description – or model – of the company's operations. It presents a summary of the financial results of the operations of the company over a specified period of time. Some beginning students may object that the operating statement is not simple in its description or summary of ordinary business operations, but as we shall see, this is not the case. *The primary purpose of the operating statement is the determination of the net profit figure, and presentation of data to support that figure.*

Figure A–1 Operating statement for XYZ Company for the (year) ended (December 31, 197X)

Gross sales			$54,000
Less: Returns and allowances			4,000
Net sales			$50,000
Cost of goods sold			
Beginning inventory at cost		$ 8,000	
Purchases at billed cost	$31,000		
Less: Purchase discounts	4,000		
Purchases at net cost	$27,000		
Plus freight-in	2,000		
Net cost of delivered purchases		29,000	
Cost of goods available for sale		$37,000	
Less: Ending inventory at cost		7,000	
Cost of goods sold			30,000
Gross margin (gross profit)			$20,000
Expenses			
Selling expenses			
Sales salaries	$ 6,000		
Advertising expense	2,000		
Delivery expense	2,000		
Total Selling Expense		$10,000	
Administrative expense			
Office salaries	$ 3,000		
Office supplies	1,000		
Miscellaneous administrative expense	500		
Total Administrative Expense		4,500	
General expense			
Rent expense	$ 1,000		
Miscellaneous general expenses	500		
Total General Expense		1,500	
Total Expenses			16,000
Net Profit from Operation			$ 4,000

Only three basic components

The basic components of an operating statement are sales, which are derived from the sale of goods or services; the costs which are incurred in the making and selling process; and the balance (called profit or loss), which is merely the difference between sales and costs. So there are only three basic elements in the statement: *sales, costs, and profit.*

Time period covered may vary

There is no single length of time which an operating statement covers. Rather, statements are prepared to satisfy the needs of a particular business. This may be at the end of each day or at the end of each week. Usually, however, an operating statement summarizes results of transactions over a period of one month, three months, six months, or a full fiscal year. Since this time period does vary with the company preparing the statement, this information is included in the heading of the statement, as follows:

Operating Statement
for
XYZ Company
For the (period) ended (date)

Management uses of operating statements

Before proceeding to a more detailed discussion of the elements of our operating statement, note some of the uses for such a statement. A glance at Figure A–1 reveals that a wealth of information is presented in a clear and concise manner. With this information, management can readily determine the *percentage of its net sales* represented by the cost of goods sold, by the gross margin, by expenses, and by the net profit. *Opening and closing inventory figures* are available, as is the amount spent during the period for the *purchase of goods for resale*. The *total expenses* are classified for the purpose of comparison with previous statements and control of these expenses.

All of this information is of vital interest to the management of a company. Assume that a particular company prepares monthly operating statements. It should be obvious that a series of these statements represents a valuable tool for the direction and control of the business. By comparing results obtained from one month to the next, management can uncover adverse trends in the sales, expense, or profit areas of the business, and take corrective action.

A skeleton statement gets down to essential details

Let us refer to Figure A–1 and begin to analyze this seemingly detailed statement. The intention at this point is to acquire first-hand knowledge of the composition of the operating statement.

As a first step, suppose we take all the items that have dollar amounts extended to the third, or right-hand, column. Using these items only the operating statement looks as follows:

Gross sales	$54,000
Less: Returns and allowances	4,000
Net sales	$50,000
Less: Cost of goods sold	30,000
Gross margin	$20,000
Less: Total expenses	16,000
Net profit (loss)	$ 4,000

Is this a complete operating statement? Note that the skeleton statement differs from Figure A–1 only in the matter of supporting detail. It is obvious that we have a complete operating statement, because all of the basic elements are included. In fact, the only items we *must* list to have a *complete* operating statement are:

Net sales	$50,000	
Less: Costs	46,000	
Net profit (loss)	$ 4,000	

These three items are the *essence* of an operating statement. All other subdivisions or details are merely useful refinements.

The next step is to define and explore the meaning of the terms that are used in the skeleton statement.

The first item is sales. But just what do we mean by sales? The term *gross sales*, as used in this discussion, is the total amount of original billing to all customers. It is inevitable, however, that there will be a certain amount of customer dissatisfaction, or just plain errors in ordering and shipping goods. This results in *returns and allowances.*

A return is the act of a customer bringing or sending back goods he has purchased. The company either refunds the purchase price or allows the customer an equal amount in credit or exchange goods.

An allowance occurs when a customer is not fully satisfied with the purchased goods for some reason, and the company grants a price reduction on the original invoice but the customer keeps the goods.

These refunds and reductions must be taken into account when the sales figure for the period is computed. We are only interested in the revenue which the company manages to retain – that is, the actual sales dollars received or which will be received. Therefore, all reductions, refunds, cancellations, and so forth – made because of returns and allowances – are deducted from the original total (gross sales) to give us the net sales figure. This may be illustrated as follows:

Gross sales	$54,000	
Less: Returns and allowances	4,000	
Net sales	$50,000	

Meaning of "cost of goods sold"
The next item appearing in the operating statement, cost of goods sold, shows the total value (at cost) of all the goods sold during the period. We will discuss the computation of *cost of goods sold* later. Meanwhile, merely note that after the cost of goods sold figure is obtained, it is subtracted from the net sales figure to get the amount of gross margin.

Meaning of "gross margin" and "expenses"
Gross margin, or gross profit, may be defined as the funds available to cover the cost of selling the goods and managing the business (and hopefully, to provide a profit after these expenses have been met).

Selling expense commonly is the major expense below the gross margin. It should be noted that in Figure A–1 all expenses are deducted from the gross margin to arrive at the net profit figure. The expenses, in this case, are the selling, administrative, and general expenses. Notice that the cost of goods purchased and sold is not included in this total expense figure—it has been deducted previously from net sales to determine gross margin.

The net profit figure at the bottom of the statement shows what the company has earned through its operations during this particular period. It is the amount left after the cost of goods sold and the expenses have been deducted from net sales.

Detailed analysis of sections of operating statement

Cost of goods sold for a wholesale or retail concern

The cost of goods sold section includes details which are used to determine the cost of goods sold ($30,000), which is placed in the third column. But just what do we mean when we say cost of goods sold? By this term we mean *the cost value of goods sold—that is, actually removed from the company's control—and not the cost value of goods on hand at any given time.*

In Figure A–1, it is obvious that beginning and ending inventory, purchases, purchase discounts, and freight-in are all necessary in the computation of cost of goods sold. If we pull the cost of goods sold section from the operating statement, it appears as follows:

Cost of goods sold		
Beginning inventory at cost		$ 8,000
Purchases at billed cost	$31,000	
Less: Purchase discounts	4,000	
Purchases at net cost	$27,000	
Plus: Freight-in	2,000	
Net cost of delivered purchases		29,000
Cost of goods available for sale		$37,000
Less: Ending inventory at cost.		7,000
Cost of goods sold		$30,000

The inventory figures merely indicate the cost of merchandise on hand at the beginning of and at the end of the period the statement covers. These figures may be obtained by a physical count of the merchandise on hand on these dates, or they may be estimated through a system of perpetual inventory bookkeeping which would show the inventory balance at any given time. The methods used in determining the inventory should be as accurate as possible, since these figures have a decided effect upon the cost of goods sold during the period, and consequently upon the net profit realized.

The net cost of delivered purchases must take into account freight charges incurred and purchase discounts received, since these items affect the cash actually spent to procure the goods and bring them to the place of business. A purchase discount is merely a reduction of the original invoice amount agreed upon at the time the goods were purchased, or which is given in consideration of prompt cash payment of the amount due. The total of such discounts is subtracted from the original invoice cost of purchases to determine the *net* cost of purchases. To this figure we add the freight charges for bringing the goods to the place of business. This gives the net cost of *delivered* purchases. When the net cost of delivered purchases is added to the *beginning* inventory at cost, we have the total cost of goods available for sale during the period. If we now subtract the *ending* inventory at cost from the cost of the goods available for sale, we obtain the cost of goods sold.[1]

Cost of goods sold for a manufacturing concern

Figure A–1 illustrates the way the proprietor of a wholesale or retail business would arrive at his cost of goods sold. Such a business would *purchase* finished goods and resell them. In a manufacturing concern, the purchases section of this operating statement would be replaced by a section called "cost of goods manufactured." This section would then take into account purchases of raw materials and parts, direct and indirect labor costs, and factory overhead charges (such as heat, light, and power) necessary in the production of the finished goods. The cost of goods manufactured would be added to the beginning finished-goods inventory, just as the net cost of delivered purchases has been, to arrive at the cost of goods available for sale. Frequently, a separate cost of goods manufactured statement is prepared, and only the total cost of production is shown in the operating statement. See Figure A–2 for an illustration of the cost of goods sold section of an operating statement for a manufacturing concern.

Expenses

Expenses typically appear below the gross margin. They usually include the costs of selling, and administering the business. They do not include the cost of goods, either purchased or produced.

There is no specific method for classifying the expense accounts or for arranging them on the operating statement. They might just as easily have been arranged alphabetically, or according to amount, with the largest being placed at the top, and so on down the line. In a business of any size, though, it is desirable to group the expenses in some manner and to use subtotals by groups for analysis and control purposes. This was done in Figure A–1.

Summary on operating statements

The statement presented in Figure A–1 contains all of the major categories in an operating statement, together with a normal amount of supporting detail. Further detail could be added to the statement under any of the major categories without changing the nature of the state-

---

[1] One important point should be noted in connection with cost of goods sold. Inventory valuation methods vary from one company to another, and these different methods may cause large relative differences in the operating statements of these companies. Consult any basic accounting textbook for descriptions of the various inventory valuation methods.

Figure A–2 Cost of goods sold section of an operating statement for a manufacturing firm

Cost of goods sold		
Finished goods inventory (beginning)	$ 20,000	
Cost of goods manufactured (Schedule 1)	100,000	
Total cost of finished goods available for sale	$120,000	
Less: Finished goods inventory (ending)	30,000	
Cost of goods sold		$ 90,000

Schedule 1. Schedule of Cost of Goods Manufactured

Beginning work in process inventory			$ 15,000
Raw materials			
Beginning raw materials inventory		$ 10,000	
Net cost of delivered purchases		80,000	
Total cost of materials available for use		$ 90,000	
Less: Ending raw materials inventory		15,000	
Cost of materials placed in production		$ 75,000	
Direct labor		20,000	
Manufacturing expenses			
Indirect labor	$4,000		
Maintenance and repairs	3,000		
Factory supplies	1,000		
Heat, light, and power	2,000		
Total manufacturing expenses		10,000	
Total manufacturing costs			105,000
Total work in process during period			$120,000
Less: Ending work in process inventory			20,000
Cost of goods manufactured			$100,000

Note: Last item, cost of goods manufactured, is used in the operating statement to determine the cost of goods sold, as above.

ment. The amount of detail normally is determined by the use to which the statement will be put. A stockholder may be presented with a sketchy operating statement, while the one prepared for internal company use may incorporate a great amount of detail.

We have already seen that the elimination of some of the detail in Figure A–1 did not affect the essential elements of the statement—net sales, costs, and net profit. Whatever further detail is added to the statement, its purpose is to help the reader to see how these three figures have been determined. A very detailed statement might easily run to several single-spaced pages, yet the nature of the operating statement would remain the same.

Computing the stockturn rate

A detailed operating statement can provide the data which is needed to compute the stockturn rate. This is a measure of the number of times the average inventory is sold during a year. Note, the stockturn rate is related to the turnover during the course of a *year, not the* length of time covered by a particular operating statement.

The stockturn rate is an especially important measure because it shows how rapidly the firm's inventory is moving. Some lines of trade typically have slower turnover than others, but a decrease in the rate of turnover in a particular business can be very alarming. For one thing, it may mean that the firm's assortment of goods is no longer as attractive as it was. Also, it may mean that more working capital will be needed to handle the same volume of sales. Most businessmen pay considerable attention to the stockturn rate, attempting to achieve more rapid turnover.

Three methods, all basically similar, can be used to compute the stockturn rate. Which method is used depends somewhat on the data which is available. These three methods are shown below and usually give approximately the same results.[2]

$$\frac{\text{Cost of goods sold}}{\text{Average inventory at cost}} \tag{1}$$

$$\frac{\text{Net sales}}{\text{Average inventory at selling price}} \tag{2}$$

$$\frac{\text{Sales in units}}{\text{Average inventory in units}} \tag{3}$$

The computation of the stockturn rate will be illustrated for formula (1), since all are similar. The only difference is that the cost figures used in formula (1) are changed to a selling price or numerical count basis in formulas (2) and (3). It is necessary, regardless of the method used, to express both the numerator and denominator of the formula in the same terms.

Using formula (1), the average inventory at cost is determined by adding the beginning and ending inventories at cost and dividing by 2. This average inventory figure is then divided *into* the cost of goods sold (expressed in cost terms) to obtain the stockturn rate.

For example, suppose the cost of goods sold for one year were $100,000. Beginning inventory was $25,000 and ending inventory $15,000. Adding the two inventory figures and dividing by 2, we obtain an average inventory of $20,000. We next divide the cost of goods sold by the average inventory ($100,000 divided by $20,000) and get a stockturn rate of 5.

Further discussion of the application of the stockturn rate is found in Chapter 24.

Operating ratios help analyze the business

The operating statement data is also used for a number of other purposes. In particular, many businessmen calculate what are called "operating ratios" from their operating statements and compare these

[2]Differences will occur because of varied markups and nonhomogeneous product assortments. In an assortment of tires, for example, those with high markups might have sold much better than those with small markups, but with formula (3) all tires would be treated equally.

ratios from one accounting period to another, as well as comparing their own operating ratios with those of competitors. Such competitive data is often available through trade associations. Each firm may report its results to the trade association, and then summary results are tabulated and distributed to the members. These ratios help management to analyze their operations and also are often used for control purposes. If some expense ratios are rising, for example, those particular costs are singled out for special attention.

Operating ratios are calculated by dividing net sales into the various operating statement items which appear below the net sales level in the statement. Net sales is used as the denominator in the operating ratio, because it is this figure with which the businessman is most concerned – that is, the revenue actually received and retained in the business.

We can see the relation of operating ratios to the operating statement if we think of there being an additional column to the right of the dollar figures in an operating statement. This additional column would contain percentage figures, using net sales as 100 percent. This idea may be illustrated as follows:

Gross sales	$540.00	
Less: Returns and allowances	40.00	
Net sales	$500.00	100%
Cost of goods sold	350.00	70
Gross margin	$150.00	30%
Expenses	100.00	20
Net profit	$ 50.00	10%

The ratio of gross margin to net sales in the above illustration shows that 30 percent of the net sales dollar is available to cover sales expenses and the administration of the business, and to provide a profit. Note that the ratio of expenses to sales, plus the ratio of profit to sales, equals the 30 percent gross margin ratio. The net profit ratio of 10 percent indicates that 10 percent of the net sales dollar is left for profit.

The usefulness of percentage ratios should be obvious. The percentages are easily derived, and much easier to work with than large dollar figures. With net sales as the base figure, they provide a useful means of comparison and control.

It should be noted that because of the interrelationship of these various categories, only a few pieces of information are necessary and the others can be derived easily. In this case, for example, knowledge of gross margin percent and net profit percent would enable the derivation of expense and cost of goods sold percentages. Furthermore, the inclusion of a single dollar amount would enable the calculation of all other dollar amounts.

Markups

A markup is the amount a firm adds to its cost to obtain its selling price. The gross margin is similar to the markup, as it is the margin available to cover the costs of selling and the management of the business, as well as to provide a profit. Gross margin and the concept of markup are related because the amount added onto the unit cost of a product by a retailer or wholesaler is expected to cover the selling and administrative expenses, and to provide a profit.

The markup approach to pricing is discussed in Chapter 24, so it will not be discussed extensively here. A simple example will illustrate the idea, however. If a retailer bought an article which cost $1 when delivered to his store, then obviously he must sell it for more than this cost if he hopes to make a profit. He might add 50 cents onto the cost of the article in order to cover his selling and other costs and, hopefully, to provide a profit. The 50 cents would be the markup.

It would also be the gross margin or gross profit on that item *if* it is sold, but it should be emphasized that it is *not* the net profit. His selling expenses might amount to 35 cents, 45 cents, or even 55 cents. In other words, there is no assurance that the markup will cover his costs. Furthermore, there is no assurance that the customers will buy at his marked-up price. This may necessitate markdowns, which are discussed later.

Markup conversions Sometimes it is convenient to talk in terms of markups on cost, while at other times markups on selling price are useful. In order to have some convention, *markup (without any clarifying comment) will mean percentage of selling price.* By this definition, the 50-cent markup on the $1.50 selling price is a markup of $33\frac{1}{3}$ percent.

Some retailers and wholesalers have developed markup conversion tables so they can readily convert from cost to selling price depending on the markup on selling price they desire. To see the interrelation, we present below two formulas which can be used to convert either type of markup to the other.

Percentage markup on selling price
$$= \frac{\text{Percentage markup on cost}}{100\% + \text{percentage markup on cost}} \tag{4}$$

Percentage markup on cost
$$= \frac{\text{Percentage markup on selling price}}{100\% - \text{Percentage markup on selling price}} \tag{5}$$

In the previous example, we had a cost of $1, a markup of 50 cents, and a selling price of $1.50. We saw that the markup on selling price was $33\frac{1}{3}$ percent, and on cost, it was 50 percent. Let us substitute these percentage figures into formulas (4) and (5) to see the process of conversion of markup from one basis to another. Assume first of all that we only know the markup on selling price, and want to convert to markup on cost. Using formula (5) we obtain:

$$\text{Percentage markup on cost} = \frac{33\frac{1}{3}\%}{100\% - 33\frac{1}{3}\%} = \frac{33\frac{1}{3}\%}{66\frac{2}{3}\%} = 50\%$$

If we know, on the other hand, only the percentage markup on cost, we could convert to markup on selling price as follows:

$$\text{Percentage markup on selling price} = \frac{50\%}{100\% + 50\%} = \frac{50\%}{150\%} = 33\frac{1}{3}\%$$

These results can be proved and summarized as follows:

$$
\begin{array}{rll}
\text{Markup } \$0.50 = & 50\% \text{ of cost or } 33\frac{1}{3}\% \text{ of selling price} \\
\text{Cost } \$1.00 = & 100\% \text{ of cost or } 66\frac{2}{3}\% \text{ of selling price} \\
\hline
\text{Selling price } \$1.50 = & 150\% \text{ of cost or } 100\% \text{ of selling price}
\end{array}
$$

It is essential to see that only the percentage figures changed, while the monetary figures of cost, markup, and selling price remained the same. Notice, too, that when the selling price is used as the basis for the computation (100 percent), then the cost percentage plus the markup percentage equal 100 percent. But when the cost of the product is used as the base figure (100 percent), it is obvious that the selling price percentage must exceed 100 percent (by the markup on cost).

Markdown ratios help control retail operations

The ratios we discussed earlier were concerned with figures on the operating statement. Another important ratio, the markdown ratio, is an analytical tool which is used by many retail merchants to measure the efficiency of various departments and their whole business. But note, it is *not directly related to the operating statement*. It requires special calculations.

A *markdown* is simply a retail price reduction which is often required because the customers will not buy some items at the originally marked-up price. This refusal to buy may be due to a variety of reasons – soiling, style changes, fading, damage caused by handling, or an original markup which was too high. To dispose of these goods, the merchant offers the merchandise at a lower price.

Markdowns are generally considered to be due to "business errors," perhaps because of poor buying, too high original markups, and other reasons. Perhaps the goods were damaged or soiled on display, but this, too, may have been due to poor buying or display. Regardless of the cause, however, markdowns are reductions in the original price and are important to managers who want to obtain some measure of the effectiveness of their operations.

Markdowns are similar to allowances in that price reductions have been made. Thus, in computing a markdown ratio, markdowns and allowances are usually added together and then divided by net sales.

This markdown ratio is computed as follows:

$$\text{Markdown \%} = \frac{\$ \text{ Markdowns} + \$ \text{ Allowance}}{\$ \text{ Net sales}} \times 100$$

The 100 is multiplied times the fraction to reduce the handling of decimal points.

Returns are *not* included in the calculation of the markdown ratio. Returns are considered as "consumer errors," not business errors, and therefore are *not* included in the computation of this measure of business efficiency.

Retailers who use markdown ratios maintain a record of the amount of markdowns and allowances in each department and then divide the total by the net sales in each department. Over a period of time, these ratios gives management a measure of the efficiency of the buyers and salespersons in the various departments.

It should be stressed again that the markdown ratio has nothing to do with the operating statement. It is not calculated directly from data on the operating statement, since the markdowns take place before the goods are sold. In fact, some goods may be marked down and still not sold. Even if the marked down items are not sold, the markdowns — that is, the reevaluations of their value — are included in the calculations in the period when they are taken.

The markdown ratio would be calculated for a whole department (or profit center), and *not* individual items. What we are seeking is a measure of the effectiveness of a whole department, not how well the department did on individual items.

QUESTIONS AND PROBLEMS

1 Distinguish between the following pairs of items which appear on operating statements:
a) Gross sales and net sales.
b) Purchases at billed cost and purchases at net cost.
c) Cost of goods available for sale and cost of goods sold.

2 How does gross margin differ from gross profit? From net profit?

3 Make a list of 10 expense items that could be classified as selling or distribution expenses, and 10 items which could be classified as administrative or general expenses.

4 Why are percentage ratios figured using net sales rather than gross sales as a base figure?

5 Explain the similarity between markups and gross margin. What connection do markdowns have with the operating statement?

6 What are the essential items on an operating statement? What is an operating statement? Of what use is an operating statement to management?

7 How is gross margin obtained? What is its significance?

8 Compute the net profit for a company with the following data:

Beginning inventory (cost)	$ 15,000
Purchases at billed cost	33,000
Sales returns and allowances	25,000
Rent	6,000
Salaries	40,000
Heat and light	18,000
Ending inventory (cost)	25,000
Freight cost (inbound)	9,000
Gross sales	130,000

Appendix: marketing arithmetic

9 From the following data, draw up a retail operating statement.

Gross sales	$525,000
Purchases at net cost	325,000
Markdowns	50,000
Opening inventory at cost	120,000
Returns and allowances	75,000
Closing inventory at cost	125,000
Expenses	115,000

10 Construct an operating statement from the following data.

Returns and allowances	$ 15,000
Expenses	20%
Closing inventory at cost	60,000
Markdowns	2%
Inward transportation	3,000
Purchases	100,000
Net profit (5%)	30,000

11 Construct an income statement on the basis of the following data and compute the gross margin percentage, the net profit percentage, and the markdown percentage.

Salary expense	$ 40,000
Inward transportation	5,000
Average inventory at cost	50,000
Closing inventory at cost	40,000
Purchases at billed cost	200,000
Markdowns	41,000
Other expense	10,000
Customer returns	10,000
Gross sales	420,000
Rent	20,000
Supplies	5,000
Advertising	15,000

12 Gilberts men's store bought 100 suits to sell at $90; 50 suits sold at the original retail price; 20 were marked down $10 from the original price; and the remainder were marked down $20 from the original price before they were finally sold. Compute the markdown percentage. The cost of the suits to Gilberts was $54 each.

13 Data given:

Markdowns	$ 10,000
Gross sales	100,000
Returns	8,000
Allowances	12,000

Compute net sales and percent of markdowns.

14 (a) What percentage markups on cost are equivalent to the following percentage markups on selling price: 20, 37½, 50, and 66.67? (b) What percentage markups on selling price are equivalent to the following percentage markups on cost: 33⅓, 20, 40, and 50?

15 What net sales volume is required to secure a stockturn rate of 20 times a year on an average inventory at cost of $100,000, with a gross margin of 30 percent?

16 If the beginning inventory at cost is $50,000 and the ending inventory is $100,000, what net sales volume is required to secure a stockturn rate of 7 if the company normally has a gross margin of 30 percent?

17 Explain why markdowns are not included in operating statements? What value are they if they are not in the statement?

18 Explain how the general manager of a department store might use the markdown ratios computed for his various departments? Would this be a fair measure? Of what?

19 Explain why operating ratios may be of greater use to management than the actual dollar and cents data.

Cases

See "Guide to the use of these cases" on page 794.

Guide to the use of these cases*

Cases can be used in many ways. And the same case may be fruitfully considered several times, for different purposes.

The following cases are organized under several headings to suggest when they might be used *for the first time*. The basic criterion for placement, however, was *not* whether the subject matter of the case fit best there, but rather whether any text principles or technical terminology to be covered later in the text were needed to read the case meaningfully. Some early cases might require some consideration of Price, for example, and might be used twice, say in regard to product planning and later pricing. But cases listed under Price can be treated more effectively *after* the Price chapters have been covered.

* Some of these cases are rewritten or edited versions of cases written by my students. I want to thank the following for their creative efforts: J. Stubbs, R. Moscote, J. Speer, D. Payeur, P. Nelson, J. Helmer, C. L. Jones, J. Genung, E. Young, W. Supernaw, C. B. Jones, D. Polson, P. Abelson, D. Metz, R. Wright, D. K. Humphries, Mary Ann Boyle, T. M. Weisenberger, A. B. Patterson, Jr., C. J. Echterling, T. E. Franklin, R. Waxman, S. Coquillard, T. H. Payne, G. Kay, K. Kelly, N. Marlet, R. A Hamrick, J. Costello, M. R. Lukes, R. Sweitzer, P. V. Ellefson, and R. K. James.

Introduction to marketing management

**1
Sweeley
Foods,
Incorporated**

Sweeley Foods, Inc., is a 105-year-old Chicago-based food processor. Its multiproduct lines have achieved widespread acceptance under the "Sweeley" brand name. The company and subsidiaries engage principally in the preparing, canning, packaging, and marketing of canned and frozen foods. Beginning with beef, the company expanded its operations to include pineapple from Hawaii and other fruits, vegetables, pickles and condiments, Alaskan salmon, and can manufacturing. Operating more than 27 processing plants in the United States, Sweeley has become one of the largest U.S. food processors, with annual sales in 1968 of $348,065,000.

Until 1941, Sweeley was a subsidiary of a major midwestern meat-packing company, and many of the present executives came up through the meat-packing industry. Sweeley's president recently said: "Al-meat's (the meat-packing firm) influence is still with us. Sweeley has always been run like a meat-packer. As long as new products indicate a potential for an increase in the company's sales volume, they are produced. Traditionally there has been little, if any, attention paid to margins. We are well aware that the profits will come through good products."

In full agreement with the multiproduct-line policy was Howard Keene, a 25-year Sweeley employee and now production manager. Mr. Keene volunteered, "Volume comes from satisfying needs. We at Sweeley will can, pack, or freeze any meat, vegetable, or fruit we think the consumer might want." He also acknowledged that much of the expansion in product lines was dictated by economics. The typical plant facilities in the industry are not fully utilized. By adding new products to use this excess capacity, costs are spread over greater volume. So the production department is regularly looking for new ways to make more effective use of its present facilities.

The wide expansion of product line coupled with Sweeley's line-forcing policy has resulted in 85 percent of Sweeley's sales coming from supermarket chain stores, such as Kroger and A&P. Smaller

795

stores are generally not willing to accept the Sweeley policy which requires that any store desiring to carry the Sweeley brand name must be willing to carry the complete line of 68 varieties of fruits, vegetables, and meats. Mr. Keene explains, "We know that only large stores can afford to invest the amount of money in inventory that it would take to be adequately supplied with our products. But, the large stores are the volume! We give the consumer the choice of any Sweeley product she wants, and the result is maximum sales." Many small retailers have voiced complaints about Sweeley's policy, but they have been considered to be too small in potential sales volume per store to be of any significance.

In 1969, a stockholders' revolt concerning low profits (in 1968, they were only $5,769) resulted in Sweeley's president and two of its five directors being removed. Thomas Speh, a lawyer previously employed as staff assistant to the chairman of the board, was elected president. One of the first things Mr. Speh decided to focus on was the erratic and inadequate level of profits generated by Sweeley in the past several years. A comparison of Sweeley's results with those of the California Packing Corporation (Calpack) and some other large competitors supports Mr. Speh's concern. In the past five years, Calpack had an average profit return on shareholder's investment of 10.8 percent, H. J. Heinz averaged 9 percent, Hunt Food 6 percent, and Sweeley 3.8 percent. Further, Sweeley's sales volume, $348,065,000 in 1968, had not increased significantly from the 1956 level of $325 million, while operating costs have soared upwards. Profits for Sweeley were about $8 million in 1956. The closest they have come since then is about $6 million, in 1964.

In his last report to the Sweeley board of directors, the outgoing president blamed his failure on an inefficient marketing department. He wrote, "Our marketing department has deteriorated. I can't exactly put my finger on it, but the overall quality of marketing personnel has dropped and morale is bad. The team just didn't perform." When Mr. Speh confronted Jerry Brown, the vice-president of marketing, with the previous statement, his reply was, "It's not our fault. I think the company made a key mistake after World War II. It expanded horizontally – by increasing its number of product offerings – while competitors like Calpack were expanding vertically, growing their own raw materials and making all of their packing materials. They can control quality and make profits in manufacturing which can be used in marketing. I lost some of my best men from frustration. We just aren't competitive enough to reach the market to the extent we should with a comparable product and price."

In further conversation with Jerry Brown, Mr. Speh learned more about the nature of Sweeley's market. Although all the firms in the food-processing industry advertise extensively to the consumer market, there has been no appreciable increase in the size of the market for processed foods. Further, consumers are not very selective. If they can't find the brand of food they are looking for, they will pick up another brand rather than go without a basic part of their diet. No firm in the industry has much effect on the price at which its products are sold. Chain store buyers are used to paying about the same case rate for any competitor's product and will not exceed it. They will, however, charge any price they wish on a given brand sold at retail, (i.e., a 48-can case of sweet peas might be purchased from any supplier for $5.83, no matter whose product it is. Generally, the shelf price for each is no more than a few pennies different, but chain stores occasionally attract customers by placing a well-known brand on "sale.")

At this point Mr. Speh is wondering why Sweeley is not as profitable as it once was. Also, he is puzzled as to why the competition is putting products on the market with low potential sales volumes. For example, one major competitor recently introduced a small line of dietary fruits and vegetables, with a potential sales volume so small that virtually every nationally known food processor had previously avoided such specialization.

Discuss Sweely's policies and what it might do to improve its present situation.

**2
United States
Maize
Company**

The United States Maize Co. is the largest of about 50 firms which specialize in the production of consumer products made from corn. In 1969, 90 percent of the company's $21 million profit on sales of $634,789,000 was made on corn flakes, corn chips, tortillas, and several varieties of canned corn. About half of the U.S. Maize's products are sold under its own brand name, while the remaining products are packaged for retailers and wholesalers, under their own brands.

Walter (Joe) Shaw, director of marketing for U.S. Maize, explained the firm's success story, "Our high sales volume is a result of U.S. Maize's products being used by our customers as part of their daily diet." In the face of strong competition, U.S. Maize has been able to achieve its impressive sales through the regular introduction of new products, which are slight variations in taste, ingredients, etc., of present ones, and efficient distribution through a vast wholesaler network. Mr. Shaw credits demand created through national and local advertising for the ease with which his salesmen are able to write orders at the wholesaler's location. The wholesaler is mainly responsible for the distribution of U.S. Maize products to as many retail outlets as will handle them.

U.S. Maize has always maintained an excellent staff of food research chemists. The company president, Mr. White, relies heavily on his chemists for new ways to use corn so that the company's sales will always be bolstered by new products.

From 1968 to 1970, the company spend $2.3 million developing a new product which the chemists expect will revolutionize the food industry by providing a more efficient packaging material.

The product, "Sol-Pak," is a transparent, edible, water-soluble, starch film. A chemically modified form of a high amylose starch from a corn hybrid, Sol-Pak was thought by the chemists to be especially valuable in the food-packaging industry. While the film is slightly hazy, soft, and stretchable, it is almost instantly soluble in hot water. (While soluble in cold water, it takes about five minutes.) Sol-Pak is a good gas and flavor barrier, and has excellent oil and grease resistance. It is stable, will not oxidize, and will not impart flavor or color to any food product when dissolved. It does not pick up moisture readily from the air and does not become tacky or sticky as long as the relative humidity is below 75 percent.

Mr. White called Joe Shaw to his office when Sol-Pak was ready to be placed on the market. He said, "Joe, you've heard about our new invention, haven't you? It's called Sol-Pak and we want you and your staff to sell it. The chemists have recommended that your target customers most likely should be packagers and distributors of portion-packed granular or powdered food preparations, drink preparations, frozen meat, frozen vegetables and fruits, and other applications where specific amounts of water are to be added as customers prepare food. Well, now it's your ball game. Go get them!"

Mr. Shaw left the office in a daze. Several questions were bothering him about his responsibility for selling Sol-Pak. While he realized the antipollution implications of the company's new product because it dissolved in water, left no hard waste, and did not require disposal, he wondered if his men were capable of selling Sol-Pak to unfamiliar markets. Shaw's assistant, Terry Clark, doubted that many consumers would be greatly impressed with a Sol-Pak–wrapped product. Further, he felt that products sold in Sol-Pak might need radically new methods of storage both at home and in the stores, since the material is flexible and will mold itself to the shape of the product.

Some cost analysis indicated that, in a typical application, the cost of using Sol-Pak would be about 15 percent higher than that of using conventional packaging materials. (Mr. White had already set the price.) Further, it appeared that the new product offered only minor improvements over competitors' earlier (unsuccessful) efforts to market water-soluble packaging materials. As a result, the sales staff doubted that very many potential customers would be willing to pay the price premium.

In a laboratory test conducted by Mr. Clark, it was discovered that Sol-Pak wrappings dissolved from contact with natural juices of frozen foods when the foods were left out to thaw. When Mr. Clark told Mr. Shaw, the marketing director replied that the chemists hadn't even bothered to clear the product with the Food and Drug Administration.

Meanwhile, U.S. Maize was moving into full-scale production in anticipation of the demand to be stimulated by the marketing department.

Discuss the role played by the marketing department of the U.S. Maize Co. in the development of "Sol-Pak." How should the marketing department have been utilized in planning the marketing of Sol-Pak? What happens now?

Mike Wren is a 26-year-old ex-Navy frogman and lifelong resident of Traverse City, Michigan, a beautiful summer resort area situated on Grand Traverse Bay along the eastern shore of Lake Michigan. The permanent population is about 20,000, and this more than trebles in the summer months.

Mike spent seven years in the Navy after high school graduation, returning home in June, 1968. Mike decided to go into business for himself, after he was unable to find other satisfactory work in the Traverse City area. He established Wren's Carpet and Furniture Cleaners. Mike felt that his accumulated savings would enable him to establish the business without borrowing any money. His estimate of required expenditures were: $2,900 for a used panel truck, $425 for a steam cleaning machine adaptable to carpets and furniture, $270 for a heavy-duty commercial vacuum cleaner, $50 for special brushes and attachments, $75 for the initial supply of cleaning fluids and compounds, and $200 for insurance and other incidental expenses. This total of $3,920 still left Mike with about $2,800 in savings to cover living expenses while getting started.

One of the reasons Mike chose this line of work is his previous work experience. From the time he was 16, Mike had worked part-time for Charles Balcom. Mr. Balcom operated the only other successful carpet-cleaning firm in Traverse City. (One other firm operated in Traverse City but was rumored to be near bankruptcy.)

Mr. Balcom prided himself on quality work and had gained a loyal clientele. Specializing in residential carpet cleaning, Balcom had been able to build a strong customer franchise. For 35 years, Balcom's major source of new business has been retailer recommendations and satisfied customers who told friends about the quality service received from Mr. Balcom. He is so highly thought of that the leading carpet and furniture stores in Traverse City always recommend Balcom's as "preventive maintenance" in quality carpet and furniture care. Often Balcom is entrusted with the keys to Traverse City's finest homes for months at a time when owners are out of town and want Balcom's services. Balcom's customers are so loyal, in fact, that a Vita-Clean national household carpet-cleaning franchise found it next to impossible to compete with him. Even price cutting was not an effective weapon against Mr. Balcom.

Mike Wren felt that he knew the business as well as Mr. Balcom, having worked for him many years. Mike was anxious to reach his $20,000-per-year sales goal because he thought this would provide him with a comfortable living in Traverse City. While aware of opportunities for carpet cleaning in businesses, office buildings, motels, etc., Mike felt that the sales volume available there was only about $7,000, because most businesses maintained their own cleaning staffs. As he saw it, his only opportunity was direct competition with Balcom.

To get started, he allocated $530 to advertise his business in the local newspaper. With this money he was able to purchase two half-page ads and have enough left over to buy daily three-line ads in the classified section, listed under Miscellaneous Residential Services, for 52 weeks. All that was left was to paint a sign on his truck and wait for business to "catch on."

Mike had occasional customers and was able to gross about $100 a week. He had, of course, expected much more. These customers were usually Balcom regulars who, for one reason or another (usually stains, spills, or house guests), weren't able to wait the two weeks required until Balcom could work them in. While these people did admit that Mike's work was of the same quality as Balcom's, they preferred Balcom's "quality care" image that had been built up over 35 years of established work. On several occasions Mike did get more work than he could handle. This happened during April and May, when resort owners were preparing for summer openings and owners of summer homes were ready to "open the cottage." The same rush repeated itself in September and October as resorts and homes were being closed for the winter. During these months, Mike was able to gross about $100–$120 a day, working 10 hours.

Toward the end of his first year in business, Mike Wren began to have thoughts about quitting. While he hated to think of the prospects of having to leave Traverse City, he couldn't see any way of making a living in the carpet and furniture cleaning business in Traverse. Mr. Balcom had the whole residential market sewed up, except in the rush seasons and for people who needed fast cleaning.

Why wasn't Mike able to reach his goal of $20,000? Is there any way Mike can stay in business?

4
Mid-State
Manufac-
turing
Company

Mid-State Manufacturing Co. is a large manufacturer of basic chemicals and polymer resins, located in Pennsylvania.

Bob Zicuti, a bright young engineer, has been working for Mid-State as a research engineer in the polymer resins laboratory. His job is to do research on established resins to find new, more profitable applications for resin products.

During the last five years, Bob has been under intense pressure from top management to come up with an idea that would open up new markets for the company's foamed polystyrene.

Two years ago, Bob developed the "spiral dome concept," a method of using the foamed polystyrene to make dome-shaped roofs and other structures. He described the procedure for making domes as follows:

> The construction of a spiral dome involves the use of a specially designed machine which bends, places, and bonds pieces of plastic foam together into a predetermined dome shape. In forming a dome, the machine head is mounted on a boom, which swings around a pivot like the hands of a clock, laying and bonding layer upon layer of foam board in a rising spherical form.

According to Bob, polystyrene foamed boards have several advantages:

1. Foam board is stiff, but capable of controlled deformation and can be bonded to itself by heat alone.

2. Foam board is extremely lightweight and easy to handle. It has good structural rigidity.
3. Foam board has excellent and permanent insulating characteristics. (In fact the major use for foamed board is as an insulator)
4. Foam board provides an "excellent" base on which to apply a variety of surface finishes.

With his fine speaking and reasoning abilities, Bob had little trouble convincing top management of the soundness of the idea.

According to a preliminary study carried out by the marketing department, the following were areas of construction that could be served by the domes:

1. Bulk storage.
2. Cold storage.
3. Educational construction.
4. Industrial tanks (covers for).
5. Light commercial construction.
6. Planetariums.
7. Recreational construction (such as a golf course starter house).

The study was based on uses for existing dome structures. Most of the existing domes are made out of concrete or some cement base material. It was estimated that considerable savings would be realized by using foam boards, due to the reduction of construction time.

Because of the new technology involved, the company decided to do its own contracting (at least for the first four to five years after starting the sales program). It felt this was necessary to make sure that no mistakes were made by inexperienced contractor crews. For example, if not applied properly, the plastic may burn.

After building a few domes to demonstrate the concept, the company contacted some leading architects across the country. Reactions were as follows:

> It is very interesting, but you know that the Fire Marshal of Detroit will never give his OK.
>
> Your tests show that foamed domes can be protected against fires, but there are no *good* tests for unconventional building materials as far as I am concerned.
>
> I like the idea, but foam board does not have the impact resistance of cement.
>
> We design a lot of recreational facilities and kids will find a way of sawing holes into the foam.
>
> Building codes around L.A. are written for wood and cement structures. Maybe when the codes change.

After this unexpected reaction, management did not know what to do. Bob still thinks the company should go ahead. He feels that a few reports of well-constructed domes in leading newspapers would go a long way toward selling the idea.

What should Mid-State do? Why did it get into the present situation?

R. R. Tank Cars, Inc., is a division of a large corporation in the transportation industry. This division manufactures railroad tank cars and dry bulk carriers, either for sale to outsiders or to the leasing division of the corporation.

Last year, the division accounted for almost one fourth of the corporation's net profit of $25 million, on a production of over 3,000 railroad cars.

The industry consists of a total of five producers of railroad tank cars, with R. R. Tank Cars, Inc., being the largest by far in terms of sales and production capacity. This advantage has forced the competitors to become extremely vigorous, especially in product innovation. But the R. R. Tank Cars engineers have always been able to place a close substitute or a superior version on the market soon after a competitive innovation.

The sales staff for the division is completely separated from the manufacturing department, with sales offices in all major transportation centers. The sales staff is extremely active and effective in terms of sales contacts, customer relations, dispersion of product information, and obtaining sales. Whenever a need arises for a new type of car, or a modification to an existing model, the sales staff contacts the design engineers at the manufacturing plant. The design engineers supply a preliminary design and cost estimates to the sales staff, so that specific details on capacity, size, cost, and so on may be shown to a potential customer.

The design engineering department is manned by a staff of very competent engineers versed in the various technical areas needed to design railroad cars. The department is responsible to the manager of the manufacturing department. As of late, this manager has received numerous complaints from the engineering department about the methods of the sales staff.

The problem came to a peak recently when the sales staff returned with a rather large order for a radically new type of tank car. The engineering department had previously provided preliminary designs and cost estimates to the sales staff, but the sales staff announced that what they had sold had little relation to the preliminary designs. Instead it was completely different from such designs.

The complaints of the engineering department can be summarized as follows:

> The sales staff comes in here and asks us for a preliminary design for a new car, and we break our backs to provide them with such information on very short notice. Then they have the gall to come back and tell us that they have sold a completely different car, for which we have done no work. It seems to me that they will sell anything the market wants, instead of what we design for them.

Another point of irritation to the engineers is the sales staff "habit" of bargaining on the prices of cars with each customer. The engineers' comment on this practice was: "Hasn't anyone around here ever heard of a standard price?"

Evaluate the engineers' views. What should be done?

Customer behavior

The Auto-Vend Co. is the largest manufacturer of coin-operated vending machines in the United States. It manufactures refrigerated, nonrefrigerated, and warming coin-operated machines for the sale of carbonated beverages, milk, ice cream, cigarettes, candy, pastry, hot food, etc., by vending-machine operators. In 1967, Auto-Vend's sales were $88,360,958, all to independent vending-machine operators who stock and service the machines in their local areas. Auto-Vend has nothing to do with the consumer level of the business, but it has been active in seeking new ways to utilize vending machines. Its suggestions have greatly aided the local operators to increase sales, and have indirectly resulted in more vending-machine sales for Auto-Vend.

The management of Auto-Vend is concerned about a trend which shows increasing sales but declining profits. Profits in 1967 were $5,015,782 but fell to $4,605,220 in 1968 on sales of $99,931,116.

As a means of generating more machine sales and a higher profit, Auto-Vend became interested in the application of vending machines to high school food service operations. The company, and much of the rest of the automatic-merchandising industry, saw a potentially profitable market in feeding millions of high school children inside the nation's 25,000 high schools. (Although they saw a potential market in elementary schools as well, Auto-Vend reasoned that high school students would be more likely to have more money and the change required to operate vending machines. Therefore, high schools became the primary target for Auto-Vend.)

Auto-Vend has estimated that the potential market for food service operators in the high schools is in the order to $300 million a year. Auto-Vend expects that about $100 million worth of new machines will be needed to service this market over a five-year period.

Roy Davis, Auto-Vend's marketing vice president, was enthusiastic as he reported, "We have identified a market and a product is ready to satisfy it. All that is needed now is desire, energy, and money to bring the two together."

Several circumstances, other than the size of the potential market, prompted Auto-Vend's decision to enter the "educational" market. Some school administrators have become increasingly upset over being in the restaurant business, with its labor problems and rising food costs. School architects, working on tight design budgets, begrudge every inch of space devoted to kitchen facilities in new buildings. A rising standard of living has made school children less content with the limited fare that most school lunchrooms offer. Furthermore, there seems to be a trend towards educational administrators turning housekeeping chores over to outside contractors.

Auto-Vend's promotion to the school market is low keyed. Except for displays at school conventions and presentations to large urban school systems, it works in the background through its customers, the food service operators, supplying them facts, case histories, and cost comparisons. Auto-Vend's sales force of 25 men is responsible for calling on all operators of vending machines, including the food service operators. It was expected that the food service operator's salesmen would be the most appropriate to approach school systems.

In spite of the prior optimism about prospects in the educational market, actual sales last year were very disappointing, and this was mainly responsible for the lack of profit growth for the company as a whole. Because of the poor results, Auto-Vend's executives shifted their focus to this market and found that a number of problems had been encountered in trying to sell the high school food market.

The major opposition came from some U.S. and state government officials, some boards of education, and organized food service employees and administrators who put up a solid front to keep vending machines out. Dr. Edgar Fuller, executive secretary of a school officials' association, said regarding vending-machine companies, "We don't want them in there and we aren't going to have them in there. Vending machines are no way to serve nutritious meals to growing children." An official of the U.S. Department of Agriculture, which subsidizes school lunch programs, was just as firm. "If you give a child free choice (that is, vending-machine food), he will end up with foods other than what would be good for him: a soft drink, and if he's affluent, maybe an order of french fries, and then the educational aspect of nutritional food wouldn't be served." On the face of it, concluded this official, vending machines in schools "wouldn't be for the good of the country." Regarding the nutrition argument, vending-machine salesmen counter by saying that school dietitians can control the school's menu, whether vending machines are used or not.

Another argument against vending machines is that they would increase the cost to children. This is an especially sensitive point where attempts are being made to feed children in low-income areas. Mrs. Agnes Mae Wuest, school lunch director for the Denver, Colorado school system and a past president of the American School Food Service Association (one of the principal "antivending" groups), put it this way: "I think vending machines can serve a nutritious meal. However, I don't think it will ever taste as good or be as psychologically beneficial to the students as a hot meal served across the counter on a plate. And certainly none of the machines can compete in price."

The matter of prices and costs were of greater importance and more complicated than had been realized by the Auto-Vend executives. In fact, they just recently learned about the National School Lunch Act (P.L. 396), administered by the School Lunch Division of the U.S. Department of Agriculture. This law was passed in 1946, to assist the states, through grants-in-aid and other means, in providing an adequate supply of foods and other facilities for the establishment, maintenance, operation, and expansion of nonprofit school lunch programs. The intention was to provide lower-cost food to more children, and various regulations were adopted to guide the program. In particular, one regulation states that a school which operates its lunch programs under a fee, concession, or contract shall not be eligible for participation, even though the school operates its program on a nonprofit basis. To get a cash subsidy of 4.5 cents per school lunch, the school must serve a "Type A" lunch, which contains specified minimums of whole milk, bread, protein-rich foods, butter or fortified margarine, vegetables, and fruit. As long as schools prepare and serve such a lunch under the terms of the act, they can have vending machines in the building — for snacks and drinks. But generally these machines have been hidden away in teachers' lounges.

Some school administrators have agreed that vending machines could supply Type A meals, so that the schools could still qualify for the federal subsidy program. But, any vending machines would have to be owned by the school or the local board of education, and *not* by outside vending-machine distributors. Moreover, they agree that if the schools owned machines, there appeared to be no reason why the cost to the students would have to be any higher with vending machines if the school were covered under the National School Lunch Act.

Mr. Davis, Auto-Vend's vice president of sales, still believes in the educational market, and therefore he cannot understand why his customers, the food service operators, have lost interest in trying to develop this market.

Some of Auto-Vend's customers, however, have expressed considerable annoyance with the recent interest in the school market. The following remark is typical: "In the past, Auto-Vend has been satisfied just to sell its machines when we asked for them. When they opened up this educational market, they really hurt our business. With all the publicity developing around the vending-machine controversy, people are starting to distrust food-vending services. I wish they had made us aware of what we were going to face." And another operator said: "I've had it with that educational market. I can't compete with subsidized programs, and I don't see why Auto-Vend keeps pushing us about that market!"

What should Mr. Davis do to improve his prospects in the educational market?

7
Sloco,
Incorporated

Mr. William Sloan is the president and only stockholder of Sloco, Inc., a small, successful enterprise engaged in the restaurant and recreation business in the small town of Jefferson, the site of the state university, (population 7,000 plus 20,000 students). Mr. Sloan attended the university in the 1930's, and during his college career paid most of his educational and living expenses by selling refreshments at all of the school's athletic events. In a truly enterprising fashion, he expanded his business by hiring local high school students to assist him. The business became so profitable that it was only natural that Mr. Sloan stay on in Jefferson after graduation, renting a small building adjacent to the campus and installing a restaurant.

Over the years, his restaurant business prospered and provided Mr. Sloan with a $36,000 profit on sales of $1,462,500 in 1969. The restaurant now consists of an attractive 40-table dining room, a large drive-in facility, and free delivery of orders to any point on the campus. The only thing that hasn't substantially changed is Mr. Sloan's clientele. He estimates that his restaurant business is still over 90 percent students, and that over three fourths of his sales are made between 6 P.M. and 1 A.M. There are several other restaurants with comparable facilities in the immediate vicinity of the campus, but none of these is as popular with the university students as his "Papa Bill's."

As a result of the restaurant's success with the student market, Mr. Sloan has aimed his entire promotional effort in that direction by advertising only through the campus newspaper and over the campus and local "rock" music radio stations. In an attempt to bolster his daytime business, from time to time Mr. Sloan has used such devices as coupon mealbooks priced at 85 percent of face value. And he features daily lunch "special" plates. Nevertheless, he concedes that he has been unable to compete with the university cafeterias for daytime business.

In 1967, when Mr. Sloan was seeking a new investment opportunity, he contacted a representative of a national manufacturer of bowling equipment and supplies about the feasibility of establishing a bowling lanes operation. Jefferson didn't have such a facility at the time, and Mr. Sloan felt that both the local and university communities would provide a receptive market. He already owned a large tract of land which would be suitable for construction of the bowling lanes. The land was next to the restaurant, and he felt that such proximity would result in each business stimulating the other.

The decision was made to go ahead with the venture, and to date the results have been nothing short of outstanding. Several local and university groups have formed bowling leagues. The university's men's and women's physical education departments schedule several bowling classes at Mr. Sloan's bowling lanes each term. And the casual bowling in the late afternoons and evenings is such that at least 12 of the 16 lanes are almost always in use. Some local radio advertising is done for the bowling lanes, but not much is considered necessary by Mr. Sloan. The success of the bowling lanes has prompted the developer of a small shopping center in the "residential" part of town to make tentative plans to include a similar facility in his new development. But, Mr. Sloan believes that competition won't hurt his business because he has more to offer in his recreation center—a restaurant and bowling.

Overjoyed by the profitability of his latest investment, Mr. Sloan decided to expand his recreational center operation even further. He noted the participation of both students and local citizens in his bowling lanes and concluded that the addition of an attractive, modern billiard parlor would also have a common appeal. There were already two "poolrooms" in Jefferson. One was modern, but about 2 miles from campus. The other one was considered to be a local "hangout" and was avoided by townspeople and students. Mr. Sloan decided that distance and atmosphere were the factors which resulted in both operations being only marginally successful. Further, he felt that by offering a billiard parlor operation, he would be able to supply yet another recreational demand of his market. He obtained a loan from a local bank and proceeded to build a third building on the rear portion of his tract of land. The billiard parlor was outfitted with 12 tables, a snack bar, wall-to-wall carpeting, and a soft-music background system.

Today, eight months later, Mr. Sloan is extremely disappointed with the billiard parlor operation. After the first two or three weeks, business steadily dropped off until at the present time only one or two tables are usually in use, even during the evening hours when business at the bowling lanes is at its peak. Promotion for the billiard parlor has been combined with promotions for the other facilities, which are still doing very well.

In an effort to discover what went wrong, Mr. Sloan interviewed several of his restaurant and bowling customers. Some typical responses were:

— a coed, "Bowling in a mini-skirt is tricky enough. There's just no way you can gracefully shoot pool in one!"
— a fraternity man, "My idea of a good date is dinner at Papa Bill's, then the movies or an evening of bowling. You just can't make a good impression by taking a girl to play pool."
— Jefferson citizen, "I've never allowed my children to enter the local pool halls. What's more, as a kid I wasn't allowed either, and thus have never learned the game. It's too late to teach an old dog new tricks!"

Mr. Sloan is considering selling the billiard equipment and installing a slot-car racetrack.

Evaluate Mr. Sloan's overall position and suggest what should be done.

Inland Steel Company

Inland Steel Co. is one of the two major producers of wide-flange beams in the Chicago area. The other major producer is the U.S. Steel Corp. (USS), which is several times larger than Inland as far as production capacity on this particular product is concerned. Bethlehem Steel Co. and USS have eastern plants which produce this product. Also, there are some small competitors in the Chicago area, and foreign competition is sometimes a factor. Generally, however, U.S. Steel and Inland Steel are the major competitors in the Chicago area because typically the mill price charged by all producers is the same and the customer must pay freight from the mill. Therefore, the large eastern mills landed price would not be competitive in the Chicago area.

Wide-flange beams are one of the principal steel products used in construction. They are the "modern" version of what are commonly known as "I-beams." USS rolls a full range of wide flanges from 6 inches to 36 inches. Inland entered the field about 15 years ago when it converted an existing mill to the production of this product. This mill is limited to flanges up to 24 inches, however. At the time of the conversion, it was estimated that customer usage of sizes over 24 inches was likely to be small. In the past few years, however, there has been a very pronounced trend toward the larger and heavier sections.

The beams produced by the various competitors are almost identical, since the customers buy according to standard dimensional and physical property specifications. In the smaller size range, there are a number of competitors, but above 14 inches only USS and Inland compete in the Chicago area. Above 24 inches, USS has not had any competition.

All the steel companies sell these beams through their own sales forces. The customer for these beams is called a structural fabricator. This fabricator typically buys unshaped beams and other steel products from the mills and shapes them according to the specifications of his customer. The fabricator's customer is the contractor or owner of a particular building or structure which is being built.

The structural fabricator typically sells his product and services on a competitive bid basis. The bidding is done on the basis of plans and specifications which are prepared by an architectural or structural engineering firm and forwarded to him by the contractor desiring the bid. Although several hundred structural fabricators compete in the Midwest, relatively few account for the majority of wide-flange tonnage. Since the price is the same from all producers, they typically buy beams on the basis of availability (i.e., availability to meet production schedules) and performance (reliability in meeting the promised delivery schedule).

Several years ago, Inland production schedulers saw that they were going to have an excess of hot-rolled plate capacity in the near future. At the same time, a new production technique was developed which would enable a steel company to weld three plates together into a section with the same dimensional and physical properties and almost the same cross section as a rolled wide-flange beam. This technical development appeared to offer two advantages to Inland: (1) it would enable Inland to use some of the excess plate capacity, and (2) larger sizes of wide-flange beams could be offered. Cost analysts showed that by using a fully depreciated plate mill and the new welding process it would be possible to produce and sell larger wide-flange beams at "competitive" prices, i.e., at the same price charged by USS.

Inland executives were excited about the possibilities because they thought customers would appreciate having a second source of supply. Also, the new approach would allow the production of up to a 60-inch depth of section and an almost 30-inch width of flange. With a little imagination, these larger sizes could offer a significant breakthrough for the construction industry.

Inland decided to go ahead with the new project. As the production capacity was being converted, the salesmen were kept well informed of the progress. They, in turn, promoted this new capability, emphasizing that soon they would be able to offer a full range of beam products. Several general information letters were sent to the trade, but no advertising was used. Moreover, the market development section of the sales department was very busy explaining the new possibilities of the process, particularly to fabricators at engineering trade associations and shows.

When the new line was finally ready to go, the reaction was disappointing. In general, the customers were wary of the new product. The structural fabricators felt they could not use it without the ap proval of their customers, because it would involve deviating from the specified rolled sections. And, as long as they could still get the rolled section, why make the extra effort for something unfamiliar, especially with no price advantage. The salesmen were also plagued with a very common question: "How can you take plate which you sell for about $121 per ton and make a product which you can sell for $122?" This question came up frequently and tended to divert the whole discussion to the cost of production rather than the way the new product might be used.

Evaluate Inland's present situation. What should it do to gain greater acceptance for its new product?

9
State
Camera
Company

State Camera Co. is located in a large, midwestern city near a major university. It sells high-quality still and movie cameras, accessories, and projection equipment, including 8 and 16MM movie projectors, 35MM slide projectors, opaque and overhead projectors, and a large assortment of projection screens. Most of the sales of this specialized equipment are made to area school boards for classroom use, to industry for use in research and sales, and to the university for use in research and instruction.

State Camera also offers a wide selection of film and a specialized film-processing service. Rather than processing film on a mass production basis, however, each roll of film is given individual attention to accentuate the particular features requested by the customer. This service is used extensively by local industries who need high-quality pictures of lab or manufacturing processes for analytical and sales work.

To encourage the school and industrial trade, State Camera offers a graphics consultation service. If a customer wishes to construct a display, whether large or small, professional advice is readily available. Along with this free service, State Camera carries a full line of graphic arts supplies.

State Camera employs four full-time store clerks and two outside salesmen. These salesmen make calls on industry, attend trade shows, make presentations for schools, and assist both present and potential customers in their use and choice of visual aids.

The people who make most of the over-the-store-counter purchases are serious amateur photographers and some professional photographers who buy in small quantities. Price discounts of up to 25 percent of the suggested retail price are given to customers who purchase more than $500 worth of goods per year. Most regular customers qualify for the discount.

About a year ago, Eastman Kodak introduced the Kodak Instamatic Camera. This camera comes in several models, each offering selected features and ranging in price from $11.95 to $140. Kodak has had great success with this camera, especially in the low-price range. The features which are especially appealing are cartridge loading ("just drop it in and shoot"), no rewinding (this is done by a spring motor), and no adjustments (camera is completely automatic). The most popular film for the Instamatic is the 35MM, 2 + 2 slide film.

The camera's major appeal is to those people who typically have had difficulty with more complicated cameras, but still enjoy taking their own pictures. Kodak claims "You get a perfect picture every time."

Because the Instamatic camera is available in discount houses, drugstores, department stores, and nearly every other possible outlet, State Camera does not carry it. However, it does sell the film cartridges, which come with a mail-in processing envelope.

Andrew Machey, the manager of State Camera, felt that with so many people taking 35MM slide pictures there ought to be a good demand for some way of viewing them. Therefore, he planned a special pre-Christmas sale of inexpensive slide projectors, viewers, and home-sized projection screens. Hoping that most of these would be purchased as Christmas gifts, Machey selected some products which offered good value and discounted the prices to competitive levels, for example, projectors at $29.95, viewers at $3.95, and screens at $11.95. To promote the sale, large signs were posted in the store windows and ads were run in a Christmas gift suggestion edition of the local newspaper. This edition appeared each Wednesday during the four weeks preceding Christmas.

At these prices and with this promotion, Machey hoped to sell at least 150 projectors and screens, and 200 viewers. When the Christmas returns were in, total sales were 22 projectors, 15 screens, and 48 viewers. He was most disappointed with these results, especially because trade estimates suggested that sales of projection equipment in this price and quality range were up 300 percent over last year.

Evaluate what happened. What should Mr. Machey do in the future?

10
Beaver
Ranch
Supply
Company*

John Roth, the owner of Beaver Ranch Supply Co., was a franchised dealer of farm implements for the David Harris Co., a major manufacturer of farm implements. He bought the business in 1954 for $45,000. In 1959, he said, "If I could sell out for half that much, I'd do it tomorrow. This business is never going to be the same again, what with competition from other David Harris dealers, the soil-bank program, and the uncertainties of the weather."

Beaver Ranch Supply Co. was located in the rural community of Beaver. Beaver was located in the western part of Nebraska, in an area which specialized in wheat and cattle. The population of 1,800 did not accurately reflect the great activity in Beaver, as it was a junc-

*This case was adapted from John D. Kline and John T. Doutt, *Case Problems of Small Business in the Rocky Mountain West,* 1961, prepared by the Bureau of Business Research, University of Colorado, under a grant from the Small Business Administration, Washington, D.C., pp. 95–100.

tion for two railroads and a crossroads for three major highways. Two other villages that were smaller in size were located about 15 miles away, and Rockmont, a city of over 100,000, was located approximately 75 miles away.

John Roth had been a wheat and livestock farmer in Iowa for 17 years before moving to Beaver. After selling his farm, Mr. Roth had $45,000 clear which he paid to Claude Remington, who had been operating the David Harris agency in Beaver for a number of years. This figure covered only the inventories, fixtures, and office and shop equipment of the business. Terms of the sale were inventory at cost, and when the actual count was made, they were found to be $10,000 higher than Mr. Remington had thought. Consequently, he took a personal note from Mr. Roth in the amount of $10,000. Mr. Roth signed a lease with Remington for $250 a month for six years for the brick showroom, the quonset-type building adjoining it, and the acre of ground on which the buildings were situated.

An arrangement was made whereby Mr. Remington was to have use of office space in the showroom to sell a sizable stock of used farm machinery which he had accumulated during his years in business. After several weeks, considerable strain developed between Mr. Roth and Mr. Remington. It soon became apparent to Mr. Roth that the sale of used farm machinery by Mr. Remington was injurious to his own business. Moreover, a little experience in the business had led Mr. Roth to believe that the sales figures Mr. Remington had shown which had induced him to purchase the business had been misrepresented and that many of the sales recorded had been on the "black market" to nonfranchised dealers in other states, who then proceeded to sell the equipment at a discount. While the David Harris Co. made every effort to stop this practice, it was being carried on by some dealers in 1954 when Mr. Roth bought the business.

Finally, the note for $10,000 which Mr. Roth had understood would be held by Mr. Remington until the business got "on its feet," had instead been discounted at the Beaver National Bank on a 90-day basis. At the end of that period the bank presented the note for payment, and if it had not been for the resources of a friend of the family who paid off the loan and made a new loan to Mr. Roth, he might have had to go out of business.

Mr. Remington was ousted from his office in the building, but his departure did not end the troubled relationship between the two men. He continued to hurt the business by sending local customers for David Harris equipment across the state line to a friend of his, who gave good prices to these out-of-state people. These low prices were based upon a number of factors: (1) the merchandise could be sold with little thought for future servicing, (2) a 5 percent volume discount was granted by the David Harris Co. to all franchised dealers who met their quota, and (3) the elimination of the state sales tax. Presumably, this merchandise was caught at the ports of entry located on the main highways leading from one state to another, but it was Mr. Roth's opinion that some farm equipment got into the state without ever having a sales tax levied on it.

Other sources of competition, by 1959, were four other implement dealers in Beaver, three dealers in the two nearby villages, none of which was a David Harris dealer, and a David Harris dealer in Rockmont. The Rockmont dealer was quite wealthy, having money from other sources, and was simply seeking ways of putting his money to good use. One of the most convenient ways he could find was the financing of farm machinery at 8 percent per annum. He reasoned that he could sell his merchandise at cost and still obtain 13 percent on sales, after allowing for the 5 percent David Harris volume discount.

One unique thing about this farm implement business was the relationship between the manufacturer and the dealer. In the fall of each year, each David Harris dealer was expected to draw up a contract for the farm machinery that he thought he would need during the coming year, but he did not have an obligation to take delivery until he actually ordered a piece of machinery. He was then given 16 months from the time of the order-release until the payment was due. In the event that only part of the order was sold, the balance owed could be extended for another 16-month period. For example, if an order-release calling for two tractors was dated March 15th, actual payment for the tractors was due July 15th of the following year. In the event that only one of the tractors was sold within this 16-month period, an adjustment would be made lengthening the time until payment for the second tractor was due.

It was important to attempt to draw up an accurate contract list, because it was difficult to get machinery during the peak spring and summer season unless it was on the contract list. Some trading was done among the David Harris dealers and was expedited by the David Harris regional representative who called every two weeks, but this was not a reliable source. Mr. Roth felt that it was impossible for the David Harris Co. to know all of the differences that existed from one region to another, and this was their way of shifting some of the risk of "outguessing" the market onto the dealer. It did have the effect of limiting a dealer somewhat, however, because if a number of his sales efforts were especially successful, then he might have difficulty obtaining delivery. On the other hand, if he overestimated his sales possibilities, he would not be eligible for the 5 percent volume discount.

The David Harris Co. was willing to finance part of a dealer's inventory in trade-in machinery, but the total amount extended to any one dealer was dependent in part on whether he was keeping up-to-date on his new machinery payments. In Mr. Roth's case, it was felt that he had already exceeded his limit, and as a result, they would grant him no further financing on used machinery until the new machinery account was cleared up. This seriously hampered the sale of new machinery, as most of it involved trade-ins. Local bank connections were, in the opinion of Mr. Roth, "cattle-minded," and not "machinery-minded," and the possibility of financing new sales through this channel seemed unlikely.

"The farm implement market is definitely changing," stated Mr.

Roth. "We have a lot more custom-cutters[1] up here this year than we had last year. That means we sell more parts but fewer pieces of equipment. They buy their equipment down in Texas where the dealers go for high volume and low markup, but we just can't do that here because our volume isn't big enough and can't be made big enough. *Life* magazine ran a story last winter about the custom-cutter and all the profits he makes, and we have certainly seen the results up here this year. Many of our local ranchers never even oiled their machines. They just let the custom-cutter come in and do it for them."

"Then there is the question of the small- and medium-sized ranch. There aren't many ranches that can afford an $8,000 combine, but some people buy them anyhow. The trend in the future is going to be towards larger farms that can utilize a major investment in machinery. And they won't be buying their equipment from a small dealer like me. These people will shop around several states before they buy. They want the best price they can get. Some implement manufacturers will sell direct to a large customer, and even though David Harris will not do this themselves, this type of competition hurts me. It's bad enough already. We get men in here from as far away as 100 miles. I had a man in here last week from Corinth, which is over 80 miles north. He wanted to buy two drills and I priced them to him at $2,000. He said he could get them in Corinth for $2,000, and that he thought he should have at least $100 discount for traveling all that way. I told him to go back to Corinth and buy them. I am not putting any money into Corinth, but his local dealer of Harris equipment is. He ought to buy in his own community and boost it."

"Yesterday I had a man in here that wanted a 30 percent discount from list price. I told him I just couldn't do it because I was only allowed 20–25 percent, depending on the item. Finally, I took him to my files and showed him exactly what the merchandise cost me, and the freight I had to pay on it. He was really surprised. He thought I had a much higher markup on the equipment. So we talked it over for a while and I cut my usual markup right in half. He took it. All they want is price.

"One of the problems of a place like this is getting the right kind of help. My parts man left me last week, and I am filling in until I find someone. Right now we don't need anyone, as slow as business is. He went down the street to one of the other implement dealers. Then my mechanic got a phone call from a David Harris agency up in Logan City. I don't know if he'll go or not. You've got to have a service department to build traffic; otherwise I think I'd turn it over to some independent garage here in town.

"I sometimes wonder if I'm making any money or not. My accountant says that I am just using up my principal. You never know how

---

[1] The term "custom-cutter" refers to men who own combines and travel through the area, cutting wheat for the land owner at some agreed price.

much you are making until you sell your used machinery and get your money out of that. We carry it at trade-in value on our monthly statements, although we try to be realistic about it on our annual reports."

Sales of new David Harris equipment have been averaging about $11,000 per month during the last few years, but inventories of new equipment have been rising, from about $40,000 in 1957 to $70,000 in 1959. Sales of used machinery have been averaging only a few thousand dollars a month, but these inventories have been rising too, from about $15,000 at trade-in value in 1957 to about $30,000 in 1959. Usually the used machinery had to be sold at lower than the trade-in price. In 1957, the business showed a net profit of almost $20,000 on total sales of $217,000, including all kinds of equipment and parts. In 1958, approximately $19,000 net profit was earned on total sales of $285,000. Mr. Roth's salary of about $6,000 was included in expenses each year. The amount owed David Harris Co. has risen from an average of about $40,000 in 1957 to approximately $90,000 in 1959. It appeared that 1959 sales would be about the same as 1957.

The organization of the Beaver Ranch Supply Co. consisted of the bookkeeper, one heavy equipment mechanic who was paid $100 per week, a delivery man paid $80 per week who also helped out in the garage, a parts man who earned $75 per week, a part-time setup man paid $1.10 per hour and a full-time salesman who was paid a 5 percent commission on both new and used machinery and who was guaranteed $75 per week.

Evaluate John Roth's marketing strategy. Should he have been more "flexible" about price discounting?

11
The American Bank of Meadville

The American Bank of Meadville, Missouri, was organized in 1898 and has been in continuous operation since that time. The bank is located in a community of about 6,500 people, which is situated 35 miles south of Kansas City. Being in Scott County, Meadville is considered to be part of the Greater Kansas City metropolitan area. The county has been experiencing rapid population growth, particularly in its northern sectors. The 1960 census gave Scott County a population of 60,000. Projected population for 1970 is 145,000. Meadville's 1960 population was 5,400. The community has four local factories which employ about 700. All other local employment is in service businesses, such as clothing, grocery, drug and hardware stores. A significant number of people commute to Kansas City to work. Four buses now shuttle workers to jobs at three Kansas City plants.

Meadville is the primary retail trade center for southern Scott County. Market studies have shown that it has an effective trade radius of about 8 miles. The American Bank has been the only bank serving the community since the early 1930's, when the Farmers and Merchants Bank was liquidated. American's footings in 1966 were about $10 million, a growth of about $1.5 million over 1964.

The largest bank in the county, with footings of $11 million, is located 10 miles northeast of Meadville in the town of Hempstead. Immediately adjacent to Hempstead is its twin city of Anderson. Both communities have a combined population of about 14,000 people. The Anderson State Bank's 1966 footings were about $7 million. The Bank of Scottsdale, located at the county seat six miles northwest of Meadville, has footings of about $3.5 million. The American Bank has no other banking competition for a distance of 25 miles to the southwest, south, and southeast.

The American Bank is controlled by a prominent local physician, Dr. Yokum. He also controls the local savings and loan association and owns much real estate in the community. He exerts considerable influence upon the operating policy of the American Bank and has seen to it that American has had a very conservative image. Likewise, he has not been a strong advocate for community growth. As recently as 1960, he said, "I'm very happy with Meadville just the way it is."

The American Bank now employs about 23 people and has 5 operating officers. The executive vice president and cashier, Mr. Martin, is about 48 years old and came to American 10 years ago from The Commerce Bank of Kansas City. The assistant to the vice president is Sam Yokum, Dr. Yokum's son, a recent political science graduate of a small men's college. The three assistant cashiers are Mr. Smith (age 54), Mrs. Conti (age 60), and Mr. Sanders (age 26). Mr. Smith handles the consumer loan department and is noted in the community for his sour disposition. Mrs. Conti handles the real estate loan department and has been experiencing some health problems the past six months. In recent years an increasing proportion of Meadville's real estate financing has been handled by Piedmont Federal Savings and Loan, located 30 miles to the south in the town of Stapleton. Mr. Sanders supervises the bookkeeping department and is noted in the community for his enthusiasm and drive. He graduated from the local high school and went to work as a teller at American. Since that time, he has taken 60 hours of accounting and similar subjects in night school at the University of Missouri at Kansas City.

American occupies a large two-story building which was remodeled in 1964. In 1966, it opened a new drive-in-walk-up facility in a shopping center on North Main Street. This facility represented an investment of about $175,000, and many in the community were surprised that "old Doc Yokum" has been persuaded to go into this venture. Hours at the bank and drive-in are similar to those of other banks in the county. And the bank offers a full line of services common to banks in the area. Its interest rates and charges are now the same as other county banks.

The officers of American can always be found in the bank. No formal plan exists for its officers to make regular visits to businesses in the community. Mr. Martin tries to get out and about town, but he has found that he must spend considerable time instructing Sam Yokum in banking matters. Both Sam's and Mr. Martin's memberships in Rotary are paid by the bank, but only Mr. Martin belongs to any other community organizations. These include the local industrial development board and the Chamber of Commerce. All bank employees are encouraged to participate in church activities and Mrs. Conti is particularly active.

The American Bank advertises in two papers having concentrated circulation in the Meadville area. The bank also advertises in an "ad" paper printed at the county seat. This paper has free countywide distribution, and all of its costs are borne by its advertisers. American has no road signs of any type and does not advertise over the county's one radio station. Recent promotional efforts have included the distribution of American Bank calendars, telephone book covers, and sending congratulation messages to area high school and college graduates. In addition, a large meeting room on the bank's second floor is made available to various local organizations. No charge is made for the use of this room. This service has not been pushed, however, and only six meetings were held in this room in the past year.

Early in 1967, a group of local business and professional men were granted a state charter to establish and operate The First State Bank of Meadville. The new bank building will be 1½ blocks north of the American Bank. The board of directors of First State have announced, through local news media, that they will aggressively pursue an energetic and progressive banking policy — to give the people of Meadville the outstanding financial services needed by a rapidly growing community.

Discuss American Bank's past strategy and what they should do now.

Product

12
B & B Floral-
Gift Shoppe

The B & B Floral-Gift Shoppe is owned and operated by Bruce and Betty Douglas (a husband and wife team). Offering hundreds of varieties and arrangements of flowers, B & B also carries small gift items intended to complement a floral arrangement. Mr. Douglas serves primarily as manager and salesclerk, while Mrs. Douglas' artistic talents lend themselves more to the selection and arrangement of appropriate flowers. Since opening in 1965, sales for B & B have been gratifying. Mr. Douglas, however, is concerned about the failure of a recent addition to his gift line.

The Douglases purchased the present operation in 1965 from Rick Allen, who had been in that location for 20 years. Called Allen's Florists, the shop was then generating about $100,000 a year in business. Bruce and Betty were confident that their previous 12 years' experience owning a smaller floral shop in a tiny (pop. 6,500) resort town less than 20 miles south would enable them to become a success in their new location.

Bruce Douglas feels their new store is in an excellent location. Situated in a residential area of a northeast Indiana community of 130,000 population, the new B & B Floral-Gift Shoppe is somewhat isolated from other neighborhood stores. It is 8 blocks to the nearest store, a drugstore, and 3½ miles to the closest shopping center. But, it is near the intersection of the major north-south and east-west thoroughfares, thereby benefiting from heavy automobile traffic.

Mr. Douglas was keenly aware of his primary customers' characteristics. This perception enabled him to direct his efforts more efficiently. As a result, B & B's sales increased steadily from $150,000 at the end of 1965 to $250,000 in 1969. Most of his regular customers were women from medium- to high-income families living in the local middle-class residential areas. Also, Mr. Douglas was pleased to see that some of his "old customers" from the resort town come to B & B, probably because a strong customer acceptance had been built on friendly service and quality floral arrangements. Those customers who stopped in less frequently were assumed to be similar to the "regulars."

The largest part of the shop's business consists of weddings, funerals, parties, dances, and other big, one-time events which utilize flowers. However, about 25 percent of the purchases are by casual buyers who like to browse and chat with the Douglases. Approximately 60 percent of the sales are telephone orders, while the remaining 40 percent are made in the shop. Almost all of the telephone orders are for special, one-time events, while the walk-in traffic is divided equally between special events and spur-of-the-moment purchases. Virtually no one buys flowers on a daily or regular basis. There is some FTD (Florist Telegraph Delivery) business, but Mr. Douglas considers this to be an added service, and it constitutes only about 5 percent of his volume.

Mr. Douglas feels that flowers are fairly homogeneous, unbranded products. Therefore, he feels that he must charge competitive prices to meet those of his 14 competitors throughout the community.

The shop was remodeled in 1969, and space for all operations was doubled. To fill in the increased display area, it was decided to add several complementary gift items, such as a famous brand of candies, high-quality flowerpots and vases, a quality line of sheep- and lambskin rungs, pen-and-pencil sets, and candles. All the new lines, except the sheep- and lambskin rugs, have taken hold and have increased in sales each month since the items were added. Sales of rugs have been very disappointing. In fact, they haven't paid their way on the basis of display area allotted (about 1/50 of the total display area).

When the busiest store traffic occurs (during a three- to four-day period before traditional flower-giving days), additional help is used. When available, Lisa and Kevin Douglas, the high school–aged children of the proprietors, fill these jobs. (It was the children who suggested that the market for sheep- and lambskin rugs was growing in their high school during the last school year.) At other times, only one of the proprietors and a full-time salesclerk handle store traffic.

Samples of everything the shop has for sale are on display. The primary activity of the salesclerk is to show customers various selections which could be used for a particular occasion and then ring up the sale. Other than store display, advertising consists only of what is printed on the delivery truck, an ad in the yellow pages of the local telephone directory, and an occasional ad (five or six times per year) in the daily newspaper. None of the advertising mentions anything but flowers, because the proprietors wish to maintain their identity as florists.

Mr. Douglas is wondering if more display area, a lower price, or extra promotion by the salesclerks might increase the movement of the sheep- and lambskin rugs. Further, he is thinking of disposing of the rugs, but isn't sure what should replace them if he did.

Evaluate the B & B Floral-Gift Shoppe's present operation and why sheep- and lambskin rugs don't sell. What strategy should it follow?

**13
Khulman
Corporation**

The Khulman Corporation was formed and incorporated by Abe Khulman in 1951 under a government contract to produce lathelike spinning machines for the production of brass cartridge cases. Soon after its formation, Mr. Khulman sensed an opportunity for greater sales within the copper and brass industries, and soon developed and manufactured several high-speed tube-forming machines and double-end tube forming-machines. In 1954, automatic tube benders and extrusion presses were added to the line. Scores of these machines have been sold over the years. By 1955, Mr. Khulman had reached a reasonably large annual sales volume of $7,629,000.

In 1956, Mr. Khulman led the industry by developing and patenting a double-end, hydraulic-operated, opposed-spindle drilling machine capable of accurate, volume production, of structural steel drilling. Automatic controls were essential to realize the machine's potential for accuracy and speed. So, in 1957, a newly developed General Electric numerical control unit was coupled to the Khulman machine. The numerical control (N/C) machine was highly successful, and purchasers were enthusiastic about the possible increases in production volume which could be achieved. In 1958, the first bridge ever constructed with beams made on numerically controlled machines was completed with the aid of Khulman machines. A crowning achievement, the Khulman Corporation's development quickly became widely known. Today, the N/C machine is the largest and most profitable part of Khulman's business, with machines located around the world. With a target market including any volume user of structural steel, Mr. Khulman has regularly been able to sell such giants as General Electric, General Motors, American Bridge, White Motors, British Motors Corporation, and Bethlehem Steel.

All N/C machines are custom-built for industrial applications. Due to the relatively high cost, considerable presale negotiation is required to determine the exact specifications required for the application. Khulman sales engineers visit the customer's site, analyze the production operations, and quote a price for a machine capable of performing the operation. The N/C machines are produced on a modular construction principle with a standard price of $60,000 for the basic machine.

Price quotations are obtained by adding to the base price the estimated cost of all custom features required by the customer. (Operator-controlled machines, in contrast, are standardized and have a standard competitive price.) Prices range from $60,000 for the basic spinning machine to $700,000 for a four-spindle N/C drilling machine. When the sales engineer quotes a price, he is also careful to include an estimate of the savings possible to the customer from installation of the Khulman machine.

The manufacturing process for the Khulman machine consists primarily of assembly operations. All custom parts which are designed by Khulman engineers are subcontracted to outside foundries and machine shops. The Khulman Corporation's machining facilities are adequate only for minor finishing operations on custom parts. Standard parts, such as motors and hydraulic cylinders, are purchased from suppliers.

As Khulman achieved success with his N/C drilling machines, several companies entered the market with machines that were slightly altered to avoid patent infringements. Mr. Khulman, however, wasn't concerned about the competition, as he thought they were reaching a different market. All of the competitors produced larger, more precise machines. For example, the Khulman machine will hold a tolerance of plus or minus 0.012 inch, while the newer machines have a guaranteed reproducible accuracy of plus or minus 0.004 inches. The Khulman machine has been correspondingly less expensive than competing machines.

As the corporation's most aggressive salesman, Abe Khulman attends most capital equipment trade shows and visits potential customers' plants around the world. The only promotion, other than personal selling, is carried on at these trade shows (Khulman N/C machines were on display at Canada's "EXPO 67" and Japan's "EXPO 70"), and at demonstrations in the Khulman plant for visiting customer representatives. Sales of the N/C machines have been good, about $4,337,000 in 1969, and the corporation presently has over a three-year backlog of orders.

Despite a substantial sales volume, however, profits for the Khulman Corp. have been declining in recent years and are expected to decline further in the future. Profit margins have decreased due to the high cost of overtime production (the plant must operate 60 hours per week to meet delivery dates), and the falling prices of N/C machines. Competing manufacturers have been able to lower costs through increased productive facilities and greater standardization of machines, and have lowered their prices. As a result, the price differential between Khulman machines and competing N/C machines has decreased. Some customers who were formerly satisfied with Khulman accuracy have switched to the more accurate competing machines. This has forced down the price of the Khulman Corporation's N/C machine and consequently has lowered profits.

Evaluate the changes that have taken place in the market for Khulman machines and how Khulman has responded to them. What should the company do now?

The Chem Glas Corporation is jointly owned by the Williams Chemical Corporation and the Alton Glass Works. Six plants produce a variety of silicone products, including silicone resins, oils, greases, rubbers and insulating compounds, and hyper-pure silicon.

In April, 1968, the Chem Glas Corporation introduced a resilient foam material, an organic rubber polymer designed to replace air in tires. At the time Chem Glas's president, Dr. Norman Bruce, was reported to have boasted, "Tire manufacturers will come running! This material finally solves the problems of the solid-material tire filler. It is durable and will spread evenly to leave tires in balance." Now, in December, 1969, Dr. Bruce is perplexed that the expected high sales volume is not being realized. In fact, it is doubtful that the corporation's minimum rate of return on investment of 6 percent will ever be reached on this product.

The new product, "Poly-fil," was the result of extensive engineering research with silicones. Since Chem Glas is jointly owned, an important objective is to increase each parent company's sales of its own products through developing new uses for silicone products. In the search for new applications of its silicones, the Chem Glas sales department came across the solid-fill tire application. Project engineer Dr. John McDermott explained how Chem Glas developed Poly-fil: "Slow leaks, punctures, and blowouts have been banes of motorists since 1893 when the automobile began riding on air. Ever since then, the tire industry has had thoughts about replacing air with something else to make a tire guaranteed safe against blowouts. Companies have tried a variety of materials from a sticky ooze to plastic foam, but these either didn't wear well or they ruined the ride. We tried silicones first and they worked, producing good resistance and complete flatproofness. But, they proved only a bridge, and we started testing other less expensive organic rubber polymers. That's when we found Poly-fil."

The production process, while not yet patented, is relatively simple. In the Poly-fil tire application, a sausage-shaped strip of the material is inserted into an ordinary tire casing in the same way that inner tubes were in the 1950's and earlier. Under heat treatment, the material expands into a spongelike substance that completely fills the casing. Since the tire contains no air, there can be no blowouts. Extensive tests have shown that tires remain solid after firing bullets into them, drilling holes through them, slashing them with knives, and driving them over spikes. Further, tread wear is not affected.

Sales efforts are aimed at manufacturers of heavy-duty tires. It was expected that construction equipment, large and small trucks, military vehicles, and other commercial users would be the best market because of their frequency of blowouts caused by travel over rough terrain. Dr. McDermott explained why passenger vehicles were not part of Poly-fil's intended market: "Foam-filled tires do not possess 100 m.p.h. capabilities. At such speeds heat buildup becomes excessive and tires may blister and thump."

Facing no competition, Chem Glas decided to use its existing sales force to introduce and sell the product. These salesmen regularly call on electronics firms and other major silicone users, and are technically competent to answer any questions about the chemical properties of Poly-fil. It was also decided that advertising would not be needed, since once a potential customer heard from the salesman about Poly-fil, it was expected that he would probably be willing to buy.

Dr. Bruce uncovered several potential problems in his review of the situation. In August, 1968, the U.S. Department of Transportation and National Bureau of Standards went on record as showing great concern about the heat buildup in solid-fill tires. (Dr. Bruce thought that this was no real problem, since Poly-fil had already been proven at 70 m.p.h.) Weight and cost were also cited as problems. Foam-filled tires weigh about twice as much as ordinary tires and cost about three times as much (for example, $110 for an average truck tire and $342 for a comparable Poly-fil). Also, they require more horsepower and improved suspension systems for operation. But, Dr. Bruce feels that these disadvantages are overcome by the avoidance of blowouts and the increased load-bearing capacity of about 10 percent.

At a recent meeting of the truck manufacturers' national trade association, Dr. Bruce reiterated his faith in the solid-fill tires. He is reported to have said, "Foam fillers have been around research labs for 10 years. But tire men have become convinced that these materials show little promise as fillers in commercial tires. So, without much support, we at Chem Glas have kept your problems in mind and have retained an enthusiasm for foam. Our interest in silicone compounds led us to believe that their resistance to heat might suit them ideally for the interiors of tires. The result is our new Poly-fil, a unique concept in tire design."

Why did Chem Glas get into its present situation? Could it have been avoided?

15
Block Phar-
maceutical
Company

The Block Pharmaceutical Company is a well-known manufacturer of high-quality cosmetics and ointments. A little over a year ago, Mr. Fine, the president of Block, was scanning the income statements for the last three quarters and did not like what he saw. At the next board meeting he stated that Block should be showing a larger profit. It was generally agreed that the reason for the profit decline was that the firm had not added any new products to its line during the last two years.

Management was directed to investigate this matter and remedy it if possible.

Mr. Fine immediately requested a report from the product-planning group and found that it had been working on a new formula for a toothpaste that might be put into production immediately if a new product were needed. Mr. Archer, the head of the research department, assured Mr. Fine that the new ingredients in this toothpaste had remarkable qualities. Clinical tests had consistently shown that the new, as yet unnamed, dentifrice cleaned teeth better and prevented decay significantly more efficiently than the many toothpastes furiously battling for prominence in the market. Based on these tests, Mr. Fine concluded that perhaps this product was what was needed and ordered work to proceed quickly to bring it to the market.

The marketing research department was asked to come up with a name that was pleasing, and a tube and carton design. The results were reported back within two months; the product was to be called "Smile" and the package would emphasize eye-pleasing pastels.

The marketing department decided to offer Smile along with its other "prestige" products in the drugstores which were carrying the rest of Block's better-quality, higher-priced products. Block's success had been built on moving quality products through these outlets, and management felt that quality-oriented customers would probably be willing to pay a bit more for a significantly better toothpaste. Block was already well established with the wholesalers selling to these retailers and experienced little difficulty obtaining distribution for Smile.

It is now six months after the introduction of Smile, and the sales results have not been good. The established wholesalers and retailers carried the product, but relatively little was purchased by final consumers. And now many retailers are requesting that Block accept returns on Smile because obviously it is not going to catch on with consumers, despite the extremely large (matching competitors) amounts of advertising which have supported Smile.

Mr. Fine has requested the marketing research department to analyze the situation and explain the disappointing results thus far. An outside survey agency interviewed several hundred consumers and has tabulated its results. These are pretty well summarized in the following quotes:

> "The stuff I'm using now tastes good. Smile tastes terrible!"
> "I never saw that brand at the supermarket I shop at."
> "I like what I'm using . . . why change?"
> "I'm not going to pay that much for any toothpaste . . . it couldn't be *that* much better!"

What recommendation would you make to Mr. Fine? Why?

**16
Dow
Chemical
Company**

Dow Chemical Company is one of the larger chemical companies in the United States, making a diversified line of organic and inorganic chemicals, plastics, bioproducts, and metals. Research has played a vital role in the company's growth.

Recently, Dow's research laboratories developed a new product in the antifreeze line—Dowtherm 209. Much research was devoted to the technical phase, involving various experiments concerned with the quality of the components in the new product.

The antifreeze commonly used now is ethylene glycol. If it leaks into the crankcase oil, it forms a thick pasty sludge that can produce bearing damage, cylinder scoring, or a dozen other costly and time-consuming troubles for both the operator and owner of heavy-duty equipment.

Dow Chemical believed that Dowtherm 209 would be very valuable to the owners of heavy-duty diesel and gasoline trucks as well as other heavy-equipment owners. Chemically, Dowtherm 209 consists of methoxy propanol, as distinguished from the conventional glycol and alcohol products. It cannot prevent leakage, but if it does get into the crankcase, it will not cause any problems.

Dowtherm 209 has been proven in the laboratory to prevent seizing of rod and main bearings, pistons, rings, and piston pins which are common with glycol leakage. The new product will not remain in the engine oil and will cut down on the sludge residue.

At first, Dow thought it had two attractive markets for this product: (1) the manufacturers of heavy-duty equipment, and (2) the users of heavy-duty equipment. Dow salesmen have made numerous calls and so far neither type of customer has been very interested. The manufacturers are reluctant to show interest in the product until it has been proven in actual use. The buyers for construction companies and other firms using heavy-duty equipment have also been hesitant. Some felt the price was far too high for the advantages offered. Others didn't understand what was wrong with the present antifreeze and dismissed the idea of paying extra for "just another" antifreeze.

The price of Dowtherm 209 is $7.98 per gallon, which is more than twice the price of regular antifreeze. The higher price is a result of higher costs in producing the product and an increment for making a better type of antifreeze.

Explain what has happened so far. What would you do if you were responsible for this product?

Place

17 Bailey Company	John Bailey graduated in business from a large midwestern university in 1962. After a year as a car salesman, he decided to go into business for himself. In an effort to locate new opportunities, John placed several advertisements in his local newspaper—in Toledo, Ohio—explaining that he was interested in becoming a sales representative in the local area. He was quite pleased to receive a number of responses. Eventually, he became the sales representative in the Toledo area for three local manufacturers: the Sampson Drill and Press Co., which manufactured portable drills; the J. C. Peterson Co., which manufactured portable sanding machines; and the Gilbert Lathe Co., which manufactured small lathes. All of these companies were relatively small and were represented in other areas by other sales representatives like John Bailey.

Bailey's main job was to *call* on industrial customers. Once he made a sale, he would send the order to the respective manufacturer, who would, in turn, ship the goods directly to the particular customer. The manufacturer would bill the customer, and Bailey would receive a commission varying from 5 percent to 10 percent of the dollar value of the sale. It was Bailey's responsibility to pay his own expenses.

Bailey called on anyone in the Toledo area who might use the products he was handling. At first, his job was relatively easy, and sales came quickly because there was little sales competition. There are many national companies making similar products, but at that time they were not well represented in the Toledo area.

In 1964, John Bailey sold $150,000 worth of drills, earning a 10 percent commission; $50,000 worth of sanding machines, also earning a 10 percent commission; and $75,000 worth of small lathes earning a 5 percent commission. He was most encouraged with his progress and was looking forward to expanding sales in the future. He was especially optimistic because he had achieved these sales volumes without overtaxing himself. In fact, he felt he was operating at about 70 percent of his capacity.

Early in 1965, however, a local manufacturer with a very good reputation – the Porter Electrical Equipment Company – decided to manufacture a line of portable drills. It had a good reputation locally, and by April of 1965 Porter had captured approximately one half of Sampson's Toledo drill market by charging a substantially lower price. Porter was using its own sales force locally, and it was likely that it would continue to do so.

The Sampson Company assured Bailey that Porter could not afford to continue to sell at such a low price and that shortly Sampson's price would be competitive with Porter's. John Bailey was not nearly as optimistic about the near-term prospects, however. He began looking for other products he could handle in the Toledo area. A manufacturer of hand trucks had recently approached him, but he was not too enthusiastic about this offer because the commission was only 2 percent on potential annual sales of $150,000.

Now John Bailey is faced with another decision. The Howard Paint Company in Cleveland, Ohio, has made what appears to be an attractive offer. They heard what a fine job he was doing in the Toledo area and felt that maybe he could help them solve their present problem. Howard is having difficulty with its whole marketing effort and would like John Bailey to take over.

The Howard Paint Company has been selling primarily to industrial customers in the Cleveland area and is faced with many competitors selling essentially the same product and charging the same low prices. Howard Paint is a small manufacturer. Last year's sales were $80,000. They would like to increase this sales volume and could handle at least double this sales volume with ease. They have offered Bailey a 12 percent commission on sales if he will take charge of their pricing, advertising, and sales efforts in the Cleveland area. John was flattered by their offer, but he is a little concerned because there would be a great deal more travelling than he is doing at present. For one thing, he would have to spend a couple of days each week in the Cleveland area, which is 110 miles distant. Further, he realizes that he is being asked to do more than just sell. But he did have some marketing courses in college and thinks the new opportunity might be challenging.

What should John Bailey do? Why?

Vanguard Vacuum Co., a nationally known manufacturer of vacuum cleaners and accessories for home use, is concerned about a downward trend in sales. Its vacuum cleaners are manufactured in a single plant located in the Allegheny Mountain region of Pennsylvania, but are distributed from 12 company-owned or -leased warehouses throughout the continental United States. Each warehouse has at least one salesman working out of it (more if the sales area requires it) to sell the product line to selected retailers in the area. The company is the second largest of six firms that dominate the vacuum cleaner market.

Vanguard produces two types of vacuum cleaners, the cannister type and the upright type, each of which is sold through the same retailers. The five cannister models range in suggested retail price from $34.88 to $59.88, and the four upright models from $56.88 to $84.88. Each model is sold with a variety of attachments and accessories, and additional accessories and replacement parts are available through all retail outlets. The bulk of the retail outlets consist of the "better" small appliance stores and department stores, although some discount houses are used in some large metropolitan areas.

Vanguard's vacuum cleaners are not changed drastically in appearance from model year to model year, and thus the brand has become nationally known for easily replaceable parts. Most of the advertising done by Vanguard has emphasized this advantage. The advertising has appeared in such national circulation magazines as *Better Homes and Gardens, Ladies' Home Journal,* and *McCall's.* Occasionally the company has purchased a minute of network television advertising time or offered its products as prizes on daytime quiz shows.

In the last few years, Vanguard vacuum sales have been declining in the face of heavy competition from manufacturers of vacuum cleaners and specialty cleaning appliances, such as rug shampooers, floor polishers, and electric brooms. Each of the specialty machines is smaller and lighter than the Vanguard vacuum cleaners equipped to do the same jobs, while competitive vacuum cleaners are different only in brand name and styling.

Vanguard's general sales manager, Mr. Charles T. Wagner, felt that Vanguard should intensify the distribution of Vanguard vacuum cleaners. Even though he realized that most potential customers put forth considerable effort to compare the price and quality of vacuum cleaners, Mr. Wagner felt that he could meet competition more effectively with more and varied outlets, while maintaining the present ones.

He was intrigued by the increase in size and move to "scrambled" merchandising of the major supermarket chains in recent years. He thought that sales of vacuum cleaners through supermarkets would be successful for the following reasons:

1. The major supermarket shopper, the housewife, is also the person who uses the family vacuum cleaner.
2. Vacuum cleaners are heavy, bulky items. Most customers drive to a supermarket and thus would be prepared to take such an item home.
3. Customers having seen Vanguard's national advertising would become even more familiar with the name through their frequent trips to the supermarket.
4. Supermarket managers would like to sell an item that could be given a much higher markup than most grocery items.

Mr. Wagner was able to persuade the managers of two large grocery chains to allow Vanguard to run tests in several stores in selected cities, for renewable periods of three months. In this test campaign, Vanguard used a 6- by 8-foot display space in each store to show the complete Vanguard line. Included were two temporary electrical outlets, a small carpeted area, and a small jar of dirtlike substance, which could be put on the carpeted area and swept up by the customer. If the customer decided to purchase a vacuum cleaner, she could ring a buzzer, and a clerk would come to take and deliver the order, placing it in the customer's car.

At the end of the first three-month period, Mr. Wagner found that no supermarket wanted to renew Vanguard's contract. Sales had averaged only about one unit per store per week. Furthermore, the supermarket managers involved in the test claimed that customers felt too inhibited to handle the vacuum cleaners in the crowded stores without the aid of a salesman. The managers also complained that people gathering around to look at the display blocked traffic in the aisles, and turnover of items displayed nearby had slowed down considerably. Several customers of the supermarket indicated their surprise at finding vacuum cleaners in a supermarket.

Mr. Wagner was disappointed with the results of the test, but felt that the supermarket might still be a good distribution outlet if Vanguard offered a larger discount to the retailer (to encourage more cooperation and demonstration assistance) and relocated the display (to reduce congestion). Further, he was puzzled by another development. In the test cities, all his regular retailer customers, except the discount houses, had served notice that they would not continue to support Vanguard's distribution efforts by offering the line in their stores. Mr. Wagner had not informed them about the test because he felt it would not affect them. He was trying to stimulate *new* business, *not* compete with the existing retailers, and was surprised at their reaction. The apparent acceptance of the trial by the discount houses was reassuring.

Mr. Wagner is wondering whether to continue to try to sell vacuum cleaners in supermarkets, offering a larger discount to the retailers. He realizes that he might lose outlets that have carried Vanguard products for years, but he feels that the potential volume generated by the high traffic in supermarkets might far outweigh the consequences.

Evaluate Vanguard's present situation and suggest what Mr. Wagner should do.

The Balfour Tool Co. is a manufacturer of industrial cutting tools. These tools include such items as lathe blades, drill press bits, and various other cutting edges used in the operation of large metal cutting, boring, or stamping machines. The president of the company, Mr. Ray Gillespie, takes great pride in the fact that his company, whose $1,342,500 sales in 1968 is small by industry standards, is recognized as a producer of the highest-quality line of cutting tools to be found.

Competition in the cutting tool industry is intense. Balfour Tool must contend with competition not only from the original manufacturers of the machines, but also from many other relatively powerful companies offering cutting tool lines as one of many diverse product lines. This situation has had the effect, over the years, of standardizing the price, specifications, and in turn, the quality, of the competing products of all manufacturers.

Approximately one year ago, Mr. Gillespie was tiring of the tremendous financial pressure of competing with companies enjoying economies of scale. At the same time, he noted that more and more potential cutting tool customers were turning to small custom tool and die shops because of specialized needs that were not met by the mass production firms. Mr. Gillespie then considered a basic change in strategy. Although he was unwilling to become strictly a custom producer, Mr. Gillespie felt that quite possibly the recent trend toward buying customized cutting edges was a good indication of the development of new markets which would be too small for the large, multiproduct-line companies to serve profitably. He thought that the new markets might be large enough so that a flexible company of Balfour Tool's size could make a good profit.

A marketing research company, Brook Marketing Research Associates, was asked to study the feasibility of serving this potential new market. The initial results were encouraging. It was estimated that Balfour Tool could increase sales by 50 percent and double profits from servicing the emerging market.

The next step taken by Balfour Tool was to develop a team of technical specialists to maintain continuous contact with potential cutting tool customers. They were supposed to identify any present or future needs which might exist in enough cases to make it possible to profitably produce a specialized product. The technical specialists were not to take orders, nor to "sell" Balfour Tool to the potential customers. Mr. Gillespie felt that only through this policy could these men easily gain access to the persons in possession of the required information.

The initial feedback from the technical specialists was most encouraging. The company, therefore, decided to constantly adapt its high-quality products to the ever changing, specialized needs of users of cutting tools and edges.

The potential customers of Balfour Tool's specialized tools are widely dispersed. The average sale per customer is not expected to exceed $150 at a time, but the sale will be repeated several times within a year. Because of the widely dispersed market and low sales volume per customer, Mr. Gillespie does not feel that selling the products direct, as would be done by small custom shops, is practical. At the present time, the Balfour Tool Company distributes 90 percent of its regular output through a large industrial supply wholesaler which serves the entire area east of the Mississippi River. This wholesaler, although very large and well known, is having trouble moving cutting tools. It is losing sales of cutting tools in some cities to newer wholesalers specializing in the cutting tool industry. The new wholesalers are able to give more technical assistance to potential customers and therefore better service. The Balfour Tool wholesaler's chief executive is convinced that the newer, less experienced concerns will either realize that a substantial profit margin cannot be maintained along with their aggressive tactics, or they will eventually go broke trying to "overspecialize."

From Mr. Gillespie's standpoint, the present wholesaler is an established landmark and has served Balfour Tool well in the past. The traditional wholesaler has been of great help to Balfour Tool in holding down Balfour Tool's inventory costs by increasing the amount of inventory maintained in the 34 branch wholesale locations operated by the wholesaler. Although he has received several complaints regarding the lack of technical asssitance given by the wholesaler's salesmen, Mr. Gillespie feels that the present wholesaler is providing the best service it can, and he discounts the complaints as "the usual trouble you get into from just doing business."

Mr. Gillespie feels that there are more pressing problems than a few complaints—profits are declining. Sales of the new cutting tool line are not nearly so high as anticipated, even though all indications are that the company's new products should serve the intended market perfectly. The high costs involved in the high-quality product line and the technical specialist research team, in conjunction with less than expected sales, have significantly reduced the firm's profits. Mr. Gillespie is seriously wondering whether it is wise to continue catering to the needs of specific target markets when the results are this discouraging. He also is contemplating an increase in advertising expenditures in the hope that customers will "pull" the new products through the channel.

Evaluate Balfour's strategy. What should Mr. Gillespie do now?

L. S. Brown and Sons is a small country store located in the crossroads town of Sevenhay, Virginia. Sevenhay serves as an accumulation center for the area's farm products. At the time of L. S. Brown and Sons' founding in 1920, Sevenhay had one other retail outlet, a gas station. The store was established by L. S. Brown, Sr., a highly respected resident of this farming area. He had served as a member of the County Board of Supervisors for 20 consecutive years until his death in 1950. L. S. Brown, Jr., has since been in charge of running the store.

Between 1920 and 1940, there were virtually no competitors within a reasonable distance of Brown's store. In fact, the nearest major trading area was Avondale, approximately 20 miles to the north. For many of the farmers, the distance was even greater, being much too time-consuming to travel by horse. (Few of the residents of Sevenhay were prosperous enough to own automobiles during these earlier days.) Brown profited from this isolation and tried to offer good service to his regular customers. The trip to Brown's store on Saturday morning had become quite a tradition for many of the farmers. Besides stocking essential foodstuffs, Brown carried clothes (mostly workclothes) and a wide assortment of other items. The farmers met on Saturday, bought their essentials, and stayed around to socialize with their neighbors.

After 1940, various small stores sprang up within a 5-mile radius of the original L. S. Brown store. In fact, another country store was established right down the street from L. S. Brown's in 1950. The owner, R. N. Hill, chose to offer the same services and product line as Brown. The only basic difference between the two stores was that Hill's was a bit more modern. Brown didn't feel that his business would suffer. The basic products were priced the same, so he felt he would maintain his favorable position through loyal patronage. Brown's main philosophy was that if you "treat the customer right, he will always be your customer." For quite a few years his philosophy paid off. Hill's eked out a meager existence until around 1955.

At that time, Hill decided to modernize his facilities and build an addition in order to double his floor space. Mr. Hill had noticed that since the automobile had become more popular in the 1950's more and more people were driving to Avondale to shop regularly. Where previously most farmers had purchased almost all durable goods from mail-order catalogs, now some were finding Avondale much more convenient for shopping. Therefore, not only did Mr. Hill add a more complete line of groceries but he also added a new department which contained a wide selection of low-priced clothing as well as a full line of hardware items. Mr. Hill felt that Sevenhay's residents were now both wealthier and more mobile, and he hoped to capitalize on their apparent change in tastes and shopping habits.

When Mr. Brown was questioned as to his reaction to Hill's move, he said, "After the novelty wears off, they will come back to where they are treated right." Brown was half right. Most of his customers still frequent his store for the traditional Saturday social, but they are not buying as much as they used to. Mr. Brown is extremely puzzled about the turn of events that has reduced his once profitable operation to a losing proposition. After all, Mr. Brown has always followed the philosophy that "if you treat the customer right, he will always be your customer."

Mr. Brown is convinced that the drop in sales is temporary, and therefore he doesn't plan any major changes. Besides, he feels the town of Sevenhay probably cannot support two stores like the new Hill's and that it would be a foolish step to "modernize" what has worked well. He does plan to begin some local advertising, however, to play up his "long years of service to the community" and the "Saturday social." He feels that his loyal customers can be brought to see that they have some obligation to "buy local," and especially from him, as compensation for providing convenient local facilities for goods *and* a meeting place.

Evaluate the evolution of retailing in Sevenhay over the years and the strategy Mr. Brown is now following. Should he do something else?

**21
Harvey
Jones**

Harvey Jones, now 55 years old, has been a salesman for over 30 years. He started selling in a department store but gave it up after 10 years to work in a lumberyard because the future looked much better in the building materials industry. After drifting from one job to another, he finally settled down and worked his way up to be the manager of a large wholesale building materials distribution warehouse in Kansas City, Kansas. In 1953, he decided to go into business for himself, selling carload lots of lumber to large retail yards in the western Missouri, eastern Kansas area.

He made arrangements to work with five large lumber mills on the West Coast. They would notify him when a carload of lumber was available to be shipped, specifying the grade, condition, and number of each size board in the shipment. Harvey was not the only man representing these mills, but he was the only one in his area. He was not obligated to take any particular number of carloads per month, but once he told the mill he wanted a particular shipment, title passed to him and he had to sell it to someone. Harvey's main function was to buy the lumber from the mill as it was being shipped, find a buyer, and have the railroad divert the car to the buyer.

Harvey has been in this business for 15 years, so he knows all of the lumberyard buyers in his area very well and is on good working terms with them. Most of his dealings are made over the telephone from his small office, but he tries to see each of them about once a month. He has been marking up the lumber between 4 to 6 percent, the standard markup, depending on the grade, and has been able to make a good living for himself and his family.

About two years ago, however, interest rates were raised for home loans and the building boom slowed down. Harvey's profits did, too, but he decided to stick it out, figuring that people still needed housing, and business would pick up again.

Six months ago, a new, aggressive salesman, much younger than Harvey, set up in the same business, covering approximately the same area but representing different mills. This new salesman charged about the same prices as Harvey, but would undersell him once or twice a week in order to get the sale. Many lumber buyers, knowing that they were dealing with a homogeneous product, seemed to be willing to buy from the least expensive source. This has hurt Harvey financially and personally, because even some of his "old friends" are willing to buy from the new man if the price is lower. The near-term outlook seems dark, as Harvey doubts if there is enough business to support two businesses like his, especially if the markup gets shaved any more.

One week ago, Harvey was contacted by a Mr. White, representing the Pope and Talbott particleboard manufacturing plant. Mr. White knew that Harvey was well acquainted with the building supply dealers in the area and wanted to know if he would like to be the sole distributor for Pope and Talbott in that area, selling carload lots, just as he did lumber. Mr. White gave Harvey several brochures on particleboard, a product introduced about 10 years ago, describing how it can be used as a cheaper and better subflooring than the standard lumber now being used. The particleboard is also made with a wood veneer so that it can be used as paneling in homes and offices. He told Harvey that the lumberyards could specify the types and grades of particleboard they wanted. Therefore, they could get exactly what they needed, unlike lumber where they choose from carloads that are already made up. Harvey knew that a carload of particleboard cost about 30 percent more than a carload of lumber and that sales would be less frequent. In fact, he knew that this product has not been as well accepted in his area as in many others, because no one has done much promotion in his area. But the 20 percent average markup looks very tempting, and the particleboard market is expanding.

Harvey has three choices:

1. Take Mr. White's offer and sell both products
2. Take the offer and drop lumber sales
3. Stay strictly with lumber and forget the offer

Mr. White is expecting an answer within another week, so Harvey has to decide soon.

Evaluate what Harvey Jones has been doing. What should he do now? Why?

22
Gold and
Company

Gold and Company is a full-line department store located in Lincoln, Nebraska. In 1963, the family-owned firm was purchased by Brandeis, Incorporated. Brandeis is a high-quality department store operation in Omaha, Nebraska, with a large downtown location and several suburban stores in successful shopping centers. It is by far the most successful store in Omaha, a position similar to that Gold's held in Lincoln before the purchase was completed.

Nathan Gold founded Gold's around the turn of the century and maintained a high-quality operation, catering to the middle and upper classes of Lincoln. Because of his long reputation as a civic leader, Nathan Gold was a respected and popular citizen. For many years he was "the man behind the city government in Lincoln."

Following the purchase by Brandeis, Gold's sales dropped considerably. In some departments, sales in 1966 were one half those of 1962. On the average, sales declined 20 percent under the new management—i.e., from 1963 to 1966.

Following the purchase by Brandeis, the entire credit function was transferred to Omaha. Only a few clerks were left at the Lincoln store. Brandeis credit cards were issued to all charge customers, replacing the former cards which were good at seven downtown Lincoln stores. Monthly statements come from the Omaha credit office and bear "Brandeis Omaha" as a return address.

For many years Gold's had given trading stamps, and the local S&H Green Stamp Redemption Center was located on the fourth floor. Stamps were discontinued almost immediately after the purchase, and S&H built a new redemption center.

Miller and Paine, the main competitor of Gold's, gives local trading stamps and has picked up much of Gold's lost sales. One advertising slogan used by Miller and Paine is: "Lincoln's only home-owned department store."

Another factor which may contribute to Gold's present situation is its downtown location. In the mid 1950's, a major shopping center was built in an outlying area of Lincoln, and many of the downtown stores opened branches there. The Gateway Center became an immediate success, in part due to the fact that it was located near to the major middle-class residential areas. This shopping center contained two department stores (Miller and Paine, and Montgomery Ward), several higher-quality shops, a large grocery store, and a large drugstore. Gold's did not locate in the center, in part because the management had believed in and was vigorously supporting the downtown area.

Parking had become quite a problem in the downtown area in the last few years. In recognition of this, Gold's just recently began offering one hour free parking with any purchase. It was hoped that this would make downtown shopping more attractive and help reverse the declining sales trend.

Gold's local manager has become increasingly concerned about his situation and has requested that customers' comments and complaints about Gold's or Gold's service be referred to him. The first returns from this request include the following:

"They have my charge account mixed up all the time and nobody here can straighten it out."

"I don't want to send my money to Omaha."

"Prices at Miller and Paine are the same and I can get stamps, too."

"They didn't lower their prices a bit when they quit their stamps."

Promotion

3
The Society
Corporation

Foster Adams helped to found Society Corp. of Muncie, Indiana, in 1957. At that time, "hope chest items" were purchased directly from independent factories and then sold directly to single, working girls. Hope chest items are goods purchased in anticipation of marriage and consist mainly of cookware, cedar chests, china, silverware, crystal, and cutlery.

In 1969, Society Corp. had a retail volume of just over $1 million per year and is consistently ranked in the top 10 companies in its field, based on sales volume. Adams owns 100 percent of the corporation's stock, and all management functions are entirely under his control. Due to his firm insistence on paying cash at all times, Society Corp. is financially secure; yearly profits rank with the best in the industry.

In 1961, Adams founded Key Associates, Inc., which has now grown to be the largest single-office finance company in Indiana, with accounts receivable of $750,000. Key offers easy financing and competitively low interest rates to its customers. Its stock is owned solely by Adams and the managers of the Society Corp. Key's primary function is financing the orders of Society and Society's subcompanies.

Society's primary source is Regal, Inc., the largest manufacturer of cookware in the world. The other primary source is the Lane Co., Inc., from whom three lines of cedar chests are purchased. Society ranks 11th in the world in sales of Lane chests (for comparison, Sears, Roebuck ranks 12th), and first in sales among its direct competitors.

Society also deals with high-prestige lines of name-brand products of crystal, silverware, and cutlery. Every Society product is made to specification and not sold in any stores, making Society the exclusive distributor. All the products are priced somewhat higher than store merchandise (but close to the prices of competing direct sales companies). This is justified by Society because it feels that it is offering products of substantially superior quality. It feels that stores could not sell such high-quality lines, since the typical consumer would not be willing to pay a premium price because she cannot differentiate among such products.

Selling efforts are concentrated on the single working girl who has completed at least a high school education, because she can save money for such things at this time in her life. Further, most girls and their mothers have traditionally felt that it is logical to begin "investing in the future" at this time. Sales "contacts" are often made in and around office buildings, where appointments are made for demonstrations ("displays") in the girl's home or apartment. And leads to other girls are always requested after each display.

Of the many competing companies, only a very few carry as complete a line of items as Society. Further, due to the competition's smaller sales volumes, they often must pay higher prices for goo? of comparable quality. Nevertheless, some competitors offer sti? competition.

A survey of salesmen's records shows that competition is beginnir? to affect Society's market by selling to girls who are still in high schoc? Therefore, by the time the girls begin working, they have already pu? chased many of their hope chest items. Further, although the gener? market is growing in size, a growing proportion of young girls atten? college rather than working. And the trend is likely to continu? Society is worried about this trend and is researching ways to cop? with it.

The firm does not advertise but relies exclusively on person? selling and community goodwill. Society considers itself to be a whol? saler that buys direct from the factory, warehouses the products, ar? then sells the products to distributors. There are two types of "sel? employed" distributors: the distributor salesmen and the subcompar? distributorships.

Distributor salesmen are hired directly by Society within th? states of Michigan, Illinois, Indiana, Kentucky, and Ohio. For then? the company supplies delivery and bookkeeping. They have no r? quired investment and are paid a commission based on the differenc? between the cost and selling price of products sold.

Outside of this five-state area, subcompany distributorships a? used. With this arrangement, the distributorship takes title to th? goods. In the usual case, a company inquires if it may buy fro? Society. Society agrees, but adds that no financing is available, ar? recommends Key. Key agrees to finance the distributorship only if? will deal exclusively in Society products and if a bond to cover fina? cial responsibility can be arranged with an insurance company. The? terms are common between wholesaler and finance company throug? out this industry. Society subcompanies presently exist in 25 stat? and account for approximately $500,000 annually.

Six full-time managers are employed by Society to supervis? Society salesmen. These managers are paid a salary plus a commi? sion on what their salesmen sell.

Society feels that price is set by competition. All competitors hav? similar prices, which are closely related to factory prices. All its con? petitors use similar markups on merchandise cost, to cover promotic? and operating costs. It appears that the consumer will see high? prices in the future, as factories are beginning to raise prices du? to higher material costs, notably in stainless steel. Society feels that? will have to raise prices, since the "limited nature of their mark? offers no other alternative."

Salesmen are currently selling 50 percent of all displays at a? average of $224 per sale. Little improvement is believed possibl? The sales volume of July and August is about equal to that of the oth? 10 months of the year. This is the result of mass hiring of colleg? students for summer jobs. These students are good salesmen fc? Society, as they have friends (girls) ready to begin jobs and get marrie?

It has been learned through experience that for every new ma?

recruited as a distributor, about $1,000 in volume is generated. The current philosophy takes this into account and states that sales growth will come through new people.

Society is now focusing on hiring more full-time managers. College student salesmen are being approached as future managers. The argument is that they are making too much money not to continue full time. Some exceptional students earn $9,000 a year working during the summer and part-time during the school year. Further, competitor's managers are being offered superior fringe benefits, profit-sharing options, and other plans designed to enhance financial security.

There are several reasons for expanding the manager force. More full-time managers should be able to recruit more college students to sell for Society. Also, they will have more time to sell directly to girls themselves, because they will have smaller territories to cover. Further, it is hoped that managers will come to have greater familiarity with their smaller territories and will be able to achieve a deeper penetration in all markets, but especially among girls who have gone on to college.

Evaluate Society Corp.'s general strategy planning and in particular its current effort to hire more sales managers.

**54
Morefiber
Wire Rope
Company**

The Morefiber Wire Rope Co. produces wire rope and cable ranging from $1/2$ inch to 4 inches in diameter. The Chicago-based company produces and sells on a national basis. Principal users of the products are manufacturing firms employing cranes and various other overhead lifts in their operations. Lately, ski resorts have become customers, as cables are used in the various lifts. However, the principal customers are still cement plants, railroad and boat yards, heavy equipment manufacturers, mining operations, construction companies, and steel manufacturers.

Morefiber employs its own sales specialists to call on the purchasing agents of potential users. All the men are qualified engineers who go through an extensive training program covering the different applications, strengths, and other technical details concerning rope and cable. Then they are assigned a region or district, the size depending on the number of customers.

Charles Roste went to work for Morefiber in 1942, immediately after receiving a civil engineering degree from Purdue University. After going through the training program, he was assigned, along with one other representative, to the Ohio, Indiana, and Michigan region. His job was to service and give technical assistance to present customers of rope and cable. He was expected to solicit new customers when the occasion arose. But his primary duties were to: (1) supply the technical assistance needed to use rope or cable in the most efficient and safe manner, (2) handle complaints, and (3) provide evaluation reports to customers' management regarding their use of cabling.

Charles Roste became one of Morefiber's most successful repre-

sentatives. His exceptional ability to handle customer complaint
and provide technical assistance was noted by many of the firm'
customers. He also brought in a considerable amount of new busines
primarily from the automobile manufacturers and ski resorts i
Michigan.

Roste's success established Michigan as Morefiber's largest-volum
state. As a result, Michigan was designated as a separate district, an
Charles Roste was assigned as the representative for the district i
1949.

Although the company's sales in Michigan have not continued t
grow in the past few years, the replacement market has been stead
and profitable. This fact is primarily due to the ability and reputatio
of Charles Roste. As one of the purchasing agents for a large autom(
bile manufacturer mentioned, "When Charles Roste makes a recom
mendation regarding use of our equipment and cabling, even if it is
competitor's cable we are using, we are sure it is for the best for ou
company. Last week, for example, a cable of one of his competitor
broke and we were going to give him a contract. He told us it was n(
a defective cable that caused the break, but rather the way we wer
using it. He told us how it should be used and what we needed to d(
to correct our operation. We took his advice and gave him the cor
tract as well!"

Four years ago, Morefiber introduced an expensive wire sling de
vice for holding cable groupings together. The sling makes operation
around the cable much safer and its use could reduce hospital an
lost-time costs due to accidents. The profit margin for the sling i
high, and Morefiber urged all its representatives to push the slin¢

The only man to sell the sling with any success has been Charle
Roste. Eighty percent of his customers are currently using the wir
sling. In other areas, sling sales are negligible.

As a result of his success, Morefiber is now considering forming
separate department for sling sales and putting Charles Roste i
charge. His duties would include traveling to the various sales dis
tricts and training other representatives in how to sell the sling. Th
Michigan district would be represented by a new man.

The question confronting Morefiber management is: Should the
gamble losing profitable customers in Michigan in hopes that slin
sales will increase?

What would you advise? Why?

**25
Sunnyside
Furniture
Company**

Mrs. Ann Alden has been operating the Sunnyside Furniture Co. fc
10 years and has slowly built the sales to $200,000 a year. Her store i
located in the downtown shopping area of a midwestern city of 150,00
population. This is basically a factory town, and she has deliberatel
selected "blue-collar" workers as her target market. She carries som
higher-priced furniture lines, but places great emphasis on budge
combinations and stresses easy credit terms.

Mrs. Alden is most concerned because she feels she has reached th limit of her sales potential; at least it would seem that way because sales have not been increasing during the last two years. Her newspaper advertising seems to attract her target customers, but many of these people come in, shop around, and then leave. Some of them come back, but the majority do not. She feels her product selections are very suitable for her target market and is concerned that her sales personnel do not close more sales with potential customers. She has discussed this matter several times with her sales personnel. They respond that they feel they ought to treat all customers alike, the way they personally would want to be treated – that is, they feel their role is merely to answer questions when asked, and not to make suggestions or help customers arrive at their selections. They feel that this would be too high-pressure.

Table 1*

In shopping for furniture I found (find) that:	Socioeconomic groups				Marital status	
	Group A	Group B	Group C	Group D	Newly-weds	Married 3–10 Yrs.
I looked at furniture in many stores before I made a purchase	78%	57%	52%	50%	66%	71%
I went (am going) to only one store and bought (buy) what I found (find) there	2	9	10	11	9	12
To make my purchase I went (am going) back to one of the stores I shopped in previously	48	45	39	34	51	49
I looked (am looking) at furniture in no more than three stores and made (will make) my purchase in one of these	20	25	24	45	37	30
No answer	10	18	27	27	6	4

**The New Consumer: Cautious or Confident?* Report #2, 1963, conducted for Kroehler Mfg. Co. by the Institute for Motivational Research.

Mrs. Alden feels her sales personnel's attitudes are interpreted as indifference by the customers who are attracted to the store by her advertising. She feels that customers must be treated on an individual basis – and that some customers need more encouragement and suggestion than others. Moreover, she feels that some customers will actually appreciate more help and suggestion than the salespeople themselves might. In support of her opinion, she showed her salesmen the accompanying table and sample design explanation from a recent

study about furniture store customers. She tried to explain to them
about the differences in socioeconomic groups and pointed out that
her store was definitely trying to cater to specific groups. She argued
that they (the salesmen) really had different attitudes than their target
customers and that as a result, the salesmen ought to cater to the needs
and desires of their customers and think less about how they would
like to be treated.

Table 2 The sample design

Socioeconomic status

Upper class (Group A) 13% of sample
  This group consisted of managers, proprietors, or executives of large businesses.
  Professionals, including doctors, lawyers, engineers, college professors and school
  administrators, research personnel. Sales personnel, including managers, execu-
  tives, and upper-income sales people above level of clerks.
  Family income over $10,000
Middle class (Group B) 37% of sample
  Group B consists of white-collar workers including clerical, secretarial, sales clerks,
  bookkeepers, etc.
    It also includes school teachers, social workers, semiprofessionals, proprietors
  or managers of small businesses; industrial foremen and other supervisory personnel.
  Family income between $5,000 and $10,000
Lower middle class (Group C) 36% of sample
  Skilled workers and semiskilled technicians were in this category along with custo-
  dians, elevator operators, telephone linemen, factory operatives, construction
  workers, and some domestic and personal service employees.
  Family income between $5,000 and $10,000
  No one in this group had above a high school education
Lower class (Group D) 14% of sample
  Nonskilled employees, day laborers. It also includes some factory operatives, domes-
  tic and service people.
  Family income under $5,000
  None had completed high school; some had only grade school education

---

*Evaluate Mrs. Alden's thinking and suggest implications for her
promotion.*

26
Gilt-Edge
Razor
Company

In the fall of 1965, the Gilt-Edge Razor Co. was experiencing market
share difficulties. For the past 70 years, since it introduced the first
safety razor, Gilt-Edge has dominated the shaving industry to the extent that it had a 72 percent share of the blade market, and a 90 percent share of the double-edged blade market, in 1965. Its "super-blue"
blades had become an institution. As of fall, 1965, the super-blue's
were the largest seller in the blade industry. Blades represent 70
percent of Gilt-Edge's $325,645,000 annual sales, with men's toiletries
and various products for women sharing the remaining 30 percent.
  In 1966, an ambitious English manufacturer introduced a stainless steel blade in the United States and managed to capture many
Gilt-Edge customers. Although it had known that the "invasion" was

imminent, Gilt-Edge had not been able to perfect its own stainless steel blade. By the time that Gilt-Edge entered the market with its own stainless steel blade, its share of the double-edged blade market had fallen to only 57 percent. The chief operating officers formally abandoned hope of regaining complete market dominance but privately entertained the hope of an innovation to recapture the market. This would be a difficult task, however, in light of the increasing aggressiveness of the British imports and two major U.S. competitors. Further, Gilt-Edge executives were surprised that the Gilt-Edge name hadn't won most customers back from other brands.

Gilt-Edge next considered the introduction of a new concept in shaving, the Raz-R-Band cartridge. The cartridge was to contain six blade edges on a continuous disposable band of stainless steel. It would eliminate the need to handle blades, and thus reduce the number of cuts and danger from exposed blades. The edge itself was the result of a new production process which produced a significantly better blade than any previously on the market. The Raz-R-Band was to be Gilt-Edge's first attempt ever to penetrate the single-edged market. Pilot tests on the product were encouraging; however, a conflict arose between some Gilt-Edge operating managers as to how the new product should be introduced. Bill Winters, the marketing manager, wasn't sure which of the courses suggested to follow, since each had its strengths.

Nick Burns, the Gilt-Edge sales manager, favored easing the product into the market. Coupled with an aggressive selling job on the retail level, Burns' plan called for introductory and informative ads. He proposed to expose the Raz-R-Band on a limited scale to see how the customers reacted to it. The salesmen would be able to get valuable information direct from their retail accounts. According to Burns, "We should go easy at first. The Raz-R-Band is a whole new idea for our customers. We've only had it in market tests for about a year. It has a new shape, size, and weight, and we don't want to get burned like we did on the stainless steel blade. We'll have to sell the idea of a disposable cartridge first. If it catches on in our introductory markets – Buffalo, Los Angeles, and New York City – then maybe we'll expand our scope a bit, say, to the northeast section of the country. Eventually, we'll go national, but for now we should keep everything scaled down until we see if we've got a winner."

Jim Lumis, the advertising manager, took a different point of view. "This Raz-R-Band is no new idea. The basic patents on the cartridge have been out since 1910. The reason it wasn't introduced before this is that they couldn't prevent the oxidation of the band in the cartridge before use. Now, we've got a polymer coating to retard it. The English showed us that the market is ripe for change. We've got an ideal opportunity to promote this "Space Age Miracle," and we ought to do it. We're already under contract to sponsor the World Series, which will be viewed nationally. I say we go national now, before Shavor and the Personal Razor Companies see what we've got. We know Shavor has a cartridge band in development, and we know that their cartridge is being designed to fit into our handle, but ours

won't fit their handle. Selling the distribution channels takes time
We must hit the customer first, and let him pull it through."

The only thing Lumis and Burns agreed on was the price. The
handle and cartridge would retail for $2.95, and a replacement car
tridge would sell for $1. This price is significantly higher than the
stainless blades now marketed, which sell for 98 cents for eigh
blades, or $1.49 for 14 blades.

*Evaluate Gilt-Edge's strategy planning and indicate what i
should do with the new product.*

27
Schering
Corporation

The Schering Corp. is a pharmaceutical manufacturer which market:
a diversified product line throughout the world. Its products includ
corticoids, cold products, antihistamines, psychopharmaceuticals
fungicides, cosmetics/toiletries, laxatives, animal health products
and medical laboratory diagnostic aids. One of the more prosperou.
of the many firms in the industry, Schering has had constantly risins
sales and profits. In 1968, the firm attained $22,944,000 net incom
from sales of $178,099,000.

Basically a manufacturer of ethical pharmaceuticals, Schering sell:
its products through wholesalers to drugstores in the United State:
and abroad. An "ethical" manufacturer typically promotes its product
to registered physicians, primarily through company salesmen wh
are more interested in persuading the doctor to prescribe Schering':
products than in getting an order. Some promotion to doctors is als
done through medical journal advertising, medical conventions
direct mail and direct-mail sampling. In contrast, "proprietary" phar
maceutical manufacturers sell their products over the counter (i.e.
without a doctor's prescription) and advertise directly to consumers
Generally, physicians frown upon medical advertising to the public
especially advertising which promises to relieve specific symptoms
As a result, pharmaceutical manufacturers tend to specialize ir
one market or the other, or to be very careful to avoid offending th
"ethical" market.

At Schering, ethical products account for about 80 percent of th
company's sales and almost all the effort of the company salesmen
However, when visiting drugstores and wholesalers, the salesmen als
will take orders for all the Schering products and are free to promot
the proprietary products. If the company salesman gets an order in a
retail store, he forwards it directly to the wholesaler for delivery from
the wholesaler's inventory. In no way is a retail order expected, sinc
the job of the salesman in the retail drugstore is to help the retaile.
move more of Schering's products.

One of Schering's most popular proprietary or over-the-counte:
(OTC) products is Coricidin, a cold product. In fact, the proprietar
line consists almost entirely of Coricidin products.

Coricidin was introduced to the market in the early 1950's. In it:
original form, it was a red tablet that relieved the symptoms of a cold
Coricidin dominated the market and sold for 98 cents a bottle for 2

tablets. The reason for the product's success was the large number of recommendations received from doctors, druggists, and through word-of-mouth from cold sufferers who used Coricidin and found it effective.

Since Coricidin reached the market, other cold products have been introduced by proprietary manufacturers, using all available advertising media to reach consumers. Some products, such as Dristan and Super Anahist, have been successful, gaining the largest market share for a year or two. None were priced above Coricidin's price of about $1, however, and all eventually succumbed to Coricidin's steady market power when the large sums spent on their initial pioneering advertising were reduced.

Schering sells all of its products, including the OTC line, to wholesalers who are instructed to sell Schering products only to retailers that maintain a certain minimum of Schering purchases. The required minimum is so small that there has been virtually no trouble arising from restricting distribution. Schering's proprietary competitors generally distribute their products in a similar manner; however, their cold products are also found in discount drug outlets and supermarkets. To maintain its image with physicians, Schering does not allow its OTC products to be sold in any outlet that does not have a registered pharmacist on the premises.

Starting in the early 1960's, Schering has extended the Coricidin line, to satisfy consumer wants and to meet competitive pressures. These new products include Coricidin "D" (a decongestant tablet that permits sinus drainage and clears the nose), Coricidin Nasal Mist, Coricidin Cough Formula, and in the children's line, Coricidin Medilets (a chewable Coricidin "red" tablet), and Coricidin Demilets (a chewable Coricidin "D" tablet).

Recently a new cold product, Contac, was introduced by Menley James, the proprietary subsidiary of the ethical manufacturer Smith, Kline, and French Laboratories. Carrying a price of $1.49 for 12 capsules, Contac has been promoted very heavily to consumers. By the end of 1969, it was believed to have more than twice the dollar sales of its closest competitor, Coricidin. However, it is likely that the total profit derived from each of the products is quite close, after all promotional expenses and manufacturing costs have been deducted from sales.

The typical retail selling prices (as of November, 1969) of the three leading cold products are shown in Table 3. The prices charged are listed for only one size, but are representative of similar price differences.

In the last few years, sales of the Coricidin line have kept pace with the expanding cold market because of the introduction of new products and aggressive promotions to drug outlets, such as special price and discount deals, and cash prizes to salespeople who recommend Coricidin.

The OTC manager at Schering is concerned for the future however, because he has noted a definite trend toward self-service for OTC products in drugstores and a substantial increase in sales of cold

Table 3

	Size	Retail price	Fair-trade price
Coricidin Regular	60 Tabs	$2.29	Not fair traded
Coricidin "D"	48 Tabs	$2.59	Not fair traded
Contac	40 Caps	$3.99	$4.95
Dristan	50 Tabs	$1.77	$1.98

products in supermarkets. He would like to make some changes but he is afraid that he won't be able to take advantage of these shifts in the marketplace without injuring Schering's position as an ethical pharmaceutical manufacturer.

Evaluate Schering's present position and suggest what should be done about the new competition.

Price

28
Wire
Specialties
Company

Wire Specialities Co., located in Minneapolis, Minnesota, is a custom producer of industrial wire products. The company had had a great deal of varied experience bending wire into many shapes, and has as well the facilities to chrome or gold-plate finished products. The company was started 10 years ago, and has slowly built its sales volume to $1 million a year. Just one year ago, Mr. Robert Thomas was appointed sales manager of the consumer products division. It was his responsibility to develop this division as a producer and marketer of the company's own branded products, as distinguished from custom orders which the industrial division produces for others.

Mr. Thomas has been working on a number of different product ideas for almost a year now, and has developed several unique designs for letter holders, flowerpot holders, key and pencil holders, and other novelties. His most promising product is a letter holder in the shape of a dog. It is very similar to one which the industrial division produced for a number of years for another company. In fact, it was experience with the seemingly amazing sales volume of this product which interested the company in the consumer market and led to the development of the consumer products division.

Mr. Thomas has sold hundreds of units of his various products to local chain stores and wholesalers on a trial basis, but each time the price has been negotiated and no firm price policy has been established. Now he is faced with the decision of what price to set on the dog-shaped letter holder which he plans to push aggressively wherever he can. Actually, he has not yet decided on exactly which channels of distribution he will use, but the trials in the local area have been encouraging, and, as noted above, the experience in the industrial division suggests that there is a large market for the product.

The manufacturing cost on this product is approximately 5 cents in it is painted black and 10 cents if it is chromed or gold-plated. Similar products have been selling at retail in the 50 cents to $1.50 range. The sales and administrative overhead to be charged to the division would amount to $15,000 a year. This would include Mr. Thomas' salary and some office expenses. It is expected that a number of other products will be developed in the near future, but for the coming year it is hoped that this letter holder will account for about half the consumer products division's sales volume.

Evaluate Mr. Thomas' marketing strategy. What price should he set?

29 Carborundum Company

As the general sales manager of the Bonded Abrasives Division of the Carborundum Co., you must make a decision shortly about how to, or whether to, meet the competitive move of the Norton Co. Norton's action seems to threaten a long-established distribution and pricing setup, and you will have to say or do something, soon.

Bonded abrasives and grinding wheels are used in almost all manufacturing operations. Of approximately $250 million annual industry-wide sales, the Norton Company's grinding wheel division accounts for approximately 35 percent, the Carborundum Co.'s bonded abrasives division accounts for approximately 25 percent, and the Bay State abrasives division of AVCO gets approximately 10 percent. The remaining 35 percent is divided among almost 60 small producers.

The three large companies are characterized by their full-line activity and excellent facilities for giving customers technical assistance. The majority of smaller producers specialize in only one commodity line (e.g., only course-grained resinoid wheels; no fine-grained wheels, no vitrified products, no diamond products, etc.) and most give no technical assistance to customers, selling only standard items to only a few industries.

The "Big 3" sell through selected industrial supply distributors (most of whom are members of one of the two major trade associations, NIDA or SIDA) who generally are specialists in material removal and finishing. Salesmen for these distributors usually are competent to handle most problems that arise. They are supported by sales representatives from the Big 3 producers, who give technical training and sales support to the distributors, as well as call on end-use customers directly. Almost all sales except to the federal government are made through distributors, regardless of who calls on the customer. The smaller producers, on the other hand, sell mostly through their own salesmen, agents, or full-line mill supply houses.

The Big 3 distributor system has evolved to meet a need. While some target markets are like the Milwaukee, Wisconsin, area with only 135 customers (most of whom are in one industry—foundries casting iron, steel, and nonferrous metals), or like Pittsburgh, with over 90 percent of sales to the basic steel industry, most markets are quite the opposite. Detroit, Michigan, with its major automobile producers and many supporting components manufacturers and their supporting "job-shops" or sub-subcontractors, has over 15,000 customers. New York, with its diversified industries, has almost 30,000 customers. These customers may use anywhere from $500 to $100,000 worth of bonded abrasives per year, with most using under $2,500. It would be prohibitively expensive for a factory representative to call on all these customers. Over the years, very close associations have grown between the Big 3 and their better distributors to fill the needs of these target markets.

The nature of the distributor setup used by the large producers has a direct bearing on the price structure. Basically, quantity discounts are given, and by combining the orders of a number of his customers, the distributor can gain additional quantity discounts while charging each customer the price which is appropriate for the quantity he is buying. The prices of various kinds of grinding wheels run all the way from as low as 50 cents to over $1,500, but the dollar value is not used directly in computing the appropriate quantity discounts. Instead, discounts are based on a system of units, with price breaks occurring at intervals of 1, 2, 5, 10, and 25 units. Each unit has a net value of somewhere between $50 and $80 depending on the item. In other words, a very large grinding wheel might be considered as many units when computing the appropriate price discount. The quantity breaks are identified by letters; i.e., a customer may buy at the A price if he purchases one unit at a time, but at C price, if he purchases five, and so forth.

The average distributor discount is 10 percent off the final customer discounted price. But, as noted above, a distributor may combine his purchases in order to entitle him to a larger discount. For example, an order combining five C quantity purchases, or an order combining three C quantity purchases and one D quantity purchase, would entitle the distributor to the E quantity price on *all* the items purchased. His customers would only be entitled to the C or D prices, however. Therefore, if a distributor were able to forecast his total sales accurately and then carry out a warehousing and bulk-breaking function, he might be able to earn up to a 45 percent discount on all of his purchases. This would occur if he catered primarily to small customers who would normally be buying A quantity while he bought at E prices. This extreme is certainly not always possible, but many distributors do earn an average 30 percent discount. This discount is considerably higher than the average that this kind of distributor would earn on his other business. Thus it is understandable why distributors would prize large volume (E quantity) customers, even though they can make only a 10 percent discount on sales to them. For each purchase a distributor would make for an E customer, he could add on all his other small purchases and obtain E prices for all.

The many smaller competitors of the Big 3 have not used the same pricing system. They are not as interested in supporting a distributor system and provide little technical and selling assistance. To offset this lack of service, they have offered significantly lower prices, often as much as 20 percent lower than the larger companies. This sub stantially lower price is *the* important selling point in those target markets where "rough-grinding" is adequate and there is a high volume of repetitive operations. Of the 35 percent of the total market held by the smaller producers, about one half is made up of sales to companies who do not need the specialized products and technical service offered by the larger companies. Some of these companies might like to buy from the larger producers, but they cannot afford the 10–20 percent price differences which are built into the price structure to cover the cost of the vareity of products and services offered.

In an effort to become more appealing to some of this high-volume repetitive business, the Norton Co. announced the "Norton Plan" on March 1, 1965. Under the terms of this plan, customers who buy a large annual volume of one single item (size, grade, or shape) may purchase directly from Norton at a special low price, low enough to beat the price competition of the small competitors.

The terms of the plan are as follows:

1. To qualify on a "per-item" basis, the minimum annual purchase requirement shall be five times E quantity (125 units).
2. No individual purchase shall be less than the minimum order quantity, computed by Norton to be the most economical manufacturing quantity (usually $\frac{1}{6}$ to $\frac{1}{8}$ the annual requirements of the customer).
3. All shipments will be direct from the Norton factory to the customer. Norton will do no warehousing of "Plan" items.
4. The customer is required to reorder whenever his inventory reaches a "reorder point" computed by Norton. This consists of the estimated "usage during delivery" stock plus a "reserve for contingencies" stock.
5. No prices will be published. Items will be priced individually by the Norton office, and price will be determined in part by quantities produced. All customers using identical items in all respects will receive identical prices.
6. Any price increases will take effect after 90 days notice. Price reductions will be effective immediately.
7. If it is determined that the customer's purchase will not total the minimum annual requirement, Norton may cancel the contract after 60 days' notice.
8. The customer may cancel the contract for any reason after 30 days' notice to Norton. He must, however, accept all work in process at time of notice. Norton may cancel the contract for any reason after 90 days' notice. Norton will fill all orders up to day of cancellation.

In the week since the plan was announced, Norton's sales force has been explaining the plan to its current large-volume customers. They have not yet had time to try to reach firms that are not now buying from them in quantity, so reaction here cannot be determined. But their distributors have expressed great dissatisfaction with the "Norton Plan." Several large distributors (over $500,000 sales per year of grinding wheels, or over $1 million per year of total abrasive sales for Norton) have threatened to drop the entire Norton line. Some have already contacted Carborundum and Bay State representatives.

Distributor's feelings may be reflected in the articles and editorials in *Industrial Distributor,* the weekly trade paper published jointly by the National Industrial Distributor's Association and the Southern Industrial Distributor's Association. The initial reaction here is that Norton has completely disregarded its network of distributors and unilaterally taken away a great "lever" for combining purchases. They feel that this move may start a trend towards downgrading or eliminating the role of the distributor and they plan to fight it. Already they are starting to prepare advertising materials and brochures stressing the importance of the functions carried out by industrial distributors, both for manufacturers and their customers.

It is now March 8, 1965, one week after Norton's announcement. You are the general sales manager, bonded abrasives division of the Carborundum Company. In the past week, you have been called at least once by nine of your best distributors, all either current or former members of Carborundum's Distributor Advisory Board. They all caution against any type of "me too" action on the part of Carborundum. You also have been asked by *Industrial Distributor* for a statement.

What would you do? Why?

30
Quik-Prints
Photo-
finishing
Corporation

Organized in 1948, the Quik-Prints Photofinishing Corp. soon became one of the four major Colorado-based photofinishers, each with annual sales of about $2.5 million.

Quik-Prints was established by three men who had had considerable experience in the photofinishing industry, working in Kodak's photofinishing division in Rochester, New York. Quik-Prints started in a small rented warehouse in Boulder, Colorado. Today it has seven company-owned plants in five cities in Colorado and western Kansas. The two color processing plants are located in Boulder and Hays, Kansas. Black-and-white processing plants are located in Boulder and Hays, as well as Pueblo, Denver, and Colorado Springs, Colorado.

Quik-Prints does all of its own processing of black-and-white films, slides, prints, and motion pictures. While they do own color processing capability, Quik-Prints has found it less costly to have most color film processed by the regional Kodak processing plant. The majority of color film sold today is Kodachrome, and Kodachrome processing is sufficiently complicated so that the cost of equipment to do the work is prohibitive for Quik-Prints. The color film processed by Quik-Prints is of the "off-brand" variety or is special work done for professional photographers. Despite this limitation in color finishing, Quik-Prints has always given its customers fast, quality service. All pictures, including those processed by Kodak, can be returned within three days of receipt by Quik-Prints.

Quik-Prints was established originally as a wholesale photofinisher, and later developed its own processing plants in an effort to achieve a greater profit margin. Its customers are drugstores, camera stores, department stores, photographic studios, and any other retail outlets where photofinishing is offered to consumers. These retailers insert film rolls, cartridges, negatives, and so on, into separate bags, marking on the outside the kind of work to be done. The customer is handed a receipt, but seldom sees the bag into which his film has been placed. The bag has the retailer's name on it, not Quik-Prints'.

Each processing plant is fronted by a small retail outlet for drop-in customers who live in the immediate vicinity of the plant. This is a minor part of Quik-Prints' business.

The company is also engaged in direct-mail photofinishing within the state of Colorado. Each processing plant in Colorado is capable of receiving direct-mail orders from consumers. All film received is handled in the same way as the other retail business.

A breakdown of the dollar volume by type of business is shown in Table 4.

Table 4

Type of business	Percent of dollar volume
Sales to retail outlets	80
Direct-mail sales	17
Retail walk-in sales	3
	100

All processing is priced at the level established by local competition. Quik-Prints establishes a retail list price, and each retailer then is offered a trade discount based on the volume of business he generates for Quik-Prints. The pricing schedule used by each of the major competitors in the Colorado-Kansas market is shown in Table 5.

Table 5

Monthly dollar volume (12-month average)	Discount (2/10 e.o.m.)
$ 0–$ 100	$33\frac{1}{3}$%
$ 101–$ 500	40 %
$ 501–$1000	45 %
$1,001–above	50 %

All direct-mail processing for final consumers is priced at the $33\frac{1}{3}$ percent discount off retail price, but this is done under a disguised name so that retailer customers are not antagonized. Retail walk-in accounts are charged the full list price for all services performed.

Retail stores offering photofinishing are served by Quik-Prints' own sales force. Each processing plant has at least three men servicing accounts. Primarily, their duties include daily visits to all accounts to pick up and deliver all photofinishing work. These salesmen also make daily trips to the Greyhound bus terminal nearby to pick up and drop off color film that is being processed by Kodak. Since the consumer does not come in contact with Quik-Prints, the firm has not found it necessary to advertise its retail business. To reach business firms, Quik-Prints has provided a listing in the Yellow Pages of all telephone books in cities and towns served by its seven plants. In addition, salesmen offer some photographic equipment to retail customers for resale. But, this business is seen only as a service and does not really generate much profit. There has been no attempt at making the consumer aware of Quik-Prints' service, since all consumers are served through retail stores.

The direct-mail portion of Quik-Prints' business is generated by regular advertisements in the Sunday pictorial sections of newspapers servicing Pueblo, Denver, Colorado Springs, and Boulder. These advertisements usually stress the low-price service, two-week turnaround, and fine quality. Quick-Prints does not use its own name for these markets. Mailers are provided for the consumer to send in to the plant being utilized. Some people in the company felt this part of the business might have great potential if pursued more aggressively.

Recently, the president of Quik-Prints, Mr. Humma, has become worried over the loss of several retail accounts in the $500–$1,000 discount range. He has been with the company since its beginning and has always stressed quality and rapid delivery of the finished product. Demanding that all plants produce the finest-quality reproductions, Mr. Humma personally conducts periodic quality tests of each plant through its direct-mail service. Plant managers are called on the carpet for any slips in quality. In order to find out what is causing the loss in retail accounts, Mr. Humma has been reviewing salesmen's reports and talking to various employees.

In their weekly reports, Quik-Prints' salesmen have reported a possible trend toward higher trade discounts being offered to retailer customers. Insty-Film, a competitor of equal size that offers the same services as Quik-Prints, is offering an additional 5 percent discount in each sales volume category. This price differential really makes a difference at some stores, because these retailers feel that all the major processors can do an equally good job. Further, they note, consumers apparently feel that the quality is acceptable, because there have been no complaints so far.

Quik-Prints has encountered price cutting before, but never by an equally well-established company. Mr. Humma cannot understand why these retailer customers would leave Quik-Prints, because it is offering higher quality and the price difference is not that large. He is considering a direct-mail and newspaper campaign to consumers to persuade them to demand Quik-Prints' quality service from their favorite retailer. Mr. Humma feels that consumers demanding quality will force retailers to stay with or return to Quik-Prints. He says: "If we can't get the business by convincing the retailer of our fine quality, we'll get it by convincing the consumer."

Evaluate Quik-Prints' strategies and Mr. Humma's present thinking. What would you do?

The Stout Manufacturing Co. of Los Angeles, California, is a leading manufacturer in the wire machinery industry. It has patents covering over 200 machine variations, but it is rare for Stout's customers to buy more than 30 different types in a year. Its machines are sold to wire and small-tubing manufacturers when they are increasing production capacity or replacing outdated equipment.

Established in 1865, the company has enjoyed a steady growth to its present position with annual sales of $27 million.

About 10 firms compete in the wire machinery market. Each is about the same size and manufactures basically similar machinery. Each of the competitors has tended to specialize in its own geographic area. Five of the competitors are in the East, three in the Midwest, and two, including Stout, on the West Coast. All of the competitors offer similar prices and sell F.O.B. their factories. Demand has been fairly strong in recent years, and as a result, all of the competitors have been satisfied to sell in their geographic areas and avoid price cutting. In fact, there is an adversion to price cutting because about 20 years ago one firm tried to win additional business and found that others immediately met the price cut but industry sales (in units) did not increase at all. Within a few years prices had returned to their earlier level, and since then, competition has tended to focus on promotion.

Stout's promotion has depended largely on company salesmen who cover the West Coast. These men usually are supported by sales engineers when the company is close to making a sale. Some advertising is run in trade journals, and direct mailings are used occasionally, but the primary promotion emphasis is on personal selling. Personal contact outside of the West Coast market, however, is through manufacturers' agents.

Mr. Andrew Lunter, president of Stout Manufacturing Co., is not satisfied with the present situation. Industry sales have begun to level off and so have Stout's sales, although Stout has continued to hold its share of the market. He would like to find a way to compete more effectively in the other regions, because he is coming to see that there is great potential outside of the West Coast if he can only find a better way of reaching it.

Stout has been acknowledged by competitors and buyers as one of the top-quality producers in the industry. Its machines have generally been somewhat superior to others in terms of reliability, durability, and productive capacity. The difference, however, has not been great enough to justify a higher price because the others are able to do the necessary job. In short, if a buyer had a choice between Stout's and another's machines at the same price, Stout would probably get the business. But it seems clear that Stout's price must be at least competitive.

The average wire machine sold by Stout (or any of the competitors) sells for about $115,000, F.O.B. shipping point. Shipping costs within any of the three major regions averages about $1,500, but then another $1,000 must be added on shipments from the West Coast to the Midwest (either way) and another $1,000 from the Midwest to the East.

Mr. Lunter is considering the possibility of expanding his market by being willing to absorb the extra freight costs which would be incurred if a midwestern or eastern customer were to buy from his West Coast location. In other words, he would absorb the additional $1,000–$2,000 in transportation costs. By so doing, he would not be cutting price in those markets, but rather reducing his net return. He felt that his competitors would not see this as price competition and therefore would not resort to cutting prices themselves. Further, he felt that such a move would be legal, because all the customers in each major region would be offered the same price.

The sales manager, Mr. Bernard Chelps, felt that the proposed freight absorption plan might actually stimulate price competition in the midwestern and eastern markets and perhaps on the West Coast. He proposed instead, that Stout hire some salesmen to work the midwestern and eastern markets, rather than relying on the manufacturers' agents. He felt that an additional three salesmen would not increase costs too much and could greatly increase the sales from these markets over that brought in by the agents. With this plan, there would be no need to absorb the freight, and therefore there would be no need to gamble on disrupting the present "status quo" with respect to competitive methods. He felt this later matter was especially important, because competition in the Midwest and East was somewhat "hotter" than on the West Coast because of the number of competitors in these regions. The situation had been rather quiet in the West, because only two firms were sharing this market.

Mr. Lunter agreed that Mr. Chelps had a point, but in view of the leveling off of industry sales, he felt that competitive situations might change drastically in the near future and that he would rather be a leader in anything that was likely to happen rather than a follower. He was impressed with Mr. Chelps's comments regarding the greater competitiveness in the other markets, however, and therefore was unsure about what should be done, if anything.

Evaluate Stout's strategy planning in the light of its market situation, and explain what it should do now.

32
Pet Food
Company

Mr. Hamilton, the sales manager of the Pet Food Co., has been approached by the buyer for a large retail grocery chain with a proposal that Pet Food manufacture a dealer brand of dog food for the chain. The retail chain, which operates in most of the states east of the Mississippi River, is offering a firm contract for monthly shipments of a total of 400,000 cans to its various regional warehouses. The contract is to run for a two-year period. The product is to be manufactured to the chain's own specifications but will be very similar to the Pet Food's most popular product. The chain plans to offer its own dealer brand at 12 cents (retail), about 3 cents a can below Pet Food's comparable brand. The price set in the contract is 9 cents per can delivered to the chain's warehouses.

The chain buyer indicates that his company will still be buying the whole Pet Food line. This is merely an additional purchase. The purchases of the Pet Food's own brands will be made through the regular wholesale channels, as usual.

Mr. Hamilton has mixed feelings about accepting the offer. To be sure, this is extra business which he probably would not get otherwise. If Pet Food turns down the offer, it is certain that the chain will interest some other pet food manufacturer, as there are many competitors. Further, the proposed price will enable Pet Food to make a net profit of about 1 cent a can on each can sold under this contract. This is by no means the same margin of profit it would get if it sold this expanded volume through its regular channels under its own brand. On the other hand, there would be no promotional cost, large quantities would be produced and handled at the same time, and there would be virtually no credit risk. Also, the orders would be definite for the next two years and this would enable the factory to stabilize its production schedule. In fact, the plant has ample capacity to produce this added volume. It will only account for about 20 per cent of the company's total volume of production.

The major drawback Mr. Hamilton sees is that the item the chain wishes to dealer brand will compete with Pet Food's own fast-moving brand. The other items in Pet Food's line are not nearly as attractive to customers, but the company carries them in order to offer a full line. It does make a profit on these other items, but not as much as on this fast-moving item. He is concerned that the dealer brand might cut into the business of this fast-moving item. This in turn might draw criticism from the company's wholesalers and might lead to some of them dropping Pet Food's line in favor of competitive lines. On the positive side, however, Mr. Hamilton recognizes that this chain does plan to go ahead with the dealer brand and that perhaps it would be desirable to be making and selling the products which inevitably will take a share of his market anyway.

Should the retail chain's offer be accepted?

Marketing management

33
Riverside
Packing
Company

The Riverside Packing Co. is a well-established manufacturer in the highly seasonal vegetable canning industry. It packs and sells canned beans, peas, carrots, corn, peas and carrots mixed, and kidney beans. Sales are made primarily through food brokers to merchant wholesalers, supermarket chains (such as Kroger, Safeway, A&P, Red Owl, etc.), cooperatives, and other outlets, mostly in the Chicago area. Of secondary importance, by volume, are sales in the immediate local market to institutions, grocery stores, and supermarkets, and sales of dented canned goods to "walk-in" customers at low prices.

Riverside is the second largest vegetable canner in the Devil's River Valley area of Wisconsin, with sales in excess of $10 million annually (exact sales data is not published by the closely held corporation). In 1964, plants were located in Riverside, Portertown, and Williamston, Wisconsin, and Clearview, Minnesota, with main offices in Riverside. The Riverside brand is used only on canned goods sold in the immediate local market; in most other cases, the goods are sold and shipped under the retailer's label, or the broker's/wholesaler's label.

Operating since 1905, Riverside has established an excellent reputation over the years for the consistent quality of its total product offering. And it is always willing to offer competitive prices. Strong channel rapport was built by Riverside's chairman of the board and chief executive officer, Mr. H. E. Edwards. Mr. Edwards, who owns controlling interest in the firm, had "worked" the Chicago area as an aggressive company salesman in the firm's earlier years before he took over from his father as president in 1931. He was an ambitious and hardworking executive, active in community affairs, and the firm prospered under his direction. He became well known within the canned food processing industry for technical/product innovations, and during World War II was appointed to a position in Washington, D.C., on the Board which formulated wartime food rationing policies.

During the "off-canning" season, Mr. Edwards traveled extensively. In connection with his travels, he arranged several significant business deals. His 1966 and 1967 trips culminated in the following two events: (1) inexpensive pineapple was imported from Formosa and marketed in the central United States through the Riverside Packing Co., primarily to expand the product line; (2) a technically advanced continuous process cooker (65-feet high) was imported from England and installed at the Riverside plant in February/March, 1968. It was the first of its kind in the United States and cut process time sharply.

Mr. Edwards retired in 1968 and named his son-in-law, the 35-year-old Mr. Evans, as his successor. Mr. Evans is intelligent and hardworking. As a member of the firm for the past seven years, he has been engaged primarily with financial matters, but more recently with marketing problems. During his tenure as financial director, the firm had received its highest credit rating ever and was able to borrow working capital ($3 million to meet seasonal seed, fertilizer, can stockage, and wage requirements) at the lowest rate ever received by the company.

The fact that the firm isn't unionized allows some competitive advantage. However, recent minimum wage law changes have increased costs. And these and other rising costs have caused profit margins to narrow. The narrowed profit margins prompted the recent closing of the Williamston plant and then the Portertown plant, as they became comparatively less efficient to operate. The remaining two plants were considerably expanded in capactiy (especially warehouse facilities), so that they could operate more profitably due to maximum use of existing processing equipment.

Shortly after Mr. Edward's retirement, Mr. Evans reviewed the company's current situation with his executives. He pointed out narrowing profit margins, debts contracted for new plant and equipment, and an increasingly competitive environment. Even considering the temporary laborsaving competitive advantage of the new cooker system, there seemed to be no way to improve the "status quo" unless the firm could sell direct, as they do in the local market, absorbing the food brokers' 5 percent commission on sales. This was the plan of action decided upon, and Mr. Burns was directed to test the new method for six months.

Mr. Burns is the only full-time salesman of the firm. Other top executives do some selling, but not much. Being a relative of Mr. Edwards', Burns is also a member of the board of directors. He is especially competent in technical matters as he has a college degree in food chemistry. Although Mr. Burns formerly did call on some important customers with the brokers' salesmen, he is not well known in the industry or even by Riverside's usual customers.

Five months later, after Mr. Burns has made several selling trips and hundreds of telephone calls, he is unwilling to continue sales efforts on his own. He is insisting that a sales staff be formed if the current operation is to continue. Orders are falling off in comparison to both expectations and the previous year's operating results. And sales of the new pineapple products are practically nil. Even in normal channels, Mr. Burns sensed a reluctance to buy, though basic consumer demand had not changed. Further, some potential customers have demanded quantity guarantees considerably larger than the firm can supply. Expanding supply would be difficult in the short run because the firm typically must contract with farmers for production acreage, to assure supplies of the type and quality they normally offer. The only success the new plan has had is in a territory where Riverside's regular broker recently retired.

Mr. Edwards, still the controlling stockholder, has scheduled a meeting in two weeks to discuss the status of Riverside's current operations.

Evaluate Mr. Evans' strategy planning. What should he tell Mr. Edwards? What should be done next?

**34
Jiffy Johns,
Incorporated**

Jiffy Johns, Inc., is a well-established family-owned and -operated company specializing in the rental of portable toilet facilities in the southern part of Florida. The portable toilets, called Jiffy Johns, are made of aluminum in the traditional outhouse design. They are made by an aluminum siding company in Tampa at a cost of $110 per unit. The toilet uses a chemical solvent to reduce odors and inhibit bacterial growth. This solvent must be changed regularly, and this is part of the service offered by Jiffy Johns, Inc.

The management of Jiffy Johns established the business 20 years ago as the Florida building boom was starting, after an analysis of the service requirements of construction firms in southern Florida. In addition to portable toilets, Jiffy Johns soon discovered that some construction firms also required on-the-site construction offices, tool sheds, and minijohns which could be raised by cranes to upper levels of multistory buildings. These products were added to the line as needed, and are easily constructed in Jiffy Johns' own warehouse.

The company's facilities consist of the warehouse and an office, both in Pompano Beach. They also have three custom-equipped tank trucks and several smaller trucks and trailers for pickup and delivery. The tank trucks are used on regular service routes to pump dry and refill with fresh chemicals each portable toilet every two or three days. At the present time, they service about 600 Jiffy Johns. Further, about 50 portable offices and tool sheds have been placed at various sites in southern Florida. The toilets rent for $35 per month, and the portable offices for $50 per month. Since there are some savings when many units are serviced at one stop, price discounts are given depending on how many units are used at a particular site.

The business has grown rapidly in recent years because more local health ordinances are requiring toilet facilities on construction sites. Some further sales growth can probably be expected for this reason, although the business naturally fluctuates depending on the activity in the construction industry.

The majority of the firm's customers seem to be well pleased with its service, and management cannot think of any way to improve the service to its present customers. Naturally, the company is always willing to provide the same service to new customers, and it carries on a regular promotion effort to this end. This effort has been concentrated on building contractors through trade journals and direct mailing. In addition, all units have large signs on both sides with the name Jiffy Johns and the local phone number. Because of the appearance of Jiffy Johns on so many construction sites, the company regularly receives inquiries from contractors and construction companies. The name Jiffy Johns has become so common in contracting circles, that even competing firms' products have been referred to as "Jiffy Johns." In fact, when informed of the true nature of the business, one caller replied: "I thought you must be the largest contractor in Florida."

The company has one full-time salesman, and the general manager also spends a portion of his time generating new accounts. However, because Jiffy John, Inc., is so well known, much of the business is conducted over the phone with people who are using or have used Jiffy Johns.

The company has several small competitors, but they offer the old-fashioned wooden outhouses. One small company, however, has entered recently with fiberglass units. Each of these competitors is much smaller than Jiffy Johns, Inc., and regularly tries to offer lower prices to take some of the company's business. Jiffy Johns has never met this price competition and has seldom lost any accounts for this reason. Generally, the company is well known for its dependable service, and some contractors even seem to enjoy making humorous references to their Jiffy Johns.

The Jiffy Johns management is now considering expanding into northern Florida and perhaps later to the Bahamas. Entry into the northern Florida market would be with approximately similar plant and equipment. A proposed warehouse in Jacksonville is expected to be able to handle another 600 Jiffy Johns and 50 portable offices, and a similar fleet of tank and delivery trucks will be needed for the service work.

The company's long-run goal is to dominate the northern market with a quality product-service package as it has done in the south. Although the Jiffy Johns name is not known in northern Florida, management hopes to be able to establish its name fairly quickly because there are no well-recognized competitors in the north. There are many small competitors currently offering this service, however. Most offer portable wooden outhouses similar to some of Jiffy Johns' competitors in the south. The general price level is lower, by about $5 to $10 a month for the portable toilet. Portable offices are generally not available from the present competitors. The lower price level seems to have been due to several rounds of price cutting in recent years, as some firms have resorted to this competitive tool in order to stay in business. Some of these firms have not been able to meet costs when prices were cut to the $25-a-month level and have gone out of business. But there still seem to be many other small competitors willing to offer their current services at these lower prices. The primary emphasis has been on low price, rather than offering better quality toilets, such as Jiffy Johns.

On the whole, new construction has not grown as fast in northern Florida as in the southern part of the state, but Jiffy Johns management expects that the passage of many more local health ordinances will have the same affect on the market as it did in the southern part of the state. Therefore, they hope that with a transfer of their know-how to this new market they will come to dominate this northern market just as they have done in the south. And if all goes well, they will move on to the Bahamas in maybe a year or two.

Evaluate Jiffy Johns, Inc.'s strategic planning for the southern market and then discuss whether it is likely to be successful in the northern market.

35	As a producer of wooden crossties, the Railway Tie Corp. of America

35
Railway Tie
Corporation
of America

As a producer of wooden crossties, the Railway Tie Corp. of America (RTCA) belongs to a large but slowly declining industry. In 1965, nation-wide use of crossties for building and rebuilding railroad track "beds" generated industry sales of slightly more than $102 million. This 1 percent decline over the previous year was attributed to failure of the major trunk-line railroads to increase the 302,000 miles of track already in use. Virtually all crossties sold today are for replacement of damaged or worn-out ties.

RTCA's gross sales are only slightly higher than the industry average of $5 million per firm. The 10 largest producers record sales of more than $5 million, while 55 smaller producers realize lower sales. Although primarily a manufacturer of wood crossties, RTCA also produces rough lumber, oak flooring, and dimension stock for the furniture industry. However, these products represent a small portion of the firm's gross sales.

In recent years, the competition for sales of crossties has become intense. Price cutting has caused the industry price to decline to $4.15 per tie, as no producer is able to effectively differentiate his product. Most companies rely on aggressive personal selling to persuade the railroads to purchase their product. No locational monopoly exists, because almost all manufacturing activity takes place in the eastern United States where the raw materials, such as red and white oak, are readily available for processing.

In 1967, in an effort to control its market and achieve higher sales and profits, RTCA undertook extensive product research to develop a crosstie that would be uniquely different and better. In collaboration with the American Railway Engineers Association, RTCA began development of a new crosstie design, trying to satisfy the two major customer concerns: service life and maintenance cost. RTCA wanted a crosstie whose special features would extend the service life of the crosstie and in the long-run reduce maintenance costs.

An investment of $51,000 in research and development gave RTCA the product it was looking for. The new crosstie was shaped like a trapezoid in its end dimensions, the broad base of which presented more load-bearing surface against the wear of the roadway ballast. The new crosstie's dimensions were: bottom 15 inches, top 9 inches, and height 7 inches. This was in contrast to the common rectangular design of 7 inches by 9 inches (base). The engineers pointed out that the broad base of the trapezoidal crosstie would extend crosstie life by more than five years. Of special interest was the new product's potential worth in supporting rails located in curves. Engineers indicated that in such locations the traditional 7-inch by 9-inch rectangular crosstie lasted at best eight years. Under identical circumstances, the trapezoidal crosstie would better resist harsh abrasion and probably serve more than 13 years.

Although the trapezoidal crosstie would require raw materials (logs) slightly larger than those used for rectangular tie production, RTCA foresters indicated that such materials were readily available from both company-owned and privately owned timber lands. The added costs of manufacturing the new crosstie was of initial concern to the firm. Subsequent analysis indicated that a revised sawing procedure would keep costs down, and applying the same pricing formula used for conventional ties led to a price per trapezoidal tie of $4.22, only slightly above the $4.15 market price for conventional ties.

The executive board of RTCA was enthusiastic. They saw great potential for the new product, because it would satisfy present customers better and enable RTCA to expand into new markets. If the new crosstie were readily accepted by the firm's regular customers, chances are it would be accepted by the other railroads with which

RTCA was not presently doing business. This would offer a "foot-in-the-door" of potential customers to whom the firm might sell its old standby, the rectangular crosstie.

RTCA utilized its existing sales force for the new product. These salesmen call directly on the railroads and have traditionally been highly trained technical people capable of providing the railroad purchasing agent and roadway engineers with technical design assistance as necessary. Often they have aided railroad design engineers in selecting special grades and species of crossties for use in heavy traffic areas. They have also consulted on custom-treated crossties for use in areas where caustic materials are transported by rail.

The decision to promote the new crosstie with existing company salesmen was followed by the development of an advertising campaign. Several general advertisements were placed in an industry trade journal. In addition, general bulletins were mailed to railroad purchasing agents, explaining the new crosstie's price and quality, but technical information was kept to a bare minimum until requested. Then the salesmen were expected to follow up such requests.

At the end of six months, Mr. Moss, the sales manager of RTCA, informed the executive board that sales of the new trapezoidal crosstie were lagging far behind expectations. The railroads were reluctant to buy the new crosstie for various reasons, several of which were repeatedly expressed: (1) The trapezoidal crosstie was a new product, quite unfamiliar to the railroads — "Why buy a new product (with all its uncertainties) when we are satisfied with the old one that has served us well in the past?" was a comment frequently heard. (2) The difference in price between the old and new product was minor and really didn't give the railroad the feeling that they were buying a new product — "A price difference of $0.07 per crosstie doesn't convince me that the performance of the old and new crossties will be any different," said one purchasing agent.

In response to the negative comments from potential customers, Mr. Moss is suggesting a price reduction coupled with the addition of more salesmen. He has been criticized for this plan by some members of the executive board who feel that a reduction in price will not help, but only aggravate, the situation.

What is the present situation in which RTCA finds itself? Should RTCA follow Mr. Moss' suggestions?

| 36 Seifert Manufacturing Company* | The Seifert Manufacturing Co. was set up in 1935 when the Mid-Continent Wholesale and Distributing Co. purchased a small clothing manufacturer in order to supply it with some of the items it sold. Both the wholesale establishment and the manufacturing firm were located in Denver, Colorado. The wholesaling firm had been formed in 1909 by |

*This case was adapted from John B. Kline and John T. Doutt, *Case Problems of Small Business in the Rocky Moutain West.* prepared by the Bureau of Business Research, University of Colorado, under a grant from the Small Business Administration, Washington, D.C., 1961, pp. 6–26.

Samuel Seifert and two cousins. Both companies are still basically family operations.

Joseph Seifert, the 37-year-old secretary-treasurer and general manager of the Seifert Manufacturing Co. has been operating the company seven years, since 1952, and has helped improve the firm's condition. He added a sales force and new product lines so that by 1959 the manufacturing and the wholesaling firms were in no way interrelated or interdependent except through common ownership. In fact, in certain lines the two companies compete almost directly, although Joe Seifert feels that his firm seeks a slightly higher-priced market. Looking into the future, Joe Seifert feels that the problem which will concern him most is that of increasing sales and developing an adequate sales force.

Seifert Manufacturing Co. offers a number of lines of men's and women's clothing. The Deseret brand is a line of women's specialty wear consisting of such things as women's cotton blouses and jeans. The Plainsman line consists of men's car coats and some sport shirts. The American Beauty line includes sweaters, skirts, sportswear, and denim jeans. Most of these garments are in the medium-price range. The company makes all items in their lines except sweaters and sports shirts. They have found that these are specialized items which some firms can make as economically as they can. Therefore, these garments, which consist of about 25 percent of their sales, are subcontracted.

Seifert has close to national distribution and faces strong competition in all areas. The company is represented by a total of 10 salesmen —4 who sell exclusively for Seifert and 6 manufacturers' agents who sell one or more additional lines. Sales are made directly to retail stores and, in most cases, salesmen are given credit for a sale in their territory whether it was a mail-order sale or a sale solicited personally by the salesman.

They try to cater to the medium-priced field. Mr. Seifert said that: "The secret in the garment business is to find a niche in the market and then fill that niche. That is what we have tried to do." Part of his basic philosophy is stated as follows:

> Back in New York City, they produce a type of merchandise that can be in a price range below ours, but the styling and quality are not always what is desired in stores where the "casual feeling" is desired. The finish quite often isn't there. In the South, they have some labor cost advantage, and they will produce a skirt there for $3.75 that might cost us $4.75 to make. At least, we will aim for a $4.75 figure and give it a finish and fit for that price that the southern or eastern skirts won't have. In the Midwest, we find a different type of competition. Many of them produce garments in a piecemeal production system that gives them high costs. Through manufacturing control, we are able to offer a garment for around $15 that competition will try to sell for as much as $25.

Mr. Seifert spends a lot of his time working between sales and production to be sure they are making the right thing at the right time

Mr. Seifert observed: "We watch our sales orders closely, and as we sense a good number, we will produce a quantity for stock. This is especially important in the early days of a season. Then there are some seasons when we just don't seem to 'hit.' This spring was one of them. Things just didn't seem to catch on, so we shut down our spring line early and moved into the fall items. And right now, although it's very early, we already have some reorders for some fall numbers. Someone has to watch these things and make the decisions of this sort."

Control of inventory and "feeling" the market are achieved largely through the use of a "Listing Book." Each day, orders for all of the different numbers in the line are accumulated and posted in this book. Then, as a cutting is made, the size of which is based on the orders listed, it is posted in a column opposite the order total. Thus, a simple calculation gives the quantity which should be on hand at any given time.

Seifert Manufacturing Co. is set up with two divisions: the manufacturing division and the sales division. The manufacturing division produces the garments and after accumulating its costs, it adds a markup to cover its own overhead and general administrative expenses as well as a small amount for profit. This factory price becomes the sales division's cost, and it adds a markup to determine Seifert's selling price. The manufacturing division commonly takes a 20 percent markup, although certain garments, such as blue jeans which are very competitive, do not permit more than a 12 percent markup. The sales division usually tries to obtain a 25 percent markup.

All salesmen are paid a 6 percent commission on all items sold with the exception of blue jeans, closeouts, and "chain store items." These latter items are produced to meet low-price competition and are sold primarily to chain stores. Only a 3 percent commission is paid on these. These commission rates are competitive with other manufacturers.

Varying degrees of control are exercised over the salesmen. Those who sell full-time for Seifert are expected to turn in a route list and a daily call report indicating firm name, location, and remarks about each call made. The manufacturers' agents, however, generally have not supplied this information.

Occasionally, but not regularly, the home office sends out bulletins. These consist of mimeographed sheets listing closeouts, new items, or special price changes. Occasionally, the sales manager or Mr. Seifert himself will add a personal note of counsel or encouragement for an individual salesman.

Some control is achieved by personal contact. Salesmen selling in the areas near Denver come into the office several times a year. In addition, Mr. Seifert makes an annual trip to California, at which time he talks to the salesmen in that area. Finally, the annual Midwest Trade Show provides a point of contact, not only with the trade but with the salesmen. All salesmen are expected to attend at their own expense.

Mr. Seifert is concerned about the quality of his salesmen. Some are good men, but he feels that improvement can be made in this area. Some men seem to be good in certain lines and not in others, or perhaps take a greater interest in certain products because of the nature of their territories, or the demands of their other lines, in the case of manufacturers' agents. The salesman in the Oklahoma and Texas area, for example, had a monthly sales range from approximately $6,000 to $52,000 in a recent year. Not all the salesmen had such extremes, but their patterns vary so that it makes it very difficult for the plant to plan its production.

From the 25 percent markup the sales division usually tries to get, several major items of expense must be paid or deducted. It is customary to grant an 8 percent cash discount to all customers who pay their bill within 10 days after the end of the month. In addition, the salesman's commission, the sales manager's salary, general administrative salary allocation, sales office expense, and advertising expense must be deducted. Advertising expense usually runs about one half of 1 percent of sales and consists primarily of selective advertising in western wear magazines, the Midwest Trade Show, and advertising allowances to retailers. These allowances range from 25 to 50 percent of the cost of the advertisement and in most cases are for local newspaper advertising in which various Seifert brand names are prominently displayed.

Salesmen are permitted to make decisions regarding the cooperative advertising allowances made in their territory, but a control is placed on this by charging their personal commission account with 7 percent of the amount of Seifert's allowance. For example, if a salesman approves cooperative advertising in the amount of $100, Seifert might pay as much as 50 percent of this amount. The salesman's commission account would then be charged 7 percent of $50, or $3.50.

Evaluate the marketing strategy being used here. What changes would you want to make if you were the sales manager of this company?

37
AAA Plastics
Company

Bob McMahon is currently employed as a sales representative for a plastics goods manufacturer. He calls primarily on large industrial accounts, such as refrigerator manufacturers, who might need large quantities of custom-made products. He is on a straight salary of $8,000 per year, plus expenses and a company car. He expects some salary increases but does not see a great long-run opportunity with this company. As a result, he is seriously considering changing jobs and investing $10,000 in the AAA Plastics Co., an established midwestern thermoplastic molder and manufacturer. Harry Mack, the present owner is nearing retirement age and has not developed anyone to run the business for him. He has agreed to sell the business to John O'Gorman, a lawyer-entrepreneur, who has invited Bob McMahon to invest and become the sales manager. Mr. O'Gorman has agreed to give Bob McMahon his current salary plus expenses, plus a bonus of 1 percent of profits. However, Bob must invest to become part of the new company. He will obtain a 5 percent interest in the business for his $10,000 investment.

The AAA Plastics Co. is well established and last year had sales of $1.5 million, but no profits. In terms of sales, cost of materials was 46 percent; direct labor, 13 percent; indirect factory labor, 15 percent; factory overhead, 13 percent; and sales overhead and general expenses, 13 percent. The company has not been making any profit for several years but has been continually adding new machines to replace those obsoleted by technological developments. The machinery is well maintained and modern, but most of it is similar to that owned by competitors. Most of the machines of the industry are standard. Special products are then made by using dies in conjunction with these machines.

Sales historically have been approximately two thirds custom-molded products (that is, made to order for other producers or merchandising concerns) and the balance proprietary items, such as housewares, and game items, such as poker chips and cribbage sets. The housewares are copies of articles initiated by others and indicate neither originality nor style. Harry Mack is in charge of the proprietary items distributed through any available wholesale channels. The custom-molded products are sold through three full-time sales engineers who receive a 5 percent commission on sales up to $10,000 and then 3 percent above that level, as well as three independent representatives working part time on a similar commission plan.

Financially, the company seems to be in fairly good condition, at least as far as book value is concerned, as the $10,000 investment would buy approximately $30,000 in assets.

Mr. O'Gorman feels that, with new management, the company offers great opportunity for profit. He expects to make some economies in the production process and hold custom-molding sales to approximately the present $1 million level. The other major expectation is that he will be able to develop the proprietary line from a sales volume of about $500,000 to $2 million a year. Bob McMahon is expected to be a real asset here because of his sales experience. This will bring the firm up to about capacity level, but of course it will entail adding additional employees. The major advantage of expanding sales would be spreading overhead. Some of the products proposed by the lawyer for the expansion of the proprietary line are listed below.

New Products for Consideration

Women's tool kit—molded housewares
Six-bottle soft drink case
Laminating printed film on housewares—molded
Short legs for furniture—molded $0.5 million minimum market
Home storage box for milk bottles $0.5 million minimum market
Step-on garbage can without liner
Importing and distributing foreign housewares
Black-nylon-handled table utensils
Extruded and embossed or formed wall coverings
Extruded and formed wall decorations—nursery rhyme figures, etc.
Formed butyrate outside house shutters
Formed inside shutters in lieu of venetian blinds

School and toy blackboards
Translucent bird houses
Formed holder for vacuum cleaner attachments
Formed household door liners
Formed "train terrain" table topography for model trains
Formed skylights
Perforated extruded sheet for industrial sale as grilles
Formed drawers for housewares sale with supports for under-furniture storage
Formed drawers for industrial sales
Formed children's furniture, including chest of formed drawers and metal angles
Extruded corrugated butyrate sheet for outdoor patio and storage covers
Extruded corrugated translucent styrene sheet for indoor room dividers
Formed restaurant tray, with surface grain
Formed lap board for studying, serving
Formed washboard
Extruded and formed traffic and street signs

There is a great deal of competition in these markets, and most retailers expect a wide margin, sometimes 40 to 50 percent, but even so, manufacturing costs are such that there is some room for promotion while still keeping the price competitive. Apparently many consumers are willing to pay for the novelty of new products.

How would you advise Bob McMahon? Explain your reasoning.

38
A. C. Gilbert Company

In the days before television became a toy-advertising medium and children's pastime, few toys were as sought as A. C. Gilbert's American Flyer trains and its chemistry and Erector sets – all first-quality, high-ticket items. In 1966, however, company management was faced with the problem of reversing a downward trend in sales and profits in an industry that had grown to a record $2.4 billion in 1965. In 1961, Gilbert's profits had shrunk to $20,011 followed by losses of $281,000 in 1962, $5.7 million in 1963, $1.9 million in 1964, and $2.9 million in 1965 – a total loss of almost $11 million.

Upon graduation from Yale in 1909, Alfred Carlton Gilbert set up the Mystro Manufacturing Co. to produce the Erector set which he had perfected. In 1916, the name became the A. C. Gilbert Co. This same year, Gilbert founded and became the first president of the Toy Manufacturers Association. A son, A. C. Jr., who graduated with honors from Yale in 1951, became assistant to his father in 1946 and president of the company in 1954. In 1961, upon the death of his father, the younger Gilbert became board chairman also.

A. C. Gilbert Co., with a reputation as a quality toymaker, was firmly among the top 10 toymakers in the 1950's, with sales topping $17 million. During this period, science achieved national attention, and Gilbert's sales of chemistry, biology, and other scientific sets dominated its sales. These sets were neatly packaged in easy-to-store metal boxes.

Gilbert toys were sold directly by the company's own sales force to hobby and toy shops and department stores. The principal advertising medium was company catalogs and window displays.

In the late 1950's, profits and sales slowly declined. But Gilbert retained its same product line and traditional marketing mix, assuming that the decline was merely temporary. In early 1961, Gilbert experienced serious financial difficulty, and John Wrather, Jr., president of Wrather Holding Co., acquired ownership of about 51 percent of Gilbert's stock. In addition to Gilbert, Wrather had among its properties real estate, hotels, oil wells, Muzak, and the rights to "Lassie," "The Lone Ranger," and "Sgt. Preston of the Yukon." A. C. Gilbert, Jr., retained the board chairmanship, but his power was clearly reduced.

Mr. Wrather named former Wrather vice president, William Quilan, president of Gilbert. In an effort to rejuvenate sales, the sales staff was increased by half, and a new marketing manager and director of international sales was hired. Despite these personnel changes, sales declined in 1962, and Gilbert experienced a loss of $281,000, attributed mostly to lower sales, the cost of preparing the 1963 line, and scrapping obsolete materials.

In 1963, the product line was expanded by 50 new toys, boosting the line to 307 items. For the first time, Gilbert offered toys for preschool children and for girls in the 6- to 14-year-old bracket as well as for boys, Gilbert's traditional market segment. Sales continued to fall and losses in 1963 amounted to $5.7 million, stemming mostly from huge returns of low-priced toys shipped on a guaranteed-sale basis to traditional outlets (nearly $3.5 million in unsold toys were in Gilbert's inventory after Christmas).

In 1964, losses were reduced as cuts in factory personnel and departments reduced administrative and operating expenses from $10 million to $4.7 million a year. Gilbert's sales force was scrapped, and manufacturers' representatives were employed to distribute its products.

In 1965, Gilbert realized that television had become the primary advertising medium and invested $2 million in sponsoring a 52-week schedule of Saturday morning cartoon shows. Sales increased to $14.9 million, the best since the 1950's, but losses were $2.9 million. The immediate cause seemed to be heavy returns of the 007 racing auto set and other racing sets. Dealer complaints stated the cars were poorly engineered, burned out after a short time, and were poorly made — looking more like toys than models. The see-through cardboard box showed only the cars, and dealers had to explain that the track was also included.

Other comments from dealers were: "Gilbert had a natural in its Erector set. Instead they neglected it. They used to offer sets up to $75, packaged in metal boxes. Now the most expensive is only $20, the parts are flimsy, and it's in an oversize box. They did the same thing to their chemistry sets. You can't store anything in those oversize see-through packages."

"Manufacturers' representatives increase dealer coverage without increasing the cost of selling but they are not liked by dealers. It used to be that you could call a Gilbert salesman and get service on a problem. Now the reps just want to get the order!"

"Gilbert timing is late. It introduced spy figures (stars from "Man from UNCLE," James Bond, etc.) on Christmas Day in 1965 – obviously too late for the selling season in which spy items were popular."

Evaluate what has been going on at Gilbert and in the toy industry. What should A. C. Gilbert Co. management do?

39 The Perlick Company	The Perlick Co., of Milwaukee, Wisconsin, has been in business for 50 years, manufacturing a line of brass and copper fittings used in the production and dispensing of beer. The product line consists of valves, casings, and connectors used in breweries, as well as tapping equipment used in taverns and restaurants. Their products are sold by several of their own salemen, who call directly on breweries, taverns, and restaurants.

Several years ago, the salesmen reported an opportunity to offer better-quality refrigeration equipment for chilling bottled and tap beer in restaurants and taverns. Following some preliminary market and engineering research, the company decided to expand its product line in this direction. It set up a "Cabinet Division" to manufacture a high-quality line of all-metal beer coolers and glass chillers. The company offered four different sizes of refrigerator cabinets, but all were basically the same style and color (black).

The same salesmen who were selling the other Perlick products had considerable success selling the new products to current customers. The salesmen had correctly seen that some of their customers' equipment had depreciated to the point where they would be very interested in new equipment. The salesmen also received some business from those setting up new establishments. But this business was more difficult to obtain because the salesmen traveled widely and were not always aware when and where new businesses were being organized. Some inquiries came to them from small ads which were placed in trade magazines appealing to restaurant and tavern operators. All such inquiries were followed up immediately by the salesmen, and the high quality of Perlick's product helped close many sales.

The cabinets were well designed from an engineering standpoint and technically superior to similar products available from competitors. (In particular, they were built more solidly. It was expected that they would outlast competitive products by four to six years. They also chilled beer faster, were more compact, and had a longer lasting finish). This higher quality enabled the cabinets to be sold for 10 to 15 percent more than competitors' products; prices ranged from $300 for the smallest size cooler to $2,400 for the largest unit.

Perlick enjoyed considerable prosperity for the first two years, since production was easily standardized on the four sizes it was producing. Further, Perlick was concentrating its sales effort in the upper Midwest to keep its selling costs low – 90 percent of sales were made in

Wisconsin, Illinois, Indiana, and Michigan. This also had the effect of reducing customers' delivered costs, because typically customers paid transportation costs from the factory. Most of Perlick's competitors sold on a nationwide basis, and many were located in other parts of the country.

Some units were sold by Perlick outside its normal selling area. These orders came in response to the small ads which were placed in leading trade magazines. The salesmen did not follow up these inquiries personally, but occasionally the telephone was used to handle closing details.

Two years after Perlick entered this business, its sales began to slip. Competitors began offering a wider variety of styles, colors, and sizes to suit the tavern and restaurant owners. Competitors' cabinets became available in black, white, blue, grey, and brown. Up to 15 different sizes were offered to meet customers' space limitations. Formica and plastic finishes were offered to supplement the metal exteriors already available. Perlick countered these offerings by extending a 10-year guarantee on the refrigeration unit, in addition to the free installation and service already provided. Sales failed to increase, however, and the sales manager recommended that the company meet the demands of customers.

The production manager maintained, however, that increasing variety in the product line would greatly increase cost. Perlick was currently producing 15 cabinets per working day, after reaching a high of 20 cabinets a day before the sales decline. The production manager estimated that if the product line were expanded as the sales manager recommended, the company would have to produce and sell an average of 45 cabinets per day to hold down its costs, while keeping quality constant.

The production manager felt that the sales manager should expand his market coverage, and perhaps also should find distributors in the present territories who could provide continuing representation, thereby supplementing the efforts of the salesmen. Basically, he felt that Perlick had developed an efficient production system, and a relatively small increase in sales would enable the company to continue profitably with its present operation. He estimated that a doubling in capital investment would be required to expand to the higher volume. This was risky, and he felt that more attention should be paid to expanding sales of the present line rather than investing in more plant and equipment to offer a wider line and greater variety.

The sales manager, on the other hand, claimed that Perlick had to remain competitive in the marketplace or the sales decline would continue. He felt that simply expanding the territory would only add to cost and not result in a significant improvement in sales. Further, he noted that the company's financial condition was good. It had the resources to increase production as he recommended, and he felt that now was the time to take action. He wanted to go on the offensive rather than wait to see what happened. Specifically, he wanted permission to expand the sales force to develop a nationwide selling program and generate the sales which would keep the expanded production facilities going. To begin with, he wanted the addition of three more salesmen and the company's commitment to expand the product line. Otherwise, he felt the morale of the salesmen would continue to decline and conditions would continue to deteriorate.

Evaluate the present situation and explain what Perlick should do.

40 XYZ Corporation

The XYZ Corp. is a large electronics manufacturer located in the eastern United States. Manufacturing a very wide range of industrial and consumer electrical and electronic components, it is also a major defense contractor. With sales of over $2 billion a year and employing more than 120,000 people, the XYZ Corp. is one of the largest electronics manufacturers in the world.

The defense manufacturing facilities are located at an industrial complex in Baltimore, Maryland. The Defense Center is divided into four main divisions: Aerospace, Surface, Underseas, and Systems Operations. Each division is headed by a vice president who reports to the Defense Center president, Mr. E. W. Briggs. Each major department within the divisions has its own marketing staff, consisting of numerous representatives who have engineering backgrounds. It has been the policy of the various marketing managers to assign specific contracts (i.e., ones the Defense Center is bidding on) to individual marketing representatives for their complete attention. It is the responsibility of these marketing representatives to obtain as much information about the contracts as possible, by whatever means they deem necessary.

The Defense Center maintains a separate sales office in Washington, D.C., under the direction of the Middle Atlantic regional manager, Mr. Clive Peters. Similar offices are located in other major cities in close proximity to other major defense installations. The purpose of these offices is to conduct as much customer contact as possbile, officially and unofficially. Each of the regional salesmen is assigned particular defense agencies as clients. Salesmen are encouraged to make as many contacts with their assigned customers as possible, whether it be on the golf course, in restaurants, or, at the customer's office. Very liberal expense accounts are assigned to the salesmen.

The Defense Center solicited all branches of the armed services and other agencies such as NASA and FAA but had been most successful in the past with the Navy. In view of this, more salesmen were assigned to cover naval offices than any of the other "targets."

Despite the complete coverage of the market by the Defense Center sales force, sales declined sharply between 1962 and 1964. During this same period, the U.S. government's expenditure on defense increased greatly. Although XYZ's products were at least as good as competitors', actual sales were far below capacity, and many workers were laid off.

XYZ competed with numerous other electronics firms for a share of the $50 billion defense budget but often bid on contracts for which other firms generally had much more experience and competence. This bidding approach was followed because it was felt it would provide a "foot in the door" to many agencies. In 1964, the XYZ Corp. stood only 44th on the list of total contract awards from the Defense Department, last among the major electronics manufacturers. Nevertheless, its reputation was good among its previous customers.

Mr. Briggs was worried about the poor performance of the Defense Center's representatives and regional salesmen. After an audit of sales efforts, several interesting things were brought to Mr. Briggs's attention. It was a common occurrence for numerous personnel to call directly on the same potential customers, because several products or contracts could be offered the same contractor at the same time. Embarrassment was often the result, as two, and on occasion three, representatives were in the same waiting room awaiting the same purchasing agent. Salesmen in the decentralized sales offices were hired and trained by those offices and therefore did not have much experience with the rest of the Defense Center's operations. All sales personnel operated on a straight salary compensation plan with very little opportunity for bonuses, except for management personnel. There appeared to be little direction of the salesmen after an account was assigned. Many of the representatives complained of having very little to do.

During the 1962–64 period of declining sales, XYZ reduced its national advertising efforts considerably in an attempt to reduce overhead costs. Institutional advertising on television was completely eliminated because of its high costs with no apparent impact on sales. Sales promotion material was also eliminated in the cost saving program. These efforts were of little concern to the Defense Center personnel, since the advertising department was located at XYZ's corporate headquarters. The only active advertising carried on at the Defense Center was precise description of the Center's production facilities included with each bid proposal submitted to a government agency or Defense Department office.

Prices on contracts were very systematically computed by the accounting department through use of sophisticated electronic data processing equipment. Each department planning to contribute any man-hours or material in support of the proposal submitted its input to the accounting department for compilation. A final price would be arrived at by applying standard labor and overhead rates in addition to the material costs. Once the price was computed by the accounting department, it was rarely questioned. XYZ Corp. was consistently underbid by its major competitors, sometimes by as much as 30 percent. It was generally felt by most marketing personnel that their prices were too high because the standard rates applied for direct labor and overhead costs were too high, but the accounting department explained that this was necessary to insure sufficient profit on the contracts.

After reviewing all of the above facts, Mr. Briggs was not sure what should be done. Perhaps more advertising would make government purchasing agents more receptive to XYZ's representatives. And perhaps the sales forces should be reorganized to avoid duplication of effort. More supervision might be desirable. Or maybe the salesmen need more incentives to encourage greater effort, for example, bonuses or commissions. He was even thinking of hiring new marketing managers with successful backgrounds in consumer goods markets where competition is as tough as that faced by the Defense Center.

Evaluate the Defense Center's strategic planning. What should be done?

Index of names

Index of names

Index of subjects

Index of subjects

Index of subjects

Index of subjects

This book has been set on Linofilm in 9 point Primer, leaded 2 points, with Helvetica Regular and Bold. Chapter numbers and titles are in 12 point Helvetica Bold. The size of the type area of the page is 26 by 48½ picas.